Edition 11

Database Processing

Fundamentals, Design, and Implementation

David M. Kroenke

David J. Auer
Western Washington University

Prentice Hall

Boston   Columbus   Indianapolis   New York   San Francisco   Upper Saddle River
Amsterdam   Cape Town   Dubai   London   Madrid   Milan   Munich   Paris   Montreal   Toronto
Delhi   Mexico City   Sao Paulo   Sydney   Hong Kong   Seoul   Singapore   Taipei   Tokyo

Executive Editor: Bob Horan
Editorial Director: Sally Yagan
AVP/Editor-in-Chief: Eric Svendsen
Assistant Editor: Kelly Loftus
Director of Marketing: Patrice Lumumba Jones
Senior Marketing Manager: Anne Fahlgren
Marketing Assistant: Susan Osterlitz
Senior Managing Editor: Judy Leale
Production Project Manager: Kelly Warsak
Senior Operations Supervisor: Arnold Vila
Operations Specialist: Ilene Kahn
Senior Art Director: Janet Slowik

Design Director: Christy Mahon
Cover and Interior Design: Karen Quigley
Manager, Rights and Permissions: Charles Morris
Manager, Cover Visual Research & Permissions: Karen Sanatar
Cover Illustration: Stockbyte/Veer/Corbis
Media Director: Lisa Rinaldi
Lead Media Project Manager: Denise Vaughn
Full-Service Project Management: Jennifer Welsch/BookMasters, Inc.
Composition: Integra Software Services
Printer/Binder: Quebecor World-Versailles
Cover Printer: Lehigh-Phoenix Color/Hagerstown
Text Font: 10/12 Kepler MM

Library of Congress Cataloging-in-Publication Data

Kroenke, David.
  Database processing: fundamentals, design, and implementation/David M. Kroenke, David J. Auer.—11th ed.
    p. cm.
  Includes bibliographical references and index.
  ISBN 978-0-13-230267-8 (casebound : alk. paper)
    1. Database management.   I. Auer, David J.   II. Title.

QA76.9.D3K7365 2009
005.74—dc22

2009011144

10 9 8 7 6 5 4 3 2

Prentice Hall
is an imprint of

www.pearsonhighered.com

ISBN 10:   0-13-230267-5
ISBN 13: 978-0-13-230267-8

Brief Contents

PART 2 ● DATABASE DESIGN   93

Chapter 3: The Relational Model and Normalization   94

PART 4 ● MULTIUSER DATABASE PROCESSING   319

Chapter 9: Managing Multiuser Databases   320

Chapter 10: Managing Databases with SQL Server 2008   351

ONLINE CHAPTER: SEE PAGE 423 FOR INSTRUCTIONS

Chapter 10A: Managing Databases with Oracle Database 11g   10A-1

ONLINE CHAPTER: SEE PAGE 425 FOR INSTRUCTIONS

Chapter 10B: Managing Databases with MySQL 5.1   10B-1

Chapter 13: Database Processing for Business Intelligence Systems   526

APPENDICES

Fundamentals, Design, and Implementation

The 11th edition of *Database Processing* refines the organization and content of this classic textbook to reflect a new teaching and professional workplace environment. The organization and topic selection of the 11th edition is designed to:

- Present an early introduction to SQL queries.
- Use a "spiral approach" to database design.
- Use a consistent, generic Information Engineering (IE) Crow's Foot E-R diagram notation for data modeling and database design.
- Provide a detailed discussion of specific normal forms within a discussion of normalization that focuses on pragmatic normalization techniques.
- Use current DBMS technology: Microsoft Access 2007, Microsoft SQL Server 2008, Oracle Database 11g, and MySQL 5.1.
- Create Web database applications based on widely used Web development technology.
- Provide an introduction to business intelligence (BI) systems.
- Discuss the dimensional database concepts used in database designs for data warehouses and OnLine Analytical Processing (OLAP).

These changes have been made because it has become obvious that the basic structure of the earlier editions (up to and including the 9th edition—the 10th edition introduced many of the changes we use in the 11th edition) was designed for a teaching environment that no longer existed. The structural changes to the book were made for several reasons:

- Unlike the early years of database processing, today's students have ready access to data modeling and DBMS products.
- Today's students are too impatient to start a class with lengthy conceptual discussions on data modeling and database design. They want to do something, see a result, and obtain feedback.
- In the current economy, students need to reassure themselves that they are learning marketable skills.

Early Introduction of SQL DML

Given these changes in the classroom environment, this book provides an early introduction to SQL data manipulation language (DML) SELECT statements. The discussion of SQL data definition language (DDL) and additional DML statements occurs in Chapters 7 and 8. By presenting SQL SELECT statements in Chapter 2, students learn early in the class how to query data and obtain results, seeing firsthand some of the ways that database technology will be useful to them.

The text assumes that students will work through the SQL statements and examples with a DBMS product. This is practical today, because nearly every student has access to Microsoft Access. Therefore, Chapters 1 and 2 and Appendix A are written to support an early introduction of Microsoft Access 2007 and the use of Access 2007 for SQL queries (Access 2007 QBE query techniques are also covered).

If a non–Access-based approach is desired, versions of SQL Server 2008, Oracle Database, and MySQL 5.1 are readily available for use. Free versions of the three major DBMS products covered in this book (SQL Server 2008 Express, Oracle Express 10g, and MySQL 5.1 Community Edition) are available for download. Further, the text can be purchased with a licensed educational version of Oracle Database 11g personal edition (this is a developer license) as well. Alternatively, a trial copy of MySQL 5.1 Enterprise Edition is also available as a download. Thus, students can actively use a DBMS product by the end of the first week of class.

> **BY THE WAY** The presentation and discussion of SQL is spread over three chapters so that students can learn about this important topic in small bites. SQL SELECT statements are taught in Chapter 2. SQL DDL and SQL DML statements are presented in Chapter 7. Correlated subqueries and EXISTS/NOT EXISTS statements are described in Chapter 8. Each topic appears in the context of accomplishing practical tasks. Correlated subqueries, for example, are used to verify functional dependency assumptions, a necessary task for database redesign.
>
> This box illustrates another feature used in this book: BTW boxes are used to separate comments from the text discussion. Sometimes they present ancillary material; other times they reinforce important concepts.

A Spiral Approach to Database Design

Today, databases arise from three sources: (1) from the integration of existing data from spreadsheets, data files, and database extracts, (2) from the development of new information systems projects, and (3) from the need to redesign an existing database to adapt to changing requirements. We believe that the fact that these three sources exist present instructors with a significant pedagogical opportunity. Rather than teach database design just once from data models, why not teach database design three times, once for each of these sources? In practice, this idea has turned out to be even more successful than expected.

Design Iteration 1: Databases from Existing Data

Considering the design of databases from existing data, if someone were to e-mail us a set of tables and say, "Create a database from them," how would we proceed? We would examine the tables in light of normalization criteria and then determine whether the new database was for query only or whether it was for query and update. Depending on the answer, we would denormalize the data, joining them together, or we would normalize the data, pulling them apart. All of which is important for students to know and understand.

Therefore, the first iteration of database design gives instructors a rich opportunity to teach normalization, not as a set of theoretical concepts, but rather as a useful toolkit for making design decisions for databases created from existing data. Additionally, the construction of databases from existing data is an increasingly common task that is often assigned to junior staff members. Learning how to apply normalization to the design of databases from existing data not only provides an interesting way of teaching normalization, it is also common and useful!

We prefer to teach and use a pragmatic approach to normalization, and present this approach in Chapter 3. However, we are aware that many instructors like to teach normalization in the context of a step-by-step normal form presentation (1NF, 2NF, 3NF, then BCNF), and Chapter 3 includes material to support this approach as well.

In today's workplace, large organizations are increasingly licensing standardized software from vendors such as SAP, Oracle, and Siebel. Such software already has a database design. But with every organization running the same software, many are learning that they can only gain a competitive advantage if they make better use of the data in those predesigned databases. Hence, students who know how to extract data and create read-only databases for reporting and data mining have obtained marketable skills in the world of ERP and other packaged software solutions.

Design Iteration 2: Data Modeling and Database Design

The second source of databases is from new systems development. Although not as common as in the past, many databases are still created from scratch. Thus, students still need to learn data modeling, and they still need to learn how to transform data models into database designs.

The IE Crow's Foot Model as a Design Standard

This edition uses a generic, standard IE Crow's Foot notation. Your students should have no trouble understanding the symbols and using the data modeling or database design tool of your choice.

IDEF1X (which was used as the preferred E-R diagram notation in the 9th edition of this text) is explained in Appendix B in case your students will graduate into an environment where it is used, or if you prefer to use it in your classes. UML is explained in Appendix C in case you prefer to use UML in your classes.

BY THE WAY The choice of a data modeling tool is somewhat problematic. The two most readily available tools, Microsoft Visio and Sun Microsystems MySQL Workbench, are database design tools, not data modeling tools. Neither can produce an N:M relationship as such (as a data model requires), but have to immediately break it into two 1:N relationships (as database design does). Therefore, the intersection table must be constructed and modeled. This confounds data modeling with database design in just the way that we are attempting to teach students to avoid.

To be fair to Visio, it is true that data models with N:M relationships can be drawn using either the standard Visio drawing tools or the Entity Relationship shapes dynamic connector. These are shown in Figure FM-01, where the N:M relationships ENTITY-ONE-to-ENTITY-THREE and ENTITY-FOUR-to-ENTITY-FIVE were drawn using the dynamic connector and show the correct line end symbols.

ENTITY-ONE and ENTITY-THREE are Visio database entity objects, and Visio stores object data such as column type, primary key, and so on, about the entities, but *not* about the relationship between them. ENTITY-FOUR and ENTITY-FIVE were drawn using the Visio rectangle drawing tool, and no database object data is stored by these shapes or the relationship between them.

Visio is at its best using the Visio relationship connector to connect entity objects. In this case, as shown in the ENTITY-ONE-to-ENTITY-TWO relationship, relationship data such as minimum and maximum cardinalities is stored in database objects and foreign keys (such as E-1-ID as FK1 in ENTITY-TWO) are automatically inserted in child

(continued)

Figure FM-01

Data Models in Microsoft Visio 2007

The Visio **relationship** connector stores relationship data (i.e., cardinalities) in the Visio file and adds foreign keys (E-1-ID as FK1 in ENTITY-TWO) automatically

The Visio **dynamic connector** can be drawn with IE Crow's Foot symbols, but it does not store relationship data in the database or add foreign keys

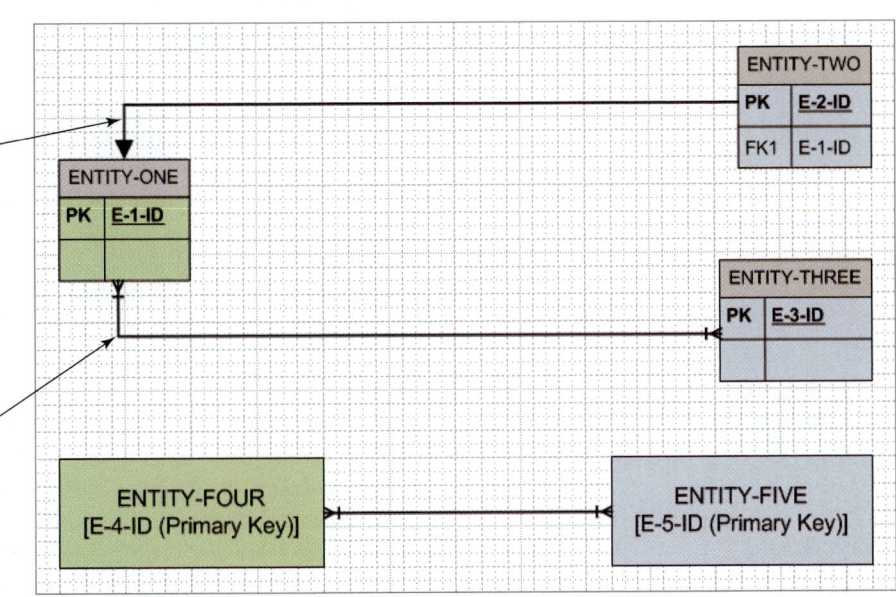

entities. However, there is no *N:M* relationship connector in Visio, so we cannot model N:M relationships using a relationship connector. Without the ability to store relationship data for N:M relationships, it is problematic to use Visio as data modeling tool while it functions well as database design tool.

There are good data modeling tools available, but they tend to be more complex and expensive. Two examples are Visible Systems' Visible Analyst and Computer Associates' ERwin Data Modeler. Visible Analyst is available in a student edition (at a modest price), and a one-year time-limitedCA ERwin Data Modeler Community Edition suitable for class use can be downloaded from www.ca.com/us/software-trials.aspx—CA has limited the number of objects that can be created by this edition to 25 entities per model, and disabled some other features (see www.ca.com/files/TechnicalDocuments/erwin-community-edition-matrix_197107.pdf), but there is still enough functionality to make this product a possible choice for class use.

Database Design from E-R Data Models

As we discuss in Chapter 6, designing a database from data models consists of three tasks: representing entities and attributes with tables and columns; representing maximum cardinality by creating and placing foreign keys; and representing minimum cardinality via constraints, triggers, and application logic.

The first two tasks are straightforward. However, designs for minimum cardinality are more difficult. Required parents are easily enforced using NOT NULL foreign keys and referential integrity constraints. Required children are more problematic. In this book, however, we simplify the discussion of this topic by limiting the use of referential integrity actions and by supplementing those actions with design documentation. See the discussion around Figure 6-28.

Although the design for required children is complicated, it is important for students to learn. It also provides a reason for students to learn about triggers as well. In any case, the discussion of these topics is much simpler than it was in prior editions because of the use of the IE Crow's Foot model and the use of ancillary design documentation.

 **THE WAY**   David Kroenke is the creator of the semantic object model (SOM). The SOM is presented in Appendix E; the E-R data model is used everywhere else in the text.

Design Iteration 3: Database Redesign

Database redesign, the third iteration of database design, is both common and difficult. As stated in Chapter 8, information systems cause organizational change. New information systems give users new behaviors, and as users behave in new ways, they require changes in their information systems.

Database redesign is by nature complex. Depending on your students, you may wish to skip it, and you can do so without loss of continuity. Database redesign is presented after the discussion of SQL DDL and DML in Chapter 7, because it requires the use of advanced SQL. It also provides a practical reason to teach correlated subqueries and EXISTS/NOT EXISTS statements.

Active Use of a DBMS Product

We assume that the students will actively use a DBMS product. The only real question becomes "which one?" Realistically, most of us have four alternatives to consider: Microsoft Access, Microsoft SQL Server, Oracle Database, or MySQL. You can use any of those products with this text, and tutorials for each of them are presented for Access 2007 (Appendix A), SQL Server 2008 (Chapter 10), Oracle Database 11g (Chapter 10A), and MySQL 5.1 (Chapter 10B). Given the limitations of class time, it is probably necessary to pick and use just one of these products. You can often devote a portion of a lecture to discussing the characteristics of each, but it is usually best to limit student work to one of them. The possible exception to this is starting the course with Microsoft Access, and then switching to a more robust DBMS product later in the course.

Using Microsoft Access 2007

The primary advantage of Microsoft Access is accessibility. Most students already have a copy, and, if not, copies are easily obtained. Many students will have used Access in their introductory or other classes. Appendix A is a tutorial on Access 2007 for students who have not used it but who wish to use it with this book.

However, Access has several disadvantages. First, as explained in Chapter 1, Access is a combination application generator and DBMS. Access confuses students because it confounds database processing with application development. Also, Access hides SQL behind its query processor and makes SQL appear as an afterthought rather than a foundation. Furthermore, as discussed in Chapter 2, Access does not correctly process some of the basic, SQL-92 standard statements in its default setup. Finally, Access does not support triggers. You can simulate triggers by trapping Windows events, but that technique is nonstandard and does not effectively communicate the nature of trigger processing.

Using Oracle, SQL Server, or MySQL

Choosing which of these products to use depends on your local situation. Oracle Database 11g, a superb enterprise-class DBMS product, is difficult to install and administer. However, if you have local staff to support your students, it can be an excellent choice. As shown in Chapter 10A, Oracle's SQL Developer GUI tool (or SQL*Plus if you are dedicated to this beloved command-line tool) is a handy tool for learning SQL, triggers, and stored procedures. In our experience, students require considerable support to install Oracle on their own computers, and you may be better off to use Oracle from a central server.

SQL Server 2008, although probably not as robust as Oracle, is easy to install on Windows machines, and it provides the capabilities of an enterprise-class DBMS product. The standard database administrator tool is the Microsoft SQL Server Management Studio GUI tool. As shown in Chapter 10, SQL Server 2008 can be used to learn SQL, triggers, and stored procedures.

MySQL 5.1, discussed in Chapter 10B is an open-source DBMS product that is receiving increased attention and market share. The capabilities of MySQL are continually being upgraded, and MySQL 5.1 supports stored procedures and triggers. MySQL also has excellent GUI tools (MySQL Query Browser and MySQL Administrator) and an excellent command-line tool (the MySQL Command Line Client). It is the easiest of the three products for students to install on their own computers. It also works with the Linux operating system, and is popular as part of the AMP (Apache-MySQL-PHP) package (known as WAMP on Windows and LAMP on Linux).

BY THE WAY   If the DBMS you use is not driven by local circumstances and you do have a choice, we recommend using SQL Server 2008. It has all of the features of an enterprise-class DBMS product, and it is easy to install and use. Another option is to start with Access 2007 if it is available, and switch to SQL Server 2008 at Chapter 7. Chapters 1 and 2 and Appendix A are written specifically to support this approach. A variant is to use Access 2007 as the development tool for forms and reports running against an SQL Server 2008 database.

If you prefer a different DBMS product, you can still start with Access 2007 and switch later in the course. You can order the text with a shrink-wrapped version of Oracle, while a trial version of SQL Server can be downloaded from Microsoft, and MySQL is so easy to download (and updated often enough) that it makes no sense to package a copy with the book.

Focus on Database Application Processing

In this edition, we clearly draw the line between *application development* per se and *database application processing*. Specifically, we have:

- Focused on specific database dependent applications:
  - Web-based, database-driven applications
  - XML-based data processing
  - Business intelligence (BI) systems applications
- Emphasized the use of commonly available, multiple OS compatible application development languages.
- Limited the use of specialized vendor-specific tools and programming languages as much as possible.

There is simply not enough room in this book to provide even a basic introduction to, for example, Visual Basic .NET and Java. Therefore, rather than attempting to introduce these languages, we leave them for other classes where they can be covered at an appropriate depth. Instead, we focus on basic tools that are relatively straightforward to learn and immediately applicable to database-driven applications. We use PHP as our Web development language, and we use the readily available Eclipse integrate development environment (IDE) as our development tool. The result is a very focused final section of the book, where we deal specifically with the interface between databases and the applications that use them.

> **BY THE WAY** Although we try to use widely available software as much as possible, there are, of course, exceptions where we must use vendor specific tools. For BI applications, for example, we draw on Microsoft Excel's PivotTable capabilities and the Microsoft SQL Server 2008 Data Mining Add-ins for Microsoft Office 2007. However, there are either alternatives to these tools (OpenOffice.org DataPilot capabilities, the Palo OLAP Server) or the tools are generally available for download.

Business Intelligence Systems and Dimensional Databases

This edition increases coverage of business intelligence (BI) systems (Chapter 13). The chapter now includes a discussion of dimensional databases, which are the underlying structure for data warehouses, data marts, and OLAP servers. It still covers data management for data warehouses and data marts and also describes reporting and data mining applications, including OLAP.

Chapter 13 includes coverage of two applications that should be particularly interesting to students. The first is RFM analysis, a reporting application frequently used by mail order and e-commerce companies. The complete RFM analysis is accomplished in Chapter 13 through the use of standard SQL statements. Additionally, this chapter includes a market basket analysis that is also performed using SQL correlated subqueries. This chapter can be assigned at any point after Chapter 8 and could be used as a motivator to illustrate the practical applications of SQL midcourse.

Overview of the Chapters in the 11th Edition

Chapter 1 sets the stage by introducing database processing, describing basic components of database systems, and summarizing the history of database processing. If the students are using Access 2007 for the first time (or need a good review), they will also need to study Appendix A at this point. Chapter 2 presents SQL SELECT statements. It also includes sections on how to submit SQL statements to Access, SQL Server, Oracle, and MySQL.

The next four chapters, Chapters 3 through 6, present the first two iterations of database design. Chapter 3 presents the principles of normalization using Boyce-Codd normal form. It describes the problems of multivalued dependencies and explains how to eliminate them. This foundation in normalization is applied in Chapter 4 to the design of databases from existing data.

Chapters 5 and 6 describe the design of new databases. Chapter 5 presents the E-R data model. Traditional E-R symbols are explained, but the majority of the chapter uses IE Crow's Foot notation. Chapter 5 provides a taxonomy of entity types, including strong, ID-dependent, weak but not ID-dependent, supertype/subtype and recursive. The chapter concludes with a simple modeling example for a university database.

Chapter 6 describes the transformation of data models into database designs by converting entities and attributes to tables and columns, by representing maximum cardinality by creating and placing foreign keys, and by representing minimum cardinality via carefully designed DBMS constraints, triggers, and application code. The primary section of this chapter parallels the entity taxonomy in Chapter 5.

Chapter 7 presents SQL DDL and DML. SQL DDL is used to implement the design of an example introduced in Chapter 6. INSERT, UPDATE, and DELETE statements are discussed, as are SQL views. Additionally, the principles of embedding SQL in program code are presented, and triggers and stored procedures are explained.

Database redesign, the third iteration of database design, is described in Chapter 8. This chapter presents SQL correlated subqueries and EXISTS/NOT EXISTS statements and uses those statements in the redesign process. Reverse engineering is described, and basic redesign patterns are illustrated and discussed.

Chapters 9, 10, 10A, and 10B consider the management of multiuser organizational databases. Chapter 9 describes database administration tasks, including concurrency, security, and backup and recovery. Chapters 10, 10A, and 10B then describe SQL Server 2008, Oracle Database 11g, and MySQL 5.1, respectively. These chapters show how to use these products to create database structures and process SQL statements. They also explain concurrency, security, and backup and recovery with each product. The discussion in Chapters 10, 10A, and 10B parallels the order of discussion in Chapter 9 as much as possible, although rearrangements of some topics are made as needed to support the discussion of a specific DBMS product.

BY THE WAY We have significantly extended our coverage of Access, SQL Server, Oracle Database, and MySQL in this book. In order to keep the bound book to a reasonable length, and to keep the cost of the book down, we have chosen to provide some materials by download from our Web site at www.pearsonhighered. com/kroenke. There you will find:

- Chapter 10A—Managing Databases with Oracle Database 11g
- Chapter 10B—Managing Databases with MySQL 5.1
- Appendix A—Getting Started with Microsoft Access 2007
- Appendix B—The IDEF1X Standard
- Appendix C—UML-Style Entity-Relationship Diagrams
- Appendix D—Data Structures for Database Processing
- Appendix E—The Semantic Object Model

Chapters 11, 12, and 13 address standards for accessing databases. Chapter 11 presents ODBC, OLE DB, ADO.NET, ASP.NET, JDBC, and Java Server Pages (JSP). It then introduces PHP (and the Eclipse IDE) and illustrates the use of PHP for the publication of databases via Web pages. Chapter 12 describes the integration of XML and database technology. The chapter begins with a primer on XML and then shows how to use the FOR XML SQL statement in SQL Server.

Chapter 13 concludes the text with a discussion of BI systems, dimensional data models, data warehouses, and data marts. It illustrates the use of SQL for RFM reporting analysis and for market basket analysis.

Supplements

This text is accompanied by a wide variety of supplements. Please visit the text's Web site at www.pearsonhighered.com/kroenke to access the instructor and student supplements described below. Please contact your Pearson sales representative for more details. All supplements were written by David Auer.

For Students

- Many of the *Sample Databases* used in this text are available in Access, Oracle, SQL Server, and MySQL format.
- Glossary

For Instructors

- The *Instructor's Resource Manual* provides sample course syllabi, teaching suggestions, and answers to end-of-chapter review, project, and case questions.
- The *Test Item File* and *TestGen* include an extensive set of test questions in multiple-choice, true/false, fill-in-the-blank, short-answer, and essay format. The difficulty level and where the topic is covered in the text are noted for each question. The Test Item File is available in Microsoft Word and in TestGen. TestGen is a comprehensive suite of tools for testing and assessment. It enables instructors to easily create and distribute tests for their courses, either by printing and distributing them through traditional methods or by online delivery via a LAN. TestGen features Screen Wizards to assist you as you move through the program, and the software is backed with full technical support. TestGen conversions for WebCT and BlackBoard course management systems are available.
- *PowerPoint Presentation Slides* feature lecture notes that highlight key terms and concepts. Instructors can customize the presentation by adding their own slides or editing the existing ones.
- The *Image Library* is a collection of the text art organized by chapter. This includes all figures, tables, and screenshots (as permission allows) to enhance class lectures and PowerPoint presentations.

Materials for Your Online Course

Prentice Hall supports our adopters using online courses by providing files ready for upload into both WebCT and BlackBoard course management systems for our testing, quizzing, and other supplements. Please contact your local Pearson sales representative for further information on your particular course.

Acknowledgments

We are grateful for the support of many people in the development of this 11th edition and previous editions. Thanks to Rick Mathieu at James Madison University for interesting and insightful discussions on the database course. Professor Doug MacLachlan from the Marketing Department at the University of Washington was most helpful in understanding the goals, objectives, and technology of data mining, particularly as it pertains to marketing. Don Nilson of the Microsoft Corporation helped us understand the importance of XML to database processing.

In addition, we wish to thank the reviewers of this edition:

Ann Aksut, *Central Piedmont Community College*

Allen Badgett, *Oklahoma City University*

Rich Beck, *Washington University*

Jeffrey J. Blessing, *Milwaukee School of Engineering*

Jason Deane, *Virginia Polytechnic Institute and State University*

Barry Flaschbart, *Missouri University of Science and Technology*

Dianne Hall, *Auburn University*

Jeff Hassett, *University of Utah*

Barbara Hewitt, *Texas A&M, Kingsville*

William Hochstettler, *Franklin University*

Nitin Kale, *University of Southern California, Los Angeles*

Johnny Li, *South University*

Mike Morris, *Southeastern Oklahoma State University*

Catherine Ricardo, *Iona College*

Kevin Roberts, *DeVry University*

Ioulia Rytikova, *George Mason University*

Christelle Scharff, *Pace University*

K. David Smith, *Cameron University*

Marcia Williams, *Bellevue Community College*

David Kroenke would like to thank our editor, Bob Horan, for his advice and assistance through four editions, so far(!), of this text. I also thank Kelly Loftus for keeping this project on track. Most importantly, I wish to thank my wife, Lynda, for her love and support through so many of these writing projects!

David Auer would like to thank David Kroenke for his generosity, insight, and support during this project. Our editor, Bob Horan; our assistant editor, Kelly Loftus; and our production project manager, Kelly Warsak, for their professionalism, insight, support, and assistance in the development of this project. My wife, Donna, for her love, encouragement, and patience while I was completing this project.

David Kroenke
Seattle, Washington

David Auer
Bellingham, Washington

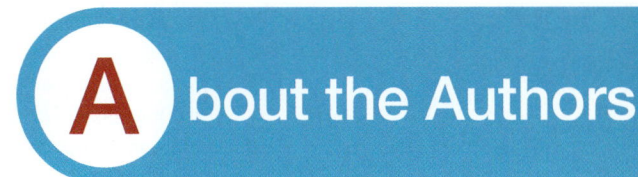

David M. Kroenke

Work Experience

David M. Kroenke has more than 35 years experience in the computer industry. He began as a computer programmer for the U.S. Air Force, working both in Los Angeles and at the Pentagon, where he developed one of the world's first DBMS products while part of a team that created a computer simulation of World War III. That simulation served a key role for strategic weapons studies during a 10-year period of the Cold War.

From 1973 to 1978, Kroenke taught in the College of Business at Colorado State University. In 1977, he published the first edition of *Database Processing,* a significant and successful textbook that, over 30 years later, you now are reading in its 11th edition. In 1978, he left Colorado State and joined Boeing Computer Services, where he managed the team that designed database management components of the IPAD project. After that, he joined with Steve Mitchell to form Mitchell Publishing and worked as an editor and author, developing texts, videos, and other educational products and seminars. Mitchell Publishing was acquired by Random House in 1986. During these years he also worked as an independent consultant, primarily as a database disaster repairman helping companies recover from failed database projects.

In 1982, Kroenke was one of the founding directors of the Microrim Corporation. From 1984 to 1987, he served as the Vice President of Product Marketing and Development and managed the team that created and marketed the DBMS product R:base 5000 as well as other related products.

For the next five years, Kroenke worked independently while he developed a new data modeling language called the *semantic object model.* He licensed this technology to the Wall Data Corporation in 1992 and then served as the Chief Technologist for Wall Data's SALSA line of products. He was awarded three software patents on this technology.

Since 1998, Kroenke has continued consulting and writing. His current interests concern the practical applications of data mining techniques on large organizational databases. An avid sailor, he wrote *Know Your Boat: The Guide to Everything That Makes Your Boat Work,* which was published by McGraw-Hill in 2002.

Consulting

Kroenke has consulted with numerous organizations during his career. In 1978, he worked for Fred Brooks, consulting with IBM on a project that became the DBMS product DB2. In 1989, he consulted for the Microsoft Corporation on a project that became Microsoft Access. In the 1990s, he worked with Computer Sciences Corporation and with General Research Corporation for the development of technology and products that were used to model all of the U.S. Army's logistical data as part of the CALS project. Additionally, he has consulted for Boeing Computer Services, the U.S. Air Force Academy, Logicon Corporation, and other smaller organizations.

Publications

- *Database Processing,* Pearson Prentice Hall, 11 editions, 1977–present (coauthor with David Auer, 11th edition)
- *Database Concepts,* Pearson Prentice Hall, four editions, 2004–present (coauthor with David Auer, third and fourth editions)

- *Using MIS*, Pearson Prentice Hall, two editions, 2006–present
- *Experiencing MIS*, Pearson Prentice Hall, two editions, 2007–present
- *MIS Essentials*, Pearson Prentice Hall, one edition, 2009
- *Know Your Boat: The Guide to Everything That Makes Your Boat Work*, McGraw-Hill, 2002
- *Management Information Systems*, Mitchell Publishing/Random House, three editions, 1987–1992
- *Business Computer Systems*, Mitchell Publishing/Random House, five editions, 1981–1990
- *Managing Information for Microcomputers*, Microrim Corporation, 1984 (coauthor with Donald Nilson)
- *Database Processing for Microcomputers*, Science Research Associates, 1985 (coauthor with Donald Nilson)
- *Database: A Professional's Primer*, Science Research Associates, 1978

Teaching

Kroenke taught in the College of Business at Colorado State University from 1973 to 1978. He also has taught part-time in the Software Engineering program at Seattle University. From 1990 to 1991, he served as the Hanson Professor of Management Science at the University of Washington. Most recently, he taught at the University of Washington from 2002 to 2008. During his career, he has been a frequent speaker at conferences and seminars for computer educators. In 1991, the International Association of Information Systems named him Computer Educator of the Year.

Education

B.S., Economics, U.S. Air Force Academy, 1968
M.S., Quantitative Business Analysis, University of Southern California, 1971
Ph.D., Engineering, Colorado State University, 1977

Personal

Kroenke is married, lives in Seattle, and has two grown children and three grandchildren. He enjoys skiing, sailing, and building small boats. His wife tells him he enjoys gardening as well.

David J. Auer

Work Experience

David J. Auer has more than 25 years experience teaching college-level business and information systems courses and for the last 15 years has worked professionally in the field of information technology. He served as a commissioned officer in the U.S. Air Force, with assignments to NORAD and the Alaskan Air Command in air defense operations. He later taught both business administration and music classes at Whatcom Community College, and business courses for the Chapman College Residence Education Center at Whidbey Island Naval Air Station. He was a founder of the Puget Sound Guitar Workshop (now in its 35th year of operations). He worked as a psychotherapist and organizational development consultant for the Whatcom Counseling and Psychiatric Clinic's Employee Assistance Program, and provided training for the Washington State Department of Social and Health Services. He has taught for Western Washington University's College of Business and Economics since 1981 and has been the college's Director of Information Systems and Technology Services since 1994.

Publications

- *Database Processing*, Pearson Prentice Hall, one edition, 2009 (coauthor with David Kroenke)
- *Database Concepts*, Pearson Prentice Hall, two editions, 2007–present (coauthor with David Kroenke)

- *Network Administrator: NetWare 4.1*, Course Technology, 1997 (coauthors Ted Simpson and Mark Ciampa)
- *New Perspectives on Corel Quattro Pro 7.0 for Windows 95*, Course Technology, 1997 (coauthors June Jamrich Parsons, Dan Oja, and John Leschke)
- *New Perspectives on Microsoft Excel 7 for Windows 95—Comprehensive*, Course Technology, 1996 (coauthors June Jamrich Parsons and Dan Oja)
- *New Perspectives on Microsoft Office Professional for Windows 95—Intermediate*, Course Technology, 1996 (coauthors June Jamrich Parsons, Dan Oja, Beverly Zimmerman, Scott Zimmerman, and Joseph Adamski)
- *The Student's Companion for Use with Practical Business Statistics* (3rd ed.), Irwin, 1993
- *Microsoft Excel 5 for Windows—New Perspectives Comprehensive*, Course Technology, 1995 (coauthors June Jamrich Parsons and Dan Oja)
- *Introductory Quattro Pro 6.0 for Windows*, Course Technology, 1995 (coauthors June Jamrich Parsons and Dan Oja)
- *Introductory Quattro Pro 5.0 for Windows*, Course Technology, 1994 (coauthors June Jamrich Parsons and Dan Oja)
- *The Student's Companion for Use with Practical Business Statistics* (2nd ed.), Irwin, 1993

Teaching

Auer has taught in the College of Business and Economics at Western Washington University from 1981 to the present. From 1975 to 1981, he taught part time for community colleges, and from 1981 to 1984 he taught part time for the Chapman College Residence Education Center System. During his career, he has taught a wide range of courses in Quantitative Methods, Production and Operations Management, Statistics, Finance and Management Information Systems. In MIS, he has taught Principles of Management Information Systems, Business Database Development, Computer Hardware and Operating Systems, and Telecommunications and Network Administration.

Education

B.A., English Literature, University of Washington, 1969
B.S., Mathematics and Economics, Western Washington University, 1978
M.A., Economics, Western Washington University, 1980
M.S., Counseling Psychology, Western Washington University, 1991

Personal

Auer is married, lives in Bellingham, Washington, and has two grown children and five grandchildren. He is active in his community, where he has been President of his neighborhood association and served on the City of Bellingham Planning and Development Commission. He enjoys music, playing acoustic and electric guitar, five-string banjo, and a bit of mandolin.

Part 1

Getting Started

The two chapters in Part 1 provide an introduction to database processing. In Chapter 1, we consider the characteristics of databases and describe important database applications. Chapter 1 also describes the various database components and provides a survey of the knowledge you need to learn from this text. The chapter also summarizes the history of database processing.

You will start working with a database in Chapter 2 and use that database to learn how to use Structured Query Language (SQL), a database-processing language, to query database data. You will learn how to query both single and multiple tables, and you will use SQL to investigate a practical example—looking for patterns in stock market data. Together, these two chapters will give you a sense of what databases are and how they are processed.

1 Introduction

Chapter Objectives

- To understand the nature and characteristics of databases.
- To survey some important and interesting database applications.
- To gain a general understanding of tables and relationships.
- To describe the components of a Microsoft Access database system and explain the functions they perform.
- To describe the components of an enterprise-class database system and explain the functions they perform.
- To define the term database management system (DBMS) and describe the functions of a DBMS.

- To define the term database and describe what is contained within the database.
- To define the term metadata and provide examples of metadata.
- To define and understand database design from existing data.
- To define and understand database design as new systems development.
- To define and understand database design in database redesign.
- To understand the history and development of database processing.

This chapter introduces database processing. We will first consider the nature and characteristics of databases and then survey a number of important and interesting database applications. Next, we will describe the components of a database system and then, in general terms, describe how databases are designed. After that, we will survey the knowledge that you need to work with databases as an application developer or as a database administrator. Finally, we conclude this introduction with a brief history of database processing.

This chapter assumes a minimal knowledge of database use. It assumes that you have used a product such as Microsoft Access to enter data into a form, to produce a report, and possibly to execute a query. If you have not done these things, you should obtain a copy of Microsoft Access 2007 and work through the tutorial in Appendix A.

The Characteristics of Databases

The purpose of a database is to help people keep track of things, and the most commonly used type of database is the **relational database**. We will discuss the relational database model in depth in Chapter 3, so for now we just need to understand a few basic facts about how a relational database helps people track things of interest to them.

First, a relational database stores data in tables. **Data** are recorded facts and numbers. A **table** has rows and columns, like those in a spreadsheet. A database usually has multiple tables, and each table contains data about a different type of thing. For example, Figure 1-1 shows a database with two tables: the STUDENT table holds data about students, and the CLASS table holds data about classes.

Each **row** of a table has data about a particular occurrence or **instance** of the thing of interest. For example, each row of the STUDENT table has data about one of four students: Cooke, Lau, Harris, and Greene. Similarly, each row of the CLASS table has data about a particular class. Because each row *records* the data for a specific instance, rows are also known as **records**. Each **column** of a table stores a characteristic common to all rows. For example, the first column of STUDENT stores StudentNumber, the second column stores LastName, and so forth.

BY THE WAY A table and a *spreadsheet* (also known as a *worksheet*) are very similar in that you can think of both as having rows, columns, and cells. The details that define a table as something different from a spreadsheet are discussed in Chapter 3. For now, the main differences you will see are that tables have column names instead of identifying letters (for example, *Name* instead of *A*) and that the rows are not necessarily numbered.

Although, in theory, you could switch the rows and columns by putting instances in the columns and characteristics in the rows, this is never done. Every database in this text, and 99.999999 percent of all databases throughout the world, store instances in rows and characteristics in columns.

A Note on Naming Conventions

In this text, table names appear in capital letters. This convention will help you to distinguish table names in explanations. However, you are not required to set table names in capital letters. Microsoft Access and similar programs will allow you to write a table name as STUDENT, student, Student, stuDent, or in some other way.

Additionally, in this text column names begin with a capital letter. Again, this is just a convention. You could write the column name Term as term, teRm, TERM, or in any other way. To ease readability, we will sometimes create compound column names in which the first letter of each element of the compound word is capitalized. Thus, in Figure 1-1, the STUDENT table has columns StudentNumber, LastName, FirstName, and EmailAddress. Again, this capitalization is just a convenient convention. However, following these or other consistent conventions will make interpretation of database structures easier. For example, you will always know that STUDENT is the name of a table and that Student is the name of a column of a table.

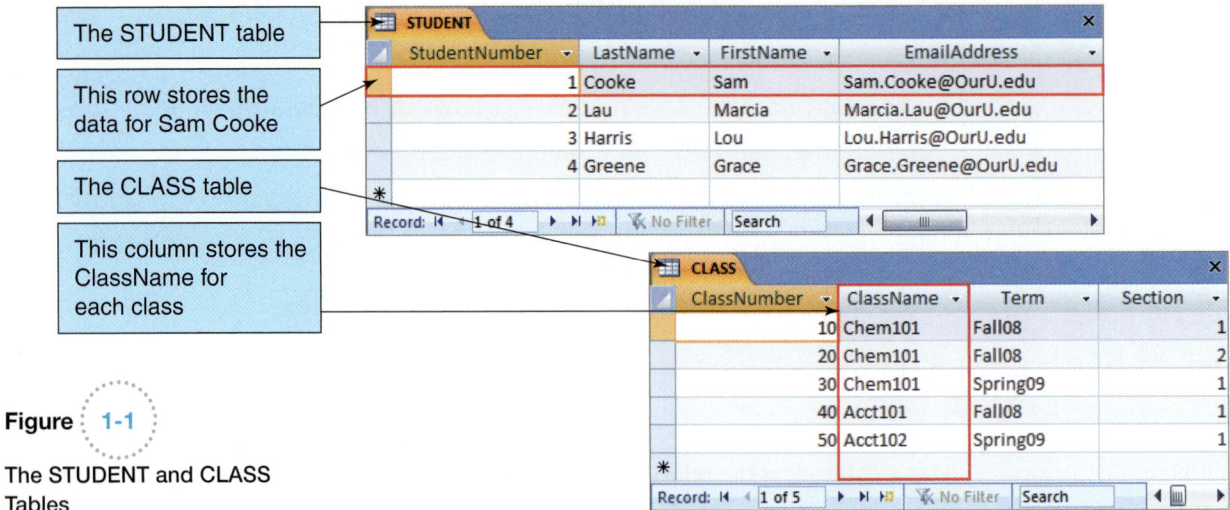

Figure 1-1

The STUDENT and CLASS Tables

A Database Has Data and Relationships

Figure 1-1 illustrates how database tables are structured to store data, but a database is not complete unless it also shows the relationships among the rows of data. To see why this is important, examine Figure 1-2. In this figure, the database contains all of the basic data shown in Figure 1-1 together with a GRADE table. Unfortunately, the relationships between the data are missing. In this format, the GRADE data are useless. It is like the joke about the sports commentator who announced: "Now for tonight's baseball scores: 2–3, 7–2, 1–0, and 4–5." The scores are useless without knowing the teams that earned them. Thus, a database contains both data and the relationships among the data.

Figure 1-3 shows the complete database that contains not only the data about students, classes, and grades, but also the relationships among the rows in those tables. For example, StudentNumber 100, who is Sam Cooke, earned a Grade of 3.7 in ClassNumber 10, which is Chem101. He also earned a Grade of 3.5 in ClassNumber 40, which is Acct101.

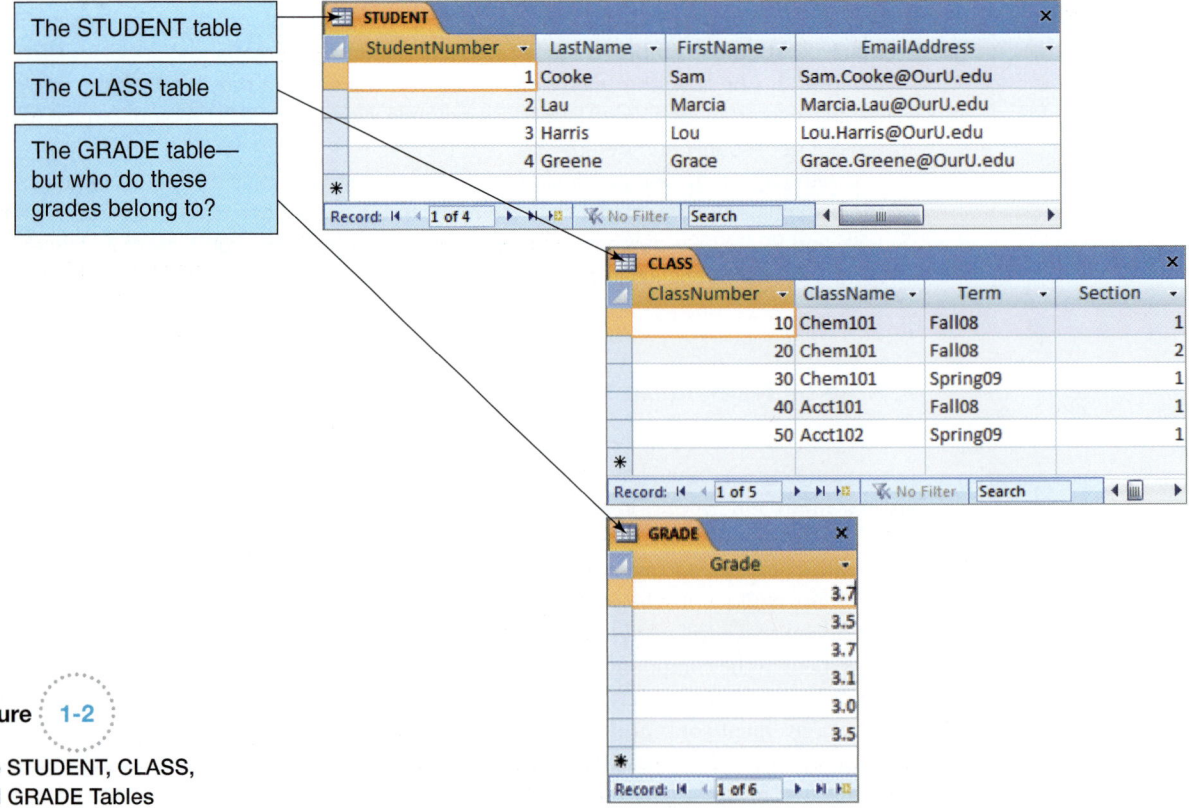

Figure 1-2

The STUDENT, CLASS, and GRADE Tables

The STUDENT table

The CLASS table

The GRADE table with foreign keys—now each grade is linked back to the STUDENT and CLASS tables

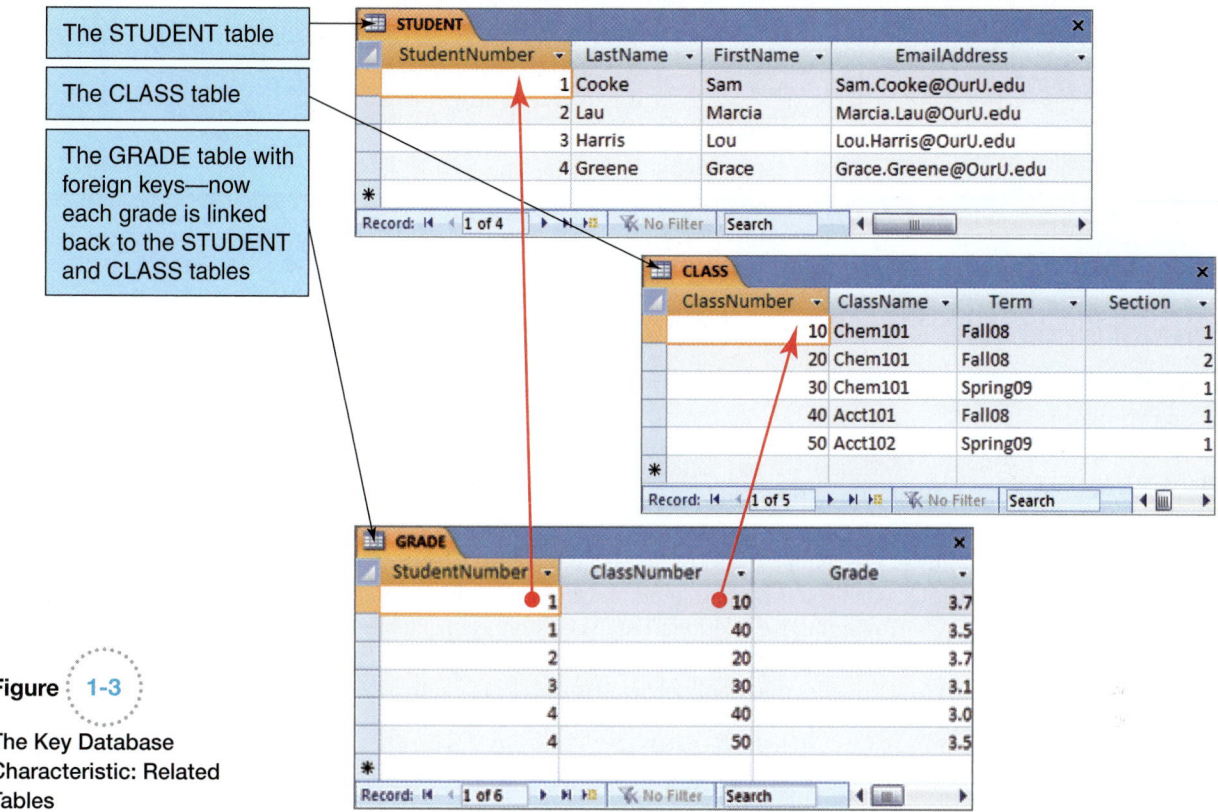

Figure 1-3

The Key Database Characteristic: Related Tables

Figure 1-3 illustrates an important characteristic of database processing. Each row in a table is uniquely indentified by a **primary key**, and the values of these keys are used to create the relationships between the tables. For example, in the STUDENT table, StudentNumber serves as the primary key. Each value of StudentNumber is unique, and uniquely indentifies on student. Thus, StudentNumber 100 identifies Sam Cooke. Similarly, ClassNumber in the CLASS table identifies each class.

By comparing Figures 1-2 and 1-3, we can see how the primary keys of STUDENT and CLASS were added to the GRADE table to provide GRADE with a primary key of (StudentNumber, ClassNumber) to uniquely identify each row. More important, in GRADE StudentNumber and ClassNumber each now serves as a **foreign key**. A foreign key provides the link between two tables. By adding a foreign key, we create a **relationship** between the two tables.

Figure 1-4 shows a Microsoft Access 2007 view of the tables and relationships shown in Figure 1-3. In Figure 1-4, primary keys in each table are marked with key symbols, and connecting lines representing the relationships are drawn from the foreign keys (in GRADE) to the corresponding primary keys (in STUDENT and CLASS). The symbols on the relationship line (the number 1 and the infinity symbol) mean that, for example, one student in STUDENT can be linked to many grades in GRADE.

Databases Create Information

In order to make decisions, we need information upon which to base those decisions. Since we have already defined *data* as recorded facts and numbers, we can now define[1] **information** as:

- Knowledge derived from data.
- Data presented in a meaningful context.
- Data processed by summing, ordering, averaging, grouping, comparing or other similar operations.

---

[1] These definitions are from David M. Kroenke's books *Using MIS* (2nd ed.) (Upper Saddle River, NJ: Prentice-Hall, 2008) and *Experiencing MIS* (2nd ed.) (Upper Saddle River, NJ: Prentice-Hall, 2009). See these books for a full discussion of these definitions, as well as a discussion of a fourth definition, "a difference that makes a difference."

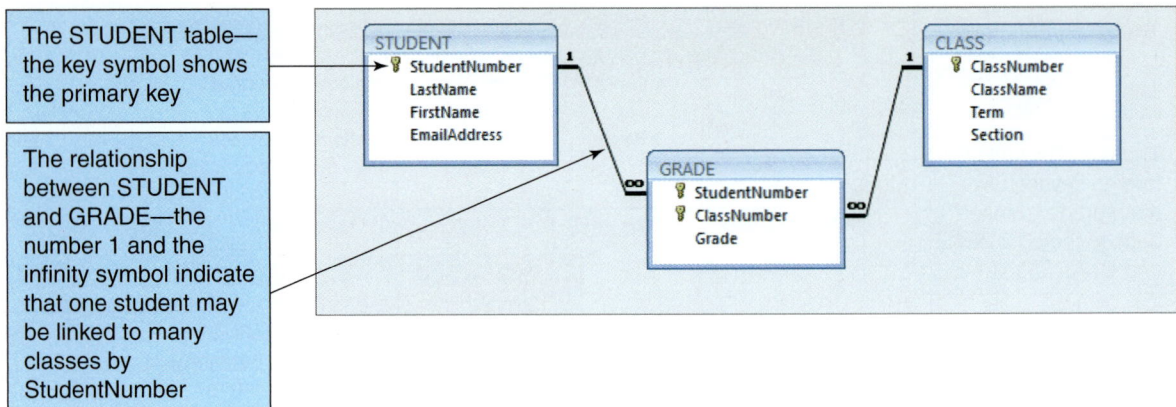

The STUDENT table—the key symbol shows the primary key

The relationship between STUDENT and GRADE—the number 1 and the infinity symbol indicate that one student may be linked to many classes by StudentNumber

Figure 1-4

Microsoft Access 2007 View of Tables and Relationships

Databases record facts and figures, so they record data. They do so, however, in a way that enables them to produce information. The data in Figure 1-3 can be manipulated to produce a student's GPA, the average GPA for a class, the average number of students in a class, and so forth. In Chapter 2, you will be introduced to a language called Structured Query Language (SQL) that you can use to produce information from database data.

To summarize, relational databases store data in tables, and they represent the relationships among the rows of those tables. They do so in a way that facilitates the production of information. We will discuss the relational database model in depth in Part 2 of this book.

Database Examples

Today, database technology is part of almost every information system. This fact is not surprising when we consider that every information system needs to store data and the relationships among those data. Still, the vast array of applications that use this technology is staggering. Consider, for example, the applications listed in Figure 1-5.

Single-User Database Applications

In Figure 1-5, the first application is used by a single salesperson to keep track of the customers she has called and the contacts that she's had with them. Most salespeople do not build their own contact manager applications; instead, they license products such as GoldMine (see *www.frontrange.com/goldmine*) or ACT! (see *www.act.com*).

Multiuser Database Applications

The next applications in Figure 1-5 are those that involve more than one user. The patient-scheduling application, for example, may have 15 to 50 users. These users will be appointment clerks, office administrators, nurses, dentists, doctors, and so forth. A database like this one may have as many as 100,000 rows of data in perhaps 5 or 10 different tables.

When more than one user employs a database application, there is always the chance that one user's work may interfere with another's. Two appointment clerks, for example, might assign the same appointment to two different patients. Special concurrency-control mechanisms are used to coordinate activity against the database to prevent such conflict. You will learn about these mechanisms in Chapter 9.

The third row of Figure 1-5 shows an even larger database application. A customer relationship management (CRM) system is an information system that manages customer contacts from initial solicitation through acceptance, purchase, continuing purchase, support, and so forth. CRM systems are used by salespeople, sales managers, customer service and support staff, and other personnel. A CRM database in a larger company might have 500 users and 10 million or more rows in perhaps 50 or more tables. According to Microsoft, in 2004 Verizon had an SQL Server customer database that contained more than 15 terabytes of data. If that data were published in books, a bookshelf 450 miles long would be required to hold them.

Enterprise resource planning (ERP) is an information system that touches every department in a manufacturing company. It includes sales, inventory, production planning, purchasing,

Application	Example Users	Number of Users	Typical Size	Remarks
Sales contact manager	Salesperson	1	2,000 rows	Products such as **GoldMine** and Act! are database centric.
Patient appointment (doctor, dentist)	Medical office	15 to 50	100,000 rows	Vertical market software vendors incorporate databases into their software products.
Customer Relationship Management (CRM)	Sales, marketing, or customer service departments	500	10 million rows	Major vendors such as Siebel and PeopleSoft build applications around the database.
Enterprise Resource Planning (ERP)	An entire organization	5,000	10 million+ rows	SAP uses a database as a central repository for ERP data.
E-commerce site	Internet users	Possibly millions	1 billion+ rows	Drugstore.com has a database that grows at the rate of 20 million rows per day!
Digital dashboard	Senior managers	500	100,000 rows	Extractions, summaries, and consolidations of operational databases.
Data mining	Business analysts	25	100,000 to millions+	Data are extracted, reformatted, cleaned, and filtered for use by statistical data mining tools.

Figure 1-5

Example Database Uses

and other business functions. SAP is the leading vendor of ERP applications, and a key element of its product is a database that integrates data from these various business functions. An ERP system may have 5,000 or more users and perhaps 100 million rows in several hundred tables.

E-Commerce Database Applications

E-commerce is another important database application. Databases are a key component of e-commerce order entry, billing, shipping, and customer support. Surprisingly, however, the largest databases at an e-commerce site are not order-processing databases. The largest databases are those that track customer browser behavior. Most of the prominent e-commerce companies, such as Amazon.com (*www.amazon.com*) and Drugstore.com (*www.drugstore.com*) keep track of the Web pages and the Web page components that they send to their customers. They also track customer clicks, additions to shopping carts, order purchases, abandoned shopping carts, and so forth.

E-commerce companies use Web activity databases to determine which Web page items are popular and successful and which are not. They also can conduct experiments to determine if a purple background generates more orders than a blue one, and so forth. Such Web usage databases are huge. For example, Drugstore.com adds 20 million rows to its Web log database each day!

Reporting and Data Mining Database Applications

Two other example applications in Figure 1-5 are digital dashboards and data mining applications. These applications use the data generated by order processing and other operational systems to produce information to help manage the enterprise. Such applications do not generate new data; instead they summarize existing data to provide insights to management. Digital dashboards and other reporting systems assess past and current performance. Data mining applications predict future performance. We will consider such applications in Chapter 15. The bottom line is that database technology is used in almost every information system and involves databases ranging in size from a few thousand rows to many millions of rows.

> **BY THE WAY** Do not assume that just because a database is small that its structure is simple. For example, consider parts distribution for a company that sells $1 million in parts per year and parts distribution for a company that sells $100 million in parts per year. Despite the difference in sales, the companies have similar databases. Both have the same kinds of data, about the same number of tables of data, and the same level of complexity in data relationships. Only the amount of data varies from one to the other. Thus, although a database for a small business may be small, it is not necessarily simple.

The Components of a Database System

As shown in Figure 1-6, a database system is typically defined to consist of four components: users, the database application, the database management system (DBMS), and the database. However, given the importance of **Structured Query Language (SQL)**, an internationally recognized standard language that is understood by all commercials DBMS products, in database processing and the fact that database applications typically send SQL statements to the DBMS for processing, we can refine our illustration of a database system to appear as shown in Figure 1-7.

Starting from the right of Figure 1-7, the **database** is a collection of related tables and other structures. The **database management system (DBMS)** is a computer program used to create, process, and administer the database. The DBMS receives requests encoded in SQL and translates those requests into actions on the database. The DBMS is a large, complicated program that is licensed from a software vendor; companies almost never write their own DBMS programs.

A **database application** is a set of one or more computer programs that serves as an intermediary between the user and the DBMS. Application programs read or modify database data by sending SQL statements to the DBMS. Application programs also present data to users in the format of forms and reports. Application programs can be acquired from software vendors, and they are also frequently written in-house. The knowledge you gain from this text will help you write database applications.

Users, the fourth component of a database system, employ a database application to keep track of things. They use forms to read, enter, and query data, and they produce reports to convey information.

Figure 1-6

The Components of a Database System

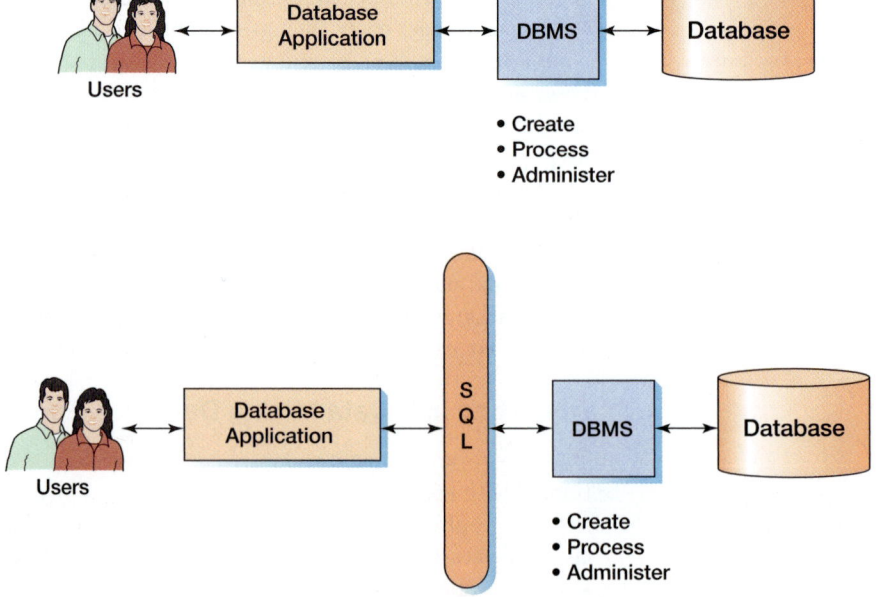

Figure 1-7

The Components of a Database System with SQL

Figure   1-8

Basic Functions of
Application Programs

- Create and process forms
- Process user queries
- Create and process reports
- Execute application logic
- Control application

Database Applications and SQL

Figure 1-7 shows the database applications that users interact with directly. Figure 1-8 lists the basic functions of database applications.

First, an application program creates and processes forms. Figure 1-9 shows a typical form for entering and processing student enrollment data for the Student-Class-Grade database shown in Figures 1-3 and 1-4. Notice that this form hides the structure of the underlying tables from the user. By comparing the tables and data in Figures 1-3 and 1-4 to the form in Figure 1-9, we can see that data from the CLASS table appears at the top of the form, while data from the STUDENT table is presented in a tabular section labeled Class Enrollment Data.

The goal of this form, like that for all data entry forms, is to present the data in a format that is useful for the users, regardless of the underlying table structure. Behind the form, the application processes the database in accordance with the users' actions. The application generates an SQL statement to insert, update, or delete data for any of the tables that underlie this form.

The second function of application programs is to process user queries. The application program first generates a query request and sends it to the DBMS. Results are then formatted and returned to the user. Applications use SQL statements and pass them to the DBMS for processing. To give you a taste of SQL, here is a sample SQL statement for processing the STUDENT table in Figure 1-1:

```
SELECT     LastName, FirstName, EmailAddress
FROM       STUDENT
WHERE      StudentNumber > 2;
```

Figure   1-9

An Example Data Entry Form

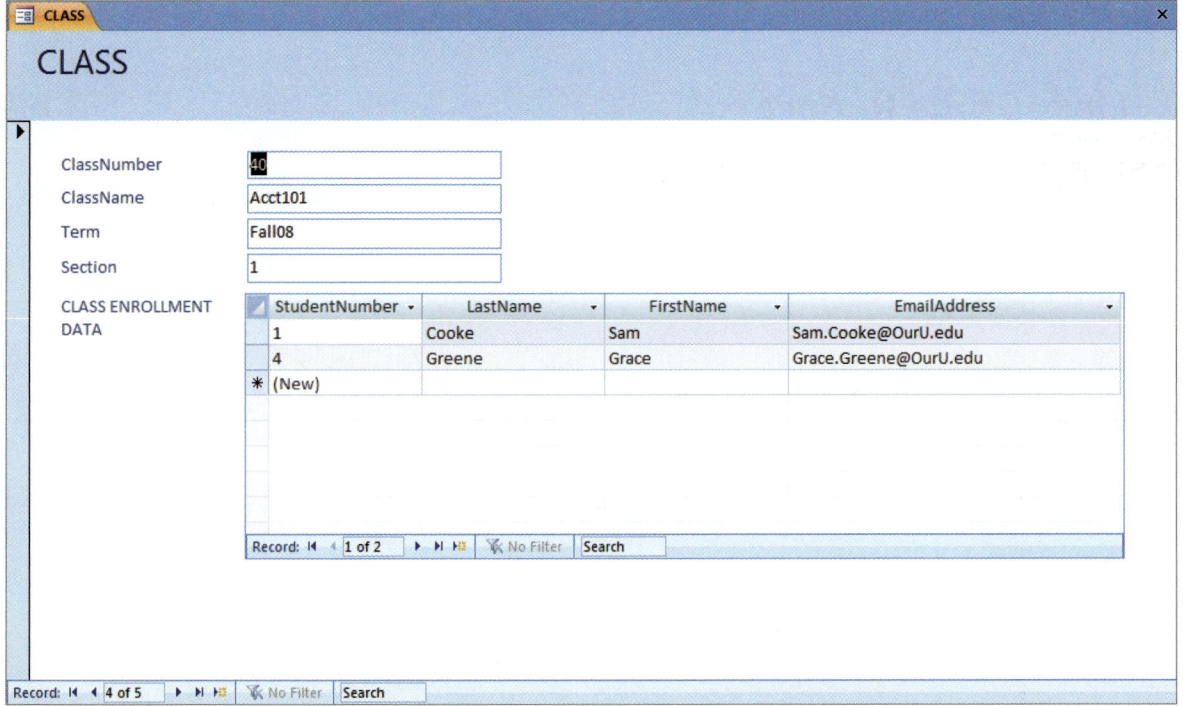

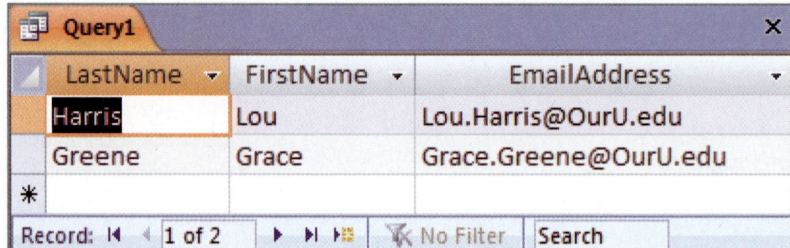

Figure 1-10

Example SQL Query Results

This SQL statement is a query statement, which asks the DBMS to obtain specific data from a database. In this case, the query asks for the last name, first name, and e-mail address of all students having a StudentNumber greater than 2. The results of this SQL statement are shown (as displayed in Microsoft Access 2007) in Figure 1-10. As shown in Figure 1-10, running this SQL statement will produce the LastName, FirstName, and EmailAddress for students Harris and Greene.

The third function of an application is to create and process reports. This function is somewhat similar to the second because the application program first queries the DBMS for data (again using SQL). The application then formats the query results as a report. Figure 1-11 shows a report that displays all the Student-Class-Grade database shown in Figure 1-3 sorted by Class Number, Section and Last Name. Notice that the report, like the form in Figure 1-9, is structured according to the users' needs, not according to the underlying table structure.

In addition to generating forms, queries, and reports, the application program takes other actions to update the database in accordance with application-specific logic. For example, suppose a user using an order-entry application requests 10 units of a particular item. Suppose further that when the application program queries the database (via the DBMS), it finds that only 8 units are in stock. What should happen? It depends on the logic of that particular application. Perhaps no units should be removed from inventory, and the user should be notified, or perhaps the 8 units should be removed and 2 more placed on back order. Perhaps some other action should be taken. Whatever the case, it is the job of the application program to execute the appropriate logic.

Finally, the last function for application programs listed in Figure 1-8 is to control the application. This is done in two ways. First, the application needs to be written so that only logical options are presented to the user. For example, the application may generate a menu with user choices. In this case, the application needs to ensure that only appropriate choices are available. Second, the application needs to control data activities with the DBMS. The application might

Figure 1-11

Example Report

Class Grade Report

Class Number	Class Name	Term	Section	Last Name	First Name	Grade
10	Chem101	Fall08	1			
				Cooke	Sam	3.7
20	Chem101	Fall08	2			
				Lau	Marcia	3.7
30	Chem101	Spring09	1			
				Harris	Lou	3.1
40	Acct101	Fall08	1			
				Cooke	Sam	3.5
				Greene	Grace	3.0
50	Acct102	Spring09	1			
				Greene	Grace	3.5

direct the DBMS, for example, to make a certain set of data changes as a unit. The application might tell the DBMS to either make all these changes or none of them. You will learn about such control topics in Chapter 9.

The DBMS

The DBMS, or database management system, creates, processes, and administers the database. A DBMS is a large, complicated product that is almost always licensed from a software vendor. One DBMS product is Microsoft Access. Other commercial DBMS products are Oracle Database, from Oracle Corporation; DB2, from IBM Corporation; SQL Server, from Microsoft Corporation; and MySQL, from Sun Microsystems.[2] Dozens of other DBMS products exist, but these five have the lion's share of the market. Figure 1-12 lists the functions of a DBMS.

A DBMS is used to create a database and to create the tables and other supporting structures inside that database. As an example of the latter, suppose that we have an EMPLOYEE table with 10,000 rows and that this table includes a column, DepartmentName, that records the name of the department in which an employee works. Furthermore, suppose that we frequently need to access employee data by DepartmentName. Because this is a large database, searching through the table to find, for example, all employees in the accounting department would take a long time. To improve performance, we can create an index (akin to the index at the back of a book) for DepartmentName to show which employees are in which departments. Such an index is an example of a supporting structure that is created and maintained by a DBMS.

The next two functions of a DBMS are to read and modify database data. To do this, a DBMS receives SQL and other requests and transforms those requests into actions on the database files. Another DBMS function is to maintain all the database structures. For example, from time to time it might be necessary to change the format of a table or another supporting structure. Developers use a DBMS to make such changes.

With most DBMS products, it is possible to declare rules about data values and have a DBMS enforce them. For example, in the Student-Class-Grade database tables in Figure 1-3, what would happen if a user mistakenly entered a value of 900 for StudentNumber in the GRADE table? No such student exists, so such a value would cause numerous errors. To prevent this situation, it is possible to tell the DBMS that any value of StudentNumber in the GRADE table must already be a value of StudentNumber in the STUDENT table. If no such value exists, the insert or update request should be disallowed. The DBMS then enforces these rules, which are called **referential integrity constraints**.

The last three functions of a DBMS listed in Figure 1-12 have to do with database administration. A DBMS controls **concurrency** by ensuring that one user's work does not inappropriately interfere with another user's work. This important (and complicated) function is discussed in Chapter 9. Also, a DBMS contains a security system that ensures that only authorized users perform authorized actions on the database. For example, users can be prevented from seeing certain data. Similarly, users' actions can be confined to making only certain types of data changes on specified data.

Finally, a DBMS provides facilities for backing up database data and recovering it from backups, when necessary. The database, as a centralized repository of data, is a valuable

Figure 1-12

Functions of a DBMS

- Create database
- Create tables
- Create supporting structures (e.g., indexes)
- Read database data
- Modify (insert, update, or delete) database data
- Maintain database structures
- Enforce rules
- Control concurrency
- Provide security
- Perform backup and recovery

---

[2] As this book goes to press, Oracle Corporation has concluded an agreement with Sun Microsystems to purchase Sun Microsystems. This will make Oracle the owner of both Oracle Database and MySQL. See http://www.sun.com/third-party/global/oracle/.

organizational asset. Consider, for example, the value of a book database to a company such as Amazon.com. Because the database is so important, steps need to be taken to ensure that no data will be lost in the event of errors, hardware or software problems, or natural or human catastrophes.

The Database

The last component in Figure 1-7 is the database. A database is a self-describing collection of integrated tables. **Integrated tables** are tables that store both data and the relationships among the data. The tables in Figure 1-3 are *integrated* because they store not just student, class, and grade data, but also data about the relationships among the rows of data.

A database is **self-describing** because it contains a description of itself. Thus, databases contain not only tables of user data, but also tables of data that describe that user data. Such descriptive data is called **metadata**, because it is data about data. The form and format of metadata varies from DBMS to DBMS. Figure 1-13 shows generic metadata tables that describe the tables and columns for the database in Figure 1-3.

You can examine metadata to determine if particular tables, columns, indexes, or other structures exist in a database. For example, the following statement queries the Microsoft SQL

Figure  **1-13**

Typical Metadata Tables

USER_TABLES Table

TableName	NumberColumns	PrimaryKey
STUDENT	3	StudentNumber
CLASS	4	ClassNumber
GRADE	3	(StudentNumber, ClassNumber)

USER_COLUMNS Table

ColumnName	TableName	DataType	Length (bytes)
StudentNumber	STUDENT	Integer	4
LastName	STUDENT	Text	25
FirstName	STUDENT	Text	25
EmailAddress	STUDENT	Text	100
ClassNumber	CLASS	Integer	4
Name	CLASS	Text	25
Term	CLASS	Text	12
Section	CLASS	SmallInteger	2
StudentNumber	GRADE	Integer	4
ClassNumber	GRADE	Integer	4
Grade	GRADE	Decimal	(2, 1)

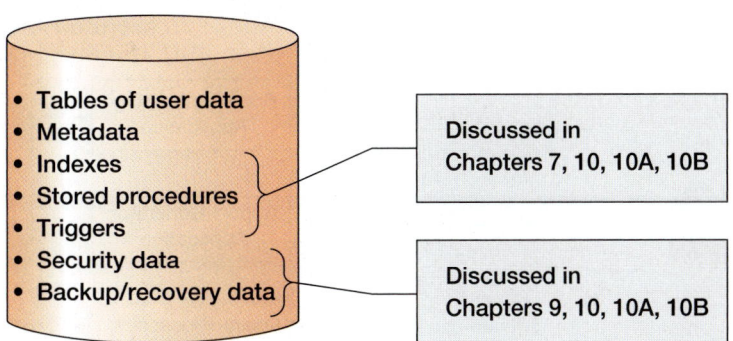

Figure 1-14

Database Contents

Server metadata table SYSOBJECTS to determine if a user table (Type = 'U') named CLASS exists in the database. If it does, the table is dropped (removed) from the database.

```
IF EXITS
     (SELECT      *
     FROM         SYSOBJECTS
     WHERE        [Name]='CLASS'
          AND     Type='U')
   DROP TABLE CLASS;
```

Do not be concerned with the syntax of this statement. You will learn what it means and how to write such statements yourself as we proceed. For now, just understand that this is one way that database administrators use metadata.

> **BY THE WAY** Because metadata is stored in tables, you can use SQL to query it, as just illustrated. Thus, by learning how to write SQL to query user tables, you will also learn how to write SQL to query metadata. To do that, you just apply the SQL statements to metadata tables rather than user tables.

In addition to user tables and metadata, databases contain other elements, as shown in Figure 1-14. These other components will be described in detail in subsequent chapters. For now, however, understand that indexes are structures that speed the sorting and searching of database data. Triggers and stored procedures are programs that are stored within the database. Triggers are used to maintain database accuracy and consistency and to enforce data constraints. Stored procedures are used for database administration tasks and are sometimes part of database applications. You will learn more about these different elements in Chapters 7, 10, 10A, and 10B.

Security data defines users, groups, and allowed permissions for users and groups. The particulars depend on the DBMS product in use. Finally, backup and recovery data are used to save database data to backup devices as well as to recover the database after failure. You will learn more about security and backup and recovery data in Chapters 9, 10, 10A, and 10B.

Personal Versus Enterprise-Class Database Systems

We can divide database systems and DBMS products into two classes: personal database systems and enterprise-class database systems.

What Is Microsoft Access?

We need to clear up a common misconception: Microsoft Access is *not* just a DBMS. Rather, it is a **personal database system**: a DBMS *plus* an application generator. Although Microsoft Access contains a DBMS engine that creates, processes, and administers the database, it also contains form, report, and query components that are the Microsoft Access application

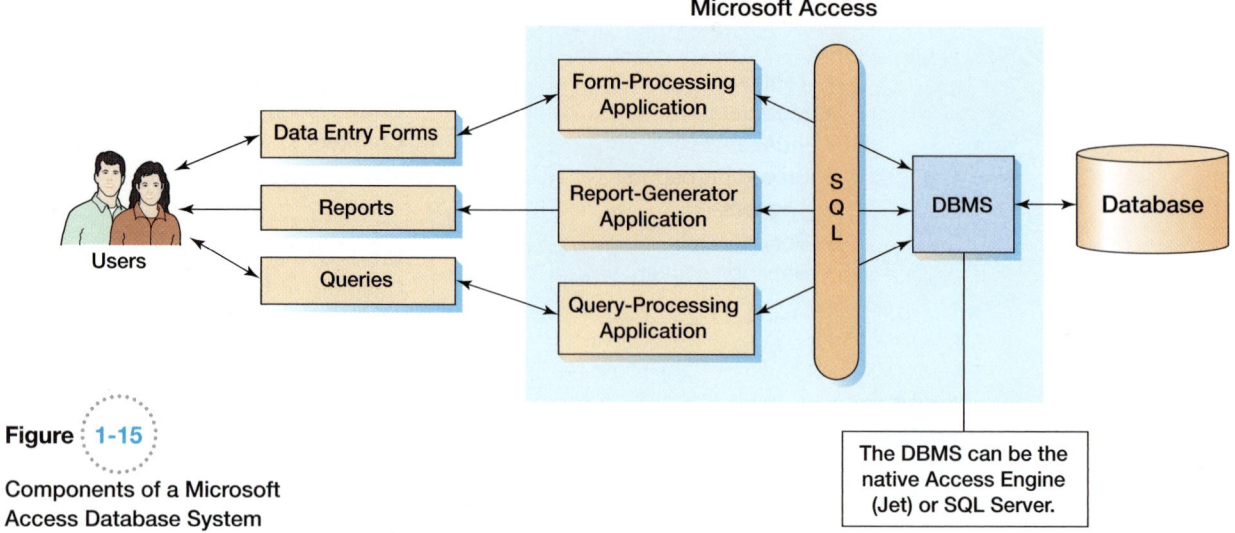

Figure 1-15

Components of a Microsoft Access Database System

generator. The components of Microsoft Access are shown in Figure 1-15, which illustrates that the Microsoft Access form, report, and query applications create SQL statements and pass them to the DBMS for processing.

Microsoft Access is a low-end product intended for individuals and small workgroups. As such, Microsoft has done all that it can to hide the underlying database technology from the user. Users interact with the application through data entry forms like the one shown in Figure 1-9. They also request reports and perform queries against the database data. Microsoft Access then processes the forms, produces the reports, and runs the queries. Internally, the application components hidden under the Access cover use SQL to call the DBMS, which is also hidden under that cover. At Microsoft, the DBMS engine within Access is called Jet. You seldom hear about Jet because Microsoft does not sell Jet as a separate product.

> **BY THE WAY** Although Microsoft Access is the best known personal database system, it is not the only one. OpenOffice Base is a personal database system distributed as part of the OpenOffice.org software suite, which is available at *www.openoffice.org*.

Although hiding the technology is an effective strategy for beginners working on small databases, it won't work for database professionals who work with applications, such as most of those described in Figure 1-5. For larger, more complex databases, it is necessary to understand the technology and components that Microsoft hides.

Nonetheless, because Microsoft Access is included in the Microsoft Office suite, it is often the first DBMS used by students. In fact, you may have already learned to use Microsoft Access in other classes you have taken, and in this book we will provide some examples using Microsoft Access 2007. If you are not familiar with Microsoft Access 2007, you should work through Appendix A, "Getting Started with Microsoft Access 2007."

> **BY THE WAY** With Microsoft Access 2000 and later versions, you can effectively replace Jet with Microsoft's enterprise-class DBMS product—SQL Server. You would do this if you wanted to process a large database or if you needed the advanced functions and features of SQL Server.

What Is an Enterprise-Class Database System?

Figure 1-16 shows the components of an **enterprise-class database system**. Here, the applications and the DBMS are not under the same cover as they are in Microsoft Access. Instead, the applications are separate from each other and separate from the DBMS.

Database Applications in an Enterprise-Class Database System

Earlier in this chapter, we discussed the basic functions of an application program, and these functions are summarized in Figure 1-8. However, as exemplified by the list in Figure 1-5, dozens of different types of database applications are available, and database applications in an enterprise-class database system introduce functions and features beyond the basics. For example, Figure 1-16 shows applications that connect to the database over a corporate network. Such applications are sometimes called *client/server applications* because the application program is a client that connects to a database server. Client/server applications often are written in programming languages such as VB.NET, C++, or Java.

A second category of applications in Figure 1-16 is e-commerce and other applications that run on a Web server. Users connect to such applications via Web browsers such as Microsoft Internet Explorer, Mozilla Firefox, and Google Chrome. Common Web servers include Microsoft's Internet Information Server (IIS) and Apache. Common languages for Web server applications are PHP, Java, and the Microsoft .NET languages such as C# and VB.NET. We will discuss some of the technology for such applications in Chapter 13.

A third category of applications is reporting applications that publish the results of database queries on a corporate portal or other Web site. Such reporting applications are often created using third-party report generation and digital dashboard products from vendors such as IBM (Cognos) and MicroStrategy (MicroStrategy 9). We will describe these applications in Chapter 15.

The last category of applications is XML Web services. These applications use a combination of the XML markup language and other standards to enable program-to-program communication. In this way, the code that comprises an application is distributed over several different computers. Web services can be written in Java or any of the .NET languages. We will discuss this important new class of applications in Chapter 13.

All of these database applications get and put database data by sending SQL statements to the DBMS. These applications may create forms and reports, or they may send their results to other programs. They also may implement application logic that goes beyond simple form and report processing. For example, an order entry application uses application logic to deal with out-of-stock items and backorders.

The DBMS in an Enterprise-Class Database Systems

As stated earlier, the DBMS manages the database. It processes SQL statements and provides other features and functions for creating, processing, and administering the database. Figure 1-17

Figure 1-16

Components of an Enterprise-class Database System

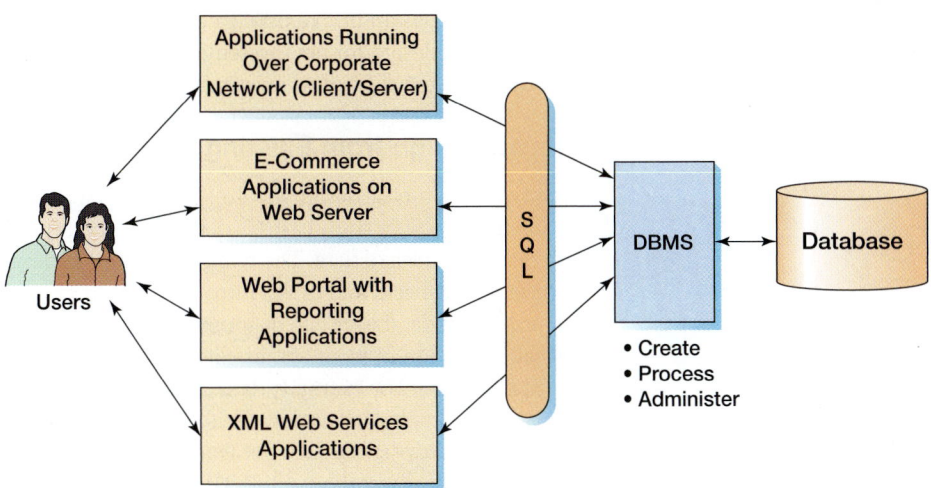

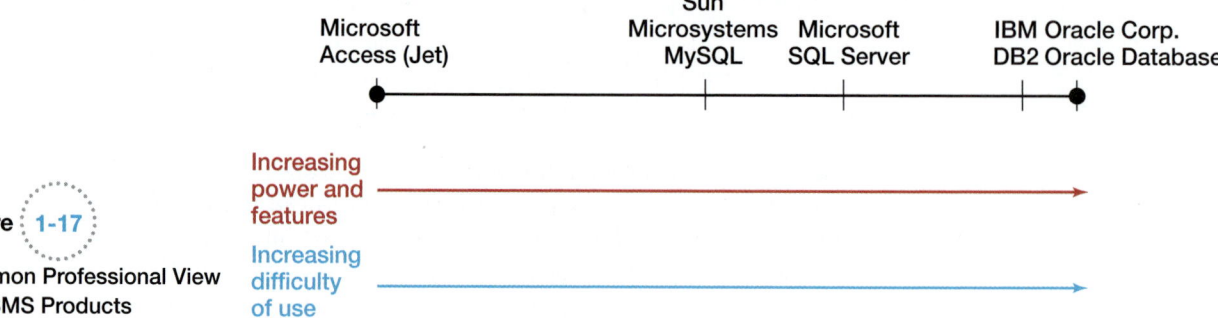

Figure 1-17

Common Professional View
of DBMS Products

presents the five most prominent DBMS products. The products are shown in order of increasing power, features, and difficulty of use.

Access (really Jet) is the easiest to use and the least powerful. Sun Microsystems MySQL is a powerful, open source DBMS frequently chosen for Web applications. Microsoft SQL Server has far more power than its stable mate Microsoft Access—it can process larger databases, faster, and it includes features for multiuser control, backup and recovery, and other administrative functions. DB2 is a DBMS product from IBM. Most people would agree that it has faster performance than SQL Server, that it can handle larger databases, and that it is also more difficult to use. Finally, the fastest and most capable DBMS is Oracle Database from the Oracle Corporation. Oracle Database can be configured to offer very high performance on exceedingly large databases that operate 24/7, year after year. Oracle Database is also far more difficult to use and administer than Microsoft SQL Server.

Database Design

Database design is both difficult and important. Determining the proper structure of tables, the proper relationships among tables, the appropriate data constraints, and other structural components is challenging, and sometimes even daunting. Consequently, the world is full of poorly designed databases. Such databases do not perform well. They may require application developers to write overly complex and contrived SQL to get wanted data, they may be difficult to adapt to new and changing requirements, or they fail in some other way.

Because database design is both difficult and important, we will devote most of the first half of this text to the topic. As shown in Figure 1-18, there are three types of database design:

- Database design from existing data
- Database design for new systems development
- Database redesign of an existing database

Database Design from Existing Data

The first type of database design involves databases that are constructed from existing data, as shown in Figure 1-19. In some cases, a development team is given a set of spreadsheets or a set of text files with tables of data. The team is required to design a database and import the data from those spreadsheets and tables into a new database.

Alternatively, databases can be created from extracts of other databases. This alternative is especially common in business intelligence (BI) systems, which include reporting and data mining applications. For example, data from an operational database, such as a CRM or ERP database, may be copied into a new database that will be used only for studies and analysis. As you will learn in Chapter 13, such databases are used in facilities called **data warehouses** and **data marts**. The data warehouse and data mart databases store data specifically organized for research and reporting purposes, and these data often are exported to other analytical tools, such as SAS's Enterprise Miner, SPSS's Clementine, or Insightful Corporation's I-Miner.

- From Existing Data (Chapters 3 and 4)
    - Analyze spreadsheets and other data tables
    - Extract data from other databases
    - Design using normalization principles
- New Systems Development (Chapters 5 and 6)
    - Create data model from application requirements
    - Transform data model into database design
- Database Redesign (Chapter 8)
    - Migrate databases to newer databases
    - Integrate two or more databases
    - Reverse engineer and design new databases using normalization principles and data model transformation

Figure 1-18

Three Types of Database Design

Note: Chapter 7 discusses database implementation using SQL. You need that knowledge before you can understand database redesign.

When creating a database from existing data, database developers must determine the appropriate structure for the new database. A common issue is how the multiple files or tables in the new database should be related. However, even the import of a single table can pose design questions. Figure 1-20 shows two different ways of importing a simple table of employees and their departments. Should this data be stored as one table or two?

Decisions such as this are not arbitrary. Database professionals use a set of principles, collectively called **normalization**, or **normal forms**, to guide and assess database designs. You will learn those principles and their role in database design in Chapter 3.

Database Design for New Systems Development

A second way that databases are designed is for the development of new information systems. As shown in Figure 1-21, requirements for a new system, such as desired data entry forms and reports, user requirements statements, use cases, and other requirements, are analyzed to create the database design.

In all but the simplest system development projects, the step from user requirements to database design is too big. Accordingly, the development team proceeds in two steps. First, the

Figure 1-19

Databases Originating from Existing Data

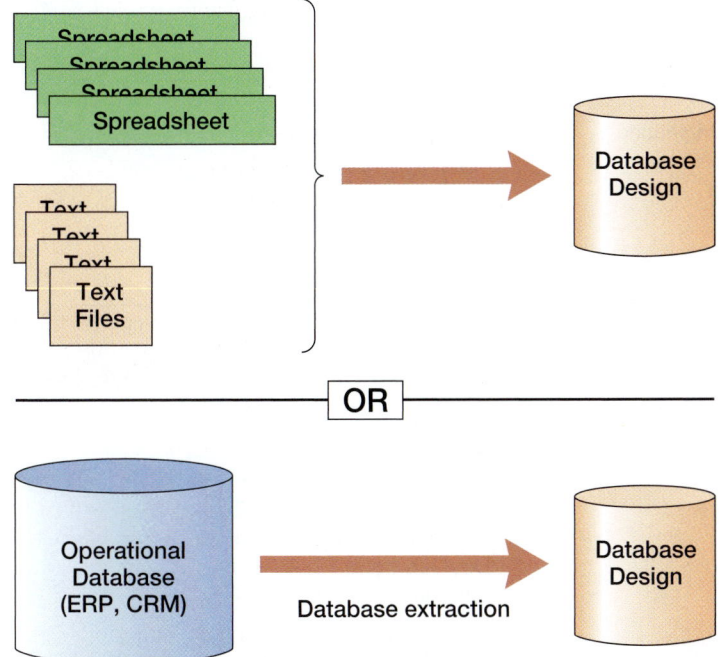

EmpNum	EmpName	DeptNum	DeptName
100	Jones	10	Accounting
150	Lau	20	Marketing
200	McCauley	10	Accounting
300	Griffin	10	Accounting

(a) One-Table Design

OR?

DeptNum	DeptName
10	Accounting
20	Marketing

EmpNum	EmpName	DeptNum
100	Jones	10
150	Lau	20
200	McCauley	10
300	Griffin	10

(b) Two-Table Design

Figure 1-20

Data Import: One or Two Tables?

team creates a **data model** from the requirements statements and then transforms that data model into a database design. You can think of a data model as a blueprint that is used as a design aid on the way to a **database design**, which is the basis for constructing the actual database in a DBMS.

In Chapter 5, you will learn about the most popular data modeling technique—**entity-relationship (ER) data modeling**. You also will see how to use the entity-relationship model to represent a variety of common form and report patterns. Then, in Chapter 6, you will learn how to transform entity-relationship data models into database designs.

Database Redesign

Database redesign also requires that databases are designed. As shown in Figure 1-22, there are two common types of database redesign.

In the first, a database is adapted to new or changing requirements. This process sometimes is called **database migration**. In the migration process, tables may be created, modified, or removed; relationships may be altered; data constraints may be changed; and so forth.

Figure 1-21

Databases Originating from New Systems Development

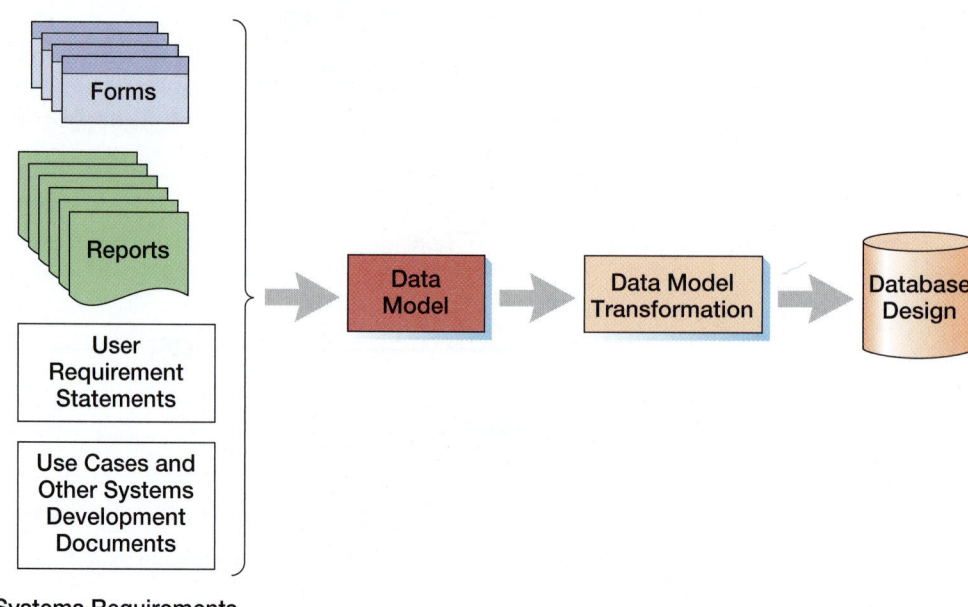

Systems Requirements

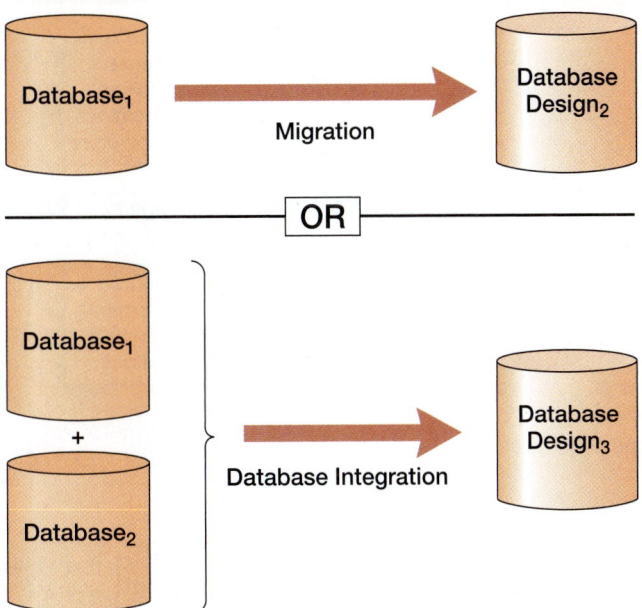

Figure 1-22

Databases Originating from
Database Redesign

The second type of database redesign involves the integration of two or more databases. This type of redesign is common when adapting or removing legacy systems. It is also common for enterprise application integration, when two or more previously separate information systems are adapted to work with each other.

Database redesign is complicated. There is no getting around that fact. If this is your first exposure to database design, your instructor may skip this topic. If this is the case, after you have gained more experience, you should reread this material. In spite of its difficulty, database redesign is important.

To understand database redesign, you need to know SQL statements for defining database structures and more advanced SQL statements for querying and updating a database. Consequently, we will not address database redesign until after Chapter 7, which presents SQL statements and techniques for creating and altering the tables that make up a database.

What You Need to Learn

In your career, you may work with database technology as either a user or as a database administrator. As a user you may be a **knowledge worker** who prepares reports, mines data, and does other types of data analysis or you may be a **programmer** who writes applications that process the database. Alternatively, you might be a **database administrator** who designs, constructs, and manages the database itself. Users are primarily concerned with constructing SQL statements to get and put the data they want. Database administrators are primarily concerned with the management of the database. The domains for each of these roles are shown in Figure 1-23.

> **BY THE WAY** The most exciting and interesting jobs in technology are always those on the leading edge. If you live in the United States and are concerned about outsourcing, a recent study by the Rand Corporation[3] indicates that the most secure jobs in the United States involve the adaptation of new technology to solve business problems in innovative ways.
>
> Right now, the leading edge involves the integration of XML, Web services, and database processing. You will need all of the fundamentals presented in this book, especially the material in Chapter 12, to work in this exciting new area.

---

[3] Karoly, Lynn A., and Constantijn W. A. Panis. *The 21st Century at Work.* (Santa Monica, CA: The Rand Corporation, 2004).

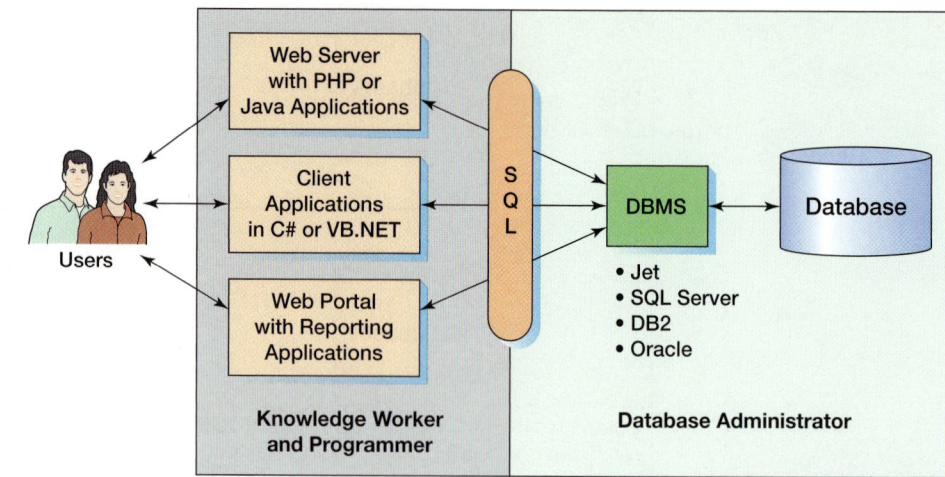

Figure 1-23

Working Domains of
Knowledge Workers,
Programmers, and Database
Administrators

Topic	Chapter	Importance to Knowledge Worker and Programmer	Importance to Database Administrator
Basic SQL	Chapter 2	1	1
Design via normalization	Chapter 3	2	1
Data modeling	Chapter 4	1	1
Data model transformation	Chapter 5	2	1
DDL SQL	Chapter 6	2	1
Constraint enforcement	Chapter 7	3	1
Database redesign	Chapter 8	3	2, but 1 for senior DBA
Database administration	Chapter 9	2	1
SQL Server, Oracle, MySQL specifics	Chapters 10, 10A, 10B	3	1
Database application technology	Chapters 13, 14, 15	1	3

1 = Very important; 2 = Important; 3 = Less important   Warning: Opinions vary, ask your instructor for his or hers.

Figure 1-24

**Priorities of What You Need
to Know**

Both users and database administrators need all of the knowledge in this text. However, the emphasis on each topic differs for the two groups. Figure 1-24 shows our opinion as to the relative importance of each topic to each group. Discuss this table with your instructor. He or she may have knowledge about your local job market that affects the relative importance of these topics.

A Brief History of Database Processing

Database processing emerged around 1970 and has been continuously evolving and changing since then. This continual change has made it a fascinating and thoroughly enjoyable field in which to work. Figure 1-25 summarizes the major eras of database processing.

The Early Years

Prior to 1970, all data were stored in separate files, most of which were kept on reels of magnetic tape. Magnetic disks and drums (magnetic cylinders that are no longer used) were exceedingly expensive and very small. Today's 1.44 megabyte floppy disk (which is now itself a technology declining in use) has more capacity than many disks of that era. Memory was expensive as well. In 1969, we were processing payroll on a computer that had just 32,000 *bytes* of memory, while the computer on which this history is being written has 2 *gigabytes* of memory.

Era	Years	Important Products	Remarks
Predatabase	Before 1970	File managers	All data were stored in separate files. Data integration was very difficult. File storage space was expensive and limited.
Early database	1970–1980	ADABAS, System2000, Total, IDMS, IMS	First products to provide related tables. CODASYL DBTG and hierarchical data models (DL/I) were prevalent.
Emergence of relational model	1978–1985	DB2, Oracle	Early relational DBMS products had substantial inertia to overcome. In time, the advantages weighed out.
Microcomputer DBMS products	1982–1992+	dBase-II, R:base, Paradox, Access	Amazing! A database on a micro. All micro DBMS products were eliminated by Microsoft Access in the early 1990s.
Object-oriented DBMS	1985–2000	Oracle ODBMS and others	Never caught on. Required relational database to be converted. Too much work for perceived benefit.
Web databases	1995–present	IIS, Apache, PHP, ASP.NET, and Java	Stateless characteristic of HTTP was a problem at first. Early applications were simple one-stage transactions. Later, more complex logic developed.
Open source DBMS products	1995–present	MySQL, PostgresQL, and other products	Open source DBMS products provide much of the functionality and features of commercial DBMS products at reduced cost.
XML and Web services	1998–present	XML, SOAP, WSDL, UDDI, and other standards	XML provides tremendous benefits to Web-based database applications. Very important today. May replace relational databases during your career. See Chapter 12.

Figure 1-25

Database History

Integrated processing was an important but very difficult problem. An insurance company, for example, wanted to relate customer account data to customer claim data. Accounts were stored on one magnetic tape, and claims were stored on another. To process claims, the data on the two tapes had to be integrated somehow.

The need for data integration drove the development of the first database technology. By 1973, several commercial DBMS products had emerged. These products were in use by the mid-1970s. The first edition of this text, copyrighted 1977, featured the DBMS products ADABAS, System2000, Total, IDMS, and IMS. Of those five, only ADABAS and IMS are still in use, and neither of them has substantial market share today.

Those early DBMS products varied in the way that they structured data relationships. One method, called **Data Language/I (DL/I)** used hierarchies or trees (see Appendix D) to represent relationships. IMS, which was developed and licensed by IBM, was based on this model. IMS had success at many organizations, particularly among large manufacturers, and is still in limited use today.

Another technique for structuring data relationships used data structures called *networks*. The CODASYL Committee (the group that developed the programming language COBOL) sponsored a subcommittee called the Database Task Group (DBTG). This subcommittee developed a standard data model that came to bear its name—the **CODASYL DBTG** model. It was an unnecessarily complicated model (everyone's favorite idea made it into the committee's design), but several successful DBMS products were developed using it. The most successful was IDMS, and its vendor, the Cullinane Corporation, was the first software company to be listed on the New York Stock Exchange. To the best of our knowledge, no IDMS database is in use today.

The Emergence and Dominance of the Relational Model

In 1970, a then little-known IBM engineer named E. F. Codd published a paper in the *Communications of the ACM*[4] in which he applied the concepts of a branch of mathematics called relational algebra to the problem of "shared data banks," as databases were then known. The results of this work are now the **relational model** for databases, and all relational database DBMS products are built on this model.

Codd's work was at first viewed as too theoretical for practical implementation. Practitioners argued that it was too slow and required so much storage that it would never be useful in the commercial world. However, the relational model and relational database DBMS products became adopted as the best way to create and manage databases.

The 1977 edition of this text featured a chapter on the relational model (which Codd himself reviewed). Many years later, Wayne Ratliff, the creator of the *dBase* series of products for personal computers, stated that he had the idea for *dBase* while reading that very chapter.[5]

> **BY THE WAY** Today, there are as many opportunities for innovation as there were for Wayne Ratliff in 1977. Perhaps you can read Chapter 12 and develop an innovative product that integrates XML and DBMS processing in a new way. Just as in 1977, no product has a lock on the future. Opportunity awaits you!

The relational model, relational algebra, and later, SQL made sense. They were not needlessly complicated; rather, they seemed to boil down the data integration problem to a few essential ideas. Over time, Codd convinced IBM management to develop relational-model DBMS products. The result was IBM's DB2 and its variants, which are still very popular today.

Meanwhile, other companies were considering the relational model as well, and by 1980 several more relational DBMS products had been released. The most prominent and important of those was Oracle Corporation's Oracle Database. Oracle achieved success for many reasons, one of which was that it would run on just about any computer and just about any operating system. (Some users complained, "Yes, and equally badly on all of them." Another, when asked "Should we sell it to communist Russia?" responded, "Only as long as they have to take the documentation with it.")

However, in addition to being able to run on many different types of machines, Oracle Database had, and continues to have, an elegant and efficient internal design. You will learn aspects of that design in the concurrency-control section in Chapter 10A. That excellent design, together with hard-driving and successful sales and marketing, has pushed Oracle to the top of the DBMS market.

Meanwhile, Gordon Moore and others were hard at work at Intel. By the early 1980s, personal computers were prevalent, and DBMS products were developed for them. Developers of microcomputer DBMS products saw the advantages of the relational model and developed their products around it. dBase was the most successful of the early products, but another product,

---

[4] Codd, E. F. "A Relational Model of Data for Large Shared Databanks," *Communications of the ACM*, June 1970, pp. 377–387.
[5] Ratliff, C. Wayne. "dStory: How I Really Developed dBASE," *Data Based Advisor*, March 1991, p. 94.

R:base, was the first to implement true relational algebra and other operations on the PC. Later, another relational DBMS product named Paradox was developed for personal computers. Eventually, Paradox was acquired by Borland.

Alas, it all came to an end when Microsoft entered the picture. Microsoft released Access in 1991 and priced it at $99. No other PC DBMS vendor could survive at that price point. Access killed R:base and Paradox, and then Microsoft bought a dBase "work-alike" product called FoxPro and used it to eliminate dBase. Microsoft has now stopped upgrading Visual FoxPro, but will continue to support it until 2014. Microsoft Access is the only major survivor of that bloodbath of PC DBMS products.

The one main challenge to Microsoft Access actually comes from the Sun Microsystems and the open source software development community, who have taken over development of OpenOffice.org, a downloadable suite of free software products that includes the personal database OpenOffice.org Base (see *www.openoffice.org*).

Post-Relational Developments

In the mid-1980s, **object-oriented programming (OOP)** emerged, and its advantages over traditional structured programming were quickly recognized. By 1990, some vendors had developed **object-oriented DBMS (OODBMS or ODBMS)** products. These products were designed to make it easy to store the data encapsulated in OOP objects. Several special-purpose OODBMS products were developed, and Oracle added OOP constructs to Oracle to enable the creation of a hybrid called an **object-relational DBMS**.

OODBMS never caught on, and today that category of DBMS products is fading away. There were two reasons for their lack of acceptance. First, using an OODBMS required that the relational data be converted from relational format to object-oriented format. By the time OODBMS emerged, billions upon billions of bytes of data were stored in relational format in organizational databases. No company was willing to undergo the expensive travail of converting those databases to be able to use the new OODBMS.

Second, object-oriented databases had no substantial advantage over relational databases for most commercial database processing. As you will see in the next chapter, SQL is not object oriented. But it works, and thousands of developers have created programs that use it. Without a demonstrable advantage over relational databases, no organization was willing to take on the task of converting their data to OODBMS format.

Meanwhile, the Internet took off. By the mid-1990s, it was clear that the Internet was one of the most important phenomena in history. It changed, forever, the ways that customers and businesses relate to each other. Early Web sites were nothing more than online brochures, but within a few years dynamic Web sites that involved querying and processing databases began to appear.

However, one substantial problem existed. HTTP is a stateless protocol; a server receives a request from a user, processes the request, and then forgets about the user and the request. Many database interactions are multistage. A customer views products, adds one or more to a shopping cart, views more products, adds more to the shopping cart, and eventually checks out. A stateless protocol cannot be used for such applications.

Over time, capabilities emerged to overcome this problem. Web application developers learned to add SQL statements to their Web applications, and soon thousands of databases were being processed over the Web. You will learn more about such processing in Chapter 11. An interesting phenomenon was the emergence of open source DBMS products. Open source products generally make the source code widely available so that a group of programmers not bound to a single company can contribute to the program. Further, some form of these products are usually offered as free downloads, although other forms or product support must be purchased from the company that owns the product.

A good example of this is the MySQL DBMS (www.mysql.com). MySQL was originally released in 1995 by the Swedish company MySQL AB. In February 2008, Sun Microsystems bought MySQL AB,[6] but MySQL continues to be available as an open source product, and the free MySQL Community Server edition can be downloaded from the MySQL Web site. MySQL has proven to be especially popular with Web site developers who need to run Web page queries

---

[6] As this book goes to press, Oracle Corporation has concluded an agreement with Sun Microsystems to purchase Sun Microsystems. This will make Oracle the owner of both Oracle Database and MySQL. See http://www.sun.com/third-party/global/oracle.

against an SQL DBMS on a Web server running the Linux operating system. We will work with MySQL in Chapter 10B.

MySQL is not the only open source DBMS product—in fact, as this is being written there are 47 listed on the Wikipedia category page *http://en.wikipedia.org/wiki/Category: Open_source_database_management_systems.*

One interesting outcome of the emergence of open source DBMS products is that companies that typically sell proprietary (closed source) DBMS products now offer free versions of their products. For example, Microsoft now offers SQL Server 2008 Express (*www.microsoft.com/ express/sql/download*), and Oracle Corporation makes its Oracle Database 10g Express Edition available for free (*www.oracle.com/technology/products/database/xe/index.html*). Although neither of these products is as complete or as powerful (for example, in terms of maximum data storage allowed) as some other versions the companies sell, they are useful for projects that require a small database. They are also ideal for students learning to use databases and SQL.

The last row in Figure 1-25 brings us to the present. In the late 1990s, XML was defined to overcome the problems that occur when HTML is used to exchange business documents. The design of the XML family of standards not only solved the problems of HTML, it also meant that XML documents were superior for exchanging views of database data. In 2002, Bill Gates said that "XML is the lingua-franca of the Internet Age." As you will learn in Chapter 12, however, two key problems that remain are (1) getting data from a database and putting it into an XML document and (2) taking data from an XML document and putting it into a database. In fact, this is where future application programmers can enter the picture.

XML database processing was given a further boost with the definition of XML Web service standards such as SOAP (not an acronym), WSDL (Web Services Description Language), UDDI (Universal Description, Discovery, and Integration), and others. Using Web services, it is possible to expose nuggets of database processing to other programs that use the Internet infrastructure. This means, for example, that in a supply chain management application, a vendor can expose portions of its inventory application to its suppliers. Further, it can do so in a standardized way.

XML Web services bring us to the edge of the IT volcano, where the magma of new technology is just now oozing out of the ground. What happens next will be, in part, up to you.

ummary

The purpose of a database is to help people keep track of things. Databases store data in tables in which each table has data about a different type of thing. Instances of the thing are stored in the rows of tables, and the characteristics of those instances are stored in columns. In this text, table names are written in all capital letters; column names are written in initial capital letters. Databases store data and the relationships among the data. Databases store data, but they are structured so that information can be created from that data.

Figure 1-5 lists many important examples of database applications. Databases can be processed by a single user or by many users. Those that support many users require special concurrency-control mechanisms to ensure that one user's work does not conflict with a second user's work.

Some databases involve just a few users and thousands of rows of data in a few tables. At the other end of the spectrum, some large databases, such as those that support ERP applications, support thousands of users and include many millions of rows in several hundred different tables.

Some database applications support e-commerce activities. Some of the largest databases are those that track users'

responses to Web pages and Web page components. These databases are used to analyze customers' responses to different Web-based marketing programs.

Digital dashboards, data mining applications, and other reporting applications use database data that is generated by transaction processing systems to help manage the enterprise. Digital dashboards and reporting systems assess past and current performance. Data mining applications predict future performance. The basic components of a database system are the database, the database management system (DBMS), one or more database applications, and users. Because Structured Query Language (SQL) is an internationally recognized language for processing databases, it can be considered a fifth component of a database system.

The functions of database applications are to create and process forms, to process user queries, and to create and process reports. Application programs also execute specific application logic and control the application. Users provide data and data changes and read data in forms, queries, and reports.

A DBMS is a large, complicated program used to create, process, and administer a database. DBMS products are almost always licensed from software vendors. Specific functions of a DBMS are summarized in Figure 1-12.

A database is a self-describing collection of integrated tables. A relational database is a self-describing collection of related tables. Tables are integrated because they store data about the relationships between rows of data. Tables are related by storing linking values of a common column. A database is self-describing because it contains a description of its contents within itself, which is known as metadata. Most DBMS products carry metadata in the form of tables. As shown in Figure 1-14, databases also contain indexes, triggers, stored procedures, security features, and backup and recovery data.

Microsoft Access is not a DBMS but rather an application generator plus a DBMS. The application generator consists of applications components that create and process forms, reports, and queries. The default Access DBMS product is called Jet, which is not licensed as a separate product. SQL Server can be substituted for Jet to support larger databases.

Enterprise database systems do not combine applications and the DBMS as Access does. Instead, applications are programs separate from each other and from the DBMS. Figure 1-16 shows four categories of database applications: client/server applications, Web applications, reporting applications, and XML Web services applications.

The five most popular DBMS products, in order of power, features, and difficulty of use, are Access (really Jet), MySQL, SQL Server, DB2, and Oracle. Jet and SQL Server are licensed by Microsoft, MySQL is licensed by Sun Microsystems, DB2 is licensed by IBM, and Oracle Database is licensed by the Oracle Corporation.

Database design is both difficult and important. Most of the first half of this text concerns database design. New databases arise in three ways: from existing data, from new systems development, and from database redesign. Normalization is used to guide the design of databases from existing data. Data models are used to create a blueprint from system requirements. The blueprint is later transformed into a database design. Most data models are created using the entity-relationship model. Database redesign occurs when an existing database is adapted to support new or changed requirements or when two or more databases are integrated.

With regards to database processing, you can have one of two roles: user or database administrator. You may be a *user* of a database/DBMS as a knowledge worker or as an application programmer. Alternatively, you might be a *database administrator* who designs, constructs, and manages the database itself. The domains of each role are shown in Figure 1-23, and the priorities as to what you need to know for each role are shown in Figure 1-24.

The history of database processing is summarized in Figure 1-25. In the early years, prior to 1970, database processing did not exist, and all data was stored in separated files. The need for integrated processing drove the development of early DBMS products. The CODASYL DBTG and DL/I data models were prevalent. Of the DBMS products used at that time, only ADABAS and IMS are still in use.

The relational model rose to prominence in the 1980s. At first, the relational model was judged to be impractical, but over time relational products such as DB2 and Oracle achieved success. During this time, DBMS products were developed for personal computers as well. dBase, R:base, and Paradox were all PC DBMS products that were eventually consumed by the success of Microsoft Access.

Object-oriented DBMS products were developed in the 1990s but never achieved commercial success. More recently, Web-based databases have been developed to support e-commerce. Open source DBMS products are readily available, forcing commercial DBMS vendors to offer limited-capacity free versions of their enterprise products. Features and functions have been implemented to overcome the stateless nature of HTTP. XML and XML Web services databases are at the leading edge of database processing.

 **ey Terms**

CODASYL DBTG	enterprise-class database system
column	entity-relationship (ER) data modeling
concurrency	foreign key
data	information
Data Language/I (DL/I)	instance
data marts	integrated tables
data model	knowledge worker
data warehouse	metadata
database	normal forms
database administrator	normalization
database application	object-oriented DBMS (OODBMS or ODBMS)
database design	object-oriented programming (OOP)
database management system (DBMS)	object-relational DBMS
database migration	personal database system

primary key   relationship
programmer   row
record   self-describing
referential integrity constraints   Structured Query Language (SQL)
relational database   table
relational model   User

eview Questions

1.1   What is the purpose of a database?

1.2   What is the most commonly used type of database?

1.3   Give an example of two related tables other than one in this book. Use the STUDENT and GRADE tables in Figure 1-3 as an example pattern for your tables. Name the tables and columns using the conventions in this book.

1.4   For the tables you created in Review Question 1.3, what are the primary keys of each table?

1.5   Explain how the two tables you provided in Review Question 1.3 are related. Which table contains the foreign key, and what is the foreign key?

1.6   Show your two tables from Review Question 1.3 without the columns that represent the relationships. Explain how the value of your two tables is diminished without the relationships.

1.7   Define the terms *data* and *information*. Explain how the two terms differ.

1.8   Give an example of information that could be determined using the two tables you provided in your answer to Review Question 1.3.

1.9   Give examples of a single-user database application and a multiuser database application other than the ones shown in Figure 1-5.

1.10 What problem can occur when a database is processed by more than one user?

1.11 Give an example of a database application that has hundreds of users and a very large and complicated database. Use an example other than one in Figure 1-5.

1.12 What is the purpose of the largest databases at e-commerce companies such as Amazon.com?

1.13 How do the e-commerce companies use these databases?

1.14 How do digital dashboard and data mining applications differ from transaction processing applications?

1.15 Explain why a small database is not necessarily simpler than a large one.

1.16 Explain the components in Figure 1-7.

1.17 What are the functions of application programs?

1.18 What is Structured Query Language (SQL), and why is it important?

1.19 What does DBMS stand for?

1.20 What are the functions of the DBMS?

1.21 Name four vendors of DBMS products.

1.22 Define the term *database*.

1.23 Why is a database considered to be self-describing?

1.24   What is metadata? How does this term pertain to a database?

1.25   What advantage is there in storing metadata in tables?

1.26   List the components of a database other than user tables and metadata.

1.27   Is Microsoft Access a DBMS? Why or why not?

1.28   Describe the components shown in Figure 1-15.

1.29   What is the function of the application generator in Access?

1.30   What is the name of the DBMS engine within Access? Why do we rarely hear about that engine?

1.31   Why does Microsoft Access hide important database technology?

1.32   Why would someone choose to replace the native Access DBMS engine with SQL Server?

1.33   Name the components of an enterprise-class database system.

1.34   Name and describe the four categories of database applications that would use an enterprise-class database system.

1.35   How do database applications get and put database data?

1.36   Name the five DBMS products described in this chapter, and compare them in terms of power, features, and ease of use.

1.37   List several consequences of a poorly designed database.

1.38   Explain two ways that a database can be designed from existing data.

1.39   What is a data warehouse? What is a data mart?

1.40   Describe the general process of designing a database for a new information system.

1.41   Explain two ways that databases can be redesigned.

1.42   What does the term *database migration* mean?

1.43   Summarize the various ways that you might work with database technology.

1.44   What job functions does a knowledge worker perform?

1.45   What job functions does a database administrator perform?

1.46   Explain the meaning of the domains in Figure 1-23.

1.47   What need drove the development of the first database technology?

1.48   What are Data Language/I and CODASYL DBTG?

1.49   Who was E. F. Codd?

1.50   What were the early objections to the relational model?

1.51   Name two early relational DBMS products.

1.52   What are some of the reasons for Oracle's success?

1.53   Name three early personal computer DBMS products.

1.54   What happened to the products in your answer to Review Question 1.53?

1.55   What was the purpose of OODBMS products? State two reasons that OODBMS products were not successful.

1.56   What characteristic of HTTP was a problem for database processing applications?

1.57   What is an open source DBMS product?

1.58   Which of the five DBMS products that you named in answering Review Question 1.36 is historically an open source DBMS product?

1.59   What has been the response of companies that sell proprietary DBMS products to the open source DBMS products? Include two examples in your answer.

1.60   What comment did Bill Gates make regarding XML?

 roject Questions

To perform the following projects you will need a computer that has Microsoft Access installed. If you have no experience working with Access, read Appendix A before you proceed.

For this set of project questions, we will create a Microsoft Access database for the Wedgewood Pacific Corporation (WPC). Founded in 1957 in Seattle, Washington, WPC has grown into an internationally recognized organization. The company is located in two buildings. One building houses the Administration, Accounting, Finance, and Human Resources departments, and the second houses the Production, Marketing, and Information Systems departments. The company database contains data about company employees, departments, company projects, company assets (for example, computer equipment), and other aspects of company operations.

In the following project questions, we will start by creating the WPC.accdb database with the following two tables:

DEPARTMENT (<u>DepartmentName</u>, BudgetCode, OfficeNumber, Phone)

EMPLOYEE (<u>EmployeeNumber</u>, FirstName, LastName, *Department*, Phone, Email)

1.61   Create a Microsoft Access database namedWPC.accdb.

1.62   Figure 1-26 shows the column characteristics for the WPC DEPARTMENT table. Using the column characteristics, create the DEPARTMENT table in the WPC.accdb database.

1.63   Figure 1-27 shows the data for the WPC DEPARTMENT table. Using Datasheet view, enter the data shown in Figure 1-27 into your DEPARTMENT table.

1.64   Figure 1-28 shows the column characteristics for the WPC EMPLOYEE table. Using the column characteristics, create the EMPLOYEE table in the WPC.accdb database.

1.65   Create the relationship and referential integrity constraint between DEPARTMENT and EMPLOYEE. Enable enforcing of referential integrity and cascading of data updates, but do *not* enable cascading of data from deleted records.

Figure  **1-26**

Database Column Characteristics for the DEPARTMENT Table

DEPARTMENT

Column Name	Type	Key	Required	Remarks
DepartmentName	Text (35)	Primary Key	Yes	
BudgetCode	Text (30)	No	Yes	
OfficeNumber	Text (15)	No	Yes	
Phone	Text (12)	No	Yes	

DepartmentName	BudgetCode	OfficeNumber	Phone
Administration	BC-100-10	BLDG01-300	360-285-8100
Legal	BC-200-10	BLDG01-200	360-285-8200
Accounting	BC-300-10	BLDG01-100	360-285-8300
Finance	BC-400-10	BLDG01-140	360-285-8400
Human Resources	BC-500-10	BLDG01-180	360-285-8500
Production	BC-600-10	BLDG02-100	360-287-8600
Marketing	BC-700-10	BLDG02-200	360-287-8700
InfoSystems	BC-800-10	BLDG02-270	360-287-8800

Figure 1-27

WPC DEPARTMENT Data

1.66 Figure 1-29 shows the data for the WPC EMPLOYEE table. Using Datasheet view, enter the first three rows of the data shown in Figure 1-29 into your EMPLOYEE table.

1.67 Using the Microsoft Access form wizard, create a data input form for the EMPLOYEE table and name it WPC Employee Data Form. Make any adjustments necessary to the form so that all data display properly. Use this form to enter the rest of the data in the EMPLOYEE table shown in Figure 1-29 into your EMPLOYEE table.

1.68 Using the Access report wizard, create a report named Wedgewood Pacific Corporation Employee Report that presents the data contained in your EMPLOYEE table sorted first by employee last name and then by employee first name. Make any adjustments necessary to the report so that all headings and data display properly. Print a copy of this report.

1.69 Using the Microsoft Access form wizard, create a form that has all of the data from both tables. When asked how you want to view your data, select *by DEPARTMENT*. Choose the default options for other questions that the wizard asks. Open your form and page through your departments.

Figure 1-28

Database Column Characteristics for the EMPLOYEE Table

1.70 Using the Access report wizard, create a report that has all of the data from both tables. When asked how you want to view your data, select *by DEPARTMENT*. For the data contained in your EMPLOYEE table in the report, specify that it will be sorted first by

EMPLOYEE

Column Name	Type	Key	Required	Remarks
EmployeeNumber	AutoNumber	Primary Key	Yes	Surrogate Key
FirstName	Text (25)	No	Yes	
LastName	Text (25)	No	Yes	
Department	Text (35)	No	Yes	
Phone	Text (12)	No	No	
Email	Text (100)	No	Yes	

EmployeeNumber	FirstName	LastName	Department	Phone	Email
[AutoNumber]	Mary	Jacobs	Administration	360-285-8110	MJacobs@WPC.com
[AutoNumber]	Rosalie	Jackson	Administration	360-285-8120	RJackson@WPC.com
[AutoNumber]	Richard	Bandalone	Legal	360-285-8210	RBandalone@WPC.com
[AutoNumber]	Tom	Caruthers	Accounting	360-285-8310	TCaruthers@WPC.com
[AutoNumber]	Heather	Jones	Accounting	360-285-8320	HJones@WPC.com
[AutoNumber]	Mary	Abernathy	Finance	360-285-8410	MAbernathy@WPC.com
[AutoNumber]	George	Smith	Human Resources	360-285-8510	GSmith@WPC.com
[AutoNumber]	Tom	Jackson	Production	360-287-8610	TJackson@WPC.com
[AutoNumber]	George	Jones	Production	360-287-8620	GJones@WPC.com
[AutoNumber]	Ken	Numoto	Marketing	360-287-8710	KNumoto@WPC.com
[AutoNumber]	James	Nestor	InfoSystems		JNestor@WPC.com
[AutoNumber]	Rick	Brown	InfoSystems	360-287-8820	RBrown@WPC.com

Figure 1-29

WPC EMPLOYEE Data

employee last name and then by employee first name. Make any adjustments necessary to the report so that all headings and data display properly. Print a copy of this report.

1.71 Explain, to the level of detail in this chapter, what is going on within Microsoft Access in Project Questions 1.67, 1.68, 1.69, and 1.70. What subcomponent created the form and report? Where is the data stored? What role do you think SQL is playing?

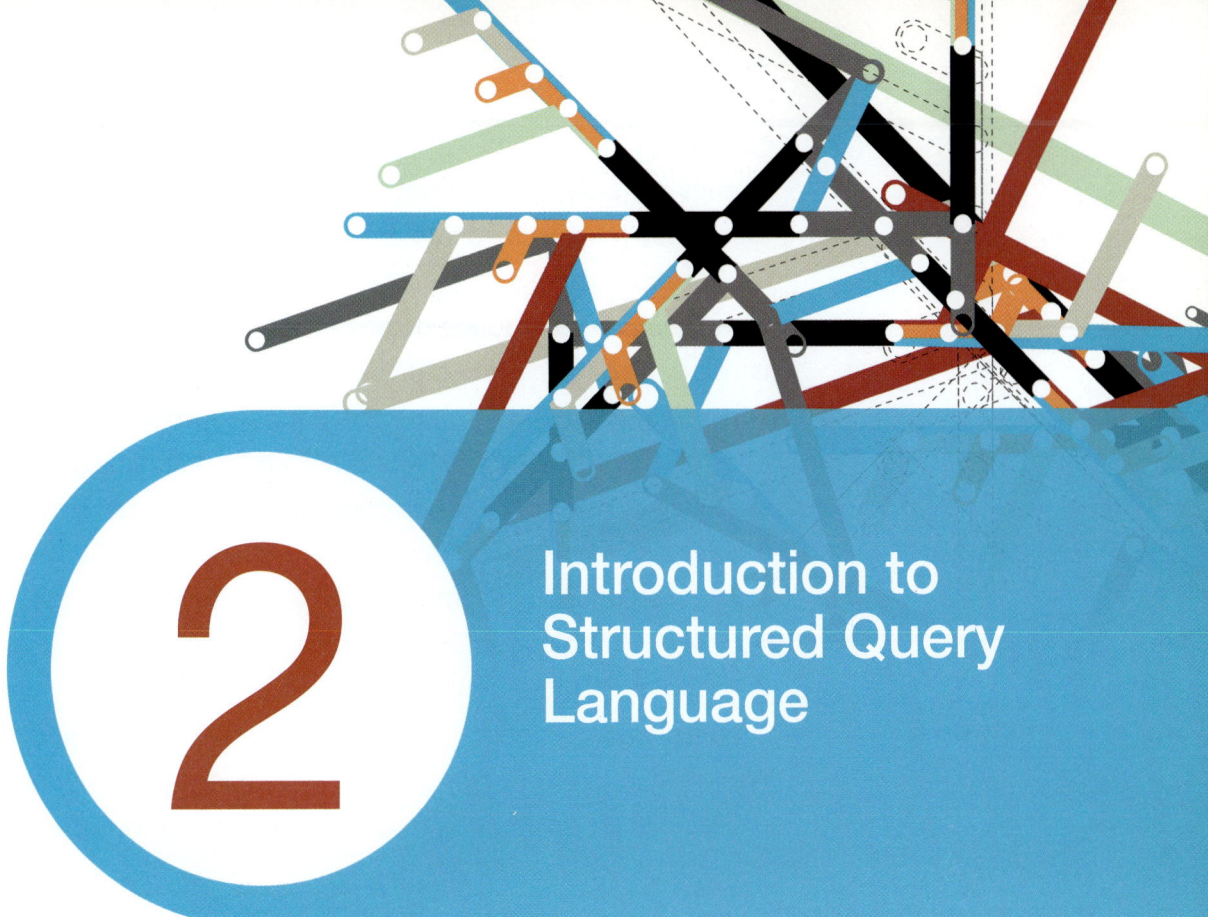

2

Introduction to Structured Query Language

Chapter Objectives

- To understand the use of extracted data sets.
- To understand the use of ad-hoc queries.
- To understand the history and significance of Structured Query Language (SQL).
- To understand the SQL SELECT/FROM/WHERE framework as the basis for database queries.
- To be able to write queries in SQL to retrieve data from a single table.
- To be able to write queries in SQL to use the SQL SELECT, FROM, WHERE, ORDER BY, GROUP BY, and HAVING clauses.

- To be able to write queries in SQL to use SQL DISTINCT, AND, OR, NOT, BETWEEN, LIKE, and IN keywords.
- To be able to use the SQL built-in functions of SUM, COUNT, MIN, MAX, and AVG with and without the use of a GROUP BY clause.
- To be able to write queries in SQL to retrieve data from a single table but restricting the data based upon data in another table (subquery).
- To be able to write queries in SQL to retrieve data from multiple tables using an SQL join.

In today's business environment, users typically use data stored in databases to produce information that can help them make business decisions. In Chapter 13, we will take an in-depth look at business intelligence (BI) systems, which are used to support management by producing information for assessment, analysis, planning, and control. In this chapter, we will see how users use ad-hoc queries, which are essentially questions that can be answered using database data. For example, in English an ad-hoc query would be "How many customers in Portland, Oregon, bought our green baseball cap?" These queries are called *ad-hoc* because they are created by the user as needed, rather than programmed into an application.

This approach to database querying has become important enough that some companies produce dedicated applications to help users who are not familiar with database structures create ad-hoc queries. One example is Open Text's LiveLink ECM BI Query product (*www.hummingbird.com/products/bi/bi_query.html*), which uses a user-friendly **graphical user interface (GUI)** to simplify the creation of ad-hoc queries. Personal databases such as Microsoft Access also have ad-hoc query tools available. Microsoft Access uses a GUI style called **query by example (QBE)** to simplify ad-hoc queries.

However, **Structured Query Language (SQL)**—the universal query language of relational DBMS products—is always behind the user-friendly GUIs. In this chapter, we will introduce SQL by learning how to write and run SQL queries. We will then return to SQL in Chapter 7 to learn how to use it for other purposes, such as how to create and add data to the databases themselves.

Cape Codd Outdoor Sports

For our work in this chapter, we will use data from Cape Codd Outdoor Sports (although based on a real outdoor retail equipment vendor, Cape Codd Outdoor Sports is a fictitious company). Cape Codd sells recreational outdoor equipment in 15 retail stores across the United States and Canada. It also sells merchandise over the Internet from a Web storefront application and via mail order. All retail sales are recorded in a sales database managed by the Oracle DBMS, as shown in Figure 2-1.

Figure 2-1

Cape Codd Retail Sales Data Extraction

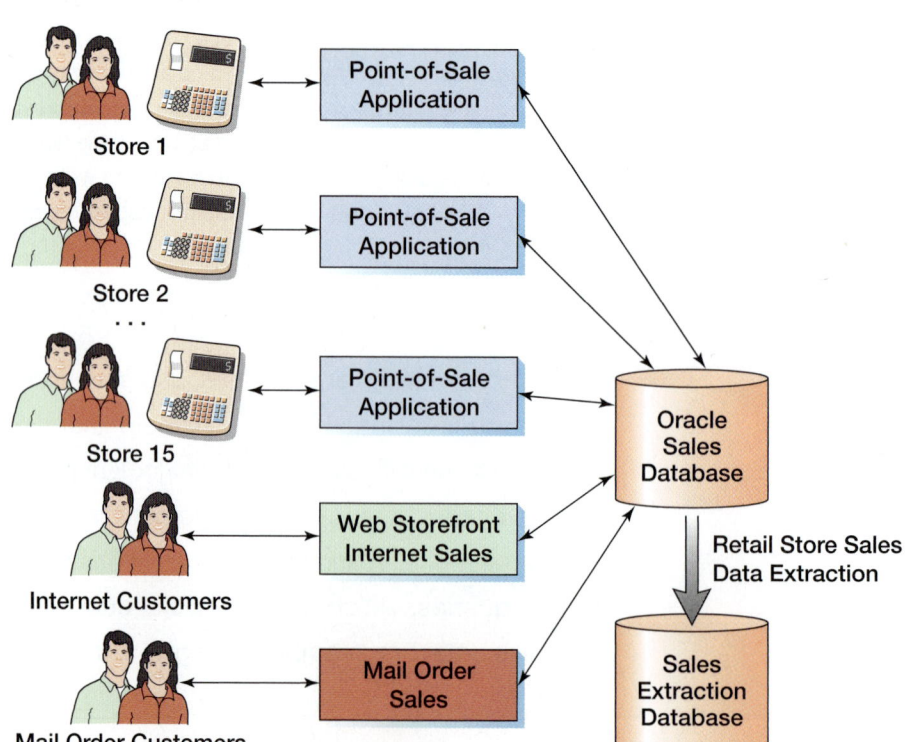

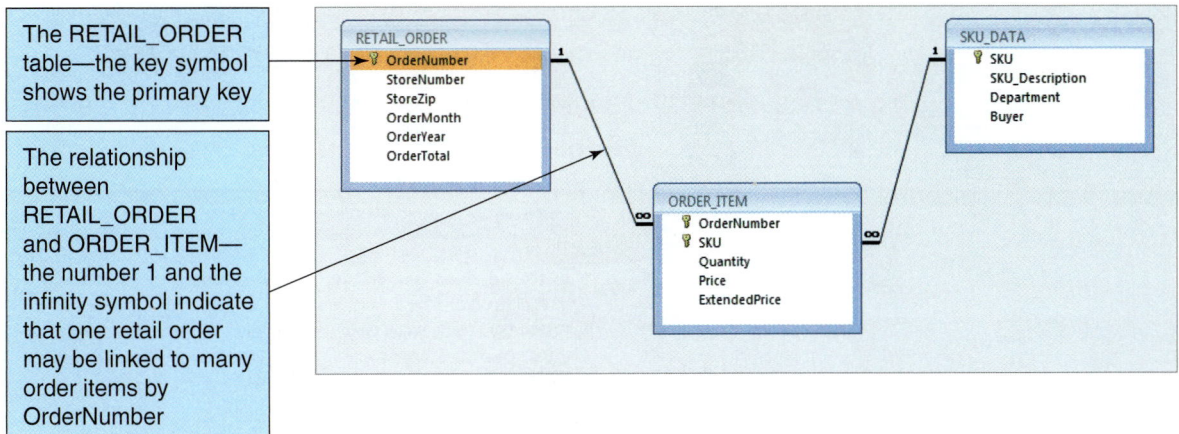

The RETAIL_ORDER table—the key symbol shows the primary key

The relationship between RETAIL_ORDER and ORDER_ITEM—the number 1 and the infinity symbol indicate that one retail order may be linked to many order items by OrderNumber

Figure 2-2

Cape Codd Extracted Retail Sales Data Database Tables and Relationships

The Retail Sales Data Extraction

Cape Codd's marketing department wants to perform an analysis of in-store sales. Accordingly, marketing analysts ask the IT department to extract retail sales data from the operational database. To perform the marketing study, they do not need all of the order data. They want just the tables and columns shown in Figure 2-2. The data types for the columns in the tables is shown in Figure 2-3.

As shown in Figures 2-2 and 2-3, three tables are needed: RETAIL_ORDER, ORDER_ITEM, and SKU_DATA. The RETAIL_ORDER table has data about each retail sales order, the ORDER_ITEM table has data about each item in an order, and the SKU_DATA table has data about each **stock-keeping unit (SKU)**. SKU is a unique identifier for each particular item that Cape Codd sells. The data stored in the tables is shown in Figure 2-4.

RETAIL_ORDER Data

As shown in Figures 2-2 and 2-3, the RETAIL_ORDER table has columns for OrderNumber, StoreNumber, StoreZip (the zip code of the store selling the order), OrderMonth, OrderYear, and OrderTotal:

RETAIL_ORDER (<u>OrderNumber</u>, StoreNumber, StoreZip, OrderMonth, OrderYear, OrderTotal)

Figure 2-3

Cape Codd Extracted Retail Sales Data Format

Table	Column	Date Type
RETAIL_ORDER	OrderNumber	Integer
	StoreNumber	Integer
	StoreZip	Character (9)
	OrderMonth	Character (12)
	OrderYear	Integer
	OrderTotal	Currency
ORDER_ITEM	OrderNumber	Integer
	SKU	Integer
	Quantity	Integer
	Price	Currency
	ExtendedPrice	Currency
SKU_DATA	SKU	Integer
	SKU_Description	Character (35)
	Department	Character (30)
	Buyer	Character (30)

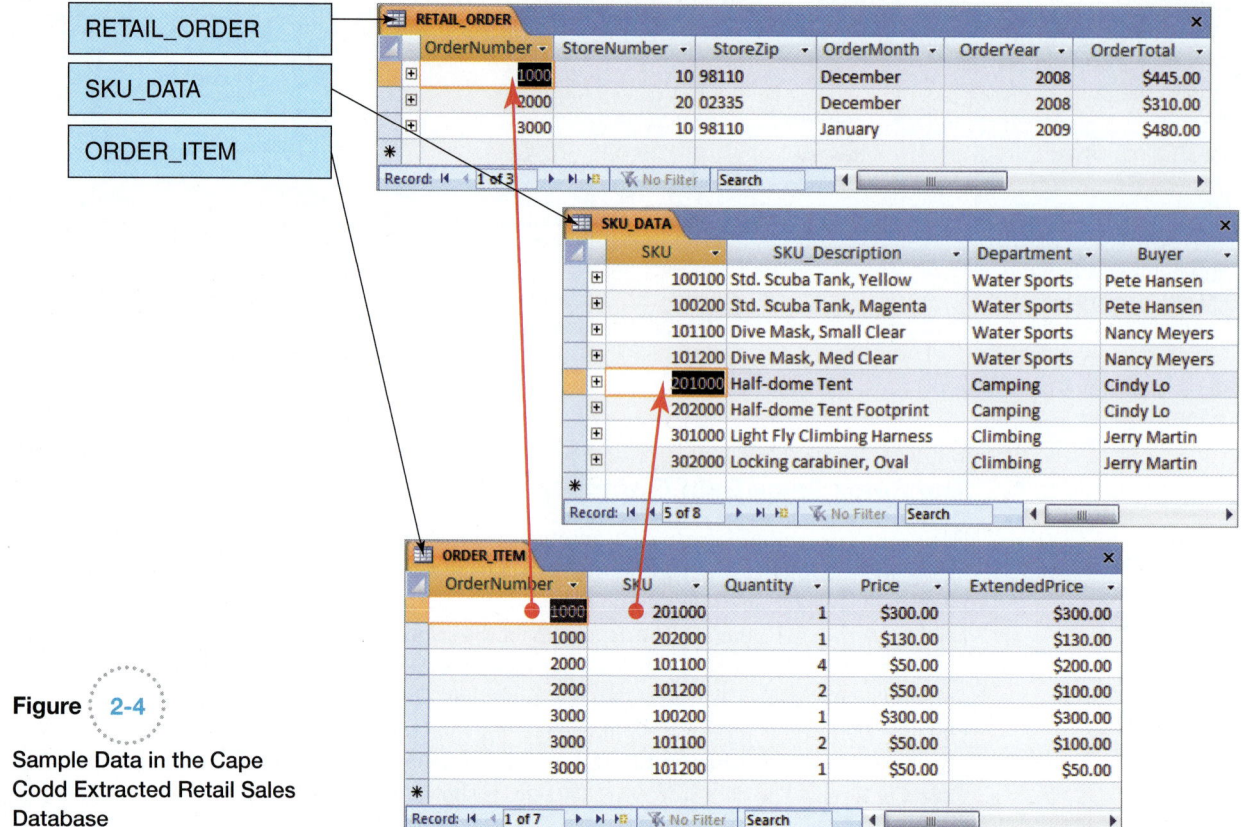

RETAIL_ORDER

SKU_DATA

ORDER_ITEM

Figure   2-4

Sample Data in the Cape Codd Extracted Retail Sales Database

Sample data for RETAIL_ORDER is shown in Figure 2-4. This extract only includes data for retail store sales, and operational data for other types of sales (and returns and other sales-related transactions) is not copied during the extraction process. Further, the data extraction process selects only a few columns of the operational data—the Point of Sale (POS) and other sales applications process far more data than that shown here. The operational database also stores the data in a different format. For example, the order data in the Oracle operational database contains a column named OrderDate that stores the data in the date format MM/DD/YYYY (e.g., 10/22/2008 for October 22, 2008). The extraction program used to populate the retail sales extracted data database converts OrderDate into two separate values of OrderMonth and OrderYear. This is done because this is the data format that marketing wants. Such filtering and data transformation are typical of a data extraction process.

ORDER_ITEM Data

As shown in Figures 2-2 and 2-3, the ORDER_ITEM table has columns for OrderNumber, SKU, Quantity, Price, and ExtendedPrice (which equals Quantity × Price):

ORDER_ITEM (OrderNumber, _SKU_, Quantity, Price, ExtendedPrice)

Thus, the ORDER_ITEM table stores an extract of the items purchased in each order. There is one row in the table for each item in an order, and this item is identified by its SKU. To understand this table, think about a sales receipt you get from a retail store. That receipt has data for one order. It includes basic order data such as the date and order total, and it has one line for each item you purchase. The rows in the ORDER_ITEM table correspond to the lines on such an order receipt.

The OrderNumber Column in ORDER_ITEM relates each row in ORDER_ITEM to the corresponding OrderNumber in the RETAIL_ORDER table. SKU indentifies the actual item purchased by its stock-keeping unit number. Further, the SKU column in ORDER_ITEM relates each row in ORDER_ITEM to its corresponding SKU in the SKU_DATA table (discussed in the next section). Quantity is the number of items of that SKU purchased in that order. Price is the price of each item, and ExtendedPrice is equal to Quantity × Price.

ORDER_ITEM data are shown in the bottom part of Figure 2-4. The first row relates to order 1000 and to SKU 201000. For SKU 201000, one item was purchased for $300.00, and the ExtendedPrice was $300.00. The second row shows the second item in order 1000. There, 1 of item 202000 was purchased for $50.00, and the ExtendedPrice is 1 × $50.00, or $50.00. This table structure of an ORDER table related to an ORDER_ITEM table is typical for sales system with many items in one order. We will discuss it in detail in Chapters 5 and 6, where we will create a data model of a complete order and then design the database for that data model.

> **BY THE WAY** You would expect the total of ExtendedPrice for all rows for a given order to equal OrderTotal in the RETAIL_ORDER table. They do not. For order 1000, for example, the sum of ExtendedPrice in the relevant rows of ORDER_ITEM is $300.00 + $130.00 = $430.00. However, the OrderTotal for order 1000 is $445.00. The difference occurs because OrderTotal includes tax, shipping, and other charges that do not appear in the data extract.

SKU_DATA Table

As shown in Figures 2-2 and 2-3, the SKU_DATA table has columns SKU, SKU_Description, Department, and Buyer:

SKU_DATA (SKU, SKU_Description, Department, Buyer)

SKU is an integer value that identifies a particular product that Cape Codd sells. For example, SKU 100100 indentifies a yellow standard-size SCUBA tank, whereas SKU 100200 identifies the magenta version of the same tank. SKU_Description contains a brief text description of each item. Department and Buyer identify the department and individual who is responsible for purchasing the product. As with the other tables, these columns are a subset of the SKU data stored in the operational database.

Data Extracts Are Common

Before we continue, realize that the data extraction process described here is not just an academic exercise. To the contrary, such extraction processes are realistic, common, and important BI system operations. Right now, hundreds of businesses worldwide are using their BI systems to create extract databases just like the one created by Cape Codd.

In the next sections of this chapter, you will learn how to write SQL statements to process the extracted data. This knowledge is exceedingly valuable and practical. Again, right now, as you read this paragraph, hundreds of people are writing SQL to create information from extracted data. The SQL you will learn in this chapter will be an essential asset to you as a knowledge worker, application programmer, or database administrator. Invest the time to learn SQL—the investment will pay great dividends later in your career.

SQL Background

SQL was developed by the IBM Corporation in the late 1970s. It was endorsed as a national standard by the **American National Standards Institute (ANSI)** in 1986 and by the **International Organization for Standardization (ISO)** (and no, that's not a typo—the acronym is *ISO,* not *IOS!*) in 1987. Subsequent versions of SQL were adopted in 1989 and 1992. The 1992 version is sometimes referred to as SQL-92, or sometimes as ANSI-92 SQL. In 1999, SQL:1999 (also referred to as SQL3), which incorporated some object-oriented concepts, was released. This was followed by the release of SQL:2003 in 2003; SQL:2006 in 2006; and, most recently, SQL:2008 in 2008. Each of these added new features or extended existing SQL features, the most important of which for us is SQL support for **Extensible Markup Language (XML)**. (XML is discussed in Chapter 12.) Our discussion in this chapter and in Chapter 7 focuses on common language features that have been in SQL since SQL-92, and some discussion of the SQL XML features is included in Chapter 12.

SQL is not a complete programming language, like Java or C#. Instead, it is called a **data sublanguage**, because it has only those statements needed for creating and processing database data and metadata. You can use SQL statements in many different ways. You can submit them directly to the DBMS for processing. You can embed SQL statements into client/server application programs. You can embed them into Web pages, and you can use them in reporting and data extraction programs. You also can execute SQL statements directly from Visual Studio. NET and other development tools.

SQL statements are commonly divided into categories, two of which are of interest to us here:

- **Data definition language (DDL)** statements, which are used for creating tables, relationships, and other structures
- **Data manipulation language (DML)** statements, which are used for querying, inserting, modifying, and deleting data

This chapter considers only DML statements for querying data. The remaining DML statements for inserting, modifying, and deleting data are discussed in Chapter 7, where we will also discuss SQL DDL statements.

SQL is ubiquitous, and SQL programming is a critical skill. Today, all DBMS products process SQL. Enterprise-class DBMSs such as Oracle Database, DB2, SQL Server, and MySQL require that you know SQL. With these products, all data manipulation is expressed using SQL.

As explained in Chapter 1, if you have used Microsoft Access, you have used SQL, even if you didn't know it. Every time you process a form, create a report, or run a query, Microsoft Access generates SQL and sends that SQL to Access' internal Jet DBMS engine. To do more than elementary database processing, you need to uncover the SQL hidden by Microsoft Access. Further, once you know SQL, you will find it easier to write a query statement in SQL rather than fight with the graphical forms, buttons, and other paraphernalia that you must use to create queries with the Microsoft Access query-by-example style GUI.

The SQL SELECT/FROM/WHERE Framework

This section introduces the fundamental statement framework for SQL query statements. After we discuss this basic structure, you will learn how to submit SQL statements to Access, SQL Server, Oracle, and MySQL. If you choose, you can then follow along with the text and process additional SQL statements as they are explained in the rest of this chapter. The basic form of SQL queries uses the **SQL SELECT/FROM/WHERE framework**. In this framework:

- The **SQL SELECT clause** specifies which *columns* are to be listed in the query results.
- The **SQL FROM clause** specifies which *tables* are to be used in the query.
- The **SQL WHERE clause** specifies which *rows* are to be listed in the query results.

Let's work through some examples so that this framework makes sense to you.

Reading Specified Columns from a Single Table

We begin very simply. Suppose we want to obtain just the values of the Department and Buyer columns of the SKU_DATA table. A SQL statement to read that data is the following:

```
SELECT     Department, Buyer
FROM       SKU_DATA;
```

Using the data in Figure 2-4, when the DBMS processes this statement the result will be:

	Department	Buyer
1	Water Sports	Pete Hansen
2	Water Sports	Pete Hansen
3	Water Sports	Nancy Meyers
4	Water Sports	Nancy Meyers
5	Camping	Cindy Lo
6	Camping	Cindy Lo
7	Climbing	Jerry Martin
8	Climbing	Jerry Martin

When SQL statements are executed, the statements transform tables. SQL statements start with a table, process that table in some way, and then place the results in another table structure. Even if the result of the processing is just a single number, that number is considered to be a table with one row and one column. As you will learn at the end of this chapter, some SQL statements process multiple tables. Regardless of the number of input tables, though, the result of every SQL statement is a single table.

Notice that SQL statements terminate with a semicolon (;) character. The semicolon is required by the SQL-92 standard. Although some DBMS products will allow you to omit the semicolon, some will not, so develop the habit of terminating SQL statements with a semicolon.

The order of the column names in the SELECT phrase determines the order of the columns in the results table. Thus, if we switch Buyer and Department in the SELECT phrase, they will be switched in the output table as well. Hence, the SQL statement:

```
SELECT      Buyer, Department
FROM        SKU_DATA;
```

produces the following result table:

	Buyer	Department
1	Pete Hansen	Water Sports
2	Pete Hansen	Water Sports
3	Nancy Meyers	Water Sports
4	Nancy Meyers	Water Sports
5	Cindy Lo	Camping
6	Cindy Lo	Camping
7	Jerry Martin	Climbing
8	Jerry Martin	Climbing

Notice that some rows are duplicated in these results. The data in the first and second row, for example, is identical. We can eliminate duplicates by using the **SQL DISTINCT keyword** as follows:

```
SELECT      DISTINCT Buyer, Department
FROM        SKU_DATA;
```

The result of this statement, where all of the duplicate rows have been removed, is:

	Buyer	Department
1	Cindy Lo	Camping
2	Jerry Martin	Climbing
3	Nancy Meyers	Water Sports
4	Pete Hansen	Water Sports

> **BY THE WAY**   The reason that SQL does not automatically eliminate duplicate rows is that it can be very time consuming to do so. To determine if any rows are duplicates, every row must be compared with every other row. If there are 100,000 rows in a table, that checking will take a long time. Hence, by default, duplicates are not removed. However, it is always possible to force their removal using the DISTINCT keyword.

Suppose that we want to view all of the columns of the SKU_DATA table. To do so, we can name each column in the SELECT statement as follows:

```
SELECT      SKU, SKU_Description, Department, Buyer
FROM        SKU_DATA;
```

The result will be a table with all of the rows and all four of the columns in SKU_DATA:

	SKU	SKU_Description	Department	Buyer
1	100100	Std. Scuba Tank, Yellow	Water Sports	Pete Hansen
2	100200	Std. Scuba Tank, Magenta	Water Sports	Pete Hansen
3	101100	Dive Mask, Small Clear	Water Sports	Nancy Meyers
4	101200	Dive Mask, Med Clear	Water Sports	Nancy Meyers
5	201000	Half-dome Tent	Camping	Cindy Lo
6	202000	Half-dome Tent Footprint	Camping	Cindy Lo
7	301000	Light Fly Climbing Harness	Climbing	Jerry Martin
8	302000	Locking carabiner, Oval	Climbing	Jerry Martin

However, SQL provides a shorthand notation for querying all of the columns of a table. The shorthand is to use an asterisk (*) to indicate that we want all the columns to be displayed:

```
SELECT      *
FROM        SKU_DATA;
```

The result will again be a table with all rows and all four of the columns in SKU_DATA:

	SKU	SKU_Description	Department	Buyer
1	100100	Std. Scuba Tank, Yellow	Water Sports	Pete Hansen
2	100200	Std. Scuba Tank, Magenta	Water Sports	Pete Hansen
3	101100	Dive Mask, Small Clear	Water Sports	Nancy Meyers
4	101200	Dive Mask, Med Clear	Water Sports	Nancy Meyers
5	201000	Half-dome Tent	Camping	Cindy Lo
6	202000	Half-dome Tent Footprint	Camping	Cindy Lo
7	301000	Light Fly Climbing Harness	Climbing	Jerry Martin
8	302000	Locking carabiner, Oval	Climbing	Jerry Martin

Reading Specified Rows from a Single Table

Suppose we want all of the *columns* of the SKU_DATA table, but we want only the *rows* for the Water Sports department. We can obtain that result by using the SQL WHERE clause as follows:

```
SELECT      *
FROM        SKU_DATA
WHERE       Department='Water Sports';
```

The result of this statement will be:

	SKU	SKU_Description	Department	Buyer
1	100100	Std. Scuba Tank, Yellow	Water Sports	Pete Hansen
2	100200	Std. Scuba Tank, Magenta	Water Sports	Pete Hansen
3	101100	Dive Mask, Small Clear	Water Sports	Nancy Meyers
4	101200	Dive Mask, Med Clear	Water Sports	Nancy Meyers

In an SQL WHERE clause, if the column contains text or date data, the comparison values must be enclosed in single quotation marks (' '). If the column contains numeric data, however, the comparison values need not be in quotes. Thus, to find all of the SKU rows with a value greater than 200,000, we would use the SQL statement (note that no comma is provided in the numeric value code):

```
SELECT      *
FROM        SKU_DATA
WHERE       SKU > 200000;
```

The result is:

	SKU	SKU_Description	Department	Buyer
1	201000	Half-dome Tent	Camping	Cindy Lo
2	202000	Half-dome Tent Footprint	Camping	Cindy Lo
3	301000	Light Fly Climbing Harness	Climbing	Jerry Martin
4	302000	Locking carabiner, Oval	Climbing	Jerry Martin

> **BY THE WAY**   SQL is very fussy about single quotes. It wants the plain, nondirectional quotes found in basic text editors. The fancy directional quotes produced by many word processors will produce errors. For example, the data value 'Water Sports' is correctly stated, but 'Water Sports' is not. Do you see the difference?

Reading Specified Columns and Rows from a Single Table

So far, we have selected certain columns and all rows and we have selected all columns and certain rows. We can combine these operations to select certain columns and certain rows by naming the columns we want and then using the SQL WHERE clause. For example, to obtain the SKU_Description and Department of all products in the Climbing department, we use the SQL query:

```
SELECT      SKU_Description, Department
FROM        SKU_DATA
WHERE       Department='Climbing';
```

The result is:

	SKU_Description	Department
1	Light Fly Climbing Harness	Climbing
2	Locking carabiner, Oval	Climbing

SQL does not require that the column used in the WHERE clause also appear in the SELECT clause column list. Thus, we can specify:

```
SELECT      SKU_Description, Buyer
FROM        SKU_DATA
WHERE       Department='Climbing';
```

where the qualifying column, Department, does not appear in the SELECT clause column list. The result is:

	SKU_Description	Buyer
1	Light Fly Climbing Harness	Jerry Martin
2	Locking carabiner, Oval	Jerry Martin

> **BY THE WAY**   Standard practice is to write SQL statements with the SELECT, FROM, and WHERE clauses on separate lines. This practice is just a coding convention, however, and SQL parsers do not require it. You could code the last SQL statement all on one line as:
>
> ```
> SELECT SKU_Description, Buyer FROM SKU_DATA WHERE Department=
> 'Climbing';
> ```
>
> All DBMS products would process the statement written in this fashion. However, the standard multiline coding convention makes SQL easier to read, and we encourage you to write your SQL according to it.

Submitting SQL Statements to the DBMS

Before continuing the explanation of SQL, it will be useful for you to learn how to submit SQL statements to specific DBMS products. That way, you can work along with the text by keying and running SQL statements as you read the discussion. The particular means by which you submit SQL statements depends on the DBMS. Here we will describe the process for Access, SQL Server, Oracle Database, and MySQL.

> **BY THE WAY**   You can learn SQL without running the queries in a DBMS, so if for some reason you do not have Access, SQL Server, Oracle Database, or MySQL readily available, do not despair. You can learn SQL without them. Chances are your instructor, like a lot of us in practice today, learned SQL without a DBMS. It is just that SQL statements are easier to understand and remember if you can run the SQL while you read. However, given that there are freely downloadable versions of Microsoft SQL Server 2008 Express Edition, Oracle Database 10g Express Edition, and Sun Microsystems MySQL Server Community Edition, you can have an installed DBMS to run these SQL examples even if you haven't purchased Microsoft Access. See Chapters 10, 10A, and 10B for specific instructions, for creating databases using each of these products. The SQL scripts needed to create the Cape Codd Outdoor Sports database used in this chapter are available at *www.pearsonhighered.com/kroenke*.

Using SQL in Microsoft Access 2007

Before you can execute SQL statements, you need a computer that has Microsoft Access installed, and you need a Microsoft Access database that contains the tables and sample data in Figure 2-4. Microsoft Access is part of many versions of the Microsoft Office suite, so it should not be too difficult to find a computer that has it.

Because Microsoft Access is commonly used in classes that use this book as a textbook, we will look how to use SQL in Microsoft Access in some detail. Before we proceed, however, we need to discuss a specific peculiarity of Microsoft Access—the limitations of the default version of SQL used in Access.

"Does Not Work with Microsoft Access ANSI-89 SQL"

As mentioned previously, our discussion of SQL is based on SQL features present in SQL standards since the ANSI SQL-92 standard (which Microsoft refers to as ANSI-92 SQL). Unfortunately, Microsoft Access 2007 still defaults to the earlier SQL-89 version—Microsoft calls it ANSI-89 SQL or Microsoft Jet SQL (after the Microsoft Jet DBMS engine used by Access). ANSI-89 SQL differs significantly from SQL-92, and, therefore, some features of the SQL-92 language will not work in Access.

Microsoft Access 2007 (and the earlier Microsoft Access 2003 version) does contain a setting that allows you to use SQL-92 instead of the default ANSI-89 SQL. Microsoft included this option to allow Access tools such as forms and reports to be used in application development for Microsoft SQL Server, which supports newer SQL standards. To set the option in Microsoft Access 2007, click the **Microsoft Office Button** and then click the **Access Options** button to open the Access Options dialog box. In the Access Options dialog box, click the **Object Designers** button to display the Access Options Object Designers page, as shown in Figure 2-5.

As shown in Figure 2-5, the **SQL Server Compatible Syntax (ANSI 92)** options control which version of SQL is used in an Access 2007 database. If you check the **This database** check box, you will use SQL-92 syntax in the current database. Or, you can check the **Default for new databases** check box to make SQL-92 syntax the default for all new databases you create. When you click the **OK** button to save the changed SQL syntax option, the SQL-Syntax Information dialog box shown in Figure 2-6 will be displayed. Read the information, and then click the **OK** button to close the dialog box.

Unfortunately, very few Microsoft Access users or organizations using Access are likely to set the Access SQL version to the SQL-92 option, and, in this chapter, we assume that Access is running in the default ANSI-89 SQL mode. One advantage of doing so is that it will help you understand the limitations of Access ANSI-89 SQL and how to cope with them.

In the discussion that follows, we use "Does Not Work with Microsoft Access ANSI-89 SQL" boxes to identify SQL commands and SQL clauses that do not work in Access ANSI-89 SQL. We also identify any workarounds that are available. Remember that the one *permanent* workaround is to choose to use the SQL-92 syntax option in the databases you create!

Nonetheless, two versions of the Microsoft Access 2007 Cape Codd Outdoor Sports database are available at *www.pearsonhighered.com/kroenke* for your use with this chapter.

Figure 2-5

The Microsoft Access 2007 Options Object Designers Page

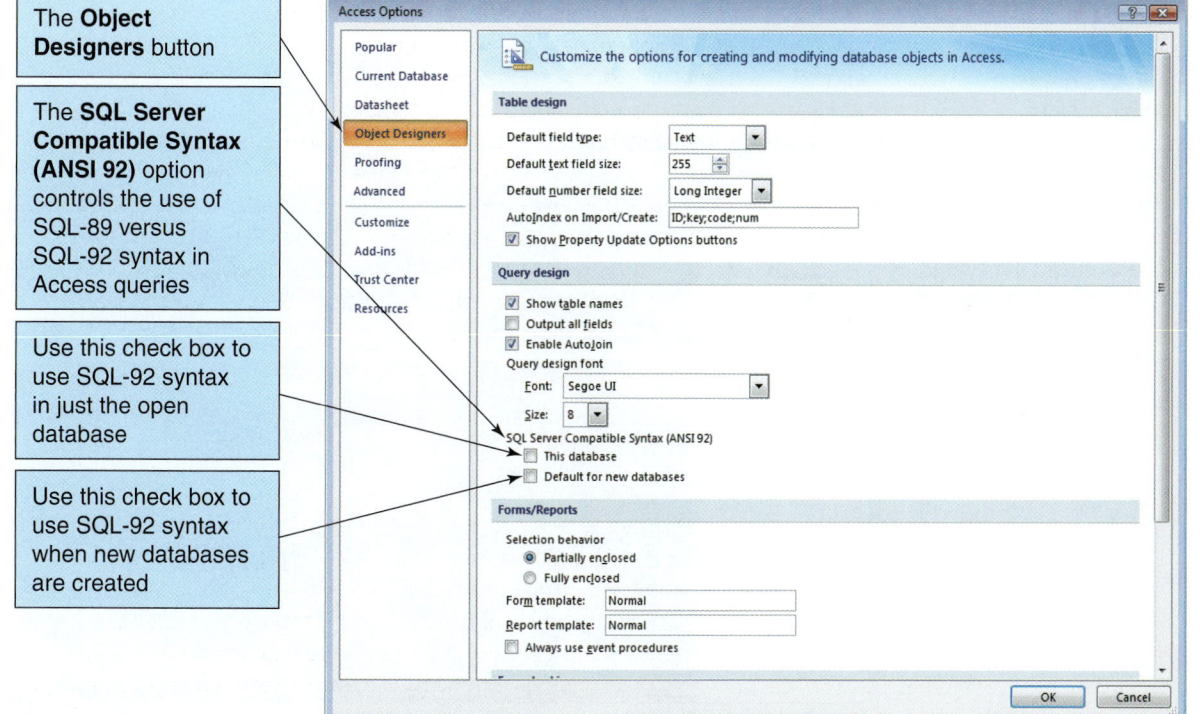

The **Object Designers** button

The **SQL Server Compatible Syntax (ANSI 92)** option controls the use of SQL-89 versus SQL-92 syntax in Access queries

Use this check box to use SQL-92 syntax in just the open database

Use this check box to use SQL-92 syntax when new databases are created

Figure  **2-6**

**The Microsoft Access 2007
SQL-Syntax Information
Dialog Box**

The Access database file named *Cape-Codd.accdb* is set to use Microsoft Access ANSI-89, whereas the Access database file name *Cape-Codd-SQL-92.accdb* is set to use Microsoft Access SQL-92. Choose the one you want to use (or use them both and compare the results!). Note that these files contain two additional tables (INVENTORY and WAREHOUSE) that we will not use in this chapter, but that you will need for the Review Questions at the end of the chapter.

Alternatively, of course, you can create your own Access database and then add the tables and data in Figures 2-3 and 2-4, as described in Appendix A. If you create your own database, look at the Review Questions at the end of the chapter and create the INVENTORY and WAREHOUSE tables shown there in addition to the RETAIL-ORDER, ORDER_ITEM and SKU tables shown in the chapter discussion. This will make sure that what you see on your monitor matches the screenshots in this chapter.

Whether you download the database file or build it yourself, you will need to do one or the other before you can proceed.

Processing SQL Statements in Microsoft Access 2007

To process an SQL statement in Microsoft Access 2007, first open the database in Access as described in Appendix A and then create a new tabbed Query window.

Opening an Access Query Window in Design View

1. Click the **Create** command tab to display the Create command groups, as shown in Figure 2-7.
2. Click the **Query Design** button.
3. The Query1 tabbed document window is displayed in Design view, along with the Show Table dialog box, as shown in Figure 2-8.

The **Create**
command tab

The **Query Design**
button

The INVENTORY and
WAREHOUSE tables
will be used in the
chapter Review
Exercises

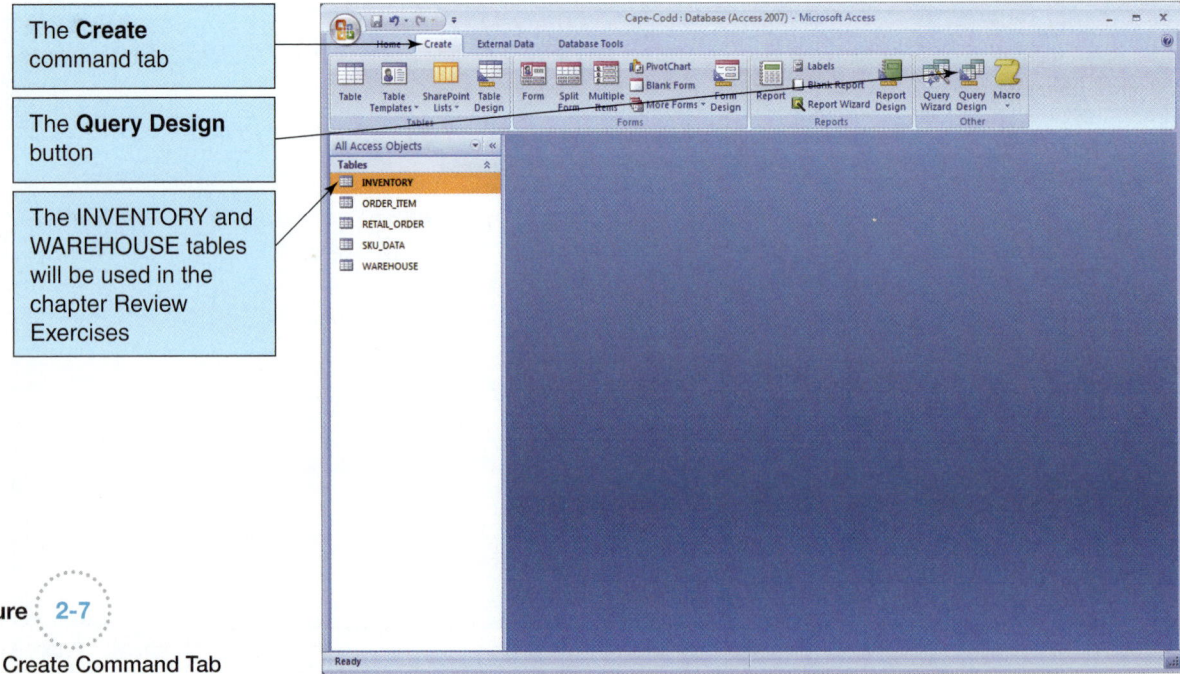

Figure **2-7**

The Create Command Tab

The **Query1** tabbed document window

The **Show Table** dialog box

Click the **Close** button

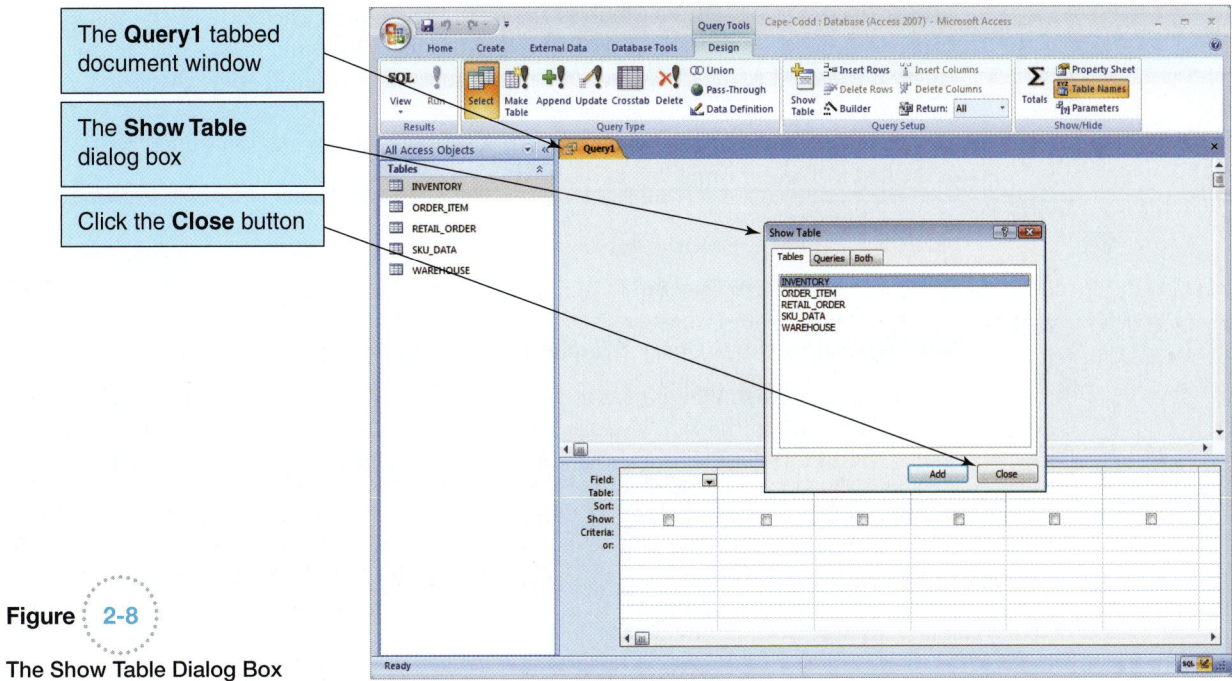

Figure 2-8

The Show Table Dialog Box

4. Click the **Close** button on the Show Table dialog box. The Query1 document window now looks as shown in Figure 2-9. This window is used for creating and editing Access queries in Design view and is used with Access QBE.

Note that in Figure 2-9, the Select button is selected in the Query Type group on the Design tab. You can tell this is so because active or selected buttons are always shown in color on the Ribbon. This indicates that we are creating a query that is the equivalent of an SQL SELECT statement.

Also note that in Figure 2-9 the View gallery is available in the Results group of the Design tab. We can use this gallery to switch between Design view and SQL view. However, we can also

Figure 2-9

The Query Tools Contextual Command Tab

The **Query Tools** tab

The **SQL View** button

The **View gallery** drop-down arrow button

The **Select** Query Type button

The **Query Type** command group

The **Query1** tabbed document window in Design view

The **Design** command tab

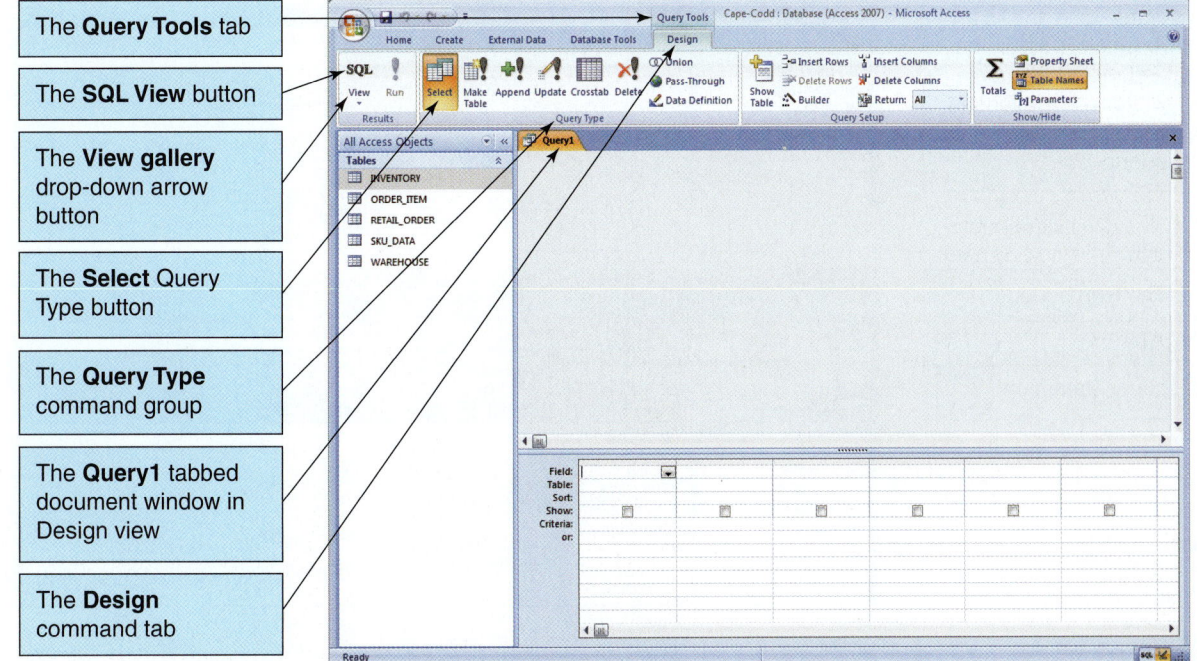

just use the displayed SQL View button to switch to SQL view. The SQL View button is being displayed because Access considers that to be the view you would most likely choose in the gallery if you used it. Access always presents a "most likely needed" view choice as a button above the View gallery.

For our example SQL query in Microsoft Access, we will use the same query that we used as the first SQL query earlier in our discussion:

```
SELECT     Department, Buyer
FROM       SKU_DATA;
```

Opening an Access SQL Query Window and Running an Access SQL Query

1. Click the **SQL View** button in the Results group on the Design tab. The Query1 window switches to the SQL view, as shown in Figure 2-10. Note the basic SQL command **SELECT;** that's shown in the window. This is an incomplete command, and running it will not produce any results.
2. Edit the SQL SELECT command to read:

```
SELECT     Department, Buyer
FROM       SKU_DATA;
```

as shown in Figure 2-11.
3. Click the **Run** button on the Design tab. The query results appear, as shown in Figure 2-12. Compare the results shown in Figure 2-12 to the SQL query results shown on page 37.

Because Microsoft Access is a personal database and includes an application generator, we can save Access queries for future use. Enterprise-level DBMS products generally do not allow us to save queries (although they do allow us to save SQL Views within the database and SQL query scripts as separate files—we will discuss these methods later).

Figure  **2-10**

The Query1 Window in SQL View

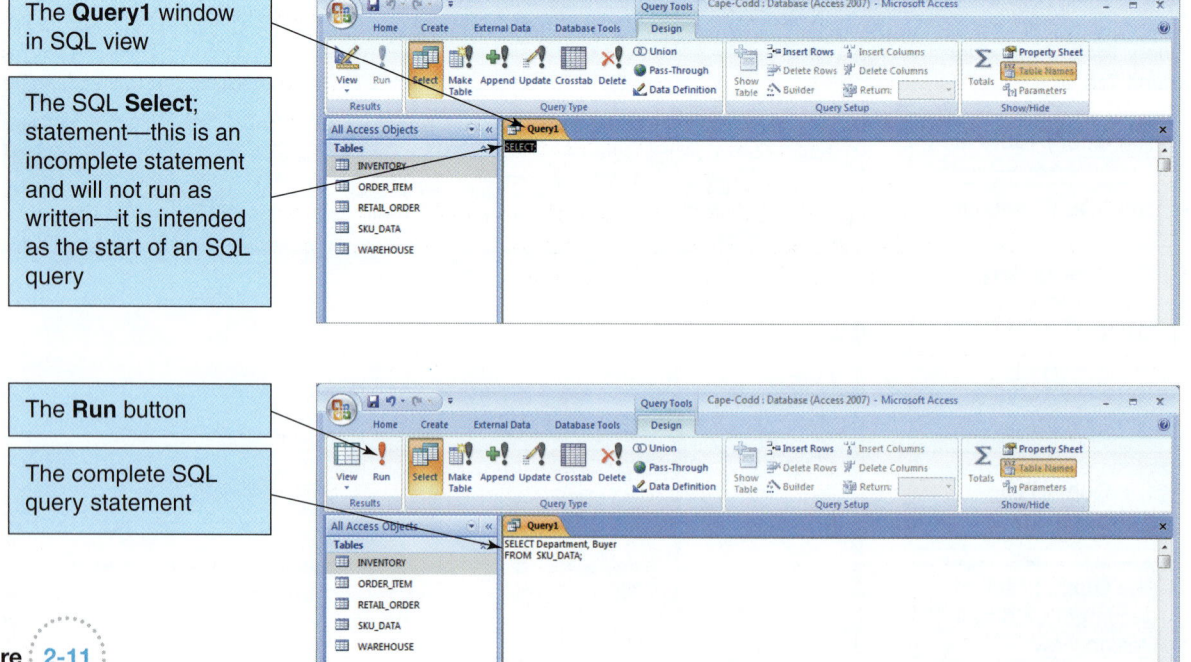

Figure 2-11

The SQL Query

The query results

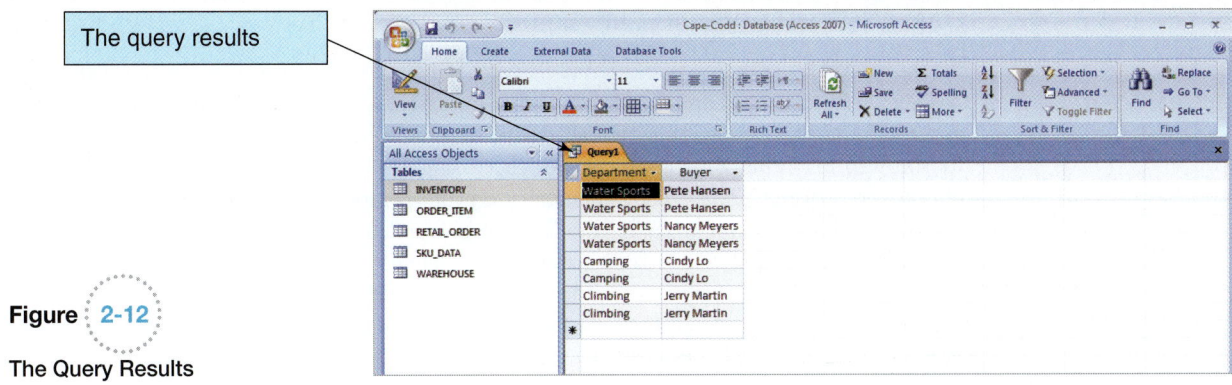

Figure 2-12

The Query Results

The **Save** button

The **Save As** dialog box

Type the query name **SQLQuery-CH02-01** here

The **OK** button

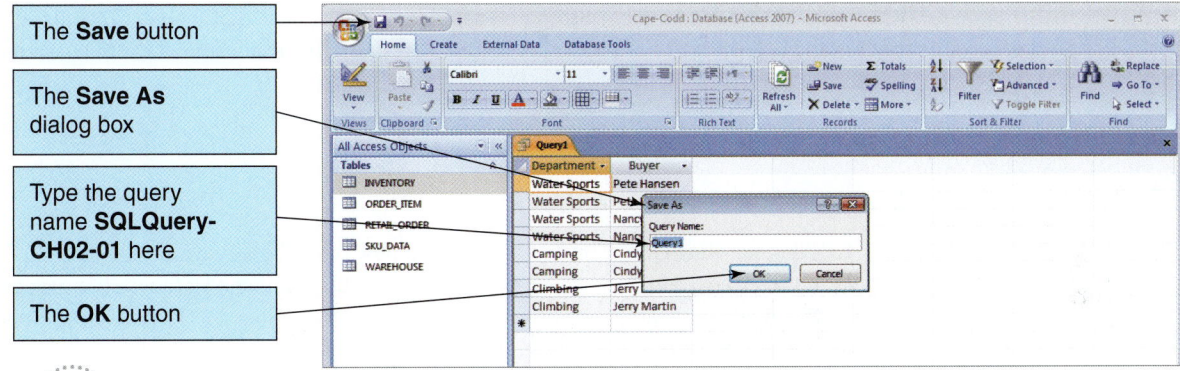

Figure 2-13

The Query Results

Saving an Access SQL Query

1. To save the query, click the **Save** button on the Quick Access Toolbar. The Save As dialog box appears, as shown in Figure 2-13.
2. Type in the query name **SQLQuery-CH02-01** and then click the **OK** button. The query is saved, and the window is renamed with the query name. As shown in Figure 2-14, the query document window is now named SQLQuery-CH02-01, and a newly created SLQQuery-CH02-01 query object appears in a Queries section of the Navigation Pane.
3. Close the SQLQuery-CH02-01 window by clicking the document window's **Close** button.
4. If Access displays a dialog box, asking whether you want to save changes to the design of the query SQLQuery-CH02-01, click the **Yes** button.

At this point, you should work through each of the other nine queries in the preceding discussion of the SQL SELECT/FROM/WHERE framework. Save each query as SQLQuery-CH02-##, where ## is a sequential number from 02 to 09.

Figure 2-14

The Named and Saved Query

The query window is now named **SQLQuery-CH02-01**

The **Queries** section of the Navigation Pane

The **SQLQuery-CH02-01** query object

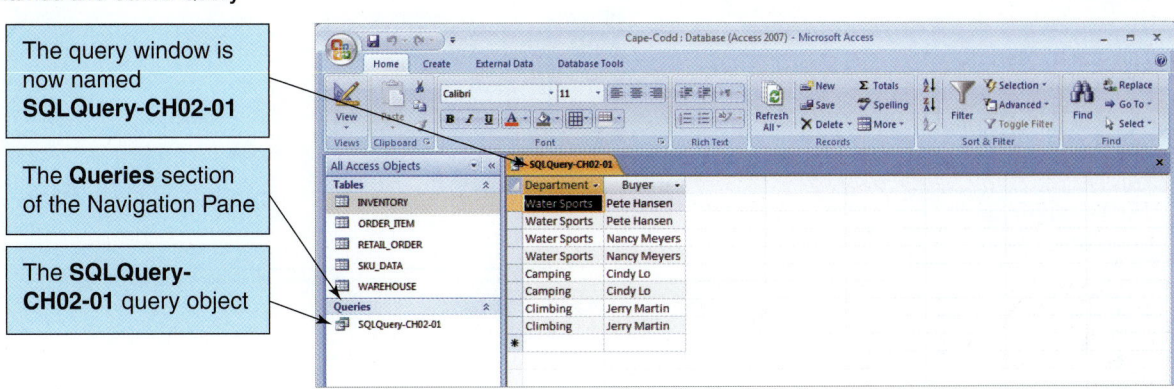

Using SQL in Microsoft SQL Server 2008

Before you can use SQL statements with Microsoft SQL Server, you need access to a computer that has SQL Server installed and that has a database with the tables and data shown in Figures 2-3 and 2-4. Your instructor may have installed SQL Server in your computer lab and entered the data for you. If so, follow his or her instructions for accessing that database. Otherwise, you will need to obtain a copy of SQL Server 2008 and install it on your computer. Read the appropriate sections of Chapter 11 about obtaining and installing SQL Server 2008.

After you have SQL Server 2008 installed, you will need to read the introductory discussion for using SQL Server in Chapter 10, starting on page 353, and create the Cape Codd database. SQL Server scripts for creating and populating the Cape Codd database tables are available on our Web site at *www.pearsonhighered.com/kroenke*.

SQL Server 2008 uses the Microsoft SQL Server 2008 Management Studio as the GUI tool for managing the SQL Server DBMS and the databases controlled by the DBMS. The Microsoft SQL Server 2008 Management Studio is installed as part of the SQL Server 2008 installation process and is discussed in Chapter 10. Figure 2-15 shows the execution of the SQL statement:

```
SELECT      Department, Buyer
FROM        SKU_DATA;
```

Running an SQL Server SQL Query

1. Click the **New Query** button to display a new tabbed query window.
2. If the Cape Codd database is not displayed in the Available Database box, select it in the Available Databases drop-down list, and then click the **Intellisense Enabled** button to *disable* Intellisense.
3. Type the SQL SELECT command:

```
SELECT      Department, Buyer
FROM        SKU_DATA;
```

in the query window, as shown in Figure 2-15.

Figure 2-15

Running an SQL Query in SQL Server Management Studio

The **New Query** button

Available Databases drop-down list—select the database here

The **Execute** button

The Cape Codd database

The Cape Codd database tables

The **Parse** button

The **IntelliSense Enabled** button

The SQL query in the tabbed query window

The **Results** tabbed window

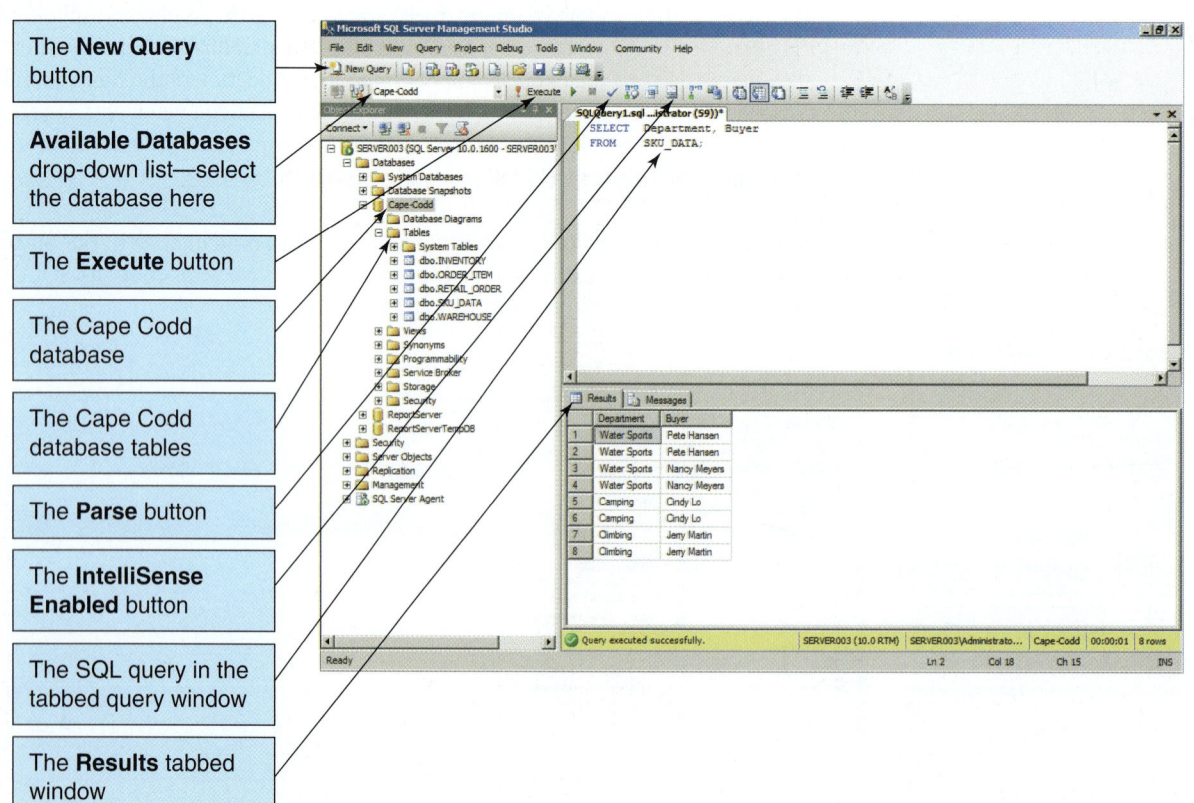

4. At this point you can check the SQL command syntax before actually running the command by clicking the **Parse** button. A Results window will be displayed in the same location shown in Figure 2-15, but with the message "Command(s) completed successfully" if the SQL command syntax is correct or with an error message if there is a problem with the syntax.

5. Click the Execute button to run the query. The results are displayed in a results window, as shown in Figure 2-15.

Note that in Figure 2-15 the Cape Codd database object in the Object Browser in the left side window of the SQL Server Management Studio has been expanded to show the tables in the Cape Codd database. Many of the functions of the SQL Server Management Studio are associated with the objects in the Object Browser and are often accessed by right-clicking the object to display a shortcut menu.

> **BY THE WAY** We are using SQL Server 2008 Enterprise edition running in Microsoft Server 2008. When we give specific sequences of steps to follow in the text or figures in this book, we use the command terminology used by SQL Server 2008 and associated utility programs in Microsoft Server 2008. If you are running a workstation operating system such as Microsoft XP or Microsoft Vista, the terminology may vary somewhat.

SQL Server 2008 is an enterprise-class DBMS product, and, as is typical of such products, does not store queries within the DBMS (it does store SQL Views, which can be considered a type of query, and we will discuss SQL Views later in this chapter). However, you can save queries as SQL script files. An **SQL script file** is a separately stored plain text file, and it usually uses a file name extension of *.sql*. An SQL script can be opened and run as an SQL command (or set of commands). Often used to create and populate databases, scripts can also be used to store a query or set of queries. Figure 2-16 shows the SQL query being saved as an SQL script.

Note that in Figure 2-16 the SQL scripts are shown in a folder named *Cape-Codd-Database*. When the Microsoft SQL Server 2008 Management Studio is installed, a new folder named *SQL Server Management Studio* is created in your Documents (My Documents in Windows XP) folder, with *Projects* as a subfolder. The Projects folder is the default location used by SQL Server 2008 for SQL script files.

Figure  **2-16**

Saving an SQL Query as an SQL Script in SQL Server Management Studio

| The **Open File** button |
| The **Save** button |
| The **Save File As** dialog box |
| The **Cape-Codd-Database** folder |
| Existing SQL scripts— these were used to create and populate the Cape-Codd database |
| Type the SQL script file name here |
| The **Save** button |

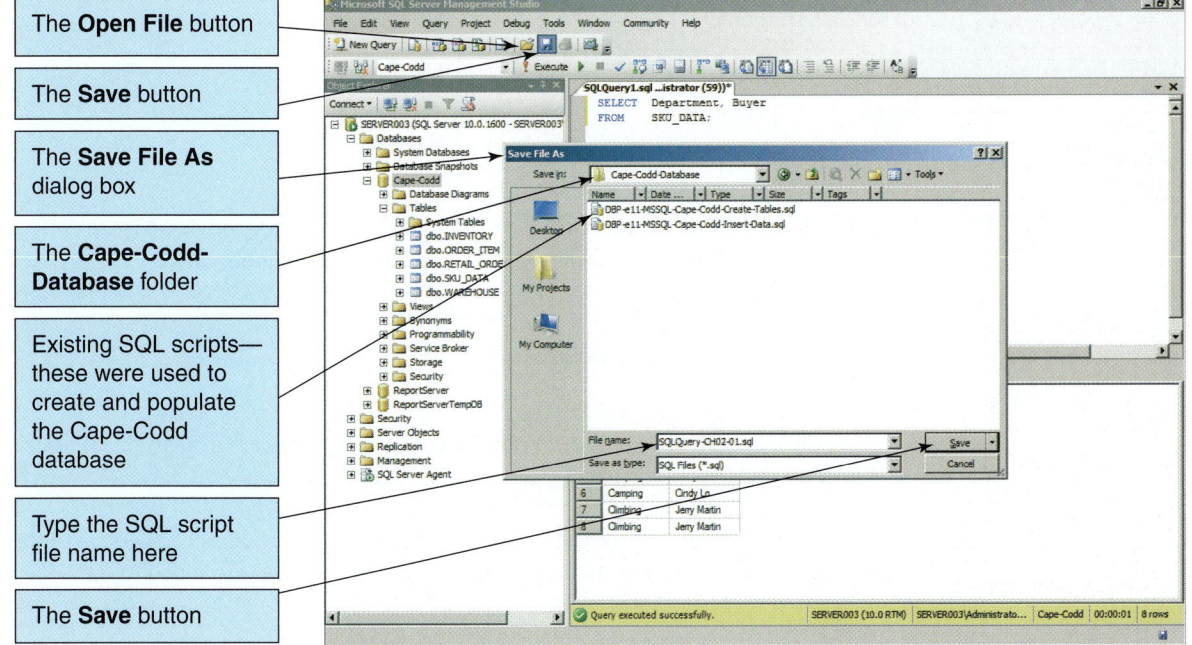

We recommend that you create a folder for each database in the Projects folder. We have created a folder named *Cape-Code-Database* to store the script files associated with the Cape Codd database.

Saving an SQL Server Query as an SQL Script

1. Click the **Save** button shown in Figure 2-16. The Save File As dialog appears, as shown in Figure 2-16.
2. Browse to the */SQL Server Management Studio/Project/Cape-Codd-Database* folder.
3. Note that there are already two SQL script names displayed in the dialog box. These are the SQL scripts that were used to create and populate the Cape Codd database tables, and they are available on our Web site at *www.pearsonhighered.com/kroenke*.
4. In the File Name text box, type the SQL script file name *SQLQuery-CH02-01*.
5. Click the **Save** button.

To rerun the saved query, you would click the **Open File** button shown in Figure 2-16 to open the Open File dialog box, open the query, and then click the **Execute** button.

At this point, you should work through each of the other nine queries in the preceding discussion of the SQL SELECT/FROM/WHERE framework. Save each query as SQLQuery-CH02-##, where ## is a sequential number from 02 to 09.

Using SQL in Oracle Database 11g

Before you can enter SQL statements to Oracle Database 11g, you need access to a computer that has Oracle installed and that has a database with the tables and data shown in Figure 2-4. Your instructor may have installed Oracle on a computer in the lab and entered the data for you. If so, follow his or her instructions for accessing that database. Otherwise, you will need to obtain a copy of Oracle Database 11g and install it on your computer. Read the appropriate sections of Chapter 10A about obtaining and installing Oracle Database 11g.

After you have installed Oracle 11g, you will need to read the introductory discussion for Oracle in Chapter 10A, starting on page 10A-5, and create the Cape Codd database. Oracle scripts for creating and populating the Cape Codd database tables are available on our Web site at *www.pearsonhighered.com/kroenke*.

Although Oracle users have been dedicated to the Oracle SQL*Plus command line tool, professionals are moving to the new Oracle SQL Developer GUI tool. This application is installed as part of the Oracle installation, and updated versions are available for free download at *www.oracle.com/technology/software/products/sql/index.html*. We will use it as our standard GUI tool for managing the databases created by the Oracle DBMS. Figure 2-17 shows the execution of the SQL statement:

```
SELECT      Department, Buyer
FROM        SKU_DATA;
```

Running an SQL Server SQL Query

1. Click the **New Connection** button and open the Cape Codd database.
2. In the tabbed SQL Worksheet, type the SQL SELECT command:

   ```
   SELECT      Department, Buyer
   FROM        SKU_DATA;
   ```

   as shown in Figure 2-17.
3. Click the **Execute** button to run the query. The results are displayed in a results window, as shown in Figure 2-17.

Note that in Figure 2-17, the Cape Codd database object in the Object Browser in the left side Connection object browser of the Oracle SQL Developer has been expanded to show the tables

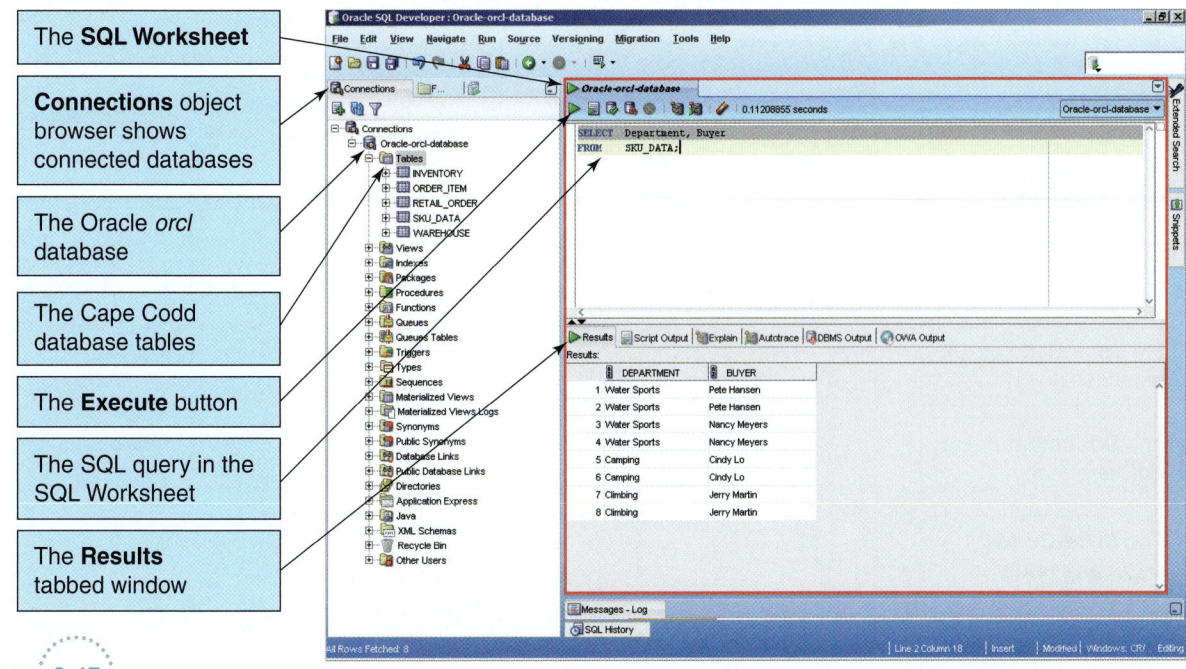

Figure 2-17

Running an SQL Query in Oracle SQL Developer

The labels shown alongside the figure:

- The **SQL Worksheet**
- **Connections** object browser shows connected databases
- The Oracle *orcl* database
- The Cape Codd database tables
- The **Execute** button
- The SQL query in the SQL Worksheet
- The **Results** tabbed window

in the Cape Codd database. Many of the functions of SQL Developer are associated with the objects in the Connections object browser and are often accessed by right-clicking the object to display a shortcut menu.

> **BY THE WAY** We are using Oracle Database 11g Enterprise edition running in Microsoft Server 2008. When we give specific sequences of steps to follow in the text or figures in this book, we use the command terminology used by Oracle Database 11g and associated utility programs in Microsoft Server 2008. If you are running a workstation operating system such as Microsoft XP, Microsoft Vista, or Linux, the terminology may vary somewhat.

Oracle 11g is an enterprise-class DBMS product, and, as is typical of such products, does not store queries within the DBMS (it does store SQL Views, which can be considered a type of query, and we will discuss SQL Views later in this chapter). However, you can save queries as SQL script files. An SQL script file is a separately stored plain text file and it usually uses a file name extension of *.sql*. An SQL script can be opened and run as an SQL command (or set of commands). Often used to create and populate databases, scripts can also be used to store a query or set of queries. Figure 2-18 shows the SQL query being saved as an SQL script.

Note that in Figure 2-18 the SQL scripts are shown in a folder named *{UserName}\ Documents\Oracle Workspace\Cape-Codd-Database*. By default, Oracle SQL Developer stores *.sql files in an obscure location within its own application files. We recommend that you create a subfolder in your Documents folder (My Documents in Windows XP) named Oracle Workspace, and then create a subfolder for each database in the Oracle Workspace folder. We have created a folder named *Cape-Code-Database* to store the script files associated with the Cape Codd database.

When we did this, a *Cape-Codd-Database Folder* button was added to the Save dialog box shown in Figure 2-18. You can easily move to the Cape-Codd-Database folder by clicking this button.

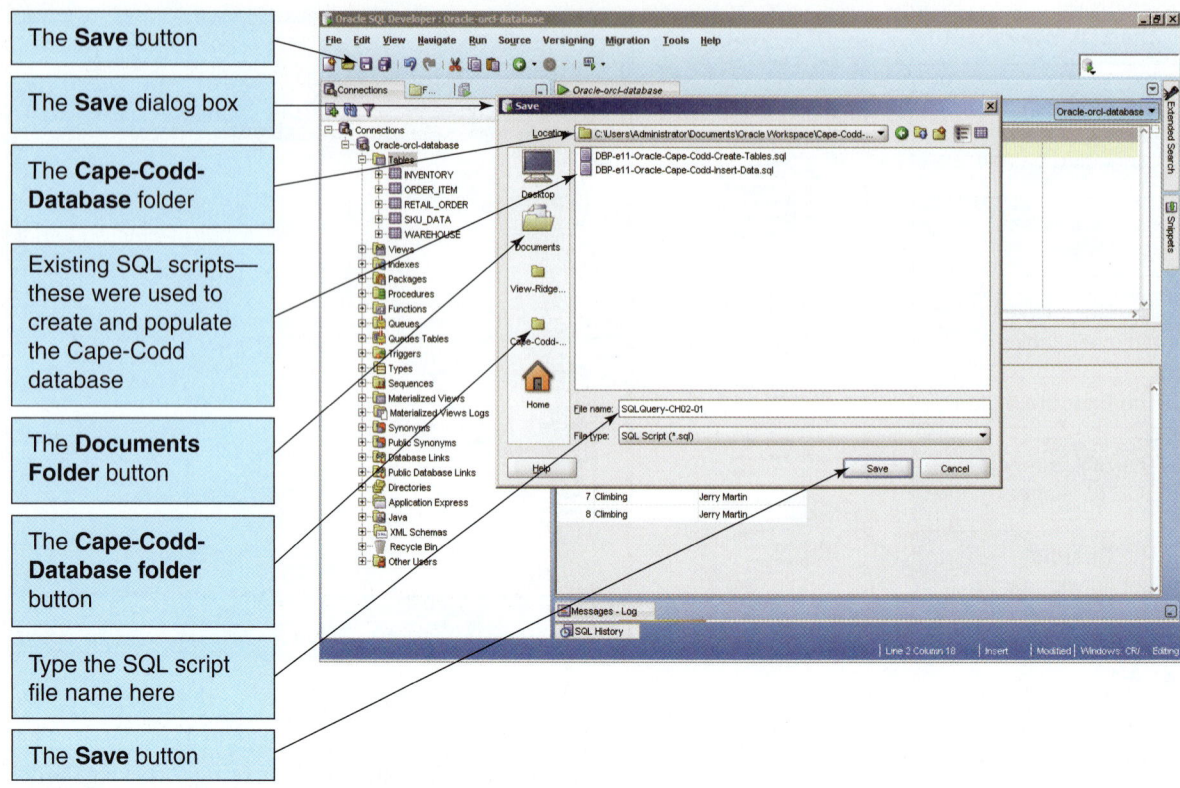

The **Save** button

The **Save** dialog box

The **Cape-Codd-Database** folder

Existing SQL scripts— these were used to create and populate the Cape-Codd database

The **Documents Folder** button

The **Cape-Codd-Database folder** button

Type the SQL script file name here

The **Save** button

Figure 2-18

Saving an SQL Query as an SQL Script in Oracle SQL Developer

Saving an SQL Script in Oracle SQL Developer

1. Click the **Save** button shown in Figure 2-18. The Save dialog appears, as shown in Figure 2-18.
2. Click the **Cape-Codd-Database Folder** button on the Save dialog box to move to the Cape-Code-Database folder. Alternatively, you can click the **Documents** button on the Save dialog box to move to the Documents folder, and then browse to the Cape-Codd-Database folder.
3. Note that there are already two SQL script names displayed in the dialog box. These are the SQL scripts that were used to create and populate the Cape Codd database tables, and they are available on our Web site at *www.pearsonhighered.com/kroenke*.
4. In the File Name text box, type the SQL script file name *SQLQuery-CH02-01.sql*.
5. Click the **Save** button.

To rerun the saved query, you would click the SQL Developer **Open File** button to open the Open File dialog box, browse to the query file, open the query file, and then click the **Execute** button.

At this point, you should work through each of the other nine queries in the preceding discussion of the SQL SELECT/FROM/WHERE framework. Save each query as SQLQuery-CH02-##, where ## is a sequential number from 02 to 09.

Using SQL in Sun Microsystems MySQL 5.1

Before you can use SQL statements with Sun Microsystems MySQL, you need access to a computer that has MySQL installed and that has a database with the tables and data shown in Figure 2-4. Your instructor may have installed MySQL in your computer lab and entered the data for you. If so, follow his or her instructions for accessing that database. Otherwise, you will need to obtain a copy of MySQL Server 5.1 and install it on your computer. Read the appropriate sections of Chapter 10B about obtaining and installing SQL Server 2008.

After you have MySQL installed, you will need to read the introductory discussion for MySQL Server in Chapter 10B, starting on page 10B-4, and create the Cape Codd database. MySQL scripts for creating and populating the Cape Codd database tables are available on our Web site at *www.pearsonhighered.com/kroenke*.

MySQL uses two tools, the MySQL Administrator and the MySQL Query Browser, as the GUI tools for managing the MySQL DBMS and the databases controlled by the DBMS. These tools must be installed separately from the MySQL DBMS, and this is discussed in Chapter 10B. SQL statements are created and run in the MySQL Query Browser, and Figure 2-19 shows the execution of the SQL statement:

```
SELECT      Department, Buyer

FROM        SKU_DATA;
```

Running an SQL Query in the MySQL Query Browser

1. To make the Cape Codd database the default schema (active database), right-click the Cape Codd schema (database) object to display the shortcut menu and then click the **Make Default** command.
2. Type the SQL SELECT command:

```
SELECT      Department, Buyer

FROM        SKU_DATA;
```

   in the **Query Toolbar text box,** as shown in Figure 2-19.
3. Click the **Execute** button to run the query. The results are displayed in a Resultset window, as shown in Figure 2-19.

Note that in Figure 2-19 the Cape Codd database object in the Object Browser in the right-side window of the MySQL Query Browser has been expanded to show the tables in the Cape Codd database. Many of the functions of the MySQL Query Browser are associated with the objects in the Object Browser and are often accessed by right-clicking the object to display a shortcut menu.

> **BY THE WAY** We are using MySQL 5.1 Community Server running in Microsoft Server 2008. When we give specific sequences of steps to follow in the text or figures in this book, we use the command terminology used for MySQL 5.1 and associated utility programs in Microsoft Server 2008. If you are running a workstation operating system such as Microsoft XP, Microsoft Vista, or Linux, the terminology may vary somewhat.

Figure 2-19

Running an SQL Query in MySQL Query Browser

The MySQL Query browser **Query Toolbar**—enter your SQL statement into the **text box** and then click the **Execute** button

The **Resultset** tabbed window

The Object Browser

The Cape Codd database

The Cape Codd database tables

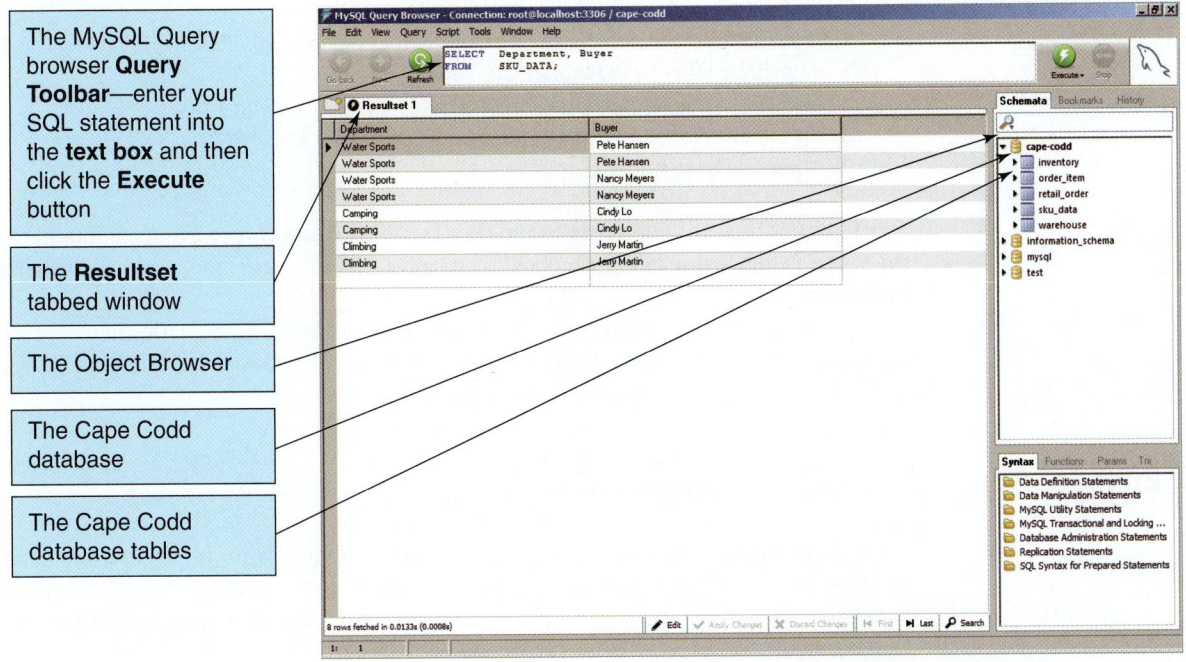

Use the **File/Save As** command to open the **Save Query to File** dialog box

The **Save Query to File** dialog box

The **Cape-Codd-Database** folder

Type the SQL Query File name here

The **Save** button

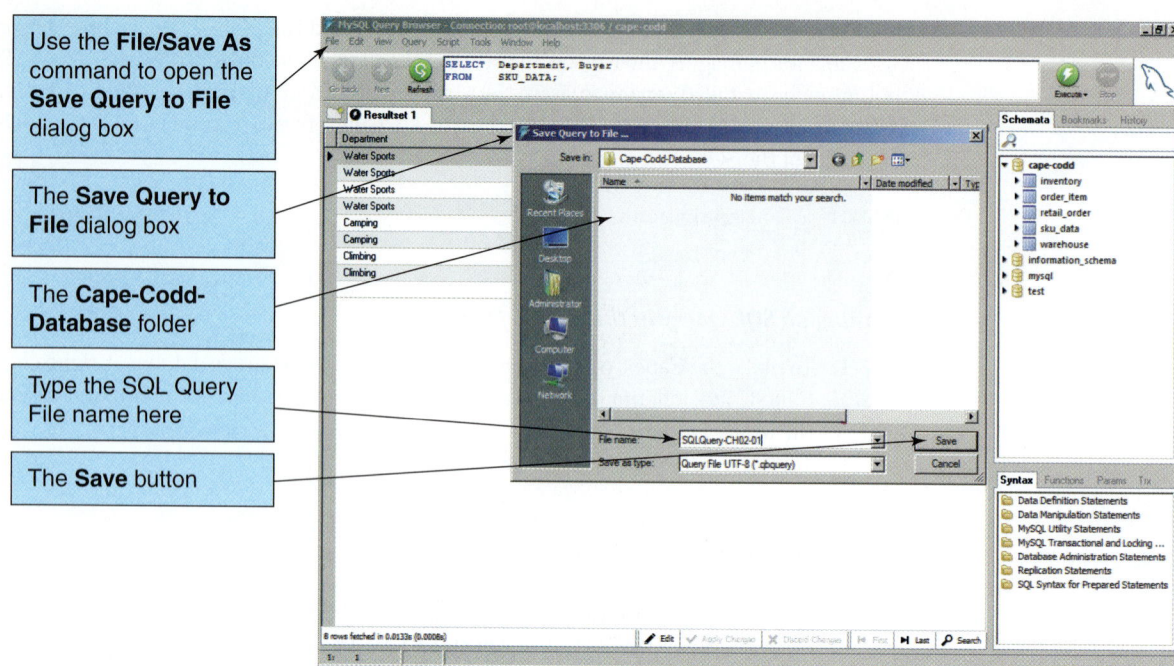

Figure 2-20

Saving an SQL Query as a MySQL Query File in MySQL Query Browser

MySQL 5.1 is an enterprise-class DBMS product, and, as is typical of such products, does not store queries within the DBMS (it does store SQL Views, which can be considered a type of query, and we will discuss SQL Views later in this chapter). However, you can save MySQL queries as **MySQL query files**. A MySQL query file is a separately stored plain text file, and it usually uses a file name extension of *.qbquery*. A MySQL query file can be opened and run as an SQL command. Figure 2-20 shows the SQL query being saved as a MySQL query file.

Note that in Figure 2-20 the query will be saved in a folder named *{UserName}\ Documents\MySQL Workspace\Cape-Codd-Database*. By default, MySQL Query Browser stores files in the user's Documents folder (My Documents in Windows XP). We recommend that you create a subfolder in your Documents folder named MySQL Workspace, and then create a subfolder for each database in the MySQL Workspace folder. We have created a folder named *Cape-Code-Database* to store the script files associated with the Cape Codd database.

Saving a MySQL Query

1. Use the **File | Save as** command as shown in Figure 2-20. The Save Query to File dialog appears, as shown in Figure 2-20.
2. Browse to the *Documents\MySQL Workspace\Cape-Codd-Database* folder.
3. In the File Name text box, type the SQL query file name *SQLQuery-CH02-01*.
4. Click the **Save** button.

To rerun the saved query, you would click the **File | Open Query** menu command to open the **Open Query from File** dialog box, then select and open the query, and finally click the **Execute** button.

At this point, you should work through each of the other nine queries in the preceding discussion of the SQL SELECT/FROM/WHERE framework. Save each query as SQLQuery-CH02-##, where ## is a sequential number from 02 to 09.

SQL Enhancements for Querying a Single Table

We started our discussion of SQL queries with SQL statements for processing a single table, and now we will add an additional SQL feature to those queries. As we proceed, you will begin to see how powerful SQL can be for querying databases and for creating information from existing data.

 **THE WAY**   The SQL results shown in this chapter were generated using Microsoft SQL Server 2008. Query results from other DBMS products will be similar, but may vary a bit.

Sorting the Results

The order of the rows produced by an SQL statement is arbitrary and determined by programs in the bowels of each DBMS. If you want the DBMS to display the rows in a particular order, you can use the **SQL ORDER BY clause**. For example, the SQL statement:

```
SELECT        *
FROM          ORDER_ITEM
ORDER BY      OrderNumber;
```

will generate the following results:

	OrderNumber	SKU	Quantity	Price	ExtendedPrice
1	1000	201000	1	300.00	300.00
2	1000	202000	1	130.00	130.00
3	2000	101100	4	50.00	200.00
4	2000	101200	2	50.00	100.00
5	3000	101200	1	50.00	50.00
6	3000	101100	2	50.00	100.00
7	3000	100200	1	300.00	300.00

We can sort by two columns by adding a second column name. For example, to sort first by OrderNumber and then by Price within OrderNumber, we use the following SQL query:

```
SELECT        *
FROM          ORDER_ITEM
ORDER BY      OrderNumber, Price;
```

The result for this query is:

	OrderNumber	SKU	Quantity	Price	ExtendedPrice
1	1000	202000	1	130.00	130.00
2	1000	201000	1	300.00	300.00
3	2000	101100	4	50.00	200.00
4	2000	101200	2	50.00	100.00
5	3000	101200	1	50.00	50.00
6	3000	101100	2	50.00	100.00
7	3000	100200	1	300.00	300.00

If we want to sort the data by Price and then by OrderNumber, we would simply reverse the order of those columns in the ORDER BY clause as follows:

```
SELECT        *
FROM          ORDER_ITEM
ORDER BY      Price, OrderNumber;
```

with the results:

	OrderNumber	SKU	Quantity	Price	ExtendedPrice
1	2000	101100	4	50.00	200.00
2	2000	101200	2	50.00	100.00
3	3000	101200	1	50.00	50.00
4	3000	101100	2	50.00	100.00
5	1000	202000	1	130.00	130.00
6	1000	201000	1	300.00	300.00
7	3000	100200	1	300.00	300.00

 **THE WAY**   Note to Microsoft Access users: Unlike the SQL Server output shown here, Microsoft Access displays dollar signs in the output of currency data.

By default, rows are sorted in ascending order. To sort in descending order, add the **SQL DESC keyword** after the column name. Thus, to sort first by Price in descending order and then by OrderNumber in ascending order, we use the SQL query:

```
SELECT          *
FROM            ORDER_ITEM
ORDER BY        Price DESC, OrderNumber ASC;
```

The result is:

	OrderNumber	SKU	Quantity	Price	ExtendedPrice
1	1000	201000	1	300.00	300.00
2	3000	100200	1	300.00	300.00
3	1000	202000	1	130.00	130.00
4	2000	101100	4	50.00	200.00
5	2000	101200	2	50.00	100.00
6	3000	101200	1	50.00	50.00
7	3000	101100	2	50.00	100.00

Because the default order is ascending, it is not necessary to specify ASC in the last SQL statement. Thus, the following SQL statement is equivalent to the previous SQL query:

```
SELECT          *
FROM            ORDER_ITEM
ORDER BY        Price DESC, OrderNumber;
```

and produces the same results:

	OrderNumber	SKU	Quantity	Price	ExtendedPrice
1	1000	201000	1	300.00	300.00
2	3000	100200	1	300.00	300.00
3	1000	202000	1	130.00	130.00
4	2000	101100	4	50.00	200.00
5	2000	101200	2	50.00	100.00
6	3000	101200	1	50.00	50.00
7	3000	101100	2	50.00	100.00

SQL WHERE Clause Options

SQL includes a number of SQL WHERE clause options that greatly expand SQL's power and utility. In this section, we consider three options: compound clauses, ranges, and wildcards.

Compound WHERE Clauses

SQL WHERE clauses can include multiple conditions by using the SQL AND, OR, IN, and NOT IN operators. For example, to find all of the rows in SKU_DATA that have a Department named Water Sports and a Buyer named Nancy Meyers, we can use the **SQL AND operator** in our query code:

```
SELECT      *
FROM        SKU_DATA
WHERE       Department='Water Sports'
    AND     Buyer='Nancy Meyers';
```

The results of this query are:

	SKU	SKU_Description	Department	Buyer
1	101100	Dive Mask, Small Clear	Water Sports	Nancy Meyers
2	101200	Dive Mask, Med Clear	Water Sports	Nancy Meyers

Similarly, to find all of the rows of SKU_DATA for either the Camping or Climbing departments, we can use the **SQL OR operator** in the SQL query:

```
SELECT      *
FROM        SKU_DATA
WHERE       Department='Camping'
    OR      Department='Climbing';
```

which gives us the following results:

	SKU	SKU_Description	Department	Buyer
1	201000	Half-dome Tent	Camping	Cindy Lo
2	202000	Half-dome Tent Footprint	Camping	Cindy Lo
3	301000	Light Fly Climbing Harness	Climbing	Jerry Martin
4	302000	Locking carabiner, Oval	Climbing	Jerry Martin

Three or more AND and OR conditions can be combined, but in such cases the **SQL IN operator** and the **SQL NOT IN operator** are easier to use. For example, suppose we want to obtain all of the rows in SKU_DATA for buyers Nancy Meyers, Cindy Lo, and Jerry Martin. We could construct a WHERE clause with two ANDs, but an easier way to do this is to use the IN operator, as illustrated in the SQL query:

```
SELECT      *
FROM        SKU_DATA
WHERE       Buyer IN ('Nancy Meyers', 'Cindy Lo', 'Jerry Martin');
```

In this format, a set of values is enclosed in parentheses. A row is selected if Buyer is equal to any one of the values provided. The result is:

	SKU	SKU_Description	Department	Buyer
1	101100	Dive Mask, Small Clear	Water Sports	Nancy Meyers
2	101200	Dive Mask, Med Clear	Water Sports	Nancy Meyers
3	201000	Half-dome Tent	Camping	Cindy Lo
4	202000	Half-dome Tent Footprint	Camping	Cindy Lo
5	301000	Light Fly Climbing Harness	Climbing	Jerry Martin
6	302000	Locking carabiner, Oval	Climbing	Jerry Martin

Similarly, if we want to find rows of SKU_DATA for which the buyer is someone *other* than Nancy Meyers, Cindy Lo, or Jerry Martin, we would use the SQL query:

```
SELECT      *
FROM        SKU_DATA
WHERE       Buyer NOT IN ('Nancy Meyers', 'Cindy Lo', 'Jerry Martin');
```

The result is:

	SKU	SKU_Description	Department	Buyer
1	100100	Std. Scuba Tank, Yellow	Water Sports	Pete Hansen
2	100200	Std. Scuba Tank, Magenta	Water Sports	Pete Hansen

Observe an important difference between IN and NOT IN. A row qualifies for an IN condition if the column is equal to *any* of the values in the parentheses. However, a row qualifies for a NOT IN condition if it is not equal to *all* of the items in the parentheses.

Ranges in SQL WHERE Clauses

SQL WHERE clauses can specify ranges of data values by using the **SQL BETWEEN keyword**. For example, the following SQL statement:

```
SELECT      *
FROM        ORDER_ITEM
WHERE       ExtendedPrice BETWEEN 100 AND 200;
```

will produce the following results:

	OrderNumber	SKU	Quantity	Price	ExtendedPrice
1	2000	101100	4	50.00	200.00
2	3000	101100	2	50.00	100.00
3	2000	101200	2	50.00	100.00
4	1000	202000	1	130.00	130.00

Notice that both the ends of the range, 100 and 200, are included in the resulting table. The preceding SQL statement is equivalent to the SQL query:

```
SELECT      *
FROM        ORDER_ITEM
WHERE       ExtendedPrice >=100
    AND     ExtendedPrice >=200;
```

And which, of course, produces identical results:

	OrderNumber	SKU	Quantity	Price	ExtendedPrice
1	2000	101100	4	50.00	200.00
2	3000	101100	2	50.00	100.00
3	2000	101200	2	50.00	100.00
4	1000	202000	1	130.00	130.00

Wildcards in SQL WHERE Clauses

The **SQL LIKE keyword** can be used in SQL WHERE clauses to specify matches on portions of column values. For example, suppose we want to find the rows in the SKU_DATA table for all buyers whose first name is *Pete*. To find such rows, we use the SQL keyword LIKE with the **SQL percent sign (%) wildcard character**, as shown in the SQL query:

```
SELECT      *
FROM        SKU_DATA
WHERE       Buyer LIKE 'Pete%';
```

When used as an SQL wildcard character, the percent symbol (%) stands for any sequence of characters. When used with the SQL LIKE keyword, the character string 'Pete%' means any sequence of characters that start with the letters *Pete*. The result of this query is:

	SKU	SKU_Description	Department	Buyer
1	100100	Std. Scuba Tank, Yellow	Water Sports	Pete Hansen
2	100200	Std. Scuba Tank, Magenta	Water Sports	Pete Hansen

Does Not Work with MS Access ANSI-89 SQL   Microsoft Access ANSI-89 SQL uses wildcards, but not the SQL-92 standard wildcards. Microsoft Access uses the **Access asterisk (*) wildcard character** instead of a percent sign to represent multiple characters.

Solution: Use the Microsoft Access asterisk (*) wildcard in place of the SQL-92 percent sign (%) wildcard in Microsoft Access ANSI-89 SQL statements. Thus, the preceding SQL query would be written as follows for Microsoft Access:

```
SELECT      *
FROM        SKU_DATA
WHERE       Buyer LIKE 'Pete*';
```

Suppose we want to find the rows in SKU_DATA for which the SKU_Description includes the word *Tent* somewhere in the description. Because the word *Tent* could be at the front, the end, or in the middle, we need to place a wildcard on both ends of the LIKE phrase, as follows:

```
SELECT      *
FROM        SKU_DATA
WHERE       SKU_Description LIKE '%Tent%';
```

This query will find rows in which the word *Tent* occurs in any place in the SKU_Description. The result is:

	SKU	SKU_Description	Department	Buyer
1	201000	Half-dome Tent	Camping	Cindy Lo
2	202000	Half-dome Tent Footprint	Camping	Cindy Lo

Sometimes we need to search for a particular value in a particular location in the column. For example, assume SKU values are coded such that a 2 in the third position from the right has some particular significance, maybe it means that the product is a variation of another product. For whatever reason, assume that we need to find all SKUs that have a 2 in the third column from the right. Suppose we try the SQL query:

```
SELECT      *
FROM        SKU_DATA
WHERE       SKU LIKE '%2%';
```

The result is

	SKU	SKU_Description	Department	Buyer
1	100200	Std. Scuba Tank, Magenta	Water Sports	Pete Hansen
2	101200	Dive Mask, Med Clear	Water Sports	Nancy Meyers
3	201000	Half-dome Tent	Camping	Cindy Lo
4	202000	Half-dome Tent Footprint	Camping	Cindy Lo
5	302000	Locking carabiner, Oval	Climbing	Jerry Martin

This is *not* what we wanted. We mistakenly retrieved all rows that had a 2 in *any* position in the value of SKU. To find the products we want, we cannot use the SQL wildcard character %. Instead, we must use the **SQL underscore (_) wildcard character**, which represents a single, unspecified character in a specific position. The following SQL statement will find all SKU_DATA rows with a value of 2 in the third position from the right:

```
SELECT      *
FROM        SKU_DATA
WHERE       SKU LIKE '%2__';
```

Observe that there are *two* underscores in this SQL query— one for the first position on the right and another for the second position on the right. This query gives us the result that we want:

	SKU	SKU_Description	Department	Buyer
1	100200	Std. Scuba Tank, Magenta	Water Sports	Pete Hansen
2	101200	Dive Mask, Med Clear	Water Sports	Nancy Meyers

Does Not Work with MS Access ANSI-89 SQL

Microsoft Access ANSI-89 SQL uses wildcards, but not the SQL-92 standard wildcards. Microsoft Access uses the **Access question mark (?) wildcard character** instead of an underscore (_) to represent a single character.

Solution: Use the Microsoft Access question mark (?) wildcard in place of the SQL-92 underscore (_) wildcard in Microsoft Access ANSI-89 SQL statements. Thus, the preceding SQL query would be written as follows for Microsoft Access:

```
SELECT      *
FROM        SKU_DATA
WHERE       SKU LIKE '*2??';
```

Furthermore, Microsoft Access can sometimes be fussy about stored trailing spaces in a text field. You may have problems with a WHERE clause like this:

```
WHERE       SKU LIKE '10?200';
```

Solution: Use a trailing asterisk (*), which allows for the trailing spaces:

```
WHERE       SKU LIKE '10?200*';
```

 **THE WAY**   The SQL wildcard percent sign (%) and underscore (_) characters are specified in the SQL-92 standard. They are accepted by all DBMS products *except Microsoft Access*. So, why does Microsoft Access use the asterisk (*) character instead of the percent sign (%) and the question mark (?) instead of the underscore? This difference probably exists because the designers of Access chose to use the same wildcard characters that Microsoft was already using in the Microsoft MS-DOS operating system.

Combing the SQL WHERE Clause and the SQL ORDER BY Clause

If we want to sort the results generated by these enhanced SQL WHERE clauses, we simply combine the SQL ORDER BY clause with the WHERE clause. This is illustrated by the following SQL query:

```
SELECT      *
FROM        ORDER_ITEM
WHERE       ExtendedPrice BETWEEN 100 AND 200
ORDER BY    OrderNumber DESC;
```

which will produce the following result:

	OrderNumber	SKU	Quantity	Price	ExtendedPrice
1	3000	101100	2	50.00	100.00
2	2000	101200	2	50.00	100.00
3	2000	101100	4	50.00	200.00
4	1000	202000	1	130.00	130.00

Performing Calculations in SQL Queries

It is possible to perform certain types of calculations in SQL query statements. One group of calculations involves the use of SQL built-in functions. Another group involves simple arithmetic operations on the columns in the SELECT statement. We will consider each in turn.

Using SQL Built-in Functions

There are five **SQL built-in functions** for performing arithmetic on table columns: **SUM**, **AVG**, **MIN**, **MAX**, and **COUNT**. Some DBMS products extend these standard built-in functions by providing additional functions. Here, we will focus only on the five standard SQL built-in functions.

Suppose we want to know the sum of OrderTotal for all of the orders in RETAIL_ORDER. We can obtain that sum by using the following SQL query:

```
SELECT      SUM(OrderTotal)
FROM        RETAIL_ORDER;
```

The result will be:

	(No column name)
1	1235.00

Recall that the result of an SQL statement is always a table. In this case, the table has one cell (the intersection of one row and one column that contains the sum of OrderTotal). But because the OrderTotal sum is not a column in a table, the DBMS has no column name to provide.

The preceding result was produced by Microsoft SQL Server 2008, and it names the column '(No column name)'. Other DBMS products take other, equivalent actions.

This result is ugly. We would prefer to have a meaningful column name, and SQL allows us to assign one using the **SQL AS keyword**. If we use the AS keyword in the query as follow:

```
SELECT       SUM(OrderTotal) AS OrderSum
FROM         RETAIL_ORDER;
```

The result of this modified query will be:

	OrderSum
1	1235.00

This result has a much more meaningful column label. The name *OrderSum* is arbitrary—we are free to pick any name that we think would be meaningful to the user of the result. We could pick *OrderTotal_Total*, *OrderTotalSum*, or any other label that we think would be useful.

The utility of the built-in functions increases when you use them with an SQL WHERE clause. For example, we can write the SQL query:

```
SELECT       SUM(ExtendedPrice) AS Order3000Sum
FROM         ORDER_ITEM
WHERE        OrderNumber=3000;
```

The result of this query is:

	Order3000Sum
1	450.00

The SQL built-in functions can be mixed and matched in a single statement. For example, we can create the following SQL statement:

```
SELECT       SUM(ExtendedPrice) AS OrderItemSum,
             AVG(ExtendedPrice) AS OrderItemAvg,
             MIN(ExtendedPrice) AS OrderItemMin,
             MAX(ExtendedPrice) AS OrderItemMax
FROM         ORDER_ITEM;
```

The result of this query is:

	OrderItemSum	OrderItemAvg	OrderItemMin	OrderItemMax
1	1180.00	168.5714	50.00	300.00

The SQL built-in COUNT function sounds similar to the SUM function, but it produces very different results. The COUNT function *counts* the number of rows, whereas the SUM function *adds* the values in a column. If we write the SQL statement:

```
SELECT       COUNT(*) AS NumberOfRows
FROM         ORDER_ITEM;
```

The result of this query is:

	NumberOfRows
1	7

This result indicates that there are seven rows in the ORDER_ITEM table. Notice that we need to provide an asterisk (*) after the COUNT function when we want to count rows. COUNT is the only built-in function that requires an asterisk. The COUNT function is also unique because it can be used on any type of data, but the SUM, AVG, MIN, and MAX functions can only be used with numeric data.

The COUNT function can produce some surprising results. For example, suppose you want to count the number of departments in the SKU_DATA table. If we use the following query:

```
SELECT      COUNT(Department) AS DeptCount
FROM        SKU_DATA;
```

The result is:

	DeptCount
1	8

which is the number of rows in the SKU_DATA table, *not* the number of unique values of Department, as shown in Figure 2-4. If we want to count the unique values of Department, we need to use the SQL DISTINCT keyword, as follows:

```
SELECT      COUNT(DISTINCT Department) AS DeptCount
FROM        SKU_DATA;
```

The result of this query is:

	DeptCount
1	3

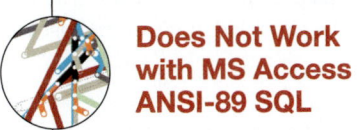

Does Not Work with MS Access ANSI-89 SQL   Microsoft Access does not support the DISTINCT keyword as part of the COUNT expression, so while the SQL command with COUNT(Department) will work, the SQL command with COUNT(DISTINCT Department) will fail.

Solution: Use an SQL subquery structure (discussed later in this chapter) with the DISTINCT keyword in the subquery itself. This SQL query works:

```
SELECT   COUNT(*) AS DeptCount
FROM     (SELECT DISTINCT Department
          FROM SKU_DATA) AS DEPT;
```

Note that this query is a bit different from the other SQL queries using subqueries we show in this text because this subquery is in the FROM clause instead of (as you'll see) the WHERE clause. Basically, this subquery builds a new temporary table named DEPT containing only distinct Department values, and the query counts the number of those values.

You should be aware of two limitations to SQL built-in functions. First, except for grouping (defined later), you *cannot* combine a table column name with an SQL built-in function. For example, what happens if we run the following SQL query?

```
SELECT      Department, COUNT(*)
FROM        SKU_DATA;
```

The result in SQL Server 2008 is:

```
Msg 8120, Level 16, State 1, Line 1
Column 'SKU_DATA.Department' is invalid in the select list because it is not contained
in either an aggregate function or the GROUP BY clause.
```

This is the specific SQL Server 2008 error message. However, you will receive an equivalent message from Access, Oracle, DB2, or MySQL.

The second problem with the SQL built-in functions that you should understand is that you cannot use them in an SQL WHERE clause. Thus, you cannot use the following SQL statement:

```
SELECT      *
FROM        RETAIL_ORDER
WHERE       OrderTotal > AVG(OrderTotal);
```

An attempt to use such a statement will also result in an error statement from the DBMS:

```
Msg 147, Level 15, State 1, Line 3
An aggregate may not appear in the WHERE clause unless it is in a subquery contained
in a HAVING clause or a select list, and the column being aggregated is an outer reference.
```

Again, this is the specific SQL Server 2008 error message, but other DBMS products will give you an equivalent error message. In Chapter 7, you will learn how to obtain the desired result of the above query using a sequence of SQL views.

SQL Expressions in SQL SELECT Statements

It is possible to do basic arithmetic in SQL statements. For example, suppose we want to compute the values of extended price, perhaps because we want to verify the accuracy of the data in the ORDER_ITEM table. To compute the extended price, we can use the SQL expression Quantity * Price in the SQL query:

```
SELECT      Quantity * Price AS EP
FROM        ORDER_ITEM;
```

The result is:

	EP
1	300.00
2	200.00
3	100.00
4	100.00
5	50.00
6	300.00
7	130.00

An **SQL expression** is basically a formula or set of values that determines the exact results of an SQL Query. We can think of an SQL expression as anything that follows an actual or implied equal to (=) character (or any other relational operator, such as greater than (>), less than (<), and so on) or that follows certain SQL keywords such as LIKE and BETWEEN. Thus, the SELECT clause in the preceding query includes the implied equal to (=) sign as *EP = Quantity * Price*. For another example, in the WHERE clause:

```
WHERE       Buyer IN ('Nancy Meyers', 'Cindy Lo', 'Jerry Martin');
```

the SQL expression consists of the three text values following the IN keyword.

Now that we know how to calculate the value of extended price, we can compare this computed value to the stored value of ExtendedPrice by using the SQL query:

```
SELECT      Quantity * Price AS EP, ExtendedPrice
FROM        ORDER_ITEM;
```

The result of this statement now allows us to visually compare the two values to ensure that the stored data are correct:

	EP	ExtendedPrice
1	300.00	300.00
2	200.00	200.00
3	100.00	100.00
4	100.00	100.00
5	50.00	50.00
6	300.00	300.00
7	130.00	130.00

Another use for SQL expressions in SQL statements is to perform string manipulation. Suppose we want to combine the Buyer and Department columns into a single column named Sponsor. If we use the SQL statement:

```
SELECT      Buyer+' in '+Department AS Sponsor
FROM        SKU_DATA;
```

the result will include a column named Sponsor that contains the combined text values:

	Sponsor	
1	Pete Hansen	in Water Sports
2	Pete Hansen	in Water Sports
3	Nancy Meyers	in Water Sports
4	Nancy Meyers	in Water Sports
5	Cindy Lo	in Camping
6	Cindy Lo	in Camping
7	Jerry Martin	in Climbing
8	Jerry Martin	in Climbing

This particular result is also ugly. We can eliminate the extra spaces by using more advanced functions. The syntax and use of such functions vary from one DBMS to another, however, and a discussion of the features of each product will take us away from the point of this discussion. To learn more, search on *string functions* in the documentation for your specific DBMS. Just to illustrate the possibilities, however, here is an SQL Server 2008 statement that strips the tailing blanks off the right-hand side of Buyer and Department:

```
SELECT      DISTINCT RTRIM(Buyer)+' in '+RTRIM(Department) AS Sponsor
FROM        SKU_DATA;
```

The result of this query is much more visually pleasing:

	Sponsor
1	Cindy Lo in Camping
2	Jerry Martin in Climbing
3	Nancy Meyers in Water Sports
4	Pete Hansen in Water Sports

Grouping in SQL SELECT Statements

In SQL queries, rows can be grouped according to common values using the **SQL GROUP BY clause**. For example, if you specify GROUP BY Department in a SELECT statement on the SKU_DATA table, the DBMS will first sort all rows by Department and then combine all of the rows having the same value into a group for that department. A grouping will be formed for each unique value of Department. For example, when we use the GROUP BY clause in the SQL query:

```
SELECT      Department, COUNT(*) AS Dept_SKU_Count
FROM        SKU_DATA
GROUP BY    Department;
```

We get the result:

	Department	Dept_SKU_Count
1	Camping	2
2	Climbing	2
3	Water Sports	4

To obtain this result, the DBMS first sorts the rows according to Department and then counts the number of rows having the same value of Department.

Here is another example of an SQL query using GROUP BY:

```
SELECT      SKU, AVG(ExtendedPrice) AS AvgEP
FROM        ORDER_ITEM
GROUP BY    SKU;
```

The result for this query is:

	SKU	AvgEP
1	100200	300.00
2	101100	150.00
3	101200	75.00
4	201000	300.00
5	202000	130.00

Here the rows have been sorted and grouped by SKU and the average ExtendedPrice for each group of SKU items has been calculated.

We can include more than one column in a GROUP BY expression. For example, the SQL statement:

```
SELECT      Department, Buyer, COUNT(*) AS Dept_Buyer_SKU_Count
FROM        SKU_DATA
GROUP BY    Department, Buyer;
```

groups rows according to the value of Department first, then according to Buyer, and then counts the number of rows for each combination of Department and Buyer. The result is:

	Department	Buyer	Dept_Buyer_SKU_Count
1	Camping	Cindy Lo	2
2	Climbing	Jerry Martin	2
3	Water Sports	Nancy Meyers	2
4	Water Sports	Pete Hansen	2

When using the GROUP BY clause, only the column or columns in the GROUP BY expression and the SQL built-in functions can be used in the expressions in the SELECT clause. The following expressions will result in an error:

```
SELECT      SKU, Department, COUNT(*) AS Dept_SKU_Count
FROM        SKU_DATA
GROUP BY    Department;
```

```
Msg 8120, Level 16, State 1, Line 1
Column 'SKU_DATA.SKU' is invalid in the select list because it is not contained
in either an aggregate function or the GROUP BY clause.
```

This is the specific SQL Server 2008 error message, but other DBMS products will give you an equivalent error message. Statements like this one are invalid because there are many values of SKU for each Department group. The DBMS has no place to put those multiple values in the result. If you do not understand the problem, try to process this statement by hand. It cannot be done.

Of course, the SQL WHERE and ORDER BY clauses can also be used with SELECT statements, as shown in the following query:

```
SELECT      Department, COUNT(*) AS Dept_SKU_Count
FROM        SKU_DATA
WHERE       SKU <>302000
GROUP BY    Department
ORDER BY    Dept_SKU_Count;
```

The result is:

	Department	Dept_SKU_Count
1	Climbing	1
2	Camping	2
3	Water Sports	4

Notice that one of the rows of the Climbing department has been removed from the count because it did not meet the WHERE clause condition. Without the ORDER BY clause, the rows would be presented in arbitrary order of Department. With it, the order is as shown. In general, to be safe, always place the WHERE clause before the GROUP BY clause. Some DBMS products do not require that placement, but others do.

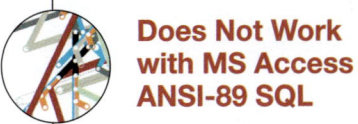

Does Not Work with MS Access ANSI-89 SQL Microsoft Access does not properly recognize the alias *Dept_SKU_Count* in the ORDER BY clause and creates a parameter query that requests an input value of as yet nonexistent Dept_SKU_Count! However, it doesn't matter whether you enter parameter values or not—click the OK button and the query will run. The results will be basically correct, but they will not be sorted correctly.

(continued)

Solution: Use the Access QBE GUI to modify the query structure. The correct QBE structure is shown in Figure 2-21. The resulting Access ANSI-89 SQL is:

```
SELECT      SKU_DATA.Department, Count(*) AS Dept_SKU_Count
FROM        SKU_DATA
WHERE       (((SKU_DATA.SKU)<>302000))
GROUP BY    SKU_DATA.Department
ORDER BY    Count(*);
```

which can be edited down to:

```
SELECT      Department, Count(*) AS Dept_SKU_Count
FROM        SKU_DATA
WHERE       SKU<>302000
GROUP BY    Department
ORDER BY    Count(*);
```

SQL provides one more GROUP BY clause feature that extends its functionality even further. The **SQL HAVING clause** restricts the groups that are presented in the result. We can restrict the previous query to display only groups having more than one row by using the SQL query:

```
SELECT      Department, COUNT(*) AS Dept_SKU_Count
FROM        SKU_DATA
WHERE       SKU <>302000
GROUP BY    Department
HAVING      COUNT (*) > 1
ORDER BY    Dept_SKU_Count;
```

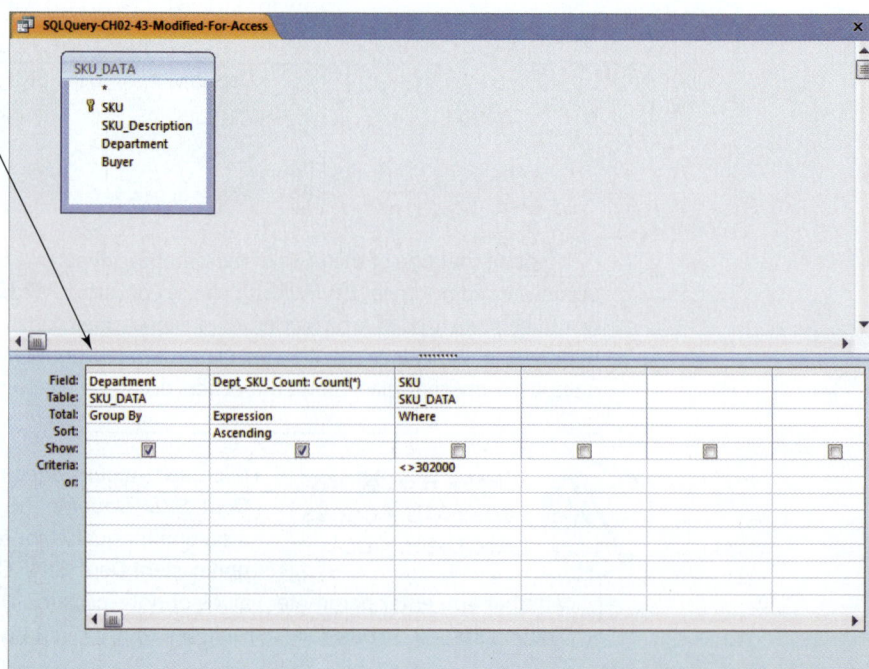

Edit the query in the QBE GUI interface so that it appears as shown here

Figure 2-21

Editing the SQL Query in the Access 2007 QBE GUI Interface

The result of this modified query is:

	Department	Dept_SKU_Count
1	Camping	2
2	Water Sports	4

Comparing this result with the previous one, the row for Climbing (which has a count of 1) has been eliminated.

Does Not Work with MS Access ANSI-89 SQL

This query fails in Microsoft Access ANSI-89 SQL for the same reason as the previous query.

Solution: See the solution described in the previous "Does Now Work with Microsoft Access ANSI-89 SQL" box. The correct Access ANSI-89 SQL for this query is:

```
SELECT      Department, Count(*) AS Dept_SKU_Count
FROM        SKU_DATA
WHERE       SKU<>302000
GROUP BY    Department
HAVING      Count(*)>1
ORDER BY    Count(*);
```

SQL built-in functions can be used in the HAVING clause. For example, the following is a valid SQL query:

```
SELECT      COUNT(*) AS SKU_Count, SUM(Price) AS TotalRev, SKU
FROM        ORDER_ITEM
GROUP BY    SKU
HAVING      SUM(Price)=100;
```

The results for this query are:

	SKU_Count	TotalRev	SKU
1	2	100.00	101100
2	2	100.00	101200

Be aware that there is an ambiguity in statements that include both WHERE and HAVING clauses. The results vary depending on whether the WHERE condition is applied before or after the HAVING. To eliminate this ambiguity, the WHERE clause is *always* applied before the HAVING clause.

Looking for Patterns in NASDAQ Trading

Before we continue our discussion of SQL, consider an example problem that will illustrate the power of the SQL just described.

Suppose that a friend tells you that she suspects the stock market tends to go up on certain days of the week and down on others. She asks you to investigate past trading data to determine if this is true. Specifically, she wants to trade an index fund called the NASDAQ 100, which is a stock fund of the 100 top companies traded on the NASDAQ stock exchange. She gives you a dataset with 20 years (1985–2004) of NASDAQ 100 trading data for analysis. Assume she gives you the data in the form of a table named NDX containing 4611 rows of data for use with a relational database (this dataset is available on the text's Web site at *www.pearsonhighered.com/kroenke*).

Investigating the Characteristics of the Data

Suppose you first decide to investigate the general characteristics of the data. You begin by seeing what columns are present in the table by issuing the SQL query:

```
SELECT     *
FROM       NDX;
```

The first five rows of that query are as follows:

	TClose	PriorClose	ChangeClose	Volume	TMonth	TDayOfMonth	TYear	TDayOfWeek	TQuarter
1	1520.46	1530.65	-10.1900000000001	24827600	January	9	2004	Friday	1
2	1530.65	1514.26	16.3900000000001	26839500	January	8	2004	Thursday	1
3	1514.26	1501.26	13	22942800	January	7	2004	Wednesday	1
4	1501.26	1496.58	4.68000000000006	22732200	January	6	2004	Tuesday	1
5	1496.58	1463.57	33.01	23629100	January	5	2004	Monday	1

Assume that you learn that the first column has the value of the fund at the close of a trading day, the second column has the value of the fund at the close of the prior trading day, and the third row has the difference between the current day's close and the prior day's close. Volume is the number of shares traded, and the rest of the data concerns the trading date.

Next, you decide to investigate the change of the stock price by issuing the SQL query:

```
SELECT     AVG(ChangeClose) AS AverageChange,
           MAX(ChangeClose) AS MaxGain,
           MIN(ChangeClose) AS MaxLoss
FROM       NDX;
```

The result of this query is:

	AverageChange	MaxGain	MaxLoss
1	0.281167028199584	399.6	-401.03

> **BY THE WAY** DBMS products have many functions for formatting query results to reduce the number of decimal points displayed, to add currency characters such as $ or £, or to make other formatting changes. However, these functions are DBMS-dependent. Search the documentation of your DBMS for the term *formatting results* to learn more about such functions.

Just out of curiosity, you decide to determine which days had the maximum and minimum change. To avoid having to key in the long string of decimal places that would be required to make an equal comparison, you use a greater than and less than comparison with values that are close:

```
SELECT     ChangeClose, TMonth, TDayOfMonth, TYear
FROM       NDX
WHERE      ChangeClose > 398
     OR    ChangeClose < -400;
```

The result is:

	ChangeClose	TMonth	TDayOfMonth	TYear
1	-401.03	January	3	1994
2	399.6	January	3	2001

This result is surprising! Is there some reason that both the greatest loss and the greatest gain both occurred on January 3? You begin to wonder if your friend might have a promising idea.

Searching for Patterns in Trading by Day of Week

You want to determine if there is a difference in the average trade by day of week. Accordingly, you create the SQL query:

```
SELECT      TDayOfWeek, AVG(ChangeClose) AS AvgChange
FROM        NDX
GROUP BY    TDayOfWeek;
```

The result is:

	TDayOfWeek	AvgChange
1	Wednesday	0.777940552017005
2	Monday	-1.03577929465299
3	Friday	0.146021739130452
4	Thursday	2.17412972972975
5	Tuesday	-0.711440677966085

Indeed, there does seem to be a difference according to the day of the week. The NASDAQ 100 appears to go down on Monday and Tuesday and then go up on the other three days of the week. Thursday, in particular, seems to be a good day to trade long.

But, you begin to wonder, is this pattern true for each year? To answer that question, you use the query:

```
SELECT      TDayOfWeek, TYear, AVG(ChangeClose) AS AvgChange
FROM        NDX
GROUP BY    TDayOfWeek, TYear
ORDER BY    TDayOfWeek, TYear DESC;
```

Because there are 20 years of data, this query results in 100 rows, of which the first 12 are shown in the following results:

	TDayOfWeek	TYear	AvgChange
1	Friday	2004	-7.2700000000001
2	Friday	2003	-2.48499999999996
3	Friday	2002	-2.19419999999997
4	Friday	2001	-19.5944
5	Friday	2000	8.8980392156863
6	Friday	1999	13.9656000000001
7	Friday	1998	5.26408163265531
8	Friday	1997	-0.194799999999989
9	Friday	1996	0.819019607843153
10	Friday	1995	0.691372549019617
11	Friday	1994	0.123725490196082
12	Friday	1993	-0.899399999999989

To simplify your analysis, you decide to restrict the number of rows to the most recent 5 years (2000–2004):

```
SELECT      TDayOfWeek, TYear, AVG(ChangeClose) AS AvgChange
FROM        NDX
WHERE       TYear > '1999'
GROUP BY    TDayOfWeek, TYear
ORDER BY    TDayOfWeek, TYear DESC;
```

Partial results from this query are as follows:

	TDayOfWeek	TYear	AvgChange
1	Friday	2004	-7.2700000000001
2	Friday	2003	-2.48499999999996
3	Friday	2002	-2.19419999999997
4	Friday	2001	-19.5944
5	Friday	2000	8.8980392156863
6	Monday	2004	33.01
7	Monday	2003	3.77416666666668
8	Monday	2002	-2.60229166666664
9	Monday	2001	-3.75270833333333
10	Monday	2000	-19.899574468085
11	Thursday	2004	16.3900000000001
12	Thursday	2003	5.70700000000002

Alas, it does not appear that day of week is a very good predictor of gain or loss. At least, not for this fund over this period of time. We could continue this discussion to further analyze this data, but by now you should understand how useful SQL can be for analyzing and processing a table. Suggested additional NDX analysis exercises are included in the SQL problems at the end of this chapter.

Querying Two or More Tables with SQL

So far in this chapter we've worked with only one table. Now we will conclude by describing SQL statements for querying two or more tables.

Suppose that you want to know the revenue generated by SKUs managed by the Water Sports department. We can compute revenue as the sum of ExtendedPrice, but we have a problem. ExtendedPrice is stored in the ORDER_ITEM table, and Department is stored in the SKU_DATA table. We need to process data in two tables, and all of the SQL presented so far operates on a single table at a time.

SQL provides two different techniques for querying data from multiple tables: subqueries and joins. Although both work with multiple tables, they are used for slightly different purposes, as you will learn.

Querying Multiple Tables with Subqueries

How can we obtain the sum of ExtendedPrice for items managed by the Water Sports department? If we somehow knew the SKU values for those items, we could use a WHERE clause with the IN keyword.

For the data in Figure 2-4, the SKU values for items in Water Sports are 100100, 100200, 101100, and 101200. Knowing those values, we can obtain the sum of their ExtendedPrice with the following SQL query:

```
SELECT      SUM(ExtendedPrice) AS Revenue
FROM        ORDER_ITEM
WHERE       SKU IN (100100, 100200, 101100, 101200);
```

The result is:

	Revenue
1	750.00

But, in general, we do not know the necessary SKU values ahead of time. However, we do have a way to obtain them from an SQL query on the data in the SKU_DATA table. To obtain the SKU values for the Water Sports department, we use the SQL statement:

```
SELECT      SKU
FROM        SKU_DATA
WHERE       Department='Water Sports'
```

The result of this SQL statement is:

	SKU
1	100100
2	100200
3	101100
4	101200

which is, indeed, the desired list of SKU values.

Now we need only combine the last two SQL statements to obtain the result we want. We replace the list of values in the WHERE clause of the first SQL query with the second SQL statement as follows:

```
SELECT      SUM(ExtendedPrice) AS Revenue
FROM        ORDER_ITEM
WHERE       SKU IN
            (SELECT     SKU
             FROM       SKU_DATA
             WHERE      Department='Water Sports');
```

The result of the query is:

	Revenue
1	750.00

which is the same result we obtained before when we know the values of SKU to use.

In the preceding SQL query, the second SELECT statement, the one enclosed in parentheses, is called a **subquery**. We can use multiple subqueries to process three or even more tables. For example, suppose we want to know the name of the buyers who manage any product purchased in January 2004. First, note that Buyer data is stored in the SKU_DATA table and OrderMonth and OrderYear data are stored in the RETAIL_ORDER table.

Now, we can use an SQL query with two subqueries to obtain the desired data as follows:

```
SELECT       Buyer

FROM         SKU_DATA

WHERE        SKU IN
             (SELECT      SKU
               FROM        ORDER_ITEM
               WHERE       OrderNumber  IN
                           (SELECT      OrderNumber
                             FROM        RETAIL_ORDER
                             WHERE       OrderMonth='January'
                                  AND    OrderYear=2009));
```

The result of this statement is:

	Buyer
1	Pete Hansen
2	Nancy Meyers
3	Nancy Meyers

To understand this statement, work from the bottom up. The bottom SELECT statement obtains the list of OrderNumbers of orders sold in January 2009. The middle SELECT statement obtains the SKU values for items sold in orders in January 2009. Finally, the top-level SELECT query obtains Buyer for all of the SKUs found in the middle SELECT statement.

Any parts of the SQL language that you have learned earlier in this chapter can be applied to a table generated by a subquery, regardless of how complicated the SQL looks. For example, we can apply the DISTINCT keyword on the results to eliminate duplicate rows. Or, we can apply the GROUP BY and ORDER BY clauses as follows:

```
SELECT       Buyer, COUNT(*) AS NumberSold

FROM         SKU_DATA

WHERE        SKU IN
             (SELECT      SKU
               FROM        ORDER_ITEM
               WHERE       OrderNumber IN
                           (SELECT      OrderNumber
                             FROM        RETAIL_ORDER
                             WHERE       OrderMonth='January'
                                  AND    OrderYear=2009))
GROUP BY     Buyer
ORDER BY     NumberSold DESC;
```

The result is:

	Buyer	NumberSold
1	Nancy Meyers	2
2	Pete Hansen	1

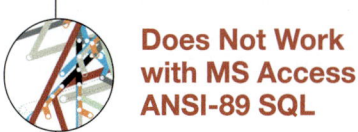

Does Not Work with MS Access ANSI-89 SQL

This query fails in Microsoft Access ANSI-89 SQL for the same reason previously described on pages 65–66.

Solution: See the solution described in the "Does Now Work with Microsoft Access ANSI-89 SQL" box on pages 65–66. The correct Access ANSI-89 SQL statement for this query is:

```
SELECT      Buyer, Count(*) AS NumberSold
FROM        SKU_DATA
WHERE       SKU IN
            (SELECT   SKU
             FROM     ORDER_ITEM
             WHERE    OrderNumber IN
                      (SELECT    OrderNumber
                       FROM      RETAIL_ORDER
                       WHERE     OrderMonth='January'
                             AND OrderYear=2009))
GROUP BY    Buyer
ORDER BY    Count(*) DESC;
```

Querying Multiple Tables with Joins

Subqueries are very powerful, but they do have a serious limitation. The selected data can only come from the top-level table. We cannot use a subquery to obtain data that arise from more than one table. To do so, we must use a join instead.

The **SQL join operator** is used to combine two or more tables by concatenating (sticking together) the rows of one table with the rows of another table. Consider how we might combine the data in the RETAIL_ORDER and ORDER_ITEM tables. We can concatenate the rows of one table with the rows of the second table with the following SQL statement:

```
SELECT       *
FROM         RETAIL_ORDER, ORDER_ITEM;
```

This statement will just stick every row of one table together with every row of the second table. For the data in Figure 2-4, the result is

	OrderNumber	StoreNumber	StoreZip	OrderMonth	OrderYear	OrderTotal	OrderNumber	SKU	Quantity	Price	ExtendedPrice
1	1000	10	98110	December	2008	445.00	3000	100200	1	300.00	300.00
2	1000	10	98110	December	2008	445.00	2000	101100	4	50.00	200.00
3	1000	10	98110	December	2008	445.00	3000	101100	2	50.00	100.00
4	1000	10	98110	December	2008	445.00	2000	101200	2	50.00	100.00
5	1000	10	98110	December	2008	445.00	3000	101200	1	50.00	50.00
6	1000	10	98110	December	2008	445.00	1000	201000	1	300.00	300.00
7	1000	10	98110	December	2008	445.00	1000	202000	1	130.00	130.00
8	2000	20	02335	December	2008	310.00	3000	100200	1	300.00	300.00
9	2000	20	02335	December	2008	310.00	2000	101100	4	50.00	200.00
10	2000	20	02335	December	2008	310.00	3000	101100	2	50.00	100.00
11	2000	20	02335	December	2008	310.00	2000	101200	2	50.00	100.00
12	2000	20	02335	December	2008	310.00	3000	101200	1	50.00	50.00
13	2000	20	02335	December	2008	310.00	1000	201000	1	300.00	300.00
14	2000	20	02335	December	2008	310.00	1000	202000	1	130.00	130.00
15	3000	10	98110	January	2009	480.00	3000	100200	1	300.00	300.00
16	3000	10	98110	January	2009	480.00	2000	101100	4	50.00	200.00
17	3000	10	98110	January	2009	480.00	3000	101100	2	50.00	100.00
18	3000	10	98110	January	2009	480.00	2000	101200	2	50.00	100.00
19	3000	10	98110	January	2009	480.00	3000	101200	1	50.00	50.00
20	3000	10	98110	January	2009	480.00	1000	201000	1	300.00	300.00
21	3000	10	98110	January	2009	480.00	1000	202000	1	130.00	130.00

Because there are three rows of retail order and seven rows of order items, there are 3 times 7, or 21, rows in this table. Notice that the retail order with OrderNumber 1000 has been combined with all seven of the rows in ORDER_ITEM_GRADE, the retail order with OrderNumber has been combined with all seven of the same rows, and, finally, that the retail order with OrderNumber 3000 has again been combined with all seven rows.

This is illogical—what we need to do is to select only those rows for which the OrderNumber of RETAIL_ORDER matches the OrderNumber in ORDER_ITEM. This is easy to do: we simply add an SQL WHERE clause to the query:

```
SELECT      *
FROM        RETAIL_ORDER, ORDER_ITEM
WHERE       RETAIL_ORDER.OrderNumber=ODRER_ITEM.OrderNumber;
```

The result is:

	OrderNumber	StoreNumber	StoreZip	OrderMonth	OrderYear	OrderTotal	OrderNumber	SKU	Quantity	Price	ExtendedPrice
1	3000	10	98110	January	2009	480.00	3000	100200	1	300.00	300.00
2	2000	20	02335	December	2008	310.00	2000	101100	4	50.00	200.00
3	3000	10	98110	January	2009	480.00	3000	101100	2	50.00	100.00
4	2000	20	02335	December	2008	310.00	2000	101200	2	50.00	100.00
5	3000	10	98110	January	2009	480.00	3000	101200	1	50.00	50.00
6	1000	10	98110	December	2008	445.00	1000	201000	1	300.00	300.00
7	1000	10	98110	December	2008	445.00	1000	202000	1	130.00	130.00

This is technically correct, but it will be easier to read if we sort the results using an ORDER BY clause:

```
SELECT      *
FROM        RETAIL_ORDER, ORDER_ITEM
WHERE       RETAIL_ORDER.OrderNumber=ORDER_ITEM.OrderNumber
ORDER BY    RETAIL_ORDER.OrderNumber, ORDER_ITEM.SKU;
```

The result is:

	OrderNumber	StoreNumber	StoreZip	OrderMonth	OrderYear	OrderTotal	OrderNumber	SKU	Quantity	Price	ExtendedPrice
1	1000	10	98110	December	2008	445.00	1000	201000	1	300.00	300.00
2	1000	10	98110	December	2008	445.00	1000	202000	1	130.00	130.00
3	2000	20	02335	December	2008	310.00	2000	101100	4	50.00	200.00
4	2000	20	02335	December	2008	310.00	2000	101200	2	50.00	100.00
5	3000	10	98110	January	2009	480.00	3000	100200	1	300.00	300.00
6	3000	10	98110	January	2009	480.00	3000	101100	2	50.00	100.00
7	3000	10	98110	January	2009	480.00	3000	101200	1	50.00	50.00

If you compare this result with the data in Figure 2-4, you will see that only the appropriate order items are associated with each retail order. You also can tell that this has been done by noticing that in each row the value of OrderNumber from RETAIL_ORDER (the first column) equals the value of OrderNumber from ORDER_ITEM (the seventh column). This was not true for our first result.

You may have noticed that we introduced a new variation in SQL statement syntax in the previous two queries, where the terms RETAIL_ORDER.OrderNumber, ORDER_ITEM. OrderNumber, and ORDER_ITEM.SKU were used. The new syntax is simply **TableName. ColumnName**, and it is used to specify exactly which table each column is linked to. RETAIL_ORDER.OrderNumber simply means the OrderNumber from the RETAIL_ORDER table. Similarly, ORDER_ITEM.OrderNumber refers to the OrderNumber in the ORDER_ITEM table, and ORDER_ITEM.SKU refers to the SKU column in the ORDER_ITEM table. You can always qualify a column name with the name of its table like this. We have not done so previously because we were working with only one table, but the SQL statements shown previously would have worked just as well with syntax like SKU_DATA.Buyer rather than just Buyer or ORDER_ITEM.Price instead of Price.

The table that is formed by concatenating two tables is called a **join**. The process of creating such a table is called **joining the two tables**, and the associated operation is called a **join operation**. When the tables are joined using an equal condition (like the one on OrderNumber), this join is called an **equijoin**. When people say *join*, 99.99999 percent of the time they mean an equijoin. This type of join is also referred to as an **inner join**.

We can use a join to obtain data from two or more tables. For example, using the data in Figure 2-4, suppose we want to show the name of the Buyer and the ExtendedPrice of the sales of all items managed by that Buyer. The following SQL query will obtain that result:

```
SELECT      Buyer, ExtendedPrice

FROM        SKU_DATA, ORDER_ITEM

WHERE       SKU_DATA.SKU=ORDER_ITEM.SKU;
```

The result is:

	Buyer	ExtendedPrice
1	Pete Hansen	300.00
2	Nancy Meyers	200.00
3	Nancy Meyers	100.00
4	Nancy Meyers	100.00
5	Nancy Meyers	50.00
6	Cindy Lo	300.00
7	Cindy Lo	130.00

Again, the result of every SQL statement is just a single table, so we can apply any of the SQL you learned for a single table to this result. For example, we can use the GROUP BY and ORDER BY clauses to obtain the total revenue associated with each buyer as shown in the following SQL query:

```
SELECT      Buyer, SUM(ExtendedPrice) AS BuyerRevenue

FROM        SKU_DATA, ORDER_ITEM

WHERE       SKU_DATA.SKU=ORDER_ITEM.SKU

GROUP BY    Buyer

ORDER BY    BuyerRevenue DESC;
```

The result is:

	Buyer	BuyerRevenue
1	Nancy Meyers	450.00
2	Cindy Lo	430.00
3	Pete Hansen	300.00

Does Not Work with MS Access ANSI-89 SQL

This query fails in Microsoft Access ANSI-89 SQL for the same reason previously described on pages 65–66.

Solution: See the solution described in the "Does Now Work with Microsoft Access ANSI-89 SQL" box on pages 65–66. The correct Access ANSI-89 SQL statement for this query is:

```
SELECT      Buyer, Sum(ORDER_ITEM.ExtendedPrice) AS BuyerRevenue

FROM        SKU_DATA, ORDER_ITEM

WHERE       SKU_DATA.SKU=ORDER_ITEM.SKU

GROUP BY    Buyer

ORDER BY    Sum(ExtendedPrice) DESC;
```

We can extend this syntax to join three or more tables. For example, suppose we want to obtain the Buyer and the ExtendedPrice and OrderMonth for all purchases of items managed by each buyer. To retrieve that data, we need to join all three tables together as shown in this SQL query:

```
SELECT      Buyer, ExtendedPrice, OrderMonth
FROM        SKU_DATA, ORDER_ITEM, RETAIL_ORDER
WHERE       SKU_DATA.SKU=ORDER_ITEM.SKU
    AND     ORDER_ITEM.OrderNumber=RETAIL_ORDER.OrderNumber;
```

The result is:

	Buyer	ExtendedPrice	OrderMonth
1	Pete Hansen	300.00	January
2	Nancy Meyers	200.00	December
3	Nancy Meyers	100.00	January
4	Nancy Meyers	100.00	December
5	Nancy Meyers	50.00	January
6	Cindy Lo	300.00	December
7	Cindy Lo	130.00	December

We can improve this result by sorting with the ORDER BY clause and grouping by Buyer with the GROUP BY clause:

```
SELECT      Buyer, OrderMonth, SUM(ExtendedPrice) AS BuyerRevenue
FROM        SKU_DATA, ORDER_ITEM, RETAIL_ORDER
WHERE       SKU_DATA.SKU=ORDER_ITEM.SKU
    AND     ORDER_ITEM.OrderNumber=RETAIL_ORDER.OrderNumber
GROUP BY    Buyer, OrderMonth
ORDER BY    Buyer, OrderMonth DESC;
```

The result is:

	Buyer	OrderMonth	BuyerRevenue
1	Cindy Lo	December	430.00
2	Nancy Meyers	December	300.00
3	Nancy Meyers	January	150.00
4	Pete Hansen	January	300.00

Joins also can be written using another syntax, the **SQL JOIN . . . ON syntax**, and there is a bit more for you to learn about joins when values are missing, but this chapter is long enough. We will finish the discussion of joins in Chapter 7. If you just cannot wait, turn to pages 260–265 for the rest of the join story.

Comparing Subqueries and Joins

Subqueries and joins both process multiple tables, but they differ slightly. As mentioned earlier, a subquery can only be used to retrieve data from the top table. A join can be used to obtain data from any number of tables. Thus, a join can do everything a subquery can do, and more. So why learn subqueries? For one, if you just need data from a single table, you might use a subquery because it is easier to write and understand. This is especially true when processing multiple tables.

In Chapter 8, however, you will learn about a type of subquery called a **correlated subquery**. A correlated subquery can do work that is not possible with joins. Thus, it is important for you to learn about both joins and subqueries, even though right now it appears that joins are uniformly superior. If you're curious, ambitious, and courageous, jump ahead and read the discussion of correlated subqueries on pages 297–301.

Summary

Wow! That was a full chapter!

Structured Query Language (SQL) was developed by IBM and has been endorsed by the ANSI SQL-92 and following standards. SQL is a data sublanguage that can be embedded into full programming languages or submitted directly to the DBMS. Knowing SQL is critical for knowledge workers, application programmers, and database administrators.

All DBMS products process SQL. Access hides SQL, but SQL Server, Oracle, DB2, and MySQL require that you use it

There are basically two kinds of SQL statements: DML and DDL statements. DML statements include statements for querying data and for inserting, updating, and deleting data. This chapter addresses only DML query statements.

The examples in this chapter are based on three tables extracted from the operational database at Cape Codd Outdoor Sports. Such database extracts are common and important. Sample data for the three tables is shown in Figure 2-4.

The basic structure of an SQL query statement is SELECT/FROM/WHERE. The columns to be selected are listed after SELECT, the table(s) to process is listed after FROM, and any restrictions on data values are listed after WHERE. In a WHERE clause, character and date data values must be enclosed in single quotes. Numeric data need not be enclosed in quotes. You can submit SQL statements directly to Access, SQL Server, Oracle, and MySQL, as described in this chapter.

This chapter explained the use of the following SQL clauses: SELECT, FROM, WHERE, ORDER BY, GROUP BY, and HAVING. This chapter explained the use of the following SQL keywords: DISTINCT, DESC, ASC, AND, OR, IN, NOT IN, BETWEEN, LIKE, % (* for Access), _ (? for Access), SUM, AVG, MIN, MAX, COUNT, AS. You should know how to mix and match these features to obtain the results you want. By default, the WHERE clause is applied before the HAVING clause.

You can query multiple tables using subqueries and joins. Subqueries are nested queries that use the SQL keywords IN and NOT IN. An SQL SELECT expression is placed inside parentheses. Using a subquery, you can display data from the top table only. A join is created by specifying multiple table names in the FROM clause. An SQL WHERE clause is used to obtain an equijoin. In most cases, equijoins are the most sensible option. Joins can display data from multiple tables. In Chapter 8, you will learn another type of subquery that can perform work that is not possible with joins.

Key Terms

ad-hoc queries
American National Standards Institute (ANSI)
Access asterisk (*) wildcard character
Access question mark (?) wildcard character
AVG
business intelligence (BI) systems
correlated subquery
COUNT
data definition language (DDL)
data manipulation language (DML)
data sublanguage
equijoin
Extensible Markup Language (XML)
graphical user interface (GUI)
inner join
International Organization for Standardization (ISO)
join

join operation
joining the two tables
MAX
MIN
MySQL query files
query by example (QBE)
SQL AND operator
SQL AS keyword
SQL BETWEEN keyword
SQL built-in functions
SQL DESC keyword
SQL DISTINCT keyword
SQL expression
SQL FROM clause
SQL GROUP BY clause
SQL HAVING clause
SQL IN operator
SQL join operator

SQL JOIN...ON syntax

SQL LIKE keyword

SQL NOT IN operator

SQL OR operator

SQL ORDER BY clause

SQL percent sign (%) wildcard character

SQL script file

SQL SELECT clause

SQL SELECT/FROM/WHERE framework

SQL Server Compatible Syntax (ANSI 92)

SQL underscore (_) wildcard character

SQL WHERE clause

stock-keeping unit (SKU)

Structured Query Language (SQL)

subquery

SUM

TableName.ColumnName syntax

Review Questions

2.1   What is a business intelligence (BI) system?

2.2   What is an ad-hoc query?

2.3   What does SQL stand for, and what is SQL?

2.4   What does SKU stand for? What is an SKU?

2.5   Summarize how data were altered and filtered in creating the Cape Codd data extraction.

2.6   Explain, in general terms, the relationships among the RETAIL_ORDER, ORDER_ITEM, and SKU_DATA tables.

2.7   Summarize the background of SQL.

2.8   What is SQL-92? How does it relate to the SQL statements in this chapter?

2.9   What features have been added to SQL in versions subsequent to the SQL-92?

2.10   Why is SQL described as a data sublanguage?

2.11   What does DML stand for? What are DML statements?

2.12   What does DDL stand for? What are DDL statements?

2.13   What is the SQL SELECT/FROM/WHERE framework?

2.14   Explain how Access uses SQL.

2.15   Explain how enterprise-class DBMS products use SQL.

The Cape Codd Outdoor Sports sale extraction database has been modified to include two additional tables, the INVENTORY table and the WAREHOUSE table. The table schemas for these tables, together with the SKU table, are as follows:

SKU_DATA (SKU, SKU_Description, Department, Buyer)

INVENTORY (SKU, Warehouse, SKU_Description, QuantityOnHand, QuantityOnOrder)

WAREHOUSE (Warehouse, Manager, Squarefeet)

The column characteristics for the WAREHOUSE table are shown in Figure 2-22, and the column characteristics for the INVENTORY table are shown in Figure 2-23. The data for the WAREHOUSE table are shown in Figure 2-24, and the data for the INVENTORY table is shown in Figure 2-25.

If at all possible, you should run your SQL solutions to the following questions against an actual database. A Microsoft Access database named Cape-Codd.accdb is available on our Web site (*www.pearsonhighered.com/kroenke*) that contains all the tables and data for the Cape Codd Outdoor Sports sales data extract database.

WAREHOUSE

Column Name	Type	Key	Required	Remarks
Warehouse	Text (30)	Primary Key	Yes	
Manager	Text (25)	No	No	
SquareFeet	Integer	No	No	

Figure 2-22

Column Characteristics for
the WAREHOUSE Table

Also available on our Web site are SQL scripts for creating and populating the tables for the Cape Codd database in SQL Server, Oracle, and MySQL.

2.16 There is an intentional flaw in the design of the INVENTORY table used in these exercises. This flaw was purposely included in the INVENTORY tables so that you can answer some of the following questions using only that table. Compare the SKU and INVENTORY tables, and determine what design flaw is included in INVENTORY. Specifically, why did we include it?

Use *only* the INVENTORY table to answer Review Questions 2.17 through 2.46:

2.17 Write an SQL statement to display SKU and SKU_Description.

2.18 Write an SQL statement to display SKU_Description and SKU.

2.19 Write an SQL statement to display Warehouse.

2.20 Write an SQL statement to display Warehouse with no duplications.

Figure 2-23

Column Characteristics for
the INVENTORY Table

2.21 Write an SQL statement to display all of the columns without using *.

WAREHOUSE

Column Name	Type	Key	Required	Remarks
SKU	Integer	Primary Key, Foreign Key	Yes	Surrogate Key
Warehouse	Text (30)	Primary Key, Foreign Key	Yes	
SKU_Description	Text (35)	No	Yes	
QuantityOnHand	Integer	No	No	
QuantityOnOrder	Integer	No	No	

Warehouse	Manager	SquareFeet
Atlanta	Jones	125,000
Chicago	Smith	100,000
New Jersey	Evans	150,000
Seattle	Rogers	130,000

Figure 2-24

Cape Codd Outdoor Sports
WAREHOUSE Data

SKU	Warehouse	SKU_Description	QuantityOnHand	QuantityOnOrder
100100	Atlanta	Std. Scuba Tank, Yellow	250	0
100100	Chicago	Std. Scuba Tank, Yellow	100	50
100100	New Jersey	Std. Scuba Tank, Yellow	100	0
100100	Seattle	Std. Scuba Tank, Yellow	200	0
100200	Atlanta	Std. Scuba Tank, Magenta	200	30
100200	Chicago	Std. Scuba Tank, Magenta	75	75
100200	New Jersey	Std. Scuba Tank, Magenta	100	100
100200	Seattle	Std. Scuba Tank, Magenta	250	0
101100	Atlanta	Dive Mask, Small Clear	0	500
101100	Chicago	Dive Mask, Small Clear	0	500
101100	New Jersey	Dive Mask, Small Clear	300	200
101100	Seattle	Dive Mask, Small Clear	450	0
101200	Atlanta	Dive Mask, Med Clear	100	500
101200	Chicago	Dive Mask, Med Clear	50	500
101200	New Jersey	Dive Mask, Med Clear	475	0
101200	Seattle	Dive Mask, Med Clear	250	250
201000	Atlanta	Half-Dome Tent	2	100
201000	Chicago	Half-Dome Tent	10	250
201000	New Jersey	Half-Dome Tent	250	0
201000	Seattle	Half-Dome Tent	0	250
202000	Atlanta	Half-Dome Tent Footprint	10	250
202000	Chicago	Half-Dome Tent Footprint	1	250
202000	New Jersey	Half-Dome Tent Footprint	100	0
202000	Seattle	Half-Dome Tent Footprint	0	200
301000	Atlanta	Light Fly Climbing Harness	300	250
301000	Chicago	Light Fly Climbing Harness	250	250
301000	New Jersey	Light Fly Climbing Harness	0	250
301000	Seattle	Light Fly Climbing Harness	0	250
302000	Atlanta	Locking Carabiner	1000	0
302000	Chicago	Locking Carabiner	1250	0
302000	New Jersey	Locking Carabiner	500	500
302000	Seattle	Locking Carabiner	0	1000

Figure  2-25

Cape Codd Outdoor Sports
INVENTORY Data

2.22   Write an SQL statement to display all of the columns using *.

2.23   Write an SQL statement to display all data on products having a QuantityOnHand greater than 0.

2.24   Write an SQL statement to display the SKU and SKU_Description for products having QuantityOnHand equal to 0.

2.25   Write an SQL statement to display the SKU, SKU_Description, and Warehouse for products having QuantityOnHand equal to 0. Sort the results in ascending order by Warehouse.

2.26   Write an SQL statement to display the SKU, SKU_Description, and Warehouse on products having QuantityOnHand equal to 0. Sort the results in descending order by Warehouse and in ascending order by SKU.

2.27   Write an SQL statement to display the SKU, SKU_Description, and Warehouse on products having QuantityOnHand equal to 0. Sort the resuts in descending order by Warehouse and in ascending order by SKU.

2.28   Write an SQL statement to display SKU and SKU_Description for all products that have a QuantityOnHand equal to 0 or a QuantityOnOrder equal to 0.

2.29   Write an SQL statement to display the SKU and SKU_Description of all items stored in the Seattle, Chicago, or New Jersey warehouse. Do not use the IN keyword.

2.30   Write an SQL statement to display the SKU and SKU_Description of all items stored in the Seattle, Chicago, or New Jersey warehouse. Use the IN keyword.

2.31   Write an SQL statement to display the SKU and SKU_Description of all items not stored in the Seattle, Chicago, or New Jersey warehouse. Do not use the NOT IN keyword.

2.32   Write an SQL statement to display the SKU and SKU_Description of all items not stored in the Seattle, Chicago, or New Jersey warehouse. Use the NOT IN keyword.

2.33   Write an SQL statement to display the SKU, SKU_Description, and QuantityOnHand for all products having a QuantityOnHand greater than 1 and less than 10. Do not use the BETWEEN keyword.

2.34   Write an SQL statement to display the SKU, SKU_Description, and QuantityOnHand for all products having a QuantityOnHand greater than 1 and less than 10. Use the BETWEEN keyword.

2.35   Write an SQL statement to show SKU and SKU_Description for all products having an SKU description starting with 'Half-dome'.

2.36   Write an SQL statement to show SKU and SKU_Description for all products having a description that includes the word 'Foot'.

2.37   Write an SQL statement to show SKU and SKU_Description for all products having a description that includes the word 'Foot'.

2.38   Write an SQL statement that uses all of the SQL built-in functions on the QuantityOnHand column. Include meaningful column names in the result.

2.39   Explain the difference between the SQL built-in functions COUNT and SUM.

2.40   Write an SQL statement to produce a single column called ItemLocation that combines the SKU_Description, the phrase "is located in," and Warehouse for all products that have a QuantityOnHand greater than 0. Do not be concerned with removing leading or trailing blanks.

2.41   Write an SQL statement to display the Warehouse and a count of QuantityOnHand, grouped by Warehouse. Name the count TotalItemsOnHand and display the results in descending order of TotalItemsOnHand.

2.42   Write an SQL statement to display the Warehouse and a count of QuantityOnHand, grouped by Warehouse. Omit all items that have a count greater than 2. Name the count TotalItemsOnHand and display the results in descending order of TotalItemsOnHand.

2.43   Write an SQL statement to display the Warehouse and a count of QuantityOnHand grouped by Warehouse. Omit all items that have a count greater than 2. Show only groups having fewer than 2 item counts. Name the count TotalItemsOnHand and display the results in descending order of TotalItemsOnHand.

2.44   In your answer to Review Question 2.44, was the WHERE clause or the HAVING clause applied first? Why?

2.45   Write an SQL statement to display the Warehouse, the sum of QuantityOnOrder and sum of QuantityOnHand, grouped by Warehouse and QuantityOnOrder. Omit all items that have a count greater than 2. Name the count of QuantityOnOrder as TotalItemsOnOrder and the count of QuantityOnHand as TotalItemsOnHand.

Use *both* the INVENTORY and WAREHOUSE tables to answer Review Questions 2.46 through 2.52:

2.46   Write an SQL statement to show the SKU and SKU_Description for all items stored in a warehouse managed by 'Smith'. Use a subquery.

2.47   Write an SQL statement to show the SKU and SKU_Description for all items stored in a warehouse managed by 'Smith'. Use a join.

2.48   Write an SQL statement to show the Warehouse and average QuantityOnHand of all items stored in a warehouse managed by 'Smith'. Use a subquery.

2.49   Write an SQL statement to show the Warehouse and average QuantityOnHand of all items stored in a warehouse managed by 'Smith'. Use a join.

2.50   Write an SQL statement to show the Warehouse, Manager, and QuantityOnHand of all items stored in a warehouse managed by 'Smith'. Use a join.

2.51   Explain why you cannot use a subquery in your answer to Review Question 2.51.

2.52   Explain how subqueries and joins differ.

Project Questions

For this set of project questions, we will continue creating a Microsoft Access database for the Wedgewood Pacific Corporation (WPC). Founded in 1957 in Seattle, Washington, WPC has grown into an internationally recognized organization. The company is located in two buildings. One building houses the Administration, Accounting, Finance, and Human Resources departments, and the second houses the Production, Marketing, and Information Systems departments. The company database contains data about company employees, departments, company projects, company assets such as computer equipment, and other aspects of company operations.

In the following project questions, we have already created the WPC.accdb database with the following two tables:

DEPARTMENT (**DepartmentName**, BudgetCode, OfficeNumber, Phone)

EMPLOYEE (**EmployeeNumber**, FirstName, LastName, *Department*, Phone, Email)

Now we will add in the following two tables:

PROJECT (**ProjectID**, Name, *Department*, MaxHours, StartDate, EndDate)

ASSIGNMENT (*ProjectID*, *EmployeeNumber*, HoursWorked)

Column Name	Type	Key	Required	Remarks
ProjectID	Number	Primary Key	Yes	Long Integer
Name	Text (50)	No	Yes	
Department	Text (35)	Foreign Key	Yes	
MaxHours	Number	No	Yes	Double
StartDate	Date/Time	No	No	
EndDate	Date/Time	No	No	

Figure 2-26

Database Column Characteristics for the PROJECT Table

2.53 Figure 2-26 shows the column characteristics for the WPC PROJECT table. Using the column characteristics, create the PROJECT table in the WPC.accdb database.

2.54 Create the relationship and referential integrity constraint between PROJECT and DEPARTMENT. Enable enforcing of referential integrity and cascading of data updates, but do *not* enable cascading of data from deleted records.

2.55 Figure 2-27 shows the data for the WPC PROJECT table. Using the Datasheet view, enter the data shown in Figure 2-27 into your PROJECT table.

2.56 Figure 2-28 shows the column characteristics for the WPC ASSIGNMENT table. Using the column characteristics, create the ASSIGNMENT table in the WPC.accdb database.

2.57 Create the relationship and referential integrity constraint between ASSIGNMENT and EMPLOYEE. Enable enforcing of referential integrity, but do *not* enable either cascading updates or the cascading of data from deleted records.

2.58 Create the relationship and referential integrity constraint between ASSIGNMENT and PROJECT. Enable enforcing of referential integrity and cascading of deletes, but do *not* enable cascading updates.

2.59 Figure 2-29 shows the data for the WPC ASSIGNMENT table. Using the Datasheet view, enter the data shown in Figure 2-29 into your ASSIGNMENT table.

2.60 In Review Questions 2.55 and 2.59, the table data was entered after referential integrity constraints were created in Review Questions 2.54, 2.57 and 2.58. Why was the data entered after the referential integrity constraints were created instead of before the constraints were created?

2.61 Using Access SQL, create and run queries to answer the following questions. Save each query using the query name format SQL-Query-02-##, where the ## sign is replaced by the letter designator of the question. For example, the first query will be saved as SQL-Query-02-A.

Figure 2-27

Sample Data for the PROJECT Table

ProjectID	Name	Department	MaxHours	StartDate	EndDate
1000	2008 Q3 Product Plan	Marketing	135	05/10/08	06/15/08
1100	2008 Q3 Portfolio Analysis	Finance	120	07/05/08	07/25/08
1200	2008 Q3 Tax Preparation	Accounting	145	08/10/08	10/25/08
1300	2008 Q4 Product Plan	Marketing	150	08/10/08	09/15/08
1400	2008 Q4 Portfolio Analysis	Finance	140	10/05/08	

Column Name	Type	Key	Required	Remarks
ProjectID	Number	Primary Key, Foreign Key	Yes	Long Integer
EmployeeNumber	Number	Primary Key, Foreign Key	Yes	Long Integer
HoursWorked	Number	No	No	Double

Figure 2-28

Database Column Characteristics for the ASSIGNMENT Table

A. What projects are in the PROJECT table? Show all information for each project.

B. What are the ProjectID, Name, StartDate, and EndDate values of projects in the PROJECT table?

C. What projects in the PROJECT table started before August 1, 2008? Show all the information for each project.

D. What projects in the PROJECT table have not been completed? Show all the information for each project.

E. Who are the employees assigned to each project? Show ProjectID, Employee-Number, LastName, FirstName, and Phone.

ProjectID	EmployeeNumber	HoursWorked
1000	1	30.0
1000	8	75.0
1000	10	55.0
1100	4	40.0
1100	6	45.0
1100	1	25.0
1200	2	20.0
1200	4	45.0
1200	5	40.0
1300	1	35.0
1300	8	80.0
1300	10	50.0
1400	4	15.0
1400	5	10.0
1400	6	27.5

Figure 1-29

Sample Data for the ASSIGNMENT Table

F. Who are the employees assigned to each project? The ProjectID, Name, and Department. Show EmployeeNumber, LastName, FirstName, and Phone.

G. Who are the employees assigned to each project? Show ProjectID, Name, Department, and Department Phone. Show EmployeeNumber, LastName, FirstName, and Employee Phone. Sort by ProjectID, in ascending order.

H. Who are the employees assigned to projects run by the marketing department? Show ProjectID, Name, Department, and Department Phone. Show EmployeeNumber, LastName, FirstName, and Employee Phone. Sort by ProjectID, in ascending order.

I. How many projects are being run by the marketing department? Be sure to assign an appropriate column name to the computed results.

J. What is the total MaxHours of projects being run by the marketing department? Be sure to assign an appropriate column name to the computed results.

K. What is the average MaxHours of projects being run by the marketing department? Be sure to assign an appropriate column name to the computed results.

L. How many projects are being run by each department? Be sure to display each DepartmentName and to assign an appropriate column name to the computed results.

2.62 Using Access QBE, create and run new queries to answer the questions in exercise 2.61. Save each query using the query name format QBE-Query-02-##, where the ## sign is replaced by the letter designator of the question. For example, the first query will be saved as QBE-Query-02-A.

The following questions refer to the NDX table of data as described starting on page 67. You can obtain a copy of this data in the Access database, DBP-e11-NDX.accdb, from the text's Web site (*www.pearsonhighered.com/kroenke*).

2.63 Write SQL queries to produce the following results:

A. The ChangeClose on Fridays.

B. The minimum, maximum, and average ChangeClose on Fridays.

C. The average ChangeClose grouped by TYear. Show TYear.

D. The average ChangeClose grouped by TYear and TMonth. Show TYear and TMonth.

E. The average ChangeClose grouped by TYear, TQuarter, TMonth shown in descending order of the average (you will have to give a name to the average in order to sort by it). Show TYear, TQuarter, and TMonth. Note that months appear in alphabetical and not calendar order. Explain what you need to do to obtain months in calendar order.

F. The difference between the maximum ChangeClose and the minimum ChangeClose grouped by TYear, TQuarter, TMonth shown in descending order of the difference (you will have to give a name to the difference in order to sort by it). Show TYear, TQuarter, and TMonth.

G. The average ChangeClose grouped by TYear shown in descending order of the average (you will have to give a name to the average in order to sort by it). Show only groups for which the average is positive.

H. Display a single field with the date in the form day/month/year. Do not be concerned with trailing blanks.

2.64 It is possible that volume (the number of shares traded) has some correlation with the direction of the stock market. Use the SQL you have learned in this chapter to investigate this possibility. Develop at least five different SQL statements in your investigation.

Marcia's Dry Cleaning is an upscale dry cleaner in a well-to-do suburban neighborhood. Marcia makes her business stand out from the competition by providing superior customer service. She wants to keep track of each of her customers and their orders. Ultimately, she wants to notify them that their clothes are ready via e-mail. To provide this service, she has developed an initial database with several tables. Three of those tables are the following:

CUSTOMER (<u>CustomerID</u>, FirstName, LastName, Phone, Email,)

ORDER (<u>InvoiceNumber</u>, *CustomerNumber*, DateIn, DateOut, TotalAmount)

ORDER_ITEM (<u>*InvoiceNumber*</u>, <u>ItemNumber</u>, Item, Quantity, UnitPrice)

In the database schema above, the primary keys are underlined and the foreign keys are shown in italics.

The database is named MDC. The column characteristics for the tables are shown in Figures 2-30, 2-31, and 2-32. The data for these tables are shown in Figures 2-33, 2-34, and 2-35.

We recommend that you create an Access 2007 database named MDC-Ch02.accdb using the database characteristics and data above, and then use this database to test your solutions to the questions in this section.

Write SQL statements and show the results based on the MDC data for each of the following:

A.   Show all data in each of the tables.

B.   List the Phone and LastName of all customers.

C.   List the Phone and LastName for all customers with a FirstName of 'Nikki'.

D.   List the Phone, DateIn, and DateOut of all orders in excess of $100.00.

E.   List the Phone and FirstName of all customers whose first name starts with 'B'.

Figure 2-30

Column Characteristics for the CUSTOMER Table

Column Name	Type	Key	Required	Remarks
CustomerID	Number	Primary Key	Yes	Long Integer
FirstName	Text (25)	No	Yes	
LastName	Text (25)	No	Yes	
Phone	Text (12)	No	No	
Email	Text (100)	No	No	

Figure 2-31

Column Characteristics for the ORDER Table

Column Name	Type	Key	Required	Remarks
InvoiceNumber	Number	Primary Key	Yes	Long Integer
CustomerNumber	Number	Foreign Key	Yes	Long Integer
DateIn	Date/Time	No	Yes	
DateOut	Date/Time	No	No	
TotalAmount	Currency	No	No	Two Decimal Places

Figure 2-32

Column Characteristics for the ORDER_ITEM Table

Column Name	Type	Key	Required	Remarks
InvoiceNumber	Number	Primary Key, Foreign Key	Yes	Long Integer
ItemNumber	Number	Primary Key	Yes	Long Integer
Item	Text (50)	No	Yes	
Quantity	Number	No	Yes	Long Integer
UnitPrice	Currency	No	Yes	Two Decimal Places

Figure 2-33

Sample Data for the CUSTOMER Table

CustomerID	FirstName	LastName	Phone	Email
1	Nikki	Kaccaton	723-543-1233	NKaccaton@somewhere.com
2	Brenda	Catnazaro	723-543-2344	BCatnazaro@somewhere.com
3	Bruce	LeCat	723-543-3455	BLeCat@somewhere.com
4	Betsy	Miller	723-654-3211	BMiller@somewhere.com
5	George	Miller	723-654-4322	GMiller@somewhere.com
6	Kathy	Miller	723-514-9877	KMiller@somewhere.com
7	Betsy	Miller	723-514-8766	BMiller@elsewhere.com

F. List the Phone and FirstName of all customers whose last name includes the characters 'cat'.

G. List the Phone, FirstName, and LastName for all customers whose second and third numbers of their phone number are 23.

Figure 2-34

Sample Data for the ORDER Table

InvoiceNumber	CustomerID	DateIn	DateOut	TotalAmount
2009001	1	04-Oct-09	06-Oct-09	$158.50
2009002	2	04-Oct-09	06-Oct-09	$25.00
2009003	1	06-Oct-09	08-Oct-09	$49.00
2009004	4	06-Oct-09	08-Oct-09	$17.50
2009005	6	07-Oct-09	11-Oct-09	$12.00
2009006	3	11-Oct-09	13-Oct-09	$152.50
2009007	3	11-Oct-09	13-Oct-09	$7.00
2009008	7	12-Oct-09	14-Oct-09	$140.50
2009009	5	12-Oct-09	14-Oct-09	$27.00

InvoiceNumber	ItemNumber	Item	Quantity	UnitPrice
2009001	1	Blouse	2	$3.50
2009001	2	Dress Shirt	5	$2.50
2009001	3	Formal Gown	2	$10.00
2009001	4	Slacks-Mens	10	$5.00
2009001	5	Slacks-Womens	10	$6.00
2009001	6	Suit-Mens	1	$9.00
2009002	1	Dress Shirt	10	$2.50
2009003	1	Slacks-Mens	5	$5.00
2009003	2	Slacks-Womens	4	$6.00
2009004	1	Dress Shirt	7	$2.50
2009005	1	Blouse	2	$3.50
2009005	2	Dress Shirt	2	$2.50
2009006	1	Blouse	5	$3.50
2009006	2	Dress Shirt	10	$2.50
2009006	3	Slacks-Mens	10	$5.00
2009006	4	Slacks-Womens	10	$6.00
2009007	1	Blouse	2	$3.50
2009008	1	Blouse	3	$3.50
2009008	2	Dress Shirt	12	$2.50
2009008	3	Slacks-Mens	8	$5.00
2009008	4	Slacks-Womens	10	$6.00
2009009	1	Suit-Mens	3	$9.00

Figure   2-35

Sample Data for the
ORDER_ITEM Table

H.   Determine the maximum and minimum TotalAmount.

I.   Determine the average TotalAmount.

J.   Count the number of customers.

K.   Group customers by LastName and then by FirstName.

L.   Count the number of customers having each combination of LastName and FirstName.

M.   Show the FirstName and LastName of all customers who have had an order with TotalAmount greater than $100.00. Use a subquery. Present the results sorted by LastName in ascending order and then FirstName in descending order.

N.   Show the FirstName and LastName of all customers who have had an order with TotalAmount greater than $100.00. Use a join. Present results sorted by LastName in ascending order and then FirstName in descending order.

O.   Show the FirstName and LastName, of all customers who have had an order with an Item named 'Dress Shirt'. Use a subquery. Present results sorted by LastName in ascending order and then FirstName in descending order.

P.   Show the FirstName and LastName of all customers who have had an order with an Item named 'Dress Shirt'. Use a join. Present results sorted by LastName in ascending order and then FirstName in descending order.

Q.   Show the FirstName, LastName, and TotalAmount of all customers who have had an order with an Item named 'Dress Shirt'. Use a join with a subquery. Present results sorted by LastName in ascending order and then FirstName in descending order.

Morgan Importing purchases antiques and home furnishings in Asia and ships those items to a warehouse facility in Los Angeles. Mr. Morgan uses a database to keep a list of items purchased, shipments, and shipment items. His database includes the following tables:

SHIPMENT (<u>ShipmentID</u>, ShipperName, ShipperInvoiceNumber, DepartureDate, Arrival-Date, InsuredValue)

SHIPMENT_ITEM (<u>*ShipmentID*</u>, <u>ShipmentItemID</u>, *ItemID*, Value)

ITEM (<u>ItemID</u>, Description, PurchaseDate, Store, City, Quantity, LocalCurrencyAmt, ExchangeRate)

In the database schema above, the primary keys are underlined and the foreign keys are shown in italics.

The database is named MI. The column characteristics for the tables are shown in Figures 2-36, 2-37, and 2-38. The data for these tables are shown in Figures 2-39, 2-40, and 2-41.

We recommend that you create an Access 2007 database named MI-Ch02.accdb using the database characteristics and data above, and then use this database to test your solutions to the questions in this section.

Write SQL statements and shown the results based on the MDC data for each of the following:

A.   Show all data in each of the tables.

B.   List the ShipmentID, ShipperName, and ShipperInvoiceNumber of all shipments.

Figure 2-36

Column Characteristics for the SHIPMENT Table

Column Name	Type	Key	Required	Remarks
ShipmentID	Number	Primary Key	Yes	Long Integer
ShipperName	Text (35)	No	Yes	
ShipperInvoiceNumber	Number	No	Yes	Long Integer
DepartureDate	Date/Time	No	No	
ArrivalDate	Date/Time	No	No	
InsuredValue	Currency	No	No	Two Decimal Places

Column Name	Type	Key	Required	Remarks
ShipmentID	Number	Primary Key, Foreign Key	Yes	Long Integer
ShipmentItemID	Number	Primary Key	Yes	Long Integer
ItemID	Number	Foreign Key	Yes	Long Integer
Quantity	Number	No	Yes	Long Integer
Value	Currency	No	Yes	Two Decimal Places

Figure 2-37

Column Characteristics for
the SHIPMENT_ITEM Table

C. List the ShipmentID, ShipperName, and ShipperInvoiceNumber for all shipments that have an insured value greater than $10,000.00.

D. List the ShipmentID, ShipperName, and ShipperInvoiceNumber of all shippers whose name starts with 'AB'.

E. Assume DepartureDate and ArrivalDate are in the format MM/DD/YY. List the ShipmentID, ShipperName, ShipperInvoiceNumber, and ArrivalDate of all shipments that departed in December.

F. Assume DepartureDate and ArrivalDate are in the format MM/DD/YY. List the ShipmentID, ShipperName, ShipperInvoiceNumber, and ArrivalDate of all shipments that departed on the tenth day of any month.

G. Determine the maximum and minimum InsuredValue.

H. Determine the average InsuredValue.

I. Count the number of shipments.

J. Show ItemID, Description, Store, and a calculated column named USCurrencyAmount that is equal to LocalCurrencyAmt multiplied by the ExchangeRate for all rows of ITEM.

K. Group item purchases by City and Store.

Figure 2-38

L. Count the number of purchases having each combination of City and Store.

Column Characteristics for
the ITEM Table

Column Name	Type	Key	Required	Remarks
ItemID	Number	Primary Key	Yes	Long Integer
Description	Text (255)	No	Yes	Long Integer
PurchaseDate	Date/Time	No	Yes	
Store	Text (50)	No	Yes	
City	Text (35)	No	Yes	
Quantity	Number	No	Yes	Long Integer
LocalCurrencyAmt	Number	No	Yes	Decimal, 18 Auto
ExchangeRate	Number	No	Yes	Decimal, 12 Auto

ShipmentID	ShipperName	ShipperInvoiceNumber	DepartureDate	ArrivalDate	InsuredValue
1	ABC Trans-Oceanic	2008651	10-Dec-08	15-Mar-09	$15,000.00
2	ABC Trans-Oceanic	2009012	10-Jan-09	20-Mar-09	$12,000.00
3	Worldwide	49100300	05-May-09	17-Jun-09	$27,500.00
4	International	399400	02-Jun-09	17-Jul-09	$7,500.00
5	Worldwide	84899440	10-Jul-09	28-Jul-09	$25,000.00
6	International	488955	05-Aug-09	11-Sep-09	$18,000.00

Figure 2-39

Sample Data for the SHIPMENT Table

M. Show the ShipperName and DepartureDate of all shipments that have an item with a value of $1,000.00 or more. Use a subquery. Present results sorted by ShipperName in ascending order and then DepartureDate in descending order.

N. Show the ShipperName and DepartureDate of all shipments that have an item with a value of $1,000.00 or more. Use a join. Present results sorted by ShipperName in ascending order and then DepartureDate in descending order.

O. Show the ShipperName and DepartureDate of all shipments that have an item that was purchased in Singapore. Use a subquery. Present results sorted by ShipperName in ascending order and then DepartureDate in descending order.

P. Show the ShipperName and DepartureDate of all shipments that have an item that was purchased in Singapore. Use a join. Present results sorted by ShipperName in ascending order and then DepartureDate in descending order.

Q. Show the ShipperName, DepartureDate of shipment, and Value for items that were purchased in Singapore. Use a combination of a join and a subquery. Present results sorted by ShipperName in ascending order and then DepartureDate in descending order.

Figure 2-40

Sample Data for the SHIPMENT_ITEM Table

ShipmentID	ShipmentItemID	ItemID	Quantity	Value
4	1	4	40	$1,200.00
4	2	3	8	$9,500.00
4	3	2	75	$4,500.00

Figure 2-41

Sample Data for the ITEM Table

ItemID	Description	PurchaseDate	Store	City	Quantity	LocalCurrencyAmt	ExchangeRate
1	QE Dining Set	07-Apr-09	Eastern Treasures	Manila	2	403405	0.01774
2	Willow Serving Dishes	15-Jul-09	Jade Antiques	Singapore	75	102	0.5903
3	Large Bureau	17-Jul-09	Eastern Sales	Singapore	8	2000	0.5903
4	Brass Lamps	20-Jul-09	Jade Antiques	Singapore	40	50	0.5903

Part 2

Database Design

The four chapters in Part 2 discuss database design principles and techniques. Chapters 3 and 4 describe the design of databases that arise from existing data sources, such as spreadsheets, text files, and database extracts. We begin in Chapter 3 by defining the relational model and discussing normalization, a process that transforms relations with modification problems. Then, in Chapter 4, we use normalization principles to guide the design of databases from existing data.

Chapters 5 and 6 examine the design of databases that arise from the development of new information systems. Chapter 5 describes the entity-relationship data model, a tool used to create plans for constructing database designs. As you will learn, such data models are developed by analysis of forms, reports, and other information systems requirements. Chapter 6 concludes this part by describing techniques for transforming entity-relationship data models into relational database designs.

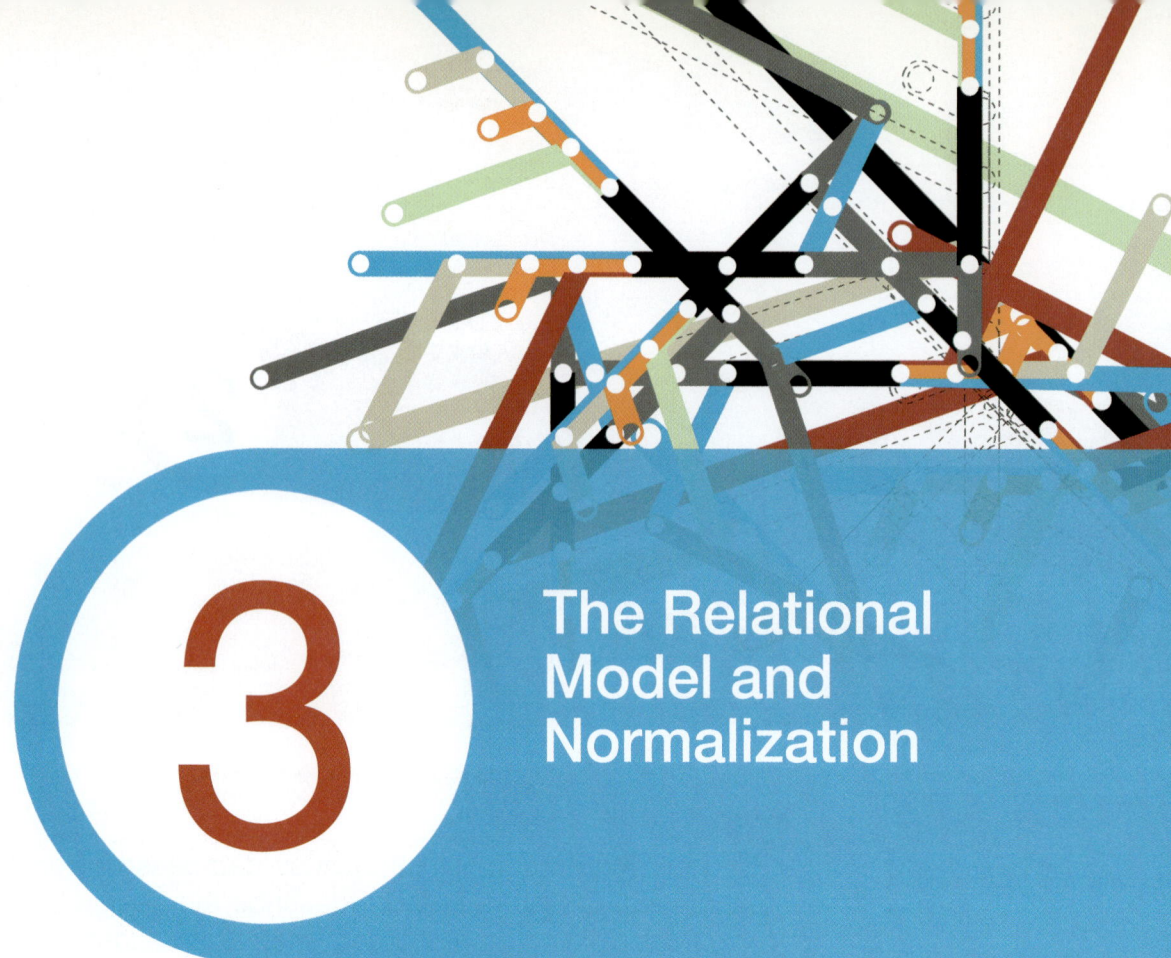

3

The Relational Model and Normalization

Chapter Objectives

- To understand basic relational terminology.
- To understand the characteristics of relations.
- To understand alternative terminology used in describing the relational model.
- To be able to identify functional dependencies, determinants, and dependent attributes.
- To identify primary, candidate, and composite keys.

- To be able to identify possible insertion, deletion, and update anomalies in a relation.
- To be able to place a relation into BCNF normal form.
- To understand the special importance of domain/key normal form.
- To be able to identify multivalued dependencies.
- To be able to place a relation in fourth normal form.

As we discussed in Chapter 1, databases arise from three sources: from existing data, from the development of new information systems, and from the redesign of existing databases. In this chapter and the next, we consider the design of databases from existing data, such as data from spreadsheets or extracts of existing databases.

The premise of Chapters 3 and 4 is that you have received one or more tables of data from some source that are to be stored in a new database. The question is: Should this data be stored as is, or should it be transformed in some way before it is stored? For example, consider the two tables in the top part of Figure 3-1. These are the SKU_DATA and ORDER_ITEM tables extracted from the Cape Codd Outdoor Sports database as used in the database in Chapter 2.

ORDER_ITEM

	OrderNumber	SKU	Quantity	Price	ExtendedPrice
1	1000	201000	1	300.00	300.00
2	1000	202000	1	130.00	130.00
3	2000	101100	4	50.00	200.00
4	2000	101200	2	50.00	100.00
5	3000	100200	1	300.00	300.00
6	3000	101100	2	50.00	100.00
7	3000	101200	1	50.00	50.00

SKU_DATA

	SKU	SKU_Description	Department	Buyer
1	100100	Std. Scuba Tank, Yellow	Water Sports	Pete Hansen
2	100200	Std. Scuba Tank, Magenta	Water Sports	Pete Hansen
3	101100	Dive Mask, Small Clear	Water Sports	Nancy Meyers
4	101200	Dive Mask, Med Clear	Water Sports	Nancy Meyers
5	201000	Half-dome Tent	Camping	Cindy Lo
6	202000	Half-dome Tent Footprint	Camping	Cindy Lo
7	301000	Light Fly Climbing Harness	Climbing	Jerry Martin
8	302000	Locking carabiner, Oval	Climbing	Jerry Martin

SKU_ITEM

	OrderNumber	SKU	Quantity	Price	SKU_Description	Department	Buyer
1	1000	201000	1	300.00	Half-dome Tent	Camping	Cindy Lo
2	1000	202000	1	130.00	Half-dome Tent Footprint	Camping	Cindy Lo
3	2000	101100	4	50.00	Dive Mask, Small Clear	Water Sports	Nancy Meyers
4	2000	101200	2	50.00	Dive Mask, Med Clear	Water Sports	Nancy Meyers
5	3000	100200	1	300.00	Std. Scuba Tank, Magenta	Water Sports	Pete Hansen
6	3000	101100	2	50.00	Dive Mask, Small Clear	Water Sports	Nancy Meyers
7	3000	101200	1	50.00	Dive Mask, Med Clear	Water Sports	Nancy Meyers

Figure 3-1

How Many Tables?

You can design the new database to store this data as two separate tables, or you can join the tables together and design the database with just one table. Each alternative has advantages and disadvantages. When you make the decision to use one design, you obtain certain advantages at the expense of certain costs. The purpose of this chapter is to help you understand those advantages and costs.

Such questions do not seem difficult, and you may be wondering why we need two chapters to answer them. In truth, even a single table can have surprising complexity. Consider, for example, the table in Figure 3-2, which shows sample data extracted from a corporate database. This simple table has three columns: the buyer's name, the SKU of the products that the buyer purchases, and the names of the buyer's college major(s). Buyers manage more than one SKU, and they can have multiple college majors.

Figure 3-2

PRODUCT_BUYER—A Very
Strange Table

PRODUCT_BUYER

	BuyerName	SKU_Managed	CollegeMajor
1	Nancy Meyers	101100	Art
2	Nancy Meyers	101100	Info Systems
3	Nancy Meyers	101200	Art
4	Nancy Meyers	101200	Info Systems
5	Pete Hansen	100100	Business
6	Pete Hansen	100200	Business

To understand why this is an odd table, suppose that Nancy Meyers is assigned a new SKU, say 101300. What addition should we make to this table? Clearly, we need to add a row for the new SKU, but if we add just one row, say the row ('Nancy Meyers', 101300, 'Art'), it will appear that she manages product 101300 as an Art major, but not as an Info Systems major. To avoid such an illogical state, we need to add two rows: ('Nancy Meyers', 101300, 'Art') and ('Nancy Meyers', 101300, 'Info Systems').

This is a strange requirement. Why should we have to add two rows of data simply to record the fact that a new SKU has been assigned to a buyer? Further, if we assign the product to Pete Hansen instead, we would only have to add one row, but if we assigned the product to a buyer who had four majors, we would have to add four new rows.

The more one thinks about the table in Figure 3-2, the more strange it becomes. What changes should we make if SKU 101100 is assigned to Pete Hansen? What changes should we make if SKU 100100 is assigned to Nancy Meyers? What should we do if all the SKU values in Figure 3-2 are deleted? Later in this chapter, you will learn that these problems arise because this table has a problem called a *multivalued dependency.* Even better, you will learn how to remove that problem.

Tables can have many different patterns; some patterns are susceptible to serious problems and other patterns are not. Before we can address this question, however, you need to learn some basic terms.

Relational Model Terminology

Figure 3-3 lists the most important terms used by the relational model. By the time you finish Chapters 3 and 4, you should be able to define each of these terms and explain how each pertains to the design of relational databases. Use this list of terms as a check on your comprehension.

Relations

So far, we have used the terms *table* and *relation* interchangeably. In fact, a relation is a special case of a table. This means that all relations are tables, but not all tables are relations. Codd

Figure   **3-3**

Important Relational
Model Terms

- Relation
- Functional dependency
- Determinant
- Candidate key
- Composite key
- Primary key
- Surrogate key
- Foreign key
- Referential integrity constraint
- Normal form
- Multivalued dependency

Characteristics of Relations
Rows contain data about an entity.
Columns contain data about attributes of the entities.
All entries in a column are of the same kind.
Each column has a unique name.
Cells of the table hold a single value.
The order of the columns is unimportant.
The order of the rows is unimportant.
No two rows may be identical.

Figure 3-4

Characteristic of Relations

defined the characteristics of a relation in his 1970 paper that laid the foundation for the relational model.[1] Those characteristics are summarized in Figure 3-4.

> **BY THE WAY** In Figure 3-4 and in this discussion, we use the term **entity** to mean some identifiable thing. A customer, a salesperson, an order, a part, and a lease are all examples of what we mean by an entity. When we introduce the entity-relationship model in Chapter 5, we will make the definition of entity more precise. For now, just think of an entity as some identifiable thing that users want to track.

Characteristics of Relations

A **relation** has a specific definition as shown in Figure 3-4. and for a table to be a relation the criteria of this definition must be met. First, the rows of the table must store data about an entity and the columns of the table must store data about the characteristics of those entities. Further, in a relation, all of the values in a column are of the same kind. If, for example, the second column of the first row of a relation has FirstName, then the second column of every row in the relation has FirstName. Also, the names of the columns are unique; no two columns in the same relation may have the same name. The EMPLOYEE table shown in Figure 3-5 meets these criteria and is a relation.

Figure 3-5

Sample EMPLOYEE Relation

EmployeeNumber	FirstName	LastName	Department	Email	Phone
100	Jerry	Johnson	Accounting	JJ@somewhere.com	834-1101
200	Mary	Abernathy	Finance	MA@somewhere.com	834-2101
300	Liz	Smathers	Finance	LS@somewhere.com	834-2102
400	Tom	Caruthers	Accounting	TC@somewhere.com	834-1102
500	Tom	Jackson	Production	TJ@somewhere.com	834-4101
600	Eleanore	Caldera	Legal	EC@somewhere.com	834-3101
700	Richard	Bandalone	Legal	RB@somewhere.com	834-3102

---

[1] Codd, E. F. "A Relational Model of Data for Large Shared Databanks," *Communications of the ACM*, June 1970, pp. 377–387.

> **BY THE WAY**   Columns in different relations may have the same name. In Chapter 2, for example, two relations had a column named SKU. When there is risk of confusion, we precede the column name with the relation name followed by a period. Thus, the name of the SKU column in the SKU_DATA relation is SKU_DATA.SKU, and column C1 of relation R1 is named R1.C1. Because relation names are unique within a database, and because column names are unique within a relation, the combination of relation name and column name uniquely identifies every column in the database.

Each cell of a relation has only a single value or item; multiple entries are not allowed. The table in Figure 3-6 is *not* a relation, because the Phone values of employees Caruthers and Bandalone store multiple phone numbers.

In a relation, the order of the rows and the order of the columns are immaterial. No information can be carried by the ordering of rows or columns. The table in Figure 3-7 is not a relation, because the entries for employees Caruthers and Caldera require a particular row arrangement. If the rows in this table were rearranged, we would not know which employee has the indicated Fax and Home numbers.

Finally, according to the last characteristic in Figure 3-4, for a table to be a relation, no two rows can be identical. As you learned in Chapter 2, some SQL statements do produce tables with duplicate rows. In such cases, you can use the DISTINCT keyword to force uniqueness. Such row duplication only occurs as a result of SQL manipulation. Tables that you design to be stored in the database should never contain duplicate rows.

> **BY THE WAY**   Do not fall into a common trap. Even though every cell of a relation must have a single value, this does not mean that all values must have the same length. The table in Figure 3-8 is a relation even though the length of the Comment column varies from row to row. It is a relation because, even though the comments have different lengths, there is only *one* comment per cell.

Alternative Terminology

As defined by Codd, the columns of a relation are called **attributes**, and the rows of a relation are called **tuples** (rhymes with "couples"). Most practitioners, however, do not use these academic-sounding terms and use the terms *column* and *row*, instead. Also, even though a table is not necessarily a relation, most practitioners mean *relation* when they say *table*. Thus, in most

Figure 3-6

Nonrelational Table—Multiple Entries per Cell

EmployeeNumber	FirstName	LastName	Department	Email	Phone
100	Jerry	Johnson	Accounting	JJ@somewhere.com	834-1101
200	Mary	Abernathy	Finance	MA@somewhere.com	834-2101
300	Liz	Smathers	Finance	LS@somewhere.com	834-2102
400	Tom	Caruthers	Accounting	TC@somewhere.com	834-1102, 834-1191, 834-1192
500	Tom	Jackson	Production	TJ@somewhere.com	834-4101
600	Eleanore	Caldera	Legal	EC@somewhere.com	834-3101
700	Richard	Bandalone	Legal	RB@somewhere.com	834-3102, 834-3191

EmployeeNumber	FirstName	LastName	Department	Email	Phone
100	Jerry	Johnson	Accounting	JJ@somewhere.com	834-1101
200	Mary	Abernathy	Finance	MA@somewhere.com	834-2101
300	Liz	Smathers	Finance	LS@somewhere.com	834-2102
400	Tom	Caruthers	Accounting	TC@somewhere.com	834-1102
				Fax:	834-9911
				Home:	723-8795
500	Tom	Jackson	Production	TJ@somewhere.com	834-4101
600	Eleanore	Caldera	Legal	EC@somewhere.com	834-3101
				Fax:	834-9912
				Home:	723-7654
700	Richard	Bandalone	Legal	RB@somewhere.com	834-3102

Figure 3-7

Nonrelational Table—Order
of Rows Matters and Kind of
Column Entries Differs in Email

Figure 3-8

Relation with Variable—Length
Column Values

conversations the terms *relation* and *table* are synonymous. In fact, for the rest of this book *table* and *relation* will be used synonymously.

Additionally, a third set of terminology also is used. Some practitioners use the terms *file, field,* and *record* for the terms *table, column,* and *row,* respectively. These terms arose from traditional data processing and are common in connection with legacy systems. Sometimes, people mix and match these terms. You might hear someone say, for example, that a relation has a certain column and contains 47 records. These three sets of terms are summarized in Figure 3-9.

EmployeeNumber	FirstName	LastName	Department	Email	Phone	Comment
100	Jerry	Johnson	Accounting	JJ@somewhere.com	834-1101	Joined the Accounting Department in March after completing his MBA. Will take the CPA exam this fall.
200	Mary	Abernathy	Finance	MA@somewhere.com	834-2101	
300	Liz	Smathers	Finance	LS@somewhere.com	834-2102	
400	Tom	Caruthers	Accounting	TC@somewhere.com	834-1102	
500	Tom	Jackson	Production	TJ@somewhere.com	834-4101	
600	Eleanore	Caldera	Legal	EC@somewhere.com	834-3101	
700	Richard	Bandalone	Legal	RB@somewhere.com	834-3102	Is a full time consultant to Legal on a retainer basis.

Table	Column	Row
Relation	Attribute	Tuple
File	Field	Record

Figure 3-9

Three Sets of Equivalent Terms

Functional Dependencies

Functional dependencies are the heart of the database design process, and it is vital for you to understand them. We first explain the concept in general terms and then examine two examples. We begin with a short excursion into the world of algebra. Suppose you are buying boxes of cookies and someone tells you that each box costs $5.00. With this fact, you can compute the cost of several boxes with the formula:

$$CookieCost = NumberOfBoxes \times \$5$$

A more general way to express the relationship between CookieCost and NumberOfBoxes is to say that CookieCost *depends upon* NumberOfBoxes. Such a statement tells us the character of the relationship between CookieCost and NumberOfBoxes, even though it doesn't give us the formula. More formally, we can say that CookieCost is **functionally dependent** on NumberOfBoxes. Such a statement can be written as:

NumberOfBoxes → CookieCost

This expression can be read as "NumberOfBoxes *determines* CookieCost." The variable on the left, here NumberOfBoxes, is called the **determinant**.

Using another formula, we can compute the extended price of a part order by multiplying the quantity of the item times its unit price, or:

$$ExtendedPrice = Quantity \times UnitPrice$$

In this case, we say that ExtendedPrice is functionally dependent on Quantity and Unit-Price, or:

(Quantity, UnitPrice) → ExtendedPrice

Here, the determinant is the composite (Quantity, UnitPrice).

Functional Dependencies That Are Not Equations

In general, a functional dependency exists when the value of one or more attributes determines the value of another attribute. Many functional dependencies exist that do not involve equations.

Consider an example. Suppose you know that a sack contains either red, blue, or yellow objects. Further, suppose you know that the red objects weigh 5 pounds, the blue objects weigh 3 pounds, and the yellow objects weigh 7 pounds. If a friend looks into the sack, sees an object, and tells you the color of the object, you can tell her the weight of the object. We can formalize this as:

ObjectColor → Weight

Thus, we can say that Weight is functionally dependent on ObjectColor and that ObjectColor determines Weight. The relationship here does not involve an equation, but the functional dependency holds. Given a value for ObjectColor, you can determine the object's weight.

If we also know that the red objects are balls, the blue objects are cubes, and the yellow objects are cubes, we can also say:

ObjectColor → Shape

Thus, ObjectColor determines Shape. We can put these two together to state:

ObjectColor → (Weight, Shape)

Thus, ObjectColor determines Weight and Shape.

Another way to represent these facts is to put them into a table:

Object Color	Weight	Shape
Red	5	Ball
Blue	3	Cube
Yellow	7	Cube

This table meets all of the conditions listed in Figure 3-4, and therefore it is a relation. You may be thinking that we performed a trick or sleight of hand to arrive at this relation, but, in truth, the only reason for having relations is to store instances of functional dependencies. If there were a formula by which we could take ObjectColor and somehow compute Weight and Shape, then we would not need the table. We would just make the computation. Similarly, if there were a formula by which we could take EmployeeNumber and compute EmployeeName and HireDate, then we would not need an EMPLOYEE relation. However, because there is no such formula, we must store the combinations of EmployeeNumber, EmployeeName, and HireDate in the rows of a relation.

Composite Functional Dependencies

The determinant of a functional dependency can consist of more than one attribute. For example, a grade in a class is determined by both the student and the class, or:

(StudentNumber, ClassNumber) → Grade

In this case, the determinant is called a **composite determinant**.

Notice that both the student and the class are needed to determine the grade. In general, if $(A, B) → C$, then neither A nor B will determine C by itself. However, if $A → (B, C)$, then it is true that $A → B$ and $A → C$. Work through examples of your own for both of these cases so that you understand why this is true.

Finding Functional Dependencies

To fix the idea of functional dependency in your mind, consider what functional dependencies exist in the SKU_DATA and ORDER_ITEM tables in Figure 3-1.

Functional Dependencies in the SKU_DATA Table

To find functional dependencies in a table, we must ask "Does any column determine the value of another column?" For example, consider the values of the SKU_DATA table in Figure 3-1:

	SKU	SKU_Description	Department	Buyer
1	100100	Std. Scuba Tank, Yellow	Water Sports	Pete Hansen
2	100200	Std. Scuba Tank, Magenta	Water Sports	Pete Hansen
3	101100	Dive Mask, Small Clear	Water Sports	Nancy Meyers
4	101200	Dive Mask, Med Clear	Water Sports	Nancy Meyers
5	201000	Half-dome Tent	Camping	Cindy Lo
6	202000	Half-dome Tent Footprint	Camping	Cindy Lo
7	301000	Light Fly Climbing Harness	Climbing	Jerry Martin
8	302000	Locking carabiner, Oval	Climbing	Jerry Martin

Consider the last two columns. If we know the value of Department, can we determine a unique value of Buyer? No, we cannot, because a Department may have more than one Buyer. In this sample data, 'Water Sports' is associated with Pete Hansen and Nancy Meyers. Therefore, Department does not functionally determine Buyer.

What about the reverse? Does Buyer determine Department? In every row, for a given value of Buyer, do we find the same value of Department? Every time Jerry Martin appears, for example, is he paired with the same department? The answer is yes. Further, every time Cindy Lo appears, she is paired with the same department. The same is true for the other buyers. Therefore, assuming that these data are representative, Buyer does determine Department, and we can write:

$$\text{Buyer} \rightarrow \text{Department}$$

Does Buyer determine any other column? If we know the value of Buyer, do we know the value of SKU? No, we do not, because a given buyer has many SKUs assigned to him or her. Does Buyer determine SKU_Description? No, because a given value of Buyer occurs with many values of SKU_Description.

BY THE WAY As stated, for the Buyer → Department functional dependency a Buyer is paired with one and only one value of Department. Notice that a buyer can appear more than once in the table, but, if so, that buyer is always paired with the same department. This is true for all functional dependencies. If A → B, then each value of A will be paired with one and only one value of B. A particular value of A may appear more than once in the relation, but, if so, it is always paired with the same value of B. Note, too, that the reverse is not necessarily true. If A → B, then a value of B may be paired with many values of A.

What about the other columns? It turns out that if we know the value of SKU, we also know the values of all of the other columns. In other words:

$$\text{SKU} \rightarrow \text{SKU\_Description}$$

because a given value of SKU will have just one value of SKU_Description. Next,

$$\text{SKU} \rightarrow \text{Department}$$

because a given value of SKU will have just one value of Department. And, finally,

$$\text{SKU} \rightarrow \text{Buyer}$$

because a given value of SKU will have just one value of Buyer.

We can combine these three statements as:

$$\text{SKU} \rightarrow (\text{SKU\_Description, Department, Buyer})$$

For the same reasons, SKU_Description determines all of the other columns, and we can write:

$$\text{SKU\_Description} \rightarrow (\text{SKU, Department, Buyer})$$

In summary, the functional dependencies in the SKU_DATA table are:

$$\text{SKU} \rightarrow (\text{SKU\_Description, Department, Buyer})$$

$$\text{SKU\_Description} \rightarrow (\text{SKU, Department, Buyer})$$

$$\text{Buyer} \rightarrow \text{Department}$$

> BY THE WAY   You cannot always determine functional dependencies from sample data. You may not have any sample data, or you may have just a few rows that are not representative of all of the data conditions. In such cases, you must ask the users who are experts in the application that creates the data. For the SKU_DATA table, you would ask questions such as, "Is a Buyer always associated with the same Department?" and "Can a Department have more than one Buyer?" In most cases, answers to such questions are more reliable than sample data. When in doubt, trust the users.

Functional Dependencies in the ORDER_ITEM Table

Now consider the ORDER_ITEM table in Figure 3-1. For convenience, here is a copy of the data in that table:

	OrderNumber	SKU	Quantity	Price	ExtendedPrice
1	1000	201000	1	300.00	300.00
2	1000	202000	1	130.00	130.00
3	2000	101100	4	50.00	200.00
4	2000	101200	2	50.00	100.00
5	3000	100200	1	300.00	300.00
6	3000	101100	2	50.00	100.00
7	3000	101200	1	50.00	50.00

What are the functional dependencies in this table? Start on the left. Does OrderNumber determine another column? It does not determine SKU, because several SKUs are associated with a given order. For the same reasons, it does not determine Quantity, Price, or ExtendedPrice.

What about SKU? SKU does not determine OrderNumber because several OrderNumbers are associated with a given SKU. It does not determine Quantity or ExtendedPrice for the same reason.

What about SKU and Price? From this data, it does appear that

SKU → Price

but that might not be true in general. In fact, we know that prices can change after an order has been processed. Further, an order might have special pricing due to a sale or promotion. To keep an accurate record of what the customer actually paid, we need to associate a particular SKU price with a particular order. Thus:

(OrderNumber, SKU) → Price

Considering the other columns, Quantity, Price, and ExtendedPrice do not determine anything else. You can decide this by looking at the sample data. You can reinforce this conclusion by thinking about the nature of sales. Would a Quantity of 2 ever determine an OrderNumber or a SKU? This makes no sense. At the grocery store, if I tell you I bought two of something, you have no reason to conclude that my OrderNumber was 1010022203466 or that I bought carrots. Quantity does not determine OrderNumber or SKU.

Similarly, if I tell you that the price of an item was $3.99, there is no logical way to conclude what my OrderNumber was or that I bought a jar of green olives. Thus, Price does not determine OrderNumber or SKU. Similar comments pertain to ExtendedPrice. It turns out that no single column is a determinant in the ORDER_ITEM table.

What about pairs of columns? We already know that

(OrderNumber, SKU) → Price

Examining the data, (OrderNumber, SKU) determines the other two columns as well. Thus:

(OrderNumber, SKU) → (Quantity, Price, ExtendedPrice)

This functional dependency makes sense. It means that given a particular order and a particular item on that order, there is only one quantity, one price, and one extended price.

Notice, too, that because ExtendedPrice is computed from the formula ExtendedPrice = (Quantity * Price) we have:

(Quantity, Price) → ExtendedPrice

In summary, the functional dependencies in ORDER_ITEM are:

(OrderNumber, SKU) → (Quantity, Price, ExtendedPrice)

(Quantity, Price) → ExtendedPrice

No single skill is more important for designing databases than the ability to identify functional dependencies. Make sure you understand the material in this section. Work problems 3.58 and 3.59 and the Marcia's Dry Cleaning and Morgan Importing projects at the end of the chapter. Ask your instructor for help if necessary. You *must* understand functional dependencies and be able to work with them.

When Are Determinant Values Unique?

In the previous section, you may have noticed an irregularity. Sometimes the determinants of a functional dependency are unique in a relation, and sometimes they are not. Consider the SKU_DATA relation, with determinants SKU, SKU_Description, and Buyer. In SKU_DATA, the values of both SKU and SKU_Description are unique in the table. For example, the SKU value 100100 appears just once. Similarly, the SKU_Description value 'Half-dome Tent' occurs just once. From this, it is tempting to conclude that values of determinants are always unique in a relation. However, this is *not* true.

For example, Buyer is a determinant, but it is not unique in SKU_DATA. The buyer 'Cindy Lo' appears in two different rows. In fact, for this sample data all of the buyers occur in two different rows.

In truth, a determinant is unique in a relation only if it determines every other column in the relation. For the SKU_DATA relation, SKU determines all of the other columns. Similarly, SKU_Description determines all of the other columns. Hence, they both are unique. Buyer, however, only determines the Department column. It does not determine SKU or SKU_Description.

The determinants in ORDER_ITEM are (OrderNumber, SKU) and (Quantity, Price). Because (OrderNumber, SKU) determines all of the other columns, it will be unique in the relation. The composite (Quantity and Price) only determines ExtendedPrice. Therefore, it will not be unique in the relation.

This fact means that you cannot find the determinants of all functional dependencies simply by looking for unique values. Some of the determinants will be unique, but some will not be. Instead, to determine if column A determines column B, look at the data and ask, "Every time that a value of column A appears is it matched with the same value of Column B?" If so, it can be a determinant of B. Again, however, sample data can be incomplete, so the best strategies are to think about the nature of the business activity from which the data arise and to ask the users.

Keys

The relational model has more keys than a locksmith. There are candidate keys, composite keys, primary keys, surrogate keys, and foreign keys. In this section, we will define each of these types of keys. Because key definitions rely on the concept of functional dependency, make sure you understand that concept before reading on.

In general, a **key** is a combination of one or more columns that is used to identify particular rows in a relation. Keys that have two columns or more are called **composite keys**.

Candidate Keys

A **candidate key** is a determinant that determines all of the other columns in a relation. The SKU_DATA relation has two candidate keys: SKU and SKU_Description. Buyer is a determinant, but it is not a candidate key because it only determines Department.

The ORDER_ITEM table has just one candidate key: (OrderNumber, SKU). The other determinant in this table, (Quantity, Price), is not a candidate key because it determines only ExtendedPrice.

Candidate keys identify a unique row in a relation. Given the value of a candidate key, we can find one and only one row in the relation that has that value. For example, given the SKU value of 100100, we can find one and only one row in SKU_DATA. Similarly, given the OrderNumber and SKU values (2000, 101100), we can find one and only one row in ORDER_ITEM.

Primary Keys

When designing a database, one of the candidate keys is selected to be the **primary key**. This term is used because this key will be defined to the DBMS, and the DBMS will use it as its primary means for finding rows in a table. A table has only one primary key. The primary key can have one column or it can be a composite.

In this text, to clarify discussions we will sometimes indicate table structure by showing the name of a table followed by the names of the table's columns enclosed in parentheses. When we do this, we will underline the column(s) that comprise the primary key. For example, we can show the structure of SKU_DATA and ORDER_ITEM as follows:

SKU_DATA (<u>SKU</u>, SKU_Description, Department, Buyer)

ORDER_ITEM (<u>OrderNumber</u>, <u>SKU</u>, Quantity, Price, ExtendedPrice)

This notation indicates that SKU is the primary key of SKU_DATA and that (OrderNumber, SKU) is the primary key of ORDER_ITEM.

> **BY THE WAY**   What do you do if a table has no candidate keys? In that case, define the primary key as the collection of all of the columns in the table. Because there are no duplicate rows in a stored relation, the combination of all of the columns of the table will always be unique. Again, while tables generated by SQL manipulation may have duplicate rows, the tables that you design to be stored should never be constructed to have duplication. Thus, the combination of all columns is always a candidate key.

Surrogate Keys

A **surrogate key** is an artificial column that is added to a table to serve as the primary key. The DBMS assigns a unique value to a surrogate key when the row is created. The assigned value never changes. Surrogate keys are used when the primary key is large and unwieldy. For example, consider the relation RENTAL_PROPERTY:

RENTAL_PROPERTY (<u>Street</u>, <u>City</u>, <u>State/Province</u>, <u>Zip/PostalCode</u>, <u>Country</u>, Rental_Rate)

The primary key of this table is (Street, City, State/Province, Zip/PostalCode, Country). As you will learn in Chapter 6, for good performance a primary key should be short and, if possible, numeric. The primary key of RENTAL_PROPERTY is neither.

In this case, the designers of the database would likely create a surrogate key. The structure of the table would then be:

RENTAL_PROPERTY (<u>PropertyID</u>, Street, City, State/Province, Zip/PostalCode, Country, Rental_Rate)

The DBMS will assign a numeric value to PropertyID when a row is created. Using that key will result in better performance than using the original key. Note that surrogate key values are artificial and have no meaning to the users. In fact, surrogate key values are normally hidden in forms and reports.

Foreign Keys

A **foreign key** is a column or composite of columns that is the primary key of a table other than the one in which it appears. The term arises because it is a key of a table *foreign* to the one in which it appears. In the following two tables, DEPARTMENT.DepartmentName is the primary key of DEPARTMENT, and EMPLOYEE.DepartmentName is a foreign key. In this text, we will show foreign keys in italics:

DEPARTMENT (<u>DepartmentName</u>, BudgetCode, ManagerName)

EMPLOYEE (<u>EmployeeNumber</u>, EmployeeLastName, EmployeeFirstName, *DepartmentName*)

Foreign keys express relationships between rows of tables. In this example, the foreign key EMPLOYEE.DepartmentName stores the relationship between an employee and his or her department.

Consider the SKU_DATA and ORDER_ITEM tables. SKU_DATA.SKU is the primary key of SKU_DATA, and ORDER_ITEM.SKU is a foreign key.

SKU_DATA (<u>SKU</u>, SKU_Description, Department, Buyer)

ORDER_ITEM (<u>OrderNumber</u>, *<u>SKU</u>*, Quantity, Price, ExtendedPrice)

Notice that ORDER_ITEM.SKU is both a foreign key and also part of the primary key of ORDER_ITEM. This condition sometimes occurs, but it is not required. In the example above, EMPLOYEE.DepartmentName is a foreign key, but is not part of the EMPLOYEE primary key. You will see some uses for foreign keys later in this chapter and the next, and you will study them at length in Chapter 6.

In most cases, we need to ensure that the values of a foreign key match a valid value of a primary key. For the SKU_DATA and ORDER_ITEM tables, we need to ensure that all of the values of ORDER_ITEM.SKU match a value of SKU_DATA.SKU. To accomplish this, we create a **referential integrity constraint**, which is a statement that limits the values of the foreign key. In this case, we create the constraint:

SKU in ORDER_ITEM must exist in SKU in SKU_DATA

This constraint stipulates that every value of SKU in ORDER_ITEM must match a value of SKU in SKU_DATA.

Normal Forms

All relations are not equal. Some are easy to process, and others are problematic. Relations are categorized into **normal forms** based on the kinds of problems that they have. Knowledge of these normal forms will help you create appropriate database designs. To understand normal forms, we need first to define modification anomalies.

Modification Anomalies

Consider the EQUIPMENT_REPAIR relation in Figure 3-10, which stores data about manufacturing equipment and equipment repairs. Suppose we delete the data for repair number 2100. When we delete this row (the second one in Figure 3-10), we remove not only data about the repair, but also data about the machine itself. We will no longer know, for example, that the machine was a Lathe and that its AcquisitionPrice was 4750.00. When we delete one row, the structure of this table forces us to lose facts about two different things, a machine and a repair. This condition is called a **deletion anomaly**.

Figure 3-10

The EQUIPMENT_REPAIR Table

	ItemNumber	Type	AcquisitionCost	RepairNumber	RepairDate	RepairCost
1	100	Drill Press	3500.00	2000	2009-05-05 ...	375.00
2	200	Lathe	4750.00	2100	2009-05-07 ...	255.00
3	100	Drill Press	3500.00	2200	2009-06-19 ...	178.00
4	300	Mill	27300.00	2300	2009-06-19 ...	1875.00
5	100	Drill Press	3500.00	2400	2009-07-05 ...	0.00
6	100	Drill Press	3500.00	2500	2009-08-17 ...	275.00

	ItemNumber	Type	AcquisitionCost	RepairNumber	RepairDate	RepairCost
1	100	Drill Press	3500.00	2000	2009-05-05 …	375.00
2	200	Lathe	4750.00	2100	2009-05-07 …	255.00
3	100	Drill Press	3500.00	2200	2009-06-19 …	178.00
4	300	Mill	27300.00	2300	2009-06-19 …	1875.00
5	100	Drill Press	3500.00	2400	2009-07-05 …	0.00
6	100	Drill Press	5500.00	2500	2009-08-17 …	275.00

Figure 3-11

The EQUIPMENT_REPAIR Table After an Incorrect Update

Now suppose we want to enter the first repair for a piece of equipment. To enter repair data, we need to know not just RepairNumber, RepairDate, and RepairCost, but also ItemNumber, Type, and AcquisitionCost. If we work in the repair department, this is a problem, because we are unlikely to know the value of AcquisitionCost. The structure of this table forces us to enter facts about two entities when we just want to enter facts about one. This condition is called an **insertion anomaly**.

Finally, suppose we want to change existing data. If we alter a value of RepairNumber, RepairDate, or RepairCost, there is no problem. But if we alter a value of ItemNumber, Type, or AcquisitionCost, we may create a data inconsistency. To see why, suppose we update the last row of the table in Figure 3-10 using the data (100, 'Drill Press', 5500, 2500, '08/17/09', 275).

Figure 3-11 shows the table after this erroneous update. The drill press has two different AcquisitionCosts. Clearly, this is an error. Equipment cannot be acquired at two different costs. If there were, say, 10,000 rows in the table, however, it might be very difficult to detect this error. This condition is called an **update anomaly**.

> **BY THE WAY** Notice that the EQUIPMENT_REPAIR table in Figures 3-10 and 3-11 duplicates data. For example, the AcquisitionCost of the same item of equipment appears several times. Any table that duplicates data is susceptible to update anomalies like the one in Figure 3-11. A table that has such inconsistencies is said to have **data integrity problems**.
>
> As you will learn in Chapter 4, to improve query speed we sometimes design a table to have duplicated data. Be aware, however, that any time we design a table this way we open the door to data integrity problems.

A Short History of Normal Forms

When Codd defined the relational model, he noticed that some tables had modification anomalies. In his second paper,[2] he defined first normal form , second normal form, and third normal form. He defined **first normal form (1NF)** as the *set of conditions for a relation* shown in Figure 3-4. Any table meeting the conditions in Figure 3-4 is therefore a relation in 1NF. Codd also noted that some tables (or, interchangeably in this book, relation) in 1NF had modification anomalies. He found that he could remove some of those anomalies by applying certain conditions. A relation that met those conditions, which we will discuss later in this chapter, was said to be in **second normal form (2NF)**. He also observed, however, that relations in 2NF could also have anomalies, and so he defined **third normal form (3NF)**, which is a set of conditions that removes even more anomalies, and which we will also discuss later in this chapter. As time went by, other researchers found still other ways that anomalies can occur, and the conditions for **Boyce-Codd Normal Form (BCNF)** was defined.

These normal forms are defined so that a relation in BCNF is in 3NF, a relation in 3NF is in 2NF, and a relation in 2NF is in 1NF. Thus, if you put a relation into BCNF, it is automatically in the lesser normal forms.

---

[2] Codd, E. F. and A. L. Dean. "Proceedings of 1971 ACM-SIGFIDET Workshop on Data Description," *Access and Control*, San Diego, California, November 11–12, 1971 ACM 1971.

Normal forms 2NF through BCNF concern anomalies that arise from functional dependencies. Other sources of anomalies were found later. They led to the definition of **fourth normal form (4NF)** and **fifth normal form (5NF)**, both of which we will discuss later in this chapter. So it went, with researchers chipping away at modification anomalies, each one improving on the prior normal form.

In 1982, Fagin published a paper that took a different tack.[3] Instead of looking for just another normal form, Fagin asked, "What conditions need to exist for a relation to have no anomalies?" In that paper, he defined **domain/key normal form (DK/NF)**. Fagin ended the search for normal forms by showing that a relation in DK/NF has no modification anomalies and, further, that a relation that has no modification anomalies is in DK/NF. DK/NF is discussed in more detail later in this chapter.

Normalization Categories

As shown in Figure 3-12, normalization theory can be divided into three major categories. Some anomalies arise from functional dependencies, some arise from multivalued dependencies, and some arise from data constraints and odd conditions.

BCNF, 3NF, and 2NF, are all concerned with anomalies that are caused by functional dependencies. A relation that is in BCNF has no modification anomalies from functional dependencies. It is also automatically in 2NF and 3NF, and, therefore, we will focus on transforming relations into BCNF. However, it is instructive to work through the progression of normal forms from 1NF to BCNF in order to understand how each normal form deals with specific anomalies, and we will do this later in this chapter.[4]

As shown in the second row of Figure 3-12, some anomalies arise because of another kind of dependency called a multivalued dependency. Those anomalies can be eliminated by placing each multivalued dependency in a relation of its own, a condition known as 4NF. You will see how to do that in the last section of this chapter.

The third source of anomalies is esoteric. These problems involve specific, rare, and even strange data constraints. Accordingly, we will not discuss them in this text.

From First Normal Form to Boyce-Codd Normal Form

Any table that meets the definition of a relation in Figure 3-4 is defined as being in 1NF. This means that the following must hold: The cells of a table must be a single value, and neither repeating groups nor arrays are allowed as values; all entries in a column must be of the same data type; each column must have a unique name, but the order of the columns in the table is not significant; no two rows in a table may be identical, but the order of the rows is not significant.

Second Normal Form

When Codd discovered anomalies in 1NF tables, he defined 2NF to eliminate some of these anomalies. A relation is 2NF if and only if *it is in 1NF* and *all non-key attributes are determined by the entire primary key*. This means that if the primary key is a composite primary key, then

Figure 3-12

Summary of Normalization Theory

Source of Anomaly	Normal Forms	Design Principles
Functional dependencies	1NF, 2NF, 3NF, BCNF	BCNF: Design tables so that every determinant is a candidate key.
Multivalued dependencies	4NF	4NF: Move each multivalued dependency to a table of its own.
Data constraints and oddities	5NF, DK/NF	DK/NF: Make every constraint a logical consequence of candidate keys and domains.

[3] Fagin, R. "A Normal Form for Relational Databases That Is Based on Domains and Keys," *ACM Transactions on Database Systems*, September 1981, pp. 387–414.
[4] See Date, C. J. *Database Systems*, 8th ed. (New York: Addison-Wesley, 2003) for a complete discussion of normal forms.

no non-key attribute can be determined by an attribute or set of attributes that make up only part of the key. Thus, if you have a relation **R (A, B, N, O, P)** with the composite key **(A, B)**, then none of the non-key attributes N, O, or P can be determined by just A or just B.

Note that the only way a non-key attribute can be dependent on part of the primary key is if there is a composite primary key. This means that relations with single-attribute primary keys are automatically in 2NF.

For example, consider the relation STUDENT_ACTIVITY (StudentID, Activity, Fee). The composite primary key is (StudentID, Activity), which allows us to determine the fee a particular student will have to pay for a particular activity. However, since fees are determined by activities, Fee is also functionally dependent on just Activity itself, and we can say that Fee is **partially dependent** on the key of the table. Thus, there is a non-key attribute determined by part of the composite primary, and the STUDENT_ACTIVITY relation is not in 2NF.

What do we do in this case? We will have to move the columns of this functional dependency into a separate relation while leaving the determinant in the original relation as a foreign key. We will end up with two relations: STUDENT_ACTIVITY (StudentID, *Activity*) and ACTIVITY_FEE (Activity, Fee). The Activity column in STUDENT_ACTIVITY becomes a foreign key.

Third Normal Form

However, the conditions necessary for 2NF do not eliminate all anomalies. To deal with additional anomalies, Codd defined 3NF. A relation is in 3NF if and only if *it is in 2NF* and *there are no non-key attributes determined by another non-key attribute*. The technical name for a non-key attribute determined by another non-key attribute is **transitive dependency**. We can therefore restate the definition of 3NF as a relation is in 3NF if and only if *it is in 2NF* and *it has no transitive dependencies*. Thus, in order for our relation **R (A, B, N, O, P)** to be in 3NF, none of the non-key attributes **N, O,** or **P** can be determined by **N, O,** or **P**.

For example, consider the relation STUDENT_HOUSING (StudentID, Building, Fee). In this case, the building fee is independent of which student is housed in the building. However, the same fee is charged for every room in a building, and therefore Building determines Fee. Thus, a non-key attribute (Fee) is functionally determined by another non-key attribute (Building).

Again, we will have to move the columns of the functional dependency into a separate relation while leaving the determinant in the original relation as a foreign key. We will end up with two relations: STUDENT_HOUSING (StudentID, *Building*) and HOUSING_FEE (Building, Fee). The Building column in STUDENT_HOUSING becomes a foreign key.

Boyce-Codd Normal Form

Some database designers normalize their relations to 3NF. Unfortunately, there are still anomalies due to functional dependences in 3NF. Together with Raymond Boyce, Codd defined BCNF to fix this situation. A relation is in BCNF if and only if *it is in 3NF* and *every determinant is a candidate key*.

For example, consider the relation STUDENT_ADVISIOR (StudentID, Major, AdvisorName), where a student (StudentID) can have one or more majors (Major), a major can have one or more faculty advisors (AdvisorName), and a faculty member advises in only one major area.

Since students can have several majors, StudentID does not determine Major. Moreover, since students can have several advisers, StudentID does not determine AdvisorName. Therefore, StudentID by itself cannot be a key. However, the composite key (StudentID, Major) determines AdvisorName, and the composite key (StudentID, AdvisorName) determines Major. This gives us (StudentID, Major) and (StudentId, AdvisorName) as two candidate keys. We can select either of these as the primary key for the relation.

Note that STUDENT_ADVISOR is in 2NF because it has no non-key attributes in the sense that every attribute is a part of at least one candidate key. This is a subtle condition, based on the fact that technically the definition of 2NF states that no *non-prime attribute* can be partially dependent on a candidate key, where a **non-prime attribute** is an attribute that is not contained in any candidate key. STUDENT_ADVISOR is in 3NF because there are no transitive dependencies in the relation.

The two candidate keys for this relation are **overlapping candidate keys**, because they share the attribute StudentID. When a table in 3NF has overlapping candidate keys, it can still have modification anomalies based on functional dependencies. In the STUDENT_ADVISOR relation, there will be modification anomalies because there is one other functional dependency in the relation: because a faculty member can be an advisor for only one major area, AdvisorName determines Major. Therefore, AdvisorName is a determinant, but not a candidate key.

Suppose that we have a student (StudentID = 300) majoring in psychology (Major = Psychology) with faculty advisor Perls (AdvisorName = Perls). Further, assume that this row is the only one in the table with the AdvisorName value of Perls. If we delete this row, we will lose all data about Perls. This is a deletion anomaly. Similarly, we cannot insert the data to represent the Economics advisor Keynes until a student majors in Economics. This is an insertion anomaly. Situations like this led to the development of BCNF.

What do we do with the STUDENT_ADVISOR relation? As before, we move the functional dependency creating the problem to another relation while leaving the determinant in the original relation as a foreign key. In this case, we will create STUDENT_ADVISOR (<u>StudentID</u>, *AdvisorName*) and ADVISOR_MAJOR (<u>AdvisorName</u>, Major). The AdvisorName column in STUDENT_ADVISOR is the foreign key.

Eliminating Anomalies from Functional Dependencies

Most modification anomalies occur because of problems with functional dependencies. You can eliminate these problems by progressively testing a relation for 1NF, 2NF, 3NF and the BCNF using the definitions of these normal forms given previously. Or, you can eliminate such problems by simply designing (or redesigning) your tables so that every determinant is a candidate key. This condition, which, of course, is the definition of BCNF, will eliminate all anomalies due to functional dependencies. We prefer this strategy, and will use it exclusively in this book.

The general normalization method is summarized in Figure 3-13. Identify every functional dependency in the relation, then identify the candidate keys. If there are determinants that are not candidate keys, then the relation is not in BCNF, and it is subject to modification anomalies. To put the relation into BCNF, follow the procedure in step 3. To fix this procedure in your mind, we will illustrate it with five different examples.

 **THE WAY**   Our process rule that a relation is in BCNF if and only if every determinant is a candidate key is summed up in a widely known phrase:

I swear to construct my tables so that all non-key columns are dependent on the key, the whole key and nothing but the key, so help me Codd!

Figure 3-13

Process for Putting a Relation into BCNF

Process for Putting a Relation into BCNF
1. Identify every functional dependency.
2. Identify every candidate key.

3. If there is a functional dependency that has a determinant that is not a candidate key:
 	
    A. Move the columns of that functional dependency into a new relation.
    B. Make the determinant of that functional dependency the primary key of the new relation.
    C. Leave a copy of the determinant as a foreign key in the original relation.
    D. Create a referential integrity constraint between the original relation and the new relation.

4. Repeat step 3 until every determinant of every relation is a candidate key.

Note: In step 3, if there is more than one such functional dependency, start with the one with the most columns.

Normalization Example 1

Consider the SKU_DATA table:

SKU_DATA (SKU, SKU_Description, Department, Buyer)

As discussed earlier, this table has three functional dependencies:

SKU → (SKU_Description, Department, Buyer)

SKU_Description → (SKU, Department, Buyer)

Buyer → Department

SKU and SKU_Description determine all of the columns in the table, so they are candidate keys. Buyer is a determinant, but it does not determine all of the other columns, and hence is not a candidate key. Hence, SKU_DATA has a determinant that is not a candidate key and is therefore not in BCNF. It will have modification anomalies.

To remove such anomalies, in step 3A we move the columns of functional dependency whose determinant is not a candidate key into a new table. In this case, we place Buyer and Department into a new table:

BUYER (Buyer, Department)

Next, in step 3B, we make the primary key of the new table the determinant of the functional dependency. In this case, Buyer becomes the primary key:

BUYER (<u>Buyer</u>, Department)

Next, following step 3C, we leave a copy of the determinant as a foreign key in the original relation. Thus, SKU_DATA becomes SKU_DATA_2:

SKU_DATA_2 (<u>SKU</u>, SKU_Description, *Buyer*)

The resulting tables are thus:

BUYER (<u>Buyer</u>, Department)

SKU_DATA_2 (<u>SKU</u>, SKU_Description, *Buyer*)

where SKU_DATA_2.Buyer is a foreign key to the BUYER table.

Both of these tables are now in BCNF and will have no anomalies due to functional dependencies. For the data in these tables to be consistent, however, we also need to define the referential integrity constraint in step 3D:

SKU_DATA_2.Buyer must exist in BUYER.Buyer

This statement means that every value in the Buyer column of SKU_DATA_2 must also exist as a value in the Buyer column of BUYER. Sample data for the resulting tables are shown in Figure 3-14.

Normalization Example 2

Now consider the EQUIPMENT_REPAIR relation in Figure 3-10. The structure of the table is:

EQUIPMENT_REPAIR (ItemNumber, Type, AcquisitionCost, RepairNumber, RepairDate, RepairCost)

Examining the data in Figure 3-8, the functional dependencies are:

ItemNumber → (Type, AcquisitionCost)

RepairNumber → (ItemNumber, Type, AcquisitionCost, RepairDate, RepairCost)

Both ItemNumber and RepairNumber are determinants, but only RepairNumber is a candidate key. Accordingly, EQUIPMENT_REPAIR is not in BCNF and is subject to modification anomalies. Following the procedure in Figure 3-13, we place the columns of the problematic functional dependency into a separate table, as follows:

ITEM (<u>ItemNumber</u>, Type, AcquisitionCost)

BUYER

	Buyer	Department
1	Cindy Lo	Camping
2	Jerry Martin	Climbing
3	Nancy Meyers	Water Sports
4	Pete Hansen	Water Sports

SKU_DATA_2

	SKU	SKU_Description	Buyer
1	100100	Std. Scuba Tank, Yellow	Pete Hansen
2	100200	Std. Scuba Tank, Magenta	Pete Hansen
3	101100	Dive Mask, Small Clear	Nancy Meyers
4	101200	Dive Mask, Med Clear	Nancy Meyers
5	201000	Half-dome Tent	Cindy Lo
6	202000	Half-dome Tent Footprint	Cindy Lo
7	301000	Light Fly Climbing Harness	Jerry Martin
8	302000	Locking carabiner, Oval	Jerry Martin

Figure 3-14

The Normalized BUYER and
SKU_DATA_2 Relations

and remove all but ItemNumber from EQUIPMENT_REPAIR (and rearrange the columns so that the primary key RepairNumber is the first column in the relation) to create:

REPAIR (RepairNumber, *ItemNumber*, RepairDate, RepairCost)

We also need to create the referential integrity constraint:

REPAIR.ItemNumber must exist in ITEM.ItemNumber

Data for these two new relations are shown in Figure 3-15.

> **BY THE WAY**   There is another, more intuitive way to think about normalization. Do you remember your eighth grade English teacher? She said that every paragraph should have a single theme. If you write a paragraph that has two themes, you should break it up into two paragraphs, each with a single theme.
>
> The problem with the EQUIPMENT_REPAIR relation is that it has two themes: one about repairs and a second about items. We eliminated modification anomalies by breaking that single table with two themes into two tables, each with a single theme. Sometimes, it is helpful to look at a table and ask, "How many themes does it have?" If it has more than one, then redefine the table so that it has a single theme.

Figure 3-15

The Normalized ITEM
and REPAIR Relations

ITEM

	ItemNumber	Type	AcquisitionCost
1	100	Drill Press	3500.00
2	200	Lathe	4750.00
3	300	Mill	27300.00

REPAIR

	RepairNumber	ItemNumber	RepairDate	RepairCost
1	2000	100	2009-05-05	375.00
2	2100	200	2009-05-07	255.00
3	2200	100	2009-06-19	178.00
4	2300	300	2009-06-19	1875.00
5	2400	100	2009-07-05	0.00
6	2500	100	2009-07-05	275.00

Normalization Example 3

Consider now the Cape Codd database ORDER_ITEM relation with the structure:

ORDER_ITEM (OrderNumber, SKU, Quantity, Price, ExtendedPrice)

with functional dependencies:

(OrderNumber, SKU) → (Quantity, Price, ExtendedPrice)

(Quantity, Price) → ExtendedPrice

This table is not in BCNF because the determinant (Quantity, Price) is not a candidate key. We can follow the same normalization practice as illustrated in examples 1 and 2, but in this case, because the second functional dependency arises from the formula ExtendedPrice = (Quantity * Price), we reach a silly result.

To see why, we follow the procedure in Figure 3-13 to create tables such that every determinant is a candidate key. This means that we move the columns Quantity, Price, and ExtendedPrice to tables of their own, as follows:

EXTENDED_PRICE (<u>Quantity</u>, <u>Price</u>, ExtendedPrice)

ORDER_ITEM (<u>OrderNumber</u>, <u>SKU</u>, *Quantity*, *Price*)

Notice that we left both Quantity and Price in the original relation as a composite foreign key. These two tables are in BCNF, but the values in the EXTENDED_PRICE table are ridiculous. They are just the results of multiplying Quantity by Price. The simple fact is that we do not need to create a table to store these results. Instead, any time we need to know ExtendedPrice we will just compute it. In fact, we can define this formula to the DBMS and let the DBMS compute the value of ExtendedPrice when necessary. You will see how to do this with Oracle, SQL Server, and MySQL in Chapters 10, 11, and 12, respectively.

Using the formula, we can remove ExtendedPrice from the table. The resulting table is in BCNF:

ORDER_ITEM (<u>OrderNumber</u>, <u>SKU</u>, Quantity, Price)

Note that Quantity and Price are no longer foreign keys. The ORDER_ITEM table with sample data now appears as shown in Figure 3-16.

Normalization Example 4

Consider the following table that stores data about student activities:

STUDENT_ACTIVITY (SID, Name, Club, Cost, AmountPaid)

where SID is a student identifier, Name is student name, Club is the name of a club, Cost is the cost of joining a club, and AmountPaid is the amount the student has paid to that club. Figure 3-17 shows sample data for this table.

SID is a unique student identifier, so we know that:

SID → Name

Figure 3-16

The Normalized ORDER_ITEM Relation

ORDER_ITEM

	OrderNumber	SKU	Quantity	Price
1	1000	201000	1	300.00
2	1000	202000	1	130.00
3	2000	101100	4	50.00
4	2000	101200	2	50.00
5	3000	100200	1	300.00
6	3000	101100	2	50.00
7	3000	101200	1	50.00

STUDENT_ACTIVITY

	SID	Name	Club	Cost	Amount Paid
1	100	Jones	Scuba	400.00	0.00
2	200	Chau	Scuba	400.00	400.00
3	200	Chau	Skiing	550.00	550.00
4	300	Garrett	Climbing	150.00	150.00
5	400	Jones	Skiing	550.00	550.00

Figure 3-17

Sample Data for the
STUDENT_ACTIVITY
Relation

However, does the functional dependency

SID → Club

exist? It does if a student belongs to just one club, but it does not if a student belongs to more than one club. Looking at the data, student Chau with SID 200 belongs to two different clubs, so SID does not determine Club. SID does not determine Cost or AmountPaid, either.

Now consider the Name column. Does Name determine SID? Is, for example, the value 'Jones' always paired with the same value of SID? No, there are two students named 'Jones', and they have different SID values. Name does not determine any other column in this table, either.

Considering the next column, Club, we know that many students can belong to a club. Therefore, Club does not determine SID or Name. Does Club determine Cost? Is the value 'Scuba', for example, always paired with the same value of Cost? From this data, it appears so, and using just this sample data, we can conclude that Club determines Cost.

However, this data is just a sample. Logically, it is possible for students to pay different costs, perhaps because they select different levels of club membership. If that were the case, then we would say that

(SID, Club) → Cost

To find out, we need to check with the users. Here, assume that all students pay the same cost for a given club. The last column is AmountPaid, and it does not determine anything.

So far, we have two functional dependencies:

SID → Name

Club → Cost

Are there other functional dependencies with composite determinants? No single column determines AmountPaid, so consider possible composite determinants for it. AmountPaid is dependent on both the student and the club the student has joined. Therefore, it is determined by the combination of the determinants Student and Club. Thus, we can say

(SID, Club) → AmountPaid

So far we have three determinants: SID, Club, and (SID, Club). Are any of these candidate keys? Do any of these determinants identify a unique row? From the data, it appears that (SID, Club) identifies a unique row and is a candidate key. Again, in real situations, we would need to check this assumption out with the users.

STUDENT_ACTIVITY is not in BCNF because columns SID and Club are both determinants, but neither is a candidate key. SID and Club are only part of the candidate key (SID, Club).

BY THE WAY   Both SID and Club are *part of* the candidate key (SID, Club). This, however, is not good enough. A determinant must have all of the same columns to be the same as a candidate key. Remember, as we stated above:

I swear to construct my tables so that all non-key columns are dependent on the key, the whole key, and nothing but the key, so help me Codd."

To normalize this table, we need to construct tables so that every determinant is a candidate key. We can do this by creating a separate table for each functional dependency as we did before. The result is:

STUDENT (SID, Name)

CLUB (Club, Cost)

PAYMENT (SID, Club, AmountPaid)

with referential integrity constraints:

PAYMENT.SID must exist in STUDENT.SID

and

PAYMENT.Club must exist in CLUB.Club

These tables are in BCNF and will have no anomalies from functional dependencies. The sample data for the normalized tables are shown in Figure 3-18.

Normalization Example 5

Now consider a normalization process that requires two iterations of step 3 in the procedure in Figure 3-13. To do this, we will extend the SKU_DATA relation by adding the budget code of each department. We call the revised relation SKU_DATA_3 and define it as follows:

SKU_DATA_3 (SKU, SKU_Description, Department, DeptBudgetCode, Buyer)

Sample data for this relation are shown in Figure 3-19.

SKU_DATA_3 has the following functional dependencies:

SKU → (SKU_Description, Department, DeptBudgetCode, Buyer)

SKU_Description → (SKU, Department, DeptBudgetCode, Buyer)

Buyer → (Department, DeptBudgetCode)

Department → DeptBudgetCode

Of the four determinants, both SKU and SKU_Description are candidate keys, but neither Department nor Buyer is a candidate key. Therefore, this relation is not in BCNF.

Figure 3-18

The Normalized STUDENT, CLUB, and PAYMENT Relations

STUDENT

	SID	Name
1	100	Jones
2	200	Chau
3	300	Garrett
4	400	Jones

CLUB

	Club	Cost
1	Climbing	150.00
2	Scuba	400.00
3	Skiing	550.00

PAYMENT

	SID	Club	AmountPaid
1	100	Scuba	0.00
2	200	Scuba	400.00
3	200	Skiing	550.00
4	300	Climbing	150.00
5	400	Skiing	550.00

SKU_DATA_3

	SKU	SKU_Description	Department	DeptBudgetCode	Buyer
1	100100	Std. Scuba Tank, Yellow	Water Sports	BC-100	Pete Hansen
2	100200	Std. Scuba Tank, Magenta	Water Sports	BC-100	Pete Hansen
3	101100	Dive Mask, Small Clear	Water Sports	BC-100	Nancy Meyers
4	101200	Dive Mask, Med Clear	Water Sports	BC-100	Nancy Meyers
5	201000	Half-dome Tent	Camping	BC-200	Cindy Lo
6	202000	Half-dome Tent Footprint	Camping	BC-200	Cindy Lo
7	301000	Light Fly Climbing Harness	Climbing	BC-300	Jerry Martin
8	302000	Locking carabiner, Oval	Climbing	BC-300	Jerry Martin

Figure 3-19

Sample Data for the SKU_DATA_3 Relation

To normalize this table, we must transform this table into two or more tables that are in BCNF. In this case, there are two problematic functional dependencies. According to the note at the end of the procedure in Figure 3-13, we take the functional dependency whose determinant is not a candidate key and has the largest number of columns first. In this case, we take the columns of

Buyer → (Department, Dept_BudgetCode)

and place them in a table of their own.

Next, we make the determinant the primary key of the new table, remove all columns except Buyer from SKU_DATA_3, and make Buyer a foreign key of the new version of SKU_DATA_3, which we will name SKU_DATA_4. The results are:

BUYER (Buyer, Department, DeptBudgetCode)

SKU_DATA_4 (SKU, SKU_Description, *Buyer*)

We also create the referential integrity constraint:

SKU_DATA_4.Buyer must exist in BUYER.Buyer

The functional dependencies from SKU_DATA_4 are:

SKU → (SKU_Description, Buyer)

SKU_Description → (SKU, Buyer)

Because every determinant of SKU_DATA_4 is also a candidate key, the relationship is now in BCNF. Looking at the functional dependencies from BUYER we find:

Buyer → (Department, DeptBudgetCode)

Department → DeptBudgetCode

BUYER is not in BCNF because Department is a determinant that is not a candidate key. In this case, we must move (Department, DeptBudgetCode) into a table of its own. Following the procedure in Figure 3-13 and breaking BUYER into two tables (DEPARTMENT and BUYER_2) gives us a set of three tables:

DEPARTMENT (Department, DeptBudgetCode)

BUYER_2 (Buyer, *Department*)

SKU_DATA_4 (SKU, SKU_Description, *Buyer*)

with referential integrity constraints:

SKU_DATA_4.Buyer must exist in BUYER_2.Buyer

BUYER_2.Department must exist in DEPARTMENT.Department

The functional dependencies from all three of these tables are:

Department → DeptBudgetCode

Buyer → Department

SKU → (SKU_Description, Buyer)

SKU_Description → SKU, Buyer

DEPARTMENT

	Department	DeptBudgetCode
1	Camping	BC-200
2	Climbing	BC-300
3	Water Sports	BC-100

BUYER_2

	Buyer	Department
1	Cindy Lo	Camping
2	Jerry Martin	Climbing
3	Nancy Meyers	Water Sports
4	Pete Hansen	Water Sports

SKU_DATA_4

	SKU	SKU_Description	Buyer
1	100100	Std. Scuba Tank, Yellow	Pete Hansen
2	100200	Std. Scuba Tank, Magenta	Pete Hansen
3	101100	Dive Mask, Small Clear	Nancy Meyers
4	101200	Dive Mask, Med Clear	Nancy Meyers
5	201000	Half-dome Tent	Cindy Lo
6	202000	Half-dome Tent Footprint	Cindy Lo
7	301000	Light Fly Climbing Harness	Jerry Martin
8	302000	Locking carabiner, Oval	Jerry Martin

Figure 3-20

The Normalized
DEPARTMENT, BUYER_2,
and SKU_DATA_4 Relations

At last, every determinant is a candidate key and all three of the tables are in BCNF. The resulting relations form these operations are shown in Figure 3-20.

Eliminating Anomalies from Multivalued Dependencies

All of the anomalies in the last section were due to functional dependencies. Anomalies can also arise from another kind of dependency—the multivalued dependency. A **multivalued dependency** occurs when a determinant is matched with a particular *set* of values.

Examples of multivalued dependencies are:

Employee → → **Degree**

Employee → → **Sibling**

PartKit → → **Part**

Such expressions are read as "Employee multi-determines Degree" and "Employee multi-determines Sibling" and "PartKit multi-determines Part." Note that multideterminants are shown with a double arrow rather than a single arrow.

In each case, the determinant is associated with a set of values. Example data for each of these multidependencies are shown in Figure 3-21. Employee Jones, for example, has degrees AA and BS. Employee Greene has degrees BS, MS, and PhD. Employee Chau has just one degree, BS. Similarly, Employee Jones has siblings (brothers and sisters) Fred, Sally, and Frank. Employee Greene has sibling Nikki, and Employee Chau has siblings Jonathan and Eileen. Finally, PartKit Bike Repair has parts Wrench, Screwdriver, and Tube Fix. Other kits have parts as shown in Figure 3-21.

Unlike functional dependencies, the determinant of a multivalued dependency can never be the primary key. In all three of the tables in Figure 3-21, the primary key consists of the

EMPLOYEE_DEGREE

	Employee	Degree
1	Chau	BS
2	Greene	BS
3	Greene	MS
4	Greene	PhD
5	Jones	AA
6	Jones	BS

EMPLOYEE_SIBLING

	Employee	Sibling
1	Chau	Eileen
2	Chau	Jonathan
3	Greene	Nikki
4	Jones	Frank
5	Jones	Fred
6	Jones	Sally

PARTKIT_PART

	PartKit	Part
1	Bike Repair	Screwdriver
2	Bike Repair	Tube Fix
3	Bike Repair	Wrench
4	First Aid	Aspirin
5	First Aid	Bandaids
6	First Aid	Elastic Band
7	First Aid	Ibuprofin
8	Vice	Extension Screw
9	Vice	Handle
10	Vice	Vice Jaw

Figure 3-21

Three Examples of Multivalued Dependencies

composite of the two columns in each table. The primary key of the EMPLOYEE_DEGREE table is the composite (Employee, Degree).

Multivalued dependencies pose no problem as long as they exist in tables of their own. None of the tables in Figure 3-21 have modification anomalies. However, if A $\rightarrow\rightarrow$ B, then any relation that contains A, B, and one or more additional columns will have modification anomalies.

For example, consider the situation if we combine the employee data in Figure 3-21 into a single EMPLOYEE_DEGREE_SIBLING table with three columns (Employee, Degree, Sibling), as shown in Figure 3-22.

Now, what actions need to be taken if student Jones earns an MBA? We must add three rows to the table. If we do not, if we only add the row ('Jones', 'MBA', 'Fred'), it will appear as if Jones is an MBA with her brother Fred, but not with her sister Sally or her other brother Frank. However, suppose Greene earns an MBA. Then we need only add one row ('Greene', 'MBA', 'Nikki'). But, if Chau earns an MBA, we need to add two rows. These are insertion anomalies. There are equivalent modification and deletion anomalies as well.

In Figure 3-22, we combined two multivalued dependencies into a single table and obtained modification anomalies. Unfortunately, we will also get anomalies if we combine a multivalued dependency with any other column, even if that other column has no multivalued dependency.

Figure 3-23 shows what happens when we combine the multivalued dependency

PartKit $\rightarrow\rightarrow$ Part

EMPLOYEE_DEGREE_SIBLING

	Employee	Degree	Sibling
1	Chau	BS	Eileen
2	Chau	BS	Jonathan
3	Greene	BS	Nikki
4	Greene	MS	Nikki
5	Greene	PhD	Nikki
6	Jones	AA	Frank
7	Jones	BS	Frank
8	Jones	AA	Fred
9	Jones	BS	Fred
10	Jones	AA	Sally
11	Jones	BS	Sally

Figure 3-22

EMPLOYEE_DEGREE_
SIBLING Relation with Two
Multivalued Dependencies

with the functional dependency

PartKit → → Price

For the data to be consistent, we must repeat the value of price for as many rows as each kit has parts. For this example, we must add three rows for the Bike Repair kit and four rows for the First Aid kit. The result is duplicated data that can cause data integrity problems.

Now you also know the problem with the relation in Figure 3-2. Anomalies exist in that table because it contains two multivalued dependencies:

BuyerName → → SKU_Managed

BuyerName → → CollegeMajor

Fortunately, it is easy to deal with multivalued dependencies: Put them into a table of their own. None of the tables in Figure 3-21 has modification anomalies, because each table consists of only the columns in a single, multivalued dependency. Thus, to fix the table in Figure 3-2, we must move BuyerName and SKU_Managed into one table and BuyerName and CollegeMajor into a second table:

PRODUCT_BUYER_SKU (BuyerName, SKU_Managed)

PRODUCT_BUYER_MAJOR (BuyerName, CollegeMajor)

The results are shown in Figure 3-24. If we want to maintain strict equivalence between these tables, we would also add the referential integrity constraint:

**PRODUCT_BUYER_SKU.BuyerName must be identical to
PRODUCT_BUYER_MAJOR.BuyerName**

Figure 3-23

PARTKIT_PART_PRICE
Relation with a Functional
Dependency and a
Multivalued Dependency

PARTKIT_PART_PRICE

	PartKit	Part	Price
1	Bike Repair	Screwdriver	14.95
2	Bike Repair	Tube Fix	14.95
3	Bike Repair	Wrench	14.95
4	First Aid	Aspirin	24.95
5	First Aid	Bandaids	24.95
6	First Aid	Elastic Band	24.95
7	First Aid	Ibuprofin	24.95
8	Vice	Extension Screw	125.00
9	Vice	Handle	125.00
10	Vice	Vice Jaw	125.00

PRODUCT_BUYER_SKU

	BuyerName	SKU_Managed
1	Nancy Meyers	101100
2	Nancy Meyers	101200
3	Pete Hansen	100100
4	Pete Hansen	100200

PRODUCT_BUYER_MAJOR

	BuyerName	College-Major
1	Nancy Meyers	Art
2	Nancy Meyers	Info Systems
3	Pete Hansen	Business

Figure 3-24

Placing the Two Multivalued Dependencies in Figure 3-2 into Separate Relations

This referential integrity constraint may not be necessary, depending on the requirements of the application.

Notice that when you put multivalued dependencies into a table of their own, they disappear. The result is just a table with two columns, and the primary key (and sole candidate key) is the composite of those two columns. When multivalued dependencies have been isolated in this way, the table is said to be in fourth normal form (4NF).

The hardest part of multivalued dependencies is finding them. Once you know they exist in a table, just move them into a table of their own. Whenever you encounter tables with odd anomalies, especially anomalies that require you to insert, modify, or delete different numbers of rows to maintain integrity, check for multivalued dependencies.

> **BY THE WAY**   You will sometimes hear people use the term *normalize* in phrases like, "that table has been normalized" or "check to see if those tables are normalized." Unfortunately, not everyone means the same thing with these words. Some people do not know about BCNF, and they will use it to mean tables in 3NF, which is a lesser form of normalization, one that allows for anomalies from functional dependencies that BCNF does not allow. Others use it to mean tables that are both BCNF and 4NF. Others may mean something else. The best choice is to use the term *normalize* to mean tables that are in both BCNF and 4NF.

Fifth Normal Form

There is a fifth normal form (5NF), also known as **Project-Join Normal Form (PJ/NF)**, which involves an anomaly where a table can be split apart but not correctly joined back together. However, the conditions under which this happens are complex, and generally if a relation is in 4NF, it is in 5NF. We will not deal with 5NF in this book. For more information about 5NF, start with the work by date cited earlier in this chapter, and the Wikipedia article at http://en.wikipedia.org/wiki/Fifth_normal_form.

Domain/Key Normal Form

As we have previously discussed in this chapter, in 1982, R. Fagin published a paper that that defined domain/key normal form (DK/NF). Fagin asked, "What conditions need to exist for a relation to have no anomalies?" He showed that a relation in DK/NF has no modification anomalies and, further, that a relation that has no modification anomalies is in DK/NF.

But what does this mean? Basically, DK/NF requires that all the constraints on the data values be logical implications of the definitions of domains and keys. To the level of detail in this text, and to the level of detail experienced by 99 percent of all database practitioners, this can be restated as follows: Every determinant of a functional dependency must be a candidate key. This, of course, is simply our definition of BCNF, and, for practical purposes, relations in BCNF are in DK/NF as well.

Summary

Databases arise from three sources: from existing data, from new systems development, and from the redesign of existing databases. This chapter and the next are concerned with databases that arise from existing data. Even though a table is a simple concept, certain tables can lead to surprisingly difficult processing problems. This chapter uses the concept of normalization to understand and possibly solve those problems. Figure 3-3 lists terms you should be familiar with.

A relation is a special case of a table; all relations are tables, but not all tables are relations. Relations are tables that have the properties listed in Figure 3-4. Three sets of terms are used to describe relation structure: (relation, attribute, tuple); (table, column, row); and (file, field, and record). Sometimes these terms are mixed and matched. In practice, the terms *table* and *relation* are commonly used synonymously, and we will do so for the balance of this text.

In a functional dependency, the value of one attribute, or attributes, determines the value of another. In the functional dependency $A \rightarrow B$, attribute A is called the determinant. Some functional dependencies arise from equations, but many others do not. The purpose of a database is, in fact, to store instances of functional dependencies that do not arise from equations.

Determinants that have more than one attribute are called composite determinants. If $A \rightarrow (B, C)$, then $A \rightarrow B$ and $A \rightarrow C$. However, if $(A, B) \rightarrow C$, then, in general, neither $A \rightarrow C$ nor $B \rightarrow C$.

If $A \rightarrow B$, the values of A may or may not be unique in a relation. However, every time a given value of A appears, it will be paired with the same value of B. A determinant is unique in a relation only if it determines every other attribute of the relation. You cannot always rely on determining functional dependencies from sample data. The best idea is to verify your conclusions with the users of the data.

A key is a combination of one or more columns used to identify one or more rows. A composite key is a key with two or more attributes. A determinant that determines every other attribute is called a candidate key. A relation may have more than one candidate key. One of them is selected to be used by the DBMS for finding rows and is called the primary key. A surrogate key is an artificial attribute used as a primary key. The value of a surrogate key is supplied by the DBMS and has no meaning to the user. A foreign key is a key in one table that references the primary key of a second table. A referential integrity constraint is a limitation on data values of a foreign key that ensures that every value of the foreign key has a match to a value of a primary key.

The three kinds of modification anomalies are insert, update, and delete. Codd and others defined normal forms for describing different table structures that lead to anomalies. A table that meets the conditions listed in Figure 3-4 is in 1NF. Some anomalies arise from functional dependencies. Three forms, 2NF, 3NF, and BCNF, are used to treat such anomalies.

In this text, we are only concerned with the best of these forms, BCNF. If a relation is in BCNF, then no anomalies from functional dependencies can occur. A relation is in BCNF if every determinant is a candidate key.

Some anomalies arise from multivalued dependencies. A multidetermines B, or $A \rightarrow \rightarrow B$, if A determines a set of values. If A multidetermines B, then any relation that contains A, B, and one or more other columns will have modification anomalies. Anomalies due to multivalued dependencies can be eliminated by placing the multivalued dependency in a table of its own. Such tables are in 4NF.

There is a 5NF, but generally tables in 4NF are in 5NF. DK/NF has been defined, but in practical terms the definition of DK/NF is the same as the definition of BCNF.

Key Terms

attribute	entity
Boyce-Codd Normal Form (BCNF)	fifth normal form (5NF)
candidate key	first normal form (1NF)
composite determinant	foreign key
composite key	fourth normal form (4NF)
data integrity problems	functionally dependent
deletion anomaly	insertion anomaly
determinant	key
domain/key normal form (DK/NF)	multivalued dependency

non-prime attribute

normal forms

overlapping candidate key

partially dependent

primary key

Project-Join Normal Form (PJ/NF)

referential integrity constraint

relation

second normal form (2NF)

surrogate key

third normal form (3NF)

transitive dependency

tuple

update anomaly

Review Questions

3.1   Name three sources for databases.

3.2   What is the basic premise of this and the next chapter?

3.3   Explain what is wrong with the table in Figure 3-2.

3.4   Define each of the terms listed in Figure 3-3.

3.5   Describe the characteristics of a table that make it a relation.

3.6   Give an example of two tables that are not relations.

3.7   Suppose that two columns in two different tables have the same column name. What convention is used to give each a unique name?

3.8   Must all the values in the same column of a relation have the same length?

3.9   Explain the three different sets of terms used to describe tables, columns, and rows.

3.10 Explain the difference between functional dependencies that arise from equations and those that do not.

3.11 Intuitively, what is the meaning of the functional dependency

PartNumber → PartWeight

3.12 Explain the following statement: "The only reason for having relations is to store instances of functional dependencies."

3.13 Explain the meaning of the expression:

(FirstName, LastName) → Phone

3.14 What is a composite determinant?

3.15 If $(A, B) \rightarrow C$, then can we also say that $A \rightarrow C$?

3.16 If $A \rightarrow (B, C)$, then can we also say that $A \rightarrow B$?

3.17 For the SKU_DATA table in Figure 3-1, explain why Buyer determines Department, but Department does not determine Buyer.

3.18 For the SKU_DATA table in Figure 3-1, explain why SKU_Description → (SKU, Department, Buyer).

3.19 If it is true that

PartNumber → PartWeight

does that mean that PartNumber will be unique in a relation?

3.20 Under what conditions will a determinant be unique in a relation?

3.21 What is the best test for determining whether a determinant is unique?

3.22 What is a composite key?

3.23   What is a candidate key?

3.24   What is a primary key?

3.25   Explain the difference between a candidate key and a primary key.

3.26   What is a surrogate key?

3.27   Where does the value of a surrogate key come from?

3.28   When would you use a surrogate key?

3.29   What is a foreign key?

3.30   The term *domestic key* is not used. If it were used, however, what do you think it would mean?

3.31   What is a normal form?

3.32   Illustrate deletion, modification, and insertion anomalies on the STUDENT_ACTIVITY relation in Figure 3-17.

3.33   Explain why duplicated data leads to data integrity problems.

3.34   What relations are in 1NF?

3.35   Which normal forms are concerned with functional dependencies?

3.36   What conditions are required for a relation to be in 2NF?

3.37   What conditions are required for a relation to be in 3NF?

3.38   What conditions are required for a relation to be in BCNF?

3.39   If a relation is in BCNF, what can we say about it with regard to 2NF and 3NF?

3.40   What normal form is concerned with multivalued dependencies?

3.41   What is the premise of Fagin's work on DK/NF?

3.42   Summarize the three categories of normalization theory.

3.43   In general, how can you transform a relation not in BCNF into ones that are in BCNF?

3.44   What is a referential integrity constraint?

3.45   Explain the role of referential integrity constraints in normalization.

3.46   Why is an un-normalized relation like a paragraph with multiple themes?

3.47   In normalization example 3, why is the EXTENDED_PRICE relation "silly"?

3.48   In normalization example 4, under what conditions is

(SID, Club) → Cost

more accurate than

Club → Cost

3.49   If a determinant is part of a candidate key, is that good enough for BCNF?

3.50   In normalization example 5, why are the following two tables not correct?

DEPARTMENT (<u>Department</u>, DeptBudgetCode, Buyer)
SKU_DATA_4 (<u>SKU</u>, SKU_Description, *Department*)

3.51   How does a multivalued dependency differ from a functional dependency?

3.52   Consider the relation:

PERSON (Name, Sibling, ShoeSize)

Assume that the following functional dependencies exist:

Name → Sibling

Name → ShoeSize

Describe deletion, modification, and insertion anomalies for this relation.

3.53   Place the PERSON relation into 4NF.

3.54   Consider the relation:

PERSON_2 (Name, Sibling, ShoeSize, Hobby)

Assume that the following functional dependencies exist:

Name → Sibling

Name → ShoeSize

Name → Hobby

Describe deletion, modification, and insertion anomalies for this relation.

3.55   Place the PERSON_2 relation into 4NF.

3.56   What is 5NF?

3.57   How do the conditions for DK/NF correspond to the conditions for BCNF?

Project Questions

3.58   Consider the table:

STAFF_MEETING (EmployeeName, ProjectName, Date)

The rows of this table record the fact that an employee from a particular project attended a meeting on a given date. Assume that a project meets at most once per day. Also, assume that only one employee represents a given project, but that employees can be assigned to multiple projects.

A.   State the functional dependencies in STAFF_MEETING.

B.   Transform this table into one or more tables in BCNF. State the primary keys, candidate keys, foreign keys, and referential integrity constraints.

C.   Is your design in part B an improvement over the original table? What advantages and disadvantages does it have?

3.59   Consider the table:

STUDENT (Number, Name, Dorm, RoomType, DormCost, Club, ClubCost, Sibling, Nickname)

Assume that students pay different dorm costs, depending on the type of room they have, but that all members of a club pay the same cost. Assume that students can have multiple nicknames.

A.   State any multivalued dependencies in STUDENT.

B.   State the functional dependencies in STUDENT.

C.   Transform this table into two or more tables such that each table is in BCNF and in 4NF. State the primary keys, candidate keys, foreign keys, and referential integrity constraints.

A. Assume that Marcia keeps a table of data about her customers. Consider just the following part of that table:

CUSTOMER (Phone, FirstName, LastName)

Explain the conditions under which each of the following are true:

1. Phone → (FirstName, LastName)
2. (Phone, FirstName) → LastName
3. (Phone, LastName) → FirstName
4. (LastName, FirstName) → Phone
5. Phone → → LastName
6. Phone → → FirstName
7. Phone → → (FirstName, LastName)

B. Is condition A.7 the same as conditions A.5 and A.6? Why or why not?

C. State an appropriate referential integrity constraint for the tables:

CUSTOMER (<u>Phone</u>, FirstName, LastName)

ORDER (<u>OrderNumber</u>, DateIn, DateOut, *Phone*)

D. Consider the tables:

CUSTOMER (Phone, <u>FirstName</u>, <u>LastName</u>)

ORDER (<u>OrderNumber</u>, DateIn, DateOut, *FirstName, LastName*)

What does the following referential integrity constraint mean?

ORDER.(FirstName, LastName) must be in CUSTOMER.(FirstName, LastName)

Is this constraint the same as the set of referential integrity constraints:

ORDER.FirstName must be in CUSTOMER.FirstName

ORDER.LastName must be in CUSTOMER.LastName

Explain why or why not.

E. Do you prefer the design in C or the design in D? Explain your reasoning.

F. Transform the following table into two or more tables in BCNF and 4NF. Indicate the primary keys, candidate keys, foreign keys, and referential integrity constraints. Make and state assumptions as necessary.

ORDER (CustomerNumber, FirstName, LastName, Phone, OrderNumber, DateIn, DateOut, ItemType, Quantity, ItemPrice, ExtendedPrice, SpecialInstructions)

G. Explain how your answer to question E changes depending on whether you assume that

CustomerNumber → (FirstName, LastName)

or

CustomerNumber → → (FirstName, LastName)

A. Morgan keeps a table of data about the stores from which he purchases. The stores are located in different countries and have different specialties. Consider the following relation:

STORE (Name, City, Country, Owner, Specialty)

Explain the conditions under which each of the following are true:

1. **Name → City**
2. **City → Name**
3. **City → Country**
4. **(Name, Country) → (City, Owner)**
5. **(City, Specialty) → Name**
6. **Owner → → Name**
7. **Name → → Specialty**

B. With regard to the relation in part A:

1. Specify which of the dependencies in part A seem most appropriate for a small import–export business.
2. Given your assumptions in B.1, transform the STORE table into a set of tables that are in both 4NF and BCNF. Indicate the primary keys, candidate keys, foreign keys, and referential integrity constraints.

C. Consider the relation:

SHIPMENT (ShipmentNumber, VendorName, VendorContact, VendorFax, DepartureDate, ArrivalDate, CountryOfOrigin, Destination, ShipmentCost, InsuranceValue, Insurer)

1. Write a functional dependency that expresses the fact that the cost of a shipment between two cities is always the same.
2. Write a functional dependency that expresses the fact the insurance value is always the same for a given vendor.
3. Write a functional dependency that expresses the fact the insurance value is always the same for a given vendor and country of origin.
4. Describe two possible multivalued dependencies in SHIPMENT.
5. State what you believe are reasonable functional dependencies for the SHIPMENT relation for a small import–export business.
6. State what you believe are reasonable multivalued dependencies for the SHIPMENT relation.
7. Using your assumptions in 5 and 6, transform SHIPMENT into a set of tables in BCNF and 4NF. Indicate the primary keys, candidate keys, foreign keys, and referential integrity constraints.

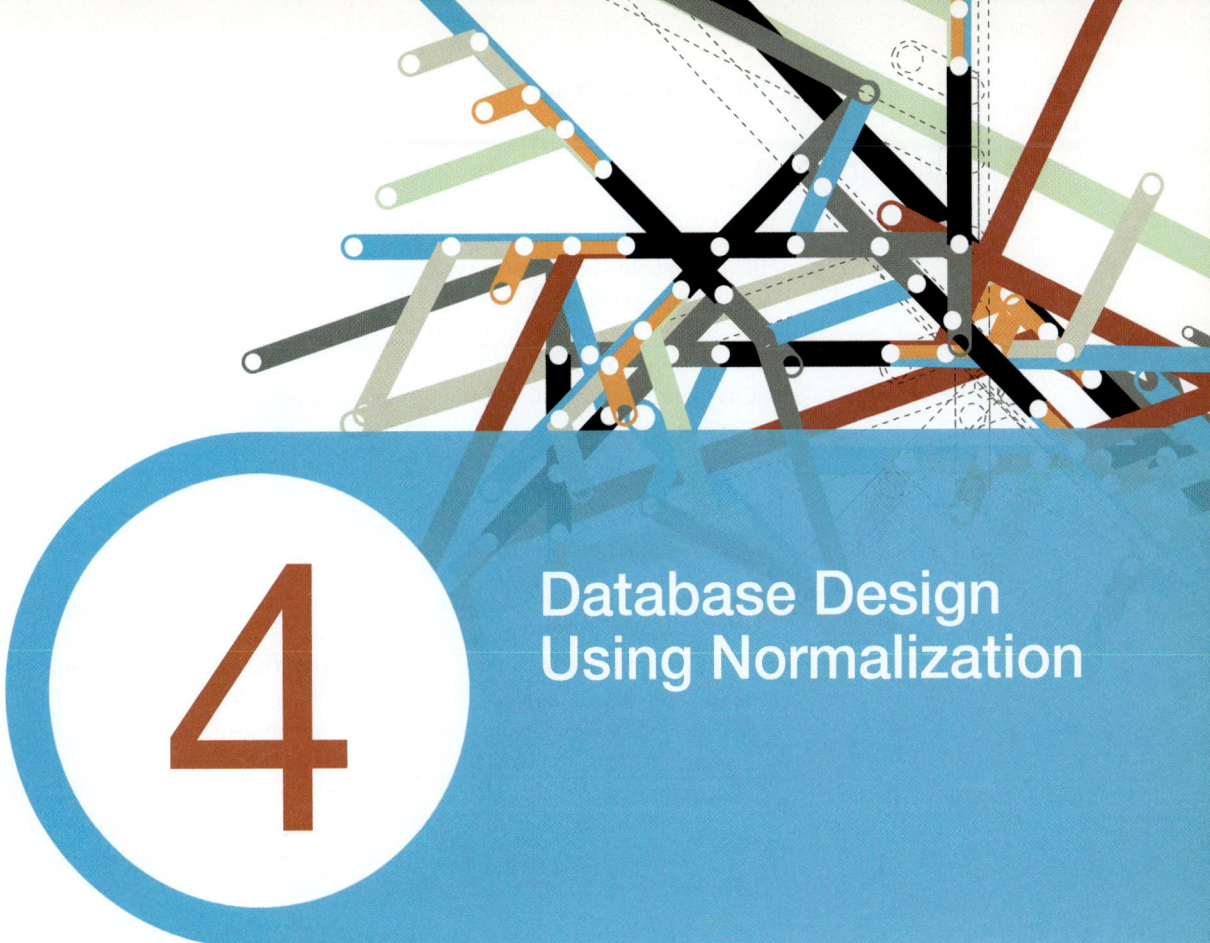

4

Database Design Using Normalization

Chapter Objectives

- To design updatable databases to store data received from another source.
- To use SQL to access table structure.
- To understand the advantages and disadvantages of normalization.
- To understand denormalization.
- To design read-only databases to store data from updateable databases.

- To recognize and be able to correct common design problems:
  - The multivalue, multicolumn problem.
  - The inconsistent values problem.
  - The missing values problem.
  - The general-purpose remarks column problem

In Chapter 3, we defined the relational model, described modification anomalies, and discussed normalization using BCNF and 4NF. In this chapter, we apply those concepts to the design of databases that are created from existing data.

The premise of this chapter is that you have received, from some source, one or more tables of data that are to be stored in a new database. The question is, should that data be stored as is, or should it be transformed in some way before it is stored? Normalization theory plays an important role, as you will see.

Assess Table Structure

When someone gives you a set of tables and asks you to construct a database to store them, your first step should be to assess the tables' structure and content. General guidelines for assessing a table's structure are summarized in Figure 4-1.

Begin by counting the number of rows in each table using the **SQL COUNT(*) function**. Then, to determine the number and type of the table's columns, use an **SQL SELECT * statement**. If your table has thousands or millions of rows, however, a full query will take considerable time. One way to limit the results of this query is to use the **SQL TOP keyword**. For example, to obtain all columns for the first 10 rows of the SKU_DATA table, you would code:

```
SELECT      TOP 10 *

FROM        SKU_DATA;
```

This query will show you all columns and data for 10 rows. If you want the top 50 rows, just use TOP 50 instead of TOP 10, and so on.

As shown in Figure 4-1, you should examine the data and determine the functional dependencies, multivalued dependencies, candidate keys, and each table's primary key. Also, look for possible foreign keys. Again, you can base your conclusions on sample data, but that data may not have all of the possible data cases. Therefore, verify your assumptions and conclusions with the users.

With regard to foreign keys, it is risky to assume that referential integrity constraints have been enforced on the data. Instead, check it yourself. For example, suppose you receive data for the following SKU_DATA and BUYER tables:

SKU_DATA (SKU, SKU_Description, Department, Buyer)

BUYER (BuyerName, Department)

After investigation, you learn that SKU is the primary key of SKU_DATA, and that Buyer-Name is the primary key of BUYER. You also think that SKU_DATA.Buyer is likely a foreign key to BUYER.BuyerName. The question is whether the following referential integrity constraint holds:

SKU_DATA.Buyer must exist in BUYER.BuyerName

You can use SQL to determine whether this is true. The following query will return any values of the foreign key that violate the constraint:

```
SELECT      Buyer

FROM        SKU_DATA

WHERE       Buyer NOT IN

            (SELECT     Buyer

              FROM        SKU_DATA, BUYER

              WHERE       SKU_DATA.Buyer = BUYER.BuyerName);
```

The subquery finds all values of Buyer for which there is a match between SKU_DATA.Buyer and BUYER.BuyerName. If there is any value of Buyer that is not in this subquery, then that

Figure 4-1

Guidelines for Assessing
Table Structure

- Count rows and examine columns
- Examine data values and interview users to determine:
    - Multivalued dependencies
    - Functional dependencies
    - Candidate keys
    - Primary keys
    - Foreign keys
- Assess validity of assumed referential integrity constraints

value will be displayed in the top query. All such values violate the referential integrity constraint.

After you have assessed the input tables, your next steps depend on whether you are creating an updatable database or a read-only database. We will consider updatable databases first.

Designing Updatable Databases

If you are constructing an updatable database, then you need to be concerned about modification anomalies and inconsistent data. Consequently, you must carefully consider normalization principles. Before we begin, let's first review the advantages and disadvantages of normalization.

Advantages and Disadvantages of Normalization

Figure 4-2 summarizes the advantages and disadvantages of normalization. On the positive side, normalization eliminates modification anomalies and reduces data duplication. Reduced data duplication eliminates the possibility of data integrity problems due to inconsistent data values. It also saves file space.

> **BY THE WAY**   Why do we say *reduce* data duplication rather than *eliminate* data duplication? The answer is that we cannot eliminate all duplicated data because we must duplicate data in foreign keys. We cannot eliminate Buyer, for example, from the SKU_DATA table, because we would then not be able to relate BUYER and SKU_DATA rows. Values of Buyer are thus duplicated in the BUYER and SKU_DATA tables.
>
> This observation leads to a second question: If we only *reduce* data duplication, how can we claim to *eliminate* inconsistent data values? Data duplication in foreign keys will not cause inconsistencies, because referential integrity constraints prohibit them. As long as we enforce such constraints, the duplicate foreign key values will cause no inconsistencies.

On the negative side, normalization requires application programmers to write more complex SQL. To recover the original data, they must write subqueries and joins to connect data stored in separate tables. Also, with normalized data, the DBMS must read two or more tables, and this can mean slower application processing.

Functional Dependencies

As you learned in Chapter 3, we can eliminate anomalies due to functional dependencies by placing all tables in BCNF. Most of the time, the problems of modification anomalies are so great that you should put your tables into BCNF. There are exceptions, however, as you will see.

Figure 4-2

Advantages and Disadvantages of Normalization

- Advantages
    - Eliminate modification anomalies
    - Reduce duplicated data
        - Eliminate data integrity problems
        - Save file space
- Disadvantages
    - More complicated SQL required for multitable subqueries and joins
    - Extra work for DBMS can mean slower applications

EQUIPMENT_REPAIR

	ItemNumber	Type	AcquisitionCost	RepairNumber	RepairDate	RepairCost
1	100	Drill Press	3500.00	2000	2009-05-05	375.00
2	200	Lathe	4750.00	2100	2009-05-07	255.00
3	100	Drill Press	3500.00	2200	2009-06-19	178.00
4	300	Mill	27300.00	2300	2009-06-19	1875.00
5	100	Drill Press	3500.00	2400	2009-07-05	0.00
6	100	Drill Press	5500.00	2500	2009-08-17	275.00

Figure 4-3

The EQUIPMENT_REPAIR Table

Normalizing with SQL

As we discussed in Chapter 3, a table is in BCNF if all determinants are candidate keys. If any determinant is not a candidate key, we must break the table into two or more tables. Consider an example. Suppose you are given the EQUIPMENT_REPAIR table in Figure 4-3 (the same table shown in Figure 3-10). In Chapter 3, we found that ItemNumber is a determinant, but not a candidate key. Consequently, we created the ITEM and REPAIR tables shown in Figure 4-4. In these tables, ItemNumber is a determinant and a candidate key of ITEM, and RepairNumber is a determinant and primary key of REPAIR; thus both tables are in BCNF.

Now, as a practical matter, how do we transform the data in the format in Figure 4-3 to that in Figure 4-4? To answer that question, we need to use the **SQL INSERT statement**. You will learn the particulars of the INSERT statement in Chapter 7. For now, we will jump ahead and use one version of it to illustrate the practical side of normalization.

First, we need to create the structure for the two new tables in Figure 4-4. If you are using Microsoft Access, you can follow the procedure in Appendix A to create the tables. Later, in Chapter 7, you will learn how to create tables using SQL, a process that works for all DBMS products.

Once the tables are created, you can fill them using the SQL INSERT command. To fill the ITEM table, we use:

```
INSERT INTO ITEM

    SELECT      DISTINCT ItemNumber, Type, AcquisitionCost
    FROM        EQUIPMENT_REPAIR;
```

Notice that we must use the DISTINCT keyword because the combination (ItemNumber, Type, AcquisitionCost) is not unique in the EQUIPMENT_REPAIR table. Once we have

Figure 4-4

The Normalized ITEM and REPAIR Relations

ITEM

	ItemNumber	Type	AcquisitionCost
1	100	Drill Press	3500.00
2	200	Lathe	4750.00
3	300	Mill	27300.00

REPAIR

	ItemNumber	RepairNumber	RepairDate	RepairCost
1	100	2000	2009-05-05	375.00
2	200	2100	2009-05-07	255.00
3	100	2200	2009-06-19	178.00
4	300	2300	2009-06-19	1875.00
5	100	2400	2009-07-05	0.00
6	100	2500	2009-08-17	275.00

created the rows in ITEM, we can then use the following INSERT command to fill the rows of REPAIR:

```
INSERT INTO REPAIR
    SELECT      ItemNumber, RepairNumber, RepairDate, RepairAmount
    FROM        EQUIPMENT_REPAIR;
```

As you can see, the SQL statements for normalizing tables are relatively simple. After this transformation, we should probably remove the EQUIPMENT_REPAIR table. For now, you can do this using the graphical tools in Access, SQL Server, Oracle, or MySQL. In Chapter 7, you will learn how to remove tables using the **SQL DROP statement**. You will also learn how to use SQL to create the referential integrity constraint:

ItemNumber in REPAIR exists in ItemNumber in ITEM

If you want to try out this example, download the Microsoft Access 2007 database Equipment-Repair-Database.accdb from the text's Web site at www.pearsonhighered.com/kroenke. This database has the EQUIPMENT_REPAIR table with data. Create the new tables (see Appendix A) and then do the normalization by executing the SQL INSERT statements illustrated.

This process can be extended to any number of tables. We will consider richer examples of it in Chapter 7. For now, however, you should have the gist of the process.

Choosing Not to Use BCNF

Although in most cases the tables in an updatable database should be placed in BCNF, in some situations BCNF is just too pure. The classic example of unneeded normalization involves zip and similar postal codes. Consider the following table for customers in the United States:

CUSTOMER (<u>CustomerID</u>, LastName, FirstName, Street, City, State, Zip)

The functional dependencies of this table are:

CustomerID → (LastName, FirstName, Street, City, State, Zip)

Zip → (City, State)

This table is not in BCNF because Zip is a determinant that is not a candidate key. We can normalize this table as follows:

CUSTOMER_2 (<u>CustomerID</u>, LastName, FirstName, Street, *Zip*)

ZIP_CODE (<u>Zip</u>, City, State)

with referential integrity constraint:

CUSTOMER_2.Zip must exist in ZIP_CODE.Zip

The tables CUSTOMER_2 and ZIP_CODE are in BCNF, but consider these tables in light of the advantages and disadvantages of normalization listed in Figure 4-2. Normalization eliminates modification anomalies, but how often does zip code data change? How often does the post office change the city and state assigned to a zip code value? Almost never. The consequences on every business and person would be too severe. So, even though the design allows anomalies to occur, in practice, they will not occur because the data never change. Consider the second advantage: Normalization reduces data duplication, and hence improves data integrity. In fact, data integrity problems can happen in the single-table example if someone enters the wrong value for City, State, or Zip. In that case, the database will have inconsistent Zip values. But, normal business processes will cause zip code errors to be noticed, and they will be corrected without problem.

Now consider the disadvantages of normalization. Two separate tables require application programs to write more complex SQL. They also require the DBMS to process two tables, which may make the applications slow. Weighing the advantages and disadvantages, most practitioners would say that the normalized data are just too pure. Zip code data would therefore be left in the original table.

In summary, when you design an updatable database from existing tables, examine every table to determine if it is in BCNF. If it is not, then the table is susceptible to modification anomalies and inconsistent data. In almost all cases, transform the table into tables that are in BCNF. However, if the data are never modified and if data inconsistencies will be easily corrected via the normal operation of business activity, then you may choose not to place the table into BCNF.

Multivalued Dependencies

Unlike functional dependencies, the anomalies from multivalued dependencies are so serious that multivalued dependencies should always be eliminated. Unlike BCNF, there is no gray area. Just place the columns of a multivalued dependency in tables of their own.

As shown in the last section, normalization is not difficult. It does mean that application programmers will have to write subqueries and joins to re-create the original data. Writing subqueries and joins, however, is *nothing* compared with the complexity of code that must be written to handle the anomalies due to multivalued dependencies.

Some experts might object to such a hard and fast rule, but it is justifiable. Although there may be a few rare, obscure, and weird cases in which multivalued dependencies are not problematic, such cases are not worth remembering. Until you have years of database design experience, always eliminate multivalued dependencies from any updatable table.

Designing Read-Only Databases

In the course of your career, you will likely be given tables of data and asked to create a read-only database. In fact, this task is commonly assigned to beginning database administrators.

Read-only databases are used in business intelligence (BI) systems for querying, reporting, and data mining applications, as you will learn in Chapter 13. Because such databases are never updated, the design guidelines and design priorities are different than those for updatable databases.

For several reasons, normalization is seldom an advantage for a read-only database. For one, if a database is never updated, then no modification anomalies can occur. Hence, considering Figure 4-2, the only reason to normalize a read-only database is to reduce data duplication. However, with no update activity, there is no risk of data integrity problems, so the only remaining reason to avoid duplicated data is to save file space.

Today, however, file space is exceedingly cheap, nearly free. So unless the database is enormous, the cost of storage is minimal. It is true that the DBMS will take longer to find and process data in large tables, so data might be normalized to speed up processing. But even that advantage is not clear-cut. If data are normalized, then data from two or more tables may need to be read, and the time required for the join may overwhelm the time savings of searching in small tables. In almost all cases, normalization of the tables in a read-only database is a bad idea.

Denormalization

Often the data for a read-only database are extracted from operational databases. Because such databases are updatable, they are probably normalized. Hence, you will likely receive the extracted data in normalized form. In fact, if you have a choice, ask for normalized data. For one, normalized data are smaller in size and can be transmitted to you more quickly. Also, if the data are normalized, it will be easier for you to reformat the data for your particular needs.

According to the last section, you probably do not want to leave the data in normalized form for a read-only database. If that is the case, you will need to **denormalize**, or join, the data prior to storage.

Consider the example in Figure 4-5. This is a copy of the normalized Student-Club-Payment data in Figure 3-18. Suppose that you are creating a read-only database that will be used to report amounts due for student club payments. If you store the data in this three-table form, every time someone needs to compare AmountPaid with Cost, he or she must join the three tables together.

STUDENT

	SID	Name
1	100	Jones
2	200	Chau
3	300	Garrett
4	400	Jones

REPAIR

	Club	Cost
1	Climbing	150.00
2	Scuba	400.00
3	Skiing	550.00

PAYMENT

	SID	Club	Amount Paid
1	100	Scuba	0.00
2	200	Scuba	400.00
3	200	Skiing	550.00
4	300	Climbing	150.00
5	400	Skiing	550.00

Figure 4-5

The Normalized STUDENT, CLUB, and PAYMENT Relations

To do this, that person will need to know how to write a three-table join, and the DBMS will need to perform the join every time the report is prepared.

You can reduce the complexity of the SQL required to read these data and also reduce DBMS processing by joining the tables once and storing the joined result as a single table. The following SQL statement will join the three tables together and store them in a new table named PAYMENT_DATA:

```
INSERT INTO PAYMENT_DATA
    SELECT   STUDENT.SID, Name, CLUB.Club, Cost, AmtPaid
    FROM     STUDENT, PAYMENT, CLUB
    WHERE    STUDENT.SID = PAYMENT.SID
      AND    PAYMENT.Club = CLUB.Club;
```

As shown in Figure 4-6, the result of this join is the same as the original STUDENT_PAYMENT table.

As you can see, denormalization is simple. Just join the data together and store the joined result as a table. By doing this when you place the data into the read-only database, you save the application programmers from having to code joins for each application, and you also save the DBMS from having to perform joins and subqueries every time the users run a query or create a report.

Figure 4-6

The Denormalized STUDENT_ACTIVITY_ PAYMENT_DATA Relation

STUDENT_ACTIVITY_PAYMENT_DATA

	SID	Name	Club	Cost	Amount Paid
1	100	Jones	Scuba	400.00	0.00
2	200	Chau	Scuba	400.00	400.00
3	200	Chau	Skiing	550.00	550.00
4	300	Garrett	Climbing	150.00	150.00
5	400	Jones	Skiing	550.00	550.00

Figure   4-7

Columns in the PRODUCT
Table

- SKU (Primary Key)
- PartNumber (Candidate key)
- SKU_Description (Candidate key)
- VendorNumber
- VendorName
- VendorContact_1
- VendorContact_2
- VendorStreet
- VendorCity
- VendorState
- VendorZip
- QuantitySoldPastYear
- QuantitySoldPastQuarter
- QuantitySoldPastMonth
- DetailPicture
- ThumbNailPicture
- MarketingShortDescription
- MarketingLongDescription
- PartColor
- UnitsCode
- BinNumber
- ProductionKeyCode

Customized Duplicated Tables

Because there is no danger of data integrity problems in a read-only database, and because the cost of storage today is miniscule, read-only databases are often designed with many copies of the same data, each copy customized for a particular application.

For example, suppose a company has a large PRODUCT table with the columns listed in Figure 4-7. The columns in this table are used by different business processes. Some are used for purchasing, some are used for sales analysis, some are used for displaying parts on a Web site, some are used for marketing, and some are used for inventory control.

The values of some of these columns, such as those for the picture images, are large. If the DBMS is required to read all of these data for every query, processing is likely to be slow. Accordingly, the organization might create several customized versions of this table for use by different applications. In an updatable database, so much duplicated data would risk severe data integrity problems, but for a read-only database there is no such risk.

Suppose for this example that the organization designs the following tables:

PRODUCT_PURCHASING (SKU, SKU_Description, VendorNumber, VendorName, VendorContact_1, VendorContact_2, VendorStreet, VendorCity, VendorState, VendorZip)

PRODUCT_USAGE (SKU, SKU_Description, QuantitySoldPastYear, QuantitySoldPastQuarter, QuantitySoldPastMonth)

PRODUCT_WEB (SKU, DetailPicture, ThumbnailPicture, MarketingShortDescription, MarketingLongDescription, PartColor)

PRODUCT_INVENTORY (SKU, PartNumber, SKU_Description, UnitsCode, BinNumber, ProductionKeyCode)

You can create these tables using the graphical design facilities of Access or another DBMS. Once the tables are created, they can be filled using INSERT commands similar to those already discussed. The only tricks are to watch for duplicated data and to use DISTINCT where necessary. See Review Question 4.10.

Common Design Problems

Although normalization and denormalization are the primary considerations when designing databases from existing data, there are four additional practical problems to consider. These are summarized in Figure 4-8.

The Multivalue, Multicolumn Problem

The table in Figure 4-7 illustrates the first common problem. Notice the columns VendorContact_1 and VendorContact_2. These columns store the names of two contacts at the part vendor. If the company wanted to store the names of three or four contacts using this strategy, it would add columns VendorContact_3, VendorContact_4, and so forth.

Consider another example for an employee parking application. Suppose the EMPLOYEE_AUTO table includes basic employee data plus columns for license numbers for up to three cars. The following is the typical table structure:

EMPLOYEE (**EmpNumber**, Name, Email, Auto1_LicenseNumber, Auto2_LicenseNumber, Auto3_LicenseNumber)

Other examples of this strategy are to store employees' children's names in columns such as Child_1, Child_2, Child_3, and so forth, for as many children as the designer of the table thinks appropriate. Or, to store a picture of a house in a real estate application in columns labeled Picture_1, Picture_2, Picture_3, and so forth.

Storing multiple values in this way is convenient, but it has two serious disadvantages. The more obvious one is that the number of possible items is fixed. What if there are three contacts at a particular vendor? Where do we put the third name if only columns VendorContact_1 and VendorContact_2 are available? Or, if there are only three columns for child names, where do we put the name of the fourth child? And so forth.

The second disadvantage occurs when querying the data. Suppose we want to know the names of employees who have a child named Gretchen. If there are three child name columns, we must write:

```
SELECT      *
FROM        EMPLOYEE
WHERE       Child_1 = 'Gretchen'
    OR      Child_2 = 'Gretchen'
    OR      Child_3 = 'Gretchen';
```

Of course, if there are seven child names . . . well, you get the picture.

These problems can be eliminated by using a second table to store the multivalued attribute. For the employee–child case, the tables are:

EMPLOYEE (**EmpNumber**, EmpLastName, EmpFirstName, Email, . . . {other data})

CHILD (**ChildFirstName**, *EmpNumber*, . . . {other data})

Figure 4-8

Practical Problems in Designing Databases from Existing Data

- Multivalue, Multicolumn Problem
- Inconsistent Values
- Missing Values
- General-Purpose Remarks Column

Using this second structure, employees can have an unlimited number of children, and storage space will be saved for employees who have no children at all. Additionally, to find all of the employees who have a child named Gretchen, we can code:

```
SELECT      *
FROM        EMPLOYEE
WHERE       EmpNumber IN
            (SELECT    EmpNumber
             FROM      CHILD
             WHERE     ChildFirstName = 'Gretchen');
```

This second query is easier to write and understand and will work regardless of the number of children that an employee has.

The alternate design does require the DBMS to process two tables, and if the tables are large and performance is a concern one can argue that the original design is better. In such cases, storing multivalues in multiple columns may be preferred. Another, less valid objection to the two-table design is as follows: "We only need space for three cars because university policy restricts each employee to registering no more than three cars." The problem with this statement is that databases often outlive policies. Next year that policy may change, and, if it does, the database will need to be redesigned. As you will learn in Chapter 8, database redesign is tricky, complex, and expensive. It is better to avoid the need for a database redesign.

> **BY THE WAY** A few years ago, people argued that only three phone number columns are needed per person: Home, Office, and Fax. Later they said, "Well, OK, maybe we need four: Home, Office, Fax, and Mobile." Today, who would want to guess the maximum number of phone numbers a person might have? Rather than guess, just store Phone in a separate table; such a design will allow each person to have from none to an unlimited number of phone numbers.

You are likely to encounter the multivalue, multicolumn problem when creating databases from nondatabase data. It is particularly common in spreadsheet and text data files. Fortunately, the preferred two-table design is easy to create, and the SQL for moving the data to the new design is easy to write.

> **BY THE WAY** The multivalue, multicolumn problem is just another form of a multivalued dependency. For the parking application, for example, rather than store multiple rows in EMPLOYEE for each auto, multiple named columns are created in the table. The underlying problem is the same, however.

Inconsistent Values

Inconsistent values are a serious problem when creating databases from existing data. It occurs because different users or different data sources may use slightly different forms of the same data value. These slight differences may be hard to detect and will create inconsistent and erroneous information.

One of the hardest such problems occurs when different users have coded the same entries differently. One user may have coded a SKU_Description as Corn, Large Can; another may have coded the same item as Can, Corn, Large; and another may have coded the entry as Large Can Corn. Those three entries all refer to the same SKU, but they will be exceedingly difficult to reconcile. These examples are not contrived; such problems frequently occur, especially when combining data from different database, spreadsheet, and file sources.

A related, but simpler, problem occurs when entries are misspelled. One user may enter *Coffee*, another may enter *Coffeee*. They will appear as two separate products.

Inconsistent data values are particularly problematic for primary and foreign key columns. Relationships will be missing or wrong when foreign key data is coded inconsistently or misspelled.

Two techniques can be used to find such problems. One is the same as the check for referential integrity shown on page 128. This check will find values for which there is no match and will find misspellings and other inconsistencies.

Another technique is to use GROUP BY on the suspected column. For example, if we suspect that there are inconsistent values on SKU_Description in the SKU_DATA table, we can code:

```
SELECT      SKU_Description, COUNT(*) as NameCount
FROM        SKU_DATA
GROUP BY    SKU_Description;
```

The result of this query for the SKU_DATA values we have been using is:

	SKU_Description	NameCount
1	Dive Mask, Med Clear	1
2	Dive Mask, Small Clear	1
3	Half-dome Tent	1
4	Half-dome Tent Footprint	1
5	Light Fly Climbing Harness	1
6	Locking carabiner, Oval	1
7	Std. Scuba Tank, Magenta	1
8	Std. Scuba Tank, Yellow	1

In this case, there are no inconsistent values, but if there were, they would stand out. If the list resulting from the select is too long, groups can be selected that have just one or two elements using HAVING. Neither check is foolproof. Sometimes, you just have to read the data.

When working with such data, it is important to develop an error reporting and tracking system to ensure that inconsistencies that users do find are recorded and fixed. Users grow exceedingly impatient with data errors that persist after they have been reported.

Missing Values

Missing values are a third problem that occurs when creating databases from existing data. A missing value, or **null value**, is a value that has never been provided. It is not the same as a blank value, because a blank value is a value that is known to be blank. A null value is not known to be anything.

The problem with null values is ambiguity. A null value can indicate one of three conditions: The value is inappropriate; the value is appropriate but unknown; or the value is appropriate and known, but no one has entered it into the database. Unfortunately, we cannot tell from a null value which of these conditions is true.

Consider, for example, a null value for the column DateOfLastChildbirth in a PATIENT table. If a row represents a male patient, then the null occurs because the value is inappropriate; a male cannot give birth. Alternatively, if the patient is a female, but the patient has never been asked for the data, then the value is appropriate, but unknown. Finally, the null value could also mean that a date value is appropriate and known, but no one has recorded it into the database.

You can use the SQL term IS NULL to check for null values. For example, to find the number of null values of Quantity in the ORDER_ITEM table, you can code:

```
SELECT       COUNT (*) as QuantityNullCount
FROM         ORDER_ITEM
WHERE        Quantity IS NULL;
```

The result of this query for the ORDER_ITEM values we have been using is:

	QuantityNullCount
1	0

In this case, there are no NULL values, but if there were, we would know how many, and then we could use a SELECT * statement to find the data of any row that has a null value.

When creating a database from existing data, if you try to define a column that has null values as the primary key, the DBMS will generate an error message. You will have to remove the nulls before creating the primary key. Also, you can tell the DBMS that a given column is not allowed to have null values, and when you import the data, if any row has a null value in that column, the DBMS will generate an error message. The particulars depend on the DBMS in use. See Chapter 10 for SQL Server 2008, Chapter 10A for Oracle Database 11g, and Chapter 10B for MySQL 5.1. You should form the habit of checking for null values in all foreign keys. Any row with a null foreign key will not participate in the relationship. That may or may not be appropriate; you will need to ask the users to find out. Also, null values can be problematic when joining tables together. You will learn how to deal with this problem in Chapter 7.

The General-Purpose Remarks Column

The general-purpose remarks column problem is common, serious, and very difficult to solve. Columns with names such as Remarks, Comments, and Notes often contain important data that are stored in an inconsistent, verbal, and verbose manner. Learn to be wary of columns with any such names.

To see why, consider customer data for a company that sells expensive items such as airplanes, rare cars, boats, or paintings. In a typical setting, someone has used a spreadsheet to track customer data. That person used a spreadsheet not because it was the best tool for such a problem, but rather because he or she had a spreadsheet program and knew how to use it.

The typical spreadsheet has columns like LastName, FirstName, Email, Phone, Address, and so forth. It almost always includes a column entitled Remarks, Comments, Notes, or something similar. The problem is that needed data are usually buried in such columns and nearly impossible to dig out. Suppose you want to create a database for a customer contact application for an airplane broker. Assume your design contains the two tables:

CONTACT (<u>ID</u>, LastName, FirstName, Address, . . . {other data}, *PlaneModel*)

AIRPLANE_MODEL (<u>Model</u>, Type, Description, . . . {other airplane data})

where CONTACT.PlaneModel is a foreign key to AIRPLANE_MODEL.Model. You want to use this relationship to determine who owns, has owned, or is interested in buying a particular model of airplane.

In the typical situation, the data for the foreign key has been recorded in the Remarks column. If you read the Remarks data, you will find entries like: 'Wants to buy a Piper Seneca II', 'Owner of a Piper Seneca II', and 'Possible buyer for a turbo Seneca'. All three of these rows should have a value of PlaneModel equal to 'Piper Seneca II', but you will pull your hair out making that determination.

Another problem with general-purpose remarks columns is that they are used inconsistently and contain multiple data items. One user may have used it to store the name of the spouse of the contact, another may have used it to store airplane models as just described, and a third day have used it to store the date the customer was last contacted. Or, the same user may have used it for all three purposes at different times!

The best solution in this case is to identify all of the different purposes of the remarks column, create new columns for each of those purposes, and then extract the data and store it into the new columns as appropriate. However, this solution can seldom be automated.

In practice, all solutions require patience and hours of labor. Learn to be wary of such columns, and don't take such jobs on a fixed-price basis!

Summary

When constructing a database from existing data, the first step is to assess the structure and content of the input tables. Count the number of rows and use the SQL SELECT TOP 10 * phrase to learn the columns in the data. Then, examine the data and determine functional dependencies, multivalued dependencies, candidate keys, each table's primary key, and foreign keys. Check out the validity of possible referential integrity constraints.

Design principles differ depending on whether an updatable or read-only database is being constructed. If the former, then modification anomalies and inconsistent data are concerns. The advantages of normalization are elimination of modification anomalies, reduced data duplication, and the elimination of data inconsistencies. The disadvantages are that more complex SQL will be required and application performance may be slower.

For updatable databases, most of the time the problems of modification anomalies are so great that all tables should be placed in BCNF. SQL for normalization is easy to write. In some cases, if the data will be updated infrequently and if inconsistencies are readily corrected by business processes, then BCNF may be too pure and the tables should be left unnormalized. The problems of multivalued dependencies are so great that they should always be removed.

Read-only databases are created for reporting, querying, and data mining applications. Creating such a database is a task commonly assigned to beginners. When designing read-only databases, normalization is less desired. If input data is normalized, it frequently needs to be denormalized by joining it together and storing the joined result. Also, sometimes many copies of the same data are stored in tables customized for particular applications.

Four common problems occur when creating databases from existing data. The multivalue, multicolumn design sets a fixed number of repeating values and stores each in a column of its own. Such a design limits the number of items allowed and results in awkward SQL query statements. A better design results from putting multiple values in a table of their own.

Inconsistent values result when data arise from different users and applications. Inconsistent foreign key values create incorrect relationships. Data inconsistencies can be detected using SQL statements, as illustrated in this chapter. A null value is not the same as a blank. A null value is not known to be anything. Null values are a problem because they are ambiguous. They can mean that a value is inappropriate; unknown; or known, but not yet been entered into the database.

The general-purpose remarks column is a column that is used for different purposes. It collects data items in an inconsistent and verbose manner. Such columns are especially problematic if they contain data needed for a foreign key. Even if they do not, they often contain data for several different columns. Automated solutions are not possible, and the correction requires patience and labor.

Key Terms

denormalize	SQL INSERT statement
null value	SQL SELECT * statement
SQL COUNT(*) function	SQL TOP keyword
SQL DROP statement	

Review Questions

4.1 Summarize the premise of this chapter.

4.2 When you receive a set of tables, what steps should you take to assess their structure and content?

4.3 Show SQL statements to count the number of rows and to list the top 15 rows of the RETAIL_ORDER table.

4.4   Suppose you receive the following two tables:

DEPARTMENT (DepartmentName, BudgetCode)

EMPLOYEE (EmpNumber, LastName, FirstName, Email, DepartmentName)

and you conclude that EMPLOYEE.DepartmentName is a foreign key to DEPART-MENT.DepartmentName. Show SQL for determining whether the following referential integrity constraint has been enforced:

DepartmentName in EMPLOYEE must exist in DepartmentName
in DEPARTMENT

4.5   Summarize how database design principles differ with regards to the design of updatable databases and the design of read-only databases.

4.6   Describe two advantages of normalized tables.

4.7   Why do we say that data duplication is only reduced? Why is it not eliminated?

4.8   If data duplication is only reduced, how can we say that the possibility of data inconsistencies has been eliminated?

4.9   Describe two disadvantages of normalized tables.

4.10 Suppose you are given the table:

EMPLOYEE_DEPARTMENT (EmpNumber, LastName, FirstName, Email, DepartmentName, BudgetCode)

and you wish to transform this table into the two tables:

EMPLOYEE (EmpNumber, LastName, FirstName, Email, DepartmentName)

and

DEPARTMENT (DepartmentName, BudgetCode)

Write the SQL statements needed for filling the EMPLOYEE and DEPARTMENT tables with data from EMPLOYEE_DEPARTMENT.

4.11 Summarize the reasons explained in this chapter for not placing zip code values into BCNF.

4.12 Describe a situation, other than the one for zip codes, in which one would choose not to place tables into BCNF. Justify your decision not to use BCNF.

4.13 According to this text, under what situations should you choose not to remove multi-valued dependencies from a relation?

4.14 Compare the difficulty of writing subqueries and joins with the difficulty of dealing with anomalies caused by multivalued dependencies.

4.15 Describe three uses for a read-only database.

4.16 How does the fact that a read-only database is never updated influence the reasons for normalization?

4.17 For read-only databases, how persuasive is the argument that normalization reduces file space?

4.18 What is denormalization?

4.19 Suppose you are given the DEPARTMENT and EMPLOYEE tables in Review Question 4.10 and asked to denormalize them into the EMPLOYEE_DEPARTMENT relation. Show the design of the EMPLOYEE_DEPARTMENT relation. Write an SQL statement to fill this table with data.

4.20 Summarize the reasons for creating customized duplicated tables.

4.21 Why are customized duplicated tables not used for updatable databases?

4.22 List four common design problems when creating databases from existing data.

4.23 Give an example of a multivalue, multicolumn table other than one discussed in this chapter.

4.24 Explain the problems in your example in Review Question 4.23.

4.25 Show how to represent the relation in your answer to Review Question 4.23 with two tables.

4.26 Show how the tables in your answer to Review Question 4.25 solve the problems you identified in Review Question 4.22.

4.27 Explain the following statement: "The multivalue, multicolumn problem is just another form of multivalued dependency." Show how this is so.

4.28 Explain ways in which inconsistent values arise.

4.29 Why are inconsistent values in foreign keys particularly troublesome?

4.30 Describe two ways to identify inconsistent values. Are these techniques certain to find all inconsistent values? What other step can be taken?

4.31 What is a null value?

4.32 How does a null value differ from a blank value?

4.33 What are three interpretations of null values? Use an example in your answer.

4.34 Show SQL for determining the number of null values in the column Name of the table EMPLOYEE.

4.35 Describe the general-purpose remarks column problem.

4.36 Give an example in which the general-purpose remarks column makes it difficult to obtain values for a foreign key.

4.37 Give an example in which the general-purpose remarks column causes difficulties when multiple values are stored in the same column. How is this problem solved?

4.38 Why should one be wary of general-purpose remarks columns?

Project Questions

The Elliot Bay Sports Club owns and operates three sports club facilities in Houston, Texas. Each facility has a large selection of modern exercise equipment, weight rooms, and rooms for yoga and other exercise classes. Elliot Bay offers 3-month and 1-year memberships. Members can use the facilities at any of the three club locations.

Elliot Bay maintains a roster of personal trainers who operate as independent consultants. Approved trainers can schedule appointments with clients at Elliot Bay facilities, as long as their client is a member of the club. Trainers also teach yoga, Pilates, and other classes. Answer the following questions, assuming you have been provided the following three tables of data (PT stands for personal trainer):

PT_SESSION (Trainer, Phone, Email, Fee, ClientLastName, ClientFirstName, ClientPhone, ClientEmail, Date, Time)

CLUB_MEMBERSHIP (ClientNumber, ClientLastName, ClientFirstName, ClientPhone, ClientEmail, MembershipType, EndingDate, Street, City, State, Zip)

CLASS (ClassName, Trainer, StartDate, EndDate, Time, DayOfWeek, Cost)

4.39   Identify possible multivalued dependencies in these tables.

4.40   Identify possible functional dependencies in these tables.

4.41   Determine whether each table is in either BCNF or in 4NF. State your assumptions.

4.42   Modify each of these tables so that every table is in BCNF and 4NF. Use the assumptions you made in your answer to question 4.41.

4.43   Using these tables and your assumptions, recommend a design for an updatable database.

4.44   Add a table to your answer to question 4.43 that would allow Elliot Bay to assign members to particular classes. Include an AmountPaid column in your new table.

4.45   Recommend a design for a read-only database that would support the following needs:

    A.   Enable trainers to ensure that their clients are members of the club.

    B.   Enable the club to assess the popularity of various trainers.

    C.   Enable the trainers to determine if they are assisting the same client.

    D.   Enable class instructors to determine if the attendees to their classes have paid.

Marcia Wilson, the owner of Marcia's Dry Cleaning, is in the process of creating databases to support the operation and management of her business. For the past year, she and her staff have been using a cash register system that collects the following data:

SALE (<u>InvoiceNumber</u>, DateIn, DateOut, Total, Phone, FirstName, LastName)

Unfortunately, during rush times, not all of the data are entered, and there are many null values in Phone, FirstName, and LastName. In some cases all three are null, in other cases one or two are null. InvoiceNumber, DateIn, and Total are never null. DateOut has a few null values. Also, occasionally during a rush, phone number and name data have been entered incorrectly. To help create her database, Marcia purchased a mailing list from a local business bureau. The mailing list includes the following data:

HOUSEHOLD (<u>Phone</u>, <u>FirstName</u>, <u>LastName</u>, Street, City, State, Zip, Apartment)

In some cases, a phone number has multiple names. The primary key is thus the composite (Phone, FirstName, LastName). There are no null values in Phone, FirstName, and LastName, but there are some null values in the address data.

There are many names in SALE that are not in HOUSEHOLD, and there are many names in HOUSEHOLD that are not in SALE.

A.   Design an updatable database for storing customer and sales data. Explain how to deal with the problems of missing data. Explain how to deal with the problems of incorrect phone and name data.

B.   Design a read-only database for storing customer and sales data. Explain how to deal with the problems of missing data. Explain how to deal with the problems of incorrect phone and name data.

Phillip Morgan, the owner of Morgan Importing, makes periodic buying trips to various countries. During the trips, he keeps notes about the items he purchases and basic data about their shipments. He hired a college student as an intern, and she transformed his notes into the spreadsheets in Figure 4-9. This is just sample data. Phillip has purchased hundreds of items over the years, and they have been shipped in dozens of different shipments.

   Phillip wants to enter the information age, thus he has decided to develop a database of his inventory. He wants to keep track of the items he has purchased, their shipments, and eventually customers and sales. To get started, he has asked you to create a database for the data in Figure 4-9.

A. Follow the procedure shown in Figure 4-1 to assess these data. List all of the multivalued dependencies, functional dependencies, candidate keys, primary keys, and foreign keys. State any assumptions you make.

B. List questions you would ask Phillip to verify your assumptions.

C. Create tables as necessary to eliminate multivalued dependencies, if any.

D. The relationship between shipment and item data could possibly be inferred by matching values in the From cells to values in the City cells. Describe two problems with that strategy.

E. Describe a change to this spreadsheet that does express the shipment–item relationship.

F. Assume that Phillip wishes to create an updatable database from these data. Design tables you think are appropriate. State all referential integrity constraints.

G. Assume that Phillip wishes to create a read-only database from these data. Design tables you think are appropriate. State all referential integrity constraints.

H. Do these data have the multivalue, multicolumn problem? If so, how will you deal with it?

I. Do these data have the inconsistent data problem? If so, how will you deal with it?

Figure 4-9

J. Do these data have a null value data problem? If so, how will you deal with it?

Spreadsheets from Morgan Imports

K. Do these data have the general-purpose remarks problem? If so, how will you deal with it?

	A	B	C	D	E	F	G	H	I
1	ShipmentNumber	Shipper	Phone	Contact	From	Departure	Arrival	Contents	InsuredValue
2	49100300	Wordwide	800-123-4567	Jose	Philippines	5/5/2009	6/17/1999	QE dining set, large bureau, porcelain lamps	$27,500
3	488955	Intenational	800-123-8898	Marilyn	Singapore	6/2/2009		Miscellaneous linen, large masks, 14 setting Willow design china	$7,500
4	84899440	Wordwide	800-123-4567	Jose	Peru	7/3/2009	7/28/2009	Woven goods, antique leather chairs	
5	399400	Intenational	800-123-8898	Marilyn	Singaporeee	8/5/2009	9/11/2009	Large bureau, brass lamps, willow design serving dishes	$18,000
6									
7									
8									
9		Item	Date	City	Store	Salesperson	Price		
10		Willow Serving Dishes	7/15/2009	Singapore	Jade Antiques	Swee Lai	$4,500		
11		Large bureau	7/17/2009	Singapore	Eastern Sales	Jeremey	$9,500		
12		Brass lamps	7/20/2009	Singapore	Jade Antiques	Mr. James	$1,200		
13		QE Dining Set	4/7/2009	Manila	E. Treasures	Gracielle	$14,300		
14									
15									

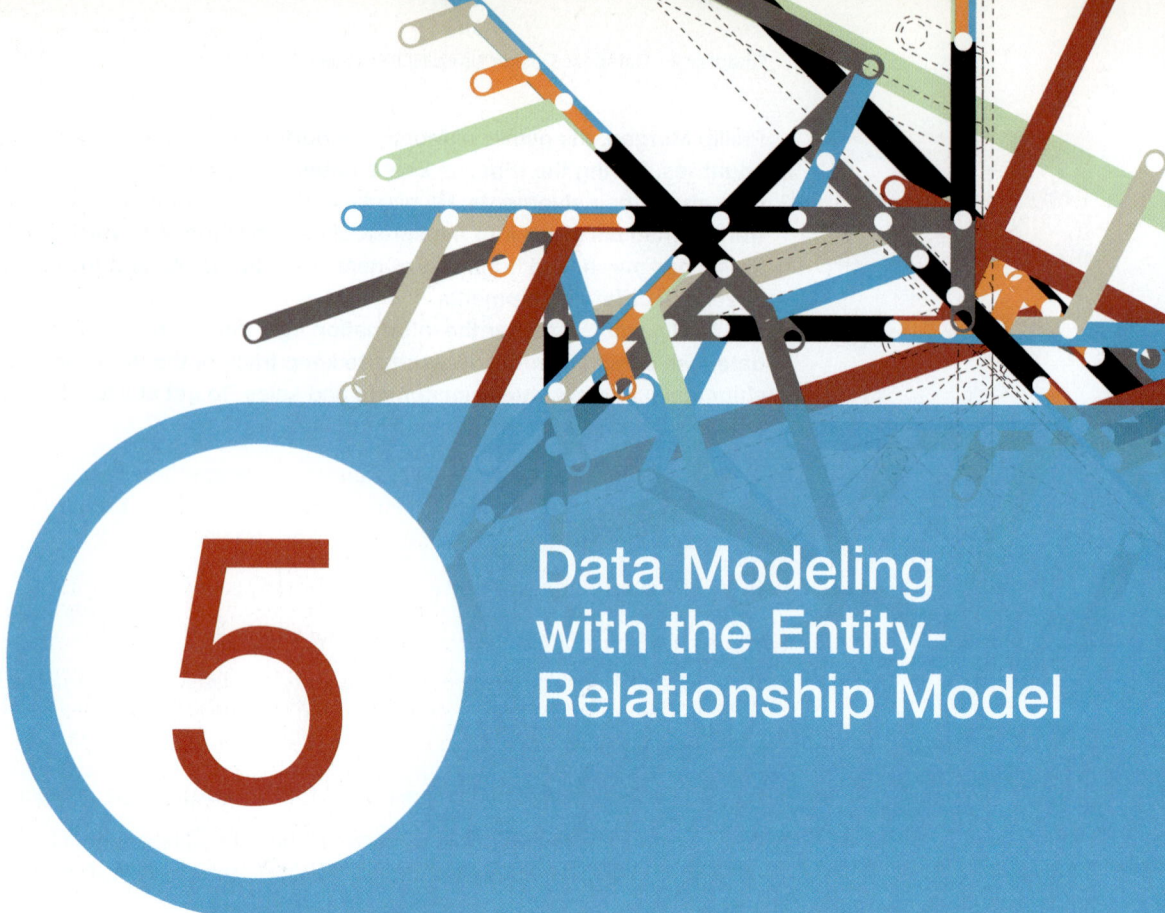

5

Data Modeling with the Entity-Relationship Model

Chapter Objectives

- To understand the two-phase data modeling/database design process.
- To understand the purpose of the data modeling process.
- To understand entity-relationship (E-R) diagrams.
- To be able to determine entities, attributes, and relationships.
- To be able to create entity identifiers.
- To be able to determine minimum and maximum cardinalities.
- To understand variations of the E-R model.
- To understand and be able to use ID-dependent and other weak entities.
- To understand and be able to use supertype/subtype entities.

- To understand and be able to use strong entity patterns.
- To understand and be able to use the ID-dependent association pattern.
- To understand and be able to use the ID-dependent multivalued attribute pattern.
- To understand and be able to use the ID-dependent archetype/instance pattern.
- To understand and be able to use the line-item pattern.
- To understand and be able to use the for-use-by pattern.
- To understand and be able to use recursive patterns.
- To understand the iterative nature of the data modeling process.
- To be able to use the data modeling process.

In this chapter and the next, we consider the design of databases that arise from the development of new information systems. As you will learn, such databases are designed by analyzing requirements and creating a data model, or blueprint, of a database that will meet those requirements. The data model is then transformed into a database design.

This chapter addresses the creation of data models using the entity-relationship data model, the most popular modeling technique. This chapter consists of three major sections. First, we explain the major elements of the entity-relationship model and briefly describe several variations on that model. Next, we examine a number of patterns in forms, reports, and data models that you will encounter when data modeling. We then illustrate the data modeling process using the example of a small database at a university. Before starting, however, you need to understand the purpose of a data model.

The Purpose of a Data Model

A **data model** is a plan, or blueprint, for a database design. By analogy, consider the construction of your dorm or apartment building. The contractor did not just buy some lumber, call for the concrete trucks, and start work. Instead, an architect constructed plans and blueprints for that building long before construction began. If, during the planning stage, it was determined that a room was too small or too large, the blueprint could be changed simply by redrawing the lines. If, however, the need for change occurs after the building is constructed, the walls, electrical system, plumbing, and so on will need to be rebuilt, at great expense and loss of time. It is easier, simpler, and faster to change the plan than it is to change a constructed building.

The same argument applies to data models and databases. Changing a relationship during the data modeling stage is just a matter of changing the diagram and related documentation. Changing a relationship after the database and applications have been constructed, however, is much more difficult. Data must be migrated to the new structure, SQL statements will need to be changed, forms and reports will need to be altered, and so forth.

The Entity-Relationship Model

Dozens of different tools and techniques for constructing data models have been defined over the years. They include the hierarchical data model, the network data model, the ANSI/SPARC data model, the entity-relationship data model, the semantic object model, and many others. Of these, the entity-relationship data model has emerged as the standard data model, and we will consider only that data model in this chapter.

The **entity-relationship (E-R) model** was first published by Peter Chen in 1976.[1] In this paper, Chen set out the basic elements of the model. Subtypes (discussed later) were added to the E-R model to create the **extended E-R model**,[2] and today it is the extended E-R model that most people mean when they use the term *E-R model*. In this text, we will use the extended E-R model.

Entities

An **entity** is something that users want to track. It is something that is readily identified in the users' work environment. Example entities are EMPLOYEE Mary Lai, CUSTOMER 12345, SALES-ORDER 1000, SALESPERSON Wally Smith, and PRODUCT A4200. Entities of a given type are grouped into an **entity class**. Thus, the EMPLOYEE entity class is the collection of all EMPLOYEE entities. In this text, entity classes are shown in capital letters.

It is important to understand the differences between an entity class and an entity instance. An entity class is a collection of entities and is described by the structure of the entities in that class. An **entity instance** of an entity class is the occurrence of a particular entity, such as CUSTOMER 12345. An entity class usually has many instances of an entity. For example, the

---

[1] Chen, Peter P. "The Entity-Relationship Model—Towards a Unified View of Data." *ACM Transactions on Database Systems*, January 1976, pp. 9–36.
[2] Teorey, T. J., D. Yang, and J. P. Fry. "A Logical Design Methodology for Relational Databases Using the Extended Entity-Relationship Model," *ACM Computing Surveys*, June 1986, pp. 197–222.

CUSTOMER Entity

CUSTOMER
CustomerNumber
CustomerName
Street
City
State
Zip
ContactName
Email

Two CUSTOMER Instances

1234	99890
Ajax Manufacturing	Jones Brothers
123 Elm Street	434 10th Street
Memphis	Boston
TN	MA
32455	01234
P_Schwartz	Fritz Billingsley
P_S@Ajax.com	Fritz@JB.com

Figure 5-1

CUSTOMER Entity and Two
Entity Instances

entity class CUSTOMER has many instances—one for each customer represented in the database. The CUSTOMER entity class and two of its instances are shown in Figure 5-1.

Attributes

Entities have **attributes** that describe their characteristics. Examples of attributes are EmployeeNumber, EmployeeName, Phone, and Email. In this text, attributes are written in both uppercase and lowercase letters. The E-R model assumes that all instances of a given entity class have the same attributes.

Figure 5-2 shows two different ways of displaying the attributes of an entity. Figure 5-2(a) shows attributes in ellipses that are connected to the entity. This style was used in the original E-R model, prior to the advent of data modeling software products. Figure 5-2(b) shows the rectangle style that is commonly used by data modeling software products today.

Identifiers

Figure 5-2

Variations on Entity Diagram
Attribute Displays

Entity instances have **identifiers**, which are attributes that name, or identify, entity instances. For example, EMPLOYEE instances can be identified by EmployeeNumber, SocialSecurityNumber,

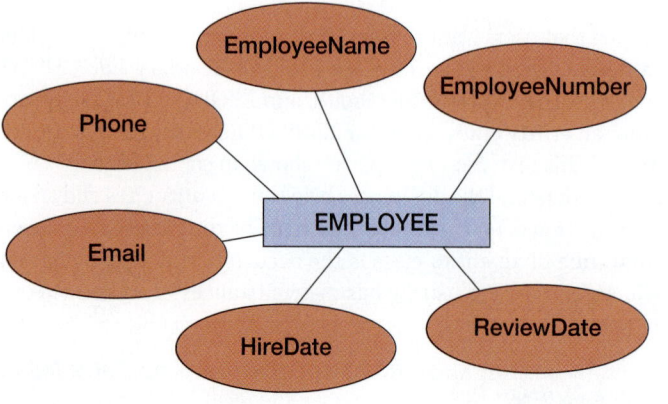

(a) Attributes in Ellipses

(b) Attributes in Rectangle

or EmployeeName. EMPLOYEE instances are not likely to be identified by attributes such as Salary or HireDate because these attributes are not normally used in a naming role. Similarly, customers can be identified by CustomerNumber or CustomerName, and sales orders can be identified by OrderNumber.

The identifier of an entity instance consists of one or more of the entity's attributes. Identifiers that consist of two or more attributes are called **composite identifiers**. Examples are (AreaCode, LocalNumber), (ProjectName, TaskName), and (FirstName, LastName, DateOfHire).

> **BY THE WAY**   Notice the correspondence of identifiers and keys. The term *identifier* is used in a data model, and the term *key* is used in a database design. Thus, entities have identifiers, and tables (or relations) have keys. Identifiers serve the same role for entities that keys serve for tables.

As shown in Figure 5-3, entities are portrayed in three levels of detail in a data model. As shown in Figure 5-3(a), sometimes the entity and all of its attributes are displayed. In such cases, the identifier of the attribute is shown at the top of the entity and a horizontal line is drawn after the identifier, However, in a large data model, so much detail can make the data model diagrams unwieldy. In those cases, the entity diagram is abbreviated by showing just the identifier, as in Figure 5-3(b), or by showing just the name of the entity in a rectangle, as shown in Figure 5-3(c). All three techniques are used in practice; the more abbreviated form in Figure 5-3(c) is used to show the big picture and overall entity relationships. The more detailed view in Figure 5-3(a) is frequently used during database design. Most data modeling software products have the ability to show all three displays.

Relationships

Entities can be associated with one another in **relationships**. The E-R model contains both relationship classes and relationship instances.[3] **Relationship classes** are associations among entity classes, and **relationship instances** are associations among entity instances. In the original E-R model, relationships could have attributes. Today, that feature is no longer used.

Relationships are given names that describe the nature of the relationship, as shown in Figure 5-4. In Figure 5-4(a), the Qualification relationship shows which employees have which skills. In Figure 5-4(b), the Assignment relationship shows which combinations of clients, architects, and projects have been created. To avoid unnecessary complexity, in this chapter, we will show the names of relationships only if there is a chance of ambiguity.

Figure 5-3

Variations on Level of Entity Attribute Displays

EMPLOYEE

EmployeeNumber
EmployeeName
Phone
Email
HireDate
ReviewDate

(a) Entity with All Attributes

EMPLOYEE

EmployeeNumber

(b) Entity with Identifier Attribute Only

EMPLOYEE

(c) Entity with No Attributes

---

[3] For brevity, we sometimes drop the word *instance* when the context makes it clear that an instance rather than an entity class is involved.

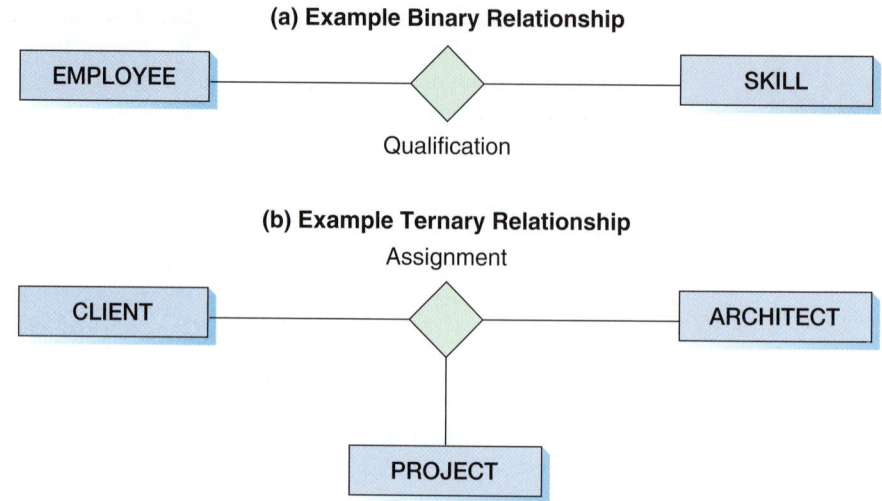

(a) Example Binary Relationship

EMPLOYEE — Qualification — SKILL

(b) Example Ternary Relationship

Assignment

CLIENT — ARCHITECT

PROJECT

Figure 5-4

Binary Versus Ternary Relationships

BY THE WAY Your instructor may believe that it is important to always show the name of a relationship. If so, be aware that you can name a relationship from the perspective of either of the entities or both. For example, you can name the relationship between DEPARTMENT and EMPLOYEE as Department Consists Of; or you can name it as Employee Works In; or you can name it both ways, using a slash between the two names, Department Consists Of/Employee Works In. Relationship names are a necessity when there are two different relationships between the same two entities.

A relationship class can involve two or more entity classes. The number of entity classes in the relationship is the **degree** of the relationship. In Figure 5-4(a), the Qualification relationship is of degree two because it involves two entity classes: EMPLOYEE and SKILL. In Figure 5-4(a), the Assignment relationship is of degree three because it involves three entity classes: CLIENT, ARCHITECT, and PROJECT. Relationships of degree two are referred to as **binary relationships**. Similarly, relationships of degree three are called **ternary relationships**.

When transforming a data model into a relational design, relationships of all degrees are treated as combinations of binary relationships. The Assignment relationship in Figure 5-4(b), for example, is decomposed into three binary relationships (can you spot them?). Most of the time, this strategy is not a problem. However, some nonbinary relationships need additional work, as you will learn in Chapter 6. All data modeling software products require you to express relationships as binary relationships.

BY THE WAY At this point, you may be wondering, "What's the difference between an entity and a table?" So far, they seem like different terms for the same thing. *The principle difference between an entity and a table is you can express a relationship between entities without using foreign keys.* In the E-R model, you can specify a relationship just by drawing a line connecting two entities. Because you are doing logical data modeling and not physical database design, you need not worry about primary and foreign keys, referential integrity constraints, and the like. Most data modeling products will allow you to consider such details if you choose to, but they do not require it.

This characteristic makes entities easier to work with than tables, especially early in a project when entities and relationships are fluid and uncertain. You can show relationships between entities before you even know what the identifiers are. For example, you can say that a DEPARTMENT relates to many EMPLOYEEs before you know any of the attributes of either EMPLOYEE or DEPARTMENT. This characteristic enables you to work from the general to the specific. First identify the entities, then think about relationships, and finally, determine the attributes.

In the entity-relationship model, relationships are classified by their **cardinality**, a word that means "count." The **maximum cardinality** is the maximum number of entity instances that can participate in a relationship instance. The **minimum cardinality** is the minimum number of entity instances that must participate in a relationship instance.

Maximum Cardinality

In Figure 5-5, the maximum cardinality is shown inside the diamond that represents the relationship. The three parts of this figure show the three basic maximum cardinalities in the E-R model.

Figure 5-5(a) shows a **one-to-one (abbreviated 1:1) relationship**. In a 1:1 relationship, an entity instance of one type is related to at most one entity instance of the other type. The Employee_Identity relationship in Figure 5-5(a) associates one EMPLOYEE instance with one BADGE instance. According to this diagram, no employee has more than one badge, and no badge is assigned to more than one employee.

The Computer_Assignment relationship in Figure 5-5(b) illustrates a **one-to-many (abbreviated 1:N) relationship**. Here, a single instance of EMPLOYEE can be associated with many instances of COMPUTER, but a COMPUTER instance is associated with just one instance of EMPLOYEE. According to this diagram, an employee can be associated with several computers, but a computer is assigned to just one employee.

The positions of the 1 and the N are significant. The 1 is close to the line connecting EMPLOYEE, which means that the 1 refers to the EMPLOYEE side of the relationship. The N is close to the line connecting COMPUTER, which means that the N refers to the COMPUTER side of the relationship. If the 1 and the N were reversed and the relationship were written N:1, an EMPLOYEE would have one COMPUTER, and a COMPUTER would be assigned to many EMPLOYEEs.

When discussing one-to-many relationships, the terms **parent** and **child** are sometimes used. The *parent* is the entity on the 1 side of the relationship, and the *child* is the entity on the many side of the relationship. Thus, in a 1:N relationship between DEPARTMENT and EMPLOYEE, DEPARTMENT is the parent and EMPLOYEE is the child (one DEPARTMENT has many EMPLOYEEs).

Figure 5-5(c) shows a **many-to-many (abbreviated N:M) relationship**. According to the Qualification relationship, an EMPLOYEE instance can be associated with many SKILL instances, and a SKILL instance can be associated with many EMPLOYEE instances. This relationship documents that fact that an employee may have many skills, and a skill may be held by many employees.

Sometimes students wonder why we do not write many-to-many relationships as N:N or M:M. The reason is that cardinality in one direction may be different than the cardinality in the other direction. In other words, in an N:M relationship, N need not equal M. An EMPLOYEE can

Figure   5-5

Three Types of Maximum Cardinality

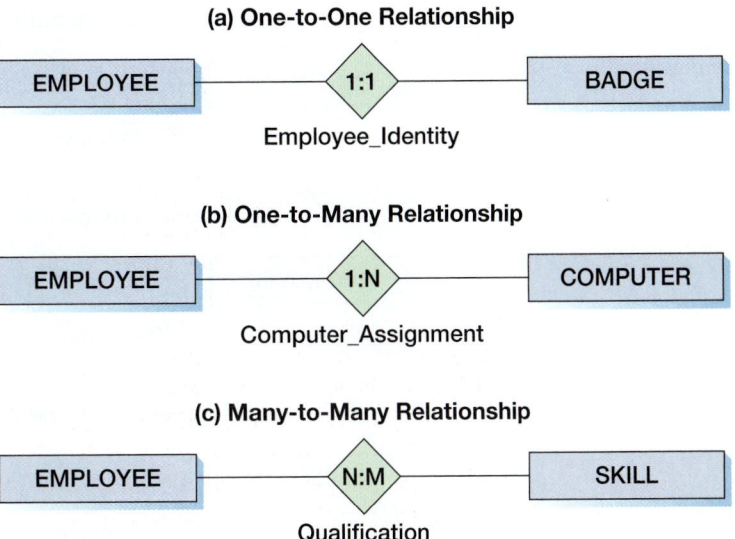

(a) One-to-One Relationship

EMPLOYEE — 1:1 — BADGE

Employee_Identity

(b) One-to-Many Relationship

EMPLOYEE — 1:N — COMPUTER

Computer_Assignment

(c) Many-to-Many Relationship

EMPLOYEE — N:M — SKILL

Qualification

have five skills, for example, but one of those skills can have three employees. Writing the relationship as N:M highlights the possibility that the cardinalities may be different.

Sometimes the maximum cardinality is an exact number. For example, for a sports team, the number of players on the roster is limited to some fixed number, say, 15. In that case, the maximum cardinality between TEAM and PLAYER would be set to 15 rather than to the more general N.

> **BY THE WAY**   Relationships like those in Figure 5-5 are sometimes called **HAS-A relationships**. This term is used because each entity instance has a relationship to a second entity instance. An employee has a badge, and a badge has an employee. If the maximum cardinality is greater than one, then each entity has a set of other entities. An employee has a set of skills, for example, and a skill has a set of employees who have that skill.

Minimum Cardinality

The minimum cardinality is the number of entity instances that must participate in a relationship. Generally, minimums are stated as either zero or one. If zero, then participation in the relationship is optional. If one, then at least one entity instance must participate in the relationship. In E-R diagrams, an optional relationship is represented by a small circle on the relationship line; a mandatory relationship is represented by a hash mark or line across the relationship line.

To better understand these terms, consider Figure 5-6. In the Employee_Identity relationship in Figure 5-6(a), the hash marks indicate that an EMPLOYEE is required to have a BADGE, and a BADGE must be allocated to an EMPLOYEE. Such a relationship is referred to as a **mandatory-to-mandatory (M-M) relationship**, because entities are required on both sides. The complete specification for the Employee_Identity relationship is that it is a 1:1, M-M relationship.

In Figure 5-6(b), the two small circles indicate that the Computer_Assignment relationship is an **optional-to-optional (O-O) relationship**. This means that an EMPLOYEE need not have a COMPUTER, and a COMPUTER need not be assigned to an EMPLOYEE. The Computer_Assignment relationship is thus a 1:N, O-O relationship.

Finally, in Figure 5-6(c) the combination of a circle and a hash mark indicates as an **optional-to-mandatory (O-M) relationship**. Here, an EMPLOYEE must be assigned to at least one SKILL, but a SKILL may not necessarily be related to any EMPLOYEE. The complete specification for the Qualification relationship is thus an N:M, O-M relationship. The position

Figure   5-6

Minimum Cardinality
Examples

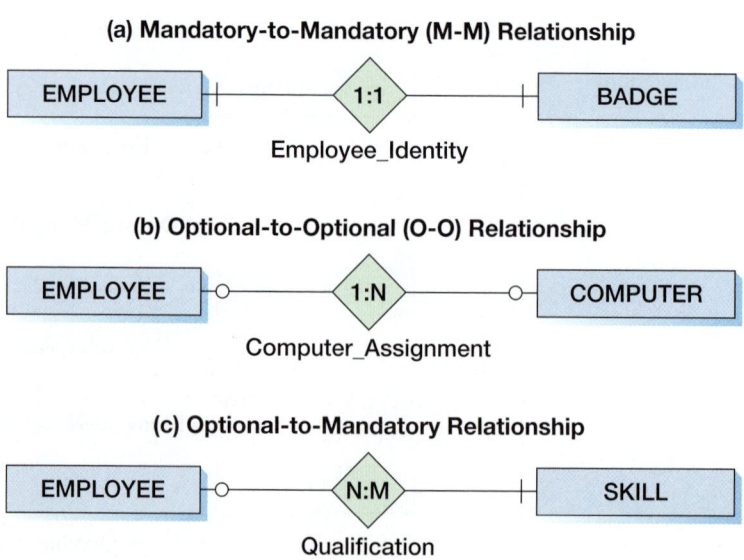

(a) Mandatory-to-Mandatory (M-M) Relationship

EMPLOYEE — 1:1 — BADGE

Employee_Identity

(b) Optional-to-Optional (O-O) Relationship

EMPLOYEE — 1:N — COMPUTER

Computer_Assignment

(c) Optional-to-Mandatory Relationship

EMPLOYEE — N:M — SKILL

Qualification

of the circle and the hash mark are important. Because the circle is in front of EMPLOYEE, it means that the employee is optional in the relationship.

BY THE WAY   Sometimes when interpreting diagrams like Figure 5-6(c) students become confused about which entity is optional and which is required. An easy way to clarify this situation is to imagine that you are standing in the diamond on the relationship line. Imagine looking toward one of the entities. If you see an oval in that direction, then that entity is optional; if you see a hash mark, then that entity is required. Thus, in Figure 5-6(c), if you stand on the diamond and look toward SKILL, you see a hash mark. This means that SKILL is required in the relationship.

A fourth option, a **mandatory-to-optional (M-O) relationship** is not shown in Figure 5-6. But, if we exchange the circle and the hash mark in Figure 5-6(c), then Qualification becomes an M-O relationship. In that case, an EMPLOYEE need not have a SKILL, but a SKILL must have at least one EMPLOYEE.

As with maximum cardinalities, in rare cases the minimum cardinality is a specific number. To represent the relationship between PERSON and MARRIAGE, for example, the minimum cardinality would be 2:Optional.

Entity-Relationship Diagrams and Their Versions

The diagrams in Figures 5-5 and 5-6 are sometimes referred to as **entity-relationship (E-R) diagrams**. The original E-R model specified that such diagrams use diamonds for relationships, rectangles for entities, and connected ellipses for attributes, as shown in Figure 5-2. You may still see examples of such E-R diagrams, and it is important for you to be able to interpret them.

For two reasons, however, this original notation is seldom used today. First, there are a number of different versions of the E-R model, and these versions use different symbols. Second, data modeling software products use different techniques. For example, Computer Associates' ERwin product uses one set of symbols, and Microsoft Visio uses a second set.

Variations of the E-R Model

At least three different versions of the E-R model are in use today. One of them, **Information Engineering (IE)**, was developed by James Martin in 1990. This model uses crow's feet to show the many side of a relationship, and it is called the **IE Crow's foot model**. It is easy to understand, and we will use it throughout this text. In 1993, the National Institute of Standards and Technology announced another version of the E-R model as a national standard. This version is called **Integrated Definition 1, Extended (IDEF1X)**.[4] This standard incorporates the basic ideas of the E-R model, but uses different graphical symbols. Although this model is a national standard, it is difficult to understand and use. As a national standard, however, it is used in government, and thus it may become important to you. Therefore, the fundamentals of the IDEF1X model are described in Appendix B.

Meanwhile, to add further complication, a new object-oriented development methodology called the **Unified Modeling Language (UML)** adopted the E-R model, but introduced its own symbols while putting an object-oriented programming spin on the model. UML notation is summarized in Appendix C.

BY THE WAY   In addition to differences due to different versions of the E-R model, there also are differences due to software products. For example, two products that both implement the IE Crow's Foot model may do so in different ways. The result is a mess. When creating a data model diagram, you need to know not just the version of the E-R model you are using, but also the idiosyncrasies of the data modeling product you use.

---

[4] *Integrated Definition for Information Modeling (IDEF1X)*. Federal Information Processing Standards Publication 184, 1993.

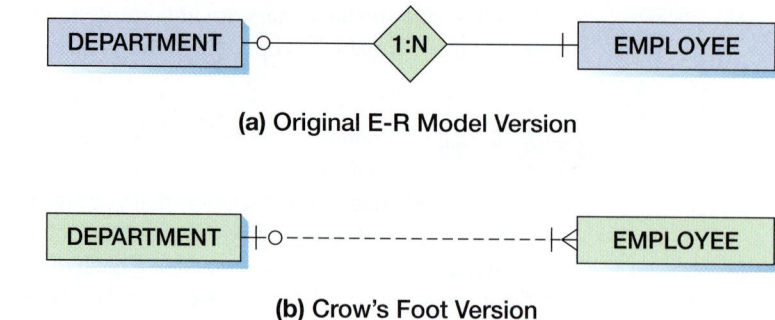

(a) Original E-R Model Version

Figure   5-7

Minimum Cardinality
Examples

(b) Crow's Foot Version

E-R Diagrams Using the IE Crow's Foot Model

Figure 5-7 shows two versions of a one-to-many, optional-to-mandatory relationship. Figure 5-7(a) shows the original E-R model version. Figure 5-7(b) shows the crow's foot model using common crow's foot symbols. Notice that the relationship is drawn as a dashed line. The reason for this will be explained later in this chapter. For now, notice the **crow's foot symbol** used to show the many side of the relationship.

The crow's foot model uses the notation shown in Figure 5-8 to indicate the relationship cardinality. The symbol closest to the entity shows the maximum cardinality, and the other symbol shows the minimum cardinality. A hash mark indicates one (and therefore also mandatory), a circle indicates zero (and thus optional), and the crow's foot symbol indicates many. Thus, the diagram in Figure 5-7(b) means that a DEPARTMENT has one or more EMPLOYEEs (the symbol shows many and mandatory), and an EMPLOYEE belongs to zero or one DEPARTMENTs (the symbol shows one and optional).

A 1:1 relationship would be drawn in a similar manner, but the line connecting to each entity should be similar to the connection shown for the one side of the 1:N relationship in Figure 5-7(b).

Figure 5-9 shows two versions of an N:M, optional to mandatory relationship. Modeling N:M relationships presents some complications. According to the original E-R model diagram shown in Figure 5-9(a), an EMPLOYEE must have at least one SKILL and may have several. At

Figure   5-8

Crow's Foot Notation

Symbol	Meaning
⊢⊢	One—Mandatory
⊢<	Many—Mandatory
⟋O⊢	One—Optional
⟋O<	Many—Optional

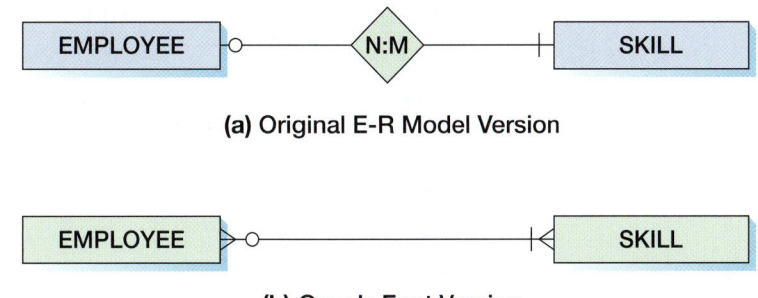

(a) Original E-R Model Version

Figure 5-9

Two Versions of an N:M
Relationship
(a) Original E-R Model Version
(b) Crow's Foot Version

(b) Crow's Foot Version

the same time, although a SKILL may or may not be held by any EMPLOYEE, a SKILL may also be held by several EMPLOYEEs. The crow's foot version in Figure 5-9(b) shows the N:M maximum cardinalities using the notation in Figure 5-8. The crow's foot symbols again indicate the minimum cardinalities for the N:M relationship.

Except for Appendices B and C, for the rest of this text we will use the IE Crow's Foot model for E-R diagrams. There are no completely standard symbols for the crow's foot notation, and we explain our symbols and notation when we first use it. You can obtain various modeling products that will produce crow's foot models, and they are easily understood and related to the original E-R model. Be aware that those other products may use the oval, hash mark, crow's foot, and other symbols in slightly differently ways. Further, your instructor may have a favorite modeling tool for you to use. If that tool does not support crow's feet, you will have to adapt the data models in this text to your tool. Making these adaptations is a good learning exercise. See, for example, exercises 5.57 and 5.58.

> **BY THE WAY** There are a number of modeling products that you can try—each will have its own idiosyncrasies. Computer Associates produces ERwin, a commercial data modeling product that handles both data modeling and database design tasks. You can download the CA ERwin Data Modeler Community Edition, which is suitable for class use, from *www.ca.com/us/software-trials.aspx*. You can use ERwin to produce either crow's foot or IDEF1X.
>
> Although it is better at creating database designs (discussed in Chapter 5) than data models, Microsoft's Visio is a possibility. A trial version is available from the Microsoft Web site at http://office.microsoft.com/en-us/visio/default.aspx.
>
> Finally, Sun Microsystems is continuing development of the MySQL Workbench, and a free (but somewhat limited) version is available at the MySQL Web site at http://dev.mysql.com/downloads/workbench/5.1.html. Although, like Microsoft Visio, it is better at database designs than data models, it is a very useful tool and the database designs it produces can be used with any DBMS, not just MySQL.

Strong Entities and Weak Entities

A **strong entity** is an entity that represents something that can exist on its own. For example, PERSON is a strong entity—we consider people to exist as individuals in their own right. Similarly, AUTOMOBILE is a strong entity. In addition to strong entities, the original version of the E-R model included the concept of a **weak entity**, which is defined as any entity whose existence depends on the presence of another entity.

ID-Dependent Entities

The E-R model includes a special type of entity called an **ID-dependent entity**. an ID-dependent entity is an entity whose identifier includes the identifier of another entity. Consider, for example, an entity for a student apartment in a building, as shown in Figure 5-10(a).

The identifier of such an entity is a composite (ApartmentNumber, BuildingName), where BuildingName is the identifier of the entity BUILDING. ApartmentNumber by itself is

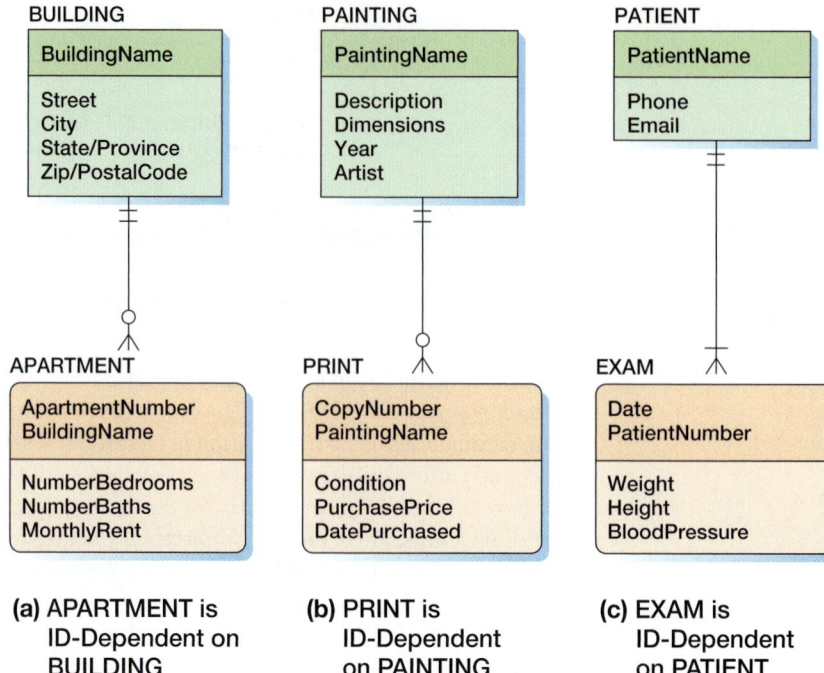

Figure 5-10

Example ID-dependent
Entities

(a) APARTMENT is
ID-Dependent on
BUILDING

(b) PRINT is
ID-Dependent
on PAINTING

(c) EXAM is
ID-Dependent
on PATIENT

insufficient to tell someone where you live. If you say you live in apartment number 5, they must ask you, "In what building?"

Figure 5-10 shows three different ID-dependent entities. In addition to APARTMENT, the entity PRINT in Figure 5-10(b) is ID-dependent on PAINTING, and the entity EXAM in Figure 5-10(c) is ID-dependent on PAINTING, and the entity EXAM in Figure 5-10(c) is ID-dependent on PATIENT.

In each of these cases, the ID-dependent entity cannot exist unless the parent (the entity on which it depends) also exists. Thus, the minimum cardinality from the ID-dependent entity to the parent is always one.

However, whether the parent is required to have an ID-dependent entity depends on the application requirements. In Figure 5-10, both APARTMENT and PRINT are optional, but EXAM is required. These restrictions arise from the nature of the application and not from any logical requirement.

As shown in Figure 5-10, in our E-R models we use an entity with rounded corners to represent the ID-dependent entity. We also use a solid line to represent the relationship between the ID-dependent entity and its parent. This type of a relationship is called an **identifying relationship**. A relationship drawn with a dashed line (refer to Figure 5-7) is used between strong entities and is called a **nonidentifying relationship** because there are no ID-dependent entities in the relationship.

ID-dependent entities pose restrictions on the processing of the database that is constructed from them. Namely, the row that represents the parent entity must be created before any ID-dependent child row can be created. Further, when a parent row is deleted, all child rows must be deleted as well.

ID-dependent entities are common. Another example is the entity VERSION in the relationship between PRODUCT and VERSION, where PRODUCT is a software product and VERSION is a release of that software product. The identifier of PRODUCT is ProductName, and the identifier of VERSION is (ProductName, ReleaseNumber). Yet another example is EDITION in the relationship between TEXTBOOK and EDITION. The identifier of TEXTBOOK is Title, and the identifier of EDITION is (Title, EditionNumber).

Non-ID-Dependent Weak Entities

All ID-dependent entities are weak entities. But, according to the original E-R model, some entities that are weak are not ID-dependent. Consider the AUTO_MODEL and VEHICLE entity classes in the database of a car manufacturer, such as Ford or Honda, as shown in Figure 5-11.

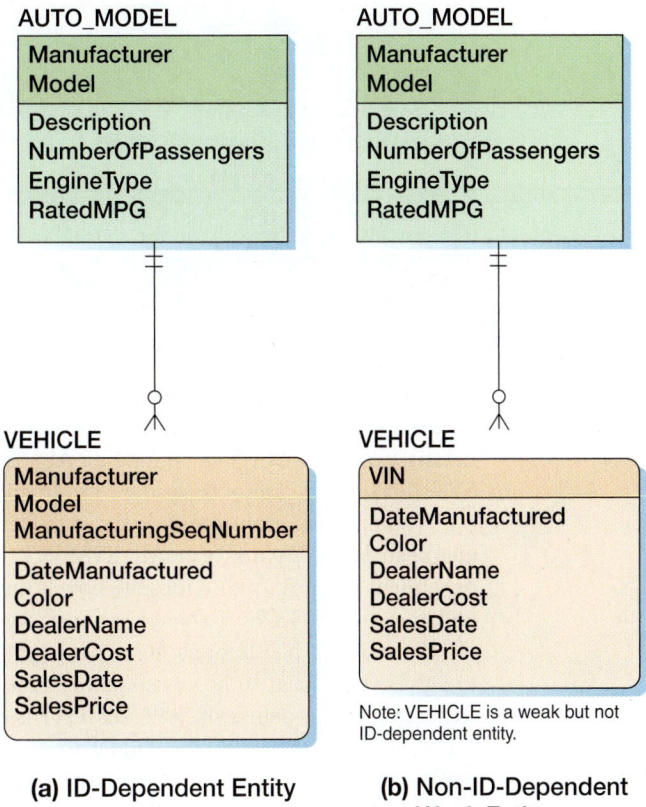

AUTO_MODEL

Manufacturer
Model

Description
NumberOfPassengers
EngineType
RatedMPG

VEHICLE

Manufacturer
Model
ManufacturingSeqNumber

DateManufactured
Color
DealerName
DealerCost
SalesDate
SalesPrice

(a) ID-Dependent Entity

AUTO_MODEL

Manufacturer
Model

Description
NumberOfPassengers
EngineType
RatedMPG

VEHICLE

VIN

DateManufactured
Color
DealerName
DealerCost
SalesDate
SalesPrice

Note: VEHICLE is a weak but not
ID-dependent entity.

(b) Non-ID-Dependent Weak Entity

Figure 5-11

Weak Entity Examples

In Figure 5-11(a), each VEHICLE is assigned a sequential number as it is manufactured. So, for the "Super SUV" AUTO_MODEL, the first VEHICLE manufactured gets a ManufacturingSeqNumber of 1, the next gets a ManufacturingSeqNumber of 2, and so on. This is clearly an ID-dependent relationship because ManufacturingSeqNumber is based on the Manufacturer and Model.

Now let's assign VEHICLE an identifier that is independent of the Manufacturer and Model. We'll use a VIN (vehicle identification number), as shown in Figure 5-11(b). Now, the VEHICLE has a unique identifier of its own and does not need to be identified by its relation to AUTO_MODEL.

This is an interesting situation. VEHICLE has an identity of its own and therefore is not ID-dependent. Yet the VEHICLE is an AUTO_MODEL, and if that particular AUTO_MODEL did not exist, the VEHICLE itself would never have existed. Therefore, VEHICLE is now a *weak but non–ID-dependent entity*.

Consider *your* car—let's say it's a Ford Mustang just for the sake of this discussion. Your individual Mustang is a VEHICLE, and it exists as a physical object and is identified by the VIN that is required for each licensed automobile. It is *not* ID-dependent on AUTO_MODEL, which in this case is Ford Mustang, for its identity. However, if the Ford Mustang had never been created as an AUTO_MODEL—a logical concept that was first designed on paper—your car would never have been built because *no* Ford Mustangs would ever have been built! Therefore, your physical individual VEHICLE would not exist without a logical AUTO_MODEL of Ford Mustang, and in a data model (which *is* what we're talking about) a VEHICLE cannot exist without a related AUTO_MODEL. This makes VEHICLE a weak but non–ID-dependent entity. Most data modeling tools cannot model non-ID-dependent entities. So, to indicate such situations, we will use a nonidentifying relationship with a note added to the data model indicating that the entity is weak, as shown in Figure 5-11(b).

Unfortunately, an ambiguity is hidden in the definition of *weak entity*, and this ambiguity is interpreted differently by different database designers (as well as different textbook authors). The ambiguity is that in a strict sense, if a weak entity is defined as any entity whose presence

Figure   5-12

Summary of ID-dependent and Weak Entities

- • An ID-dependent entity is an entity whose identifier includes the identifier of another entity.
- • Indentifying relationships are used to represent ID-dependent entities.
- • A weak entity is an entity whose existence depends on another entity.
- • All ID-dependent entities are weak.
- • Some entities are weak, but not ID-dependent. Using data modeling tools, they are shown with nonidentifying relationships, with separate documentation indicating they are weak.

in the database depends on another entity, then any entity that participates in a relationship having a minimum cardinality of one to a second entity is a weak entity. Thus, in an academic database, if a STUDENT must have an ADVISER, then STUDENT is a weak entity, because a STUDENT entity cannot be stored without an ADVISER.

This interpretation seems too broad to some people. A STUDENT is not physically dependent on an ADVISER (unlike an APARTMENT to a BUILDING), and a STUDENT is not logically dependent on an ADVISER (despite how it might appear to either the student or the adviser), and, therefore, STUDENT should be considered a strong entity.

To avoid such situations, some people interpret the definition of weak entity more narrowly. They say that to be a weak entity an entity must logically depend on another entity. According to this definition, APARTMENT is a weak entity, but STUDENT is not. An APARTMENT cannot exist without a BUILDING in which it is located. However, a STUDENT can logically exist without an ADVISER, even if a business rule requires it. Characteristics of ID-dependent and weak entities are summarized in Figure 5-12.

Subtype Entities

The extended E-R model introduced the concept of subtypes. A **subtype** entity is a special case of another entity called its **supertype**. Students, for example, may be classified as undergraduate or graduate students. In this case, STUDENT is the supertype, and UNDERGRADUATE and GRADUATE are the subtypes.

Alternatively, a student could be classified as a freshman, sophomore, junior, or senior. In that case, STUDENT is the supertype, and FRESHMAN, SOPHOMORE, JUNIOR, and SENIOR are the subtypes.

As illustrated in Figure 5-13, in our E-R models we use a circle with a line under it as a subtype symbol to indicate a supertype–subtype relationship. Think of this as a symbol for an optional (the circle) 1:1 (the line) relationship. In addition, we use a solid line to represent an ID-dependent subtype entity because each subtype is ID-dependent on the supertype. Also note that none of the line end symbols shown in Figure 5-8 are used on the connecting lines.

Figure   5-13

Example Subtype Entities

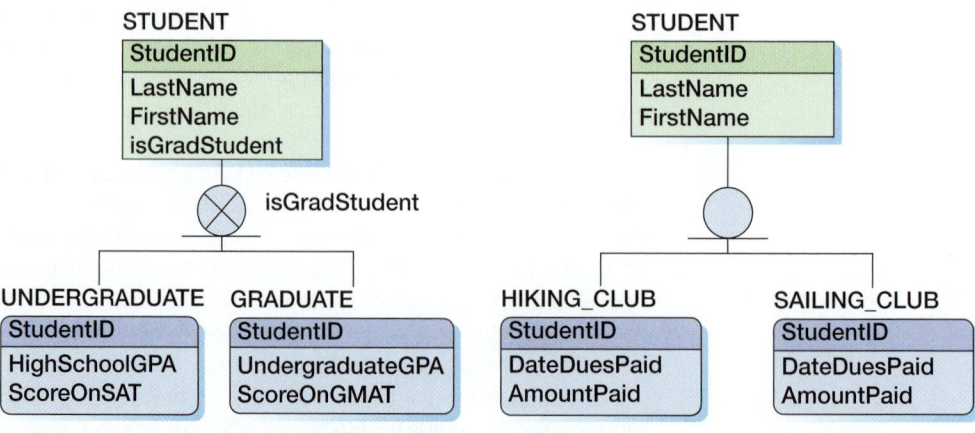

(a) Exclusive Subtypes with Discriminator   (b) Inclusive Subtypes

In some cases, an attribute of the supertype indicates which of the subtypes is appropriate for a given instance. An attribute that determines which subtype is appropriate is called a **discriminator**. In Figure 5-13(a), the attribute isGradStudent (which has only the values Yes and No) is the discriminator. In our E-R diagrams, the discriminator is shown next to the subtype symbol, as illustrated in Figure 5-13(a). Not all supertypes have a discriminator. Where a supertype does not have a discriminator, application code must be written to create the appropriate subtype.

Subtypes can be exclusive or inclusive. With **exclusive subtypes**, a supertype instance is related to at most one subtype. With **inclusive subtypes**, a supertype instance can relate to one or more subtypes. In Figure 5-13(a), the *X* in the circle means that the UNDERGRADUATE and GRADUATE subtypes are exclusive. Thus, a STUDENT can be either an UNDERGRADUATE or a GRADUATE, but not both. Figure 5-13(b) shows that a STUDENT can join either the HIKING_CLUB or the SAILING_CLUB, or both. These subtypes are inclusive (note there is no *X* in the circle). Because a supertype may relate to more than one subtype, inclusive subtypes do not have a discriminator.

The most important (some would say the only) reason for creating subtypes in a data model is to avoid value-inappropriate nulls. Undergraduate students take the SAT exam and report that score, whereas graduate students take the GMAT and report their score on that exam. Thus, the SAT score would be NULL in all STUDENT entities for graduates, and the GMAT score would be NULL for all undergraduates. Such null values can be avoided by creating subtypes.

> **BY THE WAY** The relationships that connect supertypes and subtypes are called **IS-A relationships** because a subtype is the same entity as the supertype. Because this is so, the identifier of a supertype and all its subtypes must be the same; they all represent different aspects of the same entity. Contrast this with HAS-A relationships, in which an entity has a relationship to another entity, but the identifiers of the two entities are different.

The elements of the entity-relationship model and their IE Crow's Foot representation are summarized in Figure 5-14. The identifier and attributes are shown only in the first example. Note that for 1:1 and 1:N nonidentifying relationships a relationship to a parent entity may be optional. For identifying relationships, the parent is always required.

Patterns in Forms, Reports, and E-R Models

A data model is a representation of how users view their world. Unfortunately, you cannot walk up to most computer users and ask questions like, "What is the maximum cardinality between the EMPLOYEE and SKILL entities?" Few users would have any idea of what you mean. Instead, you must infer the data model indirectly from user documents and from users' conversation and behavior.

One of the best ways to infer a data model is to study the users' forms and reports. From such documents, you can learn about entities and their relationships. In fact, the structure of forms and reports determines the structure of the data model, and the structure of the data model determines the structure of forms and reports. This means that you can examine a form or report and determine the entities and relationships that underlie it.

You can also use forms and reports to validate the data model. Rather than showing the data model to the users for feedback, an alternative is to construct a form or report that reflects the structure of the data model and obtain user feedback on that form or report. For example, if you want to know if an ORDER has one or many SALESPERSONs you can show the users a form that has a space for entering just one salesperson's name. If the user asks, "Where do I put the name of the second salesperson?" then you know that orders have at least two and possibly

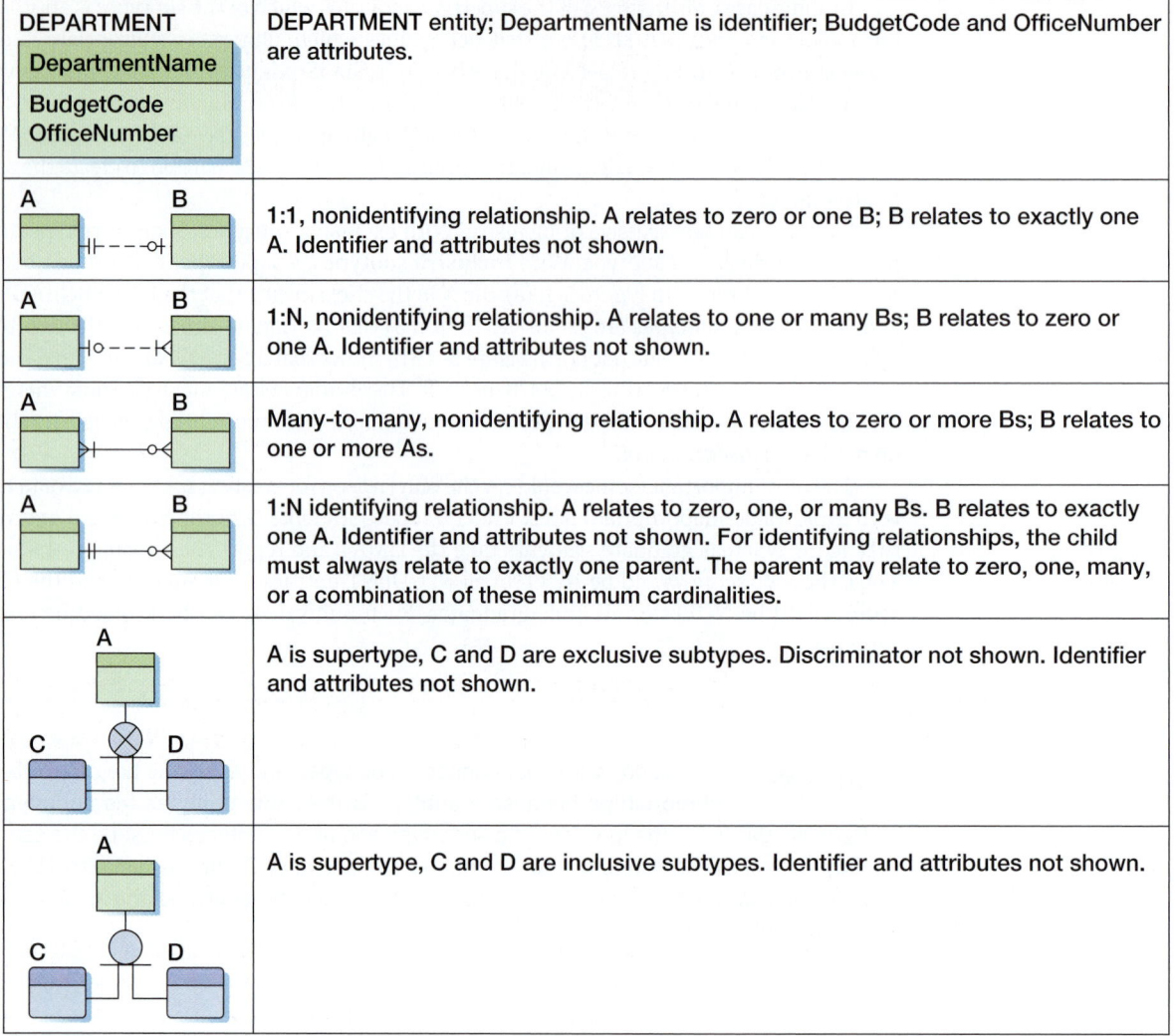

DEPARTMENT DepartmentName BudgetCode OfficeNumber	DEPARTMENT entity; DepartmentName is identifier; BudgetCode and OfficeNumber are attributes.
A B	1:1, nonidentifying relationship. A relates to zero or one B; B relates to exactly one A. Identifier and attributes not shown.
A B	1:N, nonidentifying relationship. A relates to one or many Bs; B relates to zero or one A. Identifier and attributes not shown.
A B	Many-to-many, nonidentifying relationship. A relates to zero or more Bs; B relates to one or more As.
A B	1:N identifying relationship. A relates to zero, one, or many Bs. B relates to exactly one A. Identifier and attributes not shown. For identifying relationships, the child must always relate to exactly one parent. The parent may relate to zero, one, many, or a combination of these minimum cardinalities.
A C ⊗ D	A is supertype, C and D are exclusive subtypes. Discriminator not shown. Identifier and attributes not shown.
A C ○ D	A is supertype, C and D are inclusive subtypes. Identifier and attributes not shown.

Figure   5-14

IE Crows Foot Symbol Summary

many salespeople. Sometimes, when no appropriate form or report exists, teams create a prototype form or report for the users to evaluate.

All of this means that you must understand how the structure of forms and reports determines the structure of the data model, and the reverse. Fortunately, many forms and reports fall into common patterns. If you learn how to analyze these patterns, you will be well on your way to understanding the logical relationship between forms and reports and the data model. Accordingly, in the next sections we will discuss the most common patterns in detail.

Strong Entity Patterns

Three relationships are possible between two strong entities: 1:1, 1:N, and N:M. When modeling such relationships, you must determine both the maximum and minimum cardinality. The maximum cardinality often can be determined from forms and reports. In most cases, to determine the minimum cardinality you will have to ask the users.

1:1 Strong Entity Relationships

Figure 5-15 shows a data entry form and a report that indicate a one-to-one relationship between the entities CLUB_MEMBER and LOCKER. The MEMBER_LOCKER form in Figure 5-15(a) shows data for an athletic club member, and it lists just one locker for that member. This form indicates that a CLUB_MEMBER has at most one locker. The report in Figure 5-15(b) shows the lockers in the club and indicates the member who has been allocated that locker. Each locker is assigned to one club member.

The form and report in Figure 5-15 thus suggest that a CLUB_MEMBER has one LOCKER, and a LOCKER is assigned to one CLUB_MEMBER. Hence, the relationship between them

(a) Club Membership Data Entry Form

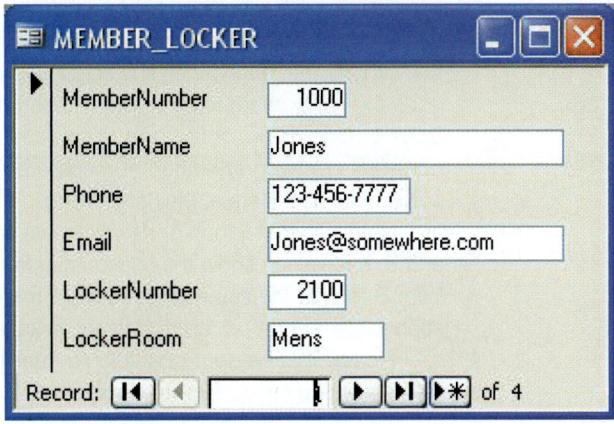

(b) Club Locker Report

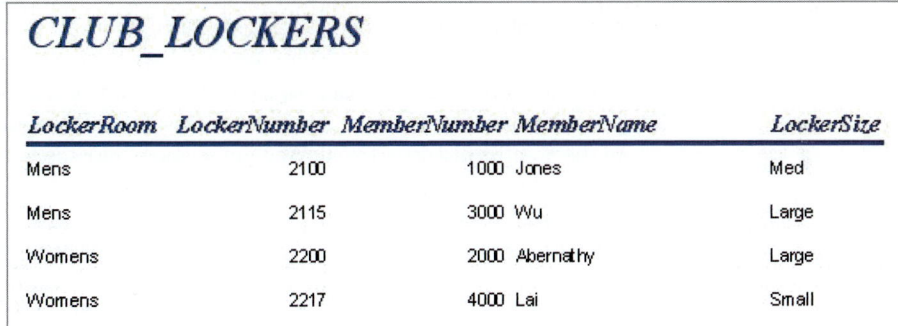

Figure 5-15

Form and Report Indicating a 1:1 Relationship

is 1:1. To model that relationship, we draw a nonidentifying relationship (meaning the relationship is strong and not ID-dependent) between the two entities, as shown in Figure 5-16. We then set the maximum cardinality to 1:1. You can tell that this is a nonidentifying relationship, because the relationship line is dashed. Also, the absence of a crow's foot indicates that the relationship is 1:1.

Regarding minimum cardinality, every club member shown in the form has a locker, and every locker shown in the report is assigned to a club member, so it appears that the relationship is mandatory to mandatory. However, this form and report are just instances; they may not show every possibility. If the club allows social, nonathletic memberships, then not every club member will have a locker. Furthermore, it is unlikely that every locker is occupied; there must be some lockers that are unused and nonallocated. Accordingly, Figure 5-16 shows this relationship as optional to optional, as indicated by the small circles on the relationship lines.

Figure 5-16

Data Model for the 1:1 Relationship in Figure 5-15

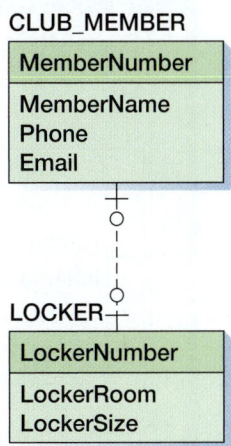

> **BY THE WAY** How do you recognize strong entities? You can use two major tests. First, does the entity have an identifier of its own? If it shares a part of its identifier with another entity, then it is an ID-dependent entity, and is therefore weak. Second, does the entity seem to be logically different from and separate from the other entities? Does it stand alone, or is it part of something else? In this case, CLUB_MEMBER and a LOCKER are two very different, separate things; they are not part of each other or of something else. Hence, they are strong.
>
> Note also that a form or report shows only one side of a relationship. Given entities A and B, a form can show the relationship from A to B, but it cannot show the relationship from B to A at the same time. To learn the cardinality from B to A, you must examine a second form or report, ask the users, or take some other action.
>
> Finally, it is seldom possible to infer minimum cardinality from a form or report. Generally, you must ask the users.

1:N Strong Entity Relationships

Figure 5-17 shows a form that lists the departments within a company. The company has many departments, so the maximum cardinality from COMPANY to DEPARTMENT is N. But what about in the opposite direction? To determine if a department relates to one or N companies, we need to examine a form or report that shows the relationship from a department to a company. However, assume that no such form or report exists. Assume that the users never view company data from the perspective of a department. We cannot ignore the issue, because we need to know whether the relationship is 1:N or N:M.

In such a case, we must ask the users or at least make a determination by thinking about the nature of the business setting. Can a department belong to more than one company? Is a department shared among companies? Because this seems unlikely, we can reasonably assume that DEPARTMENT relates to just one COMPANY. Thus, we conclude the relationship is 1:N. Figure 5-18 shows the resulting data model. Note that the many side of the relationship is indicated by the crow's foot next to DEPARTMENT.

Considering minimum cardinality, we do not know if a COMPANY must have a DEPARTMENT or if a DEPARTMENT must have a COMPANY. We will definitely need to ask the users. Figure 5-18 depicts the situation in which a DEPARTMENT must have a COMPANY, but a COMPANY need not have any DEPARTMENTs.

N:M Strong Entity Relationships

Figure 5-19(a) shows a form with data about a supplier and the parts it is prepared to supply. Figure 5-19(b) shows a report that summarizes parts and lists the companies that can supply those parts. In both cases, the relationship is many: A SUPPLIER supplies many PARTs, and a PART is supplied by many SUPPLIERs. Thus, the relationship is N:M.

Figure 5-17

Form Indicating a 1:N Relationship

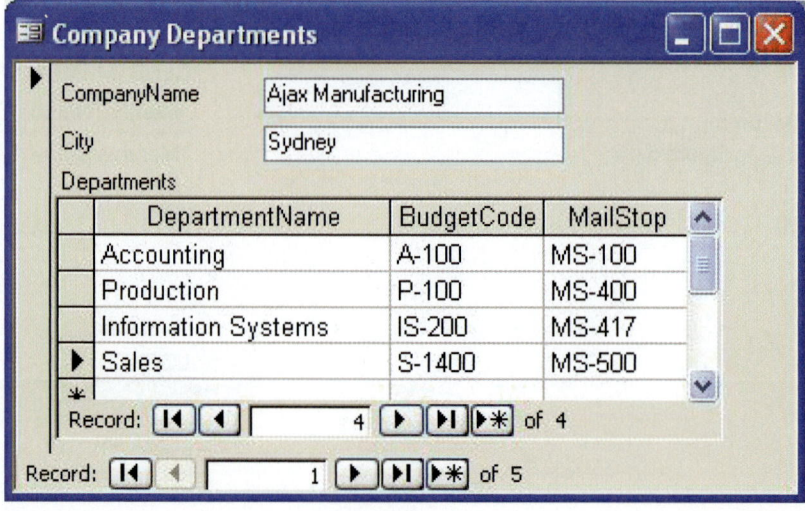

COMPANY

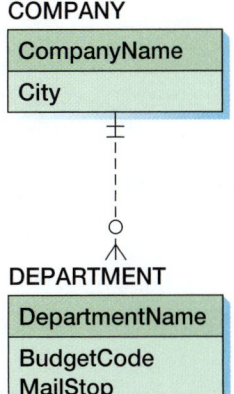

Figure 5-18

Data Model for the 1:N
Relationship in Figure 5-17

Figure 5-20 shows a data model that extends the data model in Figure 5-18 to include this new relationship. A supplier is a company, so we show the supplier entity as a COMPANY.

Because not all companies are suppliers, the relationship from COMPANY to PART must be optional. However, every part must be supplied from somewhere, so the relationship from PART to COMPANY is mandatory.

In summary, the three types of strong entity relationships are 1:1, 1:N, and N:M. You can infer the maximum cardinality in one direction from a form or report. You must examine a second form or report to determine the maximum cardinality in the other direction. If no form

Figure 5-19

Form and Report Indicating
an N:M Relationship

(a) SUPPLIERS Form

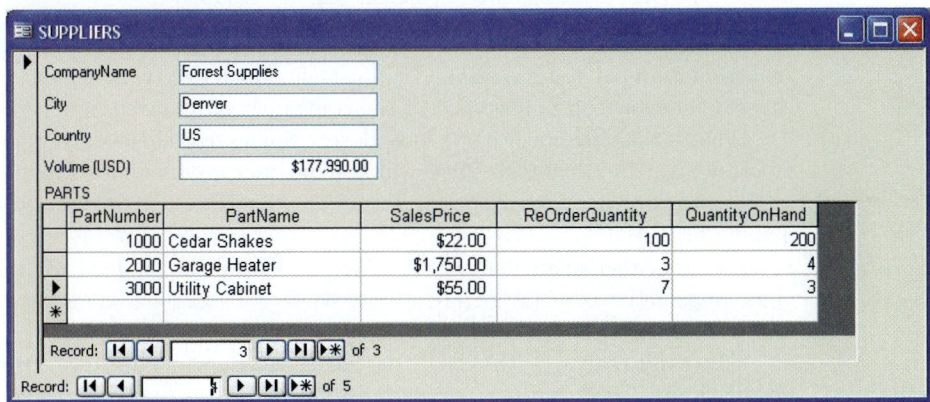

(b) PART Report

PART

Number	PartName	SalesPrice	ROQ	QOH	CompanyName	City	Country
1000	Cedar Shakes	$22.00	100	200			
					Bristol Systems	Machester	England
					ERS Systems	Vancouver	Canada
					Forrest Supplies	Denver	US
2000	Garage Heater	$1,750.00	3	4			
					Bristol Systems	Machester	England
					ERS Systems	Vancouver	Canada
					Kyoto Importers	Kyoto	Japan
					Forrest Supplies	Denver	US
3000	Utility Cabinet	$55.00	7	3			
					Ajax Manufacturing	Sydney	Australia
					Forrest Supplies	Denver	US

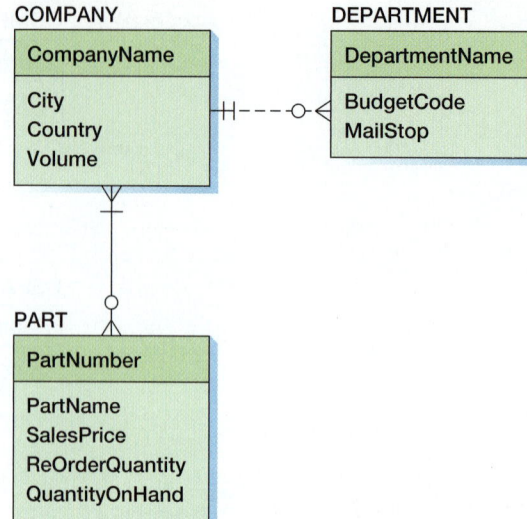

Figure 5-20

Data Model for the N:M
Relationship in Figure 5-19

or report that shows the relationship is available, you must ask the users. Generally, it is not possible to determine minimum cardinality from forms and reports.

ID-Dependent Relationships

Three principle patterns use ID-dependent entities: multivalued attribute, version/instance, and association. Because the association pattern is often confused with the N:M strong entity relationships just discussed, we will look at that pattern first.

The Association Pattern

An **association pattern** is subtly and confusingly similar to an N:M strong relationship. To see why, examine the report in Figure 5-21 and compare it with the report in Figure 5-19(b).

What is the difference? If you look closely, you'll see that the only difference is that the report in Figure 5-21 contains Price, which is the price quotation for a part from a particular supplier. The first line of this report indicates that the part Cedar Shakes is supplied by Bristol Systems for $14.00.

Price is neither an attribute of COMPANY nor is it an attribute of PART. It is an attribute of the combination of a COMPANY with a PART. Figure 5-22 shows the appropriate data model for such a case.

Here, a third entity, QUOTATION, has been created to hold the Price attribute. The identifier of QUOTATION is the combination of PartNumber and CompanyName. Note that PartNumber is the identifier of PART, and CompanyName is the identifier of COMPANY. Hence, QUOTATION is ID-dependent on *both* PART and COMPANY.

Figure 5-21

Report Indicating an
Association Pattern

Part Quotations

Number	Name	SalesPrice	ROQ	QOH	Company	City	Price
1000	Cedar Shakes	$22.00	100	200			
					Bristol Systems	Machester	$14.00
					ERS Systems	Vancouver	$12.50
					Forrest Supplies	Denver	$15.50
2000	Garage Heater	$1,750.00	3	4			
					Bristol Systems	Machester	$950.00
					ERS Systems	Vancouver	$875.00
					Kyoto Importers	Kyoto	$1,100.00
					Forrest Supplies	Denver	$915.00
3000	Utility Cabinet	$55.00	7	3			
					Ajax Manufacturing	Sydney	$37.50
					Forrest Supplies	Denver	$42.50

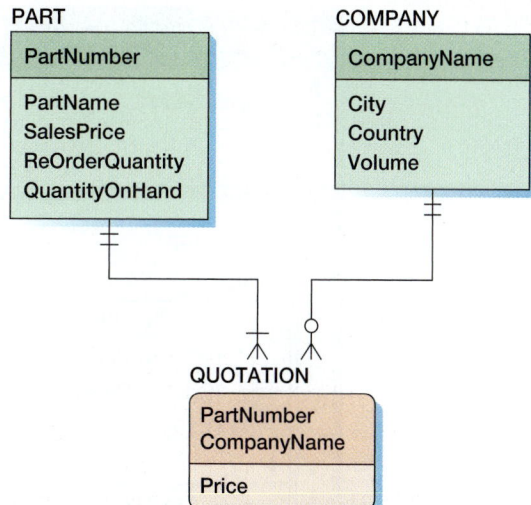

Figure 5-22

Association Pattern Data
Model for the Report in
Figure 5-21

In Figure 5-22, then, the relationships between PART and QUOTATION and between COMPANY and QUOTATION are both identifying. This fact is shown in Figure 5-22 by the solid, nondashed line that represents these relationships.

As with all identifying relationships, the parent entities are required. Thus, the minimum cardinality from QUOTATION to PART is one, and the minimum cardinality from QUOTATION to COMPANY also is one. The minimum cardinality in the opposite direction is determined by business requirements. Here, a PART must have a QUOTATION, but a COMPANY need not have a QUOTATION.

BY THE WAY   Consider the differences between the data models in Figure 5-20 and Figure 5-22. The only difference between the two is that in the latter the relationship between COMPANY and PART has an attribute, Price. Remember this example whenever you model an N:M relationship. Is there a missing attribute that pertains to the combination and not just to one of the entities? If so, you are dealing with an association, ID-dependent pattern and not an N:M, strong entity pattern.

Associations can occur among more than two entity types. Figure 5-23, for example, shows a data model for the assignment of a particular client to a particular architect for a particular

Figure 5-23

Association Pattern Data
Model for the Ternary
Relationship in Figure 5-4

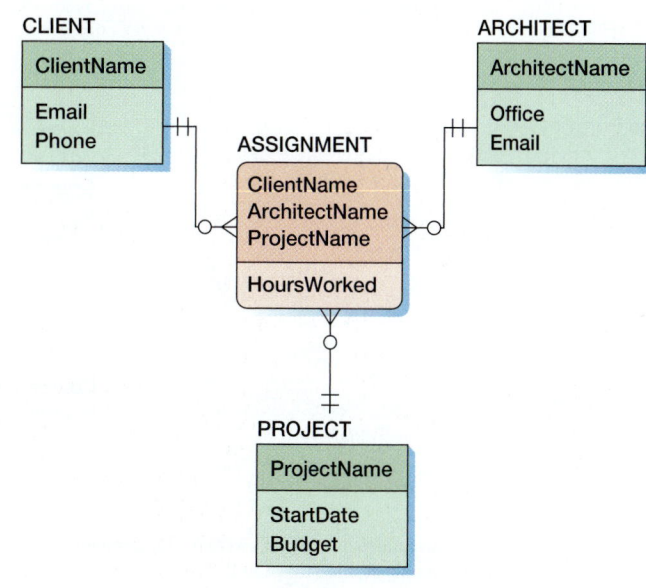

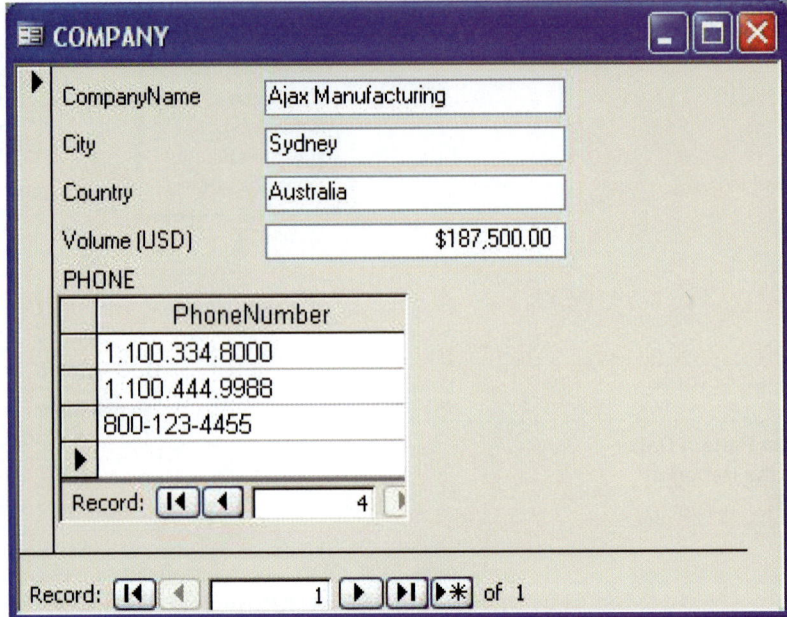

Figure 5-24

Data Entry Form with
a Multivalued Attribute

project. The attribute of the assignment is HoursWorked. This data model shows how the ternary relationship in Figure 5-4(b) can be modeled as a combination of three binary relationships.

The Multivalued Attribute Pattern

In the E-R model as used today,[5] attributes must have a single value. If the COMPANY entity has PhoneNumber and Contact attributes, then a company can have at most one value for phone number and at most one value for contact.

In practice, however, companies can have more than one phone number and one contact. Consider, for example, the data entry form in Figure 5-24. This particular company has three phone numbers; other companies might have one or two or four, or whatever. We need to create a data model that allows companies to have multiple phones, and placing the attribute PhoneNumber in COMPANY will not do it.

Figure 5-25 shows the solution. Instead of including PhoneNumber as an attribute of COMPANY, we create an ID-dependent entity, PHONE, that contains the attribute PhoneNumber. The relationship from COMPANY to PHONE is 1:N, so a company can have multiple phone numbers. Because PHONE is an ID-dependent entity, its identifier includes both CompanyName and PhoneNumber.

We can extend this strategy for as many multivalued attributes as necessary. The COMPANY data entry form in Figure 5-26 has multivalued Phone and multivalued Contact

Figure 5-25

Data Model for the Form
in Figure 5-24

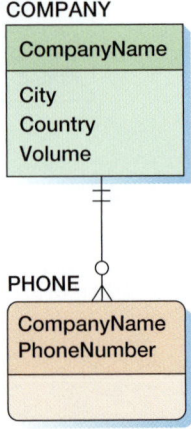

---

[5] The original E-R model allowed for multivalued attributes. Over time, that feature has been ignored, and today most people assume that the E-R model requires single-valued attributes. We will do so in this text.

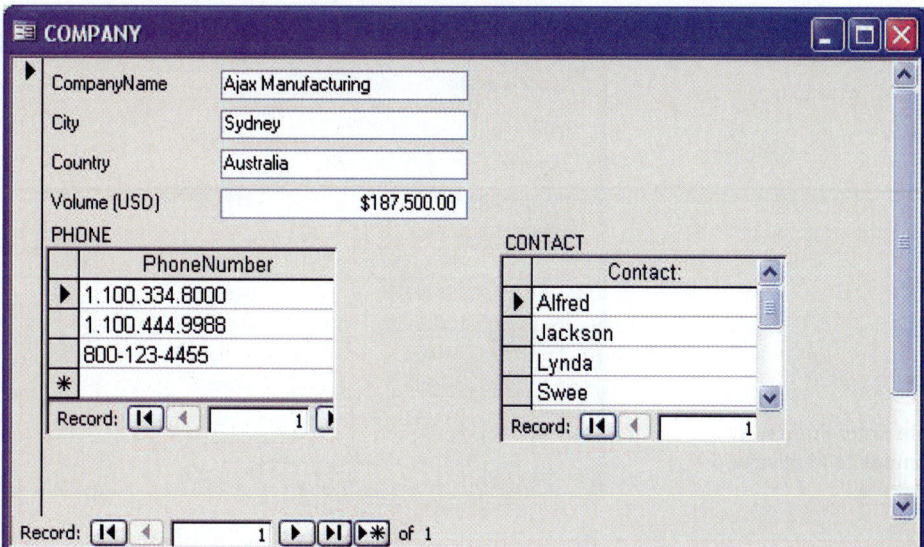

Figure 5-26

Figure 5-26

Data Entry Form with
Separate Multivalued
Attributes

attributes. In this case, we just create a separate ID-dependent entity for each multivalued attribute, as shown in Figure 5-27.

In Figure 5-27, PhoneNumber and Contact are independent. PhoneNumber is the phone number of the company and not necessarily the phone number of a contact. If PhoneNumber is not a general company phone number, but rather the phone number of a particular person at that company, then the data entry form would appear as in Figure 5-28. Here, for example, Alfred has one phone number and Jackson has another.

In this case, the attributes PhoneNumber and Contact belong together. Accordingly, we place them into a single ID-dependent entity, as shown in Figure 5-29. Notice that the identifier of PHONE_CONTACT is Contact and CompanyName. This arrangement means that a given Contact name can appear only once per company. Contacts can share phone numbers, however, as shown for employees Lynda and Swee. If the identifier of PHONE_CONTACT was PhoneNumber and CompanyName, then a phone number could occur only once per company, but contacts could have multiple numbers. Work through these examples to ensure that you understand them.

In all of these examples, the child requires a parent, which is always the case for ID-dependent entities. The parent may or may not require a child, depending on the application. A COMPANY may or may not require a PHONE or a CONTACT. You must ask the users to determine whether the ID-dependent entity is required.

Multivalued attributes are common, and you need to be able to model them effectively. Review the models in Figures 5-25, 5-27, and 5-29 and be certain that you understand their differences and what those differences imply.

Figure 5-27

Data Model for the Form
in Figure 5-26

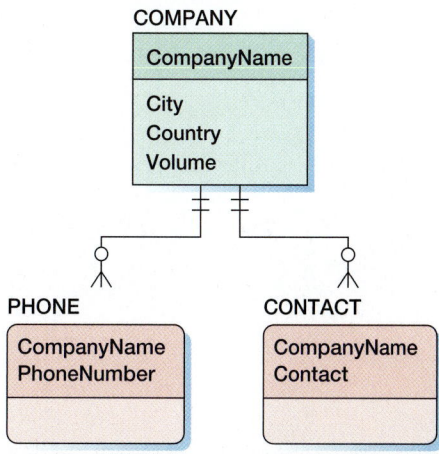

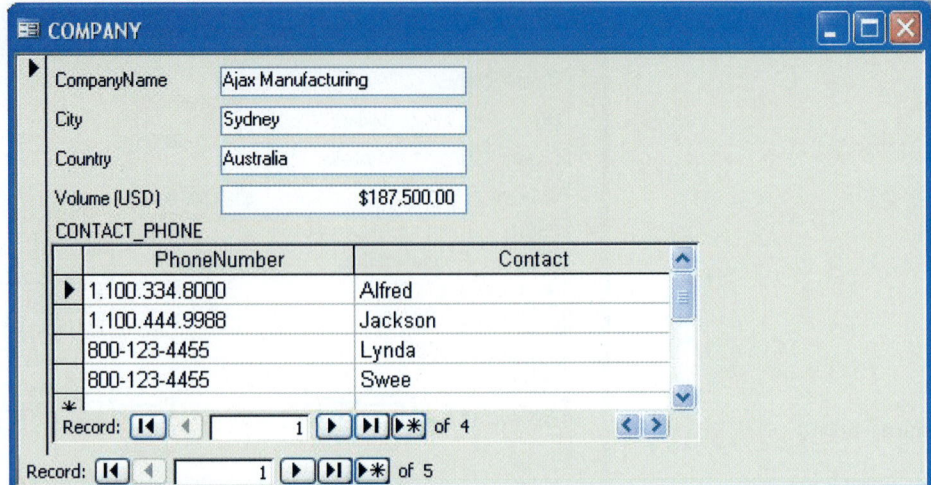

Figure 5-28

Data Entry Form with
Composite Multivalued
Attributes

The Archetype/Instance Pattern

The archetype/instance pattern occurs when one entity represents a manifestation or an instance of another entity. You have already seen one example of archetype/instance in the example of PAINTING and PRINT in Figure 5-9. The painting is the archetype, and the prints made from the painting are the instances of that archetype.

Other examples of archetype/instances are shown in Figure 5-30. One familiar example concerns classes and sections of classes. The class is the archetype, and the sections of the class are instances of that archetype. Other examples involve designs and instances of designs. A yacht manufacturer has various yacht designs, and each yacht is an instance of a particular design archetype. In a housing development, a contractor offers several different house models, and a particular house is an instance of that house model archetype.

As with all ID-dependent entities, the parent entity is required. The child entities (here SECTION, YACHT, and HOUSE) may or may not be required, depending on application requirements.

Logically, the child entity of every archetype/instance pattern is an ID-dependent entity. All three of the examples in Figure 5-30 are accurate representations of the logical structure of the underlying data. However, sometimes users will add additional identifiers to the instance entity and in the process change the ID-dependent entity to a weak entity that is not ID-dependent.

For example, although you can identify a SECTION by class name and section, colleges and universities often will add a unique identifier to SECTION, such as ReferenceNumber. In that

Figure 5-29

Data Model for the Form
in Figure 5-28

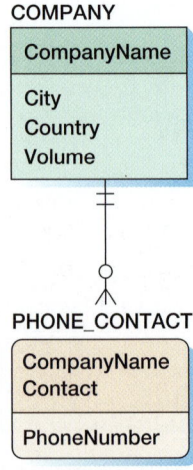

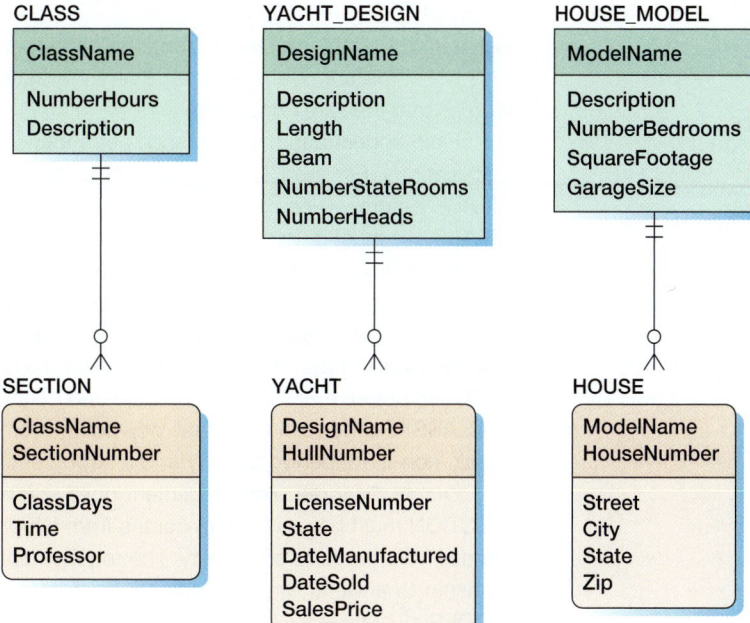

Figure **5-30**

Three Archetype/Instance
Pattern Examples

case, SECTION is no longer an ID-dependent entity, but it is still existence dependent on CLASS. Hence, as shown in Figure 5-31, SECTION is weak, but not ID-dependent.

A similar change may occur to the YACHT entity. Although the manufacturer of a yacht may refer to it by specifying the hull number of a given design, the local tax authority may refer to it by State and LicenseNumber. If we change the identifier of YACHT from (HullNumber, DesignName) to (LicenseNumber, State), then YACHT is no longer ID-dependent; it becomes a weak, non-ID-dependent entity.

Similarly, although the home builder may think of a home as the third house constructed according to the Cape Codd design, everyone else will refer to it by its address. When we change the identifier of HOUSE from (HouseNumber, ModelName) to (Street, City, State, Zip), then HOUSE becomes a weak, non-ID-dependent entity. All of these changes are shown in Figure 5-31.

Figure **5-31**

Three Weak But Not ID-
Dependent Relationships

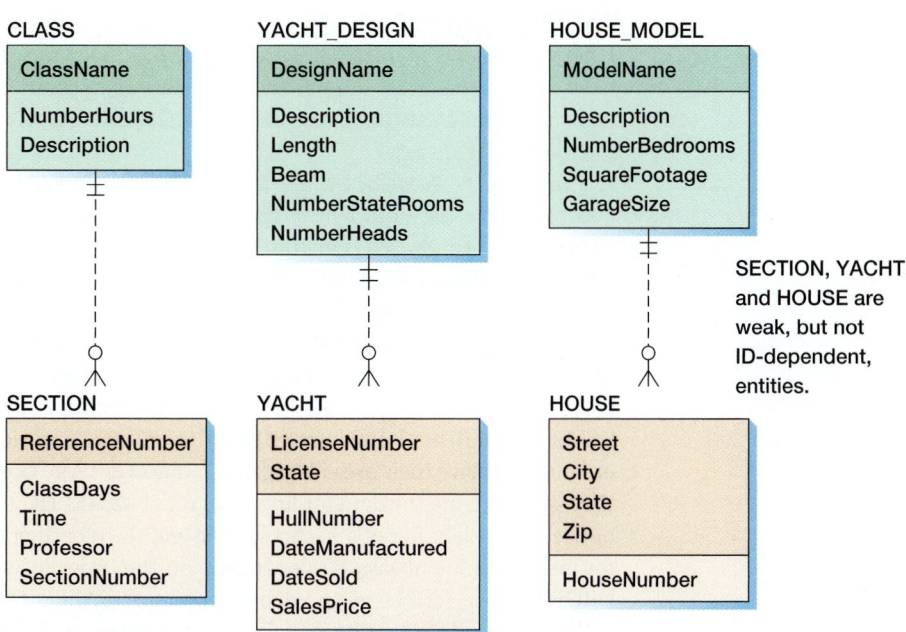

BY THE WAY Data modelers continue to debate the importance of weak, non-ID-dependent entities. Everyone agrees that they exist, but not everyone agrees that they are important.

First, understand that existence dependence influences the way we write database applications. For the CLASS/SECTION example in Figure 5-31, we must insert a new CLASS before we can add a SECTION for that class. Additionally, when we delete a CLASS, we must delete all of the SECTIONs for that CLASS as well. This is one reason that some data modelers believe that weak, non-ID-dependent entities are important.

Skeptics say that although weak, non-ID-dependent entities may exist, they are not necessary. They say that we can obtain the same result by calling SECTION strong and making CLASS required. Because CLASS is required, the application will need to insert a CLASS before a SECTION is created and delete dependent SECTIONs when deleting a CLASS. So, according to that viewpoint, there is no practical difference between a weak, non-ID-dependent entity and a strong entity with a required relationship.

Others disagree. Their argument goes something like this: The requirement that a SECTION must have a CLASS comes from a logical necessity. It has to be that way—it comes from the nature of reality. The requirement that a strong entity must have a relationship to another strong entity arises from a business rule. Initially, we say that an ORDER must have a CUSTOMER (both strong entities), and then the application requirements change and we say that we can have cash sales, meaning that an ORDER no longer has to have a CUSTOMER. Business rules change frequently, but logical necessity never changes. We need to model weak, non-ID-dependent entities so that we know the strength of the required parent rule.

And so it goes. You, with the assistance of your instructor, can make up your own mind. Is there a difference between a weak, non-ID-dependent entity and a strong entity with a required relationship? In Figure 5-31, should we call the entities SECTION, YACHT, and HOUSE strong, as long as their relationships are required? We think not; We think there is a difference. Others think differently, however.

Mixed Identifying and Nonidentifying Patterns

Some patterns involve both identifying and nonidentifying relationships. The classic example is the line-item pattern, but there are other instances of mixed patterns as well. We begin with line items.

The Line-Item Pattern

Figure 5-32 shows a typical sales order, or invoice. Such forms usually have data about the order itself, such as the order number and order date, data about the customer, data about the salesperson, and then data about the items on the order. A data model for a typical SALES_ORDER is shown in Figure 5-33.

In Figure 5-35, CUSTOMER, SALESPERSON, and SALES_ORDER are all strong entities, and they have the nonidentifying relationships you would expect. The relationship from CUSTOMER to SALES_ORDER is 1:N, and the relationship from SALESPERSON to SALES_ORDER also is 1:N. According to this model, a SALES_ORDER must have a CUSTOMER and may or may not have a SALESPERSON. All of this is readily understood.

The interesting relationships concern the line items on the order. Examine the data grid in the form in Figure 5-32. Some of the data values belong to the order itself, but other data values belong to items in general. In particular, Quantity and ExtendedPrice belong to the SALES_ORDER, but ItemNumber, Description, and UnitPrice belong to ITEM. The lines on an order do not have their own identifier. No one ever says, "Give me the data for line 12." Instead, they say, "Give me the data for line 12 of order 12345." Hence, the identifier of a line is a composite of the identifier of a particular line and the identifier of a particular order. Thus, entries for line items are always ID-dependent on the order in which they appear. In Figure 5-33, ORDER_LINE_ITEM is ID-dependent on SALES_ORDER. The identifier of the ORDER_LINE_ITEM entity is (SalesOrderNumber, LineNumber).

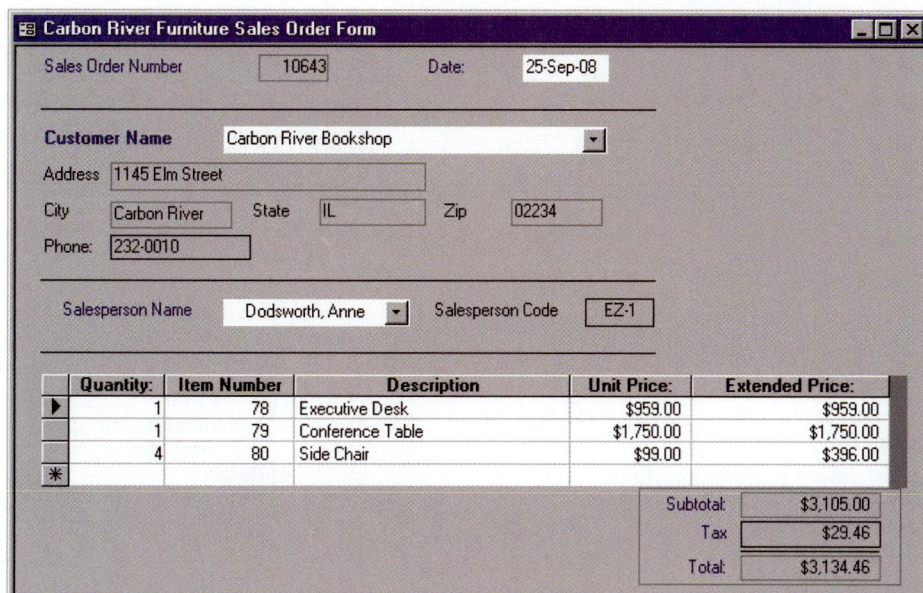

Figure 5-32

Data Entry Form for a Sales
Order

Now, and this is the part that is sometimes confusing for some students, ORDER_
LINE_ITEM is not existence dependent on ITEM. It can exist even if no item has yet been
assigned to it. Further, if an ITEM is deleted, we do not want the line item to be deleted with it.
The deletion of an ITEM may make the value of ItemNumber and other data invalid, but it
should not cause the line item itself to disappear.

Now consider what happens to a line item when an order is deleted. Unlike with the
deletion of an item, which only causes data items to become invalid, the deletion of the order
removes the existence of the line item. Logically, a line item cannot exist if its order is deleted.
Hence, line items are existence dependent on orders.

Work through each of the relationships in Figure 5-33 and ensure that you understand their
type and their maximum and minimum cardinalities. Also understand the implications of this

Figure 5-33

Data Model for the Sales
Order in Figure 5-33

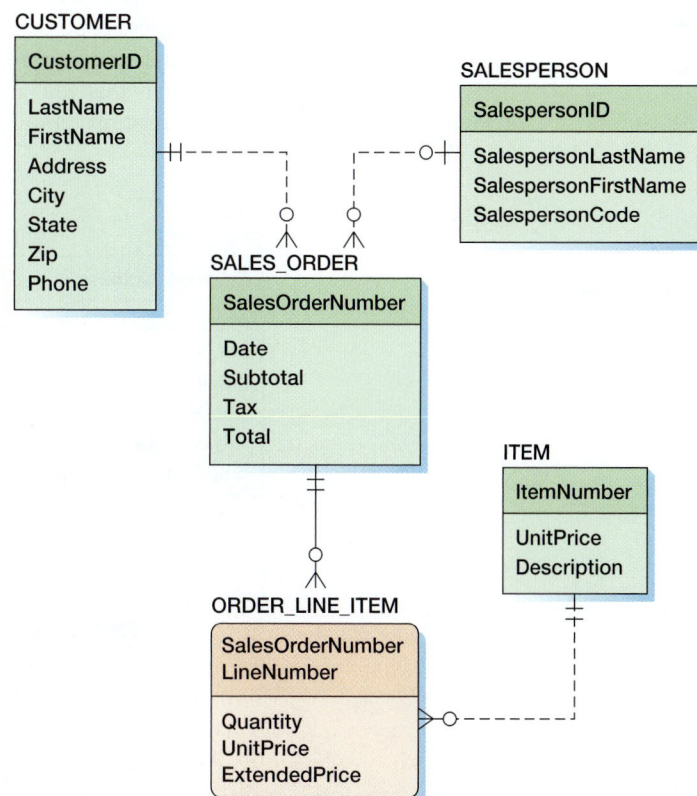

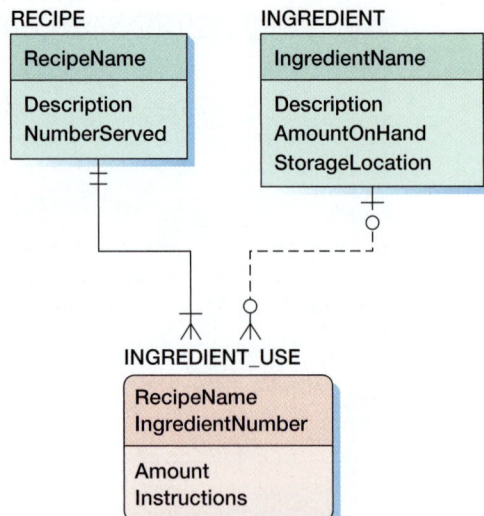

Figure 5-34

Mixed Relationship Pattern
for Restaurant Recipe

model. For example, do you see why this sales order is unlikely to be used by a company in which salespeople are on commission?

Other Mixed Patterns

Mixed identifying and nonidentifying relationships occur frequently. Learn to look for a mixed pattern when a strong entity has a multivalued composite group and when one of the elements in the composite group is an identifier of a second strong entity.

Consider, for example, baking recipes. Each recipe calls for a certain amount of a specific ingredient, such as flour, sugar, or butter. The ingredient list is a multivalued composite group, but one of the elements of that group, the name of the ingredient, is the identifier of a strong entity. As shown in Figure 5-34, the recipe and the ingredients are strong entities, but the amount and instructions for using each ingredient are ID-dependent on RECIPE.

Or, consider employees' skill proficiencies. The name of the skill and the proficiency level the employee has are a multivalued group, but the skill itself is a strong entity, as shown in Figure 5-35. Dozens of other examples are possible.

Before continuing, compare the models in Figures 5-33, 5-34, and 5-35 with the association pattern in Figure 5-22. Make sure that you understand the differences and why the model in Figure 5-24 has two identifying relationships and the models in Figures 5-33, 5-34, and 5-35 have just one.

Figure 5-35

Mixed Relationship Pattern
for Employee Skills

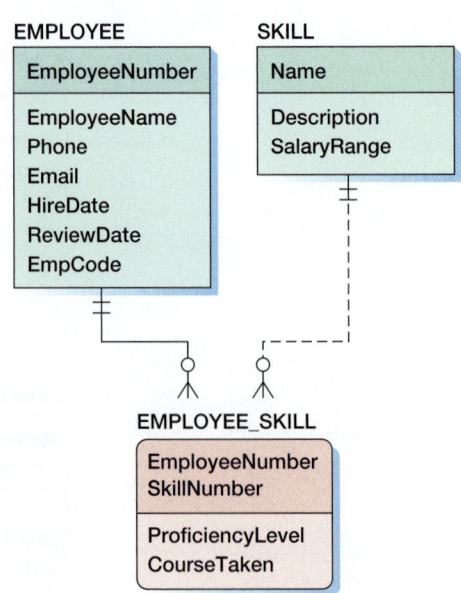

Resident Fishing License 2009 Season *State of Washington*			**License No:** **03-1123432**
Name:			
Street:			
City:		State:	Zip:
For Use by Commercial Fishers Only		For Use by Sport Fishers Only	
Vessel Number:		Number Years at This Address:	
Vessel Name:		Prior Year License Number:	
Vessel Type:			
Tax ID:			

Figure 5-36

Data Entry Form Suggesting
the Need for Subtypes

The For-Use-By Pattern

As stated earlier in this chapter, the major reason for using subtypes in a database design is to avoid value-inappropriate nulls. Some forms suggest the possibility of such nulls when they show blocks of data fields that are grayed out and labeled "For Use by *someone/something* Only." For example, Figure 5-36 shows two grayed-out sections, one for commercial fishers and another for sport fishers. The presence of these grayed-out sections indicates the need for subtype entities.

The data model for this form is shown in Figure 5-37. Observe that each grayed-out section has a subtype. Notice that the subtypes differ not only in their attributes, but that one has a relationship that the other does not have. Sometimes, the only differences between subtypes are differences in the relationships they have.

The nonidentifying relationship from VESSEL to COMMERCIAL_LICENSE is shown as 1:N, mandatory to mandatory. In fact, this form does not have sufficient data for us to conclude that the maximum cardinality from VESSEL to COMMERCIAL_LICENSE is N. This fact was determined by interviewing users and learning that one boat is sometimes used by more than one commercial fisher. The minimum cardinalities indicate a commercial fisher must have a vessel, and that only vessels that are used for licenses are to be stored in this database.

The point of this example is to illustrate how forms often suggest the need for subtypes. Whenever you see a grayed out or otherwise distinguished section of a form with the words "For use by . . . ," think "subtype."

Figure 5-37

Data Model for Form
in Figure 5-36

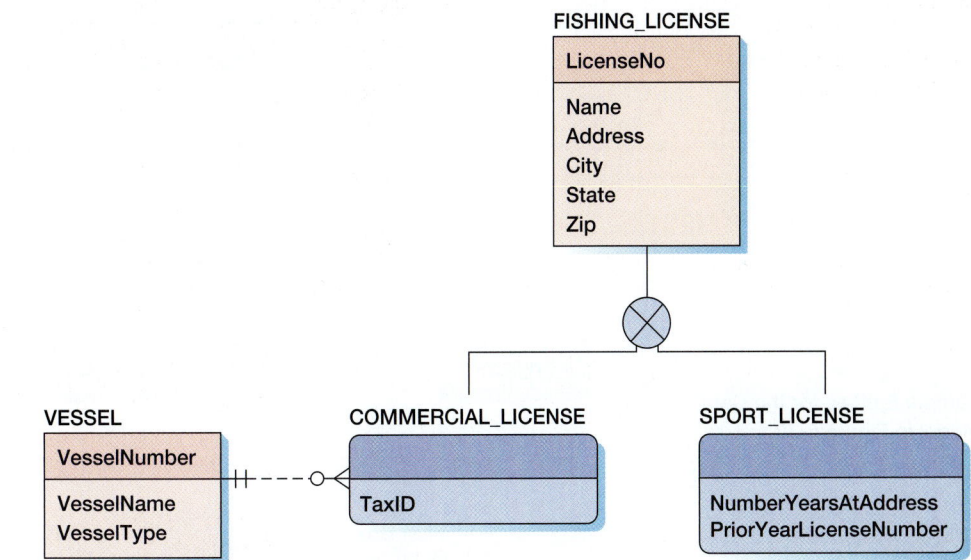

Recursive Patterns

A recursive relationship occurs when an entity type has a relationship to itself. The classic examples of recursive relationships occur in manufacturing applications, but there are many other examples as well. As with strong entities, three types of recursive relationships are possible: 1:1, 1:N, and N:M. Let's consider each.

1:1 Recursive Relationships

Suppose you are asked to construct a database for a railroad, and you need to make a model of a freight train. You know that one of the entities is BOXCAR, but how are BOXCARs related? To answer that question, envision a train. Except for the first boxcar, each has one boxcar in front and, except for the last boxcar, each boxcar has one boxcar in back. Thus, the relationship is 1:1 between boxcars, with an optional relationship for the first and last cars.

Figure 5-38 shows a data model in which each BOXCAR has a 1:1 relationship to the BOXCAR ahead. The BOXCAR entity at the head of the train has a 1:1 relationship to ENGINE. (This model assumes a train has just one engine. To model trains with multiple engines, create a second recursive relationship among engines. Construct that relationship just like the Boxcar Ahead relationship.)

Figure 5-39 shows example entity instances that illustrate this data model. Not surprisingly, this set of entity instances looks just like a train.

An alternative model is to use the relationship to represent the BOXCAR behind. Either model works. Other examples of 1:1 recursive relationships are the succession of U.S. presidents, the succession of deans in a college of business, and the order of passengers on a waiting list.

1:N Recursive Relationships

The classic example of a 1:N recursive relationship occurs in organizational charts, in which an employee has a manager who may, in turn, manage several other employees. Figure 5-40 shows an example managerial chart. Note that the relationship between employees is 1:N.

Figure 5-38

Data Model for a 1:1
Recursive Relationship

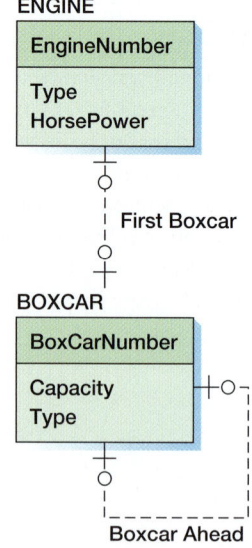

Figure 5-39

Sample Entities for the Data
Model in Figure 5-38

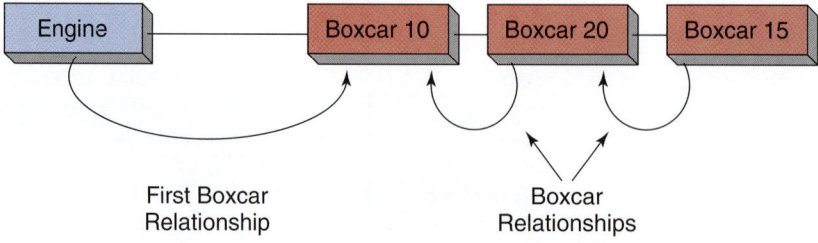

Figure 5-40

Managerial Relationships

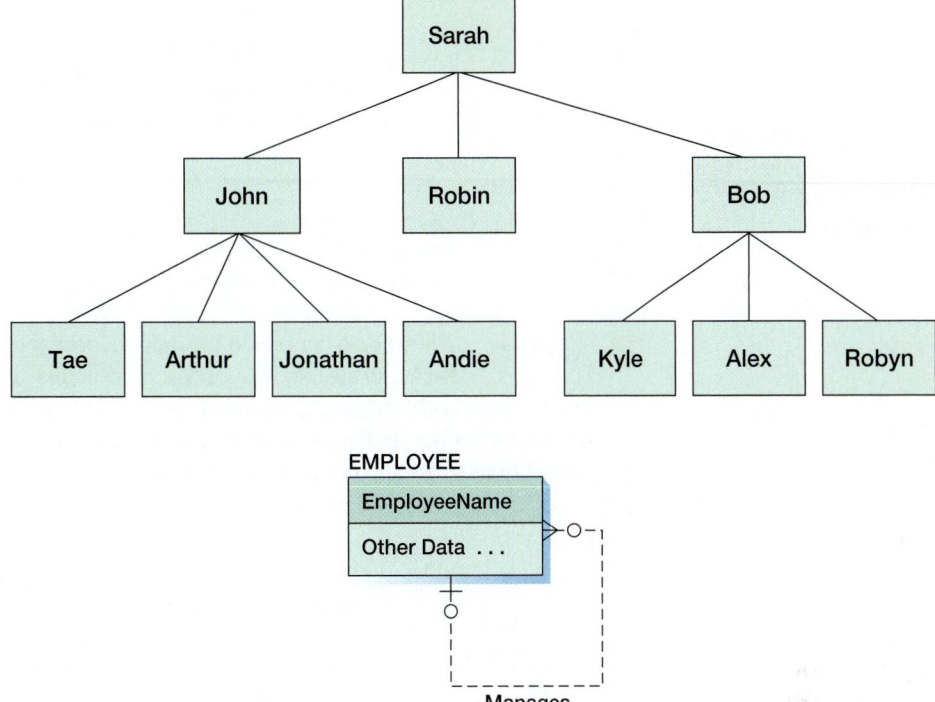

Figure 5-41

Data Model for the
Management Structure in
Figure 5-40 as a 1:N
Recursive Relationship

Figure 5-41 shows a data model for the managerial relationship. The crow's foot indicates that a manager may manage more than one employee. The relationship is optional to optional because one manager (the president) has no manager and because some employees manage no one.

Another example of a 1:N recursive relationship concerns maps. For example, a world map has a relationship to many continent maps, each continent map has a relationship to many nation maps, and so forth. A third example concerns biological parents where the relationship from PERSON to PERSON is shown by tracing either mother or father (but not both).

N:M Recursive Relationships

N:M recursive relationships occur frequently in manufacturing applications, where they are used to represent bills of materials. Figure 5-42 shows an example.

The key idea of a bill of materials is that one part is composed of other parts. A child's red wagon, for example, consists of a handle assembly, a body, and a wheel assembly, each of which is a part. The handle assembly, in turn, consists of a handle, a bolt, a washer, and a nut. The wheel assembly consists of wheels, axles, washers, and nuts. The relationship among the parts is N:M, because a part can be made up of many parts and because a part (such as washers and nuts) can be used in many parts.

The data model for a bill of materials is shown in Figure 5-43. Notice that each part has an N:M relationship to other parts. Because a part need not have any component parts, and because a part need not have any parts that contain it, the minimum cardinality is optional to optional.

Figure 5-42

Bill of Materials

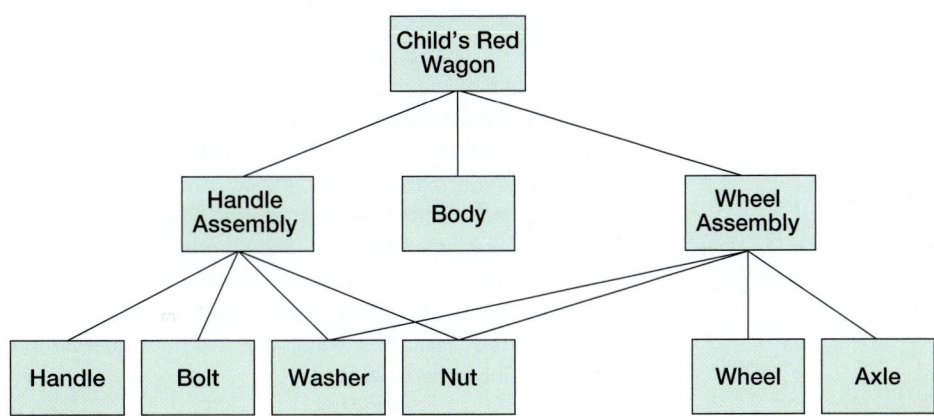

Figure 5-43

Data Model for the Bill of
Materials in Figure 5-42 as
an N:M Recursive
Relationship

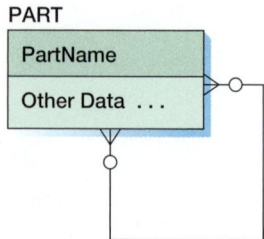

PART
PartName
Other Data . . .

BY THE WAY   What would happen to the data model if the diagram showed how many of
each part are used? Suppose, for example, that the wheel assembly requires
four washers and the handle assembly requires just one. The data model in Figure 5-43
will not be correct for this circumstance. In fact, adding Quantity to this N:M relationship
is analogous to adding Price to the N:M relationship in Figure 5-22. See question 5.67.

N:M recursive relationships can be used to model directed networks, such as the flow of
documents through organizational departments or the flow of gas through a pipeline. They also
can be used to model the succession of parents, in which mothers, fathers, and stepparents are
included.

If recursive structures seem hard to comprehend, don't fret. They may seem strange at first,
but they are not difficult. Work through some data examples to gain confidence. Make up a
train and see how the model in Figure 5-38 applies or change the example in Figure 5-40 from
employees to departments and see how the model in Figure 5-41 needs to be adjusted. Once you
have learned to identify recursive patterns, you'll find it easy to create models for them.

The Data Modeling Process

During the data modeling process, the development team analyzes user requirements and
constructs a data model from forms, reports, data sources, and user interviews. The process is
always iterative; a model is constructed from one form or report and then supplemented and
adjusted as more forms and reports are analyzed. Periodically, users are asked for additional
information, such as that needed to assess minimum cardinality. Users also review and validate
the data model. During that review, prototypes evidencing data model constructs may need to
be constructed, as explained earlier.

To give you an idea of the iterative nature of data modeling, we will consider the development of a simple data model for a university. As you read this example, strive to appreciate how
the model evolves as more and more requirements are analyzed.

BY THE WAY   One of the authors worked on a large data model for the U.S. Army's logistical system. The model contained over 500 different entity types, and it
took a team of seven people more than a year to develop, document, and validate. On
some occasions, the analysis of a new requirement indicated that the model had been
conceived incorrectly, and days of work had to be redone. The most difficult aspect of
the project was managing complexity. Knowing which entities related to which; whether
an entity had already been defined; and whether a new entity was strong, weak, a supertype, or a subtype required a global understanding of the model. Memory was of poor
help because an entity created in July could be a subtype of an entity created hundreds
of entities earlier in February. To manage the model, the team used many different administrative tools. Keep this example in mind as you read through the development of the
Highline University data model.

Figure 5-44

Highline University Sample
College Report

College of Business			
Mary B. Jefferson, Dean			
Phone: 232-1187		Campus Address:	
		Business Building, Room 100	
Department	**Chairperson**	**Phone**	**Total Majors**
Accounting	Jackson, Seymour P.	232-1841	318
Finance	HeuTeng, Susan	232-1414	211
Info Systems	Brammer, Nathaniel D.	236-0011	247
Management	Tuttle, Christine A.	236-9988	184
Production	Barnes, Jack T.	236-1184	212

Suppose the administration at a hypothetical university named Highline University wants to create a database to track colleges, departments, faculty, and students. To do this, a data modeling team has collected a series of reports as part of its requirements determination. In the next sections, we will analyze these reports to produce a data model.

The College Report

Figure 5-44 shows an example report from Highline University about one college within the university, specifically, the College of Business. This example is one instance of this report; Highline University has similar reports about other colleges, such as the College of Engineering and the College of Social Sciences. The data modeling team needs to gather enough examples to form a representative sample of all the college reports. Here, assume that the report in Figure 5-44 is representative.

Examining the report, we find data specific to the college—such as the name, dean, telephone number, and campus address—and also facts about each department within the college. These data suggest that the data model should have COLLEGE and DEPARTMENT entities with a relationship between them, as shown in Figure 5-45.

The relationship in Figure 5-45 is nonidentifying. This relationship is used because DEPARTMENT is not ID-dependent, and, logically, a DEPARTMENT is independent of a COLLEGE. We cannot tell from the report in Figure 5-44 whether a department can belong to many colleges. To answer this question, we need to ask the users or look at other forms and reports.

Assume we know from the users that a department belongs to just one college, and the relationship is thus 1:N from COLLEGE to DEPARTMENT. The report in Figure 5-44 does not show us the minimum cardinalities. Again, we must ask the users. Assume we learn from the users that a college must have at least one department, and a department must be assigned to exactly one college.

The Department Report

The Department Report shown in Figure 5-46 contains departmental data along with a list of the professors who are assigned to that department.

This report contains data concerning the department's campus address. Because these data do not appear in the DEPARTMENT entity in Figure 5-45, we need to add them, as shown

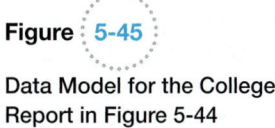

Figure 5-45

Data Model for the College
Report in Figure 5-44

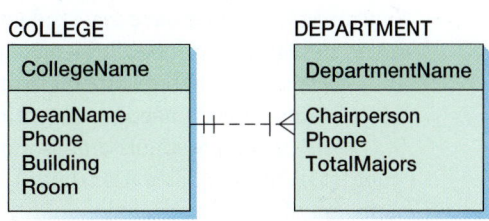

Information Systems Department
College of Business

Chairperson: Brammer, Nathaniel D
Phone: 236-0011
Campus Address: Social Science Building, Room 213

Professor	Office	Phone
Jones, Paul D.	Social Science, 219	232-7713
Parks, Mary B	Social Science, 308	232-5791
Wu, Elizabeth	Social Science, 207	232-9112

Figure 5-46

Highline University Sample
Department Report

in Figure 5-47(a). This is typical of the data modeling process. That is, entities and relationships are adjusted as additional forms, reports, and other requirements are analyzed.

Figure 5-47(a) also adds the relationship between DEPARTMENT and PROFESSOR. We initially model this as an N:M relationship, because a professor might have a joint appointment. The data modeling team must further investigate the requirements to determine whether joint appointments are allowed. If not, the relationship can be redefined as a nonidentifying 1:N, as shown in Figure 5-47(b).

Another possibility regarding the N:M relationship is that some attribute about the combination of a professor and a department is missing. If so, then an association pattern is more appropriate. At Highline, suppose the team finds a report that describes the title and employment terms for each professor in each department. Figure 5-47(c) shows an entity for such a report, named APPOINTMENT. As you would expect from the association pattern, APPOINTMENT is ID-dependent on both DEPARTMENT and PROFESSOR.

A chairperson is a professor, so another improvement on the model is to remove the Chairperson data from DEPARTMENT and replace it with a chairperson relationship. This has been done in Figure 5-47(d). In the Chairs/Chaired By relationship, the PROFESSOR is the parent entity. A professor can be a chair of zero or one departments, and a department must have exactly one professor as chair.

With the Chairs/Chaired By relationship, the attribute Chairperson is no longer needed in DEPARTMENT, so it is removed. Normally, a chairperson has his or her office in the department office; if this is the case, Phone, Building, and Room in DEPARTMENT duplicate Phone, Building, and OfficeNumber in PROFESSOR. Consequently, it might be possible to remove Phone, Building, and Room from DEPARTMENT. However, a professor may have a different phone from the official department phone, and the professor may also have an office outside of the department's office. Because of this possibility, we will leave Phone, Building, and Room in DEPARTMENT.

The Department/Major Report

Figure 5-48 shows a report of a department and the students who major in that department. This report indicates the need for a new entity called STUDENT. Because students are not ID-dependent on departments, the relationship between DEPARTMENT and STUDENT is non-identifying, as shown in Figure 5-49. We cannot determine the minimum cardinality from Figure 5-48, but assume that interviews with users indicate that a STUDENT must have MAJOR, but no MAJOR need have any students. Also, using the contents of this report as a guide, attributes StudentNumber, StudentName, and Phone are placed in STUDENT.

There are two subtleties in this interpretation of the report in Figure 5-48. First, observe that Major's Name was changed to StudentName when the attribute was placed in STUDENT. This was done because StudentName is more generic. Major's Name has no meaning outside the context of the Major relationship. Additionally, the report heading in Figure 5-48 has an ambiguity. Is the phone number for the department a value of DEPARTMENT.Phone or a value

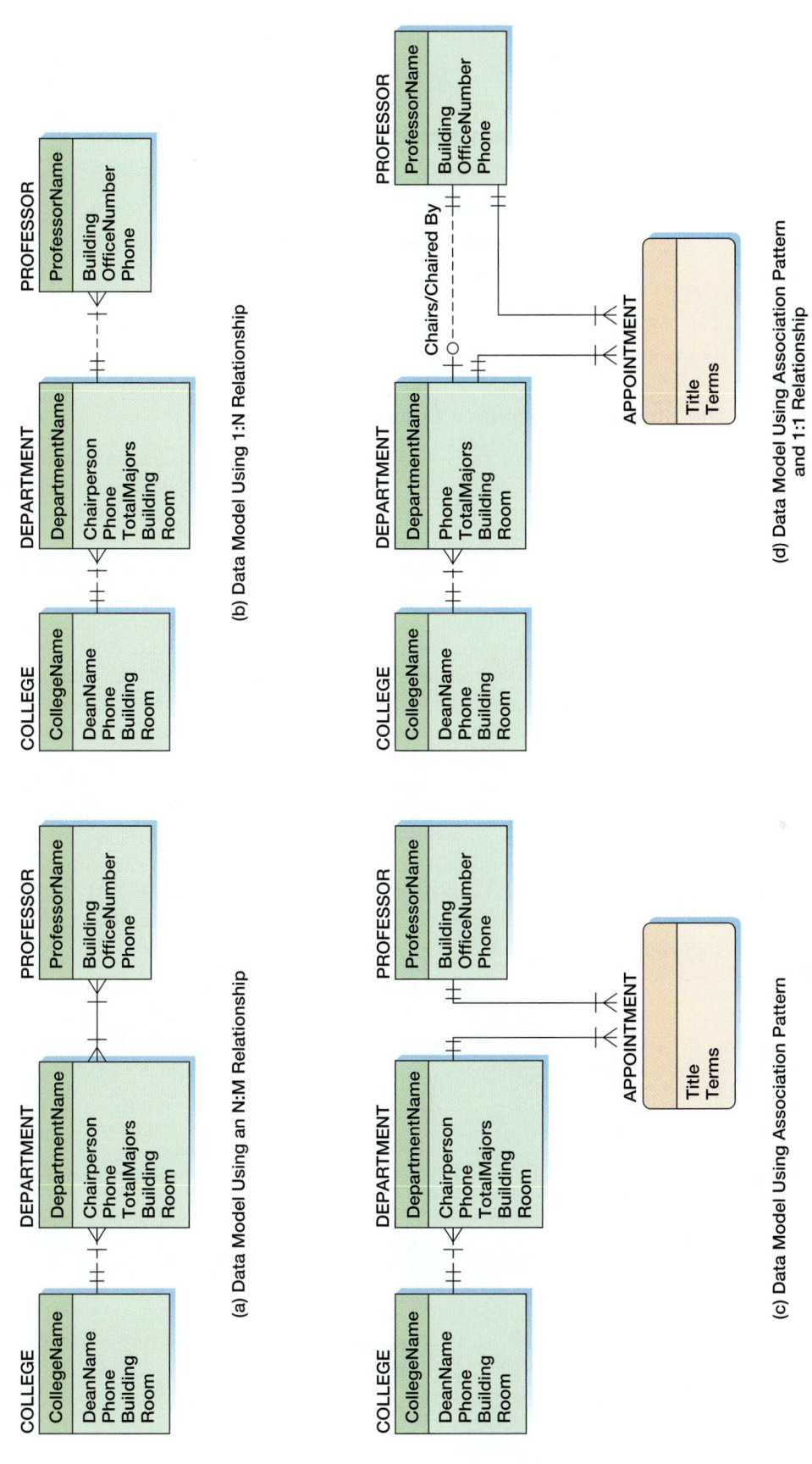

(a) Data Model Using an N:M Relationship

(b) Data Model Using a 1:N Relationship

(c) Data Model Using Association Pattern

(d) Data Model Using Association Pattern and 1:1 Relationship

Figure 5-47

Alternate Data Models for the DEPARTMENT-to-PROFESSOR Relationship

Student Major List
Information Systems Department

Chairperson: Brammer, Nathaniel D   Phone: 236-0011

Major's Name	Student Number	Phone
Jackson, Robin R.	12345	237-8713
Lincoln, Fred J.	48127	237-8713
Madison, Janice A.	37512	237-8713

Figure 5-48

Highline University Sample
Department Student Report

of PROFESSOR.Phone? The team needs to investigate this further with the users. Most likely, it is a value of DEPARTMENT.Phone.

The Student Acceptance Letter

Figure 5-50 shows the acceptance letter that Highline sends to its incoming students. The data items in this letter that need to be represented in the data model are shown in boldface. In addition to data concerning the student, this letter also contains data regarding the student's major department as well as data about the student's adviser.

We can use this letter to add an Advises/Advised By relationship to the data model. However, which entity should be the parent of this relationship? Because an adviser is a professor, it is tempting to make PROFESSOR the parent. However, a professor acts as an adviser within the context of a particular department. Therefore, Figure 5-51 shows APPOINTMENT as the parent of STUDENT. To produce the report in Figure 5-50, the professor's data can be retrieved by accessing the related APPOINTMENT entity and then accessing that entity's PROFESSOR parent. This decision is not cut-and-dried, however. One can make a strong argument that the parent of the relationship should be PROFESSOR.

According to this data model, a student has at most one adviser. Also, a student must have an adviser, but no professor (via APPOINTMENT) need advise any students. These constraints cannot be determined from any of the reports shown and will need to be verified with the users. The acceptance letter uses the title *Mr.* in the salutation. Therefore, a new attribute called Title is added to STUDENT. Observe that this Title is different from the one in APPOINTMENT. This difference will need to be documented in the data model to avoid confusion. The acceptance letter also shows the need to add new home address attributes to STUDENT.

Figure 5-49

Data Model with STUDENT
Entity

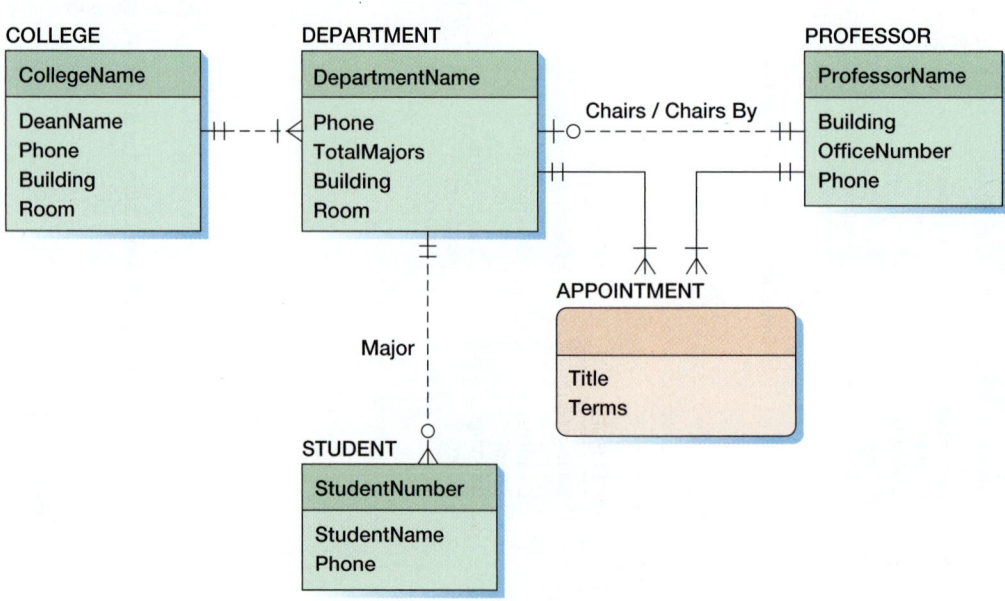

Mr. Fred Parks
123 Elm Street
Los Angeles, CA 98002

Dear Mr. Parks:

You have been admitted as a major in the **Accounting** Department at Highline University, starting in the Fall Semester, 2009. The office of the Accounting Department is located in the **Business** Building, Room **210**.

Your adviser is professor **Elizabeth Johnson**, whose telephone number is 232-**8740** and whose office is located in the **Business** Building, Room **227**. Please schedule an appointment with your adviser as soon as you arrive on campus.

Congratulations and welcome to Highline University!

Sincerely,

Jan P. Smathers
President

JPS/rkp

Figure 5-50

Highline University Sample Student Acceptance Letter

The acceptance letter reveals a problem. The name of the student is Fred Parks, but we have allocated only one attribute, StudentName, in STUDENT. It is difficult to reliably disentangle first and last names from a single attribute, so a better model is to have two attributes: StudentFirstName and StudentLastName. Similarly, note that the adviser in this letter is Elizabeth Johnson. So far, all professor names have been in the format Johnson, Elizabeth. To accommodate both forms of name, ProfessorName in PROFESSOR must be changed to the two attributes ProfessorFirstName and ProfessorLastName. A similar change is necessary for Dean-Name. These changes are shown in Figure 5-52, which is the final form of this data model.

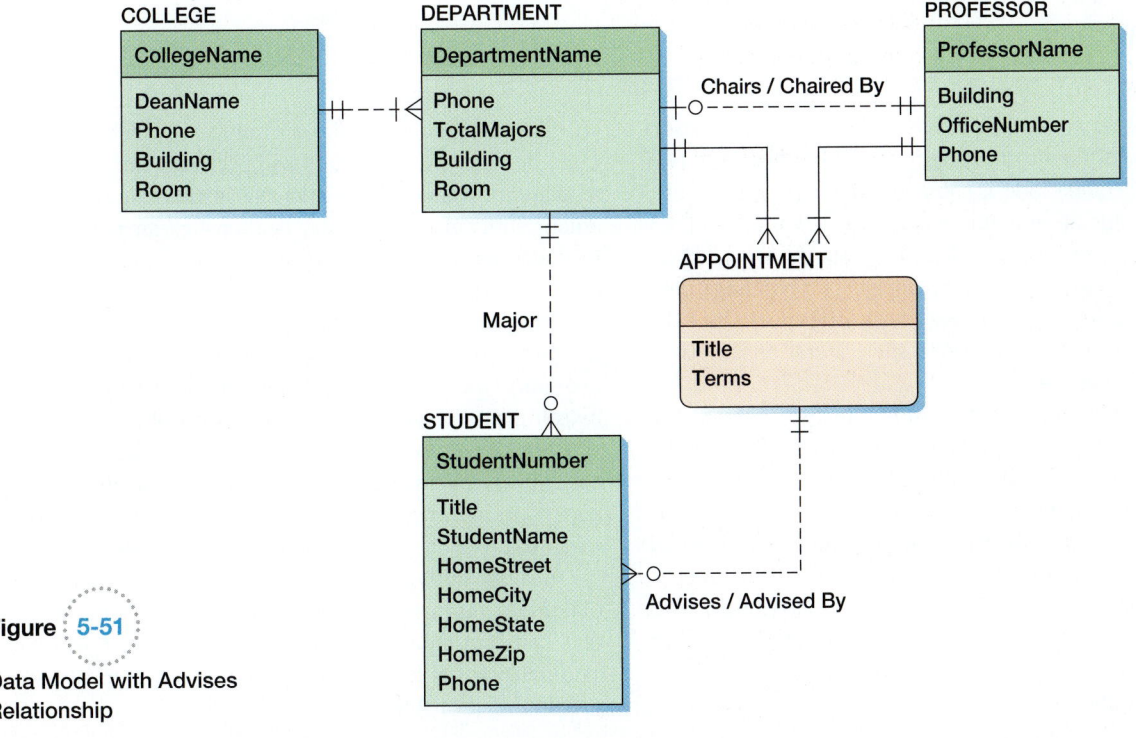

Figure 5-51

Data Model with Advises Relationship

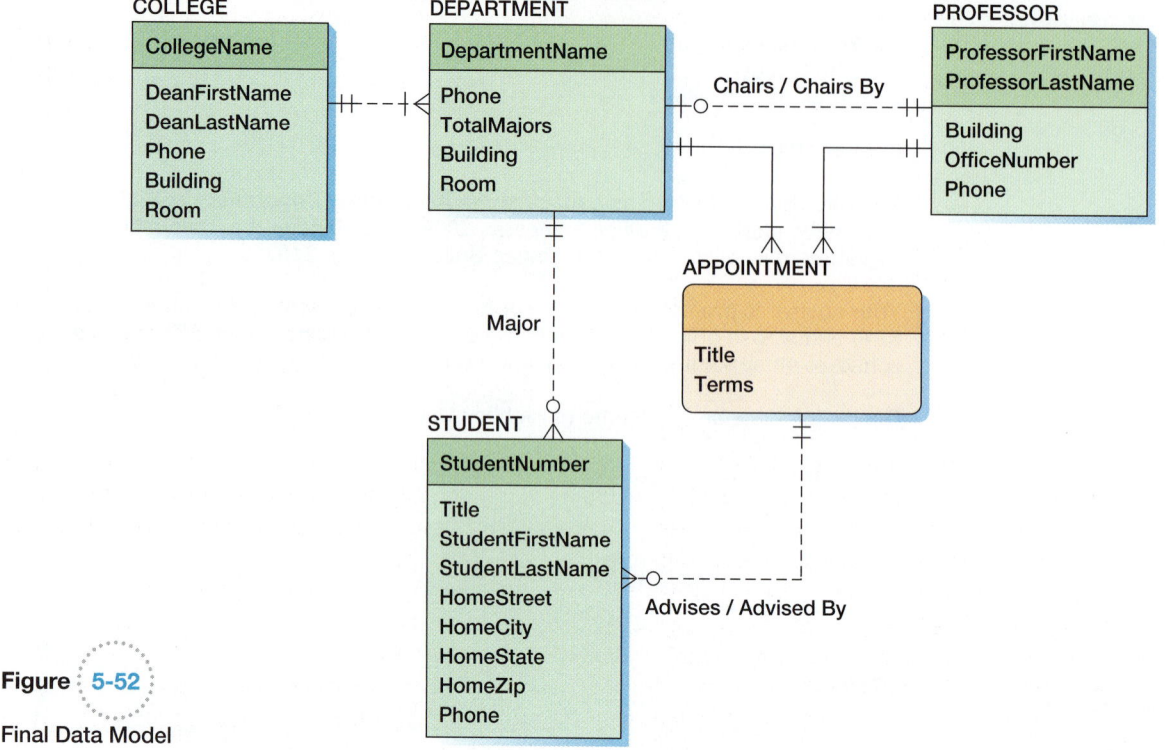

Figure 5-52

Final Data Model

This section should give you a feel for the nature of a data modeling project. Forms and reports are examined in sequence, and the data model is adjusted as necessary to accommodate the knowledge gained from each new form or report. It is very typical to revise the data model many, many times throughout the data modeling process. See question 5.68 for yet another possible revision.

Summary

When databases are developed as part of a new information systems project, the database design is accomplished in two phases. First, a data model is constructed from forms, reports, data sources, and other requirements. The data model is then transformed into a database design. A data model is a blueprint for a database design. Like blueprints for buildings, data models can be altered as necessary, with little effort. Once the database is constructed, however, such alterations are time consuming and very expensive.

The most prominent data model in use today is the entity-relationship, or E-R, data model. It was invented by Peter Chen and extended by others to include subtypes. An entity is something that users want to track. An entity class is a collection of entities of the same type and is described by the structure of the entities in the class. An entity instance is one entity of a given class. Entities have attributes that describe their characteristics. Identifiers are attributes that name entity instances. Composite identifiers consist of two or more attributes.

The E-R model includes relationships, which are associations among entities. Relationship classes are associations among entity classes, and relationship instances are associations among entity instances. Today, relationships are not allowed to have attributes. Relationships can be given names so that they can be identified.

The degree of a relationship is the number of entity types that participate in the relationship. Binary relationships have only two entity types. In practice, relationships of degrees greater than two are decomposed into multiple binary relationships.

The difference between an entity and a table is that you can express an entity relationship without specifying foreign keys. Working with entities reduces complexity and makes it easier to revise the data model as work progresses.

Relationships are classified according to their cardinality. Maximum cardinality is the maximum number of instances that can participate in a relationship instance. Minimum cardinality is the least number of entities that must participate in a relationship.

Relationships commonly have one of three maximum cardinalities: 1:1, 1:N, or N:M. In rare instances, a maximum cardinality might be a specific number, such as 1:15. Relationships commonly have one of four basic minimum cardinalities: optional to optional, mandatory to optional, optional to mandatory, or mandatory to mandatory. In rare cases, the minimum cardinality is a specific number.

Unfortunately, many variations of the E-R model are in use. The original version represented relationships with diamonds. The Information Engineering version uses a line with a crow's foot, the IDEF1X version uses another set of symbols, and UML uses yet another set. To add further complication, many data modeling products have added their own symbols. In this text, we will use the IE Crow's Foot model with symbols, as summarized in Figure 5-14. Other models and techniques are summarized in Appendices B, C, and E.

An ID-dependent entity is an entity whose identifier includes the identifier of another entity. Such entities use an identifying relationship. In such relationships, the parent is always required, but the child (the ID-dependent entity) may or may not be required, depending on application requirements. Identifying relationships are shown with solid lines in E-R diagrams.

A weak entity is an entity whose existence depends on the presence of another entity. All ID-dependent entities are weak. Additionally, some entities are weak, but not ID-dependent. Some people believe such entities are not important; others believe they are.

A subtype entity is a special case of another entity called its supertype. Subtypes may be exclusive or inclusive. Exclusive subtypes sometimes have discriminators, which are attributes that specify a supertype's subtype. The most important (and perhaps only) reason for creating subtypes in a data model is to avoid value-inappropriate nulls.

Relationships among nonsubtype entities are called HAS-A relationships. Relationships among supertype/subtype entities are called IS-A relationships.

The elements of a data model are constructed by analyzing forms, reports, and data sources. Many forms and reports fall into common patterns. In this text, we discussed the 1:1, 1:N, and N:M strong entity patterns. We also discussed three patterns that use ID-dependent relationships: association, multivalue attribute, and version/instance. Some forms involve mixed identifying and nonidentifying patterns. Line items are the classic example of mixed forms, but there are other examples as well.

The for-use-by pattern indicates the need for subtypes. In some cases, subtypes differ because they have different attributes, but they also can differ because they have different relationships. A recursive relationship occurs when an entity has a relationship to itself. The three types of recursive relationship are 1:1, 1:N, and N:M.

The data modeling process is iterative. Forms and reports are analyzed, and the data model is created, modified, and adjusted as necessary. Sometimes, the analysis of a form or report will require that earlier work be redone. *C'est la vie!*

Key Terms

association pattern	Information Engineering (IE) model
attribute	Integrated Definition 1, Extended (IDEF1X)
binary relationship	IS-A relationship
cardinality	mandatory-to-mandatory (M-M) relationship
child	mandatory-to-optional (M-O) relationship
composite identifier	many-to-many (N:M) relationship
crow's foot symbol	maximum cardinality
data model	minimum cardinality
degree	nonidentifying relationship
discriminator	one-to-many (1:N) relationship
entity	one-to-one (1:1) relationship
entity class	optional-to-mandatory (O-M) relationship
entity instance	optional-to-optional (O-O) relationship
entity-relationship (E-R) diagrams	parent
entity-relationship (E-R) model	relationship
exclusive subtype	relationship class
extended E-R model	relationship instance
HAS-A relationship	strong entity
ID-dependent entity	subtype
identifier	supertype
identifying relationship	ternary relationship
IE Crow's foot model	Unified Modeling Language (UML)
inclusive subtype	weak entity

Review Questions

5.1   Describe the two phases in designing databases that arise from the development of new information systems.

5.2   In general terms, explain how a data model could be used to design a database for a small video rental store.

5.3   Explain how a data model is like a building blueprint. What is the advantage of making changes during the data modeling stage?

5.4   Who is the author of the entity-relationship data model?

5.5   Define *entity*. Give an example of an entity (other than one presented in this chapter).

5.6   Explain the difference between an entity class and an entity instance.

5.7   Define *attribute*. Give an example attribute for the entity in your answer to Review Question 5.5.

5.8   Define *identifier*. Give an example identifier for the entity in your answer to Review Question 5.5.

5.9   Give an example of a composite identifier.

5.10 Define *relationship*. Give an example of a relationship (other than one presented in this chapter). Name your relationship.

5.11 Explain the difference between a relationship class and a relationship instance.

5.12 What is the degree of relationship? Give an example of a relationship of degree three (other than one presented in this chapter).

5.13 What is a binary relationship?

5.14 Explain the difference between an entity and a table. Why is this difference important?

5.15 What does cardinality mean?

5.16 Define the terms *maximum cardinality* and *minimum cardinality*.

5.17 Give examples of 1:1, 1:N, and N:M relationships (other than those presented in this chapter). Use the traditional diamond notation to diagram your examples.

5.18 Give an example for which the maximum cardinality must be an exact number.

5.19 Give examples of M-M, M-O, O-M, and O-O relationships (other than those presented in this chapter). Use the circle and hash mark notation on the diamond portrayal of relationships.

5.20 Explain, in general terms, how the traditional E-R model, the IE Crow's Foot version, the IDEF1X version, and the UML version differ. Which version is used primarily in this text?

5.21 Explain how the notations shown in Figure 5-7 differ.

5.22 Explain how the notations shown in Figure 5-9 differ.

5.23 What is an ID-dependent entity? Give an example of an ID-dependent entity (other than one presented in this chapter).

5.24 Explain how to determine the minimum cardinality of both sides of an ID-dependent relationship.

5.25 What rules exist when creating an instance of an ID-dependent entity? What rules exist when deleting the parent of an ID-dependent entity?

5.26   What is an identifying relationship? How is it used?

5.27   Explain why the relationship between PRODUCT and VERSION discussed on page 154 is an identifying relationship.

5.28   What is a weak entity? How do weak entities relate to ID-dependent entities?

5.29   What distinguishes a weak entity from a strong entity that has a required relationship to another entity?

5.30   Define *subtype* and *supertype*. Give an example of a subtype–supertype relationship (other than one presented in this chapter).

5.31   Explain the difference between exclusive subtypes and inclusive subtypes. Give an example of each.

5.32   What is a discriminator?

5.33   Explain the difference between IS-A and HAS-A relationships.

5.34   What is the most important reason for using subtypes in a data model?

5.35   Describe the relationship between the structure of forms and reports and the data model.

5.36   Explain two ways forms and reports are used for data modeling.

5.37   Explain why the form and report in Figure 5-15 indicate that the underlying relationship is 1:1.

5.38   Why is it not possible to infer minimum cardinality from the form and report in Figure 5-15?

5.39   Describe two tests for determining if an entity is a strong entity.

5.40   Why does the form in Figure 5-17 not indicate that the underlying relationship is 1:N? What additional information is required to make that assertion?

5.41   Explain why two forms or reports are usually needed to infer maximum cardinality.

5.42   How can you assess minimum cardinality for the entities in the form in Figure 5-17?

5.43   Explain why the form and report in Figure 5-19 indicate that the underlying relationship is N:M.

5.44   Name three patterns that use ID-dependent relationships.

5.45   Explain how the association pattern differs from the N:M strong entity pattern. What characteristic of the report in Figure 5-21 indicates that an association pattern is needed?

5.46   In general terms, explain how to differentiate an N:M strong entity pattern from an association pattern.

5.47   Explain why two entities are needed to model multivalued attributes.

5.48   How do the forms in Figures 5-26 and 5-28 differ? How does this difference affect the data model?

5.49   Describe, in general terms, the archetype/instance pattern. Why is an ID-dependent relationship needed for this pattern? Use the CLASS/SECTION example shown in Figure 5-30 in your answer.

5.50   Explain what caused the entities in Figure 5-31 to change from ID-dependent entities.

5.51   Summarize the two sides in the argument about the importance of weak, but not ID-dependent, entities.

5.52   Give an example of the line-item pattern as it could be used to describe the contents of a shipment. Assume that the shipment includes the names and quantities of various items as well as each item's insured value. Place the insurance value per item in an ITEM entity.

5.53   What entity type should come to mind when you see the words "For use by" in a form?

5.54   Give examples of 1:1, 1:N, and N:M recursive relationships (other than those presented in this chapter).

5.55   Explain why the data modeling process must be iterative. Use the Highline University example.

Project Questions

5.56   This question is for Visio users. Convert the data models in Figures 5-16, 5-20, 5-22, 5-23, 5-30, 5-33, 5-37, and 5-52 into Visio format. Use the Visio arrow notation.

5.57   This question is for Visio users. Convert the data models in Figures 5-16, 5-20, 5-22, 5-23, 5-30, 5-33, 5-37, and 5-52 into Visio format. Use the Visio version of the IE Crow's Foot model.

Answer the following questions using IE Crow's Foot notation.

5.58   Examine the subscription form shown in Figure 5-53.

Using the structure of this form, do the following:

A.   Create a model with one entity. Specify the identifier and attributes.

B.   Create a model with two entities, one for customer and a second for subscription. Specify identifiers, attributes, relationship name, type, and cardinalities.

C.   Under what conditions do you prefer the model in A to that in B?

D.   Under what conditions do you prefer the model in B to that in A?

5.59   Consider the traffic citation shown in Figure 5-54.

The rounded corners on this form provide graphical hints about the boundaries of the entities represented.

A.   Create a data model with five entities. Use the data items on the form to specify identifiers and attributes for those entities.

B.   Specify relationships among the entities. Name the relationship and give its type and cardinalities. Indicate which cardinalities can be inferred from data on the form and which need to be checked out with systems users.

Figure

Subscription Form

Fine Wood ▲▲▲▲▲Working   **To subscribe**

☐ 1 year (6 issues) for just $18—20% off the newsstand price.
(Outside the U.S. $21/year—U.S. funds, please)

☐ 2 years (12 issues) for just $34—save 24%
(Outside the U.S. $40/2 years—U.S. funds, please)

Name _____

Address_____

City_____ State _____ Zip _____

☐ My payment is enclosed. ☐ Please bill me.

Please start my subscription with ☐ *current issue* ☐ *next issue* .

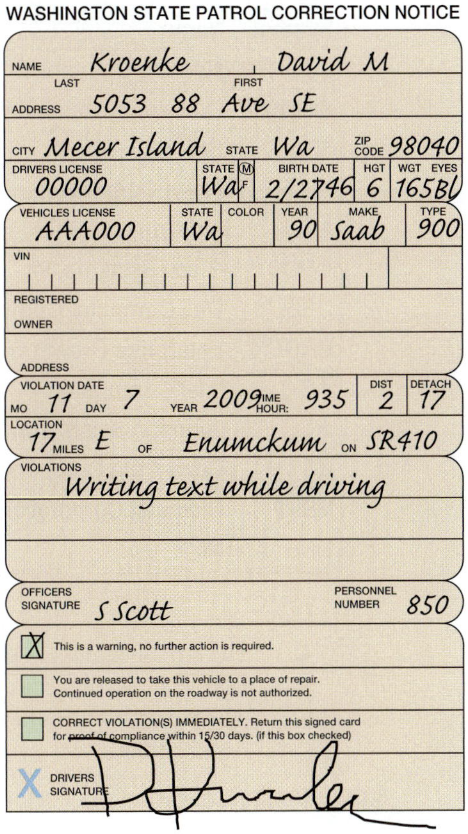
WASHINGTON STATE PATROL CORRECTION NOTICE

NAME Kroenke, David M
LAST FIRST
ADDRESS 5053 88 Ave SE
CITY Mecer Island STATE Wa ZIP CODE 98040
DRIVERS LICENSE 00000 STATE Wa M F BIRTH DATE 2/27/46 HGT 6 WGT 165 EYES Bl
VEHICLES LICENSE AAA000 STATE Wa COLOR YEAR 90 MAKE Saab TYPE 900
VIN
REGISTERED OWNER
ADDRESS
VIOLATION DATE MO 11 DAY 7 YEAR 2009 TIME HOUR: 935 DIST 2 DETACH 17
LOCATION 17 MILES E OF Enumckum ON SR410
VIOLATIONS Writing text while driving
OFFICERS SIGNATURE S Scott PERSONNEL NUMBER 850
[X] This is a warning, no further action is required.
[ ] You are released to take this vehicle to a place of repair. Continued operation on the roadway is not authorized.
[ ] CORRECT VIOLATION(S) IMMEDIATELY. Return this signed card for proof of compliance within 15/30 days. (if this box checked)
X DRIVERS SIGNATURE

Figure 5-54

Traffic Citation

5.60 Examine the list of e-mail messages in Figure 5-55.

Using the structure and example data items in this list, do the following:

A. Create a single-entity data model for this list. Specify the identifier and all entities.

B. Modify your answer to A to include entities SENDER and SUBJECT. Specify the identifiers and attributes of entities and the type and cardinalities of the relationships. Explain which cardinalities can be inferred from Figure 5-55 and which need to be checked out with users.

Figure 5-55

E-mail List

	From	Subject	Date	Size
☐	WDA2259@sailmail.com	Big Wind	5/13/2009	3 KB
☐	WDA2259@sailmail.com	Update	5/12/2009	4 KB
☐	WDA2259@sailmail.com	Re: Saturday Am	5/11/2009	4 KB
☐	WDA2259@sailmail.com	Re: Weather window!	5/10/2009	4 KB
☐	WDA2259@sailmail.com	Re: Howdy!	5/10/2009	3 KB
☐	WDA2259@sailmail.com	Still here	5/9/2009	3 KB
☐	WDA2259@sailmail.com	Re: Turle Bay	5/8/2009	4 KB
☐	WDA2259@sailmail.com	Turle Bay	5/8/2009	4 KB
☐	WDA2259@sailmail.com	Re: Hi	5/6/2009	3 KB
☐	WDA2259@sailmail.com	Sunday, Santa Maria	5/5/2009	3 KB
☐	Ki6yu@aol.com	Cabo, Thurs. Noon	5/2/2009	2 KB
☐	WDA2259@sailmail.com	turbo	5/1/2009	3 KB
☐	WDA2259@sailmail.com	on our way	4/28/2009	3 KB
☐	Tom Cooper	RE: Hola!	4/26/2009	3 KB
☐	Tom Cooper	RE: Hola!	4/24/2009	2 KB
☐	Tom Cooper	RE: Hola!	4/23/2009	3 KB

Symbol	Name	Last	Change	% Chg
$COMPX	Nasdaq Combined Composite Index	1,400.74 ▼	-4.87	-0.35%
$INDU	Dow Jones Industrial Average Index	9,255.10 ▼	-19.80	-0.21%
$INX	S&P 500 INDEX	971.14 ▼	-5.84	-0.60%
ALTR	Altera Corporation	13.45 ▼	-0.450	-3.24%
AMZN	Amazon.com, Inc.	15.62 ▲	+0.680	+4.55%
CSCO	Cisco Systems, Inc.	13.39 ▼	-0.280	-2.05%
DELL	Dell Computer Corporation	24.58 ▼	-0.170	-0.69%
ENGCX	Enterprise Growth C	14.60 ▼	-0.210	-1.42%
INTC	Intel Corporation	18.12 ▼	-0.380	-2.05%
JNJ	Johnson & Johnson	53.29 ▼	-0.290	-0.54%
KO	Coca-Cola Company	56.70 ▼	-0.580	-1.01%
MSFT	Microsoft Corporation	53.96 ▲	+1.040	+1.97%
NKE	NIKE, Inc.	57.34 ▲	+0.580	+1.02%

Figure  5-56

Stock Quotations

C. The e-mail address in the From column in Figure 5-55 is in two different styles. One style has the true e-mail address; the second style (e.g., Tom Cooper) is the name of an entry in the user's e-mail directory. Create two categories of SENDER based on these two styles. Specify identifiers and attributes.

5.61 Examine the list of stock quotes in Figure 5-56.

Using the structure and example data items in this list, do the following:

A. Create a single-entity data model for this list. Specify the identifier and attributes.

B. Modify your answer to A to include the entities COMPANY and INDEX. Specify the identifier and attributes of the entities and the type and cardinalities of the relationships. Explain which cardinalities can be inferred from Figure 5-56 and which need to be checked out with users.

C. The list in Figure 5-56 is for a quote on a particular day at a particular time of day. Suppose that the list were changed to show closing daily prices for each of these stocks and that it includes a new column: QuoteDate. Modify your model in B to reflect this change.

D. Change your model in C to include the tracking of a portfolio. Assume the portfolio has an owner name, a phone number, an e-mail address, and a list of stocks held. The list includes the identity of the stock and the number of shares held. Specify all additional entities, their identifiers and attributes, and the type and cardinality of all relationships.

E. Change your answer to part D to keep track of portfolio stock purchases and sales in a portfolio. Specify entities, their identifiers and attributes, and the type and cardinality of all relationships.

5.62 Figure 5-57 shows the specifications for single-stage air compressor products.

Note that there are two product categories that are based on Air Performance: The A models are at 125 pounds per square inch of pressure, and the E models are at 150 pounds per square inch of pressure. Using the structure and example data items in this list, do the following:

A. Create a set of exclusive subtypes to represent these compressors. The supertype will have attributes for all single-stage compressors, and the subtypes will have attributes for products having the two different types of Air Performance. Assume that there might be additional products with different types of Air Performance.

| | | | Air Performance | | | | | | Approx Ship Weight | Dimensions | | |
| | | | A @ 125 | | | E @ 150 | | | | | | |
HP	Model	Tank Gal	Pump RPM	CFM Disp	DEL'D Air	Pump RPM	CFM Disp	DEL'D Air		L	W	H
1/2	F12A-17	17	680	3.4	2.2	590	2.9	1.6	135	37	14	25
3/4	F34A-17	17	1080	5.3	3.1	950	4.7	2.3	140	37	14	25
3/4	F34A-30	30	1080	5.3	3.1	950	4.7	2.3	160	38	16	31
1	K1A-30	30	560	6.2	4.0	500	5.7	3.1	190	38	16	34
1 1/2	K15A-30	30	870	9.8	6.2	860	9.7	5.8	205	49	20	34
1 1/2	K15A-60	60	870	9.8	6.2	860	9.7	5.8	315	38	16	34
2	K2A-30	30	1140	13.1	8.0	1060	12.0	7.0	205	49	20	39
2	K2A-60	60	1140	13.1	8.0	1060	12.0	7.0	315	48	20	34
2	GC2A-30	30	480	13.1	9.1	460	12.4	7.9	270	38	16	36
2	GC2A-60	60	480	13.1	9.1	460	12.4	7.9	370	49	20	41
3	GC3A-60	60	770	21.0	14.0	740	19.9	12.3	288	38	16	36
5	GC5A-80	60	770	21.0	14.0	740	19.9	12.3	388	49	20	41
5	GC5A-60	60	1020	27.8	17.8	910	24.6	15.0	410	49	20	41
5	GC5A-80	80	1020	27.8	17.8	910	24.6	15.0	450	62	20	41
5	J5A-80	60	780	28.7	19.0	770	28.6	18.0	570	49	23	43
5	J5A-80	80	780	28.7	19.0	770	28.6	18.0	610	63	23	43

Single Stage
Set 95 to 150 PSI also available, substitute "E" for "A" in model number. i.e., K15A-30 make K15E-30

Figure 5-57

Air Compressor
Specifications

Specify the entities, identifiers, attributes, relationships, type of category cluster, and possible determinant.

B. Figure 5-58 shows a different model for the compressor data. Explain the entities, their type, the relationship, its type, and its cardinality. How well do you think this model fits the data shown in Figure 5-57?

C. Compare your answer in part A with the model in Figure 5-58. What are the essential differences between the two models? Which do you think is better?

D. Suppose you had the job of explaining the differences in these two models to a highly motivated, intelligent end user. How would you accomplish this?

5.63 Figure 5-59 shows a listing of movie times at theaters in Seattle.

Using the data in this figure as an example, do the following:

A. Create a model to represent this report using the entities MOVIE, THEATER, and SHOW_TIME. Assume that theaters may show multiple movies. Although this report is for a particular day, your data model should allow for movie times on different days as well. Specify the identifier of the entities and their attributes. Name the relationships and the type and cardinality of all relationships. Explain which cardinalities you can logically deduce from Figure 5-59 and which need to be checked out with users. Assume that distance is an attribute of THEATER.

Figure 5-58

Alternative Model for
Compressor Data

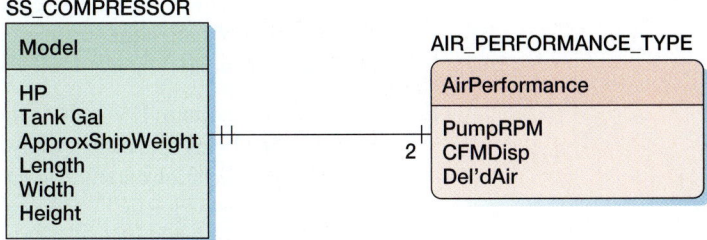

```
Movie
```

Men in Black II

Even Tommy Lee Jones at his funniest can't save Will Smith or this
goofy alien flick from sequel-itis.

Local Theaters and Showtimes

40 miles from the center of Seattle, WA Change Area
Tue, Jul 9 Wed Thu Fri Sat

Displaying 1 - 32 results, sorted by distance.

AMC Pacific Place 11 (0.5 miles)
600 Pine St, Seattle (206) 652-2404
Showtimes: 11:00 am, 12:00 pm, 12:45 pm, 1:30 pm, 2:30 pm, 3:15 pm, 4:00
pm, 5:00 pm, 5:45 pm, 6:30 pm, 7:30 pm, 8:30 pm, 9:00 pm, 10:00 pm, 10:45
pm

Neptune Theatre (3.9 miles)
1303 NE 45th, Seattle (206) 633-5545
Showtimes: 11:20 am, 1:30 pm, 3:40 pm, 5:50 pm, 8:00 pm, 10:10 pm

Regal Bellevue Galleria 11 (6.2 miles)
500 106th Ave NE, Bellevue (425) 451-7161
Showtimes: 11:00 am, 11:30 am, 1:00 pm, 1:30 pm, 3:00 pm, 3:30 pm, 5:05
pm, 5:35 pm, 7:10 pm, 7:40 pm, 9:20 pm, 9:50 pm

LCE Oak Tree Cinema (6.6 miles)
10006 Aurora Ave N., Seattle (206) 527-1748
Showtimes: 11:45 am, 2:15 pm, 4:45 pm, 7:15 pm, 9:45 pm

LCE Factoria Cinemas 8 (7.8 miles)
3505 Factoria Blvd SE, Bellevue (425) 641-9206
Showtimes: 12:00 pm, 1:00 pm, 2:15 pm, 3:15 pm, 4:30 pm, 5:45 pm, 7:30
pm, 8:15 pm, 9:45 pm, 10:30 pm

Kirkland Parkplace Cinema (8 miles)
404 Parkplace Ctr, Kirkland (425) 827-9000
Showtimes: 12:15 pm, 2:30 pm, 4:45 pm, 7:20 pm, 9:35 pm

Figure 5-59

Movie Time Listing

B.   This report was prepared for a user who is located near downtown Seattle. Suppose that it is necessary to produce this same report for these theaters, but for a user located in a Seattle suburb, such as Bellevue, Renton, Redmond, or Tacoma. In this case, distance cannot be an attribute of THEATER. Change your answer in A for this situation. Specify the entity identifiers and attributes. Name the relationships and identify the type and cardinality of all relationships.

C.   Suppose that you want to make this data model national. Change your answer to B so that it can be used for other metropolitan areas. Change your answer in A for this situation. Specify the entity identifiers and attributes. Name the relationships and identify the type and cardinality of all relationships.

D.   Modify your answer to C to include the leading cast members. Assume that the role of a cast member is not to be modeled. Specify the identifier of new entities and their attributes. Name the relationships and identify the type and cardinality of all relationships.

E.   Modify your answer to C to include the leading cast members. Assume that the role of a cast member is specified. Specify the identifier of new entities and their attributes. Name the relationships and identify the type and cardinality of all relationships.

KELLY'S RICE Cereal
Nutrition Information

SERVING SIZE: 1 OZ. (28.4 g, ABOUT 1 CUP)
SERVINGS PER PACKAGE: 13

	CEREAL	WITH ½ CUP VITAMINS A & D SKIM MILK
CALORIES	110	150*
PROTEIN	2 g	6g
CARBOHYDRATE	25 g	31g
FAT	0 g	0g*
CHOLESTEROL	0 mg	0mg*
SODIUM	290 mg	350mg
POTASSIUM	35 mg	240mg

PERCENTAGE OF U.S. RECOMMENDED
DAILY ALLOWANCES (U.S. RDA)

PROTEIN	2	10
VITAMIN A	25	30
VITAMIN C	25	25
THIAMIN	35	40
RIBOFLAVIN	35	45
NIACIN	35	35
CALCIUM	**	15
IRON	10	10
VITAMIN D	10	25
VITAMIN B₆	35	35
FOLIC ACID	35	35
PHOSPHORUS	4	15
MAGNESIUM	2	6
ZINC	2	6
COPPER	2	4

*WHOLE MILK SUPPLIES AN ADDITIONAL 30 CALORIES, 4 g FAT, AND 15 mg CHOLESTEROL.
**CONTAINS LESS THAN 2% OF THE U.S. RDA OF THIS NUTRIENT.

INGREDIENTS: RICE, SUGAR, SALT, CORN SYRUP

VITAMINS AND IRON: VITAMIN C (SODIUM ASCORBATE AND ASCORBIC ACID), NIACINAMIDE, IRON, VITAMIN B₆ (PYRIDOXINE HYDROCHLORIDE), VITAMIN A (PALMITATE), VITAMIN B₂ (RIBOFLAVIN), VITAMIN B₁ (THIAMIN HYDROCHLORIDE), FOLIC ACID, AND VITAMIN D.

FDA REPORT #6272
Date: June 30, 2009
Issuer: Kelly's Corporation
Report Title: Product Summary by Ingredient

Corn	Kelly's Corn Cereal
	Kelly's Multigrain Cereal
	Kelly's Crunchy Cereal
Corn syrup	Kelly's Corn Cereal
	Kelly's Rice Cereal
	Kelly's Crunchy Cereal
Malt	Kelly's Corn Cereal
	Kelly's Crunchy Cereal
Wheat	Kelly's Multigrain Cereal
	Kelly's Crunchy Cereal

(a)

SUPPLIERS LIST
Date: June 30, 2009

Ingredient	Supplier	Price
Corn	Wilson	2.80
	J. Perkins	2.72
	Pollack	2.83
	McKay	2.80
Wheat	Adams	1.19
	Kroner	1.19
	Schmidt	1.22
Barley	Wilson	0.85
	Pollack	0.84

(b)

Figure 5-60

Cereal Product Reports

5.64   Consider the three reports in Figure 5-60. The data are samples of data that would appear in the reports like these.

A.   Make a list of as many potential entities as these reports suggest.

B.   Examine your list to determine whether any entities are synonyms. If so, consolidate your list.

C.   Construct an IE Crow's Foot model showing relationships among your entities. Name each relationship and specify cardinalities. Indicate which cardinalities you can justify on the basis of these reports and which you will need to check out with the users.

West Side Story
Based on a conception of Jerome Robbins

Book by ARTHUR LAURENTS
Music by LEONARD BERNSTEIN
Lyrics by STEPHEN SONDHEIM

Entire Original Production Directed
and Choreographed by JEROME ROBBINS

Originally produced on Broadway by Robert E. Griffith and Harold S. Prince
by arrangement with Roger L. Stevens
Orchestration by Leonard Bernstein with Sid Ramin and Irwin Kostal

HIGHLIGHTS FROM THE COMPLETE RECORDING

Maria . . . . .KIRI TE KANAWA
Tony . . . . JOSE CARRERAS
Anita . . . . TATIANA TROYANOS
Riff . . . . KURT OLLMAN
and MARILYN HORNE singing "Somewhere"

Rosalia . . . . Louise Edeiken   Diesel . . . . Marty Nelson
Consuela. . . . . Stella Zambalis   Baby John. . . . . Stephen Bogardus
Fancisca. . . . . Angelina Reaux   A-rab . . . . Peter Thom
Action . . . . David Livingston   Snowboy . . . . .Todd Lester
Bernardo. . . .Richard Harrell

1	**Jet Song** (Riff, Action, Baby John, A-rab, Chorus)	[3'13]
2	**Something's Coming** (Tony)	[2'33]
3	**Maria** (Tony)	[2'56]
4	**Tonight** (Maria, Tony)	[5'27]
5	**America** (Anita, Rosalia, Chorus)	[4'47]
6	**Cool** (Riff, Chorus)	[4'37]
7	**One Hand, One Heart** (Tony, Maria)	[5'38]
8	**Tonight (Ensemble)** (Entire Cast)	[3'40]
9	**I Feel Pretty** (Maria, Chorus)	[3'22]
10	**Somewhere** (A Girl)	[2'34]
11	**Gee Officer Krupke** (Action, Snowboy, Diesel, A-rab, Baby John, Chorus)	[4'18]
12	**A Boy Like That** (Anita, Maria)	[2'05]
13	**I Have a Love** (Maria, Anita)	[3'30]
14	**Taunting Scene** (Orchestra)	[1'21]
15	**Finale** (Maria, Tony)	[2'40]

Figure 5-61

CD Cover

5.65   Consider the CD cover in Figure 5-61.

A.   Specify identifiers and attributes for the entities CD, ARTIST, ROLE, and SONG.

B.   Construct a crow's foot model showing relationships among these four entities. Name each relationship and specify cardinalities. Indicate which cardinalities you can justify on the basis of the CD cover and which you will need to check out with the users.

C.   Consider a CD that does not involve a musical, so there is no need for ROLE. However, the entity SONG_WRITER is needed. Create a crow's foot model for CD, ARTIST, SONG, and SONG_WRITER. Assume that an ARTIST can either be a group or an individual. Assume that some artists record individually and as part of a group.

D.   Combine the models you developed in your answers to B and C. Create new entities if necessary, but strive to keep your model as simple as possible. Specify identifiers and attributes of new entities, name new relationships, and indicate their cardinalities.

5.66   Consider the data model in Figure 5-45. How should this model be altered if the users want to keep track of how many of each part are used? Suppose, for example, that the wheel assembly requires four washers and the handle assembly requires just one, and the database must store these quantities. Hint: Adding Quantity to this N:M relationship is analogous to adding Price to the N:M relationship in Figure 5-24.

5.67   The data model in Figure 5-52 uses the attribute Room in COLLEGE and DEPARTMENT, but uses OfficeNumber in PROFESSOR. These attributes have the same kind of data, even though they have different names. Examine Figure 5-46 and explain how this situation came to be. Do you think having different names for the same attribute types is rare? Do you think it is a problem? Why or why not?

Suppose that you have been hired by Marcia's Dry Cleaning to create a database application to track customers, orders, and items. Marcia also wants to start a Frequent Cleaner's Club, whereby she will offer a 50 percent discount on every 10th customer order.

A.   Using your knowledge, create a data model for Marcia's business. Name each entity, describe its type, and indicate all attributes and identifiers. Name each relationship, describe its type, and specify minimum and maximum cardinalities.

B.   List any item in your answer to A that you believe should be checked out with Marcia and/or her employees.

Suppose that you have been hired by Morgan Importing to create a database application to track stores, purchases, shipments, and shippers. Sometimes several items are purchased from a store on a single visit, but do not assume that all of the items are placed on the same shipment. You want to track each item in a shipment and assign an insurance value to each item.

A.   Using your knowledge, create a data model for Morgan Importing. Name each entity, describe its type, and indicate all attributes and identifiers. Name each relationship, describe its type, and specify minimum and maximum cardinalities.

B.   List any item in your answer to A that you believe should be checked out with Phillip Morgan and/or his employees.

6

Transforming Data Models into Database Designs

Chapter Objectives

- To understand how to transform data models into database designs.
- To be able to identify primary keys and understand when to use a surrogate key.
- To understand the use of referential integrity constraints.
- To understand the use of referential integrity actions.
- To be able to represent ID-dependent, 1:1, 1:N, and N:M relationships as tables.

- To be able to represent weak entities as tables.
- To be able to represent supertype/subtypes as tables.
- To be able to represent recursive relationships as tables.
- To be to represent ternary relationships as tables.
- To be able to implement referential integrity actions required by minimum cardinalities.

This chapter explains the transformation of entity-relationship data models into relational database designs. This transformation consists of three primary tasks: (1) replacing entities and attributes with tables and columns; (2) representing relationships and maximum cardinalities by placing foreign keys; and (3) representing minimum cardinality by defining actions to constrain activities on values of primary and foreign keys. Steps 1 and 2 are relatively easy to understand and accomplish; step 3 may be easy or difficult, depending on the minimum cardinality type.

Create a Table for Each Entity

We begin the database design by creating a table for each entity using the steps shown in Figure 6-1. In most cases, the table is assigned the same name as the entity. Each attribute of the entity becomes a column of the table. The identifier of the entity becomes the primary key of the table. The example in Figure 6-2 shows the creation of the EMPLOYEE table from the EMPLOYEE entity. In this text, to differentiate entities from tables, we will show entities with shadowed boxes and tables with nonshadowed boxes. This notation will help clarify our discussion, but be aware that it is not standard notation across the industry.

Be certain that you understand the difference between these similar-looking graphics. The shadowed rectangle in Figure 6-2(a) represents a logical structure that has no physical existence. It is a blueprint. The nonshadowed rectangle in Figure 6-2(b) represents a database table. It is the same as the following notation that we used in Chapters 3 and 4:

EMPLOYEE (<u>EmployeeNumber</u>, EmployeeName, Phone, Email, HireDate, ReviewDate, EmpCode)

Note, too, the key symbol next to EmployeeNumber. It documents the fact that Employee Number is the table key, just as the underline does in the notation used in Chapters 3 and 4.

Figure   6-1

Steps for Transforming
a Data Model into
a Database Design

1. Create a table for each entity:
   – Specify primary key (consider surrogate keys, as appropriate)
   – Specify candidate keys
   – Specify properties for each column:
      • Null status
      • Data type
      • Default value (if any)
      • Specify data constraints (if any)
   – Verify normalization
2. Create relationships by placing foreign keys
   – Relationships between strong entities (1:1, 1:N, N:M)
   – Identifying relationships with ID-dependent entities (intersection tables, association patterns, multivalued attributes, archetype/instance patterns)
   – Relationships between a strong entity and a weak but non-ID-dependent entity (1:1, 1:N, N:M)
   – Mixed relationships
   – Relationships between supertype/subtype entities
   – Recursive relationships (1:1, 1:N, N:M)
3. Specify logic for enforcing minimum cardinality:
   – M-O relationships
   – O-M relationships
   – M-M relationships

Figure   6-2

Transforming an Entity
to a Table

EMPLOYEE

EmployeeNumber
EmployeeName
Phone
Email
HireDate
ReviewDate
EmpCode

EMPLOYEE

🔑 EmployeeNumber
EmployeeName
Phone
Email
HireDate
ReviewDate
EmpCode

(a) EMPLOYEE Entity   **(b) EMPLOYEE Table**

Selecting the Primary Key

The selection of the primary key is important. The DBMS will use the primary key to facilitate searching and sorting of table rows, and some DBMS products use it to organize table storage. DBMS products almost always create indexes and other data structures using the values of the primary key.

The ideal primary key is short, numeric, and fixed. EmployeeNumber in Figure 6-2 meets all of these conditions and is acceptable. Beware of primary keys such as EmployeeName, Email, (AreaCode, PhoneNumber), (Street, City, State, Zip), and other long character columns. In cases like these, when the identifier is not short, numeric, or fixed, consider using another candidate key as the primary key. If there are no candidate keys, or if none of them is any better, consider using a surrogate key.

A **surrogate key** is a DBMS-supplied identifier of each row of a table. Surrogate key values are unique within the table, and they never change. They are assigned when the row is created, and they are destroyed when the row is deleted. Surrogate key values are the best possible primary keys because they are designed to be short, numeric, and fixed. Because of these advantages, some organizations have gone so far as to require that surrogates be used for the primary key of every table.

Before endorsing such a policy, however, consider two disadvantages of surrogate keys. First, their values have no meaning to a user. Suppose you want to determine the department to which an employee is assigned. If DepartmentName is a foreign key in EMPLOYEE, then when you retrieve an employee row, you obtain a value such as 'Accounting' or 'Finance'. That value may be all that you need to know about department.

Alternatively, if you define the surrogate key DepartmentID as the primary key of DEPART-MENT, then DepartmentID will also be the foreign key in EMPLOYEE. When you retrieve a row of EMPLOYEE, you will get back a number such as 123499788 for the DepartmentID, a value that has no meaning to you at all. You have to perform a second query on DEPARTMENT to obtain DepartmentName.

The second disadvantage of surrogate keys arises when data are shared among different databases. Suppose, for example, that a company maintains three different SALES databases, one for each of three different product lines. Assume that each of these databases has a table called SALES_ORDER that has a surrogate key called ID. The DBMS assigns values to IDs so that they are unique within a particular database. It does not, however, assign ID values so that they are unique across the three different databases. Thus, it is possible for two different SALES_ORDER rows, in two different databases, to have the same ID value.

This duplication is not a problem until data from the different databases are merged. When that happens, to prevent duplicates, ID values will need to be changed. However, if ID values are changed, then foreign key values may need to be changed as well, and the result is a mess, or at least much work to prevent a mess.

It is, of course, possible to construct a scheme using different starting values for surrogate keys in different databases. Such a policy ensures that each database has its own range of surrogate key values. This requires careful management and procedures, however; and if the starting values are too close to one another, the ranges will overlap and duplicate surrogate key values will result.

BY THE WAY   Some database designers take the position that, for consistency, if one table has a surrogate key, all of the tables in the database should have a surrogate key. Others think that such a policy is too rigid; after all, there are good data keys, such as ProductID. If such a key exists, it should be used instead of a surrogate key. Your organization may have standards on this issue that you should follow.

Be aware that DBMS products vary in their support for surrogate keys. Access, SQL Server and MySQL provide them. SQL Server allows the designer to pick the starting value and increment of the key, and MySQL allows the designer to pick the starting value. Oracle, however, does not provide direct support for surrogate keys, but you can obtain the essence of them in a rather backhanded way, as discussed in Chapter 10A.

We use surrogate keys unless there is some strong reason not to. In addition to the advantages described here, the fact that they are fixed simplifies the enforcement of minimum cardinality, as you will learn in the last section of this chapter.

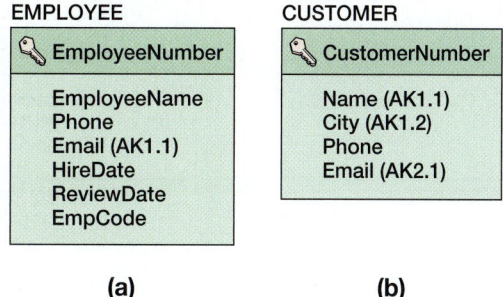

Figure 6-3

Representing Candidate (Alternative) Keys

Specifying Candidate (Alternate) Keys

The next step in creating a table is to specify candidate keys. As discussed in Chapter 3, **candidate keys** are alternative identifiers of unique rows in a table. Some products use the term **alternate key (AK)** rather than candidate key, but the two terms are synonymous. Figure 6-3 illustrates the use of alternate keys.

Figure 6-3(a) shows EMPLOYEE with a primary key of EmployeeNumber and a candidate, or alternate, key of Email. In Figure 6-3(b), CustomerNumber is the primary key of CUSTOMER, and both the composite (Name, City) and Email are candidate keys. In these diagrams, the symbol AK$n.m$ means the nth alternate key and the mth column of that alternate key. In the EMPLOYEE table, Email is labeled AK1.1 because it is the first alternate key and the first column of that key. CUSTOMER has two alternate keys. The first is a composite of two columns, which are labeled AK1.1 and AK1.2. The nomenclature Name (AK1.1) means that Name is the first column of the first alternate key, and City (AK1.2) means that City is the second column of the first alternate key. In CUSTOMER, Email is marked as AK2.1 because it is the first (and only) column of the second alternate key.

Specify Column Properties

The next step in the creation of a relation is to specify the column properties. Four properties are shown in Figure 6-1: null status, data type, default value, and data constraints.

Null Status

Null status refers to whether the column can have a null value. Typically, null status is specified by using the phrase NULL if nulls are allowed and NOT NULL if not. Thus, NULL does not mean that the column is always null; it means that null values are allowed. Because of this possible confusion, some people prefer the term NULL ALLOWED rather than NULL. Figure 6-4 shows the null status of each of the columns in the EMPLOYEE table.

BY THE WAY   The EMPLOYEE table in Figure 6-4 contains a subtlety. EmployeeNumber, the primary key, is marked NOT NULL, but Email, the alternate key, is marked NULL. It makes sense that EmployeeNumber should not be allowed to be null. If it were, and if more than one row had a null value, then EmployeeNumber would not identify a unique row. Why, however, should Email be allowed to have null values?

The answer is that alternate keys often are used just to ensure uniqueness. Marking Email as a (possibly null) alternate key means that Email need not have a value, but, if it has one, that value will be different from all other values of Email in the EMPLOYEE table. This answer is dissatisfying because it means that alternate keys are not truly alternate *primary* keys. Alas, that's the way it is. Just know that primary keys can never be null but that alternate keys can be.

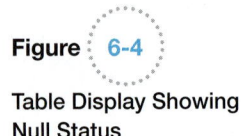

Figure 6-4

Table Display Showing Null Status

EMPLOYEE

🔑 EmployeeNumber: NOT NULL

EmployeeName: NOT NULL
Phone: NULL
Email: NULL (AK1.1)
HireDate: NOT NULL
ReviewDate: NULL
EmpCode: NULL

Data Type

The next step is to define the data type for each column. Unfortunately, each DBMS provides a different set of data types. For example, Microsoft Access has a data type called Currency; SQL Server has a data type called Money; and Oracle has no data type for currency. Instead, with Oracle, you use the numeric data type for currency values. A summary of data types for Oracle, SQL Server, and MySQL appears in Chapter 7 as Figure 7-4.

If you know which DBMS you will be using to create the database, you can use that product's data types in your design. Figure 6-5 illustrates the display of data types in a table using the data types for SQL Server (e.g., datetime is an SQL Server data type).

In fact, with many data modeling products, such as Computer Associate's ERwin, you can specify the DBMS you will use and the data modeling product will supply the appropriate set of data types. Other products are DBMS specific. On the other hand, Sun Microsystems' MySQL Workbench is intended to design databases for MySQL, and therefore uses MySQL-specific data types.

If you do not know which DBMS product you will be using, or if you want to preserve independence from a particular DBMS, you can specify the data types in a generic way. Typical generic data types are CHAR (n) for a fixed-length character string of length n; VARCHAR (n) for a variable-length character string having a maximum length of n; DATE; TIME; MONEY; INTEGER; and DECIMAL. If you work for a larger organization, that company probably has its own generic data standards. If so, you should use those data standards.

Figure 6-6 shows the EMPLOYEE table showing both data type and null status. The display becomes crowded, however; and from now on we will show tables with just column names. With most products, you can turn such displays on or off depending on the work you are doing.

> **BY THE WAY** The fact that a design tool is dedicated to one DBMS product does *not* mean that it cannot be used to design databases for other DBMSs. For example, an SQL Server database can be designed in MySQL Workbench and most of the design will be correct. You will however, have to understand the relevant differences in the DBMS products and make adjustments when creating the actual database.

Figure 6-5

Table Display Showing Data Types

EMPLOYEE

🔑 EmployeeNumber: int

EmployeeName: char(50)
Phone: char(15)
Email: char(50) (AK1.1)
HireDate: datetime
ReviewDate: datetime
EmpCode: char(18)

Figure 6-6

Table Display Showing Null Status and Data Types

EMPLOYEE

🔑 EmployeeNumber: int NOT NULL

EmployeeName: char(50) NOT NULL
Phone: char(15) NULL
Email: char(50) NULL (AK1.1)
HireDate: datetime NOT NULL
ReviewDate: datetime NULL
EmpCode: char(18) NULL

Default Value

A **default value** is a value supplied by the DBMS when a new row is created. The value can be a constant, such as the string 'New Hire' for the EmpCode column in EMPLOYEE, or it can be the result of a function, such as the date value of the computer's clock for the HireDate column.

In some cases, default values are computed using more complicated logic. The default value for a price, for example, might be computed by applying a markup to a default cost and then reducing that marked up price by a customer's discount. In such a case, an application component or a trigger (discussed in Chapter 7) will be written to supply such a value.

It is possible to use the data modeling tool to record default values, but such values often are shown in separate design documentation. Figure 6-7, for example, shows one way that default values are documented.

Data Constraints

Data constraints are limitations on data values. There are several different types. **Domain constraints** limit column values to a particular set of values. For example, EMPLOYEE.EmpCode could be limited to one of the values ['New Hire', 'Hourly', 'Salary', 'Part Time']. **Range constraints** limit values to a particular interval of values. EMPLOYEE.HireDate, for example, could be limited to dates between January 1, 1990, and December 31, 2010.

An **intrarelation constraint** limits a column's values in comparison with other columns in the same table. The constraint that EMPLOYEE.ReviewDate be at least three months after EMPLOYEE.HireDate is an intrarelation constraint. An **interrelation constraint** limits a column's values in comparison with other columns in other tables. An example for the CUSTOMER table is that CUSTOMER.Name must not be equal to BAD_CUSTOMER.Name, where BAD_ CUSTOMER is a table that contains a list of customers with credit and balance problems.

Referential integrity constraints, which we discussed in Chapter 3, are one type of interrelation constraint. Because they are so common, sometimes they are documented only when they are not enforced. For example, to save work, a design team might say that every foreign key is assumed to have a referential integrity constraint to the table that it references and that only exceptions to this rule are documented.

Verify Normalization

The last task in step 1 of Figure 6-1 is to verify table normalization. When data models are developed using forms and reports as guides, they generally result in normalized entities. This occurs because the structures of forms and reports usually reflect how users think about their data. Boundaries of a form, for example, often show the range of a functional dependency. If this is hard to understand, think of a functional dependency as a theme. A well-designed form or report will bracket themes using lines, colors, boxes, or other graphical elements. Those graphical hints will have been used by the data modeling team to develop entities, and the result will be normalized tables.

Figure ⦂ 6-7 ⦂

Sample Documentation
for Default Values

Table	Column	Default Value
ITEM	ItemNumber	Surrogate key
ITEM	Category	None
ITEM	ItemPrefix	If Category = 'Perishable' then 'P' If Category = 'Imported' then 'I' If Category = 'One-off' then 'O' Otherwise = 'N'
ITEM	ApprovingDept	If ItemPrefix = 'I' then 'SHIPPING/PURCHASING' Otherwise = 'PURCHASING'
ITEM	ShippingMethod	If ItemPrefix = 'P' then 'Next Day' Otherwise = 'Ground'

All of this, however, should be verified. You need to ask whether the resulting tables are in BCNF and whether all multivalued dependencies have been removed. If not, the tables should probably be normalized. However, as we discussed in Chapter 4, sometimes normalization is undesirable. Thus, you should also examine your tables to determine if any normalized ones should be denormalized.

Create Relationships

The result of step 1 is a set of complete, but independent, tables. The next step is to create relationships. In general, we create relationships by placing foreign keys into tables. The way in which this is done and the properties of the foreign key columns depend on the type of relationship. In this section, we consider each of the relationships described in Chapter 5: nonidentifying relationships between strong entities, identifying relationships between ID-dependent entities, relationships in mixed entity patterns, relationships between a supertype and its subtypes, and recursive relationships. We conclude this section with a discussion of special cases of ternary relationships.

Relationships Between Strong Entities

As you learned in Chapter 5, nonidentifying relationships between strong entities are characterized by their maximum cardinality. There are three types of these relationships: 1:1, 1:N, and N:M.

1:1 Relationships Between Strong Entities

After the tables corresponding to the strong entities have been designed, a 1:1 relationship between these entities can be represented in one of two ways. You can place the primary key of the first table in the second as a foreign key, or you can place the primary key of the second table in the first as a foreign key. Figure 6-8 shows the representation of the 1:1 nonidentifying relationship between CLUB_MEMBER and LOCKER. In Figure 6-8(a), MemberNumber is placed in LOCKER as a foreign key. In Figure 6-8(b), LockerNumber is placed in CLUB_MEMBER as a foreign key.

Either of these designs will work. If you have a club member's number and want his or her locker, then using the design in Figure 6-8(a) you can query the LOCKER table for the given value of MemberNumber. But, if you have the LockerNumber and want the club member's data, then using the design in Figure 6-8(a) you can query the LOCKER table for the LockerNumber, obtain the MemberNumber, and use that value to query the CLUB_MEMBER table for the rest of the club member's data.

Figure 6-8

The Two Alternatives for Representing a 1:1 Relationship Between Strong Entities

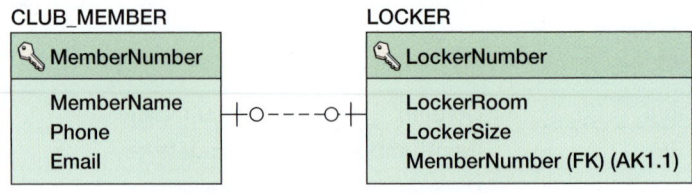

(a) With Foreign Key in LOCKER

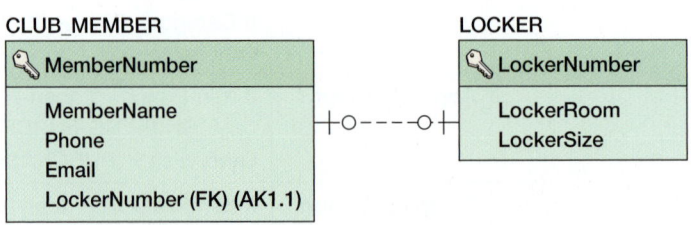

(b) With Foreign Key in CLUB_MEMBER

Follow a similar procedure to verify that the design in Figure 6-8(b) works as well. However, one data constraint applies to both designs. Because the relationship is 1:1, a given value of a foreign key can appear only once in the table. For example, in the design in Figure 6-8(a), a given value of MemberNumber can appear just once; each value must be unique in the LOCKER table. If a value of MemberNumber were to appear in two rows, then a member would be assigned to two lockers, and the relationship would not be 1:1.

To cause the DBMS to enforce the required uniqueness of the foreign key value, we define the foreign key column as unique. This can be done either directly in the column definition of the foreign key (in which case there is no designation in the table diagram) or by defining the foreign key as an alternate key. This latter technique, though common, is a bit confusing because, logically, MemberNumber is not an alternate key for LOCKER. We are just using the fact that alternate keys are unique to document the uniqueness of the foreign key in a 1:1 relationship. Depending upon the database design software being used, the alternate key designation may appear in the database design of the tables and the relationship, and this is illustrated in Figure 6-8(a). A similar technique is used on the foreign key LockerNumber in Figure 6-8(b).

Although either of the designs in Figure 6-8 will work, a design team may prefer one over the other. If the minimum cardinalities of the relationship are either M-O or O-M, then one design will be *greatly* preferred, as you will learn in the section on minimum cardinality design. Also, application requirements may mean that one design is faster than the other.

To summarize, to represent a 1:1 strong entity relationship, place the key of one table in the other table. Enforce the maximum cardinality by defining the foreign key as unique (or as an alternate key).

1:N Relationships Between Strong Entities

After the tables corresponding to the strong entities have been designed, a 1:N relationship between the entities is represented by placing the primary key of the table on the one side into the table on the many side as a foreign key. Recall from Chapter 5 that the term *parent* is used to refer to the table on the one side and the term *child* is used to refer to the table on the many side. Using this terminology, you can summarize the design of 1:N relationships by saying, "Place the primary key of the parent in the child as a foreign key." This is illustrated in Figure 6-9.

Figure 6-9(a) shows an E-R diagram for the 1:N relationship between the COMPANY and DEPARTMENT entities. The relationship is represented in the database design in Figure 6-9(b) by placing the primary key of the parent (CompanyName) in the child (DEPARTMENT) as a foreign key. Because parents have many children (the relationship is 1:N), there is no need to make the foreign key unique.

For 1:N relationships between strong entities, that's all there is to it. Just remember: "Place the primary key of the parent in the child as a foreign key."

N:M Relationships Between Strong Entities

Again, we must first create the database design tables from the data model entities, and then create the relationship. However, the situation for N:M relationships is more complicated. The

Figure 6-9

Representing a 1:N Relationship Between Strong Entities

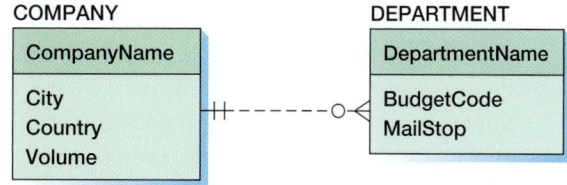

(a) 1:N Relationship Between Strong Entities

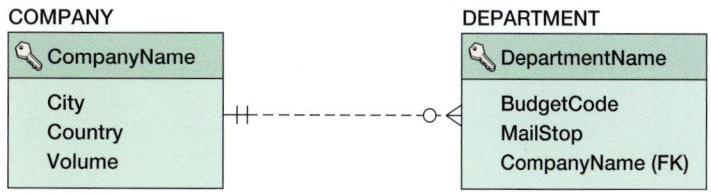

(b) Placing the Primary Key of the Parent in the Child as a Foreign Key

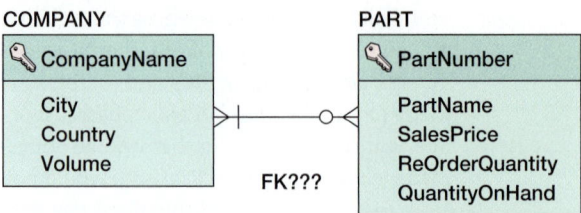

(a) The Foreign Key Has No Place in Either Table

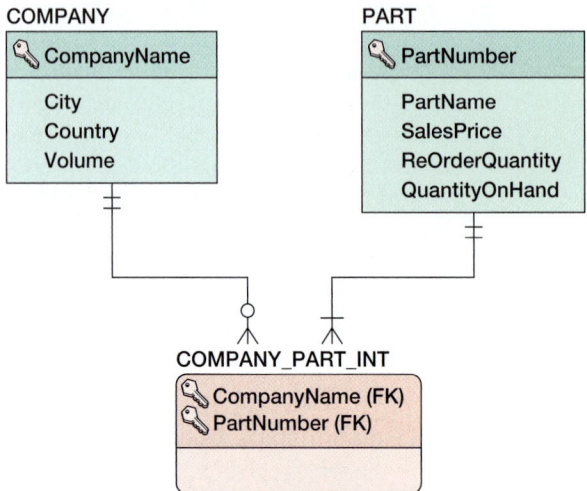

Figure 6-10

Representing an N:M
Relationship Between
Strong Entities

(b) Foreign Keys Placed in ID-Dependent Intersection Table

problem is that there is no place in either table in an N:M relationship in which to place the foreign key. Consider the example in Figure 6-10(a), which shows a relationship between COMPANY and PART that specifies which companies can supply which parts. A COMPANY may supply many PARTs, and a PART may be supplied by many different COMPANY(ies).

Suppose we try to represent this relationship by placing the primary key of one table as a foreign key in the second table, as we did for 1:N relationships. Say we place the primary key of PART in COMPANY as follows:

COMPANY (<u>CompanyName</u>, City, Country, Volume, *PartNumber*)

PART (<u>PartNumber</u>, PartName, SalesPrice, ReOrderQuantity, QuantityOnHand)

With this design, a given PartNumber may appear in many rows of COMPANY so that many companies can supply the part. But, how do we show that a company can supply many parts? There is only space to show one part. We do not want to duplicate the entire row for a company just to show a second part; such a strategy would result in unacceptable data duplication and data integrity problems. Therefore, this is not an acceptable solution, and a similar problem will occur if we try to place the primary key of COMPANY, CompanyName, into PART as a foreign key.

The solution is to create a third table, called an **intersection table**. Such a table shows the correspondences of a given company and a given part. It holds only the primary keys of the two tables as foreign keys, and this combination of keys serves as the composite primary key of the intersection table itself. The intersection holds only the key data; it contains no other user data. For the example in Figure 6-10(a) we create the following intersection table:

COMPANY_PART_INT (<u>*CompanyName*</u>, <u>*PartNumber*</u>)

The COMPANY_PART_INT table has one row for each company–part combination. Notice that both columns are part of the primary key, and that each column is a foreign key to a different table. Because both columns are keys of other tables, intersection tables are always ID dependent on both of their parent tables and the relationships with the parent tables are identifying relationships.

Thus, in Figure 6-10(b) COMPANY_PART_INT is shown as ID dependent with identifying relationship lines. Like all ID-dependent tables, the parent tables are required; COMPANY_PART_INT requires both a COMPANY and PART. The parents may or may not require an intersection table row, depending on application requirements. In Figure 6-10(b), a COMPANY need not supply a PART, but a PART must be supplied by at least one COMPANY.

> **BY THE WAY** The problem for the data models of N:M relationships between strong entity is that they have no direct representation. An N:M relationship must always be decomposed into two 1:N relationships using an intersection table in the database design. This is why products like MySQL Workbench and Visio are unable to represent N:M relationships in a data model. These products force you to make the transformation to two 1:N relationships ahead of time, during modeling. As stated in Chapter 5, however, most data modelers consider this requirement to be a nuisance because it adds complexity to data modeling when the whole purpose of data modeling is to reduce complexity to the logical essentials.

Relationships Using ID-Dependent Entities

Figure 6-11 summarizes the four uses for ID-dependent entities. We have already described the first use shown in Figure 6-11: the representation of N:M relationships. As shown in Figure 6-10, an ID-dependent intersection table is created to hold the foreign keys of the two tables participating in the relationship, and indentifying 1:N relationships are created between each table and the intersection table.

The other three uses shown in Figure 6-11 were discussed in Chapter 5, and here we will describe the creation of tables and relationships for each of these three uses.

Association Relationships

As we discussed in Chapter 5, an association relationship is subtly close to an N:M relationship between two strong entities. The only difference between the two types of relationships is that an association relationship has one or more attributes that pertain to the relationship and not to either of the entities. These attributes must be added to what would otherwise be the intersection table in the N:M relationship. Figure 6-12(a) shows the association relationship data model created in Figure 5-22. In this example, the association of a company and a part carries an attribute named Price.

The representation of such a relationship using a table is straightforward. Just create a table that is ID dependent on both of its parents and place the Price attribute in that table. The result for the example in Figure 6-12(a) is the table:

QUOTATION (*CompanyName*, *PartNumber*, Price)

This table appears in the database design in Figure 6-12(b). Like all ID-dependent relationships, the parents of an association table are required. The parents may or may not require the

Figure **6-11**

Four Uses for ID-Dependent Entities

- Representing N:M Relationships
- Association Relationships
- Multivalued Attributes
- Archetype/Instance Relationships

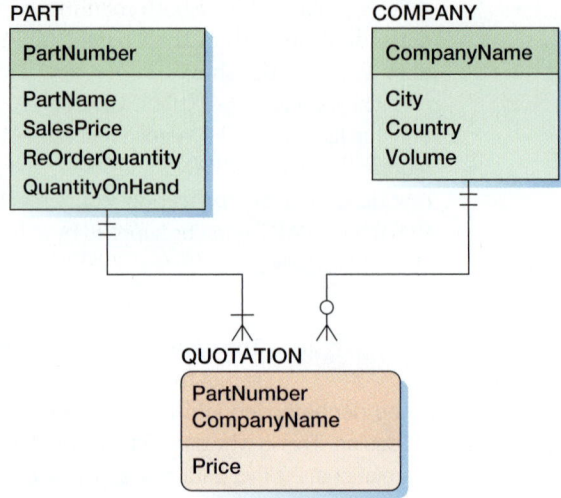

(a) Association Pattern Data Model from Figure 5-22

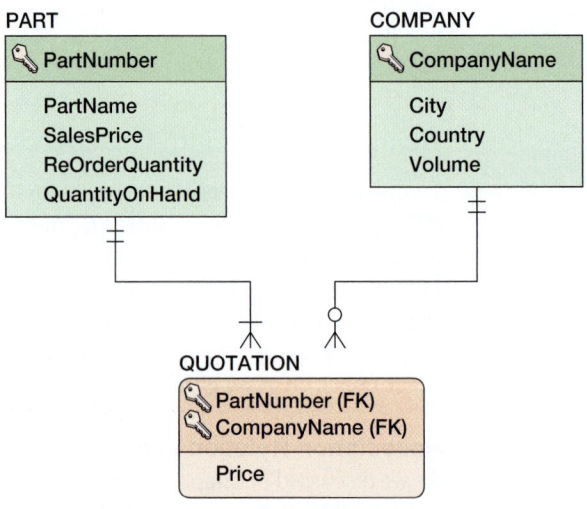

Figure 6-12

Using ID-Dependent Entities in an Association Relationship

(b) Association Pattern Database Design

rows of the association table, depending on application requirements. In Figure 6-12(b), a COMPANY need not have any QUOTATION rows, but a PART must have at least one QUOTATION row.

BY THE WAY   The table that represents the association entity looks very much like an intersection table; the only difference is the presence of the Price attribute. Because of the attribute, the need for association tables, such as QUOTATION, will appear in user requirements. Somewhere there will be a form or a report that has the attribute Price. However, the need for intersection tables never appears in the users' world. Such tables are an artifact of the relational model, and no form, report, or other user requirement will indicate the need for one.

Intersection tables complicate the construction of applications. They must be processed to obtain related rows, but they never directly appear on a form or report. In Access, they are frustratingly difficult to mangle into the form and report design tools. You will see more about this in later chapters. In any case, for now understand the key difference between association and intersection tables: Association tables have user data, but intersection tables do not.

As shown in Figure 6-13, association entities sometimes connect more than two entity types. Figure 6-13(a) shows the association relationship among the CLIENT, ARCHITECT, and PROJECT entities from the data model we created in Figure 5-23. When there are several participants in the association, the strategy just shown is simply extended. The association table will have the key of each of its parents, as shown in Figure 6-13(b). In this case, the ASSIGNMENT table has three foreign keys and one nonkey attribute, HoursWorked.

In both of these examples, it is only coincidence that the association tables have only one nonkey attribute. In general, an association table can have as many nonkey attributes as necessary to meet user requirements.

Figure 6-13

Using ID-Dependent Entities in an Association Relationship Among Three Entities

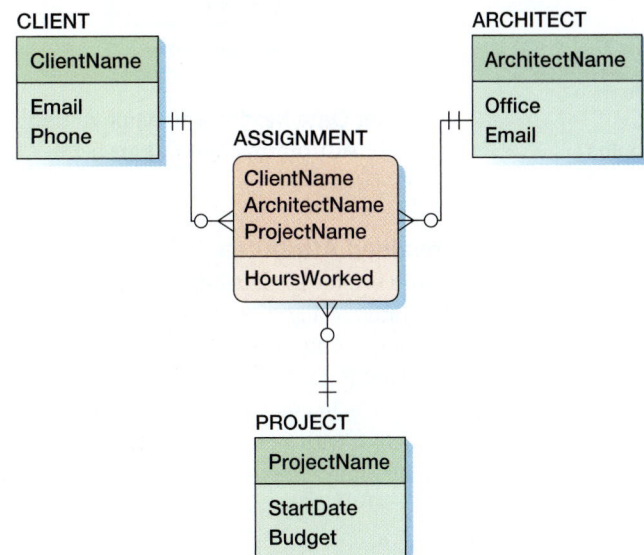

(a) Association Pattern Data Model from Figure 5-23

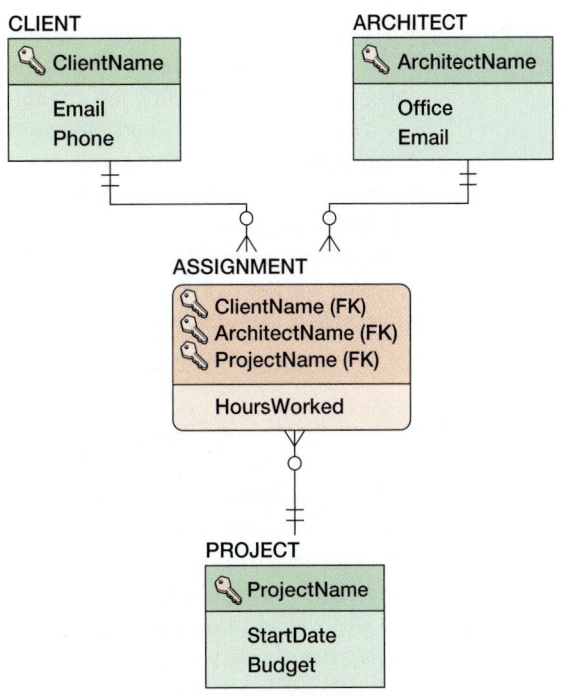

(b) Association Pattern Database Design

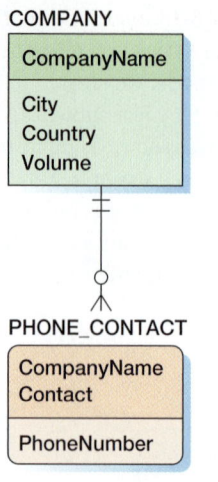

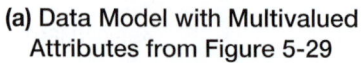

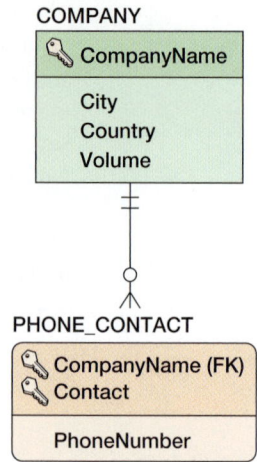

(a) Data Model with Multivalued Attributes from Figure 5-29

(b) Database Design to Store Multivalued Attributes

Figure 6-14

Using ID-Dependent Entities to Store Multivalued Attributes

Multivalued Attributes

The third use for ID-dependent entities is to represent multivalued entity attributes, and this is illustrated in Figure 6-14. Figure 6-14(a) is a copy of Figure 5-29. Here, COMPANY has a multivalued composite, (Contact, PhoneNumber), that is represented by the ID-dependent entity PHONE_CONTACT.

As shown in Figure 6-14(b), representing the PHONE_CONTACT entity is straightforward. Just replace it with a table and replace each of its attributes with a column. In this example, the CompanyName attribute is both a part of the primary key and a foreign key.

Like all ID-dependent tables, PHONE_CONTACT must have a parent row in COMPANY. However, a COMPANY row may or may not have a required PHONE_CONTACT, depending on application requirements.

> **BY THE WAY**   As you can see from these examples, it is not much work to transform an ID-dependent entity into a table. All that is necessary is to transform the entity into a table, and copy the attributes into columns.
>
> Why is it so simple? There are two reasons. First, all identifying relationships are 1:N. If they were 1:1, there would be no need for the ID-dependent relationship. The attributes could just be placed in the parent entity. Given that the relationship is 1:N, the design principle is to place the key of the parent into the child. However, the definition of an ID-dependent relationship is that part of its identifier is an identifier of its parent. Thus, by definition, the key of the parent is already in the child. Hence, it is not necessary to create a foreign key; that work has already been done during data modeling.

Archetype/Instance Pattern

As illustrated in Figure 6-15, the fourth use for ID-dependent entities and identifying relationships is the archetype/instance pattern. Figure 6-15(a), which is a copy of Figure 5-30, shows the CLASS/SECTION archetype/instance example from Chapter 5, and Figure 6-15(b) shows the relational design.

As noted in the last chapter, however, sometimes the instances of an archetype/instance pattern are given identifiers of their own. In that case, the instance entity becomes a weak, but not ID-dependent, entity. When this occurs, the relationship must be transformed using the rules of a 1:N relationship between a strong entity and a weak but non-ID-dependent entity. However, this transformation is the same as a 1:N relationship between two strong entities. This just means that the primary key of the parent table should be placed in the child table as a foreign key.

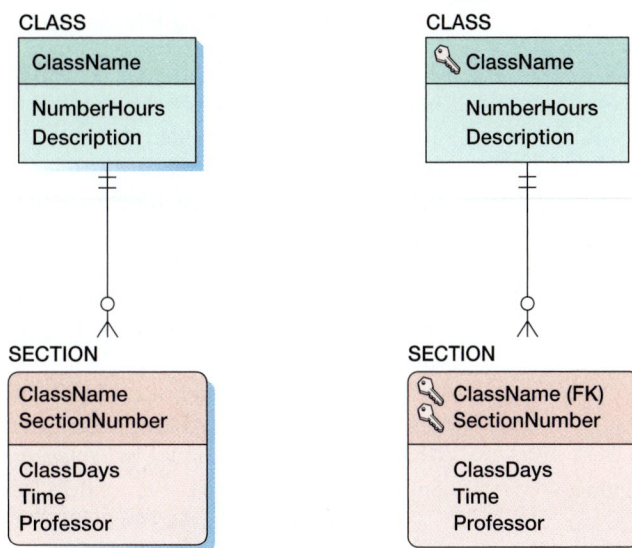

Figure 6-15

Using ID-Dependent Entities in an Archetype/Instance Pattern

(a) Data Model with Archetype/Instance Pattern from Figure 5-30

(b) Database Design for Archetype/Instance Pattern

Figure 6-16(a) shows a copy of the data model in Figure 5-31 in which SECTION has been given the identifier ReferenceNumber. In the relational database design in Figure 6-16(b), ClassName (the primary key of the parent CLASS table) has been placed in SECTION (the child table) as a foreign key.

Keep in mind, however, that even though SECTION is no longer ID-dependent, it is still weak. SECTION requires a CLASS for its existence. This means that a SECTION must always have a CLASS as its parent, and this restriction arises from logical necessity, not just from application requirements. The fact that SECTION is weak should be recorded in design documentation.

Figure 6-16

Transformation of the Archetype/Instance Pattern Using Non-ID-Dependent Weak Entities

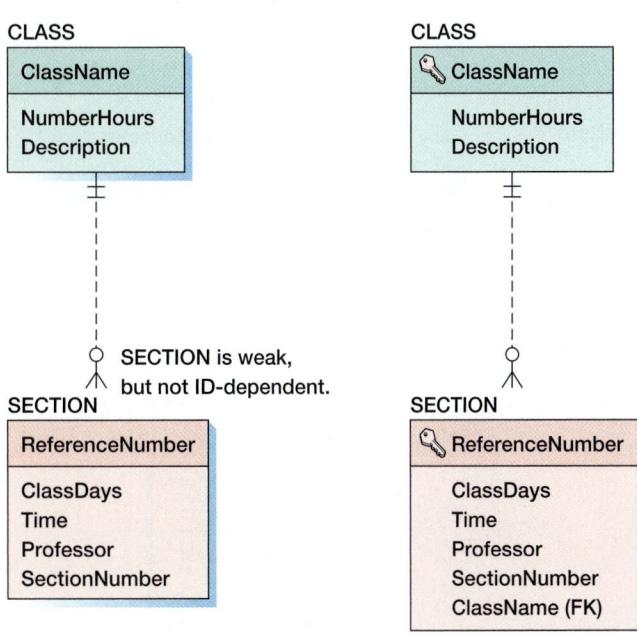

(a) Data Model with Non-ID-Dependent Weak Entity from Figure 5-31

(b) Database Design for Non-ID-Dependent Weak Entity

Relationships with a Weak Non-ID-Dependent Entity

As you learned in Chapter 5, a relationship between a strong entity and a weak but non-ID-dependent entity behaves just the same as a relationship between two strong entities. The relationship is a nonidentifying relationship, and, again, these relationships are characterized by their maximum cardinality. The previous discussion of 1:1, 1:N, and N:M relationships between strong entities also applies to these types of relationships between a strong entity and a weak but non-ID-dependent entity.

For example, what happens when the identifier of the parent of an ID-dependent entity is replaced with a surrogate key? Consider the example of BUILDING and APARTMENT, in which the identifier of APARTMENT is the composite of an apartment number and a building identifier.

Suppose that the identifier of BUILDING is (Street, City, State/Province, Country). In this case, the identifier of APARTMENT is (Street, City, State/Province, Country, ApartmentNumber). This design can be improved by replacing the long BUILDING identifier with a surrogate key. Suppose that we replace the key of BUILDING with BuildingID, a surrogate.

Now, with a surrogate key for BUILDING, what is the key of APARTMENT? When we place the key of the parent in the child, we obtain (BuildingID, ApartmentNumber). But this combination has no meaning to the user. What does an identifier of (10045898, '5C') mean to a user? Nothing. The key became meaningless when Street, City, State/Province, and Country were replaced by BuildingID in BUILDING.

We can improve the design by using the following principle: When replacing the identifier of the parent of an ID-dependent entity with a surrogate key, replace the identifier of the ID-dependent entity with its own surrogate key. The resulting table will be weak, but not ID dependent.

Relationships in Mixed Entity Designs

As you might guess, the design of mixed entity patterns is a combination of strong entities and ID-dependent entities designs. Consider the example of employees and skills in Figure 6-17. Figure 6-17(a) is a copy of Figure 5-35. Here, the entity EMPLOYEE_SKILL is ID dependent on EMPLOYEE, but it has a nonidentifying relationship to SKILL.

Figure 6-17

Transformation of the Mixed Entity Pattern

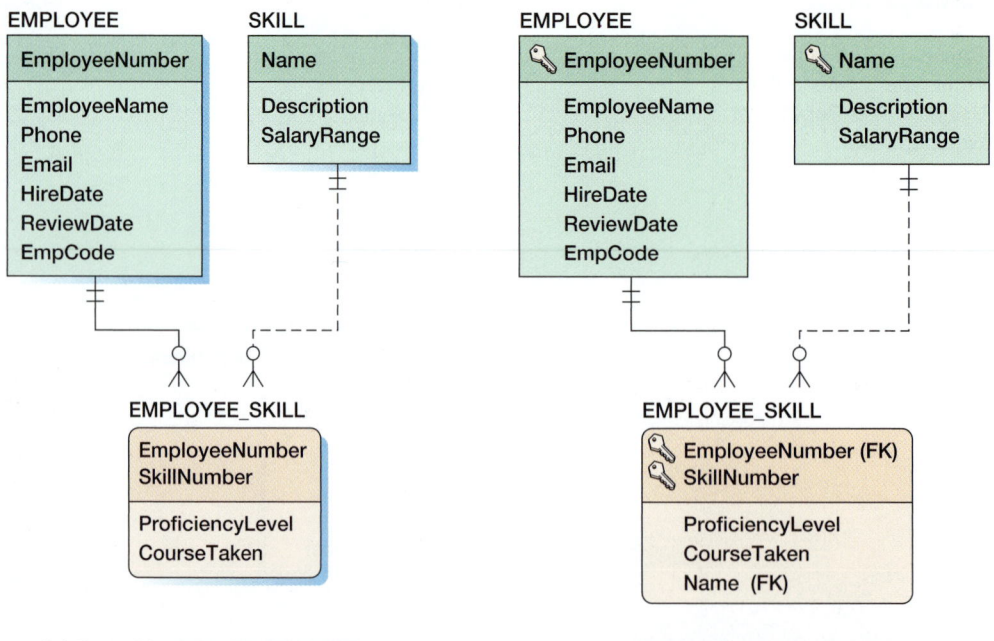

(a) Data Model with Mixed Entity Pattern from Figure 5-35

(b) Database Design for Mixed Entity Pattern

The database design of the E-R model for the data model in Figure 6-17(a) is shown in Figure 6-17(b). Notice that EmployeeNumber is both a part of the primary key of EMPLOYEE_SKILL and also a foreign key to EMPLOYEE. The 1:N nonidentifying relationship between SKILL and EMPLOYEE_SKILL is represented by placing the key of SKILL, which is Name, in EMPLOYEE_SKILL. Note that EMPLOYEE_SKILL.Name is a foreign key but not part of the primary key of EMPLOYEE_SKILL.

A similar strategy is used to transform the SALES_ORDER data model in Figure 6-18. Figure 6-19(a) is a copy of the SALES_ORDER data model originally shown in Figure 5-33. Here, the ID-dependent table, ORDER_LINE_ITEM, has SalesOrderNumber as part of its primary key and as a foreign key. It has ItemNumber as a foreign key only.

> **BY THE WAY** The design transformation process for all HAS-A relationships can be summarized by the phrase, "Place the primary key of the parent in the child as a foreign key." For strong entities, a 1:1 relationship can have either entity as the parent, hence the foreign key can go in either table. For 1:N relationships, the primary key of the parent goes in the child as the foreign key. For N:M relationships, decompose the model into two 1:N relationships by defining an intersection table and place the parent key of the parent in the child as a foreign key for each.
>
> For identifying relationships, the primary key of the parent is already in the child, so there is nothing more to do. For mixed relationships, on the identifying side, the primary key of the parent is already in the child. On the nonidentifying side, place the primary key of the parent in the child. In short, if you're going to memorize just a few rules for creating relationships, the first one is "HAS-A: Place the primary key of the parent in the child as the foreign key."

Figure 6-18

Transformation of the
SALES_ORDER Pattern

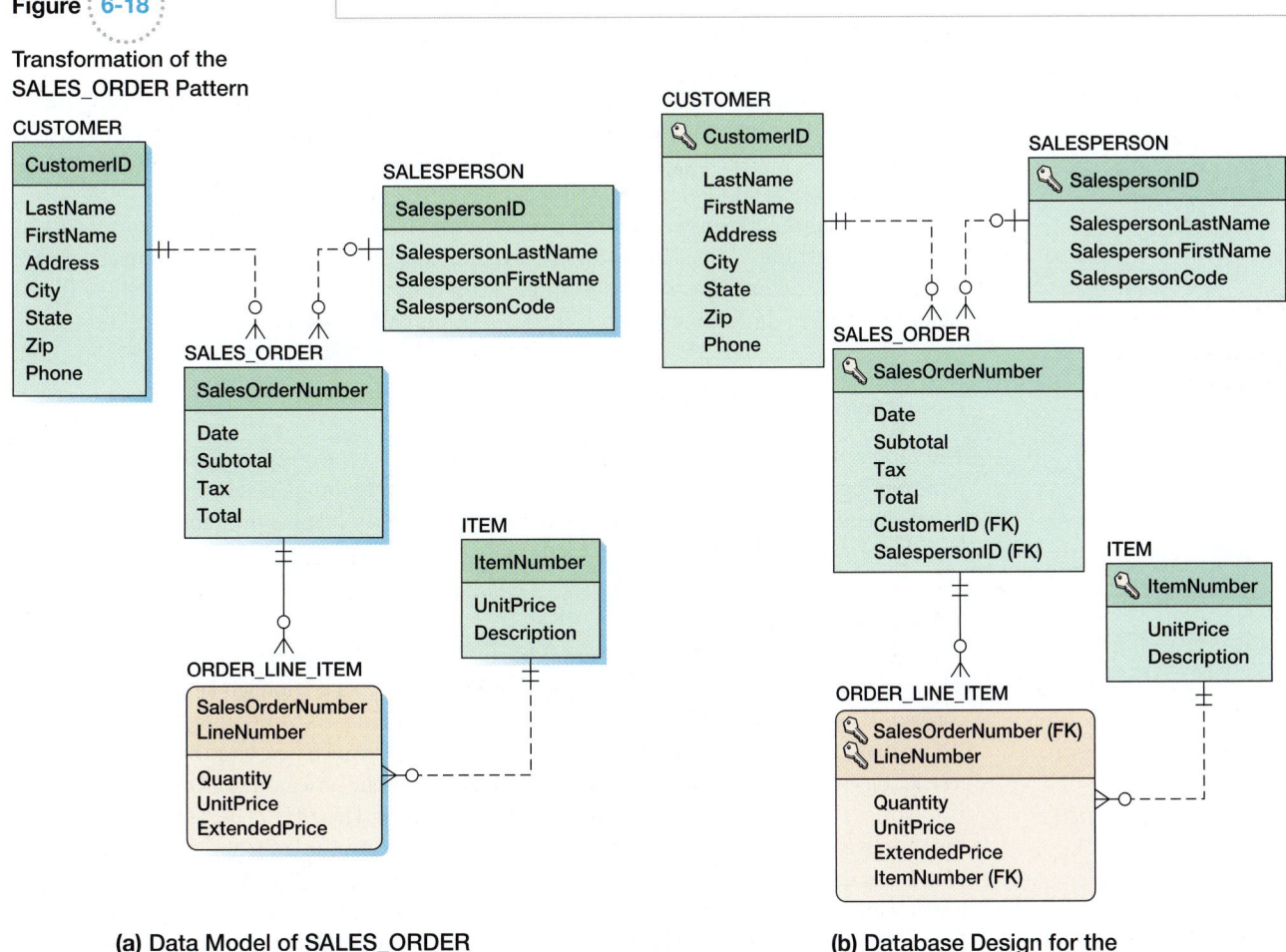

(a) Data Model of SALES_ORDER
Pattern from Figure 5-33

(b) Database Design for the
SALES_ORDER Pattern

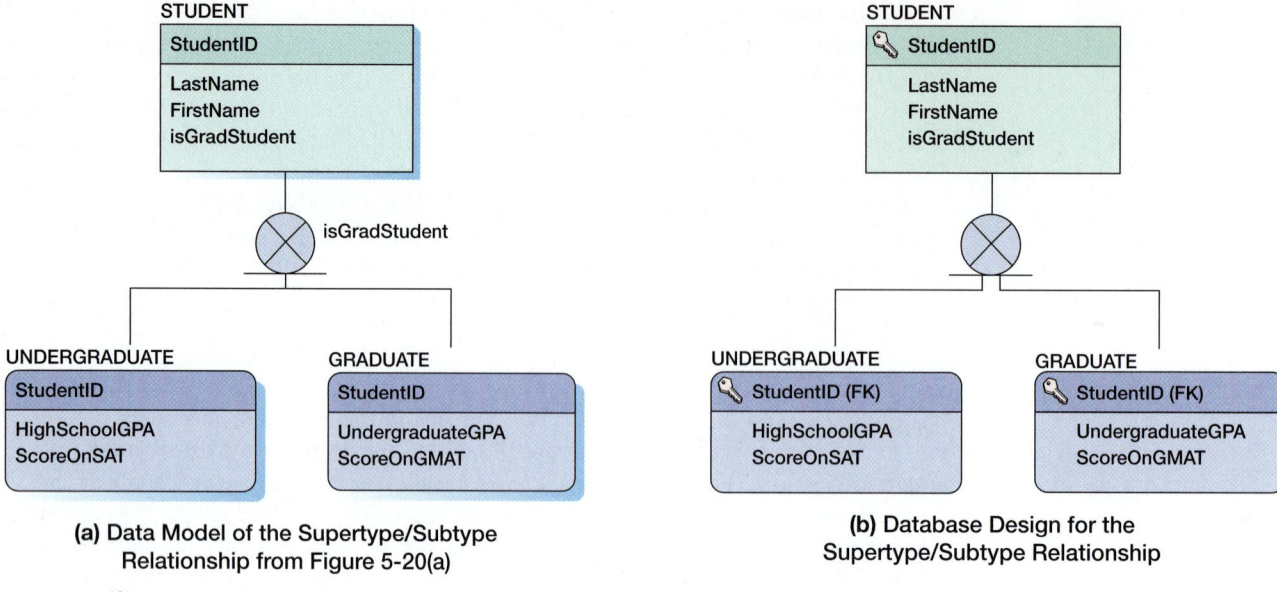

(a) Data Model of the Supertype/Subtype
Relationship from Figure 5-20(a)

(b) Database Design for the
Supertype/Subtype Relationship

Figure 6-19

Transformation of the
Supertype/Subtype Entities

Relationships Between Supertype and Subtype Entities

Representing relationships between supertype entities and their subtypes is easy. Recall that these relationships are also called IS-A relationships because a subtype and its supertype are representations of the same underlying entity. A MANAGER (subtype) is an EMPLOYEE (supertype), and a SALESCLERK (subtype) is also an EMPLOYEE (supertype). Because of this equivalence, the keys of all subtype tables are identical to the key of the supertype table.

Figure 6-19(a) shows the data model in Figure 5-13(a), an example for two subtypes of STUDENT. Notice that the key of STUDENT is StudentID and that the key of each of the subtypes also is StudentID. UNDERGRADUATE.StudentID and GRANDUATE.StudentID are both primary keys and foreign keys to their supertype.

Discriminator attributes cannot be represented in relational designs. In Figure 6-19(b), we can do nothing with isGradStudent except note in the design documentation that isGradStudent determines subtype. Application programs will need to be written to use isGradStudent to determine which subtype pertains to a given STUDENT.

Recursive Relationships

The representation of recursive relationships is just an extension of the techniques used for representing relationships between strong entities. These techniques may be a bit difficult to comprehend at first because they appear strange, but they involve principles that you have already learned.

1:1 Recursive Relationships

Consider the 1:1 recursive BOXCAR relationship in Figure 6-20(a), which is the same data model we developed in Figure 5-38. To represent the relationship, we create a foreign key in BOXCAR that contains the identifier of the boxcar ahead, as shown in Figure 6-20(b). Because the relationship is 1:1, we make the foreign key unique by defining it as unique (shown here as an alternate key). This restriction enforces the fact that a boxcar can have at most one boxcar in front of it.

Notice that both sides of the relationship are optional. This occurs because the last car on the train is ahead of no other car, and because the first car on the train has no other car ahead of it. If the data structure were circular, this restriction would not be necessary. For example, if you wanted to represent the sequence of names of the calendar months, and you wanted December to lead to January, then you could have a 1:1 recursive structure with required children.

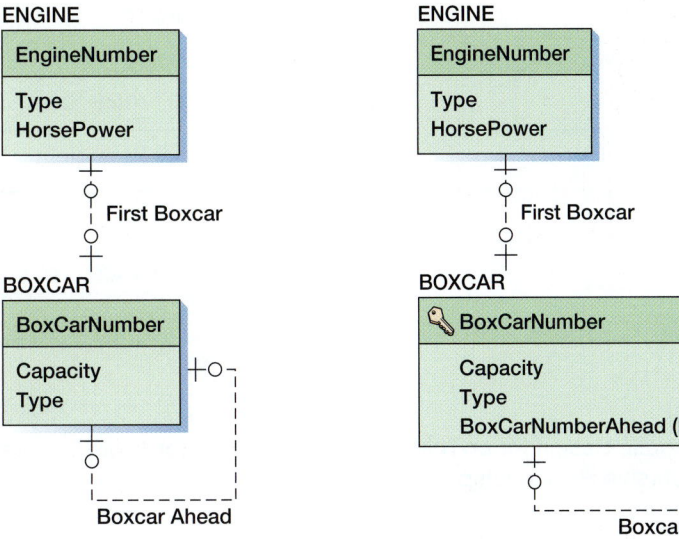

ENGINE
EngineNumber
Type
HorsePower
First Boxcar
BOXCAR
BoxCarNumber
Capacity
Type
Boxcar Ahead

Figure 6-20

Representing 1:1 Recursive Relationships

(a) Data Model for a 1:1 Recursive Relationship in Figure 5-38

(b) Database Design for a 1:1 Recursive Relationship

BY THE WAY If you find the concept of recursive relationships confusing, try this trick. Assume that you have two entities: BOXCAR_AHEAD and BOXCAR_BEHIND, each having the same attributes. Notice that there is a 1:1 relationship between these two entities. Replace each entity with its table. Like all 1:1 strong entity relationships, you can place the key of either table as a foreign key in the other table. For now, place the key of BOXCAR_AHEAD into BOXCAR_BEHIND.

Now realize that BOXCAR_AHEAD only duplicates data that reside in BOXCAR_BEHIND. The data are unnecessary. So, discard BOXCAR_AHEAD and you will have the same design as shown in Figure 6-20(b).

1:N Recursive Relationships

As with all 1:N relationships, 1:N recursive relationships are represented by placing the primary key of the parent in the child as a foreign key. Consider the Manages relationship in Figure 6-21(a), which is the data model we developed in Figure 5-41. In this case, we place the name of the manager in each employee's row. Thus, in Figure 6-21(b), the EmployeeNameMgr has been added to the EMPLOYEE table.

Notice that both the parent and the child are optional. This is true because the lowest-level employees manage no one and because the highest-level person, the CEO or other most senior person, has no manager. If the data structure were circular, this would not be the case.

Figure 6-21

Representing 1:N Recursive Relationships

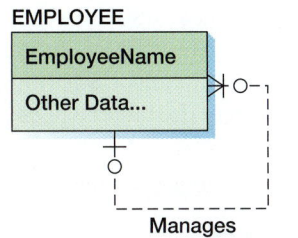

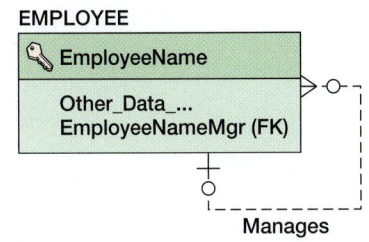

(a) Data Model for a 1:N Recursive Relationship in Figure 5-41

(b) Database Design for a 1:N Recursive Relationship

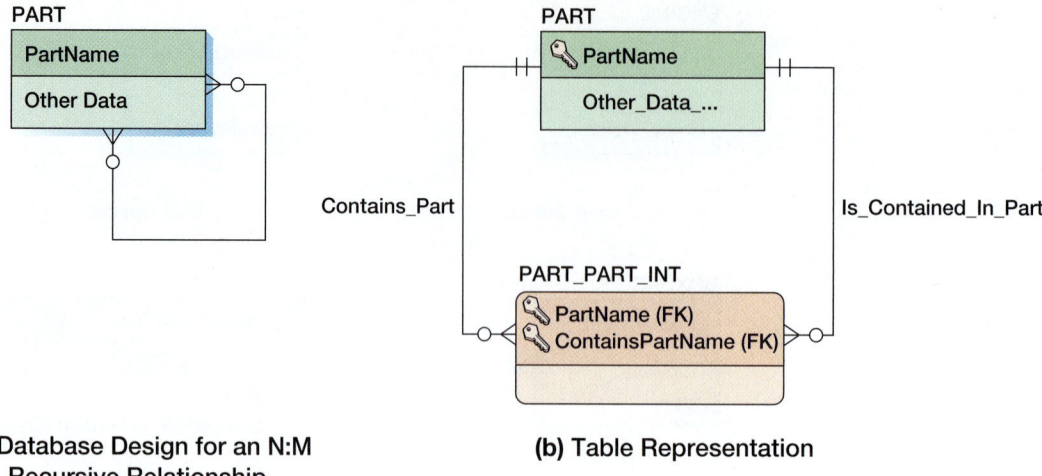

(a) Database Design for an N:M
Recursive Relationship

(b) Table Representation

Figure **6-22**

Representing N:M Recursive
Relationships

N:M Recursive Relationships

The trick for representing N:M recursive relationships is to decompose the N:M relationship into two 1:N relationships. We do this by creating an intersection table, just as we did for N:M relationships between strong entities.

Figure 6-22(a) is the data model we developed in Figure 5-43. It shows the solution to an example for a bill-of-materials problem. Each part has potentially many subordinate parts, and each part can be used as a component in potentially many other parts. To represent this relationship, create an intersection table that shows the correspondence of a part/part use. You can model upwards or downwards. If the former, the intersection table will carry the correspondence of a part and where that part is used. If the latter, the intersection table will carry the correspondence of a part and the parts that it contains. Figure 6-22(b) shows the intersection table for modeling downwards in the bill of materials.

> **BY THE WAY**   Again, if you find this to be confusing, assume that you have two different tables, one called PART and a second called CONTAINED_PART. Create the intersection table between the two tables. Note that CONTAINED_PART duplicates the attributes in PART, and is thus unnecessary. Eliminate the table and you will have the design in Figure 6-22(b).

Representing Ternary and Higher-Order Relationships

As we discussed in Chapter 5, ternary and higher-order relationships can be represented by multiple binary relationships. Most of the time, such a representation works without problem. However, in some cases, there are constraints that add complexity to the situation. For example, consider the ternary relationship among the entities ORDER, CUSTOMER, and SALESPERSON. Assume that the relationship from CUSTOMER to ORDER is 1:N and that the relationship from SALESPERSON to ORDER also is 1:N. We can represent the three-part relationship among ORDER:CUSTOMER:SALESPERSON as two separate binary relationships, one between ORDER and CUSTOMER and a second between SALESPERSON and CUSTOMER. The design of the tables will be:

CUSTOMER (<u>CustomerNumber</u>, {nonkey data attributes})

SALESPERSON (<u>SalespersonNumber</u>, {nonkey data attributes})

ORDER (<u>OrderNumber</u>, {nonkey data attributes}, *CustomerNumber, SalespersonNumber*)

SALESPERSON Table

SalespersonNumber	Other nonkey data
10	
20	
30	

CUSTOMER Table

CustomerNumber	Other nonkey data	SalespersonNumber
1000		10
2000		20
3000		30

Binary MUST Constraint

ORDER Table

OrderNumber	Other nonkey data	SalespersonNumber	CustomerNumber
100		10	1000
200		20	2000
300		10	1000
400		30	3000
500			2000

Only 20 is allowed here

Figure 6-23

Ternary Relationship with a MUST Constraint

Suppose, however, that the business has a rule that each CUSTOMER can place orders only with a particular SALESPERSON. In this case, the ternary relationship ORDER:CUSTOMER:SALESPERSON is constrained by an additional binary 1:N relationship between SALESPERSON and CUSTOMER. To represent the constraint, we need to add the key of SALESPERSON to CUSTOMER. The three relations will now be:

CUSTOMER (<u>CustomerNumber</u>, {nonkey data attributes}, *SalespersonNumber*)

SALESPERSON (<u>SalespersonNumber</u>, {nonkey data attributes})

ORDER (<u>OrderNumber</u>, {nonkey data attributes}, *CustomerNumber, SalespersonNumber*)

The constraint that a particular CUSTOMER is sold to by a particular SALESPERSON means that only certain combinations of CustomerNumber and SalespersonNumber can exist together in ORDER. Unfortunately, this constraint cannot be expressed in a relational model. It must be documented in the design, however, and enforced by program code, as shown in Figure 6-23.

A constraint that requires one entity to be combined with another entity is called a **MUST constraint**. Other similar constraints are the MUST NOT constraint and the MUST COVER constraint. In a **MUST NOT constraint**, the binary relationship indicates combinations that are not allowed to occur in the ternary relationship. For example, the ternary relationship PRESCRIPTION:DRUG:CUSTOMER shown in Figure 6-24 can be constrained by a binary relationship in the ALLERGY table that lists the drugs that a customer is not allowed to take.

In a **MUST COVER constraint**, the binary relationship indicates all combinations that must appear in the ternary relationship. For example, consider the relationship AUTO:REPAIR:TASK in Figure 6-25. Suppose that a given REPAIR consists of a number of TASKs, all of which must be performed for the REPAIR to be successful. In this case, in the relation AUTO-REPAIR, when a given AUTO has a given REPAIR, then all of the TASKs for that REPAIR must appear as rows in that relation.

None of the three types of binary constraints discussed here can be represented in the relational design. Instead, they are documented in the design and implemented in application code.

Figure 6-24

Ternary Relationship with a MUST NOT Constraint

DRUG Table

DrugNumber	Other nonkey data
10	
20	
30	
45	
70	
90	

ALLERGY Table

CustomerNumber	DrugNumber	Other nonkey data
1000	10	
1000	20	
2000	20	
2000	45	
3000	30	
3000	45	
3000	70	

Binary MUST NOT Constraint

PRESCRIPTION Table

PrescriptionNumber	Other nonkey data	*DrugNumber*	*CustomerNumber*
100		45	1000
200		10	2000
300		70	1000
400		20	3000
500			2000

Neither 20 nor 45 can appear here

Figure 6-25

Ternary Relationship with a MUST COVER Constraint

REPAIR Table

RepairNumber	Other nonkey data
10	
20	
30	
40	

TASK Table

TaskNumber	Other nonkey data	*RepairNumber*
1001		10
1002		10
1003		10
2001		20
2002		20
3001		30
4001		40

Binary MUST COVER Constraint

AUTO-REPAIR Table

InvoiceNumber	RepairNumber	TaskNumber	Other nonkey data
100	10	1001	
200	10	1002	
300	10	1003	
400	20	2001	
500	20		

2002 must appear here

Relational Representation of the Highline University Data Model

Let's consider the data model we created for Highline University in Chapter 5. Our final data model for Highline University is shown in Figure 6-26.

Using the principles we've discussed in this chapter, we can turn this into a relational database design, and the resulting database design is a straightforward application of the principles described in this chapter. The database design for Highline University is shown in Figure 6-27.

Review Figure 6-27 to ensure that you understand the representation of every relationship. Note that there are actually two foreign key references to a DepartmentName primary key column in STUDENT. The first is DepartmentName (FK), which is the foreign key linking to the DepartmentName primary key in DEPARTMENT. This relationship has the referential integrity constraint:

DepartmentName in STUDENT must exist in DepartmentName in DEPARTMENT

The second is ProfessorDepartment (FK), which is part of the composite foreign key (ProfessorDepartment, ProfessorFirstName, ProfessorLastName). This foreign key links to the primary key (DepartmentName, ProfessorFirstName, ProfessorLastName) in APPOINTMENT, and has the referential integrity constraint:

(ProfessorDepartment, ProfessorFirstName, ProfessorLastName) in STUDENT must exist in (DepartmentName, ProfessorFirstName, ProfessorLastName) in APPOINTMENT

Note that we had to change DepartmentName in APPOINTMENT to ProfessorDepartment in STUDENT because we cannot have two columns named DepartmentName in STUDENT and we had already used DepartmentName as the foreign key linking to DEPARTMENT.

This illustrates that a foreign key does not have to have the same name as the primary key it links to. As long as the referential integrity constraints are correctly specified, the foreign key name can be whatever we want it to be.

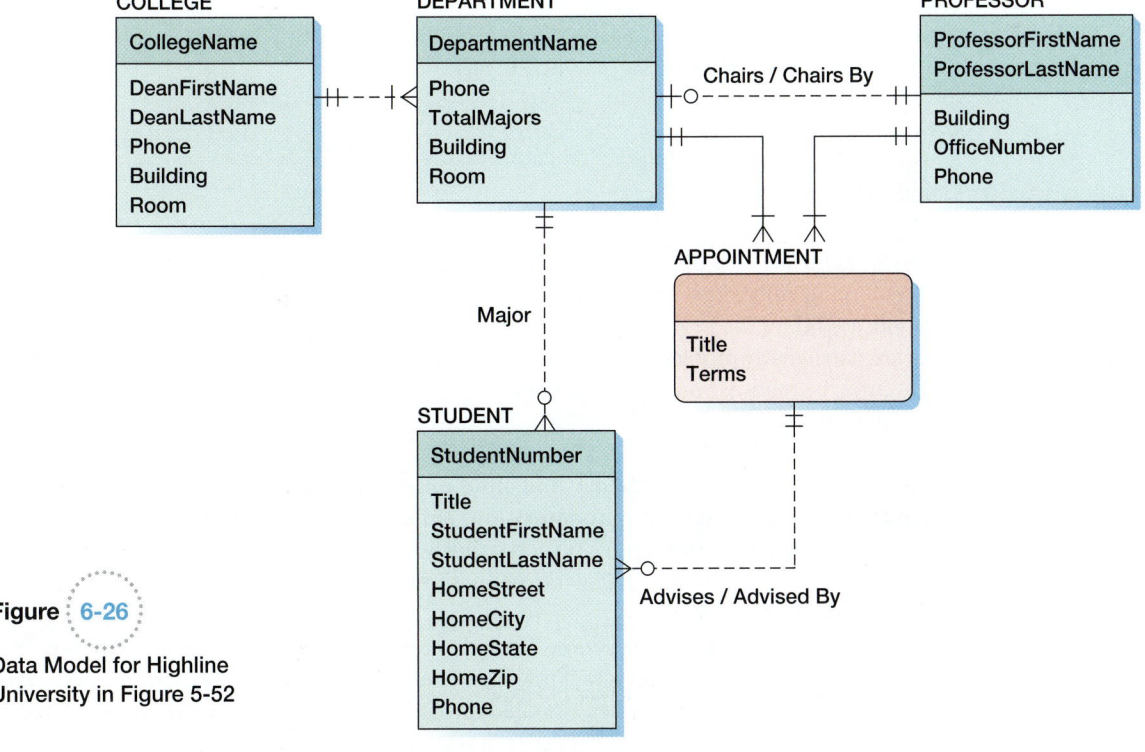

Figure 6-26

Data Model for Highline University in Figure 5-52

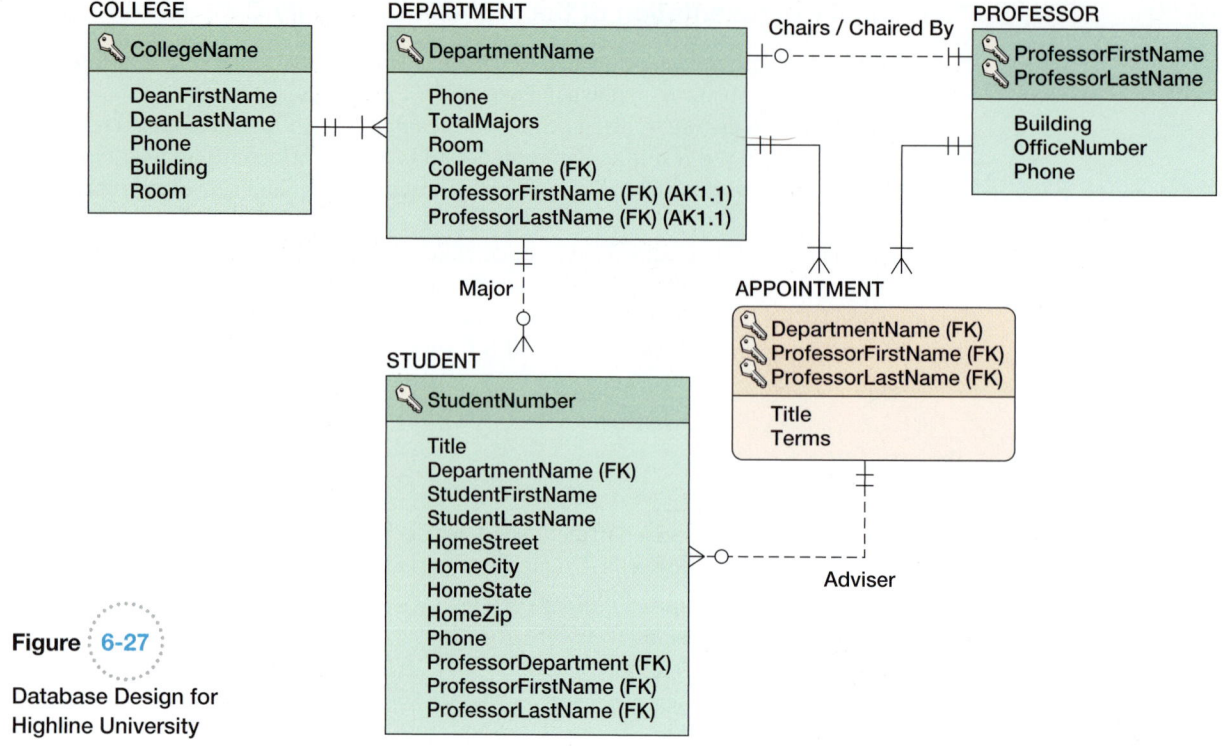

Figure 6-27

Database Design for
Highline University

In addition to the two referential integrity constraints above our database design, we will also have the following:

CollegeName in DEPARTMENT must exist in CollegeName in COLLEGE

(ProfessorFirstName, ProfessorLastName) in DEPARTMENT must exist in (Professor FirstName, ProfessorLastName) in PROFESSOR

DepartmentName in APPOINTMENT must exist in DepartmentName in DEPARTMENT

(ProfessorFirstName, ProfessorLastName) in APPOINTMENT must exist in (Professor FirstName, ProfessorLastName) in PROFESSOR

Design for Minimum Cardinality

The third and last step of transforming data models into database designs is to create a plan for enforcing minimum cardinality. Unfortunately, this step can be considerably more complicated than the first two design steps. Relationships that have required children entities are particularly problematic because we cannot enforce such constraints with database structures. Instead, as you will see, we must design procedures for execution by the DBMS or by applications.

Relationships can have one of four minimum cardinalities: **parent optional and child optional (O-O)**, **parent mandatory and child optional (M-O)**, **parent optional and child mandatory (O-M)**, or **parent mandatory and child mandatory (M-M)**. As far as enforcing minimum cardinality is concerned, no action needs to be taken for O-O relationships, and we need not consider them further. The remaining three relationships pose restrictions on insert, update, and delete activities.

Figure 6-28 summarizes the actions needed to enforce minimum cardinality. Figure 6-28(a) shows needed actions when the parent row is required (M-O and M-M relationships), and Figure 6-28(b) shows needed actions when the child row is required (O-M and M-M relationships). In

Parent Required	Action on Parent	Action on Child
Insert	None.	Get a parent. Prohibit.
Modify key or foreign key	Change children's foreign key values to match new value (**cascade update**). Prohibit.	OK, if new foreign key value matches existing parent. Prohibit.
Delete	Delete children (**cascade delete**). Prohibit.	None.

(a) Actions When the Parent Is Required

Child Required	Action on Parent	Action on Child
Insert	Get a child. Prohibit.	None.
Modify key or foreign key	Update the foreign key of (at least one) child. Prohibit.	If not last child, OK. If last child, prohibit or find a replacement.
Delete	None.	If not last child, OK. If last child, prohibit or find a replacement.

Figure 6-28

Summary of Actions to Enforce Minimum Cardinality

(b) Actions When the Child Is Required

these figures and the accompanying discussion, the term **action** means **minimum cardinality enforcement action**. We use the shorter term *action* for ease of discussion.

To discuss these rules, we will use the database design for storing data on several companies shown in Figure 6-29. In this diagram, we have a 1:N M-O relationship between COMPANY and DEPARTMENT and between DEPARTMENT and EMPLOYEE, and a 1:N M-M relationship between COMPANY and PHONE_CONTACT. In the COMPANY-to-DEPARTMENT relationship, COMPANY (on the 1 side of the relationship) is the parent entity and DEPARTMENT (on the N side of the relationship) is the child entity. In the DEPARMENT-to-EMPLOYEE relationship, DEPARTMENT (on the 1 side of the relationship) is the parent entity and EMPLOYEE (on the N

Figure 6-29

Database Design for Data on Several Companies

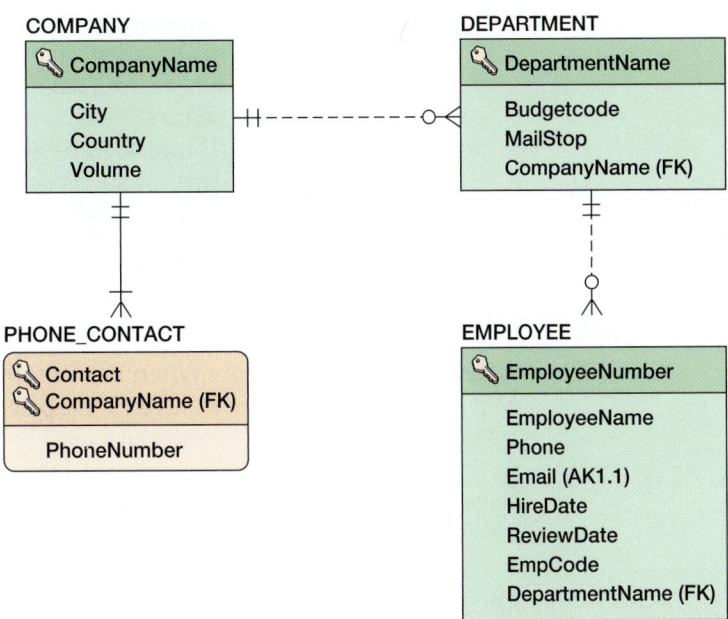

side of the relationship) is the child entity. In the COMPANY-to-PHONE_CONTACT relationship, COMPANY (on the 1 side of the relationship) is the parent entity and PHONE_CONTACT (on the N side of the relationship) is the child entity.

Actions When the Parent Is Required

When the parent is required, we need to ensure that every row of the child table has a valid, non-null value of the foreign key. To accomplish this, we must restrict actions to update or delete the parent's primary key and actions to create or modify the child's foreign key. Consider actions on the parent first.

Actions on the Parent Row When the Parent Is Required

According to Figure 6-28(a), when a new parent is created, nothing needs to be done. No child row can yet be dependent upon the new row. In our example, we can create a new DEPARTMENT and not worry about minimum cardinality enforcement.

However, consider what happens if we attempt to change the value of an existing parent row's primary key. If that row has children, then those children have a foreign key value that matches the current primary key value. If the primary key of the parent changes, then any existing children will become orphans; their foreign key values will no longer match a parent row. To prevent the creation of orphans, either the foreign key values must be changed to match the new value of the parent's primary key or the modification to the parent's primary key must be prohibited.

In our example, if a DEPARTMENT attempts to change its DepartmentName from 'Info Sys' to 'Information Systems', then any child rows that have a foreign key value of 'Info Sys' will no longer match a parent and will be orphans. To prevent orphans, either the values of the foreign key in EMPLOYEE must also be changed to 'Information Systems' or the update to the primary key in DEPARTMENT must be prohibited. The policy of propagating a change from the parent's primary key to the children's foreign key is called **cascading updates**.

Now consider what happens when there is an attempt to delete a parent. If that row has children, and if the deletion is allowed, then the children will become orphans. Hence, when such a delete attempt is made, either the children must be deleted as well or the deletion must be prohibited. Deleting the children along with the parent is called **cascading deletions**. In our example, when an attempt is made to delete a DEPARTMENT, either all related rows in EMPLOYEE must be deleted as well or the deletion must be disallowed.

> **BY THE WAY** Generally, cascading deletions are not chosen for relationships between strong entities. The deletion of a DEPARTMENT row should not force the deletion of EMPLOYEE rows. Instead, the deletion should be disallowed. To remove a DEPARTMENT row, the EMPLOYEE rows would be reassigned to a new DEPARTMENT and then the DEPARTMENT row would be deleted.
>
> However, cascading deletions are almost always chosen for weak child entities. For example, when you delete a COMPANY, you should always delete all of the weak PHONE_NUMBER rows that depend on that COMPANY.

Actions on the Child Row When the Parent Is Required

Now consider actions on the child row. If the parent is required, then when a new child row is created, the new row must have a valid foreign key value. When we create a new EMPLOYEE, for example, if DEPARTMENT is required, then the new EMPLOYEE row must have a valid value for DepartmentName. If not, the insert must be disallowed. Usually there is a default policy for assigning parents to a new row. In our example, when a new row is added to EMPLOYEE, the default policy could be to add the new employee to the department named 'Human Resources'.

With regards to modifications to the foreign key, the new value must match a value of the primary key in the parent. In EMPLOYEE, if we change DepartmentName from 'Accounting' to 'Finance', then there must already be a DEPARTMENT row with the primary key value of 'Finance'. If not, the modification must be prohibited.

If the parent row is required, there are no restrictions on the deletion of the child row. The child can go away without consequence on the parent.

> **BY THE WAY**   When the parent has a surrogate key, the enforcement actions for update are different between the parent and the child. On the parent side, the surrogate key will never change, and hence update actions can be ignored. On the child side, however, the foreign key can change if the child switches to a new parent. Hence, on the parent side, you can ignore actions when the key is a surrogate. On the child side, however, you must consider update actions even when the parent's key is a surrogate.

Actions When the Child Is Required

When the child is required, we need to ensure that there is at least one child row for the parent at all times. The last child cannot leave the parent. For example, in the DEPARTMENT-to-EMPLOYEE relationship, if a DEPARTMENT requires an EMPLOYEE, then the last EMPLOYEE cannot leave the DEPARTMENT. This has ramifications on actions on the child, as shown in Figure 6-28(b).

Enforcing required children is much more difficult than enforcing required parents. To enforce a required parent, we just need to check for a match between primary key and foreign key values. To enforce a required child, we must count the number of children that a parent has. This difference forces us to write code to enforce required children. To begin, consider the required child actions from the perspective of the parent.

Actions on the Parent Row When the Child Is Required

If the child is required, then we cannot create a new parent without also creating a relationship to a child. This means that we must either find an existing child row and change its foreign key to match that of the new parent or we must create a new child row at the same time the parent is created. If neither action can be taken, then the insertion of the new parent must be prohibited. These rules are summarized in the first row of Figure 6-28(b).

If the child is required, then to modify the parent's primary key, either the key of at least one child must also be changed or the update must be disallowed. This restriction never applies to parents with surrogate keys because their values never change.

Finally, if the child is required and the parent is deleted, no action need be taken. Because it is the child that is required, and not the parent, the parent can disappear without any consequence.

Actions on the Child Row When the Child Is Required

As shown in Figure 6-28(b), if the child is required, then no special action needs to be taken when inserting a new child. The child comes into existence without influencing any parent.

However, there are restrictions on updating the foreign key of a required child. In particular, if the child is the last child of its current parent, then the update cannot occur. If it were to occur, the current parent would be childless, and that is not allowed. Thus, a procedure must be written to determine the number of children of the current parent. If that number is two or greater, then the child foreign key value can be changed. Otherwise the update is prohibited.

A similar restriction pertains to the deletion of required children. If the child is the last child to the parent, then the deletion is not allowed. Otherwise, the child can be deleted without restriction.

Relationship Minimum Cardinality	Action to Apply	Remarks
O-O	Nothing	
M-O	Parent-required actions [Figure 6-28(a)]	Easily enforced by DBMS; define referential integrity constraint and make foreign key NOT NULL.
O-M	Child-required actions [Figure 6-28(b)]	Difficult to enforce. Requires use of triggers or other application code.
M-M	Parent-required actions and child-required actions [Figures 6-28(a) and 6-28(b)]	Very difficult to enforce. Requires a combination of complex triggers. Triggers can lock each other out. Many problems!

Figure   6-30

Actions to Apply to Enforce Minimum Cardinality

Implementing Actions for M-O Relationships

Figure 6-30 summarizes the application of the actions in Figure 6-28 for each type of minimum cardinality. As stated earlier, O-O relationships pose no restrictions and need not be considered.

M-O relationships require that the actions in Figure 6-28(a) be enforced. We need to make sure that every child has a parent and that operations on either parent or child rows never create orphans.

Fortunately, these actions are easy to enforce using facilities available in most DBMS products. It turns out that we can enforce these actions with just two limitations. First, we need to define a referential integrity constraint that ensures that every foreign key value has a match in the parent table. Second, we make the foreign key column NOT NULL. With these two restrictions, all of the actions in Figure 6-28(a) will be enforced.

Consider the DEPARTMENT-to-EMPLOYEE example. If we define the referential integrity constraint

DepartmentName in EMPLOYEE must exist in DepartmentName in DEPARTMENT

then we know that every value of DepartmentName in EMPLOYEE will match a value in DEPARTMENT. If we then make DepartmentName required, we know that every row in EMPLOYEE will have a valid DEPARTMENT.

Almost every DBMS product has facilities for defining referential integrity constraints. You will learn how to write SQL statements for that purpose in the next chapter. In those statements, you will have the option of declaring whether updates and deletions are to cascade or are to be prohibited. Once you have defined the constraint and made the foreign key NOT NULL, the DBMS will take care of all of the actions in Figure 6-28(a) for you.

> **BY THE WAY**   Recall that in a 1:1 relationship between strong entities the key of either table can be placed in the other table. If the minimum cardinality of such a relationship is either M-O or O-M, it is generally best to place the key in the optional table. This placement will make the parent required, which is easier to enforce. With a required parent, all you have to do is define the referential integrity constraint and set the foreign key to NOT NULL. However, if you place the foreign key so that the child is required, let the work begin! You will have your hands full, as you're about to see.

Implementing Actions for O-M Relationships

Unfortunately, if the child is required, the DBMS does not provide much help. There is no easy mechanism to ensure that appropriate child foreign keys exist nor is there any easy way to ensure that valid relationships stay valid when rows are inserted, updated, or deleted. You're on your own.

In most cases, required children constraints are enforced using **triggers**, which are modules of code that are invoked by the DBMS when specific events occur. Almost all DBMS products have triggers for insert, update, and delete actions. Triggers are defined for these actions on a particular table. Thus, you can create a trigger on *CUSTOMER INSERT* or a trigger on *EMPLOYEE UPDATE*, and so forth. You will learn more about triggers in the next chapter.

To see how you would use triggers to enforce required children, consider Figure 6-28(b) again. On the parent side, we need to write a trigger on insert and update on the parent row. These triggers either create the required child or they steal an existing child from another parent. If they are unable to perform one of these actions, they must cancel the insert or update.

On the child side, a child can be inserted without problem. Once a child gets a parent, however, it cannot leave that parent if it is the last or only child. Hence, we need to write update and delete triggers on the child that have the following logic: If the foreign key is null, the row has no parent, and the update or delete can proceed. If the foreign key does have a value, however, check whether the row is the last child. If so, it must either delete the parent, find a substitute child, or disallow the update or delete.

None of these actions will be automatically enforced by the DBMS. Instead, you must write code to enforce these rules. You will see generic examples of such code in the next chapter and real examples for SQL Server 2008 in Chapter 10, Oracle Database 11g in Chapter 10A, and MySQL 5.1 in Chapter 10B.

Implementing Actions for M-M Relationships

It is very difficult to enforce M-M relationships. All of the actions in both Figure 6-28(a) and Figure 6-28(b) must be enforced simultaneously. We have a needy parent and a needy child, and neither will let go of the other.

Consider, for example, what would happen if we change the relationship between DEPARTMENT and EMPLOYEE in Figure 6-29 to M-M, and the effect that would have on the creation of new rows in DEPARTMENT and EMPLOYEE. On the DEPARTMENT side, we must write an insert department trigger that tries to insert a new EMPLOYEE for the new DEPARTMENT. However, the EMPLOYEE table will have its own insert trigger. When we try to insert the new EMPLOYEE, the DBMS calls the insert employee trigger, which will prevent the insertion of an EMPLOYEE unless it has a DEPARTMENT row. But the new DEPARTMENT row does not yet exist because it is trying to create the new EMPLOYEE row, which does not exist because the new DEPARTMENT row does not yet exist, and round and round we go!

Now consider a deletion in this same M-M relationship. Suppose we want to delete a DEPARTMENT. We cannot delete a DEPARTMENT that has any EMPLOYEE children. So, before deleting the DEPARTMENT, we must first reassign (or delete) all of the employees in that department. However, when we try to reassign the last EMPLOYEE, an EMPLOYEE update trigger will be fired that will not allow the last employee to be reassigned. (The trigger is programmed to ensure that every DEPARTMENT has at least one EMPLOYEE.) We have a stalemate; the last employee cannot get out of the department, and the department cannot be deleted until all employees are gone!

This problem has several solutions, but none are particularly satisfying. In the next chapter, we will show one solution using SQL Views. That solution is complicated and requires careful programming that is difficult to test and fix. The best advice is to avoid M-M relationships if you can. If you cannot avoid them, budget your time with foreknowledge that a difficult task lies ahead.

Designing Special Case M-M Relationships

Not all M-M relationships are as bad as the last section indicates. Although M-M relationships between strong entities generally are as complicated as described, M-M relationships between strong and weak entities are often easier. For example, consider the relationship between COMPANY and PHONE_CONTACT in Figure 6-29. Because PHONE_CONTACT is an ID-dependent weak, it must have a COMPANY parent. In addition, assume that application requirements indicate that each COMPANY row must have at least one row in PHONE_CONTACT. Hence, the relationship is M-M.

However, transactions are almost always initiated from the side of the strong entity. A data entry form will begin with a COMPANY and then, somewhere in the body of the form, the data from the PHONE_CONTACT table will appear. Hence, all insert, update, and deletion activity on PHONE_CONTACT will come as a result of some action on COMPANY. Given this situation, we can ignore the Action on Child columns in Figure 6-28(a) and Figure 6-28(b), because no one will ever try to insert, modify, or delete a new PHONE_CONTACT except in the context of inserting, modifying, or deleting a COMPANY.

Because the relationship is M-M, however, we must take all of the actions in the Action on Parent columns of both Figure 6-28(a) and Figure 6-28(b). With regards to inserts on parents, we must always create a child. We can meet this need by writing a COMPANY INSERT trigger that automatically creates a new row of PHONE_CONTACT with null values for Contact and PhoneNumber.

With regard to updates and deletions, all we need to do is to cascade all of the remaining actions in Figure 6-28(a) and Figure 6-28(b). Changes to COMPANY.CompanyName will be propagated to PHONE_CONTACT.CompanyName. The deletion of a COMPANY will automatically delete that company's PHONE_CONTACT rows. This makes sense; if we no longer want data about a company, we certainly no longer want its contact and phone data.

> **BY THE WAY**   Because of the difficulty of enforcing M-M relationships, developers look for special circumstances to ease the task. Such circumstances usually exist for relationships between strong and weak entities, as described. For relationships between strong entities, such special circumstances may not exist. In this case, the M-M cardinality is sometimes just ignored. Of course, this cannot be done for applications such as financial management or operations that require careful records management, but, for an application such as airline reservations, where seats are overbooked anyway, it might be better to redefine the relationship as M-O.

Documenting the Minimum Cardinality Design

Because enforcing minimum cardinality can be complicated, and because it often involves the creation of triggers or other procedures, clear documentation is essential. Because the design for the enforcement of required parents is easier than that for required children, we will use different techniques for each.

Documenting Required Parents

Database modeling and design tools such as ERwin, Visio, and MySQL Workbench allow you to define **referential integrity (RI) actions** on each table. These definitions are useful for documenting the actions necessary for required parent. According to Figure 6-28(a), three design decisions are necessary for required parents: (1) determining whether updates to the parent's primary key should cascade or be prohibited; (2) determining whether deletions of the parent should cascade or be prohibited; and (3) identifying how a parent row is to be selected on the insert of a child.

> **BY THE WAY**   In theory, referential integrity actions can be used to document the actions to be taken to enforce required children as well as required parents. When they are used for both purposes, however, they become confusing and ambiguous. In an M-M relationship, for example, a child may have one set of rules for insert because of its required parent and another set of rules for insert because it is a required child. The insert referential integrity action will be overloaded with these two purposes, and its meaning will be ambiguous, at best. Hence, in this text, we will use referential integrity actions only for documenting required parents. We will use another technique, described next, for documenting required children.

Documenting Required Children

One easy and unambiguous way for defining the actions to enforce a required child is to use Figure 6-28(b) as a boilerplate document. Create a copy of this figure for each relationship that has a required child and fill in the specific actions for insert, update, and delete operations.

For example, consider Figure 6-31, which shows the O-M relationship between HOUSE and INSPECTION. A given house must have at least one inspection, but an inspection need not be related to any house. HOUSE has a surrogate key, HouseID, and other columns, as shown in Figure 6-31.

Because the HOUSE-to-INSPECTION relationship has a required child, we will fill out the table in Figure 6-28(b). Figure 6-32 shows the result. Here, triggers are described for HOUSE insert and INSPECTION deletion. HOUSE update actions are unneeded because HOUSE has a surrogate key, and INSPECTION update is prohibited because of the surrogate key and also because inspections are never reassigned to a different house.

Figure  6-31

HOUSE-to-INSPECTION O-M
Relationship

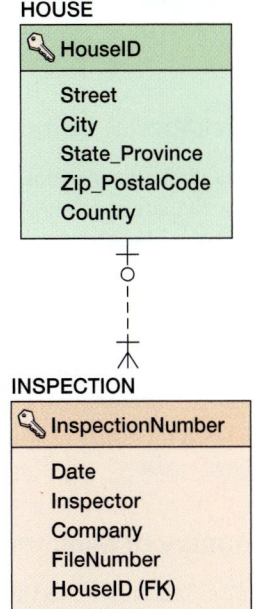

Figure 6-32

Actions to Enforce the
O-M Relationship Between
HOUSE and INSPECTION

INSPECTION Is Required	Action on HOUSE	Action on INSPECTION
Insert	Trigger to create row in INSPECTION when inserting HOUSE. Disallow HOUSE insert if INSPECTION data are not available.	None.
Modify key or foreign key	Not possible, surrogate key.	Prohibit. HOUSE has surrogate key and inspections never change to a different house.
Delete	None.	Trigger to prohibit if sole INSPECTION report.

Relationship Minimum Cardinality	Design Decisions to Be Made	Design Documentation
M-O	• Update cascade or prohibit? • Delete cascade or prohibit? • Policy for obtaining parent on insert of child	Referential integrity (RI) actions plus documentation for policy on obtaining parent for child insert.
O-M	• Policy for obtaining child on insert of parent • Primary key update cascade or prohibit? • Policy for update of child foreign key • Policy for deletion of child	Use Figure 6-28(b) as a boilerplate
M-M	All decisions for M-O and O-M above, plus how to process trigger conflict on insertion of first instance of parent/child and deletion of last instance of parent/child.	For mandatory parent, RI actions plus documentation for policy on obtaining parent for child insert. For mandatory child, use 6-28(b) as a boilerplate. Add documentation on how to process trigger conflict.

Figure  **6-33**

Summary of Design
Decisions for Minimum
Cardinality

An Additional Complication

You should be aware of an additional complication that is beyond the scope of this text. A table can participate in many relationships. In fact, there can be multiple relationships between the same two tables. You need to specify a design for the minimum cardinality of every relationship. The minimum cardinality of each relationship will vary. Some will be O-M, some will be M-O, and some will be M-M. Some of the relationships will require triggers, which may mean that you have several sets of insert, update, and delete triggers per table. This array of triggers is not only complicated to write and test, the actions of different triggers may interfere with one another during execution. You will need more experience and knowledge to design, implement, and test such complex arrays of trigger code and DBMS constraints. For now, just be aware that these problems exist.

Summary of Minimum Cardinality Design

Figure 6-33 summarizes the design for relationship minimum cardinality. It shows each type of relationship, the design decisions that need to be made, and the documentation that should be created. Use this figure as a guide.

The View Ridge Gallery Database

We conclude this chapter with an example database design problem. This design will be used throughout the rest of the text, so take the time to understand it. This particular problem was chosen because it has typical relationships and moderate complexity. It has enough challenges to make it interesting, but not so many as to make it overwhelming.

Summary of Requirements

The **View Ridge Gallery (View Ridge** or **VRG)** is a small art gallery that sells contemporary European and North American fine art, including lithographs, high-quality reproduction prints, original paintings and other artwork, and photographs. All of the lithographs, prints, and photos are signed and numbered, and the original art is usually signed. View Ridge also provides art framing services. It creates a custom frame for each artwork (rather than selling standardized, premade frames), and is known for its excellent collection of frame stock.

View Ridge emphasizes reproduction artworks of European Impressionist, Abstractionist, and Modernist artists such as Wassily Kandinsky and Henri Matisse. For original art, View Ridge

Figure 6-34

Summary of View Ridge
Gallery Database
Requirements

- Track customers and their artist interests
- Record gallery's purchases
- Record customers' art purchases
- List the artists and works that have appeared in the gallery
- Report how fast an artist's works have sold and at what margin
- Show current inventory in a Web page

concentrates on Northwest School artists, such as Mark Tobey, Morris Graves, Guy Anderson, and Paul Horiuchi, and produces shows of contemporary artists who work in the Northwest School tradition or in Northwest Maritime art. The price of new reproduction prints ranges up to $1,000, and prices for contemporary artists range from $500 to $10,000. The price of art from the Northwest School artists varies considerably, depending on the artwork itself. Small pencil, charcoal, or watercolor sketches may sell for as little as $2,000, whereas major works can range from $10,000 to $100,000. Very occasionally, View Ridge may carry Northwest School art priced up to $500,000, but art priced above $250,000 is more likely to be sold at auction by a major art auction house.

View Ridge has been in business for 30 years and has one full-time owner, three salespeople, and two workers who make frames, hang art in the gallery, and prepare artwork for shipment. View Ridge holds openings and other gallery events to attract customers to the gallery. View Ridge owns all of the art that it sells—even sales of contemporary artwork is treated as a purchase by View Ridge that then is resold to a customer. View Ridge does not take items on a consignment basis.

The requirements for the View Ridge application are summarized in Figure 6-34. First, both the owner and the salespeople want to keep track of customers' names, addresses, phone numbers, and e-mail addresses. They also want to know which artists have appeal to which customers. The salespeople use this information to determine whom to contact when new art arrives and to personalize verbal and e-mail communications with their customers.

When the gallery purchases new art, data about the artist, the nature of the work, the acquisition date, and the acquisition price are recorded. Also, on occasion, the gallery repurchases art from a customer and resells it, thus a work may appear in the gallery multiple times. When art is repurchased, the artist and work data are not reentered, but the most recent acquisition date and price are recorded. In addition, when art is sold, the purchase date, sales price, and identity of the purchasing customer are stored in the database.

Salespeople want to examine past purchase data so that they can devote more time to the most active buyers. They also sometimes use the purchase records to identify the location of artworks they have sold in the past.

For marketing purposes, View Ridge wants its database application to provide a list of artists and works that have appeared in the gallery. The owner also would like to be able to determine how fast an artist's work sells and at what sales margin. The database application also should display current inventory on a Web page that customers can access via the Internet.

The View Ridge Data Model

Figure 6-35 shows a data model for the View Ridge database. This model has two strong entities: CUSTOMER and ARTIST. In addition, the entity WORK is ID dependent on ARTIST, and the entity TRANS is ID dependent on WORK. There is also a nonidentifying relationship from CUSTOMER to TRANS.

Note that we are using the entity name TRANS instead of TRANSACTION. We are doing this because *transaction* is a **DBMS reserved word** in most (if not all) DBMS products. Using DBMS reserved words such as *table*, *column*, or other names can create problems. Similarly, we cannot use the reserved word *tran*. The word *trans*, however, is not a DBMS reserved word, and we can use it without problems. We will discuss this problem more when we discuss specific DBMS products in Chapters 10, 10A, and 10B.

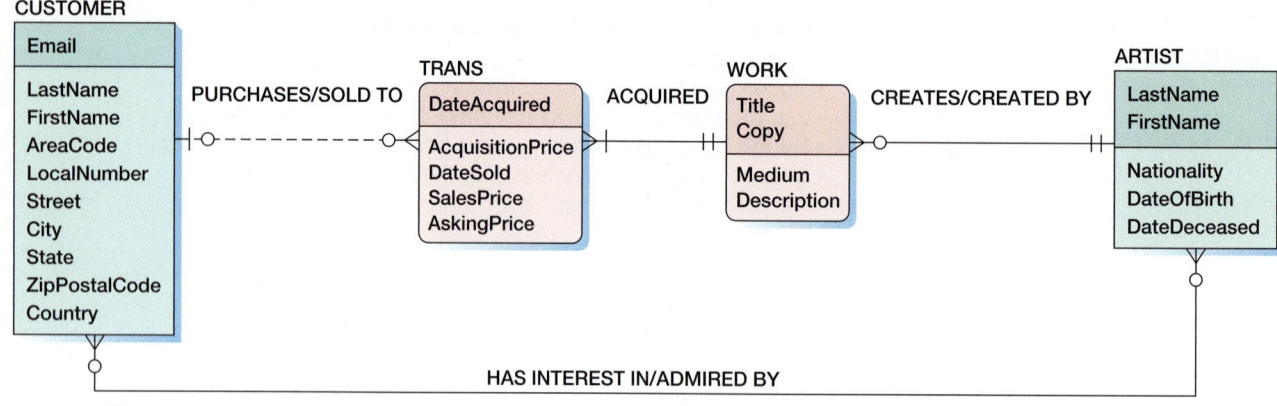

View Ridge Gallery Data Model

In the View Ridge data model, an artist may be recorded in the database even if none of his or her works has appeared in the gallery. This is done to record customer preferences for artists whose works might appear in the future. Thus, an artist may have from zero to many works.

The identifier of WORK is the composite (Title, Copy) because, in the case of lithographs and photos, there may be many copies of a given title. Also, the requirements indicate that a work may appear in the gallery many times, so there is a need for potentially many TRANS entities for each WORK. Each time a work appears in the gallery, the acquisition date and price must be recorded. Thus, each WORK must have at least one TRANS row.

A customer may purchase many works; this is recorded in the 1:N relationship from CUSTOMER to TRANS. Note that this relationship is optional in both directions. Finally, there is an N:M relationship between CUSTOMERs and ARTISTs. This is an N:M relationship between strong entities—the team searched in vain for a missing attribute that would indicate an association pattern rather than an N:M relationship.

Database Design with Data Keys

A database design for the data model in Figure 6-35 is shown in Figure 6-36. This design uses data keys, and every primary key except the composite (ARTIST.LastName, ARTIST.FirstName) has problems. The keys for WORK and TRANS are huge, and the key for CUSTOMER is doubtful; many customers may not have an e-mail address. Because of these problems, this design cries out for surrogate keys.

Initial View Ridge Gallery Database Design

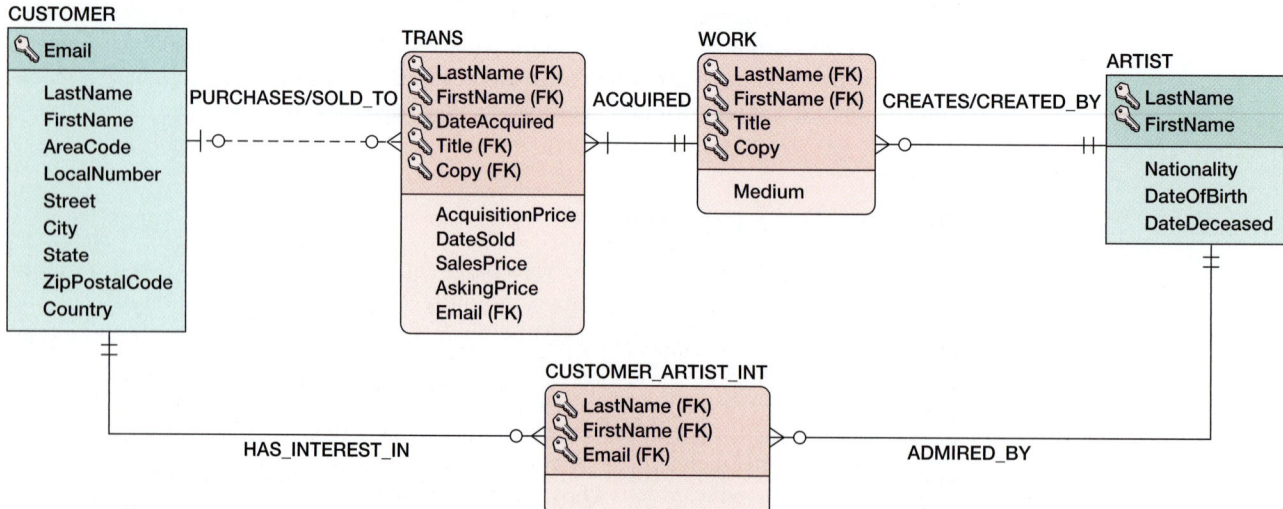

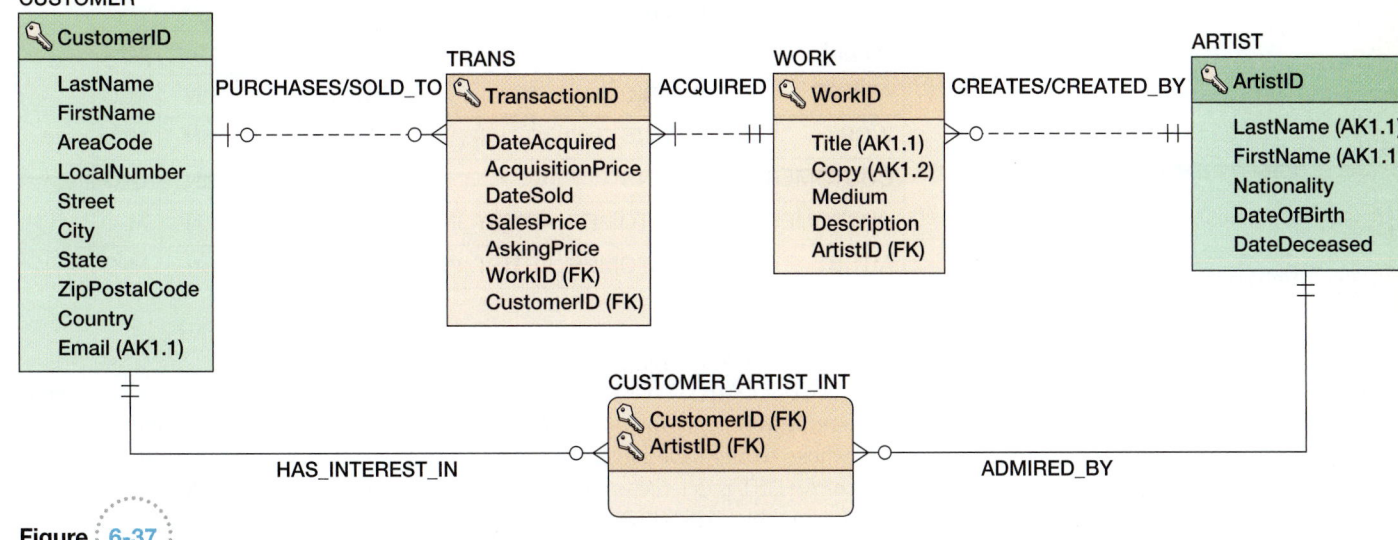

Figure 6-37

Final View Ridge Gallery
Database Design

Surrogate Key Database Design

The database design for the View Ridge database using surrogate keys is shown in Figure 6-37. Notice that two identifying relationships (TRANS-to-WORK) and (WORK-to-ARTIST) have been changed to nonidentifying relationships represented by dashed lines. This was done because once ARTIST has a surrogate key, there is no need to keep ID-dependent keys in WORK and TRANS. Realize that WORK and TRANS are both weak entities even though they are no longer ID dependent.

Notice that (LastName, FirstName) in ARTIST has been defined as an alternate key. This notation indicates that (LastName, FirstName) has a UNIQUE constraint, which ensures that artists are not duplicated in the database. Similarly, (Title, Copy) in WORK is defined as an alternate key so that a given work cannot appear more than once.

The foreign key placement is a straightforward application of the techniques described in this chapter, but note that the foreign key CustomerID in TRANS can have null values. This specification allows the creation of a TRANS row when a work is acquired, before any customer has purchased the work. All other foreign keys are required.

Minimum Cardinality Enforcement for Required Parents

According to Figure 6-28(a), for each relationship that involves a required parent, we need to decide:

- Whether to cascade or prohibit updates of the parent's primary key
- Whether to cascade or prohibit deletions of the parent
- How to obtain a parent when a new child is created.

Because there is no consistent means of documenting these actions in commercial database design products, we will use the templates in Figure 6-28 to document our decisions. Figure 6-38 summarizes the relationships in the View Ridge database design.

Because all tables have surrogate keys, there is no need for any update cascade behavior for any parent. However, some update actions on child tables must be restricted. For example, once a WORK (child) is assigned to an ARTIST (parent), it is never to change to another parent. Because this database is used to record purchases and sales, View Ridge management never wants to delete any data that are related to a transaction. From time to time, they may remove prior year's data in bulk, but they will do that using bulk data transfer and not as part of any application.

Relationship		Cardinality		
Parent	**Child**	**Type**	**MAX**	**MIN**
ARTIST	WORK	Nonidentifying	1:N	M-O
WORK	TRANS	Nonidentifying	1:N	M-M
CUSTOMER	TRANS	Nonidentifying	1:N	O-O
CUSTOMER	CUSTOMER_ARTIST_INT	Identifying	1:N	M-O
ARTIST	CUSTOMER_ARTIST_INT	Identifying	1:N	M-O

Figure 6-38

Summary of View Ridge
Database Design
Relationships

Hence, any CUSTOMER, WORK, or ARTIST row that is related to a TRANS row is never to be deleted. Note, however, that rows of CUSTOMERs who have never made a purchase and rows of ARTISTs whose works have never been carried in the gallery can be deleted. If either a CUSTOMER or ARTIST is deleted under these circumstances, the deletion will cascade to rows in the intersection table CUSTOMER_ARTIST_INT.

Finally, referential integrity actions are necessary for obtaining a parent WORK when a TRANS record is created, and a parent ARTIST when a WORK record is created. In both cases, the policy will be for the application program to provide the ID of the required parent at the time the WORK or TRANS record is created.

All these actions are documented in Figure 6-39, where each part is based on the template for required children shown in Figure 6-28(a). Note that there is no diagram for the CUSTOMER-to-TRANS relationship, because that is an O-O relationship without a required parent (or child).

Figure 6-39

Actions to Enforce Minimum
Cardinality for Required
Parents

ARTIST Is Required Parent	**Action on ARTIST (Parent)**	**Action on WORK (Child)**
Insert	None.	Get a parent.
Modify key or foreign key	Prohibit—ARTIST uses a surrogate key.	Prohibit—ARTIST uses a surrogate key.
Delete	Prohibit if WORK exists—data related to a transaction is never deleted (business rule). Allow if no WORK exists (business rule).	None.

(a) For the ARTIST-to-WORK Relationship

WORK Is Required Parent	**Action on WORK (Parent)**	**Action on TRANS (Child)**
Insert	None.	Get a parent.
Modify key or foreign key	Prohibit—WORK uses a surrogate key.	Prohibit—WORK uses a surrogate key.
Delete	Prohibit—data related to a transaction is never deleted (business rule).	None.

(b) For the WORK-to-TRANS Relationship

CUSTOMER Is Required Parent	Action on CUSTOMER (Parent)	Action on CUSTOMER_ARTITST_INT (Child)
Insert	None.	Get a parent.
Modify key or foreign key	Prohibit—CUSTOMER uses a surrogate key.	Prohibit—CUSTOMER uses a surrogate key.
Delete	Prohibit if TRANS exists—data related to a transaction is never deleted (business rule). Allow if no TRANS exists (business rule)—cascade delete children.	None.

(c) For the CUSTOMER-to-CUSTOMER_ARTIST_INT Relationship

ARTIST Is Required Parent	Action on ARTIST (Parent)	Action on CUSTOMER_ARTITST_INT (Child)
Insert	None.	Get a parent.
Modify key or foreign key	Prohibit—ARTIST uses a surrogate key.	Prohibit—ARTIST uses a surrogate key.
Delete	Prohibit if TRANS exists—data related to a transaction is never deleted (business rule). Allow if no TRANS exists (business rule)—cascade delete children.	None.

Figure 6-39
(Continued)

(d) For the ARTIST-to-CUSTOMER_ARTIST_INT Relationship

Minimum Cardinality Enforcement for the Required Child

As shown in the summary in Figure 6-38, TRANS is the only required child in the database design in Figure 6-37. The actions to enforce that required child are documented in Figure 6-40, which is based on the template in Figure 6-28(b).

TRANS Is Required Parent	Action on WORK (Parent)	Action on TRANS (Child)
Insert	INSERT trigger on WORK to create row in TRANS. TRANS will be given data for DateAcquired and AcquisitionPrice. Other columns will be null.	Will be created by INSERT trigger on WORK.
Modify key or foreign key	Prohibit—surrogate key.	Prohibit—TRANS must always refer to the WORK associated with it.
Delete	Prohibit—data related to a transaction is never deleted (business rule).	Prohibit—data related to a transaction is never deleted (business rule).

Figure 6-40

Actions to Enforce Minimum Cardinality for Required Children for the WORK-to-TRANS Relationship

According to this document, an INSERT trigger on WORK will be written to create the required child. This trigger will be fired whenever a work is first introduced at the gallery. At that time, a new TRANS row will be created to store the values for DateAcquired and AcquisitionPrice.

Changes to the primary key in WORK will not occur because it has a surrogate key. Changes to the foreign key in TRANS will not be allowed because a TRANS never switches to another work. As stated earlier, the gallery has the policy that no transaction or related data will ever be deleted. Consequently, deletions of either WORK or TRANS are not allowed.

Column Properties for the View Ridge Database Design Tables

As we discussed at the beginning of this chapter, besides naming the columns in each table, we must specify the column properties summarized in Figure 6-1 for each column: null status, data type, default value (if any), and data constraints (if any). These are shown Figure 6-41.

With this step, we have completed our database design for the View Ridge Gallery database, and now we are ready to create it as an actual, functioning database in a DBMS product. We will do so in many of the following chapters, so be certain that you understand the View Ridge Gallery database design we have built.

Figure 6-41

Database Column Properties for the View Ridge Database Design

Column Name	Type	Key	NULL Status	Remarks
ArtistID	Int	Primary Key	NOT NULL	Surrogate Key IDENTITY (1,1)
LastName	Char (25)	Alternate Key	NOT NULL	Unique (AK1.1)
FirstName	Char (25)	Alternate Key	NOT NULL	Unique (AK1.2)
Nationality	Char (30)	No	NULL	IN ('Canadian', 'English', 'French', 'German', 'Mexican', 'Russian', 'Spanish', 'United States')
DateOfBirth	Numeric (4)	No	NULL	(DateOfBirth < DateDeceased) (BETWEEN 1900 and 2999)
DateDeceased	Numeric (4)	No	NULL	(BETWEEN 1900 and 2999)

(a) Column Characteristics for the ARTIST Table

Column Name	Type	Key	NULL Status	Remarks
WorkID	Int	Primary Key	NOT NULL	Surrogate Key IDENTITY (500,1)
Title	Char (35)	Alternate Key	NOT NULL	Unique (AK1.1)
Copy	Char (12)	Alternate Key	NOT NULL	Unique (AK1.2)
Medium	Char (35)	No	NULL	
Description	Varchar (1000)	No	NULL	DEFAULT value = 'Unknown provenance'
ArtistID	Int	Foreign Key	NOT NULL	

(b) Column Characteristics for the WORK Table

Column Name	Type	Key	NULL Status	Remarks
TransactionID	Int	Primary Key	NOT NULL	Surrogate Key IDENTITY (100,1)
DateAcquired	Date	No	NOT NULL	
AcquisitionPrice	Numeric (8,2)	No	NOT NULL	
AskingPrice	Numeric (8,2)	No	NULL	
DateSold	Date	No	NULL	(DateAcquired <= DateSold)
SalesPrice	Numeric (8,2)	No	NULL	(SalesPrice > 0) AND (SalesPrice <=500000)
CustomerID	Int	Foreign Key	NULL	
WorkID	Int	Foreign Key	NOT NULL	

(c) Column Characteristics for the TRANS Table

Column Name	Type	Key	NULL Status	Remarks
CustomerID	Int	Primary Key	NOT NULL	Surrogate Key IDENTITY (100,1)
LastName	Char (25)	No	NOT NULL	
FirstName	Char (25)	No	NOT NULL	
Street	Char (30)	No	NULL	
City	Char (35)	No	NULL	
State	Char (2)	No	NULL	
ZipPostalCode	Char (9)	No	NULL	
Country	Char (50)	No	NULL	
AreaCode	Char (3)	No	NULL	
PhoneNumber	Char (8)	No	NULL	
Email	Varchar (100)	Alternate Key	NULL	Unique (AK 1.1)

(d) Column Characteristics for the CUSTOMER Table

Column Name	Type	Key	NULL Status	Remarks
ArtistID	Int	Primary Key, Foreign Key	NOT NULL	
CustomerID	Int	Primary Key, Foreign Key	NOT NULL	

(e) Column Characteristics for the CUSTOMER_ARTIST_INT Table

Figure  **6-41**

(Continued)

Summary

Transforming a data model into a database design requires three major tasks: replacing each entity with a table and each attribute with a column; representing relationships and maximum cardinality by placing foreign keys; and representing minimum cardinality by defining actions to constrain activities on values of primary and foreign keys.

During database design, each entity is replaced by a table. The attributes of the entity become columns of the table. The identifier of the entity becomes the primary key of the table, and candidate keys in the entity become candidate keys in the table. A good primary key is short, numeric, and fixed. If a good primary key is not available, a surrogate key may be used instead. Some organizations choose to use surrogate keys for all of their tables. An alternate key is the same as a candidate key and is used to ensure unique values in a column. The notation AK$n.m$ refers to the nth alternative key and the mth column in that key.

Four properties need to be specified for each table column: null status, data type, default value, and data constraints. A column can be NULL or NOT NULL. Primary keys are always NOT NULL; alternate keys can be NULL. Data types depend on the DBMS to be used. Generic data types include CHAR(n), VARCHAR(n), DATE, TIME, MONEY, INTEGER, and DECIMAL. A default value is a value to be supplied by the DBMS when a new row is created. It can be a simple value or the result of a function. Sometimes triggers are needed to supply values of more complicated expressions.

Data constraints include domain constraints, range constraints, intrarelation constraints, and interrelation constraints. Domain constraints specify a set of values that a column may have; range constraints specify an interval of allowed values; intrarelation constraints involve comparisons among columns in the same table; and interrelation constraints involve comparisons among columns in different tables. A referential integrity constraint is an example of an interrelation constraint.

Once the tables, keys, and columns have been defined, they should be checked against normalization criteria. Usually the tables will already be normalized, but they should be checked in any case. Also, it may be necessary to denormalize some tables.

The second step in database design is to create relationships by placing foreign keys appropriately. For 1:1 strong relationships, the key of either table can go in the other table as a foreign key; for 1:N strong relationships, the key of the parent must go in the child; and for N:M strong relationships, a new table, called an intersection table, is constructed that has the keys of both tables. Intersection tables never have nonkey data.

Four uses for ID-dependent entities are N:M relationships, association relationships, multivalued attributes, and archetype/instance relationships. An association relationship differs from an intersection table because the ID-dependent entity has nonkey data. In all ID-dependent entities, the key of the parent is already in the child. Therefore, no foreign key needs to be created. When an instance entity of the archetype/instance pattern is given a non-ID-dependent identifier, it changes from an ID-dependent entity to a weak entity. The tables that represent such entities must have the key of the parent as a foreign key. They remain weak entities, however. When the parent of an ID-dependent entity is given a surrogate key, the ID-dependent entity is also given a surrogate key. It remains a weak entity, however.

Mixed entities are represented by placing the key of the parent of the nonidentifying relationship into the child. The key of the parent of the identifying relationship will already be in the child. Subtypes are represented by copying the key from the supertype into the subtype(s) as a foreign key. Recursive relationships are represented in the same ways that 1:1, 1:N, and N:M relationships are represented. The only difference is that the foreign key references rows in the table in which it resides.

Ternary relationships are decomposed into binary relationships. However, sometimes binary constraints must be documented. Three such constraints are MUST, MUST NOT, and MUST COVER.

The third step in database design is to create a plan for enforcing minimum cardinality. Figure 6-28 shows the actions that need to be taken to enforce minimum cardinality for required parents and required children. The actions in Figure 6-28(a) must be taken for M-O and M-M relationships; the actions in Figure 6-28(b) must be taken for O-M and M-M relationships.

Enforcing mandatory parents can be done by defining the appropriate referential integrity constraint and by setting the foreign key to NOT NULL. The designer must specify whether updates to the parent's primary key will cascade or be prohibited, whether deletions to the parent will cascade or be prohibited, and what policy will be used for finding a parent when a new child is created.

Enforcing mandatory children is difficult and requires the use of triggers or application code. The particular actions that need to be taken are shown in Figure 6-28(b). Enforcing M-M relationships can be very difficult. Particular challenges concern the creation of the first parent/child rows and the deletion of the last parent/child rows. The triggers on the two tables interfere with one another. M-M relationships between strong and weak entities are not as problematic as those between strong entities.

In this text, the actions to enforce required parents are documented using referential integrity actions on the table design diagrams. The actions to enforce required children are documented by using Figure 6-28(b) as a boilerplate document. An additional complication is that a table can participate in many relationships. Triggers written to enforce the minimum cardinality on one relationship may interfere with triggers written to enforce the minimum cardinality on another relationship. This problem is beyond the scope of this text, but be aware that it exists. The principles for enforcing minimum cardinality are summarized in Figure 6-33.

A database design for the View Ridge Gallery is shown in Figures 6-37, 6-38, 6-39, 6-40, and 6-41. You should understand this design, because it will be used throughout the remainder of this book.

Key Terms

action	MUST constraint
alternate key (AK)	MUST COVER constraint
candidate key	MUST NOT constraint
cascading deletion	null status
cascading update	parent mandatory and child mandatory (M-M)
data constraint	parent mandatory and child optional (M-O)
DBMS reserved word	parent optional and child mandatory (O-M)
default value	parent optional and child optional (O-O)
domain constraint	range constraint
interrelation constraint	referential integrity (RI) action
intersection table	surrogate key
intrarelation constraint	trigger
minimum cardinality enforcement action	View Ridge Gallery (View Ridge or VRG)

Review Questions

6.1 Identify the three major tasks for transforming a data model into a database design.

6.2 What is the relationship between entities and tables? Between attributes and columns?

6.3 Why is the choice of the primary key important?

6.4 What are the three characteristics of an ideal primary key?

6.5 What is a surrogate key? What are its advantages?

6.6 When should you use a surrogate key?

6.7 Describe two disadvantages of surrogate keys.

6.8 What is the difference between an alternate key and a candidate key?

6.9 What does the notation LastName (AK2.2) mean?

6.10 Name four column properties.

6.11 Explain why primary keys may never be null, but alternate keys can be null.

6.12 List five generic data types.

6.13 Describe three ways that a default value can be assigned.

6.14 What is a domain constraint? Give an example.

6.15 What is a range constraint? Give an example.

6.16 What is an intrarelation constraint? Give an example.

6.17 What is an interrelation constraint? Give an example.

6.18 What tasks should be accomplished when verifying normalization of a database design?

6.19   Describe two ways to represent a 1:1 strong entity relationship. Give an example other than one in this chapter.

6.20   Describe how to represent a 1:N strong entity relationship. Give an example other than one in this chapter.

6.21   Describe how to represent an N:M strong entity relationship. Give an example other than one in this chapter.

6.22   What is an intersection table? Why is it necessary?

6.23   What is the difference between the table that represents an ID-dependent association entity and an intersection table?

6.24   List four uses for ID-dependent entities.

6.25   Describe how to represent an association entity relationship. Give an example other than one in this chapter.

6.26   Describe how to represent a multivalued attribute entity relationship. Give an example other than one in this chapter.

6.27   Describe how to represent a version/instance entity relationship. Give an example other than one in this chapter.

6.28   What happens when an instance entity is given a non-ID-dependent identifier? How does this change affect relationship design?

6.29   What happens when the parent in an ID-dependent relationship is given a surrogate key? What should the key of the child become?

6.30   Describe how to represent a mixed entity relationship. Give an example other than one in this chapter.

6.31   Describe how to represent a supertype/subtype entity relationship. Give an example other than one in this chapter.

6.32   Describe two ways to represent a 1:1 recursive relationship. Give an example other than one in this chapter.

6.33   Describe how to represent a 1:N recursive relationship. Give an example other than one in this chapter.

6.34   Describe how to represent an N:M recursive relationship. Give an example other than one in this chapter.

6.35   In general, how are ternary relationships represented? Explain how a binary constraint may impact such a relationship.

6.36   Describe a MUST constraint. Give an example other than one in this chapter.

6.37   Describe a MUST NOT constraint. Give an example other than one in this chapter.

6.38   Describe a MUST COVER constraint. Give an example other than one in this chapter.

6.39   Explain in general terms what needs to be done to enforce minimum cardinality.

6.40   Explain the need for each of the actions in Figure 6-28(a).

6.41   Explain the need for each of the actions in Figure 6-28(b).

6.42   State which of the actions in Figure 6-28 must be applied for M-O relationships, O-M relationships, and M-M relationships.

6.43   Explain what must be done for the DBMS to enforce required parents.

6.44   What design decisions must be made to enforce required parents?

6.45   Explain why the DBMS cannot be used to enforce required children.

6.46   What is a trigger? How can triggers be used to enforce required children?

6.47   Explain why the enforcement of M-M relationships is particularly difficult.

6.48   Explain the need for each of the design decisions in Figure 6-33.

6.49   Explain the implications of each of the minimum cardinality specifications in Figure 6-38.

6.50   Explain the rationale for each of the entries in the table in Figure 6-40.

Project Questions

6.51   Answer Project Question 5.58 if you have not already done so. Design a database for your model in Project Question 5.58. Your design should include a specification of tables and attributes as well as primary, candidate, and foreign keys. Also specify how you will enforce minimum cardinality. Document your minimum cardinality enforcement using referential integrity actions for a required parent, if any, and the form in Figure 6-28(b) for a required child, if any.

6.52   Answer Project Question 5.59 if you have not already done so. Design a database for your model. Your design should include a specification of tables and attributes as well as primary, candidate, and foreign keys. Also specify how you will enforce minimum cardinality. Document your minimum cardinality enforcement using referential integrity actions for required parents, if any, and the form in Figure 6-28(b) for required children, if any.

6.53   Answer Project Question 5.60 if you have not already done so. Design a database for your model in Project Question 5.60(c). Your design should include a specification of tables and attributes as well as primary, candidate, and foreign keys. Also specify how you will enforce minimum cardinality. Document your minimum cardinality enforcement using referential integrity actions for required parents, if any, and the form in Figure 6-28(b) for required children, if any.

6.54   Answer Project Question 5.61 if you have not already done so. Design a database for your model in Project Question 5.61(d). Your design should include a specification of tables and attributes as well as primary, candidate, and foreign keys. Also specify how you will enforce minimum cardinality. Document your minimum cardinality enforcement using referential integrity actions for required parents, if any, and the form in Figure 6-28(b) for required children, if any.

6.55   Answer Project Question 5.62 if you have not already done so. Design databases for your model in Project Question 5.62(a) and for the model in Figure 5-58. Your designs should include a specification of tables and attributes as well as primary, candidate, and foreign keys. Also specify how you will enforce minimum cardinality. Document your minimum cardinality enforcement using referential integrity actions for required parents, if any, and the form in Figure 6-28(b) for required children, if any.

6.56   Answer Project Question 5-63 if you have not already done so. Design a database for your model in Project Question 5-63(e). Your design should include a specification of tables and attributes as well as primary, candidate, and foreign keys. Also specify how you will enforce minimum cardinality. Document your minimum cardinality enforcement using referential integrity actions for required parents, if any, and the form in Figure 6-28(b) for required children, if any.

6.57   Answer Project Question 5-64 if you have not already done so. Design a database for your model in Project Question 5-64(c). Your design should include a specification of tables and attributes as well as primary, candidate, and foreign keys. Also specify how you will enforce minimum cardinality. Document your minimum cardinality enforcement using referential integrity actions for required parents, if any, and the form in Figure 6-28(b) for required children, if any.

6.58   Answer Project Question 5-65 if you have not already done so. Design a database for your model in Project Question 5-65(d). Your design should include a specification of tables and attributes as well as primary, candidate, and foreign keys. Also specify how you will enforce minimum cardinality. Document your minimum cardinality enforcement using referential integrity actions for required parents, if any, and the form in Figure 6-28(b) for required children, if any.

If you have not already done so, complete the Marcia's Dry Cleaning project at the end of Chapter 5. Design a database for the model in your answer. Your design should include a specification of tables and attributes as well as primary, candidate, and foreign keys. Also specify how you will enforce minimum cardinality. Document your minimum cardinality enforcement using referential integrity actions for required parents, if any, and the form in Figure 6-28(b) for required children, if any.

If you have not already done so, answer the Morgan Importing project at the end of Chapter 5. Design a database for the model in your answer. Your design should include a specification of tables and attributes as well as primary, candidate, and foreign keys. Also specify how you will enforce minimum cardinality. Document your minimum cardinality enforcement using referential integrity actions for required parents, if any, and the form in Figure 6-28(b) for required children, if any.

Part 3

Database Implementation

Part 3 consists of two chapters. Chapter 7 presents SQL data definition language statements for constructing database components and describes the SQL data manipulation statements for inserting, updating, and deleting data. You will also learn how to construct and use SQL views and how to embed SQL statements into programs. The chapter concludes with a discussion of SQL triggers and stored procedures.

Chapter 8 presents the use of SQL statements to redesign databases. It presents SQL correlated subqueries and then introduces SQL statements using the SQL EXISTS and NOT EXISTS keywords. Both of these advanced SQL statements are needed for database redesign. Chapter 8 also describes database reverse engineering, surveys common database redesign problems, and shows how to use SQL to solve database redesign problems.

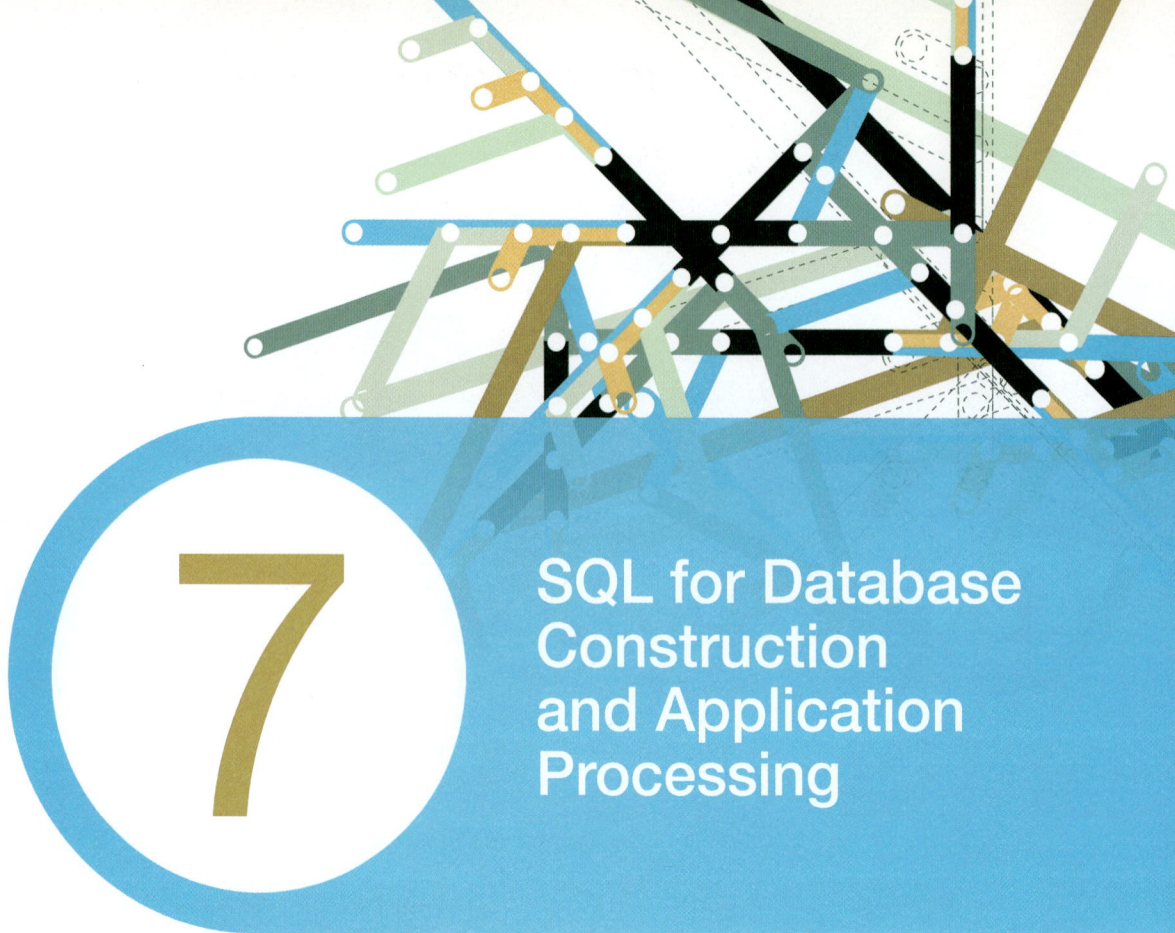

7

SQL for Database Construction and Application Processing

Chapter Objectives

- To be able to create and manage table structures using SQL statements.
- To understand how referential integrity actions are implemented in SQL statements.
- To be able to create and use SQL constraints.
- To understand several uses for SQL views.

- To be able to use SQL statements to create and use views.
- To gain an understanding of how SQL is used in an application program.
- To understand how to create and use triggers.
- To understand how to create and use stored procedures.

In Chapter 2, we introduced SQL and classified SQL statements into two categories: **data manipulation language (DML)** statements, which are used for querying, inserting, updating and deleting data, and **data definition language (DDL)** statements, which are used for creating tables, relationships, and other database structures. In Chapter 2, we discussed only DML query statements.

This chapter describes and illustrates SQL DDL statements for constructing databases and SQL DML statements for inserting, modifying, and deleting data. We will also describe how to create SQL Views, how to embed SQL statements into application programs, and how to use SQL in triggers and stored procedures.

The knowledge in this chapter is important whether you become a database administrator or an application programmer. Even if you will not construct SQL triggers or stored procedures yourself, it is important that you know what they are, how they work, and how they influence database processing.

The View Ridge Gallery Database

In Chapter 6, we introduced the View Ridge Gallery, a small art gallery that sells contemporary North American and European fine art and provides art framing services. We also developed a data model and database design for a database for the View Ridge Gallery. Our final database design for View Ridge is shown in Figure 7-1. In this chapter, we will use SQL to build the View Ridge database based on that design.

SQL DDL, DML, and a New Type of Join

Figure 7-2 summarizes the new SQL statements described in this chapter. We begin with SQL DDL statements for managing table structures, including CREATE TABLE, ALTER TABLE, and DROP TABLE. Using these statements, we will build the table structure for the View Ridge

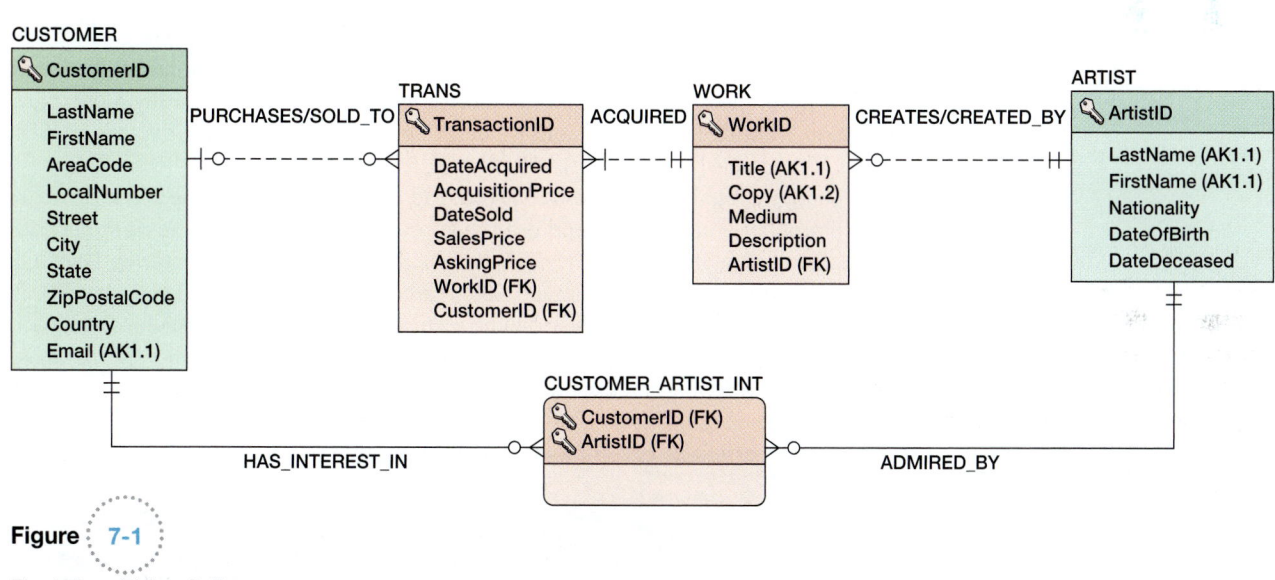

Figure 7-1

Final View Ridge Gallery
Database Design

- SQL Data Definition Language (DDL)
  - CREATE TABLE
  - ALTER TABLE
  - DROP TABLE
- SQL Data Manipulation Language (DML)
  - INSERT
  - UPDATE
  - DELETE
- Additional join forms
  - Alternative join syntax
  - Outer joins

Figure 7-2

Chapter 7 SQL Statements

database. Next, we present the three SQL DML statements for managing data: INSERT, UPDATE, and DELETE. Finally, we will add to the knowledge of joins you gained in Chapter 2 by describing a new format and offering a further discussion of SQL joins.

Managing Table Structure with SQL DDL

The **SQL CREATE TABLE statement** is used to construct tables, define columns and column constraints, and create relationships. Most DBMS products provide graphical tools for performing these tasks, and you may be wondering why you need to learn SQL to perform the same work. There are four reasons. First, creating tables and relationships with SQL is quicker than with graphical tools. Once you know how to use the SQL CREATE TABLE statement, you will be able to construct tables faster and more easily than by fussing around with buttons and graphical gimmickry. Second, some applications, particularly those for reporting, querying, and data mining, require you to create the same table repeatedly. You can do this efficiently if you create an SQL script text file with the necessary SQL CREATE TABLE statements. You then just execute the SQL script when you need to re-create a table. Third, some applications require you to create temporary tables during application work. Chapter 13 (pages 540–543) shows one such application. The only way to create tables from program code is to use SQL. Finally, SQL DDL is standardized and DBMS independent. With the exception of some data types, the same CREATE TABLE statement will work with SQL Server, Oracle, DB2, or MySQL.

Creating the View Ridge Database

Of course, before you can create any tables, you have to create the database. The SQL-92 and subsequent standards include an SQL statement for creating databases, but it is seldom used. Instead, most developers use special commands or graphical tools for creating a database. These techniques are DBMS specific, and we describe them in context in Chapters 10 (SQL Server 2008), 10A (Oracle Database 11g), 10B (MySQL 5.1), and Appendix A (Microsoft Access).

At this point, we highly recommend that you read the section on creating a new database in the DBMS product you are using and use the appropriate steps to create a new database named VRG. For illustrative purposes, we will use SQL Server 2008 in this chapter, and our SQL code will be the correct code for SQL Server 2008. The correct SQL statements for other DBMS products will be similar, but they will vary slightly. The correct SQL statements for Oracle and MySQL can be found in Chapters 10A and 10B, respectively. Figure 7-3 shows the VRG database is the SQL Server 2008 Management Studio.

The **Object Explorer**

The **VRG database** object

The VRG database object folders—when database objects such as tables are created they will be visible in these folders

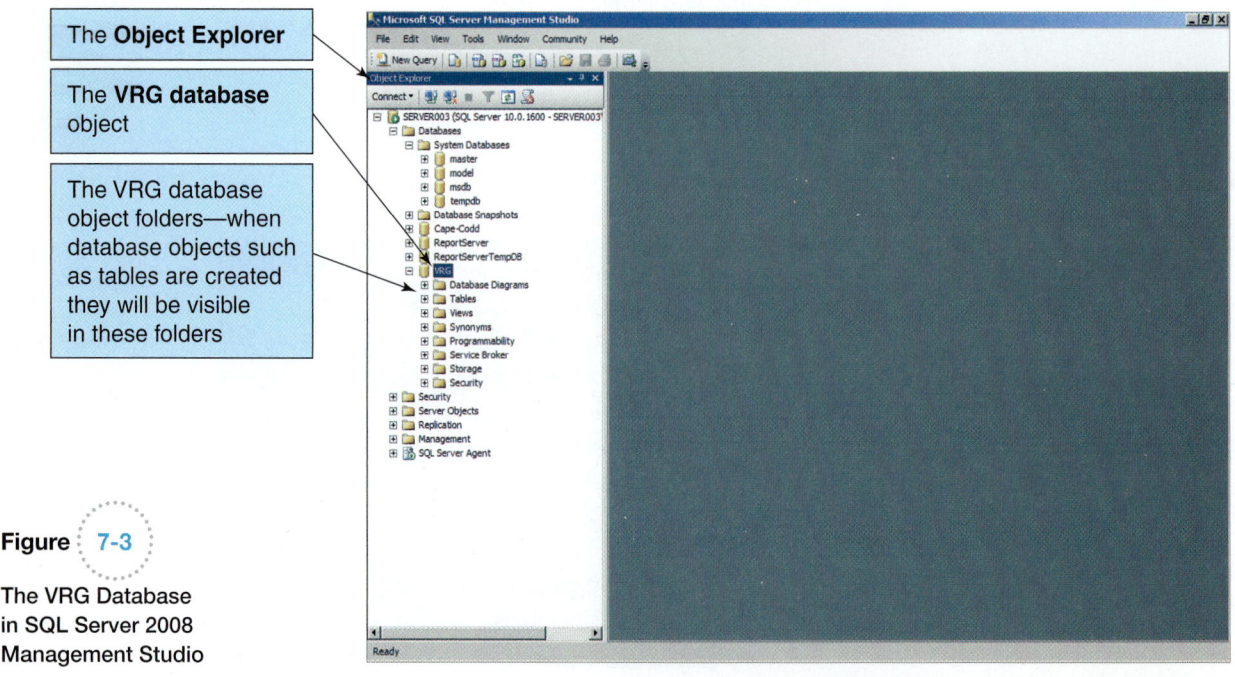

Figure 7-3

The VRG Database in SQL Server 2008 Management Studio

Using the SQL CREATE TABLE Statement

The basic format of the SQL CREATE TABLE statement is:

```
CREATE TABLE NewTableName (
    three-part column definition,
    three-part column definition,
    . . .
    optional table constraints
    . . .
);
```

The parts of the three-part column definition are the column name, the column data type, and, optionally, a constraint on column values. Thus, we can restate the CREATE TABLE format as:

```
CREATE TABLE NewTableName (
    ColumnName  DataType  OptionalConstraint,
    ColumnName  DataType  OptionalConstraint,
    . . .
    Optional table constraint
    . . .
);
```

The column and table constraints we consider in this text are **PRIMARY KEY, FOREIGN KEY, NOT NULL, NULL, UNIQUE**, and **CHECK**. Additionally, the **DEFAULT keyword** (DEFAULT is not considered a column constraint) can be used to set initial values. Finally, most variants of SQL support a property to implement surrogate primary keys. For example, SQL Server 2008 uses the **IDENTITY({StartValue},{Increment}) property**. Oracle, MySQL, and Access use somewhat different techniques for creating surrogate keys. If you are using those products, see the discussion of surrogate keys for Oracle in Chapter 10A, MySQL in Chapter 10B, or Microsoft Access in Appendix A. We will explain each of these constraints, keywords, and properties as we meet them in the context of our discussion in this chapter.

Variations in SQL Data Types

Each DBMS product has its own variant or extension of SQL, where the extensions are usually **procedural language** extensions, which are additions that allow SQL to function similarly to a procedural programming language (for example, IF . . . THEN . . . ELSE structures). Some vendors have given their variants or extended versions specific names. SQL Server's extended version of SQL is called **Transact-SQL (T-SQL)**, whereas Oracle's extended version of SQL is called **Procedural Language/SQL (PL/SQL)**. MySQL's variant, even though it, too, contains procedural extensions, is just called SQL. We will point out specific SQL syntax differences as we encounter them in our discussion. For more on T-SQL, see the SQL Server 2008 Books Online section *Transact-SQL Reference* at *http://msdn.microsoft.com/en-us/library/bb510741.aspx*. For more on PL/SQL, see the Oracle Database PL/SQL User's Guide and Reference 10g Release 2 (10.2) at *http://download.oracle.com/docs/cd/B19306_01/appdev.102/b14261/toc.htm*. For more on SQL in MySQL, see the MySQL 5.1 Reference Manual Chapter 12 on SQL Statement Syntax at *http://dev.mysql.com/doc/refman/5.1/en/sql-syntax.html*.

One source of variation in DBMS SQL stems from the different data types implemented by each vendor. The SQL standard defines a set of data types. Figure 7-4 shows a summary of common (but not all) data types for the DBMSs we have been discussing.

> **BY THE WAY**   Even though Microsoft Access reads standard SQL and the SQL used by SQL Server 2008, the results may be a bit different. For example, Microsoft Access ANSI-89 SQL coverts both the Char and VarChar SQL data types to a fixed Text data type.

Creating the ARTIST Table

We will start by considering two of the tables in the View Ridge database design we developed at the end of Chapter 6, the ARTIST table and the WORK table. These tables are shown in Figure 7-1, and Figures 7-5 and 7-6 show the database column properties for these tables. Three new features are shown in these figures.

The first is the Microsoft SQL IDENTITY property, which is used to specify surrogate keys. In the ARTIST table, the expression IDENTITY(1, 1) means that ArtistID is to be a surrogate key with values starting at 1 and incremented by 1. Thus, the value of ArtistID for the second row in ARTIST will be (1 + 1) = 2. In the WORK table, the expression IDENTITY(500, 1) means that WorkID is to be a surrogate key with values starting at 500 and incremented by 1. Thus, the value of WorkID for the second row in WORK will be (500 + 1) = 501.

The second new feature is the designation of (LastName, FirstName) in ARTIST as an alternative key. This indicates that (LastName, FirstName) is a candidate key for the ARTIST table. Alternative keys are defined using the UNIQUE constraint.

Figure   7-4

SQL Data Types in DBMS Products

Data Type	Description
Binary	Binary, length 0 to 8,000 bytes.
Char	Character, length 0 to 8,000 bytes.
Datetime	8-byte datetime. Range from January 1, 1753, through December 31, 9999, with an accuracy of three-hundredths of a second.
Image	Variable length binary data. Maximum length 2,147,483,647 bytes.
Integer	4-byte integer. Value range from –2,147,483,648 through 2,147,483,647.
Money	8-byte money. Range from –922,337,203,685,477.5808 through +922,337,203,685,477.5807, with accuracy to a ten-thousandth of a monetary unit.
Numeric	Decimal – can set precision and scale. Range -10^{38} +1 through 10^{38} –1.
Smalldatetime	4-byte datetime. Range from January 1, 1900, through June 6, 2079, with an accuracy of one minute.
Smallint	2-byte integer. Range from –32,768 through 32,767.
Smallmoney	4-byte money. Range from 214,748.3648 through +214,748.3647, with accuracy to a ten-thousandth of a monetary unit.
Text	Variable length text, maximum length 2,147,483,647 characters.
Tinyint	1-byte integer. Range from 0 through 255.
Varchar	Variable-length character, length 0 to 8,000 bytes.

(a) Common Data Types in SQL Server

Data Type	Description
BLOB	Binary large object. Up to 4 gigabytes in length.
CHAR(n)	Fixed length character field of length n. Maximum 2,000 characters.
DATE	7-byte field containing both date and time.
INTEGER	Whole number of length 38.
NUMBER(n,d)	Numeric field of length n, d places to the right of the decimal.
VARCHAR(n) or VARCHAR2(n)	Variable length character field up to n characters long. Maximum value of n = 4,000.

(b) Common Data Types in Oracle

NumericData Type	Description
BIT (M)	M = 1 to 64
TINYINT	−128 to 127
TINYINT UNSIGNED	0 to 255
BOOLEAN	0 = FALSE; 1 = TRUE
SMALLINT	−32,768 to 32,767
SMALLINT UNSIGNED	0 to 65535
MEDIUMINT	−8,388,608 to 8,388,607
MEDIUMINT UNSIGNED	0 to 16,777,215
INT or INTEGER	−2,147,483,648 to 2,147,483,647
INT UNSIGNED or INTEGER UNSIGNED	0 to 4,294,967,295
BIGINT	−9,223,372,036,854,775,808 to 9,223,372,036,854,775,807
BIGINT UNSIGNED	0 to 1,844,674,073,709,551,615
FLOAT (P)	P = Precision; 0 to 24
FLOAT (M, D)	Small (single-precision) floating-point number: M = Display width D = Number of significant digits
DOUBLE (M, B)	Normal (double-precision) floating-point number: M = Display width B = Precision; 25 to 53
DEC (M[,D]) or DECIMAL (M[,D]) or FIXED (M[,D])	Fixed-point number: M = Total number of digits D = Number of decimals
Date and Time Data Types	**Description**
DATE	YYYY-MM-DD : 1000-01-01 to 9999-12-31
DATETIME	YYYY-MM-DD HH:MM:SS
	1000-01-01 00:00:00 to 9999-12-31 23:59:59
TIMESTAMP	See documentation.
TIME	HH:MM:SS—00:00:00 to 23:59:59
YEAR (M)	M = 2 or 4 (default)
	IF 2 = 1970 to 2069 (70 to 60)
	IF 4 = 1901 to 2155
String Data Types	**Description**
CHAR (M)	M = 0 to 255
VARCHAR (M)	M = 1 to 255
BLOB (M)	BLOB = Binary Large Object; maximum 65,535 characters
TEXT (M)	Maximum 65,535 characters
TINYBLOB MEDIUMBLOB LONGBLOB TINYTEXT MEDIUMTEXT LONGTEXT	See documentation.
ENUM ('value1', 'value2', . . .)	An enumeration. Only one value, but chosen from list. See documentation.
SET ('value1', 'value2', . . .)	A set. Zero or more values, all chosen from list. See documentation.

(c) Common Data Types in MySQL

Figure   7-4

(Continued)

Column Name	Type	Key	NULL Status	Remarks
ArtistID	Int	Primary Key	NOT NULL	Surrogate Key IDENTITY (1,1)
LastName	Char (25)	Alternate Key	NOT NULL	AK1
FirstName	Char (25)	Alternate Key	NOT NULL	AK1
Nationality	Char (30)	No	NULL	
DateOfBirth	Numeric (4)	No	NULL	
DateDeceased	Numeric (4)	No	NULL	

Figure 7-5

Database Column Characteristics for the ARTIST Table

Column Name	Type	Key	NULL Status	Remarks
WorkID	Int	Primary Key	NOT NULL	Surrogate Key IDENTITY (500,1)
Title	Char (35)	No	NOT NULL	
Copy	Char (12)	No	NOT NULL	
Medium	Char (35)	No	NULL	
Description	Varchar (1000)	No	NULL	DEFAULT value = 'Unknown provenance'
ArtistID	Int	Foreign Key	NOT NULL	

Figure 7-6

Database Column Characteristics for the WORK Table

The third new feature is the use of the DEFAULT column constraint in the Description column of the WORK table. The DEFAULT constraint is used to set a value that will be inserted into each row unless some other value is specified.

Figure 7-7 describes in tabular form the M-O relationship between ARTIST and WORK shown in Figure 7-1, and Figure 7-8 [based on the template in Figure 6-28(a)] details the referential integrity actions that will be needed to enforce the minimum cardinalities in the ARTIST-to-WORK relationship.

Figure 7-9 shows the SQL CREATE TABLE statement for constructing the ARTIST table. (All of the SQL in this chapter runs on SQL Server. If you are using a different DBMS, you may need to make adjustments so consult the chapter or appendix for the DBMS you are using.) The format of CREATE TABLE is the name of the table followed by a list of all column definitions and constraints enclosed in parentheses and ending with the ubiquitous SQL semicolon (;).

As stated earlier, SQL has several column and table constraints: PRIMARY KEY, NULL, NOT NULL, UNIQUE, FOREIGN KEY, and CHECK. The PRIMARY KEY constraint is used to define the primary key of the table. Although it can be used as a column constraint, because it has to be used as a table constraint to define compound primary keys, we prefer to always use it as a table constraint, as shown in Figure 7-9. The NULL and NOT NULL column constraints are used to set the NULL status of a column, indicating whether data values are required in

Figure 7-7

The ARTIST-to-WORK Relationship

Relationship		Cardinality		
Parent	Child	Type	MAX	MIN
ARTIST	WORK	Nonidentifying	1:N	M-O

ARTIST Is Required Parent	Action on ARTIST (Parent)	Action on WORK (Child)
Insert	None.	Get a parent.
Modify key or foreign key	Prohibit—ARTIST uses a surrogate key.	Prohibit—ARTIST uses a surrogate key.
Delete	Prohibit—data related to a transaction is never deleted (business rule).	None.

Figure 7-8

Actions to Enforce Minimum Cardinality for the ARTIST-to-WORK Relationship

Figure 7-9

SQL Statements to Create the Initial Version of the ARTIST Table

```
CREATE TABLE ARTIST(
    ArtistID          Int           NOT NULL IDENTITY(1,1),
    LastName          Char(25)      NOT NULL,
    FirstName         Char(25)      NOT NULL,
    Nationality       Char(30)      NULL,
    DateOfBirth       Numeric(4)    NULL,
    DateDeceased      Numeric(4)    NULL,
    CONSTRAINT    ArtistPK          PRIMARY KEY(ArtistID),
    CONSTRAINT    ArtistAK1         UNIQUE(LastName, FirstName)
    );
```

that column. The UNIQUE constraint is used to indicate that the values of a column or columns must not use repeated values. The FOREIGN KEY constraint is used to define referential integrity constraints, and the CHECK constraint is used to define data constraints.

In the first section of the CREATE TABLE statement for the ARTIST table, each column is defined by giving its name, data type, and null status. If you do not specify the null status using NULL or NOT NULL, then NULL is assumed.

In this database, DateOfBirth and DateDeceased are years. YearOfBirth and YearDeceased would have been better column names, but that is not how the gallery personnel refer to them. Because the gallery is not interested in the month and day of an artist's birth and death, those columns are defined as Numeric (4,0), which means a four-digit number with zero places to the right of the decimal point.

The last two expressions in the SQL table definition statement in Figure 7-9 are constraints that define the primary key and a candidate, or alternate, key. As stated in Chapter 6, the primary purpose of an alternate key is to ensure uniqueness of column values. Thus, in SQL, alternate keys are defined using the UNIQUE constraint.

The format of such constraints is the word CONSTRAINT followed by a constraint name provided by the developer followed by either the PRIMARY KEY or UNIQUE keyword and then one or more columns in parentheses. For example, the following statement defines a constraint named *MyExample* that ensures that the combination of first and last name is unique:

```
CONSTRAINT MyExample UNIQUE (FirstName, LastName),
```

As stated in Chapter 6, primary key columns must be NOT NULL, but candidate keys can be NULL or NOT NULL.

> **BY THE WAY** SQL originated in the era of punch-card data processing. Punched cards had only uppercase letters, so there was no need to think about case sensitivity. When cards were replaced by regular keyboards, DBMS vendors chose to ignore the difference between uppercase and lowercase letters. Thus, CREATE TABLE, create table, and CReatE taBle are all the same in SQL. NULL, null, and Null are all the same as well.

Notice that the last line of the SQL statement in Figure 7-9 is a closed parenthesis followed by a semicolon. These characters could be placed on the line above, but dropping them to a new line is a style convention that makes it easy to determine the boundaries of CREATE TABLE statements. Also notice that column descriptions and constraints are separated by commas but that there is no comma after the last one.

BY THE WAY   Many organizations have developed SQL coding standards of their own. Such standards specify not only the format of SQL statements, but also conventions for naming constraints. For example, in the figures in this chapter we use the suffix PK on the names of all primary key constraints and the suffix FK for all foreign key constraints. Most organizations have standards that are more comprehensive. You should follow your organization's standards, even if you disagree with them. Consistent SQL coding improves organizational efficiency and reduces errors.

Creating the WORK Table and the 1:N ARTIST-to-WORK Relationship

Figure 7-10 shows SQL statements for creating the ARTIST and WORK tables and their relationship. Note that the column name Description is written as [Description], because Description is an SQL Server 2008 reserved keyword (see Chapter 10 on SQL Server 2008), and we must use the square brackets ([and]) to create a delimited identifier. This is the same reason that in Chapter 6 we decided to use the table name TRANS instead of TRANSACTION.

The only new syntax in Figure 7-10 is the FOREIGN KEY constraint at the end of WORK. Such constraints are used to define referential integrity constraints. The FOREIGN KEY constraint in Figure 7-10 is equivalent to the following referential integrity constraint:

ArtistID in WORK must exist in ArtistID in ARTIST

Note that the foreign key constraint contains two SQL clauses that implement the minimum cardinality enforcement requirements of Figure 7-8. The **SQL ON UPDATE clause** specifies whether updates should cascade form ARTIST to WORK, and the **SQL ON DELETE clause** specifies whether deletions in ARTIST should cascade to WORK.

Figure 7-10

SQL Statements to Create The ARTIST-to-WORK 1:N Relationship

```
CREATE TABLE ARTIST(
     ArtistID           Int              NOT NULL IDENTITY(1,1),
     LastName           Char(25)         NOT NULL,
     FirstName          Char(25)         NOT NULL,
     Nationality        Char(30)         NULL,
     DateOfBirth        Numeric(4)       NULL,
     DateDeceased       Numeric(4)       NULL,
     CONSTRAINT   ArtistPK              PRIMARY KEY(ArtistID),
     CONSTRAINT   ArtistAK1             UNIQUE(LastName, FirstName)
     );

CREATE TABLE WORK(
     WorkID             Int              NOT NULL IDENTITY(500,1),
     Title              Char(35)         NOT NULL,
     Copy               Char(12)         NOT NULL,
     Medium             Char(35)         NULL,
     [Description]      Varchar(1000)    NULL DEFAULT 'Unknown provenance',
     ArtistID           Int              NOT NULL,
     CONSTRAINT   WorkPK                PRIMARY KEY(WorkID),
     CONSTRAINT   WorkAK1               UNIQUE(Title, Copy),
     CONSTRAINT   ArtistFK              FOREIGN KEY(ArtistID)
                         REFERENCES ARTIST(ArtistID)
                            ON UPDATE NO ACTION
                            ON DELETE NO ACTION
     );
```

The expression ON UPDATE NO ACTION indicates that updates to the primary key for a table that has children should be prohibited (this is the standard setting for surrogate keys that should never change). The expression ON UPDATE CASCADE would indicate that updates should cascade. UPDATE NO ACTION is the default.

Similarly, the expression ON DELETE NO ACTION indicates that deletions of rows that have children should be prohibited. The expression ON DELETE CASCADE would indicate that deletions should cascade. DELETE NO ACTION is the default.

In the present case, the ON UPDATE NO ACTION is meaningless because the primary key of ARTIST is a surrogate and will never be changed. The ON UPDATE action would need to be specified for nonsurrogate data keys, however, and we show the option here so you will know how to code it.

> **BY THE WAY**   Note that you must define parent tables before child tables. In this case, you must define ARTIST before WORK. If you try to reverse the order of definition, the DBMS will generate an error message on the FOREIGN KEY constraint because it will not yet know about the ARTIST table.
>
> Similarly, you must delete tables in the opposite order. You must DROP (described later) a child before a parent. Better SQL parsers would sort out all of this so that statement order would not matter, but, alas, that's not the way it's done! Just remember the following: *Parents are first in and last out.*

Implementing Required Parent Rows

In Chapter 6, you learned that to enforce a required parent constraint you must define the referential integrity constraint and set the foreign key to NOT NULL in the child table. The SQL CREATE TABLE statement for the WORK table in Figure 7-10 does both. In this case, ARTIST is the required parent table, and WORK is the child. Thus, ArtistID in the WORK table is specified as NOT NULL (using the NOT NULL column constraint), and the ArtistFK FOREIGN KEY table constraint is used to define the referential integrity constraint. Together, these specifications thus cause the DBMS to enforce the required parent.

If the parent were not required, then we would specify ArtistID in WORK as NULL. In that case, WORK would not need to have a value for ArtistID, and thus not need a parent. However, the FOREIGN KEY constraint would still ensure that all values of ArtistID in WORK would be present in the ArtistID in ARTIST.

Implementing 1:1 Relationships

SQL for implementing 1:1 relationships is almost identical to that for 1:N relationships, as just shown. The only difference is that the foreign key must be declared as unique. For example, if the relationship were 1:1 between ARTIST and WORK (i.e., each artist could have only one work at View Ridge), then in Figure 7-10 we would add the constraint:

```
CONSTRAINT UniqueWork UNIQUE (ArtistID),
```

Note that the ARTIST-to-WORK relationship in Figure 7-1 is of course *not* 1:1, so we will *not* specify this constraint to our current SQL statements. As before, if the parent is required, then the foreign key should be set to NOT NULL. Otherwise, it should be NULL.

Casual Relationships

Sometimes it is appropriate to create a foreign key column but not specify a FOREIGN KEY constraint. In that case, the foreign key value may or may not match a value of the primary key in the parent. If, for example, you define the column DepartmentName in EMPLOYEE but do not specify a FOREIGN KEY constraint, then a row may have a value of DepartmentName that does not match a value of DepartmentName in the DEPARTMENT table.

Relationship Type	CREATE TABLE Constraints
1:N relationship, parent optional	Specify FOREIGN KEY constraint. Set foreign key NULL.
1:N relationship, parent required	Specify FOREIGN KEY constraint. Set foreign key NOT NULL.
1:1 relationship, parent optional	Specify FOREIGN KEY constraint. Specify foreign key UNIQUE constraint. Set foreign key NULL.
1:1 relationship, parent required	Specify FOREIGN KEY constraint. Specify foreign key UNIQUE constraint. Set foreign key NOT NULL.
Casual relationship	Create a foreign key column, but do not specify FOREIGN KEY constraint. If relationship is 1:1, specify foreign key UNIQUE.

Figure 7-11

Summary of Relationship Definitions Using the SQL CREATE TABLE Statement

Such relationships, which we call **casual relationships**, occur frequently in applications that process tables with missing data. For example, you might buy consumer data that includes names of consumers' employers. Assume that you have an EMPLOYER table that does not contain all of the possible companies for which the consumers might work. You want to use the relationship if you happen to have the values, but you do not want to require having those values. In that case, create a casual relationship by placing the key of EMPLOYER in the consumer data table but do *not* define a FOREIGN KEY constraint.

Figure 7-11 summarizes the techniques for creating relationships using FOREIGN KEY, NULL, NOT NULL, and UNIQUE constraints in 1:N, 1:1, and casual relationships.

Creating Default Values and Data Constraints with SQL

Figure 7-12 shows an example set of default value and example data constraints for the View Ridge database. The Description column in the WORK table is given the default value of 'Unknown provenance.' The ARTIST table and TRANS tables are assigned various data constraints.

Figure 7-12

Default Values and Data Constraints for the View Ridge Database

Table	Column	Default Value	Constraint
WORK	Description	'Unknown provenance'	
ARTIST	Nationality		IN ('Candian', 'English', 'French', 'German', 'Mexican', 'Russian', 'Spanish', 'United States'.
ARTIST	DateOfBirth		Less than DateDeceased.
ARTIST	DateOfBirth		Four digits—1 or 2 is first digit, 0 to 9 for remaining three digits.
ARTIST	DateDeceased		Four digits—1 or 2 is first digit, 0 to 9 for remaining three digits.
TRANS	SalesPrice		Greater than 0 and less than or equal to 500,000.
TRANS	DateAcquired		Less than or equal to DateSold.

In the ARTIST table, Nationality is limited to the values in the domain constraint shown, and DateOfBirth is limited by the **intrarelation constraint** (within the same table) that DateOfBirth occurs before DateDeceased. Further, DateOfBirth and DateDeceased, which as noted earlier are years, are limited to the domain defined by specifying that the first digit be a 1 or a 2 and the remaining three digits be any decimal numbers. Thus, they can have any value between 1000 and 2999. SalesPrice in the TRANS table is limited by a range constraint to a value greater than 0 but less than or equal to $500,000, and PurchaseDate is limited by an intrarelation constraint that the DateSold be no earlier than the DateAcquired (i.e., DateAcquired is less than or equal to DateSold).

Figure 7-12 shows no **interrelation constraints** between tables. Although the SQL-92 specification defined facilities for creating such constraints, no DBMS vendor has implemented those facilities. Such constraints must be implemented in triggers. An example of this is shown later in this chapter. Figure 7-13 shows the SQL statements to create the ARTIST and WORK tables modified with the appropriate default values and data constraints.

Implementing Default Values

Default values are created by specifying the DEFAULT keyword in the column definition just after the NULL/NOT NULL specification. Note how in Figure 7-13 the Description column in the WORK table is given the default value of 'Unknown provenance' using this technique.

Figure 7-13

SQL Statements to Create the ARTIST and WORK Tables with Default Values and Data Constraints

Implementing Data Constraints

The data constraints are created using the SQL CHECK Constraint. The format for the CHECK constraint is the word CONSTRAINT followed by a developer-provided constraint name followed by the word CHECK and then by the constraint specification in parentheses. Expressions in CHECK constraints are akin to those used in the WHERE clause of SQL

```
CREATE TABLE ARTIST(
       ArtistID              Int               NOT NULL IDENTITY(1,1),
       LastName              Char(25)          NOT NULL,
       FirstName             Char(25)          NOT NULL,
       Nationality           Char(30)          NULL,
       DateOfBirth           Numeric(4)        NULL,
       DateDeceased          Numeric(4)        NULL,
       CONSTRAINT    ArtistPK              PRIMARY KEY(ArtistID),
       CONSTRAINT    ArtistAK1             UNIQUE(LastName, FirstName),
       CONSTRAINT    NationalityValues     CHECK
                     (Nationality IN ('Canadian', 'English', 'French',
                      'German', 'Mexican', 'Russian', 'Spanish',
                      'United States')),
       CONSTRAINT    BirthValuesCheck      CHECK (DateOfBirth < DateDeceased),
       CONSTRAINT    ValidBirthYear        CHECK
                     (DateOfBirth LIKE '[1-2][0-9][0-9][0-9]'),
       CONSTRAINT    ValidDeathYear        CHECK
                     (DateDeceased LIKE '[1-2][0-9][0-9][0-9]')
       );

CREATE TABLE WORK(
       WorkID                Int               NOT NULL IDENTITY(500,1),
       Title                 Char(35)          NOT NULL,
       Copy                  Char(12)          NOT NULL,
       Medium                Char(35)          NULL,
       [Description]         Varchar(1000)     NULL DEFAULT 'Unknown provenance',
       ArtistID              Int               NOT NULL,
       CONSTRAINT    WorkPK                PRIMARY KEY(WorkID),
       CONSTRAINT    WorkAK1               UNIQUE(Title, Copy),
       CONSTRAINT    ArtistFK              FOREIGN KEY(ArtistID)
                        REFERENCES ARTIST(ArtistID)
                           ON UPDATE NO ACTION
                           ON DELETE NO ACTION
       );
```

statements. Thus, the SQL IN keyword is used to provide a list of valid values. The SQL NOT IN keyword also can be used for negatively expressed domain constraints (not shown in this example). The SQL LIKE keyword is used for the specification of decimal places. Range checks are specified using comparison operators such as the less than (<) and greater than (>) symbols. Because interrelation constraints are unsupported, comparisons can be made as intrarelation constraints between columns in the same table.

> **BY THE WAY**   DBMS products are inconsistent in their implementation of CHECK constraints. The use of the SQL LIKE keyword in Figure 7-13, for example, will not work with Oracle. However, Oracle implements other types of constraints. Unfortunately, you must learn the peculiarities of the DBMS you use to know how best to implement constraints.

Creating the View Ridge Database Tables

Figure 7-14 shows SQL for creating all of the tables in the View Ridge database documented at the end of Chapter 6. Read each line and be certain that you understand its function and purpose. Notice that deletions cascade for the relationships between CUSTOMER and CUSTOMER_ARTIST_INT and between ARTIST and CUSTOMER_ARTIST_INT.

Any DBMS reserved words used as table or column names need to be enclosed in square brackets ([and]), and thus converted to delimited identifiers. We have already decided to use the table name TRANS instead of TRANSACTION so that we do not use the *transaction* reserved word. The table name WORK is also a potential problem; the word *work* is a reserved word in most DBMS products, as are the column names *Description* in the WORK table and *State* in the TRANS table. Enclosing such terms in brackets signifies to the SQL parser that these terms have been provided by the developer and are not to be used in the standard way. Ironically, SQL Server can process the word WORK without problem, but Oracle cannot, while SQL Server chokes on the word TRANSACTION, but Oracle has no problem with it. Because Figure 7-14 shows SQL Server 2008 T-SQL statements, we use WORK (no brackets), [Description], and [State].

You can find a list of reserved words in the documentation for the DBMS product that you use, and we deal with some specific cases in the chapters dedicated to SQL Server 2008, Oracle, and MySQL. Be assured that if you use any keyword from the SQL syntax, such as SELECT, FROM, WHERE, LIKE, ORDER, ASC, DESC, for table or column names, you will have problems. Enclose such words in square brackets. And, of course, your life will be easier if you can avoid using such terms for tables or columns altogether.

> **BY THE WAY**   Every now and then, the DBMS might generate bizarre syntax-error messages. For example, suppose you define a table with the name ORDER. When you submit the statement SELECT * FROM ORDER, you will get very strange messages back from the DBMS.
>
> If you do receive odd messages back from statements that you know are coded correctly, think about reserved words. If a term might be reserved, enclose it in brackets and see what happens when you submit it to the DBMS. No harm is done by enclosing SQL terms in brackets.
>
> If you want to torture your DBMS, you can submit queries like SELECT [SELECT] FROM [FROM] WHERE [WHERE] < [NOT FIVE]. Most likely, you have better ways to spend your time, however. Without a doubt, the DBMS has better ways to spend its time!

Running the SQL statements in Figure 7-14 (or a specific variant in Chapter 10A for Oracle or Chapter 10B for MySQL) with your DBMS will generate all of the tables, relationships, and constraints for the View Ridge database. Figure 7-15 shows the completed table structure in SQL Server 2008 as a database diagram. It is far easier to create these tables and relationships using SQL code than by using GUI displays, which are discussed in Chapter 10 (SQL Server 2008), Chapter 10A (Oracle Database 11g), and Chapter 10B (MySQL 5.1).

```
CREATE TABLE ARTIST(
        ArtistID                Int                     NOT NULL IDENTITY(1,1),
        LastName                Char(25)                NOT NULL,
        FirstName               Char(25)                NOT NULL,
        Nationality             Char(30)                NULL,
        DateOfBirth             Numeric(4)              NULL,
        DateDeceased            Numeric(4)              NULL,
        CONSTRAINT      ArtistPK                PRIMARY KEY(ArtistID),
        CONSTRAINT      ArtistAK1               UNIQUE(LastName, FirstName),
        CONSTRAINT      NationalityValues       CHECK
                        (Nationality IN ('Canadian', 'English', 'French',
                         'German', 'Mexican', 'Russian', 'Spanish',
                         'United States')),
        CONSTRAINT      BirthValuesCheck        CHECK (DateOfBirth < DateDeceased),
        CONSTRAINT      ValidBirthYear          CHECK
                        (DateOfBirth LIKE '[1-2][0-9][0-9][0-9]'),
        CONSTRAINT      ValidDeathYear          CHECK
                        (DateDeceased LIKE '[1-2][0-9][0-9][0-9]')
        );


CREATE TABLE WORK(
        WorkID                  Int                     NOT NULL IDENTITY(500,1),
        Title                   Char(35)                NOT NULL,
        Copy                    Char(12)                NOT NULL,
        Medium                  Char(35)                NULL,
        [Description]           Varchar(1000)           NULL DEFAULT 'Unknown provenance',
        ArtistID                Int                     NOT NULL,
        CONSTRAINT      WorkPK                  PRIMARY KEY(WorkID),
        CONSTRAINT      WorkAK1                 UNIQUE(Title, Copy),
        CONSTRAINT      ArtistFK                FOREIGN KEY(ArtistID)
                                REFERENCES ARTIST(ArtistID)
                                ON UPDATE NO ACTION
                                ON DELETE NO ACTION
        );


CREATE TABLE CUSTOMER(
        CustomerID              Int                     NOT NULL IDENTITY(1000,1),
        LastName                Char(25)                NOT NULL,
        FirstName               Char(25)                NOT NULL,
        Street                  Char(30)                NULL,
        City                    Char(35)                NULL,
        [State]                 Char(2)                 NULL,
        ZipPostalCode           Char(9)                 NULL,
        Country                 Char(50)                NULL,
        AreaCode                Char(3)                 NULL,
        PhoneNumber             Char(8)                 NULL,
        Email                   Varchar(100)            Null,
        CONSTRAINT      CustomerPK              PRIMARY KEY(CustomerID),
        CONSTRAINT      EmailAK1                UNIQUE(Email)
        );
```

Figure 7-14

SQL Statements
to Create the View
Ridge Database
Table Structure

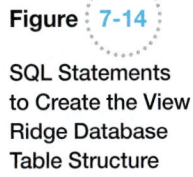

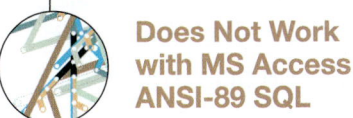

**Does Not Work
with MS Access
ANSI-89 SQL**

Microsoft Access 2007 ANSI-89 SQL, unfortunately, does not support a number of standard SQL features we have examined in this discussion. However, you *can* run a basic SQL CREATE TABLE statement in ANSI-89 SQL, and then use the Access GUI display to finish building the tables and relationships. Specifically:

1.   Although Microsoft Access supports a Number data type, it does not support the (*m, n*) extension to specify the number of digits and the number of digits to the right of the decimal place.

     Solution: You can set these values in the table Design view after the column is created.

(continued)

```
CREATE TABLE TRANS(
        TransactionID       Int             NOT NULL IDENTITY(100,1),
        DateAcquired        Datetime        NOT NULL,
        AcquisitionPrice    Numeric(8,2)    NOT NULL,
        DateSold            Datetime        NULL,
        AskingPrice         Numeric(8,2)    NULL,
        SalesPrice          Numeric(8,2)    NULL,
        CustomerID          Int             NULL,
        WorkID              Int             NOT NULL,
        CONSTRAINT  TransPK             PRIMARY KEY(TransactionID),
        CONSTRAINT  TransWorkFK         FOREIGN KEY(WorkID)
                        REFERENCES WORK(WorkID)
                            ON UPDATE NO ACTION
                            ON DELETE NO ACTION,
        CONSTRAINT  TransCustomerFK     FOREIGN KEY(CustomerID)
                        REFERENCES CUSTOMER(CustomerID)
                            ON UPDATE NO ACTION
                            ON DELETE NO ACTION,
        CONSTRAINT  SalesPriceRange  CHECK
                        ((SalesPrice > 0) AND (SalesPrice <=500000)),
        CONSTRAINT  ValidTransDate      CHECK (DateAcquired <= DateSold),
        );

CREATE TABLE CUSTOMER_ARTIST_INT(
        ArtistID            Int             NOT NULL,
        CustomerID          Int             NOT NULL,
        CONSTRAINT  CAIntPK             PRIMARY KEY(ArtistID, CustomerID),
        CONSTRAINT  CAInt_ArtistFK      FOREIGN KEY(ArtistID)
                        REFERENCES ARTIST(ArtistID)
                            ON UPDATE NO ACTION
                            ON DELETE CASCADE,
        CONSTRAINT  CAInt_CustomerFK    FOREIGN KEY(CustomerID)
                        REFERENCES CUSTOMER(CustomerID)
                            on UPDATE NO ACTION
                            ON DELETE CASCADE
        );
```

Figure 7-14

(Continued)

2. Although Microsoft Access does support an AutoNumber data type, it *always* starts at 1 and increments by 1. Further, AutoNumber *cannot* be used as an SQL data type.

   Solution: Set AutoNumber data type manually after the table is created. Any other numbering system must be supported manually or by application code.

3. Microsoft Access ANSI-89 SQL does not support the UNIQUE and CHECK column constraints, nor the DEFAULT keyword.

   Solution: Equivalent constraints and initial values can be set in the GUI table Design view.

4. Microsoft Access does completely support foreign key CONSTRAINT phrases. While the basic referential integrity constraint can be created using SQL, the ON UPDATE and ON DELETE clauses are not supported.

   Solution: ON UPDATE and ON DELETE actions can be set manually after the relationship is created.

5. Unlike SQL Server, Oracle, and MySQL, Microsoft Access does not support SQL scripts.

   Solution: You can still create tables by using the SQL CREATE command and insert data by using the SQL INSERT command (discussed later in this chapter), but you must do so one command at a time.

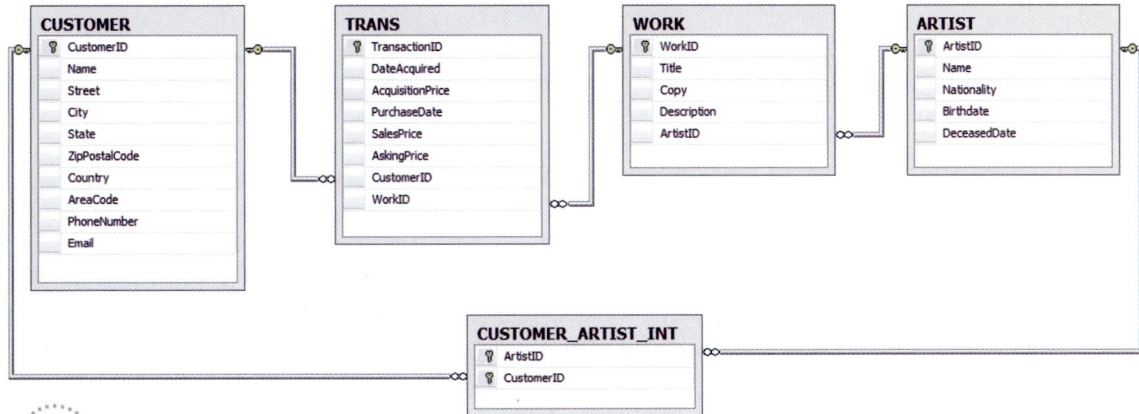

Figure 7-15

SQL Server 2008 View
Ridge Database Diagram

The SQL ALTER Statement

The **SQL ALTER statement** is an SQL DDL statement that is used to change the structure of an existing table. It can be used to add, remove, or change columns. It also can be used to add or remove constraints.

Adding and Dropping Columns

The following statement will add a column named MyColumn to the CUSTOMER table:

```
ALTER TABLE CUSTOMER ADD MyColumn Char(5) NULL;
```

You can drop an existing column with the statement:

```
ALTER TABLE CUSTOMER DROP COLUMN MyColumn;
```

Note the asymmetry in syntax; the keyword COLUMN is used with DROP but not with ADD. You can also use the ALTER statement to change column properties as well, as you will see in the next three chapters.

Adding and Dropping Constraints

The ALTER statement can be used to add a constraint as follows:

```
ALTER TABLE CUSTOMER ADD CONSTRAINT MyConstraint CHECK
     (LastName NOT IN ('RobertsNoPay'));
```

You can also use the ALTER statement to DROP a constraint:

```
ALTER TABLE CUSTOMER DROP CONSTRAINT MyConstraint;
```

> **BY THE WAY**   The SQL ALTER statement can be used to add or drop any of the SQL constraints. You can use it to create primary keys and alternate keys, to set null status, to create referential integrity constraints, and to create data constraints. In fact, another SQL coding style uses CREATE TABLE only to declare the table's columns; all constraints are added using ALTER. We do not use that style in this text, but be aware that it does exist and that your employer might require it.

The SQL DROP TABLE Statement

It is very easy to remove a table in SQL. In fact, it is far too easy. The following **SQL DROP TABLE statement** will drop the TRANS table *and all of its data:*

```
DROP TABLE TRANS;
```

Because this simple statement drops the table and all of its data, be very careful when using it. Do not code this statement on the wrong table!

The DBMS will not drop a table that is the parent in a FOREIGN KEY constraint. It will not do so even if there are no children, or even if you have coded DELETE CASCADE. Instead, to drop such a table, you must first either drop the foreign key constraint or drop the child table. Then you can delete the parent table. As mentioned earlier, parent tables must be first in and last out.

The following statements are needed to drop the CUSTOMER table:

```
DROP TABLE CUSTOMER_ARTIST_INT;
DROP TABLE TRANS;
DROP TABLE CUSTOMER;
```

Alternatively, you could drop CUSTOMER with:

```
ALTER TABLE CUSTOMER_ARTIST_INT
    DROP CONSTRAINT Customer_Artist_Int_CustomerFK;
ALTER TABLE TRANS
    DROP CONSTRAINT TransactionCustomerFK;
DROP TABLE CUSTOMER;
```

SQL DML Statements

At this point, you have learned how to query tables using SQL SELECT statements (in Chapter 2), and you know how to create, alter, and drop tables, columns, and constraints. You do not yet know, however, how to use SQL statements to insert, modify, and delete data. We consider those statements next.

The SQL INSERT Statement

The **SQL INSERT statement** is used to add rows of data to a table. The statement has a number of different options.

The SQL INSERT Statement Using Column Names

The standard version of the INSERT statement is to name the table, name the columns for which you have data, and then list the data in the following format:

```
INSERT INTO ARTIST
    (LastName, FirstName, Nationality, DateOfBirth, DateDeceased)
    VALUES ('Miro', 'Joan', 'Spanish', 1893, 1983);
```

Note that both column names and values are enclosed in parenthesis, and DBMS populated surrogate keys are not included in the statement. If you are providing data for all of the columns, if that data is in the same order as the columns in the table, and if you have no surrogate keys, then you can omit the column list.

```
INSERT INTO ARTIST VALUES ('Miro', 'Joan', 'Spanish', 1893, 1983);
```

Further, you need not provide the values in the same order as the columns in the table. If for some reason you want to provide Nationality first, you can revise the column names and the data value, as shown in the following example:

```
INSERT INTO ARTIST
    (Nationality, LastName, FirstName, DateOfBirth, DateDeceased)
    VALUES ('Spanish', 'Miro', 'Joan', 1893, 1983);
```

If you have partial values, just code the names of the columns for which you have data. For example, if you have only LastName, FirstName, and Nationality for an artist, you would use the SQL statement:

```
INSERT INTO ARTIST
    (LastName, FirstName, Nationality)
    VALUES ('Miro', 'Joan', 'Spanish');
```

You must, of course, have values for all NOT NULL columns.

Bulk INSERT

One of the most often used forms of INSERT uses an SQL SELECT statement to provide values. Suppose you have the names, nationalities, birth dates, and dates deceased of a number of artists in a table named IMPORTED_ARTIST. In this case, you can add those data to the ARTIST table with the following statement:

```
INSERT INTO ARTIST
    (LastName, FirstName, Nationality, DateOfBirth, DateDeceased)
    SELECT   (LastName, FirstName, Nationality, DateOfBirth,
             DateDeceased)
    FROM     IMPORTED_ARTIST;
```

Note that the SQL keyword VALUES is not used with this form of insert.

This syntax should seem familiar. We used it for normalization and denormalization examples in Chapters 3 and 4.

Populating the View Ridge Database Tables

Now that we know how to use the SQL INSERT statement to add rows of data to a table, we can put data into the View Ridge database. Sample data for the View Ridge database is shown in Figure 7-16.

However, we need to be careful about exactly how we enter this data into the View Ridge database. Notice that in the SQL CREATE TABLE statements in Figure 7-14 that CustomerID, ArtistID, WorkID, and TransactionID are all surrogate keys with values automatically inserted by the DBMS. This will produce sequential numbers. For example, if we insert the ARTIST table data shown in Figure 7-16(b) using the automatic ArtistID numbering from IDENTITY(1, 1), the ArtistID numbers for the 9 artist will be (1, 2, 3, 4, 5, 6, 7, 8, 9). But in Figure 7-12(b) the ArtistID numbers are (1, 2, 3, 4, 5, 11, 17, 18, 19).

This happens because the View Ridge data shown in Figure 7-16 is sample data, not the complete data for the database. Therefore, the primary key numbers for CustomerID, ArtistID, WorkID, and TransactionID are *not* sequential.

This, of course, raises the question of how to override DBMS mechanisms that provide automatic surrogate key numbering. The answer to this question varies between DBMS products (as does the method for generating the surrogate values). A discussion of this topic and the complete set of SQL INSERT statements needed to enter the data for the DBMS products discussed in the text are in Chapters 10 (SQL Server 2008), 10A (Oracle Database 11g), and 10B (MySQL 5.1). At this point, we recommend that you read the appropriate section for the DBMS product you are using and populate the View Ridge database in your DBMS.

CustomerID	LastName	FirstName	Street	City	State	ZipPostalCode
1000	Janes	Jeffrey	123 W. Elm St	Renton	WA	98055
1001	Smith	David	813 Tumbleweed Lane	Durango	CO	81201
1015	Twilight	Tiffany	88 1st Avenue	Langley	WA	98260
1033	Smathers	Fred	10899 88th Ave	Bainbridge Island	WA	98110
1034	Frederickson	Mary Beth	25 South Lafayette	Denver	CO	80201
1036	Warning	Selma	205 Burnaby	Vancouver	BC	V6Z 1W2
1037	Wu	Susan	105 Locust Ave	Atlanta	GA	30322
1040	Gray	Donald	55 Bodega Ave	Bodega Bay	CA	94923
1041	Johnson	Lynda	117 C Street	Washington	DC	20003
1051	Wilkens	Chris	87 Highland Drive	Olympia	WA	98508

CustomerID	LastName	FirstName	Country	AreaCode	PhoneNumber	Email
1000	Janes	Jeffrey	USA	425	543-2345	Jeffrey.James@somewhere.com
1001	Smith	David	USA	970	654-9876	David.Smith@somewhere.com
1015	Twilight	Tiffany	USA	360	765-5566	Tiffany.Twilight@somewhere.com
1033	Smathers	Fred	USA	206	876-9911	Fred.Smathers@somewhere.com
1034	Frederickson	Mary Beth	USA	303	513-8822	MaryBeth.Frederickson@somewhere.com
1036	Warning	Selma	Canada	604	988-0512	Selma.Warning@somewhere.com
1037	Wu	Susan	USA	404	653-3465	Susan.Wu@somewhere.com
1040	Gray	Donald	USA	707	568-4839	Donald.Gray@somewhere.com
1041	Johnson	Lynda	USA	202	438-5498	NULL
1051	Wilkens	Chris	USA	360	765-7766	Chris.Wilkens@somewhere.com

(a) CUSTOMER Table Data

Figure 7-16

Sample Data for the View Ridge Database

The SQL UPDATE Statement

The **SQL UPDATE statement** is used to change values of existing rows. For example, the following statement will change the value of City to 'New York City' for the View Ridge customer whose CustomerID is 1000 (Jeffrey Janes):

```
UPDATE       CUSTOMER
SET          City = 'New York City'
WHERE        CustomerID = 1000;
```

ArtistID	LastName	FirstName	Nationality	DateOfBirth	DateDeceased
1	Miro	Joan	Spanish	1893	1983
2	Kandinsky	Wassily	Russian	1866	1944
3	Klee	Paul	German	1879	1940
4	Matisse	Henri	French	1869	1954
5	Chagall	Marc	French	1887	1985
11	Sargent	John Singer	United States	1856	1925
17	Tobey	Mark	United States	1890	1976
18	Horiuchi	Paul	United States	1906	1999
19	Graves	Morris	United States	1920	2001

(b) ARTIST Table Data

ArtistID	CustomerID
1	1001
1	1034
2	1001
2	1034
4	1001
4	1034
5	1001
5	1034
5	1036
11	1001
11	1015
11	1036
17	1000
17	1015

ArtistID	CustomerID
17	1033
17	1040
17	1051
18	1000
18	1015
18	1033
18	1040
18	1051
19	1000
19	1015
19	1033
19	1036
19	1040
19	1051

Figure 7-16

(Continued)

(c) CUSTOMER_ARTIST_INT Table Data

WorkID	Title	Medium	Description	Copy	ArtistID
500	Memories IV	Casein rice paper collage	31 x 24.8 in.	Unique	18
511	Surf and Bird	High Quality Limited Print	Northwest School Expressionist style	142/500	19
521	The Tilled Field	High Quality Limited Print	Early Surrealist style	788/1000	1
522	La Lecon de Ski	High Quality Limited Print	Surrealist style	353/500	1
523	On White II	High Quality Limited Print	Bauhaus style of Kandinsky	435/500	2
524	Woman with a Hat	High Quality Limited Print	A very colorful Impressionist piece	596/750	4
537	The Woven World	Color lithograph	Signed	17/750	17
548	Night Bird	Watercolor on Paper	50 x 72.5 cm.—Signed	Unique	19
551	Der Blaue Reiter	High Quality Limited Print	"The Blue Rider"—Early Pointilism influence	236/1000	2
552	Angelus Novus	High Quality Limited Print	Bauhaus style of Klee	659/750	3
553	The Dance	High Quality Limited Print	An Impressionist masterpiece	734/1000	4
554	I and the Village	High Quality Limited Print	Shows Belarusian folk-life themes and symbology	834/1000	5
555	Claude Monet Painting	High Quality Limited Print	Shows French Impressionist influence of Monet	684/1000	11
561	Sunflower	Watercolor and ink	33.3 x 16.1 cm.—Signed	Unique	19
562	The Fiddler	High Quality Limited Print	Shows Belarusian folk-life themes and symbology	251/1000	5
563	Spanish Dancer	High Quality Limited Print	American realist style—From work in Spain	583/750	11
564	Farmer's Market #2	High Quality Limited Print	Northwest School Abstract Expressionist style	267/500	17

Figure 7-16

(Continued)

565	Farmer's Market #2	High Quality Limited Print	Northwest School Abstract Expressionist style	268/500	17
566	Into Time	High Quality Limited Print	Northwest School Abstract Expressionist style	323/500	18
570	Untitled Number 1	Monotype with tempera	4.3 x 6.1 in.—Signed	Unique	17
571	Yellow covers blue	Oil and collage	71 x 78 in.—Signed	Unique	18
578	Mid Century Hibernation	High Quality Limited Print	Northwest School Expressionist style	362/500	19
580	Forms in Progress I	Color aquatint	19.3 x 24.4 in.—Signed	Unique	17
581	Forms in Progress II	Color aquatint	19.3 x 24.4 in.—Signed	Unique	17
585	The Fiddler	High Quality Limited Print	Shows Belarusian folk-life themes and symbology	252/1000	5
586	Spanish Dancer	High Quality Limited Print	American Realist style—From work in Spain	588/750	11
587	Broadway Boggie	High Quality Limited Print	Northwest School Abstract Expressionist style	433/500	17
588	Universal Field	High Quality Limited Print	Northwest School Abstract Expressionist style	114/500	17
589	Color Foating in Time	High Quality Limited Print	Northwest School Abstract Expressionist style	487/500	18
590	Blue Interior	Tempera on card	43.9 x 28 in.	Unique	17
593	Surf and Bird	Gouache	26.5 x 29.75 in.—Signed	Unique	19
594	Surf and Bird	High Quality Limited Print	Northwest School Expressionist style	366/500	19
595	Surf and Bird	High Quality Limited Print	Northwest School Expressionist style	366/500	19
596	Surf and Bird	High Quality Limited Print	Northwest School Expressionist style	366/500	19

(d) WORK Table Data

Figure 7-16

(Continued)

TransactionID	DateAcquired	AcquisitionPrice	AskingPrice	DateSoldID	SalesPrice	CustomerID	WorkID
100	11/4/2005	$30,000.00	$45,000.00	12/14/2005	$42,500.00	1000	500
101	11/7/2005	$250.00	$500.00	12/19/2005	$500.00	1015	511
102	11/17/2005	$125.00	$250.00	1/18/2006	$200.00	1001	521
103	11/17/2005	$250.00	$500.00	12/12/2006	$400.00	1034	522
104	11/17/2005	$250.00	$250.00	1/18/2006	$200.00	1001	523
105	11/17/2005	$200.00	$500.00	12/12/2006	$400.00	1034	524
115	3/3/2006	$1,500.00	$3,000.00	6/7/2006	$2,750.00	1033	537
121	9/21/2006	$15,000.00	$30,000.00	11/28/2006	$27,500.00	1015	548
125	11/21/2006	$125.00	$250.00	12/18/2006	$200.00	1001	551
126	11/21/2006	$200.00	$400.00				552
127	11/21/2006	$125.00	$500.00	12/22/2006	$400.00	1034	553
128	11/21/2006	$125.00	$250.00	3/16/2007	$225.00	1036	554
129	11/21/2006	$125.00	$250.00	3/16/2007	$225.00	1036	555
151	5/7/2007	$10,000.00	$20,000.00	6/28/2007	$17,500.00	1036	561
152	5/18/2007	$125.00	$250.00	8/15/2007	$225.00	1001	562
153	5/18/2007	$200.00	$400.00	8/15/2007	$350.00	1001	563
154	5/18/2007	$250.00	$500.00	9/28/2007	$400.00	1040	564
155	5/18/2007	$250.00	$500.00				565
156	5/18/2007	$250.00	$500.00	9/27/2007	$400.00	1040	566
161	6/28/2007	$7,500.00	$15,000.00	9/29/2007	$13,750.00	1033	570
171	8/23/2007	$35,000.00	$60,000.00	9/29/2007	$55,000.00	1000	571
175	9/29/2007	$40,000.00	$75,000.00	12/18/2007	$72,500.00	1036	500
181	10/11/2007	$250.00	$500.00				578
201	2/28/2008	$2,000.00	$3,500.00	4/26/2008	$3,250.00	1040	580
202	2/28/2008	$2,000.00	$3,500.00	4/26/2008	$3,250.00	1040	581
225	6/8/2008	$125.00	$250.00	9/27/2008	$225.00	1051	585
226	6/8/2008	$200.00	$400.00				586
227	6/8/2008	$250.00	$500.00	9/27/2008	$475.00	1051	587
228	6/8/2008	$250.00	$500.00				588
229	6/8/2008	$250.00	$500.00				589
241	8/29/2008	$2,500.00	$5,000.00	9/27/2008	$4,750.00	1015	590
251	10/25/2008	$25,000.00	$50,000.00				593
252	10/27/2008	$250.00	$500.00				594
253	10/27/2008	$250.00	$500.00				595
254	10/27/2008	$250.00	$500.00				596

(e) TRANS Table Data

Figure  7-16

(Continued)

To change the value of both City and State, we would use the SQL statement:

```
UPDATE      CUSTOMER
SET         City = 'New York City', State = 'NY'
WHERE       CustomerID = 1000;
```

The DBMS will enforce all referential integrity constraints when processing UPDATE commands. For the View Ridge database, all keys are surrogate keys, but for tables with data keys the DBMS will cascade or disallow (NO ACTION) updates according to the specification in the FOREIGN KEY constraint. Also, if there is a FOREIGN KEY constraint, the DBMS will enforce the referential integrity constraint on updates to a foreign key.

Bulk Updates

It is quite easy to make bulk updates with the UPDATE statement. It is so easy, in fact, that it is dangerous. Consider the SQL UPDATE statement:

```
UPDATE      CUSTOMER
SET         City = 'New York City';
```

This statement will change the value of City for every row of the CUSTOMER table. If we had intended to change just the value for customer 1000, we would have an unhappy result—every customer would have the value 'New York City'.

You can also perform bulk updates using an SQL WHERE clause that finds multiple rows. If, for example, we wanted to change the AreaCode for every customer who lives in Denver, we would code:

```
UPDATE      CUSTOMER
SET         AreaCode = '303'
WHERE       City = 'Denver';
```

Updating Using Values from Other Tables

The SQL UPDATE statement can set a column equal to the value of a column in a different table. The View Ridge database has no appropriate example for this operation, so suppose instead that we have a table named TAX_TABLE with columns (Tax, City), where Tax is the appropriate tax rate for the City.

Now suppose we have a table named PURCHASE_ORDER that includes the columns TaxRate and City. We can update all rows for purchase orders in the city of Bodega Bay with the following SQL statement:

```
UPDATE      PURCHASE_ORDER
SET         TaxRate =
            (SELECT     Tax
              FROM      TAX_TABLE
              WHERE     TAX_TABLE.City = 'Bodega Bay')
WHERE       PURCHASE_ORDER.City = 'Bodega Bay';
```

More likely, we want to update the value of the tax rate for a purchase order without specifying the city. Say we want to update the TaxRate for purchase order number 1000. In that case, we use the slightly more complex SQL statement:

```
UPDATE          PURCHASE_ORDER
SET             TaxRate =
                (SELECT     Tax
                 FROM       TAX_TABLE
                 WHERE      TAX_TABLE.City = PURCHASE_ORDER.City)
WHERE           PURCHASE_ORDER.Number = 1000;
```

SQL SELECT statements can be combined with UPDATE statements in many different ways. We need to move on to other topics, but try these and other variations of UPDATE on your own.

The SQL DELETE Statement

The **SQL DELETE statement** is also quite easy to use. The following SQL statement will delete the row for a customer with a CustomerID of 1000:

```
DELETE      FROM CUSTOMER
WHERE       CustomerID = 1000;
```

Of course, if you omit the WHERE clause, you will delete *every* customer row, so be careful with this command as well.

The DBMS will enforce all referential integrity constraints when processing DELETE commands. For example, in the View Ridge database, you will be unable to delete a CUSTOMER row if that row has any TRANS children. Further, if a row with no TRANS children is deleted, any existing CUSTOMER_ARTIST_INT children will be deleted as well. This latter action occurs because of the CASCADE DELETE specification on the relationship between CUSTOMER and CUSTOMER_ARTIST_INT.

New Forms of Join

In Chapter 2, you learned how to perform SQL joins. Here we extend that discussion to show a different join syntax and to address ways of processing joins on tables with null values. We will be using the View Ridge database and the data in Figure 7-16 as our example, so if you want to try out these commands, you will need to have completed building and populating your VRG database based on the SQL CREATE TABLE statements and INSERT statements appropriate for your DBMS product.

The SQL JOIN ON Syntax

In Chapter 2, you learned to code joins using the following syntax:

```
SELECT      *
FROM        ARTIST, WORK
WHERE       ARTIST.ArtistID = WORK.ArtistID;
```

Another way to code this same join is:

```
SELECT      *
FROM        ARTIST JOIN WORK
    ON      ARTIST.ArtistID = WORK.ArtistID;
```

These two joins are equivalent. Some people think that the second format, which uses the **SQL JOIN ON syntax** is easier to understand than the first.

You can use the SQL JOIN ON syntax as an alternate format for joins of three or more tables, as well. If, for example, you want to obtain a list of the names of customers and the names of the artists in which they are interested, code:

```
SELECT       CUSTOMER.LastName, CUSTOMER.FirstName,
             ARTIST.LastName AS ArtistName
FROM         CUSTOMER JOIN CUSTOMER_ARTIST_INT
     ON      CUSTOMER.CustomerID = CUSTOMER_ARTIST_INT.CustomerID
             JOIN    ARTIST
                ON   CUSTOMER_ARTIST_INT.ArtistID = ARTIST.ArtistID;
```

You can make that statement even simpler by using the **SQL AS keyword** to create table aliases as well as for naming output columns:

```
SELECT       C.LastName, C.FirstName,
             A.LastName AS ArtistName
FROM         CUSTOMER AS C JOIN CUSTOMER_ARTIST_INT AS CI
     ON      C.CustomerID = CI.CustomerID
             JOIN    ARTIST AS A
                ON   CI.ArtistID = A.ArtistID;
```

When a query produces a result table with many rows, we may want to limit the number of rows that we see. We can do this using the **SQL TOP NumberOfRows syntax**, which, along with an ORDER BY clause to sort the data, produces our final SQL query statement:

```
SELECT       TOP 10 C.LastName, C.FirstName,
             A.LastName AS ArtistName
FROM         CUSTOMER AS C JOIN CUSTOMER_ARTIST_INT AS CI
     ON      C.CustomerID = CI.CustomerID
             JOIN    ARTIST AS A
                ON  CI.ArtistID = A.ArtistID
ORDER BY     C.LastName, C.FirstName;
```

The result of this statement is:

	LastName	FirstName	ArtistName
1	Frederickson	Mary Beth	Chagall
2	Frederickson	Mary Beth	Kandinsky
3	Frederickson	Mary Beth	Matisse
4	Frederickson	Mary Beth	Miro
5	Gray	Donald	Graves
6	Gray	Donald	Horiuchi
7	Gray	Donald	Tobey
8	Janes	Jeffrey	Graves
9	Janes	Jeffrey	Horiuchi
10	Janes	Jeffrey	Tobey

Outer Joins

The SQL query:

```
SELECT      C.LastName, C.FirstName, T.TransactionID, T.SalesPrice
FROM        CUSTOMER AS C JOIN TRANS AS T
    ON      C.CustomerID = T.CustomerID
ORDER BY    T.TransactionID;
```

produces the large result set shown in Figure 7-17.

This result is correct, but it only shows the names of only 8 of the 10 customers in the CUSTOMER table. What happened to the other two customers? Look closely at the data in Figure 7-16 and you will see that the two customers that do not appear in the results (Susan Wu and Lynda Johnson) are customers who have never made a purchase at the gallery. Therefore, the primary key value of these two customers does not match any foreign key value in the TRANS table, and because they have no match, they do not appear in the result of this join statement.

We can cause all of the rows in CUSTOMER to appear using what is called an **SQL outer join**. The SQL outer join syntax is shown in the query:

```
SELECT      C.LastName, C.FirstName, T.TransactionID, T.SalesPrice
FROM        CUSTOMER AS C LEFT JOIN TRANS AS T
    ON      C.CustomerID = T.CustomerID
ORDER BY    T.TransactionID;
```

Figure 7-17

Result of Join of CUSTOMER and TRANS

	LastName	FirstName	TransactionID	SalesPrice
1	Janes	Jeffrey	100	42500.00
2	Twilight	Tiffany	101	500.00
3	Smith	David	102	200.00
4	Frederickson	Mary Beth	103	400.00
5	Smith	David	104	200.00
6	Frederickson	Mary Beth	105	400.00
7	Smathers	Fred	115	2750.00
8	Twilight	Tiffany	121	27500.00
9	Smith	David	125	200.00
10	Frederickson	Mary Beth	127	400.00
11	Warning	Selma	128	225.00
12	Warning	Selma	129	225.00
13	Warning	Selma	151	17500.00
14	Smith	David	152	225.00
15	Smith	David	153	350.00
16	Gray	Donald	154	400.00
17	Gray	Donald	156	400.00
18	Smathers	Fred	161	13750.00
19	Janes	Jeffrey	171	55000.00
20	Warning	Selma	175	72500.00
21	Gray	Donald	201	3250.00
22	Gray	Donald	202	3250.00
23	Wilkens	Chris	225	225.00
24	Wilkens	Chris	227	475.00
25	Twilight	Tiffany	241	4750.00

	LastName	FirstName	TransactionID	SalesPrice
1	Wu	Susan	NULL	NULL
2	Johnson	Lynda	NULL	NULL
3	Janes	Jeffrey	100	42500.00
4	Twilight	Tiffany	101	500.00
5	Smith	David	102	200.00
6	Frederickson	Mary Beth	103	400.00
7	Smith	David	104	200.00
8	Frederickson	Mary Beth	105	400.00
9	Smathers	Fred	115	2750.00
10	Twilight	Tiffany	121	27500.00
11	Smith	David	125	200.00
12	Frederickson	Mary Beth	127	400.00
13	Warning	Selma	128	225.00
14	Warning	Selma	129	225.00
15	Warning	Selma	151	17500.00
16	Smith	David	152	225.00
17	Smith	David	153	350.00
18	Gray	Donald	154	400.00
19	Gray	Donald	156	400.00
20	Smathers	Fred	161	13750.00
21	Janes	Jeffrey	171	55000.00
22	Warning	Selma	175	72500.00
23	Gray	Donald	201	3250.00
24	Gray	Donald	202	3250.00
25	Wilkens	Chris	225	225.00
26	Wilkens	Chris	227	475.00
27	Twilight	Tiffany	241	4750.00

Figure 7-18

Result of Left Outer Join of CUSTOMER and TRANS

The result of this query is shown in Figure 7-18. Notice that the values of TransactionID and SalesPrice are NULL for all customers (Susan Wu and Lynda Johnson) who have not made purchases.

Outer joins can be either from the left or the right. If the outer join is from the left, an **SQL left outer join which uses the SQL LEFT JOIN syntax**, then all of the rows on the table on the left (or first table in the join statement) will be included in the result. If the outer join is on the right, an **SQL right outerjoin which uses the SQL RIGHT JOIN syntax**, then all rows on the table on the right (or second table in the join statement) will be included in the result.

To illustrate the use of a right outer join, we will use a modification of the preceding query we used to associate customers with transactions. With the left outer join, the NULLs showed customers who had not purchased a work. With the right outer join, the NULL will show works that have not been purchased by customers (and are therefore still in inventory and available for sale):

```
SELECT      C.LastName, C.FirstName, T.TransactionID, T.SalesPrice
FROM        CUSTOMER AS C RIGHT JOIN TRANS AS T
    ON      C.CustomerID = T.CustomerID
ORDER BY    T.TransactionID;
```

	Last Name	First Name	TransactionID	SalesPrice
1	Janes	Jeffrey	100	42500.00
2	Twilight	Tiffany	101	500.00
3	Smith	David	102	200.00
4	Frederickson	Mary Beth	103	400.00
5	Smith	David	104	200.00
6	Frederickson	Mary Beth	105	400.00
7	Smathers	Fred	115	2750.00
8	Twilight	Tiffany	121	27500.00
9	Smith	David	125	200.00
10	NULL	NULL	126	NULL
11	Frederickson	Mary Beth	127	400.00
12	Warning	Selma	128	225.00
13	Warning	Selma	129	225.00
14	Warning	Selma	151	17500.00
15	Smith	David	152	225.00
16	Smith	David	153	350.00
17	Gray	Donald	154	400.00
18	NULL	NULL	155	NULL
19	Gray	Donald	156	400.00
20	Smathers	Fred	161	13750.00
21	Janes	Jeffrey	171	55000.00
22	Warning	Selma	175	72500.00
23	NULL	NULL	181	NULL
24	Gray	Donald	201	3250.00
25	Gray	Donald	202	3250.00
26	Wilkens	Chris	225	225.00
27	NULL	NULL	226	NULL
28	Wilkens	Chris	227	475.00
29	NULL	NULL	228	NULL
30	NULL	NULL	229	NULL
31	Twilight	Tiffany	241	4750.00
32	NULL	NULL	251	NULL
33	NULL	NULL	252	NULL
34	NULL	NULL	253	NULL
35	NULL	NULL	254	NULL

Figure 7-19

Result of Right Outer Join of
CUSTOMER and TRANS

The result for this right join query is shown in Figure 7-19.

Joins that are not outer joins are called **inner joins**. All of the joins we have presented up to this discussion of outer have been inner joins, though we did not use that term. Outer joins can be combined to any level, just as inner joins can. The following SQL statement will obtain a list of every customer and the artists in which they have an interest:

```
SELECT      C.LastName, C.FirstName, A.LastName AS ArtistName
FROM        CUSTOMER AS C LEFT JOIN CUSTOMER_ARTIST_INT AS CI
    ON      C.CustomerID = CI.CustomerID
            LEFT JOIN  ARTIST AS A
                ON   CI.ArtistID = A.ArtistID;
```

	LastName	FirstName	ArtistName
3	Janes	Jeffrey	Graves
4	Smith	David	Miro
5	Smith	David	Kandinsky
6	Smith	David	Matisse
7	Smith	David	Chagall
8	Smith	David	Sargent
9	Twilight	Tiffany	Sargent
10	Twilight	Tiffany	Tobey
11	Twilight	Tiffany	Horiuchi
12	Twilight	Tiffany	Graves
13	Smathers	Fred	Tobey
14	Smathers	Fred	Horiuchi
15	Smathers	Fred	Graves
16	Frederickson	Mary Beth	Miro
17	Frederickson	Mary Beth	Kandinsky
18	Frederickson	Mary Beth	Matisse
19	Frederickson	Mary Beth	Chagall
20	Warning	Selma	Chagall
21	Warning	Selma	Sargent
22	Warning	Selma	Graves
23	Wu	Susan	NULL
24	Gray	Donald	Tobey
25	Gray	Donald	Horiuchi
26	Gray	Donald	Graves
27	Johnson	Lynda	NULL
28	Wilkens	Chris	Tobey
29	Wilkens	Chris	Horiuchi
30	Wilkens	Chris	Graves

Figure 7-20

Result of Nested Left Outer Joins

The result for this query is in Figure 7-20. Note that if we leave either LEFT keyword out of the expression the null rows will not appear in Figure 7-20. A variant of this query using right joins can also be run (if you are running these queries in a DBMS, then try it out), but note that because (as shown in the data in Figure 7-16) there is at least one customer interested in each artist, there will be no NULL values in the result. Of course, that is a significant result, showing that customers are interested in all the artists featured at the View Ridge Gallery.

> **BY THE WAY** It is easy to forget that inner joins will drop nonmatching rows. Some years ago, one of the authors had a very large organization as a consulting client. The client had a budgetary-planning application that included a long sequence of complicated SQL statements. One of the joins in that sequence was an inner join that should have been an outer join. As a result, some 3,000 employees dropped out of the budgetary calculations. The mistake was discovered only months later when the actual salary expense exceeded the budget salary expense by a large margin. The mistake was an embarrassment all the way to the board of directors.

Using SQL Views

An **SQL view** is a virtual table that is constructed from other tables or views. A view has no data of its own, but obtains data from tables or other views. Views are constructed from SQL SELECT statements using the **SQL CREATE VIEW statement**, and view names are then used just as table names would be in the FROM clause of other SQL SELECT statements. The only limitation on the SQL statements that are used to create views is that they may not contain an ORDER BY clause.[1] The sort order must be provided by the SELECT statement that processes the view.

> **BY THE WAY**   Views are a standard and popular SQL construct. Access, however, does not support them. Instead, in Access you can create a view-equivalent *query*, name it, and then save it. You can then process the query in the same ways that we process views in the following discussion.
>
> SQL Server, Oracle, and MySQL all support views, and they are an important structure with many uses. Do not conclude from Access's lack of support that views are unimportant. Read on, and, if possible, use SQL Server, Oracle, or MySQL to process the statements in this section.

The following statement defines a view named CustomerNameView on the CUSTOMER table:

```
CREATE VIEW CustomerNameView AS
        SELECT   LastName AS CustomerLastName,
                 FirstName AS CustomerFirstName
        FROM     CUSTOMER;
```

Note that the results from executing this statement will be only a system message stating the action completed. With GUI utilities such as SQL Server Management Studio, an appropriately named object will also be created.

> **BY THE WAY**   The current versions of SQL Server, Oracle, and MySQL all process the CREATE VIEW statements as written here without difficulty. However, an earlier version of SQL Server, SQL Server 2000, has a quirk: to create views, you have to remove the semicolon from the CREATE VIEW statement. We have no idea why SQL Server 2000 accepts a semicolon for all other SQL statements but will not accept one for SQL statements that create views. If, by chance, you are still using SQL Server 2000, be aware that you must remove the semicolon when writing CREATE VIEW statements.

Once the view is created, it can be used in the FROM clause of SELECT statements, just like a table. The following obtains a list of customer names in sorted order:

```
SELECT    *
FROM      CustomerNameView
ORDER BY  CustomerLastName, CustomerFirstName;
```

---

[1] This limitation appears in the SQL-92 standard, but how views are actually implemented varies by DBMS product. For example, Oracle allows views to include ORDER BY, whereas SQL Server will only allow ORDER BY in very limited circumstances.

The result for the sample data in Figure 7-16 is:

	CustomerLastName	CustomerFirstName
1	Frederickson	Mary Beth
2	Gray	Donald
3	Janes	Jeffrey
4	Johnson	Lynda
5	Smathers	Fred
6	Smith	David
7	Twilight	Tiffany
8	Warning	Selma
9	Wilkens	Chris
10	Wu	Susan

Note that the number of columns returned in the result depends on the number of columns in the view, not on the number of columns in the underlying table. In this example, the SELECT clause produces just two columns because CustomerNameView itself has just two columns.

Also notice that the columns LastName and FirstName in the CUSTOMER table have been renamed to CustomerLastName and CustomerFirstName in the view. Because of this, the ORDER BY phrase in the SELECT statement uses CustomerLastName and CustomerFirstName, not LastName and FirstName. Also, the DBMS uses the labels CustomerLastName and CustomerFirstName when producing results.

> **BY THE WAY**   If you need to change an SQL view after you have created it, use the **SQL ALTER VIEW statement**. For example, if you wanted to reverse the order of LastName and FirstName in the CustomerNameView, you would use the SQL statement:
>
> ```
> ALTER VIEW CustomerNameView AS
> SELECT     FirstName AS CustomerFirstName,
>            LastName AS CustomerLastName
> FROM       CUSTOMER;
> ```

Figure 7-21 lists the uses for SQL views. SQL views can hide columns or rows. They also can be used to display the results of computed columns, to hide complicated SQL syntax, and to layer the use of built-in functions to create results that are not possible with a single SQL statement. Additionally, SQL views can provide an alias for table names and thus hide the

Figure 7-21

Uses of SQL Views

- Hide columns or rows
- Display results of computations
- Hide complicated SQL syntax
- Layer built-in functions
- Provide level of isolation between table data and users' view of data
- Assign different processing permissions to different views of the same table
- Assign different triggers to different views of the same table

true table names from applications and users. SQL Views also are used to assign different processing permissions and different triggers to different views of the same table. We will show examples for each of these.

Using SQL Views to Hide Columns and Rows

SQL Views can be used to hide columns to simplify results or to prevent the display of sensitive data. For example, suppose the users at View Ridge want a simplified list of customers that has just names and phone numbers. The following SQL statement defines a view, BasicCustomerDataView, that will produce that list:

```
CREATE VIEW BasicCustomerDataView AS
     SELECT  LastName AS CustomerLastName,
             FirstName AS CustomerFirstName,
             AreaCode, PhoneNumber
     FROM    CUSTOMER;
```

To use this view, we can run the SQL statement:

```
SELECT       *
FROM         BasicCustomerDataView
ORDER BY     CustomerLastName, CustomerFirstName;
```

The result is:

	CustomerLastName	CustomerFirstName	AreaCode	PhoneNumber
1	Frederickson	Mary Beth	303	513-8822
2	Gray	Donald	707	568-4839
3	Janes	Jeffrey	425	543-2345
4	Johnson	Lynda	202	438-5498
5	Smathers	Fred	206	876-9911
6	Smith	David	970	654-9876
7	Twilight	Tiffany	360	765-5566
8	Warning	Selma	604	988-0512
9	Wilkens	Chris	360	876-8822
10	Wu	Susan	404	653-3465

If the management of the View Ridge Gallery wants to hide the columns AcquisitionPrice and SalesPrice in TRANS they can define a view that does not include those columns. One use for such a view is to populate a Web page.

SQL Views also can hide rows by providing a WHERE clause in the view definition. The next SQL statement defines a view of customer name and phone data for all customers with an address in Washington State:

```
CREATE VIEW BasicCustomerDataWAView AS
     SELECT   LastName AS CustomerLastName,
              FirstName AS CustomerFirstName,
              AreaCode, PhoneNumber
     FROM     CUSTOMER
     WHERE    State = 'WA';
```

To use this view, we can run the SQL statement:

```
SELECT      *
FROM        BasicCustomerDataWAView
ORDER BY    CustomerLastName, CustomerFirstName;
```

The result is:

	CustomerLastName	CustomerFirstName	AreaCode	PhoneNumber
1	Janes	Jeffrey	425	543-2345
2	Smathers	Fred	206	876-9911
3	Twilight	Tiffany	360	765-5566
4	Wilkens	Chris	360	876-8822

As desired, only customers who live in Washington are shown in this view. This limitation is not obvious from the results because State is not included in the view. This characteristic is good or bad, depending on the use of the view. It is good if this view is used in a setting in which only Washington customers matter; it is bad if the view miscommunicates that these customers are the only View Ridge customers.

Using SQL Views to Display Results of Computed Columns

Another purpose of views is to show the results of computed columns without requiring the user to enter the computation expression. For example, the following view combines the AreaCode and PhoneNumber columns and formats the result:

```
CREATE VIEW CustomerPhoneView AS
    SELECT   LastName AS CustomerLastName,
             FirstName AS CustomerFirstName,
             ('(' + AreaCode + ')' + PhoneNumber) As CustomerPhone
    FROM     CUSTOMER;
```

When the view user executes the SQL statement:

```
SELECT      *
FROM        CustomerPhoneView
ORDER BY    CustomerLastName, CustomerFirstName;
```

the results[2] will be:

	CustomerLastName	CustomerFirstName	CustomerPhone
1	Frederickson	Mary Beth	(303) 513-8822
2	Gray	Donald	(707) 568-4839
3	Janes	Jeffrey	(425) 543-2345
4	Johnson	Lynda	(202) 438-5498
5	Smathers	Fred	(206) 876-9911
6	Smith	David	(970) 654-9876
7	Twilight	Tiffany	(360) 765-5566
8	Warning	Selma	(604) 988-0512
9	Wilkens	Chris	(360) 876-8822
10	Wu	Susan	(404) 653-3465

---

[2] As you might expect, different DBMS products use a different operator for the concatenation operation in the CustomerPhoneView definition. For example, in Oracle the plus sign (+) must be replaced by double vertical bars (||) for string concatenation. See the documentation for your DBMS for more details.

Placing computations in views has two major advantages. First, it saves users from having to know or remember how to write an expression to get the results they want. Second, it ensures consistent results. If each developer who uses a computation writes his or her own SQL expression, that developer may write it differently and obtain inconsistent results.

Using SQL Views to Hide Complicated SQL Syntax

Another use of SQL views is to hide complicated SQL syntax. Using a view, developers need not enter a complex SQL statement when they want a particular result. Also, such views give the benefits of complicated SQL statements to developers who do not know how to write such statements. This use of views also ensures consistency.

For example, suppose that the View Ridge Gallery salespeople want to see which customers are interested in which artists. To display these interests, two joins are necessary: one to join CUSTOMER to CUSTOMER_ARTIST_INT and another to join that result to ARTIST. We can code an SQL statement that constructs these joins and define it as an SQL view. In fact, we already have, and we will reuse a variant of our nested left outer join example discussed earlier [we simply use equijoins (i.e., inner joins) instead of outer joins, because we are not interested in NULL values in these results] to create the CustomerInterestsView:

```
CREATE VIEW CustomerInterestsView AS
    SELECT      C.LastName AS CustomerLastName,
                C.FirstName AS CustomerFirstName,
                A.LastName AS ArtistName
    FROM        CUSTOMER AS C JOIN CUSTOMER_ARTIST_INT AS CI
        ON      C.CustomerID = CI.CustomerID
                JOIN    ARTIST AS A
                    ON  CI.ArtistID = A.ArtistID;
```

Notice the aliasing of C.LastName to CustomerLastName and A.LastName to ArtistLastName. We *must* use at least one of these column aliases, for without them the resulting table has two columns named LastName. The DBMS would not be able to distinguish one LastName from the other and would generate an error when an attempt is made to create such a view.

This is a complicated SQL statement to write, but once the view is created the result of this statement can be obtained with a simple SELECT statement. For example, the following statement shows the results sorted by CustomerLastName and Customer FirstName:

```
SELECT      *
FROM        CustomerInterestsView
ORDER BY    CustomerLastName, CustomerFirstName;
```

Figure 7-22 displays the fairly large result set. Clearly, using the view is much simpler than constructing the join syntax. Even developers who know SQL well will appreciate having a simpler SQL view with which to work.

Layering Built-in Functions

Recall from Chapter 2 that you cannot use a computation or a built-in function as part of an SQL WHERE clause. You can, however, construct a view that computes a variable and then write an

	CustomerLastName	CustomerFirstName	ArtistName
1	Frederickson	Mary Beth	Chagall
2	Frederickson	Mary Beth	Kandinsky
3	Frederickson	Mary Beth	Miro
4	Frederickson	Mary Beth	Matisse
5	Gray	Donald	Tobey
6	Gray	Donald	Horiuchi
7	Gray	Donald	Graves
8	Janes	Jeffrey	Graves
9	Janes	Jeffrey	Horiuchi
10	Janes	Jeffrey	Tobey
11	Smathers	Fred	Tobey
12	Smathers	Fred	Horiuchi
13	Smathers	Fred	Graves
14	Smith	David	Chagall
15	Smith	David	Matisse
16	Smith	David	Kandinsky
17	Smith	David	Miro
18	Smith	David	Sargent
19	Twilight	Tiffany	Sargent
20	Twilight	Tiffany	Tobey
21	Twilight	Tiffany	Horiuchi
22	Twilight	Tiffany	Graves
23	Warning	Selma	Chagall
24	Warning	Selma	Graves
25	Warning	Selma	Sargent
26	Wilkens	Chris	Tobey
27	Wilkens	Chris	Graves
28	Wilkens	Chris	Horiuchi

Figure 7-22

Result of
CustomerInterestsView

SQL statement on that view that uses the computed variable in a WHERE clause. To understand this, consider the SQL view definition for the ArtistWorkNetView:

```
CREATE VIEW ArtistWorkNetView AS
    SELECT    W.WorkID, LastName AS ArtistLastName,
              FirstName AS ArtistFirstName, Title, Copy, DateSold,
              AcquisitionPrice, SalesPrice,
              (SalesPrice - AcquisitionPrice) AS NetProfit
    FROM      TRANS AS T JOIN WORK AS W
        ON    T.WorkID = W.WorkID
              JOIN      ARTIST AS A
                  ON        W.ArtistID = A.ArtistID;
```

This SQL view joins TRANS, WORK, and ARTIST and creates the computed column NetProfit. We can now use NetProfit in an SQL WHERE clause in a query, as follows:

```
SELECT        ArtistLastName, ArtistFirstName,
              WorkID, Title, Copy, DateSold, NetProfit
FROM          ArtistWorkNetView
WHERE         NetProfit > 5000
ORDER BY      DateSold;
```

Here we are using the result of a computation in a WHERE clause, something that is not allowed in a single SQL statement. The result of the SQL SELECT statement is:

	Artist Last Name	Artist First Name	WorkID	Title	Copy	Date Sold	Net Profit
1	Horiuchi	Paul	500	Memories IV	Unique	2005-12-14 ...	12500.00
2	Graves	Morris	548	Night Bird	Unique	2006-11-28 ...	12500.00
3	Graves	Morris	561	Sunflower	Unique	2007-06-28 ...	7500.00
4	Tobey	Mark	570	Untitled Number 1	Unique	2007-09-29 ...	6250.00
5	Horiuchi	Paul	571	Yellow Covers Blue	Unique	2007-09-29 ...	20000.00
6	Horiuchi	Paul	500	Memories IV	Unique	2007-12-18 ...	32500.00

Such layering can be continued over many levels. We can define another view with another computation on the computation in the first view. For example, note that in the results above the Horiuchi work Memories IV has been acquired and sold more than once by View Ridge, and then consider the SQL view ArtistWorkTotalNetView, which will calculate the total net profit from *all* sales of each work:

```
CREATE VIEW ArtistWorkTotalNetView AS
    SELECT        ArtistLastName, ArtistFirstName,
                  WorkID, Title, Copy,
                  SUM(NetProfit) AS TotalNetProfit
    FROM          ArtistWorkNetView
    GROUP BY      ArtistLastName, ArtistFirstName,
                  WorkID, Title, Copy;
```

Now we can use TotalNetProfit in an SQL WHERE clause on the ArtistWorkTotalNet view, as follows:

```
SELECT      *
FROM        ArtistWorkTotalNetView
WHERE       TotalNetProfit > 5000
ORDER       BY TotalNetProfit;
```

In this SELECT, we are using an SQL view on an SQL view and a built-in function on a computed variable in the WHERE clause. The results are as follows:

	Artist Last Name	Artist First Name	WorkID	Title	Copy	TotalNet Profit
1	Tobey	Mark	570	Untitled Number 1	Unique	6250.00
2	Graves	Morris	561	Sunflower	Unique	7500.00
3	Graves	Morris	548	Night Bird	Unique	12500.00
4	Horiuchi	Paul	571	Yellow Covers Blue	Unique	20000.00
5	Horiuchi	Paul	500	Memories IV	Unique	45000.00

Using SQL Views for Isolation, Multiple Permissions, and Multiple Triggers

SQL Views have three other important uses. First, they can isolate source data tables from application code. To see how, suppose we define the view:

```
CREATE VIEW CustomerTable001View AS

    SELECT      *

    FROM        CUSTOMER;
```

This view assigns the alias CustomerTable001View to the CUSTOMER table. If all application code uses the CustomerTable001View in SQL statements, then the true source of the data is hidden from application programmers.

Such table isolation provides flexibility to the database administration staff. For example, suppose that at some future date the source of customer data is changed to a different table (perhaps one that is imported from a different database) named NEW_CUSTOMER. In this situation, all the database administrator needs to do is redefine CustomerTable001View using the SQL ALTER VIEW statement, as follows:

```
ALTER VIEW CustomerTable001View AS

    SELECT        *

    FROM          NEW_CUSTOMER;
```

All of the application code that uses CustomerTable001View will now run on the new data source without any problem.

The second important use for SQL views is to give different sets of processing permissions to the same table. We will discuss security in more detail in Chapters 9, 10, 10A, and 10B, but for now understand that it is possible to limit insert, update, delete, and read permissions on tables and views.

For example, an organization might define a view of CUSTOMER called CustomerReadView with read-only permissions on CUSTOMER and a second view of CUSTOMER called CustomerUpdateView with both read and update permissions. Applications that need not update the customer data would work with CustomerReadView, whereas those that need to update this data would work with CustomerUpdateView.

The final use of SQL views is to enable the definition of multiple sets of triggers on the same source data. This technique is commonly used for enforcing O-M and M-M relationships. In this case, one view has a set of triggers that prohibits the deletion of a required child and another view has a set of triggers that deletes a required child as well as the parent. The views are assigned to different applications, depending on the authority of those applications.

Updating SQL Views

Some views can be updated, others cannot. The rules by which this is determined are both complicated and dependent on the DBMS in use. To understand why this is so, consider the following two update requests on views defined in the last section:

```
UPDATE        CustomerTable001View

SET           Email = 'NewEmailAddress@elsewhere.com'

WHERE         CustomerID = 1000;
```

and

```
UPDATE        ArtistWorkTotalNetView

SET           TotalNetProfit = 23000

WHERE         ArtistLastName = 'Tobey';
```

The first request can be processed without problem because CustomerTable001View is just an alias for the CUSTOMER table. The second update, however, makes no sense at all. TotalNetProfit is a sum of a computed column. Nowhere in the database is there any such column to be updated.

Figure 7-23

Guidelines for Updating
SQL Views

> **Updatable Views:**
> - View based on a single table with no computed columns and all non-null columns present in the view
> - View based on any number of tables, with or without computed columns, and INSTEAD OF trigger defined for the view
>
> **Possibly Updatable Views:**
> - Based on a single table, primary key in view, some required columns missing from view, update and delete may be allowed. Insert is not allowed.
> - Based on multiple tables, updates may be allowed on the most subordinate table in the view if rows of that table can be uniquely identified.

Figure 7-23 shows general guidelines to determine if a view is updatable. Again, the specifics depend on the DBMS product in use. In general, the DBMS must be able to associate the column(s) to be updated with a particular row in a particular table. A way to approach this question is to ask yourself, "What would I do if I were the DBMS and I were asked to update this view? Would the request make sense, and, if so, do I have sufficient data to make the update?" Clearly, if the entire table is present and there are no computed columns, the view is updatable. Also, the DBMS will mark the view as updatable if it has an INSTEAD OF trigger defined for it, as described later.

However, if any of the required columns are missing, the view clearly cannot be used for inserts. It may be used for updates and deletes, however, as long as the primary key (or, for some DBMS products, a candidate key) is present in the view. Multitable views may be updatable on the most subordinate table. Again, this can only be done if the primary key or candidate key for that table is in the view. We will revisit this topic for SQL Server 2008 in Chapter 10, Oracle Database 11g in Chapter 10A, and MySQL 5.1 in Chapter 10B.

Embedding SQL in Program Code

SQL statements can be embedded in application programs, triggers, and stored procedures. Before we discuss those subjects, however, we need to explain the placement of SQL statements in program code.

In order to embed SQL statements in program code, two problems must be solved. The first problem is that some means of assigning the results of SQL statements to program variables must be available. Many different techniques are used. Some involve object-oriented programs, whereas others are simpler. For example, in Oracle's PL/SQL the following statement assigns the count of the number of rows in the CUSTOMER table to the variable named *rowCount*:

```
SELECT      Count(*) INTO rowCount
FROM        CUSTOMER;
```

A similar statement in SQL Server's T-SQL is:

```
SELECT      @rowCount = Count(*)
FROM        CUSTOMER;
```

In either case, the execution of this code will place the number of rows in CUSTOMER into the program variable *rowCount* or *@rowCount*.

The second problem to solve concerns a paradigm mismatch between SQL and application programming languages. SQL is table oriented; SQL SELECT statements start with one or more tables and produce a table as output. Programs, however, start with one or more variables, manipulate them, and store the result in a variable. Because of this difference, an SQL statement like the following makes no sense:

```
SELECT      LastName INTO custLastName
FROM        CUSTOMER;
```

If there are 100 rows in the CUSTOMER table, there will be 100 values of LastName. The program variable custLastName, however, is expecting to receive just one value.

To avoid this problem, the results of SQL statements are treated as **pseudofiles**. When an SQL statement returns a set of rows, a **cursor**, which is a pointer to a particular row, is established. The application program can then place the cursor on the first, last, or some other row of the SQL statement output table. With the cursor placed, values of columns for that row can be assigned to program variables. When the application is finished with a particular row, it moves the cursor to the next, prior, or some other row, and continues processing.

The typical pattern for using a cursor is as follows:

```
Open SQL (SELECT * FROM CUSTOMER);
Move cursor to first row;
    While cursor not past end of result{
        Set custLastName = LastName;
        ... other statements ...
        Advance cursor to next row;
    };
... continue processing ...
```

In this way, the rows of an SQL SELECT are processed one at a time. You will see many examples of these techniques and others like them in the chapters that follow. For now, try to gain an intuitive understanding of how SQL is embedded in program code.

Using SQL Triggers

A **trigger** is a stored program that is executed by the DBMS whenever a specified event occurs. Triggers for Oracle are written in Java or in Oracle's PL/SQL. SQL Server triggers are written in Microsoft .NET common language runtime languages such as Visual Basic.NET or Microsoft's T-SQL. MySQL triggers are written in MySQL's variant of SQL. In this chapter, we will discuss triggers in a generic manner without considering the particulars of those languages. We will discuss triggers written in DBMS-specific SQL variants in Chapters 10 (T-SQL), 10A (PL/SQL), and 10B (MySQL SQL).

A trigger is attached to a table or a view. A table or a view may have many triggers, but a trigger is associated with just one table or view. A trigger is invoked by an SQL DML INSERT, UPDATE, or DELETE request on the table or view to which it is attached. Figure 7-24 summarizes the triggers available for SQL Server 2008, Oracle Database 11g, and MySQL 5.1.

Oracle supports three kinds of triggers: BEFORE, INSTEAD OF, and AFTER. As you would expect, BEFORE triggers are executed before the DBMS processes the insert, update, or delete request. INSTEAD OF triggers are executed in place of any DBMS processing of the insert, update, or delete request. AFTER triggers are executed after the insert, update, or delete request has been processed. Altogether, nine trigger types are possible: BEFORE (Insert, Update, Delete); INSTEAD OF (Insert, Update, Delete); and AFTER (Insert, Update, Delete).

Since SQL Server 2005, SQL Server supports DDL triggers (triggers on such SQL DDL statements as CREATE, ALTER and DROP) as well as DML triggers. We will only deal with the DML triggers here, which for SQL Server 2008 are INSTEAD OF and AFTER triggers on INSERT, UPDATE, and DELETE. (Microsoft includes the FOR keyword, but this is a synonym for AFTER in Microsoft syntax). Thus, we have six possible trigger types.

MySQL Server supports only BEFORE and AFTER triggers, thus it supports only six trigger types. Other DBMS products support triggers differently. See the documentation of your product to determine which trigger types it supports.

When a trigger is invoked, the DBMS makes the data involved in the requested action available to the trigger code. For an insert, the DBMS will supply the values of columns for the

Trigger Type / DML Action	BEFORE	INSTEAD OF	AFTER
INSERT	Oracle My SQL	Oracle SQL Server	Oracle SQL Server MySQL
UPDATE	Oracle My SQL	Oracle SQL Server	Oracle SQL Server MySQL
DELETE	Oracle My SQL	Oracle SQL Server	Oracle SQL Server MySQL

Figure 7-24

Summary of SQL Triggers
by DBMS

row that is being inserted. For deletions, the DBMS will supply the values of columns for the row that is being deleted. For updates, it will supply both the old and the new values.

The way in which this is done depends on the DBMS product. For now, assume that new values are supplied by prefixing a column name with the expression *new:*. Thus, during an insert on CUSTOMER, the variable new:LastName is the value of LastName for the row being inserted. For an update, new:LastName has the value of LastName after the update takes place. Similarly, assume that old values are supplied by prefixing a column name with the expression *old:*. Thus, for a deletion, the variable old:LastName has the value of LastName for the row being deleted. For an update, old:LastName has the value of Name prior to the requested update. (This, in fact, is the strategy used by Oracle. You will see the equivalent SQL Server strategy in Chapter 10 and the way MySQL works in Chapter 10B.)

Triggers have many uses. In this chapter, we consider the four uses summarized in Figure 7-25:

- Providing default values
- Enforcing data constraints
- Updating SQL views
- Performing referential integrity actions

Using Triggers to Provide Default Values

Earlier in this chapter, you learned to use the SQL DEFAULT keyword to provide initial column values. DEFAULT works only for simple expressions, however. If the computation of a default value requires complicated logic, then an INSERT trigger must be used instead.

For example, suppose that there is a policy at View Ridge Gallery to set the value of AskingPrice equal either to twice the AcquisitionPrice or to the AcquisitionPrice plus the average net gain for sales of this art in the past, whichever is greater. The AFTER trigger in Figure 7-26 implements this policy. Note that the code in Figure 7-26 is generic. You will learn how to write specific code for SQL Server, Oracle, and MySQL in Chapters 10, 10A, and 10B respectively .

After declaring program variables, the trigger reads the TRANS table to find out how many TRANS rows exist for this work. Because this is an AFTER trigger, the new TRANS row for the

Figure 7-25

Uses for SQL Triggers

- Provide default values
- Enforce data constraints
- Update views
- Perform referential integrity actions

```
CREATE TRIGGER TRANS_AskingPriceInitialValue
      AFTER INSERT ON TRANS

DECLARE
      rowcount as int;
      sumNetProfit as Numeric(10,2);
      avgNetProfit as Numeric(10,2);

BEGIN
      /* First find if work has been here before                          */

      SELECT      Count(*) INTO rowcount
      FROM        TRANS AS T
      WHERE       T.WorkID = new:WorkID;

      IF (rowcount = 1)
      THEN
          /* This is first time work has been in gallery                  */

          new:AskingPrice = 2 * new:AcquisitionPrice;

      ELSE
          IF rowcount > 1
          THEN
              /* Work has been here before                                */

              SELECT      SUM(NetProfit) into sumNetProfit
              FROM        ArtistWorkNetView AWNV
              WHERE       AWNV.WorkID = new.WorkID
              GROUP BY    AWNV.WorkID;

              avgNetProfit = sumNetProfit / (rowcount - 1);

                  /* Now choose larger value for the new AskingPrice      */

                  IF ((new:AcquisitionPrice + avgNetProfit)
                       > (2 * new:AcquisitionPrice))
                  THEN
                      new:AskingPrice = (new:AcquisitionPrice + avgNetProfit);
                  ELSE
                      new:AskingPrice = (2 * new:AcquisitionPrice);
                  END IF;
          ELSE
              /* Error, rowcount cannot be less than 1                    */
              /* Do something!                                            */
          END IF;
      END IF;
END;
```

Figure 7-26

Trigger Code to Insert a Default Value

work will have already been inserted. Thus, the count will be one if this is the first time the work has been in the gallery. If so, the new value of SalesPrice is set to twice the AcquisitionPrice.

If the rowcount is greater than one, then the work has been in the gallery before. To compute the average gain for this work, the trigger uses the ArtistWorkNetView described on page 271 to compute Sum(NetProfit) for this work. The sum is placed in the variable sumNetProfit. Notice that the WHERE clause limits the rows to be used in the view to this particular work. The average is then computed by dividing this sum by rowcount minus one.

You may be wondering, why not use AVG(NetProfit) in the SQL statement? The answer is that the default SQL average function would have counted the new row in the computation of the average. We do not want that row to be included, so we subtract one from rowcount when the average is computed. Once the value of avgNetProfit has been computed, it is compared with twice the AcquisitionPrice; the larger result is used for the new value of AskingPrice.

Using Triggers to Enforce Data Constraints

A second purpose of triggers is to enforce data constraints. Although SQL CHECK constraints can be used to enforce domain, range, and intrarelation constraints, no DBMS vendor has implemented the SQL-92 features for interrelation CHECK constraints. Consequently, such constraints are implemented in triggers.

Suppose, for example, that the gallery has a special interest in Mexican painters and never discounts the price of their works. Thus, the SalesPrice of a work must always be at least the AskingPrice. To enforce this rule, the gallery database has an insert and update trigger on TRANS that checks to see if the work is by a Mexican painter. If so, the SalesPrice is checked against the AskingPrice. If it is less than the AskingPrice, the SalesPrice is reset to the AskingPrice. This, of course, must happen when the art work is actually being sold, and the customer charged the full amount! This is *not* a postsale accounting adjustment.

Figure 7-27 shows generic trigger code that implements this rule. This trigger will be fired after any insert or update on a TRANS row. The trigger first checks to determine if the work is by a Mexican artist. If not, the trigger is exited. Otherwise, the SalesPrice is checked against the AskingPrice; if it is less than the AskingPrice, the SalesPrice is set equal to the AskingPrice.

Figure ⦂ **7-27**

Trigger Code to Enforce an Interrelation Data Constraint

```
CREATE TRIGGER TRANS_CheckSalesPrice
      AFTER INSERT, UPDATE ON TRANS

DECLARE

      artistNationality      char (30);

BEGIN
      /* First determine if work is by a Mexican artist */

      SELECT    Nationality into artistNationality
      FROM      ARTIST AS A JOIN WORK AS W
            ON A.ArtistID = W.ArtistID
      WHERE     W.WorkID = new:WorkID;

      IF (artistNationality <> 'Mexican')
      THEN
         Exit Trigger;
      ELSE

         /* Work is by a Mexican artist - enforce constraint              */

         IF (new: SalesPrice < new:AskingPrice)
         THEN

            /* Sales Price is too low, reset it                           */

            UPDATE    TRANS
            SET       SalesPrice = new:AskingPrice;

            /* Note:  The above update will cause a recursive call on this */
            /* trigger. The recursion will stop the second time through    */
            /* because SalesPrice will be = AskingPrice.                   */

            /* At this point send a message to the user saying what's been */
            /* done so that the customer has to pay the full amount        */

         ELSE
            /* Error, artistNationality is either Mexican or it isn't      */
            /* Do something!                                               */
         END IF;
      END IF;
END;
```

This trigger will be called recursively. The update statement in the trigger will cause an update on TRANS which will cause the trigger to be called again. The second time, however, the SalesPrice will be equal to the AskingPrice, no more updates will be made, and the recursion will stop.

Using Triggers to Update Views

As stated earlier, the DBMS can update some views but not others, depending on the way the view is constructed. Applications can sometimes update the views that the DBMS cannot update by applying logic that is particular to a given business setting. In this case, the application-specific logic for updating the view is placed in an INSTEAD OF trigger.

When an INSTEAD OF trigger is declared on a view, the DBMS performs no action other than to call the trigger. Everything else is up to the trigger. If you declare an INSTEAD OF INSERT trigger on view MyView, and if your trigger does nothing but send an e-mail message, then that e-mail message becomes the result of an INSERT on the view. INSERT MyView means "Send an e-mail," and nothing more.

More realistically, consider the SQL view CustomerInterestsView on page 270 and the result of that view in Figure 7-22. This view is the result of two joins across the intersection table between CUSTOMER and ARTIST. Suppose that this view populates a grid on a user form, and further suppose that users want to make customer name corrections, when necessary, on this form. If such changes are not possible, the users will say something like, "But, hey, the name is right there. Why can't I change it?" Little do they know the trials and tribulations the DBMS went through to display those data!

In any case, if, for example, the customer LastName value happens to be unique within the database, the view has sufficient information to update the customer's last name. Figure 7-28 shows generic trigger code for such an update. The code just counts the number of customers that have the old value of LastName. If only one customer has that value, then the update is made; otherwise, an error message is generated. Notice that the update activity is on one of the tables that underlie the view. The view, of course, has no real view data. Only actual tables can be updated.

Using Triggers to Implement Referential Integrity Actions

The fourth use of triggers is to implement referential integrity actions. Consider, for example, the 1:N relationship between DEPARTMENT and EMPLOYEE. Assume that the relationship is M-M and that EMPLOYEE.DepartmentName is a foreign key to DEPARTMENT.

To enforce this constraint, we will construct two views, both based on EMPLOYEE. The first view, DeleteEmployeeView, will delete an EMPLOYEE row only if that row is not the last child in the DEPARTMENT. The second view, DeleteEmployeeDepartmentView, will delete an EMPLOYEE row, and if that row is the last EMPLOYEE in the DEPARTMENT, it will also delete the DEPARTMENT row.

An organization would make the view DeleteEmployeeView available to applications that do not have permission to delete a row in DEPARTMENT. The view DeleteEmployeeDepartmentView would be given to applications that have permission to delete both employees and departments that have no employees.

Both of the views DeleteEmployeeView and DeleteEmployeeDepartmentView have the identical structure:

```
CREATE VIEW DeleteEmployeeView
    SELECT      *
    FROM        EMPLOYEE;
CREATE VIEW DeleteEmployeeDepartmentView
    SELECT      *
    FROM        EMPLOYEE;
```

```
CREATE TRIGGER CustomerInterestView_UpdateCustomerLastName
        INSTEAD OF UPDATE ON CustomerInterestView

DECLARE

        rowcount   Int;

BEGIN

        SELECT      COUNT(*) into rowcount
        FROM        CUSTOMER
        WHERE       CUSTOMER.LastName = old:LastName

        IF (rowcount = 1)
        THEN

            /* If get here, then only one customer has this last name.   */
            /* Make the name change.                                     */

            UPDATE      CUSTOMER
            SET         CUSTOMER.LastName = new:LastName
            WHERE       CUSTOMER.LastName = old:LastName;

        ELSE

            IF (rowcount > 1 )
            THEN

                /* Send a message to the user saying cannot update because */
                /* there are too many customers with this last name.       */

            ELSE
                /* Error, if rowcount <= 0 there is an error!              */
                /* Do something!                                          */
            END IF;
        END IF;
    END;
```

Figure (7-28)

**Trigger Code to Update
an SQL View**

The trigger on DeleteEmployeeView, shown in Figure 7-29, determines if the employee is the last employee in the department. If not, the EMPLOYEE row is deleted. If however, the employee *is* the last employee in the department, *nothing* is done. Note again that the DBMS does nothing when an INSTEAD OF trigger is declared on the deletion. All activity is up to the trigger. If the employee is the last employee, then this trigger does nothing, which means that no change will be made to the database because the DBMS left all processing tasks to the INSTEAD OF trigger.

The trigger on DeleteEmployeeDepartment, shown in Figure 7-30, treats the employee deletion a bit differently. First, the trigger checks to determine if the employee is the last employee in the department. If so, the DEPARTMENT is deleted, and then, after that, the employee is deleted. Notice that the row in EMPLOYEE is deleted in either case.

Triggers such as those in Figures 7-29 and 7-30 are used to enforce the referential integrity actions for O-M and M-M relationships, as described at the end of Chapter 6. You will learn how to write them for Oracle in Chapter 10, for SQL Server in Chapter 11, and for MySQL in Chapter 12.

```
CREATE TRIGGER EMPLOYEE_DeleteCheck
      INSTEAD OF DELETE ON DeleteEmployeeView

DECLARE

      rowcount   int;

BEGIN

      /*  First determine if this is the last employee in the department */

      SELECT     Count(*) into rowcount
      FROM       EMPLOYEE
      WHERE      EMPLOYEE.EmployeeNumber = old:EmployeeNumber;

      IF (rowcount > 1)
      THEN

          /* Not last employee, allow deletion                            */

          DELETE     EMPLOYEE
          WHERE      EMPLOYEE.EmployeeNumber = old:EmployeeNumber;

      ELSE

          /* Send a message to user saying that the last employee         */
          /* in a department cannot be deleted.                           */

      END IF;

END;
```

Figure 7-29

Trigger Code to Delete All but Last Child

Using Stored Procedures

A **stored procedure** is a program that is stored within the database and compiled when used. In Oracle, stored procedures can be written in PL/SQL or in Java. With SQL Server 2005 and SQL Server 2008, stored procedures are written in T-SQL or a .NET Common Language Runtime (CLR) languages such as VisualBasic.NET, C#.NET, or C++.NET. With MySQL, stored procedures are written in MySQL's variant of SQL.

Stored procedures can receive input parameters and return results. Unlike triggers, which are attached to a given table or view, stored procedures are attached to the database. They can be executed by any process using the database that has permission to use the procedure. Differences between triggers and stored procedures are summarized in Figure 7-31.

Stored procedures are used for many purposes. Although database administrators use them to perform common administration tasks, their primary use is within database applications. They can be invoked from application programs written in languages such as COBOL, C, Java, C#, or C++. They also can be invoked from Web pages using VBScript or JavaScript. Ad hoc users can run them from DBMS management products such as SQL*Plus or SQL Developer in Oracle, SQL Server Management Studio in SQL Server, or the MySQL Query Browser in MySQL.

Advantages of Stored Procedures

The advantages of using stored procedures are listed in Figure 7-32. Unlike application code, stored procedures are never distributed to client computers. They always reside in the database and are processed by the DBMS on the database server. Thus, they are more secure than distributed

```
CREATE TRIGGER EMPLOYEE_DEPARTMENT_DeleteCheck
        INSTEAD OF DELETE ON DeleteEmployeeDepartmentView

DECLARE

        rowcount  int;

BEGIN

        /* Delete Employee row regardless of whether Department will be deleted  */

        DELETE      EMPLOYEE
        WHERE       EMPLOYEE.EmployeeNumber = old:EmployeeNumber;

        /*  First determine if this is the last employee in the department    */

        SELECT      Count(*) into rowcount
        FROM        EMPLOYEE
        WHERE       EMPLOYEE.EmployeeNumber = old:EmployeeNumber;

        IF (rowcount = 0)
        THEN

            /* Last employee in Department, delete Department                 */

            DELETE      DEPARTMENT
            WHERE       DEPARTMENT.DepartmentName = old:DepartmentName;

        END IF;

END;
```

Figure 7-30

Trigger Code to Delete Last Child and Parent When Necessary

application code, and they also reduce network traffic. Increasingly, stored procedures are the preferred mode of processing application logic over the Internet or corporate intranets. Another advantage of stored procedures is that their SQL statements can be optimized by the DBMS compiler.

When application logic is placed in a stored procedure, many different application programmers can use that code. This sharing results not only in less work, but also in standardized processing. Further, the developers best suited for database work can create the stored procedures while other developers, say, those who specialize in Web-tier programming, can do other work. Because of these advantages, it is likely that stored procedures will see increased use in the future.

Figure 7-31

Triggers Versus Stored Procedures

- Trigger
  - Module of code that is called by the DBMS when INSERT, UPDATE, or DELETE commands are issued
  - Assigned to a table or view
  - Depending on the DBMS, may have more than one trigger per table or view
  - Triggers may issue INSERT, UPDATE, and DELETE commands and thereby may cause the invocation of other triggers
- Stored Procedure
  - Module of code that is called by a user or database administrator
  - Assigned to a database, but not to a table or a view
  - Can issue INSERT, UPDATE, and DELETE commands
  - Used for repetitive administration tasks or as part of an application

Figure **7-32**

Advantages of Stored Procedures

Greater security
Decreased network traffic
SQL can be optimized
Code sharing
  Less work
  Standardized processing
  Specialization among developers

The WORK_AddWorkTransaction Stored Procedure

Figure 7-33 shows a stored procedure that records the acquisition of a work in the View Ridge database. Again, this code is generic, but the code style in Figure 7-33 is closer to that used in SQL Server rather than the more Oracle-like style that was used for the trigger examples in the prior section. If you compare the examples in both sections, you can gain a sense of the differences between code written in PL/SQL and T-SQL.

The WORK_addWorkTransaction procedure receives five input parameters and returns none. In a more realistic example, a return parameter would be passed back to the caller to indicate the success or failure of the operation. That discussion takes us away from database concepts, however, and we will omit it here. This code does not assume that the value of ArtistID that is passed to it is a valid ID. Instead, the first step in the stored procedure is to check whether the ArtistID value is valid. To do this, the first block of statements counts the number of rows that have the given ArtistID value. If the count is zero, then the ArtistID value is invalid, and the procedure writes an error message and returns.

Otherwise,[3] the procedure then checks to determine if the work has been in the View Ridge Gallery before. If so, the WORK table will already contain a row for this ArtistID, Title, and Copy. If no such row exists, the procedure creates a new WORK row. Once that has been done, it then uses a SELECT to obtain a value for the WorkID value. If the WORK row was just created, this statement is necessary to obtain the new value of the WorkID surrogate key. If the work was not created, the SELECT on WorkID is necessary to obtain the WorkID of the existing row. Once a value of WorkID has been obtained, the new row is inserted into TRANS. Notice that the system function GetDate() is used to supply a value for DateAcquired in the new row.

This procedure illustrates how SQL is embedded in stored procedures. It is not complete, because we need to do something to ensure that either all updates are made to the database or none of them are. You will learn how to do this in Chapter 9. For now, just concentrate on how SQL can be used as part of a database application.

Summary

SQL data definition language (DDL) statements are used to manage the structure of tables. This chapter presented three SQL DDL statements: CREATE TABLE, ALTER TABLE, and DROP TABLE. SQL is preferred over graphical tools for creating tables because it is faster, it can be used to create the same table repeatedly, tables can be created from program code, and it is standardized and DBMS independent.

The IDENTITY (*N, M*) data type is used to create surrogate key columns, where *N* is the starting value and *M* is the increment to be added. The SQL CREATE TABLE statement is used to define the name of the table, its columns, and constraints on columns. There are five types of constraints:

PRIMARY KEY, UNIQUE, NULL/NOT NULL, FOREIGN KEY, and CHECK.

The purposes of the first three constraints are obvious. FOREIGN KEY is used to create referential integrity constraints; CHECK is used to create data constraints. Figure 7-11 summarizes techniques for creating relationships using SQL constraints.

Simple default values can be assigned using the DEFAULT keyword. Data constraints are defined using CHECK constraints. Domain, range, and intratable constraints can be defined. Although SQL-92 defined facilities for interrelation CHECK constraints, those facilities were not implemented by DBMS vendors. Instead, interrelation constraints are enforced using triggers.

---

[3] This code does not check for more than one row having the given ArtistID, because ArtistID is a surrogate key.

```
CREATE PROCEDURE WORK_AddWorkTransaction
    (
    @ArtistID int,     /* Artist must already exist in database */
    @Title char(25),
    @Copy char(8),
    @Description varchar(1000),
    @AcquisitionPrice Numeric (6,2)
    )

/* Stored procedure to record the acquisition of a work.  If the work has    */
/* never been in the gallery before, add a new WORK row.  Otherwise, use     */
/* the existing WORK row.  Add a new TRANS row for the work and set          */
/* DateAcquired to the system date.                                          */

AS

    DECLARE @rowcount AS int
    DECLARE @WorkID AS int

    /* Check that the ArtistID is valid                                      */

    SELECT      @rowcount = COUNT(*)
    FROM        ARTIST AS A
    WHERE       A.ArtistID = @ArtistID

    IF (@rowcount = 0)
        /* The Artist does not exist in the database                         */
        BEGIN
            Print 'No artist with id of ' + Str(@artistID)
            Print 'Processing terminated.'
            RETURN
        END

    /* Check to see if the work is in the database                           */

    SELECT      @rowcount = COUNT(*)
    FROM        WORK AS W
    WHERE       W.ArtistID = @ArtistID and
                W.Title = @Title and
                W.Copy = @Copy

    IF (@rowcount = 0)
        /* The Work is not in database, so put it in.                        */
        BEGIN
            INSERT INTO WORK (Title, Copy, Description, ArtistID)
                VALUES (@Title, @Copy, @Description, @ArtistID)
        END

    /* Get the work surrogate key WorkID value                               */

    SELECT      @WorkID = W.WorkID
    FROM        WORK AS W
    WHERE       W.ArtistID = @ArtistID
        AND     W.Title = @Title
        AND     W.Copy = @Copy

    /* Now put the new TRANS row into database.                              */

    INSERT INTO TRANS (DateAcquired, AcquisitionPrice, WorkID)
        VALUES (GetDate(), @AcquisitionPrice, @WorkID)

    RETURN
```

Figure 7-33

Stored Procedure to Record
the Acquisition of a Work

The ALTER statement is used to add and remove columns and constraints. The DROP statement is used to drop tables. In SQL DDL, parents need to be created first and dropped last.

The data manipulation language (DML) SQL statements are INSERT, UPDATE, and DELETE. Each statement can be used on a single row, on a group of rows, or on the entire table.

Because of their power, both UPDATE and DELETE need to be used with care.

Some people believe the JOIN ON syntax is an easier form of join. Rows that have no match in the join condition are dropped from the join results. To keep such rows, use a LEFT OUTER or RIGHT OUTER join rather than a regular, or INNER, join.

An SQL view is a virtual table that is constructed from other tables and views. SQL SELECT statements are used to define views. The only restriction is that a view definition may not include an ORDER BY clause.

Views are used to hide columns or rows and to show the results of computed columns. They also can hide complicated SQL syntax, such as that used for joins and GROUP BY queries, and layer computations and built-in functions so that computations can be used in WHERE clauses. Some organizations use views to provide table aliases. Views also can be used to assign different sets of processing permissions to tables and to assign different sets of triggers as well. The rules for determining whether a view can be updated are both complicated and DBMS specific. Guidelines are shown in Figure 7-23.

SQL can be embedded in program code in triggers, stored procedures, and application code. To do so, there must be a way to associate SQL table columns with program variables. Also, there is a paradigm mismatch between SQL and programs. Most SQL statements return sets of rows; an application expects to work on one row at a time. To resolve this mismatch, the results of SQL statements are processed as pseudofiles using a cursor.

A trigger is a stored program that is executed by the DBMS whenever a specified event occurs on a specified table or view. In Oracle, triggers can be written in Java or in a proprietary Oracle language called PL/SQL. In SQL Server, triggers can be written in a propriety SQL Server language called TRANSACT-SQL, or T-SQL, and in Microsoft CLR languages such as Visual Basic .NET, C# .NET and C++ .NET. With MySQL, triggers can be written in MySQL's variant of SQL.

Possible triggers are BEFORE, INSTEAD OF, and AFTER. Each type of trigger can be declared for insert, update, and delete actions, so nine types of triggers are possible. Oracle supports all nine trigger types, SQL Server supports only INSTEAD OF and AFTER triggers, and MySQL supports the BEFORE and AFTER triggers. When a trigger is fired, the DBMS supplies old and new values for the update. New values are provided for inserts and updates, and old values are provided for updates and deletions. How these values are provided to the trigger depends on the DBMS in use.

Triggers have many uses. This chapter discussed four: setting default values, enforcing interrelation data constraints, updating views, and enforcing referential integrity actions.

A stored procedure is a program that is stored within the database and compiled when used. Stored procedures can receive input parameters and return results. Unlike triggers, their scope is database-wide; they can be used by any process that has permission to run the stored procedure.

Stored procedures can be called from programs written in the same languages used for triggers. They also can be called from DBMS SQL utilities. The advantages of using stored procedures are summarized in Figure 7-32.

 **ey Terms**

casual relationship
CHECK constraint
cursor
data definition language (DDL)
data manipulation language (DML)
DEFAULT keyword
FOREIGN KEY constraint
IDENTITY({StartValue},{Increment}) property
inner join
interrelation constraint
intrarelation constraint
NOT NULL constraint
NULL constraint
PRIMARY KEY constraint
procedural language
Procedural Language/SQL (PL/SQL)
pseudofile
SQL ALTER statement
SQL ALTER VIEW statement
SQL AS keyword

SQL CREATE TABLE statement
SQL CREATE VIEW statement
SQL DELETE statement
SQL DROP TABLE statement
SQL INSERT statement
SQL JOIN ON syntax
SQL LEFT JOIN syntax
SQL left outer join
SQL ON DELETE clause
SQL ON UPDATE clause
SQL outer join
SQL RIGHT JOIN syntax
SQL right outer join
SQL TOP NumberOfRows syntax
SQL UPDATE statement
SQL view
stored procedure
Transact-SQL (T-SQL)
trigger
UNIQUE constraint

Review Questions

7.1   What does DDL stand for? List the SQL DDL statements.

7.2   What does DML stand for? List the SQL DML statements.

7.3   Explain the meaning of the following expression: IDENTITY (4000, 5).

For this set of Review Questions, we will create and use a database for the Review Wedgewood Pacific Corporation (WPC) that is similar to the Microsoft Access database we created and used in Chapter 1 and Chapter 2. Founded in 1957 in Seattle, Washington, WPC has grown into an internationally recognized organization. The company is located in two buildings. One building houses the Administration, Accounting, Finance, and Human Resources departments, and the second houses the Production, Marketing, and Information Systems departments. The company database contains data about employees; departments; projects; assets, such as computer equipment; and other aspects of company operations.

The database will be named WPC and will contain the following four tables:

DEPARTMENT (<u>DepartmentName</u>, BudgetCode, OfficeNumber, Phone)

EMPLOYEE (<u>EmployeeNumber</u>, FirstName, LastName, *Department*, Phone, Email)

PROJECT (<u>ProjectID</u>, Name, *Department*, MaxHours, StartDate, EndDate)

ASSIGNMENT (<u>*ProjectID*</u>, <u>*EmployeeNumber*</u>, HoursWorked)

EmployeeNumber is a surrogate key that starts at 1 and increments by 1. ProjectID is a surrogate key that starts at 1000 and increases by 100. DepartmentName is the text name of the department, and is therefore not a surrogate key.

The WPC database has the following referential integrity constraints:

Department in EMPLOYEE must exist in Department in DEPARTMENT

Department in PROJECT must exist in Department in DEPARTMENT

ProjectID in ASSIGNMENT must exist in ProjectID in PROJECT

EmployeeNumber in ASSIGNMENT must exist in EmployeeNumber in EMPLOYEE

The relationship from **EMPLOYEE** to **ASSIGNMENT** is 1:N, M-O and the relationship from **PROJECT** to **ASSIGNMENT** is 1:N, M-O.

The database also has the following business rules:

- If an EMPLOYEE row is to be deleted and that row is connected to any ASSIGNMENT, the EMPLOYEE row deletion will be disallowed.
- If a PROJECT row is deleted, then all the ASSIGNMENT rows that are connected to the deleted PROJECT row will also be deleted.

The business sense of these rules is as follows:

- If an EMPLOYEE row is deleted (for example, if the employee is transferred), then someone must take over that employee's assignments. Thus, the application needs someone to reassign assignments before deleting the employee row.
- If a PROJECT row is deleted, then the project has been canceled, and it is unnecessary to maintain records of assignments to that project.

The column characteristics for these tables are shown in Figures 1-26 (DEPARTMENT), 1-28 (EMPLOYEE), 2-26 (PROJECT), and 2-28 (ASSIGNMENT). The data for these tables are shown in Figures 1-27 (DEPARTMENT), 1-29 (EMPLOYEE), 2-27 (PROJECT), and 2-29 (ASSIGNMENT).

If at all possible, you should run your SQL solutions to the following questions against an actual database. Because we have already created this database in Microsoft Access, you should use an SQL-oriented DBMS such as Oracle, SQL Server, or MySQL in these exercises. If that is not possible, create a new Access database named WPC-CH07.accdb, and use the SQL capabilities in these exercises. In all the exercises, use the data types appropriate for the DBMS you are using.

Answer Review Questions 7.4–7.13 without running them on your DBMS.

7.4   Write a CREATE TABLE statement for the DEPARTMENT table.

7.5   Write a CREATE TABLE statement for the EMPLOYEE table. Email is required and is an alternate key, and the default value of Department is Human Resources. Cascade updates but not deletions from DEPARTMENT to EMPLOYEE.

7.6   Write a CREATE TABLE statement for PROJECT table. The default value for MaxHours is 100. Cascade updates but not deletions from DEPARTMENT to EMPLOYEE.

7.7   Write a CREATE TABLE statement for the ASSIGNMENT table. Cascade only deletions from PROJECT to ASSIGNMENT; do not cascade either deletions or updates from EMPLOYEE to ASSIGNMENT.

7.8   Modify your answer to Review Question 7.7 to include the constraint that StartDate be prior to EndDate.

7.9   Write an alternate SQL statement that modifies your answer to question 7.7 to make the relationship between EMPLOYEE and ASSIGNMENT a 1:1 relationship.

7.10   Write an ALTER statement to add the column AreaCode to EMPLOYEE. Assume that AreaCode is not required.

7.11   Write an ALTER statement to remove the column AreaCode from EMPLOYEE.

7.12   Write an ALTER statement to make Phone an alternate key in EMPLOYEE.

7.13   Write an ALTER statement to drop the constraint that Phone is an alternate key in EMPLOYEE.

If you are using a DBMS, then at this point you should create a database named WPC and run the SQL statements from Review Questions 7.4 through 7.8 only. [Hint: write and test an SQL script, and then run the script. Save the script as *WPC-Create-Tables.sql* for future use.] Do not run your answer to Review Question 7.9! After the tables are created, run your answers to Review Questions 7.10 through 7.13. Note that after these four statements have been run, the table structure is exactly the same as it was before you ran them.

7.14   Write INSERT statements to add the data shown in Figure 1-27 to the DEPARTMENT table. Run these statements to populate the DEPARTMENT table. [Hint: write and test an SQL script, and then run the script. Save the script as *WPC-Insert-DEPARTMENT-Data.sql* for future use.]

7.15   Write INSERT statements to add the data shown in Figure 1-29 to the EMPLOYEE table. Run these statements to populate the EMPLOYEE table. [Hint: write and test an SQL script, and then run the script. Save the script as *WPC-Insert-EMPLOYEE-Data.sql* for future use.]

7.16   Write INSERT statements to add the data shown in Figure 2-27 to the PROJECT table. Run these statements to populate the PROJECT table. [Hint: write and test an SQL script, and then run the script. Save the script as *WPC-Insert-PROJECT-Data.sql* for future use.]

7.17   Write INSERT statements to add the data shown in Figure 1-29 to the ASSIGNMENT table. Run these statements to populate the ASSIGNMENT table. [Hint: write and test an SQL script, and then run the script. Save the script as WPC-Insert-ASSIGNMENT-Data.sql for future use.]

7.18   Why were the tables populated in the order shown in Review Questions 7.14–7.17?

7.19   Assume that you have a table named NEW_EMPLOYEE that has the columns Department, Email, FirstName, and LastName, in that order. Write an INSERT statement to add all of the rows from the table NEW_EMPLOYEE to EMPLOYEE. Do not attempt to run this statement!

7.20   Write an UPDATE statement to change the phone number of employee with EmployeeNumber 11 to 360-287-8810. Run this SQL statement.

7.21   Write an UPDATE statement to change the department of employee with EmployeeNumber 5 to Finance. Run this SQL statement.

7.22   Write an UPDATE statement to change the phone number of employee with EmployeeNumber 5 to 360-287-8420. Run this SQL statement.

7.23   Combine your answers to Review Questions 7.21 and 7.22 into one SQL statement. Run this statement.

7.24   Write an UPDATE statement to set the HoursWorked to 60 for every row in ASSIGNMENT having the value 10 for EmployeeNumber. Run this statement.

7.25   Assume that you have a table named NEW_EMAIL, which has new values of Email for some employees. NEW_EMAIL has two columns: EmployeeNumber and NewEmail. Write an UPDATE statement to change the values of Email in EMPLOYEE to those in the NEW_EMAIL table. Do *not* run this statement.

7.26   Write one DELETE statement that will delete all data for project '2009 Q3 Product Plan' and all of its rows in ASSIGNMENT. Do *not* run this statement.

7.27   Write a DELETE statement that will delete the row for the employee named 'Smith'. Do *not* run this statement. What happens if this employee has rows in ASSIGNMENT?

7.28   Write an SQL statement to join EMPLOYEE, ASSIGNMENT, and PROJECT using the JOIN ON syntax. Run this statement.

7.29   Write an SQL statement to join EMPLOYEE and ASSIGNMENT and include all rows of EMPLOYEE in your answer, regardless of whether they have an ASSIGNMENT. Run this statement.

7.30   What is an SQL view? What purposes do views serve?

7.31   What is the limitation on SELECT statements used in SQL views?

7.32   Write an SQL statement to create a view named EmployeePhoneView that shows the values of EMPLOYEE.LastName as EmployeeLastName, EMPLOYEE.FirstName as EmployeeFirstName, and EMPLOYEE.Phone as EmployeePhone. Run this statement, and then test the view with an SQL SELECT statement.

7.33   Write an SQL statement to create a view named FinanceEmployeePhoneView that shows the values of EMPLOYEE.LastName as EmployeeLastName, EMPLOYEE.FirstName as EmployeeFirstName, and EMPLOYEE.Phone as EmployeePhone for employees who work in the Finance department. Run this statement, and then test the view with an SQL SELECT statement.

7.34 Write an SQL statement to create a view named CombinedNameEmployeePhoneView that shows the values of EMPLOYEE.LastName, EMPLOYEE.FirstName, and EMPLOYEE.Phone as EmployeePhone, but that combines EMPLOYEE.LastName and EMPLOYEE.FirstName into one column named EmployeeName that displays the employee name first name first. Run this statement, and then test the view with an SQL SELECT statement.

7.35 Write an SQL statement to create a view named EmployeeProjectAssignmentView that shows the values of EMPLOYEE.LastName as EmployeeLastName, EMPLOYEE.First-Name as EmployeeFirstName, EMPLOYEE.Phone as EmployeePhone, and PROJECT.Name as ProjectName. Run this statement, and then test the view with an SQL SELECT statement.

7.36 Write an SQL statement to create a view named DepartmentEmployeeProjectAssign-mentView that shows the values of EMPLOYEE.LastName as EmployeeLastName, EMPLOYEE.FirstName as EmployeeFirstName, EMPLOYEE.Phone as EmployeePhone, DEPARTMENT.DepartmentName, Department.PHONE as DepartmentPhone, and PROJECT.Name as ProjectName. Run this statement, and then test the view with an SQL SELECT statement.

7.37 Write an SQL statement to create a view named ProjectHoursToDateView that shows the values of PROJECT.ProjectID, PROJECT.Name as ProjectName, PROJECT.MaxHours as ProjectMaxHour and the sum of ASSIGNMENT.HoursWorked as ProjectHoursWorkedToDate. Run this statement, and then test the view with an SQL SELECT statement.

7.38 Describe how views are used to provide an alias for tables. Why is this useful?

7.39 Explain how views can be used to improve data security.

7.40 Explain how views can be used to provide additional trigger functionality.

7.41 Give an example of a view that is clearly updatable.

7.42 Give an example of a view that is clearly not updatable.

7.43 Summarize the general idea for determining whether a view is updatable.

7.44 If a view is missing required items, what action on the view is definitely not allowed?

7.45 Explain the paradigm mismatch between SQL and programming languages.

7.46 How is the mismatch in your answer to Question 7.45 corrected?

7.47 What is a trigger?

7.48 What are PL/SQL and T-SQL? What is the MySQL equivalent?

7.49 What is the relationship between a trigger and a table or view?

7.50 Name nine possible trigger types.

7.51 Explain, in general terms, how new and old values are made available to a trigger.

7.52 Describe four uses for triggers.

7.53 Assume that the View Ridge Gallery will allow a row to be deleted from WORK if the work has never been sold. Explain, in general terms, how to use a trigger to accomplish such a deletion.

7.54   Assume that the Wedgewood Pacific Corporation will allow a row to be deleted from EMPLOYEE if the employee has no project assignments. Explain, in general terms, how to use a trigger to accomplish such a deletion.

7.55   What is a stored procedure? How do they differ from triggers?

7.56   Summarize how to invoke a stored procedure.

7.57   Summarize the key advantages of stored procedures.

roject Questions

These Project Questions extend the Wedgewood Pacific Corporation database you created and used in the Review Questions with two new tables named COMPUTER and COMPUTER_ASSIGNMENT.

The data model for these modifications is shown in Figure 7-34. The column characteristics for the COMPUTER table are shown in Figure 7-35, and those for the

Figure   7-34

WPC Data Model Extension

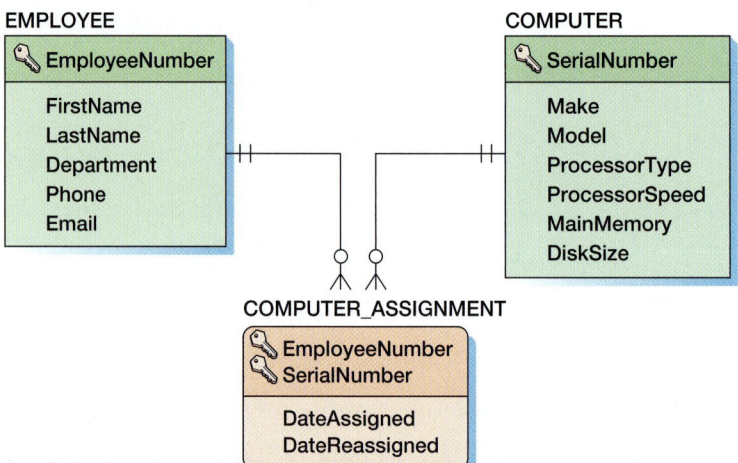

Figure   7-35

Database Column Characteristics for the COMPUTER Table

ColumnName	Type	Key	Required	Remarks
SerialNumber	Number	Primary Key	Yes	Long Integer
Make	Text (12)	No	Yes	Must be "Dell" or "Gateway" or "HP" or "Other"
Model	Text (24)	No	Yes	
ProcessorType	Text (24)	No	No	
ProcessorSpeed	Number	No	Yes	Double [3,2], Between 1.0 and 4.0
MainMemory	Text (15)	No	Yes	
DiskSize	Text (15)	No	Yes	

Figure 7-36

Database Column
Characteristics
for the
COMPUTER_
ASSIGNMENT
Table

ColumnName	Type	Key	Required	Remarks
SerialNumber	Number	Primary Key, Foreign Key	Yes	Long Integer
EmployeeNumber	Number	Primary Key, Foreign Key	Yes	Long Integer
DateAssigned	Date/Time	No	Yes	Medium Date
DateReassigned	Date/Time	No	No	Medium Date

SerialNumber	Make	Model	ProcessorType	ProcessorSpeed	MainMemory	DiskSize
9871234	HP	Compaq DC5700	Intel Core 2 Duo	2.67	1.0 GByte	80 GBytes
9871245	HP	Compaq DC5700	Intel Core 2 Duo	2.67	1.0 GByte	80 GBytes
9871256	HP	Compaq DC5700	Intel Core 2 Duo	2.67	1.0 GByte	80 GBytes
9871267	HP	Compaq DC5700	Intel Core 2 Duo	2.67	1.0 GByte	80 GBytes
9871278	HP	Compaq DC5700	Intel Core 2 Duo	2.67	1.0 GByte	80 GBytes
9871289	HP	Compaq DC5700	Intel Core 2 Duo	2.67	1.0 GByte	80 GBytes
6541001	Dell	OptiPlex 755	Intel Core 2 Quad	2.4	2.0 GBytes	160 GBytes
6541002	Dell	OptiPlex 755	Intel Core 2 Quad	2.4	2.0 GBytes	160 GBytes
6541003	Dell	OptiPlex 755	Intel Core 2 Quad	2.4	2.0 GBytes	160 GBytes
6541004	Dell	OptiPlex 755	Intel Core 2 Quad	2.4	2.0 GBytes	160 GBytes
6541005	Dell	OptiPlex 755	Intel Core 2 Quad	2.4	2.0 GBytes	160 GBytes
6541006	Dell	OptiPlex 755	Intel Core 2 Quad	2.4	2.0 GBytes	160 GBytes

Figure 7-37

WPC COMPUTER Data

COMPUTER_ASSIGNMENT table are shown in Figure 7-36. Data for the COMPUTER table are shown in Figure 7-37, and data for the COMPUTER_ASSIGNMENT table are shown in Figure 7-38.

7.58 Describe the relationships in terms of type (identifying or nonidentifying) and maximum and minimum cardinality.

7.59 Explain the need for each of the foreign keys.

7.60 Define referential integrity actions (such as ON UPDATE CASCADE) for the COMPUTER-to-COMPUTER_ASSIGNMENT relationship only. Explain the need for these actions.

7.61 Assume that COMPUTER_ASSIGNMENT in the EMPLOYEE-to-COMPUTER_ASSIGNMENT relationship is now mandatory (i.e., every employee must have at least one computer). Use Figure 6-28(b) as a boilerplate to define triggers for enforcing the required child between EMPLOYEE and COMPUTER_ASSIGNMENT. Define the purpose of any necessary triggers.

7.62 Explain the interaction between the trigger in your answer to Question 7.61 and the COMPUTER-to-COMPUTER_ASSIGNMENT relationship. What, if any, cascading behavior do you want to occur? Explain how you can test to find out if it works the way that you want it to.

SerialNumber	EmployeeNumber	DateAssigned	DateReassigned
9871234	11	15-Sep-08	21-Oct-08
9871245	12	15-Sep-08	21-Oct-08
9871256	4	15-Sep-08	
9871267	5	15-Sep-08	
9871278	8	15-Sep-08	
9871289	9	15-Sep-08	
6541001	11	21-Oct-08	
6541002	12	21-Oct-08	
6541003	1	21-Oct-08	
6541004	2	21-Oct-08	
6541005	3	21-Oct-08	
6541006	6	21-Oct-08	
9871234	7	21-Oct-08	
9871245	10	21-Oct-08	

Figure 7-38

WPC COMPUTER_ ASSIGNMENT Data

7.63 Write CREATE TABLE statements for the COMPUTER and COMPUTER_ASSIGNMENT tables in Figure 7-34 using the column characteristics shown in Figures 7-35 and 7-36. Write CHECK constraints to ensure that Make is Dell, HP, Compaq, or Other. Also, write constraints to ensure that ProcessorSpeed is between 2.0 and 5.0 (these are units of Gigahertz). Run these statements on your WPC database to extend the database structure.

7.64 Using the sample data for the COMPUTER table shown in Figure 7-37 and the COMPUTER_ASSIGNMENT table shown in Figure 7-38, write INSERT statements to add this data to these tables in the WPC database. Run these INSERT statements to populate the tables.

7.65 Create a view of COMPUTER named ComputerView that displays SerialNumber and Make and Model as one attribute named ComputerType. Place a colon and a space between Make and Model in the format: Dell: 6200 Laptop. Run this statement, and then test with an SQL SELECT statement.

7.66 Create a view called ComputerMakeView that shows the Make and average Processor-Speed for all computers. Run this statement, and then test the view with an SQL SELECT statement.

7.67 Create a view called ComputerUserView that has all of the data of COMPUTER and ASSIGNMENT. Run this statement, and then test the view with an SQL SELECT statement.

7.68 Use the view you created called ComputerView to show the computer SerialNumber, ComputerType, and Employee name. Run this statement.

7.69 Suppose you want to use a stored procedure to store a new row in COMPUTER. List the minimum list of parameters that need to be in the procedure. Describe, in general terms, the logic of the stored procedure.

Suppose that you have designed a database for Marcia's Dry Cleaning that has the following tables:

CUSTOMER (*CustomerID*, FirstName, LastName, Phone, Email)

ORDER (InvoiceNumber, *CustomerID*, DateIn, DateOut, Subtotal, Tax, TotalAmount)

ORDER_ITEM (*InvoiceNumber*, ItemNumber, *Service*, Quantity, UnitPrice, ExtendedPrice)

SERVICE (Service, Description, UnitPrice)

A. Specify NULL/NOT NULL constraints for each table column.

B. Specify alternate keys, if any.

C. State relationships as implied by foreign keys, and specify the maximum and minimum cardinality of each relationship. Justify your choices.

D. Explain how you will enforce the minimum cardinalities in your answer to part C. Use referential integrity actions for required parents, if any. Use Figure 6-28(b) as a boilerplate for required children, if any.

E. Write CREATE TABLE statements for each of the tables using your answers to parts A–D, as necessary. Set the first value of CustomerID to 100 and increment it by 5. Use FOREIGN KEY constraints to create appropriate referential integrity constraints. Set UPDATE and DELETE behavior in accordance with your referential integrity action design. Set the default value of Quantity to 1. Write a constraint that SERVICE.UnitPrice be between 1.50 and 10.00.

F. Explain how you would enforce the data constraint that ORDER_ITEM.UnitPrice be equal to SERVICE.UnitPrice, where ORDER_ITEM.Service = SERVICE.Service.

G. Write INSERT statements to insert at least three rows into each table. Use the data shown in Figures 2-33, 2-34, and 2-35 as a starting point, and create any other data needed for the revised set of tables used here.

H. Write an UPDATE statement to change values of SERVICE.Description from Mens Shirt to Mens' Shirts.

I. Write a DELETE statement(s) to delete an ORDER and all of the items on that ORDER.

J. Create a view called OrderSummaryView that contains ORDER.InvoiceNumber, ORDER.DateIn, ORDER.DateOut, ORDER_ITEM.ItemNumber, ORDER_ITEM. Service, and ORDER_ITEM.ExtendedPrice.

K. Create a view called CustomerOrderSummaryView that contains ORDER.InvoiceNumber, CUSTOMER.FirstName, CUSTOMER.LastName, CUSTOMER.Phone, ORDER.DateIn, ORDER.DateOut, ORDER.SubTotal, ORDER_ITEM.ItemNumber, ORDER_ITEM.Service, and ORDER_ITEM.ExtendedPrice.

L. Create a view called CustomerOrderHistoryView that (1) includes all columns of Customer-OrderSummaryView except ORDER_ITEM.ItemNumber and ORDER_ITEM. Service, (2) groups orders by CUSTOMER.LastName, CUSTOMER.FirstName and ORDER.InvoiceNumber in that order, and (3) sums and averages ORDER_ITEM.ExtendedPrice for each order for each customer.

M. Create a view called CustomerOrderCheckView that uses CustomerOrderHistoryView and that shows that any customers for whom the sum of ORDER_ITEM.ExtendedPrice is not equal to ORDER.SubTotal.

N. Explain, in general terms, how you will use triggers to enforce minimum cardinality actions as required by your design. You need not write the triggers, just specify which triggers you need and describe, in general terms, their logic.

Suppose that you have designed a database for Morgan Importing that has the following tables:

STORE (<u>StoreName</u>, City, Country, Phone, Fax, Email, Contact)

PURCHASE (<u>PurchaseID</u>, *StoreName*, Date, Description, Category, PriceUSD)

SHIPMENT (<u>ShipmentID</u>, *ShipperID*, ShipperInvoiceNumber, Origin, Destination, DepartureDate, Arrival Date)

SHIPMENT_ITEM (<u>*ShipmentID*</u>, <u>*PurchaseID*</u>, InsuredValue)

SHIPPER (<u>ShipperID</u>, ShipperName, Phone, Fax, Email, Contact)

A. Do you think STORE should have a surrogate key? If so, create it and make required adjustments in the design. If not, explain why not or make other adjustments to STORE and other tables that you think are appropriate.

B. Specify NULL/NOT NULL constraints for each table column.

C. Specify alternate keys, if any.

D. State relationships as implied by foreign keys, and specify the maximum and minimum cardinality of each relationship. Justify your choices.

E. Explain how you will enforce the minimum cardinalities in your answer to part D. Use referential integrity actions for required parents, if any. Use Figure 6-28(b) as a boilerplate for required children, if any.

F. Write CREATE TABLE statements for each of the tables using your answers to the parts A–E, as necessary. Set the first value of PurchaseID to 500 and increment it by 5. Set the first value of ShipmentID to 100 and increment it by 1. Use FOREIGN KEY constraints to create appropriate referential integrity constraints. Set UPDATE and DELETE behavior in accordance with your referential integrity action design. Set the default value of Insured-Value to 100. Write a constraint that STORE.Country be limited to seven countries (you can pick the seven countries you want to purchase from, but be sure to include the countries for the ITEM.City locations shown in Figure 2-41).

G. Explain how you would enforce the rule that SHIPMENT_ITEM.InsuredValue be at least as great as PURCHASE.PriceUSD.

H. Write INSERT statements to insert at least three rows into each table. Use the data shown in Figures 2-39, 2-40, and 2-41 as a starting point, and create any other data needed for the revised set of tables used here.

I. Write an UPDATE statement to change values of STORE.City from New York City to NYC.

J. Write a DELETE statement(s) to delete a SHIPMENT and all of the items on that SHIPMENT.

K. Create a view called PurchaseSummaryView that shows only PURCHASE.PurchaseID, PURCHASE.Date, PURCHASE.Description, and PURCHASE.PriceUSD.

L. Create a view called StorePurchaseHistoryView that shows STORE.StoreName, STORE.Phone, STORE.Contact, PURCHASE.PurchaseID, PURCHASE.Date, PURCHASE.Description, and PURCHASE.PriceUSD.

M. Create a view called StoreHistoryView that sums the PriceUSD column of StorePurchase-HistoryView for each store into a column named TotalPurchases.

N. Create a view called MajorSources that uses StoreHistoryView and selects only those stores that have TotalPurchases greater than 100000.

O. Explain, in general terms, how you will use triggers to enforce minimum cardinality actions as required by your design. You need not write the triggers, just specify which triggers you need and describe, in general terms, their logic.

8

Database Redesign

Chapter Objectives

- To understand the need for database redesign.
- To be able to use correlated subqueries.
- To be able to use the SQL EXISTS and NOT EXISTS keywords in correlated subqueries.
- To understand reverse engineering.
- To be able to use dependency graphs.
- To be able to change table names.
- To be able to change table columns.
- To be able to change relationship cardinalities.
- To be able to change relationship properties.
- To be able to add and delete relationships.

As stated in Chapter 1, databases arise from three sources. They can be created from existing tables and spreadsheets, they can be the result of a new systems development project, or they can be the outcome of database redesign. We have discussed the first two sources in Chapters 2 through 7. In this chapter, we will discuss the last source: database redesign.

We begin with a discussion of the need for database redesign, and then we will describe two important SQL statements: correlated subqueries and EXISTS. These statements play an important role when analyzing data prior to redesign. They also can be used for advanced queries and are important in their own right. After that discussion, we will turn to a variety of common database redesign tasks.

The Need for Database Redesign

You may be wondering, "Why do we have to redesign a database? If we build it correctly the first time, why would we ever need to redesign it?" This question has two answers. First, it is not easy to build a database correctly the first time, especially databases that arise from the development of new systems. Even if we obtain all of the users' requirements and build a correct data model, the transformation of that data model into a correct database design is difficult. For large databases, the tasks are daunting and may require several stages of development. During those stages, some aspects of the database will need to be redesigned. Also, inevitably, mistakes will be made that must be corrected.

The second answer to this question is the more important one. Reflect for a moment on the relationship between information systems and the organizations that use them. It is tempting to say that they influence each other; that is, that information systems influence organizations and that organizations influence information systems.

In truth, however, the relationship is much stronger than that. Information systems and organizations do not just influence each other; they *create* each other. When a new information system is installed, the users can behave in new ways. As the users behave in those new ways, they will want changes to the information system to accommodate their new behaviors. As those changes are made, the users will have more new behaviors, they will request more changes to the information system, and so forth, in a never-ending cycle.

This circular process means that changes to an information system are not the sad consequence of a poor implementation, but rather are a natural outcome of information system use. Therefore, the need for change to information systems never goes away; it neither can nor should be removed by better requirements definition, better initial design, better implementation, or anything else. Instead, change is part and parcel of information systems use. Thus, we need to plan for it. In the context of database processing, this means we need to know how to perform database redesign.

SQL Statements for Checking Functional Dependencies

Database redesign is not terribly difficult if the database has no data. The serious difficulties arise when we have to change a database that has data and when we want to make changes with minimum impact on existing data. Telling the users that the system now works the way they want but that all of their data were lost while making the change is not acceptable.

Often, we need to know whether certain conditions or assumptions are valid in the data before we can proceed with a change. For example, we may know from user requirements that Department functionally determines DeptPhone, but we may not know whether that functional dependency is correctly represented in all of the data.

Recall from Chapter 3 that if Department determines DeptPhone, every value of Department must be paired with the same value of DeptPhone. If, for example, Accounting has a DeptPhone value of 834-1100 in one row, it should have that value in every row in which it appears. Similarly, if Finance has a DeptPhone of 834-2100 in one row, it should have that value in all rows in which it appears. Figure 8-1 shows data that violate this assumption. In the third row, the DeptPhone for Finance is different than for the other rows; it has too many zeroes. Most likely, someone made a keying mistake when entering DeptPhone. Such errors are typical.

Now, before we make a database change, we need to find all such violations and correct them. For the small table shown in Figure 8-1, we can just look at the data, but what if the EMPLOYEE table has 4,000 rows? Two SQL statements are particularly helpful in this regard: correlated subqueries and their cousin, EXISTS/NOT EXISTS. We will consider each of these in turn.

EmployeeNumber	LastName	Email	Department	Phone
100	Johnson	JJ@somewhere.com	Accounting	834-1100
200	Abernathy	MA@somewhere.com	Finance	834-2100
300	Smathers	LS@somewhere.com	Finance	834-21000
400	Caruthers	TC@somewhere.com	Accounting	834-1100
500	Jackson	TJ@somewhere.com	Production	834-4100
600	Caldera	EC@somewhere.com	Legal	834-3100
700	Bandalone	RB@somewhere.com	Legal	834-3100

Figure 8-1

Table Showing Constraint Assumption Violation

Correlated Subqueries

A **correlated subquery** looks very much like the subqueries we discussed in Chapter 2, but, in actuality, correlated subqueries are very different. To understand the difference, consider the following subquery, which is like those in Chapter 2:

```
SELECT      A.FirstName, A.lastName
FROM        ARTIST AS A
WHERE       A.ArtistID IN
            (SELECT   W.ArtistID
             FROM     WORK W
             WHERE    W.Title = 'Blue Interior');
```

The DBMS can process such subqueries from the bottom up. That is, it can first find all of the values of ArtistID in WORK that have the title 'Blue Interior' and then process the upper query using that set of values. There is no need to move back and forth between the two SELECT statements. The result of this query is the artist Mark Tobey, as we would expect.

Searching for Multiple Rows with a Given Title

Now, to introduce correlated subqueries, suppose that someone at View Ridge Gallery proposes that the Title column of WORK be an alternate key. If you look at the data in Figure 7-16(d), you can see that while there is only one copy of 'Blue Interior', there are two or more copies of other titles, such as 'Surf and Bird'. Therefore Title cannot be an alternate key.

However, if the WORK table had 10,000 or more rows, this would be difficult to determine. In that case, we need a query that examines the WORK table and displays the Title and Copy of any works that share the same title.

If we were asked to write a program to perform such a query, our logic would be as follows: Take the value of Title from the first row in WORK and examine all of the other rows in the table. If we find a row that has the same title as the one in the first row, we know there are duplicates, so we print the Title and Copy of the first work. We continue searching for duplicate title values until we came to the end of the WORK table.

Then, we take the value of Title in the second row and compare it with all other rows in the WORK table, printing out the Title and Copy of any duplicate works. We proceed in this way until all rows of WORK have been examined.

A Correlated Subquery That Finds Rows with the Same Title

The following correlated subquery performs the action just described:

```
SELECT      W1.Title, W1.Copy
FROM        WORK AS W1
WHERE       W1.Title IN
            (SELECT     W2.Title
             FROM       WORK AS W2
             WHERE      W1.Title = W2.Title
               AND      W1.WorkID <> W2.WorkID);
```

The result of this query for the data in Figure 7-16(d) is shown in Figure 8-2.

This subquery looks deceptively similar to a regular subquery. To the surprise of many students, this subquery and the one above are drastically different. Their similarity is only superficial.

Before explaining why, first notice the notation in the correlated subquery. The WORK table is used in both the upper and the lower SELECT statements. In the upper statement, it is given the alias W1; in the lower SELECT statement, it is given the alias W2.

In essence, when we use this notation, it is as if we have made two copies of the WORK table. One copy is called W1, and the second copy is called W2. Therefore, in the last two lines of the correlated subquery, values in the W1 copy of WORK are compared with values in the W2 copy.

Figure 8-2

Results of the Check for
Duplicate Titles

	Title	Copy
1	Farmer's Market #2	267/500
2	Farmer's Market #2	268/500
3	Spanish Dancer	583/750
4	Spanish Dancer	588/750
5	Surf and Bird	142/500
6	Surf and Bird	362/500
7	Surf and Bird	365/500
8	Surf and Bird	366/500
9	Surf and Bird	Unique
10	The Fiddler	251/1000
11	The Fiddler	252/1000

The Difference Between Regular and Correlated Subqueries

Now, consider what makes this subquery so different. Unlike a regular subquery, the DBMS cannot run the bottom SELECT by itself, obtain a set of Titles, and then use that set to execute the upper query. The reason for this appears in the last two lines of the query:

```
WHERE      W1.Title = W2.Title

    AND  W1.WorkID <> W2.WorkID);
```

In these expressions, W1.Title (from the top SELECT statement) is being compared with W2.Title (from the bottom SELECT statement). The same is true for W1.WorkID and W2.WorkID. Because of this fact, the DBMS cannot process the subquery portion independent of the upper SELECT.

Instead, the DBMS must process this statement as a subquery that is *nested* within the main query. The logic is as follows: Take the first row from W1. Using that row, evaluate the second query. To do that, for each row in W2, compare W1.Title with W2.Title and W1.WorkID with W2.WorkID. If the titles are equal and the values of WorkID are not equal, return the value of W2.Title to the upper query. Do this for every row in W2.

Once all of the rows in W2 have been evaluated for the first row in W1, move to the second row in W1 and evaluate it against all the rows in W2. Continue in this way until all rows of W1 have been compared with all of the rows of W2.

If this is not clear to you, write out two copies of the WORK data from Figure 7-16(d) on a piece of scratch paper. Label one of them W1 and the second W2 and then work through the logic as described. From this, you will see that correlated subqueries always require nested processing.

A Common Trap

By the way, do not fall into the following common trap:

```
SELECT     W1.Title, W1.Copy

FROM       WORK AS W1

WHERE      W1.WorkID IN

           (SELECT     W2.WorkID

            FROM       WORK AS W2

            WHERE      W1.Title = W2.Title

              AND    W1.WorkID <> W2.WorkID);
```

The logic here seems correct, but it is not. No row will ever be displayed by this query, regardless of the underlying data. See if you can see why this is so before continuing.

The bottom query will indeed find all rows that have the same title and different WorkIDs. If one is found, it will produce the W2.WorkID of that row. But that value will then be compared with W1.WorkID. *These two values will always be different because of the condition* W1.WorkID W2.WorkID. No rows are returned because the values of the two unequal WorkIDs are used in the IN instead of the values of the two equal Titles.

Using Correlated Subqueries to Check Functional Dependencies

Correlated subqueries can be used to advantage during database redesign. As mentioned, one application of correlated subqueries is to verify functional dependencies. For example, suppose we have EMPLOYEE data like that in Figure 8-1, and we want to know whether the data conform to the functional dependency Department → DeptPhone. If so, every time a given value of Department occurs in the table, that value will be matched with the same value of DeptPhone.

The following correlated subquery will find any rows that violate this assumption:

```
SELECT      E1.Department, E1.DeptPhone
FROM        EMPLOYEE AS E1
WHERE       E1.Department IN
               (SELECT     E2.Department
                FROM       EMPLOYEE AS E2
                WHERE      E1.Department = E2.Department
                    AND    E1.DeptPhone <> E2.DeptPhone);
```

The results for the data in Figure 8-1 are:

	Department	DeptPhone
1	Finance	834-2100
2	Finance	834-21000

A listing like this can readily be used to find and fix any rows that violate the functional dependency.

EXISTS and NOT EXISTS

EXISTS and NOT EXISTS are another form of correlated subquery. We can write the last correlated subquery using the **SQL EXISTS keyword,** as follows:

```
SELECT      E1.Department, E1.DeptPhone
FROM        EMPLOYEE AS E1
WHERE       EXISTS
               (SELECT     E2.Department
                FROM       EMPLOYEE AS E2
                WHERE      E1.Department = E2.Department
                    AND    E1.DeptPhone <> E2.DeptPhone);
```

Because EXISTS is a form of a correlated subquery, the processing of the SELECT statements is nested. The first row of E1 is input to the subquery. If the subquery finds any row in E2 for which the department names are the same and the department phone numbers are different, then the EXISTS is true and the Department and DeptPhone for the first row are selected. Next, the second row of E1 is input to the subquery, the SELECT is processed, and the EXISTS is evaluated. If true, the Department and DeptPhone of the second row are selected. This process is repeated for all of the rows in E1.

Using NOT EXISTS in a Double Negative

The EXISTS keyword will be true if *any* row in the subquery meets the condition. The **SQL NOT EXISTS keyword** will be true only if *all* rows in the subquery fail the condition. Consequently, the double use of NOT EXISTS can be used to find rows that do not not match a condition. Because of the logic of a double negative, if a row does not *not match any row*, then it matches every row. For example, suppose that at View Ridge the users want to know the name of any artist that every customer is interested in. We can proceed as follows. First, produce the set of all customers who are interested in a particular artist. Then, take the complement of that set, which will be the customers who are not interested in that artist. If that complement is empty, then all customers are interested in the given artist.

> **BY THE WAY** The doubly nested NOT EXISTS pattern is famous in one guise or another among SQL practitioners. It is often used as a test of SQL knowledge in job interviews and in bragging sessions, and it can be used to advantage when assessing the desirability of certain database redesign possibilities, as you will see in the last section of this chapter. Therefore, even though this example involves some serious study, it is worth your while to understand it.

The Double NOT EXISTS Query

The following SQL statement implements the strategy just described:

```
SELECT      A.FirstName, A.LastName
FROM        ARTIST AS A
WHERE       NOT EXISTS
            (SELECT     C.CustomerID
             FROM       CUSTOMER AS C
             WHERE      NOT EXISTS
                        (SELECT     CAI.CustomerID
                         FROM       CUSTOMER_ARTIST_INT AS CAI
                         WHERE      C.CustomerID= CAI.CustomerID
                           AND      A.ArtistID = CAI.ArtistID));
```

The result of this query is an empty set, indicating that there is *no* artist that *every* customer is interested in:

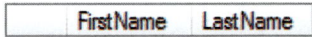

Let's see how this works. The bottom SELECT finds all of the customers who are interested in a particular artist. As you read this SELECT (the last SELECT in the query), keep in mind that this is a correlated subquery; this SELECT is nested inside the query on CUSTOMER, which is nested inside the query on ARTIST. C.CustomerID is coming from the SELECT on CUSTOMER in the middle, and A.ArtistID is coming from the SELECT on ARTIST at the top.

Now, the NOT EXISTS in the sixth line of the query will find the customers who are not interested in the given artist. If all customers are interested in the given artist, the result of the middle SELECT will be null. If the result of the middle SELECT is null, the NOT EXISTS in the third line of the query will be true, and the name of that artist will be produced, just as we want.

Consider what happens for artists who do not qualify in this query. Suppose that every customer except Tiffany Twilight is interested in the artist Joan Miro. (This is not the case for the data in Figure 7-16, but assume that it were true.) Now, for the preceding query, when Miro's row is considered, the bottom SELECT will retrieve every customer except Tiffany Twilight. In this case, because of the NOT EXISTS in the sixth line of the query, the middle SELECT will produce the CustomerID for Tiffany Twilight (because her row is the only one that does not appear in the bottom SELECT). Now, because there is a result from the middle SELECT, the NOT EXISTS in the top SELECT is false and the name Joan Miro will not be included in the output of the query. This is correct because there is a customer who is not interested in Joan Miro.

Again, take some time to study this pattern. It is a famous one, and if you become a database professional, you will certainly see it again in one form or another. In fact, you will not not see it again!

Analyzing the Existing Database

Before we proceed with a discussion of database redesign, reflect for a moment on what this task means for a real company whose operations are dependent on the database. Suppose, for example, that you work for a company such as Amazon.com. Further suppose that you have been tasked with an important database redesign assignment, say to change the primary key of the vendor table.

To begin, you may wonder, why would Amazon want to do this? It could be that in the early days, when it only sold books, Amazon used company names for vendors. But, as Amazon began to sell more types of products, company name was no longer sufficient. Perhaps there are too many duplicates, and Amazon may have decided to switch to an Amazon-created VendorID.

Now, what does it mean to switch primary keys? Besides adding the new data to the correct rows, what else does it mean? Clearly, if the old primary key has been used as a foreign key, all of the foreign keys need to be changed as well. So we need to know all of the relationships in which the old primary key was used. But what about views? Do any views use the old primary key? If so, they will need to be changed. What about triggers and stored procedures? Do any of them use the old primary key? Not to mention any application code that may break when the old key is removed.

Now, to create a nightmare, what happens if you get partway through the change process and something fails? Suppose you encounter unexpected data, and you receive errors from the DBMS while trying to add the new primary key. Amazon cannot change its Web site to display "Sorry, our database is broken—come back tomorrow (we hope)!"

This nightmare brings up many topics, most of which relate to systems analysis and design. But with regard to database processing, three principles become clear. First, as the carpenters say, "Measure twice and cut once." Before we attempt any structural changes to a database, we must clearly understand the current structure and contents of the database, and we must know what depends on what. Second, before we make any structural changes to an operational database, we must test those changes on a realistically sized test database that has all of the important test data cases. Finally, if at all possible, we need to create a complete backup of the operational database prior to making any structural changes. If all goes awry, the backup can be used to restore the database while problems are corrected. We will consider each of these important topics next.

Reverse Engineering

Reverse engineering is the process of reading a database schema and producing a data model from that schema. The data model produced is not truly a logical model because entities will be generated for every table, including entities for intersection tables that have no nonkey data and should not appear in a logical model at all. The model generated by reverse engineering is a thing unto itself, a table-relationship diagram that is dressed in entity-relationship clothes. In this text, we will call it the **reverse engineered (RE) data model**.

Figure 8-3 shows the RE database design of the View Ridge Gallery database produced by Microsoft Visio 2007 from an SQL Server 2008 Express version of the View Ridge database created in Chapter 7. Note that due to the limitations of Visio, this is a physical database design rather than a logical data model. Nonetheless, it illustrates the reverse engineering technique we are discussing.

We used Microsoft Visio here because of its general availability. This means, however, that we have to work with Visio's nonstandard database modeling notation. Note that Visio uses a directed arrow to indicate relationships (the relationship line starts at the child entity and the arrowhead points to the parent entity). Although Visio does differentiate between identifying and nonidentifying relationships in the database properties, it does not do so visually, as we have been doing. Visio also stores cardinalities as relationship properties, but it does not display them as we do with the IE Crow's Foot notation. We have added color to indicate the strong and weak entities, because Visio only uses a table structure. Note the notations PK indicating a primary key, FK indicating a foreign key, and U indicating a UNIQUE constraint (this corresponds to the AK*m.n* notation we have been using). Columns set to NOT NULL are in bold; columns set to NULL are in nonbold text. All in all, however, this is a reasonable representation of the View Ridge schema.

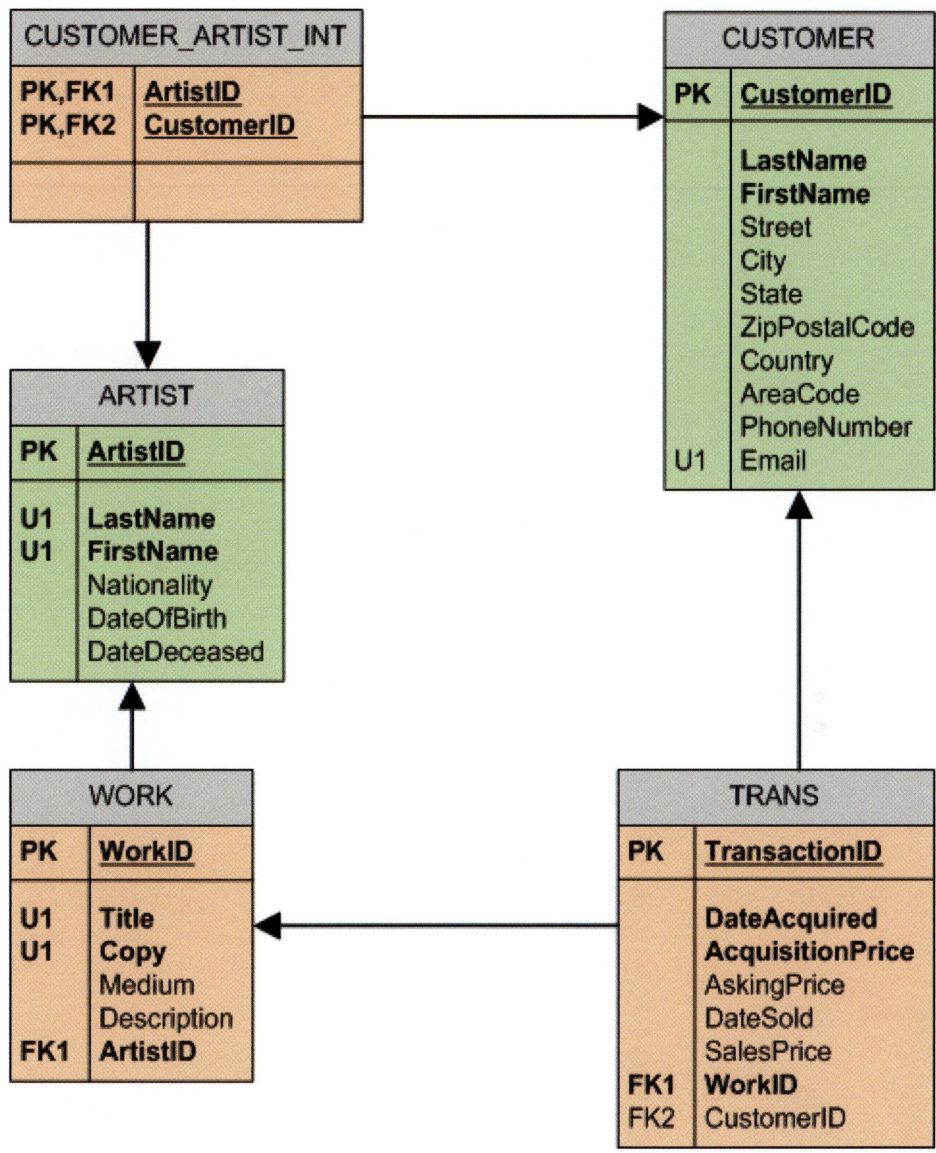

Figure 8-3

Reverse-Engineered
Database Design

Although Visio produces only a database design, and not a data model, some other design software, such as Computer Associates' ERwin, can create both logical (data model) and physical (database design) versions of the database structure. In addition to tables and views, some data modeling products will capture constraints, triggers, and stored procedures from the database.

These constructs are not interpreted, but their text is imported into the data model. With some products, the relationship of the text to the items it references also is obtained. The redesign of constraints, triggers, and stored procedures is beyond the scope of our discussion here. You should realize that they, too, are part of the database, however, and are subject to redesign.

Dependency Graphs

Before making changes to database structures, it is vitally important to understand the dependencies of those structures. What changes will impact what? For example, consider changing the name of a table. Where is the table name used? In which triggers? In which stored procedures? In which relationships? Because of the need to know all of the dependencies, many database redesign projects begin by making a **dependency graph.**

The term *graph* arises from the mathematical topic of graph theory. Dependency graphs are not graphical displays like bar charts, rather they are diagrams that consist of nodes and arcs (or lines) that connect those nodes.

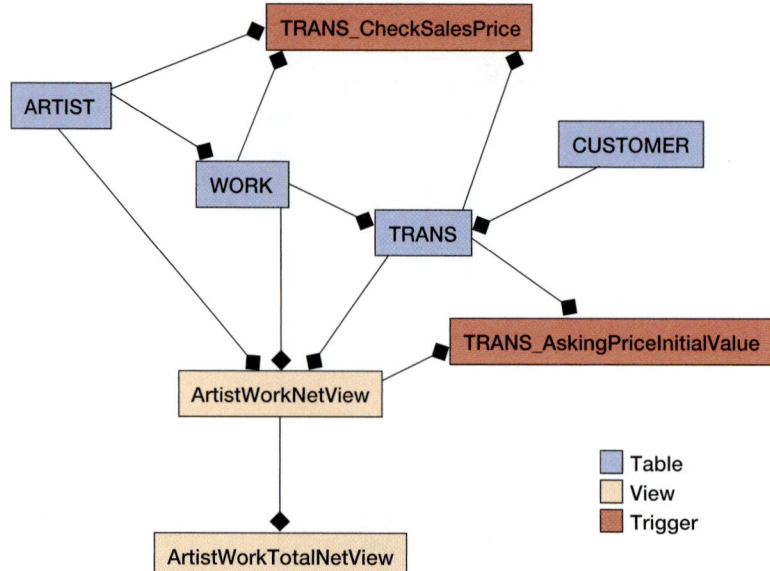

Figure   8-4

**Example Dependency
Graph (Partial)**

Figure 8-4 shows a partial dependency graph that was drawn using the results of the RE model, but manually interpreting views and triggers we developed in Chapter 7. For simplicity, this graph does not show the views and triggers of CUSTOMER, nor does it show CUSTOMER_ARTIST_INT and related structures. Also, the stored procedure WORK_AddWorkTransaction is not shown, nor are the constraints.

Even this partial diagram reveals the complexity of dependencies among database constructs. You can see that it would be wise to tread lightly, for example, when changing anything in the TRANS table. The consequences of such a change need to be assessed against two relationships, three triggers, and three views. Again, measure twice and cut once!

Database Backup and Test Databases

Because of the potential damage that can be done to a database during redesign, a complete backup of the operational database should be made prior to making any changes. Equally important, it is essential that any proposed changes be thoroughly tested. Not only must structural changes proceed successfully, but all triggers, stored procedures, and applications must also run correctly on the revised database.

Typically, at least three different copies of the database schema are used in the redesign process. One is a small test database that can be used for initial testing. The second is a large test database, which may even be a full copy of the operational database. Sometimes, there are several large test databases. Finally, there is the operational database.

A means must be created to recover all test databases to their original state during the testing process. In that way, the test can be rerun as necessary against the same starting point. Depending on the facilities of the DBMS, backup and recovery or other means are used to restore the database after a test run.

Obviously, for enterprises with very large databases, it is not possible to have a test database that is a copy of the operational database. Instead, smaller test databases need to be created, but those test databases must have all the important data characteristics of the operational database; otherwise, they will not provide a realistic test environment. The construction of such test databases is in itself a difficult and challenging job. In fact, many interesting career opportunities are available for developing test databases and database test suites.

Finally, for organizations that have very large databases, it may not be possible to make a complete copy of the operational database prior to making structural changes. In this case, the database is backed up in pieces, and the changes are made in pieces as well. This task is very difficult and requires great knowledge and expertise. It also requires weeks or months of planning. You may participate as a junior member of a team to make such a change, but you should have years of database experience before you attempt to make structural changes to such large databases. Even then, it is a daunting task.

Changing Table Names and Table Columns

In this section, we will consider alterations to tables and their columns. To accomplish these changes, we will use only SQL statements. Many DBMS products have features to facilitate changing structures other than SQL. For example, some products have graphical design tools that simplify this process. But such features are not standardized, and you should not depend on them. The statements shown in this chapter will work with any enterprise-class DBMS product, and most will work with Access as well.

Changing Table Names

At first glance, changing a table name seems like an innocent and easy operation. A review of Figure 8-4, however, shows that the consequences of such a change are greater than you would think. If, for example, we want to change the name of the table WORK to WORK_VERSION2, several tasks are necessary. The constraint that defines the relationship from WORK to TRANS must be altered, ArtistWorkNetView view must be redefined, and then the TRANS_Check-SalesPrice trigger must be rewritten to use the new name.

Furthermore, there is no SQL command to change the name of the table. Instead, the table needs to be re-created under the new name, and the old table dropped. This requirement, however, suggests a good strategy for making table name changes. First, create the new table with all attendant structures and then drop the old one once everything is working with the new table. If the table to be renamed is too large to be copied, other strategies will have to be used, but they are beyond the scope of this discussion.

This strategy has one serious problem, however. WorkID is a surrogate key. When we create the new table, the DBMS will create new values of WorkID in the new table. The new values will not necessarily match the values in the old table, which means values of the foreign key TRANS.WorkID will be wrong. The easiest way to solve this problem is first to create the new version of the WORK table and not define WorkID as a surrogate key. Then, fill the table with the current values of WORK, including the current values of WorkID. Then, change WorkID to a surrogate key.

First, we create the table by submitting an SQL CREATE TABLE WORK_VERSION2 statement to the DBMS. We make WorkID an integer, but not a surrogate key. We also must give new names to the WORK constraints. The prior constraints still exist, and if new names are not used, the DBMS will issue a duplicate constraint error when processing the CREATE TABLE statements. Examples of new constraint names are:

```
CONSTRAINT WorkV2PK PRIMARY KEY(WorkID),
CONSTRAINT WorkV2AK1 UNIQUE(Title, Copy),
CONSTRAINT ArtistV2FK FOREIGN KEY(ArtistID)
                REFERENCES ARTIST(ArtistID)
                    ON DELETE NO ACTION
                    ON UPDATE NO ACTION
```

Next, copy the data into the new table with the following SQL statement:

```
INSERT INTO WORK_VERSION2 (WorkID, Copy, Title, Medium,
    Description, ArtistID)
    SELECT    WorkID, Copy, Title, Medium, Description, ArtistID
    FROM      WORK;
```

At this point, alter the WORK_VERSION2 table to make WorkID a surrogate key. In SQL Server, the easiest way to do that is to open the graphical table designer and redefine WorkID as an IDENTITY column (there is no standard SQL for making this change). Set the Identity Seed property to the original value of 500, and SQL Server will set the next new value of WorkID to be the maximum largest value of WorkID plus one. A different strategy is used for surrogate keys with Oracle and MySQL, and these topics will be discussed in Chapters 10A and 10B.

Now all that remains is to define the two triggers. This can be done by copying the text of the old triggers and changing the name WORK to WORK_VERSION2.

At this point, test suites should be run against the database to verify that all changes have been made correctly. After that, stored procedures and applications that use WORK can be changed to run against the new table name.[1] If all is correct, then the foreign key constraint TransWorkFK and the WORK table can be dropped with the following:

```
ALTER TABLE TRANS DROP CONSTRAINT TransWorkFK;

DROP TABLE WORK;
```

The TransWorkFK constraint then can be added back to TRANS using the new name for the work table:

```
ALTER TABLE TRANS ADD CONSTRAINT TransWorkFK FOREIGN KEY(WorkID)
    REFERENCES WORK_VERSION2(WorkID)
        ON UPDATE NO ACTION
        ON DELETE NO ACTION;
```

Clearly, there is more to changing a table name than you would think. You now can see why some organizations do not allow programmers or users to employ the true name of a table. Instead, views are described that serve as table aliases, as explained in Chapter 7. If this were done here, only the views that define the aliases would need to be changed when the source table name is changed.

Adding and Dropping Columns

Adding null columns to a table is straightforward. For example, to add the null column Date-Created to WORK, we simply use the ALTER statement as follows:

```
ALTER TABLE WORK
    ADD DateCreated DateTime NULL;
```

If there are other column constraints, such as DEFAULT or UNIQUE, include them with the column definition, just as you would if the column definition were part of a CREATE TABLE statement. However, if you include a DEFAULT constraint, be aware that the default value will be applied to all new rows, but existing rows will have null values.

Suppose, for example, that you want to set the default value of DateCreated to 1/1/1900 to signify that the value has not yet been entered. In this case, you would use the ALTER statement:

```
ALTER TABLE WORK
    ADD DateCreated DateTime NULL DEFAULT '01/01/1900';
```

---

[1] The timing is important. The WORK_VERSION2 table was created from WORK. If triggers, stored procedures, and applications continue to run against WORK while the verification of WORK_VERSION2 is underway, then WORK_VERSION2 will be out–of–date. Some action will need to be taken to bring it up-to-date before switching the stored procedures and applications over to WORK_VERSION2.

This statement causes DateCreated for new rows in WORK to be set to 1/1/1900 by default. To set existing rows, you would need to execute the following query:

```
UPDATE WORK

SET       DateCreated ='01/01/1900'

WHERE     DateCreated IS NULL;
```

Adding NOT NULL Columns

To add a new NOT NULL column, first add the column as NULL. Then, use an UPDATE statement like that just shown to give the column a value in all rows. After the update, the following SQL ALTER TABLE . . . ALTER COLUMN statement can be executed to change DateCreated from NULL to NOT NULL.

```
ALTER TABLE WORK

      ALTER COLUMN DateCreated DateTime NOT NULL;
```

Note that this statement will fail if DateCreated has not been given values in all rows.

Dropping Columns

Dropping nonkey columns is easy. For example, eliminating the DateCreated column from WORK can be done with the following:

```
ALTER TABLE WORK

      DROP COLUMN DateCreated;
```

To drop a foreign key column, the constraint that defines the foreign key must first be dropped. Making such a change is equivalent to dropping a relationship, and that topic is discussed later in this chapter.

To drop the primary key, the primary key constraint first needs to be dropped. To drop that, however, all foreign keys that use the primary key must first be dropped. Thus, to drop the primary key of WORK and replace it with the composite primary key (Title, Copy, ArtistID), the following steps are necessary:

- Drop the constraint WorkFK from TRANS.
- Drop the constraint WorkPK from WORK.
- Create a new WorkPK constraint using (Title, Copy, ArtistID).
- Create a new WorkFK constraint referencing (Title, Copy, ArtistID) in TRANS.
- Drop the column WorkID.

It is important to verify that all changes have been made correctly before dropping WorkID. Once it is dropped, there is no way to recover it except by restoring the WORK table from a backup.

Changing a Column Data Type or Column Constraints

To change a column data type or to change column constraints, the column is redefined using the ALTER TABLE ALTER COLUMN command. However, if the column is being changed from NULL to NOT NULL, then all rows must have a value in that column for the change to succeed.

Also, some data type changes may cause data loss. Changing Char(50) to Date, for example, will cause loss of any text field that the DBMS cannot successfully transform into a date value. Or, alternatively, the DBMS may simply refuse to make the column change. The results depend on the DBMS product in use.

Generally, converting numeric to char or varchar will succeed. Also, converting date or money or other more specific data types to char or varchar will usually succeed. Converting char or varchar back to date, money, or numeric is risky, and it may or may not be possible.

In the View Ridge schema, if DateOfBirth had been defined as Char(4), then a risky but sensible data type change would be to modify DateOfBirth in the ARTIST table to numeric (4,0).

This would be a sensible change because all of the values in this column are numeric. Recall the check constraint that was used to define DateOfBirth (refer to Figure 7-14). The following makes that change and simplifies the CHECK constraint.

```
ALTER TABLE ARTIST
        ALTER COLUMN DateOfBirth Numeric(4,0) NULL;
ALTER TABLE ARTIST
        ADD CONSTRAINT NumericBirthYearCheck
                CHECK (Birthdate > 1900 AND Birthdate < 2100);
```

The prior check constraints on DateOfBirth should now be deleted.

Adding and Dropping Constraints

As already shown, constraints can be added and removed using the ALTER TABLE ADD CONSTRAINT and ALTER TABLE DROP CONSTRAINT statements.

Changing Relationship Cardinalities and Properties

Changing cardinalities is a common database redesign task. Sometimes, the need is to change minimum cardinalities from zero to one or from one to zero. Another common task is to change the maximum cardinality from 1:1 to 1:N or from 1:N to N:M. Another possibility, which is less common, is to decrease maximum cardinality from N:M to 1:N or from 1:N to 1:1. This latter change can only be made with data loss, as you will see.

Changing Minimum Cardinalities

The action to be taken in changing minimum cardinalities depends on whether the change is on the parent side or on the child side of the relationship.

Changing Minimum Cardinalities on the Parent Side

If the change is on the parent side, meaning that the child will or will not be required to have a parent, making the change is a matter of changing whether null values are allowed for the foreign key that represents the relationship. For example, suppose that in the 1:N relationship from DEPARTMENT to EMPLOYEE the foreign key DepartmentNumber appears in the EMPLOYEE table. Changing whether an employee is required to have a department is simply a matter of changing the null status of DepartmentNumber.

If the change is from a minimum cardinality of zero to one, then the foreign key, which would have been null, must be changed to NOT NULL. Changing a column to NOT NULL can only be done if all the rows in the table have a value. In the case of a foreign key, this means that every record must already be related. If not, all records must be changed so that all have a relationship before the foreign key can be made NOT NULL. In the previous example, every employee must be related to a department before DepartmentNumber can be changed to NOT NULL.

Depending on the DBMS product in use, the foreign key constraint that defines the relationship may have to be dropped before the change is made to the foreign key. Then the foreign key constraint can be re-added. The following SQL will work for the preceding example:

```
ALTER TABLE EMPLOYEE
        DROP CONSTRAINT DepartmentFK;
ALTER TABLE EMPLOYEE
        ALTER COLUMN DepartmentNumber Int NOT NULL;
```

```
ALTER TABLE EMPLOYEE
    ADD CONSTRAINT DepartmentFK FOREIGN KEY (DepartmentNumber)
        REFERENCES DEPARTMENT (DepartmentNumber)
            ON UPDATE CASCADE;
```

Also, cascade behavior for UPDATE and DELETE must be specified when changing the minimum cardinality from zero to one. In this example, updates are to cascade, but deletions will not (recall that the default behavior is NO ACTION).

Changing the minimum cardinality from one to zero is simple. Just change Department-Number from NOT NULL to NULL. You also may want to change the cascade behavior on updates and deletions, if appropriate.

Changing Minimum Cardinalities on the Child Side

As noted in Chapter 6, the only way to enforce a minimum cardinality other than zero on the child side of a relationship is to write triggers or application code that enforce the constraint. So, to change the minimum cardinality from zero to one, it is necessary to write the appropriate triggers. Design the trigger behavior using Figure 6-28, and then write the triggers. To change the minimum cardinality from one to zero, just drop the triggers that enforce that constraint.

In the DEPARTMENT-to-EMPLOYEE relationship example, to require each DEPARTMENT to have an EMPLOYEE triggers would need to be written on INSERT of DEPARTMENT and on UPDATE and DELETE of EMPLOYEE. The trigger code in DEPARTMENT ensures that an EMPLOYEE is assigned to the new DEPARTMENT, and the trigger code in EMPLOYEE ensures that the employee being moved to a new department or the employee being deleted is not the last employee in the relationship to its parent.

This discussion assumes that the required child constraint is enforced by triggers. If the required child constraint is enforced by application programs, then all of those programs also must be changed. Dozens of programs may need to be changed, which is one reason why it is better to enforce such constraints using triggers rather than application code.

Changing Maximum Cardinalities

The only difficulty when increasing cardinalities from 1:1 to 1:N or from 1:N to N:M is preserving existing relationships. This can be done, but it requires a bit of manipulation, as you will see. When reducing cardinalities, relationship data will be lost. In this case, a policy must be created for deciding which relationships to lose.

Changing a 1:1 Relationship to a 1:N Relationship

Figure 8-5 shows a 1:1 relationship between EMPLOYEE and PARKING_PERMIT. As we discussed in Chapter 6, the foreign key can be placed in either table for a 1:1 relationship. The action taken depends on whether EMPLOYEE is to be the parent entity in the 1:N relationship or whether PARKING_PERMIT is to be the parent.

If EMPLOYEE is to be the parent (employees are to have multiple parking permits), then the only change necessary is to drop the constraint that PARKING_PERMIT.EmployeeNumber be unique. The relationship will then be 1:N.

Figure 8-5

The EMPLOYEE-to-PARKING_PERMIT 1:1 Relationship

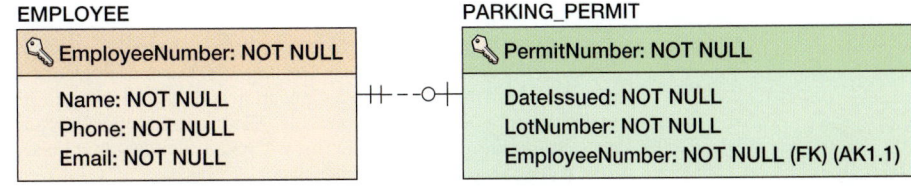

If PARKING_PERMIT is to be the parent (for example, if parking permits are to be allocated to many employees, say, for a carpool), then the foreign key and appropriate values must be moved from PARKING_PERMIT to EMPLOYEE. The following SQL will accomplish this:

```
ALTER TABLE EMPLOYEE
        ADD PermitNumber Int NULL;
UPDATE EMPLOYEE
        SET EMPLOYEE.PermitNumber =
            (SELECT   PP.PermitNumber
             FROM     PARKING_PERMIT AS PP
             WHERE    PP.EmployeeNumber = EMPLOYEE.EmployeeNumber);
```

Once the foreign key has been moved over to EMPLOYEE, the EmployeeNumber column of PARKING_PERMIT should be dropped. Next, create a new foreign key constraint to define referential integrity. So that multiple employees can relate to the same parking permit, the new foreign key must not have a UNIQUE constraint.

Changing a 1:N Relationship to an N:M Relationship

Suppose that View Ridge Gallery decides that it wants to record multiple purchasers for a given transaction. It may be that some of its art is co-owned between a customer and a bank or a trust account, for example; or perhaps it may want to record the names of both owners when a couple purchases art. For whatever reason, this change will require that the 1:N relationship between CUSTOMER and TRANS be changed to an N:M relationship.

Changing a 1:N relationship to an N:M relationship is surprisingly easy.[2] Just create the new intersection table, fill it with data, and drop the old foreign key column. Figure 8-6 shows the View Ridge database design with a new intersection table to support the N:M relationship.

Figure 8-6

View Ridge Gallery Database Design with New N:M Relationship

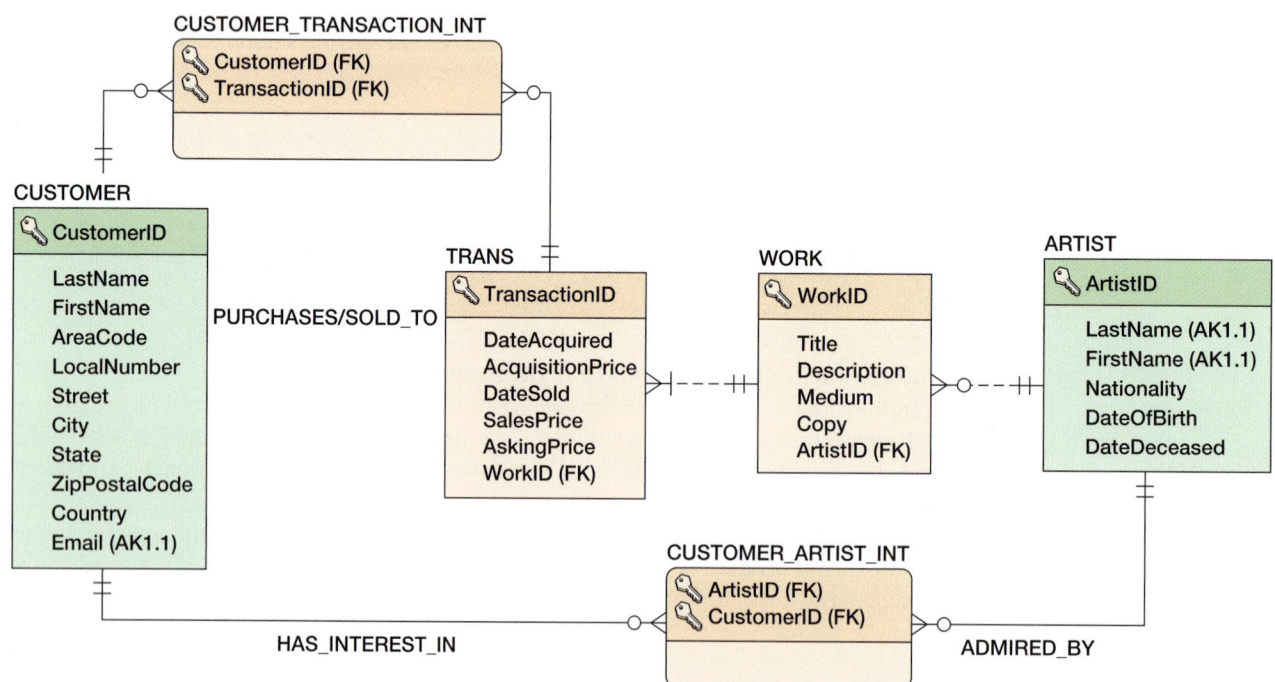

---

[2] Making the data change is easy. Dealing with the consequences of the data change with regards to views, triggers, stored procedures, and application code will be more difficult. All of these will need to be rewritten to join across a new intersection table. All forms and reports also will need to be changed to portray multiple customers for a transaction; this will mean changing text boxes to grids, for example. All of this work is time consuming, and hence expensive.

We need to create this table and then copy the values of TransactionID and CustomerID from TRANS for rows in which CustomerID is not null. First, create the new intersection table using the following SQL:

```
CREATE TABLE CUSTOMER_TRANSACTION_INT(
    CustomerID      Int     NOT NULL,
    TransactionID   Int     NOT NULL,
    CONSTRAINT      CustomerTransaction
        PK PRIMARY KEY(CustomerID, TransactionID),
    CONSTRAINT Customer_Transaction_Int_Trans_FK
        FOREIGN KEY (TransactionID) REFERENCES TRANS(TransactionID),
    CONSTRAINT Customer_Transaction_Int_Customer_FK
        FOREIGN KEY (CustomerID) REFERENCES CUSTOMER(CustomerID)
    );
```

Note that there is no cascade behavior for updates because CustomerID is a surrogate key. There is no cascade behavior for deletions because of the business policy never to delete data that involve transactions. The next task is to fill the table with data from the TRANS table using the following SQL statement:

```
INSERT INTO CUSTOMER_TRANSACTION_INT (CustomerID, TransactionID)
    SELECT    CustomerID, TransactionID
    FROM      TRANS
    WHERE     CustomerID IS NOT NULL;
```

Once all of these changes have been made, the CustomerID column of TRANS can be dropped.

Reducing Cardinalities (with Data Loss)

It is easy to make the structural changes to reduce cardinalities. To reduce an N:M relationship to 1:N, we just create a new foreign key in the relation that will be the child and fill it with data from the intersection table. To reduce a 1:N relationship to 1:1, we just make the values of the foreign key of the 1:N relationship unique and then define a unique constraint on the foreign key. In either case, the most difficult problem is deciding which data to lose.

Consider the reduction of N:M to 1:N. Suppose, for example, that the View Ridge Gallery decides to keep just one artist interest for each customer. Thus, the relationship will then be 1:N from ARTIST to CUSTOMER. Accordingly, we add a new foreign key column ArtistID to CUSTOMER and set up a foreign key constraint to ARTIST on that customer. The following SQL will accomplish this:

```
ALTER TABLE CUSTOMER
    ADD ArtistID Int NULL;
ALTER TABLE CUSTOMER
    ADD CONSTRAINT ArtistInterestFK FOREIGN KEY (ArtistID)
        REFERENCES ARTIST(ArtistID);
```

Updates need not cascade because of the surrogate key, and deletions cannot cascade because the customer may have a valid transaction and ought not to be deleted just because an artist interest goes away.

Now which of a customer's potentially many artist interests should be preserved in the new relationship? The answer depends on the business policy at the gallery. Here, suppose we decide simply to take the first artist interest:

```
UPDATE      CUSTOMER
SET         ArtistID =
            (SELECT     Top 1 ArtistID
             FROM       CUSTOMER_ARTIST_INT AS CAI
             WHERE      CUSTOMER.CustomerID = CAI.CustomerID);
```

The SQL Top 1 phrase is used to return the first qualifying row.

All views, triggers, stored procedures, and application code need to be changed to account for the new 1:N relationship. Then the constraints defined on CUSTOMER_ ARTIST_INT can be dropped. Finally, the table CUSTOMER_ARTIST_INT can be dropped.

To change a 1:N to a 1:1 relationship, we just need to remove any duplicate values of the foreign key of the relationship and then add a unique constraint on the foreign key. See question 8.51.

Adding and Deleting Tables and Relationships

Adding new tables and relationships is straightforward. Just add the tables and relationships using CREATE TABLE statements with FOREIGN KEY constraints, as shown before. If an existing table has a child relationship to the new table, add a FOREIGN KEY constraint using the existing table.

For example, if a new table, COUNTRY, were added to the View Ridge database with the primary key Name and if CUSTOMER.Country is to be used as a foreign key in the new table, a new FOREIGN KEY constraint would be defined in CUSTOMER:

```
ALTER TABLE CUSTOMER
      ADD CONSTRAINT CountryFK FOREIGN KEY (Country)
          REFERENCES COUNTRY(Name)
              ON UPDATE CASCADE;
```

Deleting relationships and tables is just a matter of dropping the foreign key constraints and then dropping the tables. Of course, before this is done, dependency graphs must be constructed and used to determine which views, triggers, stored procedures, and application programs will be affected by the deletions.

As described in Chapter 4, another reason to add new tables and relationships or to compress existing tables into fewer tables is for normalization and denormalization. We will not address that topic further in this chapter, except to say that normalization and denormalization are common tasks during database redesign.

Forward Engineering(?)

You can use a variety of different data modeling products to make database changes on your behalf. To do so, you first reverse engineer the database, make changes to the RE data model, and then invoke the forward-engineering functionality of the data modeling tool.

We will not consider forward engineering here because it hides the SQL that you need to learn. Also, the specifics of the forward-engineering process are product dependent.

Because of the importance of making data model changes correctly, many professionals are skeptical about using an automated process for database redesign. Certainly, it is necessary to test the results thoroughly before using forward engineering on operational data. Some products will show the SQL they are about to execute for review before making the changes to the database.

Database redesign is one area in which automation may not be the best idea. Much depends on the nature of the changes to be made and the quality of the forward-engineering features of the data modeling product. Given the knowledge you have gained in this chapter, you should be able to make most redesign changes by writing your own SQL. There is nothing wrong with that approach!

Summary

Database redesign is the third way in which databases can arise. Redesign is necessary both to fix mistakes made during the initial database design and also to adapt the database to changes in system requirements. Such changes are common because information systems and organizations do not just influence each other—they create each other. Thus, new information systems cause changes in systems requirements.

Correlated subqueries and EXISTS/NOT EXISTS are important SQL statements. They can be used to answer advanced queries. They also are useful during database redesign for determining whether specified data conditions exist. For example, they can be used to determine whether possible functional dependencies exist in the data.

A correlated subquery appears deceptively similar to a regular subquery. The difference is that a regular subquery can be processed from the bottom up. In a regular subquery, results from the lowest query can be determined and then used to evaluate the upper-level queries. In contrast, in a correlated subquery, the processing is nested; that is, a row from an upper-level query statement is compared with rows in a lower-level query. The key distinction of a correlated subquery is that the lower-level SELECT statements use columns from upper-level statements.

EXISTS and NOT EXISTS are specialized forms of correlated subqueries. When these are used, the upper-level query produces results, depending on the existence or nonexistence of rows in lower-level queries. An EXISTS condition is true if any row in the subquery meets the specified conditions; a NOT EXISTS condition is true only if all rows in the subquery do not meet the specified condition. NOT EXISTS is useful for queries that involve conditions that must be true for all rows, such as a "customer who has purchased all products." The double use of NOT EXISTS is a famous SQL pattern that often is used to test a person's knowledge of SQL.

Before redesigning a database, the existing database needs to be carefully examined to avoid making the database unusable by partially processing a database change. The rule is to measure twice and cut once. Reverse engineering is used to create a data model of the existing database. This is done to better understand the database structure before proceeding with a change. The data model produced, called a reverse engineered (RE) data model, is not a true data model, but is a thing unto itself. Most data modeling tools can perform reverse engineering. The RE data model almost always has missing information; such models should be carefully reviewed.

All of the elements of a database are interrelated. Dependency graphs are used to portray the dependency of one element on another. For example, a change in a table can potentially impact relationships, views, indexes, triggers, stored procedures, and application programs. These impacts need to be known and accounted for before making database changes.

A complete backup must be made to the operational database prior to any database redesign changes. Additionally, such changes must be thoroughly tested, initially on small test databases and later on larger test databases that may even be duplicates of the operational databases. The redesign changes are made only after such extensive testing has been completed.

Database redesign changes can be grouped into different types. One type involves changing table names and table columns. Changing a table name has a surprising number of potential consequences. A dependency graph should be used to understand these consequences before proceeding with the change. Nonkey columns are readily added and deleted. Adding a NOT NULL column must be done in three steps: first, add the column as NULL; then add data to every row; and then alter the column constraint to NOT NULL. To drop a column used as a foreign key, the foreign key constraint must first be dropped.

Column data types and constraints can be changed using the ALTER TABLE . . . ALTER COLUMN statement. Changing the data type to char or varchar from a more specific type, such as date, is usually not a problem. Changing a data type from char or varchar to a more specific type can be a problem. In some cases, data will be lost or the DBMS may refuse the change.

Constraints can be added or dropped using the ALTER TABLE . . . ADD/DROP CONSTRAINT statement. Use of this statement is easier if the developers have provided their own names for all constraints.

Changing minimum cardinalities on the parent side of a relationship is simply a matter of altering the constraint on the foreign key from NULL to NOT NULL or from NOT NULL to NULL. Changing minimum cardinalities on the child side of a relationship can be accomplished only by adding or dropping triggers that enforce the constraint.

Changing maximum cardinality from 1:1 to 1:N is simple if the foreign key resides in the correct table. In that case, just remove the unique constraint on the foreign key column. If the foreign key resides in the wrong table for this change, move the foreign key to the other table and do not place a unique constraint on that table.

Changing a 1:N relationship to an N:M relationship requires building a new intersection table and moving the primary key and foreign key values to the intersection table. This aspect of the change is relatively simple. It is more difficult to change all of the views, triggers, stored procedures, application programs, and forms and reports to use the new intersection table.

Reducing cardinalities is easy, but such changes may result in data loss. Prior to making such reductions, a policy must be determined to decide which data to keep. Changing N:M to 1:N involves creating a foreign key in the parent table and moving one value from the intersection table into that foreign key. Changing 1:N to 1:1 requires first eliminating duplicates in the foreign key and then setting a uniqueness constraint on that key. Adding and deleting relationships can be accomplished by defining new foreign key constraints or by dropping existing foreign key constraints.

Most data modeling tools have the capacity to perform forward engineering, which is the process of applying data model changes to an existing database. If forward engineering is used, the results should be thoroughly tested before using it on an operational database. Some tools will show the SQL that they will execute during the forward-engineering process. Any SQL generated by such tools should be carefully reviewed. All in all, there is nothing wrong with writing database redesign SQL statements by hand rather than using forward engineering.

Key Terms

correlated subquery
dependency graph
reverse engineered (RE) data model

SQL EXISTS keyword
SQL NOT EXISTS keyword

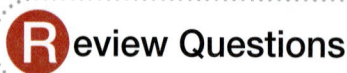

Review Questions

8.1   Explain, one more time, the three ways that databases arise.

8.2   Describe why database redesign is necessary.

8.3   Explain the following statement in your own words: "Information systems and organizations create each other." How does this relate to database redesign?

8.4   Suppose that a table contains two nonkey columns: AdviserName and AdviserPhone. Further suppose that you suspect that AdviserPhone → AdviserName. Explain how to examine the data to determine if this supposition is true.

8.5   Write a subquery, other than one in this chapter, that is not a correlated subquery.

8.6   Explain the following statement: "The processing of correlated subqueries is nested, whereas that of regular subqueries is not."

8.7   Write a correlated subquery, other than one in this chapter.

8.8   Explain how the query in your answer to Review Question 8.5 differs from the query in your answer to Review Question 8.7.

8.9   Explain what is wrong with the correlated subquery on page 299.

8.10   Write a correlated subquery to determine whether the data support the supposition in Review Question 8.4.

8.11   Explain the meaning of the SQL keyword EXISTS.

8.12   Answer Review Question 8.10, but use the SQL EXISTS keyword.

8.13   Explain how the words *any* and *all* pertain to the SQL keywords EXISTS and NOT EXISTS.

8.14   Explain the processing of the query on page 301.

8.15   Using the View Ridge Gallery database, write a query that will display the names of any customers who are interested in all artists.

8.16   Explain how the query in your answer to Review Question 8.15 works.

8.17   Why is it important to analyze the database before implementing database redesign tasks? What can happen if this is not done?

8.18   Explain the process of reverse engineering.

8.19   Why is it important to carefully evaluate the results of reverse engineering?

8.20   What is a dependency graph? What purpose does it serve?

8.21   Explain the dependencies for WORK in the graph in Figure 8-4.

8.22   What sources are used when creating a dependency graph?

8.23   Explain two different types of test databases that should be used when testing database redesign changes.

8.24   Explain the problems that can occur when changing the name of a table.

8.25   Describe the process of changing a table name.

8.26   Considering Figure 8-4, describe the tasks that need to be accomplished to change the name of the table WORK to WORK_VERSION2.

8.27   Explain how views can simplify the process of changing a table name.

8.28   Under what conditions is the following SQL statement valid?

```
INSERT      INTO T1      (A, B)
            SELECT       (C, D) FROM T2;
```

8.29   Show an SQL statement to add an integer column C1 to the table T2. Assume that C1 is NULL.

8.30   Extend your answer to Review Question 8.29 to add C1 when C1 is to be NOT NULL.

8.31   Show an SQL statement to drop the column C1 from table T2.

8.32   Describe the process for dropping primary key C1 and making the new primary key C2.

8.33   Which data type changes are the least risky?

8.34   Which data type changes are the most risky?

8.35   Write an SQL statement to change a column C1 to Char(10) NOT NULL. What conditions must exist in the data for this change to be successful?

8.36   Explain how to change the minimum cardinality when a child that was required to have a parent is no longer required to have one.

8.37   Explain how to change the minimum cardinality when a child that was not required to have a parent is now required to have one. What condition must exist in the data for this change to work?

8.38   Explain how to change the minimum cardinality when a parent that was required to have a child is no longer required to have one.

8.39   Explain how to change the minimum cardinality when a parent that was not required to have a child is now required to have one.

8.40   Describe how to change the maximum cardinality from 1:1 to 1:N. Assume that the foreign key is on the side of the new child in the 1:N relationship.

8.41   Describe how to change the maximum cardinality from 1:1 to 1:N. Assume that the foreign key is on the side of the new parent in the 1:N relationship.

8.42   Assume that tables T1 and T2 have a 1:1 relationship. Assume that T2 has the foreign key. Show the SQL statements necessary to move the foreign key to T1. Make up your own names for the primary and foreign keys.

8.43   Explain how to transform a 1:N relationship into an N:M relationship.

8.44   Suppose that tables T1 and T2 have a 1:N relationship. Show the SQL statements necessary to fill an intersection T1_T2_INT. Make up your own names for the primary and foreign keys.

8.45   Explain how the reduction of maximum cardinalities causes data loss.

8.46   Using the tables in your answer to Review Question 8.44, show the SQL statements necessary to change the relationship back to 1:N. Assume that the first row in the qualifying rows of the intersection table is to provide the foreign key. Use the keys and foreign keys from your answer to Review Question 8.44.

8.47   Using the results of your answer to Review Question 8.46, explain what must be done to convert this relationship to 1:1. Use the keys and foreign keys from your answer to Review Question 8.46.

8.48   In general terms, what must be done to add a new relationship?

8.49   Suppose that tables T1 and T2 have a 1:N relationship, with T2 as the child. Show the SQL statements necessary to remove table T1. Make your own assumptions about the names of keys and foreign keys.

8.50   What are the risks and problems of forward engineering?

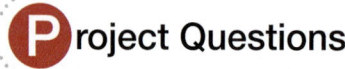 **P**roject Questions

8.51   Suppose that the table EMPLOYEE has a 1:N relationship to the table PHONE_NUMBER. Further suppose that the primary key of EMPLOYEE is EmployeeID and the columns of PHONE_NUMBER are PhoneNumberID (a surrogate key), AreaCode, Local-Number, and EmployeeID (a foreign key to EMPLOYEE). Alter this design so that EMPLOYEE has a 1:1 relationship to PHONE_NUMBER. For employees having more than one phone number, keep only the first one.

8.52   Suppose that the table EMPLOYEE has a 1:N relationship to the table PHONE_NUMBER. Further suppose that the key of EMPLOYEE is EmployeeID and the columns of PHONE_NUMBER are PhoneNumberID (a surrogate key), AreaCode, LocalNumber, and EmployeeID (a foreign key to EMPLOYEE). Write all SQL statements necessary to redesign this database so that it has just one table. Explain the difference between the result of question 8.51 and the result of this question.

8.53   Consider the following table:

TASK (EmployeeID, EmpLastName, EmpFirstName, Phone, OfficeNumber, ProjectName, Sponsor, WorkDate, HoursWorked)

with the following possible functional dependencies:

EmployeeID → (EmpLastName, EmpFirstName, Phone, OfficeNumber)
ProjectName → Sponsor

A.   Write SQL statements to display the values of any rows that violate these functional dependencies.

B.   If no data violate these functional dependencies, can we assume that they are valid? Why or why not?

C.   Assume that these functional dependencies are true and that the data have been corrected, as necessary, to reflect them. Write all SQL statements necessary to redesign this table into a set of tables in BCNF and 4NF. Assume that the table has data values that must be appropriately transformed to the new design.

Assume that Marcia has created a database with the tables described at the end of Chapter 7:

CUSTOMER (**CustomerID**, FirstName, LastName, Phone, Email)

ORDER (**InvoiceNumber**, *CustomerID*, DateIn, DateOut, Subtotal, Tax, TotalAmount)

ORDER_ITEM (*InvoiceNumber*, ItemNumber, *Service*, Quantity, UnitPrice, ExtendedPrice)

SERVICE (**Service**, Description, UnitPrice)

Assume that all relationships have been defined, as implied by the foreign keys in this table list.

A.   Create a dependency graph that shows dependencies among these tables. Explain how you need to extend this graph for views and other database constructs such as triggers and stored procedures.

B.   Using your dependency graph, describe the tasks necessary to change the name of the ORDER table to CUST_ORDER.

C.   Write all SQL statements to make the name change described in part B.

D.   Suppose that Marcia decides to allow multiple customers per order (for customers' spouses, for example). Modify the design of these tables to accommodate this change.

E.   Code SQL statements necessary to redesign the database, as described in your answer to part D.

F.   Suppose that Marcia considers changing the primary key of CUSTOMER to (FirstName, LastName). Write correlated subqueries to display any data that indicate that this change is not justifiable.

G.   Suppose that (FirstName, LastName) can be made the primary key of CUSTOMER. Make appropriate changes to the table design with this new primary key.

H.   Code all SQL statements necessary to implement the changes described in part G.

Morgan
Importing

Assume that Morgan has created a database with the tables described at the end of Chapter 7 (Note that STORE uses the surrogate key StoreID):

STORE (<u>StoreID</u>, StoreName, City, Country, Phone, Fax, Email, Contact)

PURCHASE (<u>PurchaseID</u>, *StoreID*, Date, Description, Category, PriceUSD)

SHIPMENT (ShipmentID, *ShipperID*, ShipperInvoiceNumber, Origin, Destination, DepartureDate, ArrivalDate)

SHIPMENT_ITEM (*<u>ShipmentID</u>*, *<u>PurchaseID</u>*, InsuredValue)

SHIPPER (<u>ShipperID</u>, ShipperName, Phone, Fax, Email, Contact)

Assume that all relationships have been defined as implied by the foreign keys in this table list.

A.   Create a dependency graph that shows dependencies among these tables. Explain how you need to extend this graph for views and other database constructs, such as stored procedures.

B.   Using your dependency graph, describe the tasks necessary to change the name of the SHIPMENT table to MORGAN_SHIPMENT.

C.   Write all SQL statements to make the name change described in part B.

D.   Suppose that Morgan decides to allocate some purchases to more than one shipment. Make design changes in accordance with this new fact. You will need to make assumptions about how purchases are divided and allocated to shipments. State your assumptions.

E.   Code SQL statements to implement your redesign recommendations in your answer to part D.

F.   Suppose that Morgan considers changing the primary key of PURCHASE to (StoreID, Date). Write correlated subqueries to display any data that indicate that this change is not justifiable.

G.   Suppose that (StoreID, Date) can be made the primary key of PURCHASE. Make appropriate changes to the table design.

H.   Code all SQL statements necessary to implement the changes described in part G.

Part 4

Multiuser Database Processing

The four chapters in Part 4 introduce and discuss the major problems of multiuser database processing and describe the features and functions for solving those problems offered by two important DBMS products. We begin in Chapter 9 with a description of database administration and the major tasks and techniques for multiuser database management. The next three chapters illustrate the implementation of these concepts using SQL Server 2008 (Chapter 10), Oracle Database 11g (Chapter 10A), and MySQL 5.1 (Chapter 10B).

9 Managing Multiuser Databases

Chapter Objectives

- To understand the need for and importance of database administration.
- To understand the need for concurrency control, security, and backup and recovery.
- To learn about typical problems that can occur when multiple users process a database concurrently.
- To understand the use of locking and the problem of deadlock.
- To learn the difference between optimistic and pessimistic locking.

- To know the meaning of an ACID transaction.
- To learn the four 1992 ANSI standard isolation levels.
- To understand the need for security and specific tasks for improving database security.
- To know the difference between recovery via reprocessing and recovery via rollback/rollforward.
- To understand the nature of the tasks required for recovery using rollback/rollforward.
- To know basic administrative and managerial DBA functions.

Although multiuser databases offer great value to the organizations that create and use them, they also pose difficult problems for those same organizations. For one, multiuser databases are complicated to design and develop because they support many overlapping user views.

Additionally, as discussed in the last chapter, requirements change over time, and those changes necessitate other changes to the database structure. Such structural changes must be carefully planned and controlled so that a change made for one group does not cause problems for another. In addition, when users process a database concurrently, special controls are needed to ensure that the actions of one user do not inappropriately influence the results for another. This topic is both important and complicated, as you will see.

In large organizations, processing rights and responsibilities need to be defined and enforced. What happens, for example, when an employee leaves the firm? When can the employee's records be deleted? For the purposes of payroll processing, records can be deleted after the last pay period. For the purposes of quarterly reporting, they can be deleted at the end of the quarter. For the purposes of end-of-year tax record processing, they can be deleted at the end of the year. Clearly, no department can unilaterally decide when to delete that data. Similar comments pertain to the insertion and changing of data values. For these and other reasons, security systems need to be developed that enable only authorized users to take authorized actions at authorized times.

Databases have become key components of organizational operations, and even key components of an organization's value. Unfortunately, database failures and disasters do occur. Thus, effective backup and recovery plans, techniques, and procedures are essential.

Finally, over time, the DBMS itself will need to be changed to improve performance by incorporating new features and releases and to conform with changes made in the underlying operating system. All of this requires attentive management.

To ensure that these problems are addressed and solved, most organizations have a database administration office. We begin with a description of the tasks of that office. We then describe the combination of software and manual practices and procedures that are used to perform those tasks. In the next three chapters, we will discuss and illustrate features and functions of SQL Server 2008, Oracle Database 11g, and MySQL 5.1, respectively, for dealing with these issues.

Database Administration

The terms **data administration** and **database administration** are both used in practice. In some cases, the terms are considered to be synonymous; in other cases, they have different meanings. Most commonly, the term *data administration* refers to a function that applies to an entire organization; it is a management-oriented function that concerns corporate data privacy and security issues. In contrast, the term *database administration* refers to a more technical function that is specific to a particular database, including the applications that process that database. This chapter addresses database administration.

Databases vary considerably in size and scope, from single-user personal databases to large interorganizational databases, such as airline reservation systems. All of these databases have a need for database administration, although the tasks to be accomplished vary in complexity. For personal databases, individuals follow simple procedures for backing up their data, and they keep minimal records for documentation. In this case, the person who uses the database also performs the database administration functions, even though he or she is probably unaware of it.

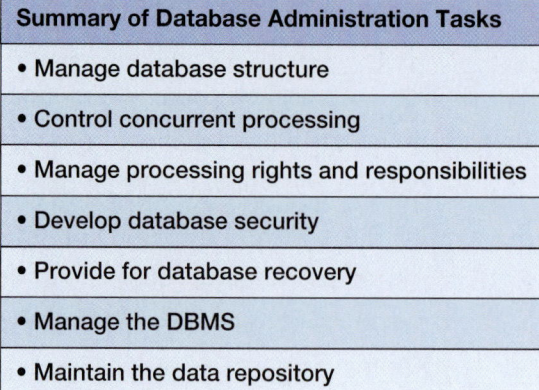

Figure 9-1

Summary of Database
Administration Tasks

For multiuser database applications, database administration becomes both more important and more difficult. Consequently, it generally has formal recognition. For some applications, one or two people are given this function on a part-time basis. For large Internet or intranet databases, database administration responsibilities are often too time consuming and too varied to be handled even by a single full-time person. Supporting a database with dozens or hundreds of users requires considerable time as well as both technical knowledge and diplomatic skills. Such support usually is handled by an office of database administration. The manager of the office is often known as the **database administrator**. In this case, the acronym **DBA** refers to either the office or the manager.

The overall responsibility of the DBA is to facilitate the development and use of the database. Usually, this means balancing the conflicting goals of protecting the database and maximizing its availability and benefit to users. Specific tasks are shown in Figure 9-1. We consider each of these tasks in the following sections.

Managing the Database Structure

Managing the database structure includes participating in the initial database design and implementation as well as controlling and managing changes to the database. Ideally, the DBA is involved early in the development of the database and its applications; participates in the requirements study; helps evaluate alternatives, including the DBMS to be used; and helps design the database structure. For large organizational applications, the DBA usually is a manager who supervises the work of technically oriented database design personnel.

Creating the database involves several different tasks. First, the database is created and disk space is allocated for database files and logs. Then tables are generated, indexes are created, and stored procedures and triggers are written. We will discuss examples of all of these tasks in the next three chapters. Once the database structures are created, the database is filled with data.

Configuration Control

After a database and its applications have been implemented, changes in requirements are inevitable, as described in Chapter 8. Such changes can arise from new needs, from changes in the business environment, from changes in policy, and from changes in business processes that evolve with system use. When changes to requirements necessitate changes to the database structure, great care must be used, because changes to the database structure seldom involve just one application.

Hence, effective database administration includes procedures and policies by which users can register their needs for changes, the entire database community can discuss the impacts of the changes, and a global decision can be made whether to implement proposed changes. Because of the size and complexity of a database and its applications, changes sometimes have unexpected results. Thus, the DBA must be prepared to repair the database and to gather sufficient information to diagnose and correct the problem that caused the damage. The database is most vulnerable to failure after its structure has been changed.

Participate in Database and Application Development
• Assist in requirements stage and data model creation
• Play an active role in database design and creation

Facilitate Changes to Database Structure
• Seek communitywide solutions
• Assess impact on all users
• Provide configuration control forum
• Be prepared for problems after changes are made
• Maintain documentation

Figure 9-2

Summary of DBA's Responsibilities for Managing Database Structure

Documentation

The DBA's final responsibility in managing the database structure is documentation. It is extremely important to know what changes have been made, how they were made, and when they were made. A change in the database structure may cause an error that is not revealed for six months; without proper documentation of the change, diagnosing the problem is next to impossible. Considerable work may be required to identify the point at which certain symptoms first appeared. For this reason, it also is important to maintain a record of the test procedures and test runs made to verify a change. If standardized test procedures, test forms, and recordkeeping methods are used, recording the test results does not have to be time consuming.

Although maintaining documentation is tedious and unfulfilling, the effort pays off when disaster strikes and the documentation is the difference between a quick problem solution and a confused muddle of activity. Today, several products are emerging that ease the burden of documentation. Many CASE tools, for example, can be used to document logical database designs. Version-control software can be used to track changes. Data dictionaries provide reports and other outputs that present database data structures.

Another reason for carefully documenting changes in the database structure is so that historical data are used properly. If, for example, marketing wants to analyze three-year-old sales data that have been in the archives for two years, it will be necessary to know what structure was current at the time the data were last active. Records that show the changes in the structure can be used to answer that question. A similar situation arises when a six-month-old backup copy of data must be used to repair a damaged database (although this should not happen, it sometimes does). The backup copy can be used to reconstruct the database to the state it was in at the time of the backup. Then, transactions and structural changes can be made in chronological order to restore the database to its current state. Figure 9-2 summarizes the DBA's responsibilities for managing the database structure.

Concurrency Control

Concurrency control measures are taken to ensure that one user's work does not inappropriately influence another user's work. In some cases, these measures ensure that a user gets the same result when processing with other users that he or she would have received if processing alone. In other cases, it means that the user's work is influenced by other users, but in an anticipated way. For example, in an order-entry system, a user should be able to enter an order and get the same result, regardless of whether there are no other users or hundreds of other users. In contrast, a user who is printing a report of the most current inventory status may want to obtain in-process data changes from other users, even if there is a danger that those changes may later be cancelled.

Unfortunately, no concurrency control technique or mechanism is ideal for every circumstance. All involve trade-offs. For example, a program can obtain very strict concurrency control by locking the entire database, but no other programs will be able to do anything while it runs. This is strict protection, but at a high cost. As you will see, other measures are available that are more difficult to program or enforce but that allow more throughput. Still other measures are available that maximize throughput but have a low level of concurrency control. When designing multiuser database applications, you will need to choose among these trade-offs.

The Need for Atomic Transactions

In most database applications, users submit work in the form of **transactions**, which are also known as **logical units of work (LUWs)**. A transaction (or LUW) is a series of actions to be taken on the database so that either all of them are performed successfully or none of them are performed at all, in which case the database remains unchanged. Such a transaction is sometimes called *atomic* because it is performed as a unit.

Consider the following sequence of database actions that could occur when recording a new order:

1. Change a customer's row, increasing AmountDue.
2. Change a salesperson's row, increasing CommissionDue.
3. Insert a new order row into the database.

Suppose that the last step failed, perhaps because of insufficient file space. Imagine the confusion if the first two changes were made but the third one was not. The customer would be billed for an order never received, and a salesperson would receive a commission on an order that was never sent to the customer. Clearly, these three actions need to be taken as a unit—either all of them should be done or none of them should be done.

Figure 9-3 compares the results of performing these activities as a series of independent steps [Figure 9-3(a)] and as an atomic transaction [Figure 9-3(b)]. Notice that when the steps are carried out atomically and one fails, no changes are made in the database. Also note that the commands Start Transaction, Commit Transaction, and Rollback Transaction are issued by the application program to mark the boundaries of the transaction logic. You will learn more about these commands later in this chapter and in Chapters 10, 10A, and 10B.

Concurrent Transaction Processing

When two transactions are being processed against a database at the same time, they are termed **concurrent transactions**. Although it may appear to the users that concurrent transactions are being processed simultaneously, this cannot be true because the CPU of the machine processing the database can execute only one instruction at a time. Usually, transactions are interleaved, which means that the operating system switches CPU services among tasks so that some portion of each transaction is carried out in a given interval. This switching among tasks is done so quickly that two people seated at browsers side by side, processing the same database, may believe that their two transactions are completed simultaneously; in reality, however, the two transactions are interleaved.

Figure 9-4 shows two concurrent transactions. User A's transaction reads Item 100, changes it, and rewrites it in the database. User B's transaction takes the same actions, but on Item 200. The CPU processes User A's transactions until it encounters an I/O interrupt or some other delay for User A. The operating system shifts control to User B. The CPU now processes User B's transactions until an interrupt, at which point the operating system passes control back to User A. To the users, the processing appears to be simultaneous, but it is interleaved, or concurrent.

The Lost Update Problem

The concurrent processing illustrated in Figure 9-4 poses no problems because the users are processing different data. But suppose that both users want to process Item 100. For example,

Figure 9-3

Need for Transaction
Processing

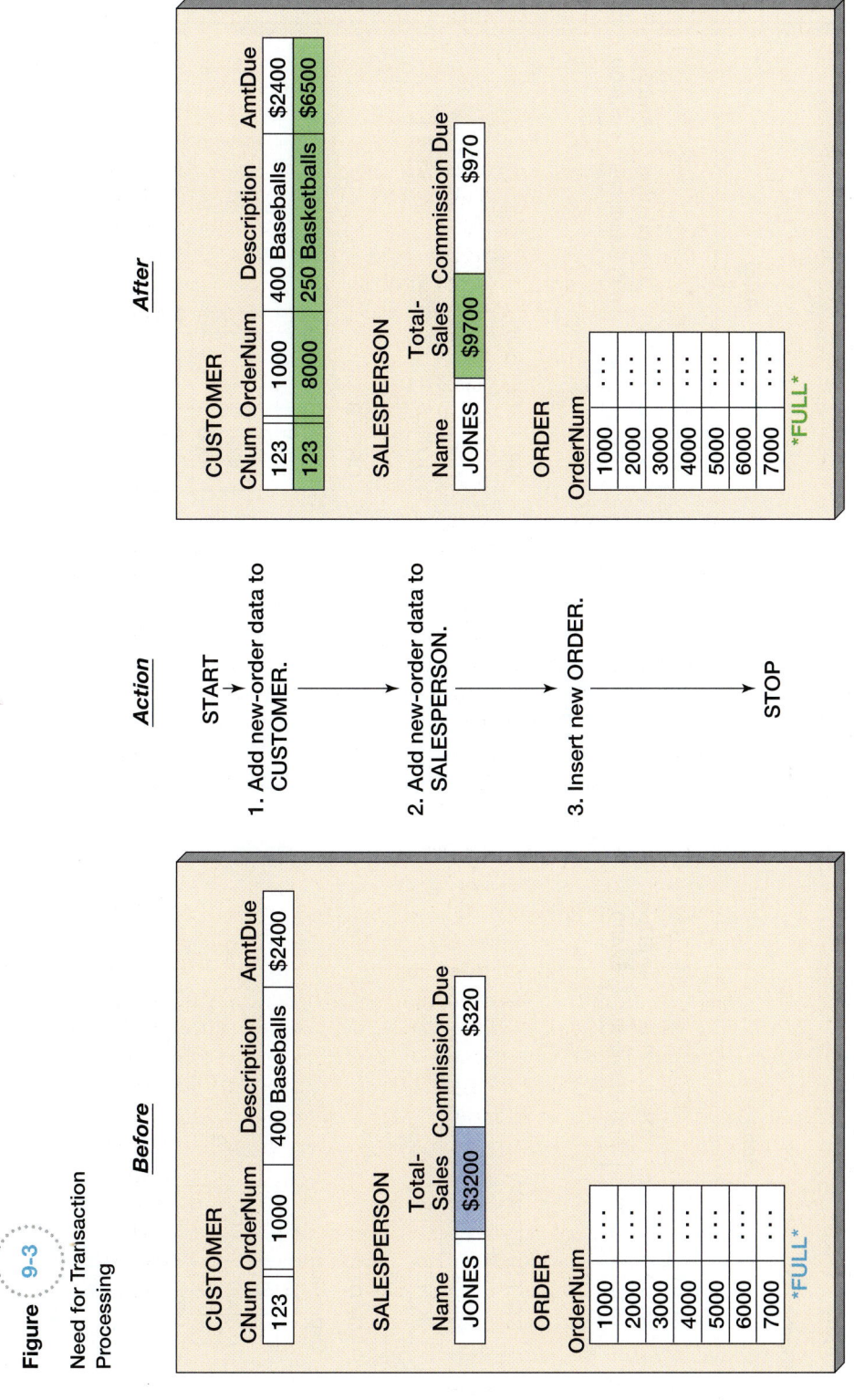

(a) Errors Introduced Without Transaction

Figure 9-3

(Continued)

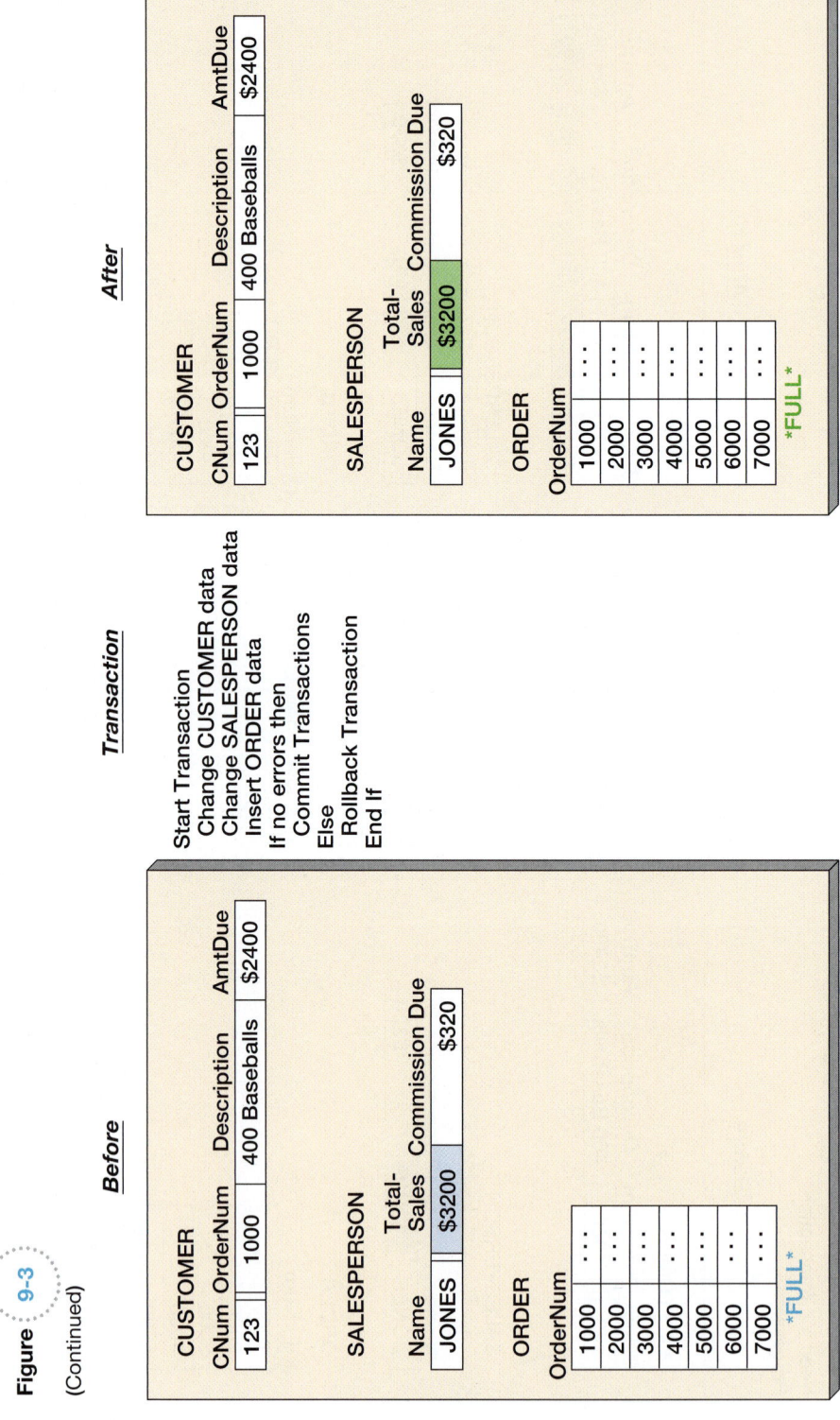

Before

CUSTOMER

CNum	OrderNum	Description	AmtDue
123	1000	400 Baseballs	$2400

SALESPERSON

Name	Total-Sales	Commission Due
JONES	$3200	$320

ORDER

OrderNum
1000	...
2000	...
3000	...
4000	...
5000	...
6000	...
7000	...

FULL

Transaction

Start Transaction
Change CUSTOMER data
Change SALESPERSON data
Insert ORDER data
If no errors then
  Commit Transactions
Else
  Rollback Transaction
End If

After

CUSTOMER

CNum	OrderNum	Description	AmtDue
123	1000	400 Baseballs	$2400

SALESPERSON

Name	Total-Sales	Commission Due
JONES	$3200	$320

ORDER

OrderNum
1000	...
2000	...
3000	...
4000	...
5000	...
6000	...
7000	...

FULL

(b) Atomic Transaction Prevents Errors

User A

1. Read item 100.
2. Change item 100.
3. Write item 100.

User B

1. Read item 200.
2. Change item 200.
3. Write item 200.

Order of processing at database server

1. Read item 100 for A.
2. Read item 200 for B.
3. Change item 100 for A.
4. Write item 100 for A.
5. Change item 200 for B.
6. Write item 200 for B.

Figure   9-4

Concurrent-Processing
Example

User A wants to order five units of Item 100, and User B wants to order three units of the same item. Figure 9-5 illustrates the problem.

User A reads a copy of Item 100's record into memory. According to the record, there are 10 items in inventory. Then User B reads another copy of Item 100's record into a different section of memory. Again, according to the record, there are 10 items in inventory. Now User A takes five, decrements the count of items in its copy of the data to five, and rewrites the record for Item 100. Then User B takes three, decrements the count in its copy of the data to seven, and rewrites the record for Item 100. The database now shows, incorrectly, that there are seven Item 100s in inventory. To review: We started with 10 in inventory, User A took five, User B took three, and the database shows that seven are in inventory. Clearly, this is a problem.

Both users obtained data that were correct at the time they obtained them. But when User B read the record, User A already had a copy that it was about to update. This situation is called the **lost update problem**, or the **concurrent update problem**. A similar problem is the **inconsistent read problem**. With this problem, User A reads data that have been processed by a portion of a transaction from User B. As a result, User A reads incorrect data.

Figure   9-5

Lost-Update Problem

User A

1. Read item 100
   (item count is 10).
2. Reduce count of items by 5.
3. Write item 100.

User B

1. Read item 100
   (item count is 10).
2. Reduce count of items by 3.
3. Write item 100.

Order of processing at database server

1. Read item 100 (for A).
2. Read item 100 (for B).
3. Set item count to 5 (for A).
4. Write item 100 for A.
5. Set item count to 7 (for B).
6. Write item 100 for B.

Note: The change and write in steps 3 and 4 are lost.

One remedy for the inconsistencies caused by concurrent processing is to prevent multiple applications from obtaining copies of the same record when the record is about to be changed. This remedy is called **resource locking**.

Resource Locking

One way to prevent concurrent processing problems is to disallow sharing by locking data that are retrieved for update. Figure 9-6 shows the order of processing using a **lock** command.

Because of the lock, User B's transaction must wait until User A is finished with the Item 100 data. Using this strategy, User B can read Item 100's record only after User A has completed the modification. In this case, the final item count stored in the database is two, as it should be. (We started with ten, User A took five, and User B took three, leaving two.)

Lock Terminology

Locks can be placed either automatically by the DBMS or by a command issued to the DBMS from the application program. Locks placed by the DBMS are called **implicit locks**; those placed by command are called **explicit locks**. Today, almost all locking is implicit. The program declares the behavior it wants, and the DBMS places locks accordingly. You will learn how to do that later in this chapter.

In the preceding example, the locks were applied to rows of data. Not all locks are applied at this level, however. Some DBMS products lock groups of rows within a table, some lock entire tables, and some lock the entire database. The size of a lock is referred to as **lock granularity**. Locks with large granularity are easy for the DBMS to administer, but frequently cause conflicts. Locks with small granularity are difficult to administer (the DBMS has to track and check many more details), but conflicts are less common.

Locks also vary by type. An **exclusive lock** locks the item from any other access. No other transaction can read or change the data. A **shared lock** locks the item from change but not from read. That is, other transactions can read the item as long as they do not attempt to alter it.

Figure 9-6

Concurrent Processing with Explicit Locks

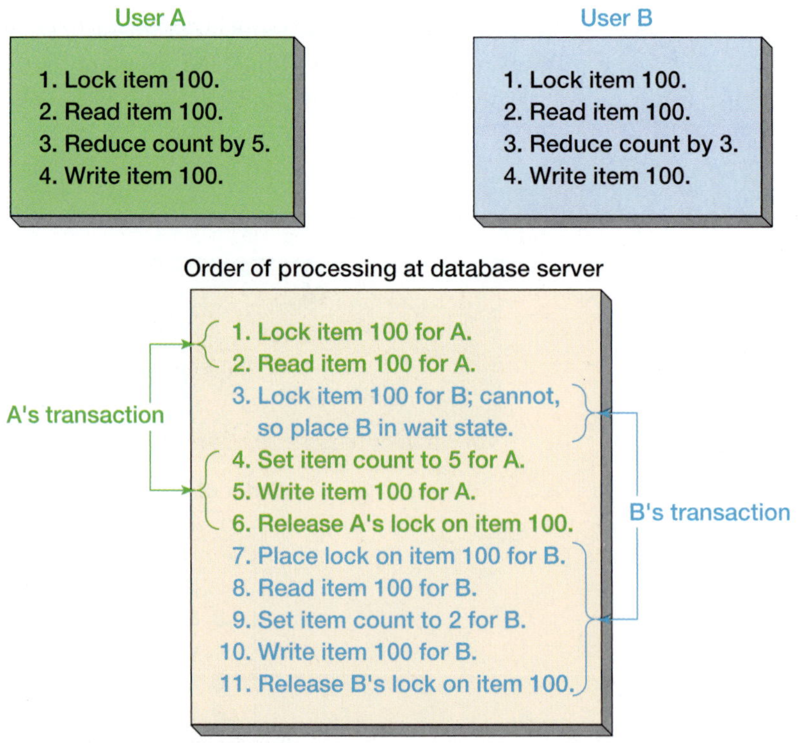

User A

1. Lock item 100.
2. Read item 100.
3. Reduce count by 5.
4. Write item 100.

User B

1. Lock item 100.
2. Read item 100.
3. Reduce count by 3.
4. Write item 100.

Order of processing at database server

A's transaction

1. Lock item 100 for A.
2. Read item 100 for A.
3. Lock item 100 for B; cannot, so place B in wait state.
4. Set item count to 5 for A.
5. Write item 100 for A.
6. Release A's lock on item 100.
7. Place lock on item 100 for B.
8. Read item 100 for B.
9. Set item count to 2 for B.
10. Write item 100 for B.
11. Release B's lock on item 100.

B's transaction

Serializable Transactions

When two or more transactions are processed concurrently, the results in the database should be logically consistent with the results that would have been achieved had the transactions been processed in an arbitrary, serial fashion. A scheme for processing concurrent transactions in this way is said to be **serializable**.

Serializability can be achieved by a number of different means. One way is to process the transaction using **two-phased locking**. With this strategy, transactions are allowed to obtain locks as necessary, but once the first lock is released, no other lock can be obtained. Transactions thus have a **growing phase**, during which the locks are obtained, and a **shrinking phase**, during which the locks are released.

A special case of two-phased locking is used with a number of DBMS products. With it, locks are obtained throughout the transaction, but no lock is released until the COMMIT or ROLLBACK command is issued. This strategy is more restrictive than two-phase locking requires, but it is easier to implement.

Consider an order-entry transaction that processes data in the CUSTOMER, SALESPERSON, and ORDER tables. To avoid concurrency problems, the order-entry transaction issues locks on CUSTOMER, SALESPERSON, and ORDER, as needed; makes all database changes; and then releases all locks.

Deadlock

Although locking solves one problem, it introduces another. Consider what can happen when two users want to order two items from inventory. Suppose that User A wants to order some paper, and if she can get the paper, she wants to order some pencils. Then suppose that User B wants to order some pencils, and if he can get the pencils, he wants to order some paper. The order of processing is shown in Figure 9-7.

In this figure, Users A and B are locked in a condition known as **deadlock**, or sometimes as the **deadly embrace**. Each user is waiting for a resource that the other has locked. This problem can be solved either by preventing the deadlock from occurring or by allowing the deadlock to occur and then breaking it.

Deadlock can be prevented in several ways. One way is to require users to issue all lock requests at one time. In Figure 9-7, if User A had locked both the paper and the pencil records at the beginning, deadlock would not occur. A second way to prevent deadlock is to require all application programs to lock resources in the same order.

Figure 9-7

Deadlock

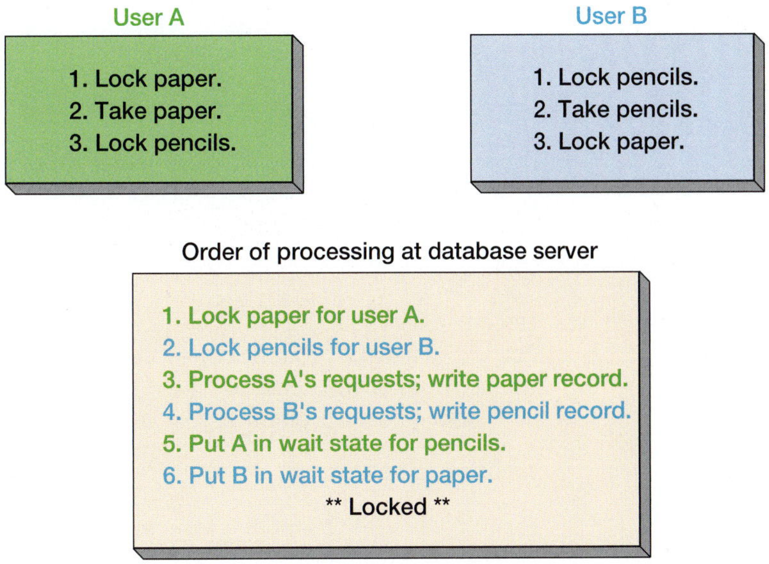

User A

1. Lock paper.
2. Take paper.
3. Lock pencils.

User B

1. Lock pencils.
2. Take pencils.
3. Lock paper.

Order of processing at database server

1. Lock paper for user A.
2. Lock pencils for user B.
3. Process A's requests; write paper record.
4. Process B's requests; write pencil record.
5. Put A in wait state for pencils.
6. Put B in wait state for paper.
   ** Locked **

> **BY THE WAY** Even if all the applications do not lock resources in the same order, deadlock will be prevented for those that do. Sometimes this policy is implemented with an organizational programming standard such as "Whenever processing rows from tables in a parent-child relationship, lock the parent row before the child rows." This policy will at least reduce the likelihood of deadlock and thus save the DBMS from having to recover from some deadlocked transactions.

Almost every DBMS has algorithms for breaking deadlock, when it does occur. First, the DBMS must detect that it has occurred. Then, the typical solution is to cancel one of the transactions and remove its changes from the database. You will see variants of this with Oracle, SQL Server, and MySQL in the next three chapters.

Optimistic Versus Pessimistic Locking

Locks can be invoked in two basic styles. With **optimistic locking**, the assumption is made that no conflict will occur. Data are read, the transaction is processed, updates are issued, and then a check is made to see if conflict occurred. If not, the transaction is finished. If conflict did occur, the transaction is repeated until it processes with no conflict. With **pessimistic locking**, the assumption is made that conflict will occur. Locks are issued, the transaction is processed, and then the locks are freed.

Figures 9-8 and 9-9 show examples of each style for a transaction that is reducing the quantity of the pencil row in PRODUCT by five. Figure 9-8 shows optimistic locking. First, the data are read and the current value of Quantity of pencils is saved in the variable OldQuantity. The transaction is then processed, and assuming that all is OK, a lock is obtained on PRODUCT. (In fact, the lock might be only for the pencil row or it might be at a larger level of granularity, but the principle is the same.) After obtaining the lock, an SQL statement is issued to update the pencil row with a WHERE condition that the current value of Quantity equals OldQuantity. If no other transaction has changed the Quantity of the pencil row, then this UPDATE will be successful. If another transaction has changed the Quantity of the pencil row, the UPDATE will fail. In either case, the lock is released. If the transaction failed, the process is repeated until the transaction finishes with no conflict.

Figure 9-8

Optimistic Locking

```
SELECT    PRODUCT.Name, PRODUCT.Quantity
FROM      PRODUCT
WHERE     PRODUCT.Name = 'Pencil'

Set NewQuantity = PRODUCT.Quantity - 5

{process transaction - take exception action if NewQuantity < 0, etc.

Assuming all is OK: }

LOCK PRODUCT

UPDATE    PRODUCT
SET       PRODUCT.Quantity = NewQuantity
WHERE     PRODUCT.Name = 'Pencil'
    AND PRODUCT.Quantity = OldQuantity

UNLOCK    PRODUCT

{check to see if update was successful;
if not, repeat transaction}
```

(a)

```
LOCK      PRODUCT

SELECT    PRODUCT.Name, PRODUCT.Quantity
FROM      PRODUCT
WHERE     PRODUCT.Name = 'Pencil'

Set NewQuantity = PRODUCT.Quantity - 5

{process transaction - take exception action if NewQuantity < 0, etc.

Assuming all is OK: }

UPDATE    PRODUCT
SET       PRODUCT.Quantity = NewQuantity
WHERE     PRODUCT.Name = 'Pencil'

UNLOCK    PRODUCT

{no need to check if update was successful}
```

(b)

Figure 9-9

Pessimistic Locking

Figure 9-9 shows the logic for the same transaction using pessimistic locking. Here, a lock is obtained on PRODUCT before any work is begun. Then, values are read, the transaction is processed, the UPDATE occurs, and PRODUCT is unlocked.

The advantage of optimistic locking is that locks are held for much less time than with pessimistic locking, because locks are obtained only after the transaction has finished. If the transaction is complicated or if the client is slow (due to transmission delays, the client doing other work, or the user getting a cup of coffee or shutting down without exiting the browser), optimistic locking can dramatically improve throughput. This advantage will be especially true if the lock granularity is large—say, the entire PRODUCT table.

The disadvantage of optimistic locking is that if there is a lot of activity on the pencil row, the transaction may have to be repeated many times. Thus, transactions that involve a lot of activity on a given row (purchasing a popular stock, for example) are poorly suited for optimistic locking.

In general, the Internet is a wild and woolly place, and users are likely to take unexpected actions, such as abandoning transactions in the middle. So, unless Internet users have been prequalified (by enrolling in an online brokerage stock purchase plan, for example), optimistic locking is the better choice in that environment. On intranets, however, the decision is more difficult. Optimistic locking is probably still preferred unless some characteristic of the application causes substantial activity on particular rows or if application requirements make reprocessing transactions particularly undesirable.

Declaring Lock Characteristics

As you can see, concurrency control is a complicated subject; determining the level, type, and placement of the lock is difficult. Sometimes, too, the optimum locking strategy depends on which transactions are active and what they are doing. For these and other reasons, database application programs do not generally explicitly issue locks as shown in Figures 9-8 and 9-9. Instead, they mark transaction boundaries and then declare the type of locking behavior they want the DBMS to use. In this way, the DBMS can place and remove locks and even change the level and type of locks dynamically.

Figure 9-10 shows the pencil transaction with transaction boundaries marked with BEGIN TRANSACTION, COMMIT TRANSACTION, and ROLLBACK TRANSACTION statements. These boundaries are the essential information that the DBMS needs to enforce the different locking strategies. If the developer now declares via a system parameter that he or she wants optimistic locking, the DBMS will implicitly set locks for that locking style. If, however, the developer declares pessimistic locking, the DBMS will set the locks differently.

```
BEGIN TRANSACTION

SELECT      PRODUCT.Name, PRODUCT.Quantity
FROM        PRODUCT
WHERE       PRODUCT.Name = 'Pencil'

Set NewQuantity = PRODUCT.Quantity - 5

{process transaction - take exception action if NewQuantity < 0, etc.}

UPDATE      PRODUCT
SET         PRODUCT.Quantity = NewQuantity
WHERE       PRODUCT.Name = 'Pencil'

{continue processing transaction} . . .



IF {transaction has completed normally} THEN

     COMMIT TRANSACTION

ELSE

     ROLLBACK TRANSACTION

END IF

Continue processing other actions not part of this transaction . . .
```

Figure 9-10

Marking Transaction Boundaries

Consistent Transactions

Sometimes, you will see the acronym ACID applied to transactions. An **ACID transaction** is one that is *a*tomic, *c*onsistent, *i*solated, and *d*urable. Atomic and durable are easy to define. As you just learned, an **atomic** transaction is one in which either all of the database actions occur or none of them do. A **durable** transaction is one in which all committed changes are permanent. Once a durable change is committed, the DBMS takes responsibility for ensuring that the change will survive system failures.

The terms **consistent** and **isolated** are not as definitive as the terms atomic and durable. Consider the following SQL UPDATE statement:

```
UPDATE          CUSTOMER

SET             AreaCode = '425'

WHERE           ZipCode = '98050';
```

Suppose that there are 500,000 rows in the CUSTOMER table, and that 500 of them have ZipCode equal to '98050'. It will take some time for the DBMS to find those 500 rows. During that time, other transactions may attempt to update the AreaCode or ZipCode fields of CUSTOMER. If the SQL statement is consistent, such update requests will be disallowed. Hence, the update will apply to the set of rows as they existed at the time the SQL statement started. Such consistency is called **statement-level consistency**.

Now, consider a transaction that contains two SQL UPDATE statements:

```
BEGIN TRANSACTION

    UPDATE      CUSTOMER

    SET         AreaCode = '425'

    WHERE       ZipCode = '98050';

    {other transaction work}
```

```
UPDATE      CUSTOMER
SET         Discount = 0.05
WHERE       AreaCode = '425';
{other transaction work}
COMMIT TRANSACTION
```

In this context, what does *consistent* mean? Statement-level consistency means that each statement independently processes rows consistently, but that changes from other users to these rows might be allowed during the interval between the two SQL statements. **Transaction-level consistency** means that all rows impacted by either of the SQL statements are protected from changes during the entire transaction.

Observe that transaction-level consistency is so strong that, for some implementations of it, a transaction will not see its own changes. In this example, the second SQL statement may not see rows changed by the first SQL statement.

Thus, when you hear the term *consistent*, look further to determine which type of consistency is meant. Be aware as well of the potential trap of transaction-level consistency.

Transaction Isolation Level

The term *isolated* has several different meanings. To understand those meanings, we need first to define several new terms.

A **dirty read** occurs when a transaction reads a row that has been changed but for which the change has not yet been committed to the database. The danger of a dirty read is that the uncommitted change can be rolled back. If so, the transaction that made the dirty read will be processing incorrect data.

Nonrepeatable reads occur when a transaction rereads data it has previously read and finds modifications or deletions caused by a committed transaction. Finally, **phantom reads** occur when a transaction rereads data and finds new rows that were inserted by a committed transaction since the prior read.

The 1992 SQL standard defines four **isolation levels** that specify which of these problems are allowed to occur. Using these levels, the application programmer can declare the type of isolation level he or she wants, and the DBMS will create and manage locks to achieve that level of isolation.

As shown in Figure 9-11, the read uncommitted isolation level allows dirty reads, nonrepeatable reads, and phantom reads to occur. With read-committed isolation, dirty reads are disallowed. The repeatable-read isolation level disallows both dirty reads and nonrepeatable reads. The serializable isolation level will not allow any of these three problems to occur.

Generally, the more restrictive the level, the less the throughput, though much depends on the workload and how the application programs are written. Moreover, not all DBMS products support all of these levels. You will learn how SQL Server, Oracle and MySQL support isolation levels in the next three chapters.

Figure 9-11

Summary of Transaction
Isolation Levels

		Isolation Level			
		Read Uncommitted	**Read Committed**	**Repeatable Read**	**Serializable**
Problem Type	**Dirty Read**	Possible	Not Possible	Not Possible	Not Possible
	Nonrepeatable Read	Possible	Possible	Not Possible	Not Possible
	Phantom Read	Possible	Possible	Possible	Not Possible

Cursor Type

A **cursor** is a pointer into a set of rows. Cursors are usually defined using SQL SELECT statements. For example, the following statement defines a cursor named TransCursor that operates over the set of rows indicated by the following SELECT statement:

```
DECLARE CURSOR TransCursor AS

    SELECT     *

    FROM       TRANS

    WHERE      PurchasePrice > '10000';
```

As explained in Chapter 7, after an application program opens a cursor, it can place the cursor somewhere in the result set. Most commonly, the cursor is placed on the first or last row, but other possibilities exist.

A transaction can open several cursors—either sequentially or simultaneously. Additionally, two or more cursors may be open on the same table; either directly on the table or through an SQL view on that table. Because cursors require considerable memory, having many cursors open at the same time for, say, a thousand concurrent transactions, will consume considerable memory. One way to reduce cursor burden is to define reduced-capability cursors and use them when a full-capability cursor is not needed.

Figure 9-12 lists four cursor types used in the Windows environment (cursor types for other systems are similar). The simplest cursor is forward only. With it, the application can only move forward through the records. Changes made by other cursors in this transaction and by other transactions will be visible only if they occur to rows ahead of the cursor.

The next three types of cursors are called **scrollable cursors**, because the application can scroll forward and backward through the records. A **static cursor** takes a snapshot of a relation and processes that snapshot. Changes made using this cursor are visible; changes from other sources are not visible.

A **keyset cursor** combines some of the features of static cursors with some of the features of dynamic cursors. When the cursor is opened, a primary key value is saved for each row. When the application positions the cursor on a row, the DBMS uses the key value to read the current value of the row. Inserts of new rows by other cursors (in this transaction or in other transactions) are not visible. If the application issues an update on a row that has been deleted by a different cursor, the DBMS creates a new row with the old key value and places the updated values in the new row (assuming that all required fields are present). Unless the isolation level of the transaction is a dirty read, only committed updates and deletions are visible to the cursor.

A **dynamic cursor** is a fully featured cursor. All inserts, updates, deletions, and changes in row order are visible to a dynamic cursor. As with keyset cursors, unless the isolation level of the transaction is a dirty read, only committed changes are visible.

The amount of overhead and processing required to support a cursor is different for each type of cursor. In general, the cost goes up as we move down the cursor types shown in Figure 9-12. To improve DBMS performance, the application developer should create cursors that are just powerful enough to do the job. It is also very important to understand how a particular DBMS implements cursors and whether cursors are located on the server or on the client. In some cases, it might be better to place a dynamic cursor on the client than to have a static cursor on the server. No general rule can be stated because performance depends on the implementation used by the DBMS product and the application requirements.

A word of caution: If you do not specify the isolation level of a transaction or do not specify the type of cursors you open, the DBMS will use a default level and default types. These defaults may be perfect for your application, but they also may be terrible. Thus, even though these issues can be ignored, their consequences cannot be avoided. You must learn the capabilities of your DBMS product.

CursorType	Description	Comments
Forward only	Application can only move forward through the recordset.	Changes made by other cursors in this transaction or in other transactions will be visible only if they occur on rows ahead of the cursor.
Static	Application sees the data as they were at the time the cursor was opened.	Changes made by this cursor are visible. Changes from other sources are not visible. Backward and forward scrolling allowed.
Keyset	When the cursor is opened, a primary key value is saved for each row in the recordset. When the application accesses a row, the key is used to fetch the current values for the row.	Updates from any source are visible. Inserts from sources outside this cursor are not visible (there is no key for them in the keyset). Inserts from this cursor appear at the bottom of the recordset. Deletions from any source are visible. Changes in row order are not visible. If the isolation level is dirty read, then committed updates and deletions are visible; otherwise only committed updates and deletions are visible.
Dynamic	Changes of any type and from any source are visible.	All inserts, updates, deletions, and changes in recordset order are visible. If the isolation level is dirty read, then uncommitted changes are visible. Otherwise, only committed changes are visible.

Figure 9-12

Summary of Cursor Types

Database Security

The goal of database security is to ensure that only authorized users can perform authorized activities at authorized times. This goal is difficult to achieve, and to make any progress at all the database development team must determine the processing rights and responsibilities of all users during the project's requirements specification phase. These security requirements can then be enforced using the security features of the DBMS and additions to those features written into the application programs.

Processing Rights and Responsibilities

Consider, for example, the needs of View Ridge Gallery. The View Ridge database has three types of users: sales personnel, management personnel, and system administrators. View Ridge designed processing rights for each as follows: Sales personnel are allowed to enter new customer and transaction data, to change customer data, and to query any of the data. They are not allowed to enter new artist or work data. They are never allowed to delete data.

Management personnel are allowed all of the permissions of sales personnel, plus they are allowed to enter new artist and work data and to modify transaction data. Even though management personnel have the authority to delete data, they are not given that permission in this application. This restriction is made to prevent the possibility of accidental data loss.

	CUSTOMER	**TRANSACTION**	**WORK**	**ARTIST**
Sales personnel	Insert, change, query	Insert, query	Query	Query
Management personnel	Insert, change, query	Insert, change, query	Insert, change, query	Insert, change, query
System administrator	Grant rights, modify structure	Grant rights, modify structure	Grant rights, modify structure	Grant rights, modify structure

Figure 9-13

Processing Rights at View Ridge Gallery

The system administrator can grant processing rights to other users; and he or she can change the structure of the database elements such as tables, indexes, stored procedures, and the like. The system administrator is not given rights to process the data. Figure 9-13 summarizes these processing rights.

> **BY THE WAY** You may be wondering what good it does to say that the system administrator cannot process the data when that person has the ability to grant processing rights. He or she can just grant the right to change data to him- or herself. Although this is true, the granting of those rights will leave an audit trail in the database log. Clearly, this limitation is not foolproof, but it is better than just allowing the system administrator (or DBA) full access to all rights in the database.

The permissions in this table are not given to particular people, but rather are given to groups of people. Sometimes these groups are termed **roles**, because they describe people acting in a particular capacity. The term **user groups** is also used. Assigning permission to roles (or user groups) is typical, but not required. It would be possible to say, for example, that the user identified as "Benjamin Franklin" has certain processing rights. Note, too, that when roles are used, it is necessary to have a way to allocate users to roles. When "Mary Smith" signs on to the computer, there must be some way to determine which role or roles she has. We will discuss this further in the next section.

In this discussion, we have used the phrase **processing rights and responsibilities**. As this phrase implies, responsibilities go with processing rights. If, for example, the manager modifies transaction data, the manager has the responsibility to ensure that these modifications do not adversely impact the gallery's operation, accounting, and so forth.

Processing responsibilities cannot be enforced by the DBMS or by the database applications. Instead, they are encoded in manual procedures and explained to users during systems training. These are topics for a systems development text, and we will not consider them further here—except to reiterate that *responsibilities* go with *rights*. Such responsibilities must be documented and enforced.

According to Figure 9-1, the DBA has the task of managing processing rights and responsibilities. As this implies, these rights and responsibilities will change over time. As the database is used and as changes are made to the applications and to the structure of the DBMS, the need for new or different rights and responsibilities will arise. The DBA is a focal point for the discussion of such changes and for their implementation.

Once processing rights have been defined, they can be implemented at many levels: operating system, network, Web server, DBMS, and application. In the next two sections, we will consider DBMS and application implementation. The other levels are beyond the scope of this text.

DBMS Security

The terminology, features, and functions of DBMS security depend on the DBMS product in use. Basically, all such products provide facilities that limit certain actions on certain objects to certain users. A general model of DBMS security is shown in Figure 9-14.

A USER can be assigned to one or more ROLEs (or USER GROUPs), and a ROLE can have one or more USERs. An OBJECT is an element of a database, such as a table, view, or stored procedure. PERMISSION is an association entity among USER, ROLE, and OBJECT. Hence, the relationships from USER to PERMISSION, ROLE to PERMISSION, and OBJECT to PERMISSION are all 1:N, M-O.

When a user signs on to the database, the DBMS limits the user's actions to the permissions defined for that user and to the permissions for roles to which that user has been assigned. Determining whether someone actually is who they claim to be is a difficult task, in general. All commercial DBMS products use some version of user name and password verification, even though such security is readily circumvented if users are careless with their identities.

Users can enter their name and password, or, in some applications, the name and password is entered on the user's behalf. For example, the Windows user name and password can be passed directly to the DBMS. In other cases, an application program provides the name and password. Internet applications usually define a group such as "Unknown Public" and assign anonymous users to that group when they sign on. In this way, companies, such as Dell, need not enter every potential customer into their security system by name and password.

SQL Server, Oracle, and MySQL security systems are variations of the model in Figure 9-14. You will learn about them in Chapters 10, 10A, and 10B, respectively.

DBMS Security Guidelines

Guidelines for improving security in database systems are listed in Figure 9-15. First, the DBMS must always be run behind a firewall. However, the DBA should plan security with the assumption that the firewall has been breached. The DBMS, the database, and all applications should be secure even if the firewall fails.

DBMS vendors, including IBM, Oracle, Microsoft, and Sun Microsystems are constantly adding product features to improve security and reduce vulnerability. Consequently, organizations using DBMS products should continually check the vendors' Web sites for service packs and fixes; any service packs or fixes that involve security features, functions, and processing should be installed as soon as possible.

The installation of new service packs and fixes is not quite as simple as described here. The installation of a service pack or fix can break some applications, particularly some licensed software that requires specific service packs and fixes to be installed (or not installed). It may be necessary to delay installation of DBMS service packs until vendors of licensed software have upgraded their products to work with the new versions. Sometimes just the possibility that a licensed application *might* fail after a DBMS service pack or fix is applied is sufficient reason to delay the fix. But, the DBMS is still vulnerable during this period. Pick your regret!

Figure  **9-14**

A Model of DBMS Security

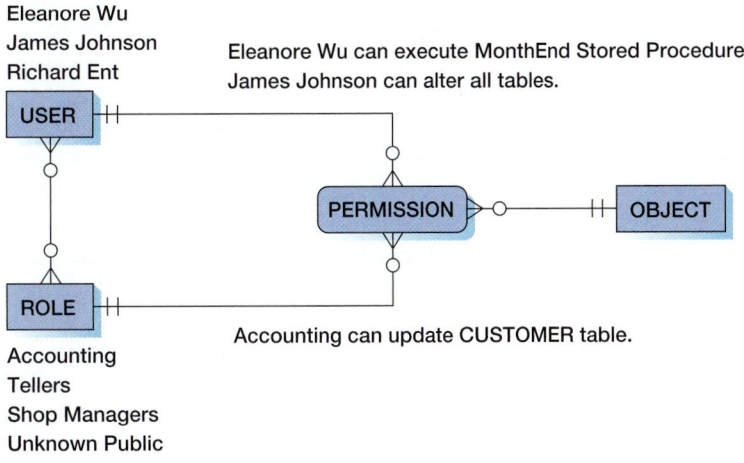

> - Run DBMS behind a firewall, but plan as though the firewall has been breached
>
> - Apply the latest operating system and DBMS service packs and fixes
>
> - Use the least functionality possible
>   - Support the fewest network protocols possible
>   - Delete unnecessary or unused system stored procedures
>   - Disable default logins and guest users, if possible
>   - Unless required, never allow users to log on to the DBMS interactively
>
> - Protect the computer that runs the DBMS
>   - No user allowed to work at the computer that runs the DBMS
>   - DBMS computer physically secured behind locked doors
>   - Visits to the room containing the DBMS computer should be recorded in a log
>
> - Manage accounts and passwords
>   - Use a low privilege user account for the DBMS service
>   - Protect database accounts with strong passwords
>   - Monitor failed login attempts
>   - Frequently check group and role memberships
>   - Audit accounts with null passwords
>   - Assign accounts the lowest privileges possible
>   - Limit DBA account privileges
>
> - Planning
>   - Develop a security plan for preventing and detecting security problems
>   - Create procedures for security emergencies and practice them

Figure 9-15

Summary of DBMS
Security Guidelines

Additionally, database features and functions that are not required by the applications should be removed or disabled from the DBMS. For example, if TCP/IP is used to connect to the DBMS, other communications protocols should be removed. This action reduces the pathways by which unauthorized activity can reach the DBMS. Further, all DBMS products are installed with system-stored procedures that provide services such as starting a command file, modifying the system registry, initiating e-mail, and the like. Any of these stored procedures that are not needed should be removed. If all users are known to the DBMS, default logins and guest user accounts should be removed as well. Finally, unless otherwise required, users should never be allowed to log on to the DBMS in interactive mode. They should always access the database via an application.

In addition, the computer(s) that runs the DBMS must be protected. No one other than authorized DBA personnel should be allowed to work at the keyboard of the computer that runs the DBMS. The computer running the DBMS should be physically secured behind locked doors, and access to the facility housing the computer should be controlled. Visits to the DBMS computer room should be recorded in a log.

Accounts and passwords should be assigned carefully and continually managed. The DBMS itself should run on an account that has the lowest possible operating system privileges. In that way, if an intruder were to gain control of the DBMS, the intruder would have limited authority on that local computer or network. Additionally, all accounts within the DBMS should be protected by **strong passwords**. Such passwords have at least 15 characters and contain upper- and lowercase letters; numbers; special characters, such as +, @, #, ***; and unprintable key combinations (certain Alt + key combinations).

The DBA should frequently check the accounts that have been assigned to groups and roles to ensure that all accounts and roles are known, authorized, and have the correct permissions. Further, the DBA should audit accounts with null passwords. The users of such accounts should be required to protect those accounts with strong passwords. Also, as a general rule, accounts should be granted the lowest privileges possible.

As stated, the privileges for the DBA should normally not include the right to process the users' data. If the DBA grants him- or herself that privilege, the unauthorized grant operation will be visible in the database log.

In the spring of 2003, the Slammer worm invaded thousands of sites running SQL Server. Microsoft had previously released a patch to SQL Server that prevented this attack. Sites that had installed the patch had no problems. The moral: Install security patches to your DBMS as promptly as possible. Create a procedure for regularly checking for such patches.

Finally, the DBA should participate in security planning. Procedures both for preventing and detecting security problems should be developed. Furthermore, procedures should be developed for actions to be taken in case of a security breach. Such procedures should be practiced. The importance of security in information systems has increased dramatically in recent years. DBA personnel should regularly search for security information on the Web in general and at the DBMS vendor's Web site.

Application Security

Although DBMS products such as Oracle, SQL Server, and MySQL do provide substantial database security capabilities, those capabilities are generic. If the application requires specific security measures such as "No user can view a row of a table or of a join of a table that has an employee name other than his or her own," the DBMS facilities will not be adequate. In these cases, the security system must be augmented by features in database applications.

For example, as you will learn in Chapter 11, application security in Internet applications is often provided on the Web server. Executing application security on this server means that sensitive security data need not be transmitted over the network.

To understand this better, suppose that an application is written so that when users click a particular button on a browser page, the following query is sent to the Web server and then to the DBMS:

```
SELECT          *
FROM            EMPLOYEE;
```

This statement will, of course, return all EMPLOYEE rows. If the application security policy only permits employees to access their own data, then a Web server could add the following WHERE clause to this query:

```
SELECT          *
FROM            EMPLOYEE
WHERE           EMPLOYEE.Name = '<% = SESSION(("EmployeeName)")%>';
```

An expression like this one will cause the Web server to fill the employee's name into the WHERE clause. For a user signed in under the name 'Benjamin Franklin', the statement that results from this expression is:

```
SELECT          *
FROM            EMPLOYEE
WHERE           EMPLOYEE.Name = 'Benjamin Franklin';
```

Because the name is inserted by a program on the Web server, the browser user does not know that it is occurring, and cannot interfere with it even if he or she did.

Such security processing can be done as shown here on a Web server, but it also can be done within the application programs themselves or written as stored procedures or triggers to be executed by the DBMS at the appropriate times.

This idea can be extended by storing additional data in a security database that is accessed by the Web server or by stored procedures and triggers. That security database could contain, for example, the identities of users paired with additional values of WHERE clauses. For example, suppose that the users in the personnel department can access more than just their own data. The predicates for appropriate WHERE clauses could be stored in the security database, read by the application program, and appended to SQL SELECT statements as necessary.

Many other possibilities exist for extending DBMS security with application processing. In general, however, you should use the DBMS security features first. Only if they are inadequate for the requirements should you add to them with application code. The closer the security enforcement is to the data, the less chance there is for infiltration. Also, using the DBMS security features is faster, cheaper, and probably results in higher-quality results than developing your own.

The SQL Injection Attack

Whenever data from the user are used to modify an SQL statement, an **SQL injection attack** is possible. For example, in the prior section, if the value of EmployeeName used in the SELECT statement is not obtained via a secure means, such as from the operating system rather from a Web form, there is the chance that the user can inject SQL into the statement.

For example, suppose that users are asked to enter their names into a Web form textbox. Suppose that a user enters the value *'Benjamin Franklin' OR TRUE* for his or her name. The SQL statement generated by the application will then be the following:

```
SELECT      *
FROM        EMPLOYEE
WHERE       EMPLOYEE.Name = 'Benjamin Franklin' OR TRUE;
```

Of course, the value TRUE is true for every row, so every row of the EMPLOYEE table will be returned! Thus, any time user input is used to modify an SQL statement, that input must be carefully edited to ensure that only valid input has been received and that no additional SQL syntax has been entered.

Database Backup and Recovery

Computer systems fail. Hardware breaks. Programs have bugs. Human procedures contain errors, and people make mistakes. All of these failures can and do occur in database applications. Because a database is shared by many people and because it often is a key element of an organization's operations, it is important to recover it as soon as possible.

Several problems must be addressed. First, from a business standpoint, business functions must continue. During the failure, customer orders, financial transactions, and packing lists must be completed somehow, even manually. Later, when the database application is operational again, the data from those activities must be entered into the database. Second, computer operations personnel must restore the system to a usable state as quickly as possible and as close as possible to what it was when the system crashed. Third, users must know what to do when the system becomes available again. Some work may need to be reentered, and users must know how far back they need to go.

When failures occur, it is impossible simply to fix the problem and resume processing. Even if no data are lost during a failure (which assumes that all types of memory are nonvolatile—an unrealistic assumption), the timing and scheduling of computer processing are too complex to be accurately re-created. Enormous amounts of overhead data and processing would be required for the operating system to be able to restart processing precisely where it was interrupted. It is simply not possible to roll back the clock and put all of the electrons in the same configuration they were in at the time of the failure. Two other approaches are possible: **recovery via reprocessing** and **recovery via rollback/rollforward**.

Recovery via Reprocessing

Because processing cannot be resumed at a precise point, the next best alternative is to go back to a known point and reprocess the workload from there. The simplest form of this type of recovery is to periodically make a copy of the database (called a **database save**) and to keep a record of all transactions that have been processed since the save. Then, when there is a failure, the operations staff can restore the database from the save and then reprocess all the transactions. Unfortunately, this simple strategy is normally not feasible. First, reprocessing transactions takes the same amount of time as processing them in the first place did. If the computer is heavily scheduled, the system may never catch up.

Second, when transactions are processed concurrently, events are asynchronous. Slight variations in human activity, such as a user reading an e-mail before responding to an application prompt, can change the order of the execution of concurrent transactions. Therefore, whereas Customer A got the last seat on a flight during the original processing, Customer B may get the last seat during reprocessing. For these reasons, reprocessing is normally not a viable form of recovery from failure in concurrent processing systems.

Recovery via Rollback/Rollforward

A second approach is to periodically make a copy of the database (the database save) and to keep a log of the changes made by transactions against the database since the save. Then, when there is a failure, one of two methods can be used. Using the first method, called **rollforward**, the database is restored using the saved data, and all valid transactions since the save are reapplied. (We are not reprocessing the transactions because the application programs are not involved in the rollforward. Instead, the processed changes, as recorded in the log, are reapplied.)

The second method is **rollback**. With this method, we undo changes made by erroneous or partially processed transactions by undoing the changes they have made in the database. Then, the valid transactions that were in process at the time of the failure are restarted.

Both of these methods require that a **log** of the transaction results be kept. This log contains records of the data changes in chronological order. Transactions must be written to the log before they are applied to the database. That way, if the system crashes between the time a transaction is logged and the time it is applied, at worst there is a record of an unapplied transaction. If, however, the transactions were to be applied before they were logged, it would be possible (as well as undesirable) to change the database but have no record of the change. If this happened, an unwary user might reenter an already completed transaction. In the event of a failure, the log is used both to undo and to redo transactions, as shown in Figure 9-16.

To undo a transaction, the log must contain a copy of every database record (or page) before it was changed. Such records are called **before images**. A transaction is undone by applying before images of all of its changes to the database.

To redo a transaction, the log must contain a copy of every database record (or page) after it was changed. These records are called **after images**. A transaction is redone by applying after images of all of its changes to the database. Possible data items in a transaction log are shown in Figure 9-17.

In this example log, each transaction has a unique name for identification purposes. Furthermore, all of the images for a given transaction are linked together with pointers. One pointer points to the previous change made by this transaction (the reverse pointer), and the other points to the next change made by this transaction (the forward pointer). A zero in the pointer field means that this is the end of the list. The DBMS recovery subsystem uses these pointers to locate all of the records for a particular transaction. Figure 9-17 shows an example of the linking of log records.

Other data items in the log are the time of the action; the type of operation (START marks the beginning of a transaction and COMMIT terminates a transaction, releasing all locks that were in place); the object acted on, such as record type and identifier; and, finally, the before images and the after images.

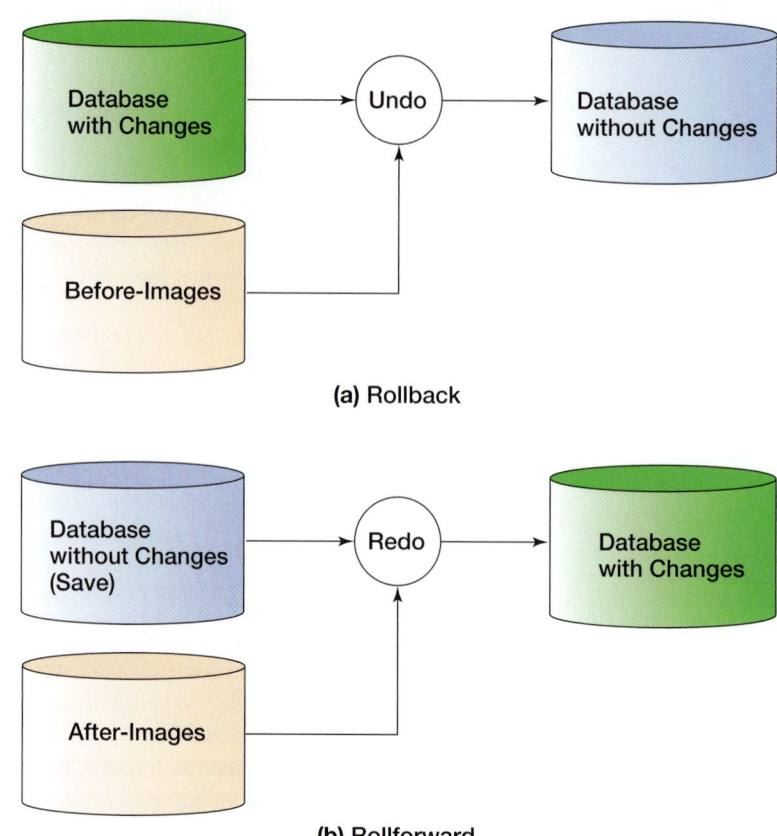

(a) Rollback

(b) Rollforward

Figure 9-16

Undo and Redo Transactions

Relative Record Number	Transaction ID	Reverse Pointer	Forward Pointer	Time	Type of Operation	Object	Before-Image	After-Image
1	OT1	0	2	11:42	START			
2	OT1	1	4	11:43	MODIFY	CUST 100	(old value)	(new value)
3	OT2	0	8	11:46	START			
4	OT1	2	5	11:47	MODIFY	SP AA	(old value)	(new value)
5	OT1	4	7	11:47	INSERT	ORDER 11		(value)
6	CT1	0	9	11:48	START			
7	OT1	5	0	11:49	COMMIT			
8	OT2	3	0	11:50	COMMIT			
9	CT1	6	10	11:51	MODIFY	SP BB	(old value)	(new value)
10	CT1	9	0	11:51	COMMIT			

Figure 9-17

Example Transaction Log

Given a log with before images and after images, the undo and redo actions are straightforward. To undo the transaction in Figure 9-18, the recovery processor simply replaces each changed record with its before image.

When all of the before images have been restored, the transaction is undone. To redo a transaction, the recovery processor starts with the version of the database at the time the transaction started and applies all of the after images. As stated, this action assumes that an earlier version of the database is available from a database save.

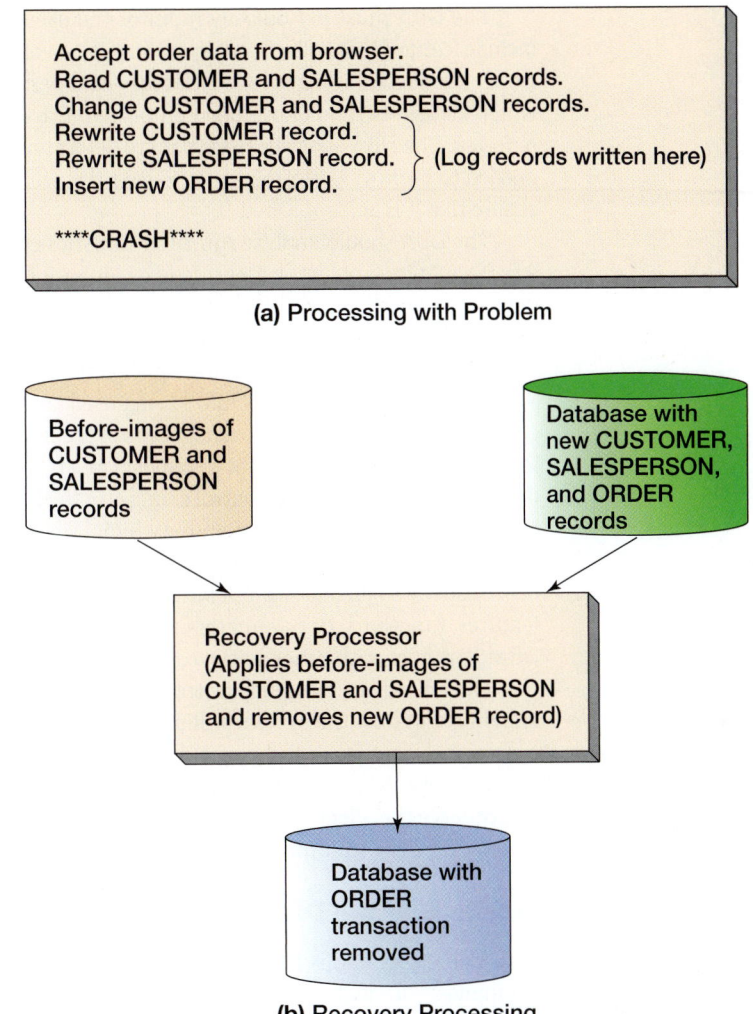

(a) Processing with Problem

(b) Recovery Processing

Figure 9-18

Recovery Example

Restoring a database to its most recent save and reapplying all transactions may require considerable processing. To reduce the delay, DBMS products sometimes use checkpoints. A **checkpoint** is a point of synchronization between the database and the transaction log. To perform a checkpoint, the DBMS refuses new requests, finishes processing outstanding requests, and writes its buffers to disk. The DBMS then waits until the operating system notifies it that all outstanding write requests to the database and to the log have been successfully completed. At this point, the log and the database are synchronized. A checkpoint record is then written to the log. Later, the database can be recovered from the checkpoint and only after images for transactions that started after the checkpoint need be applied.

Checkpoints are inexpensive operations, and it is feasible to take three or four (or more) per hour. In this way, no more than 15 or 20 minutes of processing need be recovered. Most DBMS products perform automatic checkpoints, making human intervention unnecessary.

You will see specific examples of backup and recovery techniques for SQL Server, Oracle, and MySQL in the next three chapters. For now, you only need to understand the basic ideas and to realize that it is the responsibility of the DBA to ensure that adequate backup and recovery plans have been developed and that database saves and logs are generated as required.

Managing the DBMS

In addition to managing data activity and the database structure, the DBA must manage the DBMS itself. The DBA should compile and analyze statistics concerning the system's performance and identify potential problem areas. Keep in mind that the database is serving many user groups. The DBA needs to investigate all complaints about the system's response time, accuracy, ease of use, and so forth. If changes are needed, the DBA must plan and implement them.

The DBA must periodically monitor the users' activity on the database. DBMS products include features that collect and report statistics. For example, some of these reports may indicate which users have been active, which files—and perhaps which data items—have been used, and which access methods have been employed. Error rates and types also can be captured and reported. The DBA analyzes these data to determine whether a change to the database design is needed to improve performance or to ease the users' tasks. If change is necessary, the DBA will ensure that it is accomplished.

The DBA should analyze run-time statistics on database activity and performance. When a performance problem is identified (by either a report or a user's complaint), the DBA must determine whether a modification of the database structure or system is appropriate. Examples of possible structural modifications are establishing new keys, purging data, deleting keys, and establishing new relationships among objects.

When the vendor of the DBMS being used announces new product features, the DBA must consider them in light of the overall needs of the user community. If the DBA decides to incorporate the new DBMS features, the developers must be notified and trained in their use. Accordingly, the DBA must manage and control changes in the DBMS as well as in the database structure.

Other changes in the system for which the DBA is responsible vary widely, depending on the DBMS product as well as on other software and hardware in use. For example, changes in other software (such as the operating system or the Web server) may mean that some DBMS features, functions, or parameters must be changed. The DBA must therefore also tune the DBMS product with other software in use.

The DBMS options (such as transaction isolation levels) are initially chosen when little is known about how the system will perform in the particular user environment. Consequently, operational experience and performance analysis over a period of time may reveal that changes are necessary. Even if the performance seems acceptable, the DBA may want to alter the options and observe the effect on performance. This process is referred to as *tuning*, or *optimizing*, the system. Figure 9-19 summarizes the DBA's responsibilities for managing the DBMS product.

Maintaining the Data Repository

Consider a large and active Internet database application, such as those used by e-commerce companies—for instance, an application that is used by a company that sells clothing over the Internet. Such a system may involve data from several different databases, dozens of different Web pages, and hundreds, or even thousands, of users.

Suppose that the company using this application decides to expand its product line to include the sale of sporting goods. Senior management of this company might ask the DBA to develop an estimate of the time and other resources required to modify the database application to support this new product line.

To respond to this request, the DBA needs accurate metadata about the database, about the database applications and application components, about the users and their rights and privileges, and about other system elements. The database does carry some of this metadata in system tables, but this metadata is inadequate to answer the questions posed by senior management. The DBA needs additional metadata about COM and ActiveX objects, script procedures and functions, Active Server Pages (ASPs), style sheets, document type definitions, and the like. Furthermore, although

Figure 9-19

Summary of the DBA's Responsibilities for Managing the DBMS

- Generate database application performance reports
- Investigate user performance complaints
- Assess need for changes in database structure or application design
- Modify database structure
- Evaluate and implement new DBMS features
- Tune the DBMS

DBMS security mechanisms document users, groups, and privileges, they do so in a highly structured, and often inconvenient, form.

For all of these reasons, many organizations develop and maintain **data repositories**, which are collections of metadata about databases, database applications, Web pages, users, and other application components. The repository may be virtual in that it is composed of metadata from many different sources: the DBMS, version-control software, code libraries, Web page generation and editing tools, and so forth. Or, the data repository may be an integrated product from a CASE tool vendor or from a company such as Microsoft or Oracle.

Either way, the time for the DBA to think about constructing such a facility is long before senior management asks questions. In fact, the repository should be constructed as the system is developed and should be considered an important part of the system deliverables. If such a facility is not constructed, the DBA will always be playing catch-up—trying to maintain the existing applications, adapting them to new needs, and somehow gathering together the metadata to form a repository.

The best repositories are **active repositories**—they are part of the systems development process in that metadata is created automatically as the system components are created. Less desirable, but still effective, are **passive repositories**, which are filled only when someone takes the time to generate the needed metadata and place it in the repository.

The Internet has created enormous opportunities for businesses to expand their customer bases and increase their sales and profitability. The databases and database applications that support these companies are an essential element of that success. Unfortunately, the growth of some organizations will be stymied by their inability to grow their applications or adapt them to changing needs. Often, building a new system is easier than adapting an existing one. Building a new system that integrates with an old one while it replaces that old one can be very difficult.

 ummary

Multiuser databases pose difficult problems for the organizations that create and use them, and most organizations have created an office of database administration to ensure that such problems are solved. In this text, the term *database administrator* refers to the person or office that is concerned with a single database. The term *data administrator* is used to describe a management function that is concerned with the organization's data policy and security. Major functions of the database administrator are listed in Figure 9-1.

The database administrator (DBA) participates in the initial development of database structures and in providing configuration control when requests for changes arise. Keeping accurate documentation of the structure and changes to it is an important DBA function.

The goal of concurrency control is to ensure that one user's work does not inappropriately influence another user's work. No single concurrency control technique is ideal for all circumstances. Trade-offs need to be made between the level of protection and throughput. A transaction, or logical unit of work (LUW), is a series of actions taken against the database that occurs as an atomic unit; either all of them occur or none of them do. The activity of concurrent transactions is interleaved on the database server. In some cases, updates can be lost if concurrent transactions are not controlled. Another concurrency problem concerns inconsistent reads.

To avoid concurrency problems, database elements are locked. Implicit locks are placed by the DBMS; explicit locks are issued by the application program. The size of the locked resource is called lock granularity. An exclusive lock prohibits other users from reading the locked resource; a shared lock allows other users to read the locked resource, but they cannot update it. Two transactions that run concurrently and generate results that are consistent with the results that would have occurred if they had run separately are referred to as serializable transactions. Two-phased locking, in which locks are acquired in a growing phase and released in a shrinking phase, is one scheme for serializability. A special case of two-phase locking is to acquire locks throughout the transaction, but not to free any lock until the transaction is finished.

Deadlock, or the deadly embrace, occurs when two transactions are each waiting on a resource that the other transaction holds. Deadlock can be prevented by requiring transactions to acquire all locks at the same time. Once deadlock occurs, the only way to cure it is to abort one of the transactions (and back out of partially completed work). Optimistic locking assumes that no transaction conflict will occur and deals with the consequences if it does. Pessimistic locking assumes that conflict will occur and so prevents it ahead of time with locks. In general, optimistic locking is preferred for the Internet and for many intranet applications.

Most application programs do not explicitly declare locks. Instead, they mark transaction boundaries with BEGIN, COMMIT, and ROLLBACK transaction statements and declare the concurrent behavior they want. The DBMS then places locks for the application that will result in the desired behavior.

An ACID transaction is one that is atomic, consistent, isolated, and durable. *Durable* means that database changes are permanent. *Consistency* can mean either statement-level or transaction-level consistency. With transaction-level consistency, a transaction may not see its own changes. The 1992 SQL standard defines four transaction isolation levels: read uncommitted, read committed, repeatable read, and serializable. The characteristics of each are summarized in Figure 9-11.

A cursor is a pointer into a set of records. Four cursor types are prevalent: forward only, static, keyset, and dynamic. Developers should select isolation levels and cursor types that are appropriate for their application workload and for the DBMS product in use.

The goal of database security is to ensure that only authorized users can perform authorized activities at authorized times. To develop effective database security, the processing rights and responsibilities of all users must be determined.

DBMS products provide security facilities. Most involve the declaration of users, groups, objects to be protected, and permissions or privileges on those objects. Almost all DBMS products use some form of user name and password security. Security guidelines are listed in Figure 9-15. DBMS security can be augmented by application security.

In the event of system failure, the database must be restored to a usable state as soon as possible. Transactions in process at the time of the failure must be reapplied or restarted. Although in some cases recovery can be done by reprocessing, the use of logs and rollback and rollforward is almost always preferred. Checkpoints can be taken to reduce the amount of work that needs to be done after a failure.

In addition to these tasks, the DBA manages the DBMS product itself, measuring database application performance and assessing the need for changes in database structure or DBMS performance tuning. The DBA also ensures that new DBMS features are evaluated and used as appropriate. Finally, the DBA is responsible for maintaining the data repository.

 **ey Terms**

ACID transaction	lock
active repository	lock granularity
after image	log
atomic	logical unit of work (LUW)
before image	lost update problem
checkpoint	nonrepeatable reads
concurrent transaction	optimistic locking
concurrent update problem	passive repository
consistent	pessimistic locking
cursor	phantom reads
data administration	processing rights and responsibilities
data repository	recovery via reprocessing
database administration	recovery via rollback/rollforward
database administrator	resource locking
database save	role
DBA	rollback
deadlock	rollforward
deadly embrace	scrollable cursor
dirty read	serializable
durable	shared lock
dynamic cursor	shrinking phase
exclusive lock	SQL injection attack
explicit lock	statement-level consistency
growing phase	static cursor
implicit lock	strong password
inconsistent read problem	transaction
isolated	transaction-level consistency
isolation levels	two-phased locking
keyset cursor	user group

ⓡeview Questions

9.1   Briefly describe five difficult problems for organizations that create and use multiuser databases.

9.2   Explain the difference between a database administrator and a data administrator.

9.3   List seven important DBA tasks.

9.4   Summarize the DBA's responsibilities for managing database structure.

9.5   What is configuration control? Why is it necessary?

9.6   Explain the meaning of the word *inappropriately* in the phrase "one user's work does not inappropriately influence another user's work."

9.7   Explain the trade-off that exists in concurrency control.

9.8   Define an atomic transaction and explain why atomicity is important.

9.9   Explain the difference between concurrent transactions and simultaneous transactions. How many CPUs are required for simultaneous transactions?

9.10   Give an example, other than the one in this text, of the lost update problem.

9.11   Explain the difference between an explicit and an implicit lock.

9.12   What is lock granularity?

9.13   Explain the difference between an exclusive lock and a shared lock.

9.14   Explain two-phased locking.

9.15   How does releasing all locks at the end of the transaction relate to two-phase locking?

9.16   In general, how should the boundaries of a transaction be defined?

9.17   What is deadlock? How can it be avoided? How can it be resolved once it occurs?

9.18   Explain the difference between optimistic and pessimistic locking.

9.19   Explain the benefits of marking transaction boundaries, declaring lock characteristics, and letting the DBMS place locks.

9.20   Explain the use of BEGIN, COMMIT, and ROLLBACK TRANSACTION statements.

9.21   Explain the meaning of the expression ACID transaction.

9.22   Describe statement-level consistency.

9.23   Describe transaction-level consistency. What disadvantage can exist with it?

9.24   What is the purpose of transaction isolation levels?

9.25   Explain the read uncommitted isolation level. Give an example of its use.

9.26   Explain the read committed isolation level. Give an example of its use.

9.27   Explain the repeatable read isolation level. Give an example of its use.

9.28   Explain the serializable isolation level. Give an example of its use.

9.29   Explain the term *cursor*.

9.30   Explain why a transaction may have many cursors. Also, how is it possible that a transaction may have more than one cursor on a given table?

9.31   What is the advantage of using different types of cursors?

9.32   Explain forward-only cursors. Give an example of their use.

9.33   Explain static cursors. Give an example of their use.

9.34   Explain keyset cursors. Give an example of their use.

9.35   Explain dynamic cursors. Give an example of their use.

9.36   What happens if you do not declare the transaction isolation level and the cursor type to the DBMS? Is this good or bad?

9.37   Explain the necessity of defining processing rights and responsibilities. How are such responsibilities enforced?

9.38   Explain the relationships among USER, ROLE, PERMISSION, and OBJECT for a generic database security system.

9.39   Should the DBA assume a firewall when planning security?

9.40   What should be done with unused DBMS features and functions?

9.41   Explain how to protect the computer that runs the DBMS.

9.42   With regard to security, what actions should the DBA take on user accounts and passwords?

9.43   List two elements of a database security plan.

9.44   Describe the advantages and disadvantages of DBMS-provided and application-provided security.

9.45   What is an SQL injection attack and how can it be prevented?

9.46   Explain how a database could be recovered via reprocessing. Why is this generally not feasible?

9.47   Define *rollback* and *rollforward*.

9.48   Why is it important to write to the log before changing the database values?

9.49   Describe the rollback process. Under what conditions should it be used?

9.50   Describe the rollforward process. Under what conditions should it be used?

9.51   What is the advantage of taking frequent checkpoints of a database?

9.52   Summarize the DBA's responsibilities for managing the DBMS.

9.53   What is a data repository? A passive data repository? An active data repository?

9.54   Explain why a data repository is important. What is likely to happen if one is not available?

Project Questions

9.55   Visit *www.oracle.com* and search for "Oracle Security Guidelines." Read articles at three of the links that you find and summarize them. How does the information you find compare with that in Figure 9-15?

9.56   Visit *www.msdn.microsoft.com* and search for "SQL Server Security Guidelines." Read articles at three of the links that you find and summarize them. How does the information you find compare with that in Figure 9-15?

9.57   Visit *www.mysql.com* and search for "MySQL Security Guidelines." Read articles at three of the links that you find and summarize them. How does the information you find compare with that in Figure 9-15?

9.58   Use Google *(www.google.com)* or another search engine and search the Web for "Database Security Guidelines." Read articles at three of the links that you find and summarize them. How does the information you find compare with that in Figure 9-15?

9.59   Answer the following questions for the View Ridge Gallery database discussed in Chapter 7 with the tables shown in Figure 7-15.

A.   Suppose that you are developing a stored procedure to record an artist who has never been in the gallery before, a work for that artist, and a row in the TRANS table to record the date acquired and the acquisition price. How will you declare the boundaries of the transaction? What transaction isolation level will you use?

B.   Suppose that you are writing a stored procedure to change values in the CUSTOMER table. What transaction isolation level will you use?

C.   Suppose that you are writing a stored procedure to record a customer's purchase. Assume that the customer's data are new. How will you declare the boundaries of the transaction? What isolation level will you use?

D.   Suppose that you are writing a stored procedure to check the validity of the intersection table. Specifically, for each customer, your procedure should read the customer's transaction and determine the artist of that work. Given the artist, your procedure should then check to ensure that an interest has been declared for that artist in the intersection table. If there is no such intersection row, your procedure should create one. How will you set the boundaries of your transaction? What isolation level will you use? What cursor types (if any) will you use?

Marcia's Dry Cleaning

Assume that Marcia has hired you as a database consultant to develop an operational database having the following four tables (the same tables described at the end of Chapter 7):

CUSTOMER (*CustomerID*, FirstName, LastName, Phone, Email)

ORDER (*InvoiceNumber*, *CustomerID*, DateIn, DateOut, Subtotal, Tax, TotalAmount)

ORDER_ITEM (*InvoiceNumber*, ItemNumber, *Service*, Quantity, UnitPrice, ExtendedPrice)

SERVICE (Service, Description, UnitPrice)

A.   Assume that Marcia's has the following personnel: two owners, a shift manager, a part-time seamstress, and two salesclerks. Prepare a two-to-three-page memo that addresses the following points:

   1. The need for database administration.
   2. Your recommendation as to who should serve as database administrator. Assume that Marcia's is not sufficiently large to need or afford a full-time database administrator.
   3. Using Figure 9-1 as a guide, describe the nature of database administration activities at Marcia's. As an aggressive consultant, keep in mind that you can recommend yourself for performing some of the DBA functions.

B.   For the employees described in part A, define users, groups, and permissions on data in these four tables. Use the security scheme shown in Figure 9-13 as an example. Create a table like that in Figure 9-12. Don't forget to include yourself.

C.   Suppose that you are writing a stored procedure to create new records in SERVICE for new services that Marcia's will perform. Suppose that you know that while your procedure is running another stored procedure that records new or modifies existing customer orders and order line items can also be running. Additionally, suppose that a third stored procedure that records new customer data also can be running.

1. Give an example of a dirty read, a nonrepeatable read, and a phantom read among this group of stored procedures.
2. What concurrency control measures are appropriate for the stored procedure that you are creating?
3. What concurrency control measures are appropriate for the two other stored procedures?

Assume that Morgan has hired you as a database consultant to develop an operational database having the same tables described at the end of Chapter 7 (Note that STORE uses the surrogate key StoreID):

STORE (<u>StoreID</u>, StoreName, City, Country, Phone, Fax, Email, Contact)

PURCHASE (<u>PurchaseID</u>, *StoreName*, Date, Description, Category, PriceUSD)

SHIPMENT (<u>ShipmentID</u>, ShipDate, ShipperName, ShipperInvoiceNumber, Origin, Destination)

SHIPMENT_ITEM (<u>*ShipmentID*</u>, <u>*PurchaseID*</u>, InsuredValue)

SHIPPER (<u>ShipperName</u>, Phone, Fax, Email, Contact)

A. Assume that Morgan personnel are the owner (Morgan), an office administrator, one full-time salesperson, and two part-time salespeople. Morgan and the office administrator want to process data in all tables. Additionally, the full-time salesperson can enter purchase and shipment data. The part-time employees can only read shipment data; they are not allowed to see InsuredValue, however. Prepare a three-to-five-page memo for the owner that addresses the following issues:

1. The need for database administration at Morgan.
2. Your recommendation as to who should serve as database administrator. Assume that Morgan is not sufficiently large that it needs or can afford a full-time database administrator.
3. Using Figure 9-1 as a guide, describe the nature of database administration activities at Morgan. As an aggressive consultant, keep in mind that you can recommend yourself for performing some of the DBA functions.

B. For the employees described in part A, define users, groups, and permissions on data in these five tables. Use the security scheme shown in Figure 9-13 as an example. Create a table like that in Figure 9-12. Don't forget to include yourself.

C. Suppose that you are writing a stored procedure to record new purchases. Suppose that you know that while your procedure is running, another stored procedure that records shipment data can be running, and a third stored procedure that updates shipper data can also be running.

1. Give an example of a dirty read, a nonrepeatable read, and a phantom read among this group of stored procedures.
2. What concurrency control measures are appropriate for the stored procedure that you are creating?
3. What concurrency control measures are appropriate for the two other stored procedures?

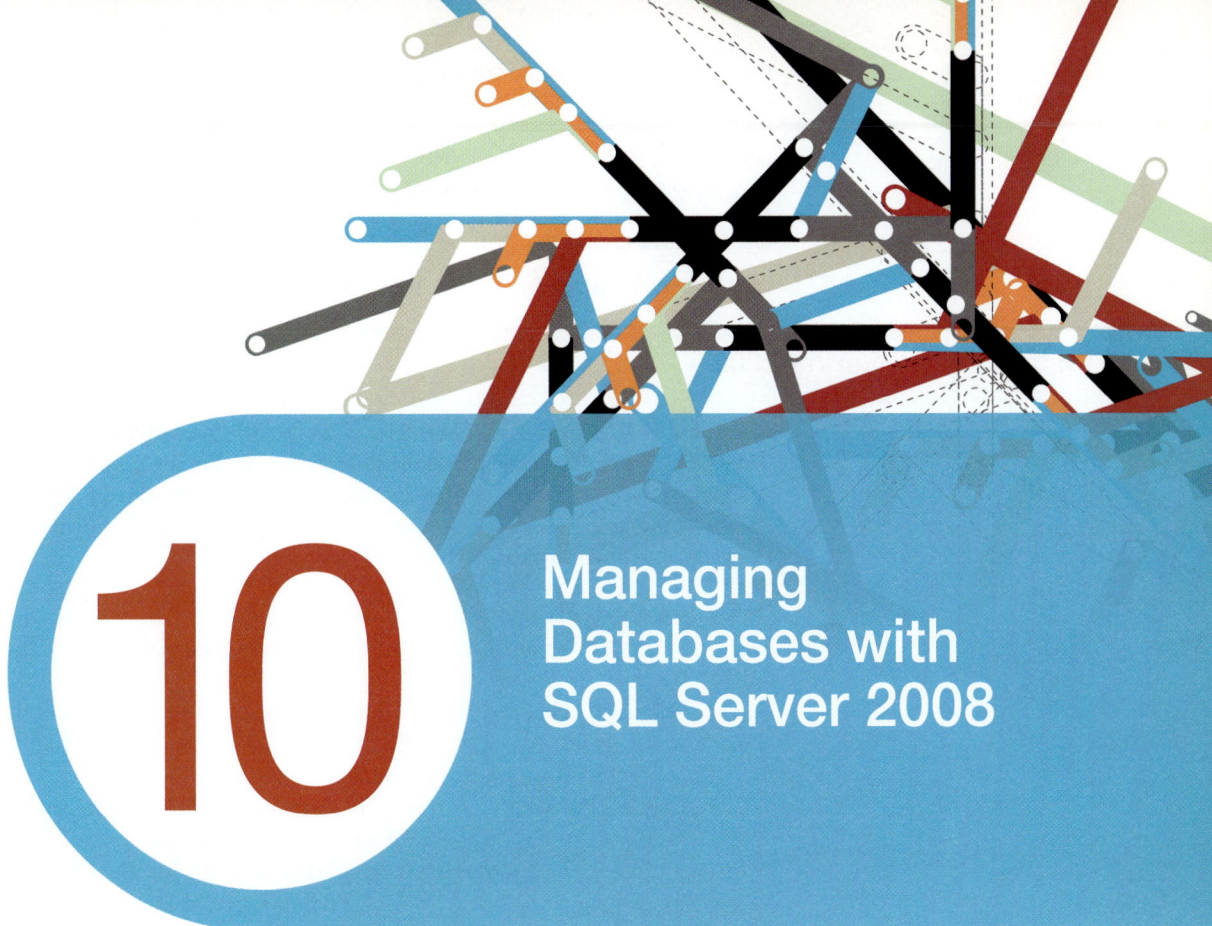

10

Managing Databases with SQL Server 2008

Chapter Objectives

- To be able to install SQL Server and create a database.
- To be able to use SQL Server's graphical utilities.
- To be able to submit both SQL DDL and DML via the Microsoft SQL Server Management Studio.
- To understand the purpose and role of stored procedures and know how to create simple stored procedures.

- To understand the purpose and role of triggers and know how to create simple stored procedures.
- To understand how SQL Server implements concurrency control.
- To understand the fundamental features of SQL Server backup and recovery facilities.

This chapter describes the basic features and functions of Microsoft SQL Server 2008. The discussion uses the View Ridge Gallery database from Chapter 7, and it parallels the discussion of the database administration tasks in Chapter 9. The presentation is similar in scope and orientation to that of Oracle Database 11g in Chapter 10A and MySQL 5.1 in Chapter 10B.

SQL Server 2008 is a large and complicated product. In this one chapter, we will only be able to scratch the surface. Your goal should be to learn sufficient basics so that you can continue learning on your own or in other classes.

The topics and techniques discussed here also apply to the earlier SQL Server 2005, although the exact functions of the SQL Server 2005 Management Studio vary a bit from the SQL Server 2008 version. The material you learn in this chapter will be applicable to that older version.

Installing SQL Server 2008

Microsoft SQL Server is an enterprise-class DBMS that has been around for many years. In 2005, SQL Server 2005 was released, followed by SQL Server 2008 in 2008. SQL Server 2008 is available in several versions, which can be reviewed at the Microsoft SQL Server 2008 Web site (*www.microsoft.com/sqlserver/2008/en/us/editions.aspx*). For our purposes, there are three editions you need to be aware of:

- **Enterprise Edition.** This is the most powerful and feature-laden version. It handles as many CPUs as the computer's operating system will support and includes data warehouse capabilities.
- **Standard Edition.** This is the basic commercial version. It does not have the complete feature set of the Enterprise Edition. It handles up to four CPUs and does not include data warehouse capabilities.
- **Express Edition.** This free, feature-limited version is available for download. It supports one CPU, 1 GByte of memory, and a maximum database size of 4 GBytes. Despite its limitations, it is a great learning tool when the Express Advanced version, which includes the SQL Server 2008 Management Studio and a basic reporting services package, is used (and did we mention that it's free?).

The SQL Server Express Edition was introduced with SQL Server 2005, and SQL Server 2008 includes the **SQL Server 2008 Express** version. The SQL Server Express Editions seem to be designed to compete with Sun Microsystems MySQL (see Chapter 10B). MySQL, while not having as many features as SQL Server, is an open-source database that has had the advantage of being available for free via download over the Internet. It has become widely used and very popular as a DBMS, supporting Web sites running the Apache Web server.

SQL Server 2008 Express Advanced is the version of SQL Server 2008 Express that contains an advanced feature package. The advanced features package includes Microsoft's GUI SQL Server management tool and support for SQL Server Reporting Services. Both of these features are well worth having (otherwise you will need to download the management tool separately), so download and install the version with the advanced features package.

For SQL Server 2008 Express, you can start at the SQL Server 2008 homepage at *www.microsoft.com/sqlserver/2008/en/us/default.aspx*. To install SQL Server 2008 Express Edition with Advanced Services, you need to download four programs:

1. **Microsoft .NET Framework version 3.5 Service Pack 1**. Before installing any of the SQL Server products, you must install the Microsoft .NET Framework 3.5 SP1.
2. **Microsoft Windows Installer 4.5**. Before installing any of the SQL Server products, you must install Windows Installer 4.5.
3. **Microsoft Windows PowerShell 1.0**. Before installing any of the SQL Server products, you must install Windows PowerShell 1.0.
4. **Microsoft SQL Server 2008 Express Advanced**. Note that **Microsoft SQL Server 2008 Management Studio** is included in the download of Microsoft SQL Server 2008 Express Advanced. If you choose to download the basic version of SQL Server 2008 Express, you must download and install this program separately. Microsoft SQL Server 2008 Management Studio is the graphical management utility for the SQL Server 2008 Express edition. While SQL Server 2008 was originally a command–line-oriented program, SQL Server 2008 Management Studio makes it much easier to work with SQL Server.

SQL Server 2008 Express is one of several Express Editions available from Microsoft. For more information on the Microsoft Express series of products, a good place to start is *www.microsoft.com/express*.

Although SQL Server 2008 Express Advanced can handle most of the topics in this book, it cannot handle advanced business intelligence (BI) systems topics, which are discussed in Chapter 13. For that you will need the Enterprise Edition. An 180-day trial version can be downloaded from Microsoft (*www.microsoft.com/sqlserver/2008/en/us/trial-software.aspx*).

You may also want to download and install the following software from the SQL Server 2008 Feature Pack depending on whether SQL Server 2008 is installed on your workstation or a separate server (start at *www.microsoft.com/sqlserver/2008/en/us/trial-software.aspx* and click the **Download it now** button to ensure that you are taken to the most current set of software):

- Microsoft Core XML Services (MSXML) 6.0
- Microsoft SQL Server 2008 Command Line Utilities
- Microsoft SQL Server 2008 Native Client
- Microsoft SQL Server Driver for PHP (Listed as Microsoft SQL Server 2005 Driver for PHP
- Microsoft SQL Server 2008 Data Mining Add-ins for Microsoft Office 2007

Be aware that SQL Server 2008 is an enterprise-class DBMS and, as such, is much more complex than Microsoft Access. Further, it does not include application development tools, such as form and report generators.

Regardless of which version of SQL Server 2008 you are going to use, you should install it now. You should then check for the latest service packs and patches to make sure your installation is as secure as possible.

The Microsoft SQL Server 2008 Management Studio

After you install SQL Server 2008, you can start working with SQL Server by opening the Microsoft SQL Server Management Studio. In this book, we are running SQL Server 2008 Enterprise Edition in Microsoft Server 2008. To open the Microsoft SQL Server Management Studio in Windows Server 2008 or in the Windows Vista operating system, select **Start | All Programs | Microsoft SQL Server 2008 | SQL Server Management Studio Express**.[1] The Microsoft SQL Server Management Studio **Connect to Server dialog box** appears, as shown in Figure 10-1.

Figure  **10-1**

The Connect to Server Dialog Box

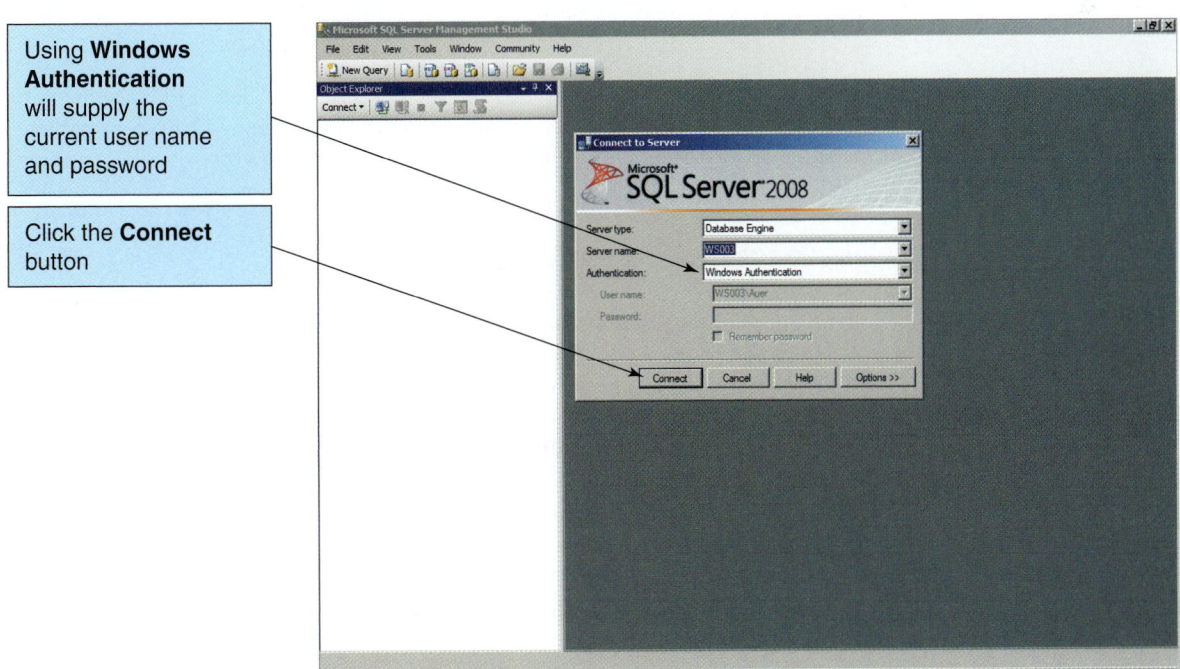

Using **Windows Authentication** will supply the current user name and password

Click the **Connect** button

---

[1] If you're using the Windows XP operating system, select **Start | All Programs | Microsoft SQL Server 2008 | SQL Server Management Studio**.

The **Object Explorer** shows SQL Server 2008 objects and the folders that are used to contain and organize those objects

The **System Databases** folder contains database objects for the databases automatically created by SQL Server 2008

The **Cape-Codd Database** object

The **ReportServer** and **ReportServerTempDB** database objects hold databases used by SQL Server 2008 Reporting Services

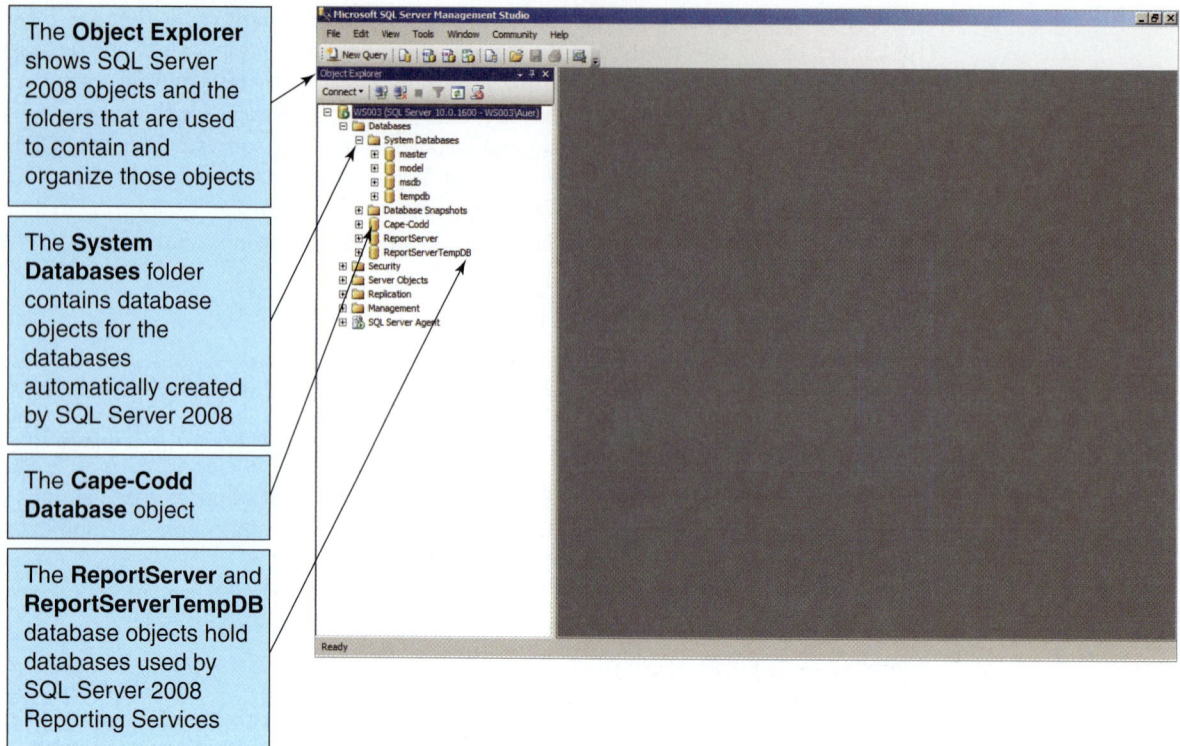

Figure 10-2

The Microsoft SQL Server Management Studio Window

After you have done this, find the folder icon labeled Databases in the Object Explorer, as shown in Figure 10-2. Click the plus sign to open it, and then open the System Database folder the same way. As shown in Figure 10-2, objects representing the databases managed by the SQL Server 2008 DBMS are displayed in these folders. For example, you can see the Cape Codd database that we used in our discussion of SQL queries in Chapter 2. We normally keep the System Databases folder closed because we usually do not work with these databases.

Creating an SQL Server 2008 Database

Now that the SQL Server 2008 is installed and the Microsoft SQL Server Management Studio is open, we can create a new database. We will create a database named **VRG** for the View Ridge Gallery database we designed in Chapter 6, and for which we wrote the SQL statements in Chapter 7.

Creating an SQL Server 2008 Database

1. Right-click the **Databases** folder in the Object Explorer to display a shortcut menu, as shown in Figure 10-3.
2. Click the **New Database** command to display the New Database dialog box, as shown in Figure 10-4.
3. Type the database name **VRG** in the Database Name text box, and then click the **OK** button. The database is created and the VRG database object is displayed in the Object Explorer, as shown in Figure 10-5. Click the plus (+) button to display the VRG folders, also shown in Figure 10-5.
4. Right-click the **VRG** database object to display a shortcut menu, and then click the **Properties** command. The Database Properties – VRG dialog box is displayed, as shown in Figure 10-5.
5. In the **Database Properties – VRG** dialog box, click the **Files** page object, as shown in Figure 10-5. The database files associated with the VRG database are displayed.
6. Click the **OK** button in the Database Properties – VRG dialog box to close the dialog box.

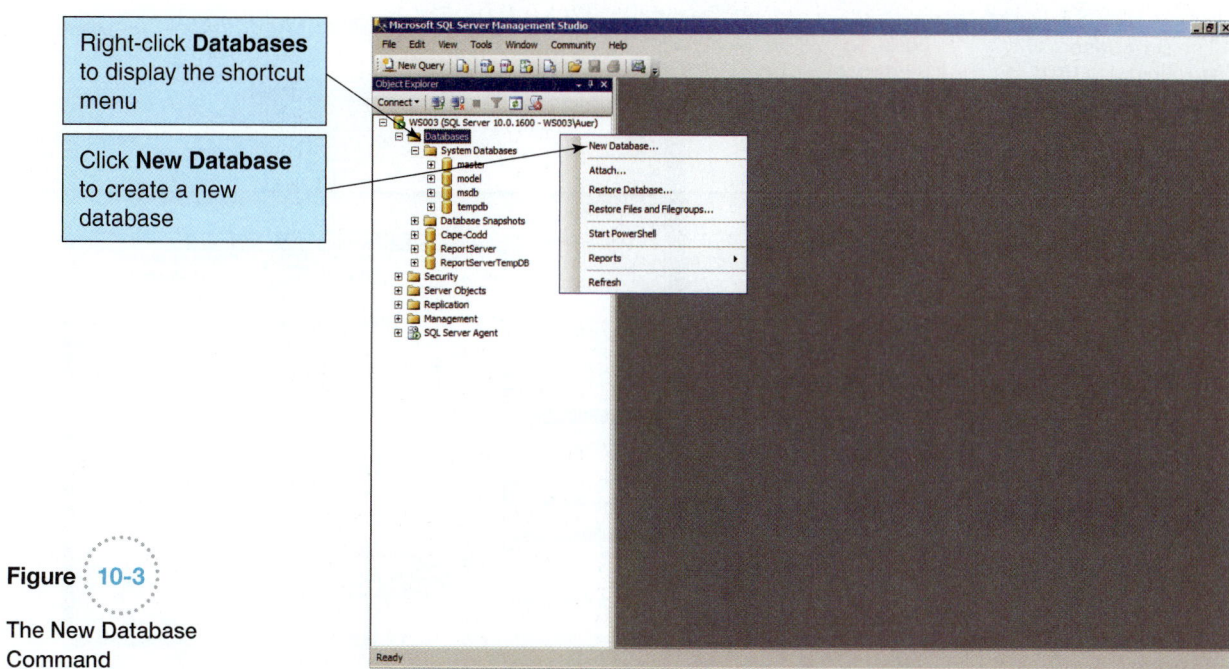

Figure  10-3

The New Database Command

If you look at the database files listed for the VRG database in the New Database dialog box in Figure 10-4, and displayed again on the Files page of the Database Properties – VRG dialog box, as shown in Figure 10-5, you will see that by default SQL Server creates one data file (logical name VRG) and one log file (logical name VRG_log) for each database. You can create multiple files for both data and logs and assign particular tables and logs to particular files and file groups. However, all of this is beyond the scope of our current discussion, however. To learn more about it on your own, use the SQL Server 2008 help system.

Figure 10-4

Naming the New Database

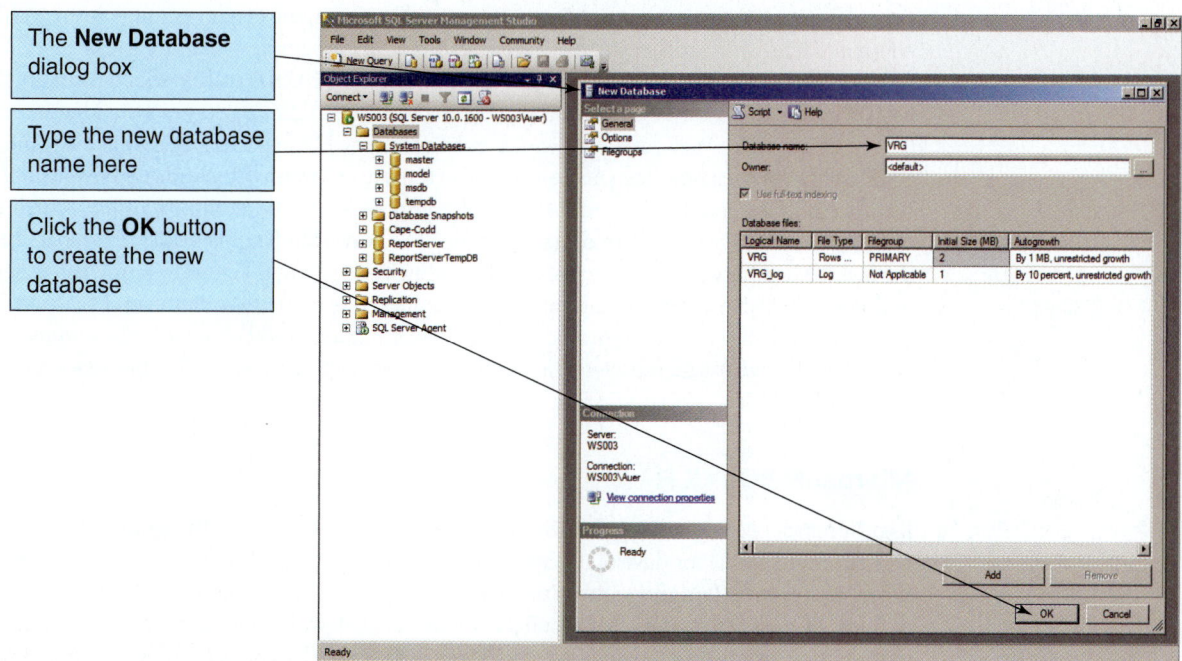

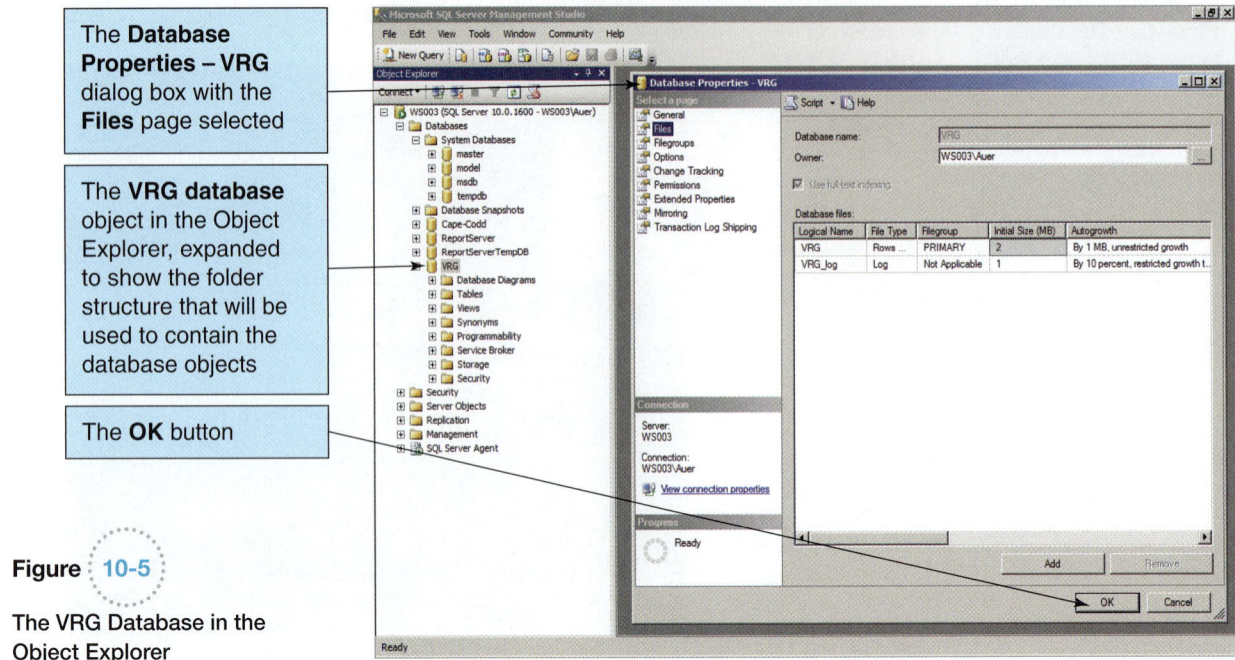

The **Database Properties – VRG** dialog box with the **Files** page selected

The **VRG database** object in the Object Explorer, expanded to show the folder structure that will be used to contain the database objects

The **OK** button

Figure 10-5

The VRG Database in the Object Explorer

SQL Server 2008 Utilities

Now that we have created the VRG database itself, we need to create the table and relationship structure of the database, and then populate the tables with data. What SQL Server 2008 utilities or tools shall we use to do this? It turns out that we have several choices.

SQL CMD and Microsoft PowerShell

In the beginning, there were the command-line utilities. A **command-line utility** is strictly text based. You are presented with a symbolic prompt to show you where to enter your commands. You type in a command (only one at a time) and press the [Enter] key to execute it. The results are displayed as plaintext (with some rudimentary character-based line- and box-drawing capabilities) in response. All major computer operating systems have their version of a command-line utility. For personal computer users using a Microsoft operating system, the classic example is the MS-DOS command line, which still exists in Windows as the CMD program.

For SQL Server, the classic command-line tool is the **SQL CMD utility**, which is still available as part of the Microsoft SQL Server 2008 Command Line Utilities package in the Microsoft SQL Server 2008 Feature Pack discussed earlier in this chapter. However, the functionality of the SQL CMD utility has been now been made available in the newer **Microsoft Windows PowerShell** utility. Microsoft PowerShell is a very powerful command-line and scripting utility, which runs command equivalents called **cmdlets**. By loading the **PowerShell sqlps utility**, the capabilities of the SQL CMD utility are made available in PowerShell, as shown in Figure 10-6. You can easily see that PowerShell carries on the command-line tradition (for more information on Microsoft Windows PowerShell, start at *www.microsoft.com/windowsserver2003/technologies/management/powershell/default.mspx*, and then search the Microsoft Web site for specific information on SQL Server PowerShell).

Microsoft SQL CLR

If you are an applications developer using Microsoft Visual Studio as your **Integrated Development Environment (IDE)** for developing applications that use SQL Server, you will probably be using the **SQL Common Language Runtime (CLR)** technology that is built into SQL Server. SQL CLR enables SQL Server to provide Microsoft .NET CLR support, which allows application components written in programming languages such as Visual Basic .NET (VB.NET) to be stored and run in

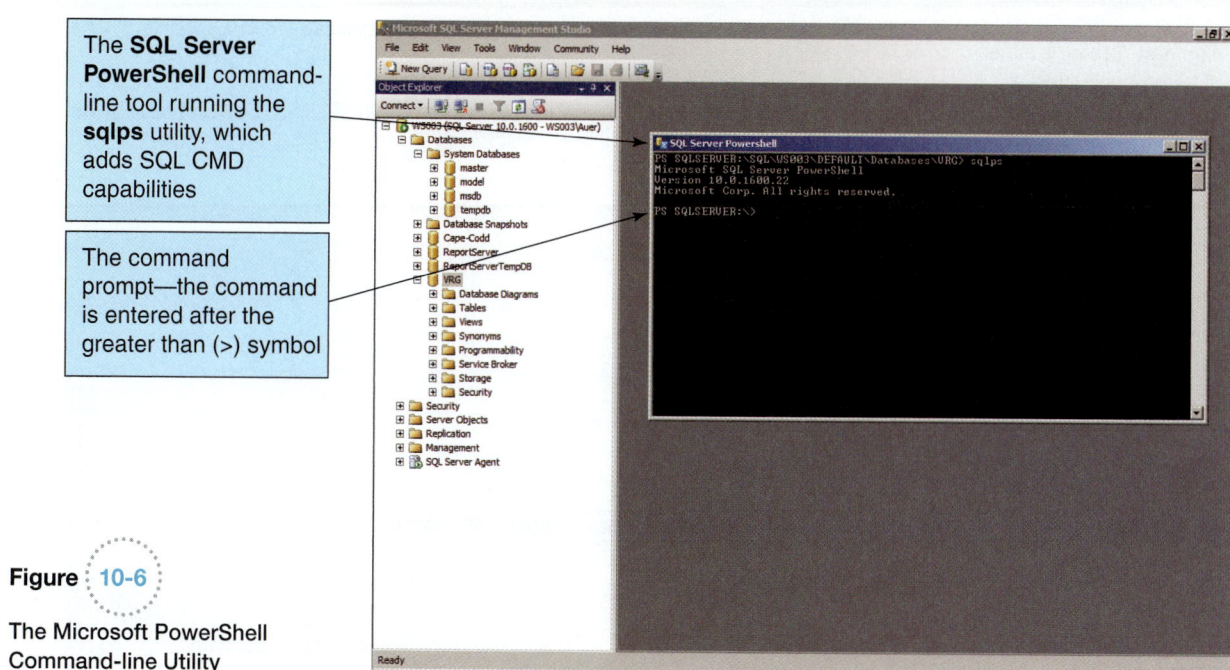

The **SQL Server PowerShell** command-line tool running the **sqlps** utility, which adds SQL CMD capabilities

The command prompt—the command is entered after the greater than (>) symbol

Figure 10-6

The Microsoft PowerShell Command-line Utility

SQL Server. Now database triggers and stored procedures (discussed in Chapter 7 and later in this chapter) can be written in VB.NET or C#.NET instead of standard SQL. SQL CLR is beyond the scope of this book, but you may use it in a class on applications development.

SQL Server 2008 GUI Displays

Although command-line utilities can be powerful, they can also be tedious and ugly. That's why GUI applications such as Windows were created in the first place. And popular personal databases such as Microsoft Access have certainly put GUI features to good use. Therefore, we have to ask "Is there a GUI display for SQL Server 2008?" The answer, of course, is "yes, there is." In fact, we are already using it. The Microsoft SQL Server Management Studio is the GUI display for SQL Server 2008.

Can we use the Microsoft SQL Server Management Studio the same way we use Microsoft Access to build tables using the GUI? Again, the answer is "yes." Figure 10-7 shows the start of a new table currently named Table_1. The column data shown are for the first column (ArtistID) in the VRG database ARTIST table described in Chapter 7. The design interface shown is very similar to Microsoft Access—basic column specifications are entered in a row in the top pane and specific column properties are set in the bottom pane. And, like Microsoft Access, the GUI will actually create an SQL statement and run that statement in the DBMS.

SQL Server 2008 SQL Statements and SQL Scripts

Because we have already argued that you need to know how to write and use SQL statements instead of relying on GUI tools, we come back to simply using SQL as the basis of our work. But we do not want to use a command-line utility, and we are not going to use the GUI tool in GUI mode, so what's left?

The answer is that the Microsoft SQL Server Management Studio provides us with an excellent SQL editing environment. This lets us take advantage of GUI capabilities while still working with text-based SQL statements. We do this by opening an SQL Query window, but using it more generally as an "SQL statement editor" window.

Opening an SQL Server 2008 SQL Statement Editor Window

1. Click the **VRG Database** object in the Object Browser to select it.
2. Click the **New Query** button. A new tabbed SQL Query window is displayed, and the SQL Editor toolbar appears, as shown in Figure 10-8.

The new **Table_1** table is being built using a GUI similar to Microsoft Access

Enter column names, data types, and whether not NULL values are allowed in this row

Enter column properties such as IDENTITY parameters in this window

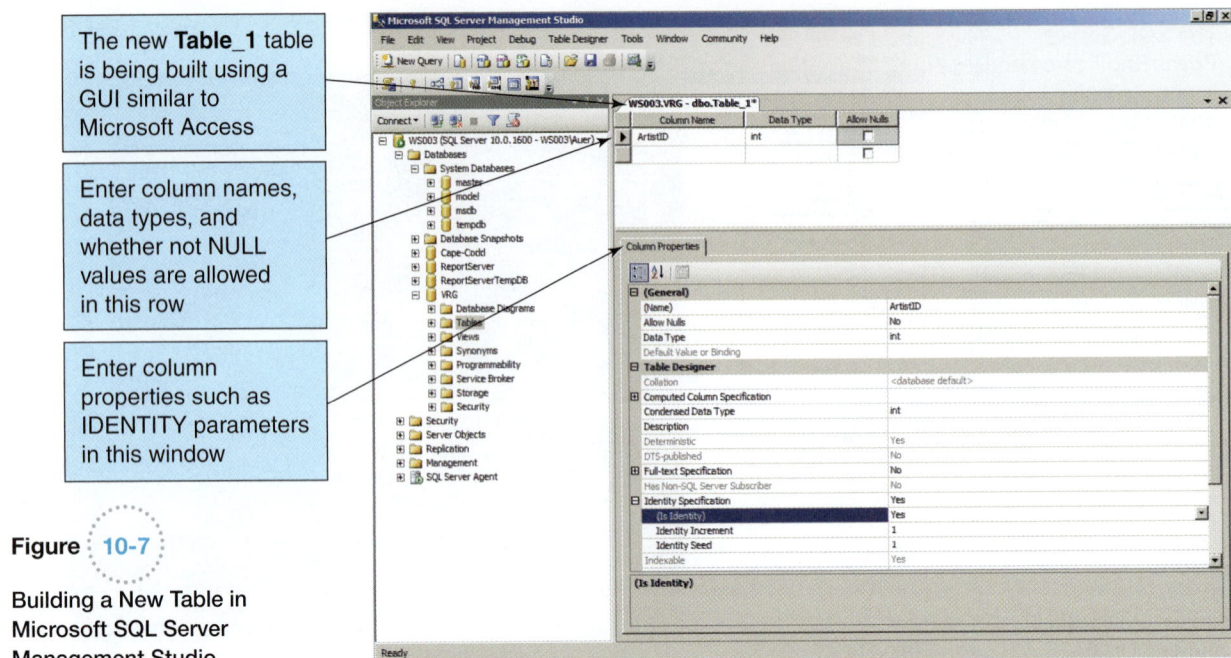

Figure 10-7

Building a New Table in Microsoft SQL Server Management Studio

3. Click the **Intellisense Enabled** button to *disable* Intellisense. Intellisense is an object-search feature that, while useful for experienced developers, can be more confusing than helpful if you do not know how to use it. In this book, we will not use Intellisense, but if you want to learn more about it, you can read about it in SQL Server 2008 Books Online.

If the tabbed document window looks familiar, it is because it is the same window we used for SQL Server 2008 SQL queries in Chapter 2. We are simply using it for a slightly different purpose. This SQL editing environment will be our tool of choice.

One advantage of using this SQL editor is the ability to save and reuse SQL scripts. For SQL Server, **SQL scripts** are plaintext files labeled with the *.sql* file extension. We can save, open, and

Figure 10-8

The Microsoft SQL Server Management Studio SQL Editor

The **New Query** button

The **SQL Editor** toolbar

Available Databases dropdown list—select the database here

The **Execute** button

The **Parse** button

The **Intellisense Enabled** button

The SQL statement tabbed window

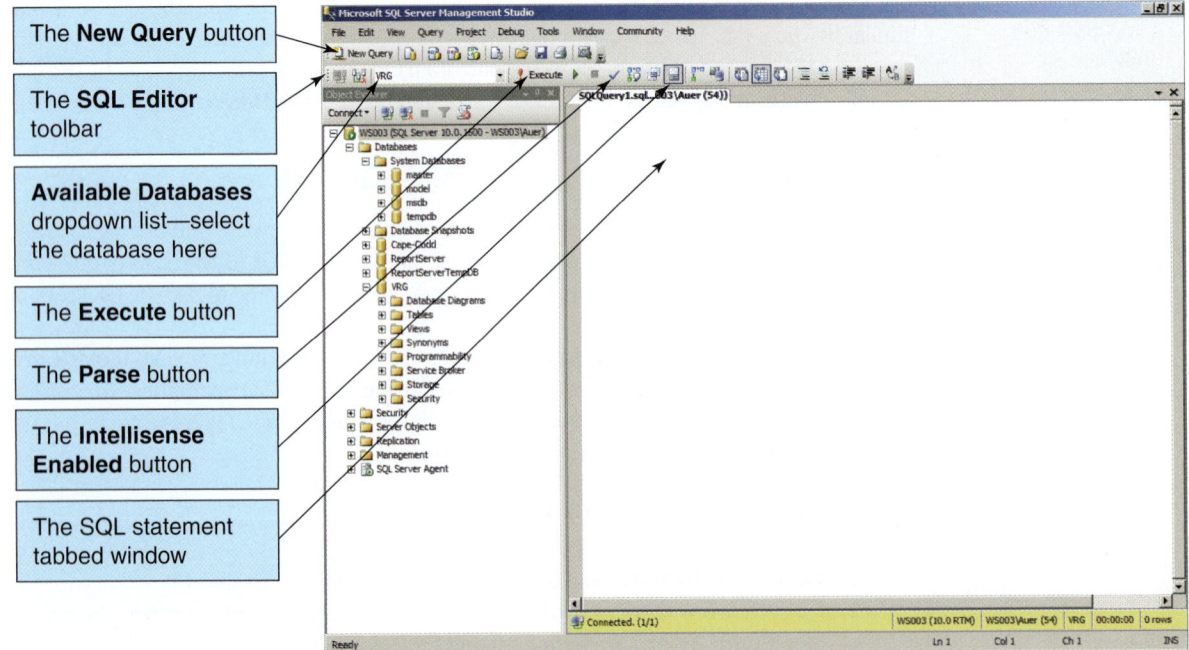

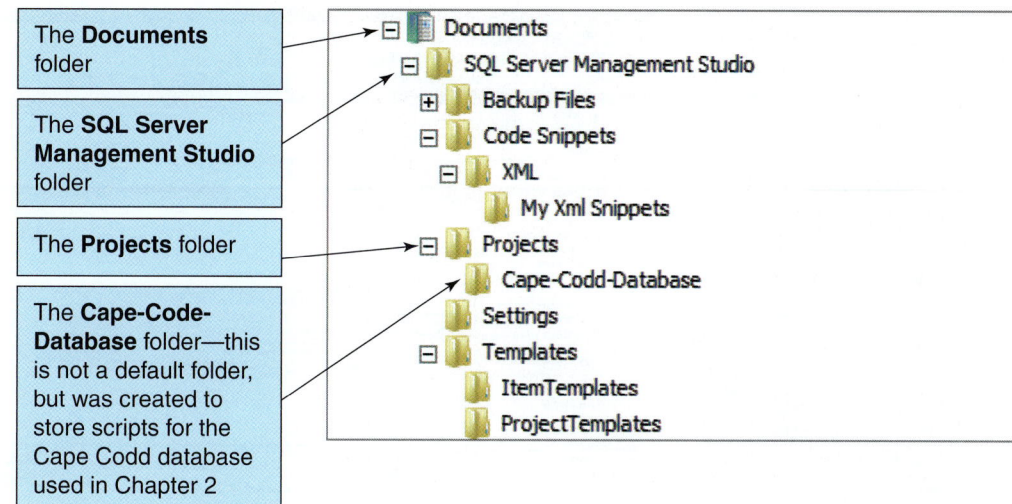

Figure 10-9

The Microsoft SQL
Server Management
Studio Folder Structure

run (and rerun) SQL scripts. As shown in Figure 10-9, when the SQL Server Management Studio is installed, the installation process creates a set of folders in the user's Documents folder. By default, scripts are stored in the Projects folder. However, in order to organize our work we can create subfolders for various database projects. This is illustrated by the Cape-Codd-Database folder that was created to store the scripts (including scripts containing SQL queries) that we used with the Cape Codd Outdoor Sports database in Chapter 2.

An SQL script is composed of one or more SQL statements, which can include SQL script comments. **SQL script comments** are lines of text that do not run when the script is executed, but are used to document the purpose and contents of the script. Each comment line begins with the characters /* and ends with the characters */.

Creating and Saving an SQL Script

Figure 10-10

Entering SQL statements
in the SQL Editor

1. In the open tabbed SQL Query window, type the SQL comments shown in Figure 10-10.
2. Click the **Save** button. The Save File As dialog box is displayed, as shown in Figure 10-11.

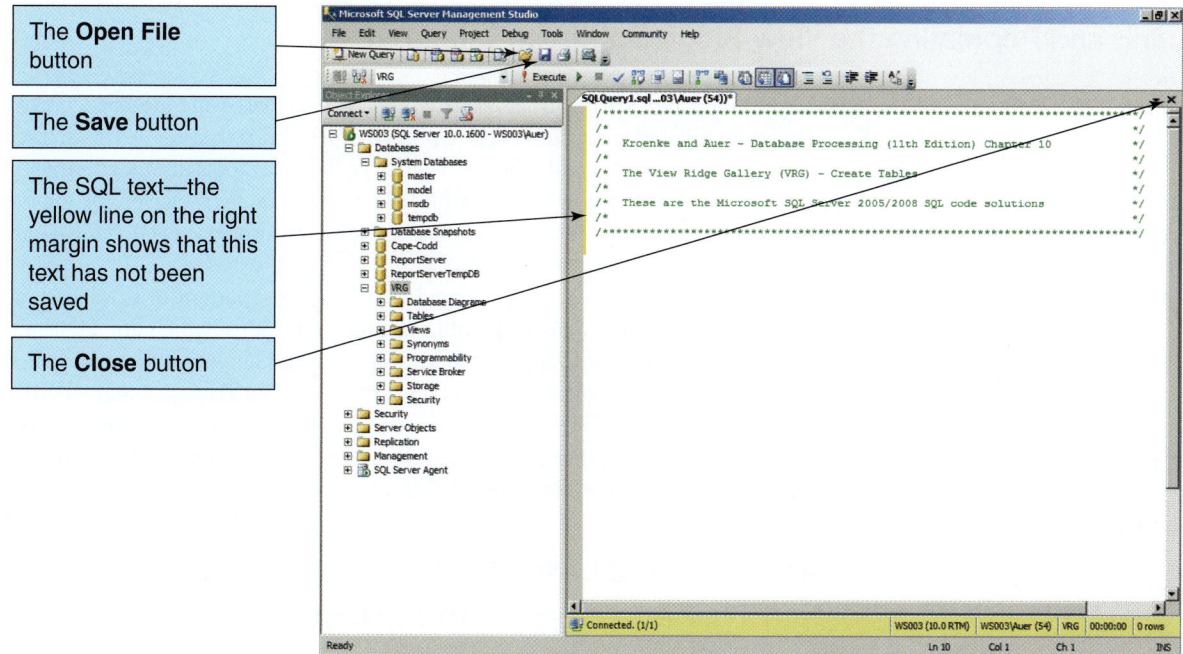

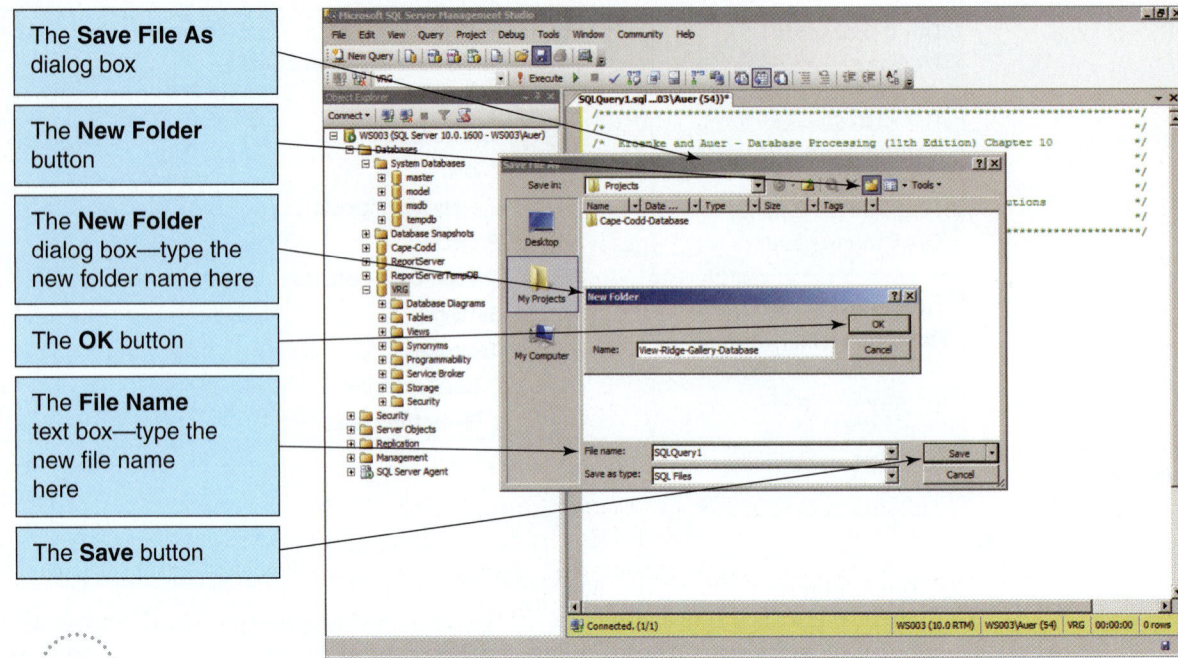

The **Save File As** dialog box

The **New Folder** button

The **New Folder** dialog box—type the new folder name here

The **OK** button

The **File Name** text box—type the new file name here

The **Save** button

Figure 10-11

Saving the SQL Script in a New Folder

3. Click the **New Folder** button in the Save File As dialog box. The New Folder dialog box is displayed, as shown in Figure 10-11.
4. Type the folder name **View-Ridge-Gallery-Database** into the Name text box of the New Folder dialog box.
5. Click the **OK** Button on the New Folder dialog box.
6. Type the file name **VRG-Create-Tables** in the File Name text box of the Save File As dialog box.
7. Click the **OK** Button on the Save File As dialog box. The script is saved, the colored line on the right-hand margin of the text is changed to green, and the tab is renamed with the new file name.
8. Click the document **Close** button shown in Figure 10-10 to close the script window.

Creating and Populating the View Ridge Database Tables

As we have seen, tables and other SQL Server structures can be created and modified in two ways. The first is to write SQL code using either the CREATE or ALTER SQL statements we discussed in Chapter 7. The second is to use the SQL Server 2008 GUI display tools discussed earlier in this chapter. Although either method will work, CREATE statements are preferred for the reasons described in Chapter 7. Some professionals choose to create structures via SQL but then modify them with the GUI tools.

As discussed in Chapter 7, each DBMS product has its own variant or extension of SQL, where the extensions are usually **procedural language** extensions, which are additions that allow SQL to function similarly to a procedural programming language (for example, IF . . . THEN . . . ELSE structures). Microsoft's SQL Server version is called **Transact-SQL (T-SQL)**. We will point out specific Transact-SQL syntax as we encounter it in our discussion. For more on Transact-SQL, see the SQL Server 2008 Books Online article "Transact-SQL Reference" at *http://msdn.microsoft.com/en-us/library/bb510741.aspx*.

Creating the View Ridge Database Table Structure

The SQL Server 2008 version of the SQL CREATE TABLE statements for the View Ridge database in Chapter 7 are shown in Figure 10-12.

Note that we are using the table name TRANS rather than TRANSACTION in Figure 10-12. This was done because TRANSACTION is a **reserved word** in SQL Server 2008.[2] Even if you make TRANSACTION a **delimited identifier** by placing the name in square brackets, as in [TRANSACTION], SQL Server still becomes confused when executing the logic of stored procedures and triggers. Life became much simpler for applications using this database when the table TRANSACTION was renamed to TRANS (which is not a Transact-SQL keyword, although TRAN is). WORK is not currently a Transact-SQL reserved word, but it is an ODBC reserved word (OBDC will be discussed in Chapter 11). Still, SQL Server is less sensitive to it, and therefore we can use it in delimited identifier form, enclosed in square brackets, as [WORK].

SQL Server supports surrogate keys, and the surrogate key columns are created using the **Transact-SQL IDENTITY property** with the primary key of the ARTIST, [WORK], CUSTOMER, and TRANS tables. The IDENTITY property has the syntax IDENTITY (seed, increment), where *seed* is the starting value for the surrogate key and *increment* is the value added to the previous surrogate key value each time a new value is created.

Creating the VRG Table Structure Using SQL Statements

1. In the SQL Server Management Studio, click the **Open File** button shown in Figure 10-10 to open the Open File dialog box.
2. Click the file name **VRG-Create-Tables.sql** to select the file.
3. Click the **Open** button in the Open File dialog box. The script is opened for use in a tabbed document window in the SQL editor.

Figure  **10-12**

The SQL Statements to Create the VRG Table Structure

```
CREATE TABLE ARTIST (
     ArtistID              Int              NOT NULL IDENTITY(1,1),
     LastName              Char(25)         NOT NULL,
     FirstName             Char(25)         NOT NULL,
     Nationality           Char(30)         NULL,
     DateOfBirth           Numeric(4)       NULL,
     DateDeceased          Numeric(4)       NULL,
     CONSTRAINT   ArtistPK              PRIMARY KEY(ArtistID),
     CONSTRAINT   ArtistAK1             UNIQUE(LastName, FirstName),
     CONSTRAINT   NationalityValues     CHECK
                     (Nationality IN ('Canadian', 'English', 'French',
                      'German', 'Mexican', 'Russian', 'Spanish',
                      'United States')),
     CONSTRAINT   BirthValuesCheck      CHECK (DateOfBirth < DateDeceased),
     CONSTRAINT   ValidBirthYear        CHECK
                     (DateOfBirth LIKE '[1-2][0-9][0-9][0-9]'),
     CONSTRAINT   ValidDeathYear        CHECK
                     (DateDeceased LIKE '[1-2][0-9][0-9][0-9]')
     );

CREATE TABLE WORK (
     WorkID                Int              NOT NULL IDENTITY(500,1),
     Title                 Char(35)         NOT NULL,
     Copy                  Char(12)         NOT NULL,
     Medium                Char(35)         NULL,
     [Description]         Varchar(1000)    NULL DEFAULT 'Unknown provenance',
     ArtistID              Int              NOT NULL,
     CONSTRAINT   WorkPK                PRIMARY KEY(WorkID),
     CONSTRAINT   WorkAK1               UNIQUE(Title, Copy),
     CONSTRAINT   ArtistFK              FOREIGN KEY(ArtistID)
                          REFERENCES ARTIST(ArtistID)
                              ON UPDATE NO ACTION
                              ON DELETE NO ACTION
     );
```

---

[2] For a complete list of SQL Server 2008 reserved keywords, OBDC reserved keywords (ODBC is discussed in Chapter 13) and potential future SQL Server keywords, see the SQL Server 2008 Books Online article on *Reserved Keywords (Transact-SQL)* at *http://msdn.microsoft.com/en-us/library/ms189822.aspx*.

```
CREATE TABLE CUSTOMER (
        CustomerID              Int             NOT NULL IDENTITY(1000,1),
        LastName                Char(25)        NOT NULL,
        FirstName               Char(25)        NOT NULL,
        Street                  Char(30)        NULL,
        City                    Char(35)        NULL,
        [State]                 Char(2)         NULL,
        ZipPostalCode           Char(9)         NULL,
        Country                 Char(50)        NULL,
        AreaCode                Char(3)         NULL,
        PhoneNumber             Char(8)         NULL,
        Email                   Varchar(100)    Null,
        CONSTRAINT  CustomerPK              PRIMARY KEY(CustomerID),
        CONSTRAINT  EmailAK1                UNIQUE(Email)
        );

CREATE TABLE TRANS (
        TransactionID           Int             NOT NULL IDENTITY(100,1),
        DateAcquired            Datetime        NOT NULL,
        AcquisitionPrice        Numeric(8,2)    NOT NULL,
        DateSold                Datetime        NULL,
        AskingPrice             Numeric(8,2)    NULL,
        SalesPrice              Numeric(8,2)    NULL,
        CustomerID              Int             NULL,
        WorkID                  Int             NOT NULL,
        CONSTRAINT  TransPK                 PRIMARY KEY(TransactionID),
        CONSTRAINT  TransWorkFK             FOREIGN KEY(WorkID)
                        REFERENCES WORK(WorkID)
                            ON UPDATE NO ACTION
                            ON DELETE NO ACTION,
        CONSTRAINT  TransCustomerFK     FOREIGN KEY(CustomerID)
                        REFERENCES CUSTOMER(CustomerID)
                            ON UPDATE NO ACTION
                            ON DELETE NO ACTION,
        CONSTRAINT  SalesPriceRange  CHECK
                        ((SalesPrice > 0) AND (SalesPrice <=500000)),
        CONSTRAINT  ValidTransDate      CHECK (DateAcquired <= DateSold),
        );

CREATE TABLE CUSTOMER_ARTIST_INT(
        ArtistID                Int             NOT NULL,
        CustomerID              Int             NOT NULL,
        CONSTRAINT  CAIntPK                 PRIMARY KEY(ArtistID, CustomerID),
        CONSTRAINT  CAInt_ArtistFK          FOREIGN KEY(ArtistID)
                        REFERENCES ARTIST(ArtistID)
                            ON UPDATE NO ACTION
                            ON DELETE CASCADE,
        CONSTRAINT  CAInt_CustomerFK    FOREIGN KEY(CustomerID)
                        REFERENCES CUSTOMER(CustomerID)
                            ON UPDATE NO ACTION
                            ON DELETE CASCADE
        );
```

Figure 10-12

(Continued)

4. Click the **Intellisense Enabled** button to disable Intellisense.
5. Type in the SQL statements shown in Figure 10-12. Be sure to save the script often, and save the script a final time after you have finished entering all the SQL statements.
6. Scroll to the top of the script. The completed SQL script to create the VRG table structure appears as shown in Figure 10-13.
7. Make sure the database name **VRG** is shown in the Available Databases drop-down list as shown in Figure 10-13. If it isn't, click the Available Databases drop-down list arrow and select VRG.
8. Click the **Parse** button shown in Figure 10-13. A message window appears below the tabbed document window. If this window contains the message "The command(s)

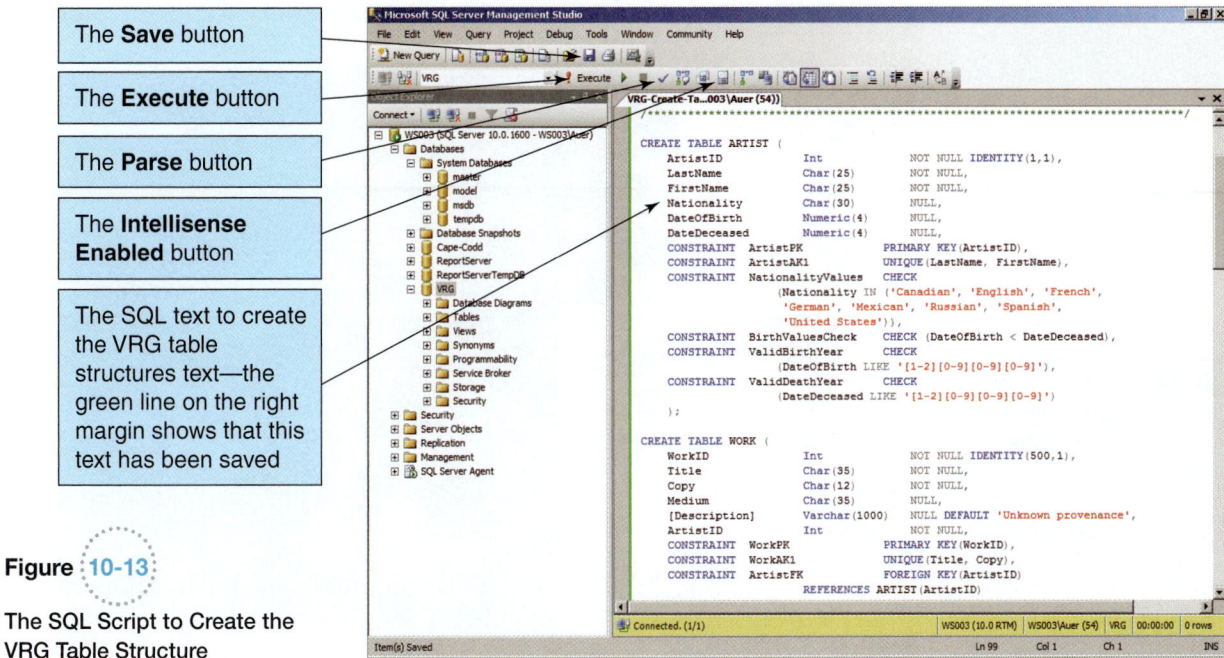

The **Save** button

The **Execute** button

The **Parse** button

The **Intellisense Enabled** button

The SQL text to create the VRG table structures text—the green line on the right margin shows that this text has been saved

Figure 10-13

The SQL Script to Create the VRG Table Structure

completed successfully." there are probably no errors in the script. However, if any error messages are displayed, then you have errors in your SQL statements. Correct any errors. Repeat this step until you see the message "The command(s) completed successfully."

9. Click the **Save** button to save your debugged SQL script.
10. Click the **Execute** button shown in Figure 10-14. The tables are created, and the Results message "The command(s) completed successfully." appears.
11. Expand the VRG Tables folder to see the VRG tables, as shown in Figure 10-14.
12. Click the document window **Close** button to close the SQL script.

Now we have created the VRG table and relationship structure. By the way, in Figure 10-14 *dbo* stands for database owner. That will be you if you installed SQL Server and created this database.

Figure 10-14

The VRG Database Tables

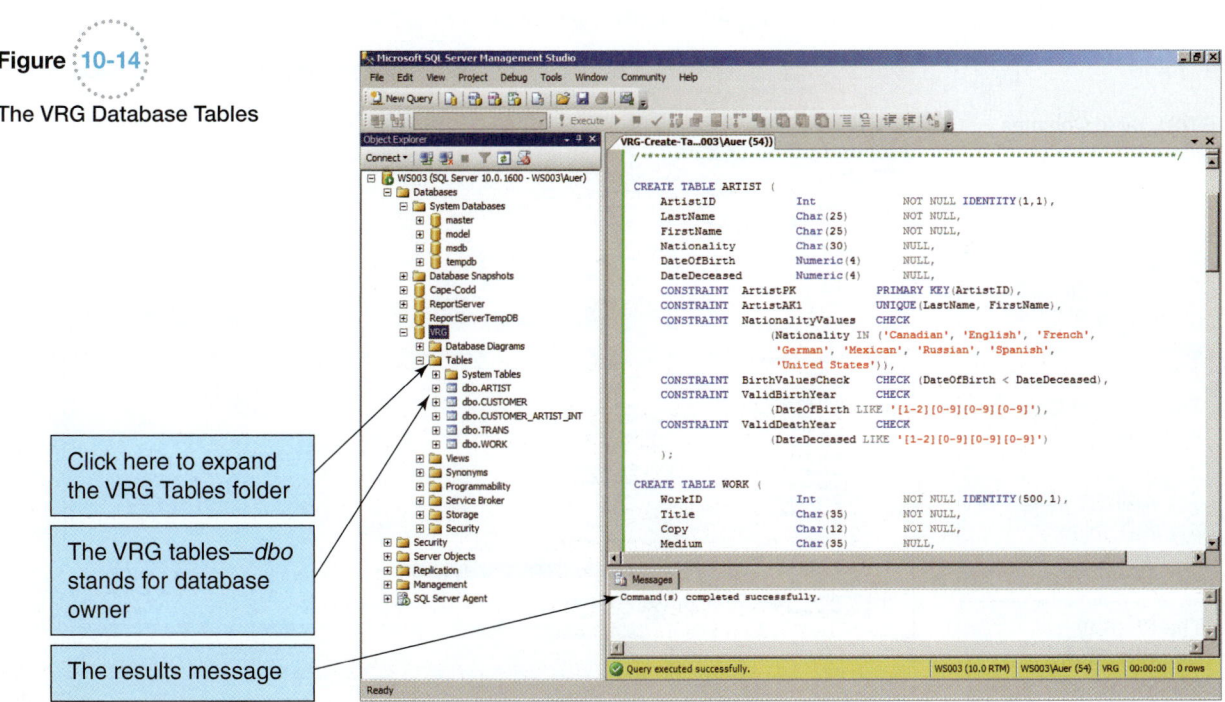

Click here to expand the VRG Tables folder

The VRG tables—*dbo* stands for database owner

The results message

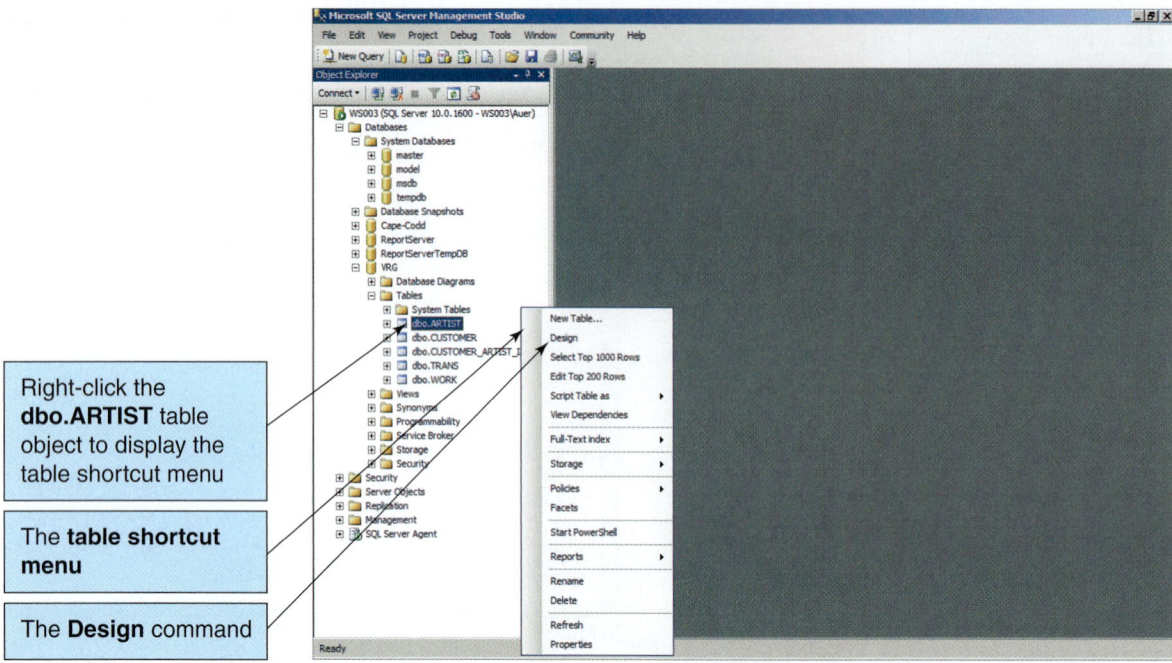

Right-click the **dbo.ARTIST** table object to display the table shortcut menu

The **table shortcut menu**

The **Design** command

Figure 10-15

The Table Shortcut Menu

Reviewing Database Structures in the SQL Server GUI Display

After building the table structure using SQL statements, we can inspect the results using the SQL Server GUI tools. Let's take a look at the ARTIST table, particularly at the properties of the ArtistID primary key.

Viewing the ARTIST Table Structure in the GUI Display

1. In the SQL Server Management Studio Object Browser, right-click the **dbo.ARTIST** table object to open the table shortcut menu, as shown in Figure 10-15.
2. In the table shortcut menu, click the **Design** command. The ARTIST table design is displayed in a tabbed document window, as shown in Figure 10-16, with the Identity Specification properties expanded. Compare this figure to Figure 10-7.
3. Click the document window **Close** button to close the ARTIST table's columns and column properties tabbed window.

Figure 10-16

The ARTIST Table Columns and Column Properties

The **ARTIST** table column name, data types, and NULL status

The **Primary Key symbol**

The ARTIST table **ArtistID** column properties

The **Identity Specification properties**

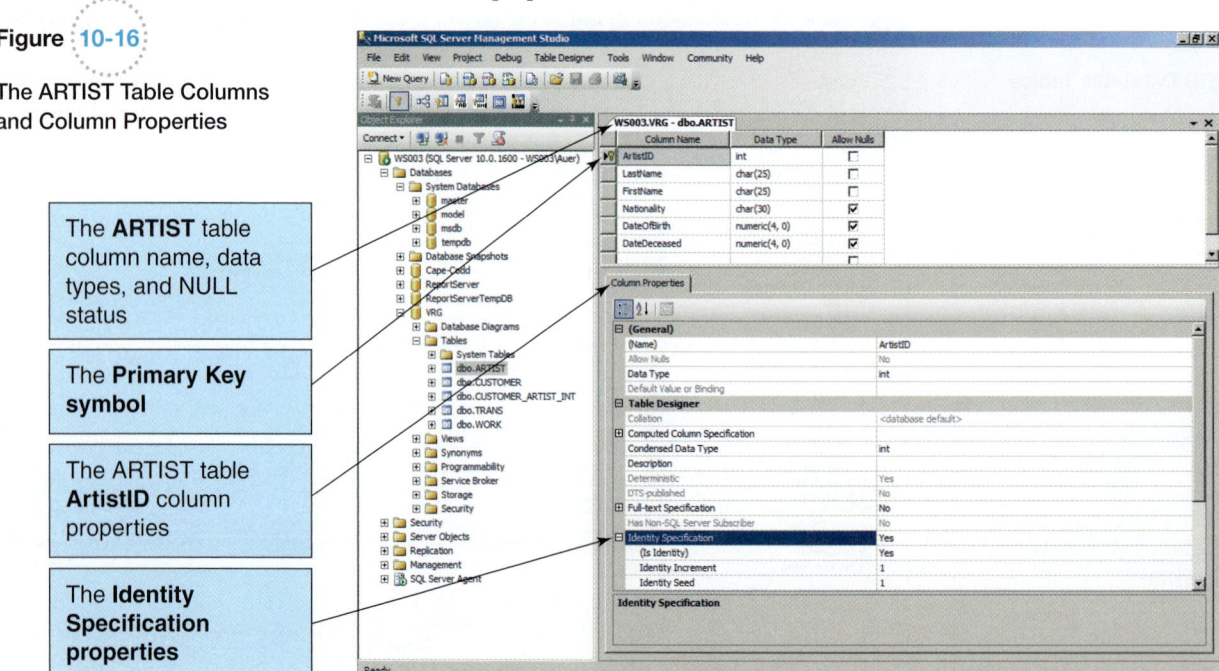

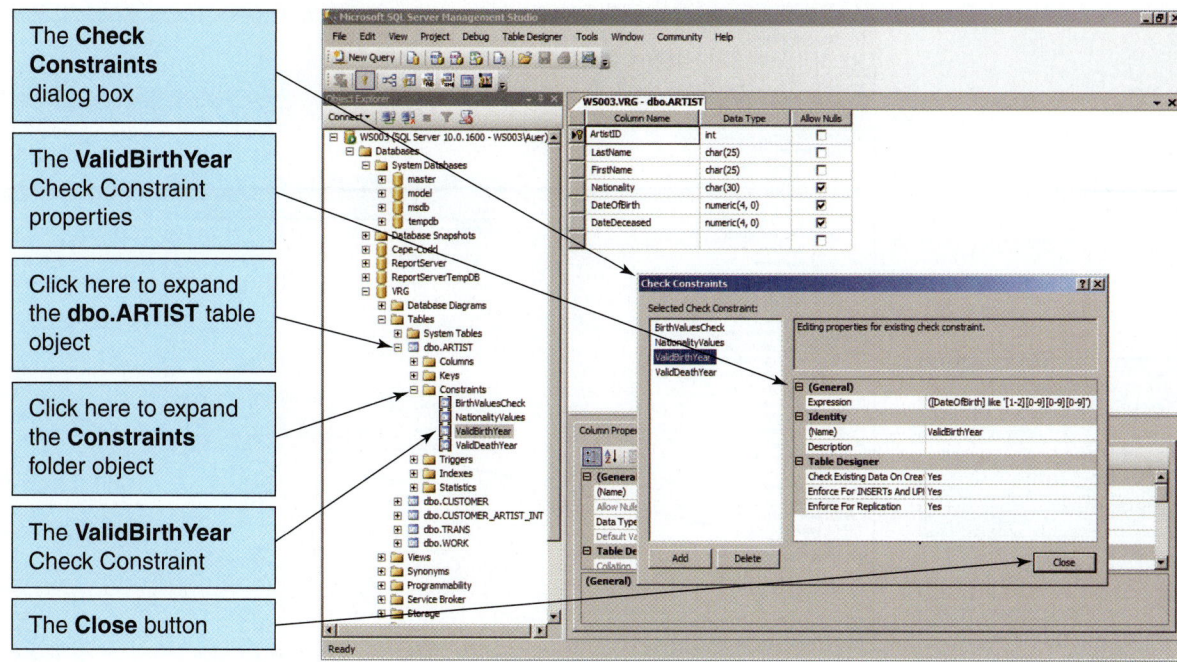

The **Check Constraints** dialog box

The **ValidBirthYear** Check Constraint properties

Click here to expand the **dbo.ARTIST** table object

Click here to expand the **Constraints** folder object

The **ValidBirthYear** Check Constraint

The **Close** button

Figure 10-17

The ARTIST Table Check Constraints

We can also inspect the constraints on the ARTIST table. We'll take a look at the ValidBirthYear constraint we coded into our SQL CREATE TABLE statements.

Viewing the ARTIST Table Constraints in the GUI Display

1. In the SQL Server Management Studio Object Browser, expand the **dbo.ARTIST** table object.
2. Expand the **Constraints** folder. The ARTIST table constraint objects are displayed in the Object Browser.
3. Right-click the **ValidBirthYear** constraint object to display the shortcut menu.
4. Click the **Modify** command in the shortcut menu. The Check Constraints dialog box appears, as shown in Figure 10-17.
5. Note that the check constraint itself is located in the Expression text box of the (General) properties group, and it can be edited there if needed. At this point, however, there is no need to change the constraint.
6. Click the **Close** button to close the Check Constraints dialog box.
7. Click the document window **Close** button to close the ARTIST table's columns and column properties tabbed window.
8. Contract (minimize) the **dbo.ARTIST** table object display.

Clearly, it is easier to key the constraint into SQL statements than it would be to type it as shown in this window!

Throughout this chapter, you may see dialog boxes similar to the one shown in Figure 10-17 that have properties that reference something about replication. All such references refer to distributed SQL Server databases in which data are placed in two or more databases and updates to them are coordinated in some fashion. We will not consider that topic here, so ignore any references to replication. You can learn more by searching for the replication topic in the SQL Server 2008 documentation.

To ensure that the VRG database relationships were created correctly, let's create a database diagram for the VRG database. We can then use that diagram as the basis for checking the relationships among the various tables.

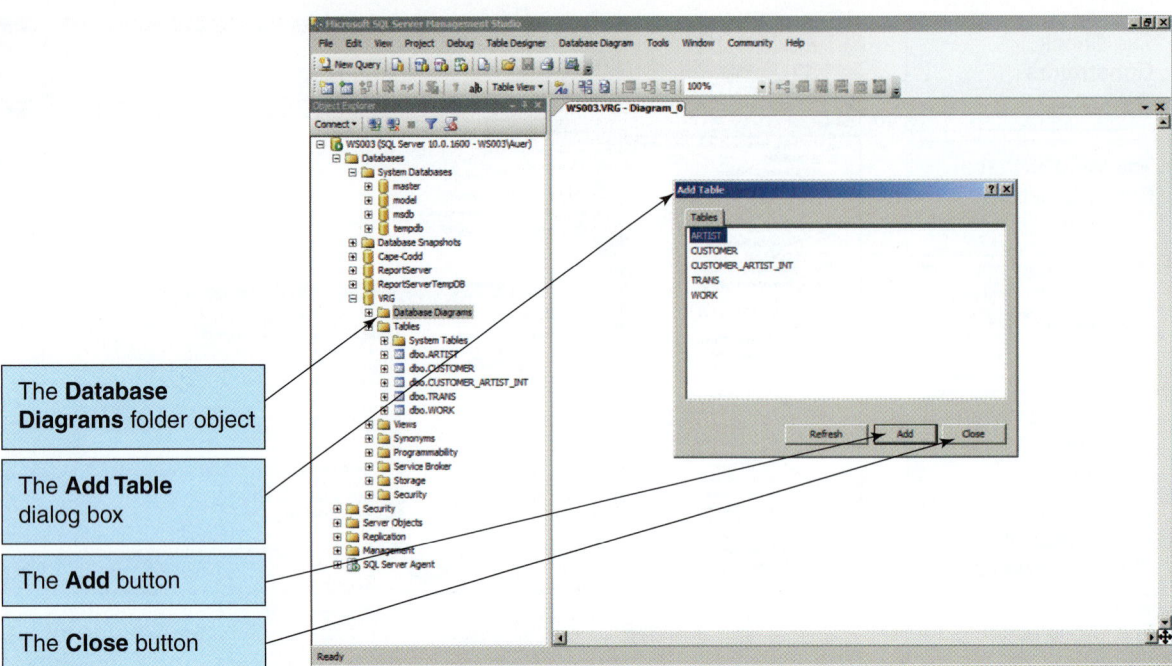

The **Database Diagrams** folder object

The **Add Table** dialog box

The **Add** button

The **Close** button

Figure

The Add Table Dialog Box

Creating an SQL Server Database Diagram

1. In the SQL Server Management Studio Object Browser, right-click the **VRG Database Diagrams** folder object to display the shortcut menu.
2. Click the **Install Diagram Support** command on the shortcut menu.
3. A Microsoft SQL Server Management Studio dialog box appears asking if you want to create some objects that support database diagrams. Of course you do! Isn't that the command you just gave? Click the **Yes** button!
4. Right-click the **VRG Database Diagrams** folder object to display the shortcut menu.
5. Click the **New Database Diagram** command on the shortcut menu. The Add Table dialog box appears, as shown in Figure 10-18.
6. Click the **Add** button to add the highlighted ARTIST table to the database diagram.
7. Repeat step 6 for each of the other four tables in the VRG database
8. Click the **Close** button to close the Add Table dialog box.
9. Rearrange the VRG tables in the database diagram until it appears as shown in Figure 10-19.
10. Click the **Save** button, and name the diagram **VRG-Database-Diagram**.
11. Expand the **VRG Database Diagrams** folder object to display the VRG-Database-Diagram object, which is shown in Figure 10-20.

Now we can use the VRG database diagram to view the properties of a relationship. We will take a look at the relationship between ARTIST and WORK, checking the referential integrity constraint and the cascading update and deletion behavior between ARTIST and WORK.

Viewing Relationship Properties

1. Right-click the **ARTIST** table in the VRG Database Diagram to display the shortcut menu as shown in Figure 10-20. Note how many actions are available from this short-cut menu.
2. Click the **Relationships** command to display the Foreign Key Relationships dialog box, as shown in Figure 10-21.
3. Expand the **Tables and Columns Specifications** property section, as shown in Figure 10-21.

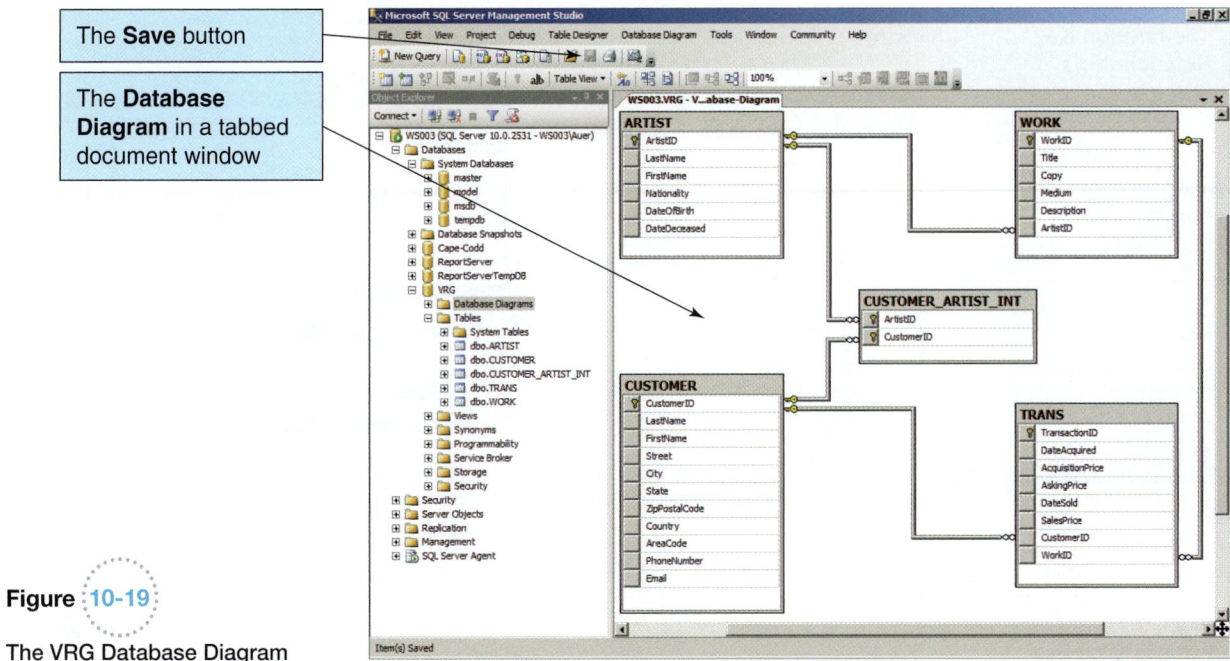

Figure 10-19

The VRG Database Diagram

4. In Figure 10-21, note that the Tables and Columns Specifications property section details the *primary and foreign keys* in the relationship between the two tables.

5. In Figure 10-21, note that the Check Existing Data On Creation Or Re-Enabling property is enabled. This is the *referential integrity constraint* between the ArtistID column in WORK and the ArtistID column in ARTIST.

6. In the Foreign Key Relationships dialog box, expand the **INSERT and UPDATE Specification**, and then scroll down until it is visible. The property settings indicate that neither updates to the primary key of ARTIST nor deletions of rows in ARTIST will cause any cascading actions in the WORK table.

7. Click the **Close** button to close the Foreign Key Relationships dialog box.

8. Click the **Close** button to close the VRG Database Diagram.

9. Contract (minimize) the **System Databases** folder.

Figure 10-20

The Database Diagram Table
Shortcut Menu

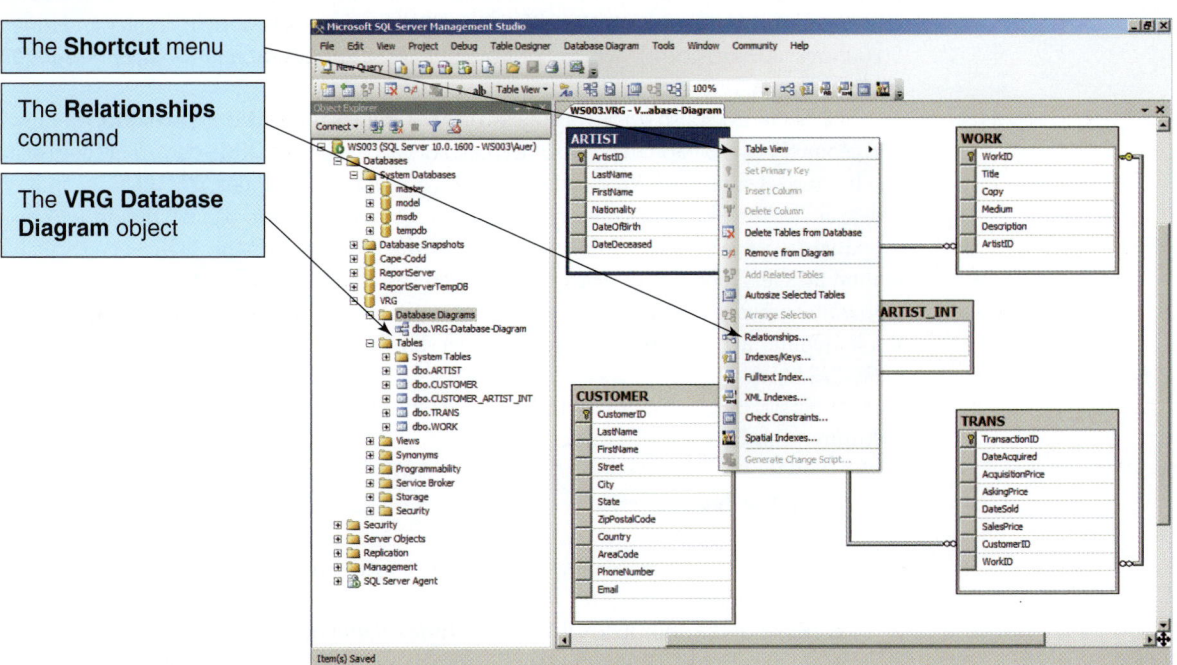

The **Foreign Key Relationships** dialog box

The enabled referential integrity constraint between WORK and ARTIST

The expanded **Table and Columns Specification** properties

The **Close** button

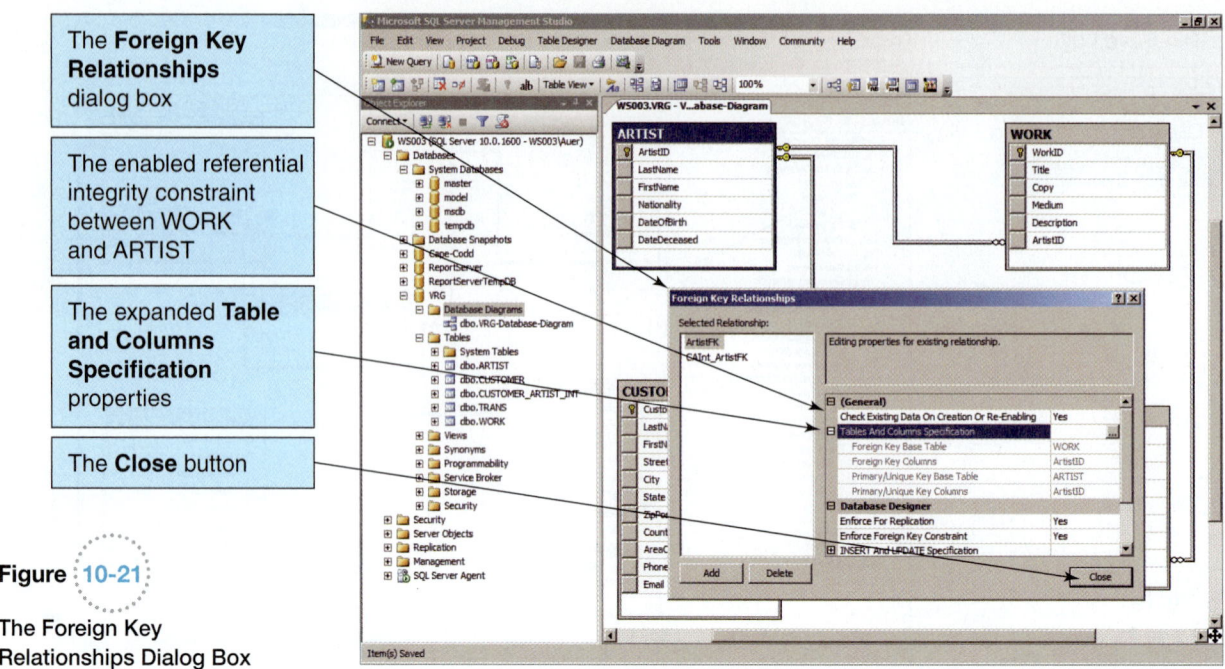

Figure 10-21

The Foreign Key Relationships Dialog Box

Indexes

As discussed in Appendix D, an **index** is a special data structure that is created to improve database performance. SQL Server automatically creates an index on all primary and foreign keys. A developer can also direct SQL Server to create an index on other columns that are frequently used in WHERE clauses or on columns that are used for sorting data when sequentially processing a table for queries and reports.

SQL Server supports two kinds of indexes for tables: clustered and nonclustered. With a **clustered index**, the data are stored in the bottom level of the index and in the same order as that index. With a **nonclustered index**, the bottom level of an index does not contain data; it contains pointers to the data. Because rows can be sorted only in one physical order at a time, only one clustered index is allowed per table. Retrieval is faster with clustered indexes than nonclustered indexes. Updating is normally faster as well with clustered indexes, but not if there are many updates in the same spot in the middle of the relation. For more information on clustered and nonclustered indexes, see the SQL Server 2008 Books Online article "Tables and Index Data Structures Architecture," which is available at *http://msdn.microsoft.com/en-us/library/ms180978.aspx*.

SQL Server 2008 also supports indexes on XML data (see the discussion of XML in Chapter 12) and geometry or geographic spatial data types. For each column of XML data, four types of indexes can be created: a primary XML index, a PATH secondary XML index, a VALUE secondary XML index, and a PROPERTY secondary XML index. For each column of spatial data, we can create a spatial index. For more information on XML indexes, see the SQL Server 2008 Books Online article "Tables and Index Data Structures Architecture" (*http://msdn.microsoft.com/en-us/library/ms180978.aspx*). For more information on spatial indexes, see the SQL Server 2008 Books Online article "Spatial Indexing Overview" (*http://msdn.microsoft.com/en-us/library/bb964712.aspx*).

To illustrate how to create indexes, we will create a new index on the ZipPostalCode column in the CUSTOMER table.

Creating a New Index

1. In the SQL Server Management Studio Object Browser, expand the **dbo.CUSTOMER** table object.
2. Expand the dbo.CUSTOMER table **Index** folder object to display the existing indexes.
3. Right-click the **Index** folder object to display the shortcut menu.

The **New Index** dialog box

The **General** page

The **Index name** text box

The **Index type** drop-down list

The **Unique** checkbox

The **Add** button

The expanded **Indexes** folder

The clustered index icon

The nonclustered index icon

The **OK** button

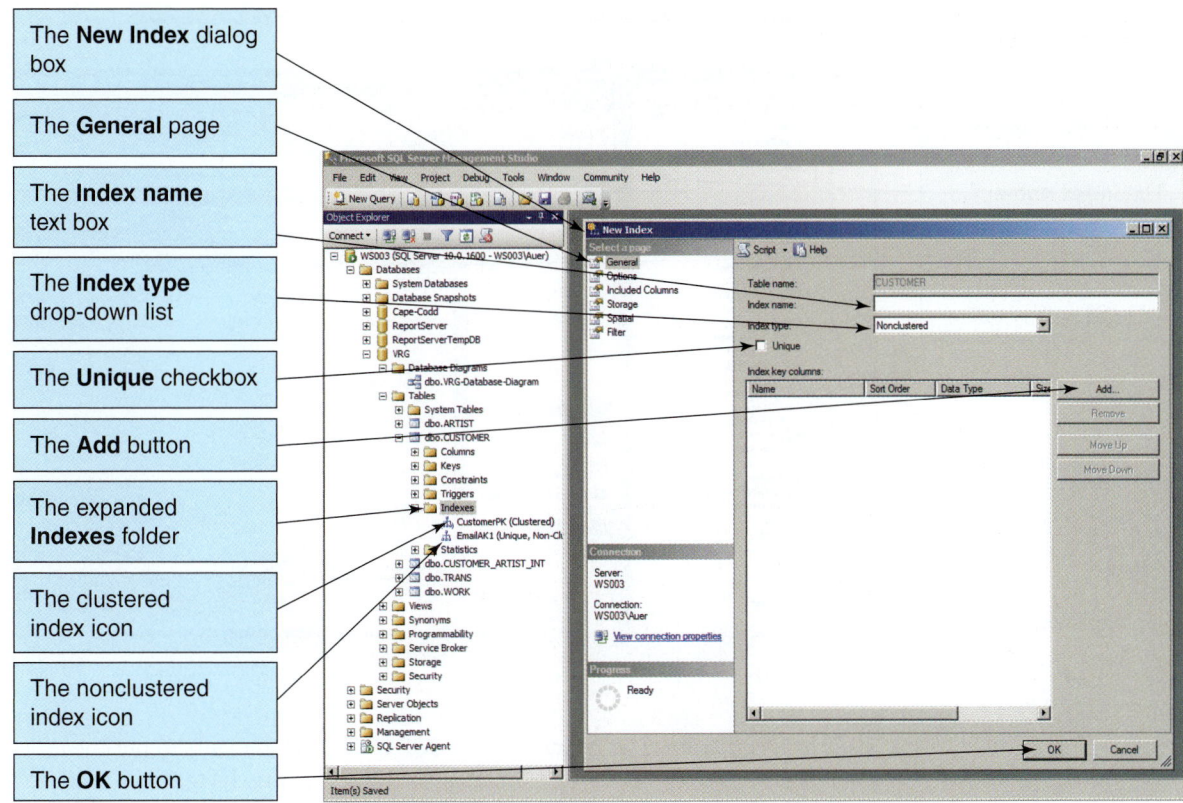

Figure 10-22

The New Index Dialog Box

4. Click the **New Index** command on the shortcut menu. The New Index dialog box appears, as shown in Figure 10-22.

5. Type the name **ZipPostalCodeIndex** in the Index Name text box of the New Index dialog box.

6. Click the **Add** button on the New Index dialog box to display the Select Columns from 'dbo.CUSTOMER' dialog box.

7. Click the **check box** for the ZipPostalCode column in the Select Columns from 'dbo.CUSTOMER' dialog box.

8. Click the **OK** button on the Select Columns from 'dbo.CUSTOMER' dialog box. The New Index dialog box now appears as shown in Figure 10-23.

9. Click the **OK** button in the New Index dialog box to create the ZipPostalCodeIndex. The ZipPostalCodeIndex nonclustered index object appears in the Indexes folder of the dbo.CUSTOMER table in the Object Browser.

10. Collapse the **dbo.CUSTOMER** table structure in the Object Browser.

Populating the VRG Tables with Data

You can enter data into SQL Server either by entering data into a table grid in the Microsoft SQL Server Management Studio GUI display or by using SQL INSERT statements. The Microsoft SQL Server Management Studio GUI display is more useful for occasional data edits than for populating all the tables of a new database. You can open a table grid for data entry by a right-clicking the table name to display a shortcut menu, then click the Edit Top 200 Rows command.

However, we will use the same method for populating the VRG database tables that we used to create the table structure: an SQL script. But before we do that, we need to address the surrogate key values issue raised in Chapter 7. The data shown in Figure 7-16 is sample data, and the primary key values of CustomerID, ArtistID, WorkID, and TransactionID shown in that figure are nonsequential. Yet, the IDENTITY(m,n) property that we use to populate SQL Server surrogate primary keys creates sequential numbering.

The **New Index** dialog box

The **General** page

The **Index name**

The included columns

The **OK** button

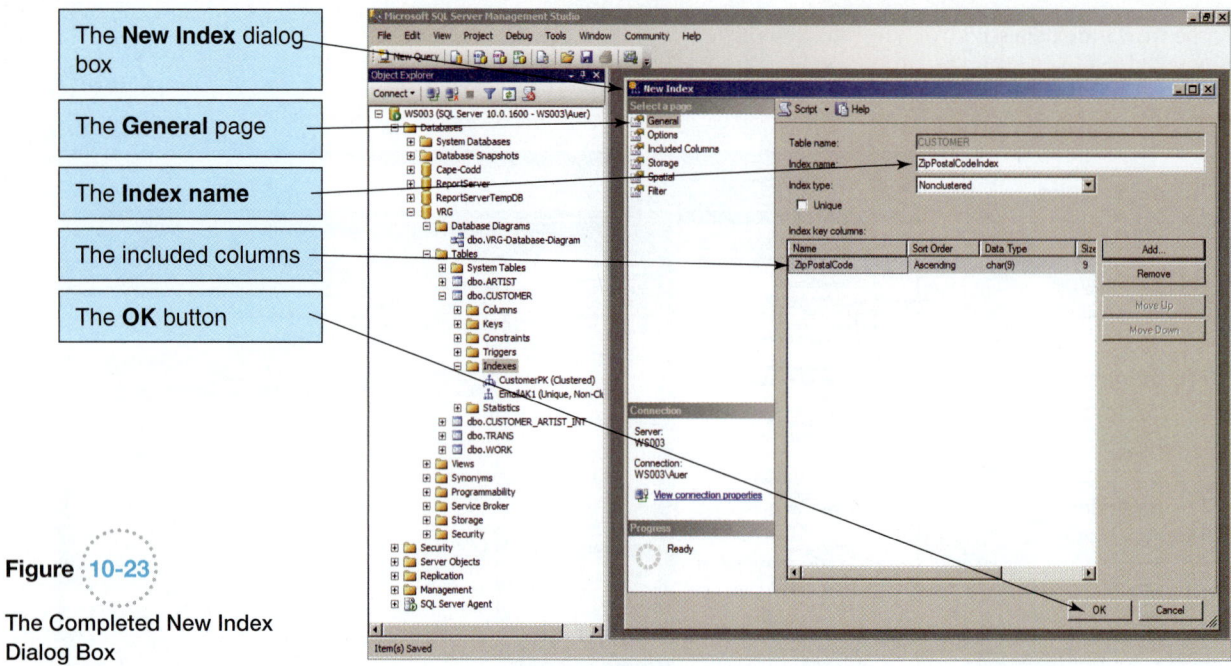

Figure 10-23

The Completed New Index Dialog Box

This means that if we write and execute SQL INSERT statements to put the artist data shown in Figure 7-12(b) into the ARTIST table, the values of ArtistID that will be added to the table will be (1, 2, 3, 4, 5, 6, 7, 8, 9) instead of the values of (1, 2, 3, 4, 5, 11, 17, 18, 19) listed in the figure. How can we enter the needed nonsequential values?

The answer is the **Transact-SQL IDENTITY_INSERT property**. When IDENTITY_INSERT is set to OFF (the default setting), only the SQL Server DBMS can enter data into the controlled ID column in the table. When IDENTITY_INSERT is set to ON, values can be input into the controlled column in the table. However, IDENTITY_INSERT can only be set to ON for only one table at a time. Futher, IDENTITY_INSERT requires the use of a column list containing the name of the surrogate key in each INSERT command.

Thus, instead of using an SQL INSERT statement that automatically enters the surrogate value, such as:

```
INSERT INTO ARTIST VALUES('Miro', 'Joan', 'Spanish', 1893, 1983);
```

we have to use a set of SQL statements similar to the following:

```
SET IDENTITY_INSERT dbo.ARTIST ON
INSERT INTO ARTIST
    (ArtistID, LastName, FirstName, Nationality,
    DateOfBirth, DateDeceased)
    VALUES (1, 'Miro', 'Joan', 'Spanish', 1893, 1983);
SET IDENTITY_INSERT dbo.ARTIST OFF
```

Note how we set INDENTITY_INSERT to ON, insert the date, and then set IDENTITY_INSERT to OFF. Of course this is a lot of work if we are inserting one row of data at a time, but when used in an SQL script that inserts a lot of data into a table it makes sense. So, we will use an SQL script.

The set of SQL INSERT statements needed to populate the VRG database with the View Ridge Gallery data shown in Figure 7-16 is shown in Figure 10-24. Create and save a new SQL script named **VRG-Table-Data.sql** based on Figure 10-24, testing it with the **Parse** command (use the Parse button) until you have corrected any errors. Save the corrected script, and then run the script (use the **Execute** button) to populate the tables. Close the script window after the script has been successfully run.

```
/******************************************************************************/
/*                                                                          */
/*      Kroenke and Auer - Database Processing (11th Edition) Chapter 10     */
/*                                                                          */
/*      The View Ridge Gallery (VRG) Database - Insert Data                 */
/*                                                                          */
/*      These are the Microsoft SQL Server 2005/2008 SQL code solutions     */
/*                                                                          */
/******************************************************************************/
/*                                                                          */
/*      This file contains the initial data for each table.                 */
/*                                                                          */
/*      NOTE:  We will have a problem entering the surrogate key values shown in */
/*      the text.                                                           */
/*                                                                          */
/*      The database table structure was set up using the SQL Server T-SQL */
/*      keyword IDENTITY to create surrogate keys. This means that by default */
/*      we cannot enter values into any column defined with IDENTITY.       */
/*                                                                          */
/*      But that means we cannot enter the primary key values as shown.     */
/*      To work around this, we will use the T-SQL command IDENTITY_INSERT. */
/*                                                                          */
/*      When IDENTITY_INSERT is set to OFF (the default), only the DBMS     */
/*      can enter data into the controlled column in the table.             */
/*                                                                          */
/*      When IDENTITY_INSERT is set to ON, values can be input into the     */
/*      controlled column in the table. However, IDENTITY_INSERT can only be set */
/*      to ON for only one table at a time. Futher, IDENTITY_INSERT requires */
/*      the use of a column list containing the name of the surrogate key in each */
/*      INSERT command.                                                     */
/*                                                                          */
/******************************************************************************/

/*      Be sure IDENTITY_INSERT is OFF for all tables.                      */

SET IDENTITY_INSERT dbo.CUSTOMER OFF
SET IDENTITY_INSERT dbo.ARTIST OFF
SET IDENTITY_INSERT dbo.WORK OFF
SET IDENTITY_INSERT dbo.TRANS OFF


/******************************************************************************/

/*      INSERT data for CUSTOMER                                            */

/*      Set IDENTITY_INSERT to ON for CUSTOMER;                             */
/*      reset it to OFF after CUSTOMER data is inserted.                     */

SET IDENTITY_INSERT dbo.CUSTOMER ON

INSERT INTO CUSTOMER
        (CustomerID, LastName, FirstName, Street, City, State, ZipPostalCode, Country,
         AreaCode, PhoneNumber, Email)
        VALUES (
        1000, 'Janes', 'Jeffrey', '123 W. Elm St', 'Renton', 'WA', '98055', 'USA',
        '425', '543-2345', 'Jeffrey.Janes@somewhere.com');
```

Figure 10-24

The SQL Statements to
Populate the VRG Tables

```
INSERT INTO CUSTOMER
      (CustomerID, LastName, FirstName, Street, City, State, ZipPostalCode, Country,
      AreaCode, PhoneNumber, Email)
      VALUES (
      1001, 'Smith', 'David', '813 Tumbleweed Lane', 'Loveland', 'CO', '81201', 'USA',
      '970', '654-9876', 'David.Smith@somewhere.com');
INSERT INTO CUSTOMER
      (CustomerID, LastName, FirstName, Street, City, State, ZipPostalCode, Country,
      AreaCode, PhoneNumber, Email)
      VALUES (
      1015, 'Twilight', 'Tiffany', '88 1st Avenue', 'Langley', 'WA', '98260', 'USA',
      '360', '765-5566', 'Tiffany.Twilight@somewhere.com');
INSERT INTO CUSTOMER
      (CustomerID, LastName, FirstName, Street, City, State, ZipPostalCode, Country,
      AreaCode, PhoneNumber, Email)
      VALUES (
      1033, 'Smathers', 'Fred', '10899 88th Ave', 'Bainbridge Island', 'WA', '98110', 'USA'
      '206', '876-9911', 'Fred.Smathers@somewhere.com');
INSERT INTO CUSTOMER
      (CustomerID, LastName, FirstName, Street, City, State, ZipPostalCode, Country,
      AreaCode, PhoneNumber, Email)
      VALUES (
      1034,'Frederickson','Mary Beth','25 South Lafayette', 'Denver', 'CO', '80201', 'USA',
      '303', '513-8822', 'MaryBeth.Frederickson@somewhere.com');
INSERT INTO CUSTOMER
      (CustomerID, LastName, FirstName, Street, City, State, ZipPostalCode, Country,
      AreaCode, PhoneNumber, Email)
      VALUES (
      1036, 'Warning', 'Selma', '205 Burnaby', 'Vancouver', 'BC', 'V6Z 1W2', 'Canada',
      '604', '988-0512', 'Selma.Warning@somewhere.com');
INSERT INTO CUSTOMER
      (CustomerID, LastName, FirstName, Street, City, State, ZipPostalCode, Country,
      AreaCode, PhoneNumber, Email)
      VALUES (
      1037, 'Wu', 'Susan', '105 Locust Ave', 'Atlanta', 'GA', '30322', 'USA',
      '404', '653-3465', 'Susan.Wu@somewhere.com');
INSERT INTO CUSTOMER
      (CustomerID, LastName, FirstName, Street, City, State, ZipPostalCode, Country,
      AreaCode, PhoneNumber, Email)
      VALUES (
      1040, 'Gray', 'Donald','55 Bodega Ave', 'Bodega Bay', 'CA', '94923', 'USA',
      '707', '568-4839', 'Donald.Gray@somewhere.com');
INSERT INTO CUSTOMER
      (CustomerID, LastName, FirstName, Street, City, State, ZipPostalCode, Country,
      AreaCode, PhoneNumber)
      VALUES (
      1041, 'Johnson', 'Lynda', '117 C Street', 'Washington', 'DC', '20003', 'USA',
INSERT INTO CUSTOMER
      (CustomerID, LastName, FirstName, Street, City, State, ZipPostalCode, Country,
      AreaCode, PhoneNumber, Email)
      VALUES (
      1051, 'Wilkens', 'Chris', '87 Highland Drive', 'Olympia', 'WA', '98508', 'USA',
      '360', '765-7766', 'Chris.Wilkens@somewhere.com');

SET IDENTITY_INSERT dbo.CUSTOMER OFF
```

Figure 10-24

(Continued)

```
/****************************************************************************/

/*    INSERT data for ARTIST                                            */

/*    Set IDENTITY_INSERT to ON for ARTIST;                             */
/*    reset it to OFF after ARTIST data is inserted.                    */

SET IDENTITY_INSERT dbo.ARTIST ON

INSERT INTO ARTIST
      (ArtistID, LastName, FirstName, Nationality, DateOfBirth, DateDeceased)
      VALUES (
      1, 'Miro', 'Joan', 'Spanish', 1893, 1983);
INSERT INTO ARTIST
      (ArtistID, LastName, FirstName, Nationality, DateOfBirth, DateDeceased)
      VALUES (
      2, 'Kandinsky', 'Wassily', 'Russian', 1866, 1944);
INSERT INTO ARTIST
      (ArtistID, LastName, FirstName, Nationality, DateOfBirth, DateDeceased)
      VALUES (
      3, 'Klee', 'Paul', 'German', 1879, 1940);
INSERT INTO ARTIST
      (ArtistID, LastName, FirstName, Nationality, DateOfBirth, DateDeceased)
      VALUES (
      4, 'Matisse', 'Henri', 'French', 1869, 1954);
INSERT INTO ARTIST
      (ArtistID, LastName, FirstName, Nationality, DateOfBirth, DateDeceased)
      VALUES (
      5, 'Chagall', 'Marc', 'French', 1887, 1985);
INSERT INTO ARTIST
      (ArtistID, LastName, FirstName, Nationality, DateOfBirth, DateDeceased)
      VALUES (
      11, 'Sargent', 'John Singer', 'United States', 1856, 1925);
INSERT INTO ARTIST
      (ArtistID, LastName, FirstName, Nationality, DateOfBirth, DateDeceased)
      VALUES (
      17, 'Tobey', 'Mark', 'United States', 1890, 1976);
INSERT INTO ARTIST
      (ArtistID, LastName, FirstName, Nationality, DateOfBirth, DateDeceased)
      VALUES (
      18, 'Horiuchi', 'Paul', 'United States', 1906, 1999);
INSERT INTO ARTIST
      (ArtistID, LastName, FirstName, Nationality, DateOfBirth, DateDeceased)
      VALUES (
      19, 'Graves', 'Morris', 'United States', 1920, 2001);

SET IDENTITY_INSERT dbo.ARTIST OFF
```

Figure 10-24

(Continued)

```
/**************************************************************************/
/*      INSERT data for CUSTOMER_ARTIST_INT                       */

/*      IDENTITY_INSERT OFF is NOT needed for CUSTOMER_ARTIST_INT -      */
/*      There are NO surrogate keys in CUSTOMER_ARTIST_INT.             */

INSERT INTO CUSTOMER_ARTIST_INT VALUES (1, 1001);
INSERT INTO CUSTOMER_ARTIST_INT VALUES (1, 1034);
INSERT INTO CUSTOMER_ARTIST_INT VALUES (2, 1001);
INSERT INTO CUSTOMER_ARTIST_INT VALUES (2, 1034);
INSERT INTO CUSTOMER_ARTIST_INT VALUES (4, 1001);
INSERT INTO CUSTOMER_ARTIST_INT VALUES (4, 1034);
INSERT INTO CUSTOMER_ARTIST_INT VALUES (5, 1001);
INSERT INTO CUSTOMER_ARTIST_INT VALUES (5, 1034);
INSERT INTO CUSTOMER_ARTIST_INT VALUES (5, 1036);
INSERT INTO CUSTOMER_ARTIST_INT VALUES (11, 1001);
INSERT INTO CUSTOMER_ARTIST_INT VALUES (11, 1015);
INSERT INTO CUSTOMER_ARTIST_INT VALUES (11, 1036);
INSERT INTO CUSTOMER_ARTIST_INT VALUES (17, 1000);
INSERT INTO CUSTOMER_ARTIST_INT VALUES (17, 1015);
INSERT INTO CUSTOMER_ARTIST_INT VALUES (17, 1033);
INSERT INTO CUSTOMER_ARTIST_INT VALUES (17, 1040);
INSERT INTO CUSTOMER_ARTIST_INT VALUES (17, 1051);
INSERT INTO CUSTOMER_ARTIST_INT VALUES (18, 1000);
INSERT INTO CUSTOMER_ARTIST_INT VALUES (18, 1015);
INSERT INTO CUSTOMER_ARTIST_INT VALUES (18, 1033);
INSERT INTO CUSTOMER_ARTIST_INT VALUES (18, 1040);
INSERT INTO CUSTOMER_ARTIST_INT VALUES (18, 1051);
INSERT INTO CUSTOMER_ARTIST_INT VALUES (19, 1000);
INSERT INTO CUSTOMER_ARTIST_INT VALUES (19, 1015);
INSERT INTO CUSTOMER_ARTIST_INT VALUES (19, 1033);
INSERT INTO CUSTOMER_ARTIST_INT VALUES (19, 1036);
INSERT INTO CUSTOMER_ARTIST_INT VALUES (19, 1040);
INSERT INTO CUSTOMER_ARTIST_INT VALUES (19, 1051);

/**************************************************************************/
/*      INSERT data for WORK                                      */

/*      Set IDENTITY_INSERT to ON for WORK;                       */
/*      reset it to OFF after WORK data is inserted.              */

SET IDENTITY_INSERT dbo.WORK ON

INSERT INTO WORK (WorkID, Title, Copy, Medium, Description, ArtistID)
      VALUES (
      500, 'Memories IV', 'Unique', 'Casein rice paper collage', '31 x 24.8 in.', 18);
INSERT INTO WORK (WorkID, Title, Copy, Medium, Description, ArtistID)
      VALUES (
      511, 'Surf and Bird', '142/500', 'High Quality Limited Print',
      'Northwest School Expressionist style', 19);
INSERT INTO WORK (WorkID, Title, Copy, Medium, Description, ArtistID)
      VALUES (
      521, 'The Tilled Field', '788/1000', 'High Quality Limited Print',
      'Early Surrealist style', 1);
INSERT INTO WORK (WorkID, Title, Copy, Medium, Description, ArtistID)
      VALUES (
      522, 'La Lecon de Ski', '353/500', 'High Quality Limited Print',
      'Surrealist style', 1);
```

Figure 10-24

(Continued)

```
INSERT INTO WORK (WorkID, Title, Copy, Medium, Description, ArtistID)
        VALUES (
        523, 'On White II', '435/500', 'High Quality Limited Print',
        'Bauhaus style of Kandinsky', 2);
INSERT INTO WORK (WorkID, Title, Copy, Medium, Description, ArtistID)
        VALUES (
        524, 'Woman with a Hat', '596/750', 'High Quality Limited Print',
        'A very colorful Impressionist piece', 4);
INSERT INTO WORK (WorkID, Title, Copy, Medium, Description, ArtistID)
        VALUES (
        537, 'The Woven World', '17/750', 'Color lithograph', 'Signed', 17);
INSERT INTO WORK (WorkID, Title, Copy, Medium, Description, ArtistID)
        VALUES (
        548, 'Night Bird', 'Unique', 'Watercolor on Paper',
        '50 x 72.5 cm. - Signed', 19);
INSERT INTO WORK (WorkID, Title, Copy, Medium, Description, ArtistID)
        VALUES (
        551, 'Der Blaue Reiter', '236/1000', 'High Quality Limited Print',
        'The Blue Rider-Early Pointilism influence', 2);
INSERT INTO WORK (WorkID, Title, Copy, Medium, Description, ArtistID)
        VALUES (
        552, 'Angelus Novus', '659/750', 'High Quality Limited Print',
        'Bauhaus style of Klee', 3);
INSERT INTO WORK (WorkID, Title, Copy, Medium, Description, ArtistID)
        VALUES (
        553, 'The Dance', '734/1000', 'High Quality Limited Print',
        'An Impressionist masterpiece', 4);
INSERT INTO WORK (WorkID, Title, Copy, Medium, Description, ArtistID)
        VALUES (
        554, 'I and the Village', '834/1000', 'High Quality Limited Print',
        'Shows Belarusian folk-life themes and symbology', 5);
INSERT INTO WORK (WorkID, Title, Copy, Medium, Description, ArtistID)
        VALUES (
        555, 'Claude Monet Painting', '684/1000', 'High Quality Limited Print',
        'Shows French Impressionist influence of Monet', 11);
INSERT INTO WORK (WorkID, Title, Copy, Medium, Description, ArtistID)
        VALUES (
        561, 'Sunflower', 'Unique', 'Watercolor and ink',
        '33.3 x 16.1 cm. - Signed', 19);
INSERT INTO WORK (WorkID, Title, Copy, Medium, Description, ArtistID)
        VALUES (
        562, 'The Fiddler', '251/1000', 'High Quality Limited Print',
        'Shows Belarusian folk-life themes and symbology', 5);
INSERT INTO WORK (WorkID, Title, Copy, Medium, Description, ArtistID)
        VALUES (
        563, 'Spanish Dancer', '583/750', 'High Quality Limited Print',
        'American realist style - From work in Spain', 11);
INSERT INTO WORK (WorkID, Title, Copy, Medium, Description, ArtistID)
        VALUES (
        564, 'Farmer''s Market #2',   '267/500', 'High Quality Limited Print',
        'Northwest School Abstract Expressionist style', 17);
INSERT INTO WORK (WorkID, Title, Copy, Medium, Description, ArtistID)
        VALUES (
        565, 'Farmer''s Market #2',   '268/500', 'High Quality Limited Print',
         'Northwest School Abstract Expressionist style', 17);
INSERT INTO WORK (WorkID, Title, Copy, Medium, Description, ArtistID)
        VALUES (
        566, 'Into Time', '323/500', 'High Quality Limited Print',
        'Northwest School Abstract Expressionist style', 18);
```

Figure 10-24

(Continued)

```
INSERT INTO WORK (WorkID, Title, Copy, Medium, Description, ArtistID)
      VALUES (
      570, 'Untitled Number 1', 'Unique', 'Monotype with tempera',
      '4.3 x 6.1 in. Signed', 17);
INSERT INTO WORK (WorkID, Title, Copy, Medium, Description, ArtistID)
      VALUES (
      571, 'Yellow Covers Blue', 'Unique', 'Oil and collage',
      '71 x 78 in. - Signed', 18);
INSERT INTO WORK (WorkID, Title, Copy, Medium, Description, ArtistID)
      VALUES (
      578, 'Mid-Century Hibernation', '362/500', 'High Quality Limited Print',
      'Northwest School Expressionist style', 19);
INSERT INTO WORK (WorkID, Title, Copy, Medium, Description, ArtistID)
      VALUES (
      580, 'Forms in Progress I', 'Unique', 'Color aquatint',
      '19.3 x 24.4 in. - Signed', 17);
INSERT INTO WORK (WorkID, Title, Copy, Medium, Description, ArtistID)
      VALUES (
      581, 'Forms in Progress II', 'Unique', 'Color aquatint',
      '19.3 x 24.4 in. - Signed', 17);
INSERT INTO WORK (WorkID, Title, Copy, Medium, Description, ArtistID)
      VALUES (
      585, 'The Fiddler', '252/1000', 'High Quality Limited Print',
      'Shows Belarusian folk-life themes and symbology', 5);
INSERT INTO WORK (WorkID, Title, Copy, Medium, Description, ArtistID)
      VALUES (
      586, 'Spanish Dancer', '588/750', 'High Quality Limited Print',
      'American Realist style - From work in Spain', 11);
INSERT INTO WORK (WorkID, Title, Copy, Medium, Description, ArtistID)
      VALUES (
      587, 'Broadway Boggie', '433/500', 'High Quality Limited Print',
      'Northwest School Abstract Expressionist style', 17);
INSERT INTO WORK (WorkID, Title, Copy, Medium, Description, ArtistID)
      VALUES (
      588, 'Universal Field', '114/500', 'High Quality Limited Print',
      'Northwest School Abstract Expressionist style', 17);
INSERT INTO WORK (WorkID, Title, Copy, Medium, Description, ArtistID)
      VALUES (
      589, 'Color Floating in Time', '487/500', 'High Quality Limited Print',
      'Northwest School Abstract Expressionist style', 18);
INSERT INTO WORK (WorkID, Title, Copy, Medium, Description, ArtistID)
      VALUES (
      590, 'Blue Interior', 'Unique', 'Tempera on card', '43.9 x 28 in.', 17);
INSERT INTO WORK (WorkID, Title, Copy, Medium, Description, ArtistID)
      VALUES (
      593, 'Surf and Bird', 'Unique', 'Gouache', '26.5 x 29.75 in. - Signed', 19);
INSERT INTO WORK (WorkID, Title, Copy, Medium, Description, ArtistID)
      VALUES (
      594, 'Surf and Bird', '362/500', 'High Quality Limited Print',
      'Northwest School Expressionist style', 19);
```

Figure 10-24

(Continued)

```
INSERT INTO WORK (WorkID, Title, Copy, Medium, Description, ArtistID)
      VALUES (
      595, 'Surf and Bird', '365/500', 'High Quality Limited Print',
      'Northwest School Expressionist style', 19);
INSERT INTO WORK (WorkID, Title, Copy, Medium, Description, ArtistID)
      VALUES (
      596, 'Surf and Bird', '366/500', 'High Quality Limited Print',
      'Northwest School Expressionist style', 19);

SET IDENTITY_INSERT dbo.WORK OFF

/***************************************************************************/

/*    INSERT data for TRANS                                             */

/*    Set IDENTITY_INSERT to ON for TRANS;                             */
/*    reset it to OFF after TRANS data is inserted.                    */

SET IDENTITY_INSERT dbo.TRANS ON

INSERT INTO TRANS (TransactionID, DateAcquired, AcquisitionPrice,
      AskingPrice, DateSold, SalesPrice, CustomerID, WorkID)
      VALUES (
      100, '11/4/2005', 30000.00, 45000.00, '12/14/2005', 42500.00, 1000, 500);
INSERT INTO TRANS (TransactionID, DateAcquired, AcquisitionPrice,
      AskingPrice, DateSold, SalesPrice, CustomerID, WorkID)
      VALUES (
      101, '11/7/2005', 250.00, 500.00, '12/19/2005', 500.00, 1015, 511);
INSERT INTO TRANS (TransactionID, DateAcquired, AcquisitionPrice,
      AskingPrice, DateSold, SalesPrice, CustomerID, WorkID)
      VALUES (
      102, '11/17/2005', 125.00, 250.00, '01/18/2006', 200.00, 1001, 521);
INSERT INTO TRANS (TransactionID, DateAcquired, AcquisitionPrice,
      AskingPrice, DateSold, SalesPrice, CustomerID, WorkID)
      VALUES (
      103, '11/17/2005', 250.00, 500.00, '12/12/2006', 400.00, 1034, 522);
INSERT INTO TRANS (TransactionID, DateAcquired, AcquisitionPrice,
      AskingPrice, DateSold, SalesPrice, CustomerID, WorkID)
      VALUES (
      104, '11/17/2005', 250.00, 250.00, '01/18/2006', 200.00, 1001, 523);
INSERT INTO TRANS (TransactionID, DateAcquired, AcquisitionPrice,
      AskingPrice, DateSold, SalesPrice, CustomerID, WorkID)
      VALUES (
      105, '11/17/2005', 200.00, 500.00, '12/12/2006', 400.00, 1034, 524);
INSERT INTO TRANS (TransactionID, DateAcquired, AcquisitionPrice,
      AskingPrice, DateSold, SalesPrice, CustomerID, WorkID)
      VALUES (
      115, '03/03/2006', 1500.00, 3000.00, '06/07/2006', 2750.00, 1033, 537);
INSERT INTO TRANS (TransactionID, DateAcquired, AcquisitionPrice,
      AskingPrice, DateSold, SalesPrice, CustomerID, WorkID)
      VALUES (
      121, '09/21/2006', 15000.00, 30000.00, '11/28/2006', 27500.00, 1015, 548);
INSERT INTO TRANS (TransactionID, DateAcquired, AcquisitionPrice,
      AskingPrice, DateSold, SalesPrice, CustomerID, WorkID)
      VALUES (
      125, '11/21/2006', 125.00, 250.00, '12/18/2006', 200.00, 1001, 551);
```

Figure 10-24

(Continued)

```
INSERT INTO TRANS (TransactionID, DateAcquired, AcquisitionPrice,
    AskingPrice, WorkID)
    VALUES (
    126, '11/21/2006', 200.00, 400.00, 552)
INSERT INTO TRANS (TransactionID, DateAcquired, AcquisitionPrice,
    AskingPrice, DateSold, SalesPrice, CustomerID, WorkID)
    VALUES (
    127, '11/21/2006', 125.00, 500.00, '12/22/2006', 400.00, 1034, 553);
INSERT INTO TRANS (TransactionID, DateAcquired, AcquisitionPrice,
    AskingPrice, DateSold, SalesPrice, CustomerID, WorkID)
    VALUES (
    128, '11/21/2006', 125.00, 250.00, '03/16/2007', 225.00, 1036, 554);
INSERT INTO TRANS (TransactionID, DateAcquired, AcquisitionPrice,
    AskingPrice, DateSold, SalesPrice, CustomerID, WorkID)
    VALUES (
    129, '11/21/2006', 125.00, 250.00, '03/16/2007', 225.00, 1036, 555);
INSERT INTO TRANS (TransactionID, DateAcquired, AcquisitionPrice,
    AskingPrice, DateSold, SalesPrice, CustomerID, WorkID)
    VALUES (
    151, '05/7/2007', 10000.00, 20000.00, '06/28/2007', 17500.00, 1036, 561);
INSERT INTO TRANS (TransactionID, DateAcquired, AcquisitionPrice,
    AskingPrice, DateSold, SalesPrice, CustomerID, WorkID)
    VALUES (
    152, '05/18/2007', 125.00, 250.00, '08/15/2007', 225.00, 1001, 562);
INSERT INTO TRANS (TransactionID, DateAcquired, AcquisitionPrice,
    AskingPrice, DateSold, SalesPrice, CustomerID, WorkID)
    VALUES (
    153, '05/18/2007', 200.00, 400.00, '08/15/2007', 350.00, 1001, 563);
INSERT INTO TRANS (TransactionID, DateAcquired, AcquisitionPrice,
    AskingPrice, DateSold, SalesPrice, CustomerID, WorkID)
    VALUES (
    154, '05/18/2007', 250.00, 500.00, '09/28/2007', 400.00, 1040, 564);
INSERT INTO TRANS (TransactionID, DateAcquired, AcquisitionPrice,
    AskingPrice, WorkID)
    VALUES (
    155, '05/18/2007', 250.00, 500.00, 565);
INSERT INTO TRANS (TransactionID, DateAcquired, AcquisitionPrice,
    AskingPrice, DateSold, SalesPrice, CustomerID, WorkID)
    VALUES (
    156, '05/18/2007', 250.00, 500.00, '09/27/2007', 400.00, 1040, 566);
INSERT INTO TRANS (TransactionID, DateAcquired, AcquisitionPrice,
    AskingPrice, DateSold, SalesPrice, CustomerID, WorkID)
    VALUES (
    161, '06/28/2007', 7500.00, 15000.00, '09/29/2007', 13750.00, 1033, 570);
INSERT INTO TRANS (TransactionID, DateAcquired, AcquisitionPrice,
    AskingPrice, DateSold, SalesPrice, CustomerID, WorkID)
    VALUES (
    171, '08/23/2007', 35000.00, 60000.00, '09/29/2007', 55000.00, 1000, 571);
INSERT INTO TRANS (TransactionID, DateAcquired, AcquisitionPrice,
    AskingPrice, DateSold, SalesPrice, CustomerID, WorkID)
    VALUES (
    175, '09/29/2007', 40000.00, 75000.00, '12/18/2007', 72500.00, 1036, 500);
INSERT INTO TRANS (TransactionID, DateAcquired, AcquisitionPrice,
    AskingPrice, WorkID)
    VALUES (
    181, '10/11/2007', 250.00, 500.00, 578);
```

Figure 10-24

(Continued)

```
INSERT INTO TRANS (TransactionID, DateAcquired, AcquisitionPrice,
        AskingPrice, DateSold, SalesPrice, CustomerID, WorkID)
        VALUES (
        201, '02/28/2008', 2000.00, 3500.00, '04/26/2008', 3250.00, 1040, 580);
INSERT INTO TRANS (TransactionID, DateAcquired, AcquisitionPrice,
        AskingPrice, DateSold, SalesPrice, CustomerID, WorkID)
        VALUES (
        202, '02/28/2008', 2000.00, 3500.00, '04/26/2008', 3250.00, 1040, 581);
INSERT INTO TRANS (TransactionID, DateAcquired, AcquisitionPrice,
        AskingPrice, DateSold, SalesPrice, CustomerID, WorkID)
        VALUES (
        225, '06/8/2008', 125.00, 250.00, '09/27/2008', 225.00, 1051, 585);
INSERT INTO TRANS (TransactionID, DateAcquired, AcquisitionPrice,
        AskingPrice, WorkID)
        VALUES (
        226, '06/8/2008', 200.00, 400.00, 586);
INSERT INTO TRANS (TransactionID, DateAcquired, AcquisitionPrice,
        AskingPrice, DateSold, SalesPrice, CustomerID, WorkID)
        VALUES (
        227, '06/8/2008', 250.00, 500.00, '09/27/2008', 475.00, 1051, 587);
INSERT INTO TRANS (TransactionID, DateAcquired, AcquisitionPrice,
        AskingPrice, WorkID)
        VALUES (
        228, '06/8/2008', 250.00, 500.00, 588)
INSERT INTO TRANS (TransactionID, DateAcquired, AcquisitionPrice,
        AskingPrice, WorkID)
        VALUES (
        229, '06/8/2008', 250.00, 500.00, 589)
INSERT INTO TRANS (TransactionID, DateAcquired, AcquisitionPrice,
        AskingPrice, DateSold, SalesPrice, CustomerID, WorkID)
        VALUES (
        241, '08/29/2008', 2500.00, 5000.00, '09/27/2008', 4750.00, 1015, 590)
INSERT INTO TRANS (TransactionID, DateAcquired, AcquisitionPrice,
        AskingPrice, WorkID)
        VALUES (
        251, '10/25/2008', 25000.00, 50000.00, 593);
INSERT INTO TRANS (TransactionID, DateAcquired, AcquisitionPrice,
        AskingPrice, WorkID)
        VALUES (
        252, '10/27/2008', 250.00, 500.00, 594);
INSERT INTO TRANS (TransactionID, DateAcquired, AcquisitionPrice,
        AskingPrice, WorkID)
        VALUES (
        253, '10/27/2008', 250.00, 500.00, 595);
INSERT INTO TRANS (TransactionID, DateAcquired, AcquisitionPrice,
        AskingPrice, WorkID)
        VALUES (
        254, '10/27/2008', 250.00, 500.00, 596);

SET IDENTITY_INSERT dbo.TRANS OFF

/*************************************************************************
```

Figure 10-24

(Continued)

Creating Views

SQL views were discussed in Chapter 7. One view we created there was *CustomerInterestsView*. In SQL Server 2008, views can be created in the Microsoft SQL Server Management Studio by using either an SQL statement (as we have done to create and populate the VRG tables) or by using the GUI Display (by right-clicking the Views folder to display a shortcut menu and then clicking the New View command.) *CustomerInterestsView* can be created with the SQL statement:

```
CREATE VIEW CustomerInterestsView AS
    SELECT    C.LastName AS CustomerLastName,
              C.FirstName AS CustomerFirstName,
              A.LastName AS ArtistName
    FROM      CUSTOMER AS C JOIN CUSTOMER_ARTIST_INT AS CI
        ON    C.CustomerID = CI.CustomerID
        JOIN    ARTIST AS A
            ON  CI.ArtistID = A.ArtistID;
```

Figure 10-25 shows this SQL CREATE VIEW statement in an SQL script named VRG-Create-Views.sql in the Microsoft SQL Server Management Studio. We'll step through creating and testing this view.

Creating a New View

1. In the Microsoft SQL Server Management Studio Object Explorer, click the **New Query** button to open a new tabbed SQL document window.
2. Click the **Intellisense Enabled** button to disable the Intellisense feature.
3. Type the SQL statements, but not the comments, shown in Figure 10-25.
4. Click the **Parse** button. If there are any SQL coding errors detected, fix them.
5. Click the **Execute** button.
6. Expand the **Views** folder in the VRG database object. Note that the dbo.CustomerInterestsView object has been added to the VRG database, as shown in Figure 11-25.
7. To save this CREATE VIEW statement as part of an SQL script, add the comments shown in Figure 11-25 and then save the script as **VRG-Create-Views.sql**.
8. Click the document window **Close** button to close the window.

We can now look at the view in a GUI display.

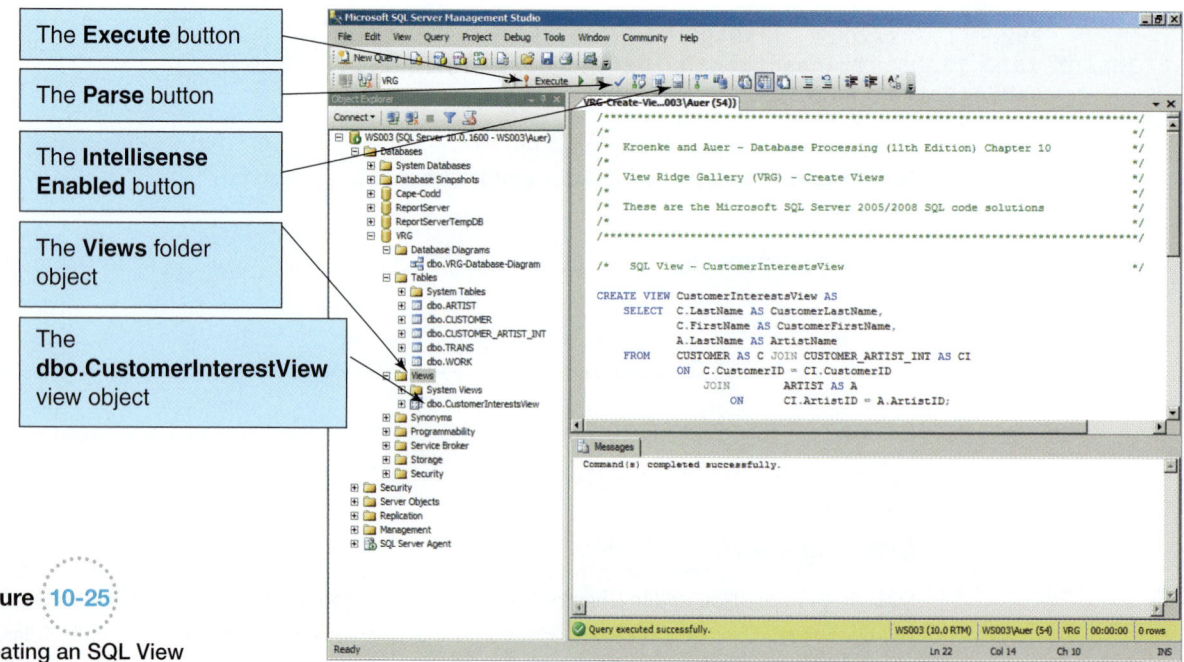

The **Execute** button

The **Parse** button

The **Intellisense Enabled** button

The **Views** folder object

The **dbo.CustomerInterestView** view object

Figure 10-25

Creating an SQL View

Figure 10-26

Viewing an SQL View in the
GUI Display

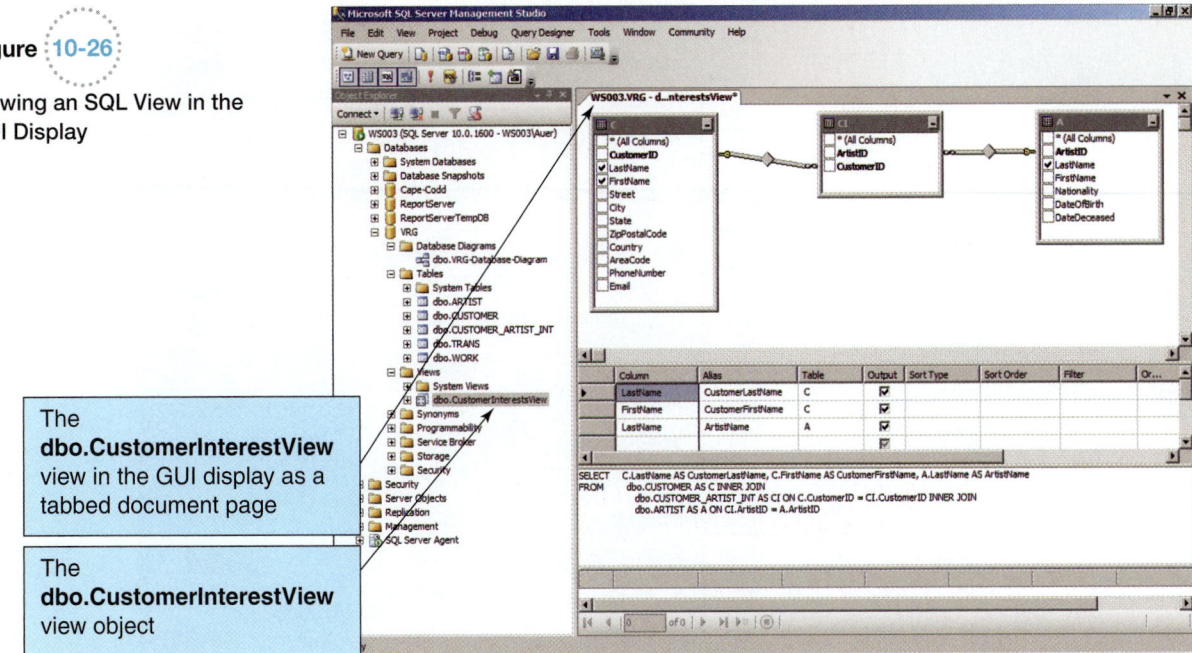

The **dbo.CustomerInterestView** view in the GUI display as a tabbed document page

The **dbo.CustomerInterestView** view object

Viewing an Existing View in the SQL Server GUI Display

1. Right-click the **dbo.CustomerInterests** view object in the Object Browser to display a shortcut menu.
2. Click the **Design** command on the shortcut menu. The dbo.CustomerInterestView is displayed in a new tabbed document window in the GUI display format.
3. Rearrange the components of the view in the GUI display so that it appears as shown in Figure 10-26.
4. Click the **Save** button to save the reconfigured view GUI display.
5. Click the document window **Close** button to close the GUI display window.
6. Collapse the **Views** folder in the Object Browser.

As explained in Chapter 7, SQL views are used like tables in other SQL statements. For example, to see all the data in the view, we use the SQL SELECT statement:

```
SELECT          *
FROM            CustomerInterestsView
ORDER BY        CustomerLastName, CustomerFirstName;
```

The result is shown in Figure 10-27.

SQL Server Application Logic

An SQL Server database can be processed from an application in a number of different ways. The first is one that we are already familiar with—SQL scripts. For security, however, such files should only be used during application development and testing and never on an operational database.

Another way is to create application code using a Microsoft .NET language such as C#.NET, C++.NET, VB.NET, or some other programming language and then invoke SQL Server DBMS commands from those programs. The modern way to do this is to use a library of object classes, create objects that accomplish database work, and then process those objects by setting object properties and invoking object methods.

	CustomerLastName	CustomerFirstName	ArtistName
1	Frederickson	Mary Beth	Chagall
2	Frederickson	Mary Beth	Kandinsky
3	Frederickson	Mary Beth	Miro
4	Frederickson	Mary Beth	Matisse
5	Gray	Donald	Tobey
6	Gray	Donald	Horiuchi
7	Gray	Donald	Graves
8	Janes	Jeffrey	Graves
9	Janes	Jeffrey	Horiuchi
10	Janes	Jeffrey	Tobey
11	Smathers	Fred	Tobey
12	Smathers	Fred	Horiuchi
13	Smathers	Fred	Graves
14	Smith	David	Chagall
15	Smith	David	Matisse
16	Smith	David	Kandinsky
17	Smith	David	Miro
18	Smith	David	Sargent
19	Twilight	Tiffany	Sargent
20	Twilight	Tiffany	Tobey
21	Twilight	Tiffany	Horiuchi
22	Twilight	Tiffany	Graves
23	Warning	Selma	Chagall
24	Warning	Selma	Graves
25	Warning	Selma	Sargent
26	Wilkens	Chris	Tobey
27	Wilkens	Chris	Graves
28	Wilkens	Chris	Horiuchi

Figure 10-27

Result of Using the View CustomerInterestView

Application logic can be embedded in triggers. As you learned in Chapter 7, triggers can be used to set default values, to enforce data constraints, to update views, and to enforce referential integrity constraints. In this chapter, we will describe four triggers, one for each of the four trigger uses. These triggers will be invoked by SQL Server when the specified actions occur.

Finally, another way of processing an SQL Server database is to create stored procedures, as described in Chapter 7. These stored procedures can then be invoked from application programs or from Web pages using languages such as VBScript or PHP. Stored procedures can also be executed from the SQL Server Management Studio. This should be done only when the procedures are being developed and tested, however. As described in Chapter 9, for security reasons, no one other than authorized members of the DBA staff should be allowed to interactively process an operational database.

In this chapter, we will describe and illustrate two stored procedures. Here, we will test those procedures by invoking them from the SQL Server Management Studio, and some of our output will be designed specifically for this environment. Again, this should be done only during development and testing. You will learn how to invoke these stored procedures from application code in Chapter 11.

Transact-SQL

Transact-SQL (T-SQL) is Microsoft's variant of SQL with additional procedural language added for use in stored procedures and triggers. We will use certain elements of Transact-SQL in such code, and therefore we need to discuss them at this point. Information on these and other Transact-SQL language components can be found at the Microsoft SQL Server Language Reference at *http://msdn.microsoft.com/en-us/library/ms166026(SQL.90).aspx*.

Transact-SQL identifies variables and parameters with an @ symbol. Thus, WorkID is a column name, but @WorkID is a Transact-SQL variable or parameter. A **parameter** is a value that is passed to a stored procedure when it is called. A **variable** is a value used within a stored procedure or trigger itself. Comments in Transact-SQL are either enclosed in /* and */ signs or follow **two dashes (- -)** if they are restricted to one line.

BY THE WAY   Transact-SQL statements in procedures and triggers can be written with or without the ending semicolon (;) required in nonprocedural SQL statements. For consistency, we will continue to use semicolons for SQL statements, but we will not use them for some of the other procedural elements discussed in the following sections.

Transact-SQL Control-of-flow Statements

The **Transact-SQL control-of-flow language** contains procedural language components that let you control exactly which parts of your code are used and the conditions required for their use. These components include IF . . . ELSE, BEGIN . . . END, WHILE, RETURN, and other keywords that can be used to direct the operations of a block of code. The **IF . . . ELSE keywords** are used to test for a condition, and then direct which blocks of code are used based on the result of that test. Note that the END keyword is *not* used as part of this construct in Transact-SQL, although it is commonly used here in many other programming languages. The **BEGIN . . END keywords** define a block of Transact-SQL statements so that more than one statement can be executed. Without this grouping, only one SQL statement can be used in either the IF or ELSE section of an IF . . . ELSE conditional branching. The **WHILE keyword** is used to create loops in Transact-SQL, where a section of code is repeated as long as ("while") some condition is true. The **RETURN keyword** is used to exit a block of code and terminate whatever code structure (stored procedure or trigger) is running. In this case, control is "returned" to the DBMS.

As an example, let's consider a new customer at the View Ridge Gallery who needs to have customer data entered into the CUSTOMER table and artist interest data entered into the CUSTOMER_ARTIST_INT table. The new customer is Michael Bench, with phone number 206-876-8822, e-mail address Michael.Bench@somewhere.com, and an interest in French artists.

Before we enter Michael's data, we need to check to see whether he is already in the database. To do this, we can use the following Transact-SQL code:

```
DECLARE    @RowCount    AS    Int
-- Check to see if Customer already exists in database
SELECT     @RowCount = COUNT(*)
FROM       CUSTOMER
WHERE      LastName = 'Bench'
    AND    FirstName = 'Michael'
    AND    AreaCode = '206'
    AND    PhoneNumber = '876-8822'
    AND    Email = 'Michael.Bench@somewhere.com';
-- IF @RowCount > 0 THEN Customer already exists.
IF (@RowCount > 0)
    BEGIN
        PRINT ' The Customer is already in the database. '
        RETURN
    END
```

```
-- IF (@RowCount = 0) THEN Customer does not exist in database.
ELSE
    BEGIN
    -- Insert new Customer data.
        INSERT INTO dbo.CUSTOMER
            (LastName, FirstName, AreaCode, PhoneNumber,
            Email)
            VALUES('Bench', 'Michael', '206', '876-8822',
            'Michael.Bench@somewhere.com');
            PRINT ' The new Customer is now in the database. '
    END
```

This block of SQL code illustrates the use of all of the control-of-flow keywords we have discussed except WHILE. The WHILE keyword is used in code loops, and one use of a code loop is in an SQL cursor.

Transact-SQL Cursor Statements

As we discussed in Chapter 7, a cursor is used so that SQL results stored in a table can be processed one row at a time. The **Transact-SQL cursor** is Microsoft's implementation of a cursor. Related cursor keywords include DECLARE, OPEN, FETCH, CLOSE, and DEALLOCATE. The **DECLARE CURSOR keywords** are used to create a cursor, whereas the **OPEN CURSOR keywords** start the use of the cursor. The **FETCH keyword** is used to retrieve row data. The **CLOSE CURSOR keywords** are used to exit the use of a cursor, and the **DEALLOCATE CURSOR keywords** remove the cursor from the DBMS. When using a cursor, the WHILE keyword is used to control how long the cursor is active.

Let's consider Michael Bench's interest in French artists. The ARTIST table has two French artists—Henri Matisse and Marc Chagall. Therefore, we need to add new rows to CUSTOMER_ARTIST_INT, both of which will contain Michael's CustomerID number (now that he has one) and each of which contain the ArtistID for one of these artists. To do this, we can use the following Transact-SQL code:

```
DECLARE        @ArtistID      AS      Int
DECLARE        @CustomerID    AS      Int
-- GET the CustomerID surrogate key value.
SELECT         @CustomerID = CustomerID
FROM           CUSTOMER
WHERE          LastName = 'Bench'
        AND    FirstName = 'Michael'
        AND    AreaCode = '206'
        AND    PhoneNumber = '876-8822'
        AND    Email = 'Michael.Bench@somewhere.com';
-- Create intersection record for each appropriate Artist.
-- Create cursor ArtistCursor
DECLARE ArtistCursor CURSOR FOR
        SELECT     ArtistID
        FROM       ARTIST
        WHERE      Nationality = 'French';
-- Process each appropriate Artist
OPEN ArtistCursor
    FETCH NEXT FROM ArtistCursor INTO @ArtistID
        WHILE @@FETCH_STATUS = 0
```

```
      BEGIN

        INSERT INTO CUSTOMER_ARTIST_INT

          (ArtistID, CustomerID)

          VALUES(@ArtistID, @CustomerID)

      PRINT ' New CUSTOMER_ARTIST_INT row added. '

      PRINT ' ArtistID = '+CONVERT(Char(6), @ArtistID)

      PRINT ' CustomerID = '+CONVERT(Char(6), @CustomerID)

          FETCH NEXT FROM ArtistCursor INTO @ArtistID

      END

CLOSE ArtistCursor

-- Remove cursor ArtistCursor

DEALLOCATE ArtistCursor
```

In this code, the ArtistCursor loops through the set of ArtistID values for French artists as long as ("while") the value of @@FETCH_STATUS is equal to 0. The **Transact-SQL @@FETCH_STATUS function** returns a value based on whether the FETCH NEXT statement actually returned a value from the next row. If there is no next row, then @@FETCH_STATUS returns 0.

Transact-SQL Output Statements

The two previous code segments also illustrate the use of the **Transact-SQL PRINT command**. This command will send a message to the SQL Server Management Console Messages window. We will use this output as a proxy for the real output that would be returned to an application, as it would be in most situations. Note that the actual output to be printed is marked by a single quote at the beginning and the end. Also note the use of the CONVERT function. The **Transact-SQL CONVERT function** is used to change one data type to another. In this case, we can only print character strings, so numbers such as ArtistID must be converted to character strings using the CONVERT function. Character strings can be combined by using the plus sign (+), and this is also shown in the code segments above.

Stored Procedures

With SQL Server 2000, stored procedures must be written in Transact-SQL. Starting with the release of SQL Server 2005, stored procedures and triggers can be written in any of the .NET or Common Language Runtime languages such as Visual Basic .NET, Visual C# .NET, and Visual C++ .NET. Transact-SQL continues to be supported and will have improved features and functions for error handling as well as other language upgrades. The Transact-SQL shown here will operate in SQL Server 2005 and SQL 2008, but in the long run, however, Visual Basic .NET, Visual C# .NET, or Visual C++ .NET will become better choices for stored procedures and triggers.

As with other database structures, you can write a stored procedure in an SQL script text file and process the commands using the SQL Server Management Studio. However, there is one little gotcha. The first time you create a stored procedure in an SQL script, you use the **SQL CREATE PROCEDURE statement**. Subsequently, if you change the procedure, use the **SQL ALTER PROCEDURE statement**. Otherwise, you will get an error message saying that the procedure already exists when you execute the modified procedure code.

You can also create a stored procedure within the SQL Server Management Studio by Enterprise Manager by expanding a database's Programmability folder object, right-clicking Stored Procedures, and selecting New Stored Procedure. If you do this, however, SQL Server simply opens an editable draft template in a tabbed document window.

The Stored Procedure InsertCustomerAndInterests

In our preceding discussion of Transact-SQL, we used as our example the need to enter data for a new customer and the artists of interest to that customer. The code segments we wrote were very specifically tied to the data we used, and thus of limited use. Is there a way to write a general block of code that could be used for more than one customer? Yes, and that block of code is a stored procedure.

Figure 10-28 shows the SQL code for the InsertCustomerAndInterests stored procedure. This stored procedure generalizes our previous code and can be used to insert data for any new customer into CUSTOMER, and then store data for that customer in CUSTOMER_ARTIST_INT, linking the customer to all artists having a particular nationality.

Five parameters are input to the procedure: @NewLastName, @NewFirstName, @NewAreaCode, @NewPhoneNumber, and @Nationality. The first four parameters are the new customer data, and the fourth one is the nationality of the artists for which the new customer has an interest. The stored procedure also uses three variables: @RowCount, @ArtistID, and @CustomerID.

Figure 10-28

The SQL Statements for the InsertCustomerAndInterests Stored Procedure

```
CREATE PROCEDURE InsertCustomerAndInterests
            @NewLastName       Char(25),
            @NewFirstName      Char(25),
            @NewAreaCode       Char(3),
            @NewPhoneNumber    Char(8),
            @NewEmail          Varchar(100),
            @Nationality       Char(30)
AS
    DECLARE    @RowCount    AS  Int
    DECLARE    @ArtistID    AS  Int
    DECLARE    @CustomerID  AS  Int

    -- Check to see if Customer already exists in database

    SELECT @RowCount = COUNT(*)
    FROM   dbo.CUSTOMER
    WHERE  LastName = @NewLastName
       AND FirstName = @NewFirstName
       AND AreaCode = @NewAreaCode
       AND PhoneNumber = @NewPhoneNumber
       AND Email =  @NewEmail;

    -- IF @RowCount > 0 THEN Customer already exists.
    IF (@RowCount > 0)
        BEGIN
            PRINT '********************************************************'
            PRINT ''
            PRINT '    The Customer is already in the database. '
            PRINT ''
            PRINT '    Customer Last Name          =  '+@NewLastName
            PRINT '    Customer First Name         =  '+@NewFirstName
            PRINT ''
            PRINT '********************************************************'
            RETURN
        END
    -- IF @RowCount = 0 THEN Customer does not exist in database.
    ELSE
        BEGIN
        -- Insert new Customer data.
            INSERT INTO dbo.CUSTOMER
                (LastName, FirstName, AreaCode, PhoneNumber, Email)
                VALUES(
                @NewLastName, @NewFirstName, @NewAreaCode,
                @NewPhoneNumber, @NewEmail);
        -- Get new CustomerID surrogate key value.
            SELECT @CustomerID = CustomerID
            FROM   dbo.CUSTOMER
            WHERE  LastName = @NewLastName
               AND FirstName = @NewFirstName
               AND AreaCode = @NewAreaCode
               AND PhoneNumber = @NewPhoneNumber
               AND Email =  @NewEmail;
```

```
                PRINT   '*****************************************************'
                PRINT   ''
                PRINT   '    The new Customer is now in the database. '
                PRINT   ''
                PRINT   '    Customer Last Name          =   '+@NewLastName
                PRINT   '    Customer First Name         =   '+@NewFirstName
                PRINT   ''
                PRINT   '*****************************************************'
-- Create intersection record for each appropriate Artist.
DECLARE ArtistCursor CURSOR FOR
        SELECT ArtistID
        FROM    dbo.ARTIST
        WHERE   Nationality=@Nationality
--Process each appropriate Artist
OPEN    ArtistCursor
    FETCH NEXT FROM ArtistCursor INTO @ArtistID
            WHILE @@FETCH_STATUS = 0
            BEGIN
                INSERT INTO dbo.CUSTOMER_ARTIST_INT
                    (ArtistID, CustomerID)
                    VALUES(@ArtistID, @CustomerID);
                    PRINT   '*************************************************'
                    PRINT   ''
                    PRINT   '   New CUSTOMER_ARTIST_INT row added. '
                    PRINT   ''
                    PRINT   '    ArtistID    =   '+CONVERT(Char(6), @ArtistID)
                    PRINT   '    CustomerID  =   '+CONVERT(Char(6), @CustomerID)
                    PRINT   ''
                    PRINT   '*************************************************'
            FETCH NEXT FROM ArtistCursor INTO @ArtistID
            END
    CLOSE   ArtistCursor
    DEALLOCATE      ArtistCursor
END
```

Figure 10-28

(Continued)

These variables are used to store values of the number of the row, the value of the ArtistID primary key, and the value of the CustomerID primary key, respectively.

The first task performed by this stored procedure is to determine whether the customer already exists. If the value of @RowCount in the first SELECT statement is greater than zero, then a row for that customer already exists. In this case, nothing is done, and the stored procedure prints an error message and exits (using the RETURN command). As stated earlier, the error message is visible in the Microsoft SQL Server Management Studio, but it generally would not be visible to application programs that invoked this procedure. Instead, a parameter or other facility needs to be used to return the error message back to the user via the application program. Discussion of that topic is beyond the scope of the present discussion, but we will send message back to the Microsoft SQL Server Management Studio to mimic such actions and provide a means to make sure our stored procedures are working correctly.

If the customer does not already exist, the procedure inserts the new data into the table dbo.CUSTOMER and then a new value of CustomerID is read into the variable @CustomerID. Internally, SQL Server adds a prefix to the table name that shows the name of the user who created it. Here, the prefix dbo is used to ensure that the CUSTOMER table created by the database owner (dbo) is processed. Without the dbo prefix, if the user invoking the stored procedure had created a table named CUSTOMER, then the user's table and not the dbo's table would be used.

The purpose of the second SELECT in Figure 10-28 is to obtain the value of the surrogate key CustomerID that was created by the INSERT statement. Another option is to use the **SQL Server function @@Identity**, which provides the value of the most recently created surrogate key value. Using this function, you could replace the second SELECT statement with the expression:

```
SET @CustomerID = @@Identity
```

To create the appropriate intersection table rows, an SQL cursor named ArtistCursor is created on an SQL statement that obtains all ARTIST rows where Nationality equals the parameter @Nationality. The cursor is opened and positioned on the first row by calling FETCH NEXT, and then the cursor is processed in a WHILE loop. In this loop, statements between BEGIN and END are iterated until SQL Server signals the end of the data by setting the value of the SQL Server function @@FETCH_STATUS to zero. At each iteration of the WHILE loop, a new row is inserted into the intersection table CUSTOMER_ ARTIST_INT. The FETCH NEXT statement at the end of the block moves the cursor to the next row.

To create the InsertCustomerAndInterests stored procedure in the VRG database, create a new SQL script named VRG-Create-Stored-Procedures.sql containing the SQL code in Figure 10-28. Include a beginning comments section similar to the one shown in Figure 10-10. Use the Parse button to check your SQL code, and after it parses correctly save the completed code before running it. Finally, check to make sure that the VRG database is selected in the Available Databases list, and then use the Execute button to create the stored procedure.

To invoke the InsertCustomerAndInterests stored procedure for Michael Bench, we use the following SQL statement:

```
EXEC InsertCustomerAndInterests
    @NewLastName = 'Bench', @NewFirstName = 'Michael',
    @NewAreaCode = '206', @NewPhoneNumber = '876-8822',
    @NewEmail = 'Michael.Bench@somewhere.com',
    @Nationality = 'French';
```

> **BY THE WAY**   Before we test any new functionality of a database such as a stored procedure or a trigger, it is always a good idea to refresh content in database in the Microsoft SQL Server Management Studio. This can be done by using the Refresh command in the object shortcut menu. For example, after creating the Insert-CustomerAndInterests stored procedure, right-click the VRG Stored Procedures folder in the Programmability folder and then click the Refresh command. Then expand the Stored Procedures folder and make sure the stored procedure object (shown as dbo.InsertCustomerWithInterests) is visible before running any test data.

Figure 10-29 shows the execution of the stored procedure in the SQL Server Management Studio. Notice how our sections of PRINT commands have produced the necessary output so that we can see what actions were taken. If we now wanted to check the tables themselves, we could do so, but that is not necessary at this point. In the output in Figure 10-29, we see that customer Michael Bench has been added to the CUSTOMER table and that new rows (a total of two, although we would have to scroll through the output to see that there are no more than two) have been inserted into the CUSTOMER_ARTIST_INT table.

> **BY THE WAY**   You can include the preceding EXEC InsertCustomerAndInterests statement in your VRG-Create-Stored-Procedures.sql script and run it from there. When there are multiple SQL statements in an open SQL script file, you can still run them one at a time by highlighting the SQL statement that you want to use. The Microsoft SQL Server Management Studio will then only apply actions such as parsing (using the Parse button) and executing (using the Execute button) to the highlighted SQL statement.
>
> This is a good trick to know, because it allows you to store multiple SQL statements (for example, a set of queries) in one SQL script for convenience but still control which statements are actually executed. Even better, note that if you highlight more than one SQL statement then the highlighted *set* of commands can be controlled the same way.

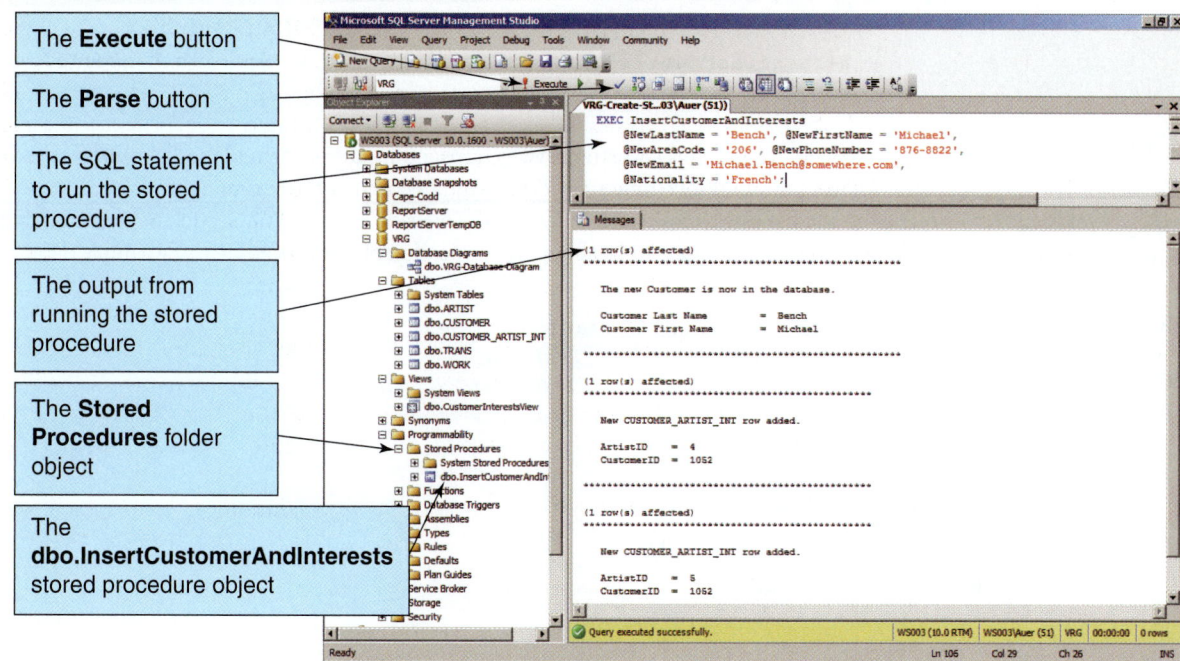

The **Execute** button

The **Parse** button

The SQL statement to run the stored procedure

The output from running the stored procedure

The **Stored Procedures** folder object

The **dbo.InsertCustomerAndInterests** stored procedure object

Figure 10-29

Running InsertCustomerAndInterests Stored Procedure

The Stored Procedure InsertCustomerWithTransaction

Now we will write a stored procedure that inserts data for a new customer, records a purchase, and creates an entry in the CUSTOMER_ARTIST_INT table. We will name this stored procedure *InsertCustomerWithTransaction*, and the necessary SQL code is shown in Figure 10-30. This procedure receives seven parameters having data about the new customer and about the customer's purchase. We will use this procedure to discuss transaction processing in SQL Server 2008.

The first action is to see whether the customer already exists. If so, the procedure exits with an error message. If the customer does not exist, this procedure then starts a transaction with the **Transact-SQL BEGIN TRANSACTION command**. Recall from Chapter 9 that transactions ensure that all of the database activity is committed atomically; either all of the updates occur or none of them do. The transaction begins, and the new customer row is inserted. The new value of CustomerID is obtained, as shown in the InsertCustomerWithInterests stored procedure. Next, the procedure checks to determine whether ArtistID, WorkID, and TransactionID are valid. If any are invalid, the transaction is rolled back using the **Transact-SQL ROLLBACK TRANSACTION command**.

If all the surrogate key values are valid, two actions in the transaction are completed. First, an UPDATE statement updates DateSold, SalesPrice, and CustomerID in the appropriate TRANS row. DateSold is set to system date via the **Transact-SQL Getdate( ) function**, SalesPrice is set to the value of @TransSalesPrice, and CustomerID is set to the value of @CustomerID. Second, a row is added to CUSTOMER_ARTIST_INT to record the customer's interest in this artist.

If everything proceeds normally to this point, the transaction is committed using the **Transact-SQL COMMIT TRANSACTION command**. After, and only after, the transaction is committed, we print the results messages.

To create the InsertCustomerWithTransaction stored procedure in the VRG database, add the SQL code in Figure 10-30 to your VRG-Create-Stored-Procedures.sql script. Include a comment to separate the code sections in this script file. Use the highlighting technique described in the preceding by the Way section to parse and execute the SQL code.

To use the InsertCustomerWithTransaction stored procedure, we will record the following purchase by our next new customer, Melinda Gliddens, who just bought a print of John Singer Sargent's *Spanish Dancer* for $350.00. The SQL statement is:

```
EXEC InsertCustomerWithTransaction

    @NewCustomerLastName = 'Gliddens',

    @NewCustomerFirstName = 'Melinda',

    @NewCustomerAreaCode = '360',

    @NewCustomerPhoneNumber = '765-8877',
```

```
                           @NewCustomerEmail = 'Melinda.Gliddens@somewhere.com',

                           @ArtistLastName = 'Sargent', @WorkTitle = 'Spanish Dancer',

                           @WorkCopy = '588/750', @TransSalesPrice = 350.00;
```

Figure 10-30

The SQL Statements for the InsertCustomer WithTransaction Stored Procedure

To execute this EXEC InsertCustomerWithTransaction statement, add the SQL statement to your VRG-Create-Stored-Procedures.sql script. Include a comment to separate the new SQL statement. Use the highlighting technique described in the preceding By the Way section to parse and execute the SQL statement. Figure 10-31 shows the invocation of this procedure using sample data.

```
CREATE PROCEDURE InsertCustomerWithTransaction
                @NewCustomerLastName        Char(25),
                @NewCustomerFirstName       Char(25),
                @NewCustomerAreaCode        Char(3),
                @NewCustomerPhoneNumber     Char(8),
                @NewCustomerEmail           Varchar(100),
                @ArtistLastName             Char(25),
                @WorkTitle                  Char(35),
                @WorkCopy                   Char(12),
                @TransSalesPrice            Numeric(8,2)

AS
    DECLARE     @RowCount       AS  Int,
                @ArtistID       AS  Int,
                @CustomerID     AS  Int,
                @WorkID         AS  Int,
                @TransactionID  AS  Int

    -- Check to see if Customer already exists in database

    SELECT      @RowCount = COUNT(*)
    FROM        dbo.CUSTOMER
    WHERE       LastName = @NewCustomerLastName
        AND     FirstName = @NewCustomerFirstName
        AND     AreaCode = @NewCustomerAreaCode
        AND     PhoneNumber = @NewCustomerPhoneNumber
        AND     Email =   @NewCustomerEmail;

    -- IF @RowCount > 0 THEN Customer already exists.
    IF  (@RowCount > 0)
        BEGIN
            PRINT '*********************************************************'
            PRINT ''
            PRINT '   The Customer is already in the database. '
            PRINT ''
            PRINT '   Customer Last Name     =  '+@NewCustomerLastName
            PRINT '   Customer First Name    =  '+@NewCustomerFirstName
            PRINT ''
            PRINT '*********************************************************'
            RETURN
        END
    -- IF @RowCount = 0 THEN Customer does not exist in database.
    ELSE
        -- Start transaction - Rollback everything if unable to complete it.
        BEGIN TRANSACTION
            -- Insert new Customer data.
            INSERT INTO dbo.CUSTOMER
                (LastName, FirstName, AreaCode, PhoneNumber, Email)
                VALUES(
                @NewCustomerLastName, @NewCustomerFirstName,
                @NewCustomerAreaCode, @NewCustomerPhoneNumber, @NewCustomerEmail);
            -- Get new CustomerID surrogate key value.
```

```
SELECT      @CustomerID = CustomerID
FROM        dbo.CUSTOMER
WHERE       LastName = @NewCustomerLastName
   AND      FirstName = @NewCustomerFirstName
   AND      AreaCode = @NewCustomerAreaCode
   AND      PhoneNumber = @NewCustomerPhoneNumber
   AND      Email =   @NewCustomerEmail;

-- Get ArtistID surrogate key value, check for validity.
SELECT      @ArtistID = ArtistID
FROM        dbo.ARTIST
WHERE       LastName = @ArtistLastName;

IF @ArtistID IS NULL
   BEGIN
      PRINT '*********************************************************'
      PRINT ''
      PRINT '    Invalid ArtistID '
      PRINT ''
      PRINT '*********************************************************'
      ROLLBACK TRANSACTION
      RETURN
   END

-- Get WorkID surrogate key value, check for validity.
SELECT      @WorkID = WorkID
FROM        dbo.WORK
WHERE       ArtistID = @ArtistID
   AND      Title = @WorkTitle
   AND      Copy = @WorkCopy;

IF @WorkID IS NULL
   BEGIN
      PRINT '*********************************************************'
      PRINT ''
      PRINT '    Invalid WorkID '
      PRINT ''
      PRINT '*********************************************************'
      ROLLBACK TRANSACTION
      RETURN
   END

-- Get TransID surrogate key value, check for validity.
SELECT      @TransactionID = TransactionID
FROM        dbo.TRANS
WHERE       WorkID = @WorkID
   AND      SalesPrice = NULL;

IF @TransactionID IS NULL
   BEGIN
      PRINT '*********************************************************'
      PRINT ''
      PRINT '    Invalid TransactionID '
      PRINT ''
      PRINT '*********************************************************'
      ROLLBACK TRANSACTION
      RETURN
   END
```

Figure 10-30

(Continued)

```
        -- All surrogate key values of OK, complete the transaction
        BEGIN
            -- Update TRANS row
            UPDATE dbo.TRANS
            SET     DateSold = GETDATE(),
                    SalesPrice = @TransSalesPrice,
                    CustomerID = @CustomerID
            WHERE   TransactionID = @TransactionID;
            -- Create CUSTOMER_ARTIST_INT row
            INSERT INTO dbo.CUSTOMER_ARTIST_INT (CustomerID, ArtistID)
                    VALUES(@CustomerID, @ArtistID);
        END
-- Commit the Transaction
COMMIT TRANSACTION
        -- The transaction is completed. Print output
        BEGIN
            -- Print Customer results.
            PRINT '*********************************************************'
            PRINT ''
            PRINT '   The new Customer is now in the database. '
            PRINT ''
            PRINT '   Customer Last Name  =   '+@NewCustomerLastName
            PRINT '   Customer First Name =   '+@NewCustomerFirstName
            PRINT ''
            PRINT '*********************************************************'
            -- Print Transaction result
            PRINT ''
            PRINT '   Transaction complete. '
            PRINT ''
            PRINT '   TransactionID       = '+CONVERT(Char(6), @TransactionID)
            PRINT '   ArtistID            = '+CONVERT(Char(6), @ArtistID)
            PRINT '   WorkID              = '+CONVERT(Char(6), @WorkID)
            PRINT '   Sales Price         = '+CONVERT(Char(12), @TransSalesPrice)
            PRINT ''
            PRINT '*********************************************************'
            -- Print CUSTOMER_ARTIST_INT update
            PRINT ''
            PRINT '   New CUSTOMER_ARTIST_INT row added. '
            PRINT ''
            PRINT '   ArtistID            = '+CONVERT(Char(6), @ArtistID)
            PRINT '   CustomerID          = '+CONVERT(Char(6), @CustomerID)
            PRINT ''
            PRINT '*********************************************************'
        END
-- ***** End of stored procedure InsertCustomerWithTransaction *****
```

Figure 10-30

(Continued)

> **BY THE WAY**   If we now look at the SQL code that has actually been stored for these two stored procedures (by right-clicking the stored procedure object and then choosing Modify), we will find that SQL Server has added the following lines before the code we wrote:
>
> ```
> USE [VRG]
> GO
> /****** Object: StoredProcedure [ {StoredProcedureName} ]
>      Script Date: {Date and Time created or altered} ******/
> SET ANSI_NULLS ON
> GO
> SET QUOTED_IDENTIFIER ON
> GO
> ```
>
> The **Transact-SQL USE [{DatabaseName}] command** tells the stored procedure to use the VRG database when it is called. This is the SQL command equivalent of selecting the database name in the Available Databases drop-down list in the Microsoft SQL Server Management Studio.
>
> The **Transact-SQL SET ANSI_NULLS ON command** specifies how SQL server handles comparisons of NULL values using equals (=) and not equals (<>) (for more information, see *http://msdn.microsoft.com/en-us/library/ms188048.aspx*). The **Transact-SQL SET QUOTED_IDENTIFIER ON command** specifies that object identifiers (table names, column names, etc.) can be enclosed in double quotes ("), which allows the use of SQL reserved words as objects names. For example, we could run the SQL statement:
>
> ```
> SELECT "Select"
> FROM "FROM"
> WHERE "Where" = 'San Francisco';
> ```
>
> Note that literals (San Francisco) are still enclosed in single quotes. For more information, see *http://msdn.microsoft.com/en-us/library/ms174393.aspx*.
>
> Finally, the **GO command** is not a Transact-SQL statement, but rather a command used by the Microsoft SQL Server Management Studio (and other SQL utilities) to mark the end of a batch of commands so that the utility can process sections of the code (as marked by the GO commands) separately instead of all at once. Declared variables (@RowCount) only exist within a section of code delineated by the GO statement and are cleared after that group of statements is run. For more information, see *http://msdn.microsoft.com/en-us/library/ms188037.aspx*.

Triggers

SQL Server 2008 supports the INSTEAD OF and AFTER triggers, but not a BEFORE trigger. A table may have one or more AFTER triggers for insert, update, and delete actions; AFTER triggers may not be assigned to views. A view or table may have at most one INSTEAD OF trigger for each triggering by an insert, an update, or delete action.

In SQL Server, triggers can roll back the transactions that caused them to be fired. When a trigger executes a ROLLBACK or ROLLBACK TRANSACTION command (two versions of the same command), all work done by the transaction that caused the trigger to be fired will be rolled back. If the trigger contains instructions after the ROLLBACK command, those instructions will be executed. However, any instructions in the transaction after the statement that caused the trigger to be fired will not be executed.

The **Execute** button

The **Parse** button

The SQL statement to run the stored procedure

The output from running the stored procedure

The **Stored Procedures** folder object

The **dbo.InsertCustomerWithTransaction** stored procedure object

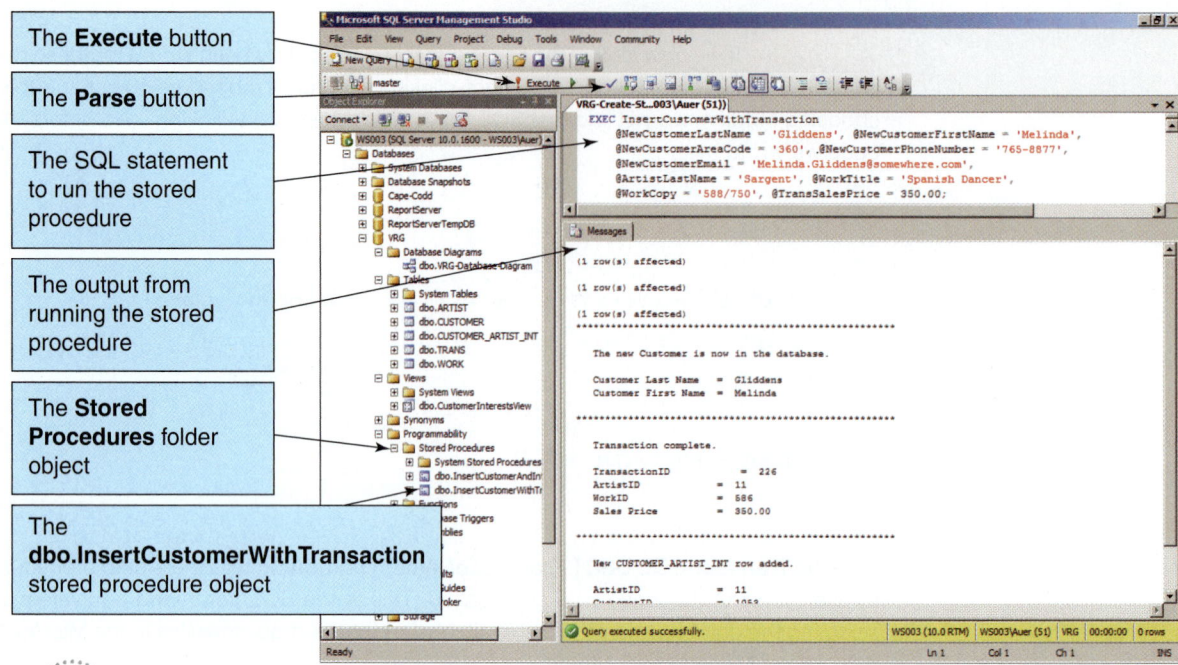

Figure 10-31

Running InsertCustomerWithTransaction Stored Procedure

For insert and update triggers, the new values for every column of the table being processed will be stored in a pseudotable named *inserted*. If, for example, a new row is being added to the ARTIST table, the pseudotable *inserted* will have five columns: LastName, FirstName, Nationality, DateOfBirth, and DateDeceased. Similarly, for update and delete commands, the old values for every column of the table being updated or deleted will be stored in the pseudotable named *deleted*. You will see how to use these pseudotables in the examples that follow.

The next four sections illustrate four triggers for each of the trigger functions described in Chapter 7. The best way to create these triggers is by keying them into an SQL script (using CREATE TRIGGER or ALTER TRIGGER as the first statement) in the Microsoft SQL Server Management Studio SQL editor. You can create a trigger by right-clicking the Triggers folder object for each table, but this only creates a skeleton trigger template for you to edit. It is better to create and test your own SQL script. For the VRG database, use an SQL script named VRG-Create-Triggers.sql, with introductory comments and comment lines to separate the triggers and the SQL statements used to test them. Use the previously discussed highlighting technique to control which SQL statement is actually being run.

A Trigger for Setting Default Values

Triggers can be used to set default values that are more complex than those that can be set with the Default constraint on a column definition. For example, the View Ridge Gallery has a pricing policy that says that the default AskingPrice of an artwork depends on whether the piece has been in the gallery before. If not, the default AskingPrice is twice the AcquisitionPrice. If the artwork has been in the gallery before, the default price is the larger of twice the AcquisitionPrice or the AcquisitionPrice plus the average net gain of the work in the past. The TRANS_AfterInsertSetAskingPrice trigger shown in Figure 10-32 implements this pricing policy.

Note the use of the AFTER keyword in this trigger code. We can use the keywords FOR or AFTER here, but both of these indicate an AFTER trigger—SQL Server does not support BEFORE triggers.

In the trigger, after the variables are declared, the new values of WorkID and AcquisitionPrice are obtained from the *inserted* pseudo table. Then, a SELECT FROM dbo.TRANS is executed to count the number of rows with the given WorkID. This trigger uses the system function @@rowCount, which contains the number of rows processed in the preceding Transact-SQL statement. Its value must be checked immediately after the statement is executed or saved in a variable to be checked later. Here, the trigger immediately uses the value of @@rowCount.

```
CREATE TRIGGER TRANS_AfterInsertSetAskingPrice
    ON TRANS
    AFTER INSERT

AS
BEGIN
    SET NOCOUNT ON;

    DECLARE     @PriorRowCount      AS Int,
                @WorkID             AS Int,
                @TransactionID      AS Int,
                @AcquisitionPrice   AS Numeric(8,2),
                @NewAskingPrice     AS Numeric(8,2),
                @SumNetProfit       AS Numeric(8,2),
                @AvgNetProfit       AS Numeric(8,2)

    SELECT @TransactionID = TransactionID,
           @AcquisitionPrice = AcquisitionPrice,
           @WorkID = WorkID
    FROM   inserted;

    -- First find if work has been here before.

    SELECT      *
    FROM        dbo.TRANS AS T
    WHERE       T.WorkID = @WorkID;

    -- Since this is an AFTER trigger, @@Rowcount includes the new row.

    SET @PriorRowCount = (@@Rowcount - 1)

    IF (@PriorRowCount = 0)
        -- This is first time work has been in the gallery.
        -- Set @NewAskingPrice to twice the acquisition cost.
        SET @NewAskingPrice = (2 * @AcquisitionPrice)

    ELSE
        -- The work has been here before
        -- We have to determine the value of @NewAskingPrice
        BEGIN
            SELECT      @SumNetProfit = SUM(NetProfit)
            FROM        dbo.ArtistWorkNetView AWNV
            WHERE       AWNV.WorkID = @WorkID
            GROUP BY    AWNV.WorkID;

            SET @AvgNetProfit = (@SumNetProfit / @PriorRowCount);

                -- Now choose larger value for the new AskingPrice.

            IF ((@AcquisitionPrice + @AvgNetProfit)
                    > (2 * @AcquisitionPrice))
                SET @NewAskingPrice = (@AcquisitionPrice + @AvgNetProfit)
            ELSE
                SET @NewAskingPrice = (2 * @AcquisitionPrice)
        END
```

Figure 10-32

The SQL Statements
for the TRANS_After
InsertSetAskingPrice
Trigger

```
-- Update TRANS with the value of AskingPrice
UPDATE dbo.TRANS
SET    AskingPrice = @NewAskingPrice
WHERE  TransactionID = @TransactionID;

-- The INSERT is completed. Print output
BEGIN
    PRINT '*****************************************************'
    PRINT ''
    PRINT '    INSERT complete. '
    PRINT ''
    PRINT '    TransactionID     =  '+CONVERT(Char(6), @TransactionID)
    PRINT '    WorkID            =  '+CONVERT(Char(6), @WorkID)
    PRINT '    Acquisition Price =  '+CONVERT(Char(12), @AcquisitionPrice)
    PRINT '    Asking Price      =  '+CONVERT(Char(12), @NewAskingPrice)
    PRINT ''
    PRINT '*****************************************************'
END
END
```

Figure 10-32

(Continued)

The variable @PriorRowCount is set to @@rowCount minus one because this is an AFTER trigger, and the new row will already be in the database. The expression (@@rowCount-1) is the correct number of qualifying TRANS rows that were in the database prior to the insert.

We test to see if the work is new. If so, @NewAskingPrice is then set to twice the AcquisitionPrice. If the work has been in the gallery before, we must calculate which value of @NewAskingPrice to use. Thus, if @PriorRowCount is greater than zero, there were TRANS rows for this work in the database, and the ArtistWorkNet view (see pages 270–271) is used to obtain the sum of the WorkNetProfit for the work. The AVG built-in function cannot be used because it will compute the average using @@rowCount rather than @PriorRowCount. Next, the two possible values of @AskingNewPrice are compared, and @NewAskingPrice is set to the larger value. Finally, an update is made to TRANS to set the computed value of @newPrice for AskingPrice.

> **BY THE WAY** In the two stored procedures we discussed in the previous section, the @@rowCount function could have been used instead of counting rows using COUNT(*) to set the value of the variable @RowCount. Just remember to check it or store it immediately after the SQL statement is executed.

To test the trigger, we will begin by obtaining a new work for the View Ridge Gallery. Because Melinda Gliddens just bought the only copy of the print John Singer Sargent's *Spanish Dancer*, we will replace it:

```
INSERT INTO WORK VALUES(
    'Spanish Dancer', '635/750', 'High Quality Limited Print',
    'American Realist style - From work in Spain', 11);

-- Obtain the new WorkID

SELECT      WorkID

FROM        dbo.WORK

WHERE       ArtistID = 11
    AND     Title = 'Spanish Dancer'
    AND     Copy = '635/750';

-- Use the new WorkID value (597 in this case)

INSERT INTO TRANS (DateAcquired, AcquisitionPrice, WorkID)

VALUES ('06/8/2008', 200.00, 597);
```

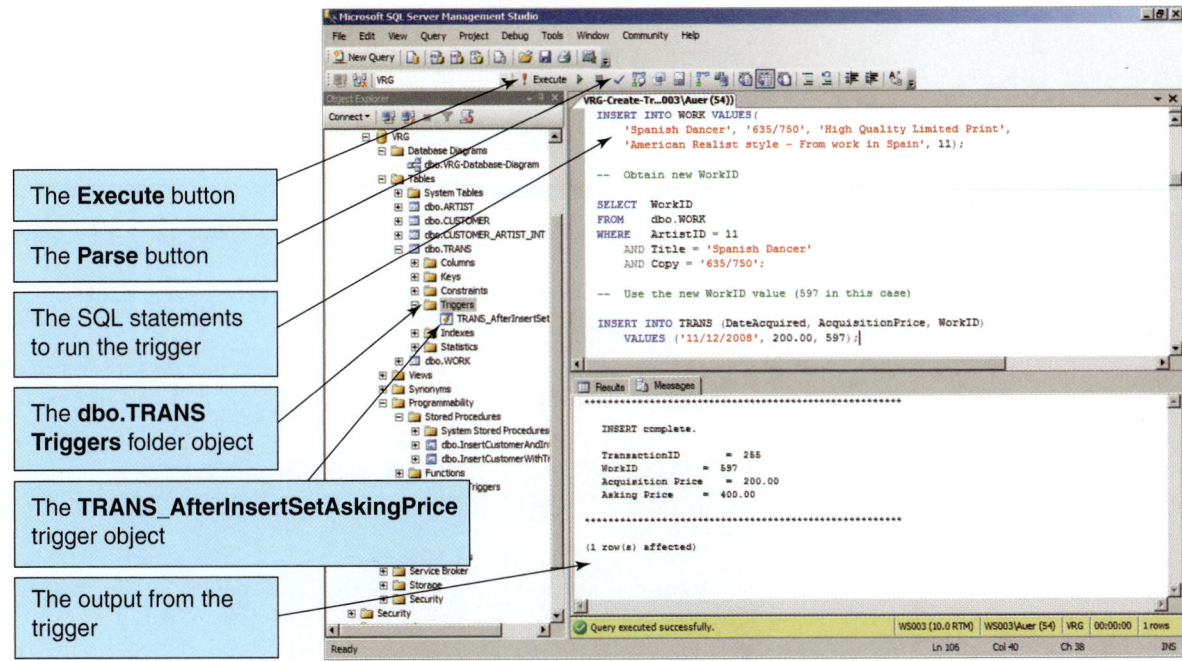

The **Execute** button

The **Parse** button

The SQL statements to run the trigger

The **dbo.TRANS Triggers** folder object

The **TRANS_AfterInsertSetAskingPrice** trigger object

The output from the trigger

Figure 10-33

Results of the TRANS_AfterInsertSetAsking Price Trigger

Figure 10-33 shows the results of the events triggered by the INSERT statement on TRANS. Note that the asking price for the new work (400.00) has been set to twice the acquisition cost (200.00), which is the correct value for a work that has not previously been in the gallery. This trigger provides useful functionality for the gallery. It saves the gallery personnel considerable manual work in implementing their pricing policy and likely improves the accuracy of the results as well.

> **BY THE WAY** At the beginning of the trigger code, you will see the command "SET NOCOUNT ON;" You may have noticed that when, for example, you execute INSERT statements SQL Server generates the message "(1 row(s) affected)" after each INSERT statement so that this message appears in the Microsoft SQL Server Management Studio Messages window. This is useful if you are actually watching these actions (it tells you that the intended action successfully completed), but it is meaningless when a trigger is firing based on an application action. Further, the time it takes to generate these messages can slow performance down in some cases. Therefore, we set NOCOUNT to ON so that these messages are not generated by trigger actions.

A Trigger for Enforcing a Data Constraint

The View Ridge Gallery needs to track problem-customer accounts; these are customers who have either not paid promptly or who have presented other problems to the gallery. When a customer who is on the problem list attempts to make a purchase at the gallery, the gallery wants the transaction to be rolled back and a message displayed. Note that this feature requires an intertable CHECK constraint between the TRANS table and the CUSTOMER table, which, as we discussed in Chapter 7, requires a trigger to implement.

To enforce this policy and the corresponding constraint, we need to add a column to the CUSTOMER table named isProblemAccount. This column will use the **SQL Server Bit data type**, which can have the values NULL, 0, and 1. Zero indicates a good account, whereas a 1 indicates a problem account. And it looks like our new customer Melinda Gliddens had trouble with her previous payment, so we set her isProblemAccount value to 1:

```
ALTER TABLE dbo.CUSTOMER
     ADD isProblemAccount   Bit NULL DEFAULT '0';
```

```
UPDATE       dbo.CUSTOMER
   SET       isProblemAccount = 0;

UPDATE       dbo.CUSTOMER
   SET       isProblemAccount = 1
   WHERE     LastName = 'Gliddens'
      AND    FirstName = 'Melinda';

SELECT       CustomerID, LastName, FirstName, isProblemAccount
FROM         dbo.CUSTOMER;
```

The results of the SELECT statement are:

	CustomerID	LastName	FirstName	isProblemAccount
1	1000	Janes	Jeffrey	0
2	1001	Smith	David	0
3	1015	Twilight	Tiffany	0
4	1033	Smathers	Fred	0
5	1034	Frederic...	Mary Beth	0
6	1036	Warning	Selma	0
7	1037	Wu	Susan	0
8	1040	Gray	Donald	0
9	1041	Johnson	Lynda	0
10	1051	Wilkens	Chris	0
11	1052	Bench	Michael	0
12	1053	Gliddens	Melinda	1

Now we will create a trigger on TRANS named TRANS_CheckIsProblemAccount. With this trigger, when a customer makes a purchase the trigger determines whether the customer is flagged by the value of the isProblemAccount data in the CUSTOMER table. If so, the transaction is rolled back and a message is displayed. The trigger code in Figure 10-34 enforces this policy.

Note one interesting feature of the trigger code in Figure 10-34. As noted there, this trigger will fire for every update on TRANS, including updates fired by another trigger such as TRANS_After-InsertSetAskingPrice. But in that trigger, no customer is involved. Therefore, before completing the rest of this trigger, we have to be sure that there is actually a customer participating in a transaction whose account status needs to be checked. This is done by the line:

```
IF (@CustomerID IS NULL) RETURN
```

Note that we only want to exit the TRANS_CheckIsProblemAccount trigger if there is no customer, not rollback the transaction that fired the trigger. When writing multiple triggers, remember that they may be run from other actions besides the one that you originally created them to handle.

OK, here comes Melissa to make another purchase—let's see what happens.

```
UPDATE    TRANS
SET       DateSold = '11/18/2008',
          SalesPrice = 475.00,
          CustomerID = 1056
WHERE     TransactionID = 229;
```

```sql
CREATE TRIGGER TRANS_CheckIsProblemAccount
    ON dbo.TRANS
    FOR UPDATE

AS
BEGIN
    SET NOCOUNT ON;

    DECLARE    @TransactionID     AS Int,
               @CustomerID        AS Int,
               @isProblemAccount  AS Bit

    SELECT @TransactionID = TransactionID,
           @CustomerID  = CustomerID
    FROM   inserted;

    /* This trigger will fire for every update of TRANS.
     * This includes updates without a Customer participating,
     * such as an update of AskingPrice using the
     * TRANS_AfterInsertSetAskingPrice tigger.
     * Therefore, make sure there is a Customer particpating
     * in the Update of TRANS/
     */

    -- Check if Customer ID is NULL and if so RETURN.
    -- Do not ROLLBACK the transaction, just don't complete this trigger.

    IF (@CustomerID IS NULL) RETURN

    -- Valid CustomerID.
    -- Obtain value of @isProblemAcocunt.

    SELECT    @isProblemAccount = isProblemAccount
    FROM      dbo.CUSTOMER AS C
    WHERE     C.CustomerID = @CustomerID;

    IF (@isProblemAccount = 1)
        -- This is a problem account.
        -- Rollback the transaction and send message.
        BEGIN
            ROLLBACK TRANSACTION
            PRINT '*******************************************************'
            PRINT ''
            PRINT '    Transaction canceled.'
            PRINT ''
            PRINT '    CustomerID        = '+CONVERT(Char(6), @CustomerID)
            PRINT ''
            PRINT '    Refer customer to the manager immediately.'
            PRINT ''
            PRINT '*******************************************************'
            RETURN
```

Figure 10-34

The SQL Statements for the
TRANS_CheckIsProblem
Account Trigger

```
    ELSE
        -- This is a good account
        -- Let the transaction stand.
        BEGIN
            PRINT '*************************************************'
            PRINT ''
            PRINT '    Transaction complete.'
            PRINT '    TransactionID   = '+CONVERT(Char(6), @TransactionID)
            PRINT '    CustomerID      = '+CONVERT(Char(6), @CustomerID)
            PRINT ''
            PRINT '    Thank the customer for their business.'
            PRINT ''
            PRINT '*************************************************'
        END
    END
```

Figure 10-34

(Continued)

The resulting output is shown in Figure 10-35. Looks like Melinda is off to talk to the manager about her account!

> **BY THE WAY** Using a table of valid or invalid values is more flexible and dynamic than placing such values in a CHECK constraint. For example, consider the CHECK constraint on Nationality values in the ARTIST table. If the gallery manager wants to expand the nationality of allowed artists, the manager will have to change the CHECK constraint using the ALTER TABLE statement. In reality, the gallery manager will have to hire a consultant to change this constraint.
>
> A better approach is to place the allowed values of Nationality in a table, say, ALLOWED_NATIONALITY. Then, write a trigger like that shown in Figure 10-34 to enforce the constraint that new values of Nationality exist in ALLOWED_NATIONALITY. When the gallery owner wants to change the allowed artists, the manager would simply add or remove values in the ALLOWED_NATIONALITY table.

Figure 10-35

Results of the
TRANS_CheckIsProblem
Account

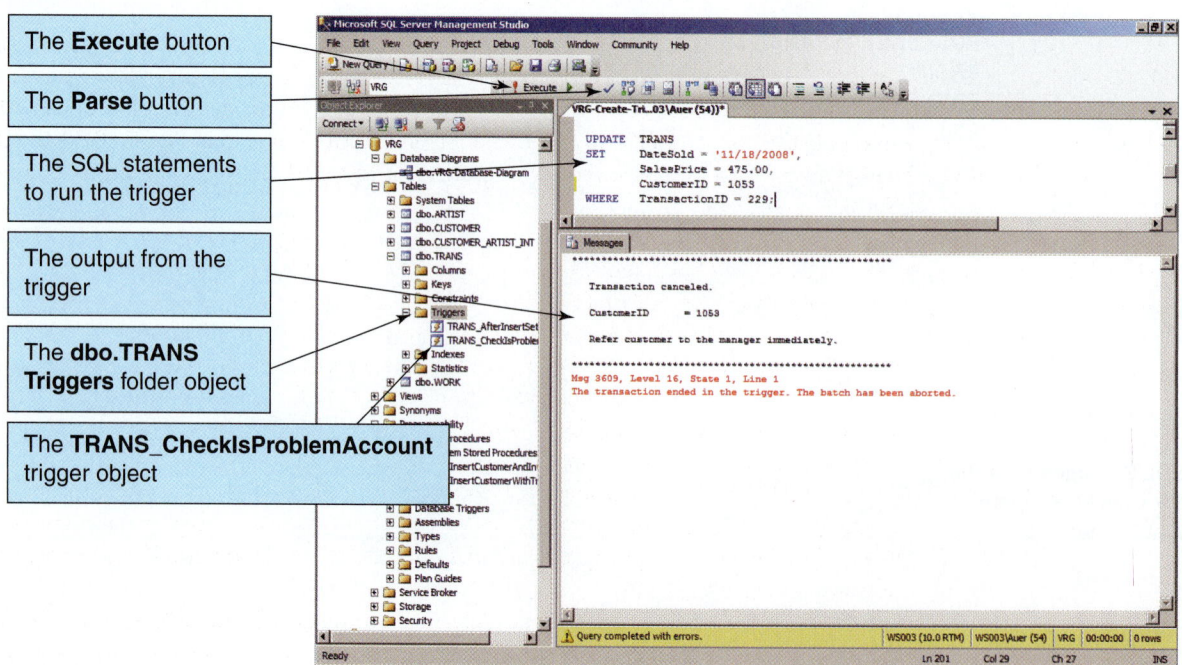

A Trigger for Updating a View

In Chapter 7, we discussed the problem of updating views. One such problem concerns updating views created via joins; it is normally not possible for the DBMS to know how to update tables that underlie the join. However, sometimes application-specific knowledge can be used to determine how to interpret a request to update a joined view.

Consider the view CustomerInterestsView shown in Figure 10-25. It contains rows of CUSTOMER and ARTIST joined over their intersection table. CUSTOMER.LastName is given the alias CustomerLastName, CUSTOMER.FirstLastName is given the alias CustomerFirstName, and ARTIST.LastName is given the alias ArtistName. A request to change the last name of a customer in CustomerInterests can be interpreted as a request to change the last name of the underlying CUSTOMER table. Such a request, however, can be processed only if the value of CUSTOMER.LastName is unique. If not, the request cannot be processed.

The INSTEAD OF trigger shown in Figure 10-36 implements this logic. First, the new and old values of the CustomerLastName column in CustomerInterestsView are obtained. Then, a correlated subquery is used to determine whether the old value of CUSTOMER.LastName is unique. If so, the name can be changed, but otherwise, no update can be made.

This trigger needs to be tested against cases in which the last name is unique and cases in which the last name is not unique. Figure 10-37 shows the case in which the customer name was unique. View Ridge Gallery's two newest customers, Michael Bench and Melissa Gliddens, just got married after meeting at a View Ridge Gallery opening, and Melissa wants to change her last name. To do this, we use the SQL statement:

```
UPDATE    dbo.CustomerInterestsView

SET       CustomerLastName = 'Bench'

WHERE     CustomerLastName = 'Gliddens';
```

Note that the UPDATE command was issued against the view. As indicated in the Messages pane, Melissa is now Melissa Bench.

A Trigger for Enforcing a Required Child Constraint

The VRG database design includes an M-M relationship between WORK and TRANS. Every WORK must have a TRANS to store the price of the work and the date the work was acquired, and every TRANS must relate to a WORK parent. Figure 10-38 shows the tasks that must be accomplished to enforce this constraint; it is based on the boilerplate shown in Figure 6-28(b).

Because the CREATE TABLE statement for TRANS in Figure 10-13 defines TRANS.WorkID as NOT NULL and defines the FOREIGN KEY constraint without cascading deletions, the DBMS will ensure that every TRANS has a WORK parent. So, we need not be concerned with enforcing the insert on TRANS or the deletion on WORK. As stated in Figure 10-38, the DBMS will do that for us. Also, we need not be concerned with updates to WORK.WorkID because it is a surrogate key.

Three constraints remain that must be enforced by triggers: (1) ensuring that a TRANS row is created when a new WORK is created; (2) ensuring that TRANS.WorkID never changes; and (3) ensuring that the last TRANS child for a WORK is never deleted.

We can enforce the second constraint by writing a trigger on the update of TRANS that checks for a change in WorkID. If there is such a change, the trigger can roll back the change.

With regards to the third constraint, View Ridge Gallery has a business policy that no TRANS data ever be deleted. Thus, we need not only to disallow the deletion of the last child, we need to disallow the deletion of any child. We can do this by writing a trigger on the deletion of TRANS that rolls back any attempted deletion. (If the gallery allowed TRANS deletions, we could enforce the deletion constraint using views, as shown in Chapter 7, Figures 7-29 and 7-30.) The triggers for enforcing the second and third constraints are simple, and we leave them as exercises 11.28 and 11.29.

However, the first constraint is a problem. Now, we could write a trigger on the WORK INSERT to create a default TRANS row, but this trigger will be called before the application has

```sql
CREATE TRIGGER CIV_ChangeCustomerLastName
    ON dbo.CustomerInterestsView
    INSTEAD OF UPDATE

AS
BEGIN
    SET NOCOUNT ON;

    DECLARE     @NewCustomerLastName    AS Char(25),
                @OldCustomerLastName    AS Char(25)

    -- Get values of new and old names.
    SELECT      @NewCustomerLastName = CustomerLastName
    FROM        inserted;

    SELECT      @OldCustomerLastName = CustomerLastName
    FROM        deleted;

    -- Count number of synonyms is CUSTOMER.
    SELECT      *
    FROM        dbo.CUSTOMER AS C1
    WHERE       C1.LastName = @OldCustomerLastName
        AND     EXISTS
                (SELECT     *
                 FROM       dbo.CUSTOMER AS C2
                 WHERE      C1.LastName = C2.LastName
                    AND     C1.CustomerID <> C2.CustomerID);

    IF (@@rowCount = 0)
        -- The Customer last name is unique.
        -- Update the Customer record.
        BEGIN
            UPDATE  dbo.CUSTOMER
            SET     LastName = @NewCustomerLastName
            WHERE   LastName = @OldCustomerLastName;

            -- Print update message.
            PRINT '*********************************************************'
            PRINT ''
            PRINT '   The Customer last name has been changed.'
            PRINT ''
            PRINT '   Former Customer Last Name    = '+@OldCustomerLastName
            PRINT ''
            PRINT '   Upddated Customer Last Name  = '+@NewCustomerLastName
            PRINT ''
            PRINT '*********************************************************'
        END
```

Figure 10-36

The SQL Statements for
the CIV_ChangeCustomer
LastName Trigger

```
ELSE
    -- The Customer name is not unique.
    -- Rollback the transaction and send message.
    BEGIN
        ROLLBACK
        PRINT '*********************************************************'
        PRINT ''
        PRINT '    Transaction canceled.'
        PRINT ''
        PRINT '    Customer Last Name  = '+@NewCustomerLastName
        PRINT ''
        PRINT '    The customer last name is not unique.'
        PRINT ''
        PRINT '*********************************************************'
    END
END
```

Figure 10-36

(Continued)

a chance to create the TRANS row itself. The trigger would create a TRANS row and then the application may create a second one. To guard against the duplicate, we could then write a trigger on TRANS to remove the row the WORK trigger created in those cases when the application creates its own trigger. However, this solution is awkward, at best.

A better design is to require the applications to create the WORK and TRANS combination via a view. For example, we can create a view named WorkAndTransView (we will add the code into our VRG-Create-Views.sql script and execute it from there):

```
CREATE VIEW WorkAndTransView AS
    SELECT      Title, Copy, Medium, [Description], ArtistID,
                DateAcquired, AcquisitionPrice
    FROM        WORK AS W JOIN TRANS AS T
        ON      W.WorkID = T.WorkID;
```

Figure 10-37

Results of the
CIV_ChangeCustomer
LastName Trigger

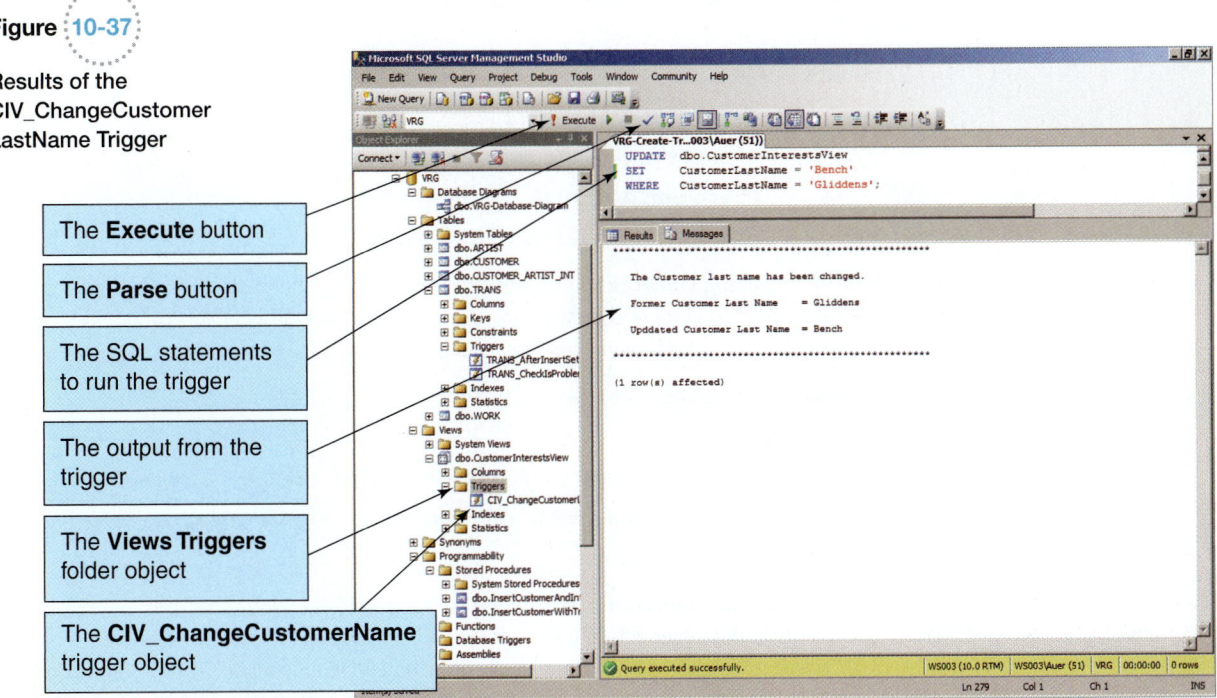

The **Execute** button

The **Parse** button

The SQL statements
to run the trigger

The output from the
trigger

The **Views Triggers**
folder object

The **CIV_ChangeCustomerName**
trigger object

WORK Is Required Parent TRANS Is Required Child	Action on WORK (Parent)	Action on TRANS (Child)
Insert	Create a TRANS row.	New TRANS must have a valid WorkID (enforced by DBMS).
Modify key or foreign key	Prohibit—WORK uses a surrogate key.	Prohibit—TRANS uses a surrogate key, and TRANS cannot change to a different WORK.
Delete	Prohibit—Cannot delete a WORK with and TRANS children (enforced by DBMS by lack of CASCADE DELETE).	Cannot delete the last child. [Actually, data related to a transaction is never deleted (business rule)].

Figure 10-38

Actions to Enforce Minimum Cardinality for the WORK-to-TRANS Relationship

The DBMS will not be able to process an insert on this view. We can, however, define an INSTEAD OF trigger to process the insert. Our trigger, named WATV_InsertTransactionWithWork, will create both a new row in WORK and the new required child in TRANS. The code for this trigger is shown in Figure 10-39. Note that with this solution applications must not be allowed to insert WORK rows directly. They must always insert them via the view WorkAndTransView.

To test our trigger, we will add a new work to the VRG database. Melissa, now Mrs. Michael Bench, has worked out her account problems with the View Ridge Gallery and completed her purchase of the print of Horiuchi's *Color Floating in Time*.

```
UPDATE    dbo.CUSTOMER
SET       isProblemAccount = 0
WHERE     LastName    = 'Bench'
   AND    FirstName   = 'Melinda';


UPDATE    TRANS
SET       DateSold = '11/18/2008',
          SalesPrice = 475.00,
          CustomerID = 1053
          WHERE    TransactionID = 229;
```

Note that the preceding UPDATE statement fired the TRAN_CheckIsProblemAccount trigger, but since Melinda is now a good customer again, the transaction was accepted. Now we will restock a copy of *Color Floating in Time* into the gallery.

```
INSERT INTO WorkAndTransView
    VALUES(
    'Color Floating in Time', '493/750', 'High Quality Limited Print',
    'Northwest School Abstract Expressionist style', 18,
    '02/05/2009', 250.00);
```

The results of the transaction are shown in Figure 10-39. Note that the WATV_Insert-TransactionWithWork trigger actually sets off two other triggers. First it fires the INSERT trigger TRANS_AfterInsertSetAskingPrice, which then fires the UPDATE trigger TRANS_CheckProblem Account trigger. Because no customer is involved in this transaction, the TRANS_CheckProblem

```
CREATE TRIGGER WATV_InsertTransactionWithWork
   ON dbo.WorkAndTransView
   INSTEAD OF INSERT

AS
BEGIN
   SET NOCOUNT ON;

   DECLARE     @TransactionID      AS Int,
               @WorkID             AS Int,
               @Title              AS Char(35),
               @Copy               AS Char(12),
               @Medium             AS Char(35),
               @Description        AS Varchar(1000),
               @ArtistID           AS Int,
               @DateAcquired       AS DateTime,
               @AcquisitionPrice   AS Numeric(8,2),
               @AskingPrice        AS Numeric(8,2)

   -- Get available values from Insert on the view.
   SELECT      @Title = Title, @Copy = Copy, @Medium = Medium,
               @Description = [Description],
               @ArtistID = ArtistID, @DateAcquired =DateAcquired,
               @AcquisitionPrice = AcquisitionPrice
   FROM        inserted;

   -- Insert new row into WORK.
   INSERT INTO WORK VALUES(
               @Title, @Copy, @Medium, @Description, @ArtistID);

   -- Get new WorkID surrogate key value using @@Identity funcion.
   SET @WorkID = @@Identity;

   -- Insert new row into TRANS.
   -- Note that INSERT will trigger TRANS_AfterInsertSetAskingPrice.
   INSERT INTO TRANS (DateAcquired, AcquisitionPrice, WorkID)
               VALUES(
               @DateAcquired, @AcquisitionPrice, @WorkID);

   -- Get new TransactionID surrogate key value.
   SET @TransactionID = @@Identity;

   -- Get new AskingPrice set by TRANS_AfterInsertSetAskingPrice.
   SELECT      @AskingPrice = AskingPrice
   FROM        TRANS
   WHERE       TransactionID = @TransactionID;

   -- Print results message.
   PRINT '********************************************************'
   PRINT ''
   PRINT '   The new work has been inserted into WORK and TRANS.'
   PRINT ''
   PRINT '   TransactionID      = '+CONVERT(Char(6), @TransactionID)
   PRINT '   WorkID             = '+CONVERT(Char(6), @WorkID)
   PRINT '   ArtistID           = '+CONVERT(Char(6), @ArtistID)
   PRINT '   Title              = '+@Title
   PRINT '   Copy               = '+@Copy
   PRINT '   Medium             = '+@Medium
   PRINT '   Description        = '+@Description
   PRINT '   DateAcquired       = '+CONVERT(Char(12), @DateAcquired)
   PRINT '   Acquisition Price  = '+CONVERT(Char(12), @AcquisitionPrice)
   PRINT '   Asking Price       = '+CONVERT(Char(12), @AskingPrice)
   PRINT '********************************************************'
   END
```

Figure 10-39

The SQL Statements
for the WATV_Insert
TransactionWithWork
Trigger

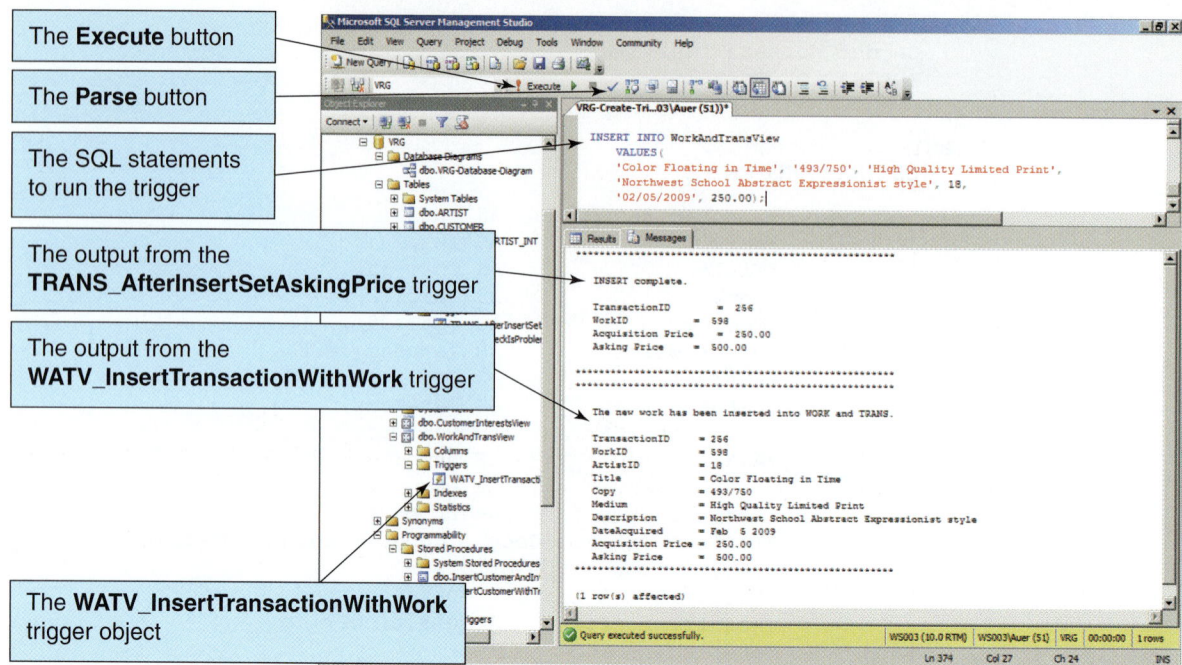

The **Execute** button

The **Parse** button

The SQL statements to run the trigger

The output from the **TRANS_AfterInsertSetAskingPrice** trigger

The output from the **WATV_InsertTransactionWithWork** trigger

The **WATV_InsertTransactionWithWork** trigger object

Figure 10-40

Results of the WATV_InsertTransaction WithWork Trigger

Account returns control without completing the trigger (see the previous discussion of the code for this trigger). However, the TRANS_AfterInsertSetAskingPrice trigger does run and sets the new asking price for the new work. Therefore, the results of two triggers show up in the output in Figure 10-40 and the new work does now have an asking price.

BY THE WAY   If we look at the SQL code that has actually been stored for these triggers, we will again find that SQL Server has added some lines before the code we wrote:

```
USE [VRG]
GO
/****** Object:  Trigger [ {StoredProcedureName} ]
     Script Date: {Date and Time created or altered} ******/
SET ANSI_NULLS ON
GO
SET QUOTED_IDENTIFIER ON
GO
```

This is essentially the same code used for stored procedures. However, we should also note that there is an important use of the GO command when running scripts. Triggers are run only *once* for a set of operations, such as typically found in a script, not for each individual command.

For example, suppose that in our last trigger example we had decided to use an SQL script to input the data for three copies of *Color Floating in Time* at once as follows (note the change in the value of Copy):

```
INSERT INTO WorkAndTransView
    VALUES(
    'Color Floating in Time', '493/750', 'High Quality Limited Print',
    'Northwest School Abstract Expressionist style', 18,
    '02/05/2009', 250.00);
```

```
INSERT INTO WorkAndTransView

    VALUES(
    'Color Floating in Time', '494/750', 'High Quality Limited Print',
    'Northwest School Abstract Expressionist style', 18,
    '02/05/2009', 250.00);

INSERT INTO WorkAndTransView

    VALUES(
    'Color Floating in Time', '495/750', 'High Quality Limited Print',
    'Northwest School Abstract Expressionist style', 18,
    '02/05/2009', 250.00);
```

In this case, the WATV_InsertTransactionWithWork trigger only fires *once*! But this is not what we want—we want it to fire once per INSERT. This is where the GO command comes in handy, and we will use the following code:

```
INSERT INTO WorkAndTransView

    VALUES(
    'Color Floating in Time', '493/750', 'High Quality Limited Print',
    'Northwest School Abstract Expressionist style', 18,
    '02/05/2009', 250.00);

GO

    INSERT INTO WorkAndTransView

    VALUES(
    'Color Floating in Time', '494/750', 'High Quality Limited Print',
    'Northwest School Abstract Expressionist style', 18,
    '02/05/2009', 250.00);

GO

    INSERT INTO WorkAndTransView

    VALUES(
    'Color Floating in Time', '495/750', 'High Quality Limited Print',
    'Northwest School Abstract Expressionist style', 18,
    '02/05/2009', 250.00);

GO
```

Now the each statement is considered its own "batch of commands," and the trigger fires three times, as we intended.

Concurrency Control

SQL Server 2008 provides a comprehensive set of capabilities to control concurrent processing. Many choices and options are available, and the resulting behavior is determined by the interaction of three factors: the transaction isolation level, the cursor concurrency setting, and locking hints provided in the SELECT clause. Locking behavior also depends on whether the cursor is processed as part of a transaction, whether the SELECT statement is part of a cursor, and whether INSERT, UPDATE, or DELETE commands occur inside of transactions or independently.

Figure 10-41 summarizes the concurrency control options. In this section, we will just describe the basics. For more information, see the article "Set Transaction Isolation Level" at *http://msdn.microsoft.com/en-us/library/ms173763(SQL.90).aspx.*

With SQL Server, developers do not place explicit locks. Instead, developers declare the concurrency control behavior they want, and SQL Server determines where to place the locks.

Type	Scope	Options
Tranaction isolation level	Connection—all transactions	READ UNCOMMITTED READ COMMITTED REPEATABLE READ SNAPSHOT SERIALIZABLE
Cursor concurrency	CURSOR statements	READ_ONLY SCROLL_LOCKS OPTIMSTIC
Locking hints	SELECT statements	READCOMMITTED READUNCOMMITTED REPEATABLERAD SERIALIZABLE NOLOCK HOLDLOCK And many more...

Figure 10-41

Concurrency Options for
SQL Server 2008

Locks are applied on rows, pages, keys, indexes, tables, and even on the entire database. SQL Server determines what level of lock to use and may promote or demote a lock level while processing. It also determines when to place the lock and when to release it, depending on the declarations made by the developer.

Transaction Isolation Level

The broadest level of concurrency settings is the **transaction isolation level**. As shown in Figure 10-41, there are five transaction isolation level options, listed in ascending level of restriction. Four of these options are the four you studied in Chapter 9, and they are the SQL-92 standard levels. A new level, SNAPSHOT, is unique to SQL Server. With the **SNAPSHOT transaction isolation level**, the data read by an SQL statement will be the same as the data that existed and were committed at the start of the transaction. SNAPSHOT does not request locks during reads (except during database recovery) and does not prevent other transactions from writes. With SQL Server, READ COMMITED is the default isolation level, although it is possible to make dirty reads by setting the isolation level to READ UNCOMMITTED. However, the exact behavior of READ UNCOMMITTED now depends on the setting of the READ_COMMITTED_SNAPSHOT option. See the article "Set Transaction Isolation Level" at *http://msdn.microsoft.com/en-us/library/ms173763(SQL.90).aspx* for a complete discussion.

An SQL to set the isolation level can be issued anyplace Transact-SQL is allowed, prior to any other database activity. An example Transact-SQL statement to set the isolation level of, say, REPEATABLE READ is:

```
SET TRANSACTION ISOLATION LEVEL REPEATABLE READ;
```

Cursor Concurrency

The second way in which the developer can declare locking characteristics is with cursor concurrency. Possibilities are read only, optimistic, and pessimistic, here called **SCROLL_LOCK**. As described in Chapter 9, with optimistic locking, no lock is obtained until the user updates the data. At that point, if the data have been changed since they were read, the update is refused. Of course, the application program must specify what to do when such a refusal occurs. See the SQL Server 2008 documentation on "Declare Cursor" at *http://msdn.microsoft.com/en-us/library/ms180169(SQL.90).aspx* for a complete discussion.

SCROLL_LOCK is a version of pessimistic locking. With it, an update lock is placed on a row when the row is read. If the cursor is opened within a transaction, the lock is held until the transaction commits or rolls back. If the cursor is outside of a transaction, the lock is dropped when the next row is read. Recall from Chapter 9 that an update lock blocks another update lock, but it does not block a shared lock. Thus, other connections can read the row with shared locks.

As described in Chapter 9, the default cursor concurrency setting depends on the cursor type. It is read only for static and forward only cursors, and it is optimistic for dynamic and keyset cursors.

Cursor concurrency is set with the DECLARE CURSOR statement. An example to declare a dynamic SCROLL_LOCK cursor on all rows of the TRANS table is as follows:

```
DECLARE MyCursor CURSOR DYNAMIC SCROLL_LOCKS

FOR

    SELECT   *

    FROM     dbo.TRANS;
```

Locking Hints

Locking behavior can be further modified by providing locking hints in the WITH parameter of the FROM clause in SELECT statements. Figure 11-41 lists several of the locking hints available with SQL Server. The first four hints override the transaction isolation level; the next two influence the type of lock issued. For a full list of locking hints, see the documentation at *http://msdn.microsoft.com/en-us/library/ms187373.aspx*.

Consider the following statements:

```
SET TRANSACTION ISOLATION LEVEL REPEATABLE READ;

DECLARE MyCursor CURSOR DYNAMIC SCROLL_LOCKS

FOR

    SELECT   *

    FROM     dbo.TRANS WITH READUNCOMMITTED NOLOCK;
```

Without the locking hints, the cursor MyCursor would have REPEATABLE READ isolation and would issue update locks on all rows read. The locks would be held until the transaction committed. With the locking hints, the isolation level for this cursor becomes READ UNCOMMITTED. Furthermore, the specification of NOLOCK changes this cursor from DYNAMIC to READ_ONLY.

Consider another example:

```
SET TRANSACTION ISOLATION LEVEL REPEATABLE READ;

DECLARE MyCursor CURSOR DYNAMIC SCROLL_LOCKS

FOR

    SELECT   *

    FROM     dbo.TRANS WITH HOLDLOCK;
```

Here, the locking hint will cause SQL Server to hold update locks on all rows read until the transaction commits. The effect is to change the transaction isolation level for this cursor from REPEATABLE READ to SERIALIZABLE.

In general, the beginner is advised not to provide locking hints. Rather, until you have become an expert, set the isolation level and cursor concurrency to appropriate values for your transactions and cursors and leave it at that. In fact, the SQL Server 2008 documentation specifically suggests relying on the SQL Server query optimizer and only using locking hints when absolutely necessary.

SQL Server 2008 Security

We discussed security in general terms in Chapter 9. Here, we will summarize how those general ideas pertain to SQL Server security. Starting with SQL Server 2005 and continuing with SQL Server 2008, Microsoft introduced a more complex version of the model of DBMS security shown in Figure 9-14. The SQL Server 2008 model is shown in Figure 10-42.

As usual, security consists of authentication and authorization. As shown in Figure 10-1, we have to log into SQL Server itself first, and we log in using one of the server logins illustrated in Figure 10-14. This login will be a member of one or more server roles, and each of these roles has specific permission at the server level.

Figure 10-42

SQL Server 2008
Security Model

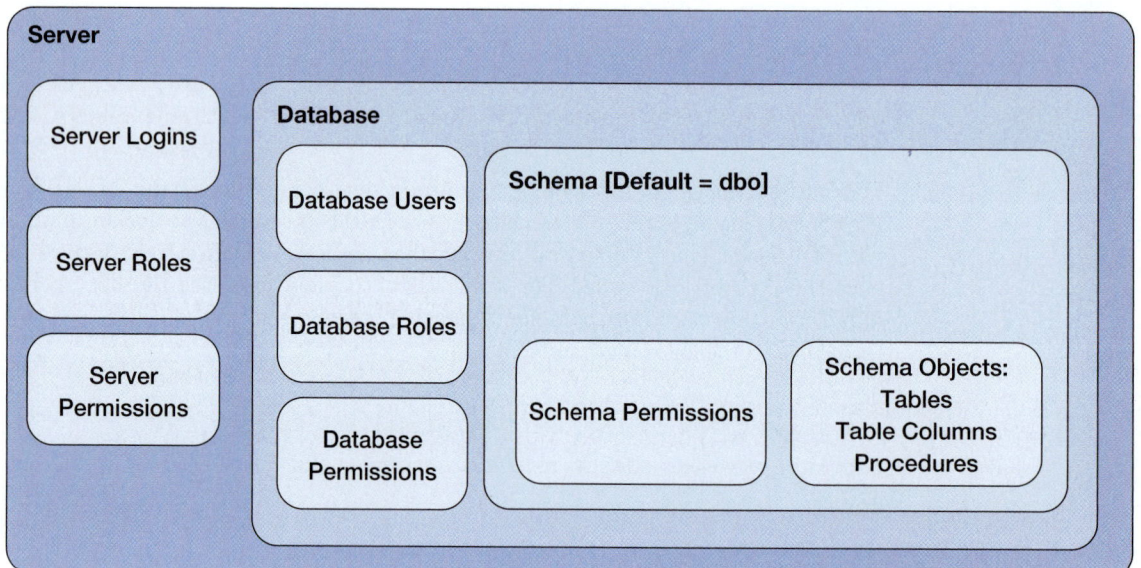

Figure 10-43

Server Logins and
Server Roles

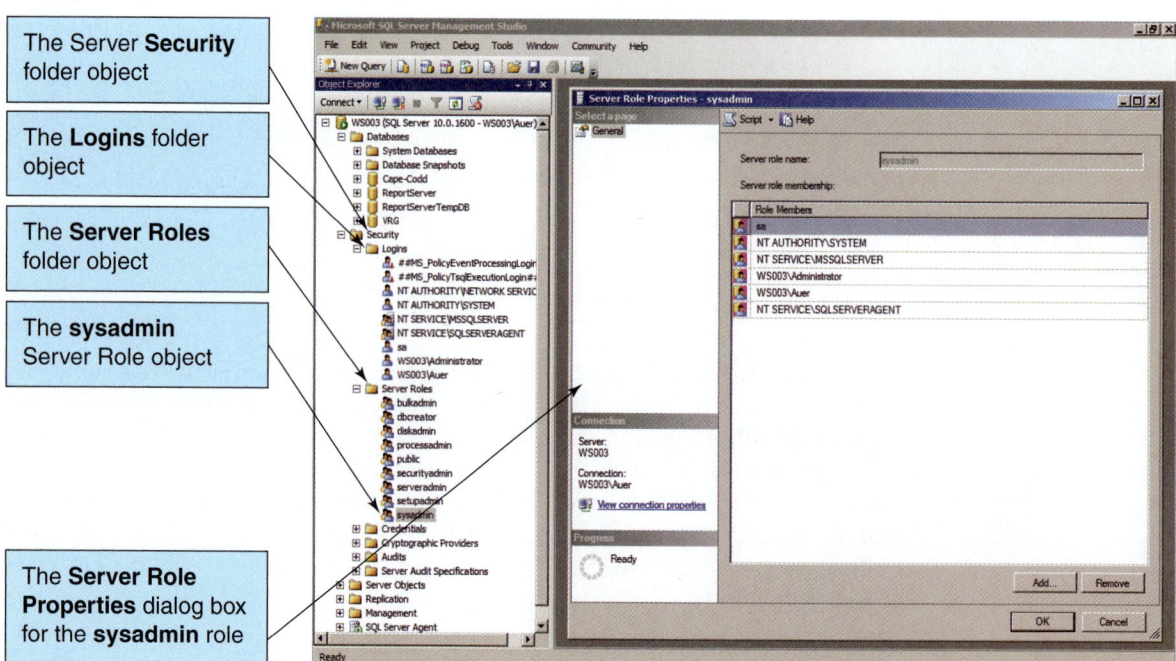

We are currently logged into SQL Server 2008 (on a computer running the Windows Server 2008 operating system and named WS003) as the login WS003\Auer (see Figure 10-1), which means that we logged in based on the local computer user account *Auer*, and, as shown in Figure 10-43, that login is assigned to the sysadmin role. This means that the user auer has all the privileges of an SQL Server 2008 systems administrator (which is everything!). SQL Server 2008 logins can either be based on Windows operating system security (recommended by Microsoft), SQL–Server-specific logins (see the *sa* login in Figure 10-43—*sa* is the SQL Server system administrator account and if you use it be sure to set a secure password for it), or both (which is how our SQL Server 2008 instance is set up).

To see the server permissions that the login *Auer* has, we look at the Permissions page of the Server Properties dialog box (right-click the SQL Server object at the top of the Object Explorer, and then click the Properties command). Figure 10-44 shows the effective properties for the login *Auer*.

This gives us an overview of the SQL Server authorization model. **SQL Server principals** (either **server principals**, such as logins and server roles, or **database principals**, such users and database roles) are granted permissions to **SQL Server securable objects** (databases, schemas, tables, procedures, etc.). The new concept here is the schema. An **SQL Server schema** is a named container for SQL Server. In other words, SQL objects such as tables and stored procedures are now held in a container called a schema. A schema can be owned by any SQL server principal. The main advantage is that schema ownership can be transferred, and thus a database principal can be deleted without the loss of the objects owned by that principal. For more information, see "Owner–Schema Separation" at *http://msdn.microsoft.com/en-us/library/ms190387.aspx*. The default schema, the one an object will automatically be assigned to, is the **dbo schema**. In earlier versions of SQL Server, dbo (database owner) was only a *user*, now dbo is a also a *schema name*.

As an example, let's create a login for use by the View Ridge Gallery.

Creating a New Login

1. Expand the **Security** folder object in the Object Explorer so that the Logins folder object is displayed.
2. Right-click the **Logins** folder object to display the shortcut menu.

Figure 10-44

Effective Server Permissions for the Login *WS003/Auer*

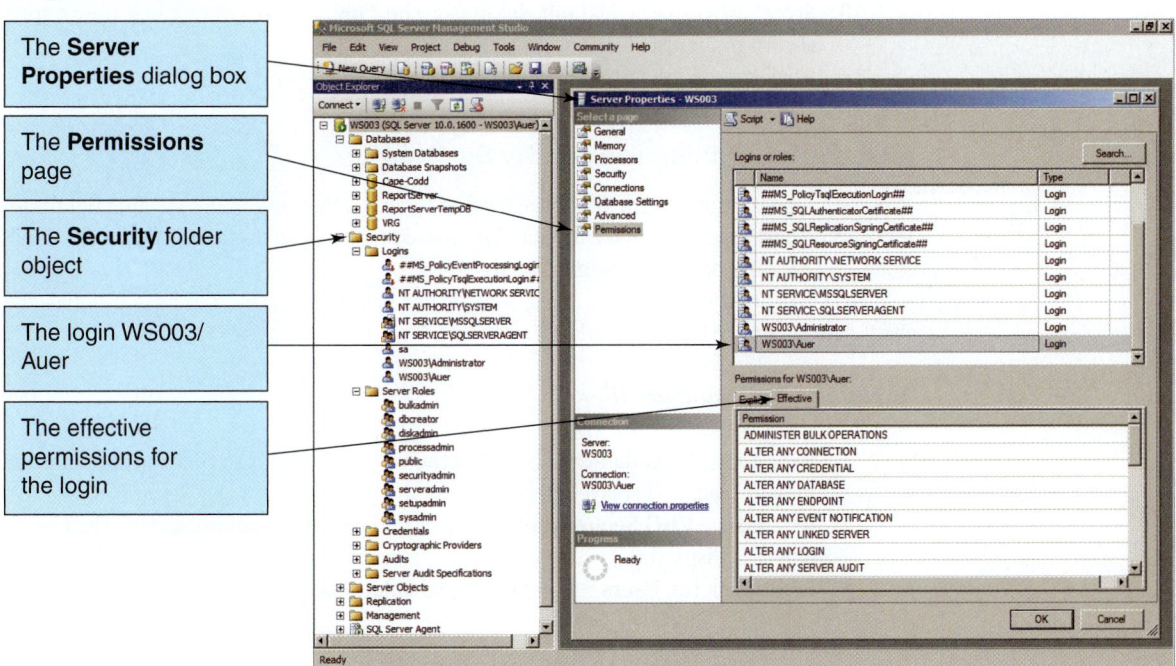

| The **Server Properties** dialog box |
| The **Permissions** page |
| The **Security** folder object |
| The login WS003/Auer |
| The effective permissions for the login |

The **Security** folder object

The **Logins** folder object

The **Login - New** dialog box

The **OK** button

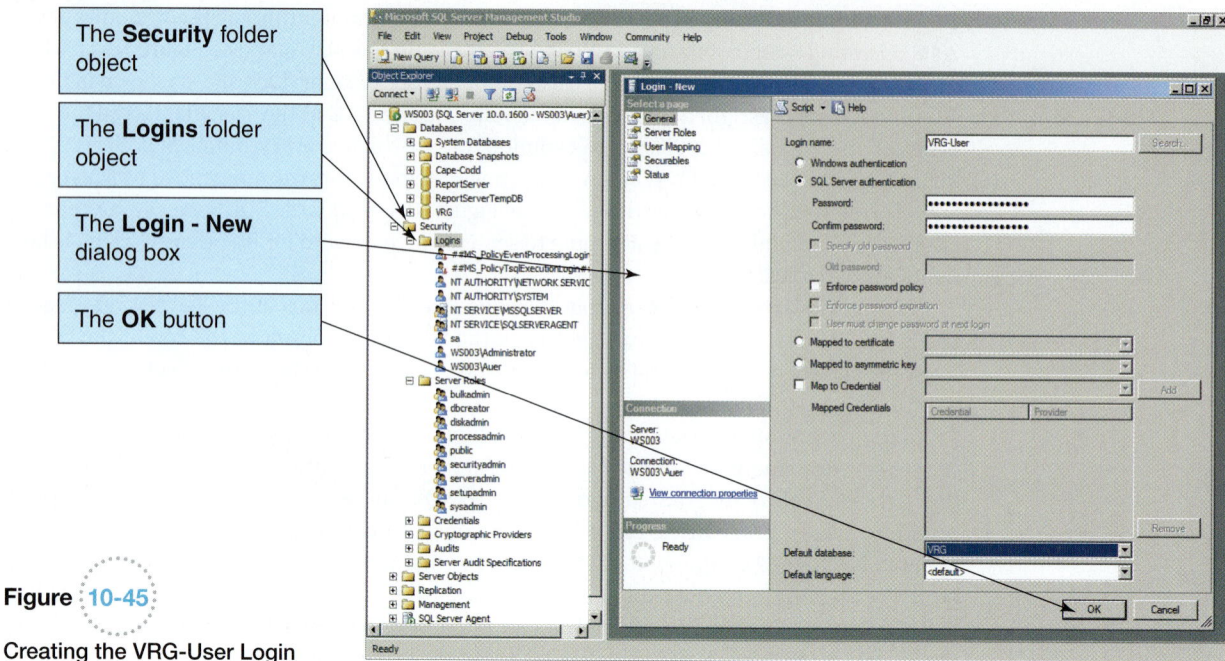

Figure 10-45

Creating the VRG-User Login

3. In the shortcut menu, click the **New Login** command. The Login – New dialog box is displayed.
4. The completed new login data is shown in Figure 10-45. Use that figure for reference in the following steps.
5. In the Login name text box, type in the login name **VRG-User**.
6. Click the **SQL Server authentication** radio button to enable the use of SQL Server authentication mode.
7. In the Password text box, type the password **VRG-User+password**.
8. In the Confirm password text box, type the password **VRG-User+password**.
9. Uncheck the **Enforce password policy** check box to disable enforcing password policy, disable enforcing password expiration, and disable forcing a password change. **NOTE:** This step is to simplify the use of this login in our test environment only. Do *not* do this in a production environment.
10. Select **VRG** as the Default database. The Login – New dialog box now appears, as shown in Figure 10-45.
11. Click the **OK** button. The new login is created.

SQL Server Database Security Settings

Now we need to move to the database level of security. Here we create specific database users and assign database roles (and associated permissions) to those users. SQL Server 2008 database roles and permissions are shown in Figure 10-46.

To illustrate the use of a database specific user, we will create a database user based on the VRG-User login we have created for use by the View Ridge Gallery.

Creating a New Database User

1. Expand the **VRG** database object in the Object Explorer so that the database Security folder object is displayed.
2. Expand the **VRG Security** folder object in the Object Explorer so that the Users folder object is displayed.
3. Right-click the **Users** folder object to display a shortcut menu.

Fixed Database Role	Database-Specific Permissions	DBMS Server Permissions
db_accessadmin	Permissions granted: ALTER ANY USER, CREATE SCHEMA Permissions granted with GRANT option: CONNECT	Permissions granted: VIEW ANY DATABASE
db_backupoperator	Permissions granted: BACKUP DATABASE, BACKUP LOG, CHECKPOINT	Permissions granted: VIEW ANY DATABASE
db_datareader	Permissions granted: SELECT	Permissions granted: VIEW ANY DATABASE
db_datawriter	Permissions granted: DELETE. INSERT, UPDATE	Permissions granted: VIEW ANY DATABASE
db_ddladmin	Permissions granted: See SQL Server 2005 documentation	Permissions granted: VIEW ANY DATABASE
db_denydatareader	Permissions denied: SELECT	Permissions granted: VIEW ANY DATABASE
db_denydatawriter	Permissions denied: DELETE, INSERT, UPDATE	Permissions granted: VIEW ANY DATABASE
db_owner	Permissions granted with GRANT option: CONTROL	Permissions granted: VIEW ANY DATABASE
db_securityadmin	Permissions granted: ALTER ANY APPLICATION ROLE, ALTER ANY ROLE, CREATE SCHEMA, VIEW DEFINITION	Permissions granted: VIEW ANY DATABASE

Note: For the definitions of each of the SQL Server permissions shown in the table, consult the SQL Server documentation.

Figure 10-46

SQL Server 2008 Fixed
Database Roles

4. In the shortcut menu, click the **New User** command. The Database User – New dialog box is displayed.
5. The completed new login data is shown in Figure 10-47. Use that figure for reference in the following steps.
6. In the User name text box, type in the user name **VRG-Database-User**.
7. In the Login name text box, type in the login name **VRG-User**. **NOTE**: You can also browse to the correct login name using the Browse button shown in Figure 10-47.
8. In the Database role membership list, check **db_owner**.
9. The Database User – New dialog box now appears, as shown in Figure 10-47.
10. Click the **OK** button. The new login is created.

Now we have completed creating the needed logins and database users for the VRG database. We will use these in other chapters when we develop applications based on this database.

Figure 10-47

Creating the VRG-Database-User Database User

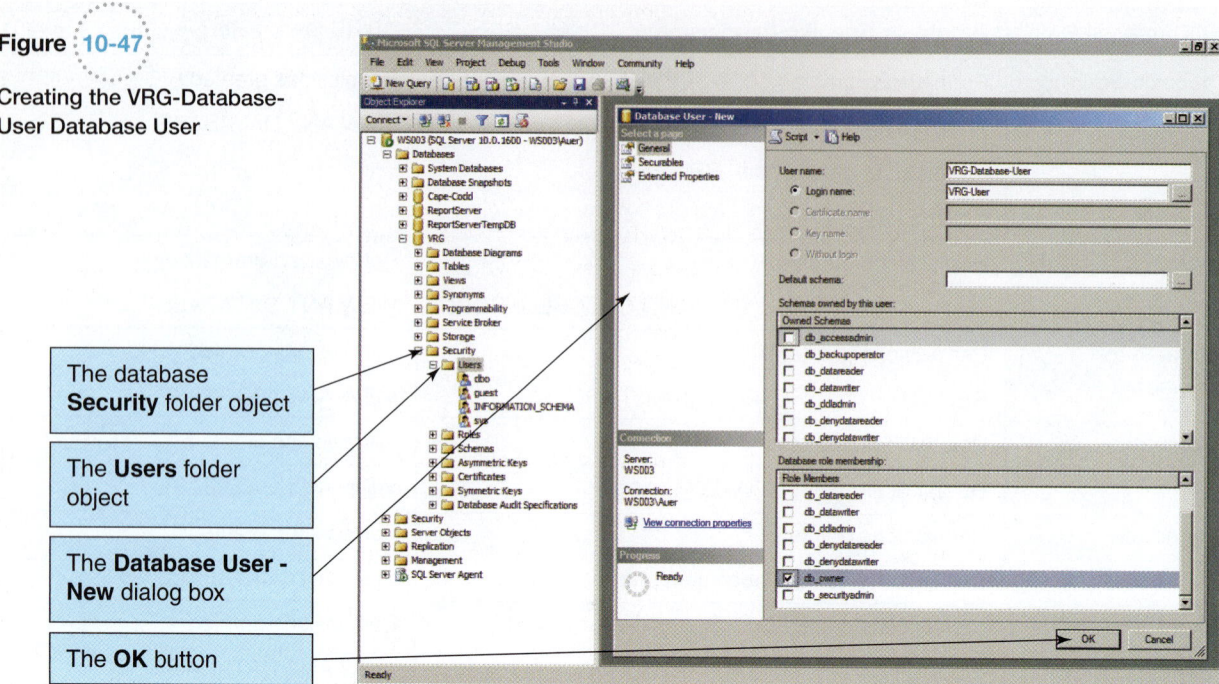

The database **Security** folder object

The **Users** folder object

The **Database User - New** dialog box

The **OK** button

SQL Server 2008 Backup and Recovery

When you create an SQL Server 2008 database, both data and log files are created. As explained in Chapter 9, these files should be backed up periodically. When backups are available, it is possible to recover a failed database by restoring it from a prior database save and applying changes in the log.

To recover a database with SQL Server, the database is restored from a prior database backup and log after images are applied to the restored database. When the end of the log is reached, changes from any transaction that failed to commit are then rolled back.

It is also possible to process the log to a particular point in time or to a transaction mark. For example, the following statement causes a mark labeled NewCust to be placed into the log every time this transaction is run:

```
BEGIN TRANSACTION NewCust WITH MARK;
```

If this is done, the log can be restored to a point either just before or just after the first NewCust mark or the first NewCust mark after a particular point in time. The restored log can then be used to restore the database. Such marks consume log space, however, so they should not be used without good reason.

Backing Up a Database

SQL Server 2008 supports several types of backup. We can, for example, choose to do a full backup, a differential backup, or a transaction log backup. A **full backup** backs up the complete database and the transaction logs. A **differential backup** backs up up only the changes since the last full backup, which is useful if a full backup takes a long time. This allows us to make periodic full backups (for example, once a week) and still capture daily changes to the database using differential backups. A **transaction log backup** backs up only the current transaction log. This is useful in keeping a series of transaction log files backed up more currently than even our differential backups. For example, we may do a transaction log backup every 6 hours.

Here, we will make a complete backup of the VRG database. Other backup options may require the use of backup device objects and management policies. A full discussion of these topics is beyond the scope of this book. For more information, see the Microsoft SQL Server 2008 Books Online at *http://msdn.microsoft.com/en-us/library/ms130214.aspx*.

Backing Up the VRG Database

1. Right-click the **VRG** database object in the Object Explorer to display a shortcut menu.
2. In the shortcut menu, click the **Tasks** command, then click the **Backup** command. The Back Up Database – VRG dialog box is displayed, as shown in Figure 10-48.
3. SQL Server 2008 has already set up all the backup options correctly for a simple full backup of the database.
4. Click the **OK** button. The database backup is created.

We could use the same backup task we just ran to make differential backups if we wanted—we would simply choose Differential instead of Full as the backup type.

In a more production-oriented backup system, the transaction log needs to be periodically backed up to ensure that its contents are preserved. Further, the transaction log must be backed up before it can be used to recover a database. Backups can be made either to disk or to tape—our backup was just made to disk. When possible, the backups should be made to devices other than those that store the operational database and log. Backing up to removable devices allows the backups to be stored in a location physically removed from the database data center. This is important for recovery in the event of disasters caused by floods, hurricanes, earthquakes, and the like.

SQL Server Recovery Models

SQL Server supports three recovery models: simple, full, and bulk logged. With the simple recovery model, no logging is done. The only way to recover a database is to restore the database to the last backup. Changes made since that last backup are lost. The simple recovery model can be used for a database that is never changed—one having the names and locations of the occupants of a full graveyard, for example—or for one that is used for read-only analysis of data that are copied from some other transactional database.

Figure  10-48

Backing Up the VRG Database

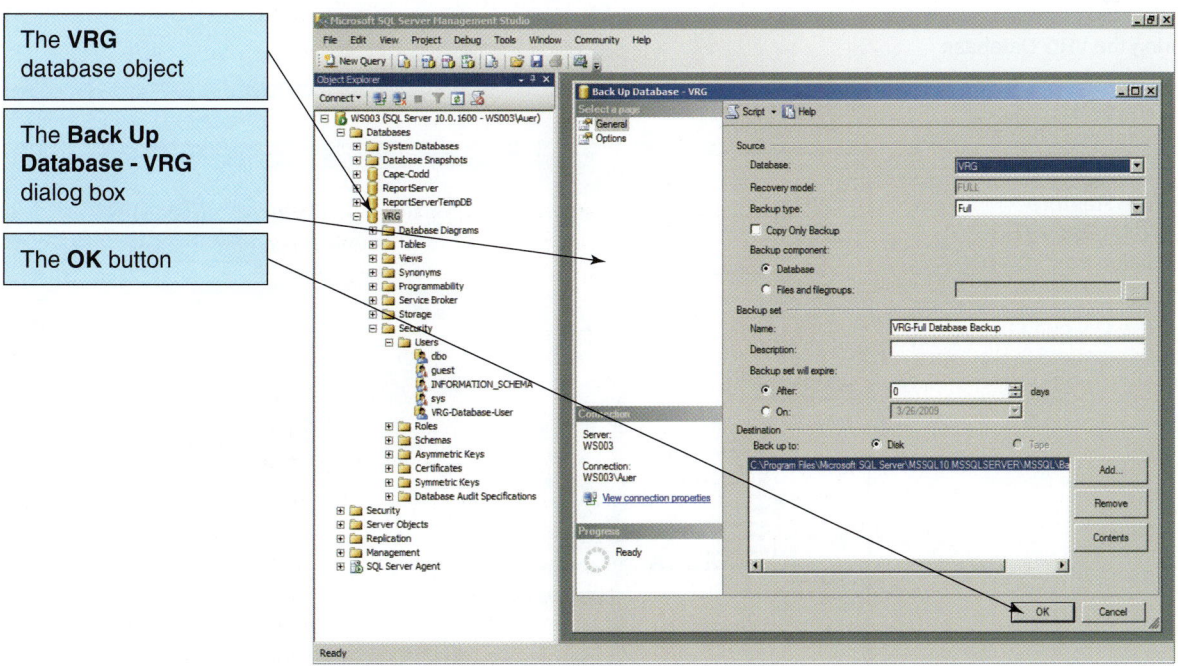

The **VRG** database object

The **Back Up Database - VRG** dialog box

The **OK** button

With full recovery, all database changes are logged. With bulk-logged database recovery, all changes are logged except those that cause large log entries. With bulk-logged recovery, changes to large text and graphic data items are not recorded to the log, actions such as CREATE INDEX are not logged, and some other bulk-oriented actions are not logged. An organization uses bulk-logged recovery if conserving log space is important and if the data used in the bulk operations are saved in some other way.

Restoring a Database

If the database and log files have been properly backed up, restoring the database is straight-forward.

Restoring the VRG Database

1. Right-click the **VRG** database object in the Object Explorer to display a shortcut menu.
2. In the shortcut menu, click the **Tasks** command, then click the **Restore** command. The Restore Database – VRG dialog box is displayed, as shown in Figure 10-49.
3. SQL Server 2008 has already set up all the backup options correctly for a simple full backup of the database.
4. If we were going to actually restore the VRG database, we would click the OK button at this point, and the database backup would be restored. However there is no need to do so at this point, so click the **Cancel** button.

You can use backup and restore to transfer a database to another computer or user (for example, to your professor!). Just do a full backup of the database you want to share to a file, say, the file *MyBackup*. Then, create a new database on another computer and name it whatever you want. Then, restore the database using the file MyBackup.

Database Maintenance Plans

You can create a database maintenance plan to facilitate the making of database and log back-ups, among other tasks, using SQL Server policy management. This topic, however, is beyond the scope of this book. For more information, see the Microsoft SQL Server 2008 Books Online at *http://msdn.microsoft.com/en-us/library/ms130214.aspx*.

Figure  **10-49**

Restoring the VRG Database

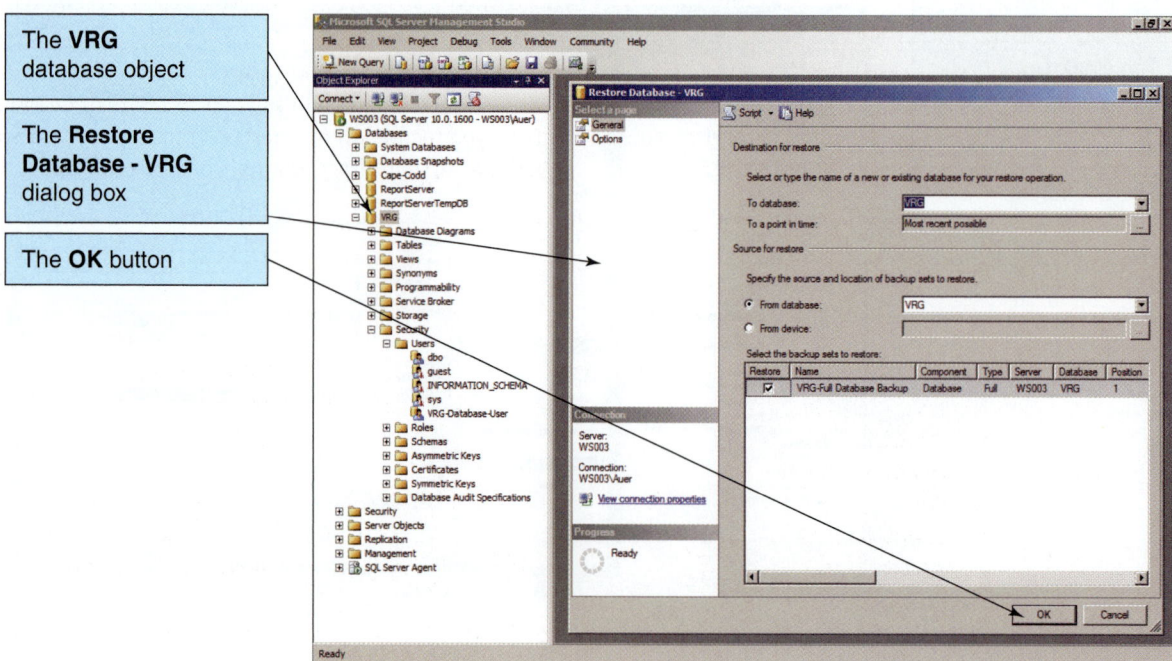

The **VRG** database object

The **Restore Database - VRG** dialog box

The **OK** button

Topics Not Discussed in This Chapter

Several important SQL Server topics are beyond the scope of this discussion. For one, SQL Server provides utilities to measure database activity and performance. The DBA can use these utilities when tuning the database. Another facility not described here is connecting Access to SQL Server. You can check the Access documentation for more information about this topic.

SQL Server 2008 provides facilities to support distributed database processing (called **replication** in SQL Server). Although very important in its own right, distributed database processing is beyond the scope of this text. Finally, SQL Server has facilities for processing database views in the form of XML documents. We will discuss those facilities in Chapter 14.

 ummary

SQL Server 2008 can be installed on computers running Windows XP, Windows Vista, Windows Server 2003, or Windows Server 2008. Tables, views, indexes, and other database structures can be created in two ways. One is to use the graphical design tools, which are similar to those in Microsoft Access. The other is to write SQL statements to create the structures and then submit them to SQL Server via the SQL Server Management Studio utility. SQL Server supports all of the SQL DDL that you have learned in this text, including the IDENTITY keyword for defining surrogate keys. The only change required for the View Ridge schema was to change the name of the TRANSACTION table to TRANS.

Indexes are special data structures used to improve performance. SQL Server automatically creates an index on all primary and foreign keys. Additional views can be created using CREATE INDEX or the Manage Index graphical tool. SQL Server supports clustered and nonclustered indexes.

SQL Server supports a language called Transact-SQL, which surrounds basic SQL statements with programming constructs such as parameters, variables, and logic structures, such as IF, WHILE, and so forth.

SQL Server databases can be processed from application programs coded in standard programming languages, such as Visual Basic .NET, Visual C# .NET, or Visual C++ .NET or application logic can be placed in stored procedures and triggers. Stored procedures can be invoked from standard languages or from VBScript and JScript in Web pages. In this chapter, stored procedures were invoked from the SQL Server Query Manager. This technique should be used only during development and testing.

For security reasons, no one should process an SQL Server operational database in interactive mode. This chapter demonstrated SQL Server triggers for computing default values, for enforcing a data constraint, for updating a view, and for enforcing a mandatory child referential integrity constraint.

Three factors determine the concurrency control behavior of SQL Server: the transaction isolation level, the cursor concurrency setting, and locking hints provided in the SELECT clause. These factors are summarized in Figure 10-41. Behavior also changes depending on whether actions occur in the context of transactions or cursors or independently. Given these behavior declarations, SQL Server places locks on behalf of the developer. Locks may be placed at many levels of granularity and may be promoted or demoted as work progresses.

SQL Server supports log backups and both complete and differential database backups. Three recovery models are available: simple, full, and bulk logged. With simple recovery, no logging is done nor are log records applied. Full recovery logs all database operations and applies them for restoration. Bulk-logged recovery omits certain transactions that would otherwise consume large amounts of space in the log.

 ey Terms

/* and */ signs
BEGIN . . . END keywords
CLOSE CURSOR keywords
clustered index
cmdlets
command-line utility
Connect to Server dialog box
database principals
dbo schema
DEALLOCATE CURSOR keywords

DECLARE CURSOR keywords
delimited identifier
differential backup
FETCH keyword
full backup
GO command
IF . . . ELSE keywords
index
Integrated Development Environment (IDE)
Microsoft SQL Server

Microsoft SQL Server 2008 Management Studio
Microsoft Windows PowerShell
nonclustered index
OPEN CURSOR keywords
parameter
PowerShell sqlps utility
replication
reserved word
RETURN keyword
SCROLL_LOCK
server principals
SNAPSHOT transaction isolation level
SQL ALTER PROCEDURE statement
SQL CMD utility
SQL Common Language Runtime (CLR)
SQL CREATE PROCEDURE statement
SQL script
SQL script comment
SQL Server 2008 Express
SQL Server 2008 Express Advanced
SQL Server bit data type
SQL Server function @@Identity
SQL Server principals
SQL Server schema
SQL Server securable objects

transaction isolation level
Transact-SQL (T-SQL)
Transact-SQL @@FETCH_STATUS function
Transact-SQL BEGIN TRANSACTION
   command
Transact-SQL COMMIT TRANSACTION
   command
Transact-SQL control-of-flow language
Transact-SQL CONVERT function
Transact-SQL cursor
Transact-SQL GETDATE( ) function
Transact-SQL IDENTITY property
Transact-SQL IDENTITY_INSERT property
Transact-SQL PRINT command
Transact-SQL ROLLBACK TRANSACTION
   command
Transact-SQL SET ANSI_NULLS ON command
Transact-SQL SET QUOTED_IDENTIFIER ON
   command
Transact-SQL USE [{DatabaseName}]
   command
transaction log backup
two dashes (- -)
variable
WHILE keyword

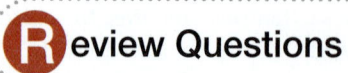

eview Questions

If you have not already installed SQL Server 2008 (or do not otherwise have it available to you), you need to install a version of it at this point.
   Review Questions 10.1–10.9 are based on a database named MEDIA that is used to record data about photographs that are stored in the database.

10.1   Create a database named MEDIA in SQL Server 2008. Use the default settings for file sizes, names, and locations.

10.2   Write an SQL statement to create a table named PICTURE with columns Name, Description, DateTaken, and FileName. Assume that Name is char(20), Description is varchar(200), DateTaken is smalldate, and FileName is char(45). Also assume that Name and DateTaken are required. Use Name as the primary key. Set the default value of Description to '(None)'.

10.3   Use the Microsoft SQL Server Management Studio to submit the SQL statement in Review Question 10.2 to create the PICTURE table in the MEDIA database.

10.4   Write a CREATE TABLE statement to create the table SLIDE_SHOW (ShowID, Name, Description, Purpose). Assume that ShowID is a surrogate key. Set the data type of Name and Description however you deem appropriate. Set the data type of Purpose to char (15) and limit it to the set of values ('Home', 'Office', 'Family', 'Recreation', 'Sports', 'Pets'). Execute your CREATE TABLE statement using Query Analyzer.

10.5   Use the Microsoft SQL Server Management Studio to create the table SHOW_PICTURE_INT as an intersection table between PICTURE and SLIDE_SHOW. Create appropriate relationships between PICTURE and SHOW_PICTURE_INT and between SLIDE_SHOW and SHOW_PICTURE_INT. Set the referential integrity properties to disallow any deletion of a SLIDE_SHOW row that has any SHOW_PICTURE_INT rows related to it. Set the referential integrity properties to cascade deletions when a PICTURE is deleted. Cascade updates to PICTURE.Name.

10.6   Write an SQL statement to create a view name PopularShows that has SLIDE_SHOW.Name and PICTURE.Name for all slide shows that have a Purpose of either 'Home' or 'Pets'. Execute this statement using the Microsoft SQL Server Management Studio.

10.7   Use the Microsoft SQL Server Management Studio GUI tools to determine that PopularShows was constructed correctly. Modify this view to include PICTURE.Description and FileName.

10.8   Can the SQL DELETE statement be used with the PopularShows view? Why or why not?

10.9   Under what circumstances can PopularShows be used for inserts and modifications?

Review Questions 10.10–10.25 are about terms and concepts discussed in this chapter.

10.10   In Figure 10-28, what is the purpose of the @RowCount variable?

10.11   In Figure 10-28, why is the SELECT statement that begins SELECT @CustomerID necessary?

10.12   Explain how you would change the stored procedure in Figure 10-28 to connect the customer to all artists who either (a) were born before 1900 or (b) had a null value for DateOfBirth.

10.13   Explain the purpose of the transaction shown in Figure 10-30.

10.14   What happens if an incorrect value of Copy is input to the stored procedure in Figure 10-30?

10.15   In Figure 10-30, what happens if the ROLLBACK statement is executed?

10.16   In Figure 10-30, why is SUM used instead of AVG?

10.17   What are the three primary factors that influence SQL Server locking behavior?

10.18   Explain why the strategy for storing CHECK constraint values in a separate table is better than implementing them in a table-based constraint. How can this strategy be used to implement the constraint on ARTIST.Nationality?

10.19   Explain why the view CustomerInterestsView in Figure 10-25 is not updatable. Describe the logic of the INSTEAD OF UPDATE trigger in Figure 10-36.

10.20   Explain what limitation must be enforced for the trigger in Figure 10-36 to be effective.

10.21   Explain the meaning of each of the transaction isolation levels under Options shown in Figure 10-41.

10.22   Explain the meaning of each of the cursor concurrency settings listed in Figure 10-41.

10.23   What is the purpose of locking hints?

10.24   What is the difference between complete and differential backups? Under what conditions are complete backups preferred? Under what conditions are differential backups preferred?

10.25   Explain the differences between simple, full, and bulk-logged recovery models. Under what conditions would you choose each one?

Project Questions

In the Chapter 7 Review Questions, we introduced the Wedgewood Pacific Corporation (WPC) and developed the WPC database. Two of the tables that are used in the WPC database are:

> DEPARTMENT (<u>DepartmentName</u>, BudgetCode, OfficeNumber, Phone)
>
> EMPLOYEE (<u>EmployeeNumber</u>, FirstName, LastName, *Department*, Phone, Email)

Assume that the relationship between these tables is M-M, and use them as the basis for your answers to Review Questions 10.26 through 10.28.

10.26 Code an SQL Server trigger to enforce the constraint that an employee can never change his or her department.

10.27 Code an SQL Server trigger to allow the deletion of a department if it only has one employee. Assign the last employee to the Human Resources department.

10.28 Design a system of triggers to enforce the M-M relationship. Use Figure 10-38 as an example, but assume that departments with only one employee can be deleted. Assign the last employee in a department to Human Resources.

Review Question 10.29 is based on the View Ridge Gallery database discussed in this chapter.

10.29 If you have not already installed SQL Server 2008 (or do not otherwise have it available to you), you need to install a version of it at this point. Write SQL statements to accomplish the following tasks and submit them to SQL Server 2008 via the Microsoft SQL Server Management Studio.

A. Create an SQL Server 2008 database named VRG.

B. Create the VRG database tables shown in Figure 10-13, except do not create the NationalityValues constraint.

C. Populate your database with the sample data from Figure 10-24.

D. Create all the VRG views discussed in the Chapter 7 section on SQL views.

E. Write a stored procedure to read the ARTIST table and display the artist data using the Transact-SQL PRINT command.

F. Write a stored procedure that reads the ARTIST and WORK tables, and that accepts the name of the artist to display as an input parameter. Your procedure should then display the data for that artist, followed by a display of all the works for that artist stored in WORK.

G. Write a stored procedure to update customer phone data. Assume that your stored procedure receives LastName, FirstName, PriorAreaCode, NewAreaCode, Prior PhoneNumber, and NewPhoneNumber. Your procedure should first ensure that there is only one customer with the values of (LastName, FirstName, PriorArea-Code, PriorPhoneNumber). If not, produce an error message and quit. Otherwise, update the customer data with the new phone number data, and print a results message.

H. Create a table named ALLOWED_NATIONALITY with one column, called Nation. Place the values of all nationalities currently in the VRG database into the table. Write a trigger that will check to determine whether a new or updated value of Nationality resides in this table. If not, write an error message and roll back the insert or change. Use the Microsoft SQL Server Management Studio to demonstrate that your trigger works.

I. Create a view having all of the data from the WORK and TRANS tables except for the surrogate keys. Write and insert an INSTEAD OF trigger on this view that will create a new row in both WORK and TRANS. Use the Microsoft SQL Server Management Studio to demonstrate that your trigger works. Hint: Recall that you can issue an INSERT command on WORK and TRANS without specifying a value for the surrogate key. SQL Server will provide it.

Answer questions A through M for Marcia's Dry Cleaning at the end of Chapter 7, page 293 if you have not already done so. Use the SQL Server data types in your answer.

A. Using SQL Server 2008 and the Microsoft SQL Server Management Studio, execute all of the SQL statements that you created in your answers to A through M for Marcia's Dry Cleaning at the end of Chapter 7.

B. Assume that the relationship between ORDER and ORDER_ITEM is M-M. Design triggers to enforce this relationship. Use Figure 10-38 and the discussion of that figure as an example, but assume that Marcia does allow ORDERs and their related ORDER_ITEM rows to be deleted. Use the deletion strategy shown in Figures 7-29 and 7-30 for this case.

C. Write and test the triggers you designed in part B.

Answer questions A through N for Morgan Importing at the end of Chapter 7, page 294, if you have not already done so. Use the SQL Server data types in your answer.

A. Using SQL Server 2008 and the Microsoft SQL Server Management Studio, execute all of the SQL statements that you created in your answers to A through N for Morgan Importing at the end of Chapter 7.

B. Assume that the relationship between SHIPMENT and SHIPMENT_ITEM is M-M. Design triggers to enforce this relationship. Use Figure 10-38 and the discussion of that figure as an example, but assume that Morgan does allow SHIPMENTs and their related SHIPMENT_ITEM rows to be deleted. Use the deletion strategy shown in Figures 7-29 and 7-30 for this case.

C. Write and test the triggers you designed in part B.

10A

Managing Databases with Oracle Database 11g

Chapter Objectives

- To be able to install Oracle Database 11g and create a database.
- To be able to use Oracle Database 11g's Web-based Enterprise Manager Database Control utility.
- To be able to use Oracle Database 11g's graphical utilities.
- To be able to create and use Oracle Database 11g namespaces.
- To be able to submit both SQL DDL and DML via the SQL Developer utility.

- To understand the purpose and role of stored procedures and learn how to create simple stored procedures.
- To understand the purpose and role of triggers and learn how to create simple stored procedures.
- To understand how Oracle Database 11g implements concurrency control.
- To understand the fundamental features of Oracle Database 11g backup and recovery facilities.

A complete version of this chapter is available on the textbook's Web site:

www.pearsonhighered.com/kroenke

10B

Managing Databases with MySQL 5.1

Chapter Objectives

- To be able to install MySQL and create a database.
- To be able to use MySQL's graphical utilities.
- To be able to submit both SQL DDL and DML via the MySQL Query Browser.
- To understand the purpose and role of stored procedures and know how to create simple stored procedures.

- To understand the purpose and role of triggers and know how to create simple stored procedures.
- To understand how MySQL implements concurrency control.
- To understand the fundamental features of MySQL backup and recovery facilities.

A complete version of this chapter is available on the textbook's Web site:

www.pearsonhighered.com/kroenke

Part 5

Database Access Standards

The three chapters in this section examine standards for database application processing. We begin in Chapter 11 by discussing database access standards, including ODBC, ADO.NET and ASP.NET in Microsoft's .NET Framework, and the Java-based JDBC and Java Server Pages (JSP) technologies. Even though some of these standards are no longer on the leading edge of database processing, many applications still use them, and you will likely encounter them in your career. Chapter 11 then describes the use of the popular PHP scripting language to create Web pages that access the View Ridge Gallery database.

Chapter 12 discusses one of the most important developments in information technology today, the confluence of database processing and document processing. This chapter introduces you to XML and XML Schema. Chapter 13 discusses business intelligence (BI) systems and the data warehouse and data mart databases that support them.

11

The Web Server Environment

Chapter Objectives

- To understand the nature and characteristics of the data environment that surrounds Internet technology database applications.
- To learn the purpose, features, and facilities of ODBC.
- To understand the characteristics of the Microsoft .NET Framework
- To understand the nature and goals of OLE DB.
- To learn the characteristics and object model of ADO.NET.

- To understand the characteristics of JDBC and the four types of JDBC drivers.
- To understand the nature of JSP and know the differences between JSP and ASP.NET.
- To understand HTML and PHP.
- To be able to construct Web database applications pages using PHP.

This chapter discusses some traditional standard interfaces and current tools for accessing database servers. ODBC, or the Open Database Connectivity standard, was developed in the early 1990s to provide a product-independent interface to relational and other tabular data. In the mid-1990s, Microsoft announced OLE DB, which is an object-oriented interface that encapsulates data-server functionality. Microsoft then developed Active Data Objects (ADO), which is a set of objects for utilizing OLE DB that is designed for use by any language, including VBScript, and JScript. This technology was used in Active Server Pages (ASP), which were the basis of Web database applications. In 2002, Microsoft introduced the .NET Framework, which included ADO.NET (the successor to ADO) and ASP.NET (the successor to ASP) components. Today, the .NET Framework is the basis for all application development using Microsoft technology.

As an alternative to the Microsoft technologies, Sun Microsystems developed the Java platform, which includes the Java programming language, Java Database Connectivity (JDBC) and Java Server Pages (JSP).

While the .NET and Java technologies are important development platforms, there are additional technologies that have been developed by other companies and open-source projects. We will use two of these independently developed tools in this chapter—the Eclipse integrated development environment (IDE) and the PHP scripting language.

However, before considering these standards, we need to gain some perspective on the data environment that surrounds the Web server in Internet technology database applications.

The Web Database Processing Environment

The environment in which today's database applications reside is rich and complicated. As shown in Figure 11-1, a typical Web server needs to publish applications that involve data of dozens of different data types. So far in this text, we have considered only relational databases, but as you can see from this figure, there are many other data types as well.

Consider the problems that the developer of Web server applications has when integrating these data. The developer may need to connect to an Oracle database; a DB2 mainframe database; a nonrelational database, such as IMS, IBM's older DBMS product; file-processing

Figure 11-1

The Variety of Data Types in Web Database Applications

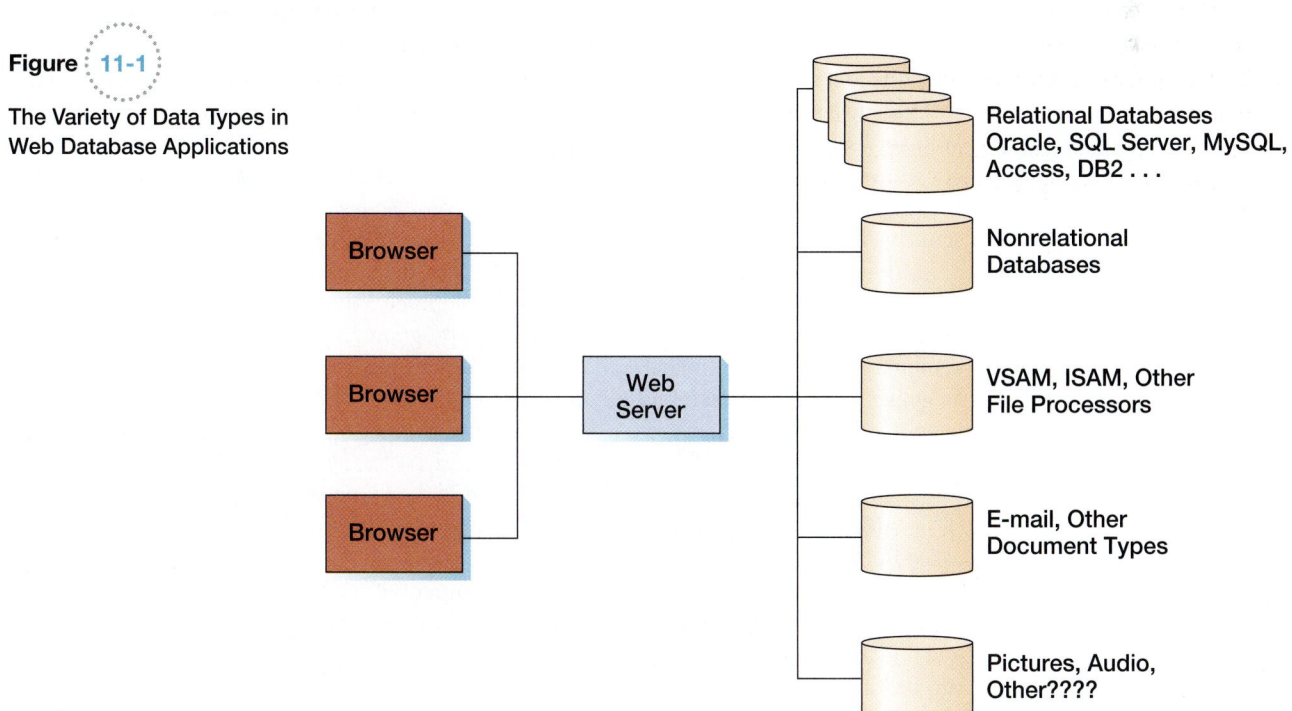

data, such as VSAM and ISAM; e-mail directories; and so forth. Each one of these products has a different programming interface that the developer must learn. Further, these products evolve, thus new features and functions will be added over time that will increase the developer's challenge.

Several standard interfaces have been developed for accessing database servers. Every DBMS product has an **application program interface (API)**. An API is a collection of objects, methods, and properties for executing DBMS functions from program code. Unfortunately, each DBMS has its own API, and APIs vary from one DBMS product to another. To save programmers from having to learn to use many different interfaces, the computer industry has developed standards for database access.

The **Open Database Connectivity (ODBC)** standard was developed in the early 1990s to provide a DBMS-independent means for processing relational database data. In the mid-1990s, Microsoft announced **OLE DB**, which is an object-oriented interface that encapsulates data-server functionality. OLE DB was designed not just for access to relational databases, but also for accessing many other types of data as well. As a **Component Object Model (COM)** interface, OLE DB is readily accessible to programmers, using such programming languages as C, C#, and Java. However, OLE DB is not as accessible to users of Visual Basic (VB) and scripting languages. Therefore, Microsoft developed **Active Data Objects (ADO)**, which is a set of objects for utilizing OLE DB that is designed for use by any language, including Visual Basic (VB), VBScript, and JScript. ADO has now been followed by **ADO.NET** (pronounced "A-D-O-dot-NET"), which is an improved version of ADO developed as part of Microsoft's .NET (pronounced "dot-NET") initiative and a component of the .NET Framework.

ADO technology is used in **Active Server Pages (ASP)** Web pages to create Web-based database applications. ASP is a combination of Hypertext Markup Language (HTML) and VBScript or JScript that can read and write database data and transmit it over public and private networks, using Internet protocols. ASP runs on Microsoft's Web server product, **Internet Information Services (IIS)**. When ADO.NET was introduced, Microsoft also introduced **ASP.NET**. ASP.NET is the successor to ASP, and is the preferred Web page technology in the .NET Framework.

Of course, there are other connectivity methods and standards besides those propagated by Microsoft. The main alternatives to ADO.NET technology are based on or associated with Sun Microsystems' **Java platform**, and include the **Java programming language**, **Java Database Connectivity (JBDC)**, **Java Data Objects (JDO)** and **JavaServer Pages (JSP)**.

JavaServer Pages (JSP) technology is a combination of HTML and Java that accomplishes the same function as ASP.NET by compiling pages into Java servlets. JSP may connect to databases using Java Database Connectivity (JDBC). JSP is often used on the open-source **Apache Web server**.

However, the defining characteristic of the Java-related technology is that you must use Java as the programming language. You cannot even use JavaScript, Java's somewhat related scripting language cousin. If you know (or want to learn) Java, this if fine.

While the Microsoft .NET Framework and the Sun Microsystems Java platform are two major players in Web database application development, there are other options. One such product is PHP, which is an open-source Web page programming language, and another favorite combination of Web developers is the Apache Web server with the MySQL DBMS and the PHP language. This combination is called **AMP** (Apache-MySQL-PHP). When running on the Linux operating system, it's it is referred to as **LAMP**; when running on the Windows operating system, it's it is referred to as **WAMP**. And because PHP works with all DBMS products, we will use it in this book. Other possibilities include the Perl and Python languages (both of which can be the "P" in AMP, LAMP and WAMP), and the Ruby language with its Web development framework called Ruby on Rails.

In a Web-based database processing environment, if the Web server and the DBMS can run on the same computer, the system has **two-tier architecture**. (One tier is for the browsers, and one is for the Web server/DBMS computer.) Alternatively, the Web server and DBMS can run on different computers, in which case the system has **three-tier architecture**. High-performance applications might use many Web server computers, and in some systems several computers can run the DBMS, as well. In the latter case, if the DBMS computers are processing the same databases, the system is referred to as a *distributed database*.

The ODBC Standard

The ODBC standard was created to address the data access problem that concerns relational databases and data sources that are table-like, such as spreadsheets. As shown in Figure 11-2, ODBC is an interface between the Web server (or other database application) and the DBMS. It consists of a set of standards by which SQL statements can be issued and results and error messages can be returned. As shown in Figure 11-2, developers can call the DBMS using native DBMS interfaces (which are APIs) if they want to (sometimes they do this to improve performance), but the developer who does not have the time or desire to learn many different DBMS native libraries can use the ODBC instead.

The ODBC standard is an interface by which application programs can access and process databases and tabular data in a DBMS-independent manner. This means, for example, that an application that uses the ODBC interface could process an Oracle database, an SQL Server database, a spreadsheet, or any other ODBC-compliant database without making any coding changes. The goal is to allow a developer to create a single application that can access databases supported by different DBMS products without needing to be changed, or even recompiled.

ODBC was developed by a committee of industry experts from the X/Open and SQL Access Group committees. Several such standards were proposed, but ODBC emerged as the winner, primarily because it had been implemented by Microsoft and is an important part of Windows. Microsoft's initial interest in support of such a standard was to allow products such as Microsoft Excel to access database data from a variety of DBMS products without having to be recompiled. Of course, Microsoft's interests have changed since the introduction of OLE DB and ADO.NET.

ODBC Architecture

Figure 11-3 shows the components of the ODBC standard. The application program, driver manager, and DBMS drivers all reside on the application server computer. The drivers send requests to data sources, which reside on the database server. According to the standard, an **ODBC data source** is the database and its associated DBMS, operating system, and network platform. An ODBC data source can be a relational database; it can also be a file server, such as BTrieve, or even a spreadsheet.

The application issues requests to create a connection with a data source; to issue SQL statements and receive results; to process errors; and to start, commit, and roll back transactions.

Figure  **11-2**

Role of the ODBC Standard

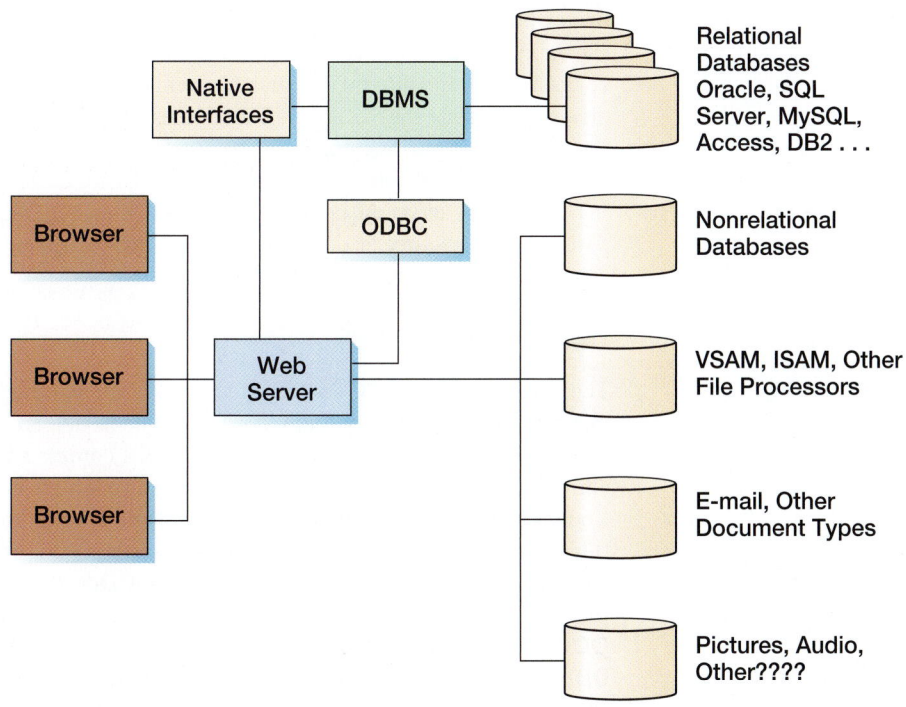

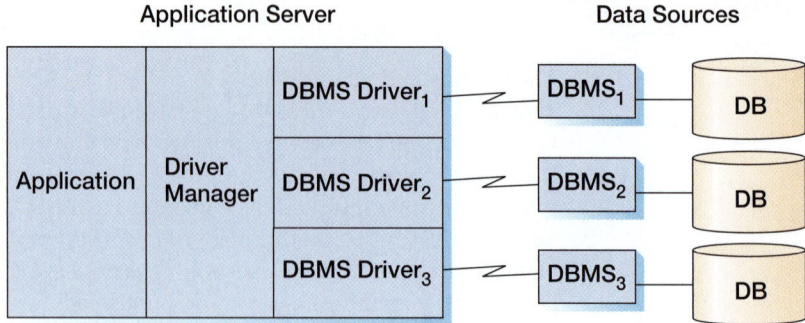

Application Server   **Data Sources**

Application can process a database using any of the three
DBMS products.

Figure 11-3

ODBC Architecture

ODBC provides a standard means for each of these requests, and it defines a standard set of error codes and messages.

The **ODBC driver manager** serves as an intermediary between the application and the DBMS drivers. When the application requests a connection, the driver manager determines the type of DBMS that processes a given ODBC data source and loads that driver into memory (if it is not already loaded). The driver manager also processes certain initialization requests and validates the format and order of ODBC requests that it receives from the application. For Windows, the driver manager is provided by Microsoft.

An **ODBC driver** processes ODBC requests and submits specific SQL statements to a given type of data source. Each data source type has a different driver. For example, there are drivers for SQL Server, for Oracle, for MySQL, for Access, and for all of the other products whose vendors have chosen to participate in the ODBC standard. Drivers are supplied by DBMS vendors and by independent software companies.

It is the responsibility of the driver to ensure that standard ODBC commands execute correctly. In some cases, if the data source is itself not SQL compliant, the driver may need to perform considerable processing to fill in for a lack of capability at the data source. In other cases, when the data source supports full SQL, the driver need only pass the request through for processing by the data source. The driver also converts data source error codes and messages into the ODBC standard codes and messages.

ODBC identifies two types of drivers: single tier and multiple tier. An **ODBC single-tier driver** processes both ODBC calls and SQL statements. An example of a single-tier driver is shown in Figure 11-4(a). In this example, the data are stored in Xbase files (the format used by FoxPro, dBase, and others). Because Xbase file managers do not process SQL, it is the job of the driver to translate the SQL request into Xbase file-manipulation commands and to transform the results back into SQL form.

An **ODBC multiple-tier driver** processes ODBC calls, but passes the SQL requests directly to the database server. Although it may reformat an SQL request to conform to the dialect of a particular data source, it does not process the SQL. An example of the use of a multiple-tier driver is shown in Figure 11-4(b).

Conformance Levels

The creators of the ODBC standard faced a dilemma. If they chose to describe a standard for a minimal level of capability, many vendors would be able to comply. But if they did so, the standard would represent only a small portion of the complete power and expressiveness of ODBC and SQL. However, if the standard addressed a very high level of capability, only a few vendors would be able to comply with the standard, and it would become unimportant. To deal with this dilemma, the committee wisely chose to define levels of conformance to the standard. The committee defined two types of conformance: ODBC conformance and SQL conformance.

ODBC Conformance Level

ODBC conformance levels are concerned with the features and functions that are made available through the driver's application program interface (API). A driver API is a set of functions

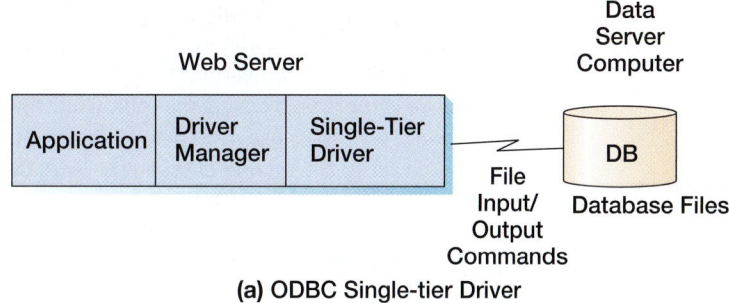

(a) ODBC Single-tier Driver

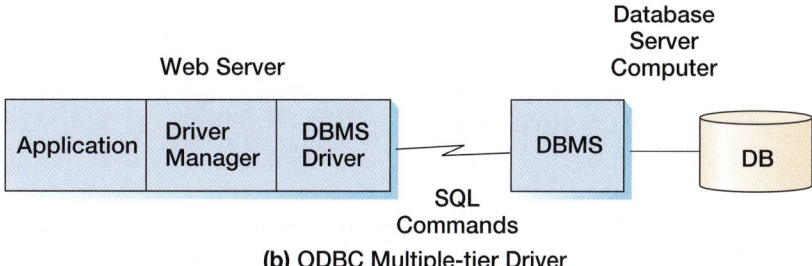

Figure 11-4

ODBC Driver Types

(b) ODBC Multiple-tier Driver

that the application can call to receive services. Figure 11-5 summarizes the three levels of ODBC conformance that are addressed in the standard. In practice, almost all drivers provide at least Level 1 API conformance, so the core API level is not too important.

An application can call a driver to determine which level of ODBC conformance it provides. If the application requires a level of conformance that is not present, it can terminate the session in an orderly fashion and generate appropriate messages to the user. Or, the application can be written to use higher-level conformance features if they are available and to work around the missing functions if a higher level is not available.

Figure 11-5

Summary of ODBC Conformance Levels

Core API
- Connect to data sources
- Prepare and execute SQL statements
- Retrieve data from a result set
- Commit or roll back transactions
- Retrieve error information

Level 1 API
- Core API
- Connect to data sources with driver-specific information
- Send and receive partial results
- Retrieve catalog information
- Retrieve information about driver options, capabilities, and functions

Level 2 API
- Core and Level 1 API
- Browse possible connections and data sources
- Retrieve native form of SQL
- Call a translation library
- Process a scrollable cursor

For example, drivers at the Level 2 API must provide a scrollable cursor. Using conformance levels, an application could be written to use cursors if they are available; but if they are not, to work around the missing feature, it would select needed data using very restrictive WHERE clauses. Doing this would ensure that only a few rows were returned at a time to the application, and it would process those rows using a cursor that it maintained itself. Performance would likely be slower in the second case, but at least the application would be able to successfully execute.

SQL Conformance Level

ODBC SQL conformance levels specify which SQL statements, expressions, and data types a driver can process. Three SQL conformance levels are defined, as summarized in Figure 11-6. The capability of the minimum SQL grammar is very limited, and most drivers support at least the core SQL grammar.

As with ODBC conformance levels, an application can call the driver to determine what level of SQL conformance it supports. With that information, the application can then determine which SQL statements can be issued. If necessary, the application can then terminate the session or use alternative, less-powerful means of obtaining the data.

Creating an ODBC Data Source Name

An **ODBC data source** is an ODBC data structure that identifies a database and the DBMS that processes it. Data sources identify other types of data, such as spreadsheets and other non-database tabular data stores, but we are not concerned with that use here.

Figure 11-6

Summary of SQL
Conformance Levels

Minimum SQL Grammar
- CREATE TABLE, DROP TABLE
- Simple SELECT (does not include subqueries)
- INSERT, UPDATE, DELETE
- Simple expressions (A > B + C)
- CHAR, VARCHAR, LONGVARCHAR data types

Core SQL Grammar
- Minimum SQL Grammar
- ALTER TABLE, CREATE INDEX, DROP INDEX
- CREATE VIEW, DROP VIEW
- GRANT, REVOKE
- Full SELECT (includes subqueries)
- Aggregate functions such as SUM, COUNT, MAX, MIN, AVG
- DECIMAL, NUMERIC, SMALLINT, INTEGER, REAL, FLOAT, DOUBLE PRECISION data types

Extended SQL Grammar
- Core SQL Grammar
- Outer joins
- UPDATE and DELETE using cursor positions
- Scalar functions such as SUBSTRING, ABS
- Literals for date, time, and timestamp
- Batch SQL statements
- Stored procedures

The three types of data sources are file, system, and user. A **file data source** is a file that can be shared among database users. The only requirement is that the users have the same DBMS driver and privilege to access the database. The data source file can be e-mailed or otherwise distributed to possible users. A **system data source** is one that is local to a single computer. The operating system and any user on that system (with proper privileges) can use a system data source. A **user data source** is available only to the user who created it.

In general, the best choice for Internet applications is to create a system data source on the Web server. Browser users then access the Web server, which in turn uses the system data source to set up a connection with the DBMS and the database.

We need a system data source for the View Ridge Gallery VRG database so that we can use it in a Web database processing application. To create a system data source in a Windows operating system, you use the **ODBC Data Source Administrator**.[1]

Opening the ODBC Data Source Administrator in Windows XP or Windows Vista

1. Open the Windows Control Panel by clicking the **Start** button and then **Control Panel**.
2. Switch the Control Panel to **Classic View** if necessary.
3. In the Control Panel window, double-click **Administrative Tools**.
4. In the Administrative Tools window, double-click the **Data Sources (ODBC)** shortcut icon.

Opening the ODBC Data Source Administrator in Windows Server 2008

1. Click the **Start** button and then click the **All Programs** button.
2. Click the **Administrative Tools** folder to open it.
3. Click the **Data Sources (ODBC)** program.

We can now use the ODBC Data Source Administrator to create a system data source named VRG for use with SQL Server 2008:

Creating the VRG System Data Source

1. In the ODBC Data Source Administrator, click the **System DSN** tab and then click the **Add** button.
2. In the Create New Data Source dialog box, click the **Data Sources (ODBC)** program.
3. Select the **SQL Server Native Client 10**, as shown in Figure 11-7.
4. Click the **Finish** button. The Create New Data Source to SQL Server dialog box appears.
5. In the Create New Data Source to SQL Server dialog box, enter the information shown in Figure 11-8 (note that the database server is selected from the Server drop-down list) and then click the **Finish** button.
6. The completed VRG system data source is shown in Figure 11-9. Click the **OK** button to close the ODBC Data Source Administrator.

We will use the VRG DSN later in this chapter to process the SQL Server database created in Chapter 10. Similarly, if you are using either the Oracle or MySQL DBMS, you should create an appropriate system data source for use with your Oracle or MySQL version of the View Ridge Gallery database.

---

[1] If you are using a 64-bit Windows operating system, be aware that there are two different ODBC Data Source Administrator programs provided—one for 32-bit applications and one for 64-bit applications. The ODBC Data Source Administrator used if you follow the steps in the text is the 64-bit version. However, if you are running a 32-bit DBMS (for example, the 32-bit version of SQL Server 2008 Express Advanced), then you must use the 32-bit version of the ODBC Data Source Administrator. In the 64-bit of Vista, this is the odbcad32.exe program located at C:\Windows\sysWOW64\odbcad32.exe.

436   **Part 5**   Database Access Standards

Select **System DSN** and click the Add button

The **MySQL ODBC 5.1 Driver**

Select the **SQL Server Native Client 10.0**

Click the **Finish** button

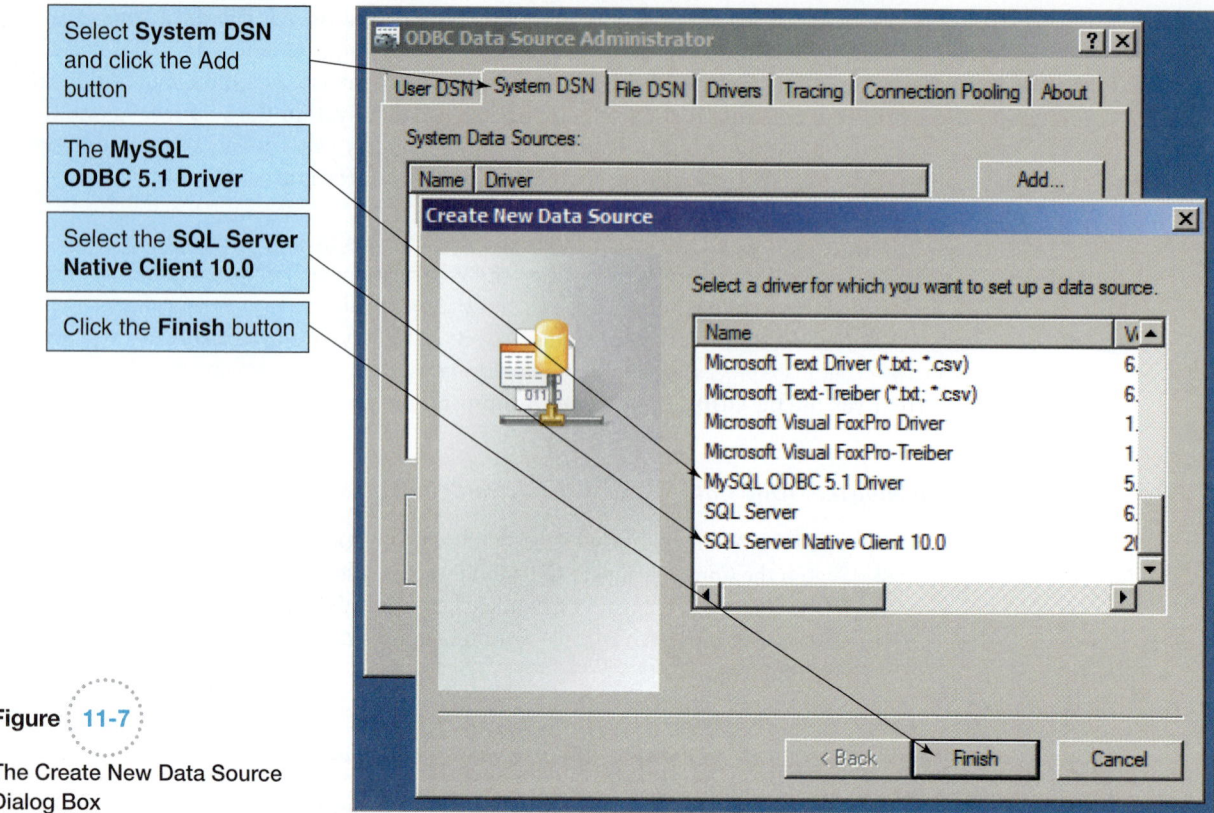

Figure 11-7

The Create New Data Source Dialog Box

Figure 11-8

The Create New Data Source to SQL Server Dialog Box

Type in the name for this System DSN: **VRG**

Type in a description

The drop-down list arrow button—select the SQL server from the drop-down list—if the list is empty, type in the name of the server itself, not the SQL Server instance name

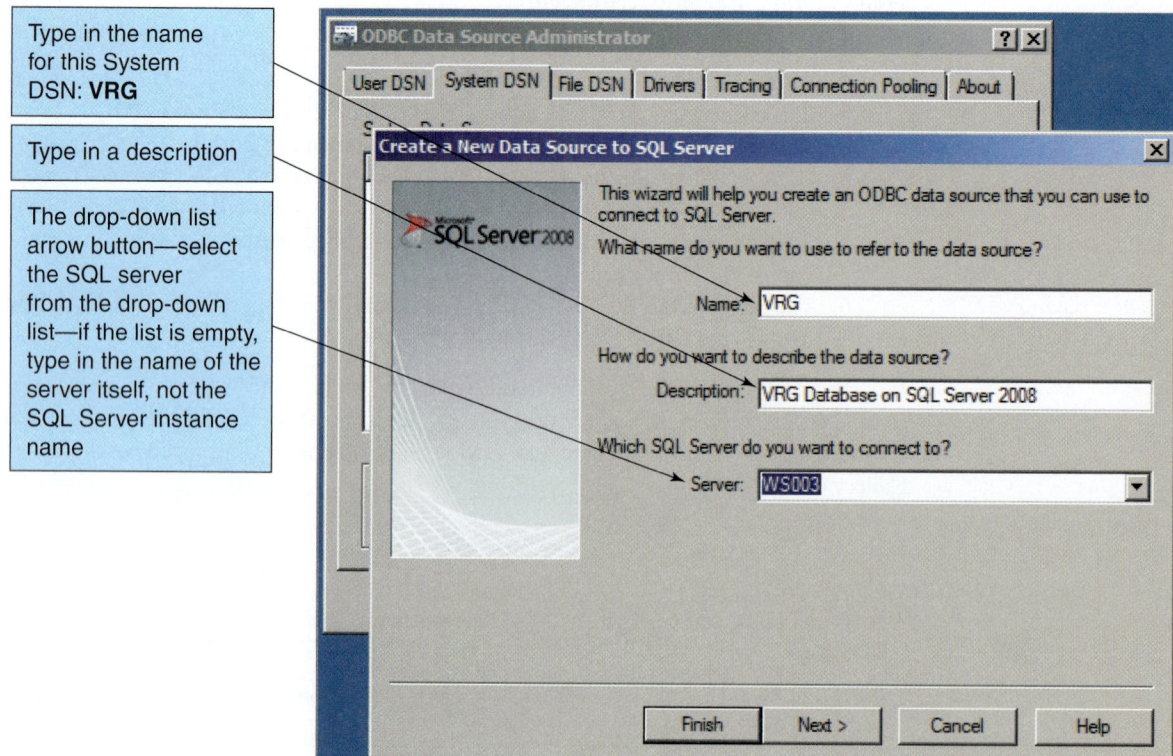

The VRG system data source

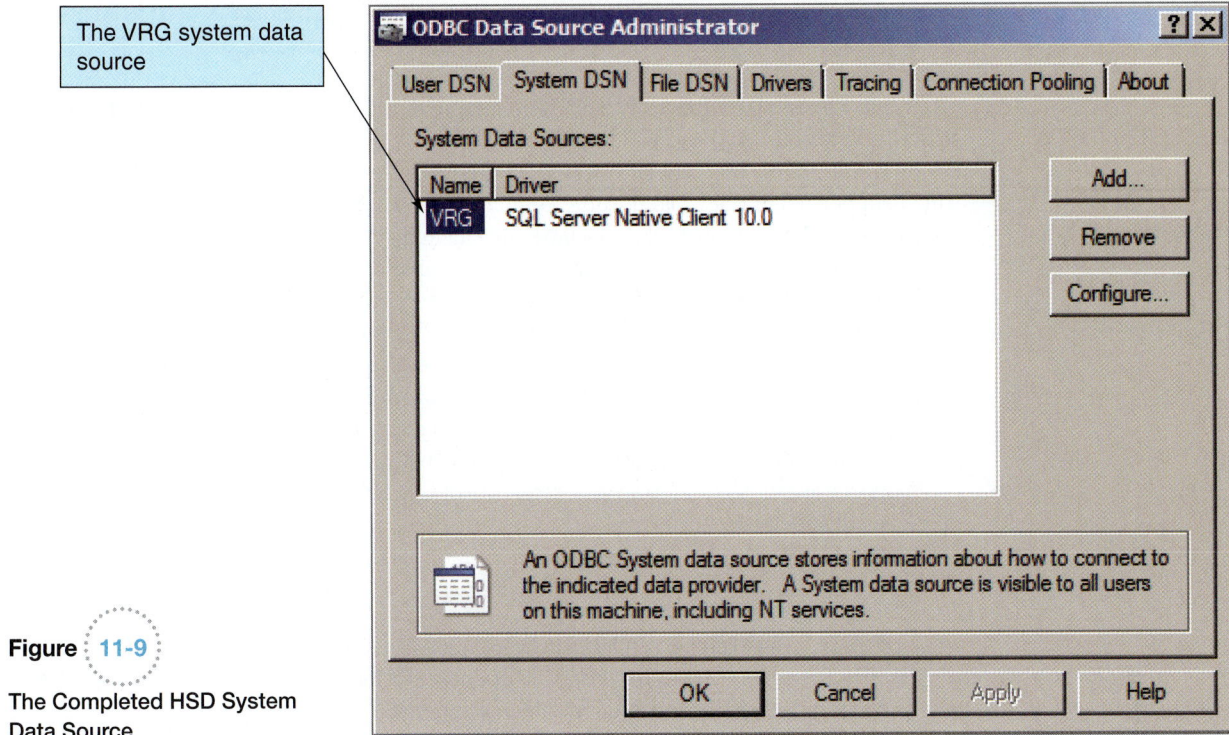

Figure 11-9

The Completed HSD System Data Source

The Mircosoft .NET Framework and ADO.NET

The **NET Framework** is Microsoft's comprehensive application development platform. Web database applications tools are included in the .NET Framework. Originally released as the .NET Framework 1.0 in January 2002, the current version is the .NET Framework 3.5 SP1 (and this is the version needed for use with SQL Server 2008).

As shown in Figure 11-10, the .NET Framework can best be visualized as a set of building blocks stacked on top of each other. Each additional block adds additional functionality to the

Figure 11-10

The Microsoft .NET Framework Structure

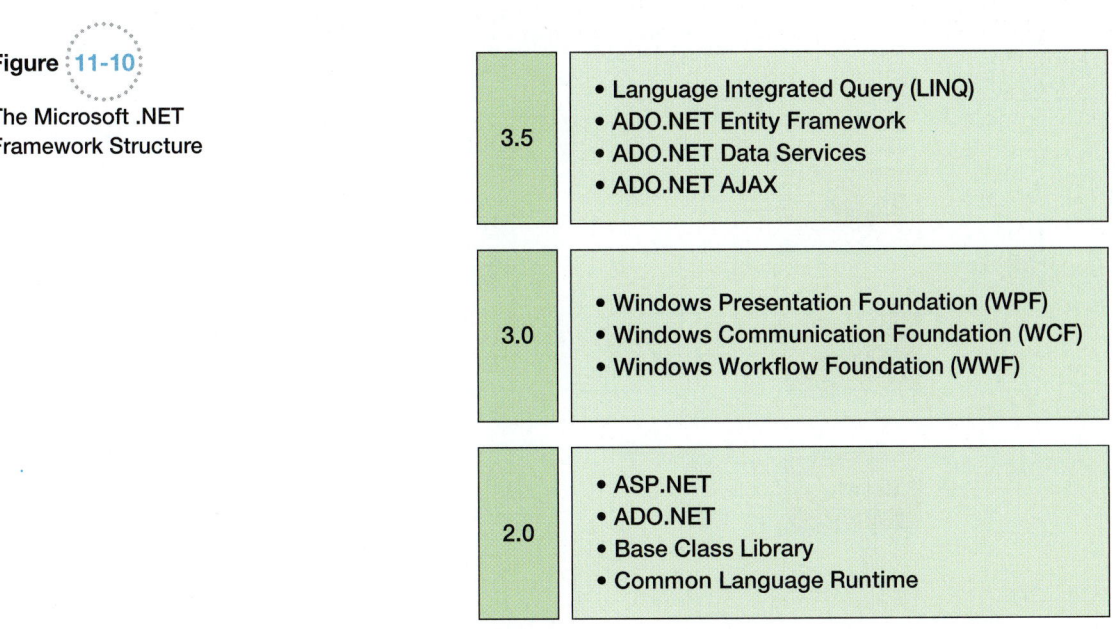

components already existing in previous blocks, and if earlier components need to be updated this is done by service packs to the older blocks. Thus, .NET Framework 2.0 SP2 and .NET Framework SP2 are included as part of .NET Framework 3.5 SP1.

While Figure 11-10 does not show every feature of the .NET Framework 3.5 SP1, the basic structure is easy to see. The .NET Framework 2.0 is now the basic layer and contains the most basic features. These include the **Common Language Runtime** and the **Base Class Library**, which support all of the programming languages (for example, VB.NET and Visual C#.NET) used with the .NET Framework. This layer also includes the ADO.NET and ASP.NET components, which are needed for Web database applications.

The .NET Framework 3.0 added a set of components that are not of interest to us here. We are more concerned with the features added in .NET Framework 3.5 and 3.5 SP1. Note that several extensions to ADO.NET have been included, such as the **ADO.NET Entity Framework**, which supports Microsoft's emerging **Entity Data Model (EDM)** data modeling technology, as well as the **Language Integrated Query (LINQ)** component, which allows SQL queries to be programmed directly into application programs in a simple manner.

Now that we understand the basic structure of the .NET Framework, we can look at some of the pieces in detail.

> **BY THE WAY**   The Microsoft Entity Data Model (EDM) is similar in concept to the Semantic Object Model discussed in Appendix E of this book. A discussion of the EDM can be found at msdn.microsoft.com/en-us/library/aa697428(VS.80).aspx.

OLE DB

ODBC has been a tremendous success and has greatly simplified some database development tasks. However, it does have some disadvantages, and in particular one substantial disadvantage that Microsoft addressed by creating OLE DB. Figure 11-11 shows the relationship among OLE DB, ODBC, and other data types. OLE DB is one of the foundations of data access in the Microsoft world. As such, it is important to understand the fundamental ideas of OLE DB, even if you will

Figure  11-11

The Role of OLE DB

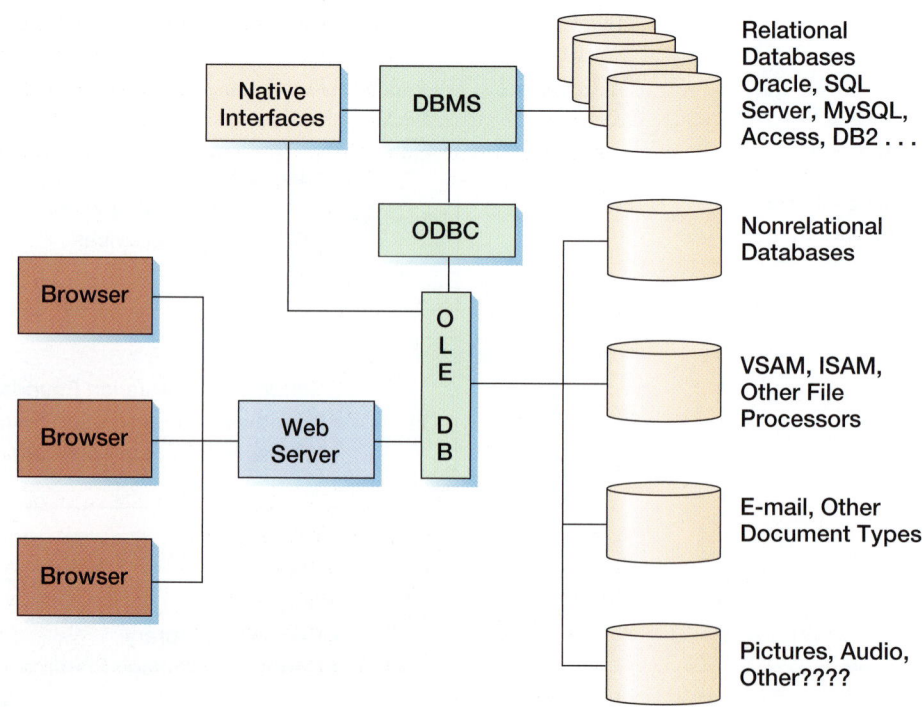

only work with the ADO.NET interface that lies on top of it because, as you will see, OLE DB remains as a data provider to ADO.NET. In this section, we present essential OLE DB concepts, and use them to introduce some important object-oriented programming topics.

OLE DB provides an object-oriented interface to data of almost any type. DBMS vendors can wrap portions of their native libraries in OLE DB objects to expose their product's functionality through this interface. OLE DB can also be used as an interface to ODBC data sources. Finally, OLE DB was developed to support the processing of nonrelational data as well.

OLE DB is an implementation of the Microsoft **Object Linking and Embedding (OLE)** object standard. OLE DB objects are Component Object Model (COM) objects and support all required interfaces for such objects. Fundamentally, OLE DB breaks the features and functions of a DBMS up into COM objects. Some objects support query operations; others perform updates; others support the creation of database schema constructs, such as tables, indexes, and views; and still others perform transaction management, such as optimistic locking.

This characteristic overcomes a major disadvantage of ODBC. With ODBC, a vendor must create an ODBC driver for almost all DBMS features and functions in order to participate in ODBC at all. This is a large task that requires a substantial investment. With OLE DB, however, a DBMS vendor can implement portions of a product. One could, for example, implement only the query processor, participate in OLE DB, and hence be accessible to customers using ADO.NET. Later, the vendor could add more objects and interfaces to increase OLE DB functionality.

This text does not assume that you are an object-oriented programmer, so we need to develop a few concepts. In particular, you need to understand abstractions, methods, properties, and collections. An **abstraction** is a generalization of something. ODBC interfaces are abstractions of native DBMS access methods. When we abstract something, we lose detail, but we gain the ability to work with a broader range of types.

For example, a **recordset** is an abstraction of a relation. In this abstraction, a recordset is defined to have certain characteristics that will be common to all recordsets. Every recordset, for instance, has a set of columns, which in this abstraction is called Fields. Now, the goal of abstraction is to capture everything important but to omit details that are not needed by users of the abstraction. Thus, Oracle relations may have some characteristics that are not represented in a recordset; the same might be true for relations in SQL Server, DB2, and in other DBMS products. These unique characteristics will be lost in the abstraction, but if the abstraction is a good one, no one will care.

Moving up a level, a **rowset** is the OLE DB abstraction of a recordset. Now, why does OLE DB need to define another abstraction? Because OLE DB addresses data sources that are not tables but that do have *some of* the characteristics of tables. Consider all of the e-mail addresses in your personal e-mail file. Are those addresses the same as a relation? No, but they do share some of the characteristics that relations have. Each address is a semantically related group of data items. Like rows of a table, it is sensible to go to the first one, move to the next one, and so forth. But, unlike relations, they are not all of the same type. Some addresses are for individuals, others are for mailing lists. Thus, any action on a recordset that depends on everything in the recordset being the same kind of thing cannot be used on a rowset.

Working from the top down, OLE DB defines a set of data properties and behaviors for rowsets. Every rowset has those properties and behaviors. Furthermore, OLE DB defines a recordset as a subtype of a rowset. Recordsets have all of the properties and behaviors that rowsets have, plus they have some that are uniquely characteristic of recordsets.

Abstraction is both common and useful. You will hear of abstractions of transaction management or abstractions of querying or abstractions of interfaces. This simply means that certain characteristics of a set of things are formally defined as a type.

An object-oriented programming **object** is an abstraction that is defined by its properties and methods. For example, a recordset object has an AllowEdits property and a RecordsetType property and an EOF property. These **properties** represent characteristics of the recordset abstraction. An object also has actions that it can perform that are called **methods**. A recordset has methods such as Open, MoveFirst, MoveNext, and Close. Strictly speaking, the definition of an object abstraction is called an **object class**, or just a *class*. An instance of an object class, such as a particular recordset, is called an *object*. All objects of a class have the same methods and the same properties, but the values of the properties vary from object to object.

The last term we need to address is *collection*. A **collection** is an object that contains a group of other objects. A recordset has a collection of other objects called Fields. The collection has properties and methods. One of the properties of all collections is Count, which is the number of objects in the collection. Thus, recordset.Fields.Count is the number of fields in the collection. In OLE DB, collections are named as the plural of the objects they collect. Thus, there is a Fields collection of Field objects, an Errors collection of Error objects, a Parameters collection of Parameters, and so forth. An important method of a collection is an iterator, which is a method that can be used to pass through or otherwise identify the items in the collection.

Goals of OLE DB

The major goals for OLE DB are listed in Figure 11-12. First, as mentioned, OLE DB breaks DBMS functionality and services into object pieces. This partitioning means great flexibility for both **data consumers** (users of OLE DB functionality) and **data providers** (vendors of products that deliver OLE DB functionality). Data consumers take only the objects and functionality they need; a wireless device for reading a database can have a very slim footprint. Unlike with ODBC, data providers need only implement a portion of DBMS functionality. This partitioning also means that data providers can deliver capabilities in multiple interfaces.

This last point needs expansion. An object interface is a packaging of objects. An **interface** is specified by a set of objects and the properties and methods that they expose. An object need not expose all of its properties and methods in a given interface. Thus, a recordset object would expose only read methods in a query interface, but would expose create, update, and delete methods in a modification interface.

How the object supports the interface, or the **implementation**, is completely hidden from the user. In fact, the developers of an object are free to change the implementation whenever they want. Who will know? But they may not ever change the interface without incurring the justifiable disdain of their users!

OLE DB defines standardized interfaces. Data providers, however, are free to add interfaces on top of the basic standards. Such extensibility is essential for the next goal, which is to provide an object interface to any data type. Relational databases can be processed through OLE DB objects that use ODBC or that use the native DBMS drivers. OLE DB includes support for the other types as indicated.

The net result of these design goals is that data need not be converted from one form to another, nor need they be moved from one data source to another. The Web server shown in

Figure 11-12

The Goals of OLE DB

- Create object interfaces for DBMS functionality pieces
    - Query
    - Update
    - Transaction management
    - Etc.
- Increase flexibility
    - Allow data consumers to use only the objects they need
    - Allow data providers to expose pieces of DBMS functionality
    - Providers can deliver functionality in multiple interfaces
    - Interfaces are standardized and extensible
- Object interface over any type of data
    - Relational database
    - ODBC or native
    - Nonrelational database
    - VSAM and other files
    - E-mail
    - Other
- Do not force data to be converted or moved from where they are

Figure 11-11 can utilize OLE DB to process data in any of the formats, right where the data reside. This means that transactions may span multiple data sources and may be distributed on different computers. The OLE DB provision for this is the **Microsoft Transaction Manager (MTS)**; however, discussion of the MTS is beyond the scope of this text.

OLE DB Terminology

As shown in Figure 11-13, OLE DB has two types of data providers. **Tabular data providers** present their data via rowsets. Examples are DBMS products, spreadsheets, and ISAM file processors, such as dBase and FoxPro. Additionally, other types of data, such as e-mail, can also be presented in rowsets. Tabular data providers bring data of some type into the OLE DB world.

A **service provider**, in contrast, is a transformer of data. Service providers accept OLE DB data from an OLE DB tabular data provider and transform it in some way. Service providers are both consumers and providers of transformed data. An example of a service provider is one that obtains data from a relational DBMS and then transforms them into XML documents. Both data and service providers process rowset objects. A rowset is equivalent to what we called a **cursor** in Chapter 9, and in fact the two terms are frequently used synonymously.

For database applications, rowsets are created by processing SQL statements. The results of a query, for example, are stored in a rowset. OLE DB rowsets have dozens of different methods, which are exposed via the interfaces listed in Figure 11-14.

IRowSet provides object methods for forward-only sequential movement through a rowset. When you declare a forward-only cursor in OLE DB, you are invoking the IRowSet interface. The IAccessor interface is used to bind program variables to rowset fields.

The IColumnsInfo interface has methods for obtaining information about the columns in a rowset. IRowSet, IAccessor, and IColumnsInfo are the basic rowset interfaces. Other interfaces are defined for more advanced operations such as scrollable cursors, update operations, direct access to particular rows, explicit locks, and so forth.

Figure 11-13

Two Types of OLE DB Data Providers

- Tabular data provider
  - Exposes data via rowsets
  - Examples: DBMS, spreadsheets, ISAMs, e-mail
- Service provider
  - Transforms data through OLE DB interfaces
  - Both a consumer and a provider of data
  - Examples: query processors, XML document creator

Figure 11-14

Rowset Interfaces

- IRowSet
  - Methods for sequential iteration through a rowset
- IAccessor
  - Methods for setting and determining bindings between rowset and client program variables
- IColumnsInfo
  - Methods for determining information about the columns in the rowset
- Other interfaces
  - Scrollable cursors
  - Create, update, delete rows
  - Directly access particular rows (bookmarks)
  - Explicitly set locks
  - And so on

ADO and ADO.NET

Because OLE DB is an object-oriented interface, it is particularly suited to object-oriented languages such as VB.NET and Visual C#.NET. Many database application developers, however, program in scripting languages such as VBScript or JScript (Microsoft's version of JavaScript). To meet the needs of these programmers, Microsoft developed **Active Data Objects (ADO)** as a cover over OLE DB objects, as shown in Figure 11-15. ADO enabled programmers to use almost any language to access OLE DB functionality.

ADO is a simple object model that overlies the more complex OLE DB object model. ADO can be called from scripting languages, such as JScript and VBScript, and it can also be called from more powerful languages, such as Visual Basic .NET, Visual C#.NET, Visual C++.NET, and even Java. Because ADO is easier to understand and use than OLE DB, ADO was (and still is) often used for database applications.

ADO.NET is a new, improved, and greatly expanded version of ADO that was developed as part of Microsoft's .NET initiative. It incorporates the functionality of ADO and OLE DB, but adds much more. In particular, ADO.NET facilitates the transformation of XML documents (discussed in Chapter 12) to and from relational database constructs. ADO.NET also provides the ability to create and process in-memory databases called *datasets*. Figure 11-16 shows the role of ADO.NET.

The ADO.NET Object Model

Now we need to look at ADO.NET in more detail. As shown in Figure 11-17, an **ADO.NET Data Provider** is a class library that provides ADO.NET services. There are .NET Framework Data Providers for ODBC, OLE DB, SQL Server, and EDM applications, which means that ADO.NET works with not only the ODBC and OLE DB data access methods we've discussed in this chapter, but directly with SQL Server and .NET language applications that use EDM as well.

Figure  **11-15**

The Role of ADO

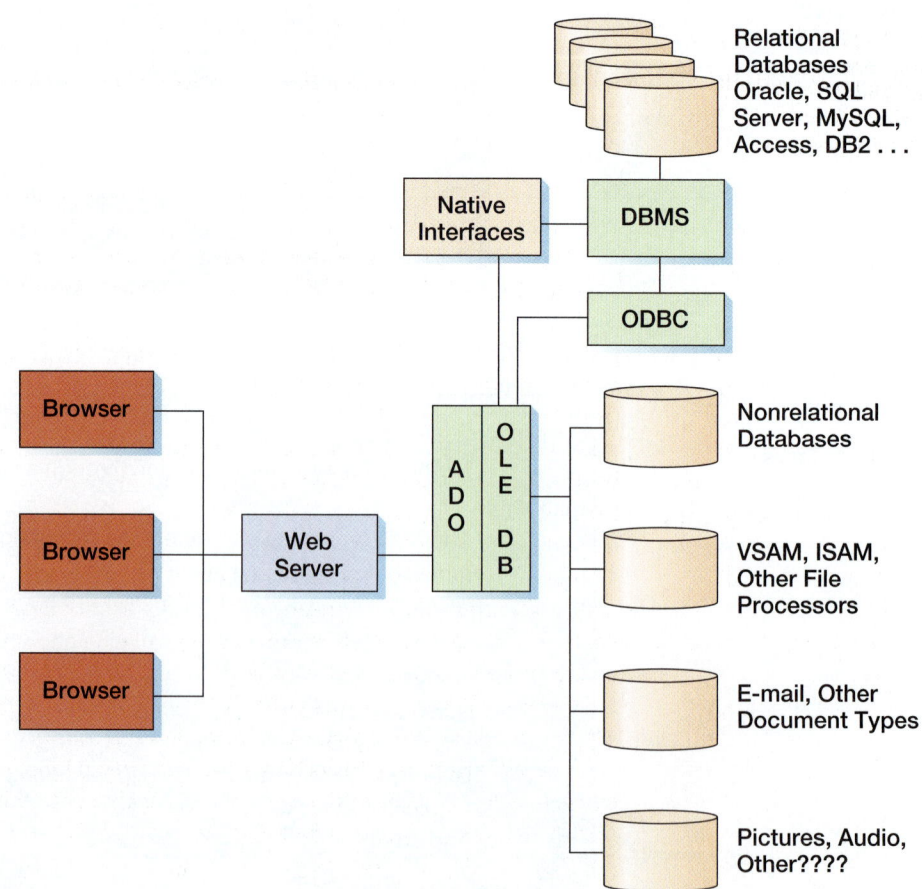

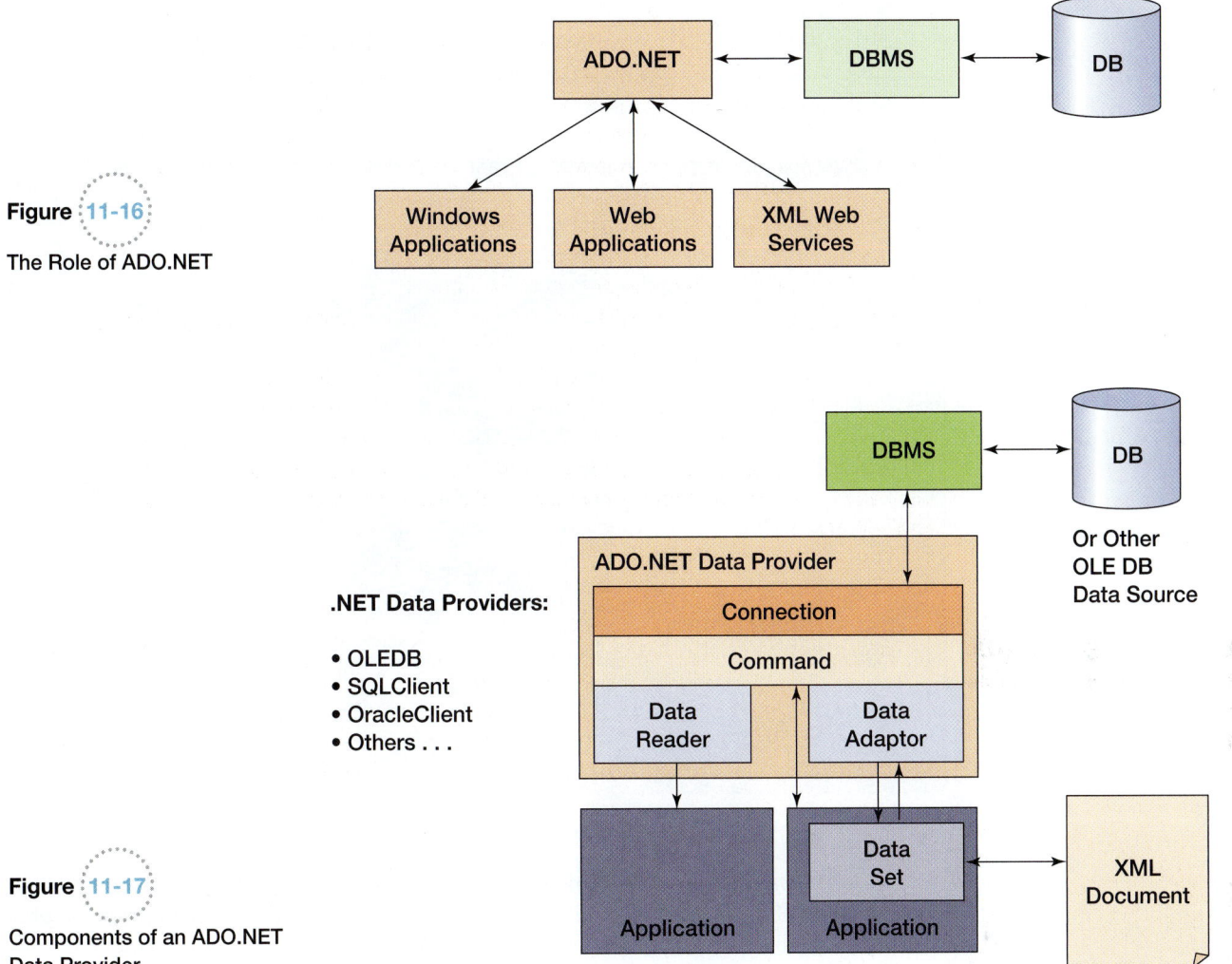

Figure 11-16

The Role of ADO.NET

Figure 11-17

Components of an ADO.NET
Data Provider

A simplified version of the ADO.NET object model is shown in Figure 11-18. The ADO.NET object classes are grouped into Data Providers and Data Sets.

The **ADO.NET Connection object** is responsible for connecting to the data source. It is basically the same as the ADO Connection object, except that ODBC is not used as a data source.

The **ADO.NET DataSet** is a representation of the data stored in the computer memory as a set of data separate from the one in the DBMS. The DataSet is distinct and disconnected from the DBMS data. This allows commands to be run against the DataSet instead of the actual data. DataSet data can be constructed from data in multiple databases, and they can be managed by different DBMS products. The DataSet contains the DataTableCollection and the DataRelationCollection. A more detailed version of the ADO.NET dataset object model is shown in Figure 11-19.

The **DataTableCollection** mimics DBMS tables with **DataTable objects**. DataTable objects include a **DataColumnsCollection**, a **DataRowCollection**, and **Constraints**. Data values are stored in DataRow collections in three forms: **original values**, **current values**, and **proposed values**. Each DataTable object has a **PrimaryKey property** to enforce row uniqueness. The Constraints collection uses two constraints. The **ForeignKeyConstraint** supports referential integrity, and the **UniqueConstraint** supports data integrity.

The **DataRelationCollection** stores **DataRelations**, which act as the relational links between tables. Note again that referential integrity is maintained by the ForeignKeyConstraint in the Constraints collection. Relationships among DataSet tables can be processed just as relationships in a database can be processed. A relationship can be used to compute the values of a column, and DataSet tables can also have views.

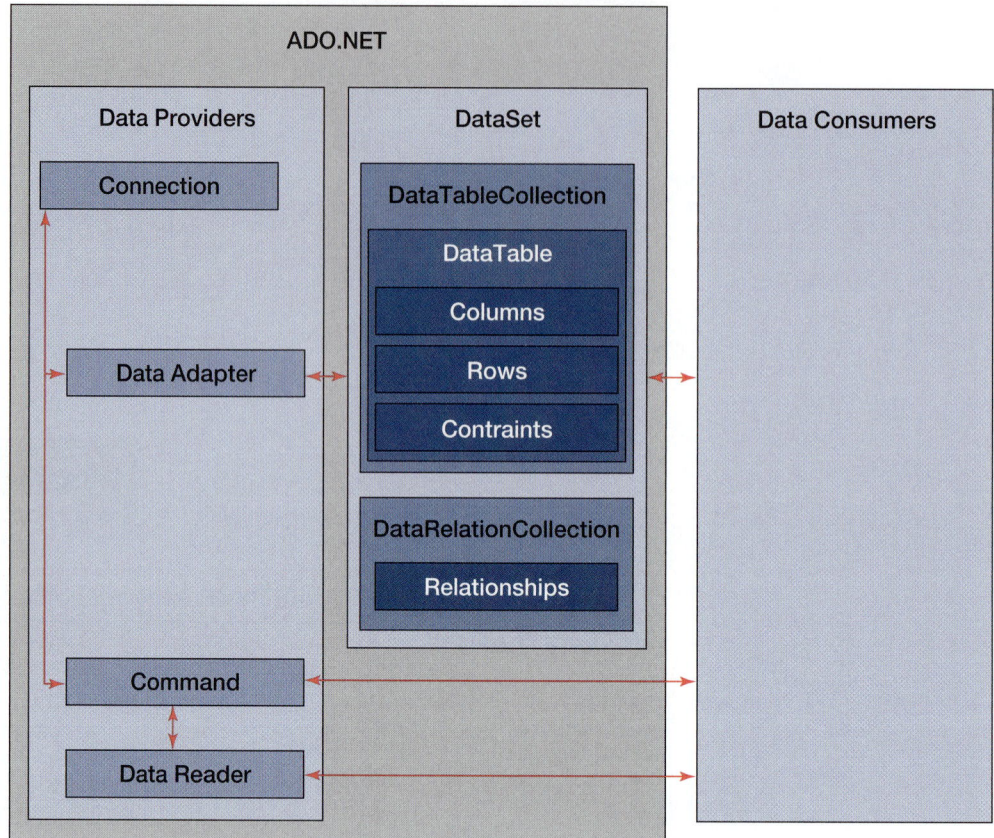

Figure 11-18

The ADO.NET
Object Model

The **ADO.NET Command object** shown in Figures 11-17 and 11-18 is used as an SQL statement or stored procedure and is run on data in the DataSet. The **ADO.NET DataAdapter object** is the link between a Connection object and a DataSet object. The DataAdapter uses four Command objects: the **SelectCommand object**, the **InsertCommand object**, the **UpdateCommand object**, and the **DeleteCommand object**. The SelectCommand object gets data from a DBMS and places it in a DataSet. The other commands send changes in the DataSet back to the DBMS data.

The **ADO.NET DataReader** is similar to a cursor that provides read-only, forward-only data transfers from a data source, and can only be used through an Execute method of a Command.

Looking ahead to Chapter 12 on XML, we see some of the advantages of ADO.NET over ADO. Once a DataSet is constructed, its contents can be formatted as an XML document with a single command. Similarly, an XML Schema document for the DataSet can also be produced with a single command. This process works in reverse as well. An XML Schema document can be used to create the structure of a DataSet, and the DataSet data can then be filled by reading an XML document.

> **BY THE WAY** You may be wondering, "Why is all of this necessary? Why do we need an in-memory database?" The answer lies in database views like that shown in Chapter 12 in Figure 12-14. There is no standardized way to describe and process such data structures. Because it involves two multivalue paths through the data, SQL cannot be used to describe the data. Instead, we must execute two SQL statements and somehow patch the results to obtain the view.
>
> Views like that shown in Figure 12-14 have been processed for many years, but only by private, proprietary means. Every time such a structure needs to be processed, a developer designs programs for creating and manipulating the data in memory and for

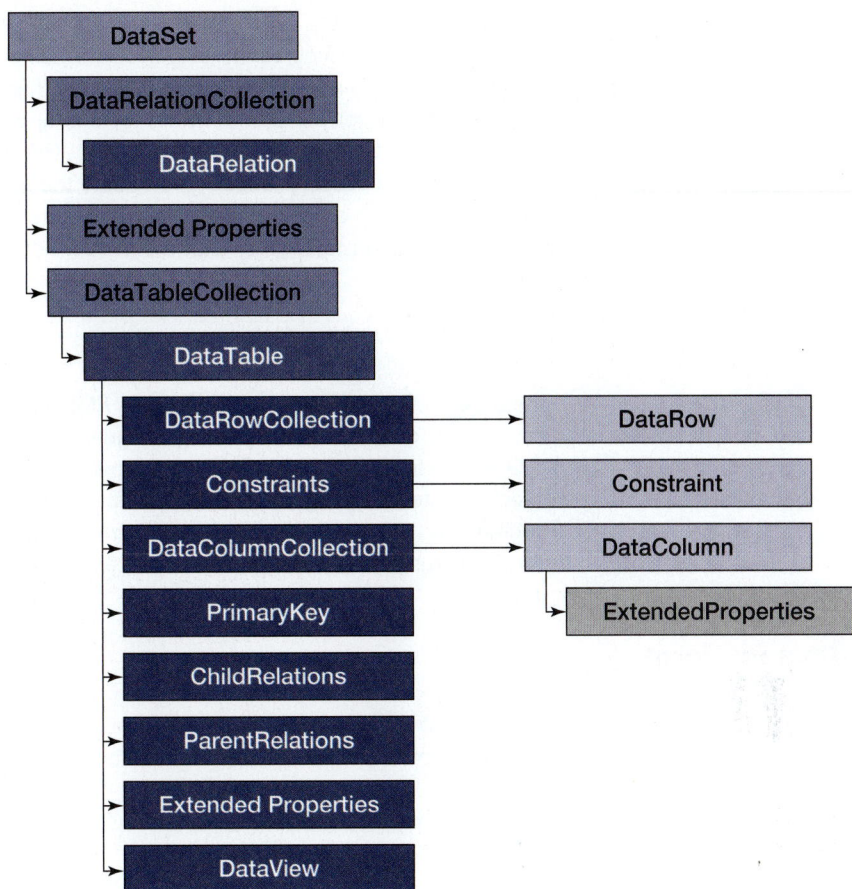

Figure 11-19

The ADO.NET DataSet
Object Model

saving them to the database. Object-oriented programmers define a class for this data structure and create methods to serialize objects of this class into the database. Other programmers use other means. The problem is that every time a different view is designed, a different scheme must be designed and developed to process the new view.

As Microsoft developed .NET technology, it became clear that a generalized means was needed to define and process database views and related structures. Microsoft could have defined a new proprietary technology for this purpose, but thankfully it did not. Instead, it recognized that the concepts, techniques, and facilities used to manage regular databases can be used to manage in-memory databases as well. The benefit to you is that all of the concepts and techniques that you have learned to this point for processing regular databases can also be used to process datasets.

DataSets do have a downside, and a serious one for some applications. Because DataSet data are disconnected from the regular database, only optimistic locking can be used. The data are read from the database, placed into the DataSet, and processed there. No attempt is made to propagate changes in the DataSet back to the database. If, after processing, the application later wants to save all of the DataSet data into a regular database, it needs to use optimistic locking. If some other application has changed the data, either the DataSet will need to be reprocessed or the data change will be forced onto the database, causing the lost update problem.

Thus, DataSets cannot be used for applications in which optimistic locking is problematic. For such applications, the ADO.NET Command object should be used instead. But for applications in which conflict is rare or for those in which reprocessing after conflict can be accommodated, DataSets provide significant value.

> **BY THE WAY**   ASP.NET connects to the DBMS using the default user name ASP.NET. Oracle requires any user name that has operating system authentication to begin with the letters OPS$. Thus, for this application to run, there must be an account named OPS$ASPNET in the Oracle VRG database, and that account must have privileges necessary to read and update the View Ridge tables in VRG. If you do not want to use the default name ASPNET, you can cause ASP.NET to pass the user's credentials through to Oracle. That technique, however, is beyond the scope of this discussion.

> **BY THE WAY**   The only way to use Oracle's XML facilities is to write in Java, an object-oriented programming language. Further, the only way to process ADO.NET is from one of the .NET languages, all of which, like Visual Basic .NET, are object-oriented languages. Thus, if you do not yet know object-oriented design and programming, and if you want to work in the emerging world of database processing, you should run, not walk, to your nearest object-oriented design and programming class!

The Java Platform

Having looked at the Microsoft .NET Framework in some detail, we will now turn our attention to the Java platform and look at its components.

JDBC

Originally, and contrary to many sources, JDBC originally did *not* stand for Java Database Connectivity. According to Sun Microsystems—the inventor of Java and the source of many Java-oriented products—JDBC was not an acronym; it just stood for JDBC. At this point in time, however, we can even find the name Java Database Connectivity (JBDC) on Sun's Web site (see *http://java.sun.com/javase/technologies/database/*)! Still, because we use acronyms in this book after introducing the full term, we will use *JDBC*.

A JDBC driver is available for almost every conceivable DBMS product. Sun maintains a directory of them available through *http://java.sun.com/products/jdbc/overview.html*). Some of the drivers are free, and almost all of them have an evaluation edition that can be used for free for a limited period of time. The JDBC driver for MySQL is the MySQL Connector/J, which is available at *http://dev.mysql.com/downloads/connector/j/5.1.html*.

Driver Types

As summarized in Figure 11-20, Sun defines four JDBC driver types. Type 1 drivers are JDBC–ODBC bridge drivers, which provide an interface between Java and regular ODBC drivers. Most ODBC drivers are written in C or C++. For reasons unimportant to us here, there are incompatibilities between Java and C/C++. Bridge drivers resolve these incompatibilities and allow access to ODBC data sources from Java. Because we use ODBC in the chapter, if you are using MySQL you will want to download the MySQL Connector/ODBC driver from *http://dev.mysql.com/downloads/connector/odbc/5.1.html*.

Drivers of Types 2 through 4 are written entirely in Java; they differ only in how they connect to the DBMS. Type 2 drivers connect to the native API of the DBMS. For example, they call Oracle using the standard (non-ODBC) programming interface to Oracle. Drivers of Types 3 and 4 are intended for use over communications networks. A Type 3 driver translates JDBC calls into a DBMS-independent network protocol. This protocol is then translated into the network protocol used by a particular DBMS. Finally, Type 4 drivers translate JDBC calls into DBMS-specific network protocols.

To understand how drivers Types 2 through 4 differ, you must first understand the difference between a *servlet* and an *applet*. As you probably know, Java was designed to be portable. To accomplish portability, Java programs are not compiled into a particular machine language,

Driver Type	Characteristics
1	JDBC–ODBC bridge. Provides a Java API that interfaces to an ODBC driver. Enables processing of ODBC data sources from Java.
2	A Java API that connects to the native-library of a DBMS product. The Java program and the DBMS must reside on the same machine, or the DBMS must handle the intermachine communication, if not.
3	A Java API that connects to a DBMS-independent network protocol. Can be used for servlets and applets.
4	A Java API that connects to a DBMS-dependent network protocol. Can be used for servlets and applets.

Figure 11-20

Summary of JDBC Driver Types

but instead are compiled into machine-independent bytecode. Sun, Microsoft, and others have written **bytecode interpreters** for each machine environment (Intel 386, Alpha, and so on). These interpreters are referred to as **Java virtual machines**.

To run a compiled Java program, the machine-independent bytecode is interpreted by the virtual machine at run time. The cost of this, of course, is that bytecode interpretation constitutes an extra step, so such programs can never be as fast as programs that are compiled directly into machine code. This may or may not be a problem, depending on the application's workload.

An **applet** is a Java bytecode program that runs on the application user's computer. Applet bytecode is sent to the user via HTTP and is invoked using the HTTP protocol on the user's computer. The bytecode is interpreted by a virtual machine, which is usually part of the browser. Because of portability, the same bytecode can be sent to a Windows, a UNIX, or an Apple computer.

A **servlet** is a Java program that is invoked via HTTP on the Web server computer. It responds to requests from browsers. Servlets are interpreted and executed by a Java virtual machine running on the server.

Because they have a connection to a communications protocol, Type 3 and Type 4 drivers can be used in either applet or servlet code. Type 2 drivers can be used only in situations where the Java program and the DBMS reside on the same machine or where the Type 2 driver connects to a DBMS program that handles the communications between the computer running the Java program and the computer running the DBMS.

Thus, if you write code that connects to a database from an applet (two-tier architecture), only a Type 3 or Type 4 driver can be used. In these situations, if your DBMS product has a Type 4 driver, use it; it will be faster than a Type 3 driver.

In three-tier or *n*-tier architecture, if the Web server and the DBMS are running on the same machine, you can use any of the four types of drivers. If the Web server and the DBMS are running on different machines, Type 3 and Type 4 drivers can be used without a problem. Type 2 drivers can also be used if the DBMS vendor handles the communications between the Web server and the DBMS. The MySQL Connector/J, the Java connector that you can download from *http://dev.mysql.com/downloads/connector/j/5.1.html* is a Type 4 driver.

Using JDBC

Unlike ODBC, JDBC does not have a separate utility for creating a JDBC data source. Instead, all of the work to define a connection is done in Java code via the JDBC driver. The coding pattern for using a JDBC driver is as follows:

1. Load the driver.
2. Establish a connection to the database.
3. Create a statement.
4. Do something with the statement.

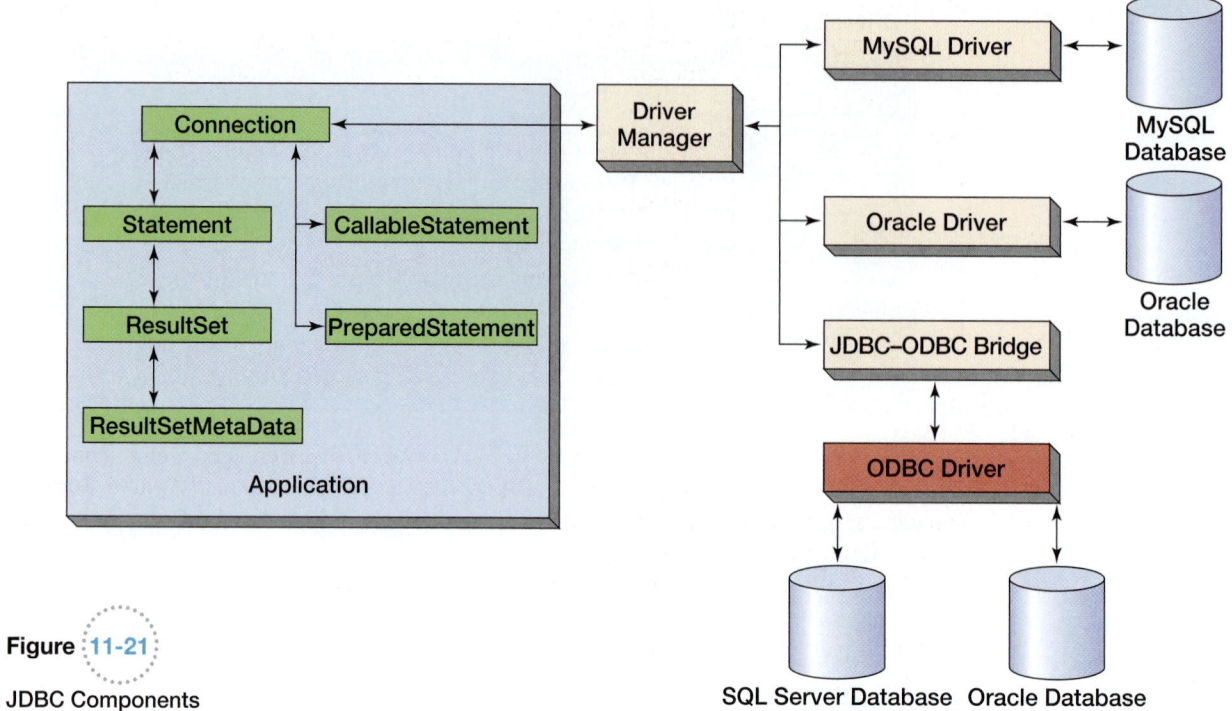

Figure 11-21

JDBC Components

To load the driver, you must first obtain the driver library and install it in a directory. You need to ensure that the directory is named in the CLASSPATH for both the Java compiler and for the Java virtual machine. The name of the DBMS product to be used and the name of the database are provided at step 2. Figure 11-21 summarizes the JDBC components.

Note that Java is used to create the application shown in the figure, and because Java is an object-oriented programming language, we see a set of objects in the application that are similar to those we have discussed for ADO.NET. The application creates a **JDBC Connection object**, **JDBC Statement objects**, a **JDBC ResultSet object**, and a **JDBC ResultSetMetaData object**. Calls from these objects are routed via the **JDBC Driver Manager** to the proper driver. Drivers then process their databases. Notice that the Oracle database in this figure could be processed via either a JDBC–ODBC bridge or via a pure JDBC driver.

> **BY THE WAY** By the way, most of this technology arose in the UNIX world. UNIX is case sensitive, and almost everything you enter here also is case sensitive. Thus, *jdbc* and *JDBC* are *not* the same.

Prepared Statement objects and **Callable Statement objects** can be used to invoke compiled queries and stored procedures in the database. Their use is similar to the use of ADO.NET Command objects discussed previously in this chapter. It is possible to receive values back from procedures as well. Start at *http://java.sun.com/javase/reference/index.jsp* for more information.

Java Server Pages (JSP) and Servlets

Java Server Pages (JSP) technology provides a means to create dynamic Web pages using HTML (and XML) and the Java programming language. With Java, the capabilities of a complete object-oriented language are directly available to the Web page developer. This is similar to what can be done using ASP.NET using the Microsoft .NET languages.

Because Java is machine independent, JSP is also machine independent. With JSP, you are not locked into using Windows and IIS. You can run the same JSP page on a Linux server, on a Windows server, and on others as well. The official specification for JSP can be found at *http://java.sun.com/products/jsp/*.

JSP pages are transformed into standard Java language and then compiled just like a regular program. In particular, they are transformed into Java servlets, which means that JSP pages are transformed into subclasses of the HTTPServlet class behind the scenes. JSP code thus has access to the HTTP request and response objects and also to their methods and to other HTTP functionality.

Apache Tomcat

The Apache Web server does not support servlets. However, the Apache Foundation and Sun cosponsored the Jakarta Project that developed a servlet processor named **Apache Tomcat** (now in version 6). You can obtain the source and binary code of Tomcat from the Apache Tomcat Web site at *http://tomcat.apache.org/*.

Tomcat is a servlet processor that can work in conjunction with Apache or as a stand-alone Web server. Tomcat has limited Web server facilities, however; so it is normally used in stand-alone mode only for testing servlets and JSP pages. For commercial production applications, Tomcat should be used in conjunction with Apache. If you are running Tomcat and Apache separately on the same Web server, they need to use different ports. The default port for a Web server is 80, and Apache normally uses it. When used in stand-alone mode, Tomcat is usually configured to listen to port 8080, though this, of course, can be changed.

Figure 11-22 shows the process by which JSP pages are compiled. When a request for a JSP page is received, a Tomcat (or other) servlet processor finds the compiled version of the page and checks to determine whether it is current. It does this by looking for an uncompiled version of the page having a creation date and time later than the compiled page's creation date and time. If the page is not current, the new page is parsed and transformed into a Java source file, and that source file is then compiled. The servlet is then loaded and executed. If the compiled JSP page is current, then it is loaded into memory, if not already there, and then executed. If it is in memory, it is simply executed.

 **THE WAY** The downside of such automatic compilation is that if you make syntax errors and forget to test your pages, the first user to access your page will receive the compiler errors!

Unlike CGI files and some other Web server programs, only one copy of a JSP page can be in memory at a time. Further, pages are executed by one of Tomcat's threads, not by an independent process. This means that much less memory and processor time are required to execute a JSP page than to execute a comparable CGI script.

Web Database Processing with PHP

At this point in our discussion, it is time to build an actual Web database application and apply both some of the knowledge from this chapter and some new techniques yet to be discussed. We have already created an ODBC data source for the View Ridge Gallery database, and now we will use it to look at Web database processing. Although we have introduced technologies such as ADO.NET, ASP.NET, Java, and JSP, these technologies are complex subjects and beyond the scope of this book. Further, these technologies tend to become vendor specific—you're either working

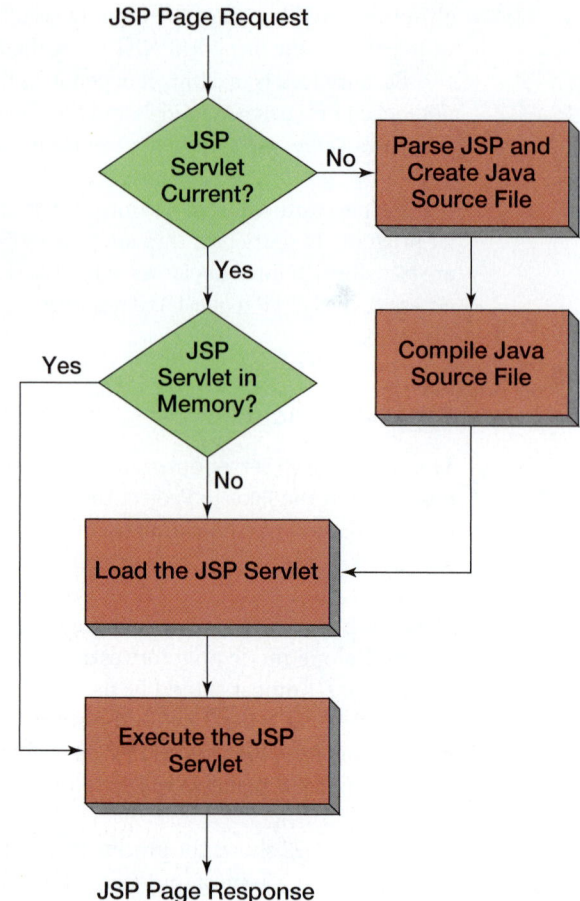

Figure 11-22

JSP Compilation Process

in a Microsoft-centric world with .NET technologies and ASPs , or a Sun Microsystems–centric world with Java and JSPs.

In this book, we will take a vendor-neutral approach and use technologies that can be used with any operating system or DBMS. We will use the **PHP** language. PHP, which is an abbreviation for **PHP: Hypertext Processor** (and that was previously known as the *Personal Hypertext Processor*), is a scripting language that can be embedded in Web pages. Although PHP started as purely a scripting language, it now also has object-oriented programming elements, but we will not cover those in this book.

PHP is extremely popular. In the summer of 2007, more than 2 million Internet domains had servers running PHP,[2] and the March 2008 TIOBE Programming Community Index ranked PHP as the fourth most popular programming language (following, in order, Java, C, and Visual Basic).[3] PHP is easy to learn and can be used in most Web server environments and with most databases. As an added bonus, it is an open-source product available for free download from the PHP Web site (*www.php.net*).

While Microsoft would probably prefer that you use ASP.NET for Web applications, there is still good information on using PHP in a Microsoft environment on the Microsoft Web site (for example, see *PHP on IIS7* at php.iis.net). Oracle and MySQL enthusiastically support PHP. Oracle publishes the *Oracle Database 2 Day + PHP Developer's Guide* (available in both HTML and PDF format at *www.oracle.com/pls/db111/homepage*), which is an excellent reference for using PHP with Oracle Database 11g. Since PHP is often the P in AMP, LAMP and WAMP, many books are available discussing the combination of PHP and MySQL, and the MySQL Web site contains basic documentation on using PHP with MySQL (for example, see *dev.mysql.com/doc/refman/5.1/en/apis-php.html*).

---

[2] See *www.php.net/usage.php*.
[3] See *www.tiobe.com/index.php/content/paperinfo/tpci/index.html*.

Web Database Processing with PHP and Eclipse

To start, we need a Web server to store the Web pages that we will build and use. We could use the Apache HTTP Server (available from the Apache Software Foundation at *www.apache.org*). This is the most widely used Web server, and there is a version that will run on just about every operating system in existence. However, because we have been using the Windows operating system for the DBMS products shown in this book, we will build a Web site using the Microsoft IIS Web server. One advantage of using this Web server for users of the Windows XP Professional and the Windows Vista operating systems is that IIS is included with the operating system: IIS version 5.1 is included with Windows XP, and IIS version 7.0 is included with Vista. IIS is not installed by default but can easily be installed at any time. This means that any user can practice creating and using Web pages on his or her own workstation.

> **BY THE WAY** This discussion of Web database processing has been written to be as widely applicable as possible. With minor adjustments to the following steps, you should be able to use the Apache Web server if you have it available. Whenever possible, we have chosen to use products and technologies that are available for many operating systems.

When IIS is installed, it creates an **inetpub folder** on the C: drive as C:\inetpub. Within the inetpub folder is the **wwwroot folder**, which is where IIS stores the most basic Web pages used by the Web server. Figure 11-22 shows this directory structure in Windows Server 2008 after IIS has been installed, with the files in the wwwroot folder displayed in the file pane.

IIS is managed using a program called **Internet Information Services Manager** in Windows Vista and Server 2008, as shown in Figure 11-24. The location of the program icon varies depending on the operating system. In Windows Vista, open **Control Panel** and then open **Administrative Tools**. The shortcut icon for Internet Information Services Manager is located in Administrative Tools. For Windows Server 2008, use **Start | Administrative Tools | Internet Information Services (IIS) Manager**.

Figure 11-23

The IIS wwwroot Folder in Windows Server 2008

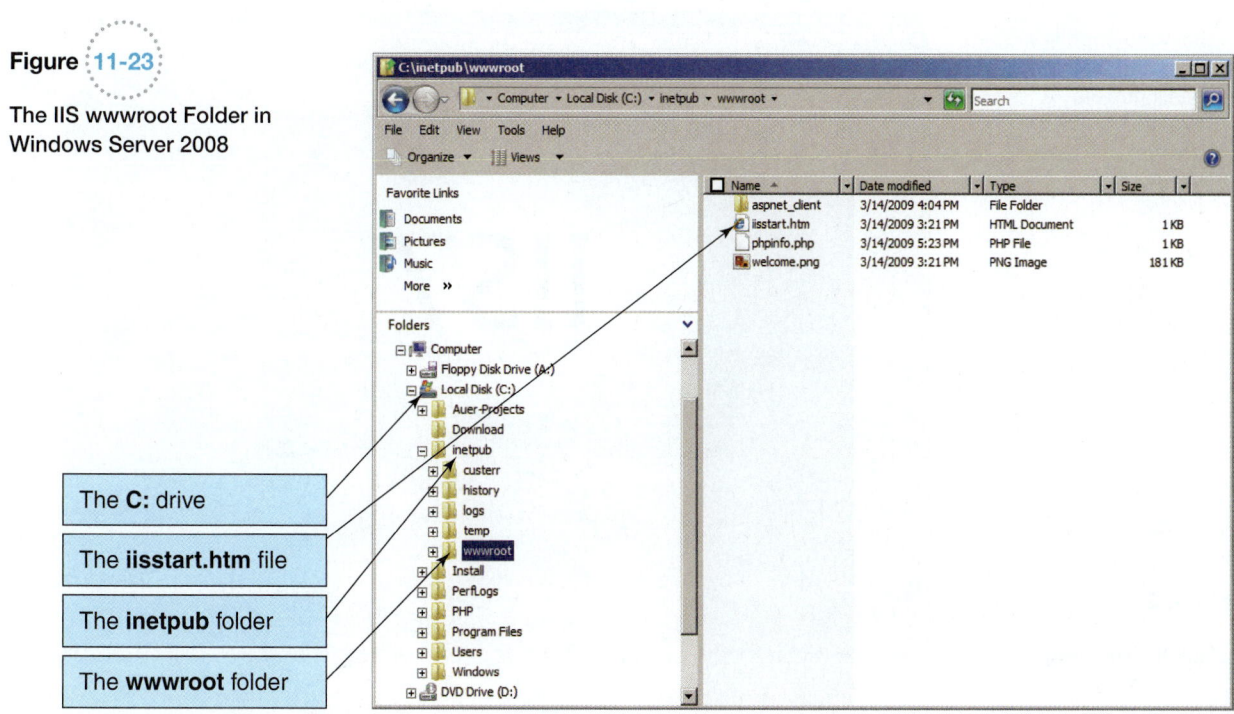

The **C:** drive

The **iisstart.htm** file

The **inetpub** folder

The **wwwroot** folder

Note that the files shown in the **Default Web Site folder** in Figure 11-23 are the same files that are in the wwwroot folder in Figure 11-24—they are the default files created by IIS when it is installed. In Windows Vista and Windows Server 2008, the file **iisstart.htm** generates the Web page that Internet Explorer (or any other Web browser) contacting this Web server over the Internet will see displayed.

To test the Web server installation, open your Web browser, type in the URL **http://localhost**, and press the **Enter** key. For Windows Server 2008, the Web page shown in Figure 11-25 appears. If the appropriate Web page isn't displayed in your Web browser, your Web server is not properly installed.

Figure 11-24

Managing IIS with the Internet Information Services Manager

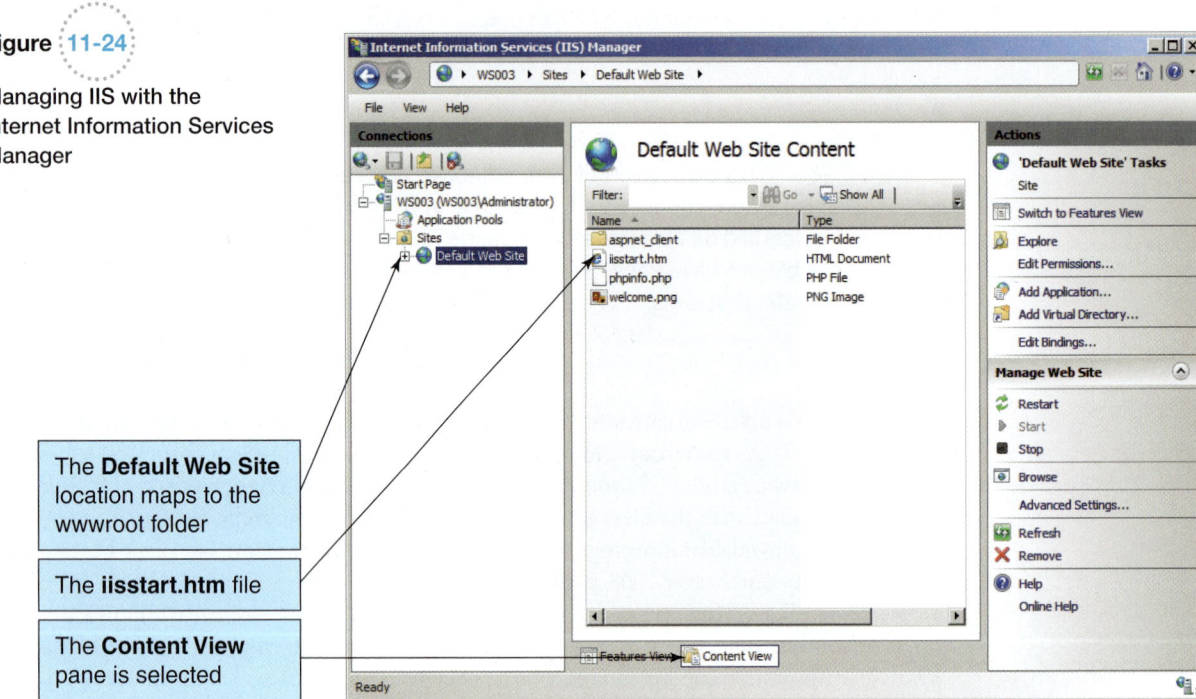

The **Default Web Site** location maps to the wwwroot folder

The **iisstart.htm** file

The **Content View** pane is selected

This Web page is generated by the iisstart.htm file

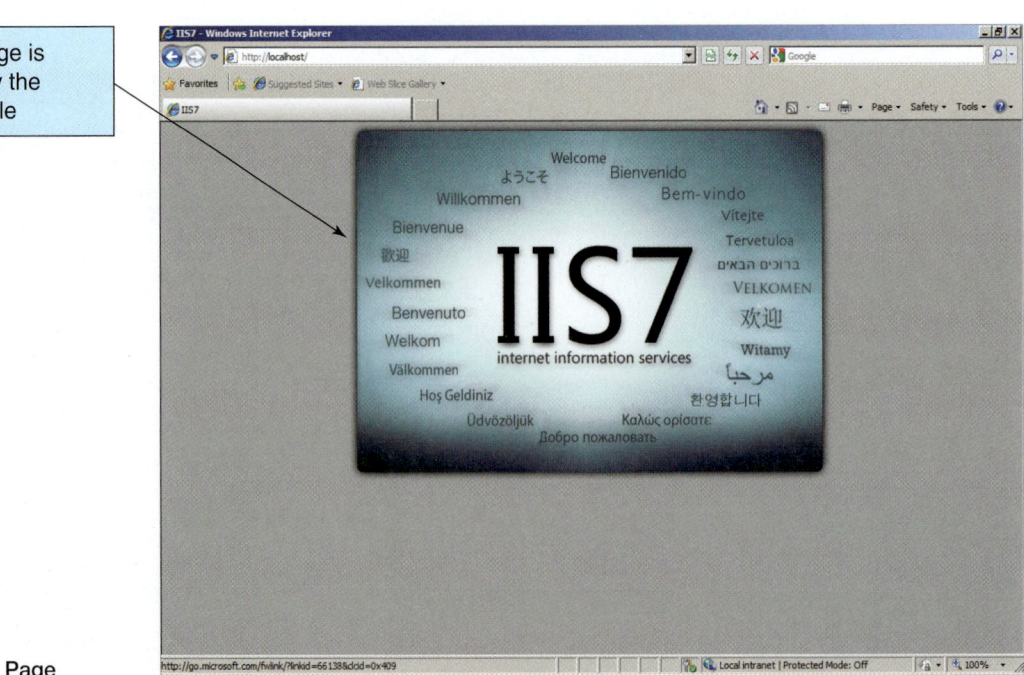

Figure 11-25

The Default IIS Web Page

Now we will set up a small Web site that can be used for Web database processing of the View Ridge Gallery VRG database. First, we will create a new folder named DBP (Database Processing) under the wwwroot folder. This new folder will be used to hold all the Web pages developed in discussions and exercises in this book. Second, we will create a subfolder of DBC named VRG. This folder will hold the VRG Web site. You create these folders using Windows Explorer.

Getting Started with HTML Web Pages

The most basic Web pages are created using **Hypertext Markup Language (HTML)**. The term *hypertext* refers to the fact that you can include links to other objects, such as Web pages, maps, pictures, and even audio and video files in a Web page, and when you click the link, you are immediately taken to that other object, and it is displayed in your Web browser. HTML itself is a standard set of **HTML syntax rules** and **HTML document tags** that can be interpreted by Web browsers to create specific onscreen displays.

Tags are usually paired, with a specific beginning tag and a matching ending tag that includes the backslash character (/). Thus, a paragraph of text is tagged as <p>{*paragraph text here*}</p>, and a main heading is tagged as <h1>{*heading text here*}</h1>. Some tags do not need a separate end tag because they are essentially self-contained. For example, to insert a horizontal line on a Web page, you use the horizontal rule tag, <hr />. Note that such single, self-contained tags must include the backslash character as part of the tag.

The rules of HTML are defined as standards by the **World Wide Web Consortium (W3C)**, and the details of current and proposed standards can be found at *www.w3c.org* (this site also has several excellent tutorials on HTML[4]). The W3C Web site has current standards for HTML; **Extensible Markup Language (XML)**, which we will discuss in Chapter 14; and a hybrid of the two called **XHTML**. A full discussion of these standards is beyond the scope of this text; this chapter uses the current HTML 4.01 standard (usually in what is called the "strict" form).

In this chapter, we will create a simple HTML homepage for the View Ridge Gallery Web site and place it in the VRG folder. We will discuss some of the numerous available Web page editors shortly, but all you really need to create Web pages is a simple text editor. For this first Web page, we will use the Microsoft Notepad ASCII text editor, which has the advantage of being supplied with every version of the Windows operating system.

The index.html Web Page

The name for the file we are going to create is **index.html**. We need to use the name *index.html* because it is a special name as far as Web servers are concerned. The file name index.html is one of only a few file names that *most* Web servers automatically display when a URL request is made without a specific file reference, and thus it will become the new default display page for our Web database application. However, note the phrase "*most* Web servers" in the last sentence. Although Apache and IIS 7.0 (as shown in Figure 11-26) are configured to recognize index.html, IIS 5.1 is not. If you are using Windows XP and IIS 5.1, you need to add index.html to the list of recognized files using the Internet Information Services management program.

Creating the index.html Web Page

Now we can create the index.html Web page, which consists of the basic HTML statements shown in Figure 11-27. Figure 11-28 shows the HTML code in Notepad.

---

[4] To learn more about HTML, go to the Web site of the World Wide Web Consortium (W3C) at *www.w3.org*. For good HTML tutorials, see David Raggett's "Getting Started with HTML" tutorial at *www.w3.org/MarkUp/Guide*, his "More Advanced Features" tutorial at *www.w3.org/MarkUp/Guide/Advanced.html*, and his "Adding a Touch of Style" tutorial at *www.w3.org/MarkUp/Guide/Style.html*.

The Features View
Default Document
settings page

The **index.html**
file name is already
listed

The **Features View**
pane is selected

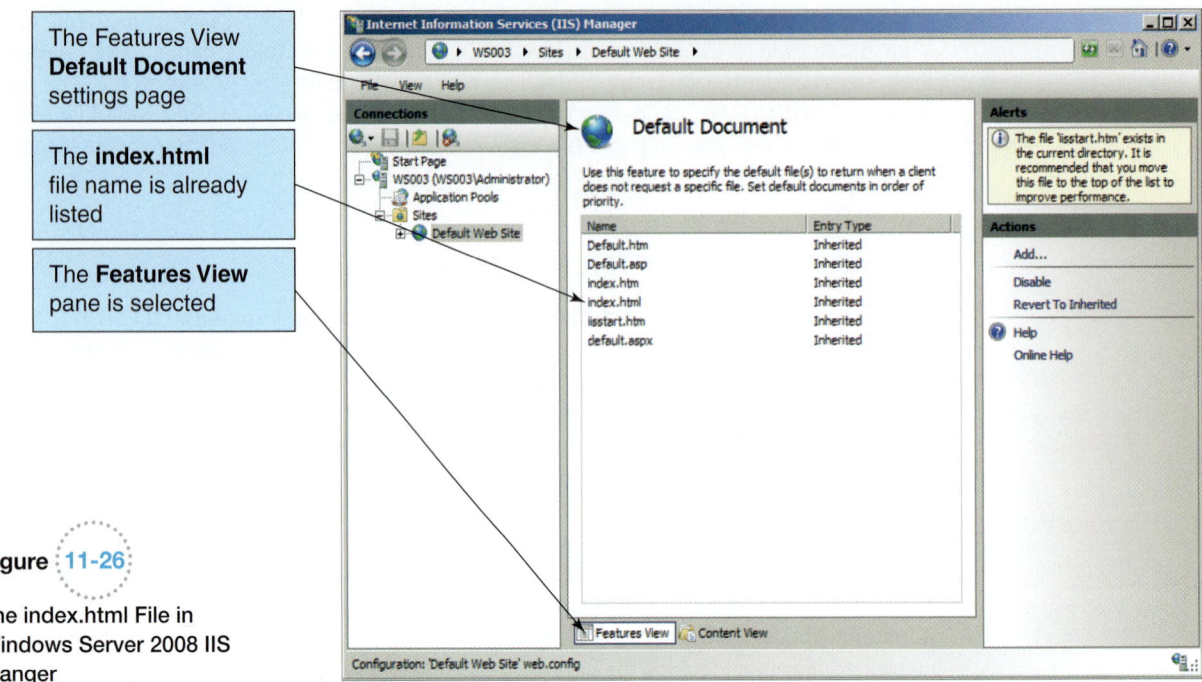

Figure 11-26

The index.html File in
Windows Server 2008 IIS
Manger

Figure 11-27

The HTML Code for the
index.html File in the VRG
Folder

```html
<!DOCTYPE html PUBLIC "-//W3C//DTD HTML 4.01 Strict//EN"
"http://www.w3.org/TR/html4/strict.dtd">
<html>
     <head>
          <meta http-equiv="Content-Type" content="text/html; charset=ISO-8859-1" />
          <title>View Ridge Gallery Demonstration Pages Home Page</title>
     </head>
     <body>
          <h1 style="text-align: center; color: blue">
               Database Processing (11th Edition)
          </h1>
          <h2 style="text-align: center; font-weight: bold">
               David M. Kroenke
          </h2>
          <h2 style="text-align: center; font-weight: bold">
               David J. Auer
          </h2>
          <hr />
          <h2 style="text-align: center; color: blue">
               Welcome to the View Ridge Gallery Home Page
          </h2>
          <hr />
          <p>Chapter 11 Demonstration Pages From Figures in the Text:</p>
          <p>Example 1:   
               <a href="ReadArtist.php">
                    Display the ARTIST Table (LastName, FirstName, Nationality)
               </a>
          </p>
          <hr />
     </body>
</html>
```

The **index.html** HTML code—note how indentation is used to keep the code organized and readable

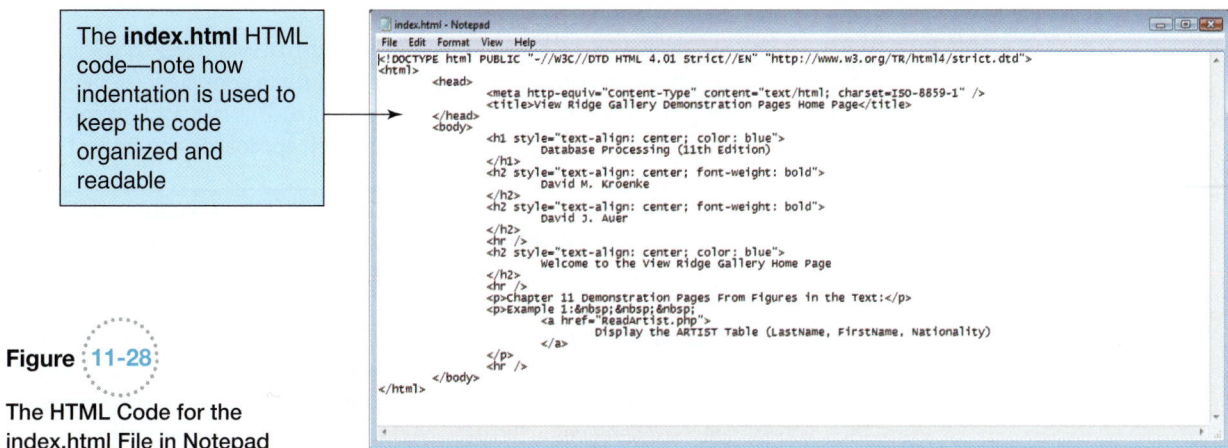

Figure 11-28

The HTML Code for the index.html File in Notepad

BY THE WAY   In the HTML code for index.html, the HTML code segment:

```
<!DOCTYPE html PUBLIC "-//W3C//DTD HTML 4.01 Strict//EN"
"http://www.w3.org/TR/html4/strict.dtd">
```

is an HTML/XML **document type declaration (DTD)**, which is used to check and validate the contents of the code that you write. DTDs are discussed later in this chapter. For now, just include the code as it is written.

If we now use either the URL *http://localhost/DBC/VRG* (if the Web server is on the same computer we're working on) or the URL http://{*Web server DNS Name or IP Number*}/ DBC/WPC (if the Web server is on another computer), we get the Web page shown in Figure 11-29.

This IP number indicates that the Web server is on a separate computer—if the Web server is on your computer itself, use the URL *http://localhost/ DBP/VRG*

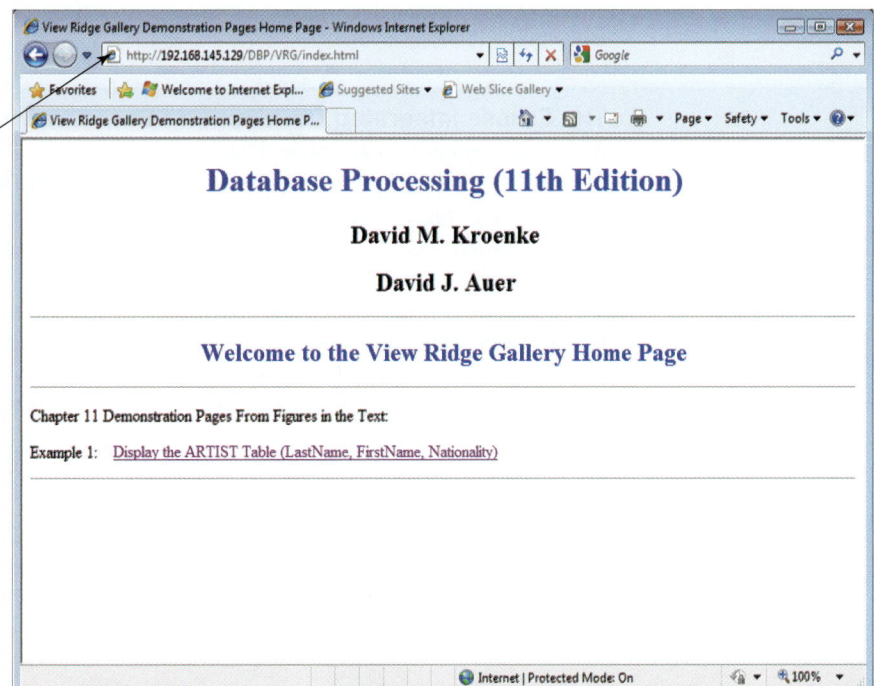

Figure 11-29

The index.html Web Page in VRG

> **BY THE WAY**   If you are working on a single computer, with the DBMS, Web server, and development tools all installed together, you will see a consistent user interface. It may be Windows XP, Windows Vista, or a version of Linux. This is, in fact, typical of small development platforms, and allows you to easily test each application component as you create it.
>
> In a larger production environment, however, the Web server and database server (which may or may not be the same physical server) are separate from the developer's workstation. In this case you, as the developer, will see different user interfaces depending on which computer you're using.
>
> We are illustrating this latter setup in this chapter. Our Web server (IIS) and DBMS server (SQL Server 2008) are on one server running Windows Server 2008. Our development tools (the IE 8 Web browser and the Eclipse IDE) are on a separate workstation running Windows Vista. Thus, you will see the differences in the user interface depending on whether the work is being done on the server (for example, in Figures 11-23 through 11-26) or on the workstation (for example, Figure 11-29).

Using PHP

Now that we have our basic Web site set up, we will expand its capabilities with a Web development environment that allows us to connect Web pages to our database. Several technologies allow us to do this. Developers using Microsoft products usually work with the .NET framework and use ASP.NET technology. Developers who use the Apache Web server may prefer creating JSP files in the JavaScript scripting language or using the Java programming language in the Java Enterprise Edition (Java EE) environment.

The PHP Scripting Language

In this chapter, we will use PHP, available as this is being written in version 5.2.9. and available for free download from the PHP Web site (*www.php.net*). You should download the latest version for you operating system and install PHP on your computer. There is documentation on the PHP Web site, and good discussion can also be found by searching the Web for "PHP installation." Setting up PHP usually requires several steps (not just running an installation routine), so take some time and be sure you have PHP running correctly. Also be sure to enable PHP Data Objects (PDO)—this is not done automatically.

The Eclipse Integrated Development Environment (IDE)

Although a simple text editor such as Notepad is fine for simple Web pages, as we start creating more complex pages we will move to an **Integrated Development Environment (IDE)**. An IDE is intended to be a complete development framework, with all the tools you need in one place. An IDE gives you the most robust and user-friendly means of creating and maintaining your Web pages.

If you are working with Microsoft products, you will most likely use Visual Studio (or the Visual Studio 2008 Express Editions, available at for free from *www.microsoft.com/express/*). In fact, if you've installed SQL Server 2008 Express Advanced or any non-Express version of the product, you have already installed some Visual Studio 2008 components. These are installed to support SQL Server Reporting Services, and are sufficient for creating basic Web pages. If you are working with JavaScript or Java, you might prefer the NetBeans IDE (downloadable from *www.netbeans.org*).

For this chapter, we will again turn to the open-source development community and use the **Eclipse IDE**. Eclipse provides a framework that can be modified by add-in modules for many purposes. For PHP, we can use Eclipse as modified for the **Eclipse PDT (PHP Development Tools) Project**, which is specifically intended to provide a PHP development environment in

The **DBP-e11-VRG** project—Eclipse organizes work into projects

The **index.html** HTML code—note how color coding has been added to indentation to keep the code organized and readable

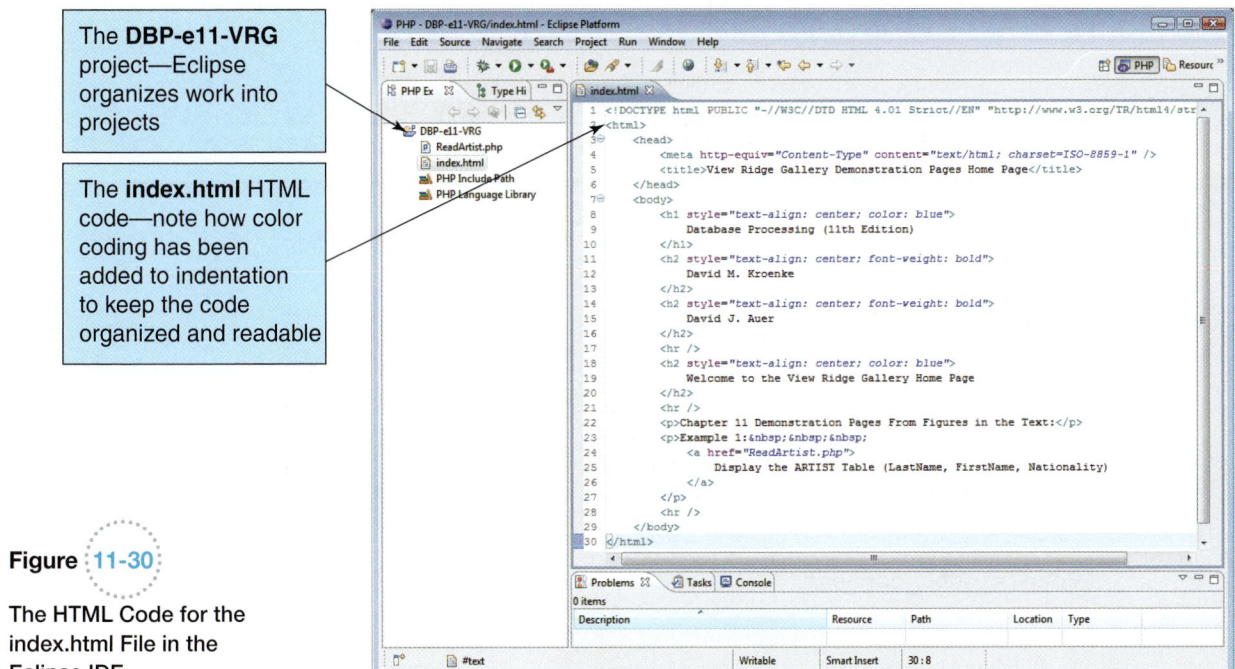

Figure 11-30

The HTML Code for the index.html File in the Eclipse IDE

Eclipse (see *www.eclipse.org/pdt/* for general information and *http://download.eclipse.org/ tools/pdt/downloads/* for downloadable files—download the current stable build for your operating system).[5]

Figure 11-29 shows the index.html file as created in the Eclipse IDE. Compare this version with the Notepad version in Figure 11-30.

The ReadArtist.php File

Now that we have our basic Web site set up, we will start to integrate PHP into the Web pages. First, we will create a page to read data from a database table and display the results in a Web page. Specifically, we will create a Web page in the VRG folder named ReadArtist.php to run the SQL query:

```
SELECT LastName, FirstName, Nationality FROM ARTIST;
```

This page displays the result of the query, without the table's surrogate key of ArtistID, in a Web page. The HTML and PHP code for ReadArtist.php is shown in Figure 11-31, and the same code is shown in Eclipse in Figure 11-32.

Now if you use the URL *http://localhost/DBP/VRG* in your Web browser and then click the **Example 1: Display the ARTIST Table (No surrogate key)** link on that page, the Web page shown in Figure 11-33 is displayed.

The ReadArtist.php code blends HTML (executed on the user's workstation) and PHP statements (executed on the Web server). In Figure 11-30, the statements included between the **<?php** and **?>** tags are program code that is to be executed on the Web server computer. All

---

[5] As noted on the PDT download page, you also need to install the Java Runtime Environment (as of this writing, it's JRE 6 Update 11 from Sun Microsystems, at *http://java.sun.com/javase/downloads/index.jsp*). Also note that the Windows version of Eclipse does not install like most Windows program: You need to create a folder named Eclipse in the Program Files folder on your C: drive (the full path name will be C:\Program Files\Eclipse), unzip the Eclipse PDT files in that directory, and create a desktop shortcut to Eclipse.exe.

```
<!DOCTYPE HTML PUBLIC "-//W3C//DTD HTML 4.01 Frameset//EN">
<html>
      <head>
            <meta http-equiv="Content-Type" content="text/html; charset=UTF-8">
            <title>ReadArtist PHP Page</title>
            <style type="text/css">
                  h1 {text-align: center; color: blue}
                  h2 {font-family: Ariel, sans-serif; text-align: left; color: blue}
                  p.footer {text-align: center}
                  table.output {font-family: Ariel, sans-serif}
            </style>
      </head>
      <body>
      <?php
            // Get connection
            $DSN = "VRG";
            $User = "VRG-User";
            $Password = "VRG-User+password";

            $Conn = odbc_connect($DSN, $User, $Password);

            // Test connection
            if (!$Conn)
            {
                  exit ("ODBC Connection Failed: " . $Conn);
            }
            // Create SQL statement
            $SQL = "SELECT LastName, FirstName, Nationality FROM ARTIST";

            // Execute SQL statement
            $RecordSet = odbc_exec($Conn,$SQL);

            // Test existence of recordset
            if (!$RecordSet)
                  {
                        exit ("SQL Statement Error: " . $SQL);
                  }
      ?>
            <!-- Page Headers -->
            <h1>
                  The View Ridge Gallery ARTIST Table
            </h1>
            <hr />
            <h2>
                  ARTIST
            </h2>
      <?php
```

Figure 11-31

The HTML and PHP Code
for ReadArtist.php

```
                        // Table headers
                        echo "<table class='output' border='1'>
                             <tr>
                                     <th>LastName</th>
                                     <th>FirstName</th>
                                     <th>Nationality</th>
                             </tr>";

                        // Table data
                        while($RecordSetRow = odbc_fetch_array($RecordSet))
                             {
                             echo "<tr>";
                             echo "<td>" . $RecordSetRow['LastName'] . "</td>";
                             echo "<td>" . $RecordSetRow['FirstName'] . "</td>";
                             echo "<td>" . $RecordSetRow['Nationality'] . "</td>";
                             echo "</tr>";
                             }
                        echo "</table>";

                        // Close connection
                        odbc_close($Conn);
             ?>

                        <br />
                        <hr />
                        <p class="footer">
                             <a href="../VRG/index.html">
                                     Return to View Ridge Gallery Home Page
                             </a>
                        </p>
                        <hr />
                    </body>
                  </html>
```

Figure 11-31

(Continued)

The **ReadArtist.php** code—PHP code is enclosed in the **<?php** and **?>** symbols, which are displayed in red in Eclipse

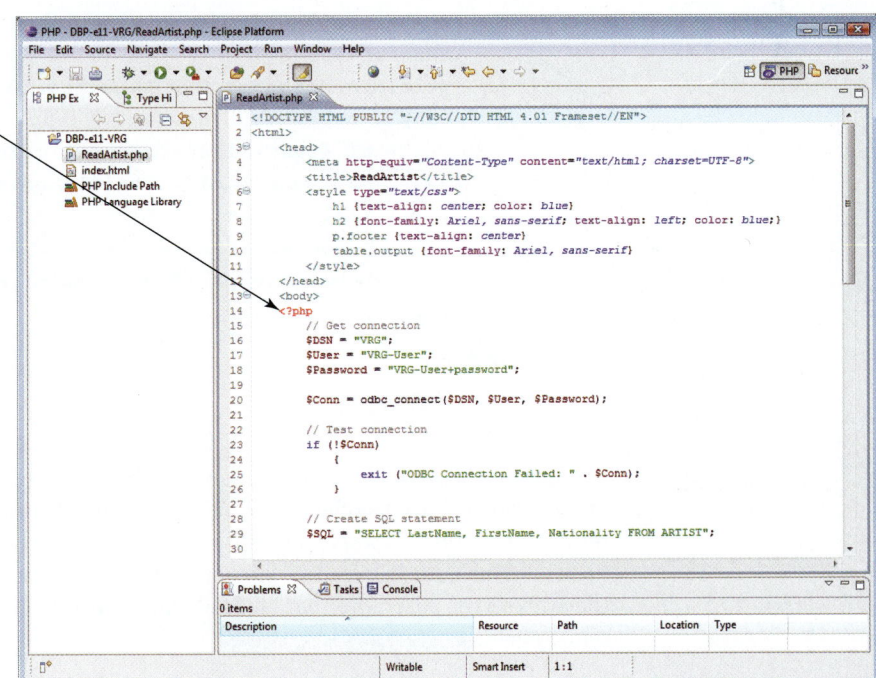

Figure 11-32

The HTML and PHP Code for ReadArtist.php in Eclipse

This IP number indicates that the Web server is on a separate computer—if the Web server is on your computer itself, use the URL *http://localhost/ DBP/VRG*

Click to return to the View Ridge Gallery Home Page

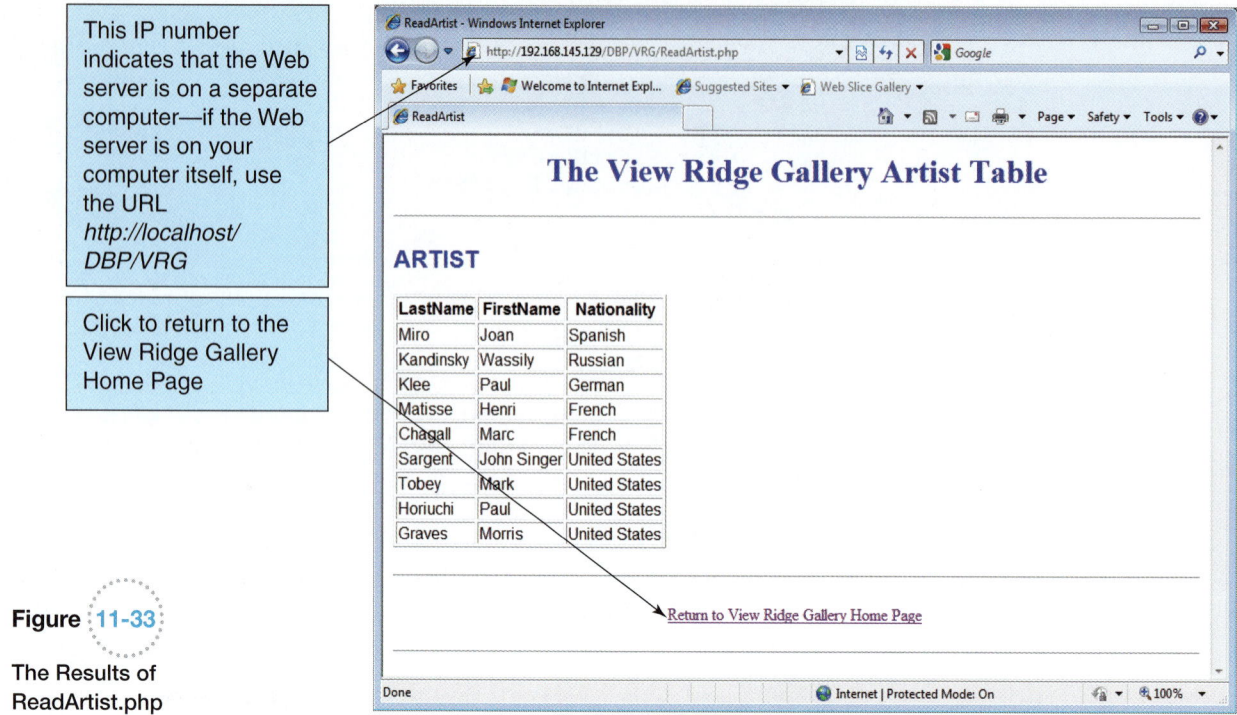

Figure 11-33

The Results of ReadArtist.php

the rest of the code is HTML that is generated and sent to the browser client. In Figure 11-30, the statements:

```
<!DOCTYPE HTML PUBLIC "-//W3C//DTD HTML 4.01 Frameset//EN">

<html>

    <head>

        <meta http-equiv="Content-Type" content="text/html;
        charset=UTF-8">
        <title>ReadArtist PHP Page</title>
        <style type="text/css">
            h1 {text-align: center; color: blue}
            h2 {font-family: Ariel, sans-serif; text-align:
            left; color: blue}
            p.footer {text-align: center}
            table.output {font-family: Ariel, sans-serif}
        </style>

    </head>

    <body>
```

are normal HTML code. When sent to the browser, these statements set the title of the browser window to ReadSeminar PHP Page; define styles to be used by the headings,[6] the results table, and the footer; and cause other HTML-related actions. The next group of statements are included between <?php and ?> and, thus, are PHP code that will be executed on the Web server. Also note that all PHP statements, like SQL statements, must end with a semicolon (;).

---

[6] Styles are used to control the visual presentation of the Web page and are defined in the HTML section between the <style> and </style> tags. For more information about styles, see David Raggett's "Adding a Touch of Style" tutorial at *www.w3.org/MarkUp/Guide/Style.html*.

Creating a Connection to the Database

In the HTML and PHP code in Figure 11-31, the following PHP code is embedded in the HTML code to create and test a connection to the database:

```php
<?php

    // Get connection

    $DSN = "VRG";
    $User = "VRG-User";
    $Password = "VRG-User+password";

    $Conn = odbc_connect($DSN, $User, $Password);

    // Test connection

    if (!$Conn)

    {

        exit ("ODBC Connection Failed: " . $Conn);

    }
```

After it runs, the variable $Conn can be used to connect to the ODBC data source VRG. Note that all PHP variables start with the dollar sign symbol ($).

> **BY THE WAY** Be sure to use comments to document your Web pages. PHP code segments with two forward slashes (//) in front of them are comments. This symbol is used to define single-line comments. In PHP, comments can also be inserted in blocks between the symbols /* and */, whereas in HTML comments *must* be inserted between the symbols <!-- and -->.

The connection is used to open the VRG ODBC data source. Here, the user ID of VRG-User and the password of VRG-User+password that we created in Chapters 10 for SQL Server 2008 are being used to authenticate to the DBMS. If you are using Oracle or MySQL, use the ODBC data source name, user name, and user password as you created it for your database.

The test of the connection is contained in the code segment:

```php
    // Test connection

    if (!$Conn)

    {

        exit ("ODBC Connection Failed: " . $Conn);

    }
```

In English, this statement says, "IF the connection Conn does not exist, THEN print the error message 'ODBC Connection Failed' followed by the contents of the variable $Conn." Note that the code (!$Conn) means NOT $Conn—in PHP the exclamation point symbol (!) means NOT.

At this point, a connection has been established to the DBMS via the ODBC data source, and the database is open. The $Conn variable can be used whenever a connection to the database is needed.

Creating a RecordSet

Given the connection with an open database, the following code segment from Figure 11-31 will store an SQL statement in the variable $SQL and then use the PHP odbc_exec command to run that SQL statement against the database to retrieve the query results and store them in the variable $RecordSet:

```php
    // Create SQL statement
    $SQL = "SELECT LastName, FirstName, Nationality FROM ARTIST";

    // Execute SQL statement
    $RecordSet = odbc_exec($objConn, $SQL);
```

```
        // Test existence of recordset
        if (!$RecordSet)
            {
                exit ("SQL Statement Error: " . $SQL);
            }
?>
```

Note that you need to test the results to be sure the PHP command executed correctly.

Displaying the Results

Now that the record set name $RecordSet has been created and populated, we can process the $RecordSet collection with the following code:

```html
<!-- Page Headers -->
<h1>
    The View Ridge Gallery ARTIST Table
</h1>
<hr />
<h2>
    ARTIST
</h2>
```
```php
<?php
    // Table headers
    echo "<table class='output' border='1'>
        <tr>
            <th>LastName</th>
            <th>FirstName</th>
            <th>Nationality</th>
        </tr>";
    // Table data
    while($RecordSetRow = odbc_fetch_array($RecordSet))
            {
            echo "<tr>";
            echo "<td>" . $RecordSetRow['LastName'] . "</td>";
            echo "<td>" . $RecordSetRow['FirstName'] . "</td>";
            echo "<td>" . $RecordSetRow['Nationality'] . "</td>";
            echo "</tr>";
            }
    echo "</table>";
```

The HTML section defines the page headers, and the PHP section defines how to display the SQL results in a table format. Note the use of the PHP command *echo* to allow PHP to use HTML syntax within the PHP code section. Also note that a loop is executed to iterate through the rows of the RecordSet using the PHP variable $RecordSetRow.

Disconnecting from the Database

Now that we have finished running the SQL statement and displaying the results, we can end our ODBC connection to the database with the code:

```php
    // Close connection
    odbc_close($Conn);
?>
```

The basic page we have created here illustrates the basic concepts of using ODBC and PHP to connect to a database and process data from that database in a Web database processing application. We can now build on this foundation by studying PHP command syntax and incorporating additional PHP features into our Web pages.[7]

Challenges for Web Database Processing

Web database application processing is complicated by an important characteristic of HTTP. Specifically, HTTP is stateless; it has no provision for maintaining sessions between requests. Using HTTP, a client at a browser makes a request of a Web server. The server services the client request, sends results back to the browser, and forgets about the interaction with that client. A second request from that same client is treated as a new request from a new client. No data are kept to maintain a session or connection with the client.

This characteristic poses no problem for serving content, either static Web pages or responses to queries of a database. However, it is not acceptable for applications that require multiple database actions in an atomic transaction. Recall from Chapter 6 that in some cases, a group of database actions needs to be grouped into a transaction, with all of them committed to the database or none of them committed to the database. In this case, the Web server or other program must augment the base capabilities of HTTP.

For example, IIS provides features and functions for maintaining data about sessions between multiple HTTP requests and responses. Using these features and functions, the application program on the Web server can save data to and from the browser. A particular session will be associated with a particular set of data. In this way, the application program can start a transaction, conduct multiple interactions with the user at the browser, make intermediate changes to the database, and commit or roll back all changes when ending the transaction. Other means are used to provide for sessions and session data with Apache.

In some cases, the application programs must create their own methods for tracking session data. PHP does include support for sessions—see the PHP documentation for more information.

The particulars of session management are beyond the scope of this chapter. However, you should be aware that HTTP is stateless, and, regardless of the Web server, additional code must be added to database applications to enable transaction processing.

Web Page Examples with PHP

The following three examples extend our discussion of using PHP Web pages in Web database applications. These examples focus mainly on the use of PHP and not as much on the graphics, presentation, or workflow. If you want a flashy, better-behaving application, you should be able to modify these examples to obtain that result. Here, just learn how PHP is used.

All of these examples process the View Ridge Gallery database. In all of them we use the VRG database in each DBMS as we constructed it for SQL Server, Oracle, and MySQL in Chapters 10, 10A, and 10B, respectively. For simplicity, we connect to each using an ODBC system data source—VRG for SQL Server, VRG-Oracle for Oracle, and VRG-MySQL for MySQL. And if we use the same user name and password in each DBMS, we need to only change the ODBC data source name to switch between DBMSs! That is amazing, and exactly what the originators of ODBC hoped for when they created the ODBC specification.

Note, however, that although we are using ODBC functions, PHP actually provides a specific set for most DBMS products. These sets are generally more efficient than ODBC, and if you

---

[7] For more information on PHP, see the PHP documentation at *www.php.net/docs.php*.

are working with a specific DBMS you will want to explore the PHP function set for it.[8] As an example of this, note that we connected to the database using

```
// Get connection
$DSN = "VRG";
$User = "VRG-User";
$Password = "VRG-User+password";
$Conn = odbc_connect($DSN, $User, $Password);
```

If we are using MySQL, however, we can use:

```
// Get connection
$Host = "localhost";
$User = "VRG-User";
$Password = "VRG-User+password";
$Database = "VRG";

$Conn = mysqli_connect($Host, $User, $Password, $Database);
```

Similarly, SQL Server uses the *sqlsrv_connect* function (using the Microsoft PHP driver described in footnote 8), and Oracle uses the *oci_connect* function.

PHP 5.2 also supports object-oriented programming and a new data abstraction layer called **PHP Data Objects (PDO)** that provides a common syntax for accessing DBMS products. There is a lot of power in PHP, and we will barely scratch the surface here.

However, before proceeding with our examples, we need to add some links to our VRG homepage. The necessary code is shown in Figure 11-34. If you are working through these examples (and you should be), be sure to make these changes.

Example 1: Updating a Table

The previous example of a PHP Web page just read data. This next example shows how to update table data by adding a row to a table with PHP. Figure 11-35 shows a data entry form that will capture artist name and nationality and create a new row. This form has three data entry fields: the First Name and Last Name fields are text boxes where the user types in the artist's name and the Nationality field has been implemented as a drop-down list to control the possible values and to make sure they are spelled correctly. When the user clicks Save New Artist, the artist is added to the database; and if the results are successful, the acknowledgment Web page in Figure 11-36 is displayed. The See Revised Artist List link will invoke the ReadArtist.php page, which will display the ARTIST table with the new row, as shown in Figure 11-37. We have tested these pages by adding the American artist Guy Anderson (born 1906, deceased 1998), who is a member of the Northwest School.

This processing necessitates two PHP pages. The first, shown in Figure 11-38, is the data entry form with three fields: artist last name, artist first name, and artist nationality.

It also contains the form tag:

```
<form action="InsertNewArtist.php" method="POST">
```

This tag defines a form section on the page, and the section will be set up to obtain data entry values. This form has only one data entry value: the table name. The **POST method** refers to a process that causes the data in the form (here, the last name, the first name, and the selected nationality) to be delivered to the PHP server so it can be used in an array variable named $_POST. Note that $_POST is an array, and can thus have multiple values. An alternative method is GET, but POST can carry more data, and this distinction is not too important to us here. The

---

[8] Microsoft has created an updated set of functions for SQL Server If you are going to use the SQL Server specific functions, you should download the SQL Server Driver for PHP. As this book goes to press, although this driver works with both SQL Server 2005 and SQL Server 2008, it is still referred to as the SQL Server 2005 Driver for PHP on the Microsoft SQL Feature Pack Web page at *www.microsoft.com/downloads/details.aspx?FamilyId= 228DE03F-3B5A-428A-923F-58A033D316E1&displaylang=en*. Documentation is available at *msdn.microsoft.com/en-us/library/cc296189.aspx*.

```
<p>Chapter 11 Demonstration Pages From Figures in the Text:</p>
        <p>Example 1:   
            <a href="ReadArtist.php">
                    Display the ARTIST Table (LastName, FirstName, Nationality)
            </a>
        </p>
<!-- *********** New text starts here ***********  -->
        <p>Example 2:   
            <a href="NewArtistForm.html">
                Add a New Artist to the ARTIST Table
            </a>
        </p>
        <p>Example 3:   
            <a href="ReadArtistPDO.php">
                    Display the ARTIST Table Using PHP PDO
            </a>
        </p>
        <p>Example 4:   
            <a href="NewCustomerWithInterestsForm.html">
                Add a New Customer to the CUSTOMER Table Using PHP PDO
            </a>
        </p>

<!-- *********** New text ends here ***********  -->
        <hr />
```

Figure 11-34

Modifications to the VRG
index.html Homepage

second parameter of the form tag is *action*, which is set to InsertNewArtist.php. This parameter tells the Web server that when it receives the response from this form it should store the data values in the $_POST array and pass control to the InsertNewArtist.php page.

The rest of the page is standard HTML, with the addition of the <select><option> . . . </option></select> structure for creating a drop-down list in the form. Note that the name of the select is Nationality.

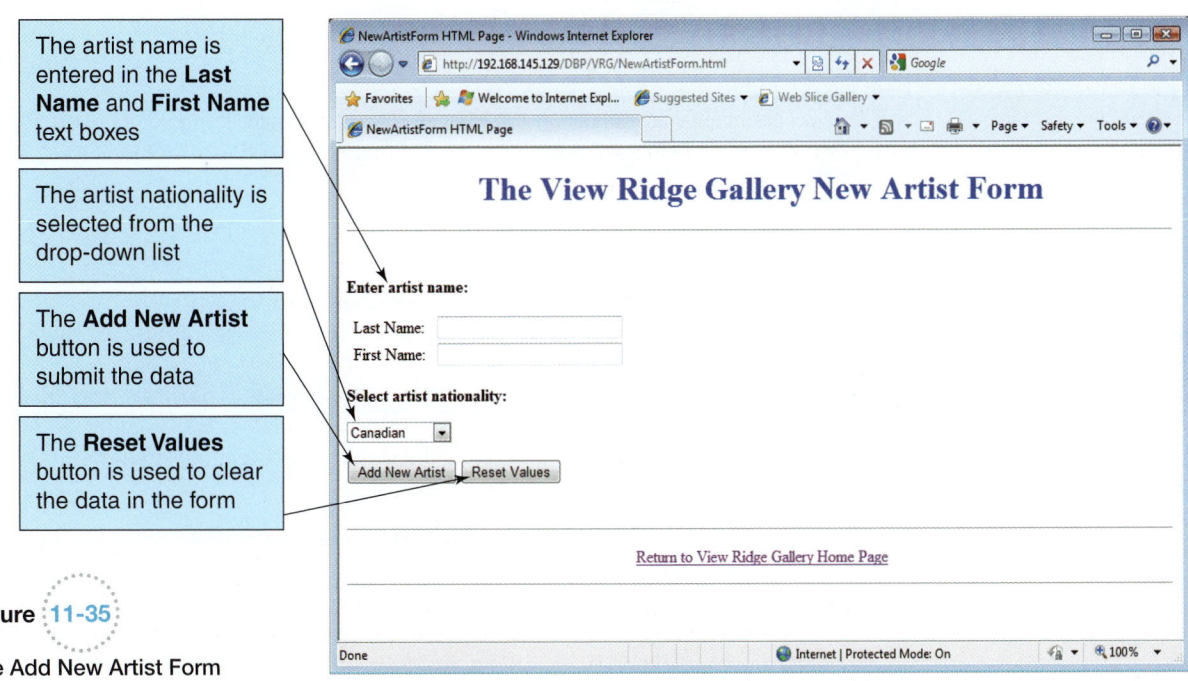

The artist name is entered in the **Last Name** and **First Name** text boxes

The artist nationality is selected from the drop-down list

The **Add New Artist** button is used to submit the data

The **Reset Values** button is used to clear the data in the form

Figure 11-35

The Add New Artist Form

The New Artist
Added message is
displayed along with
the artist data

Click this link to see
the ARTIST table with
the new artist data

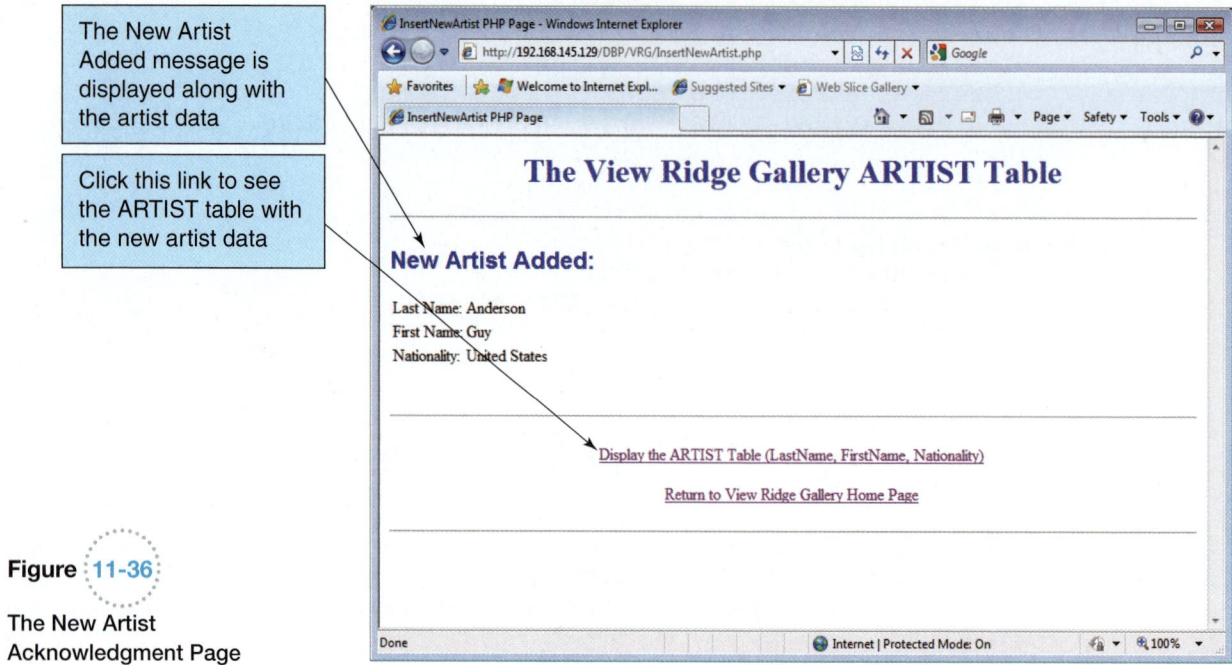

Figure 11-36

The New Artist
Acknowledgment Page

Figure 11-37

The ARTIST Table with the
New Artist

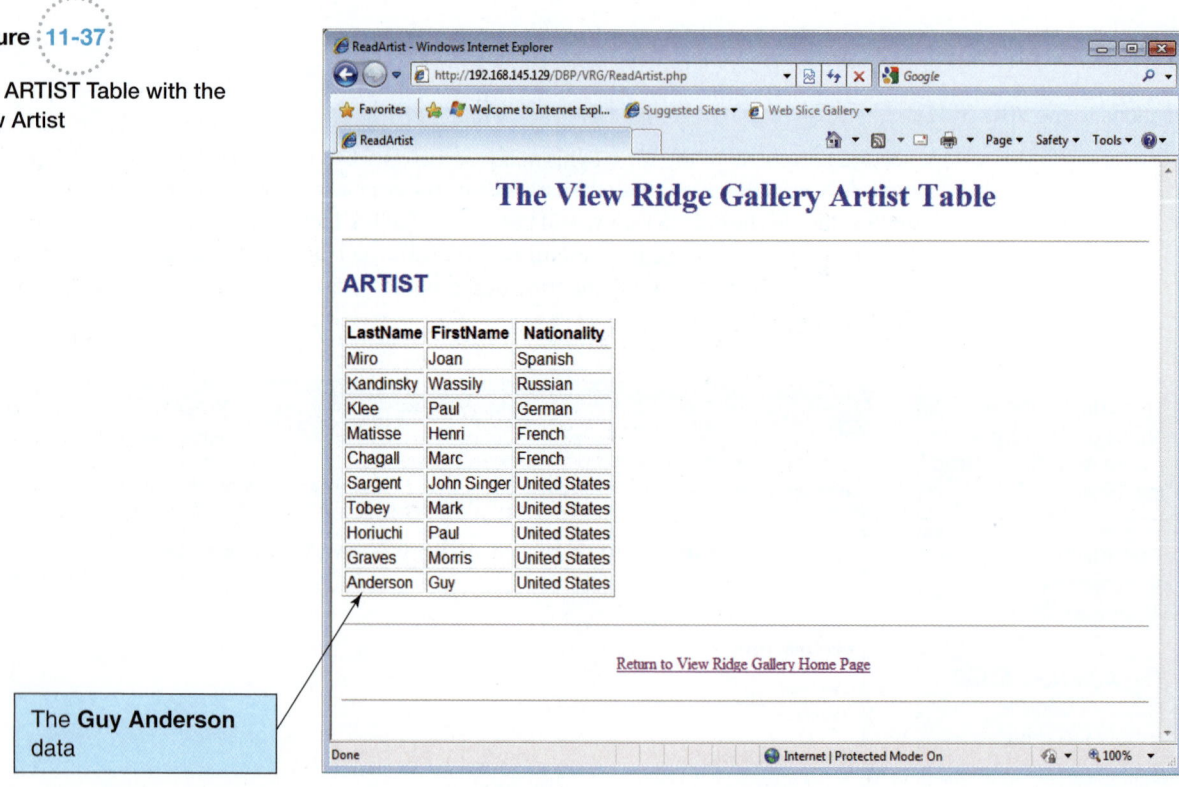

The **Guy Anderson**
data

When the user clicks the Add New Artist button, these data are to be processed by the InsertNewArtist.php page.

Figure 11-39 shows the InsertNewArtist.php, the page that will be invoked when the response is received from the form. Note that the variable values for the INSERT statement are obtained from the $_POST[] array. First, we create short variable names for the $_POST

```html
<!DOCTYPE html PUBLIC "-//W3C//DTD HTML 4.01 Strict//EN"
"http://www.w3.org/TR/html4/strict.dtd">
<html>
    <head>
        <meta http-equiv="Content-Type" content="text/html; charset=UTF-8">
        <title>NewArtistForm HTML Page</title>
        <style type="text/css">
            h1 {text-align: center; color: blue}
            h2 {font-family: Ariel, sans-serif; text-align: left; color: blue}
            p.footer {text-align: center}
            table.output {font-family: Ariel, sans-serif}
        </style>
    </head>
    <body>
        <form action="InsertNewArtist.php" method="POST">
        <!--  Page Headers -->
        <h1>
            The View Ridge Gallery New Artist Form
        </h1>
        <hr />
        <br />
        <p>
            <b>Enter artist name:</b>
        </p>
        <table>
            <tr>
                <td> Last Name:  </td>
                <td>
                    <input type="text" name="LastName" size="25" />
                </td>
            </tr>
            <tr>
                <td> First Name:  </td>
                <td>
                    <input type="text" name="FirstName" size="25" />
                </td>
            </tr>
        </table>
        <p>
            <b>Select artist nationality:</b>
        </p>
        <select name="Nationality">
            <option value="Canadian">Canadian</option>
            <option value="English">English</option>
            <option value="French">French</option>
            <option value="German">German</option>
            <option value="Mexican">Mexican</option>
            <option value="Russian">Russian</option>
            <option value="Spanish">Spanish</option>
            <option value="United States">United States</option>
        </select>
        <br />
        <p>
            <input type="submit" value="Add New Artist" />
            <input type="reset" value="Reset Values" />
        </p>
        </form>
        <br />
        <hr />
        <p class="footer">
            <a href="../VRG/index.html">
                Return to View Ridge Gallery Home Page
            </a>
        </p>
        <hr />
    </body>
</html>
```

Figure 11-38

The HTML Code for
NewArtistForm.html

```html
<!DOCTYPE HTML PUBLIC "-//W3C//DTD HTML 4.01 Frameset//EN">
<html>
    <head>
        <meta http-equiv="Content-Type" content="text/html; charset=UTF-8">
        <title>InsertNewArtist PHP Page</title>
        <style type="text/css">
            h1 {text-align: center; color: blue}
            h2 {font-family: Ariel, sans-serif; text-align: left; color: blue}
            p.footer {text-align: center}
            table.output {font-family: Ariel, sans-serif}
        </style>
    </head>
    <body>
    <?php
        // Get connection
            $DSN = "VRG";
            $User = "VRG-User";
            $Password = "VRG-User+password";

            $Conn = odbc_connect($DSN, $User, $Password);

        // Test connection
        if (!$Conn)
            {
                exit ("ODBC Connection Failed: " . $Conn);
            }
        // Create short variable names
        $LastName = $_POST["LastName"];
        $FirstName = $_POST["FirstName"];
        $Nationality = $_POST["Nationality"];

        // Create SQL statement
        $SQL = "INSERT INTO ARTIST(LastName, FirstName, Nationality) ";
        $SQL .= "VALUES('$LastName', '$FirstName', '$Nationality')";

        // Execute SQL statement
        $Result = odbc_exec($Conn, $SQL);

        // Test existence of result
        echo "<h1>
            The View Ridge Gallery ARTIST Table
        </h1>
        <hr />";
        if ($Result){
            echo "<h2>
            New Artist Added:
        </h2>
```

Figure 11-39

The HTML and PHP
Code for Insert
NewArtist.php

```
        <table>
          <tr>";
          echo "<td>Last Name:</td>";
          echo "<td>" . $LastName . "</td>";
          echo "</tr>";
          echo "<tr>";
          echo "<td>First Name:</td>";
          echo "<td>" . $FirstName . "</td>";
          echo "</tr>";
          echo "<tr>";
          echo "<td>Nationality:</td>";
          echo "<td>" . $Nationality . "</td>";
          echo "</tr>";
        echo "</table><br />";
        }
        else {
          exit ("SQL Statement Error: " . $SQL);
        }

    // Close connection
    odbc_close($Conn);
?>
    <br />
    <hr />
    <p class="footer">
      <a href="../VRG/ReadArtist.php">
        Display the ARTIST Table (LastName, FirstName, Nationality)
      </a>
    </p>
    <p class="footer">
      <a href="../VRG/index.html">
        Return to View Ridge Gallery Home Page
      </a>
    </p>
    <hr />
  </body>
</html>
```

Figure 11-39

(Continued)

version of the name, and then we use these short variable names to create the SQL INSERT statement. Thus:

```
// Create short variable names

$LastName = $_POST["LastName"];
$FirstName = $_POST["FirstName"];
$Nationality = $_POST["Nationality"];

// Create SQL statement

$SQL = "INSERT INTO ARTIST(LastName, FirstName, Nationality) ";
$SQL .= "VALUES('$LastName', '$FirstName', '$Nationality')";
```

Note the use of the **PHP concatenation operator (.=)** (a combination of a period and an equals sign) to combine the two sections of the SQL INSERT statement. As another example, to create a variable named $AllOfUs with the value *me, myself, and I* we would use:

```
$AllOfUs = "me, ";

$AllOfUs .= "myself, ";

$AllOfUs .= "and I";
```

Most of the code is self-explanatory, but make sure you understand how it works.

Example 2: Using PHP Data Objects (PDO)

Our next example is an exercise in using PHP Data Objects (PDO). Here we are re-creating the ReadArtist.php page, but using PDO to do it. We call the new Web page ReadArtistPDO.php, and it is shown in Figure 11-40. The PHP code to create the page is shown in Figure 11-41, and you should compare this PHP code to the PHP code for ReadArtist.php in Figure 11-31.

PHP PDO will become important as newer versions of PHP are released. The power of PHP PDO is that the only line of PHP code that needs to be changed when using a different DBMS product is the one that establishes the connection to the database. In Figure 11-41 this is the line:

```
$PDOconnection = new PDO("odbc:$DSN", $User, $Password);
```

Example 3: Invoking a Stored Procedure

We created a stored procedure named InsertCustomerAndInterest for the SQL Server, Oracle, and MySQL versions of the VRG database in Chapters 10, 10A, and 10B, respectively. In all cases, the stored procedure accepts a new customer's last name, first name, area code, local number, e-mail, and the nationality of all artists in whom the customer is interested. It then creates a new row in CUSTOMER and adds appropriate rows to the CUSTOMER_ARTIST_INT table.

To invoke the stored procedure using a PHP page using PDO, we create a Web form page to collect the necessary data, as shown in Figure 11-42. Then, when the user clicks Add New Customer, we want to invoke a PHP page that uses PDO to call the stored procedure with the form data. So that the user can verify that the new data have been entered correctly, the PHP

Figure

The Results of
ReadArtistPDO.php

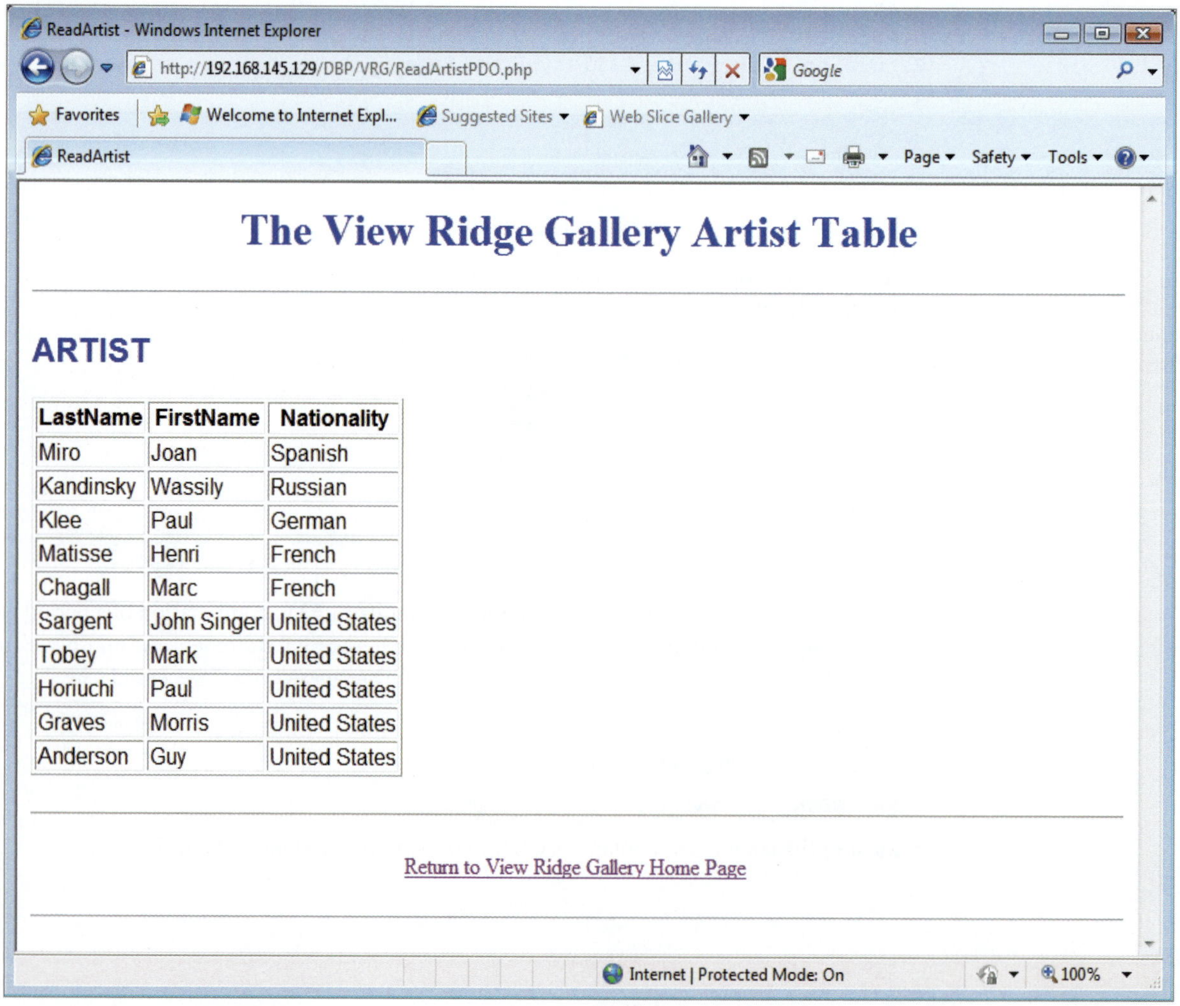

The View Ridge Gallery Artist Table

ARTIST

LastName	FirstName	Nationality
Miro	Joan	Spanish
Kandinsky	Wassily	Russian
Klee	Paul	German
Matisse	Henri	French
Chagall	Marc	French
Sargent	John Singer	United States
Tobey	Mark	United States
Horiuchi	Paul	United States
Graves	Morris	United States
Anderson	Guy	United States

Return to View Ridge Gallery Home Page

```
<!DOCTYPE HTML PUBLIC "-//W3C//DTD HTML 4.01 Frameset//EN">
<html>
    <head>
        <meta http-equiv="Content-Type" content="text/html; charset=UTF-8">
        <title>ReadArtist</title>
        <style type="text/css">
            h1 {text-align: center; color: blue}
            h2 {font-family: Ariel, sans-serif; text-align: left; color: blue;}
            p.footer {text-align: center}
            table.output {font-family: Ariel, sans-serif}
        </style>
    </head>
    <body>
    <?php
        // Get connection
        $DSN = "VRG";
        $User = "VRG-User";
        $Password = "VRG-User+password";

        $PDOconnection = new PDO("odbc:$DSN", $User, $Password);

        // Test connection
        if (!$PDOconnection)
            {
                exit ("ODBC Connection Failed: " . $PDOconnection);
            }

        // Create SQL statement
        $SQL = "SELECT LastName, FirstName, Nationality FROM ARTIST";

        // Execute SQL statement
        $RecordSet = $PDOconnection->query($SQL);

        // Test existence of recordset
        if (!$RecordSet)
            {
                exit ("SQL Statement Error: " . $SQL);
            }
    ?>
        <!-- Page Headers -->
        <h1>
            The View Ridge Gallery Artist Table
        </h1>
        <hr />
        <h2>
            ARTIST
        </h2>
    <?php

        // Table headers
        echo "<table class='output' border='1'
                <tr>
                    <th>LastName</th>
                    <th>FirstName</th>
                    <th>Nationality</th>
                </tr>";
```

Figure 11-41

The HTML and PHP Code
for ReadArtistPDO.php

```php
                     //Table data
                     while($RecordSetRow = $RecordSet->fetch())
                         {
                             echo "<tr>";
                                 echo "<td>" . $RecordSetRow['LastName'] . "</td>";
                                 echo "<td>" . $RecordSetRow['FirstName'] . "</td>";
                                 echo "<td>" . $RecordSetRow['Nationality'] . "</td>";
                             echo "</tr>";
                         }
                     echo "</table>";

                     // Close connection
                     $PDOconnection = null;
                 ?>
                     <br />
                     <hr />
                     <p class="footer">
                         <a href="../VRG/index.html">
                             Return to View Ridge Gallery Home Page
                         </a>
                     </p>
                     <hr />
                 </body>
             </html>
```

Figure  **11-41**

(Continued)

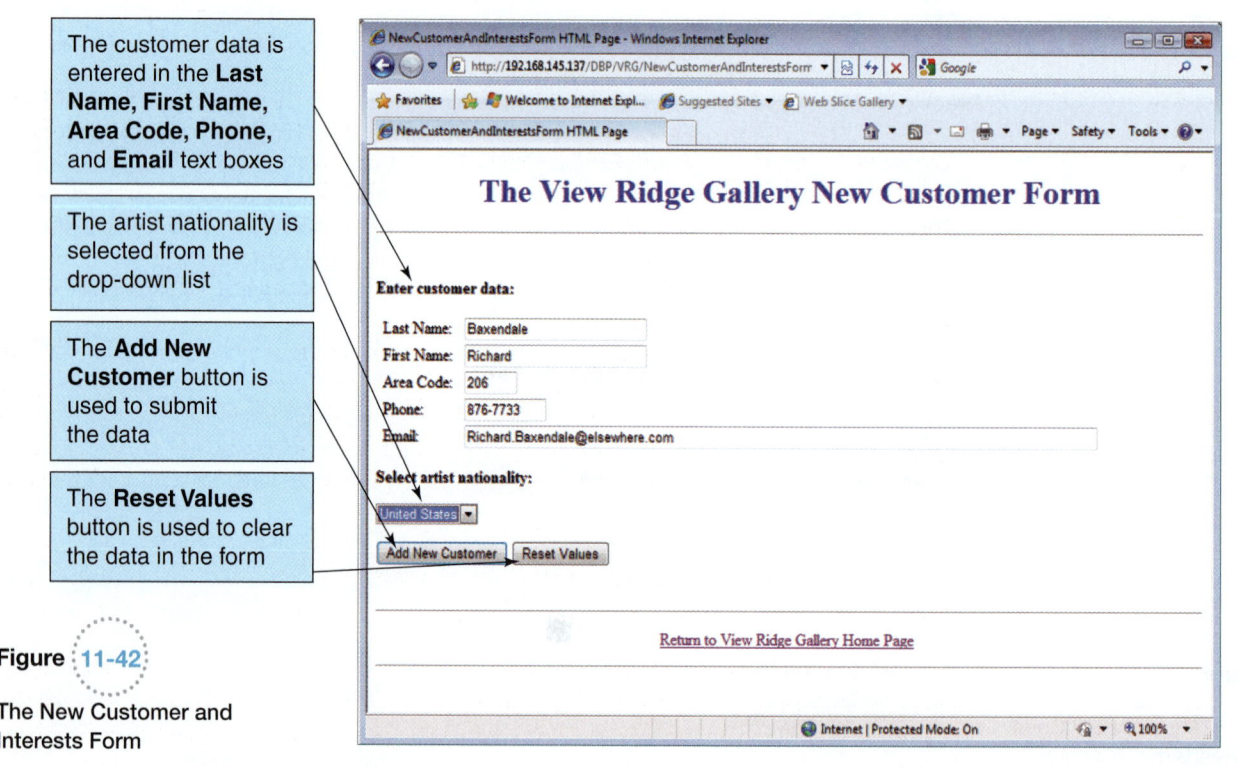

The customer data is entered in the **Last Name, First Name, Area Code, Phone,** and **Email** text boxes

The artist nationality is selected from the drop-down list

The **Add New Customer** button is used to submit the data

The **Reset Values** button is used to clear the data in the form

Figure 11-42

The New Customer and Interests Form

then queries a view that joins customer names with artist names and nationalities. The result is shown in Figure 11-43. In this case, we are adding Richard Baxendale, with phone number 206-876-7733 and e-mail address Richard.Baxendale@elsewhere.com. Richard is interested in United States artists.

Figure 11-44 shows the code for the NewCustomerAndInterestsForm.html page used to generate the data-gathering form. The form invokes the InsertNewCustomerAndInterestsPDO.php page code shown in Figure 11-45.

The New Customer and Artist Interests added message is displayed along with the customer and artist interest data

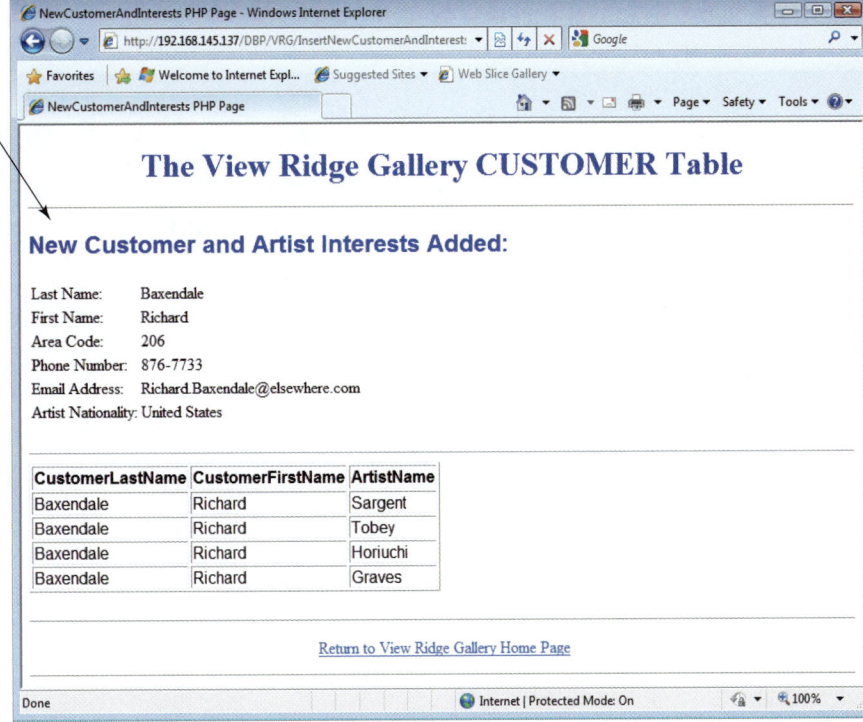

Figure 11-43

The New Customer
Acknowledgment Page

In Figure 11-45, note that the PDO statements take the form of *$Variable01 = $Variable02 ->* {PDO command}(*$Variable03*). For example, in the PDO statement $RecordSet = $PDO-connection-> query($SQL), we are using the PDO command query to send the contents of the variable $SQL to the database through the connection named $PDOconnection, and the storing the results in the variable $RecordSet. Note that while PDO standardizes the PDO command set itself, the exact SQL statements used various DBMS products will vary, and even PHP code using PDO has to be modified for those differences. For example, SQL Server uses EXEC to call a stored procedure, while MySQL uses CALL.

This PHP page is very straightforward, but it is interesting because it includes two SQL statements. First, we use an SQL CALL statement to invoke the stored procedure and pass the necessary parameters to it. Then we use an SQL SELECT statement to retrieve the values we need for the construction of our Web page acknowledging the addition of a new customer. The rest of the page reuses the same elements we have used in the previous examples.

It is also interesting that in this page we have made use of both an SQL view (CustomerInterestsView) and an SQL stored procedure (InsertCustomerAndInterests). This page illustrates the power of both these SQL structures and how we can use them in a Web database processing environment.

These examples give you an idea of the uses of PHP. The best way to learn more is to write some pages yourself. This chapter has shown all the basic techniques that you will need. You have worked hard to get to this point, and if you are able to understand enough to create some of your own pages, you have come very far indeed since Chapter 1!

```
<!DOCTYPE html PUBLIC "-//W3C//DTD HTML 4.01 Strict//EN"
"http://www.w3.org/TR/html4/strict.dtd">
<html>
   <head>
       <meta http-equiv="Content-Type" content="text/html; charset=UTF-8">
       <title>NewCustomerAndInterestsForm HTML Page</title>
       <style type="text/css">
          h1 {text-align: center; color: blue}
          h2 {font-family: Ariel, sans-serif; text-align: left; color: blue}
          p.footer {text-align: center}
          table.output {font-family: Ariel, sans-serif}
       </style>
   </head>
   <body>
       <form action="InsertNewCustomerAndInterestsPDO.php" method="POST">
          <!-- Page Headers -->
          <h1>
              The View Ridge Gallery New Customer Form
          </h1>
          <hr />
          <br />
          <p>
              <b>Enter customer data:</b>
          </p>
          <table>
             <tr>
                <td> Last Name:  </td>
                <td>
                   <input type="text" name="LastName" size="25" />
                </td>
             </tr>
             <tr>
                <td> First Name:  </td>
                <td>
                   <input type="text" name="FirstName" size="25" />
                </td>
             </tr>
             <tr>
                <td> Area Code:  </td>
                <td>
                   <input type="text" name="AreaCode" size="3" />
                </td>
             </tr>
             <tr>
                <td> Phone:  </td>
                <td>
                   <input type="text" name="PhoneNumber" size="8" />
                </td>
             </tr>
             <tr>
                <td> Email:  </td>
                <td>
                   <input type="text" name="Email" size="100" />
                </td>
             </tr>
```

Figure 11-44

The HTML Code for
NewCustomerAnd
InterestsForm.html

```
                          </table>
                          <p>
                             <b>Select artist nationality:</b>
                          </p>
                          <select name="Nationality">
                             <option value="Canadian">Canadian</option>
                             <option value="English">English</option>
                             <option value="French">French</option>
                             <option value="German">German</option>
                             <option value="Mexican">Mexican</option>
                             <option value="Russian">Russian</option>
                             <option value="Spanish">Spanish</option>
                             <option value="United States">United States</option>
                          </select>
                          <br />
                          <p>
                             <input type="submit" value="Add New Customer" />
                             <input type="reset" value="Reset Values" />
                          </p>
                       </form>
                       <br />
                       <hr />
                       <p class="footer">
                          <a href="../VRG/index.html">
                             Return to View Ridge Gallery Home Page
                          </a>
                       </p>
                       <hr />
                    </body>
                 </html>
```

Figure

(Continued)

```html
<!DOCTYPE HTML PUBLIC "-//W3C//DTD HTML 4.01 Strict//EN"
"http://www.w3.org/TR/html4/strict.dtd">
<html>
    <head>
        <meta http-equiv="Content-Type" content="text/html; charset=UTF-8">
        <title>NewCustomerAndInterests PHP Page</title>
        <style type="text/css">
            h1 {text-align: center; color: blue}
            h2 {font-family: Ariel, sans-serif; text-align: left; color: blue}
            p.footer {text-align: center}
            table.output {font-family: Ariel, sans-serif}
        </style>
    </head>
    <body>
<?php
    // Get connection
    $DSN = "VRG";
    $User = "VRG-User";
    $Password = "VRG-User+password";

    $PDOconnection = new PDO("odbc:$DSN", $User, $Password);

    // Test connection
    if (!$PDOconnection)
    {
        exit ("ODBC Connection Failed: " . $PDOconnection);
    }
    // Create short variable names
    $LastName = $_POST["LastName"];
    $FirstName = $_POST["FirstName"];
    $AreaCode = $_POST["AreaCode"];
    $PhoneNumber = $_POST["PhoneNumber"];
    $Email = $_POST["Email"];
    $Nationality = $_POST["Nationality"];

    // Create SQL statement to call the Stored Procedure
    $SQLSP = "EXEC InsertCustomerAndInterests ";
    $SQLSP .= "'$LastName', '$FirstName', '$AreaCode','$PhoneNumber', ";
    $SQLSP .= "'$Email', '$Nationality'";


    // Execute SQL statement
    $Result = $PDOconnection->exec($SQLSP);

    // Test existence of $Result
    if (!$Result)
        {
            exit ("SQL Statement Error: " . $SQLSP);
        }
```

Figure 11-45

The HTML and PHP Code
for InsertNewCustomer
AndInterestsPDO.php

```php
// Create SQL statement to retrieve additions to
// CUSTOMER_ARTIST_INT table
$SQL = "SELECT * FROM CustomerInterestsView ";
$SQL .= "WHERE CustomerLastName = '$LastName' ";
$SQL .= "AND CustomerFirstName = '$FirstName'";


// Execute SQL statement
$RecordSet = $PDOconnection->query($SQL);

// Test existence of $RecordSet
if (!$RecordSet)
    {
        exit ("SQL Statement Error: " . $SQL);
    }

echo "<h1>
        The View Ridge Gallery CUSTOMER Table
    </h1>
    <hr />";

    echo "<h2>
        New Customer and Artist Interests Added:
    </h2>
    <table>
        <tr>";
        echo "<td>Last Name:</td>";
        echo "<td>" . $LastName . "</td>";
        echo "</tr>";
        echo "<tr>";
        echo "<td>First Name:</td>";
        echo "<td>" . $FirstName . "</td>";
        echo "</tr>";
        echo "<tr>";
        echo "<td>Area Code:</td>";
        echo "<td>" . $AreaCode . "</td>";
        echo "</tr>";
        echo "<tr>";
        echo "<td>Phone Number:</td>";
        echo "<td>" . $PhoneNumber . "</td>";
        echo "</tr>";
        echo "<tr>";
        echo "<td>Email Address:</td>";
        echo "<td>" . $Email . "</td>";
        echo "</tr>";
        echo "<tr>";
        echo "<td>Artist Nationality:</td>";
        echo "<td>" . $Nationality . "</td>";
        echo "</tr>";
    echo "</table><br /><hr />";
```

Figure 11-45

(Continued)

```
                      // Table headers
                      echo "<table class='output' border='1'>
                        <tr>
                            <th>CustomerLastName</th>
                            <th>CustomerFirstName</th>
                            <th>ArtistName</th>
                        </tr>";

                      // Table data
                      while($RecordSetRow = $RecordSet->fetch())
                        {
                        echo "<tr>";
                        echo "<td>" . $RecordSetRow['CustomerLastName'] . "</td>";
                        echo "<td>" . $RecordSetRow['CustomerFirstName'] . "</td>";
                        echo "<td>" . $RecordSetRow['ArtistName'] . "</td>";
                        echo "</tr>";
                        }
                      echo "</table>";

                      // Close connection
                      $PDOconnection = null;
                  ?>
                      <br />
                      <hr />
                      <p class="footer">
                        <a href="../VRG-MYSQL/index.html">
                            Return to View Ridge Gallery Home Page
                        </a>
                      </p>
                      <hr />
                  </body>
              </html>
```

Figure 11-45

(Continued)

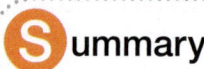

Summary

Today, database applications reside in rich and complicated environments. In addition to relational databases, there are nonrelational databases, VSAM and other file-processing data, e-mail, and other types of data. To ease the job of the application programmer, various standards have been developed. The ODBC standard is for relational databases; the OLE DB standard is for relational databases and other data sources. ADO was developed to provide easier access to OLE DB data for the non-object-oriented programmer.

ODBC, or the Open Database Connectivity standard, provides an interface by which database applications can access and process relational data sources in a DBMS-independent manner. ODBC was developed by an industry committee and has been implemented by Microsoft and many other vendors. ODBC consists of an applications program, a driver manager, DBMS drivers, and data source components. Single- and multiple-tier drivers are defined. The three data source names are file, system, and user. System data sources are recommended for Web servers. The process of defining a system data source name involves specifying the type of driver and the identity of the database to be processed.

The Microsoft .NET Framework is Microsoft's comprehensive application development framework. the current version is .NET Framework 3.5 SP1, which is built on top of the .NET Framework 2.0 and .NET Framework 3.0 (and their service pack updates). It includes ADO.NET, ASP.NET, CLR, and the Base Class Library. Enhancements specific to .NET Framework 3.5 include the ADO.NET Entity Framework, which supports the EDM, and LINQ.

OLE DB is one of the foundations of the Microsoft data access world. It implements the Microsoft OLE and COM standards, and it is accessible to object-oriented programs through those interfaces. OLE DB breaks the features and functions of a DBMS into objects, thus making it easier for vendors to implement portions of functionality. Key object terms are *abstraction, methods, properties,* and *collections.* A rowset is an abstraction of a recordset, which, in turn, is an abstraction of a relation. Objects are defined by properties that specify their characteristics and by methods, which are the actions they can perform. A collection is an object that contains a group of other objects. An interface is a set of objects and the properties and methods they expose in that interface. Objects may expose different properties and methods in different interfaces. An implementation is how an object accomplishes its tasks. Implementations are hidden from the outside world and may be changed without impacting the users of the objects. An interface ought not to be changed, ever.

Tabular data providers present data in the form of rowsets. Service providers transform data into another form; such providers are both consumers and providers of data. A rowset is equivalent to a cursor. Basic rowset interfaces are IRowSet, IAccessor, and IColumnsInfo. Other interfaces are defined for more advanced capabilities.

ADO.NET is a new, improved, and greatly expanded version of ADO that was developed for the Microsoft .NET initiative. ADO.NET incorporates all of the functionality of ADO, but adds much more. In particular, ADO.NET facilitates the transformation of XML documents to and from database data. Most important, ADO.NET introduces the concept of DataSets, which are in-memory, fully functioned, independent databases.

A .NET data provider is a library of classes that provides ADO.NET services. A data provider data reader provides fast, forward-only access to data. A Command object can be processed to execute SQL and also to invoke stored procedures in a manner similar to but improved from that in ADO. The major new concept of ADO.NET is the DataSet. A DataSet is an in-memory database that is disconnected from any regular database but that has all the important characteristics of a regular database. DataSets can have multiple tables, relationships, referential integrity rules, referential integrity actions, views, and the equivalent of triggers. DataSet tables may have surrogate key columns (called auto-increment columns) and primary keys and may be declared unique.

DataSets are disconnected from the database(s) from which they are constructed, and they may be constructed from several different databases and possibly managed by different DBMS products. After a DataSet is constructed, an XML document of its contents and an XML Schema of its structure are easily produced. Further, the process works in reverse as well. XML Schema documents can be read to create the structure of the DataSet, and XML documents can be read to fill the DataSet.

DataSets are needed to provide a standardized, nonproprietary means to process database views. They are especially important for the processing of views with multiple multivalue paths. The potential downside of DataSets is that because they are disconnected, any updates against the databases they access must be performed using optimistic locking. In the case of conflict, either the DataSet must be reprocessed or the data change must be forced onto the database, causing the lost update problem.

JDBC is an alternative to ODBC and ADO that provides database access to programs written in Java. A JDBC driver is available for almost every conceivable DBMS product. Sun defines four driver types. Type 1 drivers provide a bridge between Java and ODBC. Types 2, 3, and 4 are written entirely in Java. Type 2 drivers rely on the DBMS product for intermachine communication, if any. Type 3 drivers translate JDBC calls into a DBMS-independent network protocol. Type 4 drivers translate JDBC calls into a DBMS-dependent network protocol.

An applet is a compiled Java bytecode program that is transmitted to a browser via HTTP and is invoked using the HTTP protocol. A servlet is a Java program that is invoked on the server to respond to HTTP requests. Type 3 and Type 4 drivers can be used for both applets and servlets. Type 2 drivers can be used only in servlets, and only then if the DBMS and Web server are on the same machine or if the DBMS vendor handles the intermachine communication between the Web server and the database server.

There are four steps when using JDBC: (1) load the driver; (2) establish a connection to the database; (3) create a statement; and (4) execute the statement.

Java Server Pages (JSP) technology provides a means to create dynamic Web pages using HTML (and XML) and Java. JSP pages provide the capabilities of a full object-oriented language to the page developer. Neither VBScript nor JavaScript can be used in a JSP page. JSP pages are compiled into machine-independent bytecode.

JSP pages are compiled as subclasses of the HTTPServlet class. Consequently, small snippets of code can be placed in a JSP page, as well as complete Java programs. To use JSP, the Web server must implement the Java Servlet 2.1+ and JSP 1.0+ specifications. Apache Tomcat, an open-source product from the Jakarta Project, implements these specifications. Tomcat can work in conjunction with Apache or as a stand-alone Web server for testing purposes.

When using Tomcat (or any other JSP processor), the JDBC drivers and JSP pages must be located in specified directories. When a JSP page is requested, Tomcat ensures that the most recent page is used. If an uncompiled newer version is available, Tomcat will automatically cause it to be parsed and compiled. Only one JSP page can be in memory at a time, and JSP requests are executed as a thread of the servlet processor, not as a separate process. The Java code in a JSP page can invoke a compiled Java bean, if desired.

PHP (PHP: Hypertext Processor) is a scripting language that can be embedded in Web pages. PHP is extremely popular and easy to learn, and it can be used in most Web server environments and with most databases.

For creating complex pages, you need an Integrated Development Environment (IDE). An IDE gives you the most robust and user-friendly means of creating and maintaining Web pages. Microsoft Visual Studio, NetBeans for Java users, and the open-source Eclipse IDE are all good IDEs. Eclipse provides a framework that can be modified by add-in modules. For PHP, there is a modification of Eclipse called the Eclipse PDT Project that is specifically intended to provide a PHP development environment.

PHP now includes object-oriented features and PHP Data Objects (PDO), which simplify connecting Web pages to databases.

Key Terms

?>
<?php
abstraction
Active Data Objects (ADO)
ADO.NET
ADO.NET Command object
ADO.NET Connection object
ADO.NET Data Provider
ADO.NET DataAdapter object
ADO.NET DataReader
ADO.NET DataSet
ADO.NET Entity Framework
AMP
Apache Tomcat
Apache Web server
applet
application program interface (API)
ASP.NET
Base Class Library
bytecode interpreter
Callable Statement object
collection
Common Language Runtime (CLT)
Component Object Model (COM)
Constraints
current values
cursor
data consumer
data provider
DataRelations
DataRelationCollection
DataTable object
DataTableCollection
Default Web Site folder
DeleteCommand object
document type declaration (DTD)
DataColumns Collection
DataRow Collection
Eclipse IDE
Eclipse PDT (PHP Development Tools) Project
Entity Data Model (EDM)
Extensible Markup Language (XML)
File data source
ForeignKeyConstraint
HTML document tags
HTML syntax rules
http://localhost
Hypertext Markup Language (HTML)
iisstart.htm
implementation
index.html
inetpub folder

InsertCommand object
Integrated Development Environment (IDE)
interface
Internet Information Services (IIS)
Internet Information Services Manager
Java Data Objects (JDO)
Java Database Connectivity (JBDC)
Java platform
Java programming language
Java Server Page (JSP)
Java virtual machine
JDBC Connection object
JDBC DriverManager
JDBC ResultSet object
JDBC ResultSetMetaData object
JDBC Statement object
LAMP
Language Integrate Query (LINQ)
localstart.asp
method
Microsoft Transaction Manager (MTS)
.NET Framework
object
object class
ODBC conformance levels
ODBC data source
ODBC Data Source Administrator
ODBC driver
ODBC driver manager
ODBC multiple-tier driver
ODBC single-tier driver
ODBC SQL conformance levels
Object Linking and Embedding (OLE)
OLE DB
Open Database Connectivity (ODBC)
original values
PHP
PHP concatenation operator (.=)
PHP Data Objects (PDO)
PHP: Hypertext Processor
POST method
Prepared Statement objects
PrimaryKey property
properties
proposed values
recordset
rowset
SelectCommand object
service provider
servlet
system data source
Tabular data providers

three-tier architecture

two-tier architecture

UniqueConstraint

UpdateCommand object

user data source

WAMP

World Wide Web Consortium (W3C)

wwwroot folder

Review Questions

11.1   Describe why the data environment is complicated.

11.2   Explain how ODBC, OLE DB, and ADO are related.

11.3   Explain the author's justification for describing Microsoft standards. Do you agree?

11.4   Name the components of the ODBC standard.

11.5   What role does the driver manager serve? Who supplies it?

11.6   What role does the DBMS driver serve? Who supplies it?

11.7   What is a single-tier driver?

11.8   What is a multiple-tier driver?

11.9   Do the uses of the term *tier* in the three-tier architecture and its use in ODBC have anything to do with each other?

11.10   Why are conformance levels important?

11.11   Summarize the three ODBC API conformance levels.

11.12   Summarize the three SQL grammar conformance levels.

11.13   Explain how the three types of data sources differ.

11.14   Which data source type is recommended for Web servers?

11.15   What are the two tasks to be accomplished when setting up an ODBC data source name?

11.16   What is the Microsoft .NET Framework. What basic elements does it include?

11.17   What is the current version of the .NET Framework, and what new features does it include?

11.18   Why is OLE DB important?

11.19   What disadvantage of ODBC does OLE DB overcome?

11.20   Define abstraction and explain how it relates to OLE DB.

11.21   Give an example of abstraction involving rowset.

11.22   Define object properties and methods.

11.23   What is the difference between an object class and an object?

11.24   Explain the role of data consumers and data providers.

11.25   What is an interface?

11.26   What is the difference between an interface and an implementation?

11.27   Explain why an implementation can be changed but an interface should not be changed.

11.28   Summarize the goals of OLE DB.

11.29   Explain the difference between a tabular data provider and a service provider. Which transforms OLE DB data into XML documents?

11.30   In the context of OLE DB, what is the difference between a rowset and a cursor?

11.31   What is ADO.NET?

11.32   What is a data provider?

11.33   What is a data reader?

11.34   How can ADO.NET be used to process a database without using DataReaders or DataSets?

11.35   What is an ADO.NET DataSet?

11.36   How do ADO.Net DataSets differ conceptually from databases?

11.37   List the primary structures of an ADO.NET DataSet, as described in this chapter.

11.38   How do ADO.NET DataSets solve the problem of views with multivalue paths?

11.39   What is the chief disadvantage of ADO.NET DataSets? When is this likely to be a problem?

11.40   Why, in database processing, is it important to become an object-oriented programmer?

11.41   What is an ADO.NET Connection?

11.42   What is a DataAdapter?

11.43   What is the purpose of the SelectCommand property of a DataAdapter?

11.44   How is a data table relationship constructed in ADO.NET?

11.45   How is referential integrity defined in ADO.NET? What referential integrity actions are possible?

11.46   Explain how original, current, and proposed values differ.

11.47   How does an ADO.NET DataSet allow for trigger processing?

11.48   What is the purpose of the UpdateCommand property of a DataAdapter?

11.49   What are the purposes of the InsertCommand and DeleteCommand of a DataAdapter?

11.50   Explain the flexibility inherent in the use of the InsertCommand, UpdateCommand, and DeleteCommand properties.

11.51   What is the one major requirement for using JDBC?

11.52   What does JDBC stand for?

11.53   What are the four JDBC driver types?

11.54   Explain the purpose of Type 1 JDBC drivers.

11.55   Explain the purpose of Types 2, 3, and 4 JDBC drivers.

11.56   Define applet and servlet.

11.57   Explain how Java accomplishes portability.

11.58   List the four steps of using a JDBC driver.

11.59   What is the purpose of Java Server Pages?

11.60   Describe the differences between ASP and JSP.

11.61   Explain how JSP pages are portable.

11.62   What is the purpose of Tomcat?

11.63   Describe the process by which JSP pages are compiled and executed. Can a user ever access an obsolete page? Why or why not?

11.64   Why are JSP programs preferable to CGI programs?

11.65   What is Hypertext Markup Language (HTML), and what function does it serve?

11.66   What are HTML document tags, and how are they used?

11.67 What is the World Wide Web Consortium (W3C)?

11.68 Why is index.hmtl a significant file name?

11.69 What is PHP, and what function does it serve?

11.70 How is PHP code designated in a Web page?

11.71 How are comments designated in PHP code?

11.72 How are comments designated in HMTL code?

11.73 What is an Integrated Development Environment (IDE), and how is it used?

11.74 What is the Eclipse IDE?

11.75 What is the Eclipse PDT Project?

11.76 Show a snippet of PHP code for creating a connection to a database. Explain the meaning of the code.

11.77 Show a snippet of PHP code for creating a RecordSet. Explain the meaning of the code.

11.78 Show a snippet of PHP code for displaying the contents of a RecordSet. Explain the meaning of the code.

11.79 Show a snippet of PHP code for disconnecting from the database. Explain the meaning of the code.

11.80 With respect to HTTP, what does *stateless* mean?

11.81 Under what circumstances does statelessness pose a problem for database processing?

11.82 In general terms, how are sessions managed by database applications when using HTTP?

11.83 What are PHP Data Objects (PDO)?

11.84 What is the significance of PDOs?

11.85 Show two snippets of PHP Code that compare creating a connection to a database in standard PHP and in PDO. Discuss the similarities and differences in the code.

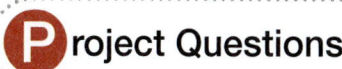 **P**roject Questions

11.86 In this exercise you will create a Web page in the DBP folder and link it to the VRG Web page in the VRG folder.

    A. Figure 11-46 shows the HTML code for a Web page for the DBP folder. Note that the page is called index.html, the same name as the Web page in the VRG folder. This is not a problem because the files are in different folders. Create the index.html Web page in the DBP folder.

    B. Figure 11-47 shows some additional HTML to be added near the end of the code for the VRG Web page in the file index.html in the VRG folder. Update the VRG index.html file with the code.

    C. Try out the pages. Type **http://localhost/DBP** into your Web browser to display the DBP homepage. From there, you should be able to move back and forth between the two pages by using the hyperlinks on each page. *Note:* You may need to click the Refresh button on your Web browser when using the VRG home page to get the hyperlink back to the DBP home page to work properly.

11.87 Microsoft expends much effort to promote the .NET Framework. It does not directly receive revenue from these standards. IIS is free with Windows XP and 2000. Microsoft's Web sites have numerous articles to help developers learn more about these standards, and all of the information is free. Why do you think Microsoft does this? What goal is served?

```html
<!DOCTYPE html PUBLIC "-//W3C//DTD HTML 4.01 Strict//EN"
"http://www.w3.org/TR/html4/strict.dtd">
<html>
      <head>
            <meta http-equiv="Content-Type" content="text/html; charset=ISO-8859-1" />
            <title>DBP-e11 Home Page</title>
      </head>
      <body>
            <h1 style="text-align: center; color: blue">
                  Database Processing (11th Edition) Home Page
            </h1>
            <hr />
            <h3 style="text-align: center">
                  Use this page to access Web-based materials from Chapter 11 of:
            </h3>
            <h2 style="text-align: center; color: blue">
                  Database Processing (11th Edition)
            </h2>
            <p style="text-align: center; font-weight: bold">
                  David M. Kroenke
            </p>
            <p style="text-align: center; font-weight: bold">
                  David J. Auer
            </p>
            <hr />
            <h3>Chapter 11 Demonstration Pages From Figures in the Text:</h3>
            <p>
                  <a href="VRG/index.html">
                        View Ridge Gallery Demonstration Pages
                  </a>
            </p>
            <hr />
      </body>
</html>
```

Figure 11-46

The HTML Code for the index.html File in the DBP Folder

```html
<p>Example 4:   
      <a href="NewCustomerWithInterestsForm.html">
            Add a New Customer to the CUSTOMER Table Using PHP PDO
      </a>
</p>
<hr />
<!-- *********** NEW CODE STARTS HERE ***********  -->
<p style="text-align: center">
      <a href="../index.html">
            Return to the Database Processing Home Page
      </a>
</p>
<hr />
<!-- *********** NEW CODE ENDS HERE ***********  -->
</body>
</html>
```

Figure 11-47

HTML Modifications for the index.html File in the VRG Folder

Marcia's Dry Cleaning

If you have not already done so, answer questions A through G for Marcia's Dry Cleaning at the end of Chapter 7 (page 293). Use SQL Server, Oracle, or MySQL to implement your database.

A.   Add a new folder to the DBP Web site named MDC. Create a Web page for Marcia's Dry Cleaning in this folder, using the file name index.html. Link this page to the DBP Web page.

B.   Create an appropriate ODBC data source for your database.

C.   Add a new column Status to ORDER. Assume that Status can have the values ['Waiting', 'In-process', 'Finished', 'Pending'].

D.   Create a view called CustomerOrder that has the columns LastName, FirstName, Phone, InvoiceNumber, Date, Total, and Status.

E.   Code a PHP page to display CustomerOrder. Using your sample database, demonstrate that your page works.

F.   Code two HTML/PHP pages to receive a date value AsOfDate and to display rows of CustomerOrder for orders having DateIn greater than or equal to AsOfDate. Using your sample database, demonstrate that your pages work.

G.   Code two HTML/PHP pages to receive customer Phone, LastName, and FirstName and to display rows for customers having that Phone, LastName, and FirstName. Using your sample database, demonstrate that your pages work.

H.   Write a stored procedure that receives values for InvoiceNumber and NewStatus and that sets the value of Status to NewStatus for the row having the given value of Invoice Number. Generate an error message if no row has the given value of InvoiceNumber. Using your sample database, demonstrate that your stored procedure works.

I.   Code two HTML/PHP pages to invoke the stored procedure created in task H. Using your sample database, demonstrate that your page works.

Morgan Importing

If you have not already done so, answer questions A through H for Morgan Importing at the end of Chapter 7 (page 294). Use SQL Server, Oracle, or MySQL to implement your database.

A.   Add a new folder to the DBP Web site named MI. Create a Web page for Morgan Importing in this folder, using the file name index.html. Link this page to the DBP Web page.

B.   Create an appropriate ODBC data source for your database.

C.   Create a view called StorePurchases that has the columns StoreName, City, Country, Email, Contact, Date, Description, Category, and PriceUSD.

D.   Code a PHP page to display StorePurchases. Using your sample database, demonstrate that your page works.

E.   Code two HTML/PHP pages to receive a date value AsOfDate and display rows of StorePurchases for purchases having Date greater than or equal to AsOfDate. Using your sample database, demonstrate that your pages work.

F.   Code two HTML/PHP pages to receive values of Country and Category and display rows of StorePurchases having values for input Country and Category values. Using your sample database, demonstrate that your pages work.

G.   Write a stored procedure that receives values for PurchaseID and NewPriceUSD and sets the value of PriceUSD to NewPriceUSD for the row having the given value of PurchaseID. Generate an error message if no row has the given value of PurchaseID. Using your sample database, demonstrate that your stored procedure works.

H.   Code two HTML/PHP pages to invoke the stored procedure created in task G. Using your sample database, demonstrate that your page works.

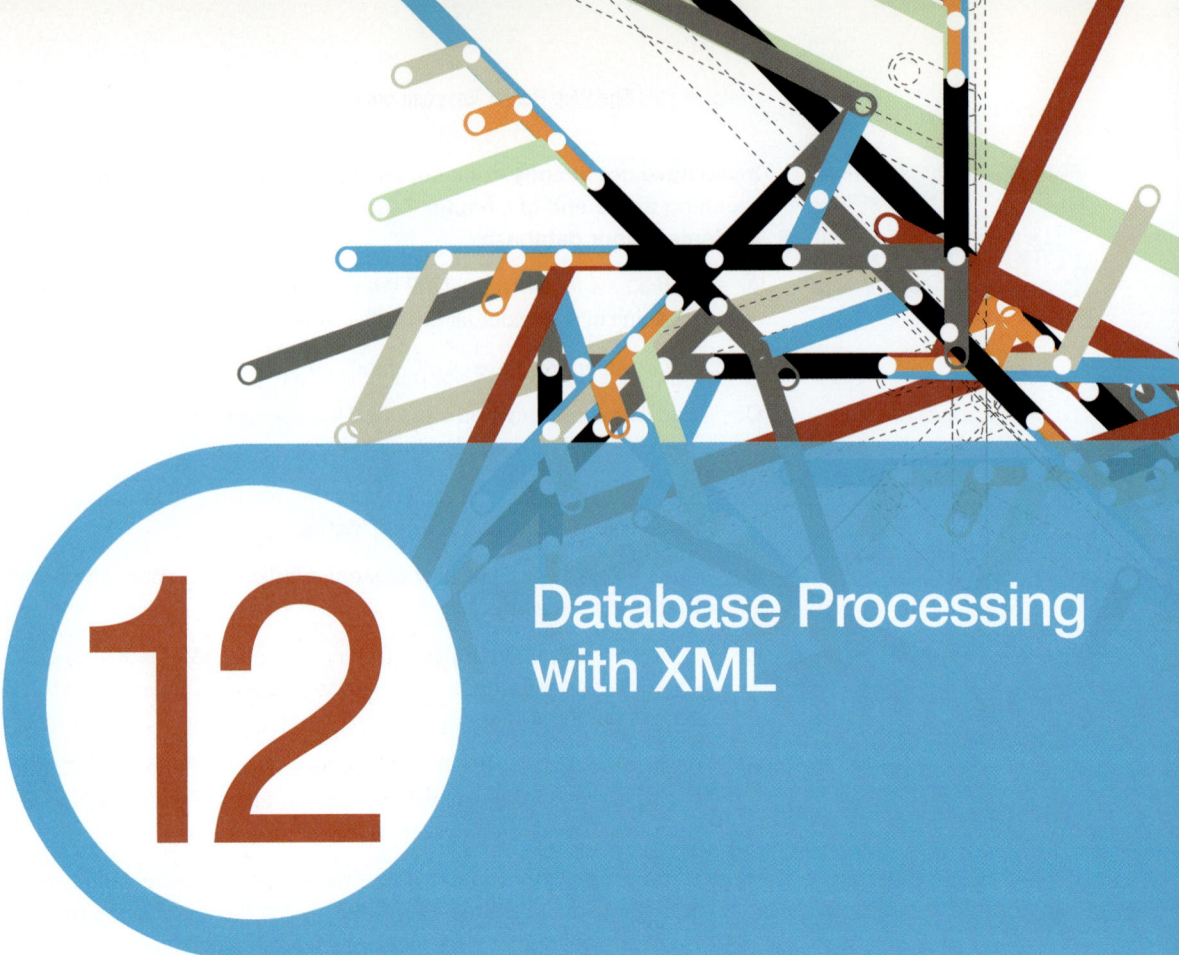

12

Database Processing with XML

Chapter Objectives

- Understand the importance of XML.
- Learn the elements of XML, including XML documents, document type declarations (DTDs), and XML stylesheets.
- Understand the role of XSLT in materializing XML documents.
- Learn the basic concepts of XML Schema and understand their importance to database processing.
- Understand XML documents.
- Learn the basic concepts of using the SQL SELECT . . . FOR XML statement.

This chapter considers one of the most important, if not *the* most important, developments in information systems technology today. It discusses the confluence of two information technology subject areas: database processing and document processing. For more than 20 years, these two subject areas developed independently of one another. With the advent of the Internet, however, they crashed together in what some industry pundits called a technology train wreck. The result is still being sorted out, with new products, product features, technology standards, and development practices emerging every month.

The Importance of XML

Database processing and document processing need each other. Database processing needs document processing for transmitting database views; document processing needs database processing for storing and manipulating data. However, even though these technologies need each other, it took the popularity of the Internet to make that need obvious. As Web sites evolved, organizations wanted to use Internet technology to display and update data from organizational databases. Web developers began to take a serious interest in SQL, database performance, database security, and other aspects of database processing.

As the Web developers invaded the database community, database practitioners wondered, "Who are these people and what do they want?" Database practitioners began to learn about HTML, the language used to mark up documents for display by Web browsers. At first, the database community scoffed at HTML because of its limitations, but they soon learned that HTML was the output of a more robust document markup language called **Standard Generalized Markup Language (SGML)**. SGML was clearly important, just as important to document processing as the relational model was to database processing. Obviously, this powerful language had some role to play in the display of database data, but what role?

In the early 1990s, the two communities began to meet, and the result of their work is a series of standards that concerns a language called **Extensible Markup Language (XML)**. XML is a subset of SGML, but additional standards and capabilities have been added to XML, and today XML technology is a hybrid of document processing and database processing. In fact, as XML standards evolved, it became clear that the communities had been working on different aspects of the same problem for many years. They even used the same terms, but with different meanings. You will see later in this chapter how the term *schema* is used in XML for a concept that is completely different from the use of *schema* in the database world.

XML provides a standardized yet customizable way to describe the content of documents. As such, it can be used to describe any database view, but in a standardized way. As you will learn, unlike SQL views, XML views are not limited to one multivalued path.

In addition, when used with the XML Schema standard, XML documents can automatically be generated from database data. Further, database data can automatically be extracted from XML documents. Even more, there are standardized ways of defining how document components are mapped to database schema components, and vice versa.

Meanwhile, the rest of the computing community began to take notice of XML. **SOAP**, which originally meant **Simple Object Access Protocol**, was defined as an XML-based standard for providing remote procedure calls over the Internet. Initially, SOAP assumed the use of HTTP as a transport mechanism. When Microsoft, IBM, Oracle, and other large companies joined forces in support of the SOAP standard, this assumption was removed, and SOAP was generalized to become a standard protocol for sending messages of any type, using any protocol. With this change, SOAP no longer meant Simple Object Access Protocol, so now SOAP is just a name, and not an acronym.

Today, XML is used for many purposes. One of the most important is its use as a standardized means to define and communicate documents for processing over the Internet. XML plays a key role in Microsoft's .NET initiative; and in 2001 Bill Gates called XML the "*lingua franca* of the Internet age."

We will begin the discussion of XML by describing its use for displaying Web pages. As you will learn, however, XML uses go far beyond Web page display. In fact, Web page display is one of the least important applications of XML. We begin with page display only because it is an easy way to introduce XML documents. After that, we will explain the XML Schema standard and discuss its use for database processing.

As you read this chapter, keep in mind that this area is at the leading edge of database processing. Standards, products, and product capabilities are changing frequently. You can keep abreast of these changes by checking the following Web sites: *www.w3c.org*, *www.xml.org*, *http://msdn.microsoft.com*, *www.oracle.com*, *www.ibm.com*, and *www.mysql.com*. Learning as much as you can about XML and database processing is one of the best ways you can prepare yourself for a successful career in database processing.

XML as a Markup Language

As a markup language, XML is significantly better than HTML in several ways. For one, XML provides a clean separation between document structure, content, and materialization. XML has facilities for dealing with each, and they cannot be confounded, as they are with HTML.

Additionally, XML is standardized, but as its name implies, the standards allow for extension by developers. With XML, you are not limited to a fixed set of elements such as <title>, <h1>, and <p>; you can create your own.

Third, XML eliminates the inconsistent tag use that is possible (and popular) with HTML. For example, consider the following HTML:

```
<h2>Hello World</h2>
```

Although the <h2> tag can be used to mark a level-two heading in an outline, it can be used for other purposes, too, such as causing "Hello World" to be displayed in a particular font size, weight, and color. Because a tag has potentially many uses, we cannot rely on tags to discern the structure of an HTML page. Tag use is too arbitrary; <h2> may mean a heading, or it may mean nothing at all.

As you will see, the structure of an XML document can be formally defined. Tags are defined in relationship to one another. In XML, if we find the tag <street>, we know exactly what data we have, where that data belongs in the document, and how that tag relates to other tags.

XML Document Type Declarations

Figure 12-1 shows a sample XML document. Notice that the document has two sections. The first section defines the structure of the document; it is referred to as the **document type declaration (DTD)**. The second part is the document data.

The DTD begins with the word DOCTYPE and specifies the name of this type of document, which is customer. Then, it specifies the content of the customer document. The customer document consists of two groups: name and address. The name group consists of two elements: firstname and lastname. Firstname and lastname are defined as #PCDATA, which means that they are strings of character data. Next, the address element is defined to have four elements: street, city, state, and zip. Each of these is also defined as character data. The plus sign after street indicates that one value is required and that multiple values are possible.

Figure 12-1

XML Document with Internal DTD

```
<?xml version="1.0" encoding="UTF-8"?>
<!DOCTYPE Customer [
    <!ELEMENT Customer (CustomerName, Address)>
    <!ELEMENT CustomerName (FirstName, LastName)>
    <!ELEMENT FirstName (#PCDATA)>
    <!ELEMENT LastName (#PCDATA)>
    <!ELEMENT Address (Street+, City, State, Zip)>
    <!ELEMENT Street (#PCDATA)>
    <!ELEMENT City (#PCDATA)>
    <!ELEMENT State (#PCDATA)>
    <!ELEMENT Zip (#PCDATA)>
]>
<Customer>
    <CustomerName>
        <FirstName>Jeffery</FirstName>
        <LastName>Janes</LastName>
    </CustomerName>
    <Address>
        <Street>123 W. Elm St.</Street>
        <City>Renton</City>
        <State>WA</State>
        <Zip>98055</Zip>
    </Address>
</Customer>
```

Figure 12-2

XML Document with
External DTD

```xml
<?xml version="1.0" encoding="UTF-8"?>
<!DOCTYPE CustomerList SYSTEM "C:\inetpub\wwwroot\DBP\VRG\CustomerList.dtd">
<CustomerList>
    <Customer>
        <CustomerName>
            <FirstName>David</FirstName>/>
            <LastName>Smith</LastName>/>
        </CustomerName>
        <Address>
            <Street>813 Tumbleweed Lane</Street>/>
            <City>Durango</City>/>
            <State>CO</State>/>
            <Zip>81201</Zip>/>
        </Address>
    </Customer>
</CustomerList>
```

The data instance of customer shown in Figure 12-1 conforms to the DTD; hence, this document is said to be a **type-valid** XML document. If it did not conform to the DTD, it would be a **not-type-valid** document. Documents that are not-type-valid can still be perfectly good XML; they just do not conform to their type description. For example, if the document in Figure 12-1 had two city elements, it would be valid XML, but it would be not-type-valid.

Although DTDs are almost always desirable, they are not required in XML documents. Documents that have no DTD are by definition not-type-valid, because there is no type to validate them against.

The DTD does not need to be contained inside the document. Figure 12-2 shows a customer document in which the DTD is obtained from the file C:\inetpub\wwwroot\DBP\VRG\CustomerList.dtd. In this case, the DTD is located on the computer that stores this document. DTDs can also be referenced by URL Web addresses. The advantage of storing the DTD externally is that many documents can be validated against the same DTD.

The creator of a DTD is free to choose any elements he or she wants. Hence, XML documents can be extended, but in a standardized and controlled way.

Materializing XML Documents with XSLT

The XML document shown in Figure 12-1 shows both the document's structure and content. Nothing in the document, however, indicates how it is to be materialized. The designers of XML created a clean separation among structure, content, and format. The most popular way to materialize XML documents is to use XSLT, or Extensible Style Language: Transformations. XSLT is a powerful and robust transformation language. It can be used to materialize XML documents into HTML, and it can be used for many other purposes as well.

One common application of XSLT is to transform an XML document in one format into a second XML document in another format. A company can, for example, use XSLT to transform an XML order document in its own format into an equivalent XML order document in its customer's format. We will be unable to discuss many of the features and functions of XSLT here. See *www.w3.org* for more information.

XSLT is a declarative transformation language. It is declarative because you create a set of rules that govern how the document is to be materialized instead of specifying a procedure for materializing document elements. It is transformational because it transforms the input document into another document.

Figure 12-3(a) shows the CustomerList.dtd, which is a DTD for a document that has a list of customers, and Figure 12-3(b) shows the CustomerListDoucment.xml,which is an XML document that is type-valid on that DTD. The DOCTYPE statement in Figure 12-3(b) points to a file that contains the DTD shown in Figure 12-3(a). The next statement in the XML document indicates the location of another document, called a stylesheet. Shown in the

Figure 12-3

CustomerList DTD and
Example Document

```
<?xml version="1.0" encoding="UTF-8"?>
<!ELEMENT CustomerList (Customer+)>
<!ELEMENT Customer (CustomerName, Address)>
<!ELEMENT CustomerName (FirstName, LastName)>
<!ELEMENT FirstName (#PCDATA)>
<!ELEMENT LastName (#PCDATA)>
<!ELEMENT Address (Street+, City, State, Zip)>
<!ELEMENT Street (#PCDATA)>
<!ELEMENT City (#PCDATA)>
<!ELEMENT State (#PCDATA)>
<!ELEMENT Zip (#PCDATA)>
```

(a) CustomerList.dtd DTD

```
<?xml version="1.0" encoding="UTF-8"?>
<!DOCTYPE CustomerList SYSTEM "C:\inetpub\wwwroot\DBP\VRG\CustomerList.dtd">
<?xml-stylesheet type="text/xsl" href="C:\inetpub\wwwroot\DBP\VRG\CustomerListStylesheet.xls"?>
<CustomerList>
    <Customer>
        <CustomerName>
            <FirstName>Jeffery</FirstName>
            <LastName>Janes</LastName>
        </CustomerName>
        <Address>
            <Street>123 W. Elm St.</Street>
            <City>Renton</City>
            <State>WA</State>
            <Zip>98055</Zip>
        </Address>
    </Customer>
    <Customer>
        <CustomerName>
            <FirstName>David</FirstName>
            <LastName>Smith</LastName>
        </CustomerName>
        <Address>
            <Street>813 Tumbleweed Lane</Street>
            <City>Durango</City>
            <State>CO</State>
            <Zip>81201</Zip>
        </Address>
    </Customer>
</CustomerList>
```

(b) CustomerListDocument.xml with Two Customers

CustomerListStylesheet.xsl in Figure 12-4, a **stylesheet** is used by XSLT to indicate how to transform the elements of the XML document into another format. Here, those elements will transform it into an HTML document that will be acceptable to a browser.

The XSLT processor copies the elements of the stylesheet until it finds a command in the format {*item, action*}. When it finds such a command, it searches for an instance of the indicated item; when it finds one, it takes the indicated action. For example, when the XSLT processor encounters

```
<xsl:for-each select = "CustomerList/Customer">
```

it starts a search in the document for an element named CustomerList. When it finds such an element, it looks further within the customerlist element for an element named Customer. If a match is found, it takes the actions indicated in the loop that ends with </xsl:for-each> (third from the bottom of the stylesheet). Within the loop, styles are set for each element in the CustomerList document.

```xml
<?xml version="1.0" encoding="UTF-8"?>
<xsl:stylesheet version="1.0" xmlns:xsl="http://www.w3.org/1999/XSL/Transform"
    xmlns:fo="http://www.w3.org/1999/XSL/Format">
  <xsl:output method="html"/>
  <xsl:template match="/">
    <html>
      <head>
        <title>CustomerListStylesheet</title>
        <style type="text/css">
          h1 {text-align:center; color:blue}
          body {font-family:ariel, sans-serif; font-size:12pt; background-color:#FFFFFF}
          div.customername {font-weight:bold; background-color:#3399FF;
              color:#FFFFFF; padding:4px}
          div.customerdata {font-size:10pt; font-weight:bold; background-color:#87CEFA;
              color:#000000; margin-left:20px; margin-bottom:20px}
          p.footer {text-align:center}
        </style>
      </head>
      <body>
        <h1>
          View Ridge Gallery Customer List
        </h1>
        <hr/>
        <xsl:for-each select="CustomerList/Customer">
          <div class="customername">
            <xsl:value-of select="CustomerName/LastName"/>,
            <xsl:value-of select="CustomerName/FirstName"/>
          </div>
          <br />
          <div class="customerdata">
            <xsl:for-each select="Address/Street">
              <xsl:value-of select="node()"/>
            </xsl:for-each>
            <br />
            <xsl:value-of select="Address/City"/>,
            <xsl:value-of select="Address/State"/>
            <br />
            <xsl:value-of select="Address/Zip"/>
          </div>
        </xsl:for-each>
        <hr />
        <p class="footer">
          <a href="../VRG/index.html">
            Return to View Ridge Gallery Home Page
          </a>
        </p>
        <hr />
      </body>
    </html>
  </xsl:template>
</xsl:stylesheet>
```

Figure 12-4

The
CustomerListStylesheet.xsl
XSL Stylesheet

The examples we have created are based on the View Ridge Gallery database that we have used in previous chapters. Here, we are creating an XML document that can be viewed using a Web browser to display the list of customers at the View Ridge Gallery. As shown in Figure 12-5(a), we have revised the View Ridge Gallery home page we created in Chapter 11 to include a link to the XML document. Clicking the link displays the Web page shown in Figure 12-5(b), which is the result of applying the stylesheet in Figure 12-4 to the document in Figure 12-3(b). The actual code generated by the XSL stylesheet for display on the Web page is shown in Figure 12-5(c). Read through the document and the stylesheet and see how the results in Figure 12-5(c) are generated.

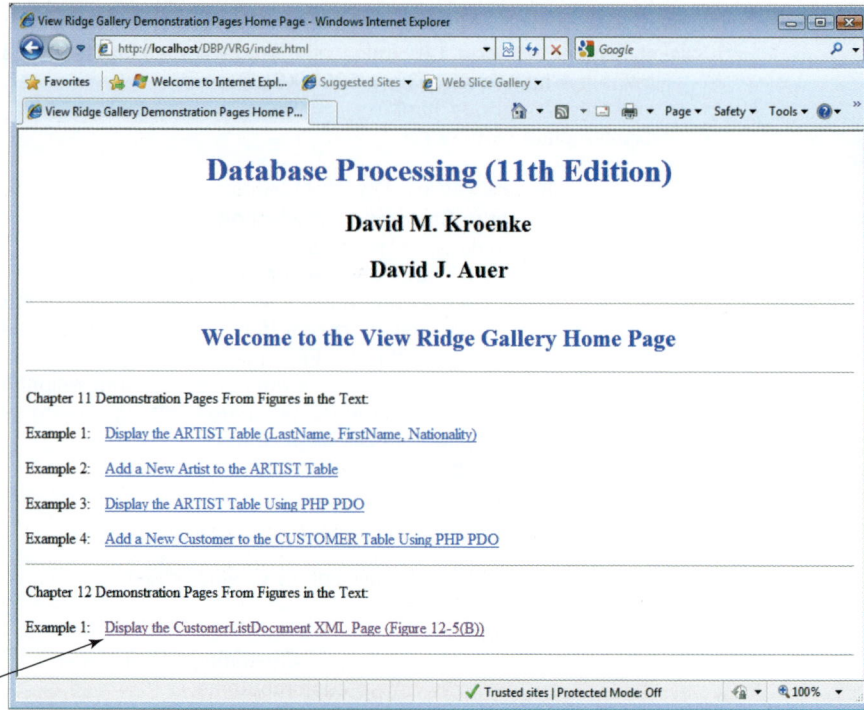

Use this link to display the XML document in a Web browser

(a) The View Ridge Gallery Home Page

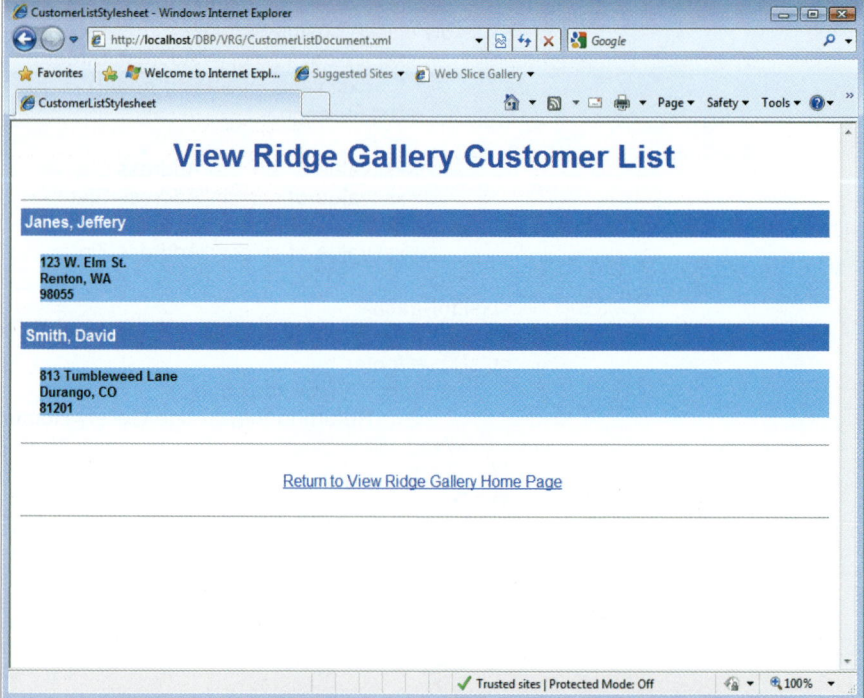

Figure 12-5

HTML Result from Application of an XSL Stylesheet

(b) The CustomerList Web Page as Displayed in Web Browser

XSLT processors are context oriented; each statement is evaluated in the context of matches that have already been made. Thus, the following statement:

```
<xsl:value-of select = "name/lastname"/>
```

operates in the context of the CustomerList/Customer match that was made above. There is no need to code

```
<xsl:select = "CustomerList/Customer/CustomerName/LastName"/>
```

because the context has already been set to customerlist/customer. In fact, if the select were coded in this second way, nothing would be found. Similarly,

```
<xsl:select "LastName"/>
```

results in no match, because lastname occurs only in the context CustomerList/Customer/CustomerName, and not in the context CustomerList/Customer.

BY THE WAY   The nature of XSLT processing is: "When you find one of these, do this." Thus, the document in Figure 12-4 says, for each customer that you find under the tag customerlist, do the following: output an HTML <div> . . . </div> section and then some HTML with the value that you find in the document for CustomerName/LastName. Then, output more HTML and the value that you find for CustomerName/FirstName. Then, for each Address/Street you find, output some HTML along with the value of the Address/Street you just found, and so forth.

XSL can output anything. Instead of outputting HTML, it could be writing Russian or Chinese or algebraic equations. XSL is simply a transformation facility for structured documents such as XML documents.

This context orientation explains the need for the following statement (in the center of the style sheet):

```
xsl:value-of select = "node()"/>
```

The context at the location of this statement has been set to CustomerList/Customer/Address/Street. Hence, the current node is a street element, and this expression indicates that the value of that node is to be produced.

Observe, too, that a small transformation has been made by the stylesheet. The original document has FirstName followed by LastName, but the output stream has LastName followed by FirstName.

The XML document in Figure 12-3(b) is transformed into HTML using the XSL stylesheet in Figure 12-4. Figure 12-5(a) shows the revised VRG Home page, which now has a link to display the XML document. When this transformed document is input to a browser, the browser will materialize it, as shown in Figure 12-5(b).

Browsers have built-in XSLT processors. You need only supply the document to the browser; it will locate the stylesheet and apply it to the document for you. The results will be like those shown in Figure 12-5(b).

XML Schema

DTDs were the XML community's first attempt at developing a document structure specification language. DTDs work, but they have some limitations, and embarrassingly, DTD documents are not XML documents. To correct these problems, the W3C Committee defined another specification language called **XML Schema**. Today, XML Schema is the preferred method for defining document structure.

XML Schemas are XML documents. This means that you use the same language to define an XML Schema as you would use to define any other XML document. It also means that you can validate an XML Schema document against its schema, just as you would any other XML document.

If you are following this discussion, then you realize that there is a chicken-and-the-egg problem here. If XML Schema documents are themselves XML documents, what document is used to validate them? What is the schema of all of the schemas? There is such a document; the mother of all schemas is located at *www.w3.org*. All XML Schema documents are validated against this document.

XML Schema is a broad and complex topic. Dozens of sizable books have been written just on XML Schema alone. Clearly, we will not be able to discuss even the major topics of XML Schema in this chapter. Instead, we will focus on a few basic terms and concepts and show how those terms and concepts are used with database processing. Given this introduction, you will then be able to learn more on your own.

> **BY THE WAY**   XML Schema validation requires thinking at two meta levels. To understand why, recall that metadata is data about data. The statement *CUSTOMER contains column CustomerLastName Char(25)* is metadata. Extending this idea, the statement *SQL has a data type Char(n) for defining character data of length n* is data about metadata, or meta-metadata.
>
> XML has the same meta levels. An XML document has a structure that is defined by an XML Schema document. The XML Schema document contains metadata, because it is data about the structure of other XML documents. But an XML Schema document has its own structure that is defined by another XML Schema. That XML Schema document is data about metadata, or meta-metadata.
>
> The XML case is elegant. You can write a program to validate an XML document (but don't—use one of the hundreds that already exist). Once you have such a program, you can validate any XML document against its XML Schema document. The process is exactly the same, regardless of whether you are validating an XML document, an XML Schema document, or a document at any other level.

XML Schema Validation

Figure 12-6(a) shows a simple XML Schema document that can be used to represent a single row from the ARTIST table at View Ridge Gallery. The second line indicates what schema is to be used to validate this document. Because this is an XML Schema document, it is to be validated against the mother of all schemas, the one at *www.w3.org*. This same reference will be used in all XML Schemas, in every company, worldwide. (By the way, this reference address is used only for identification purposes. Because this schema is so widely used, most schema validation programs have their own built-in copy of it.)

This first statement not only specifies the document that is to be used for validation, it also establishes a labeled namespace. Namespaces are a complicated topic in their own right, and we will not discuss them in this chapter other than to explain the use of labels. In this first statement, the label *xs* is defined by the expression: xmlns:xs. The first part of that expression stands for *xml n*amespace, and the second part defines the label *xs*. Notice that all of the other lines in the document use the label xs. The expression *xs:complexType* simply tells the validating program to look into the namespace called xsd (here, the one specified as *www.w3.org/2001/XMLSchema*) to find the definition of the term *complexType*.

Figure 12-6

Use of an XML Schema

```xml
<?xml version="1.0" encoding="UTF-8"?>
<xs:schema xmlns:xs="http://www.w3.org/2001/XMLSchema" elementFormDefault="qualified"
attributeFormDefault="unqualified">
    <xs:element name="Artist">
        <xs:annotation>
            <xs:documentation>
                This is the XML Schema document the VRG ARTIST table
            </xs:documentation>
        </xs:annotation>
        <xs:complexType>
            <xs:sequence>
                <xs:element name="LastName"/>
                <xs:element name="FirstName"/>
                <xs:element name="Nationality"/>
                <xs:element name="DateOfBirth" minOccurs="0"/>
                <xs:element name="DateDeceased" minOccurs="0"/>
            </xs:sequence>
            <xs:attribute name="ArtStyle"/>
        </xs:complexType>
    </xs:element>
</xs:schema>
```

(a) XML Schema Document

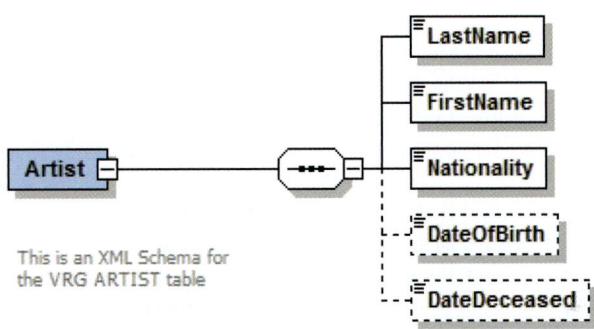

This is an XML Schema for
the VRG ARTIST table

(b) Graphical Representation of the XML Schema

```xml
<?xml version="1.0" encoding="UTF-8"?>
<Artist xmlns:xsi="http://www.w3.org/2001/XMLSchema-instance"
xsi:noNamespaceSchemaLocation="C:\inetpub\wwwroot\DBP\VRG\VRG-ARTIST-001.xsd" ArtStyle="Modern" >
    <LastName>Miro</LastName>
    <FirstName>Joan</FirstName>
    <Nationality>Spanish</Nationality>
    <DateOfBirth>1893</DateOfBirth>
    <DateDeceased>1983</DateDeceased>
</Artist>
```

(c) Schema-Valid XML Document

The name of the label is up to the designer of the document. You could change xmlns:xs to xmlns:xsd or to xmlns:mylabel, and you would set xsd or mylabel to point to the w3 document. Documents can have multiple namespaces, but that topic is beyond the scope of this discussion.

Elements and Attributes

As shown in Figure 12-6(a), schemas consist of elements and attributes. Elements are either simple or complex. Simple elements have a single data item. In Figure 12-6(a), the elements LastName, FirstName, Nationality, DateOfBirth, and DateDeceased are all simple elements.

Complex elements contain other elements that can be either simple or complex. In Figure 12-6(a), the Artist element is complexType. It contains a sequence of five simple elements: LastName, FirstName, Nationality, DateOfBirth, and DateDeceased. Later you will see examples of complex types that contain other complex types.

Complex types can have attributes. Figure 12-6(a) defines the attribute ArtStyle. The creator of an XML document uses this attribute to specify a characteristic about an artist; in this case, his or her style. The example document in Figure 12-6(c) specifies the ArtStyle for this artist (Miro) as Modern.

> **BY THE WAY**   Elements and attributes both carry data, and you may be wondering when
> to use one or the other. As a general rule, for database/XML applications,
> use elements to store data and attributes to store metadata. For example, define an
> ItemPrice element to store the value of a price, and define a Currency attribute to store
> the currency type of that price, such as USD, Aus$, or Euros.
>
> The XML standards do not require that elements and attributes be used in this way.
> It is a matter of style, and in subsequent sections we will show how it is possible to
> cause SQL Server to place all of the column values in attributes, to place all of them in
> elements, or to mix them up so that some columns are placed in attributes and others
> are placed in elements. Thus, these decisions are a matter of design choice rather than
> XML standard.

By default, the cardinality of both simple and complex elements is 1.1, meaning that a single value is required and no more than a single value can be specified. For the schema in Figure 12-6(a), the minOccurs = "0" expressions indicate that the defaults are being overridden for Birthdate and DeceasedDate so that they need not have a value. This is similar to the NULL constraint in SQL schema definitions.

Figure 12-6(b) shows the XML Schema in a diagram format as drawn by Altova's XMLSpy XML editing tool (see http://www.altova.com/xml-editor/). Being able to see an XML Schema as a diagram often makes it easier to interpret exactly what the XML Schema is specifying. In this diagram, note that required elements (NOT NULL in SQL terms) are indicated with solid lines and box outlines, while optional elements (NULL in SQL terms) are indicated by dashed line and box outlines.

> **BY THE WAY**   You can find out more about this excellent product from a small company,
> which is not yet owned by Microsoft or some other behemoth corporation,
> from the Web site *www.altova.com*. A 30-day trial version is available. You can process
> all of the XML code in this chapter using XMLSpy, and the XML code for this chapter is
> available on this text's Web site at *www.pearsonhighered.com/kroenke*.

Figure 12-6(c) shows an XML document that is valid on the schema shown in Figure 12-6(a). Observe that the value of the ArtStyle attribute is given with the heading of the Artist element. Also note that a namespace of *xsi* is defined. This namespace is used just once—for the noNamespaceSchemaLocation attribute. Do not be concerned about the name of this attribute; it is simply a means of telling the XML parser where to find the XML Schema for this document. Focus your attention on the relationship of the structure of the document and the description in the XML Schema.

Flat Versus Structured Schemas

Figure 12-7 shows an XML Schema and an XML document that represent the columns of the CUSTOMER table in the View Ridge database. As shown in Figure 12-7(a), CustomerID, LastName, and FirstName are required, but all of the other elements are required.

XML Schemas like the one shown in Figure 12-7(a) are sometimes called *flat*, because all of the elements reside at the same level. Figure 12-7(b) shows a diagram of the XML Schema as drawn by XMLSpy, and this diagram graphically depicts why this schema is called flat. The XML document in Figure 12-7(c) contains one of the rows of the CUSTOMER table.

If you think about the elements in Figure 12-7(a) for a moment, you will realize that something about the semantics of them has been left out. In particular, the group {Street, City, State, ZipPostalCode, Country} is part of an Address theme. Also, the group {AreaCode, PhoneNumber} is part of a Phone theme. As you know, in the relational model, all columns are considered equal, and there is no way to represent these themes.

```xml
<?xml version="1.0" encoding="UTF-8"?>
<xs:schema xmlns:xs="http://www.w3.org/2001/XMLSchema" elementFormDefault="qualified"
attributeFormDefault="unqualified">
    <xs:element name="Customer">
        <xs:annotation>
            <xs:documentation>This is the XML Schema for the VRG CUSTOMER table</xs:documentation>
        </xs:annotation>
        <xs:complexType>
            <xs:sequence>
                <xs:element name="CustomerID" type="xs:int"/>
                <xs:element name="LastName" type="xs:string"/>
                <xs:element name="FirstName" type="xs:string"/>
                <xs:element name="Street" type="xs:string" minOccurs="0"/>
                <xs:element name="City" type="xs:string" minOccurs="0"/>
                <xs:element name="State" type="xs:string" minOccurs="0"/>
                <xs:element name="ZipPostalCode" type="xs:string" minOccurs="0"/>
                <xs:element name="Country" type="xs:string" minOccurs="0"/>
                <xs:element name="AreaCode" type="xs:string" minOccurs="0"/>
                <xs:element name="PhoneNumber" type="xs:string" minOccurs="0"/>
                <xs:element name="EmailAddress" type="xs:string" minOccurs="0"/>
            </xs:sequence>
        </xs:complexType>
    </xs:element>
</xs:schema>
```

(a) XML Schema with Flat Structure

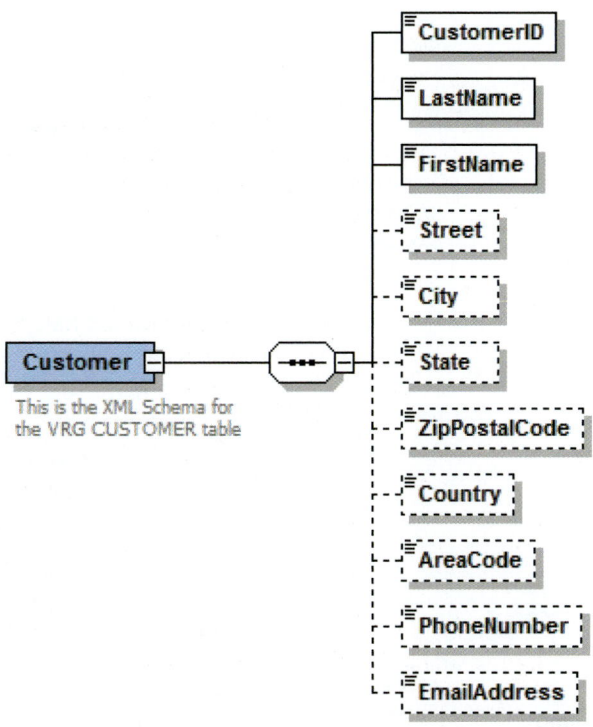

Figure 12-7

Example of a Flat Structure

(b) Graphical Representation of the XML Schema

```
<?xml version="1.0" encoding="UTF-8"?>
<Customer xmlns:xsi="http://www.w3.org/2001/XMLSchema-instance"
xsi:noNamespaceSchemaLocation="C:\inetpub\wwwroot\DBP\VRG\DBP-e11-Figure-12-07-A.xsd">
        <CustomerID>1000</CustomerID>
        <LastName>Janes</LastName>
        <FirstName>Jeffery</FirstName>
        <Street>123 W. Elm St.</Street>
        <City>Renton</City>
        <State>WA</State>
        <ZipPostalCode>98055</ZipPostalCode>
        <Country>USA</Country>
        <AreaCode>425</AreaCode>
        <PhoneNumber>543-2345</PhoneNumber>
        <EmailAddress>Jeffery.Janes@somewhere.com</EmailAddress>
</Customer>
```

Figure 12-7
(Continued)

(c) Schema-Valid XML Document

With XML, however, such groups can be modeled. The schema shown in Figure 12-8(a) structures the appropriate columns into an Address complexType and other columns into a Phone complexType. A graphical display of this schema is shown in Figure 12-8(b). An XML document for one of the rows of CUSTOMER expressed in this format is shown in Figure 12-8(c).

Such schemas are sometimes called **structured schemas** because they add structure to table columns. Such a model captures additional user meaning, so it is superior to the relational model from a descriptive standpoint.

```
<?xml version="1.0" encoding="UTF-8"?>
<xs:schema xmlns:xs="http://www.w3.org/2001/XMLSchema" elementFormDefault="qualified"
attributeFormDefault="unqualified">
    <xs:complexType name="AddressType">
        <xs:sequence>
            <xs:element name="Street" type="xs:string"/>
            <xs:element name="City" type="xs:string"/>
            <xs:element name="State" type="xs:string"/>
            <xs:element name="ZipPostalCode" type="xs:string"/>
            <xs:element name="Country" type="xs:string" minOccurs="0"/>
        </xs:sequence>
    </xs:complexType>
    <xs:complexType name="PhoneType">
        <xs:sequence>
            <xs:element name="AreaCode" type="xs:string"/>
            <xs:element name="PhoneNumber" type="xs:string"/>
        </xs:sequence>
    </xs:complexType>
    <xs:element name="Customer">
        <xs:annotation>
            <xs:documentation>
                This is the structured XML Schema for the VRG CUSTOMER table
            </xs:documentation>
        </xs:annotation>
        <xs:complexType>
            <xs:sequence>
                <xs:element name="CustomerID" type="xs:int"/>
                <xs:element name="LastName" type="xs:string"/>
                <xs:element name="FirstName" type="xs:string"/>
                <xs:element name="Address" type="AddressType" minOccurs="0"/>
                <xs:element name="Phone" type="PhoneType" minOccurs="0"/>
                <xs:element name="EmailAddress" type="xs:string" minOccurs="0"/>
            </xs:sequence>
        </xs:complexType>
    </xs:element>
</xs:schema>
```

Figure 12-8

Example of a Structured Schema

(a) Structured XML Schema

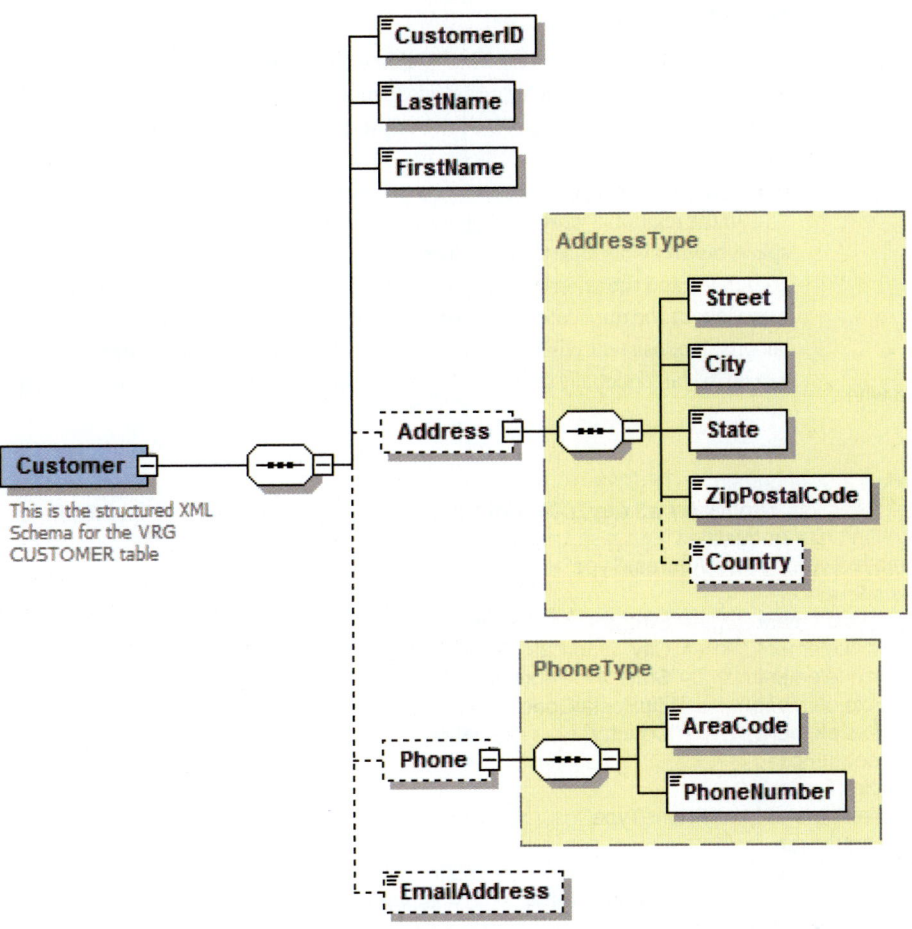

(b) Graphical Representation of the Schema

```xml
<?xml version="1.0" encoding="UTF-8"?>
<Customer xmlns:xsi="http://www.w3.org/2001/XMLSchema-instance"
xsi:noNamespaceSchemaLocation="C:\inetpub\wwwroot\DBP\VRG\DBP-e11-Figure-12-08-A.xsd">
    <CustomerID>1000</CustomerID>
    <LastName>Janes</LastName>
    <FirstName>Jeffery</FirstName>
    <Address>
        <Street>123 W. Elm St.</Street>
        <City>Renton</City>
        <State>WA</State>
        <ZipPostalCode>98055</ZipPostalCode>
        <Country>USA</Country>
    </Address>
    <Phone>
        <AreaCode>425</AreaCode>
        <PhoneNumber>543-2345</PhoneNumber>
    </Phone>
    <EmailAddress>Jeffery.Janes@somewhere.com</EmailAddress>
</Customer>
```

Figure 12-8

(Continued)

(c) Schema-Valid XML Document

Note that in this structured XML Schema, Address and Phone remain as optional (NULL values allowed) in Customer. This maintains the optional status of these columns in the CUSTOMER table. However, in the Address complexType {Street, City, State, ZipPostalCode) are required (NOT NULL). Similarly, in the Phone complexType, {AreaCode, Phone Number} are required. These conditions can be read as "IF there is Address data for a customer, it MUST include the street address, city, state and zip / postal code," and "IF there is Phone data for a customer, it MUST include both the area code and phone number."

Global Elements

Suppose that we want to use XML Schema to represent a document that extends the customer data in Figure 12-8 to include the salesperson assigned to that customer. Further, suppose that both customers and salespeople have address and phone data. We can use the techniques shown thus far to represent this new customer structure, but, if we do so, we will duplicate the definition of Phone and Address.

In the relational world, we worry about duplication of data, not so much because of wasted file space, but more because there is always the chance of inconsistent data when one copy of the data is changed and the other copy is not changed. Similarly, in the document-processing world, people worry about the duplicate definition of elements because there is always the chance that they will become inconsistent when one is changed and the other is not. As shown in Figure 12-9, elements can be declared globally and then reused to eliminate the definition duplication.

Figure 12-9

Example of a Schema with Global Elements

```xml
<?xml version="1.0" encoding="UTF-8"?>
<xs:schema xmlns:xs="http://www.w3.org/2001/XMLSchema" elementFormDefault="qualified"
attributeFormDefault="unqualified">
    <xs:complexType name="AddressType">
        <xs:sequence>
            <xs:element name="Street" type="xs:string"/>
            <xs:element name="City" type="xs:string"/>
            <xs:element name="State" type="xs:string"/>
            <xs:element name="ZipPostalCode" type="xs:string"/>
            <xs:element name="Country" type="xs:string" minOccurs="0"/>
        </xs:sequence>
    </xs:complexType>
    <xs:complexType name="PhoneType">
        <xs:sequence>
            <xs:element name="AreaCode" type="xs:string"/>
            <xs:element name="PhoneNumber" type="xs:string"/>
        </xs:sequence>
    </xs:complexType>
    <xs:element name="Customer">
        <xs:annotation>
            <xs:documentation>
                This is the structured XML Schema for the VRG database with SALESPERSON added
            </xs:documentation>
        </xs:annotation>
        <xs:complexType>
            <xs:sequence>
                <xs:element name="CustomerID" type="xs:int"/>
                <xs:element name="LastName" type="xs:string"/>
                <xs:element name="FirstName" type="xs:string"/>
                <xs:element name="Address" type="AddressType" minOccurs="0"/>
                <xs:element name="Phone" type="PhoneType" minOccurs="0" maxOccurs="3"/>
                <xs:element name="EmailAddress" type="xs:string" minOccurs="0"/>
                <xs:element name="Salesperson">
                    <xs:complexType>
                        <xs:sequence>
                            <xs:element name="SalespersonID" type="xs:int"/>
                            <xs:element name="LastName" type="xs:string"/>
                            <xs:element name="FirstName" type="xs:string"/>
                            <xs:element name="Address" type="AddressType"/>
                            <xs:element name="Phone" type="PhoneType"/>
                        </xs:sequence>
                    </xs:complexType>
                </xs:element>
            </xs:sequence>
        </xs:complexType>
    </xs:element>
</xs:schema>
```

(a) XML Schema with Global PhoneType Element

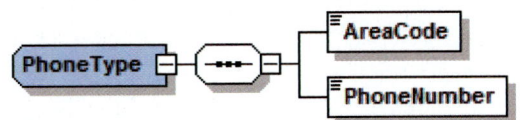

**(b) Graphical Representation of the PhoneType
Global Element**

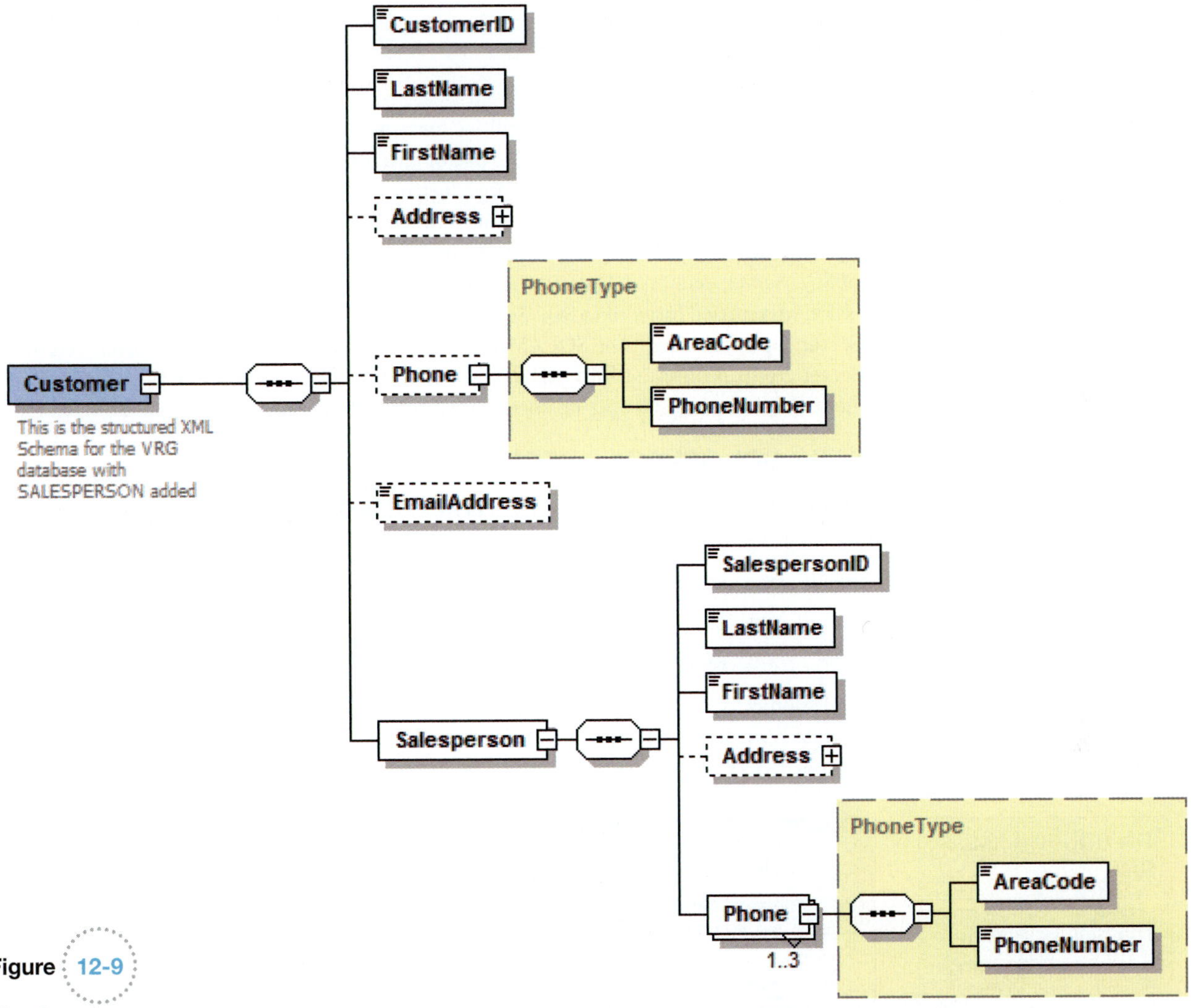

Figure 12-9

(Continued)

(c) Graphical Representation of the XML Schema

In Figure 12-9(a), for example, the Address group is defined as the global element AddressType, and the Phone group is defined as the global element PhoneType. According to the XML Schema standard, these are global elements because they reside at the top level of the schema.

If you examine Figure 12-9(a) further, you will see that both Customer and Salesperson within Customer use the AddressType and PhoneType global definitions. They are referenced by the notations *type = "AddressType"* and *type = "PhoneType."* By using these global definitions, if either PhoneType or AddressType is changed, the definition of Customer and Salesperson will inherit the change.

One other change in this figure is that the cardinality of the Phone group of Salesperson has been set to 1..3. This notation means that at least one Phone group is required and as many as three are allowed. As you learned in Chapter 5, representing such multivalued attributes in the entity-relationship model requires the definition of an ID-dependent entity. That entity will later be transformed into a table in the relational model. We will ignore this issue here. This notation is shown only so that you can see how multivalued elements are documented in an XML Schema.

Figure 12-9(b) shows how XMLSpy graphically represents the PhoneType global element, and Figure 12-9(c) illustrates the way that the PhoneType reference is shown for Customer and Salesperson.

> **BY THE WAY** In the VRG table structure we specified in Chapter 7 and used in Chapter 10, Chapter 10A, and Chapter 10B, there is no SALESPERSON table defined. The XML Schema in Figure 12-9, however, suggests how we could add a SALESPERSON table to the VRG database.

Creating XML Documents from Database Data

Oracle, SQL Server, and MySQL have facilities for generating XML documents from database data. The Oracle XML features require the use of Java. Because we do not assume that you are a Java programmer, we will not discuss those features further in this chapter. If you are a Java programmer, you can learn more about Oracle's XML features at *www.oracle.com*.

The facilities in Oracle, SQL Server, and MySQL are undergoing rapid development. In the case of SQL Server, version 7.0 added the expression FOR XML to SQL SELECT syntax. That expression was carried forward to SQL Server 2000. In 2002, the SQL Server group extended the SQL Server capabilities with the SQLXML class library. SQLXML, which was produced by the SQL Server group, is different from ADO.NET. All of these features and functions were merged together in SQL Server 2005 and are carried forward in SQL Server 2008.

Using the SQL SELECT . . . FOR XML Statement

SQL Server 2008 uses the **SQL SELECT . . . FOR XML statement** to work with XML. Consider the following SQL statement:

```
SELECT     *
FROM       ARTIST
    FOR    XML RAW;
```

The expression FOR XML RAW tells SQL Server to place the values of the columns as attributes in the resulting XML document. Figure 12-10(a) shows an example of as FOR XML RAW query in the Microsoft SQL Server Management Studio. The results of the query are displayed in a single cell.

The SQL FOR XML RAW query

The SQL FOR XML RAW query results—click this cell to display the results in a separate window

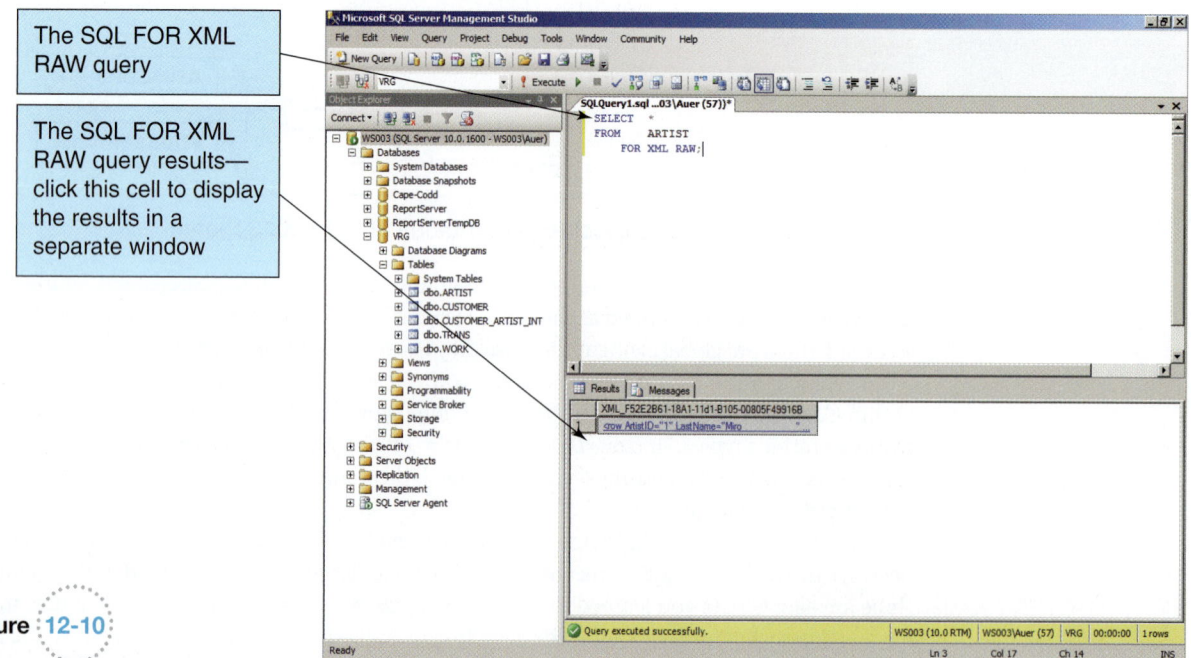

Figure 12-10

FOR XML RAW Examples

(a) FOR XML RAW Query

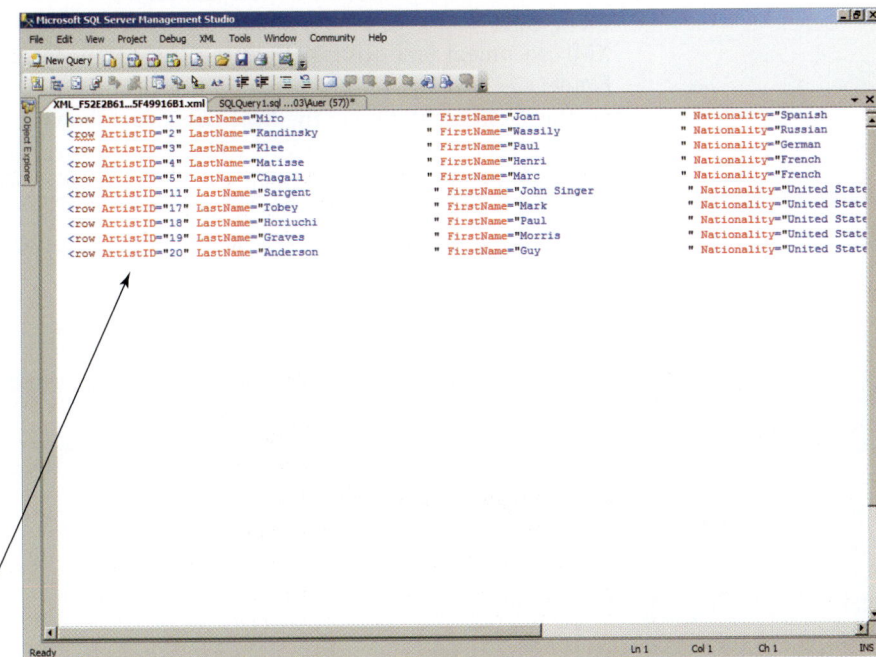

(b) FOR XML RAW Results in the Microsoft SQL Server Management Studio

<row ArtistID="1" LastName="Miro" FirstName="Joan"
        Nationality="Spanish"   DateOfBirth="1893" DateDeceased="1983" />
<row ArtistID="2" LastName="Kandinsky" FirstName="Wassily"
        Nationality="Russian " DateOfBirth="1866" DateDeceased="1944" />
<row ArtistID="3" LastName="Klee" FirstName="Paul"
        Nationality="German" DateOfBirth="1879" DateDeceased="1940" />
<row ArtistID="4" LastName="Matisse" FirstName="Henri"
        Nationality="French" DateOfBirth="1869" DateDeceased="1954" />
<row ArtistID="5" LastName="Chagall" FirstName="Marc"
        Nationality="French" DateOfBirth="1887" DateDeceased="1985" />
<row ArtistID="11" LastName="Sargent" FirstName="John Singer"
        Nationality="United States" DateOfBirth="1856" DateDeceased="1925" />
<row ArtistID="17" LastName="Tobey" FirstName="Mark"
        Nationality="United States" DateOfBirth="1890" DateDeceased="1976" />
<row ArtistID="18" LastName="Horiuchi" FirstName="Paul"
        Nationality="United States" DateOfBirth="1906" DateDeceased="1999" />
<row ArtistID="19" LastName="Graves" FirstName="Morris"
        Nationality="United States" DateOfBirth="1920" DateDeceased="2001" />
<row ArtistID="20" LastName="Anderson" FirstName="Guy"
        Nationality="United States" />

Figure 12-10

(Continued)   **(c) FOR XML RAW Results in XML Document**

Clicking this cell displays the results as shown in Figure 12-10(b). As expected, each column is placed as an attribute of the element named *row*. The complete output, edited as it would appear in an XML document (and with extra spaces in the attribute values removed) is shown in Figure 12-10(c).

It is also possible to cause SQL Server to place the values of the columns into elements rather than attributes by using FOR XML AUTO, ELEMENTS. For example, we can display the data in the ARTIST table using the SQL query:

```
SELECT      *
FROM        ARTIST
    FOR   XML AUTO, ELEMENTS;
```

Figure 12-11(a) shows the query in the Microsoft SQL Server Management Studio, and Figure 12-11(b) shows the full results in a separate tabbed window. Here, each attribute value appears as a separate element. The complete output, edited as it would appear in an XML document (and with MyData tags added to contain the entire data set) is shown in Figure 12-11(c). The XML Schema for this document is shown in Figure 12-11(d), and the graphical representation of the XML Schema is shown in Figure 12-11(e).

Using another option, FOR XML EXPLICIT, you can cause SQL Server to place some columns into elements and others into attributes. For example, you might decide to place all column values except surrogate key values into elements and all surrogate key values into attributes. The justification for this design is that surrogate key values have no meaning to the users, so they are more

The SQL FOR XML AUTO, ELEMENTS query

The SQL FOR XML AUTO, ELEMENTS query results—click this cell to display the results in a separate window

Figure 12-11

FOR XML AUTO, ELEMENTS Examples

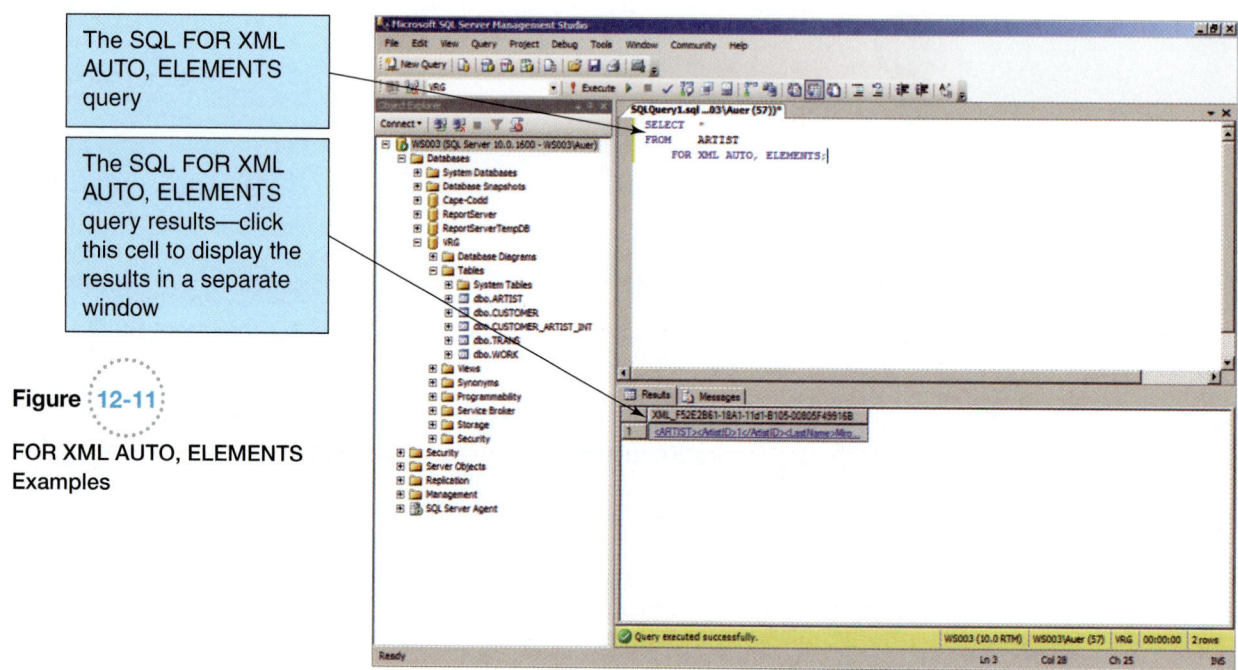

(a) FOR XML AUTO, ELEMENTS Query

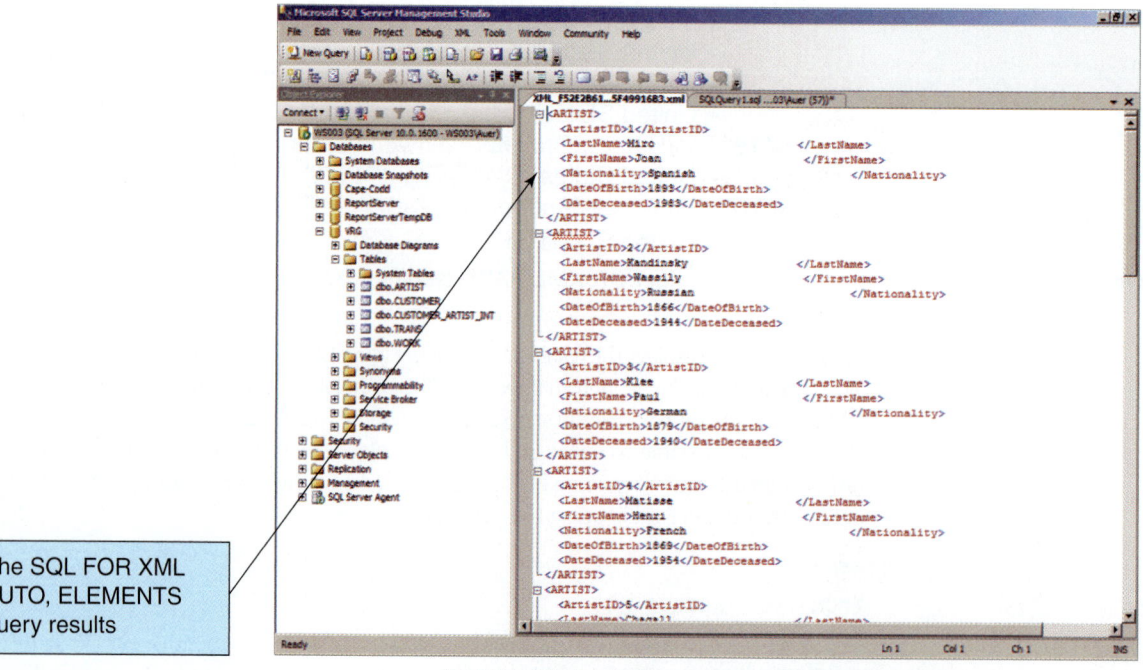

The SQL FOR XML AUTO, ELEMENTS query results

(b) FOR XML AUTO, ELEMENTS Results in the Microsoft SQL Server Management Studio

```xml
<?xml version="1.0" encoding="UTF-8"?>
<MyData xmlns:xsi="http://www.w3.org/2001/XMLSchema-instance"
xsi:noNamespaceSchemaLocation="C:\inetpub\wwwroot\DBP\VRG\DBP-e11-Figure-12-11-D.xsd">
    <ARTIST>
        <ArtistID>1</ArtistID>
        <LastName>Miro              </LastName>
        <FirstName>Joan             </FirstName>
        <Nationality>Spanish            </Nationality>
        <DateOfBirth>1893</DateOfBirth>
        <DateDeceased>1983</DateDeceased>
    </ARTIST>
    <ARTIST>
        <ArtistID>2</ArtistID>
        <LastName>Kandinsky           </LastName>
        <FirstName>Wassily          </FirstName>
        <Nationality>Russian             </Nationality>
        <DateOfBirth>1866</DateOfBirth>
        <DateDeceased>1944</DateDeceased>
    </ARTIST>
    <ARTIST>
        <ArtistID>3</ArtistID>
        <LastName>Klee              </LastName>
        <FirstName>Paul             </FirstName>
        <Nationality>German              </Nationality>
        <DateOfBirth>1879</DateOfBirth>
        <DateDeceased>1940</DateDeceased>
    </ARTIST>
    <ARTIST>
        <ArtistID>4</ArtistID>
        <LastName>Matisse            </LastName>
        <FirstName>Henri            </FirstName>
        <Nationality>French              </Nationality>
        <DateOfBirth>1869</DateOfBirth>
        <DateDeceased>1954</DateDeceased>
    </ARTIST>
    <ARTIST>
        <ArtistID>5</ArtistID>
        <LastName>Chagall            </LastName>
        <FirstName>Marc             </FirstName>
        <Nationality>French              </Nationality>
        <DateOfBirth>1887</DateOfBirth>
        <DateDeceased>1985</DateDeceased>
    </ARTIST>
    <ARTIST>
        <ArtistID>11</ArtistID>
        <LastName>Sargent            </LastName>
        <FirstName>John Singer          </FirstName>
        <Nationality>United States          </Nationality>
        <DateOfBirth>1856</DateOfBirth>
        <DateDeceased>1925</DateDeceased>
    </ARTIST>
    <ARTIST>
        <ArtistID>17</ArtistID>
        <LastName>Tobey              </LastName>
        <FirstName>Mark             </FirstName>
        <Nationality>United States          </Nationality>
        <DateOfBirth>1890</DateOfBirth>
        <DateDeceased>1976</DateDeceased>
    </ARTIST>
```

Figure 12-11

(Continued)

```
<ARTIST>
    <ArtistID>18</ArtistID>
    <LastName>Horiuchi            </LastName>
    <FirstName>Paul            </FirstName>
    <Nationality>United States            </Nationality>
    <DateOfBirth>1906</DateOfBirth>
    <DateDeceased>1999</DateDeceased>
</ARTIST>
<ARTIST>
<ArtistID>19</ArtistID>
    <LastName>Graves            </LastName>
    <FirstName>Morris            </FirstName>
    <Nationality>United States            </Nationality>
    <DateOfBirth>1920</DateOfBirth>
    <DateDeceased>2001</DateDeceased>
</ARTIST>
<ARTIST>
    <ArtistID>20</ArtistID>
    <LastName>Anderson            </LastName>
    <FirstName>Guy            </FirstName>
    <Nationality>United States            </Nationality>
</ARTIST>
</MyData>
```

(c) FOR XML AUTO, ELEMENTS Results in XML Document

```
<?xml version="1.0" encoding="UTF-8"?>
<xs:schema xmlns:xs="http://www.w3.org/2001/XMLSchema" elementFormDefault="qualified"
attributeFormDefault="unqualified">
    <xs:element name="MyData">
        <xs:annotation>
            <xs:documentation>
                This is the XML Schema document for the VRG ARTIST table
            </xs:documentation>
        </xs:annotation>
        <xs:complexType>
            <xs:sequence>
                <xs:element name="ARTIST" maxOccurs="unbounded">
                    <xs:complexType>
                        <xs:sequence>
                            <xs:element name="ArtistID" type="xs:int"/>
                            <xs:element name="LastName"/>
                            <xs:element name="FirstName"/>
                            <xs:element name="Nationality"/>
                            <xs:element name="DateOfBirth" minOccurs="0"/>
                            <xs:element name="DateDeceased" minOccurs="0"/>
                        </xs:sequence>
                    </xs:complexType>
                </xs:element>
            </xs:sequence>
        </xs:complexType>
    </xs:element>
</xs:schema>
```

Figure 12-11

(Continued)

(d) XML Schema

like metadata than data. The means by which this is done is beyond the scope of this discussion. See FOR XML EXPLICIT in the SQL Server documentation for more information.

Multitable SELECT with FOR XML

FOR XML SELECT statements are not limited to single-table SELECTs—they can be applied to joins as well. For example, we can use the following SQL join query to produce a list of VRG customers and the artists they are interesting in:

Figure 12-11

(Continued)

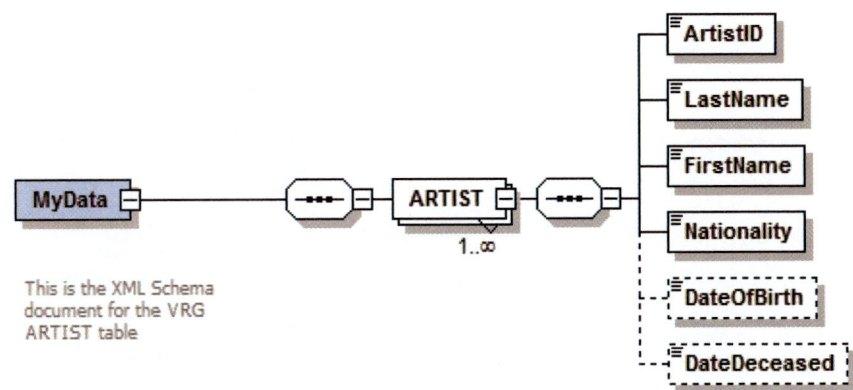

This is the XML Schema
document for the VRG
ARTIST table

(e) Graphical Representation of the XML Schema

```
SELECT      CUSTOMER.LastName AS CustomerLastName,
            CUSTOMER.FirstName AS CustomerFirstName,
            ARTIST.LastName AS ArtistName
FROM        CUSTOMER,
            CUSTOMER_ARTIST_INT ,
            ARTIST
WHERE       CUSTOMER.CustomerID = CUSTOMER_ARTIST_INT.CustomerID
    AND     CUSTOMER_ARTIST_INT.ArtistID = ARTIST.ArtistID
ORDER BY    CUSTOMER.LastName, ARTIST.LastNAme
    FOR     XML AUTO, ELEMENTS;
```

Figure 12-12

FOR XML AUTO, ELEMENTS
Example Displaying
Customer and Artist
Interests

Figure 12-12(a) shows the query in the Microsoft SQL Server Management Studio, and
Figure 12-12(b) shows the full results in a tabbed window. Figure 12-12(c) shows results in
an XML document.

SQL Server uses the order of the tables in the FROM clause to determine the hierarchical
placement of the elements in the generated XML document. Here, the top-level element is

The SQL FOR XML
AUTO, ELEMENTS
query

The SQL FOR XML
AUTO, ELEMENTS
query results—click
this cell to display the
results in a separate
window

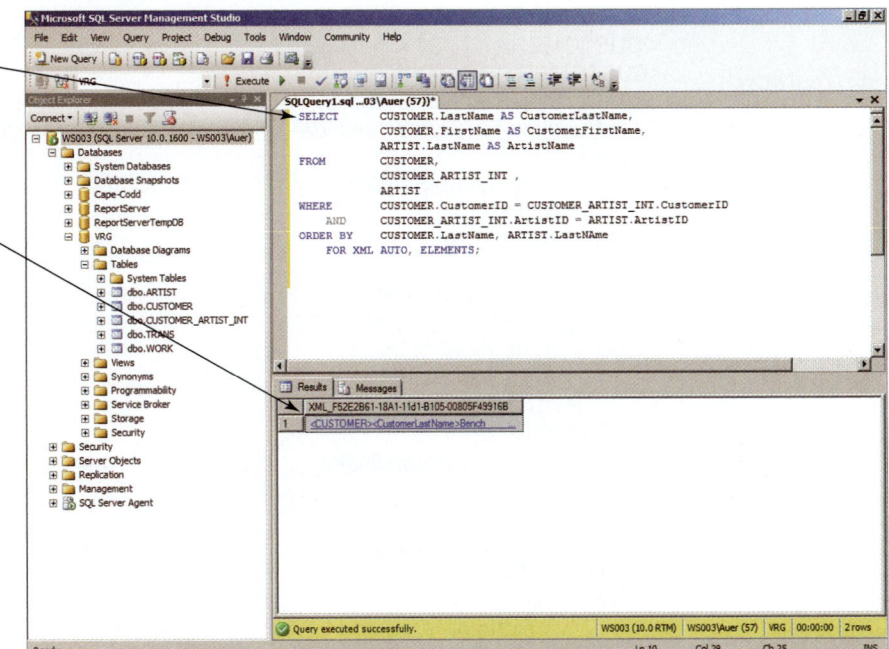

(a) FOR XML AUTO, ELEMENTS Query

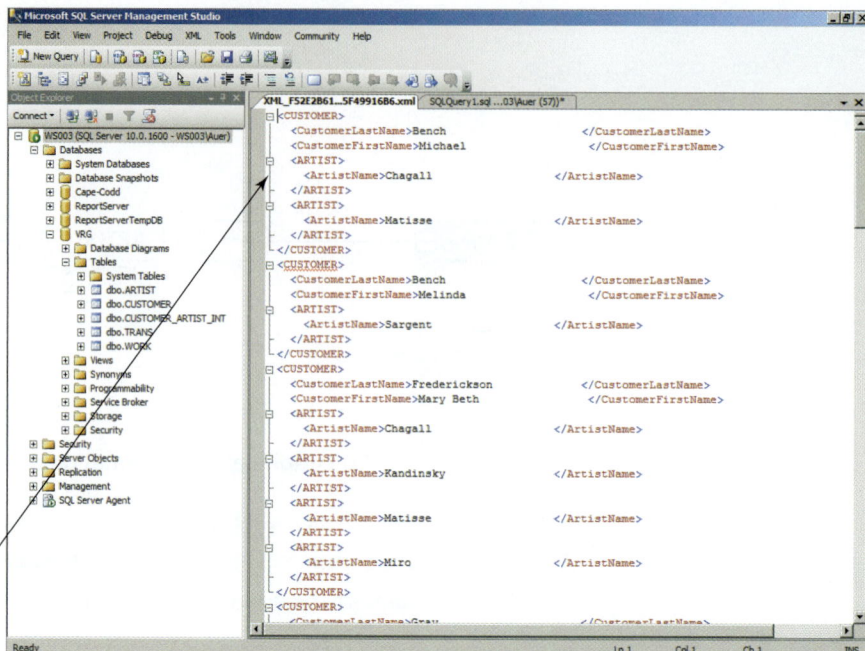

The SQL FOR XML AUTO, ELEMENTS query results

(b) FOR XML AUTO, ELEMENTS Results in the
Microsoft SQL Server Management Studio

```xml
<?xml version="1.0" encoding="UTF-8"?>
<MyData xmlns:xsi="http://www.w3.org/2001/XMLSchema-instance"
xsi:noNamespaceSchemaLocation="C:\inetpub\wwwroot\DBP\VRG\DBP-e11-Figure-12-13-A.xsd">
    <CUSTOMER>
        <CustomerLastName>Bench              </CustomerLastName>
        <CustomerFirstName>Michael            </CustomerFirstName>
        <ARTIST>
            <ArtistName>Chagall          </ArtistName>
        </ARTIST>
        <ARTIST>
            <ArtistName>Matisse          </ArtistName>
        </ARTIST>
    </CUSTOMER>
    <CUSTOMER>
        <CustomerLastName>Bench              </CustomerLastName>
        <CustomerFirstName>Melinda            </CustomerFirstName>
        <ARTIST>
            <ArtistName>Sargent          </ArtistName>
        </ARTIST>
    </CUSTOMER>
    <CUSTOMER>
        <CustomerLastName>Frederickson       </CustomerLastName>
        <CustomerFirstName>Mary Beth          </CustomerFirstName>
        <ARTIST>
            <ArtistName>Chagall          </ArtistName>
        </ARTIST>
        <ARTIST>
            <ArtistName>Kandinsky        </ArtistName>
        </ARTIST>
        <ARTIST>
            <ArtistName>Matisse          </ArtistName>
        </ARTIST>
        <ARTIST>
            <ArtistName>Miro             </ArtistName>
        </ARTIST>
    </CUSTOMER>
```

Figure 12-12
(Continued)

```
<CUSTOMER>
    <CustomerLastName>Gray                </CustomerLastName>
    <CustomerFirstName>Donald              </CustomerFirstName>
    <ARTIST>
        <ArtistName>Graves          </ArtistName>
    </ARTIST>
    <ARTIST>
        <ArtistName>Horiuchi          </ArtistName>
    </ARTIST>
    <ARTIST>
        <ArtistName>Tobey          </ArtistName>
    </ARTIST>
</CUSTOMER>
<CUSTOMER>
    <CustomerLastName>Janes                </CustomerLastName>
    <CustomerFirstName>Jeffrey              </CustomerFirstName>
    <ARTIST>
        <ArtistName>Graves          </ArtistName>
    </ARTIST>
    <ARTIST>
        <ArtistName>Horiuchi          </ArtistName>
    </ARTIST>
    <ARTIST>
        <ArtistName>Tobey          </ArtistName>
    </ARTIST>
</CUSTOMER>
<CUSTOMER>
    <CustomerLastName>Smathers                </CustomerLastName>
    <CustomerFirstName>Fred              </CustomerFirstName>
    <ARTIST>
        <ArtistName>Graves          </ArtistName>
    </ARTIST>
    <ARTIST>
        <ArtistName>Horiuchi          </ArtistName>
    </ARTIST>
    <ARTIST>
        <ArtistName>Tobey          </ArtistName>
    </ARTIST>
</CUSTOMER>
<CUSTOMER>
    <CustomerLastName>Smith                </CustomerLastName>
    <CustomerFirstName>David              </CustomerFirstName>
    <ARTIST>
        <ArtistName>Chagall          </ArtistName>
    </ARTIST>
    <ARTIST>
        <ArtistName>Kandinsky          </ArtistName>
    </ARTIST>
    <ARTIST>
        <ArtistName>Matisse          </ArtistName>
    </ARTIST>
    <ARTIST>
        <ArtistName>Miro          </ArtistName>
    </ARTIST>
    <ARTIST>
        <ArtistName>Sargent          </ArtistName>
    </ARTIST>
</CUSTOMER>
```

Figure 12-12

(Continued)

```
<CUSTOMER>
    <CustomerLastName>Twilight              </CustomerLastName>
    <CustomerFirstName>Tiffany              </CustomerFirstName>
    <ARTIST>
        <ArtistName>Graves          </ArtistName>
    </ARTIST>
    <ARTIST>
        <ArtistName>Horiuchi          </ArtistName>
    </ARTIST>
    <ARTIST>
        <ArtistName>Sargent          </ArtistName>
    </ARTIST>
    <ARTIST>
        <ArtistName>Tobey          </ArtistName>
    </ARTIST>
</CUSTOMER>
<CUSTOMER>
    <CustomerLastName>Warning              </CustomerLastName>
    <CustomerFirstName>Selma              </CustomerFirstName>
    <ARTIST>
        <ArtistName>Chagall          </ArtistName>
    </ARTIST>
    <ARTIST>
        <ArtistName>Graves          </ArtistName>
    </ARTIST>
    <ARTIST>
        <ArtistName>Sargent          </ArtistName>
    </ARTIST>
</CUSTOMER>
<CUSTOMER>
    <CustomerLastName>Wilkens              </CustomerLastName>
    <CustomerFirstName>Chris              </CustomerFirstName>
    <ARTIST>
        <ArtistName>Graves          </ArtistName>
    </ARTIST>
    <ARTIST>
        <ArtistName>Horiuchi          </ArtistName>
    </ARTIST>
    <ARTIST>
        <ArtistName>Tobey          </ArtistName>
    </ARTIST>
</CUSTOMER>
</MyData>
```

Figure 12-12
(Continued)

(c) FOR XML AUTO, ELEMENTS Results in XML Document

CUSTOMER, and the next element is ARTIST. The CUSTOMER_ARTIST_INT table does not appear in the generated document because no column from that table appeared in the SQL SELECT statement.

You can write the expression FOR XML AUTO, XMLDATA to cause SQL Server to produce an XML Schema statement in front of the XML document that it writes. The schema produced, however, involves topics that we will not cover in this chapter, so we will not do that.

An XML Schema for the XML document shown in Figure 12-12(c) is shown in Figure 12-13(a), and Figure 12-13(b) shows the graphical display of this same schema. Observe that the MyData element can have an unbounded number of CUSTOMER elements, and each CUSTOMER can have an unbounded number of ARTIST elements, one for each artist interest. In this figure, the notation $1..\infty$ means that at least one CUSTOMER is required and an unlimited number will be allowed.

An XML Schema for All CUSTOMER Purchases

Suppose now that we want to produce a document that has all of the customer purchase data. To do that, we need to join CUSTOMER to TRANS to WORK to ARTIST and select the appropriate data. The following SQL statement produces the required data:

```
SELECT        CUSTOMER.CustomerID,

              CUSTOMER.LastName AS CustomerLastName,

              CUSTOMER.FirstName AS CustomerFirstName,

              TRANS.TransactionID, SalesPrice,

              WORK.WorkID, Title, Copy,

              ARTIST.ArtistID, ARTIST.LastName AS ArtistName

FROM          CUSTOMER, TRANS, [WORK], ARTIST

WHERE         CUSTOMER.CustomerID = TRANS.CustomerID

    AND       TRANS.WorkID = WORK.WorkID

    AND       WORK.ArtistID = ARTIST.ArtistID

ORDER BY      CUSTOMER.LastName, ARTIST.LastName

    FOR       XML AUTO, ELEMENTS;
```

Figure 12-13

Customer and Artist
Interests

```
<?xml version="1.0" encoding="UTF-8"?>
<xs:schema xmlns:xs="http://www.w3.org/2001/XMLSchema" elementFormDefault="qualified"
attributeFormDefault="unqualified">
    <xs:element name="MyData">
        <xs:annotation>
            <xs:documentation>
                This XML Schema is for the VRG Customer Artist Interest data
                generated by an SQL XML FOR AUTO, ELEMENTS query
            </xs:documentation>
        </xs:annotation>
        <xs:complexType>
            <xs:sequence>
                <xs:element name="CUSTOMER" maxOccurs="unbounded">
                    <xs:complexType>
                        <xs:sequence>
                            <xs:element name="CustomerLastName"/>
                            <xs:element name="CustomerFirstName"/>
                            <xs:element name="ARTIST" minOccurs="0" maxOccurs="unbounded">
                                <xs:complexType>
                                    <xs:sequence>
                                        <xs:element name="ArtistName"/>
                                    </xs:sequence>
                                </xs:complexType>
                            </xs:element>
                        </xs:sequence>
                    </xs:complexType>
                </xs:element>
            </xs:sequence>
        </xs:complexType>
    </xs:element>
</xs:schema>
```

(a) XML Schema

This XML Schema is for the
VRG Customer Artist
Interest data generated by
an SQL XML FOR AUTO,
ELEMENTS query

(b) Graphical Representation of the XML Schema

Figure 12-14(a) shows the query in the Microsoft SQL Server Management Studio, and Figure 12-14(b) shows the full results in a tabbed window. Figure 12-14(c) shows *partial* results in an XML document (this is a very long xml document).

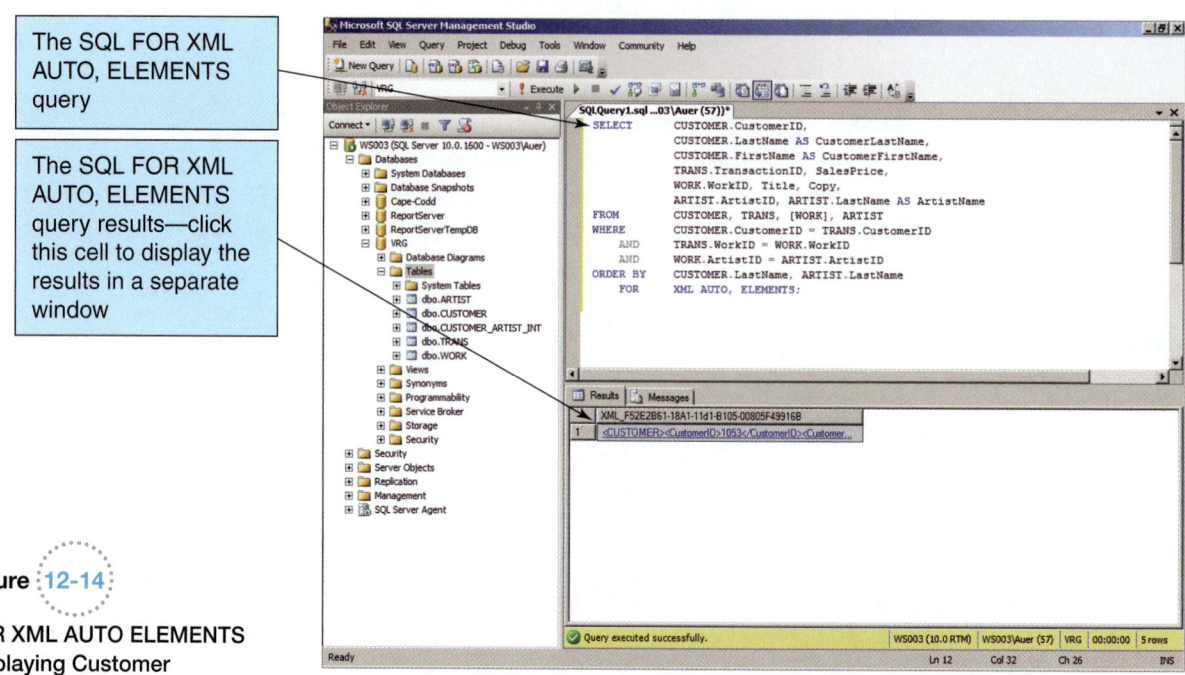

The SQL FOR XML AUTO, ELEMENTS query

The SQL FOR XML AUTO, ELEMENTS query results—click this cell to display the results in a separate window

Figure 12-14

FOR XML AUTO ELEMENTS Displaying Customer Purchases

(a) FOR XML AUTO, ELEMENTS Query

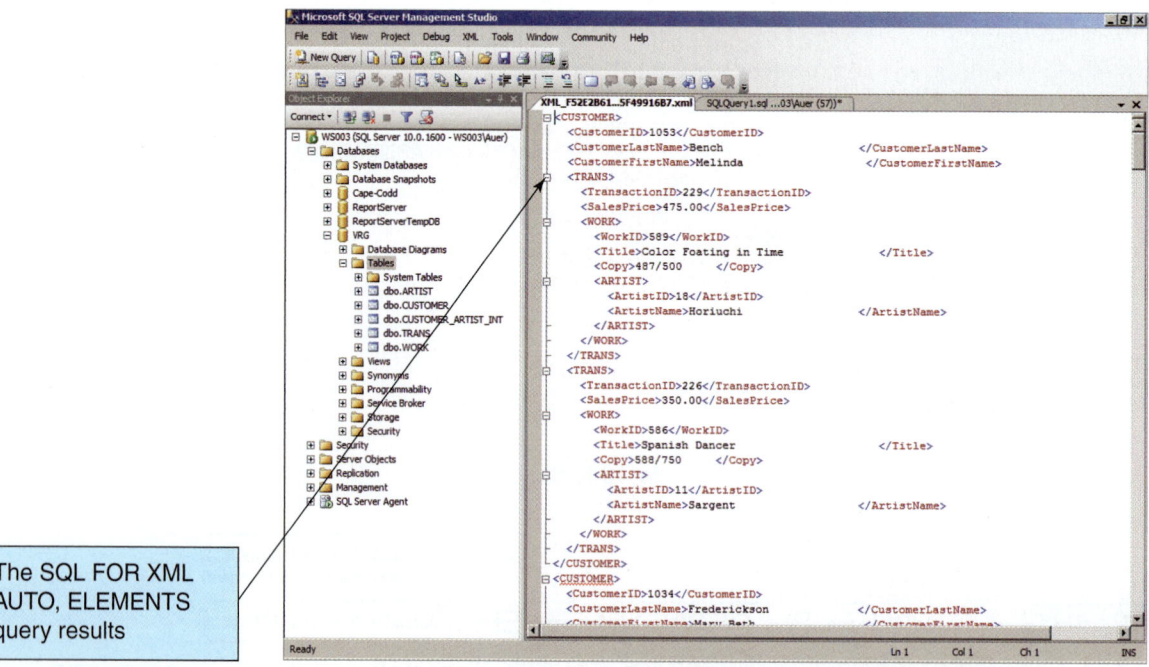

The SQL FOR XML AUTO, ELEMENTS query results

(b) FOR XML AUTO, ELEMENTS Results in the Microsoft SQL Server Management Studio

```
<?xml version="1.0" encoding="UTF-8"?>
<MyData xmlns:xsi="http://www.w3.org/2001/XMLSchema-instance"
xsi:noNamespaceSchemaLocation="C:\inetpub\wwwroot\DBP\VRG\DBP-e11-Figure-12-15-A.xsd">
    <CUSTOMER>
        <CustomerID>1053</CustomerID>
        <CustomerLastName>Bench              </CustomerLastName>
        <CustomerFirstName>Melinda              </CustomerFirstName>
        <TRANS>
            <TransactionID>229</TransactionID>
            <SalesPrice>475.00</SalesPrice>
            <WORK>
                <WorkID>589</WorkID>
                <Title>Color Foating in Time         </Title>
                <Copy>487/500     </Copy>
                <ARTIST>
                    <ArtistID>18</ArtistID>
                    <ArtistName>Horiuchi          </ArtistName>
                </ARTIST>
            </WORK>
        </TRANS>
        <TRANS>
            <TransactionID>226</TransactionID>
            <SalesPrice>350.00</SalesPrice>
            <WORK>
                <WorkID>586</WorkID>
                <Title>Spanish Dancer              </Title>
                <Copy>588/750     </Copy>
                <ARTIST>
                    <ArtistID>11</ArtistID>
                    <ArtistName>Sargent            </ArtistName>
                </ARTIST>
            </WORK>
        </TRANS>
    </CUSTOMER>
    <CUSTOMER>
        <CustomerID>1034</CustomerID>
        <CustomerLastName>Frederickson        </CustomerLastName>
        <CustomerFirstName>Mary Beth            </CustomerFirstName>
        <TRANS>
            <TransactionID>105</TransactionID>
            <SalesPrice>400.00</SalesPrice>
            <WORK>
                <WorkID>524</WorkID>
                <Title>Woman with a Hat          </Title>
                <Copy>596/750     </Copy>
                <ARTIST>
                    <ArtistID>4</ArtistID>
                    <ArtistName>Matisse            </ArtistName>
                </ARTIST>
            </WORK>
        </TRANS>
        <TRANS>
        <TransactionID>127</TransactionID>
        <SalesPrice>400.00</SalesPrice>
        <WORK>
            <WorkID>553</WorkID>
            <Title>The Dance                </Title>
            <Copy>734/1000     </Copy>
            <ARTIST>
                <ArtistID>4</ArtistID>
                <ArtistName>Matisse          </ArtistName>
            </ARTIST>
        </WORK>
        </TRANS>
```

Figure 12-14

(Continued)

```
<TRANS>
    <TransactionID>103</TransactionID>
    <SalesPrice>400.00</SalesPrice>
    <WORK>
        <WorkID>522</WorkID>
        <Title>La Lecon de Ski          </Title>
        <Copy>353/500    </Copy>
        <ARTIST>
            <ArtistID>1</ArtistID>
            <ArtistName>Miro           </ArtistName>
        </ARTIST>
    </WORK>
</TRANS>
</CUSTOMER>
```

Figure 12-14
(Continued)

(c) FOR XML AUTO, ELEMENTS Partial Results in XML Document

Figure 12-15(a) shows an XML Schema document for this SQL statement, and a graphical view of it is shown in Figure 12-15(b). According to the XML Schema in Figure 12-15(b), a CUSTOMER has from zero to unlimited TRANS elements, a TRANS element has exactly one WORK element, and a WORK element has exactly one ARTIST element.

A Schema with Two Multivalue Paths

Suppose now that we want to construct an XML document that has all of the View Ridge Gallery customer data. We cannot construct such a view from a single SQL statement because it has two multivalued paths. We need one SQL statement to obtain all of the customer purchase data and a second SQL statement to obtain all of the customer/artist interests.

XML Schema does not have this limitation, however. An XML document may have as many multivalued paths as the application requires. In our case, all we need to do is to combine the schemas in Figure 12-13(a) and Figure 12-15(a). While we're at it, we can also add the surrogate keys for each of the underlying tables.

The result of combining these results (using cut and paste in XMLSpy!) is shown in Figure 12-16. Observe that in Figure 12-16(b) MyData may have from one to an unlimited number of CUSTOMER elements, and that each such element may have from zero to many TRANS and from zero to many ArtistInterests elements. All of the simple elements in this schema are required.

Why Is XML Important?

At this point, you should have some idea of the nature of XML and the XML standards. You know that XML makes a clear separation between structure, content, and materialization. Structure is defined by either a DTD or an XML Schema document. Content is expressed in an XML document, and the materializations of a document are expressed in an XSL document. You also understand that SQL statements can be used to create XML documents, but only as long as those documents involve at most one multivalue path. If more than one such path exists in the document, multiple SQL statements need to be issued to fill the document in some fashion.

You may be asking, "These are interesting ideas, but why do they matter? What's so important about all of this?" The answer to these questions is that XML processing provides a standardized facility to describe, validate, and materialize any database view.

Consider the View Ridge Gallery. Suppose that the gallery wants to share all of its customer data with another gallery, maybe because of a joint sales program. If both galleries agree on an XML Schema like the one shown in Figure 12-17, they can prepare customer data documents in accordance with that schema. Before sending a document, they can run an automated process to validate the document against the schema. In this way, only correct data are transmitted. Of course, this process works in both directions. Not only can View Ridge ensure that it is sending only valid documents; by validating the documents it

```
<?xml version="1.0" encoding="UTF-8"?>
<xs:schema xmlns:xs="http://www.w3.org/2001/XMLSchema" elementFormDefault="qualified"
attributeFormDefault="unqualified">
    <xs:element name="MyData">
        <xs:annotation>
            <xs:documentation>
                This XML Schema is for the VRG Customer Purchase data generated
                by an SQL XML FOR AUTO, ELEMENTS query
            </xs:documentation>
        </xs:annotation>
        <xs:complexType>
            <xs:sequence>
                <xs:element name="CUSTOMER" maxOccurs="unbounded">
                    <xs:complexType>
                        <xs:sequence>
                            <xs:element name="CustomerID" type="xs:int"/>
                            <xs:element name="CustomerLastName"/>
                            <xs:element name="CustomerFirstName"/>
                            <xs:element name="TRANS" minOccurs="0" maxOccurs="unbounded">
                                <xs:complexType>
                                    <xs:sequence>
                                        <xs:element name="TransactionID" type="xs:int"/>
                                        <xs:element name="SalesPrice"/>
                                        <xs:element name="WORK">
                                            <xs:complexType>
                                                <xs:sequence>
                                                    <xs:element name="WorkID" type="xs:int"/>
                                                    <xs:element name="Title"/>
                                                    <xs:element name="Copy"/>
                                                    <xs:element name="ARTIST">
                                                        <xs:complexType>
                                                            <xs:sequence>
                                                                <xs:element name="ArtistID" type="xs:int"/>
                                                                <xs:element name="ArtistName"/>
                                                            </xs:sequence>
                                                        </xs:complexType>
                                                    </xs:element>
                                                </xs:sequence>
                                            </xs:complexType>
                                        </xs:element>
                                    </xs:sequence>
                                </xs:complexType>
                            </xs:element>
                        </xs:sequence>
                    </xs:complexType>
                </xs:element>
            </xs:sequence>
        </xs:complexType>
    </xs:element>
</xs:schema>
```

(a) XML Schema

Figure 12-15

Customer Purchases

receives it can ensure that it is receiving only valid documents. Best of all, the programs for document validation are publicly available and free to the galleries. The galleries do not need to write program code for validation.

Additionally, each gallery can develop its own set of XSL documents to materialize the customer data documents in whatever ways they want. View Ridge can develop one XSL document to display the data on a customer's computer, another to display it on salespersons' computers, another to display it on mobile devices when art buyers are on the road, and so forth. Given these XSLs, customer data can be displayed regardless of whether it came from one gallery or the other.

Now, broaden this idea from two small businesses to an industry. Suppose, for example, that the real estate industry agrees on an XML Schema document for property listings. Every real

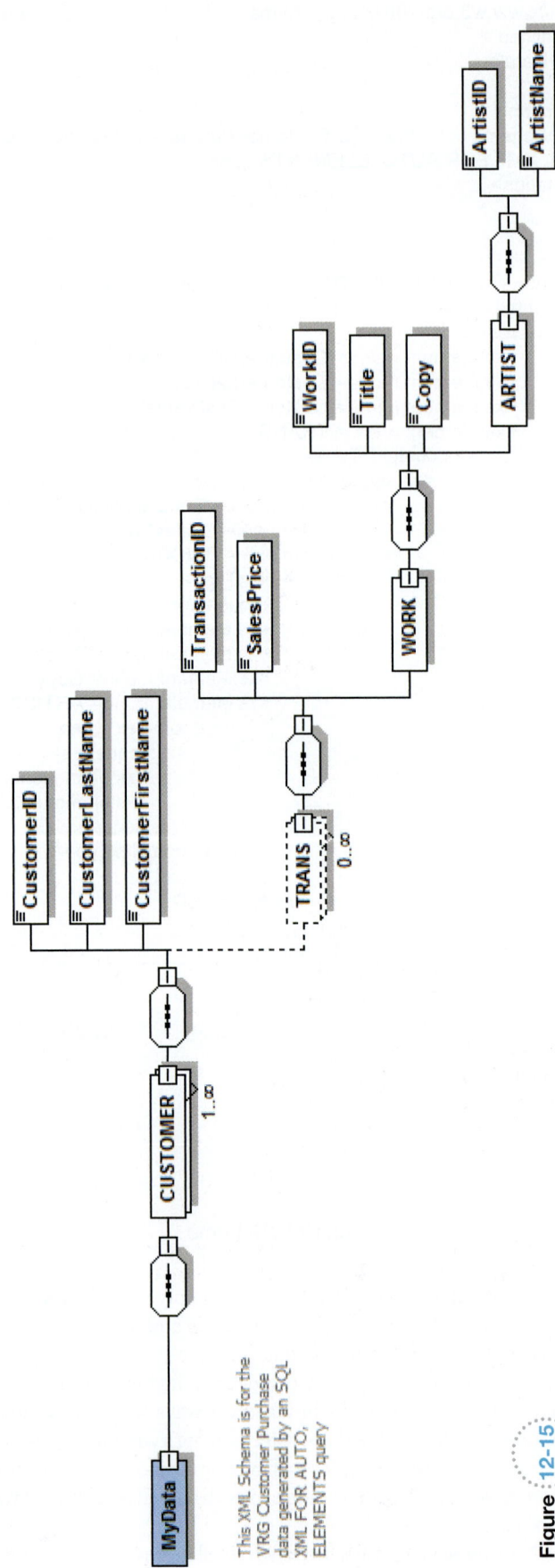

This XML Schema is for the
VRG Customer Purchase
data generated by an SQL
XML FOR AUTO,
ELEMENTS query

(b) Graphical Representation of the XML Schema

Figure 12-15

(Continued)

```xml
<?xml version="1.0" encoding="UTF-8"?>
<!-- edited with XMLSpy v2006 rel. 3 sp2 (http://www.altova.com) by David Auer (David J. Auer Consultation and
Training) -->
<xs:schema xmlns:xs="http://www.w3.org/2001/XMLSchema" elementFormDefault="qualified"
attributeFormDefault="unqualified">
    <xs:element name="MyData">
        <xs:annotation>
            <xs:documentation>
                This XML Schema is for VRG Customer data with two multivalue paths
            </xs:documentation>
        </xs:annotation>
        <xs:complexType>
            <xs:sequence>
                <xs:element name="CUSTOMER" maxOccurs="unbounded">
                    <xs:complexType>
                        <xs:sequence>
                            <xs:element name="CustomerID" type="xs:int"/>
                            <xs:element name="LastName"/>
                            <xs:element name="FirstName"/>
                            <xs:element name="TRANS" minOccurs="0" maxOccurs="unbounded">
                                <xs:complexType>
                                    <xs:sequence>
                                        <xs:element name="TransactionID" type="xs:int"/>
                                        <xs:element name="SalesPrice"/>
                                        <xs:element name="WORK">
                                            <xs:complexType>
                                                <xs:sequence>
                                                    <xs:element name="WorkID" type="xs:int"/>
                                                    <xs:element name="Title"/>
                                                    <xs:element name="Copy"/>
                                                    <xs:element name="ARTIST">
                                                        <xs:complexType>
                                                            <xs:sequence>
                                                                <xs:element name="ArtistID" type="xs:int"/>
                                                                <xs:element name="LastName"/>
                                                                <xs:element name="FirstName"/>
                                                            </xs:sequence>
                                                        </xs:complexType>
                                                    </xs:element>
                                                </xs:sequence>
                                            </xs:complexType>
                                        </xs:element>
                                    </xs:sequence>
                                </xs:complexType>
                            </xs:element>
                            <xs:element name="ArtistInterests" minOccurs="0" maxOccurs="unbounded">
                                <xs:complexType>
                                    <xs:sequence>
                                        <xs:element name="ArtistID" type="xs:int"/>
                                        <xs:element name="LastName"/>
                                        <xs:element name="LastName"/>
                                        <xs:element name="Nationality"/>
                                        <xs:element name="DateOfBirth"" minOccurs="0"/>
                                        <xs:element name="DateDeceased"" minOccurs="0"/>
                                    </xs:sequence>
                                </xs:complexType>
                            </xs:element>
                        </xs:sequence>
                    </xs:complexType>
                </xs:element>
            </xs:sequence>
        </xs:complexType>
    </xs:element>
</xs:schema>
```

(a) XML Schema

Figure 12-16

View Ridge Gallery
Customer View with Two
Multivalue Paths

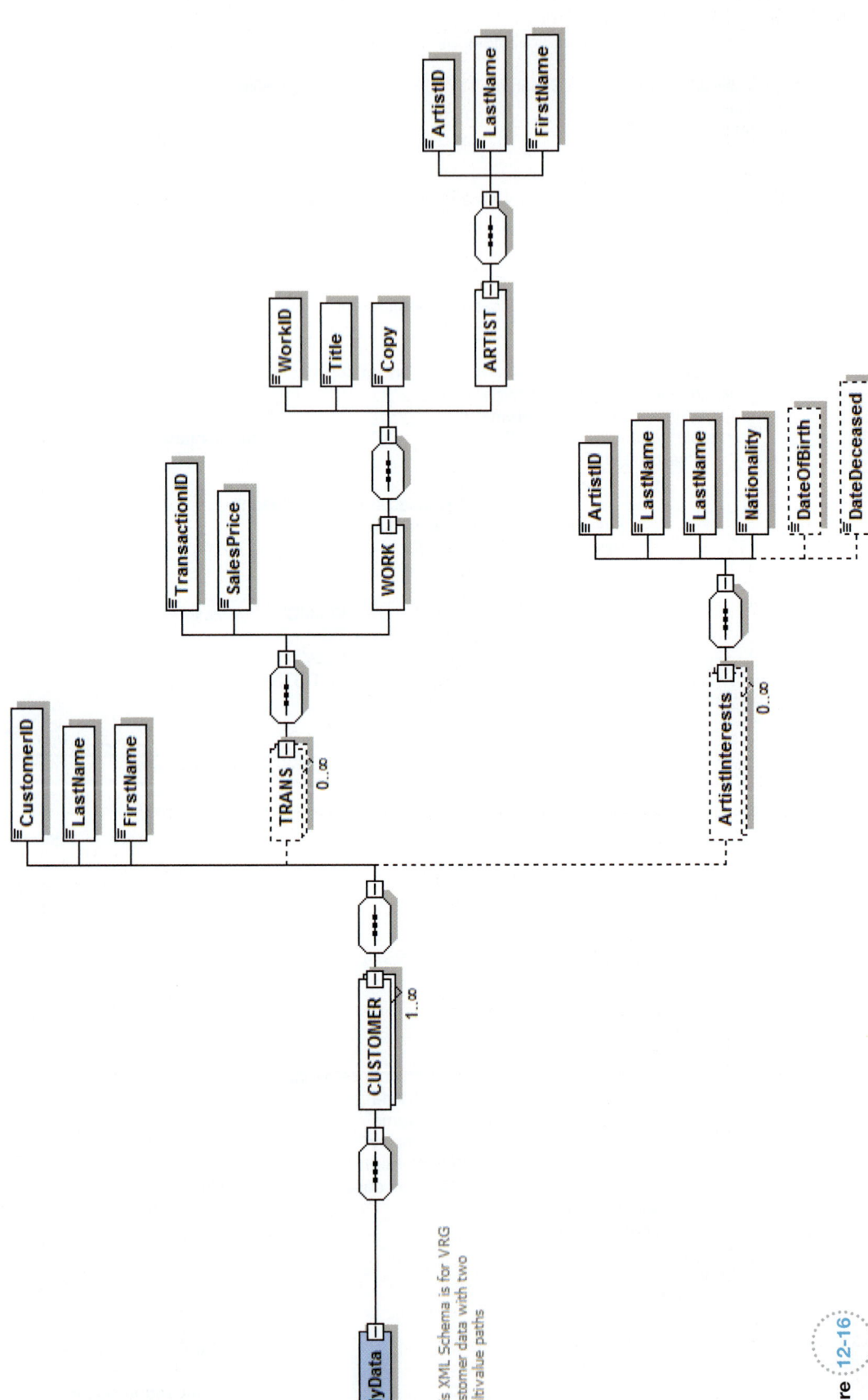

This XML Schema is for VRG
Customer data with two
multivalue paths

(b) Graphical Representation of the XML Schema

Figure 12-16
(Continued)

Industry Type	Example Standards
Accounting	• American Institute of Certified Public Accountants (AICPA): Extensible Financial Reporting Markup Language (XFRML) [OASIS Cover page] • Open Applications Group, Inc (OAG)
Architecture and Construction	• Architecture, Engineering, and Construction XML Working Group (aecXML Working Group) • ConSource.com: Construction Manufacturing and Distribution Extensible Markup Language (cmdXML)
Automotive	• Automotive Industry Action Group (AIAG) • Global Automedia • MSR: Standards for Information Exchange in the Engineering Process (MEDOC) • The Society of Automotive Engineers (SAE): XML for the Automotive Industry–SAE J2008 [OASIS Cover page] • Open Applications Group, Inc (OAG)
Banking	• Banking Industry Technology Secretariat (BITS): [OASIS Cover page] • Financial Services Technology Consortium (FSTC): Bank Internet Payment System (BIPS) [OASIS Cover page] • Open Applications Group, Inc (OAG)
Electronic Data Interchange	• Data Interchange Standards Association (DISA): [OASIS Cover page] • EEMA EDI/EC Work Group[OASIS Cover page] • European Committee for Standardization/Information Society Standardization System (CEN/ISSS; The European XML/EDI Pilot Project) [OASIS Cover page] • XML/EDI Group [OASIS Cover page]
Human Resources	• DataMain: Human Resources Markup Language (hrml) • HR-XML Consortium [OASIS Cover page]: JobPosting, CandidateProfile, Resume • Open Applications Group (OAG): Open Applications Group Interface Specification (OASIS) [OASIS Cover page] • Tapestry.Net: JOB Markup Language (JOB) • Open Applications Group, Inc (OAG)
Insurance	• ACORD: Property and Casualty [OASIS Cover page], Life (XMLife) [OASIS Cover page] • Lexica: iLingo

Figure 12-17

Example XML Industry Standards

estate company that can produce data in the format of the schema can then exchange listings with every other real estate company. Given the schema, each company can ensure that it is transmitting valid documents, and it can also ensure that it is receiving valid documents. Further, each company can develop its own set of XSL documents to materialize property listings in whatever way it wants. Once the XSL documents have been prepared, any listing from any participating agent can be displayed in the local agency's materializations. Figure 12-17 lists some XML standards work that is under way in various industries.

For another example, consider business-to-business e-commerce. Suppose that Wal-Mart wants to send orders to its vendors in a particular standardized format and that it wants to receive shipment responses to those orders in another particular standardized format. To do this, Wal-Mart can develop an XML Schema for Order documents and another for Shipment documents. It can then publish those XML Schemas on a Web site accessible to its vendors. In this way, all vendors can determine how they will receive orders from Wal-Mart and how they should send their Shipment notifications back.

Industry Type	Example Standards
Real Estate	• OpenMLS: Real Estate Listing Management System (OpenMLS) [OASIS Cover page] • Real Estate Transaction Standard working group (RETS): Real Estate Transaction Standard (RETS) [OASIS Cover page]
Software	• IBM: [OASIS Cover page] • Flashline.com: Software Component Documentation DTD • Flashline.com • INRIA: Koala Bean Markup Language (KBML) [OASIS Cover page] • Marimba and Microsoft: Open Software Description Format (OSD) [OASIS Cover page] • Object Management Group (OMG) [OASIS Cover page]
Workflow	• Internet Engineering Task Force (IETF): Simple Workflow Access Protocol (SWAP) [OASIS Cover page] • Workflow Management Coalition (MfMC): Wf-XML [OASIS Cover page]

Figure 12-17

(Continued)

The schemas can be used by Wal-Mart and all of its vendors to ensure that they are sending and receiving only valid XML documents. Further, Wal-Mart can develop XSL documents to cause the Order and Shipment documents to be transformed into the specific formats needed by its accounting, operations, marketing, and general management departments.

These XSL documents work for any Order or Shipment from any of its vendors. In all of these cases, once the XML Schema documents have been prepared and the XSL documents have been written, all validation and materialization is done via automated processes. Thus, there is no need for any human to touch the Order document between its origination at Wal-Mart and the picking of the inventory at the supplier.

So, the only challenge that remains is to populate the XML documents with database data in accordance with the relevant XML Schema. SQL can be used to populate schemas that have only one multivalue path, but this is too restrictive, and newer technologies like ADO.NET ease the transformation of database data into XML documents. SQL can also be used to ease the transformation of XML documents into database data.

Additional XML Standards

As you know, XML was developed as a series of standards. So far, we have mentioned XML, XSL, XSLT, and XML Schema. There are a number of other XML standards that you may encounter, and some of these are listed in Figure 12-18. You can find the standards, their documentation, and some tutorials on the *www.w3.org* and *www.xml.org* Web sites.

In addition to the four standards discussed in this chapter, XPath is a standard for addressing elements within documents. In Figure 12-4, expressions like

```
<xsl: value-of-select = "name/lastname"/>
```

use XPath to locate a particular element in the document. XPath includes concepts from another standard, XPointer, which was developed to provide a sophisticated means for documents to reference elements in other documents.

SAX and *DOM* refer to different methods of parsing XML documents. The process of parsing consists of reading a document, breaking it into components, and responding to those components in some way—perhaps storing them into a database. XML parsers also validate documents against the DTDs and XML Schemas.

To use the SAX API, a program that is working on an XML document—an XSLT processor, for example—invokes the SAX-compliant parser and passes it the name of the document to

Standard	Description
XML	Extensible Markup Language. A document markup language that started the following:
XSL	XSLT Stylesheet. The document that provides the {match, action} pairs and other data for XSLT to use when transforming an XML document.
XSLT	A program (or process) that applies XSLT Stylesheets to an XML document to produce a transformed XML document.
XML Schema	An XML-compliant language for constraining the structure of an XML document. Extends and replaces DTDs. Under development and *very* important to database processing.
XPath	A sublanguage within XSLT that is used to identify parts of an XML document to be transformed. Can also be used for calculations and string manipulation. Comingled with XSLT.
XPointer	A standard for linking one document to another. XPath has many elements from XPointer.
SAX	Simple API (application program interface) for XML. An event-based parser that notifies a program when the elements of an XML document have been encountered during document parsing.
DOM	Document Object Model. An API that represents an XML document as a tree. Each node of the tree represents a piece of the XML document. A program can directly access and manipulate a node of the DOM representation.
XQuery	A standard for expressing database queries as XML documents. The structure of the query uses XPath facilities, and the result of the query is represented in an XML format. Under development and likely to be important in the future.
XML Namespaces	A standard for allocating terminology to defined collections. X:Name is interpreted as the element Name as defined in namespace X. Y:Name is interpreted as the element Name as defined in namespace Y. Useful for disambiguating terms.

Figure 12-18

Important XML
Standards

parse. The SAX parser processes the document and calls back objects within the XSLT processor whenever particular structures are encountered. A SAX parser, for example, calls the XSLT parser when it encounters a new element, passing the name of the element, its content, and other relevant items.

The DOM API works from a different paradigm. A DOM-compliant parser processes the entire XML document and then creates a tree representation of it. Each element of the document is a node on the tree. The XSLT processor can then call the DOM parser to obtain particular elements using XPath or a similar addressing scheme. DOM requires the entire document to be processed at one time and may require an unreasonable amount of storage for very large documents. If the document is large, SAX is the better choice. However, if all of the document contents need to be available for use at once, DOM is the only choice.

XQuery is an emerging standard for expressing generalized queries on XML documents. You can think of XQuery as SQL for XML documents. When it becomes available, this standard will be very important to the database/XML world. Visit *www.w3.org/XML/Query/* for more on XQuery.

The last XML standard we will mention, XML Namespaces, is very important because it is used to combine different vocabularies into the same XML Schema. It can be used to define and support domains and to disambiguate terms. The need for the latter occurs when a document contains synonyms. For example, consider a document that has two different uses for the term *Instrument*. Suppose that one use of this term refers to musical instruments and has subelements {Manufacturer, Model, Material}, as in {Horner, Bflat Clarinet, Wood}, and a second use of this term refers to electronic instruments and has subelements {Manufacturer, Model, Voltage}, as in {RadioShack, Ohm-meter, 12-volt}. The author of the XML Schema for such a document can define two different namespaces that each contain one of these definition. Then, the complexType definition for each of these definitions of Instrument can be prefixed by the label of the namespace, as was done in our schema documents when we used the label xsd. There is more to XML Namespaces, and you will undoubtedly learn more as you work with XML.

The XML Standards Committee continues its important work, and more standards will be developed as the needs arise. At present, work is underway for developing security standards. Keep checking *www.w3.org* for more information.

Summary

The confluence of database processing and document processing is one of the most important developments in information systems technology today. Database processing and document processing need each other. Database processing needs document processing for the representation and materialization of database views. Document processing needs database processing for the permanent storage of data.

SGML is as important to document processing as the relational model is to database processing. XML is a series of standards that were developed jointly by the database processing and document processing communities. XML provides a standardized yet customizable way to describe the contents of documents. XML documents can automatically be generated from database data, and database data can be automatically extracted from XML documents.

Although XML can be used to materialize Web pages, this is one of its least important uses. More important is its use for describing, representing, and materializing database views. XML is on the leading edge of database processing; see *www.w3.org* and *www.xml.org* for the latest developments.

XML is a better markup language than HTML, primarily because XML provides a clear separation between document structure, content, and materialization. Also, XML tags are not ambiguous.

The content of XML documents can be described by Document Type Declarations (DTDs) and by XML Schemas. An XML document that conforms to its DTD is called type-valid. A document can be well formed and not be type-valid, either because it violates the structure of its DTD or because it has no DTD.

XML documents are transformed when an XSLT processor applies an XSL document to the XML document. A common transformation is to convert the XML document into HTML format. In the future, other transformations will

be more important. For example, XSL documents can be written to transform the same Order document into different formats needed by different departments, say for sales, accounting, or production. XSLT processing is context oriented; given a particular context, an action is taken when a particular item is located. Today, most browsers have built-in XSLT processors.

XML Schema is a standard for describing the content of an XML document. XML Schema can be used to define custom vocabularies. Documents that conform to an XML Schema are called schema-valid. Unlike DTDs, XML Schema documents are themselves XML documents and can be validated against their schema, which is maintained by W3C.

Schemas consist of elements and attributes. There are two types of elements: simple and complex. Simple elements have one data value. ComplexType elements can have multiple elements nested within them. ComplexTypes may also have attributes. The elements contained in a ComplexType may be simple or other ComplexTypes. ComplexTypes may also define element sequences. A good rule of thumb is that elements represent data and attributes represent metadata, although this is not part of any XML standard.

XML Schemas (and documents) may have more structure than the columns of a table. Groups, such as Phone and Address, can be defined. An XML Schema that has all elements at the same level is a flat schema. Structured schemas are those that have defined subgroups, such as Phone and Address. To avoid definition duplication, elements can be defined globally. Duplication is undesirable because there is the risk that definitions will become inconsistent if a change is made to one definition and not the other.

Oracle, SQL Server, and MySQL can produce XML documents from database data. The Oracle facilities require the use of Java; see *www.oracle.com* for more information. SQL Server supports an add-on expression to the SQL SELECT statement, the FOR XML expression. FOR XML can be used to produce XML documents in which all data are expressed as attributes or as elements. FOR XML can also write an XML Schema description as well as the XML document. Using FOR XML EXPLICIT, the developer can place some columns into elements and others into attributes.

When interpreting multitable selects, the FOR XML processor uses the order of the tables to determine the hierarchical order of elements in the document. FOR XML can be used to produce XML documents with one multivalue path. Documents with more than one multivalue path must be patched together in the application by some means.

XML is important because it facilitates the sharing of XML documents (and hence database data) among organizations. After an XML Schema has been defined, organizations can ensure that they are receiving and sending only schema-valid documents. Additionally, XSL documents can be coded to transform any schema-valid XML document, from any source, into other standardized formats. These advantages become even more important as industry groups standardize their own XML Schemas. XML also facilitates business-to-business processing. This chapter concludes with a brief description of additional XML standards: XPath, SAX, DOM, XQuery, and XML Namespaces.

Key Terms

document type declaration (DTD)
Extensible Markup Language (XML)
not-type-valid
Simple Object Access Protocol
SOAP
SQL SELECT . . . FOR XML statement

Standard Generalized Markup Language (SGML)
structured schemas
stylesheet
type-valid
XML Schema

Review Questions

12.1 Why do database processing and document processing need each other?

12.2 How are HTML, SGML, and XML related?

12.3 Explain the phrase "standardized but customizable."

12.4 What is SOAP? What did it stand for originally? What does it stand for today?

12.5 What are the problems in interpreting a tag such as <h2> in HTML?

12.6 What is a DTD, and what purpose does it serve?

12.7 What is the difference between a well-formed XML document and a type-valid XML document?

12.8 Why is it too limiting to say that XML is just the next version of HTML?

12.9 How are XML, XSL, and XSLT related?

12.10 Explain the use of the pattern {item, action} in the processing of an XSL document.

12.11 What is the purpose of XML Schema?

12.12 How does XML Schema differ from DTD?

12.13 What is a schema-valid document?

12.14 Explain the chicken-and-egg problem concerning the validation of XML Schema documents.

12.15 Explain the difference between simple and complex elements.

12.16 Explain the difference between elements and attributes.

12.17 What is a good basic rule for using elements and attributes to represent database data?

12.18   Give an example, other than one in this text, of a flat XML Schema.

12.19   Give an example, other than one in this text, of a structured XML Schema.

12.20   What is the purpose of global elements?

12.21   What requirement is necessary for processing XML documents with Oracle?

12.22   Explain the difference between FOR XML RAW and FOR XML AUTO, ELEMENTS.

12.23   When would you use FOR XML EXPLICIT?

12.24   What is the importance of the order of tables in a SQL statement that uses FOR XML?

12.25   Explain, in your own words, why SQL with FOR XML cannot be used to construct an XML document having two multivalue paths.

12.26   Why is the limitation in Review Question 12.25 important?

12.27   Explain, in your own words, why XML is important to database processing.

12.28   Why is XML Schema important for interorganizational document sharing?

12.29   What is XPath?

12.30   How does DOM differ from SAX?

12.31   What is XQuery? What is it used for?

12.32   What is XML Namespaces? What is its purpose?

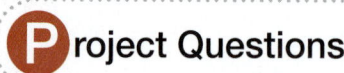 **roject Questions**

12.33   Create a DTD and XML document like that shown in Figure 12-1 to represent the first row in the ARTIST table (see Figure 7-12).

12.34   Using Figure 12-4 as an example, create an XSL document to materialize the document in your answer to Question 12.1. Materialize your document using a browser.

12.35   Create an XML Schema document for a row of TRANS. Place TransactionID as an attribute. Group acquisition data into a complexType, and group sales data into a second complexType. Use Figure 12-7 as an example.

12.36   Create an XML Schema for artists and the customers who are interested in them. Use Figure 12-13 as an example.

12.37   Create an XML Schema for artist, work, transaction, and customer data. Use Figure 12-15 as an example and include your answer to Project Question 12.35 in the schema.

12.38   Create an XML Schema for all artist data. Use Figure 12-16 and your answer from Project Question 12.35.

If you have not already done so, answer parts A through G for Marcia's Dry Cleaning at the end of Chapter 7 (page 293). Use SQL Server, Oracle, or MySQL.

A. Using Figure 12-1 as an example, create an XML document with a DTD for a row of the CUSTOMER table.

B. Using Figure 12-4 as an example, create an XSL document to materialize the document you created in part A. Show your document in a browser.

C. Create an XML Schema document for a join of CUSTOMER and ORDER data. Assume that the document has one customer and from zero to many orders for that customer. Use Figure 12-13 as an example.

D. Write an SQL statement with FOR XML that will produce the document you created in part C.

E. Create an XML Schema document that has all of the data for a given customer. How many multivalue paths does this schema have?

F. Explain how the XML Schema document you created in part E can be used to advantage by Marcia's Dry Cleaning.

If you have not already done so, answer parts A through H for Morgan Importing at the end of Chapter 7 (page 294). Use SQL Server, Oracle, or MySQL.

A. Using Figure 12-1 as an example, create an XML document with a DTD for a row of the PURCHASE table.

B. Using Figure 12-4 as an example, create an XSL document to materialize the document you created in part A. Show your document in a browser.

C. Create an XML Schema document for a join of STORE and PURCHASE data. Assume that the document has one store and from zero to many purchases for that store. Use Figure 12-13 as an example.

D. Write an SQL statement with FOR XML that will produce the document you created in part C.

E. Create an XML Schema document that has all of the data for a given purchase. How many multivalue paths does this schema have?

F. Explain how the XML Schema document you created in part E can be used to advantage by Morgan Importing.

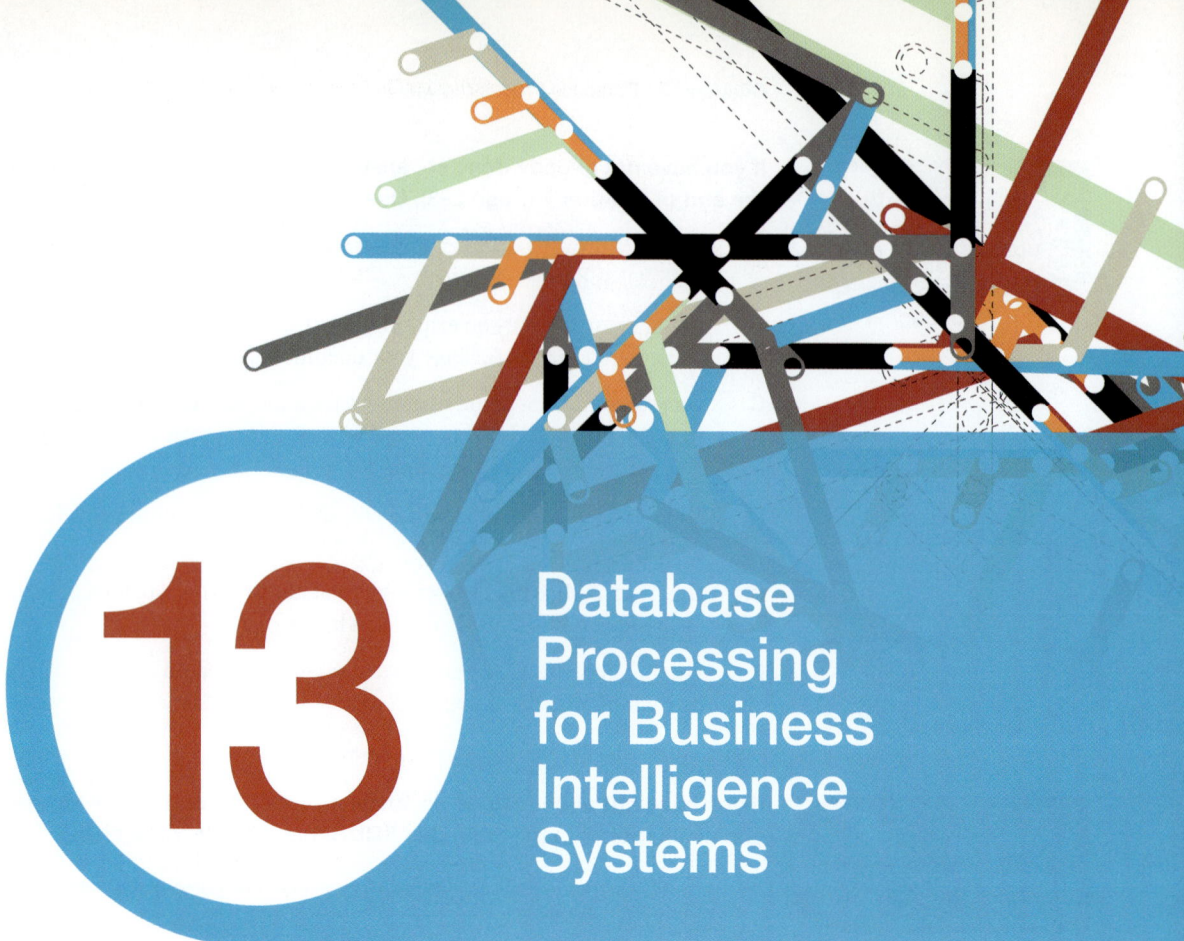

13

Database Processing for Business Intelligence Systems

Chapter Objectives

- To learn the basic concepts of data warehouses and data marts.
- To learn the basic concepts of dimensional databases.

- To learn the basic concepts of business intelligence (BI) systems.
- To learn the basic concepts of OnLine Analytical Processing (OLAP) and data mining.

Business Intelligence Systems

Business intelligence (BI) systems (also referred to as **decision support systems (DSSs)**) are information systems that assist managers and other professionals in the analysis of current and past activities and in the prediction of future events. Unlike transaction processing systems, they do not support operational activities, such as the recording and processing of orders. Instead, BI systems are used to support management assessment, analysis, planning, control, and, ultimately, decision making.

The Relationship Between Operational and BI Systems

Figure 13-1 summarizes the relationship among operational and business intelligence systems. **Operational systems**—such as sales, purchasing, and inventory control systems—support primary business activities. They use a DBMS to both read data from and store data in the operational database. They are also known as **transactional systems** or **online transaction processing (OLTP) systems**, because they record the ongoing stream of business transactions.

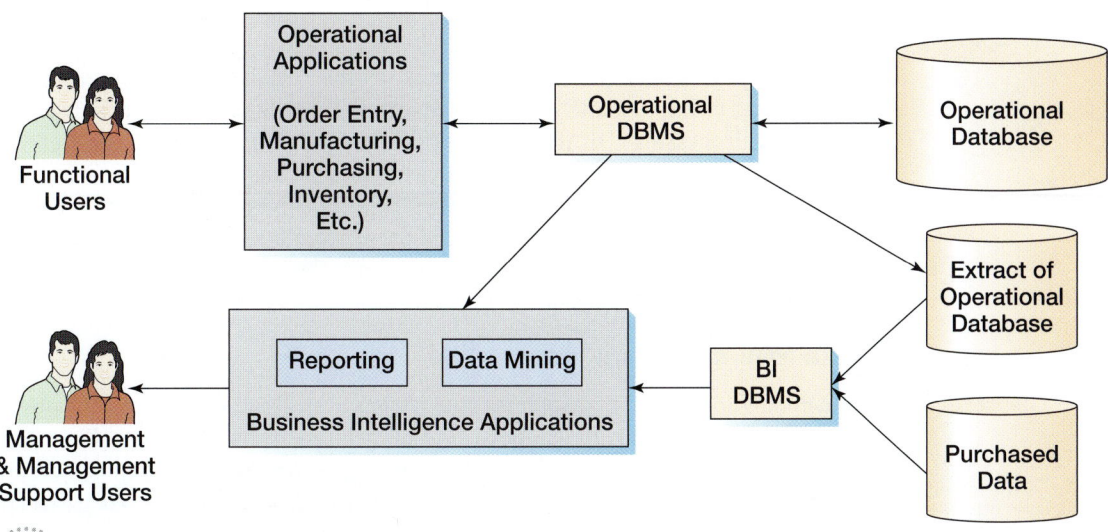

Instead of supporting the primary business activities, BI systems support management's analysis and decision-making activities. BI systems obtain data from three possible sources. First, they read and process data existing in the operational database—they use the operational DBMS to obtain such data, but they do not insert, modify, or delete operational data. Second, BI systems process data that are extracted from operational databases. In this situation, they manage the extracted database using a BI DBMS, which may be the same as or different from the operational DBMS. Finally, BI systems read data purchased from data vendors.

Reporting Systems and Data Mining Applications

BI systems fall into two broad categories: reporting systems and data mining applications. **Reporting systems** sort, filter, group, and make elementary calculations on operational data. **Data mining applications**, in contrast, perform sophisticated analyses on data, analyses that usually involve complex statistical and mathematical processing. The characteristics of BI applications are summarized in Figure 13-2.

- Reporting
    - Filter, sort, group, and make simple calculations
    - Summarize current status
    - Compare current status to past or predicted status
    - Classify entities (customers, products, employees, etc.)
    - Report delivery crucial
- Data Mining
    - Often employ sophisticated statistical and mathematical techniques
    - Used for:
        - What-if analyses
        - Predictions
        - Decisions
    - Results often incorporated into some other report or system

Reporting Systems

Reporting systems filter, sort, group, and make simple calculations. All reporting analyses can be performed using standard SQL, although extensions to SQL, such as those used for **OnLine Analytical Processing (OLAP)**, are sometimes used to ease the task of report production.

Reporting systems summarize the current status of business activities and compare that status with past or predicted future activities. Report delivery is crucial. Reports must be delivered to the proper users on a timely basis, in the appropriate format. For example, reports may be delivered on paper, via a Web browser, or in some other format.

Data Mining Applications

Data mining applications use sophisticated statistical and mathematical techniques to perform what-if analyses, to make predictions, and to facilitate decision making. For example, data mining techniques can analyze past cell phone usage and predict which customers are likely to switch to a competing phone company. Or, data mining can be used to analyze past loan behavior to determine which customers are most (or least) likely to default on a loan.

Report delivery is not as important for data mining systems as it is for reporting systems. First, most data mining applications have only a few users, and those users have sophisticated computer skills. Second, the results of a data mining analysis are usually incorporated into some other report, analysis, or information system. In the case of cell phone usage, the characteristics of customers who are in danger of switching to another company may be given to the sales department for action. Or, the parameters of an equation for determining the likelihood of a loan default may be incorporated into a loan approval application.

Data Warehouses and Data Marts

According to Figure 13-1, some BI systems read and process operational data directly from the operational database. Although this is possible for simple reporting systems and small databases, such direct reading of operational data is not feasible for more complex applications or larger databases. Those larger applications usually process a separate database constructed from an extract of the operational database.

Operational data are difficult to read for several reasons. For one, querying data for BI applications can place a substantial burden on the DBMS and unacceptably slow the performance of operational applications. Additionally, operational data have problems that limit their use for BI applications. Further, the creation and maintenance of BI systems require programs, facilities, and expertise that are not normally available from operations.

Because of these problems, many organizations have chosen to develop data warehouses and data marts to support BI applications. Before we consider the components of data warehouses and data marts, let's first consider some of the problems of using operational data for BI processing.

Components of a Data Warehouse

To overcome the problems just described, many organizations have created **data warehouses**, which are database systems that have data, programs, and personnel that specialize in the preparation of data for BI processing. Data warehouse databases differ from operational databases because the data warehouse data are frequently denormalized. Data warehouses vary in scale and scope. They can be as simple as a sole employee processing a data extract on a part-time basis or as complex as a department with dozens of employees maintaining libraries of data and programs.

Figure 13-3 shows the components of a data warehouse. Data are read from operational databases by the **Extract, Transform, and Load (ETL) system**. The ETL system then cleans and prepares the data for BI processing. This can be a complex process.

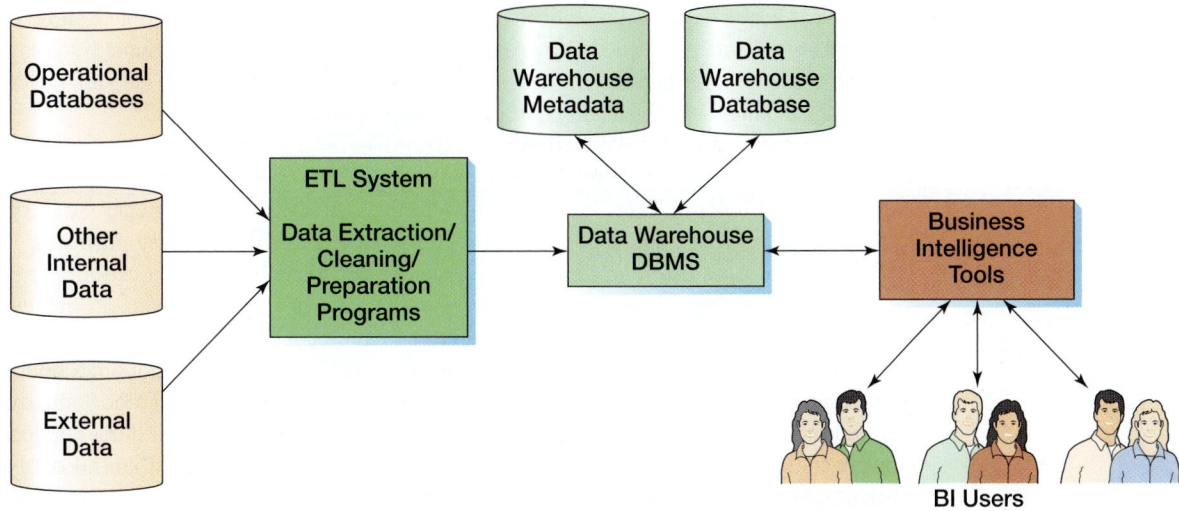

Figure 13-3

Components of a Data
Warehouse

First, the data may be problematic, which we will discuss in the next section. Second, data may need to be changed or transformed for use in a data warehouse. For example, the operational systems may store data about countries using standard two-letter country codes, such as US (United States) and CA (Canada). However, applications using the data warehouse may need to use the country names in full. Thus, the data transformation **{CountryCode→CountryName}** will be needed before the data can be loaded into the data warehouse.

The ETL stores the extracted data in a data warehouse database using a data warehouse DBMS, which can be different from the organization's operational DBMS. For example, an organization might use Oracle for its operational processing, but use SQL Server for its data warehouse. Other organizations might use SQL Server for operational processing and data management programs from statistical package vendors such as SAS or SPSS in the data warehouse.

Metadata concerning the data's source, format, assumptions and constraints, and other facts are kept in a **data warehouse metadata database**. The data warehouse DBMS extracts and provides data to BI tools, such as data mining programs.

> **BY THE WAY**   Problematic operational data that have been cleaned in the ETL system can also be used to update the operational system to fix the original data problems.

Problems with Operational Data

Most operational databases have problems that limit their usefulness to all but the simplest BI applications. Figure 13-4 lists the major problem categories.

Figure 13-4

Problems of Using
Transaction Data for
Business Intelligence

- Dirty data
- Missing values
- Inconsistent data
- Data not integrated
- Wrong format
    - Too fine
    - Not fine enough
- Too much data
    - Too many attributes
    - Too much volume

First, although data that are critical for successful operations must be complete and accurate, data that are only marginally necessary need not be. For example, some operational systems gather customer demographic data during the ordering process. But, because such data are not needed to fill, ship, or bill orders, the quality of the demographic data suffers.

Problematic data are termed **dirty data**. Examples are a value of "G" for customer sex and a value of "213" for customer age. Other examples are a value of "999-999-9999" for a U.S. phone number, a part color of "gren," and an e-mail address of "WhyMe@somewhereelseintheuniverse.who." All of these values pose problems for reporting and data mining purposes.

Purchased data often contain missing elements. In fact, most data vendors state the percentage of missing values for each attribute in the data they sell. An organization buys such data because, for some uses, some data are better than no data at all. This is especially true for data items whose values are difficult to obtain, such as the number of adults in a household, household income, dwelling type, and the education of primary income earner. Some missing data are not too much of a problem for reporting applications. For data mining applications, however, a few missing or erroneous data points can actually be worse than no data at all, because they bias the analysis.

Inconsistent data, the third problem in Figure 13-4, is particularly common for data that have been gathered over time. When an area code changes, for example, the phone number for a given customer before the change will differ from the customer's phone number after the change. Part codes can change, as can sales territories. Before such data can be used, it must be recoded for consistency over the period of the study.

Some data inconsistencies occur because of the nature of the business activity. Consider a Web-based order entry system used by customers around the world. When the Web server records the time of order, which time zone does it use? The server's system clock time is irrelevant to an analysis of customer behavior. Any standard time such as Universal Time Coordinate (UTC) time is also meaningless. Somehow, Web server time must be adjusted to the time zone of the customer.

Another problem is **nonintegrated data**. Suppose, for example, that an organization wants to report on customer order and payment behavior. Unfortunately, order data are stored in a CRM system developed by Siebel, whereas payment data are recorded in a PeopleSoft financial management database. To perform the analysis, the data must somehow be integrated.

Data can also be too fine or too coarse. With regards to the former, suppose that we want to analyze the placement of graphics and controls on an order entry Web page. It is possible to capture the customers' clicking behavior in what is termed **click-stream data**. However, click-stream data include *everything* the customer does. In the middle of the order stream there may be data for clicks on the news, e-mail, instant chat, and the weather. Although all of this data might be useful for a study of consumer computer behavior, it will be overwhelming if all we want to know is how customers respond to an ad located on the screen. Because the data are too fine, the data analysts must throw millions and millions of clicks away before they can proceed.

Data can also be too coarse. A file of order totals cannot be used for a market basket analysis, which identifies items that are commonly purchased together. Market basket analyses require item-level data; we need to know which items were purchased with which others. This doesn't mean the order total data are useless; it can be adequate for other analyses, it just won't do for a market basket analysis.

If the data are too fine, they can be made coarser by summing and combining. An analyst and a computer can sum and combine such data. If the data are too coarse, however, they cannot be separated into their constituent parts.

The final problem listed in Figure 13-4 concerns data volume. We can have an excess of columns, rows, or both. Suppose that we want to know the attributes that influence customers' responses to a promotion. Between customer data stored within the organization and customer data that can be purchased, we might have a hundred or more different attributes, or columns, to consider. How do we select among them? Because of a phenomenon called the **curse of dimensionality**, the more attributes there are, the easier it is to build a model that fits the sample data but that is worthless as a predictor. For this and other reasons, the number of attributes should be reduced and one of the major activities in data mining concerns the efficient and effective selection of variables.

Finally, we may have too many instances, or rows, of data. Suppose that we want to analyze click-stream data on CNN.com. How many clicks does this site receive per month? Millions upon millions! To meaningfully analyze such data, we need to reduce the number of instances. A good solution to this problem is statistical sampling. However, developing a reliable sample requires specialized expertise and information system tools.

Purchasing Data for Vendors

Data warehouses often include data that are purchased from outside sources. A typical example is customer credit data. Figure 13-5 lists some of the consumer data than can be purchased from the KnowledgeBase Marketing company in their AmeriLINK database of consumer data (*www2.kbm1.com/Documents/AmeriLINK_brochure.pdf*). An amazing, and from a privacy standpoint frightening, amount of data is available just from this one vendor.

Data Warehouses Versus Data Marts

You can think of a data warehouse as a distributor in a supply chain. The data warehouse takes data from the data manufacturers (operational systems and purchased data), cleans and processes them, and locates the data on the shelves, so to speak, of the data warehouse. The people who work in a data warehouse are experts at data management, data cleaning, data transformation, and the like. However, they are not usually experts in a given business function.

A **data mart** is a collection of data that is smaller than that in the data warehouse and that addresses a particular component or functional area of the business. A data mart is like a retail store in a supply chain. Users in the data mart obtain data that pertain to a particular business function from the data warehouse. Such users do not have the data management expertise that data warehouse employees have, but they are knowledgeable analysts for a given business function. Figure 13-6 illustrates these relationships.

The data warehouse takes data from the data producers and distributes the data to three data marts. One data mart analyzes click-stream data for the purpose of designing Web pages.

The second analyzes store sales data and determines which products tend to be purchased together. This information is used to train salespeople on the best way to up-sell customers. The third data mart analyzes customer order data for the purpose of reducing labor for item picking from the warehouse. A company such as Amazon.com, for example, goes to great lengths to organize its warehouses to reduce picking expenses.

When the data mart structure shown in Figure 13-6 is combined with the data warehouse architecture shown in Figure 13-3, the combined system is known as an **enterprise data warehouse (EDW) architecture**. In this configuration, the data warehouse maintains all

Figure 13-5

The AmeriLINK Database Contains Data on 230 Million Americans

- Name, Address, Phone
- Age, Gender
- Ethnicity, Religion
- Income
- Education
- Marital Status, Life Stage
- Height, Weight, Hair and Eye Color
- Spouse Name, Birth Date, etc.
- Kids' Names and Birth Dates
- Voter Registration
- Home Ownership
- Vehicles
- Magazine Subscriptions
- Catalog Orders
- Hobbies
- Attitudes

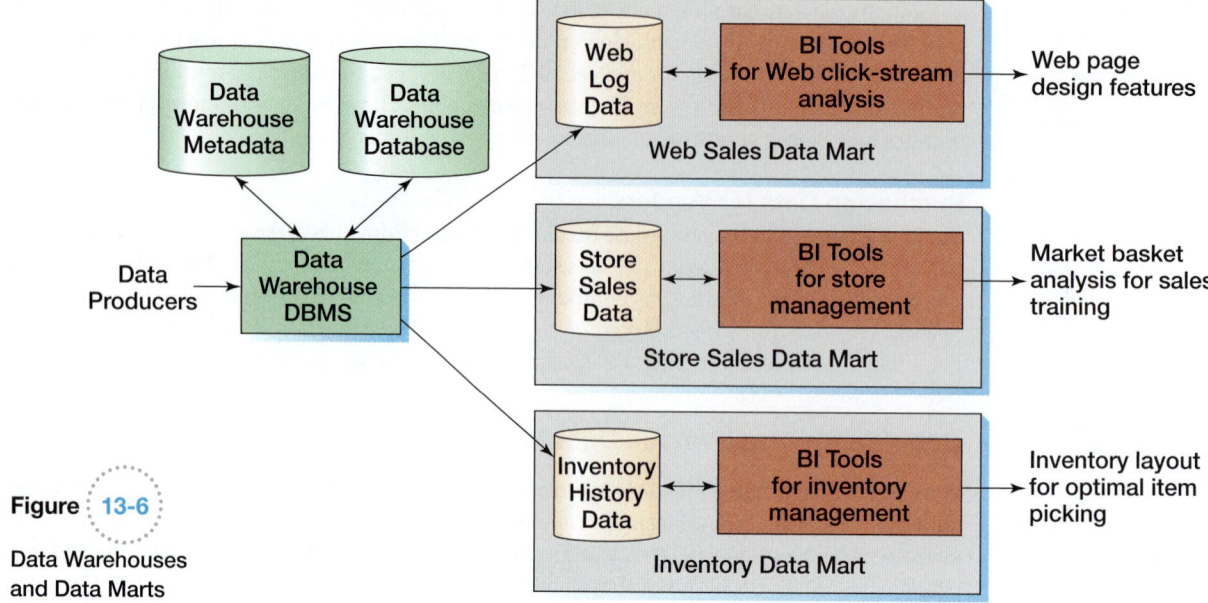

Figure 13-6

Data Warehouses
and Data Marts

enterprise BI data and acts as the authoritative source for data extracts provided to the data marts. The data marts receive all their data from the data warehouse—they do not add or maintain any additional data.

Of course, it is expensive to create, staff, and operate data warehouses and data marts, and only large organizations with deep pockets can afford to operate a system such as an EDW. Smaller organizations operate subsets of this system. For example, they may have just a single data mart for analyzing marketing and promotion data.

Dimensional Databases

The databases in a data warehouse or data mart are built to a different type of database design than the normalized relational databases used for operational systems. The data warehouse databases are built in a design called a **dimensional database** that is designed for efficient data queries and analysis. A dimensional database is used to store historical data rather than just the current data stored in an operational database. Figure 13-7 compares operational databases and dimensional databases.

Because dimensional databases are used for the analysis of historical data, they must be designed to handle data that change over time. For example, a customer may have moved from one residence to another in the same city or may have moved to a completely different city and state. This type of data arrangement is called a **slowly changing dimension**, and in order to track such changes a dimensional database must have a **date dimension** or **time dimension** as well.

Figure 13-7

Characteristics
of Operational
and Dimensional
Databases

Operational Database	Dimensional Database
Used for structured transaction data processing	Used for unstructured analytical data processing
Current data are used	Current and historical data are used
Data are inserted, updated, and deleted by users	Data are loaded and updated systematically, not by users

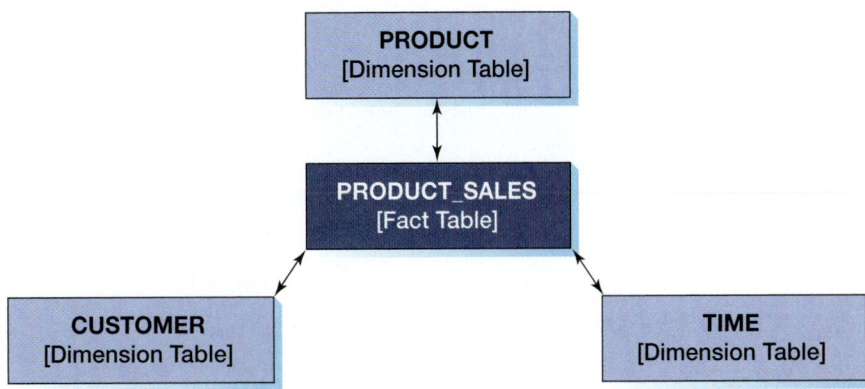

Figure 13-8

The Star Schema

The Star Schema

Rather than using the normalized database designs used in operational databases, a dimensional database uses a star schema. A **star schema**, so named because, as shown in Figure 13-8, it visually resembles a star, with a **fact table** at the center of the star and **dimension tables** radiating out from the center. The fact table is always fully normalized, but dimension tables may be non-normalized.

> **BY THE WAY** There is a more complex version of the star schema called the *snowflake schema*. In the snowflake schema, each dimension table is normalized, which may create additional tables attached to the dimension tables.

To illustrate a star schema for a dimensional database, we will build a small (very small) data warehouse for Heather Sweeney Designs (HSD), a Texas company specializing in products for kitchen-remodeling services. HSD puts on seminars to attract customers and sell books and videos in addition to doing actual design work. A database design for HSD is shown in Figure 13-9, and an SQL Server database diagram for the HSD database is shown in Figure 13-10. The actual dimensional database for BI use at HSD is named *HSD-DW*, and it is shown in Figure 13-11. The SQL statements needed to create the tables in the HSD-DW database are shown in Figure 13-12, and the data for the HSD-DW database are shown in Figure 13-13. Compare the HSD-DW dimensional database model in Figure 13-11 to the HSD database diagram shown in Figure 13-10 and note how data in the HSD database have been used in the HSD-DW schema.

> **BY THE WAY** Note that in the HSD-DW database the CUSTOMER table has a surrogate primary key named CustomerID, which has an integer value, whereas in the HSD database the primary key EmailAddress was used. There are two reasons for this. First, the primary key EmailAddress used in the HSD database is simply too cumbersome for a data warehouse, so we switched to the preferable small and numeric surrogate key. Second, we do not use individual EmailAddress values in the HSD-DW database, only values of EmailDomain, which is not unique and cannot be used as a primary key.

A fact table is used to store **measures** of business activity, which are quantitative or factual data about the entity represented by the fact table. For example, in the HSD-DW database, the fact table is PRODUCT_SALES:

PRODUCT_SALES (<u>TimeID</u>, <u>CustomerID</u>, <u>ProductNumber</u>, Quantity, UnitPrice, Total)

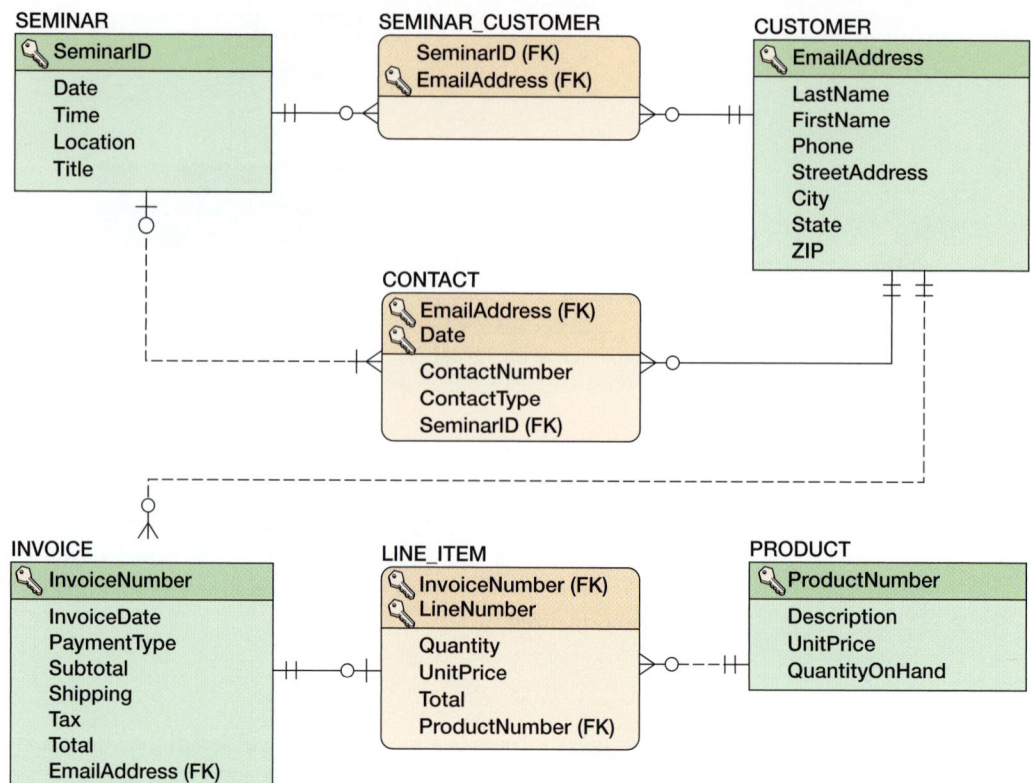

Figure 13-9

The HSD Database Design

In this table:

- Quantity is quantitative data that record how many of the item were sold.
- UnitPrice is quantitative data that record the dollar price of each item sold.
- Total (= Quantity * UnitPrice) is quantitative data that record the total dollar value of the sale of this item.

Figure 13-10

The HSD Database Diagram

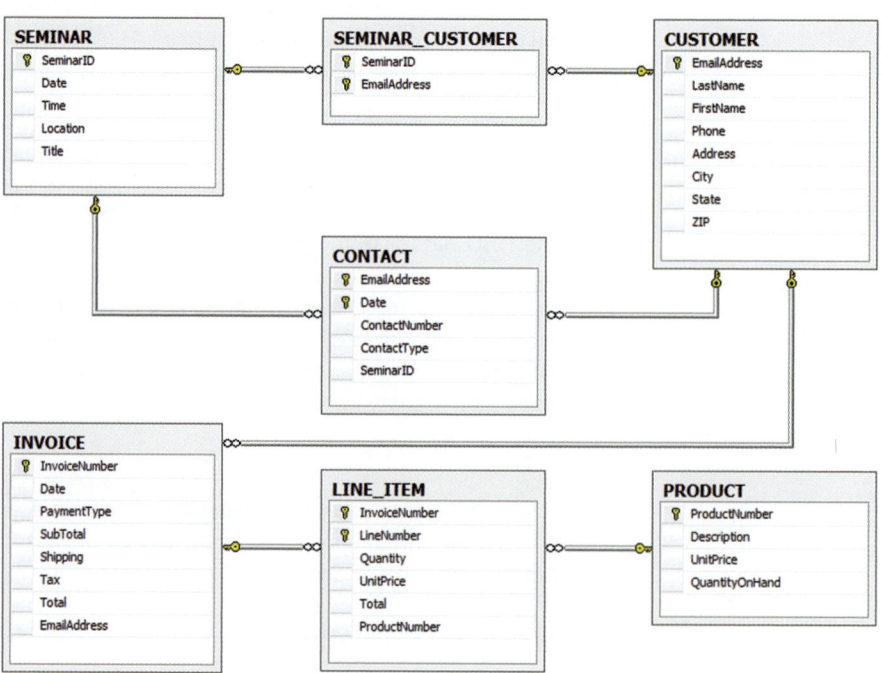

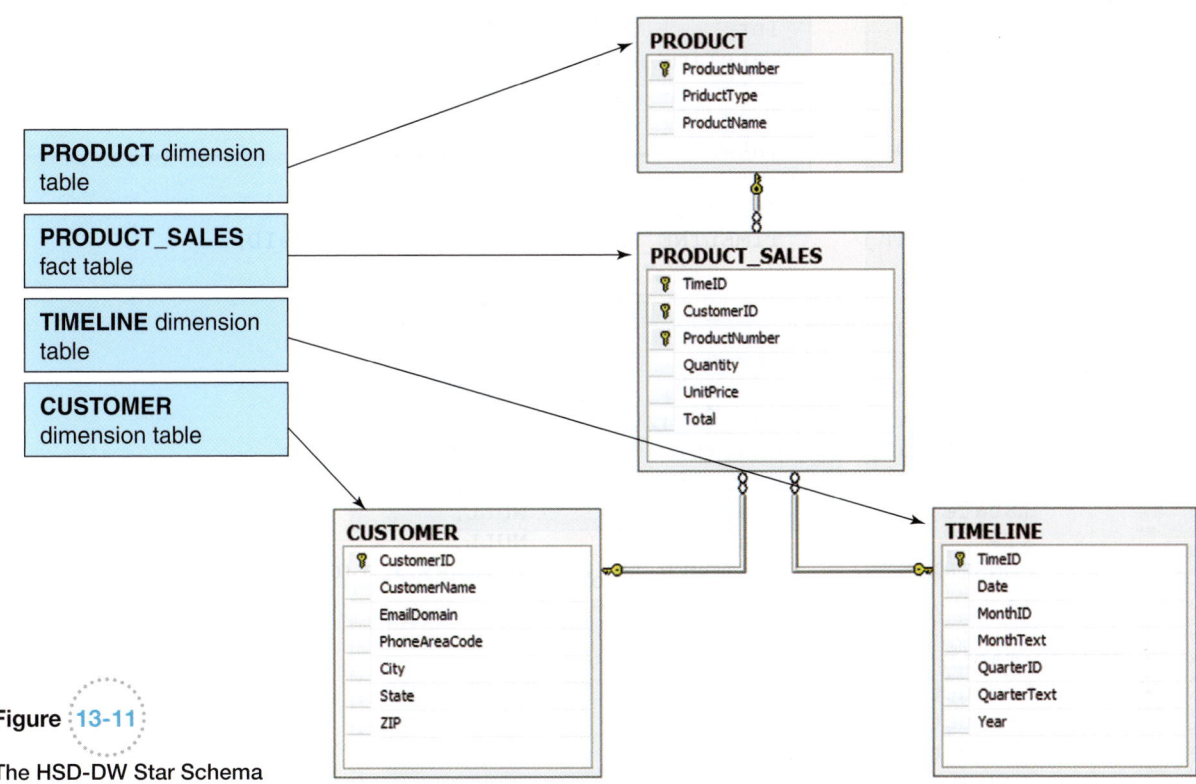

PRODUCT dimension table

PRODUCT_SALES fact table

TIMELINE dimension table

CUSTOMER dimension table

Figure 13-11

The HSD-DW Star Schema

The measures in the PRODUCT_SALES table are for *units of product per day.* We do not use individual sale data (which would be based on InvoiceNumber), but rather data summed for each customer for each day. For example, if you could compare the HSD database INVOICE data for Ralph Able for 6/5/08, you would see that Ralph made two purchases on that date (InvoiceNumber 35013 and InvoiceNumber 35016). In the HSD-DW database, however, these two purchases are summed into the PRODUCT_SALES data for Ralph (CustomerID = 3) for 6/5/08 (TimeID = 39604).

> **BY THE WAY** The TimeID values are the sequential *serial values* used in Microsoft Excel to represent dates. Starting with 01-JAN-1900 as date value 1, the date value is increased by 1 for each calendar day. Thus, 05-JUN-2008 = 39604. For more information, search "Date formats" in the Excel help system.

A dimension table is used to record values of attributes that describe the fact measures in the fact table, and these attributes are used in queries to select and group the measures in the fact table. Thus, CUSTOMER records data about the customers referenced by CustomerID in the SALES table, TIMELINE provides data that can be used to interpret the SALES event in time (which month? which quarter?), and so on. A query to summarize product units sold by Customer (CustomerName) and Product (ProductName) would be:

```
SELECT    C.CustomerNumber, C.CustomerName,
          C.ProductNumber, P.ProductName,
          SUM(PS.Quantity) AS TotalQuantity
FROM      CUSTOMER C, PRODUCT_SALES PS, PRODUCT P
WHERE     C.CustomerID = PS.CustomerID
  AND     P.ProductNumber = PS.ProductNumber
GROUP BY  C.CustomerNumber, C.CustomerName,
          P.ProductNumber, P.ProductName
ORDER BY  C.CustomerNumber, P.ProductNumber;
```

Figure 13-18

RFM Analysis

- Simple report-based customer classification scheme
- Score customers on recentness, frequency, and monetary size of orders
- Typically, divide each criterion into 5 groups and score from 1 to 5

RFM Analysis

As discussed earlier, **RFM analysis** is a way of analyzing and ranking customers according to their purchasing patterns. It is a simple technique that considers how *recently* (**R**) a customer ordered, how *frequently* (**F**) a customer orders, and how much *money* (**M**) the customer spends per order. RFM is summarized in Figure 13-18.

To produce an RFM score, we need only two things: customer data and sales data for each purchase (the date of the sale and the total amount of the sale) made by each customer. If you look at the SALES_FOR_RFM table and its associated CUSTOMER and TIMELINE dimension tables in Figure 13-17, you see that we have exactly those data: The SALE_FOR_RFM table is the starting point for RFM analysis in the HSD-DW BI system.

To produce an RFM score, customer purchase records are first sorted by the date of their most recent (R) purchase. In a common form of this analysis, the customers are divided into five groups, and a score of 1 to 5 is given to customers in each group. Thus, the 20 percent of the customers having the most recent orders are given an R score of 1, the 20 percent of the customers having the next most recent orders are given an R score of 2, and so forth, down to the last 20 percent, who are given an R score of 5.

The customers are then resorted on the basis of how frequently they order. The 20 percent of the customers who order most frequently are given an F score of 1, the next 20 percent most frequently ordering customers are given a score of 2, and so forth, down to the least frequently ordering customers, who are given an F score of 5.

Finally, the customers are sorted again according to the amount of their orders. The 20 percent who have ordered the most expensive items are given an M score of 1, the next 20 percent are given an M score of 2, and so forth, down to the 20 percent who spend the least, who are given an M score of 5.

Figure 13-19 shows sample RFM data for Heather Sweeney Designs. (Note that these data have *not* been calculated and are for illustrative purposes only.) The first customer, Ralph Able, has a score of {1 1 2}, which means that he has ordered recently and orders frequently. His M score of 2 indicates, however, that he does not order the most expensive goods. From these scores, the salespeople can surmise that Ralph is a good customer but that they should attempt to up-sell Ralph to more expensive goods.

Susan Baker (RFM score of {2 2 3}) is above average in terms of how frequently she shops and how recently she has shopped, but her purchases are average in value. Sally George (RFM score of {3 3 3}) is truly in the middle. Jenny Tyler (RFM score of {5 1 1}) is a problem. Jenny has not ordered in some time, but, in the past, when she did order, she ordered frequently, and her orders were of the highest monetary value. These data suggest that Jenny might be going to another vendor. Someone from the sales team should contact her immediately. However, no one on the sales team should be talking to Chantel Jacobs (RFM score of {5 5 5}). She has not

Figure 13-19

The RFM Score Report

Each customer is ranked for **R** (recent), **F** (frequent), and **M** (money) characteristics—1 is highest (best) and 5 is lowest (worst) score

Customer	RFM Score		
	R	F	M
Able, Ralph	1	1	2
Baker, Susan	2	2	3
George, Sally	3	3	3
Tyler, Jenny	5	1	1
Jacobs, Chantel	5	5	5

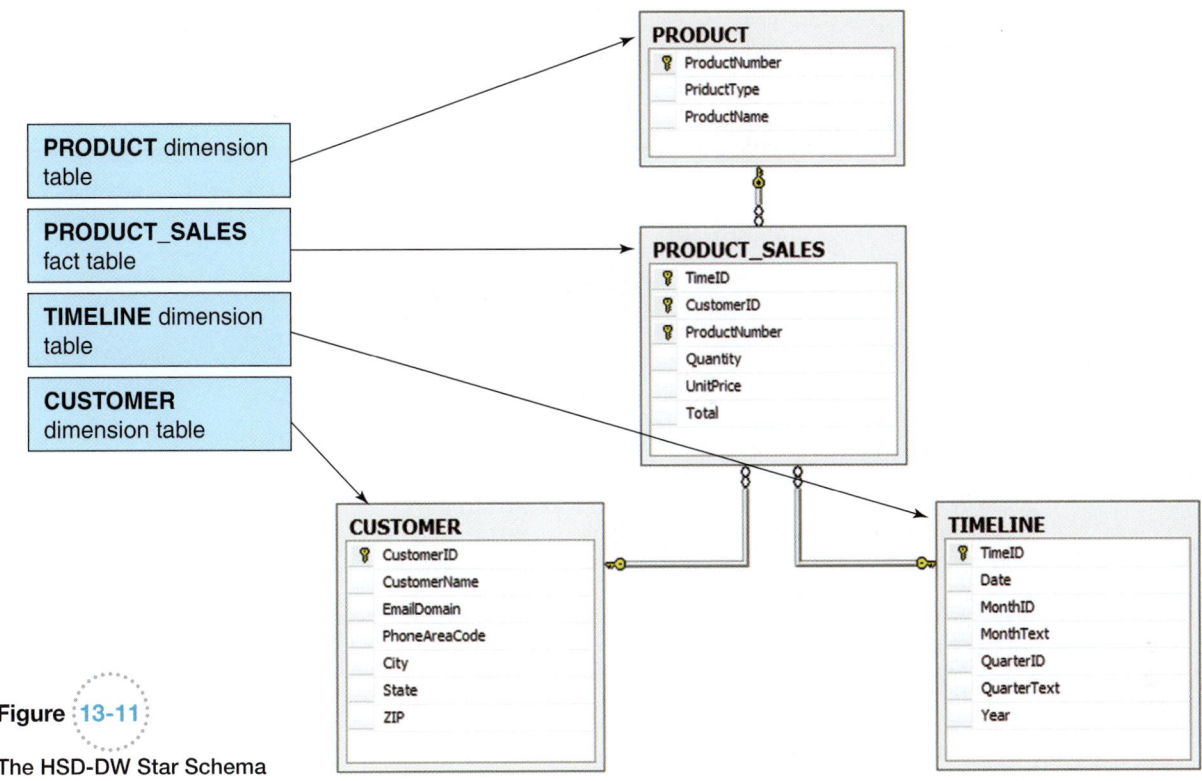

PRODUCT dimension table

PRODUCT_SALES fact table

TIMELINE dimension table

CUSTOMER dimension table

Figure 13-11

The HSD-DW Star Schema

The measures in the PRODUCT_SALES table are for *units of product per day*. We do not use individual sale data (which would be based on InvoiceNumber), but rather data summed for each customer for each day. For example, if you could compare the HSD database INVOICE data for Ralph Able for 6/5/08, you would see that Ralph made two purchases on that date (InvoiceNumber 35013 and InvoiceNumber 35016). In the HSD-DW database, however, these two purchases are summed into the PRODUCT_SALES data for Ralph (CustomerID = 3) for 6/5/08 (TimeID = 39604).

> **BY THE WAY** The TimeID values are the sequential *serial values* used in Microsoft Excel to represent dates. Starting with 01-JAN-1900 as date value 1, the date value is increased by 1 for each calendar day. Thus, 05-JUN-2008 = 39604. For more information, search "Date formats" in the Excel help system.

A dimension table is used to record values of attributes that describe the fact measures in the fact table, and these attributes are used in queries to select and group the measures in the fact table. Thus, CUSTOMER records data about the customers referenced by CustomerID in the SALES table, TIMELINE provides data that can be used to interpret the SALES event in time (which month? which quarter?), and so on. A query to summarize product units sold by Customer (CustomerName) and Product (ProductName) would be:

```
SELECT    C.CustomerNumber, C.CustomerName,
          C.ProductNumber, P.ProductName,
          SUM(PS.Quantity) AS TotalQuantity
FROM      CUSTOMER C, PRODUCT_SALES PS, PRODUCT P
WHERE     C.CustomerID = PS.CustomerID
   AND    P.ProductNumber = PS.ProductNumber
GROUP BY  C.CustomerNumber, C.CustomerName,
          P.ProductNumber, P.ProductName
ORDER BY  C.CustomerNumber, P.ProductNumber;
```

```
CREATE TABLE TIMELINE(
        TimeID          Int             NOT NULL,
        [Date]          DateTime        NOT NULL,
        MonthID         Int             NOT NULL,
        Month           Char(15)        NOT NULL,
        QuarterID       Int             NOT NULL,
        Quarter         Int             NOT NULL,
        [Year]          Char(10)        NOT NULL,
        CONSTRAINT      TIMELINE_PK     PRIMARY KEY(TimeID)
        );

CREATE TABLE CUSTOMER(
        CustomerID      Int             NOT NULL,
        CustomerName    Char(75)        NOT NULL,
        EmailDomain     VarChar(100)    NOT NULL,
        PhoneAreaCode   Char(6)         NOT NULL,
        City            Char(35)        NULL,
        [State]         Char(2)         NULL,
        ZIP             Char(10)        NULL,
        CONSTRAINT      CUSTOMER_PK     PRIMARY KEY(CustomerID)
        );

CREATE TABLE PRODUCT(
        ProductNumber   Char(35)        NOT NULL,
        ProductType     Char(25)        NOT NULL,
        ProductName     VarChar(75)     NOT NULL,
        CONSTRAINT      PRODUCT_PK      PRIMARY KEY(ProductNumber)
        );

CREATE TABLE PRODUCT_SALES(
        TimeID          Int             NOT NULL,
        CustomerID      Int             NOT NULL,
        ProductNumber   Char(35)        NOT NULL,
        Quantity        Int             NOT NULL,
        UnitPrice       Numeric(9,2)    NOT NULL,
        Total           Numeric(9,2)    NULL,
        CONSTRAINT      PRODUCT_SALES_PK
                           PRIMARY KEY (TimeID,CustomerID,ProductNumber),
        CONSTRAINT      PS_TIMELINE_FK FOREIGN KEY(TimeID)
                           REFERENCES TIMELINE(TimeID)
                               ON UPDATE NO ACTION
                               ON DELETE NO ACTION,
        CONSTRAINT      PS_CUSTOMER_FK FOREIGN KEY(CustomerID)
                           REFERENCES CUSTOMER(CustomerID)
                               ON UPDATE NO ACTION
                               ON DELETE NO ACTION,
        CONSTRAINT      PS_PRODUCT_FK FOREIGN KEY(ProductNumber)
                           REFERENCES PRODUCT(ProductNumber)
                               ON UPDATE NO ACTION
                               ON DELETE NO ACTION
        );
```

Figure 13-12

The HSD-DW
SQL Statements

The results of this query are shown in Figure 13-14.

In Chapter 6, we discussed how an N:M relationship is created in a database as two 1:N relationships by use of an intersection table. We also discussed how additional attributes can be added to the intersection table in an association relationship.

(a) TIMELINE Dimension Table

	TimeID	Date	MonthID	MonthText	QuarterID	QuarterText	Year
1	39370	2007-10-15 00:00:00.000	10	October	3	Qtr3	2007
2	39380	2007-10-25 00:00:00.000	10	October	3	Qtr3	2007
3	39436	2007-12-20 00:00:00.000	12	December	3	Qtr3	2007
4	39532	2008-03-25 00:00:00.000	3	March	1	Qtr1	2008
5	39534	2008-03-27 00:00:00.000	3	March	1	Qtr1	2008
6	39538	2008-03-31 00:00:00.000	3	March	1	Qtr1	2008
7	39541	2008-04-03 00:00:00.000	4	April	2	Qtr2	2008
8	39546	2008-04-08 00:00:00.000	4	April	2	Qtr2	2008
9	39561	2008-04-23 00:00:00.000	4	April	2	Qtr2	2008
10	39575	2008-05-07 00:00:00.000	5	May	2	Qtr2	2008
11	39589	2008-05-21 00:00:00.000	5	May	2	Qtr2	2008
12	39604	2008-06-05 00:00:00.000	6	June	2	Qtr2	2008

(b) CUSTOMER Dimension Table

	CustomerID	CustomerName	EmailDomain	PhoneAreaCode	City	State	ZIP
1	1	Jacobs, Nancy	somewhere.com	817	Fort Worth	TX	76110
2	2	Jacobs, Chantel	somewhere.com	817	Fort Worth	TX	76112
3	3	Able, Ralph	somewhere.com	210	San Antonio	TX	78214
4	4	Baker, Susan	elsewhere.com	210	San Antonio	TX	78216
5	5	Eagleton, Sam	elsewhere.com	210	San Antonio	TX	78218
6	6	Foxtrot, Kathy	somewhere.com	972	Dallas	TX	75220
7	7	George, Sally	somewhere.com	972	Dallas	TX	75223
8	8	Hullett, Shawn	elsewhere.com	972	Dallas	TX	75224
9	9	Pearson, Bobbi	elsewhere.com	512	Austin	TX	78710
10	10	Ranger, Terry	elsewhere.com	512	Austin	TX	78712
11	11	Tyler, Jenny	somewhere.com	972	Dallas	TX	75225
12	12	Wayne, Joan	elsewhere.com	817	Fort Worth	TX	76115

(c) PRODUCT Dimension Table

	ProductNumber	ProductType	ProductName
1	BK001	Book	Kitchen Remodeling Basics For Everyone
2	BK002	Book	Advanced Kitchen Remodeling For Everyone
3	VB001	Video Companion	Kitchen Remodeling Basics Video Companion
4	VB002	Video Companion	Advanced Kitchen Remodeling Video Companion
5	VB003	Video Companion	Kitchen Remodeling Dallas Style Video Companion
6	VK001	DVD Video	Kitchen Remodeling Basics
7	VK002	DVD Video	Advanced Kitchen Remodeling
8	VK003	DVD Video	Kitchen Remodeling Dallas Style
9	VK004	DVD Video	Heather Sweeny Seminar Live in Dallas on 25-OCT-07

(d) PRODUCT_SALES Fact Table

	TimeID	CustomerID	ProductNumber	Quantity	UnitPrice	Total
1	39370	3	VB001	1	7.99	7.99
2	39370	3	VK001	1	14.95	14.95
3	39380	4	BK001	1	24.95	24.95
4	39380	4	VB001	1	7.99	7.99
5	39380	4	VK001	1	14.95	14.95
6	39436	7	VK004	1	24.95	24.95
7	39532	4	BK002	1	24.95	24.95
8	39532	4	VK002	1	14.95	14.95
9	39532	4	VK004	1	24.95	24.95
10	39534	6	BK002	1	24.95	24.95
11	39534	6	VB003	1	9.99	9.99
12	39534	6	VK002	1	14.95	14.95
13	39534	6	VK003	1	19.95	19.95
14	39534	6	VK004	1	24.95	24.95
15	39534	7	BK001	1	24.95	24.95
16	39534	7	BK002	1	24.95	24.95
17	39534	7	VK003	1	19.95	19.95
18	39534	7	VK004	1	24.95	24.95
19	39538	9	BK001	1	24.95	24.95
20	39538	9	VB001	1	7.99	7.99
21	39538	9	VK001	1	14.95	14.95
22	39541	11	VB003	2	9.99	19.98
23	39541	11	VK003	2	19.95	39.90
24	39541	11	VK004	2	24.95	49.90
25	39546	1	BK001	1	24.95	24.95
26	39546	1	VB001	1	7.99	7.99
27	39546	1	VK001	1	14.95	14.95
28	39546	5	BK001	1	24.95	24.95
29	39546	5	VB001	1	7.99	7.99
30	39546	5	VK001	1	14.95	14.95
31	39561	3	BK001	1	24.95	24.95
32	39575	9	VB002	1	7.99	7.99
33	39575	9	VK002	1	14.95	14.95
34	39589	8	VB003	1	9.99	9.99
35	39589	8	VK003	1	19.95	19.95
36	39589	8	VK004	1	24.95	24.95
37	39604	3	BK002	1	24.95	24.95
38	39604	3	VB001	1	7.99	7.99
39	39604	3	VB002	2	7.99	15.98
40	39604	3	VK001	1	14.95	14.95
41	39604	3	VK002	2	14.95	29.90
42	39604	11	VB002	2	7.99	15.98
43	39604	11	VK002	2	14.95	29.90
44	39604	12	BK002	1	24.95	24.95
45	39604	12	VB003	1	9.99	9.99
46	39604	12	VK002	1	14.95	14.95
47	39604	12	VK003	1	19.95	19.95
48	39604	12	VK004	1	24.95	24.95

Figure 13-13

The HSD-DW Table Data

In a star schema, the fact table is an association table—it is an intersection table for the relationships between the dimension tables with additional measures also stored in it. And, as with all other intersection tables, the key of the fact table is a composite key made up of all the foreign keys to the dimension tables.

Illustrating the Dimensional Model

When you think of the word *dimension*, you might think of "two dimensional" or "three dimensional." And the dimensional models can be illustrated by using a two-dimensional matrix and a three-dimensional cube. Figure 13-15 shows the SQL query results from Figure 13-14, displayed as a two-dimensional matrix of Product (using ProductNumber) and Customer (using CustomerID), with each cell showing the number of units of each product purchased by each customer. Note how ProductNumber and CustomerID define the two dimensions of the matrix: CustomerID labels what would be the *x*-axis, and ProductNumber labels the *y*-axis.

Figure 13-16 shows a three-dimensional cube with the same ProductNumber and CustomerID dimensions, but now with the added Time dimension on the *z*-axis. Now instead of occupying a two-dimensional box, the total quantity of products purchased by each customer on each day occupies a small three-dimensional cube, and all these small cubes combine to form a large cube.

As human beings, we can visualize two-dimensional matrices and three-dimensional cubes. Although we cannot visualize models with four, five, and more dimensions, BI systems and dimensional databases can handle such models.

Multiple Fact Tables and Conformed Dimensions

Data warehouse systems build dimensional models, as needed, to analyze BI questions, and the HSD-DW star schema in Figure 13-11 would be just one schema in a set of schemas. Figure 13-17 shows an extended HSD-DW schema.

#	CustomerID	CustomerName	ProductNumber	ProductName	TotalQuantity
1	1	Jacobs, Nancy	BK001	Kitchen Remodeling Basics For Everyone	1
2	1	Jacobs, Nancy	VB001	Kitchen Remodeling Basics Video Companion	1
3	1	Jacobs, Nancy	VK001	Kitchen Remodeling Basics	1
4	3	Able, Ralph	BK001	Kitchen Remodeling Basics For Everyone	1
5	3	Able, Ralph	BK002	Advanced Kitchen Remodeling For Everyone	1
6	3	Able, Ralph	VB001	Kitchen Remodeling Basics Video Companion	2
7	3	Able, Ralph	VB002	Advanced Kitchen Remodeling Video Companion	2
8	3	Able, Ralph	VK001	Kitchen Remodeling Basics	2
9	3	Able, Ralph	VK002	Advanced Kitchen Remodeling	2
10	4	Baker, Susan	BK001	Kitchen Remodeling Basics For Everyone	1
11	4	Baker, Susan	BK002	Advanced Kitchen Remodeling For Everyone	1
12	4	Baker, Susan	VB001	Kitchen Remodeling Basics Video Companion	1
13	4	Baker, Susan	VK001	Kitchen Remodeling Basics	1
14	4	Baker, Susan	VK002	Advanced Kitchen Remodeling	1
15	4	Baker, Susan	VK004	Heather Sweeny Seminar Live in Dallas on 25-OCT-07	1
16	5	Eagleton, Sam	BK001	Kitchen Remodeling Basics For Everyone	1
17	5	Eagleton, Sam	VB001	Kitchen Remodeling Basics Video Companion	1
18	5	Eagleton, Sam	VK001	Kitchen Remodeling Basics	1
19	6	Foxtrot, Kathy	BK002	Advanced Kitchen Remodeling For Everyone	1
20	6	Foxtrot, Kathy	VB003	Kitchen Remodeling Dallas Style Video Companion	1
21	6	Foxtrot, Kathy	VK002	Advanced Kitchen Remodeling	1
22	6	Foxtrot, Kathy	VK003	Kitchen Remodeling Dallas Style	1
23	6	Foxtrot, Kathy	VK004	Heather Sweeny Seminar Live in Dallas on 25-OCT-07	1
24	7	George, Sally	BK001	Kitchen Remodeling Basics For Everyone	1
25	7	George, Sally	BK002	Advanced Kitchen Remodeling For Everyone	1
26	7	George, Sally	VK003	Kitchen Remodeling Dallas Style	1
27	7	George, Sally	VK004	Heather Sweeny Seminar Live in Dallas on 25-OCT-07	2
28	8	Hullett, Shawn	VB003	Kitchen Remodeling Dallas Style Video Companion	1
29	8	Hullett, Shawn	VK003	Kitchen Remodeling Dallas Style	1
30	8	Hullett, Shawn	VK004	Heather Sweeny Seminar Live in Dallas on 25-OCT-07	1
31	9	Pearson, Bobbi	BK001	Kitchen Remodeling Basics For Everyone	1
32	9	Pearson, Bobbi	VB001	Kitchen Remodeling Basics Video Companion	1
33	9	Pearson, Bobbi	VB002	Advanced Kitchen Remodeling Video Companion	1
34	9	Pearson, Bobbi	VK001	Kitchen Remodeling Basics	1
35	9	Pearson, Bobbi	VK002	Advanced Kitchen Remodeling	1
36	11	Tyler, Jenny	VB002	Advanced Kitchen Remodeling Video Companion	2
37	11	Tyler, Jenny	VB003	Kitchen Remodeling Dallas Style Video Companion	2
38	11	Tyler, Jenny	VK002	Advanced Kitchen Remodeling	2
39	11	Tyler, Jenny	VK003	Kitchen Remodeling Dallas Style	2
40	11	Tyler, Jenny	VK004	Heather Sweeny Seminar Live in Dallas on 25-OCT-07	2
41	12	Wayne, Joan	BK002	Advanced Kitchen Remodeling For Everyone	1
42	12	Wayne, Joan	VB003	Kitchen Remodeling Dallas Style Video Companion	1
43	12	Wayne, Joan	VK002	Advanced Kitchen Remodeling	1
44	12	Wayne, Joan	VK003	Kitchen Remodeling Dallas Style	1
45	12	Wayne, Joan	VK004	Heather Sweeny Seminar Live in Dallas on 25-OCT-07	1

Figure 13-14

The HSD-DW Query Results

In Figure 13-17, a second fact table named SALES_FOR_RFM has been added:

SALES_FOR_RFM (TimeID, CustomerID, InvoiceNumber, PreTaxTotalSale)

This table shows that fact table primary keys do not need to be composed solely of foreign keys that link to dimension tables. In SALES_FOR_RFM, the primary key includes the InvoiceNumber attribute. This attribute is necessary because the composite key (TimeID, CustomerID) will not be unique and thus cannot be the primary key. Note that SALES_FOR_RFM links to the same CUSTOMER and TIMELINE dimension tables as PRODUCT_SALES. This is done to maintain consistency within the data warehouse, and when a dimension table links to two or more fact tables it is called a **conformed dimension**.

Why would we add a fact table named SALES_FOR_RFM? To explain that, we need to discuss reporting systems.

Figure 13-15

The Two-Dimensional
ProductNumber–CustomerID
Matrix

Each cell shows the total quantity of each product that has been purchased by each customer

ProductNumber	CustomerID											
	1	2	3	4	5	6	7	8	9	10	11	12
BK001	1		1	1			1		1			
BK002			1	1		1	1					1
VB001	1		2	1	1				1			
VB002			2						1		2	
VB003						1		1			2	1
VK001	1		2	1	1				1			
VK002			2	1		1			1		2	1
VK003						1	1	1			2	1
VK004				1		1	2	1			2	1

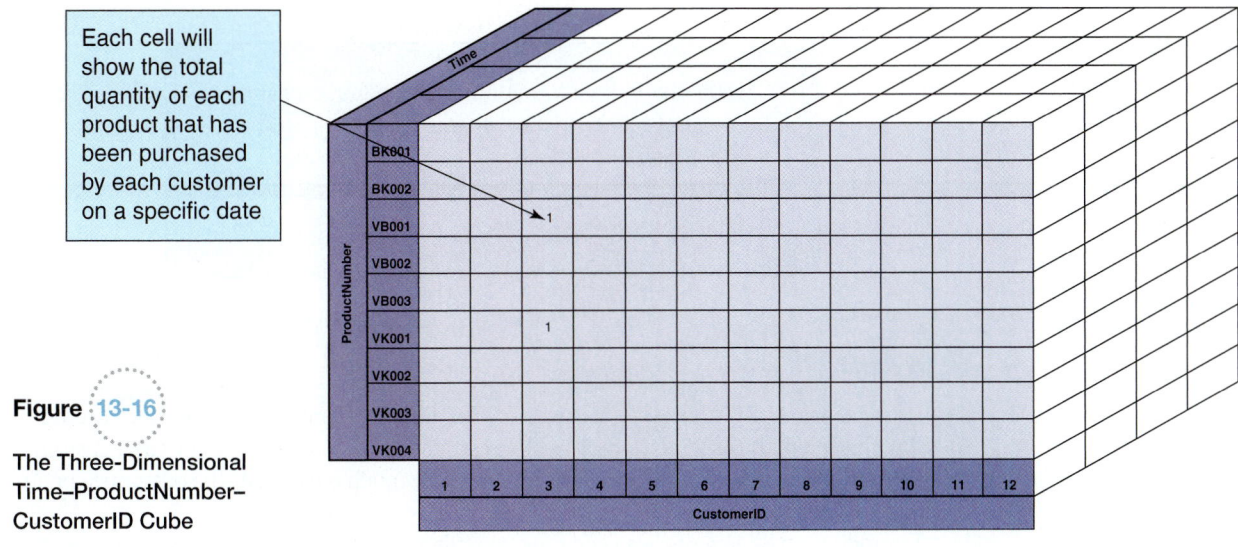

Figure 13-16

The Three-Dimensional Time–ProductNumber–CustomerID Cube

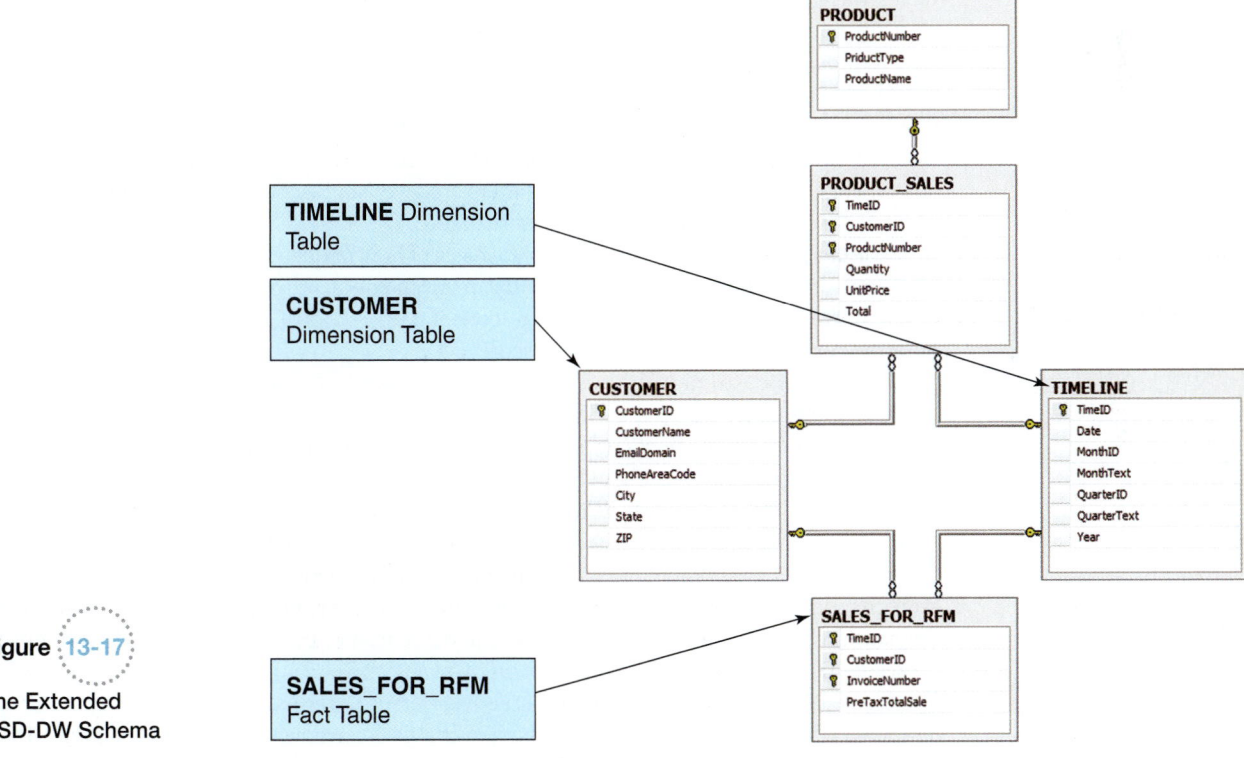

Figure 13-17

The Extended HSD-DW Schema

Reporting Systems

The purpose of a reporting system is to create meaningful information from disparate data sources and to deliver that information to the proper users on a timely basis. As stated earlier, reporting systems differ from data mining because they create information using the simple operations of sorting, filtering, grouping, and making simple calculations. We begin this section with a description of a typical reporting problem: RFM analysis.

Figure 13-18

RFM Analysis

- Simple report-based customer classification scheme
- Score customers on recentness, frequency, and monetary size of orders
- Typically, divide each criterion into 5 groups and score from 1 to 5

RFM Analysis

As discussed earlier, **RFM analysis** is a way of analyzing and ranking customers according to their purchasing patterns. It is a simple technique that considers how *recently* (**R**) a customer ordered, how *frequently* (**F**) a customer orders, and how much *money* (**M**) the customer spends per order. RFM is summarized in Figure 13-18.

To produce an RFM score, we need only two things: customer data and sales data for each purchase (the date of the sale and the total amount of the sale) made by each customer. If you look at the SALES_FOR_RFM table and its associated CUSTOMER and TIMELINE dimension tables in Figure 13-17, you see that we have exactly those data: The SALE_FOR_RFM table is the starting point for RFM analysis in the HSD-DW BI system.

To produce an RFM score, customer purchase records are first sorted by the date of their most recent (R) purchase. In a common form of this analysis, the customers are divided into five groups, and a score of 1 to 5 is given to customers in each group. Thus, the 20 percent of the customers having the most recent orders are given an R score of 1, the 20 percent of the customers having the next most recent orders are given an R score of 2, and so forth, down to the last 20 percent, who are given an R score of 5.

The customers are then resorted on the basis of how frequently they order. The 20 percent of the customers who order most frequently are given an F score of 1, the next 20 percent most frequently ordering customers are given a score of 2, and so forth, down to the least frequently ordering customers, who are given an F score of 5.

Finally, the customers are sorted again according to the amount of their orders. The 20 percent who have ordered the most expensive items are given an M score of 1, the next 20 percent are given an M score of 2, and so forth, down to the 20 percent who spend the least, who are given an M score of 5.

Figure 13-19 shows sample RFM data for Heather Sweeney Designs. (Note that these data have *not* been calculated and are for illustrative purposes only.) The first customer, Ralph Able, has a score of {1 1 2}, which means that he has ordered recently and orders frequently. His M score of 2 indicates, however, that he does not order the most expensive goods. From these scores, the salespeople can surmise that Ralph is a good customer but that they should attempt to up-sell Ralph to more expensive goods.

Susan Baker (RFM score of {2 2 3}) is above average in terms of how frequently she shops and how recently she has shopped, but her purchases are average in value. Sally George (RFM score of {3 3 3}) is truly in the middle. Jenny Tyler (RFM score of {5 1 1}) is a problem. Jenny has not ordered in some time, but, in the past, when she did order, she ordered frequently, and her orders were of the highest monetary value. These data suggest that Jenny might be going to another vendor. Someone from the sales team should contact her immediately. However, no one on the sales team should be talking to Chantel Jacobs (RFM score of {5 5 5}). She has not

Figure 13-19

The RFM Score Report

Each customer is ranked for **R** (recent), **F** (frequent), and **M** (money) characteristics—1 is highest (best) and 5 is lowest (worst) score

Customer	RFM Score		
	R	F	M
Able, Ralph	1	1	2
Baker, Susan	2	2	3
George, Sally	3	3	3
Tyler, Jenny	5	1	1
Jacobs, Chantel	5	5	5

ordered for some time, she doesn't order frequently, and when she does order, she only buys inexpensive items and not many of them.

Producing the RFM Report

Like most reports, an RFM report can be created using a series of SQL expressions. This section presents two SQL Server stored procedures that produce RFM scores. Figure 13-20 shows the five tables that are used.

The CUSTOMER_SALES table contains the raw data that is used in the RFM calculations. CUSTOMER_RFM contains CustomerID and the final R, F, and M scores. The remaining three tables, CUSTOMER_R, CUSTOMER_F, and CUSTOMER_M are used to store intermediate results. Note that all CustomerID columns are NOT NULL.

The stored procedure shown in Figure 13-21 is used to calculate and store the R, F, and M scores. It begins by deleting the results from any prior analysis from the CUSTOMER_R, CUSTOMER_F, and CUSTOMER_M tables. It then calls three procedures for computing the R, F, and M scores. Finally, it stores the R, F, and M scores in the CUSTOMER_RFM table. Only this table is needed for reporting purposes.

Figure 13-20

SQL Server Tables
for RFM Analysis

```sql
CREATE TABLE CUSTOMER_SALES (
    CustomerID          Int         NOT NULL,
    TransactionID       Int         NOT NULL,
    TransactionDate     DateTime    NOT NULL,
    OrderAmt            Money       NOT NULL,
    CONSTRAINT      Customer_Sales_PK
                        PRIMARY KEY(TransactionID)
    );

CREATE TABLE CUSTOMER_RFM (
    CustomerID          Int         NOT NULL,
    R                   SmallInt    NULL,
    F                   SmallInt    NULL,
    M                   SmallInt    NULL,
    CONSTRAINT      Customer_RFM_PK
                        PRIMARY KEY(CustomerID)
    );

CREATE TABLE CUSTOMER_R (
    CustomerID          Int         NOT NULL,
    MostRecentOrderDate DateTime    NULL,
    R                   SmallInt    NULL,
    CONSTRAINT      Customer_R_PK
                        PRIMARY KEY(CustomerID)
    );

CREATE TABLE CUSTOMER_F (
    CustomerID          Int         NOT NULL,
    OrderCount          Int         NULL,
    R                   SmallInt    NULL,
    CONSTRAINT      Customer_F_PK
                        PRIMARY KEY(CustomerID)
    );

CREATE TABLE CUSTOMER_M (
    CustomerID          Int         NOT NULL,
    AverageOrderAmount  Money       NULL,
    R                   SmallInt    NULL,
    CONSTRAINT      Customer_M_PK
                        PRIMARY KEY(CustomerID)
    );
```

```
CREATE PROCEDURE RFM_Analysis

AS

/*** Delete any existing RFM data   ***/
DELETE FROM CUSTOMER_R;
DELETE FROM CUSTOMER_F;
DELETE FROM CUSTOMER_M;

/*** Compute R, F, M Scores  **********/
Exec Calculate_R;
Exec Calculate_F;
Exec Calculate_M;

/*** Display Results  ****************/
SELECT      R_Score, Count(*) AS R_Count
FROM        CUSTOMER_R
GROUP BY    R_Score;

SELECT      F_Score, Count(*) AS F_Count
FROM        CUSTOMER_F
GROUP BY    F_Score;

SELECT      M_Score, Count(*) AS M_Count
FROM        CUSTOMER_M
GROUP BY    M_Score;

/***  Store Results  *****************/
INSERT INTO CUSTOMER_RFM (CustomerID)
      (SELECT  CustomerID
       FROM CUSTOMER_SALES);

UPDATE CUSTOMER_RFM
SET    R =
       (SELECT R_Score
        FROM CUSTOMER_R
        WHERE CUSTOMER_RFM.CustomerID = CUSTOMER_R.CustomerID);

UPDATE CUSTOMER_RFM
SET    F =
       (SELECT F_Score
        FROM CUSTOMER_F
        WHERE CUSTOMER_RFM.CustomerID = CUSTOMER_F.CustomerID);

UPDATE CUSTOMER_RFM
SET    M =
       (SELECT M_Score
        FROM CUSTOMER_M
        WHERE CUSTOMER_RFM.CustomerID = CUSTOMER_M.CustomerID);
```

Figure 13-21

The RFM_Analysis Stored Procedure

The Calculate_R stored procedure shown in Figure 13-22 illustrates how the R score is calculated. This procedure first places the date of each customer's most recent order into the MostRecentOrderDate column. Then, it uses the **SQL Top ... Percent option** of SQL SELECT statements to set the R_Score values. The first UPDATE statement sets the value of R_Score to 1 for the top 20 percent of customers (after they have been sorted in descending order according to MostRecentOrderDate). Then, it sets the R_Score to 2 for the top 25 percent of

```
CREATE PROCEDURE Calculate_R

AS

/*** Compute R_Score   ********************************/

INSERT INTO CUSTOMER_R (CustomerID, MostRecentOrderDate)
       (SELECT  CustomerID, Max (TransactionDate)
        FROM CUSTOMER_SALES
        GROUP BY CustomerID);

UPDATE     CUSTOMER_R
SET        R_Score = 1
WHERE      CustomerID IN
           (Select Top 20 Percent CustomerID
            FROM CUSTOMER_R
            ORDER BY MostRecentOrderDate DESC);

UPDATE     CUSTOMER_R
SET        R_Score = 2
WHERE      CustomerID IN
           (Select Top 25 PERCENT CustomerID
            FROM CUSTOMER_R
            WHERE R_Score IS NULL
            ORDER BY MostRecentOrderDate DESC);

UPDATE     CUSTOMER_R
SET        R_Score = 3
WHERE      CustomerID IN
           (Select Top 33 PERCENT CustomerID
            FROM CUSTOMER_R
            WHERE R_Score IS NULL
            ORDER BY MostRecentOrderDate DESC);

UPDATE     CUSTOMER_R
SET        R_Score = 4
WHERE      CustomerID IN
           (Select Top 50 PERCENT CustomerID
            FROM CUSTOMER_R
            WHERE R_Score IS NULL
            ORDER BY MostRecentOrderDate DESC);

UPDATE     CUSTOMER_R
SET        R_Score = 5
WHERE      CustomerID IN
           (Select CustomerID
            FROM CUSTOMER_R
            WHERE R_Score IS NULL);
```

Figure 13-22

**The Calculate_R
Stored Procedure**

customers who have a null value for R_Score in descending order of MostRecentOrderDate. The procedure continues to set the R values for all customers. The Calculate_F and Calculate_M procedures are similar and will be left to you as exercise 13.57.

Figure 13-23 shows how the CUSTOMER_RFM table is used for reporting purposes. Figure 13-23 shows a SELECT on CUSTOMER_RFM that was prepared using a database of more than 5,000 customers and over 1 million transactions. The preparation of the CUSTOMER_RFM table required less than 30 seconds on a moderately powered personal computer.

The results in Figure 13-23 are interesting, but unless this information is delivered to the correct users, it will be of no ultimate value to the organization. For example, the 12th row in

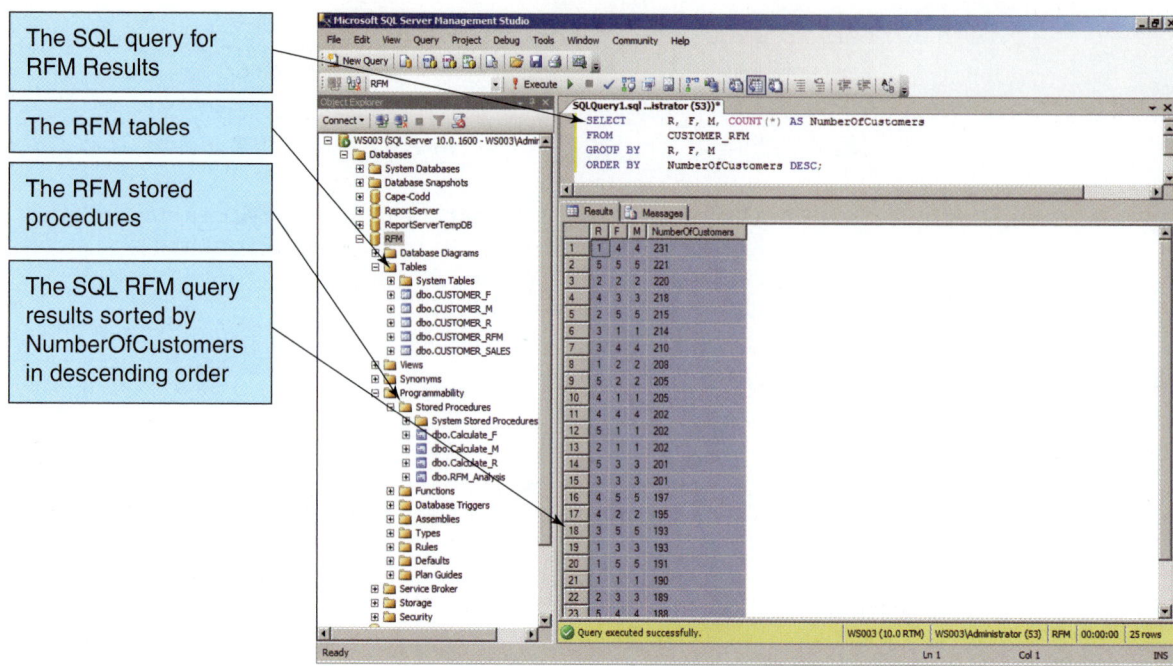

The SQL query for RFM Results

The RFM tables

The RFM stored procedures

The SQL RFM query results sorted by NumberOfCustomers in descending order

Figure 13-23

Example RFM Results

this figure shows that 202 customers have an RFM score of {5 1 1}. These customers order frequently, they order items of high monetary value, but they have not ordered recently. The company may be in danger of losing them. Somehow this report and the customers who have these scores (see Review Question 13.32) need to be made available to the appropriate sales personnel. To understand the modern means for accomplishing this, we will consider the components of a reporting system.

Reporting System Components

Figure 13-24 shows the major components of a reporting system. Data from disparate data sources are read and processed. As shown, reporting systems can obtain data from operational databases, from data warehouses, and from data marts. Some data are generated within the organization, other data are obtained from public sources, and still other data may be purchased from data utilities.

Figure 13-24

Components of a Reporting System

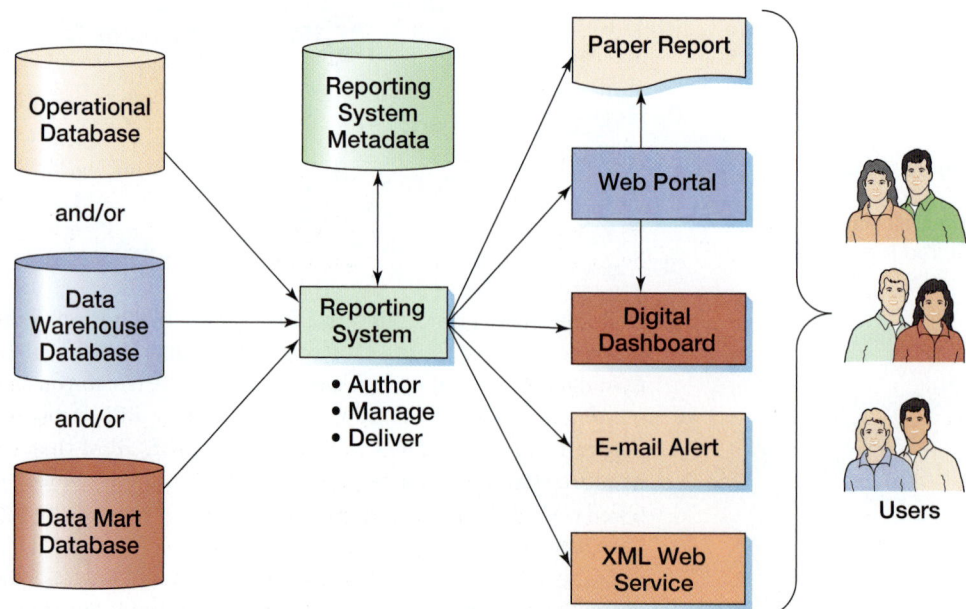

Figure 13-25

Report Characteristics

Type	Media	Mode
Static	Paper	Push
Dynamic	Web portal	Pull
Query	Digital dashboard	
OnLine Analytical Processing (OLAP)	E-mail/alert	
	XML Web service and application specific	

A reporting system maintains a database of reporting metadata. The metadata describes reports, users, groups, roles, events, and other entities involved in the reporting activity. The reporting system uses the metadata to prepare and deliver appropriate reports to the proper users in the correct format on a timely basis.

As shown in Figure 13-24, reports can be prepared in a variety of formats. Figure 13-25 lists report characteristics.

Report Types

Some reports are **static**. They are prepared once from the underlying data, and they do not change. A report of last year's sales, for example, is a static report. Other reports are **dynamic**; at the time of their creation, the reporting system reads the latest, most current data and generates the report using those fresh data. Reports on today's sales or on current stock prices are dynamic reports.

Query reports are prepared in response to information entered by users. Google is an example of a query report. You enter the keywords you want to search for, and the reporting system within Google searches its database and generates a response that is particular to your query. Within an organization, a query report could be generated to show current inventory levels. The user enters item numbers, and the reporting system responds with inventory levels of those items at various stores and warehouses.

Another type of report is an OLAP, or OnLine Analytical Processing, report. OLAP reports enable the user to dynamically change the report-grouping structures. An OLAP reporting application is illustrated later in this chapter.

Report Media

Today, reports are delivered via many different channels. Some reports are printed on paper, others are created in formats such as PDF that can be printed or viewed electronically. Other reports are delivered via Web portals. An organization might place sales reports on the sales department's Web portal and a report on customers serviced on the customer service department's Web portal.

A **digital dashboard** is an electronic display that is customized for a particular user. Companies such as Yahoo! and MSN offer digital dashboard services. Users of these services can define the content they want to see—say, a local weather forecast, a list of stock prices, and a list of news sources—and the vendor constructs the customized display for each user. Such pages are called My Yahoo! or My MSN, or some similar title. Other dashboards are particular to an organization. Executives at a manufacturing organization, for example, might have a dashboard that shows up-to-the-minute production and sales activities.

Reports can also be delivered via **alerts**. Users can declare that they wish to be notified of news and events by e-mail or on their cell phone. Of course, some cell phones are capable of displaying Web pages and can use digital dashboards as well.

Finally, reports can be delivered to other information systems. The modern way to do this is to publish reports as an XML Web service. This style of reporting is particularly useful for interorganizational information systems, such as supply chain management.

Report Modes

The final report characteristic in Figure 13-25 is report mode. A **push report** is sent to users based on a predetermined schedule. Users receive the report without any activity on their part. A **pull report** is one that users must request. To obtain a pull report, a user goes to a Web portal or digital dashboard and clicks a link or button to cause the reporting system to produce and deliver the report.

Report System Functions

As shown in Figure 13-25, the **reporting system** serves three functions: authoring, management, and delivery.

Report Authoring
Report authoring involves connecting to the required data sources, creating the report structure, and formatting the report. Figures 13-26 and 13-27 show the use of SQL Server Business Intelligence Development Studio to author a report that publishes the results of an RFM analysis done in SQL Server. The SQL Server Business Intelligence Development Studio is a version of Microsoft Visual Studio .NET that is included with SQL Server 2008 (it is one of the tools in the SQL Server 2008 Express Advanced as well as being included in all major versions of SQL Server 2008).

In Figure 13-26, the developer has specified a database that contains the CUSTOMER_RFM table and has just entered the SQL statement shown in Figure 13-23. You can see the SQL statement in the lower-center portion of this display.

In Figure 13-27, the report author creates the format of the report by specifying the headings and selecting the format for the data items. In a more complicated report, the author would specify the sorting and grouping of data items, as well as page headers and footers. The developer uses the property list in the right-hand side of the display in Figure 13-27 to set the values for item

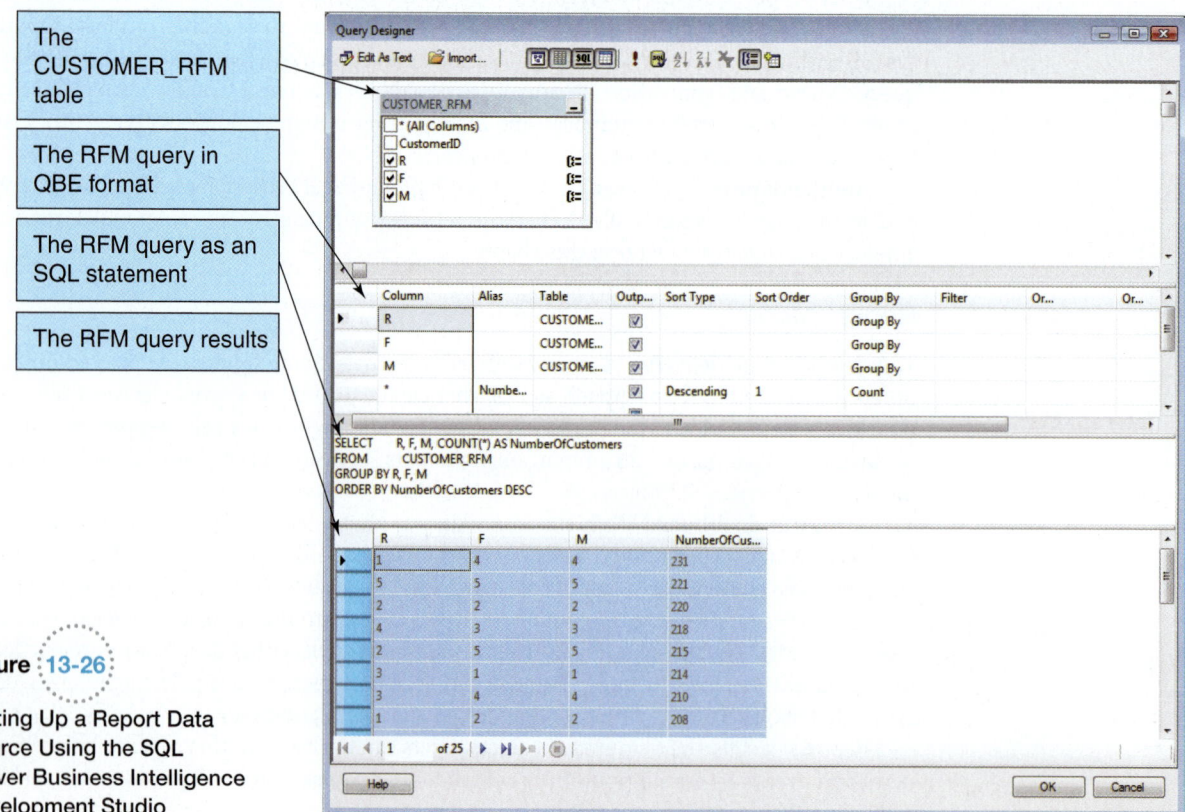

Figure 13-26

Setting Up a Report Data Source Using the SQL Server Business Intelligence Development Studio

Figure 13-27

Formatting a Report Using the SQL Server Business Intelligence Developement Studio

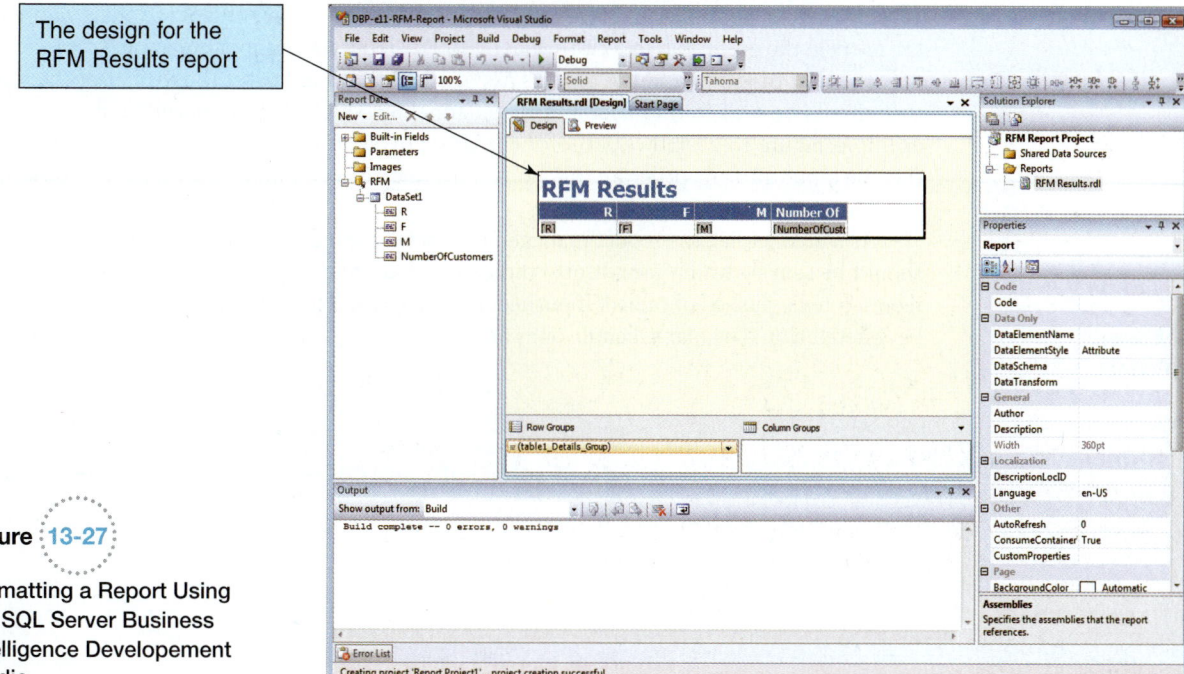

The design for the RFM Results report

properties. The final report, as it appears in a browser window, is shown in Figure 13-28. To learn more about this application, search for "reporting services" at *www.microsoft.com.*

Report Management

The purpose of **report management** is to define who receives what reports, when, and by what means. Most report management systems enable the report administrator to define user accounts and user groups and to assign particular users to particular groups. For example, all of the salespeople would be assigned to the sales group, all of the executives would be assigned to the executive group, and so forth. All of these data are stored in the reporting system metadata shown in Figure 13-24.

Reports created using the report authoring system are assigned to groups and users. Assigning reports to groups saves the administrator work; when a report is created, changed,

Figure 13-28

The RFM Report in a Web Browser

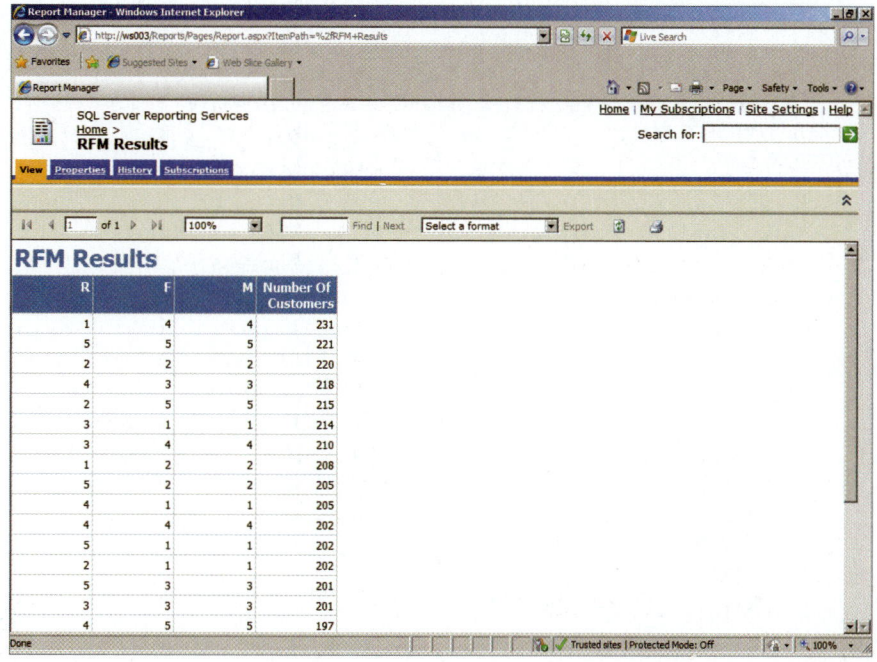

or removed, the administrator need only change the report assignments to the group. All of the users in the group will inherit the changes. The report assignment metadata includes not only the user or group and the reports assigned, but also indicates the format of the report that should be sent to that user and the channel by which the report will be delivered. For example, Figure 13-29 shows part of the RFM report materialized in XML. The XML file can then be input into any program that consumes XML and manipulated via XSL, as described in Chapter 12.

As stated earlier, the report management metadata indicates which format of the report should be sent to which user. It also indicates what channel is to be used and whether the report is to be pushed or pulled. If pushed, the administrator declares whether the report is to be generated on a regular schedule or as an alert.

Figure 13-29

The RFM Report in XML Format

```xml
<?xml version="1.0" encoding="UTF-8"?>
<MyData xmlns:xsi="http://www.w3.org/2001/XMLSchema-instance"
    xsi:noNamespaceSchemaLocation="C:\inetpub\wwwroot\DBP\VRG\DBP-e11-Figure-13-29-B.xsd">
    <CUSTOMER_RFM>
        <R>1</R>
        <F>4</F>
        <M>4</M>
        <NumberOfCustomers>231</NumberOfCustomers>
    </CUSTOMER_RFM>
    <CUSTOMER_RFM>
        <R>5</R>
        <F>5</F>
        <M>5</M>
        <NumberOfCustomers>221</NumberOfCustomers>
    </CUSTOMER_RFM>
    <CUSTOMER_RFM>
        <R>2</R>
        <F>2</F>
        <M>2</M>
        <NumberOfCustomers>220</NumberOfCustomers>
    </CUSTOMER_RFM>
    <CUSTOMER_RFM>
        <R>4</R>
        <F>3</F>
        <M>3</M>
        <NumberOfCustomers>218</NumberOfCustomers>
    </CUSTOMER_RFM>
    <CUSTOMER_RFM>
        <R>2</R>
        <F>5</F>
        <M>5</M>
        <NumberOfCustomers>215</NumberOfCustomers>
    </CUSTOMER_RFM>
    <CUSTOMER_RFM>
        <R>3</R>
        <F>1</F>
        <M>1</M>
        <NumberOfCustomers>214</NumberOfCustomers>
    </CUSTOMER_RFM>
    <CUSTOMER_RFM>
        <R>3</R>
        <F>4</F>
        <M>4</M>
        <NumberOfCustomers>210</NumberOfCustomers>
    </CUSTOMER_RFM>
    <CUSTOMER_RFM>
        <R>1</R>
        <F>2</F>
        <M>2</M>
        <NumberOfCustomers>208</NumberOfCustomers>
    </CUSTOMER_RFM>
</MyData>
```

Report Delivery

The **report delivery** function of a reporting system pushes reports or allows them to be pulled based on the report management metadata. Reports can be delivered via an e-mail server, a Web portal, XML Web services, or by other program-specific means. The report delivery system uses the operating system and other program security components to ensure that only authorized users receive authorized reports. It also ensures that push reports are produced at appropriate times.

For query reports, the report delivery system serves as an intermediary between the user and the report generator. It receives user query data, such as the item numbers in an inventory query, passes the query data to the report generator, receives the resulting report, and delivers the report to the user.

OLAP

OLAP provides the ability to sum, count, average, and perform other simple arithmetic operations on groups of data. OLAP systems produce **OLAP reports**. An OLAP report is also called an **OLAP cube**. This is a reference to the dimensional data model, and some OLAP products show OLAP displays using three axes, like a geometric cube. The remarkable characteristic of an OLAP report is that it is dynamic: The format of an OLAP report can be changed by the viewer, hence the term *online* in the name OnLine Analytical Processing.

OLAP uses the dimensional database model discussed earlier in this chapter, so it is not surprising to learn that an OLAP report has measures and dimensions. A measure is a dimensional model *fact*—the data item of interest that is to be summed or averaged or otherwise processed in the OLAP report. For example, sales data may be summed to produce Total Sales or averaged to produce Average Sales. The term *measure* is used because you are dealing with quantities that have been or can be measured and recorded. A dimension, as you have already learned, is an attribute or a characteristic of a measure. Purchase date (TimeID), customer location (City), and sales region (ZIP or State) are all examples of dimensions, and in the HSD-DW database, you saw how the time dimension is important.

In this section we will generate an OLAP report by using an SQL query from the HSD-DW database and a Microsoft Excel **PivotTable**.

> **BY THE WAY** We use Microsoft SQL Server and Microsoft Excel to illustrate this discussion of OLAP reports and PivotTables. For other DBMS products, such as MySQL, you can use the DataPilot feature of the Calc spreadsheet application in the OpenOffice.org product suite (see *www.openoffice.org*).

Now we can either create an Excel-formatted table in an Excel worksheet:

- Copy the SQL query results into an Excel worksheet.
- Add column names to the results.
- Format the query results as an Excel table (optional).
- Select the Excel range containing the results with column names.

Or connect to a DBMS data source:

- Click the PivotTable button in the Tables group of the Insert ribbon.
- Specify that the PivotTable should be in a new worksheet.
- Select the column variables (Column Labels), row variables (Row Labels), and the measure to be displayed (Values).

We can use an SQL query if we copy the data into an Excel worksheet. The SQL query, as used in SQL Server, is:

```sql
SELECT      C.CustomerID, CustomerName, C.City,
            P.ProductNumber, P.ProductName,
            T.[Year], T.QuarterText,
            SUM(PS.Quantity) AS TotalQuantity
FROM        CUSTOMER C, PRODUCT_SALES PS, PRODUCT P, TIMELINE T
WHERE       C.CustomerID = PS.CustomerID
   AND      P.ProductNumber = PS.ProductNumber
   AND      T.TimeID = PS.TimeID
GROUP BY    C.CustomerID, C.CustomerName, C.City,
            P. ProductNumber, P.ProductName,
            T.QuarterText, T.[Year]
ORDER BY    C.CustomerName, T.[Year], T.QuarterText;
```

However, because SQL Server (and other SQL-based DBMS products, such as Oracle and MySQL) can store views but not queries, we need to create and use an SQL view if we are going to use an Excel-data connection. The SQL query to create the HSDDWProductSalesView, as used in SQL Server, is:

```sql
CREATE VIEW HSDDWProductSalesView AS
   SELECT      C.CustomerID, C.CustomerName, C.City,
               P.ProductNumber, P.ProductName,
               T.[Year], T.QuarterText,
               SUM(PS.Quantity) AS TotalQuantity
   FROM        CUSTOMER C, PRODUCT_SALES PS, PRODUCT P, TIMELINE T
   WHERE       C.CustomerID = PS.CustomerID
      AND      P.ProductNumber = PS.ProductNumber
      AND      T.TimeID = PS.TimeID
   GROUP BY    C.CustomerID, C.CustomerName, C.City,
               P. ProductNumber, P.ProductName,
               T.QuarterText, T.[Year];
```

Figure 13-30 shows the OLAP report as an Excel PivotTable. Here, the measure is quantity sold, and the dimensions are ProductNumber and City. This report shows how quantity varies by product and city. For example, four copies of VB003 (Kitchen Remodeling Dallas Style Video Companion) were sold in Dallas, but none were sold in Austin.

We generated the OLAP report in Figure 13-30 by using a simple SQL query and Microsoft Excel, but many DBMS and BI products include more powerful and sophisticated tool. For example, SQL Server includes SQL Server Analysis Services.[1] It is possible to display OLAP cubes in many ways besides with Excel. Some third-party vendors provide more sophisticated graphical displays, and OLAP reports can be delivered just like any of the other reports described for report management systems.

---

[1] Up to this point in this book, we have been able to do everything in this book using SQL Server 2008 Express. Unfortunately, SQL Server Express Edition does not include SQL Server Analysis Services, so you will have to use the SQL Server Standard Edition or better if you want to use the SQL Server Analysis Services. Although OLAP reports *can* be done without SQL Server Analysis Services, Server Analysis Services adds a lot of functionality, and the Microsoft SQL Server 2008 Data Mining Add-ins for Microsoft Office 2007 (used in this text) will not function without it.

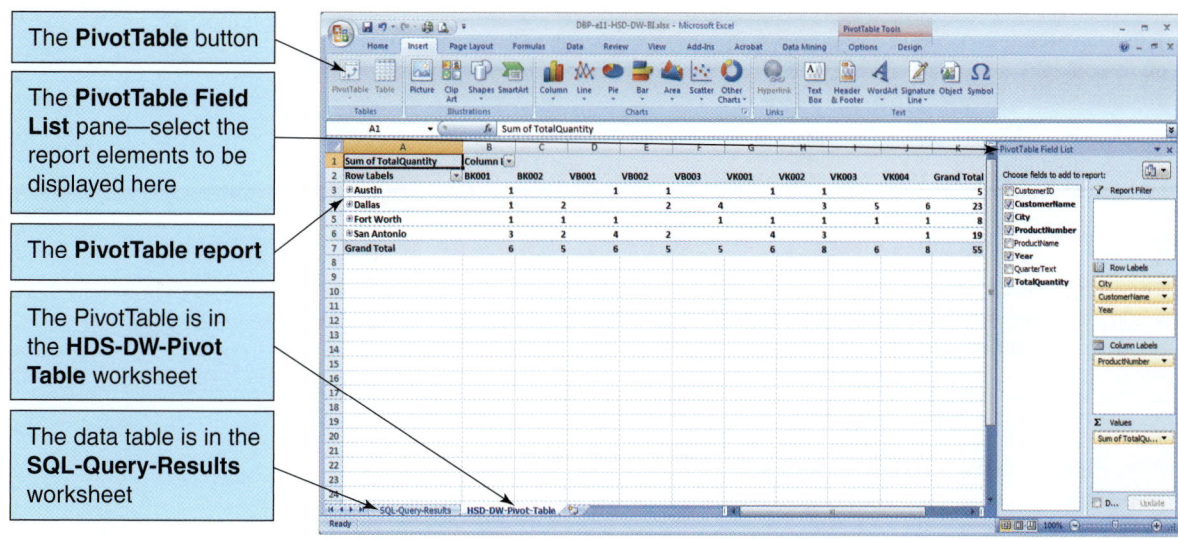

The **PivotTable** button

The **PivotTable Field List** pane—select the report elements to be displayed here

The **PivotTable report**

The PivotTable is in the **HDS-DW-Pivot Table** worksheet

The data table is in the **SQL-Query-Results** worksheet

Figure 13-30

OLAP ProductNumber by City Report

The distinguishing characteristic of an OLAP report is that the user can alter the format of the report. Figure 13-30 shows an alteration in which the user added two additional dimensions, customer and year, to the horizontal display. Quantity sold is now broken out by customer and, in one case, by year. With an OLAP report, it is possible to **drill down** into the data—that is, to further divide the data into more detail. In Figure 13-31, for example, the user has drilled down into the San Antonio data to display all customer data for that city and to display year sales data for Ralph Able.

In an OLAP report, it is also possible to change the order of the dimensions. Figure 13-32 shows city quantities as vertical data, and ProductID quantities as horizontal data. This OLAP report shows quantity sold by city, by product, customer, and year.

Both displays are valid and useful, depending on the user's perspective. A product manager might like to see product families first (ProductID) and then location data (city). A sales manager might like to see location data first and then product data. OLAP reports provide both perspectives, and the user can switch between them while viewing a report.

Unfortunately, all of this flexibility comes at a cost. If the database is large, doing the necessary calculating, grouping, and sorting for such dynamic displays will require substantial computing power. Although standard, commercial DBMS products do have the features and functions required to create OLAP reports, they are not designed for such work. They are designed to provide rapid response to transaction processing applications such as order entry or manufacturing planning.

Accordingly, special-purpose products called **OLAP servers** have been developed to perform OLAP analyses. As shown in Figure 13-33, an OLAP server reads data from an operational database, performs preliminary calculations, and stores the results of those calculations in an OLAP database. For performance and security reasons, the OLAP server and the DBMS usually run on separate computers. The OLAP server would normally be located in the data warehouse or a data mart.

Figure 13-31

OLAP ProductNumber by City, Customer, and Year Report

The City = San Antonio data are also showing customer data

The Customer = Able, Ralph data are also showing year data

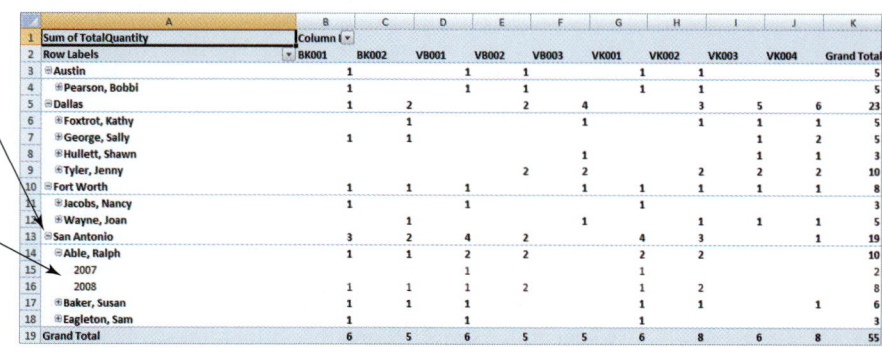

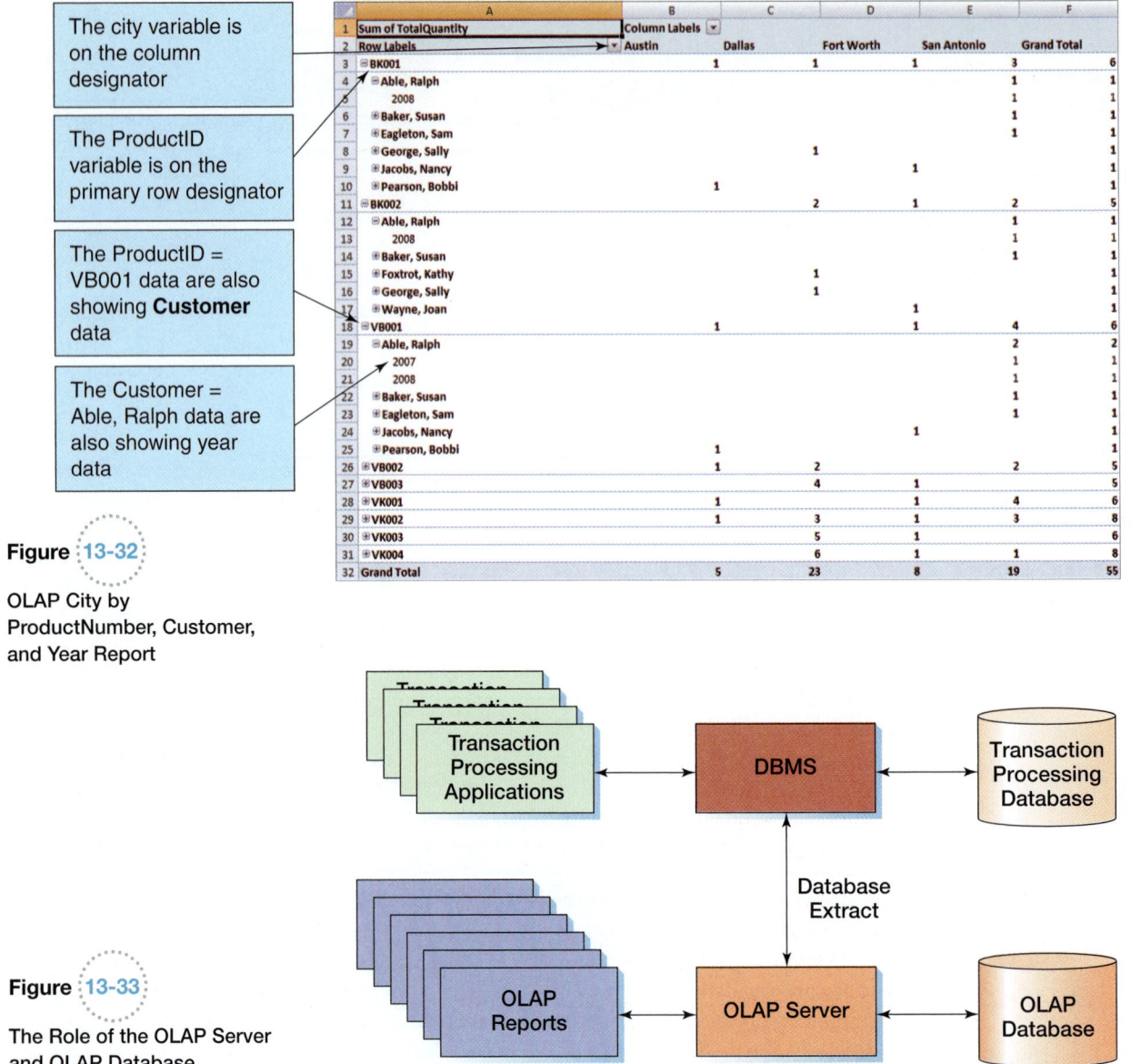

Figure 13-32

OLAP City by ProductNumber, Customer, and Year Report

Annotations:
- The city variable is on the column designator
- The ProductID variable is on the primary row designator
- The ProductID = VB001 data are also showing **Customer** data
- The Customer = Able, Ralph data are also showing year data

Sum of TotalQuantity Row Labels	Austin	Dallas	Fort Worth	San Antonio	Grand Total
⊟ BK001	1	1	1	3	6
⊟ Able, Ralph				1	1
2008				1	1
⊞ Baker, Susan				1	1
⊞ Eagleton, Sam				1	1
⊞ George, Sally		1			1
⊞ Jacobs, Nancy			1		1
⊞ Pearson, Bobbi	1				1
⊟ BK002		2	1	2	5
⊟ Able, Ralph				1	1
2008				1	1
⊞ Baker, Susan				1	1
⊞ Foxtrot, Kathy		1			1
⊞ George, Sally		1			1
⊞ Wayne, Joan			1		1
⊟ VB001	1		1	4	6
⊟ Able, Ralph				2	2
2007				1	1
2008				1	1
⊞ Baker, Susan				1	1
⊞ Eagleton, Sam				1	1
⊞ Jacobs, Nancy			1		1
⊞ Pearson, Bobbi	1				1
⊞ VB002	1	2		2	5
⊞ VB003		4	1		5
⊞ VK001	1		1	4	6
⊞ VK002	1	3	1	3	8
⊞ VK003		5	1		6
⊞ VK004		6	1	1	8
Grand Total	5	23	8	19	55

Figure 13-33

The Role of the OLAP Server and OLAP Database

[Diagram: Transaction Processing Applications ↔ DBMS ↔ Transaction Processing Database; Database Extract; OLAP Reports ↔ OLAP Server ↔ OLAP Database]

Data Mining

Instead of the basic calculations filtering, sorting, and grouping used in reporting applications, data mining involves the application of sophisticated mathematical and statistical techniques to find patterns and relationships that can be used to classify data and predict future outcomes. As shown in Figure 13-34, data mining represents the convergence of several phenomena. Data mining techniques have emerged from the statistical and mathematics disciplines and from the artificial intelligence and machine-learning communities. In fact, data mining terminology is an odd combination of terms used by these different disciplines.

Data mining techniques take advantage of developments for processing enormous databases that have emerged in the past dozen or so years. Of course, all these data would not have been generated were it not for fast and inexpensive computers, and, without such computers, the new techniques would be impossible to compute.

Most data mining techniques are sophisticated and difficult to use. However, such techniques are valuable to organizations, and some business professionals, especially those in finance and marketing, have developed expertise in their use. Almost all data mining techniques require specialized software. Popular data mining products are Enterprise Miner from SAS Corporation, Clementine from SPSS, and Insightful Miner from Insightful Corporation.

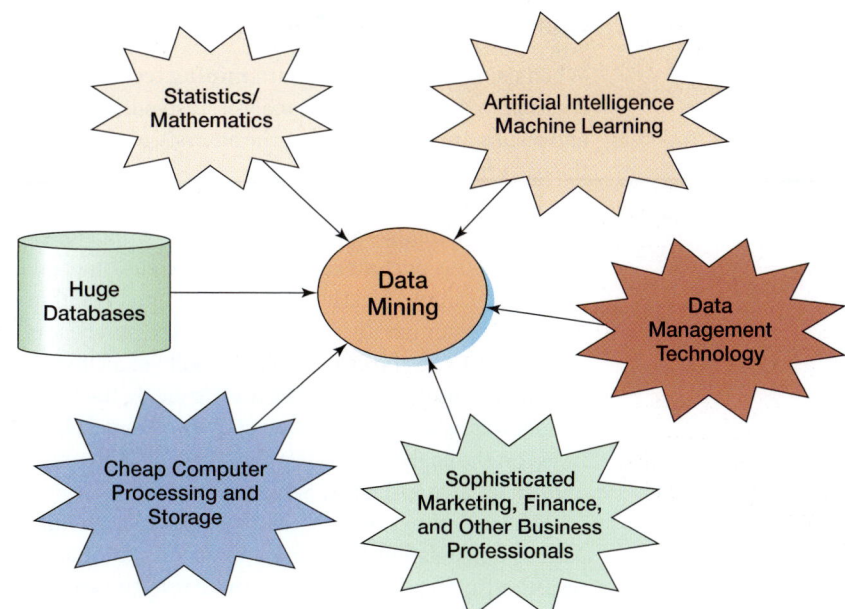

Figure 13-34

Convergence of Disciplines
for Data Mining

However, there is a movement to make data mining available to more users. For example, Microsoft has created the Microsoft SQL Server 2008 Data Mining Add-ins for Office 2007.[2] Figure 13-35 shows Excel 2007 with the Data Mining command tab and command groups. With this add-in, data stored in Excel are sent to SQL Server Analysis Services for processing, and the results are returned to Excel for display.

Data mining techniques fall into two broad categories: unsupervised and supervised.

The **Data Mining** command tab

The **Cluster Analysis** button

The connection to SQL Server 2008 Analysis Services

The data table is in the SQL-Query-Results worksheet

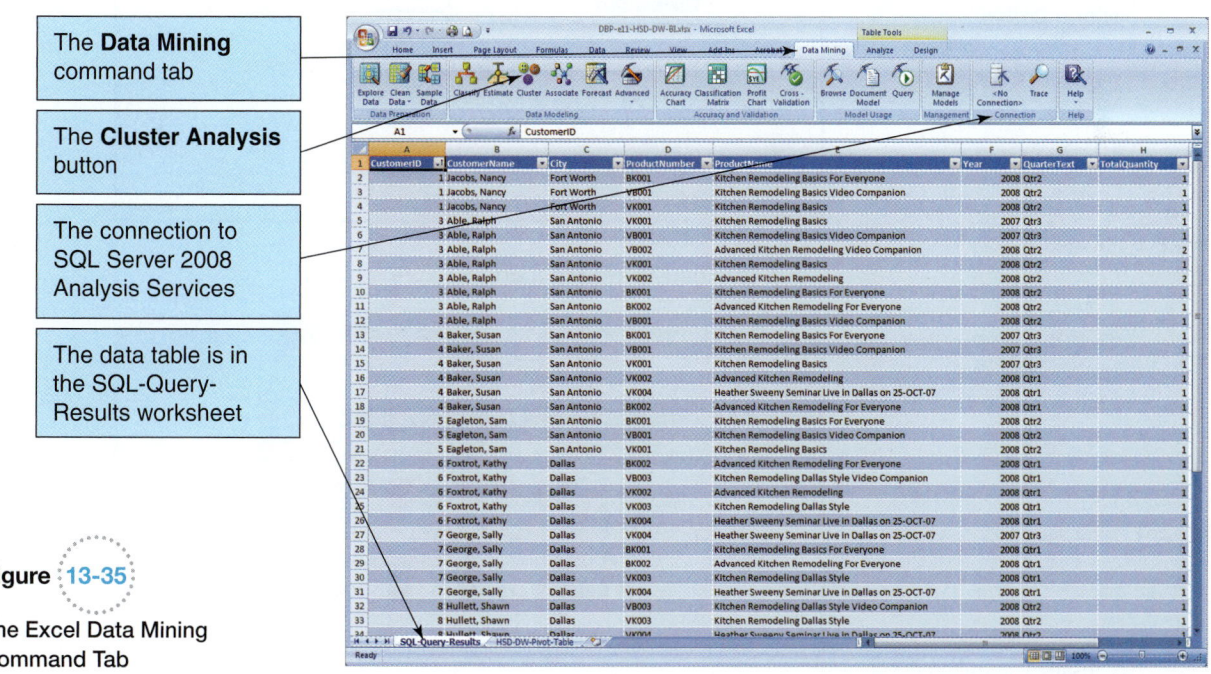

Figure 13-35

The Excel Data Mining
Command Tab

[2] For more information, and to download the Microsoft SQL Server 2005 Data Mining Add-ins for Office 2007 package, go to *www.microsoft.com/sql/technologies/dm/addins.mspx* or directly to the download Web page at *www.microsoft.com/downloads/details.aspx?FamilyId=7c76e8df-8674-4c3b-a99b-55b17f3c4c51&displaylang=en*. The Microsoft SQL Server 2008 Data Mining Add-ins for Office 2007 are available at *www.microsoft.com/ sqlserver/2008/en/us/data-mining.aspx* . Note, however, that these add-ins will not work with SQL Server Express Edition. You have to have a version of SQL Server with SQL Server Analysis Services.

Unsupervised Data Mining

When using **unsupervised data mining** techniques, analysts do not create a model or hypothesis prior to beginning the analysis. Instead, the data mining technique is applied to the data, and results are observed. After the analysis, explanations and hypotheses are created to explain the patterns found.

One commonly used unsupervised technique is **cluster analysis**. With cluster analysis, statistical techniques are used to identify groups of entities that have similar characteristics. A common use for cluster analysis is to find customer groups in order and customer demographic data. For example, Heather Sweeney Designs could use cluster analysis to determine which groups of customers are associated with the purchase of specific products.

Figure 13-36 shows part of the results of a cluster analysis using the same HSD-DW data table in Microsoft Excel that we used to create the OLAP reports. In this case, the cluster analysis tool was asked to generate exactly two clusters based on the ProductID and City variables. Based on the analysis, it is clear that there are different sales patterns for the Dallas area and the non-Dallas area (primarily San Antonio).

These findings were obtained solely by data analysis. No model was used to find these patterns and relationships. The analysis speaks for itself. It is up to the analyst to form hypotheses, after the fact, to explain why these results were obtained.

Figure 13-36

The Cluster Analysis Results

The **Cluster Diagram** tab

The Shading Variable is City and the cluster with **City = Dallas** is shaded

Cluster 1 is based on **City = Dallas**

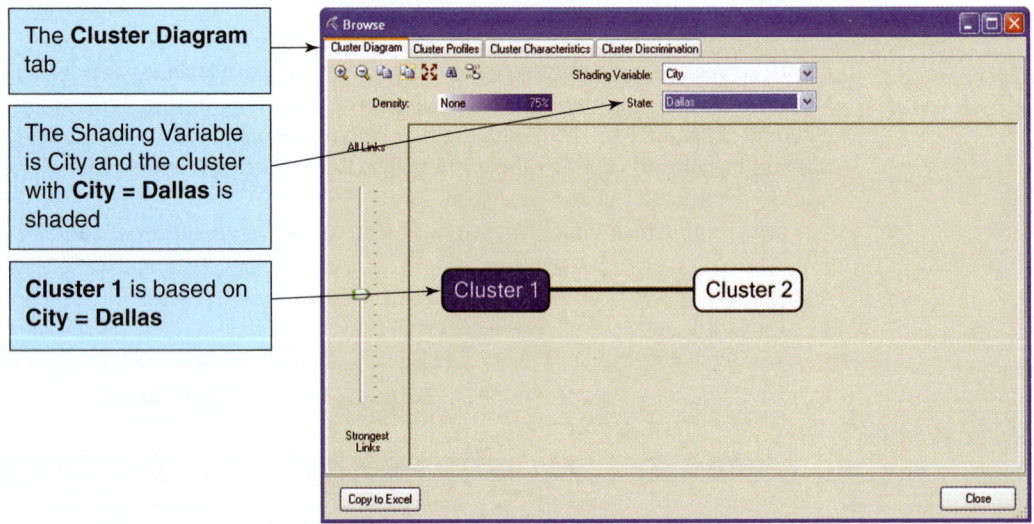

(a) The Cluster Diagram

The **Cluster Profiles** tab

Cluster 2 is based on **City = San Antonio**

Cluster 1 is based on **City = Dallas**

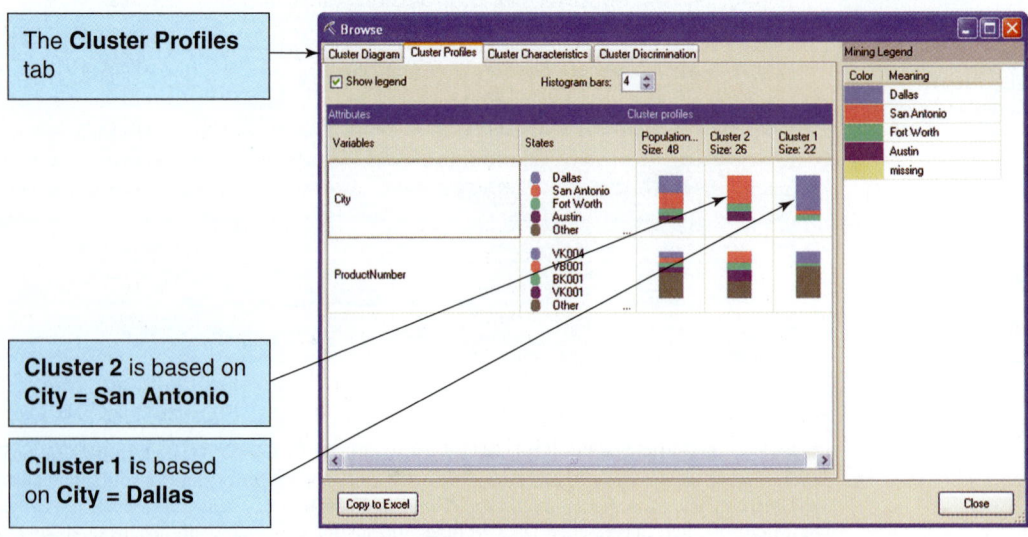

(b) The Cluster Profiles

Supervised Data Mining

With **supervised data mining**, data miners develop a model prior to the analysis and then apply statistical techniques to the data to estimate parameters of the model. For example, suppose that marketing experts at a communications company believe that the use of cell phone weekend minutes is determined by the age of the customer and the number of months the customer has had the cell phone account. A data mining analyst would then run an analysis called a **regression analysis** to determine the coefficients of the equation of that model. A possible result is:

$$CellPhoneWeekendMinutes = 12 + (17.5 * CustomerAge) + (23.7 * NumberMonthsOfAccount)$$

As you will learn in your statistics classes, considerable skill is required to interpret the quality of such a model. The regression tool will create an equation; whether the equation is a good predictor of future cell phone usage depends on t values, confidence intervals, and related statistical techniques.

Three Popular Data Mining Techniques

Three popular data mining techniques are decision trees, logistic regression, and neural networks. **Decision tree analysis** classifies customers or other entities of interest into two or more groups according to past history. **Logistic regression** produces equations that offer probabilities that particular events will occur. Common applications of logistic regression are using donor characteristics to predict the likelihood of a donation in a given period and using customer characteristics to predict the likelihood that customers will switch to another vendor.

Neural networks are complex statistical prediction techniques. The name is a misnomer. Although there is some loose similarity between the structure of a neural network and a network of biological neurons, the similarity is only superficial. Data mining neural networks are just a technique for creating very complex mathematical functions for making predictions.

These three techniques, like almost all data mining techniques, require specialized software. Popular data mining products are Enterprise Miner from the SAS Corporation, Clementine from SPSS, and Insightful Miner from the Insightful Corporation. All of these products have facilities for importing data from relational databases, and, as a database professional, you may be asked to prepare data for input to a data mining product. Typically, this work involves joining relations together into a large flat file and then filtering the data for particular data cases. Simple SQL is used to create such files.

Market Basket Analysis

However, **market basket analysis** is a data mining technique that can be readily implemented with pure SQL. What is market basket analysis?

Suppose that you run a dive shop and one day you realize that one of your salespeople is much better at up-selling your customers. Any of your sales associates can fill a customer's order, but this one salesperson is especially able to sell customers items in addition to those for which they ask. One day you ask him how he does it.

"It's simple," he says, "I just ask myself what is the next product they'd want to buy. If someone buys a dive computer, I don't try to sell her fins. If she's buying a dive computer, she's already a diver, and she already has fins. But, look, these dive computer displays are hard to read. A better mask makes it easier to read the display and get the full benefits from the dive computer."

A market basket analysis is a data mining technique for determining such patterns. A market basket analysis shows the products that customers tend to purchase at the same time. Several different statistical techniques can be used to generate a market basket analysis. Here we will discuss a technique that involves conditional probabilities.

Figure 13-37 shows hypothetical data from 1,000 transactions at a dive shop. The first row of numbers under each column is the total number of transactions that include the product in that column. For example, the 270 in the first row of Mask means that 270 of the 1,000 transactions include the purchase of a mask. The 120 under Dive Computer means that 120 of the 1,000 purchased transactions included a dive computer.

We can use the numbers in the first row to estimate the probability that a customer will purchase an item. Because 270 out of 1,000 transactions included a mask, we can estimate the

1,000 Transactions	Mask	Tank	Fins	Weights	Dive Computer
	270	200	280	130	120
Mask	20	20	150	20	50
Tank	20	80	40	30	30
Fins	150	40	10	60	20
Weights	20	30	60	10	10
Dive Computer	50	30	20	10	5
No Additional Product	10	–	–	–	5

Support = P (A & B)   Example: P (Fins & Mask) = 150 / 1000 = .15
Confidence = P (A | B)   Example: P (Fins | Mask) = 150 / 270 = .55556
Lift = P (A | B)/ P (A) Example: P (Fins | Mask) / P (Fins) = .55556 / .28 = 1.98
   Note: P (Mask | Fins) / P (Mask) = 150 / 280 / .27 = 1.98

Figure 13-37

Market Basket Example

likelihood that a customer will buy a mask to be 270/1,000, or .27. Similarly, the likelihood of a tank purchase is 200/1,000, or .2, and that for fins is 280/1,000, or .28.

The remaining rows in this table show the occurrences of transactions that involve two items. For example, the last column indicates that 50 transactions included both a dive computer and a mask, 30 transactions included a dive computer and a tank, 20 included a dive computer and fins, 10 included a dive computer and weights, 5 included a dive computer with another dive computer (meaning the customer bought two dive computers), and 5 transactions had a dive computer and no other product.

These data are interesting, but we can refine the analysis by computing additional factors. Marketing professionals define **support** as the probability that two items will be purchased together. From these data, the support for fins and mask is 150 out of 1,000, or .15.

Confidence is defined as the probability of buying one product given that a customer purchased another product. The confidence of fins, given that the customer has already purchased a mask, is the number of purchases of fins and masks out of the number of purchases of masks. Thus, in this example, the confidence is 150 out of 270, or .55556. The confidence that a customer purchases a tank, given that the customer has purchased fins, is 40 out of 280, or .14286.

Lift is defined as the ratio of confidence divided by the base probability of an item purchase. The lift for fins given a mask is the probability that a customer buys fins, given the customer has purchased a mask, divided by the overall probability that the customer buys fins. If the lift is greater than one, then the probability of buying fins goes up when a customer buys a mask; if the lift is less than one, the probability of buying fins goes down when a customer buys a mask.

For the data in Figure 13-37, the lift for fins given a mask purchase is .55556/.28, or 1.98. This means that when someone purchases a mask, the likelihood he or she will also purchase fins almost doubles. The lift for fins given a dive computer purchase is 20/120 (the confidence of fins, given a dive computer) divided by .28. The probability that someone buys fins (280 of the 1,000 transaction involved fins) is 20/120 (or .16667), and .16667/.28 is .59524. Therefore, the lift for fins given a dive computer is just under .6, meaning that when a customer buys a dive computer, the likelihood that he or she will buy fins decreases.

Surprisingly, as shown in the last line of Figure 13-37, lift is symmetric. If the lift of fins given mask is 1.98, then the lift of mask given fins is also 1.98.

Using SQL for Market Basket Analysis

All of the major data mining products have features and functions to perform market basket analysis. These products, however, are expensive; you can perform a market basket analysis with basic SQL, if necessary.

```
CREATE VIEW TwoItemBasket AS
        SELECT     T1.Item AS FirstItem,
                   T2.Item AS SecondItem
        FROM       TRANS_DATA T1, TRANS_DATA T2
        WHERE      T1.TransactionID = T1.TransactionID
            AND    T1.ItemID <> T2.ItemID;
```

Figure 13-38

SQL Statement for Creating a Two-item Market Basket

The key SQL statement is shown in Figure 13-38. That SQL statement processes a relation named TRANS_DATA that stores line-item data. Here, suppose that TRANS_DATA has a column TransactionID that stores an identifier of a transaction, and ItemID that stores the identifier of an item in that transaction. A given transaction may have multiple items, so the key of TRANS_DATA is (TransactionID, ItemID). TRANS_DATA has other data, such as ItemPrice, Qty, and ExtendedPrice, but those data are unnecessary for a market basket analysis, and we ignore them here.

The SQL statement in Figure 13-38 creates a view of all items that have appeared together in two or more transactions. You can then compute support in a view using the following statement:

```
CREATE VIEW ItemSupport AS

    SELECT     FirstItem, SecondItem, COUNT(*) as SupportCount

    FROM       TwoItemBasket

    GROUP BY   FirstItem, SecondItem;
```

This view produces the count of transactions in which each pair of items appears. You can divide the SupportCount in each row by the total number of transactions to obtain support for the two items. You can then use standard SQL to compute confidence and lift for each pair of items. See Project Questions 13.58 and 13.60.

ummary

Business intelligence (BI) systems assist managers and other professionals in the analysis of current and past activities and in the prediction of future events. BI applications are of two major types: reporting applications and data mining applications. Reporting applications make elementary calculations on data; data mining applications use sophisticated mathematical and statistical techniques.

BI applications obtain data from three sources: operational databases, extracts of operational databases, and purchased data. BI systems sometimes have their own DBMS, which may or may not be the operational DBMS. Characteristics of reporting and data mining applications are listed in Figure 13-2.

Direct reading of operational databases is not feasible for all but the smallest and simplest BI applications and databases for several reasons. Querying operational data can unacceptably slow the performance of operational systems, operational data have problems that limit their usefulness for BI applications, and BI system creation and maintenance requires programs, facilities, and expertise that are normally not available for an operational database.

Problems with operational data are listed in Figure 13-4. Because of these problems with operational data, many organizations have chosen to create and staff data warehouses and data marts. Data warehouses extract and clean operational data and store the revised data in data warehouse databases. Organizations may also purchase and manage data obtained from data vendors. Data warehouses maintain metadata that describes the source, format, assumptions, and constraints about the data they contain. A data mart is a collection of data that is smaller than that held in a data warehouse and that addresses a particular component or functional area of the business. In Figure 13-6, the data warehouse distributes data to three smaller data marts. Each data mart services the needs of a different aspect of the business.

Operational databases and dimensional databases have different characteristics, as shown in Figure 13-7. Dimensional databases use a star schema with a fully normalized fact table that connects to dimension tables that may be non-normalized. Dimensional databases must deal with slowly changing dimensions, and therefore a time dimension is important in a dimensional database. Fact tables hold measures of interest, and dimension tables hold attribute values used in queries. The star schema can be extended with additional fact tables, dimension tables, and conformed dimensions.

The purpose of a reporting system is to create meaningful information from disparate data sources and to deliver that information to the proper users on a timely basis. Reports are produced by sorting, filtering, grouping, and making simple calculations on the data. RFM analysis is a typical reporting application. Customers are grouped and classified according to how recently they have placed an order (R), how frequently they order (F), and how much money (M) they spend on orders. The result of an RFM analysis is three scores. In a typical analysis, the scores range from 1 to 5. An RFM score of {1 1 4} indicates that the customer has purchased recently, purchases frequently, but does not purchase large-dollar items. An RFM report can be produced using simple SQL. Figures 13-21 and 13-22 show stored procedures for computing these scores.

For the RFM data to add value to the organization, an RFM report must be prepared and delivered to the appropriate users. The components of a modern reporting system are shown in Figure 13-24. Reporting systems maintain metadata that supports the three basic report functions: authoring, managing, and delivering reports. The metadata includes information about users, user groups, and reports and data about which users are to receive which reports, in what medium, and when. As shown in Figure 13-24, reports vary by type, media, and mode.

OnLine Analytical Processing (OLAP) is a generic category of reporting applications that enable users to dynamically restructure reports. A measure is the data item of interest. A dimension is a characteristic of a measure. An OLAP cube is an arrangement of measures and dimensions. With OLAP, users can drill down and exchange the order of dimensions. Because of the high processing requirements, some organizations designate separate computers to function as OLAP servers.

Data mining is the application of mathematical and statistical techniques to find patterns and relationships and to classify and predict. Data mining has arisen in recent years because of the confluence of factors shown in Figure 13-34.

With unsupervised data mining, analysts do not create models or hypotheses prior to the analysis. Results are explained after the analysis has been performed. With supervised techniques, hypotheses are formed and tested before the analysis. Three popular data mining techniques are decision trees, logistic regression, and neural networks.

Although most data mining techniques require special-purpose software, one data mining technique, market basket analysis, can be performed by using only SQL. According to market basket analysis terminology, the *support* for two products is the frequency that they appear together in a transaction. The *confidence* is the conditional probability that one item will be purchased given that another item has already been purchased. *Lift* is confidence divided by the base probability that an item will be purchased.

An SQL join statement can be written to create a view showing products that have appeared together in a transaction. That view can then be processed to compute support, and the support view can then be processed to compute confidence and lift.

Key Terms

alert	dirty data
business intelligence (BI) system	drill down
click-stream data	dynamic report
cluster analysis	enterprise data warehouse (EDW) architecture
confidence	Extract, Transform, and Load (ETL) System
conformed dimension	F score
curse of dimensionality	fact table
data mart	lift
data mining application	logistic regression
data warehouse	M score
data warehouse metadata database	market basket analysis
date dimension	measure
decision support system (DSS)	neural network
decision tree analysis	nonintegrated data
digital dashboard	OLAP cube
dimension table	OLAP report
dimensional database	OLAP server

OnLine Analytical Processing (OLAP)
online transaction processing (OLTP) system
operational system
PivotTable
pull report
push report
query report
R score
regression analysis
report authoring
report delivery
report management

reporting system
RFM analysis
slowly changing dimension
SQL Top . . . Percent option
star schema
static report
supervised data mining
support
time dimension
transactional system
unsupervised data mining
Web portal

Review Questions

13.1 What are BI systems?

13.2 How do BI systems differ from transaction processing systems?

13.3 Name and describe the two main categories of BI systems.

13.4 What are the three sources of data for BI systems?

13.5 Explain the difference in processing between reporting and data mining applications.

13.6 Describe three reasons why direct reading of operational data is not feasible for BI applications.

13.7 Summarize the problems with operational databases that limit their usefulness for BI applications.

13.8 What are dirty data? How do dirty data arise?

13.9 Why is server time not useful for Web-based order entry BI applications?

13.10 What is click-stream data? How is it used in BI applications?

13.11 Why are data warehouses necessary?

13.12 Why do the authors describe the data in Figure 13-5 as "frightening"?

13.13 Give examples of data warehouse metadata.

13.14 Explain the difference between a data warehouse and a data mart. Use the analogy of a supply chain.

13.15 What is the enterprise data warehouse (EDW) architecture?

13.16 Describe the differences between operational databases and dimensional databases.

13.17 What is a star schema?

13.18 What is a fact table? What type of data are stored in fact tables?

13.19 What is a measure?

13.20 What is a dimension table? What type of data are stored in dimension tables?

13.21 What is a slowly changing dimension?

13.22 Why is the time dimension important in a dimensional model?

13.23 What is a conformed dimension?

13.24 State the purpose of a reporting system.

13.25 What do the letters *RFM* stand for in RFM analysis?

13.26 Describe, in general terms, how to perform an RFM analysis.

13.27 Explain the characteristics of customers having the following RFM scores: {1 1 5}, {1 5 1}, {5 5 5}, {2 5 5}, {5 1 2}, {1 1 3}.

13.28 In the RFM analysis in Figures 13-20 through 13-21, what role does the CUSTOMER_RFM table serve? What role does the CUSTOMER_R table serve?

13.29 Explain the purpose of the following SQL statement from Figure 13-21:

```
INSERT INTO CUSTOMER_R (CustomerID, MostRecentOrderDate)
    (SELECT    CustomerID, MAX(TransactionDate)
     FROM      CUSTOMER_SALES
     GROUP BY  CustomerID);
```

13.30 Explain the purpose and operation of the following SQL statement from Figure 13-22:

```
UPDATE    CUSTOMER_R
SET       R_Score = 1
WHERE     CustomerID IN
          (SELECT TOP 20 PERCENT CustomerID
           FROM       CUSTOMER_R
           ORDER BY   MostRecentOrderDate DESC
           GROUP BY   CustomerID);
```

13.31 Explain the purpose and operation of the following SQL statement from Figure 13-22:

```
UPDATE    CUSTOMER_R
SET       R_Score = 2
WHERE     CustomerID IN
          (SELECT TOP 25 PERCENT CustomerID
           FROM       CUSTOMER_R
           WHERE      R_Score IS NULL
           ORDER BY   MostRecentOrderDate DESC);
```

13.32 Write an SQL statement to query the CUSTOMER_RFM table and display the CustomerID values for all customers having an RFM score of {5 1 1} or {4 1 1}. Why are these customers important?

13.33 Name and describe the purpose of the major components of a reporting system.

13.34 What are the major functions of a reporting system?

13.35 Summarize the types of reports described in this chapter.

13.36 Describe the various media used to deliver reports.

13.37 Summarize the modes of reports described in this chapter.

13.38 Name three tasks of report authoring.

13.39 Describe the major tasks in report management. Explain the role of report metadata in report management.

13.40 Describe the major tasks in report delivery.

13.41 What does OLAP stand for?

13.42 What is the distinguishing characteristic of OLAP reports?

13.43 Define *measure, dimension,* and *cube.*

13.44   Give an example, other than one in this text, of a measure, two dimensions related to your measure, and a cube.

13.45   What is drill down?

13.46   Explain two ways that the OLAP report in Figure 13-31 differs from that in Figure 13-30.

13.47   What is the purpose of an OLAP server?

13.48   Define *data mining*.

13.49   Explain the difference between unsupervised and supervised data mining. Give examples, other than one in this text, of unsupervised and supervised data mining.

13.50   For the HSD-DW cluster analysis results shown in Figure 13-36, give an explanation for the two clusters. Use the report data and data descriptions for the HSD-DW data in the text to describe which cities and products are primarily associated with each cluster. [Hint: Study the City and ProductNumber results in Figure 13-36(b).]

13.51   Name three popular data mining techniques. What is the purpose of logistic regression? What is the purpose of a neural network?

Use the data in Figure 13-37 to answer Review Questions 13.52 through 13.57.

13.52   What is the probability that someone will buy a tank?

13.53   What is the support for buying a tank and fins? What is the support for buying two tanks?

13.54   What is the confidence for fins given that a tank has been purchased?

13.55   What is the confidence for a second tank given that a tank has been purchased?

13.56   What is the lift for fins given that a tank has been purchased?

13.57   What is the lift for a second tank given that a tank has been purchased?

 roject Questions

13.58   Using the code in Figure 13-22 as an example, write the procedures Calculate_F and Calculate_M that are called from the Calculate_RFM stored procedure in Figure 13-21.

For questions 13.59 through 13.61, use Oracle, SQL Server, or MySQL.

13.59   Write a stored procedure to calculate support. Use the TRANS_DATA table described on page 557 and the TwoItemBasket view shown in Figure 13-38. Place your results in a view name SupportView.

13.60   Write a stored procedure to calculate confidence. Use the TRANS_DATA table described on page 557 and the SupportView. Place your results in a view named ConfidenceView.

13.61   Write a stored procedure to compute lift. Use the TRANS_DATA table described on page 557 to compute unconditional probabilities and use the ConfidenceView for Confidence.

13.62   Based on the discussion of the Heather Sweeney Designs operational database (HSD) and dimensional database (HSD-DW) in the text, answer the following questions.

    A.   Using the SQL statements shown in Figure 13-12, create the HSD-DW database in a DBMS.

    B.   What possible transformations of data were made before HSD-DW was loaded with data? List some possible transformations, showing the original format of the HSD data and how they appear in the HSD-DW database.

C.   Write the complete set of SQL statements necessary to load the transformed data into the HSD-DW database.

D.   Populate the HSD-DW database, using the SQL statements you wrote to answer part C.

E.   Figure 13-39 shows the SQL code to create the SALES_FOR_RFM fact table shown in Figure 13-17. Using those statements, add the SALES_FOR_RFM table to your HSD-DW database.

F.   What possible transformations of data are necessary to load the SALES_FOR_RFM table? List any possible transformations, showing the original format of the HSD data and how they appear in the HSD-DW database.

G.   Write an SQL query similar to the one shown on page 535 that uses the total dollar amount of each day's product sales as the measure (instead of the number of products sold each day).

H.   Write the SQL view equivalent of the SQL query you wrote to answer part G.

I.   Create the SQL view you wrote to answer part H in your HSD-DW database.

J.   Create an Excel 2007 workbook named *HSD-DW-BI-Exercises.xlsx*.

K.   Using either the results of your SQL query from part H (copy the results of the query into a worksheet in the HSD-DW-BI.xlsx workbook and then format this range as a worksheet table) or your SQL view from part K (create an Excel data connection to the view), create an OLAP report similar to the OLAP report shown in Figure 13-32. (Hint: If you need help with the needed Excel actions, search in the Excel help system for more information.)

L.   Heather Sweeney is interested in the effects of payment type on sales in dollars.

   1.   Modify the design of the HSD-DW dimensional database to include a PAYMENT_TYPE dimension table.

   2.   Modify the HSD-DW database to include the PAYMENT_TYPE dimension table.

   3.   What data will be used to load the PAYMENT_TYPE dimension table? What data will be used to load foreign key data into the PRODUCT_SALES fact table? Write the complete set of SQL statements necessary to load these data.

   4.   Populate the PAYMENT_TYPE and PRODUCT_SALES tables, using the SQL statements you wrote to answer part 3.

Figure 13-39

The HSD-DW SALES_FOR_RFM SQL Statements

```
CREATE TABLE SALES_FOR_RFM(
        TimeID              Int                 NOT NULL,
        CustomerID          Int                 NOT NULL,
        InvoiceNumber       Int                 NOT NULL,
        PreTaxTotalSale     Numeric(9,2)        NOT NULL,
        CONSTRAINT          SALES_FOR_RFM_PK
                            PRIMARY KEY (TimeID, CustomerID, InvoiceNumber),
        CONSTRAINT          SRFM_TIMELINE_FK FOREIGN KEY(TimeID)
                                REFERENCES TIMELINE(TimeID)
                                    ON UPDATE NO ACTION
                                    ON DELETE NO ACTION,
        CONSTRAINT          SRFM_CUSTOMER_FK FOREIGN KEY(CustomerID)
                                REFERENCES CUSTOMER(CustomerID)
                                    ON UPDATE NO ACTION
                                    ON DELETE NO ACTION
        );
```

5. Create the SQL queries or SQL views needed to incorporate the PaymentType attribute.

6. Create an Excel 2007 OLAP report to show the effect of payment type on product sales in dollars.

13.63 The following questions require that you have completed question 13.61 and that you have a version of SQL Server 2005 or SQL Server 2008 that includes SQL Server Analysis Services.

A. Download and install the correct version of the Microsoft SQL Server Data Mining add-ins for Microsoft Office 2007 for your version of SQL Server.

B. Use the data mining add-in in Excel 2007 to do a cluster analysis of the HSD-DW data results from your SQL query results from question 13.61(I) or SQL view from questions 13.62(J) and 13.62(K). Use only the City and ProductNumber attributes in your analysis. Interpret you results.

Assume that Marcia uses a database that includes the following three tables:

CUSTOMER (<u>CustomerID</u>, FirstName, LastName, Phone, Email)

ORDER (<u>InvoiceNumber</u>, CustomerID, DateIn, DateOut, Subtotal, Tax, TotalAmount)

ORDER_ITEM (<u>*InvoiceNumber*</u>, <u>ItemNumber</u>, *Service*, Quantity, UnitPrice, ExtendedPrice)

(ORDER_ITEM.Service is a foreign key to the SERVICE table, but the SERVICE table is not needed for these exercises.)

A. Describe how an RFM analysis could be useful in Marcia's business.

B. Using the four tables in Figure 13-20, write a set of stored procedures to compute an RFM analysis on Marcia's data.

C. Show SQL to process the table generated in your answer to B to display the names and e-mail data for all customers having an RFM score of {5 1 1} or {4 1 1}.

D. Describe in general terms how a market basket analysis can be used on the items in a dry cleaning order.

E. Using the instructions in questions 13.58 through 13.60, write stored procedures to perform a market basket analysis on the items in a dry cleaning order.

The tables we have used for Morgan Importing have no natural application for either RFM or market basket analysis, at least not to Morgan. However, consider the following three tables from the standpoint of a shipper:

SHIPMENT (<u>ShipmentID</u>, ShipDate, *ShipperName*, ShipperInvoiceNumber, Origin,
          Destination)

SHIPMENT_ITEM (*<u>ShipmentID</u>*, *<u>PurchaseID</u>*, InsuredValue)

SHIPPER (<u>ShipperName</u>, Phone, Fax, Email, Contact)

If we substitute CUSTOMER for SHIPPER, we can create the structure of a database that would record customers and shipments and items they've shipped with us. The modified tables are:

SHIPMENT (<u>ShipperInvoiceNumber</u>, ShipDate, *CustomerID*, Origin, Destination,
          Subtotal, Tax, Total)

SHIPMENT_ITEM (*<u>ShipperInvoiceNumber</u>*, <u>ItemNumber</u>, ShippingCost)

CUSTOMER (<u>CustomerID</u>, CustomerName, Phone, Fax, Email, Contact)

where CustomerID is a surrogate key for the customer data. Use these revised tables to answer the following questions.

A.   Describe how an RFM analysis could be useful to the shipper.

B.   Using the four tables in Figure 13-20, write a set of stored procedures to compute an RFM analysis for shipments.

C.   Show SQL to process the table generated in your answer to B to display the names and e-mail data for all customers having an RFM score of {5 1 1} or {4 1 1}.

D.   Describe in general terms how a market basket analysis can be used on the items in a shipment.

E.   Using the instructions in questions 13.58 through 13.60, write stored procedures to perform a market basket analysis on the items in a shipment.

Online Appendices

Complete versions of these appendices are available on the textbook's Web site:

www.pearsonhighered.com/kroenke

Appendix A

Getting Started with Microsoft Access 2007

Appendix B

The IDEF1X Standard

Appendix C

UML-Style Entity-Relationship Diagrams

Appendix D

Data Structures for Database Processing

Appendix E

The Semantic Object Model

Bibliography

Web Links

News

CNET News.com: *www.news.com*
Advisor: *www.advisor.com*
Intelligent Enterprise: *www.intelligententerprise.com*
ZDNet: *www.zdnet.com*

Data Mining

KDnuggets: *www.kdnuggets.com*
Google Dating Mining Directory: *directory.google.com/Top/Computers/Software/Databases/ Data_Warehousing/Decision_Support_Tools*
Insightful Miner 3: *www.insightful.com/products/iminer*
SAS Enterprise Miner: *www.sas.com/technologies/analytics/datamining/miner*
SPSS Clementine: *www.spss.com/Clementine*
Microsoft SQL Server 2008 Data Mining Add-Ins for Office 2007: *www.microsoft.com/ sqlserver/2008/en/us/data-mining-addins.aspx*

DBMS and Other Vendors

Oracle Database 11g: *www.oracle.com/database/index.html*
SQL Server 2008: *www.microsoft.com/sqlserver/2008/en/us/default.aspx*
MySQL: *www.mysql.com*
Eclipse IDE: *www.eclipse.org*
PHP: *http://us.php.net*
NetBeans: *www.netbeans.org/index.html*
Microsoft Express Editions: *www.microsoft.com/Express*

Standards

JDBC: *http://java.sun.com/products/jdbc* and *http://en.wikipedia.org/wiki/JDBC*
ODBC: *www.liv.ac.uk/middleware/html/odbc.html* and *http://en.wikipedia.org/wiki/Open_ Database_Connectivity*
Worldwide Web Consortium (W3C): *www.w3.org*
XML: *www.w3.org/XML*, *www.xml.org*, and *http://en.wikipedia.org/wiki/XML*

Classic Articles and References

ANSI X3. *American National Standard for Information Systems—Database Language SQL.* ANSI, 1992.
Bruce, T. *Designing Quality Databases with IDEF1X Information Models.* New York: Dorset House, 1992.
Chamberlin, D. D., et al. "SEQUEL 2: A Unified Approach to Data Definition, Manipulation, and Control." *IBM Journal of Research and Development* 20 (November 1976).
Chen, P. "The Entity-Relationship Model: Toward a Unified Model of Data." *ACM Transactions on Database Systems* 1 (March 1976).

Chen, P. *Entity-Relationship Approach to Information Modeling.* E-R Institute, 1981.

Coar, K. A. L. *Apache Server for Dummies.* Foster City, CA: IDG Books, 1997.

Codd, E. F. "A Relational Model of Data for Large Shared Data Banks." *Communications of the ACM* 25 (February 1970).

Codd, E. F. "Extending the Relational Model to Capture More Meaning." *Transactions on Database Systems* 4 (December 1979).

Date, C. J. *An Introduction to Database Systems,* 8th ed. Upper Saddle River, NJ: Pearson Education, 2003.

Embley, D. W. "NFQL: The Natural Forms Query Language." *ACM Transactions on Database Systems* 14 (June 1989).

Eswaran, K. P., J. N. Gray, R. A. Lorie, and I. L. Traiger. "The Notion of Consistency and Predicate Locks in a Database System." *Communications of the ACM* 19 (November 1976).

Fagin, R. "A Normal Form for Relational Databases That Is Based on Domains and Keys." *Transactions on Database Systems* 6 (September 1981).

Fagin, R. "Multivalued Dependencies and a New Normal Form for Relational Databases." *Transactions on Database Systems* 2 (September 1977).

Hammer, M., and D. McLeod. "Database Description with SDM: A Semantic Database Model." *Transactions on Database Systems* 6 (September 1981).

Keuffel, W. "Battle of the Modeling Techniques." *DBMS Magazine* (August 1996).

Kroenke, D. "Waxing Semantic: An Interview." *DBMS Magazine* (September 1994).

Moriarty, T. "Business Rule Analysis." *Database Programming and Design* (April 1993).

Muller, R. J. *Database Design for Smarties: Using UML for Data Modeling.* San Francisco: Morgan Kaufmann, 1999.

Nijssen, G., and T. Halpin. *Conceptual Schema and Relational Database Design: A Fact-Oriented Approach.* Upper Saddle River, NJ: Prentice Hall, 1989.

Nolan, R. *Managing the Data Resource Function.* St. Paul: West Publishing, 1974.

Ratliff, C. Wayne, "dStory: How I Really Developed dBASE." *Data Based Advisor* (March 1991).

Rogers, D. "Manage Data with Modeling Tools." *VB Tech Journal* (December 1996).

Ross, R. *Principles of the Business Rule Approach.* Boston: Addison-Wesley, 2003.

Zloof, M. M. "Query by Example." *Proceedings of the National Computer Conference, AFIPS* 44 (May 1975).

Useful Books

Berry, M., and G. Linoff. *Data Mining Techniques for Marketing, Sales, and Customer Support.* New York: Wiley, 1997.

Celko, J. *SQL for Smarties,* 2d ed. San Francisco: Morgan Kaufmann, 2000.

Celko, J. *SQL Puzzles and Answers.* San Francisco: Morgan Kaufmann, 1997.

Fields, D. K., and M. A. Kolb. *Web Development with Java Server Pages.* Greenwich, CT: Manning Press, 2000.

Harold, E. R. *XML: Extensible Markup Language.* New York: IDG Books Worldwide, 1998.

Kay, M. *XSLT: Programmer's Reference.* Birmingham, UK: WROX Press, 2000.

Loney, K. *Oracle Database 11g: The Complete Reference.* Berkeley, CA: Osborne/McGraw-Hill, 2008.

Muench, S. *Building Oracle XML Applications.* Sebastopol, CA: O'Reilly, 2000.

Muller, R. J. *Database Design for Smarties: Using UML for Data Modeling.* San Francisco: Morgan Kaufmann, 1999.

Mundy, J., W. Thornthwaite, and R. Kimball, *The Microsoft Data Warehouse Toolkit.* Indianapolis, IN: Wiley, 2006.

Pyle, D. *Data Preparation for Data Mining.* San Francisco: Morgan Kaufmann, 1999.

While this section defines many of the key terms in the book, it is not meant to be exhaustive. Terms related to a specific DBMS product, for example, should be referenced in the chapter dedicated to that product. These references can be found in the index. Similarly, SQL concepts are included, but details of SQL commands and syntax should be referenced in the chapter that discusses those details.

.NET Framework. Microsoft's comprehensive application development platform. It includes such components as ADO.NET and ASP.NET.

/* and */. The symbols used to indicate a comment line in an SQL script in SQL Server 2008, Oracle Database 11g, and MySQL 5.1.

<?php and ?>. The symbols used to indicate blocks of PHP code in Web pages.

Abstraction. A generalization of something that hides some unimportant details but enables work with a wider class of types. A recordset is an abstraction of a relation. A rowset is an abstraction of a recordset.

ACID transaction. ACID stands for "*atomic, consistent, isolated,* and *durable.*" An *atomic* transaction is one in which all of the database changes are committed as a unit; either all are done, or none are. A *consistent* transaction is one in which all actions are taken against rows in the same logical state. An *isolated* transaction is one that is protected from changes by other users. A *durable* transaction is one that is permanent after it is committed to the database, regardless of subsequent failures. There are different levels of consistency and isolation. *See also* transaction-level consistency, statement-level consistency, and transaction isolation level.

Active Data Objects (ADO). An implementation of OLE DB that is accessible via object- and non-object-oriented languages. It is used primarily as a scripting-language (JScript, VBScript) interface to OLE DB.

Active repository. Parts of the systems development processes where metadata is created automatically as the system components are created. *See* data repository.

Active Server Pages (ASP). A file containing markup language, server script, and client script that is processed by the Active Server Processor in Microsoft Internet Information Server (IIS).

Ad-hoc query A query created by a user as and when needed, as compared to a predefined and stored query.

ADO.NET. A data access technology that is part of Microsoft's .NET initiative. ADO.NET provides the capabilities of ADO, but with a different object structure. ADO.NET also includes new capabilities for the processing of datasets. *See also* ADO.NET DataSet.

ADO.NET Command object. The ADO.NET object that mimics an SQL statement or stored procedure. It is run against the data in the DataSet.

ADO.NET Connection object. The ADO.NET object responsible for connecting to a data source.

ADO.NET Data Provider. A class library that provides ADO.NET services. There are Data Providers for ODBC, OLE.DB, SQL Server, and EDM applications.

ADO.NET DataAdapter object. The ADO.NET object that is the connector between a Connection object and a DataSet object. It uses four command objects: SelectCommand, InsertCommand, UpdateCommand, and DeleteCommand.

ADO.NET DataReader. An ADO.NET object that is similar to a read-only, forward-only cursor, and which can only be used by an ADO.NET Command object 's Execute method.

ADO.NET DataSet. A representation of data from a database that is stored in computer memory for immediate use. It is distinct and disconnected from the data in the database.

ADO.NET Entity Framework. An extension to ADO.NET that supports the Microsoft EDM. *See* Entity Data Model (EDM).

After image. A record of a database entity (normally a row or a page) after a change. Used in recovery to perform rollforwards.

Alert. In reporting systems, a type of report that is triggered by an event.

Alternate key. In entity-relationship models, a synonym for candidate key.

American National Standards Institute (ANSI). The American standards organization that creates and publishes the SQL standards. *See* Structured Query Language (SQL).

AMP. An abbreviation for Apache, MySQL, and PHP/Pearl/Python. *See* Apache Web Server, PHP.

Anomaly. An undesirable consequence of a data modification. The term is used in normalization discussions. With an insertion anomaly, facts about two or more different themes must be added to a single row of a relation. With a deletion anomaly, facts about two or more themes are lost when a single row is deleted.

API. *See* application program interface (API).

Apache Tomcat. An application server that works in conjunction with the Apache Web server. *See* Apache Web server.

Apache Web server. A popular Web server that runs on most operating systems, particularly Windows and Linux.

Applet. A compiled, machine-independent Java bytecode program that is run by the Java virtual machine embedded in a browser.

Application. A business computer system that processes a portion of a database to meet a user's information needs. It consists of menus, forms, reports, queries, Web pages, and application programs.

Application program. A custom-developed program for processing a database. It can be written in a standard procedural language, such as Java, C#, Visual Basic .NET, or C++, or in a language unique to the DBMS, such as PL/SQL or T-SQL.

Application program interface (API). A set of program procedures or functions that can be called to invoke a set of services. The API includes the names of the procedures and functions and a description of the name, purpose, and data type of parameters to be provided. For example, a DBMS product can provide a library of functions to call for database services. The names of procedures and their parameters constitute the API for that library.

Archetype/version object. A two-object structure that represents multiple versions of a standardized item; for example, a SOFTWARE-PRODUCT (the archetype) and PRODUCT-RELEASE (the version of the archetype). The identifier of the version always includes the identifier of the archetype object.

ASP. *See* Active Server Pages (ASP).

ASP.NET. The updated version of ASP for the .NET Framework. *See* Active Server Pages (ASP), .NET Framework.

Association object. An object that represents the combination of at least two other objects and that contains data about that combination. It is often used in contracting and assignment applications.

Association pattern. In database design, a table pattern where an intersection table contains additional attributes beyond the attributes that make up the composite primary key.

Asterisk (*) wildcard character. A character used in Access 2007 queries to represent one or more unspecified characters. *See* SQL percent sign (%) wildcard character.

Atomic. A set of actions that is completed as a unit. Either all of the actions are completed, or none of them are.

Atomic transaction. A group of logically related database operations that is performed as a unit. Either all of the operations are performed, or none of them are.

Attribute. (1) A column of a relation; also called a *column, field,* or *data item.* (2) A property in an entity.

Authorization rules. A set of processing permissions that describes which users or user groups can take particular actions against particular portions of the database.

AUTO_INCREMENT attribute. In MySQL, the data attribute used to create surrogate keys.

AutoNumber. In Access 2007, the data type used to create surrogate keys.

AVG. In SQL, a function that averages up a set of numbers. *See* SQL built-in functions.

Base Class Library. A component of the Microsoft .NET Framework that provides support for the programming languages used with the .NET Framework.

Base domain. In IDEF1X, a domain definition that stands alone. Other domains may be defined as subsets of a base domain.

Before image. A record of a database entity (normally a row or a page) before a change. Used in recovery to perform rollback.

BI. *See* business intelligence (BI) systems.

Binary relationship. A relationship between exactly two entities or tables.

Boyce-Codd normal form (BCNF). A relation in which every determinant is a candidate key.

Branch. A subelement of a tree that may consist of one or many nodes.

Buffer. An area of memory used to hold data. For a read, data are read from a storage device into a buffer; for a write, data are written from the buffer to storage.

Business intelligence (BI) systems. Information systems that assist managers and other professionals in the analysis of current and past activities and in the prediction of future events. Two major categories of BI systems are reporting systems and data mining systems.

Bytecode interpreter. For an applications written in Java, the program used by a specific operating system to execute the application. Bytecode interpreters are known as Java virtual machines. *See* Java virtual machine.

Candidate key. An attribute or group of attributes that identifies a unique row in a relation. One of the candidate keys is chosen to be the primary key.

Cardinality. In a binary relationship, the maximum or minimum number of elements allowed on each side of the relationship. The maximum cardinality can be 1:1, 1:N, N:1, or N:M. The minimum cardinality may be optional-optional, optional-mandatory, mandatory-optional, or mandatory-mandatory.

Cascading deletion. A referential integrity action specifying that when a parent row is deleted, related child rows should be deleted as well.

Cascading update. A referential integrity action specifying that when the key of a parent row is updated, the foreign keys of matching child rows should be updated as well.

Casual relationship. A relationship that is created without a foreign key constraint. This is useful if the tables are missing data values.

Categorization cluster. In IDEF1X, a group of mutually exclusive category entities. *See also* complete category cluster.

Category entity. In IDEF1X, a subtype that belongs to a category cluster.

CHECK constraint. In SQL, a constraint that specifies what data values are allowed in a particular column.

Checkpoint. The point of synchronization between a database and a transaction log. All buffers are force-written to external storage. The term is sometimes used in other ways by DBMS vendors.

Child. An entity or row on the many side of a one-to-many relationship.

Class attributes. In the uniform modeling language (UML), attributes that pertain to the class of all entities of a given type.

Click-stream data. Data about a customer's clicking behavior on a Web page; such data are often analyzed by e-commerce companies.

Cluster analysis. A form of unsupervised data mining in which statistical techniques identify groups of entities that have similar characteristics.

Collection. An object that contains a group of other objects. Examples are the ADO Names, Errors, and Parameters collections.

Column. A logical group of bytes in a row of a relation or a table. The meaning of a column is the same for every row of the relation.

COM. *See* Component Object Model (COM).

Command line utility. A character user interface program that presents a command prompt to the user. The user then types a command and presses the Enter key for execution. Each major DBMS product has a command line utility.

Commit. A command issued to the DBMS that makes database modifications permanent. After the command has been processed, database changes are written to the database and to a log so that they will survive system crashes and other failures. A commit is usually used at the end of an atomic transaction. Contrast this with rollback.

Common Language Runtime (CLT). A component of the Microsoft .NET Framework that provides support for the programming languages used with the .NET Framework.

Complete category cluster. A category cluster in which all possible category entities are defined. The generic entity must also be one of the category entities.

Component Object Model (COM). A Microsoft specification for the development of object-oriented programs.

Composite determinant. In functional dependencies, a determinant consisting of two or more attributes.

Composite identifier. In data modeling, an identifier consisting of two or more attributes.

Composite key. In database design, a key with two or more attributes.

Composite primary key. In database design and actual databases, a primary key with two or more attributes.

Computed value. A column of a table that is computed from other column values. Values are not stored, but are computed when they are to be displayed.

Concurrency. A condition in which two or more transactions are processed against the database at the same time. In a single CPU system, the changes are interleaved; in a multi-CPU system, the transactions may be processed simultaneously, and the changes on the database server are interleaved.

Concurrent processing. The sharing of the CPU among several transactions. The CPU is allocated to each transaction in a round robin or in some other fashion for a certain period of time. Operations are performed so quickly that they appear to users to be simultaneous. In local area networks (LANs) and other distributed applications, concurrent processing is used to refer to the (possibly simultaneous) processing of applications on multiple computers.

Concurrent transactions. Two transactions that are being processed at the same time.

Concurrent update problem. An error condition in which one user's data changes are overwritten by another user's data changes. Same as lost update problem.

Confidence. In market basket analysis, the probability of a customer's buying one product, given that the customer has purchased another product.

Conformed dimension. In a dimensional database design, a dimension table that has relationships to two or more fact tables.

Connection relationship. In IDEF1X, a HAS-A relationship.

Consistency. Two or more concurrent transactions are consistent if the result of their processing is the same as it would have been if they had been processed in some serial order.

Consistent. In an ACID transaction, either statement-level or transaction-level consistency. *See* ACID transaction, consistency, statement-level consistency, and transaction-level consistency.

Consistent backup. A backup file from which all uncommitted changes have been removed.

Correlated subquery. A type of subquery in which an element in the subquery refers to an element in the containing query. A subquery that requires nested processing.

Crow's foot model. Formally known as the Information Engineering (IE) Crow's Foot model, it is a system of symbology used to construct E-R diagrams in data modeling and database design,

Crow's foot symbol. A symbol in the IE Crow's Foot E-R model that indicates a many side of the relationship. It visually resembles a bird's foot, and thus the name *crow's foot*.

Control-of-flow statements. Procedural program statements that direct execution of the program depending upon an existing condition. Control-of-flow statements include, for example, IF..THEN..ELSE logic and DO WHILE logic.

COUNT. In SQL, a function that counts the number of rows in a query result. *See* SQL built-in functions.

Curse of dimensionality. In data mining applications, the phenomenon that the more attributes there are, the easier it is to build a model that fits the sample data but that is worthless as a predictor.

Cursor. An indicator of the current position in a pseudofile for an SQL SELECT that has been embedded in a program; it shows the identity of the current row.

Cursor type. A declaration on a cursor that determines how the DBMS places implicit locks. Four types of cursor discussed in this text are forward only, snapshot, keyset, and dynamic.

Data. The values stored in database tables.

Data administration. The enterprise-wide function that concerns the effective use and control of the organization's data assets. Data administration may be handled by an individual, but it is usually handled by a group. Specific functions include setting data standards and policies and providing a forum for conflict resolution. *See also* database administrator (DBA).

Data consumer. A user of OLE DB functionality.

Data definition language (DDL). A language used to describe the structure of a database. SQL DDL is that portion of SQL that is used to create, modify, and drop database structures.

Data dictionary. A user-accessible catalog of database and application metadata. The contents of an *active* data dictionary are automatically updated by the DBMS whenever changes are made in the database or application structure. The contents of a *passive* data dictionary must be updated manually when changes are made.

Data integrity. The state of a database in which all constraints are fulfilled. Usually refers to interrelation constraints in which the value of a foreign key is required to be present in the table having that foreign key as its primary key.

Data integrity problems. A table that has inconsistencies that create insert, update, or deletion anomalies is said to have *data integrity problems*.

Data manipulation language (DML). A language used to describe the processing of a database. SQL DML is that portion of SQL that is used to query, insert, update, and modify data.

Data mart. A facility similar to a data warehouse, but with a restricted domain. Often, the data are restricted to particular types, business functions, or business units.

Data mining application. Business intelligence systems that use sophisticated statistical and mathematical techniques to perform what-if analyses, to make predictions, and to facilitate decisions. Contrast with reporting systems.

Data model. A model of the users' data requirements usually expressed in terms of the entity-relationship model.

Data provider. A provider of OLE DB functionality. Examples are tabular data providers and service data providers.

Data repository. Collections of metadata about databases, database applications, Web pages, users, and other application components.

Data sublanguage. A language for defining and processing a database to be embedded in programs written in another language, in most cases a procedural language such as Java, C#, Visual Basic, or C++. A data sublanguage is an incomplete programming language because it contains only constructs for data access.

Data warehouse. A store of enterprise data that is designed to facilitate management decision making. A data warehouse includes not only data, but also metadata, tools, procedures, training, personnel information, and other resources that make access to the data easier and more relevant to decision makers.

Data warehouse metadata. In a data warehouse, metadata concerning the data, its source, its format, its assumptions and constraints, and other facts about the data.

Data warehouse metadata database. The database used to store the data warehouse metadata.

Database. A self-describing collection of integrated records.

Database administration. The function that concerns the effective use and control of a particular database and its related applications.

Database administrator (DBA). The person or group responsible for establishing policies and procedures to control and protect a database. The database administrator works within guidelines set by data administration to control the database structure, manage data changes, and maintain DBMS programs.

Database application. An application that uses a database to store the data needed by the application.

Database data. The portion of a database that contains data of interest and use to the application end users. *See* data.

Database design. A diagram that represents that database as it will be implemented in a DBMS product.

Database management system (DBMS). A set of programs used to define, administer, and process the database and its applications.

Database redesign. The process of changing the structure of a database to adapt the database to changing requirements or to fix it so that it has the structure it should have had in the first place.

Database save. A copy of database files that can be used to restore the database to some previous consistent state.

Database schema. In MySQL, the functional equivalent of a database in Microsoft Access or SQL Server.

Dataset. In ADO.NET, an in-memory collection of tables that is not connected to any database. Datasets have relationships, referential integrity constraints, referential integrity actions, and other important database characteristics. They are processed by ADO.NET objects. A single dataset may be materialized as tables, as an XML document, or as an XML Schema.

DBA. *See* database administrator (DBA).

DBMS. *See* database management system (DBMS).

DBMS reserved word. A word that has a special meaning in the DBMS and should not be used as a table, column, or other name in a database.

DDL. *See* data definition language (DDL).

Deadlock. A condition that can occur during concurrent processing in which each of two (or more) transactions is waiting to access data that the other transaction has locked. Also called a deadly embrace.

Deadly embrace. *See* deadlock.

Decision support system (DSS). One or more applications designed to help managers make decisions. An earlier name for business intelligence (BI).

Decision tree analysis. A form of unsupervised data mining that classifies entities of interest into two or more groups according to values of attributes that measure the entities' past history.

DEFAULT keyword. In SQL, the work used to specify a default value for an attribute.

Default value. A value assigned to an attribute if there is no other value assigned to it when a new row is created in a table.

Default namespace. In an XML Schema document, the namespace that is used for all unlabeled elements.

Degree. For relationships in the entity-relationship model, the number of entities participating in the relationship. In almost all cases, such relationships are of degree two.

Deletion anomaly. In a relation, the situation in which the removal of one row of a table deletes facts about two or more themes.

Delimited identifier. A reserved word placed in special symbols to distinguish it from the DBMS reserved word so that it can be used as a table, column, or other name in a database.

Denormalize. To intentionally create a set of database tables that are not normalized to BCNF and 4NF.

Dependency graph. A network of nodes and lines that represents the logical dependencies among tables, views, triggers, stored procedures, indexes, and other database constructs.

Determinant. One or more attributes that functionally determine another attribute or attributes. In the functional dependency $(A, B) \rightarrow C$, the attributes (A, B) are the determinant.

Differential backup. A backup file that contains only changes made since a prior backup.

Digital dashboard. In reporting systems, a display that is customized for a particular user. Typically, a digital dashboard has links to many different reports.

Dimension table. In a star schema dimensional database, the tables that connect to the central fact table. Dimension tables hold attributes used in the organizing queries in analyses such as those of OLAP cubes.

Dimensional database. A database design that is used for data warehouses and is designed for efficient queries and analysis. It contains a central fact table connected to one or more dimension tables.

Dirty data. In a business intelligence system, data with errors. Examples are a value of "G" for customer sex and a value of "213" for customer age. Other examples are a value of "999-999-9999" for a U.S. phone number, a part color of "gren," and an e-mail address of "WhyMe@somewhereelseintheuniverse.who." Dirty data pose problems for reporting and data mining applications.

Dirty read. Reading data that has been changed but not yet committed to the database. Such changes may later be rolled back and removed from the database.

Discriminator. In the entity-relationship model, an attribute of a supertype entity that determines which subtype pertains to the supertype.

DK/NF. *See* domain/key normal form.

DML. *See* data manipulation language (DML).

Document Object Model (DOM). An API that represents an XML document as a tree. Each node of the tree represents a piece of the XML document. A program can directly access and manipulate a node of the DOM representation.

Document type declaration (DTD). A set of markup elements that defines the structure of an XML document.

DOM. *See* Document Object Model.

Domain. A named set of all possible values that an attribute can have. Domains can be defined by listing allowed values or by defining a rule for determining allowed values.

Domain/key normal form (DK/NF). A relation in which all constraints are logical consequences of domains and keys.

Drill down. User-directed disaggregation of data used to break higher-level totals into components.

DTD. *See* document type declaration.

Durable. In an ACID transaction, the database changes are permanent. *See* ACID transaction.

Dynamic cursor. A fully featured cursor. All inserts, updates, deletions, and changes in row order are visible to a dynamic cursor.

Dynamic report. In reporting systems, a report that reads the most current data at the time of the report's creation. Contrast with static report.

Eclipse IDE. A popular open-source integrated development environment.

Eclipse PDT (PHP Development Tools) Project. A version of the Eclipse IDE customized for use with PHP. *See* Eclipse IDE, PHP.

Enterprise-class database system. A DBMS product capable of supporting the operating requirement of large organizations.

Enterprise data warehouse (EDW) architecture. A data warehouse architecture that links specialized data marts to a central data warehouse for data consistency and efficient operations.

Entity. (1) In the entity-relationship model, a representation of something that users want to track. *See also* entity class and entity instance. (2) In a generic sense, something that users want to track. In the relational model, an entity is stored in one row of a table.

Entity class. In the entity-relationship model, a collection of entities of a given type; for example, EMPLOYEE and DEPARTMENT. The class is described by its attributes.

Entity Data Model (EDM). An emerging Microsoft data modeling technology that is part of the .NET Framework.

Entity instance. A particular occurrence of an entity; for example, Employee 100 and the Accounting Department. An entity instance is described by values of its attributes.

Entity-relationship (E-R) data modeling. Creating a data model using E-R diagrams. *See* entity-relationship (E-R) diagram

Entity-relationship (E-R) diagram. A graphic used to represent entities and their relationships. In the traditional E-R model, entities are shown as squares or rectangles, and relationships are shown as diamonds. The cardinality of the relationship is shown inside the diamond. In the crow's foot model, entities are shown in rectangles, and relationships are shown by lines between the rectangles. Attributes are generally listed within the rectangle. The many side of many relationships is represented by a crow's foot.

Entity-relationship (E-R) model. A set of constructs and conventions used to create data models. The things in the users' world are represented by entities, and the associations among those things are represented by relationships. The results are usually documented in an entity-relationship (E-R) diagram.

Enumerated list. A list of allowed values for a domain, attribute, or column.

Equijoin. The process of joining relation A containing attribute A1 with B containing attribute B1 to form relation C, so that for each row in C, A1 = B1. Both A1 and B1 are represented in C.

E-R diagram. *See* entity-relationship diagram.

Exclusive lock. A lock on a data resource such that no other transaction can either read or update that resource.

Existence-dependent entity. Same as a weak entity. An entity that cannot appear in the database unless an instance of one or more other entities also appears in the database. A subclass of existence-dependent entities is ID-dependent entities.

Explicit lock. A lock requested by command from an application program.

Extensible Markup Language. *See* XML.

Extensible Style Language. *See* XSLT.

Extract. A portion of an operational database downloaded to a local area network (LAN) or personal computer for local processing. Extracts are created to reduce communication cost and time when querying and creating reports from data created by transaction processing.

Extract, Transform, and Load (ETL) system. The portion of a data warehouse that converts operation data to data warehouse data.

F score. In RFM analysis, the "how frequently" score, which reflects how often a customer makes a purchase. *See* RFM Analysis.

Fact table. In a dimensional database, the central table that contains numerical values.

Field. (1) A logical group of bytes in a record such as Name or PhoneNumber. (2) In the relational model, a synonym for attribute.

Fifth normal form (5NF). A normal form necessary to eliminate an anomaly where a table can be split apart but not correctly joined back together. Also know as Project-Join Normal Form (PJ/NF)

File data source. An ODBC data source stored in a file that can be e-mailed or otherwise distributed among users.

First normal form (1NF). Any table that fits the definition of a relation.

Flat file. A file that has only a single value in each field. The meaning of the columns is the same in every row.

Foreign key. An attribute that is a key of one or more relations other than the one in which it appears. Used to represent relationships.

FOREIGN KEY constraint. In SQL, the constraint used to create relationships and referential integrity between tables.

Fourth normal form (4NF). A relation in Boyce-Codd normal form in which there are no multivalued dependencies or in which all attributes participate in a single multivalued dependency.

Functional dependency. A relationship between attributes in which one attribute or group of attributes determines the value of another. The expression $X \rightarrow Y$ means that given a value of X, we can determine the value of Y. A given value of X may appear in a relation more than once, but if so, it is always paired with the same value of Y. Also, if $X \rightarrow (Y, Z)$, then $X \rightarrow Y$ and $X \rightarrow Z$. However, if $(X, Y) \rightarrow Z$, then, in general X Not $\rightarrow Z$ and Y Not $\rightarrow Z$.

Generic entity. In IDEF1X, an entity that has one or more category clusters. The generic entity takes the role of a supertype for the category entities in the category cluster.

Graphical User Interface (GUI). A user interface that uses graphical elements for interaction with a user.

Granularity. The size of the database resource that is locked. Locking the entire database is large granularity; locking a column of a particular row is small granularity.

Growing phase. The first stage in two-phase locking in which locks are acquired but not released.

HAS-A relationship. A relationship between two entities or objects that are of different logical types; for example, EMPLOYEE HAS-A(n) AUTO. Contrast this with an IS-A relationship.

HTML. *See* Hypertext Markup Language.

HTML document tags. The tags in HTML documents that indicate the structure of the document.

HTML syntax rules. The standards that are used to create HTML documents.

HTTP. *See* Hypertext Transfer Protocol.

Http://localhost. For a Web server, a reference to the user's computer.

Hypertext Markup Language (HTML). A standardized set of text tags for formatting text, locating images and other nontext files, and placing links or references to other documents.

Hypertext Transfer Protocol (HTTP). A standardized means for using TCP/IP to communicate over the Internet.

ID-dependent entity. An entity whose identifier contains the identifier of a second entity. For example, APPOINTMENT is ID-dependent on CLIENT, where the identifier of APPOINTMENT is (Date, Time, ClientNumber) and the identifier of CLIENT is ClientNumber. An ID-dependent entity is weak, meaning that it cannot logically exist without the existence of that second entity. Not all weak entities are ID-dependent, however.

IDEF1X (Integrated Definition 1, Extended). A version of the entity-relationship model, adopted as a national standard, but difficult to understand and use. Most organizations use a simpler E-R version like the crow's foot model.

Identifier. An attribute that names, or identifies, and entity.

Identifying connection relationship. In IDEF1X, a 1:1 or 1:N HAS-A relationship in which the child entity is ID-dependent on the parent.

Identifying relationship. A relationship that is used when the child entity is ID-dependent upon the parent entity.

IDENTITY ({StartValue}, {Increment}) property [MSSQL]. For SQL Server 2008, the attribute that is used to create a surrogate key.

IIS. *See* Internet Information Server.

Implementation. In object-oriented programming, a set of objects that instantiates a particular object-oriented interface.

Implicit lock. A lock that is automatically placed by the DBMS.

Import. A function of the DBMS; to read a file of data in bulk.

Inclusive subtype. In data modeling and database design, a subtype that allows a supertype entity to be associated with more than one subtype.

Inconsistent backup. A backup file that contains uncommitted changes.

Inconsistent read problem. In a transaction, a series of reads of a set of rows in which some of the rows have been updated by a second transaction and some of the rows have not been updated by that second transaction. Can be prevented by two-phase locking and other strategies.

Index. Data created by the DBMS to improve access and sorting performance. Indexes can be constructed for a single column or groups of columns. They are especially useful for columns used by WHERE clauses, for conditions in joins, and for sorting.

Index.html. A default Web page name provided by most Web servers.

Inetpub folder. In Windows operating systems, the root folder for the IIS Web server.

Information. (1) Knowledge derived from data, (2) data presented in a meaningful context, or (3) data processed by summing, ordering, averaging, grouping, comparing, or other similar operations.

Information Engineering (IE) model. An E-R model developed by James Martin.

Inner join. Synonym for join. Contrast with outer join.

Insertion anomaly. In a relation, the condition that exists when, to add a complete row to a table, one must add facts about two or more logically different themes.

Instance failure. A failure in the operating system or hardware that causes the DBMS to fail.

Integrated Development Environment (IDE). An application that provideds a programmer or application developer with a complete set of development tools in one package.

Integrated tables. Database tables that store both data and the relationships among the data.

Interface. (1) The means by which two or more programs call each other; the definition of the procedural calls between two or more programs. (2) In object-oriented programming, the design of a set of objects that includes the objects' names, methods, and attributes.

International Organization for Standardization (ISO). The international standards organization that works of SQL standards, among others.

Internet Information Server (IIS). A Microsoft product that operates as an HTTP server.

Internet Information Services Manger. The application used to manage Microsoft's IIS Web server.

Intersection table. A table (relation) used to represent a many-to-many relationship. It contains the keys of the tables (relations) in the relationship. The relationships from the parent tables to the intersection tables must have a minimum cardinality of either mandatory-optional or mandatory-mandatory.

Interrelation constraint. A data constraint between two tables.

Intrarelation constraint. A data constraint within one table.

IS-A relationship. A relationship between a supertype and a subtype. For example, EMPLOYEE and ENGINEER have an IS-A relationship.

Isolation level. *See* transaction isolation level.

Java. An object-oriented programming language that has better memory management and bounds checking than C++. It is used primarily for Internet applications, but it also can be used as a general-purpose programming language. Java compilers generate Java bytecode that is interpreted on client computers. Many believe that Microsoft C# is a near-copy of Java.

Java Database Connectivity (JDBC). A standard interface by which application programs written in Java can access and process SQL databases (or table structures such as spreadsheets and text tables) in a DBMS-independent manner. While originally it did not stand for Java Database Connectivity, it does now and is an acronym.

Java platform. The complete set of Java tools provided by Sun Microsystems.

Java Server Pages (JSP). A combination of HTML and Java that is compiled into a Java servlet that is a subclass of the HttpServlet class. Java code embedded in a JSP has access to HTTP objects and methods. JSPs are used similarly to ASPs, but they are compiled rather than interpreted, as ASP pages are.

Java servlet. *See* servlet.

Java virtual machine. A Java bytecode interpreter that runs on a particular machine environment; for example, Intel 386 or Alpha. Such interpreters are usually embedded in browsers, included with the operating system, or included as part of a Java development environment.

JavaScript. A proprietary scripting language owned by Netscape. The Microsoft version is called JScript; the standard version is called ECMAScript-262. These are easily learned interpreted languages that are used for both Web server and Web client application processing. Sometimes written as *Java Script.*

JDBC. *See* Java Database Connectivity (JDBC).

Join. A relational algebra operation on two relations, A and B, which produces a third relation, C. A row of A is concatenated with a row of B to form a new row in C if the rows in A and B meet a restriction concerning their values. Normally, the restriction is that one or more columns of A equal one or more columns of B. For example, suppose that A1 is an attribute in A, and B1 is an attribute in B. The join of A with B in which A1 = B1 will result in a relation, C, having the concatenation of rows in A and B in which the value of A1 equals the value of B1. In theory, restrictions other than equality are allowed; a join could be made in which A1 < B1. Such nonequal joins are not used in practice, however.

Join operation. In SQL, the process of combining data rows from two tables. *See* join.

JScript. A proprietary scripting language owned by Microsoft. The Netscape version is called JavaScript; the standard version is called ECMAScript-262. These are easily learned interpreted languages used for both Web server and Web client application processing.

JSP. *See* Java Server Page.

Key. (1) A group of one or more attributes identifying a unique row in a relation. Because relations may not have duplicate rows, every relation must have at least one key, which is the composite of all of the attributes in the relation. A key is sometimes called a logical key. (2) With some relational DBMS products, an index on a column used to improve access and sorting speed. It is sometimes called a physical key.

Labeled namespace. In an XML Schema document, a namespace that is given a name (label) within the document. All elements preceded by the name of the labeled namespace are assumed to be defined in that labeled namespace.

LAMP. A version of AMP that runs on Linux. *See* AMP.

Language Integrated Query (LINQ). A Microsoft .NET Framework component that allows SQL queries to be run directly from application programs.

Logical unit of work (LUW). An equivalent term for transaction. *See* transaction.

LEFT OUTER join. A join that includes all the rows of the first table listed in the SQL statement (the "left" table) regardless of whether or not they have a matching row in the other table.

Lift. In market basket analysis, confidence divided by the base probability of an item purchase.

Lock. The process of allocating a database resource to a particular transaction in a concurrent-processing system. The size of the resource locked is known as the lock granularity. With an exclusive lock, no other transaction may read or write the resource. With a shared lock, other transactions may read the resource, but no other transaction may write it.

Lock granularity. The size of a locked data element. The lock of a column value of a particular row is a small granularity lock, and the lock of an entire table is a large granularity lock.

Log. A file containing a record of database changes. The log contains before-images and after-images.

Logistic regression. A form of supervised data mining that estimates the parameters of an equation to calculate the odds that a given event will occur.

Lost update problem. Same as concurrent update problem.

M score. In RFM analysis, the "how much money" score, which reflects how much a customer spends per purchase. *See* RFM Analysis.

Many-to-many (N:M) relationship. A relationship in which one parent entity instance (or row in the parent table) can be associated with many child entity instances (or rows in the child table). At the same time, one child entity instance (or row in the child table) can be associated with many parent entity instances (or rows in the parent table). In an actual database, these relationships are tansformed into two one-to-many relationships between the original entities (tables) and an intersection table.

Market basket analysis. A type of data mining that estimates the correlations of items that are purchased together. *See also* confidence and lift.

MAX. In SQL, a function that determines the largest value in a set of numbers. *See* SQL built-in functions.

Maximum cardinality. (1) In a binary relationship in the entity-relationship model, the maximum number of entities on each side of the relationship. Common values are 1:1, 1:N, and N:M. (2) In a relationship in the relational model, the maximum number of rows on each side of the relationship. Common values are 1:1 and 1:N. An N:M relationship is not possible in the relational model.

Measure. In OLAP, the source data for the cube—data that are displayed in the cells. It may be raw data or it may be functions of raw data, such as SUM, AVG, or other computations.

Media failure. A failure that occurs when the DBMS is unable to write to a disk. Usually caused by a disk head crash or other disk failure.

Metadata. Data concerning the structure of data that are used to describe tables, columns, constraints, indexes, and so forth. Metadata is data about data.

Method. A program attached to an object-oriented programming (OOP) object. A method can be inherited by lower-level OOP objects.

Microsoft SQL Server 2008 Management Studio. The GUI utility that is used with Microsoft SQL Server 2008.

Microsoft Windows PowerShell. A Microsoft command line utility.

MIN. In SQL, a function that determines the smallest value in a set of numbers. *See* SQL built-in functions.

Minimum cardinality. (1) In a binary relationship in the entity-relationship model, the minimum number of entities required on each side of a relationship. (2) In a binary relationship in the relational model, the minimum number of rows required on each side of a relationship. Common values of minimum cardinality for both definitions are optional to optional (O-O), mandatory to optional (M-O), optional to mandatory (O-M), and mandatory to mandatory (M-M).

Minimum cardinality enforcement actions. Activities that must be taken to preserve minimum cardinality restrictions. Summarized in Figure 6-28. *See also* referential integrity (RI) actions.

Modification anomaly. In a relation, the situation that exists when the storage of one row records facts about two or more entities or when the deletion of one row removes facts about two or more entities.

Multivalued dependency. A condition in a relation with three or more attributes in which independent attributes appear to have relationships they do not have. Formally, in a relation R (A, B, C), having key (A, B, C) where A is matched with multiple values of B (or of C or both), B does not determine C, and C does not determine B. An example is the relation EMPLOYEE (EmpNumber, EmpSkill, DependentName), where an employee can have multiple values of EmpSkill and DependentName. EmpSkill and DependentName do not have any relationship, but they do appear to in the relation.

MUST constraint. A constraint that requires one entity to be combined with another entity.

MUST COVER constraint. The binary relationship indicates all combinations that must appear in the ternary relationship.

MUST NOT constraint. The binary relationship indicates combinations that are not allowed to occur in the ternary relationship.

MySQL Query Browser. The GUI utility used with MySQL 5.1.

Natural join. A join of a relation A having attribute A1 with relation B having attribute B1, where A1 equals B1. The joined relation, C, contains either column A1 or B1, but not both. Contrast this with equijoin.

Neural networks. A form of supervised data mining that estimates complex mathematical functions for making predictions. The name is a misnomer. Although there is some loose similarity between the structure of a neural network and a network of biological neurons, the similarity is only superficial.

N:M. The abbreviation for a many-to-many relationship between two entities or relations.

Nonidentifying connection relationships. In IDEF1X, 1:1 and 1:N HAS-A relationships that do not involve ID-dependent entities.

Nonidentifying relationship. In data modeling, a relationship between two entities such that one is *not* ID-dependent on the other. *See* identifying relationship.

Nonintegrated data. Data that are stored in two incompatible information systems.

Non-prime attribute. In normalization, an attribute that is not contained in any candidate key.

Nonrepeatable reads. The situation that occurs when a transaction reads data it has previously read and finds modifications or deletions caused by a committed transaction.

Nonspecific IDEF1X relationships. In IDEF1X, an N:M relationship.

Normal form. A rule or set of rules governing the allowed structure of relations. The rules apply to attributes, functional dependencies, multivalue dependencies, domains, and constraints. The most important normal forms are first normal form, second normal form, third normal form, Boyce-Codd normal form, fourth normal form, fifth normal form, and domain/key normal form.

Normalization. (1) The process of constructing one or more relations such that in every relation the determinant of every functional dependency is a candidate key (BCNF). (2) The process of removing multivalued dependencies (4NF). (3) In general, the process of evaluating a relation to determine whether it is in a specified normal form and of converting it to relations in that specified normal form, if necessary.

NOT NULL constraint. In SQL, a constraint that specifies that a column must contain a value in every row.

Not-type-valid document. An XML document that either does not conform to its Document Type Declaration (DTD) or does not have a DTD. *See also* type-valid document and schema-valid document.

NULL constraint. In SQL, a constraint that specifies that a column may have empty cells in some or all rows.

Null status. Whether the column has a NULL constraint or a NOT NULL constraint. *See* NOT NULL constraint, and NULL constraint.

Null value. An attribute value that has never been supplied. Such values are ambiguous and can mean that (a) the value is unknown, (b) the value is not appropriate, or (c) the value is known to be blank.

Object class. In object-oriented programming, a set of objects with a common structure. *See* object-oriented programming (OOP).

Object Linking and Embedding (OLE). Microsoft's object standard. OLE objects are Component Object Model (COM) objects and support all required interfaces for such objects.

Object persistence. In object-oriented programming, the characteristic that an object can be saved to nonvolatile memory, such as a disk. Persistent objects exist between executions of a program.

Object-oriented DBMS (OODBMS or ODBMS). A DBMS that can store the objects similar to those used in OOP. *See* object-oriented programming (OOP).

Object-oriented programming (OOP). A programming methodology that defines objects and the interactions between them to create application programs.

Object-relational DBMS. DBMS products that support both relational and object-oriented programming data structures, such as Oracle.

ODBC. *See* Open Database Connectivity standard.

ODBC conformance level. In ODBC, definitions of the features and functions that are made available through the driver's application program interface (API). A driver API is a set of functions that the application can call to receive services. There are three conformance levels: Core API, Level 1 API, and Level 2 API.

ODBC data source. In the ODBC standard, a database and its associated DBMS, operating system, and network platform.

ODBC Data Source Administrator. The application used to create ODBC data sources.

ODBC Driver. In ODBC, a program that serves as an interface between the ODBC driver manager and a particular DBMS product. Runs on the client machines in a client-server architecture.

ODBC Driver Manager. In ODBC, a program that serves as an interface between an application program and an ODBC driver. It determines the required driver, loads it into memory, and coordinates activity between the application and the driver. On Windows systems, it is provided by Microsoft.

ODBC multiple-tier driver. In ODBC, a two-part driver, usually for a client-server database system. One part of the driver resides on the client and interfaces with the application; the second part resides on the server and interfaces with the DBMS.

ODBC single-tier driver. In ODBC, a database driver that accepts SQL statements from the driver manager and processes them without invoking another program or DBMS. A single-tier driver is both an ODBC driver and a DBMS. It is used in file-processing systems.

ODBC SQL conformance levels. ODBC SQL conformance levels specify which SQL statements, expressions, and data types an OBDC driver can process. Three SQL conformance levels are defined: Minimum SQL Grammar, Core SQL Grammar, Extended SQL Grammar.

OLAP. *See* OnLine Analytical Processing.

OLAP cube. In OLAP, a presentation structure having axes upon which data dimensions are placed. Measures of the data are shown in the cells of the cube. Also called a hypercube.

OLAP report. The output of an OLAP analysis in tabular format. For example, this can be an Excel Pivot Table. *See* OLAP cube.

OLAP server. A server specifically developed to perform OLAP analyses.

OLE DB. The COM-based foundation of data access in the Microsoft world. OLE DB objects support the OLE object standard. ADO is based on OLE DB.

1:N. The abbreviation for a one-to-many relationship between two entities or relations.

OnLine Analytical Processing (OLAP). A form of dynamic data presentation in which data are summarized, aggregated, deaggregated, and viewed in the frame of a table or a cube.

Online transaction processing (OLTP) system. An operational database system available for, and dedicated to, transaction processing.

One-to-many (1:N) relationship. A relationship in which one parent entity instance (or row in the parent table) can be associated with many child entity instances (or rows in the child table). At the same time, one child entity instance (or row in the child table) can be associated with only one parent entity instance (or row in the parent table).

One-to-one (1:1) relationship. A relationship in which one parent entity instance (or row in the parent table) can be associated with only one child entity instance (or row in the child table). At the same time, one child entity instance (or row in the child table) can be associated with only one parent entity instance (or row in the parent table).

Open Database Connectivity standard (ODBC). A standard interface by which application programs can access and process relational databases, spreadsheets, text files, and other table-like structures in a DBMS or in a program-independent manner. The driver manager portion of ODBC is incorporated into Windows. ODBC drivers are supplied by DBMS vendors, Microsoft, and by third-party software developers.

Operational system. A database system in use for the operations of the enterprise, typically an OLTP system, *See* Online transaction processing (OLTP) system.

Optimistic locking. A locking strategy that assumes no conflict will occur, processes a transaction, and then checks to determine whether conflict did occur. If conflict did occur, no changes are made to the database and the transaction is repeated. *See also* pessimistic locking.

Oracle SQL Developer. The GUI utility for Oracle Database 11g.

Outer join. A join in which all of the rows of a table appear in the join result, regardless of whether they have a match in the join condition. In a left outer join, all of the rows in the left-hand relation appear; in a right outer join, all of the rows in the right-hand relation appear.

Overlapping candidate keys. Two candidate keys are said to be overlapping candidate keys if they have one or more attributes in common.

Parameter. A data value that is passed as input to a stored procedure or other application.

Parent. An entity or row on the one side of a one-to-many relationship.

Parent mandatory and child mandatory (M-M). A relationship where the minimum cardinality of the parent is 1 and the minimum cardinality of the child is 1.

Parent mandatory and child optional (M-O). A relationship where the minimum cardinality of the parent is 1 and the minimum cardinality of the child is 0.

Parent optional and child mandatory (O-M). A relationship where the minimum cardinality of the parent is 0 and the minimum cardinality of the child is 1.

Parent optional and child optional (O-O). A relationship where the minimum cardinality of the parent is 0 and the minimum cardinality of the child is 0.

Partially dependent. In normalization, a condition where an attribute is dependent on only part of a composite primary key instead of on the whole key.

Passive repository. Repositories that are filled only when someone takes the time to generate the needed metadata and place it in the repository. *See* data repository.

Persistent object. In object-oriented programming, an object that has been written to persistent storage.

Personal database system. A DBMS product intended for use by an individual or small workgroup. Such products typically include application development tools such as form and report generators in addition to the DBMS. For example, Microsoft Access 2007.

Pessimistic locking. A locking strategy that prevents conflict by locking data resources, processing the transaction, and then unlocking the data resources. *See also* optimistic locking and deadlock.

Phantom reads. The situation that occurs when a transaction reads data it has previously read and finds new rows that were inserted by a committed transaction.

PHP. *See* PHP: Hypertext Processor.

PHP Data Objects (PDO). A consistent data-access specification for PHP that allows a programmer to use the same functions independent of which DBMS is being used.

PHP: Hypertext Processor (PHP). A Web page scripting language used to create dynamic Web pages. It now includes an object-oriented programming component and PHP Data Objects (PDO). *See* PHP Data Objects (PDO).

PL/SQL. *See* Procedural Language/SQL.

POST method. In PHP, a method of passing data values from one Web page to another for processing.

PowerShell sqlps utility [MSSQL]. In SQL Server 2008, an add-in to the Microsoft PowerShell command line utility that allows it to work with SQL Server.

Primary key. A candidate key selected to be the key of a relation; the primary key is used as a foreign key for representing relationships.

PRIMARY KEY constraint. In SQL, a constraint statement used to create a primary key for a table.

Prepared Statement objects.

Procedural language. A programming language where each step necessary to obtain a result must to specified. The language may have the ability to contain sets of steps in structures called procedures or subprocedures.

Procedural Language/SQL (PL/SQL). An Oracle-supplied language that augments SQL with programming language structures such as while loops, if-then-else blocks, and other such constructs. PL/SQL is used to create stored procedures and triggers.

Processing rights and responsibilities. Organizational policies regarding which groups can take which actions on specified data items or other collections of data.

Program/data independence. The condition existing when the structure of the data is not defined in application programs. Rather, it is defined in the database and then the application programs obtain it from the DBMS. In this way, changes can be made in the data structures that may not necessarily be made in the application programs.

Programmer. A person who creates application programs in a programming language.

Project-Join normal form (PJ/NF). Another name for 5NF. *See* Fifth normal form (5NF).

Property. Same as attribute.

Prototype. A quickly developed demonstration of an application or portion of an application.

Pull report. In reporting systems, a report that must be requested by users.

Push report. In reporting systems, a report that is sent to users according to a schedule.

QBE. *See* query by example.

Query. A request for database data that meets specific criteria. This can be thought of as asking the database a question and getting an answer in the form of the data returned.

Query by example (QBE). A style of query interface, first developed by IBM but now used by Microsoft Access 2007 and other DBMS products, that enables users to express queries by providing examples of the results they seek.

Question mark (?) wildcard character. A character used in Access 2007 queries to represent a single unspecified characters. *See* SQL underscore (_) wildcard character.

R score. In RFM analysis, the "how recently" score, which reflects how recently a customer made a purchase. *See* RFM Analysis.

Range constraint. In SQL, a constraint that specifies that data values must be within a specific range of values.

Read committed. A level of transaction isolation that prohibits dirty reads but allows nonrepeatable reads and phantom reads.

Read uncommitted. A level of transaction isolation that allows dirty reads, nonrepeatable reads, and phantom reads.

Record. (1) In a relational model, a synonym for row and tuple. (2) A group of fields pertaining to the same entity; used in file-processing systems.

Recordset. An ADO.NET object that encapsulates a relation; created as the result of the execution of an SQL statement or a stored procedure.

Recovery via reprocessing. Recovering a database by restoring the last full backup, and then recreating each transaction since the backup.

Recovery via rollback/rollforward. Recovering a database by restoring the last full backup, and then using data stored in a transaction log to modify the database as needed by either adding transactions (roll forward) or removing erroneous transactions (rollback).

Recursive relationship. A relationship among entities or rows of the same type. For example, if CUSTOMERs refer to other CUSTOMERs, the relationship is recursive.

ReDo files. In Oracle, backups of rollback segments used for backup and recovery. ReDo files may be online or off-line.

Referential integrity (RI) actions. In general, rules that specify the activities that must take place when insert, update, or delete actions occur on either the parent or child entities in a relationship. In this text, we use referential integrity actions only to document activities needed to preserve required parents. Other actions can be defined as part of the database design. See minimum cardinality enforcement actions and Figure 6-28.

Referential integrity constraint. A relationship constraint on foreign key values. A referential integrity constraint specifies that the values of a foreign key must be a subset of the values of the primary key to which it refers.

Regression analysis. A form of supervised data mining in which the parameters of equations are estimated by data analysis.

Relation. A two-dimensional array containing single-value entries and no duplicate rows. Values for a given entity are shown in rows; values of attributes of that entity are shown in columns. The meaning of the columns is the same in every row. The order of the rows and columns is immaterial.

Relational data model. A data model in which data are stored in relations, and relationships between rows are represented by data values.

Relational database. A database consisting of relations. In practice, relational databases contain relations with duplicate rows. Most DBMS products include a feature that removes duplicate rows when necessary and appropriate. Such a removal is not done as a matter of course because it can be time-consuming to enforce.

Relational schema. A set of relations with interrelation constraints.

Relationship. An association between two entities or rows.

Relationship cardinality constraint. A constraint on the number of rows that can participate in a relationship. Minimum cardinality constraints determine the number of rows that must participate; maximum cardinality constraints specify the largest number of rows that can participate.

Relationship class. An association between entity classes.

Relationship instance. (1) An association between entity instances, (2) a specific relationship between two tables in a database.

Repeatable read. A level of transaction isolation that disallows both dirty reads and nonrepeatable reads. Phantom reads can occur.

Replication. For both Oracle, SQL Server, and MySQL, a term that refers to databases that are distributed on more than one computer.

Report. A formatted set of information created to meet a user's need.

Report authoring. In a reporting system, connecting to the data source, creating the report structure, and formatting the report.

Report delivery. In a reporting system, pushing the reports to users, or allowing them to pull the reports as needed.

Report management. In a reporting system, defining who receives which reports, when, and by what means.

Reporting system. A business intelligence system that processes data by filtering, sorting, and making simple calculations. OLAP is a type of reporting system. Contrast with data mining systems.

Repository. A collection of metadata about database structure, applications, Web pages, users, and other application components. Active repositories are maintained automatically by tools in the application-development environment. Passive repositories must be maintained manually.

Reserved word. A word that has a special meaning in the DBMS or ODBC, and should not be used as a table, column, or other name in a database. See DBMS reserved word.

Resource locking. *See* lock.

Reverse-engineered (RE) data model. The structure that results from reverse engineering. It is not really a data model, because it includes physical structures such as intersection tables. It is, instead, a thing unto itself; midway between a data model and a relational database design.

Reverse engineering. The process of reading the structure of an existing database and creating a reverse-engineered data model from that schema.

RFM analysis. A type of reporting system in which customers are classified according to how recently (R), how frequently (F), and how much money (M) they spend on their orders.

RIGHT OUTER constraint. A join that include all the rows of second table listed in the SQL statement (the "right" table) regardless of whether or not they have a matching row in the other table.

Role. In database administration, a defined set of permissions that can be assigned to users or groups.

Rollback. The process of recovering a database in which before-images are applied to the database to return to an earlier checkpoint or other point at which the database is logically consistent.

Rollforward. The process of recovering a database by applying after-images to a saved copy of the database to bring it to a checkpoint or other point at which the database is logically consistent.

Root. (1) In MySQL, the name of the DBMS administrator account. (2) The top record, row, or node in a tree. A root does not have a parent.

Row. A group of columns in a table. All the columns in a row pertain to the same entity. A row is the same as a tuple and a record.

Rowset. In OLE DB, an abstraction of data collections such as recordsets, e-mail addresses, and nonrelational and other data.

SAX. Simple API (Application Program Interface) for XML. An event-based parser that notifies a program when the elements of an XML document have been encountered during document parsing.

Schema. (1) In MySQL, a synonym for *database*. (2) A complete logical view of the database.

Schema-valid document. An XML document that conforms to its XML Schema definition.

SCN. *See* system change number.

Scrollable cursor. A cursor type that enables forward and backward movement through a recordset. Three scrollable cursor types discussed in this text are snapshot, keyset, and dynamic.

Second normal form (2NF). A relation in first normal form in which all nonkey attributes are dependent on all of the key attributes.

Self-describing. In a database, the characteristic of including data about the database in the database itself. Thus, the data that defines a table is included in a database along with the data that is contained in that table. This descriptive data is called *metadata*. *See* table, relation, and metadata.

Semantic object model. The constructs and conventions used to create a model of the users' data. The things in the users' world are represented by semantic objects (sometimes called objects). Relationships are modeled in the objects, and the results are usually documented in object diagrams.

Sequence. The Oracle Database 11g SQL statement used to create surrogate key values.

Serializable. A level of transaction isolation that disallows dirty reads, nonrepeatable reads, and phantom reads.

Service provider. An OLE DB data provider that transforms data. A service provider is both a data consumer and a data provider.

Servlet. A compiled, machine-independent Java bytecode program that is run by a Java virtual machine located on a Web server.

SGML. *See* Standard Generalized Markup Language.

Shared lock. A lock against a data resource in which only one transaction may update the data, but many transactions can concurrently read that data.

Shrinking phase. In two-phase locking, the stage at which locks are released but no lock is acquired.

Sibling. A record or node that has the same parent as another record or node.

Simple Object Access Protocol. A standard used for remote procedure calls. It uses XML for definition of the data and HTTP for transport. Contrast with SOAP.

Slowly changing dimension. In a dimensional database, a data column with values that change occasionally but irregularly over time, For example, a customer's address or phone number.

Snowflake schema. In a dimensional database or an OLAP database, the structure of tables such that dimension tables may be several levels away from the table storing the measure values. Such dimension tables are usually normalized. Contrast with star schema.

SOAP. Originally, Simple Object Access Protocol. Today, it is a protocol for remote procedure calls that differs from the Simple Object Access Protocol because it involves transport protocols in addition to HTTP. It is no longer an acronym.

Software development kit (SDK). A group of development tools provided to programmers to help them create applications.

SQL. *See* Structured Query Language.

SQL AND operator. The SQL operator used to combine conditions in an SQL WHERE clause.

SQL built-in functions. In SQL, the functions COUNT, SUM, AVG, MAX, or MIN.

SQL CMD utility. A command line utility used with SQL Server 2008.

SQL CREATE TABLE statement. The SQL command used to create a database table.

SQL CREATE VIEW statement. The SQL command used to create a database view.

SQL FROM clause. The part of an SQL SELECT statement that specifies conditions used to determine which tables are used in a query.

SQL GROUP BY clause. The part of an SQL SELECT statement that specifies conditions for grouping rows when determining the query results.

SQL HAVING clause. The part of an SQL SELECT statement that specifies conditions used to determine which rows are in the qroupings in a GROUP BY clause.

SQL OR operator. The SQL operator used to specify alternate conditions in an SQL WHERE clause.

SQL ORDER BY clause. The part of an SQL SELECT statement that specifies how the query results should be sorted when they are displayed.

SQL percent sign (%) wildcard character. The standard SQL wildcard character used to specify multiple characters. Microsoft Access 2007 uses an asterisk (*) character instead of the underscore character.

SQL script. A set of SQL statements that are intended to be executed as a group.

SQL script comment. A comment in an SQL script. *See* SQL script.

SQL script file. A file that holds an SQL script for repeated use. *See* SQL script.

SQL SELECT clause. The part of an SQL SELECT statement that specifies which columns are in the query results.

SQL SELECT * statement. A variant of an SQL SELECT query that returns all columns for all tables in the query.

SQL SELECT . . . for XML statement. A variant of an SQL SELECT query that returns the query results in XML format.

SQL SELECT/FROM/WHERE framework. The basic structure of an SQL query. *See* SQL SELECT clause, SQL FROM clause, SQL WHERE clause, SQL ORDER BY clause, SQL GROUP BY clause, SQL HAVING clause, SQL AND operator, and SQL OR operator.

SQL underscore (_) wildcard character. The standard SQL wildcard character used to specify a single character. Microsoft Access 2007 uses a question mark (?) character instead of the underscore character.

SQL WHERE clause. The part of an SQL SELECT statement that specifies conditions used to determine which rows are in the query results.

SQL view. A relation that is constructed from a single SQL SELECT statement. SQL views have at most one multivalued path. The term *view* in most DBMS products, including Access, Oracle, and SQL Server, means SQL view.

SQL*Plus. A command line utility in Oracle Database 11g.

Standard Generalized Markup Language (SGML). A standard means for tagging and marking the format, structure, and content of documents. HTML is an application of SGML. XML is a subset of SGML.

Star schema. In a dimensional database or an OLAP database, the structure of tables such that every dimension table is adjacent to the table storing the measure values. In the star schema, the dimension tables are often not normalized. Contrast with snowflake schema.

Statement-level consistency. All rows impacted by a single SQL statement are protected from changes made by other users during the execution of the statement. Contrast with transaction-level consistency.

Static cursor. A cursor that takes a snapshot of a relation and processes that snapshot.

Static report. In reporting systems, a report that is prepared once from underlying data and does not change when the underlying data change. Contrast with dynamic report.

Stock-keeping unit (SKU). A unique identifier for each product available from a vendor.

Stored procedure. A collection of SQL statements stored as a file that can be invoked by a single command. Usually, DBMS products provide a language for creating stored procedures that augments SQL with programming language constructs. Oracle provides PL/SQL for this purpose; SQL Server provides T-SQL; MySQL also adds procedural capabilities, but does not use a separate name for these additions. With some products, stored procedures can be written in a standard language such as Java. Usually, stored procedures are stored within the database itself.

Strong entity. In an entity-relationship model, any entity whose existence in the database does not depend on the existence of any other entity. *See also* ID-dependent entity and weak entity.

Strong password. A password that meets requirements intended to make it difficult to unencrypt.

Structured Query Language (SQL). A language for defining the structure and processing of a relational database. It can be used as a stand-alone language or it may be embedded in application programs. SQL has been adopted as a national standard by the American National Standards Institute (ANSI). The most common version used today is SQL-92, the version adopted by ANSI in 1992. SQL was originally developed by IBM.

Structured schema. An XML schema that is not flat.

Stylesheet. A document used by XSLT to indicate how to transform the elements of an XML document into another format.

Subquery. In SQL, a SELECT statement within another SELECT statement.

Subtype. In generalization hierarchies, an entity or object that is a subspecies or subcategory of a higher-level type, called a supertype. For example, ENGINEER is a subtype of EMPLOYEE.

SUM. In SQL, a function that adds up a set of numbers. *See* SQL built-in functions.

Supertype. In generalization hierarchies, an entity or object that logically contains subtypes. For example, EMPLOYEE is a supertype of ENGINEER, ACCOUNTANT, and MANAGER.

Supervised data mining. A form of data mining in which an analyst creates a prior model or hypothesis and then uses the data to test that model or hypothesis.

Support. In market basket analysis, the probability that two items will be purchased together.

Surrogate key. A unique, system-supplied identifier used as the primary key of a relation. It is created when a row is created, it never changes, and it is destroyed when the row is deleted. The values of a surrogate key have no meaning to the users and are usually hidden within forms and reports.

System change number (SCN). In Oracle, a database-wide value that is used to order changes made to database data. The SCN is incremented whenever database changes are committed.

System data source. An ODBC data source that is local to a single computer and can be accessed by that computer's operating system and select users of that operating system.

Table. A database structure of rows and columns to create cells that hold data values. Also known as a *relation* in a relational database, although strictly only tables that meet specific conditions can be called relations. *See* relation.

TableName.ColumnName syntax. A syntax used to indicate which table a column is associated with. For example, CUSTOMER.LastName indicates the LastName column in the CUSTOMER table.

Tabular data provider. An OLE DB data provider that presents data in the form of rowsets.

Ternary relationship. A relationship between three entities.

Third normal form (3NF). A relation in second normal form that has no transitive dependencies.

Three-tier architecture. A system of computers having a database server, a Web server, and one or more client computers. The database server hosts a DBMS, the Web server hosts an HTTP server, and the client computer hosts a browser. Each tier can run a different operating system.

Time dimension. A required dimension table in a dimensional database. The time dimension allows the data to be analyzed over time.

Transaction. (1) A group of actions that is performed on the database automatically; either all actions are committed to the database, or none of them are. (2) In general, the record of an event in the business world.

Transaction isolation level. The degree to which a database transaction is protected from actions by other transactions. The 1992 SQL standard specified four isolation levels: Read Uncommitted, Read Committed, Repeatable Reads, and Serializable.

Transaction-level consistency. All rows impacted by any of the SQL statements in a transaction are protected from changes during the entire transaction. This level of consistency is expensive to enforce and reduces throughput. It may also mean that a transaction cannot see its own changes. Contrast with statement-level consistency.

Transact-SQL (T-SQL). A Microsoft-supplied language that is part of SQL Server. It augments SQL with programming language structures such as while loops, if-then-else blocks, and other such constructs. Transact-SQL is used to create stored procedures and triggers.

Transitive dependency. In a relation having at least three attributes, for example, R (A, B, C), the situation in which A determines B, B determines C, but B does not determine A.

Transactional system. A database dedicated to processing transactions such as product sales and orders. It is designed to make sure that only complete transactions are recorded in the database.

Tree. A collection of records, entities, or other data structures in which each element has at most one parent, except for the top element, which has no parent.

Trigger. A special type of stored procedure that is invoked by the DBMS when a specified condition occurs. BEFORE triggers are executed before a specified database action, AFTER triggers are executed after a specified database action, and INSTEAD OF triggers are executed in place of a specified database action. INSTEAD OF triggers are normally used to update data in SQL views.

T-SQL. *See* Transact-SQL.

Tuple. Same as row.

Two dashes (- -). Symbology to indicate a single line comment in a stored procedure or a trigger in SQL Server 2008, Oracle Database 11g, and MySQL 5.1.

Two-phase locking. The procedure by which locks are obtained and released in two phases. During the growing phase, the locks are obtained; during the shrinking phase, the locks are released. After a lock is released, no other lock will be granted that transaction. Such a procedure ensures consistency in database updates in a concurrent-processing environment.

Two-tier architecture. In a Web-based database processing environment, the Web server and the DBMS are running on the same computer. One tier is for the Web browsers, and one is for the Web server/DBMS computer.

Type domain. In IDEF1X, a domain that is defined as a subset of a base domain or another type of domain.

Type-valid document. An XML document that conforms to its Document Type Declaration (DTD). Contrast with not-type-valid document.

UML. *See* Unified Modeling Language.

Unified Modeling Language (UML). A set of structures and techniques for modeling and designing object-oriented programs and applications. It is a set of tools for object-oriented development that has led to a development methodology. UML incorporates the entity-relationship model for data modeling.

UNIQUE constraint. In SQL, a constraint that specifies that the values in a column must be unique.

Unsupervised data mining. A form of data mining in which analysts do not create a prior model or hypothesis, but rather let the data analysis reveal a model.

Updatable view. An SQL view that can be updated. Such views are usually very simple, and the rules that allow updating are normally quite restrictive. Nonupdatable views can be made updatable by writing application-specific INSTEAD OF triggers.

User. A person using an application.

User data source. An ODBC data source that is available only to the user who created it.

User group. A group of users. *See* user.

Variable. A value that may be assigned or calculated by a stored procedure or a trigger in SQL Server 2008, Oracle Database 11g, and MySQL 5.1.

VBScript. An easily learned, interpreted language used for both Web server and Web client applications processing.

WAMP. AMP running on a Windows operating system. *See* AMP.

Weak entity. In an entity-relationship model, an entity whose logical existence in the database depends on the existence of another entity. All ID-dependent entities are weak, but not all weak entities are ID-dependent.

Web portal. A Web page designed to be an entrance point for a Web site. It may display information from several sources, and may require authentication to access.

World Wide Web Consortium (W3C). The group that creates, maintains, revises, and publishes standards for the World Wide Web including HTML, XML, and XHTML.

Wwwroot folder. The root folder or directory of a Web site on a Microsoft IIS Web server.

x..y cardinality format [UML]. The symbology format used in UML E-R diagrams to document minimum and maximum cardinalities. X records the minimum cardinality, and y records the maximum cardinality.

XHTML. The Extensible Hypertext Markup Language. A reformulation of HTML to XML standards of well-formed documents.

XML (Extensible Markup Language). A standard markup language that provides a clear separation between structure, content, and materialization. It can represent arbitrary hierarchies and hence can be used to transmit any database view.

XML Namespaces. A standard for assigning names to defined collections. X:Name is interpreted as the element Name as defined in namespace X. Y:Name is interpreted as the element Name as defined in namespace Y. Useful for disambiguating terms.

XML Schema. An XML document that defines the structure of other XML documents. Extends and replaces Document Type Declarations (DTDs).

XPath. A sublanguage within XSLT that is used to identify parts of an XML document to be transformed. Can also be used for calculations and string manipulation. Commingled with XSLT.

XPointer. A standard for linking one document to another. XPath has many elements from XPointer.

XQuery. A standard for expressing database queries as XML documents. The structure of the query uses XPath facilities, and the result of the query is represented in an XML format. Currently under development and likely to be important in the future.

XSL (XSLT Stylesheet). The document that provides the {match, action} pairs and other data for XSLT to use when transforming an XML document.

XSLT (Extensible Style Language: Transformations). A program (or process) that applies XSLT Stylesheets to an XML document to produce a transformed XML document.

ndex